	Italy	Japan	Luxembourg	Netherlands	Spain	Sweden	Switzerland	United Kingdom	United States
	36	37.5	33	40/35	35	30			
	15	20	0	0	25	0			
	15	10	0	0	10	0			
	10	10	0	0	12	0	0	—	0
	12.5	10	0	0	10	0	—	0	5
	15	10	0	0	15	—	5	0	0
	12	10	0	0	—	0	10	0/12	10
	15	10	0	—	10	0	5	0	0
	10	20	—	0	10	0	35	0	0
	10	—	0	0	10	0	10	10	10
	—	10	0	0	12	0	12.5	10	15
	10	10	0	0	25	0	0	0	0
	0/15	10	0	0	10	0	0/30	0	0
	15	10	0	0	10	0	10	0	0
	15	10	0	0	10	0	0	0	0
	15	10	0	0	15	0	15	10	15
	15	15	0	0	15	0	10	15	15
	10	10	0	0	20	0	10	10	10

1992
INTERNATIONAL
TAX SUMMARIES

1992 INTERNATIONAL TAX SUMMARIES

A GUIDE FOR PLANNING AND DECISIONS

Coopers & Lybrand International Tax Network

David T. Wright, Editor

JOHN WILEY & SONS, INC.

New York · Chichester · Brisbane · Toronto · Singapore

Coopers & Lybrand (International) is an association of professional firms that practice in many countries throughout the world. The firms provide a broad range of financial and consulting services.

As prominent indigenous firms, they are able to combine a detailed knowledge of local customs, regulations and requirements with the resources and skills of an international network of firms conducting their practices in accordance with agreed standards and procedures.

Member and Associated firms of Coopers & Lybrand (International) currently practice in 112 countries through 710 offices, with over 65,000 partners and staff worldwide.

The tax summaries in this volume are designed to provide a general understanding of the principal features of the tax systems of the countries concerned. Information contained in them should be used for guidance only. The summaries are not intended to be comprehensive, and no specific action should be taken on the basis of information contained in them without consultation.

The Library of Congress has cataloged this serial publication as follows:

International tax summaries / Coopers & Lybrand International
  Tax Network.—   — New York : Wiley,
    v. ; 24-28 cm.
  Annual.
  Began in 1982
  Description based on: 1984.
  "A guide for planning and decisions."
  ISSN 8755-1551 = International tax summaries.

   1. Income tax—Law and legislation. 2. Corporations—Taxation—Law and legislation. 3. Taxation—Law and legislation. I. Coopers & Lybrand.

K4505.4.I54   343.04—dc19   84-647140
             [342.3] AACR 2 MARC-S
Library of Congress   [8512]

ISBN 0-471-55933-4

Printed and bound by Courier Companies, Inc.

10 9 8 7 6 5 4 3 2 1

INTRODUCTION

The 1992 edition of the *International Tax Summaries* presents an overview of the tax systems of 110 countries in which member and associated firms of Coopers & Lybrand (International) have practice offices or in which they have correspondent firms. The tax information, which features both individual and corporate income tax laws, has been provided by members of the Coopers & Lybrand International Tax Network. This edition of *International Tax Summaries* reflects the tax systems as of July 31, 1991 unless otherwise indicated. The tax summaries are updated annually.

To assist in the comparison of the tax systems of different countries and to provide a method of retrieving information quickly, the significant tax attributes of each of the countries generally include and are ordered as follows:

INCOME TAXES ON CORPORATIONS

1. Rates
2. Local Income Taxes
3. Capital Gains Taxes
4. Branch Profits Taxes
5. Foreign Tax Reliefs
6. Classification of Corporations
7. Payment of Taxes
8. Other Matters

INCOME TAXES ON INDIVIDUALS

9. Rates
10. Local Income Taxes
11. Capital Gains Taxes
12. Foreign Tax Reliefs
13. Tax Period
14. Other Matters

INCOME TAXES ON NONRESIDENTS

15. Liability to Tax
16. Rates

The last two sections may be of particular interest. The best approaches for investing in 80 countries are discussed in the section entitled "Selection of Business Entity by Nonresidents." Specimen tax computations that illustrate the information provided in the summaries have been prepared for 47 countries.

Of the countries included in this edition, those marked with an asterisk (*) do not impose income taxes.

Coopers & Lybrand
International Tax Network

TAX INFORMATION SUMMARIES IN THIS EDITION

The individual members of the Coopers & Lybrand International Tax Network who provided the information about their respective countries are noted in most cases.

* Countries that do not impose income taxes.

1992
INTERNATIONAL
TAX SUMMARIES

ANGOLA

INCOME TAXES ON CORPORATIONS

1. Rates

Corporations doing business in Angola are subject to income tax on taxable profits, at the rate of 35%. It may be reduced to 23% or 30% if the Ministry of Finance considers the business activity fundamental to the Angolan economy.

The amount of final taxable income ("materia colectavel") also is subject to a surtax ("imposto de resistência popular"), based on 11 income levels:

☐ Normal rate of 2% and average rate of 0.8% for provisional taxable income ("rendimento colectavel") between 150,000 Nkz and 250,000 Nkz;

☐ Normal rate of 28% and average rate of 19.099% for income between 45,000,000 Nkz and 50,000,000 Nkz.

2. Local Income Taxes

None.

4. Branch Profits Taxes

Branches of foreign companies are liable for tax on profits obtained in Angola in exactly the same way as Angolan companies.

5. Foreign Tax Reliefs

In the case of commercial or civil companies in a commercial form with head-office or effective management in Angola, the income tax and the surtax "imposto de resistencia popular" will be based on a third of the gross profits earned overseas.

7. Payment of Taxes

In a system of provisional tax payments, which is the case of groups A and B (see item 33), taxpayers must pay their taxes in three equal installments, due in January, April, and July.

The provisional determination of the following year's tax is made until December 10, the base being the amount corresponding to 50% of the previous year's taxable profit, should this amount exist, or the minimum income, should there be no taxable profit or should this amount not be known.

The correction of the provisional payment is carried out until September 15, the differences then collectable or refundable.

In the case of an "accidental activity" of contractual nature, the tax is paid in one single installment, after the determination is processed in the foreseen terms.

INCOME TAXES ON INDIVIDUALS

9. Rates

Income from employment is taxed on employment income tax ("IRT—Imposto Sobre os Rendimentos do Trabalho").

With respect to rates, the law distinguishes the following:

- [ ] Employees: 14 income levels, taxed at rates varying between a minimum of 1% for monthly income up to 6,000 Nkz and a maximum of 37,740 Nkz, to 40% on the excess of 200,000 Nkz for income above this amount;
- [ ] Free professionals: 11 income levels, taxed at rates varying between 3% for annual income up to 72,000 Nkz and 229,640 Nkz, to 60% on the excess of 1,000,000 Nkz for income above this amount.

With respect to copyrights, the rates are more progressive, varying according to the annual income and whether attributed to inheritors (family or strangers).

10. Local Income Taxes

None.

13. Tax Period

The tax year is the calendar year.

INCOME TAXES ON NONRESIDENTS

15. Liability to Tax

Nonresidents, whether individuals or corporations, engaged in any trade or business activity are subject to the same fiscal treatment as residents.

If books of accounts are not properly kept in relation to the activity in Angola, taxation is based on the estimated profit, which may reach 30% of the value of the contracts that are executed in Angola.

Employees are, in principle, subject to the payment of employment income tax (IRT) in respect of activity carried out in Angola.

16. Rates

The tax rates applicable to nonresidents are the same as for residents. Total taxes on corporations can reach approximately 18% of the gross value.

OTHER SIGNIFICANT TAXES

21. Sales (Value Added)

In Angola, there is a tax on production and consumption, which is applied to approximately 100 listed products, whether these are produced or imported by Angola.

The tax amount results from the application of *ad valorem* rates varying between 5% and 80%, according to the type of merchandise.

There are, however, cases in which the taxation is applied by means of *specific rates*, also variable. In these cases, the tax amount is calculated as a function of indexes such as volume, weight, dimension, engine capacity, etc.

22. Inheritance and Gift Taxes

Inheritance and gift tax is based on the free transmission of real and personal property and certain rights, between people or by "mortis causa."

Rates vary with the value of the goods transmitted and the degree of relationship of the person to whom the transmission is made, with a minimum rate of 3% and a maximum rate of 33%.

23. Taxes on Payrolls (Social Security)

Employers pay, as a contribution for the social security system, a percentage of 5% of the total amount of salaries and additional remunerations paid. Employees pay 2% of their salaries and additional remunerations earned.

24. Taxes on Natural Resources

Oil industries and geological and mining activities are subject to a special taxation system.

25. Other Taxes

The Angolan tax system integrates other taxes, which according to its growing importance are import duties, property tax, and tax on the transfer of real estate (SISA).

□ Import duties are levied on imported goods and are contained in a list approved by the Council of Ministers. The rate varies between 3% and 80%, according to the type of merchandise on which it is levied.

□ Property tax is levied on income from real estate, in the case of rent, based on the actual revenue from which other charges are deducted; in other cases, the law foresees an estimated value. The tax rate is 30%.

☐ Tax on the transfer of real estate is a tax levied generally on the transmission of a property right, or of parts of that right on real estate. The rate is normally 10%.

COMPUTATION OF TAXABLE INCOME

27. Depreciation and Depletion

Depreciation rates are defined by the tax authorities and are contained in a table published by the Tax Authorities.

28. Treatment of Dividends

Dividends received are considered as income for the year. However, the capital tax on dividends is deducted from the income tax due. Capital tax on dividends is known usually as withholding tax on dividend distributions. It is applicable when dividends are attributed to shareholders, resident or not.

32. Tax Periods

The tax period is the calendar year.

33. Other Matters

Taxpayer Categories. Businesses in the A category must keep full, reliable accounting records. B category businesses must keep only certain accounting records. In the case of A businesses, taxable income is determined on the basis of the profit shown by the accounts adjusted for revenue or cost items not accepted for fiscal purposes. In the case of B businesses, profit is estimated on the basis of some indicators provided by the taxpayer or used by the tax authorities.

RELATED CONSIDERATIONS

34. Incentives and Grants

The Angolan Law foresees the concession of certain fiscal incentives to taxpayers whose business activity is considered innovative and of particular importance for the country's economic development.

These incentives may take the form of exemptions or reduction of rates, in order to stimulate the investment and reinvestment of profits.

35. Exchange Controls

Exchange operations are subject to a very strict control by the "Banco Nacional de Angola," being subject to a regime of prior authorizations.

36. Investment Restrictions on Nonresidents

Foreign investments are subject to a special regime, always depending on the Government's authorization. However, only the areas considered by law as inaccessible to private initiative are forbidden.

SELECTION OF BUSINESS ENTITY BY NONRESIDENTS

Foreign investors may operate in Angola through "mixed companies," associations, and private companies, in the form of joint stock companies or limited liability companies and joint ventures.

Specialists should be consulted in order to obtain knowledge on the advantages and disadvantages of each of the forms of association, in the Angolan market.

ARGENTINA

INCOME TAXES ON CORPORATIONS

1. Rates

The tax rate applicable to the taxable income of Argentine corporations is 20%. This rate also applies to stock-issuing partnerships.

Dividends paid in cash or in kind (other than stock dividends) to shareholders are subject to a flat 10% tax withholding if the shareholder is an individual domiciled within Argentina (who has provided identification). If the shareholder is a nonresident (individual or legal entity), or an individual who has not provided identification, the withholding tax is 20%.

The Source Principle. Argentine tax legislation is based on the "source" principle, under which it only taxes income from sources within Argentina (i.e., derived from capital, rights or property located, employed, or utilized in Argentina; stemming from trading activities carried out or personal services rendered in Argentina; and income earned by Argentine residents from occasional personal services abroad) and from assets and rights held in Argentina.

2. Local Income Taxes

None.

3. Capital Gains Taxes

Capital gains are added to other taxable income and taxed at the standard corporate rate.

4. Branch Profit Taxes

The income tax rate for branches and other permanent establishments belonging to foreign companies or nonresidents is 36% of their taxable income. There are no other differences between the tax treatment of branches and that of corporations.

5.   Foreign Tax Reliefs

Argentine corporations are not granted any relief from Argentine income tax in connection with foreign taxes paid. Nevertheless, as Argentina's taxes are levied on the basis of the source principle (see item 1), profits obtained by Argentine corporations from sources outside Argentina are not taxed.

7.   Payment of Taxes

Taxpayers may recognize 37.5% of the tax on debits to bank current accounts, charged to them during the fiscal period by banks, as a tax credit against their income tax.

Corporations are required to make 11 monthly prepayments towards their income tax liabilities. Each one of these prepayments is equivalent to 8.5% of the previous year's net income tax liability and must be paid only if (and to the extent that) its amount exceeds the corresponding assets tax prepayment. (See item 20, "Assets Tax".

For purposes of the final determination of income tax, the prepayments made during the year are index-linked in the taxpayer's favor from the date of deposit to the fiscal closing date (using the wholesale price index for the end of the second last month in both cases).

If the cumulative amounts collected monthly from a payer exceed certain thresholds set monthly by the Tax Department, they are subject to income tax withholding at source. The withholding rate depends on the type of income involved. Sample rates are 1% for sales of assets (2% if the recipient is not a registered taxpayer), 6% for most interest, rents, and royalties (25% if the recipient is not a registered taxpayer).

The annual tax return is filed with the Tax Authority by the twentieth day of the fifth month after the closing date of the fiscal year, which is also the deadline for paying any income tax due.

The mere default in paying taxes calls for the payment of interest to the Tax Authority at the rate of 7% per month.

If it is deemed that the taxpayer is at fault, fines ranging between 50% and 100% of the index-linked tax payment omitted due to inaccuracies in the tax returns or failure to file may be imposed on the taxpayer. If it is deemed that the taxpayer has behaved in a deceitful way, the fines vary between double and ten times the index-adjusted tax payment omitted.

Under the penal tax law that came into effect on March 8, 1990, any stratagem or deceit that could be detrimental to the Tax Department's assets may be punished with prison sentences of up to three years (crime of danger) or up to six years (crime involving the result). The penal tax law entails trial before the criminal courts of the directors, syndics, professionals, advisors, and others, including the persons presumably involved in a tax crime, before the administrative and judicial discussion of the tax differences and fines that might be determined by the Tax Department.

The system of index adjustment and default interest, as well as that involving fines for omissions for which the taxpayer involved is to blame or has been deceitful, and prison terms is applicable with slight variations not only with regard to corporate income taxes but also for all other national, provincial, and municipal taxes.

INCOME TAXES ON INDIVIDUALS

9. Rates

Resident individuals are taxed at progressive rates, whose present level (July 1991) ranges from 6% on the first Å 12,779,000 (approximately US$ 1,280) to 30% on taxable income over Å 1,073,456,000 (approximately US$ 10,730). The rungs of the tax scale are subject to monthly adjustments in the same way as the personal allowances. Individuals who have been resident in Argentina at least six months of the year may claim personal allowances, which are adjusted monthly for inflation. The approximate July 1991 annual levels are:

Personal Allowances		Approx. US $ Equivalent
(A) Basic exemption	Å 42,007,000	US$ 4,200
(B) Earned income allowance	52,509,000	5,250
(C) Spouse	21,004,000	2,100
(D) Children and other dependents (each)	10,502,000	1,050

Individuals may also deduct their contributions to social security funds, medical plan premiums up to 15% of the sum of (A), (C), and (D), life insurance premiums up to Å 8,849,000 at the July 1991 level (approximately US$ 880), private retirement insurance premiums up to Å 12,314,000 at the June 1991 level (approximately US$ 1,230), and donations up to 10% of taxable income. There is no provision for filing joint returns, so husband and wife must keep their incomes separate and file separate returns. Salaries and wages are subject to income tax withholding at source (P.A.Y.E.).

10. Local Income Taxes

None.

11. Capital Gains Taxes

Capital gains (obtained by individuals on assets not included in the net worth of sole proprietorships) are not subject either to income tax or to capital gains tax, because the capital gains tax (which applied to individuals with certain types of capital gains and was levied at the rate of 15%) was repealed effective January 1, 1990.

Instead, a 1.5% tax on the selling price of real estate transfers by individuals has been introduced.

12. Foreign Tax Reliefs

Foreign taxes paid by Argentine residents on income from occasional activities abroad are deemed prepayments for Argentine income tax purposes, subject to certain limitations.

13. Tax Period

Individual taxpayers must file their returns on a calendar-year basis.

INCOME TAXES ON NONRESIDENTS

15. Liability to Tax

As stated in item 1, the source principle also applies to nonresidents; that is, only income from Argentine sources is taxable.

16. Rates

Dividends paid to nonresident shareholders in cash or in kind (except for fully paid stock dividends and capital distributions stemming from accounting revaluations) by companies or stock-issuing partnerships are subject to income tax withholding at the flat rate of 20%. The remittance of profits by branches, or other permanent establishments belonging to foreign companies, is not taxed, but the branch is taxed on its profits at 36% (item 4). The portion of the taxable income of a general partnership or limited liability partnership (or that corresponding to the general partners in a stock-issuing partnership) that corresponds to nonresidents is subject to a 36% income tax withholding upon either its distribution or five months after the closing date, whichever occurs first.

Any other Argentine source profits paid to nonresident beneficiaries (including those collected in Argentina before the beneficiaries have established permanent residence in Argentina) are subject to a flat 32.4% income tax withholding (36% on an assumed net income of 90%) if the profits are not covered by any other special provision (see item 17).

17. Withholding Tax Rates

Under the special provisions covering payments to nonresident beneficiaries, fees covering technical assistance, engineering, or consulting services actually rendered in Argentina but not otherwise available in Argentina are subject to an effective withholding tax rate of 21.6%, provided the underlying contracts fulfill the requirements of the technological transfer law. Royalties and other types of consideration covered by contracts fulfilling the requirements of the technological transfer law are subject to an effective withholding rate of 28.8%. Royalties paid to nonresidents under copyrights registered with the National Copyright Board are taxed at the effective rate of 12.6%. Interest paid on credits to finance imports of depreciable movable assets except automobiles is exempt from the tax. Other interest payments, in general, are taxed at the effective rate of 14.4%

There are special rules that establish the taxable portion of income deemed to be of Argentine source (without allowing any proof to the contrary). This applies to payments to nonresident individuals working temporarily in Argentina, and payments for international freight services, container services, international news services, underwriting premiums, and license fees for the use of films.

Subject to the specific provisions of tax treaties, the withholding tax percentages on outward remittances may be summarized as follows:

	Dividends	Interest	Fees for Services Not Obtainable in Argentina (1)	Royalties (1)
Nontreaty countries	20%	14.4%	21.6%	28.8%
Treaty countries:				
Austria	15	12.5	15	15
Bolivia	(2)	(2)	(2)	(2)
Brazil	(2)	(2)	(2)	(2)
Chile	(2)	(2)	(2)	(2)
France	15	(3)	18	18
Italy	15	(3)	18 (4)	18 (4)
Sweden	(1)	(1)	15	15
West Germany	15	15 (5)	15	15

Notes:
(1) Provided the related royalty agreement has been registered with the National Institute of Industrial Technology.
(2) The rates for nontreaty countries apply because the source principle is recognized for purposes of the treaty.
(3) The rates for nontreaty countries apply because the maximum rate set by the treaty is higher.
(4) Reduced to 10% for copyrights.
(5) Reduced to 10% in cases involving credits for equipment sales, bank loans, and financing of public works.

On the basis of the clause that bars discrimination against nonresidents contained in nearly all the tax treaties, it could now be alleged that tax withholdings from dividends should not exceed the 10% withholding tax rate applicable to resident shareholders.

Negotiations are under way for signing treaties for avoiding double taxation with Belgium, Canada, Finland, Japan, Rumania, Soviet Union, Spain, and the United States.

20. Other Matters

Assets Tax. Corporations, branches of foreign companies, joint partnerships, and sole proprietors are subject to a tax on the assets reported by them at the end of the fiscal year. Individuals and undivided estates that own rural properties not being used by sole proprietorships also are subject to this tax, solely in connection with those properties reported at the end of the calendar year.

The tax is 1%, but it has been increased to 2% for the first fiscal year after February 19, 1991.

The income tax determined for the same fiscal year is recognizable as a tax credit for purposes of the assets tax. In the case of branches, which pay income tax at the 36% rate, the tax credit is limited to 20% of the taxable income, so as to place branches on a par with corporations. The portion of income tax potentially recognizable as a credit for assets tax purposes but exceeding the amount determined for the latter tax for the same fiscal year does not lead to any credit balance or refund in the taxpayer's favor.

Taxpayers are required to make 11 monthly payments towards their final assets tax liability as from the sixth month of their fiscal year. The annual tax return is filed with the Tax Authority by the twentieth day of the fifth month after the closing date of the fiscal year, which also is the deadline for paying any assets tax due.

There is an exemption for assets permanently located abroad and shares or partnership interests in entities subject to the same tax. Other excludable assets include investments in the construction of properties (other than those deemed inventories) and purchases of first-hand depreciable movable assets (excluding motorcars), in the year in which the investment has been made and the next year. In the case of rural real estate property, the law allows a 25% reduction in the value of unimproved land, which has been increased to 50% for the fiscal year ended after February 19, 1991.

In the case of insurance companies, banks, and consignees, the tax basis is 40% of the sum of the assets (recognizing a tacit deduction of 60% to cover their liabilities). No other taxpayers are allowed to take a deduction for real or assumed liabilities.

Tax on Debits to Bank Current Accounts. Charges to current accounts with banks carry a 1.2% tax. This is a tax on the holder of the account, payable through withholding by the banks. A reduced rate of 0.2% applies in a few cases, such as cooperatives, brokers, etc.

Of the tax paid, 37.5% may be recognized as a tax credit for income tax purposes (see item 7), and a further 37.5% as a tax credit for VAT purposes (see item 21), with the remaining 25% representing a direct expense for the taxpayer.

OTHER SIGNIFICANT TAXES

21. Sales (Value Added)

VAT has a very broad scope, as it is levied at all stages of production and trading, including retailing, as well as on a wide range of services. The standard rate is 16% as of February 21, 1991.

Telephone services provided to ultimate consumers or to business entities not subject to VAT are taxed at a reduced rate of 11%. All other telephone services, as well as telecommunication services in general and the supply of gas, electricity, running water, and drainage and sanitation services, are taxed at the rate of 25%.

All sales of movable assets on the domestic market are taxed unless specifically exempt under the law. Effective February 1, 1990, practically the only exemptions regarding movable assets concern publications (books, pamphlets, periodicals, magazines, etc.), water in its natural state, milk, and bread provided they are sold to ultimate consumers or certain non-profit entities. Medicines for human use also are exempt, but only when sold by wholesale druggists and chemist stores. Property sales are taxed (including the value of the land) only when undertaken by building companies (when the full or partial construction or sale of the property is undertaken with a profit motive) or companies that had earmarked the properties for activities subject to VAT and had recognized fiscal credits for the construction thereof in the past ten years).

The leasing and rendering of services in general is subject to VAT as well, with very few exceptions. The latter include insurance, banking, financial placements and services, cargo and passenger transport, property rentals, most educational and health services, stock exchange transactions, admissions to sporting events and artistic events or performances, the services of directors and syndics of corporations, employees' salaries, and news agency services.

Exports are not subject to VAT, and exporters may, in addition, recognize a tax credit for the VAT billed to them on the goods exported. Imports are subject to VAT at the rates corresponding to the items involved.

Tax payments are determined monthly by deducting the fiscal credits arising from the tax billed by suppliers of inputs (including fixed assets) connected with taxable revenue (or those stemming from the tax paid upon the customs clearance of imported inputs) from the fiscal debits (computed on taxable revenues at the applicable rate).

There is a system under which registered taxpayers are required to bill and collect an excess tax equivalent to 16% of a flat estimated profit of 50% (i.e., 8% in addition to the standard 16% tax) from their purchasers who are not registered for VAT.

Taxpayers whose sales during the year 1990 have been less than A 405 million (approximately US$ 72,000) have the option to register or not.

There is also a system of standard withholding or collections under which responsible parties of a certain financial size are required to withhold from their registered suppliers (and pay over to the Tax Department on their behalf) 45% or

75% of the VAT contained in the invoices they have received and to collect 3% of the selling price from their customers towards the VAT that such customers are ultimately required to pay.

Those responsible for paying VAT may recognize 37.5% of the tax on debits to bank current accounts charged to them during the period by the banks with which they deal as a payment on account of their VAT liability.

The deadline for paying the net tax liability arising from each monthly computation is around the twentieth of the following month.

23. Taxes on Payrolls (Social Security)

The main social security rates levied in Argentina are:

	Employer Contributions	Employee Withholdings
Pension Fund	13%	13%
Family subsidy fund	9%	—
Health scheme	6%	3%
National Housing Fund	5%	—

The obligatory legal bonus of one month's salary per year is subject to similar contributions.

24. Taxes on Natural Resources

Exploitation of Oil and Gas Resources. In explaining the taxes applicable to businesses engaged in oil and gas exploration, extraction, and operation, it is necessary to distinguish between: 1) the holders of exploration permits and operating concessions taxed in accordance with Law 17319 of 1987; 2) companies that enter into "Risk Contracts for the Exploration and Exploitation of Hydrocarbons," covered by Law 21778 enacted in April 1978; and 3) companies that are granted the right to exploit, explore, and develop given areas pursuant to Law 17319 but within the special conditions arising from Law 23696 enacted in 1989 (the State Reform Law) and various decrees issued in 1989 and 1990.

The special tax system envisaged by article 56 of Law 17319 included a special income tax (55% of the profits obtained), against which the taxpayers could credit the amounts paid in respect of the fixed charge per square kilometer, oil and gas royalties, and provincial or municipal taxes. Nevertheless, in practice this tax system has hardly been applied.

The tax system applicable to "risk contracts," which is governed by Law 21778, entails the application of the general tax rules, coupled with such special benefits as the possibility of taking up 100% depreciation for the value of certain depreciable assets used for exploration purposes in the first year they are put into service. It should be mentioned that under the system of Law 21778 the contractor does not acquire the right of ownership to the oil and gas extracted even though its compensation is fixed on the basis thereof.

The concessions granted latterly by YPF (the State Oil Company), which are based on Law 17319 and the series of decrees issued in 1989 and 1990, specifically exclude the application of the special 55% tax envisaged by that law and declare that the awardees are subject to the general tax rules. Incidentally, these adjudications specifically call for the concessionaire to pay the State a fixed charge per square kilometer and a 12% royalty on the well-head value of the production computed (which may be reduced if the operation is not profitable) and grant the concessionaires the right to dispose freely of the oil and gas produced.

25. Other Taxes

Land and Property Taxes. Land and property taxes are levied by the provinces and the Municipality of Buenos Aires, based on the assessed valuation of the property. Rates vary from one jurisdiction to another. The assessed valuation is usually below the current market value.

Stamp Duty. Stamp duty is levied by the Federal District and the provinces on documents supporting legal transactions, such as deeds, mortgages, contracts, letters accepting proposals, etc.

The rates and rules for assessment are determined in each jurisdiction. Sample rates are 1% for public and private instruments (including insurance policies) and promissory notes, 0.5% for joint venture agreements, and 0.75% to 2.5% for conveyances of real estate. There are rules designed to avoid double taxation in the case of documents supporting transactions involving two or more jurisdictions.

The Federal District (city of Buenos Aires) also levies stamp duty on financial transactions that accrue interest or indexing, but foreign currency transactions settled through the official exchange market and transactions between different companies belonging to the same economic group are exempt. The tax ranges up to 6% per annum (apportioned on a daily basis) on the principal plus interest and indexing.

Tax on the Purchase and Sale of Foreign Exchange. This is a 0.6% tax on transactions involving the purchase or sale of foreign currency by banks or authorized exchange brokers. The tax is borne by the other party, but withheld by the bank or broker. There is a reduced rate of 0.4% for foreign trade transactions.

Excise Taxes. These nationwide federal taxes are levied on the manufacturers or importers of tobacco, spirits, alcoholic beverages, tires, fuel, and lubricants, and on the manufacturers, importers, bottlers, packagers, and finishers (including the persons for whose account such jobs are undertaken) of toiletries, luxury articles (such as jewelry and furs), soft drinks, syrups, extracts and concentrates, television sets, tape recorders, record players, radiograms, automobiles, magnetic tapes, phonograph records, and photographic plates and film, etc. as well as on premiums charged by insurance companies.

Excise taxes on nationally made automobiles (4% in most cases) have been suspended up to December 31, 1991, and those on imported automobiles (previously 21.5%) have been eliminated.

Excise taxes are paid on the basis of sworn returns or through stamps affixed to the products sold; rates vary considerably, ranging up to 70% of the retail selling price (including the tax itself) in the case of cigarettes.

Tax on Transfer of Liquid Fuels and Other Petroleum and Natural Gas By-Products.   This tax on the transfer of liquid fuels and other petroleum and natural gas by-products is applied to only one stage of the traffic in them. The parties responsible for paying it are oil refiners, importers, and traders. The tax is settled on the basis of unit amounts per liter or cubic meter. Exports are exempt from this tax.

Taxes on Gross Revenue.   These taxes are levied by the provinces and the city of Buenos Aires on the gross receipts from business activities and services rendered within their respective jurisdictions. Deductions from gross sales are usually allowed for discounts, returns and excise taxes, as well as VAT. Export transactions and trading in government securities are exempt in the city of Buenos Aires and most of the provinces. Banks and other financial entities may deduct interest and indexing payable on deposits for purposes of determining the tax basis. The rates vary from one province to another. The standard rate levied by the city of Buenos Aires is 3%, while the following differential rates also apply: 1% for primary production activities, 1.5% for manufacturing and processing activities, 4.5% for moneylenders and pawnbrokers, 4.5% for financial and certain other entities, and 15% for entertainment halls. The rates in the province of Buenos Aires and other provinces are similar.

Tax on Transfer of Securities.   This is a 0.75% or 0.5% national tax on the transfer of ownership for valuable consideration of shares, bonds (including Government bonds), debentures, and other securities. The tax is not levied on original subscriptions and payments of securities, on the distribution of fully paid stock dividends or stock corresponding to the capitalization of accounting revaluation surpluses, or on swap operations and pledges covering securities transactions.

The transfer of securities is also currently subject to an additional emergency tax of 0.75% or 0.5% depending on the circumstances.

Tax on Transfer of Real Estate.   The rate of tax is 1.5%, and the tax is levied on the selling price of property sales effected by individuals, when the sales are not subject to income tax.

National Highway Fund Tax.   This tax, suspended in April 1991, was levied on sales of new cars and trucks. The manufacturers and importers of cars and trucks were responsible for paying this 7% tax on the retail sales prices (based on the manufacturer's list price) or the import price including all related expenses and taxes.

Tax on Interest on and Indexing of Fixed-Term Deposits. This is a 4.2% national tax on interest and indexing of fixed-term deposits by banks and finance companies, which are required to withhold the tax.

Tax on Financial Services. This tax is levied on banks and other authorized financial entities. The tax rate is 6%. The tax basis is the monthly net income according to the financial statements (before income tax) plus amounts accrued in respect of employee compensation and compensation payable to temporary staff, as well as related social security contributions.

COMPUTATION OF TAXABLE INCOME

27. Depreciation and Depletion

Depreciation for tax purposes is normally determined using the straight-line method, at rates varying with the asset classification, and based on their probable useful life. Other depreciation systems may be used provided they are justifiable from a technical point of view. Depletion charges may be computed on the basis of units extracted, in relation to the estimated productive capacity. The Tax Department may also authorize other technically justifiable methods for computing depletion charges.

28. Treatment of Dividends

Dividends in cash or in kind that are paid to nonresident beneficiaries are subject to a 20% income tax withholding. Those distributed in fully paid shares are, however, exempt. Dividends distributed to stockholders who are individuals resident in Argentina are subject to a 10% withholding tax if they identify themselves; otherwise they are subject to a 20% income tax withholding. This withholding tax must also be paid on any dividends not claimed within 90 days of their being placed at the disposal of the stockholders.

Stockholders do not include dividends received in their income tax returns to determine their net taxable income.

29. Loss Carryovers

Net operating losses may be carried forward to offset future years' taxable income. Such operating losses may be adjusted for inflation based on the variation in the wholesale price index between the fiscal year in which they arose and that in which they are used.

For fiscal years in progress on October 11, 1985 and earlier, the availability of loss carryforwards is ten years; thereafter five years, except that under a recent amendment no offset of losses may be recognized in fiscal years ending in 1988 or 1989. For fiscal years ending in 1990, offset is restricted to 50% of the taxable income of that year. In connection with this restriction, the statute of limitations has been lifted for any loss carryforwards that it would otherwise have been possible to use to offset taxable income arising in fiscal years ending in 1988 and 1989.

There is no provision for loss carrybacks.

30. Transactions between Related Parties

Juridical acts made between a "local foreign capital company" and the nonresident individual or foreign company that controls it directly or indirectly are treated for all legal and tax purposes as having been made between two independent parties, provided the terms and consideration involved conform to normal practice for such transactions conducted on an arm's-length basis, subject to the following limitations:

- [ ] Loans. The transaction must not be challenged by the Argentine Central Bank (which has 30 days to do so after being advised of the related details), based on the specific conditions of the operation or the inadequate level of indebtedness of the borrower.
- [ ] Contracts Covered by the Technological Transfer Law. Subject to its rules.

If the conditions for treating transactions between related parties as though they had been conducted on an independent basis are not met, the considerations involved must be treated in accordance with the rules governing capital contributions and profit distributions.

The term "local foreign capital company" signifies a company domiciled in Argentina that is owned by nonresident individuals or foreign companies that directly or indirectly own more than 49% of the local company's capital, or directly or indirectly hold sufficient voting power to prevail at stockholders' or partners' meetings.

Argentine law provides for the tax-free reorganization of corporations, partnerships, and sole proprietorships, accomplished through merger, consolidation, divisive reorganization, or acquisition of assets, provided certain requirements are met.

31. Consolidation of Income

The Argentine tax laws and regulations contain no provisions regarding the preparation of consolidated tax returns. However, the Tax Department holds an interpretation that they are not allowed.

32. Tax Periods

Individuals are required to use the calendar year. For purposes of the income tax and assets tax, corporations, branches, and so on, must use a fiscal period that ties in with their financial reporting date. Once the annual fiscal year-end has been established, the closing date may not be changed without permission from the Tax Department. Other taxes are filed on a calendar-year basis (or on a monthly basis).

33. Other Matters

Determination of Net Income. In general, only income of Argentine source is taxed. For determining the net income subject to tax, the law permits the deduction from gross taxable income of all necessary expenses incurred in order to obtain, maintain, preserve, and collect it, as well as the expenses incurred to maintain and preserve the source that produces the taxable income.

Revaluation of Fixed Assets. Because of inflation, annual revaluations of fixed assets are recognized for purposes relating to the computation of depreciation charges and the adjustment of the carrying value of the assets. Such revaluations are achieved by applying official wholesale price level indices published by the Tax Department to the basic depreciation and carrying value of the assets, computed on the historical cost basis.

Revaluation of Inventories. For tax purposes, inventories must be valued following certain rules. In the case of commercial and industrial entities, the general criterion consists in valuing the closing inventory of each item at the most recent purchase or production price (restated using the inflation index for the intervening period between the month in which such purchase or production took place and the closing month of the fiscal year).

Price-Level Adjustments. These adjustments must be recognized for tax purposes by companies, partnerships, branches of foreign firms, and other types of associations and sole proprietorships. They aim at achieving a more equitable tax basis both for income tax and assets tax purposes, based on the reasoning that under unstable currency conditions it is inequitable to levy taxes on an entity's nominal profits because they are not representative of the real variation in its net worth. The general principle consists in computing the adjustment on the difference between the initial balances of assets exposed to inflation and liabilities, using the factor corresponding to the variation in the wholesale price index over the fiscal year. (There are detailed rules as to the asset and liability items includible and excludible for purposes of the adjustment.)

When the assets subject to adjustment are higher than the corresponding liabilities, the adjustment represents a loss due to inflation and is fully deductible in the fiscal year involved. When the reverse occurs, there is a gain due to inflation. Additional partial inflation adjustments must also be recognized for major changes in underlying assets; for example, capital increases or decreases, dividend distributions, fixed asset acquisitions, and foreign investments.

RELATED CONSIDERATIONS

34. Incentives and Grants

The following individuals and entities are exempt from income tax: diplomatic representatives if reciprocal treatment is given to Argentine diplomats, cooperatives, religious institutions, trade unions, and educational, charitable, and scientific institutions.

The following types of income are exempt: interest on savings accounts with banks and finance companies; income from government securities and gains on their sale; gains arising from the revaluation of receivables (due to exchange variances or pursuant to agreements between the parties, etc.) to the extent that they exceed the losses stemming from similar revaluations of liabilities, but excluding revaluations of trading transactions whose financing term is less than 180 days. These exemptions do not apply to taxpayers recognizing price-level adjustments for tax purposes (see item 33).

In the case of export transactions, the various domestic tax refunds or reimbursements collected by the exporters are exempt from income tax.

Taxpayers who acquire new depreciable movable assets (with the exception of imported motorcars) before October 31, 1992 have the option of depreciating them fully for tax purposes in the year in which they are put into service.

Income tax exemptions and allowances may not be claimed if they would lead indirectly to a transfer of revenue to any foreign taxing authority (except in a few, specific cases).

The entire amount of investments—made either directly or through the purchase of shares, bonds, etc.—for the reclamation of *arid or swampy land for farming use* may also be recognized as an allowance for income tax purposes.

There is an attractive system of incentives covering *investments in afforestation plans* that merit the approval of the National Forestry Institute. It consists basically in the granting of fiscal credits—in the nature of subsidies—that are transferable to third parties and may be used to pay any national taxes, so they are of equal interest to all potential investors, regardless of individual tax brackets or situations. The credits are determined on the basis of a fixed sum per hectare set annually by the Economy Ministry depending on the species of trees planted and the geographical area involved; this amount varies between 20% and 70% of the updated afforestation costs estimated by the Institute, without taking into consideration the actual cost incurred by each producer. Credits take the form of certificates issued and delivered to the recipients by the Institute based on their fulfillment of the afforestation plans, and their face value is adjustable for inflation based on the wholesale price index. Amounts received in respect of these fiscal credits are exempt from all national taxes and are not subject to any expense apportionment for these fiscal credits. The same law provides for the updating of the plantation costs deductible for income tax purposes upon sale of the timber, based on the wholesale price index.

There are various industrial development incentives for new investments in certain industries, such as steel mills, petrochemicals, cellulose and paper, wine, cold storage, and mining, as well as firms engaging in international tenders, and industries located in certain geographic areas, such as the provinces of Tucuman, San Juan, Catamarca, La Rioja, San Luis, the North-Western and North-Eastern provinces and Patagonia. These incentives vary according to the industry and region involved, but in general include varying reductions in income tax, assets tax, and VAT, exemption from stamp duty and relief from customs duty on fixed assets and spare parts imported, for varying periods of time.

Other Incentives. A 1981 law provides for *exemption from income tax* for 10 years for persons or companies domiciled in continental *Patagonia* (this includes most of the provinces of Rio Negro, Neuquen, Chubut and Santa Cruz, except for the fertile valley areas). This exemption does not apply to certain lines of business, such as banks, oil, mining, public works contractors, insurance companies, and aluminium producers. Tierra del Fuego enjoys exemption from income tax, assets tax, excise tax, and VAT, as well as significant customs benefits.

Emergency Curtailments of a Temporary Nature. Law 23,697, enacted September 1989, The Economic Emergency Law, suspended all subsidies and grants existing on that date for 180 days (renewed for a further 180-day period). In the case of the industrial and mining promotion regulations, all benefits granted under existing regulations in force were subjected to a 50% suspension. Therefore, from October 1, 1989 until September 30, 1990, the investees enjoying promotional benefits had to pay 50% of the VAT for which they previously enjoyed a waiver under the promotional regulations. As regards income tax and capital tax (or tax on assets), the suspensions of promotional benefits cover 25% of the taxes for the next two fiscal closings after September 1989. Nevertheless, the taxes thus paid will lead to a credit in the investor's or investee's favor, against the State, to be settled through the issuance of fiscal credit bonds, which the parties concerned may subsequently use for paying taxes or duty, or endorse over to suppliers once the economic emergency is over.

The Economic Emergency Law also has suspended the approval of new promotional projects.

35. Exchange Controls

In December 1989, the Argentine Government lifted all exchange controls and adopted a single foreign exchange market, on which the rate fluctuates according to supply and demand. Previously, differential rates were in existence, as well as exchange controls, with frequent changes in the related regulations. There is a forward exchange market.

Effecive April 1, 1991, the National Government passed a law (No. 23928) declaring the convertibility of the austral at a rate of Å 10,000 equals US$ 1. In this connection, the Argentine Central Bank has undertaken to maintain backing for the currency, to be held in gold and freely available devisen.

Private individuals may freely hold foreign currency, keep accounts in foreign currency with local banks, collect interest in foreign currency, etc.

36. Investment Restrictions on Nonresidents

The rules covering foreign investment are contained in the Foreign Investment Law of 1976 (Law 21,382), which has been significantly amended to simplify and speed up the formalities connected with the registration of these investments.

The principal foreign investment regulations are summarized as follows:

- [ ] There is no legal obligation to register foreign investments.
- [ ] All foreign capital investments should be registered with the Foreign Investments Under-Secretariat, which reports to the Economy Ministry, in order that the foreign currency amount of each investment can be recognized as entitled to repatriation, even in the event of the existence of exchange controls.
- [ ] Foreign investments, in general, are entitled to the same rights and subject to the same obligations as national investments.
- [ ] Transitory contributions of foreign capital connected with the performance of leasing, construction, service, or other contracts spanning less than five years are subject to the applicable contractual and general legal provisions, rather than to the foreign investment regulations, although the investors may elect treatment under this law.
- [ ] Regardless of the amount of foreign capital invested or the industry sector in which it is made, the investment may be made without application to the National Executive Power or the Foreign Investments Under-Secretariat for any prior approval, even if the investment leads to the denationalization of the investee, notwithstanding the regulations that apply under laws governing the specific activity toward which the investment is destined.
- [ ] The formalities for registering foreign investments are simple, as it is sufficient to submit a letter to the competent authority informing it of the details relating to the foreign investor and the local investee, the amount of the investment, the activities to be conducted, and the currency in which the investment has been made, without having to submit any additional documentation.
- [ ] If the foreign capital investment is effected through debt for equity swaps or the conversion of debentures, debt securities, negotiable instruments, or other debt obligations incurred by companies, for purposes of the investment registration, the payment and transfer should be permitted under the Argentine Central Bank exchange regulations.
- [ ] Foreign investors may remit the profits or dividends arising from their registered investments in Argentine (based on inflation-adjusted financial statements), subject to payment of the applicable income tax withholding. No further tax applies due to the fact that the remittance stems from a registered foreign capital investment.
- [ ] Foreign investors may repatriate the foreign currency amount of their invested capital at any time after three years have elapsed since the investment, unless a longer term has been set in the investment contract.

Foreign investors may use any of the legal forms of organization envisaged by Argentine law.

Local foreign capital companies may make use of short-, medium-, and long-term domestic credit facilities granted by local financial organizations, under conditions similar to those applicable to local national capital companies.

SELECTION OF BUSINESS ENTITY BY NONRESIDENTS

On the whole, foreign investors setting up operations in Argentina tend to favor S.A. or branch operations. The choice depends largely on the size of the contemplated investment. The statutory reporting requirements and controls imposed on the S.A. (corporation) make that form more expensive and complicated but, on the other hand, smooth branch operations depend largely on the confidence placed in the appointed manager and deputy manager.

SPECIMEN TAX COMPUTATION

	₳	₳

Fiscal Year Ended June 30, 1991
Computation:

	₳	₳
Net profit before income tax (as determined for historical accounting purposes)		4,600,000
Add		
Provision for contingencies at year-end	250,000	
Royalties not yet paid to an affiliated company at filing date	1,650,000	
Revaluation of inventories at year-end	1,500,000	3,400,000
		8,000,000
Less		
Tax purpose adjustment for inflation*	987,000	
Adjustment for fixed asset depreciation	250,000	
Provision for contingencies at beginning of year	30,000	
Revaluation of inventories at beginning of year	200,000	

Foreign-source income (exchange gain plus interest)	1,780,000	3,247,000
Taxable net income		4,753,000
Corporate income tax (at 20%)		950,000

Notes: Inflation between June 30, 1990 and June 30, 1991, was 118%; between October 31, 1990 and June 30, 1991, it was 60%; and between January 31, 1991 and June 30, 1991, it was 43%. Cash dividends approved and paid on October 31, 1990: Å 250,000. Fixed asset purchased on January 31, 1991: Å 100,000.
(*) The adjustment for inflation is calculated as follows:

	Å	Å
Total assets at beginning of year (July 1, 1990)		2,210,000
Less: Assets not entering into the calculation		
Net book value of fixed assets	500,000	
Bank deposits abroad (as they generate foreign-source income)	510,000	1,010,000
		1,200,000
Plus: Adjustment of asset valuation		
Revaluation of inventories		200,000
Assets subject to inflation adjustment		1,400,000
Less: Total liabilities at beginning of year	430,000	
Provision for contingencies	(30,000)	400,000
Net worth subject to inflation adjustment		1,000,000
Principal inflation adjustment: loss Å 1,000,000 × 118%	1,180,000	
Additional inflation adjustments: profit		
—On dividends: Å 250,000 × 60% = 150,000		
—On purchases of fixed assets: Å 100,000 × 43% = 43,000	193,000	
Total inflation adjustment: loss	987,000	

AUSTRALIA

INCOME TAXES ON CORPORATIONS

1. Rates

The rate of tax applicable to the taxable income of corporations is 39%.

The taxable income of a resident corporation includes foreign-source income (however, see item 5) and net capital gains (see item 3).

2. Local Income Taxes

None.

3. Capital Gains Taxes

A general capital gains system applies to assets acquired on or after September 20, 1985. Under the system, capital gains and losses are recognized when assets are disposed or deemed to be disposed (whether by sale, gift, grant of an interest, etc.) Corporations ceasing to be residents of Australia are deemed to dispose of certain assets at that time (individuals may defer the time of disposal by lodging an election with the tax authorities). Capital gains are calculated after allowing for inflation (i.e., the cost base of the asset is increased by reference to increases in the consumer price index), but capital losses are calculated without any such indexing. Any net capital gain for the year (being the aggregate of capital gains less allowable capital losses) is included in the taxpayer's income for income tax purposes and, in the case of corporations, is taxed at regular rates. Any net capital loss for the year is carried forward to offset future capital gains, or may be transferred by a resident corporation to another resident corporation within the same wholly owned corporate group (but subject to certain restrictions).

4. Branch Profits Taxes

The taxable income of a nonresident corporation is subject to the same rate of income tax as is applicable to resident corporations. However, also see items 15, 17, 18, and 28.

5. Foreign Tax Reliefs

Except for certain salary and wage income and certain dividend and branch income (see below), foreign-source income derived by resident corporations and individuals is included in taxable income and is liable to Australian income tax.

Credits are allowed against Australian tax for the foreign tax paid by an Australian resident on foreign-source income. Generally, foreign-source income is aggregated on a worldwide basis into four separate classes, namely: certain foreign interest income, passive income (dividends, rent), offshore banking income, and other foreign-source income. Where expenses and other deductions relating to a class of foreign-source income from activities carried on by the taxpayer exceed the amount of income, the excess (i.e., the loss) cannot offset foreign-source income of another class but is "quarantined." Credits are separately calculated on the basis of three classes of income: passive income, certain offshore banking income, and other foreign-source income. In each case, the credit allowed for foreign taxes paid will not exceed the amount of Australian tax payable with respect to that foreign income. Excess credits can be carried forward for up to five years but cannot be carried back. Excess credits also are transferable between resident corporations within the same wholly owned corporate group, subject to various restrictions.

In some circumstances where interest income is recharacterized and remitted to Australia as dividends, the dividends are treated as interest income for foreign tax credit purposes.

An Australian resident corporation receiving assessable dividends from overseas subsidiaries is allowed credits for underlying foreign company tax on the profits from which the dividends are paid, as well as for foreign withholding tax imposed on the dividends. The credit for underlying tax is allowed for unlimited tiers of subsidiary companies, provided that each company has a 10% controlling interest in the company immediately below it and the Australian parent has a direct or indirect interest of at least 5% in the voting shares of each company. Rules identify the profits from which a dividend will be treated as paid.

Salary and wages earned overseas by an Australian resident and subject to tax in the country of source are fully exempt from Australian income tax where derived in performing services overseas for a continuous period of at least three months. Tax on other nonexempt income is calculated by applying a notional average rate of tax payable on the sum of exempt income and nonexempt income.

"Tax sparing" relief (i.e., the granting of credits for taxes foregone by the foreign country) may be provided under a tax treaty between Australia and the country concerned or granted under regulations on a country-by-country basis.

Effective the 1990–1991 year, Australia has a system of taxing certain income of controlled foreign corporations (CFCs) on an accruals basis. The main features of the system are as follows:

☐ Dividends received by Australian corporations from non-portfolio investments (i.e., those involving voting interests of at least 10%) from corporations resident in "listed" (comparable tax) countries are exempt from Australian corporate tax. Dividends received by Australian corporations from non-portfolio investments in corporations resident in "unlisted" (low-tax) countries also may be exempt to the extent that the dividends are paid from profits that, in broad terms, have borne tax in Australia or a listed country.

☐ If a resident corporation has a branch in a "listed" (comparable tax) country, the income (including certain types of capital gains) of the branch is exempt from Australian corporate tax—with the exception of income that is not taxed in a listed country or income that benefits from certain overseas tax concessions (e.g., non-taxation of capital gains or concessionary rates of tax on income such as interest, royalties, or shipping profits).

☐ Certain income of CFCs and nonresident trusts is subject to "accruals taxation," i.e., attributed to Australian shareholders and taxed in their hands at the time it is derived by the overseas-resident corporation or trust. A nonresident corporation is a CFC if five or fewer resident shareholders together with their associates own or can acquire or control an interest (whether direct or indirect) of 50% or more in the corporation or can effectively control the corporation by whatever means. The categories of income of a CFC that would be attributed would vary depending on whether the CFC is resident in a listed or unlisted country and whether any income is excluded by reason of the active income test or other criteria. Affected income generally will be attributed to those Australian residents who, with associates, have a 10% or more interest (direct or indirect) in the CFC or effective control of the CFC. Different rules apply in attributing certain income of nonresident trusts to Australian residents who have directly or indirectly transferred value to the trusts. Relief is available for any foreign tax relating to attributed income.

☐ An exemption applies for certain dividends from investments in nonresident corporations where the income of the nonresident corporation has already been attributed to resident shareholders under the accruals taxation system (see above).

6. Classification of Corporations

Corporations are classified for Australian tax purposes in two ways: (1) as a resident or nonresident corporation, and (2) as a public or private corporation. A resident corporation is one that is incorporated in Australia, or carries on business in Australia and has either:

☐ Its central management and control in Australia.
☐ Its voting power controlled by shareholders who are residents of Australia.

The distinction between resident and nonresident corporations is important for a variety of reasons. Australian residents are subject to tax on their worldwide income and worldwide capital gains, whereas nonresidents are only subject to tax on their Australian-source income and their capital gains on certain Australian-related assets (see item 5 for certain exceptions). The distinction also affects the treatment of dividend income and liability to Australian tax on capital gains from dispositions of stock in corporations held by nonresident shareholders (see items 1, 4, 15, and 16).

Both resident and nonresident corporations are divided into public and private corporations. Broadly, public corporations are those whose shares are listed on a stock exchange anywhere in the world or are subsidiaries of listed corporations, providing 75% of the paid-up capital, voting power, and dividend rights are held by more than 20 persons throughout the year. All other corporations are private.

Private corporations are subject to anti-avoidance provisions concerning payments and loans to shareholders, directors, and associates of shareholders and directors. Furthermore, a private corporation may not be entitled to the intercompany dividend rebate in respect to the unfranked portion of dividends paid to the corporation on or after May 26, 1988 (see item 28).

7. Payment of Tax

Tax collection arrangements for corporations consist of a single installment of tax, due from most corporations by the twenty-eighth day of the first month after the end of the financial year (i.e., by July 28 in the case of a June year-end company), equal to 85% of the tax paid for the previous year or the taxpayer's estimate of actual tax liability for 1990–1991. The balance of tax owing will be due from most corporations by the fifteenth day of the ninth month following the end of the financial year (i.e., by March 15 in the case of a June year-end company). Corporations with a substituted accounting period in lieu of the following June 30 will be required to pay the single (85%) installment by the twenty-eighth day of the first month after the end of the substituted accounting period (but the due day will not be earlier than January 28) and the balance by the fifteenth day of the ninth month following the end of the substituted accounting period (but the due date will not be earlier than September 15).

INCOME TAXES ON INDIVIDUALS

9. Rates

Income tax rates on total income, including dividends, of a resident individual for the year ending June 30, 1992 are generally as follows:

Taxable Income		Tax on	Percentage
Over	Not Over	Lower Amount	on Excess
A$ 5,400	A$20,700	A$ 0	20%
20,700	36,000	3,060	38
36,000	50,000	8,874	46
50,000		15,314	47

The rates mentioned above do not apply where a resident has any net capital gain (see item 3). Instead, a single rate of tax is calculated and is applied to each dollar of taxable income (including the net capital gain). This rate is calculated to generate a total tax liability equivalent to that obtained by:

☐ Applying the ordinary tax rate to the "reduced" income (i.e., all taxable income other than the net capital gain); and

☐ Adding five times the additional tax that would arise at the ordinary rates if one-fifth of the net capital gain were added to that reduced income.

Modified tax rates also apply in the case of farmers and other primary producers, artists, composers, inventors, performers, and production associates and children under 18 on the last day of the year of income.

For income tax rates applicable to individuals who are nonresidents throughout the year, see item 16.

Residents are entitled to an imputation rebate in respect of the franked portion of dividends received from resident corporations (see item 28). In addition, there are some minor rebates. If taxable income exceeds specified thresholds, residents are required to pay a levy of 1.25% of taxable income to fund the government health insurance scheme ("Medicare"). For the year ended June 30, 1992, the income threshold before application of the Medicare levy will be A$11,745 for single persons and A$19,674 for married couples and sole parents (A$2,100 is added to the threshold for each dependent child or student).

Salaries and wages are subject to tax deductions at source. Every person who earns in excess of A$1,000 from other than salary and wages must pay provisional tax. Provisional tax for 1991–1992 will generally be payable in a lump sum on March 31, 1992 or on the issuance of a notice of assessment, whichever is later. However, certain taxpayers will be required to pay provisional tax by quarterly installments.

An additional system of deducting tax at source (the prescribed payments system) operates whereby persons making payments for building or construction industry work, road transport, motor vehicle repair, cleaning, joinery or cabinetmaking, or architectural, surveying, engineering, or other professional building services will in some situations be required to report such payments monthly to the tax authorities and to deduct tax at a flat rate unless an exemption or rate variation certificate is held by the payee. In the main, these requirements apply only where the payer is in the same industry as the payee; however, persons paying for construction-related work associated with projects costing over A$10,000 and persons paying for road transport where the arrangement involves the regular daily exclusive use of the payee's vehicle will have responsibilities under the system even though the payer is not engaged in those industries. Tax deducted is credited against the final income tax liability of the payee.

10. Local Income Taxes

None.

11. Capital Gains Taxes

See item 3.

12. Foreign Tax Reliefs

See item 5.

13. Tax Period

June 30 is the standard tax year-end. It is unusual for an individual to obtain permission to adopt a different year-end.

INCOME TAXES ON NONRESIDENTS

15. Liability to Tax

In general, any income derived by a nonresident from sources in Australia is subject to Australian income tax or withholding tax (see items 17 and 18) but subject to certain exemptions and the terms of any applicable tax treaty.

A foreign entity that is a resident of a country with which Australia has a tax treaty (see item 17) will be subject to Australian income tax on trading income only if it has a permanent establishment in Australia. Except for New Zealand, a foreign entity that has a permanent establishment in Australia will be taxed only on those profits sourced in Australia and attributable to the permanent establishment. In the case of New Zealand, Australian income tax will be imposed on all of the entity's Australian-source profits, whether or not attributable to the permanent establishment. An entity that is resident in a nontreaty country will pay Australian income tax on all its Australian-source income.

Trustees who distribute Australian-source income of a trust to a nonresident beneficiary (other than dividends and interest subject to withholding tax) are assessable on that income and will normally retain sufficient funds to meet the assessment. If the nonresident beneficiary lodges an Australian tax return, credit will be given for the tax paid by the trustee.

Any net capital gains accruing to a nonresident on the disposition of ''taxable Australian assets'' are subject to Australian tax under the capital gains system (see item 3) unless exempted under the terms of a relevant tax treaty. Taxable Australian assets include such items as land and buildings in Australia, any assets that have been used by the nonresident in carrying on business through a permanent establishment in Australia, an interest in a resident trust, and shares in resident private corporations. Shares in resident public corporations do not represent taxable Australian assets unless the nonresident and/or associates hold at least 10% of certain issued share capital of the corporation at some time within the five-year period preceding disposition of the shares.

16. Rates

Nonresident corporations are taxed on their Australian-source income at the rate of 39% (note exceptions in items 17, 18, and 28).

The Australian-source income of a nonresident individual is not taxed at the same rates that apply to a resident. Where the income of a nonresident individual does not include any net capital gain from taxable Australian assets (see item 15), the income tax rates applicable to Australian-source income (other than income discussed in items 17 and 18) for the year ended June 30, 1992 are:

Taxable Income		Tax on Lower Amount	Percentage on Excess
Over	Not Over		
A$ 0	A$20,700	A$ 0	29%
20,700	36,000	6,003	38
36,000	50,000	11,817	46
50,000		18,257	47

The tax rates set out above are modified (see item 9) where the income of a nonresident individual includes any net capital gain from taxable Australian assets, and in the case of nonresidents under the age of 18.

17. Withholding Tax Rates

Listed below are the withholding rates that generally apply to dividends, interest, and royalties. Variations from this general regime are:

☐ Franked dividends. To the extent that dividends paid to a nonresident have been franked by tax paid at the corporate level (refer to item 28), the dividends are not subject to Australian income tax (i.e., neither regular rates nor withholding tax).

☐ Unfranked dividends. The unfranked portion (if any) of a dividend paid to a nonresident is subject to withholding tax. The withholding tax rate is generally 30% where the dividend income does not fall within the Dividend Article of an applicable tax treaty (e.g., where the dividend income is effectively connected with a nonresident's permanent establishment in Australia or where there is no applicable treaty).

☐ Interest and royalties. Interest and royalty income effectively connected with a nonresident's permanent establishment in Australia will be taxed at the income tax rates noted in item 16.

☐ Other exemptions apply which are too numerous to list in detail. The specific treaty should be reviewed in each case.

Withholding Tax on Outward Remittances

	Unfranked Dividends	Interest	Royalties (1)
Nontreaty countries	30% (2)	10%	(3)
Treaty countries:			
Austria	15	10	10%
Belgium	15	10	10
Canada	15	10 (4)	10
China	15	10	10
Denmark	15	10	10
Fiji	20	10	15
Finland	15	10	10
France	15	10	10
Germany (5)	15	10	10
Greece	*	*	*
Hungary (6)	15	10	10
India (6)	15	10 (4)	10 (7)
Ireland	15	10	10
Israel	*	*	*
Italy	15	10	10
Japan	15	10	10
Kiribati	20	10	15
Korea	15	10 (4)	15
Malaysia	15	10 (4)	15
Malta	15	10 (4)	10
Netherlands	15	10	10
New Zealand	15	10	15
Norway	15	10	10
Papua New Guinea	15	10	10
Philippines	15/25	10 (4)	25
Poland (6)	15	10	10
Singapore	15	10	10 (8)
Spain	*	*	*
Sri Lanka (6)	15	10	10
Sweden	15	10	10
Switzerland	15	10	10
Thailand	15/20	10 (4)	15
Yugoslavia	*	*	*
United Kingdom	15	10	10
United States	15	10	10

* These treaties are under negotiation, and no information is currently available.

Notes:

(1) The rates do not apply to "natural resource" royalties, which are taxed at standard rates.

(2) In the case of Papua New Guinea, the withholding tax on unfranked dividends is 15%.

(3) Taxed as normal income, no special withholding tax rate applies.

(4) Although the maximum withholding tax rate on interest is greater than 10%, the 10% rate generally is used as the appropriate rate in respect of interest paid to a nonresident by an Australian resident.

(5) This treaty is the subject of renegotiation.

(6) As of September 1, 1991, these treaties have not yet entered force.

(7) Depending on the category of royalty, this may increase to 20%.

(8) The special rate of 10% does not apply to "natural resource" and "cultural" type royalties, which are taxed at standard rates.

18. Special Withholding Provisions

Although interest paid to overseas lenders is normally subject to withholding tax of 10%, there are some exceptions including:

☐ Interest payments on overseas borrowings by a State government (or a Federal or State government authority) where the loan funds were contracted for prior to July 1, 1986 and were not used in direct competition with the private sector.

☐ Interest on public (or widely spread) securities issued overseas by a resident corporation, where a certificate is obtained by the corporation from the Australian tax authorities. This exemption is available also for interest on widely spread securities issued overseas (under contractual obligations entered into on or after July 2, 1986) by State governments or Federal or State government authorities, where a certificate is obtained.

☐ Pure offshore banking. Interest paid on offshore borrowings of a person who has been declared by the Treasurer to be an offshore banking unit is exempt from interest withholding tax where the deposits accepted or borrowings are lent only to nonresidents.

☐ Interest on certain borrowings under contractual obligations entered into prior to May 20, 1983 may qualify for exemption from interest withholding tax under the previous "Australian entity" exemption provisions. (However, additional restrictions have been imposed effective July 1, 1986).

In addition to ordinary interest, certain other amounts are treated as interest for withholding tax purposes:

☐ Amounts paid on the purchase or redemption of certain discounted or deferred interest securities, DINGO bonds, etc.

□ Amounts paid to the nonresident acceptor of a bill of exchange (or issuer of a promissory note) to compensate that person for an amount payable on presentation of the bill or note.

□ Payments under hire purchase, or similar agreements made with nonresidents for the use of property.

In the case of a trustee distributing Australian source-trust income to a nonresident, see item 15.

Special provisions govern the taxation of income received by nonresidents from:

□ Shipping. Taxed at the applicate rate (e.g., for corporations, see item 1) on 5% of the amounts received for carrying passengers, goods, etc.

□ Insurance. Taxed at the applicable rate (e.g., for corporations see item 1) on 10% of gross premium income.

□ Film and video tape royalties. Taxed at 10% of gross royalties.

Australia has a treaty with Greece covering only international air transport.

OTHER SIGNIFICANT TAXES

21. Sales (Value Added)

Sales tax is imposed on all goods which are manufactured in, or imported into, Australia for use or consumption in Australia unless specifically exempted. The tax is a single stage tax which is designed to fall on sales by manufacturers or wholesalers to retailers. Sales tax is payable on "sale value," which is the equivalent of a fair wholesale price. The liability to account for sales tax falls principally on three classes of persons: manufacturers, wholesalers, and importers. In addition, retailers who sell goods under indirect marketing arrangements (i.e., through agents or from another person's retail premises) are liable for sales tax. Persons who make royalty payments may be liable for sales tax if the royalties relate to goods. Persons involved in installing inground swimming pools can be liable for the tax.

Goods are subject to sales tax at the rate of 10%, 20%, or 30% unless they are exempt. The following is a list of typical goods falling into these categories:

Goods	Category
Most food, clothing, books, magazines and newspapers, building materials, medicine, agricultural and mining equipment, aids to manufacture, and exported goods	Exempt
Household goods and appliances, confectionery, and certain non-alcoholic beverages and cordials	10%
General rate applying to goods which are neither exempt nor taxable at 10%, or 30%, including nonluxury motor vehicles,	

office equipment and stationery, soft drinks, most beers, alcoholic wine, spirits, toys, sporting goods, cleaning products, pet food, video and sound tapes and records	20%
Jewelry, furs, watches, clocks, electronic home entertainment equipment: such as televisions, record players, radios, and certain luxury motor vehicles	30%

Sales tax paid on goods used in a business forms part of the cost of those goods. Thus, in relation to revenue items it becomes an allowable deduction for income tax purposes or, in the case of plant, forms part of the amount subject to depreciation. (However, most plant and equipment used in manufacturing activities is exempt from sales tax being "aids to manufacture.")

22. Inheritance and Gift Taxes

None. However, a lifetime gift of property may represent capital gain to the donor where the property has increased in value while in the hands of the donor. Capital gains are not generally treated as arising on death (except where property other than money passes to a tax-exempt institution such as a charity, church, etc.). However, a capital gain may be recognized if assets are sold by the executor or beneficiaries.

23. Taxes on Payrolls (Social Security)

The Australian social security system provides a wide range of pension, unemployment, and other benefits. As these are funded from consolidated revenue, neither employers nor employees are required to make separate contributions.

Each state or territory imposes a payroll tax of up to 7% on salaries and wages paid. Various exemption thresholds apply from state to state (ranging from A$300,000 to A$500,000), and full rates phase in as payrolls increase beyond these thresholds. Groups of businesses are entitled to only one exemption threshold for the group.

24. Taxes on Natural Resources

A resources rent tax is imposed on oil and gas produced from certain offshore fields. Oil subject to the tax is not subject to excise duty.

Each state imposes a tax in the form of a rental or royalty on mineral and oil leases whether for exploration or development and extraction.

25. Other Taxes

Land and Property. Each state and municipality imposes an annual tax based on the value of land owned.

Stamp Duty. Each state and territory imposes duties, usually ad valorem, on transfers of property, particularly real estate. Duties also are imposed on certain transactions (e.g., insurance, hiring arrangements, and leases).

Financial Transaction Duties.   All states and territories impose a tax on the receipts of financial institutions and debits made to certain bank accounts.

Customs and Excise.   The federal government imposes excise duties on a narrow range of products, including oil, petroleum products, beer, spirits, and tobacco.

Australia has adopted many international customs agreements, including those relating to valuation, anti-dumping, and tariff classification. The customs tariff is comparatively protectionist by international standards, although a gradual program of tariff reduction has begun. By 1996, most goods will be subject to rates of 5%. Motor vehicle tariff rates will phase down to 15% by the year 2000.

Exceptions to these rates are: textiles, clothing, and footwear, which will remain subject to quantitative restrictions (quotas) until March 1993. Customs duty rates applying to these goods, which can exceed 100%, will then phase down so that by the year 2000 they will be at levels of 10%, 15%, or 25%, depending on the goods involved.

Fringe Benefits Tax.   A separate federal tax is imposed on all employers, whether resident or nonresident (except public benevolent institutions), with respect to the total taxable values of specified fringe benefits provided to employees (or associates), including employer-provided cars, free or low interest loans, residential accommodations, expenses paid on behalf of employees, and goods and services provided by employers. The tax applies to benefits provided in relation to employees who are residents of Australia (except where the relevant salary or wages of the employee is exempt from Australian income tax) and to nonresident employees whose salary or wages from the employment has an Australian source.

The rate of tax on the aggregate taxable value of benefits is 47% for the year ending March 31, 1992. The rate will increase to 48.25% effective April 1, 1992.

Fringe benefits tax is self-assessed, without need for any notice of assessment from the taxation authorities. Each employer must calculate the amount of tax which is due and pay that amount and file a return no later than the 28th day following the end of the fringe benefits tax year (i.e., by April 28). Quarterly installments are payable in most cases during the course of the year.

COMPUTATION OF TAXABLE INCOME

26. Capital Gains

See item 3.

27. Depreciation and Depletion

Plant.   For plant acquired under a contract entered into after May 25, 1988, the rates of depreciation are based on the estimated lives of the assets increased, in most cases, by a loading of 20%. Depreciation may be calculated by either the straight-line or reducing-balance methods. Reducing-balance rates are automatically 50% higher than straight-line rates. Plant purchased by the taxpayer between July 19, 1982 and May 25, 1988 is usually eligible for write-off over three or five years.

Effective July 1, 1991, it is proposed that taxpayers be given the option of accounting for depreciation on the basis of pools of items of plant subject to the same depreciation rate. The pool would be treated as a single item of plant and depreciated accordingly using the reducing-balance method.

The Government also has indicated that it proposes to introduce legislation allowing an immediate deduction for expenditure on items of depreciable plant acquired on or after July 1, 1991 if the value of the item of plant does not exceed $300 or the estimated effective life of the item is less than three years.

Buildings. Depreciation is allowable on the following buildings:

☐ Income-Producing Nonresidential Buildings. The cost of construction work commenced between July 19, 1982 and August 21, 1984 on constructing, extending, or altering most income-producing, nonresidential buildings qualifies for a 2.5% per annum prime cost deduction to either the owner, lessee, or a successor-in-title. For construction commenced after August 21, 1984, the allowable deduction is 4% per annum. For construction commenced after September 15, 1987, the allowable deduction will generally be 2.5% per annum.

☐ Income-Producing Residential Buildings. The cost of construction work commenced after July 17, 1985 on constructing, extending, or altering most income-producing residential buildings qualifies for an annual 4% prime cost deduction. For construction commenced after September 15, 1987, the allowable deduction will generally be 2.5% per annum.

☐ Traveller Accommodations. Construction expenditures on qualifying traveller accommodations qualify for a 2.5% per annum deduction if construction commenced between August 22, 1979, and August 21, 1984. Where construction commenced after August 21, 1984, the allowable deduction is 4% per annum. For construction commenced after September 15, 1987, the allowable deduction will generally be 2.5% per annum.

☐ Buildings Used in Mining. These buildings may attract special tax write-offs.

Mining. Generally, expenditures incurred in prospecting, exploring, developing, and operating a mine or oil or gas well, whether of a capital nature or otherwise, are deductible. Under current rules, capital costs incurred in developing or operating the mine will be deductible over the life of the mine or on a 10% straight-line basis, whichever gives the greater deductions. Most plant acquired under contracts entered into after May 25, 1988 cannot be written off as mining expenditure but instead is depreciated (see "plant" above). Capital costs incurred in the past may be deductible on a different basis. Subject to some restrictions, exploration and prospecting costs (including the cost of plant) are deductible in full in the year incurred. Excess expenditures may be carried forward indefinitely until recouped. Mineral transport costs (i.e., the capital costs of installing a railway, road, pipeline, or other facility) are deductible in 10 equal annual amounts or, at the election of the taxpayer, over 20 years.

Research and Development Expense. The cost of plant and equipment used exclusively for scientific research is deductible over three years. Most other scientific research expenditures are deductible in full in the year incurred. Tax incentives for industrial research and development are outlined in item 34.

Patent Amortization and Licensing Costs. Costs of research and development leading to a patented invention or design, and the cost of purchased patents may qualify for the tax incentives for research and development outlined in item 34. Otherwise, if the patent is registered in Australia, the costs may be written off over the life of the patent (normally 16 years). The legal fees or similar costs of obtaining a patent are deductible in full.

28. Treatment of Dividends

An imputation system applies to most dividends paid by resident corporations. Prior to payment of a dividend, corporations must determine the proportion of the dividend that is to be franked (i.e., carry a credit for Australian tax paid at the corporate level). Shareholders must be notified of the franked amount of dividend and the amount of imputed credit for corporate taxes paid.

Resident corporations must include in their assessable income the amount of all dividends received. Resident public corporations (see item 6) generally receive a rebate of tax in respect of dividends received from other resident corporations so that, effectively, no tax is paid on local dividend income whether those dividends are franked or not. However, special rules apply to life insurance funds. Resident private corporations receiving local dividends paid after May 25, 1988 by a company not within the same wholly owned group are generally entitled to a rebate of tax only in respect of the franked amount of those dividends. Resident corporations are not required to include in assessable income the imputed credit attached to franked dividends received. However, the franked amount of dividends received is taken into account in determining the ability of the corporation to frank the dividends that it pays to its own shareholders.

Resident individuals must include in their assessable income all dividends received and also, in the case of franked dividends, the imputed credit attached to those dividends. Resident individuals are entitled to a rebate of tax equal to the imputed credit attached to franked dividends received.

Dividends paid by resident corporations are not included in the assessable income of a nonresident, whether or not the nonresident has a permanent establishment in Australia. However, the unfranked portion (if any) of a dividend paid to a nonresident is subject to withholding tax (refer to item 17).

29. Loss Carryovers

The seven-year loss carryforward restriction (which previously has applied to most tax losses other than primary production losses) has been removed in respect of tax losses incurred in 1989–1990 and subsequent income years. Unlimited carryforward will apply to such losses. However, tax losses may not be carried back. In the case of corporations, there must be a continuity of ownership or continuity of business in order to obtain a deduction for the past year's losses or losses incurred in any part of the current year. Certain capital mining expenditures and exploration expenditures (see item 27) may be carried forward indefinitely.

Foreign-source losses are quarantined according to the class of the income (see item 5).

Within a corporate group, each company is assessed income tax separately from any other company in the group. However, domestic losses incurred in 1984–1985 and subsequent years can be transferred between two resident companies where one company entirely owns the other or both are wholly owned by some other company. The group/company relationship must be satisfied throughout the year the loss was incurred, the year of transfer, and any years between.

The amount of the loss transferred cannot exceed the sum of the taxable income and certain net exempt income of the recipient company and to effect the loss transfer, a joint election must be lodged with the tax authorities by the time of lodgment of the tax return of the transferee company.

Separate elections are available (where the group company relationship has been satisfied) to transfer a net capital loss (see item 3) or excess foreign tax credits (see item 5) from one resident company to another resident company within the same wholly owned group. Various amendments have been made to the capital loss transfer provisions, which impose a restriction on the amount of capital losses that can be transferred after August 15, 1989.

Mining and Petroleum Corporations.   General mining and petroleum companies are allowed an annual election to have excess deductions from exploration and development expenditures actually incurred in 1985–1986 and subsequent income years transferred within the ordinary group loss provisions described in the preceding paragraphs.

30. Transactions between Related Parties

The various double-tax treaties contain provisions under which transactions between related parties may be adjusted to the price that would have prevailed on an arm's-length basis. Australian legislation has complementary provisions dealing with transfer pricing and other tax avoidance arrangements.

31. Consolidation of Income

There is no provision for the filing of consolidated tax returns by related corporations or individuals. However, subject to various restrictions, tax losses, capital losses, and excess foreign tax credits may be transferred between resident companies under 100% common ownership (see item 29).

32. Tax Periods

Generally, June 30 is the mandatory year-end for all taxpayers (both individual and corporate). In limited circumstances where reasonable cause can be shown, the tax authorities may allow the adoption of an alternate date.

Where a corporation is granted approval by the tax authorities to adopt a regular year-end other than June 30 that consent will specify whether that alternative accounting period is to substitute for the income year ending on the June 30 following the balance date or the income year ending on the June 30 preceding the balance date. Where a corporation is granted a substituted accounting period, the general result is that income earned in that accounting period is treated for income tax purposes as if it were earned in the income year for which it substitutes.

33. Other Matters

Deductions for Taxes Other than Income Taxes.   In computing the liability for income tax, businesses may deduct payroll tax, land, and property taxes, and natural resources royalties and rentals, but not fringe benefits tax (see item 25). Sales tax and stamp duty are treated as part of the cost of the goods acquired.

Inventory Valuation.   For tax purposes, inventories may be valued at cost, market selling value, or replacement price. At the election of the taxpayer, a different valuation method may be used for different items of the same class of inventory. Under circumstances such as obsolescence, values below the permitted three may be used if deemed reasonable by the Commissioner.

Average cost or FIFO is generally used to determine cost. Other methods are available, but the LIFO method is not permitted unless it approximates actual physical flows. Absorption costing rather than direct costing must be used to determine cost.

Interest on Amounts Owing to Foreign Investors.   Tax deductions are restricted for interest expenses relating to thinly capitalized foreign investment in Australia. This restriction is effective from July 1, 1987, but limited deferrals apply for some pre-existing arrangements.

The debt taken into account is the aggregate of interest-bearing amounts owed by an Australian company or business enterprise (including branch offices, partnerships, trusts, and investments in Australia by individuals) to foreign investors or their nonresident associates, including back-to-back loans through third parties. For these purposes, a foreign controller means a nonresident who together with nonresident associates holds directly or indirectly at least 15% of the equity, income or control of an Australian enterprise, etc.

The restriction on tax deductions for interest will apply where the total relevant debt is more than three times the foreign investors' equity in the enterprise, etc., for the financial year. For foreign investment in the banking and non-bank financial intermediary sector, the restrictions will be triggered where the debt/equity ratio exceeds 6:1. Where the relevant ratio is exceeded, a tax deduction for interest paid on the debt will, to the extent of the excess, be disallowed to the company or business. An alternative test may be applied to measure debt on a weighted average for those days on which the debt/equity ratio is exceeded. Equity and debt carry extended meanings for the purposes of these tests, and interests in underlying reserves and unappropriated profits may be taken into account.

Debt Resulting from Corporate Restructures, etc. With few exceptions, tax deductions are denied for interest on debt (including arm's-length debt and local debt as well as foreign debt) that becomes owing in connection with the acquisition by a company of an asset from another company that has a common foreign controller. For these purposes, a foreign controller is a nonresident who together with nonresident associates holds directly or indirectly 50% or more of the equity, income, or control of the company.

Bad Debts. Provisions for doubtful accounts are not deductible. Bad debts are deductible only in the year actually written off. Any recovery after a debt has been written off is included in assessable income. To obtain a deduction for a bad debt incurred in previous years, a corporation must demonstrate a continuity of ownership or a continuity of business.

Entertainment Expenses. Income tax deductions are not allowed for most entertainment expenses.

Partnerships. The members of a partnership include their individual share of the partnership profit or loss in their own tax returns. The partnership entity is not subject to tax, although it is required to file a tax return.

Joint Ventures. Joint venturers include as income the sales proceeds of their individual share of production in their own tax returns and deduct their individual expenditures. A joint venture itself is not subject to tax nor required to file an income tax return.

Trusts. The beneficiaries must include in assessable income their entitlement to the income of the trust. The trustee is subject to tax at the rate of 47% (plus medicare levy) on any undistributed income of the trust for the 1991–1992 income year. Public trading trusts and certain other unit trusts are treated as corporations for tax purposes.

Employee Benefit Provisions. Provisions for employee benefits (annual leave, sick leave, long service leave, etc.) are not deductible. Deductions for these expenses are allowable only when payments are made to the employee.

RELATED CONSIDERATIONS

34. Incentives and Grants

Venture Capital. A full tax deduction is available for capital subscribed by the taxpayer to a licensed management and investment company for a period of at least four years. Partial deductions are allowed for shares held for a period greater than two years. The capital is to be used by the company to invest in a range of target businesses, such as those utilizing new technologies and with the potential for rapid growth. Subscriptions in excess of the approved capital of the licensed management and investment company do not receive a tax deduction.

Australian Film Industry. For capital expenditures incurred under a contract entered into after May 25, 1988 on producing or contributing to the production of a new Australian film, a taxpayer who acquires an interest in a film copyright may qualify for a deduction in the year of expenditure of 100% of the expenditure incurred. Various conditions must be met in order to receive this tax concession, and all returns from the investment will be treated as income.

Exports. As an incentive to the development of exports, the government currently provides a cash grant (maximum A$250,000) of 50% of eligible market development expenditures. This grant is taxable.

Industrial Research and Development Incentives. A 150% tax deduction is available until June 30, 1993 (the tax deduction will be reduced to 125% effective July 1, 1993) to resident companies for eligible expenditures in excess of A$50,000 on research and development (R&D) in Australia. A sliding-scale deduction applies for expenditures between A$20,000 and A$50,000.

The tax concession covers basic research, applied research, and experimental development (using the results of earlier research or experience) to create new or improved materials, devices, products, processes, or services. Production and marketing expenses do not qualify. Expenditures on plant and equipment exclusively used in R&D are eligible for the 150% tax deduction over three years. Companies unable to take advantage of the taxation incentive may qualify for certain cash grants.

Assistance to Industry. The Federal Government provides bounties and subsidies to manufacturers of a number of Australian-produced goods.

Most states provide various forms of assistance to industries locating in those states, especially in decentralized regions.

35. Exchange Controls

From July 1, 1990, as a result of changes in the taxation treatment of foreign-source income (see item 5), existing exchange control regulations were lifted.

Individuals and corporations are no longer required to obtain a tax clearance certificate or complete a declaration form when international payments are made. However, exports and imports of Australian and foreign cash of more than $5,000 must be reported to the special Cash Transactions Reports Agency.

Certain transactions, regardless of their value, must be reported to the Cash Transactions Reports Agency. Such transactions, known as "suspect transactions," are those that may be relevant to the investigation or prosecution of taxation or criminal offences.

36. Investment Restrictions on Nonresidents

In most cases, nonresidents may make portfolio and interest-bearing investments in Australia without formality, but they should be aware of the Foreign Takeovers Act and government foreign investment policy.

A nonresident, a foreign corporation, a resident corporation controlled from outside Australia, or a trustee of a trust estate in which a substantial beneficial interest is held by a foreign interest may not acquire, without approval from the Foreign Investment Review Board, the assets of an Australian business or more than 15% of the capital of a resident corporation. Two or more such foreign interests may not acquire a total of 40% or more of a resident corporation without such approval.

Proposals by foreign interests to acquire shares in an Australian corporation that would increase, or alter the ownership of, a substantial interest in the corporation must be transmitted to the Foreign Investment Review Board. However, where the total assets of the business subject to acquisition are less than A$5 million (or A$3 million if more than 50% of the business assets are held in the form of Australian rural land), the government generally does not interfere where the proposals fall within the scope of the Foreign Takeovers Act.

More stringent requirements apply to civil aviation, media, new mineral developments (excluding oil and gas), urban real estate (contingent upon Foreign Investment Review Board approval), and industries considered important to Australia's interests.

Tax deductions are restricted in relation to thinly capitalized foreign investment and are denied on debt resulting from corporate restructures (see item 33).

SELECTION OF BUSINESS ENTITY BY NONRESIDENTS

Nonresident investors usually operate in Australia either through a branch or by forming a local subsidiary corporation. In addition to general commercial considerations, a variety of Australian and/or home country tax factors may influence the choice between branch or subsidiary. Some Australian tax matters that can be relevant are as follows:

□ *Australian Branch of Nonresident Corporation*. In general, except where varied by a relevant tax treaty, a branch operation will only be subject to Australian income tax on Australian-source income and capital gains on certain Australian-related assets including capital gains on land and buildings in Australia, plant, equipment, and goodwill of the branch business. Branch profits derived in the 1991–1992 year are taxable at 39% (see item 1) except in the case of local dividend income. Franked dividend income is not subject to tax, while unfranked dividend income will generally be subject to withholding tax at 30%. No additional tax is levied on remittances of branch profits. However, Australian withholding tax is imposed on foreign interest charged to the branch, and royalties charged to the branch may also be subject to Australian tax (see item 18). Tax deductions for interest expenses charged to the branch may be restricted where the debt/equity ratio exceeds 3:1 at any time in a year (see item 33). Foreign equity will generally be the interest-free amount shown in the branch accounts as standing to the credit of Head Office. Foreign debt will include the amount of interest-bearing debt in the branch accounts. Losses of a branch of a nonresident corporation cannot be transferred for Australian tax purposes against profits of other corporations within the same corporate group.

A nonresident corporation cannot frank dividends paid to shareholders for Australian tax purposes. Accordingly, any Australian residents who hold shares in the nonresident corporation will not receive imputed credits for Australian tax paid by the corporation. If branch operations are transferred to a wholly owned local subsidiary, a rollover election is available to defer recognition of capital gains on branch assets transferred to the local corporation.

□ *Australian-Resident Corporation*. In general, an Australian-resident corporation is subject to Australian income tax on worldwide income and capital gains. The tax rate applicable to income of the 1991–1992 year is 39% (see item 1). A rebate of tax may be allowed on dividend income from other resident corporations (see item 28), and credits are allowed for foreign taxes paid on foreign income.

Where dividends paid to nonresident investors by the resident corporation have been franked (see item 28), the dividends are not subject to Australian tax. Any unfranked portion of dividends paid will be subject to withholding tax, generally at a 15% or 30% rate (see item 18). Royalties paid to nonresidents by the resident corporation may be subject to Australian tax, and withholding tax will generally apply to interest paid to nonresidents (see item 18). Tax deductions for interest expenses of the local corporation will be restricted where the debt/equity ratio in relation to substantial foreign investors and their associates exceeds 3:1 at any time in a year (see item 33). Only interest-bearing debt and similar accommodation will be taken into account for the purpose of this ratio, and equity will generally include direct interest in share capital reserves and unappropriated profits. Thus trading losses will reduce the equity. Special rules apply for the debt/equity ratio where there is an onshore company with wholly owned onshore subsidiaries. Losses may be transferred by election against profits of other resident corporations within the same wholly owned group (see item 29).

Any Australian residents who receive franked dividends from the resident corporation may be entitled to imputed credits for Australian tax paid by the corporation.

AUSTRIA

INCOME TAXES ON CORPORATIONS

1. Rates

As of 1989, the corporate tax rate is set uniformly at 30% of taxable income or, in the case of limited liability to tax, at 30% of taxable income earned within Austria.

Example:

Profit before corporate tax	AUS 1,000
30% corporation tax	300
Net income (to be retained or distributed)	AUS 700

2. Local Income Taxes

Trade tax is payable by every enterprise carrying on a business in Austria, regardless of its form of organization or nationality, unless specifically exempted by law; for example, certain state or federal organizations, charities, and savings banks. Trade tax is deductible from corporation tax income. Trade tax is computed on the following basis:

☐ The profits for the tax year. The tax rate varies in each federal state and amounts to about 13.5% of profit as computed for income and corporation tax purposes, with certain specified adjustments.

3. Capital Gains Taxes

Capital gains are fully included in taxable income and are taxed at corporation income tax rate.

As of 1989, capital gains on sales of shares in foreign companies (sales of more than 25% of the foreign company) are exempt from Austrian corporate income taxes under certain circumstances.

4. Branch Profits Taxes

Branches of a foreign corporation are subject to corporation tax in Austria on their income earned in Austria. Losses may be carried forward for seven years (see item 29).

5. Foreign Tax Reliefs

In general, taxation of foreign income is based on the regulations for avoiding double taxation. A special tax relief is called Schachtelbeguenstigung (Intercorporate Privilege). If a corporation holds at least 25% of a foreign corporation's shares for more than one year, dividends of this foreign corporation distributed to the company are not subject to tax in Austria.

At present, unilateral tax credits do not exist in Austria. In exceptional cases, however, the Ministry of Finance allows such tax credits.

INCOME TAXES ON INDIVIDUALS

9. Rates

As of January 1, 1989, the income tax rates for an individual (married or unmarried) without children are:

Taxable Income		Tax on	Percentage
Over	Not Over	Lower Amount	on Excess
AUS 0	AUS 50,000	AUS 0	10%
50,000	150,000	5,000	22
150,000	300,000	22,000	32
300,000	700,000	48,000	42
700,000		168,000	50

There is a general tax allowance of AUS 5,000.

Example:

Income for the year		AUS 700,000	100%
Income tax (see table above)	AUS243,000		
Less deduction	(5,000)	238,000	34%
Income after tax		AUS 462,000	66%

An individual's tax liability is reduced by the following tax credits and allowances (which do not apply to nonresidents):

	1991
Married couple if only one spouse has earned income	AUS 4,000
—plus for each child	1,800
Tax allowance for employees	AUS 1,500
Transport allowance for employees	4,000
Special deduction for pensioners	5,500

The income tax payable by individuals on dividend distributions by Austrian companies is reduced by 50% of the normal tax rate.

A payroll withholding tax is imposed on an individual's employment income. If the individual has other types of income, he or she is, therefore, required to file an income tax return. The employee's annual salary is divided into 14 parts from which the tax is withheld at source (see specimen tax computation).

In place of child allowance deductions, nontaxable subsidies of AUS 1,300 per child per month are provided for all taxpayers with dependent children until the age of nine years. For children aged ten or older, the taxpayers receive AUS 1,550 per child per month.

All individuals having their place of abode or their normal residence for more than six months in the tax year in the territory of the Federal Republic of Austria are fully liable; all others are only partly liable.

10. Local Income Taxes

The rules determining liability for trade taxes (item 2) apply to individually owned enterprises as well as to corporations.

11. Capital Gains Taxes

Capital gains on the sale of nonbusiness property, including shares, are tax-free if the property has been held for at least one year (ten years for real estate).

Gains from the sale of a house or flat are tax-free if the house or flat has been used as the main domicile for at least two years.

If an individual owns more than 10% of a company's shares, any capital gain on the sale of those shares is taxable and is taxed at one-half the ordinary income tax rate (i.e., maximum rate of 25%).

If an individual has held a participation in a partnership for at least seven years, the capital gain on the sale of the interest is taxed at one-half the ordinary income tax rate (i.e., maximum rate of 25%).

12. Foreign Tax Reliefs

Taxation of foreign income follows the regulations for avoiding double taxation.

13. Tax Period

The calendar year is the normal tax period (see item 32).

INCOME TAXES ON NONRESIDENTS

15. Liability to Tax

Natural persons having neither their place of abode nor their normal residence in the territory of the Federal Republic of Austria are taxable only on their Austrian-source income. Corporations having neither their site nor management in Austria are also taxable only on Austrian-source income. "Operating and other business expenses'' and ''allowable expenses'' that are economically related to Austrian-source income may be deducted. Nonresidents are not allowed to deduct ''special personal expenses'' or ''extraordinary expenses.''

In Austria, the following types of income of nonresidents are subject to limited income taxation:

☐ Income from agriculture and forestry.

☐ Income from self-employment performed in Austria or using an Austrian permanent establishment.

☐ Income from an enterprise engaged in trade or business, if a branch or a permanent establishment is in existence in Austria or if an authorized representative of the business is domiciled in Austria on a permanent basis.

☐ Income from commercial and technical advice performed within the country, personnel leasing, sports, arts (also if no permanent establishment is in existence).

☐ Income from employment (salaries to nonresidents).

☐ Certain investment income, if Austrian income tax is levied by withholding tax at source or if it comprises interest income from mortgages.

☐ Rental income from domestic real estate and from rights.

☐ Capital gains on real estate transactions (if taxable) and on the sale of certain participations.

16. Rates

The same tax rates apply to nonresidents as to residents.

17. Withholding Tax Rates

Tax is withheld at a special rate of 20% on the following categories of income:

☐ Income from employment and directors' fees.

☐ Income derived from the practice of an art or sport, from commercial and technical advice, or from personnel leasing.

☐ Income received for the right to use copyrights, patents, plans, designs, know-how, licensing fees.

Such withholding constitutes a final tax.

19. Tax Treaties

The following treaties between Austria and other countries are in force:

	Dividends	Interest (1)	Royalties
Nontreaty countries	25%	10% up to 50%	20%
Treaty countries:			
Argentina	15	12.5	15
Australia	15	10	10
Belgium	15	15	0, 10 (2)
Brazil	15	15	10, 15, 25 (3)
Bulgaria	0	0	0
Canada	15	15	0, 10 (4)
Cyprus	10	0	0
Czechoslovakia	10	0	5
Denmark	10	0	0, 10 (2)
Egypt	10	0	0
Finland	10	0	0, 10 (2)
France	15	0	0, 10 (2)
Germany (5)	normal	normal	0
Greece	normal	0, 10 (2)	0, 10 (2)
Hungary	10	0	0
India	normal	normal	normal
Indonesia	10, 15 (6)	10	10
Ireland	0, 10 (6)	0	0, 10 (2)
Israel	25	15	0, 10 (4)
Italy	15	10	0, 10 (2)
Japan	10, 20 (7)	10	10
Korea	10, 15 (8)	10	10
Liechtenstein	15	10	5, 10 (9)
Luxembourg	5, 15 (6)	0	0, 10 (2)
Malaysia	5, 10 (6)	15	10
Malta	15	5	0, 10 (9)
Netherlands	5, 15 (6)	0	0, 10 (2)
Norway	15	0	0, 10 (2)
Pakistan	10, 25 (6)	normal	20
Poland	10	0	0
Philippines	10, 25 (8)	15	15
Portugal	15	10	5, 10 (2)
Romania	15	10	10
Spain	10, 15 (7)	5	5
Soviet Union	0	0	0
Sweden	10	0	0, 10 (2)
Switzerland	5	5	5
Thailand	10, 25 (6)	10, 25 (10)	15
Tunisia	10, 20 (6)	10	10, 15 (4)
Turkey	25, 35 (11)	15	10
United Kingdom	5, 15 (6)	0	0, 10 (2)
United States	5, 12.5 (12)	0	0

Notes:

(1) Interest from bank accounts received by individuals (non-business income) is subject to a 10% withholding tax. In all other cases, refund of withholding tax of 10% may be claimed.

Interest on debt secured by mortgage on real estate is assessed at normal income tax rates (up to 50%) for individuals or at corporation tax rate (30%) for corporations.

(2) Higher rate if recipient owns over 50% of shares.

(3) Rate of 10% applies to special rights; rate of 5% to trademarks; rate of 15% in other cases.

(4) Lower rate applies to special rights.

(5) A new double taxation treaty is under negotiation.

(6) Lower rate applies if recipient owns 25% or more of payor.

(7) Lower rate applies if recipient owns 50% or more of payor.

(8) Lower rate applies if recipient owns 10% or more of payor.

(9) Lower rate applies to industrial companies.

(10) Rate of 10% applies to banks and insurance companies; rate of 25% applies to other companies; normal rate in other cases.

(11) Austria's withholding rate is 25% in all cases. Turkey's withholding rate is 35% if the Austrian recipient owns less than 25% of payor.

(12) Lower rate generally applies if foreign recipient has no branch and owns 95% or more of payor.

OTHER SIGNIFICANT TAXES

21. Sales (Value Added)

An Austrian buyer must pay the net sales price plus a 20% value added tax, which is listed separately on the supplier's invoice. The buyer, in effect, pays the supplier's tax burden. The amount is thereafter deductible from the buyer's own value added tax liability. Upon transferring these purchased goods (often further processed) to the next customer, the buyer-now-seller lists a 20% value added tax for that transaction on the invoice presented to the customer, and the process is repeated. The ultimate retail consumer absorbs the final burden. Among others, exports and certain services for foreigners (agents, advertising services, etc.) are exempt from value added tax. Import transactions are subject to a value added tax called "Einfuhr-umsatzsteuer," which in general is levied at the same rate as the internal tax.

On certain products, value added tax is reduced to 10%. This applies to basic foods, printed material such as magazines and newspapers. Value added tax of 32% is imposed on passenger cars and certain luxury goods.

22. Inheritance and Gift Taxes

The tax rate varies from 2% to 60%, depending upon the value of the inheritance or the gift and upon the relationship of the beneficiary to the deceased or the donor. An exemption of between AUS 1,500 and AUS 130,000 is provided, depending upon the degree of the relationship. The law provides for many other exemptions; for example, household goods, objects of historical value, etc.

Austria has signed a treaty to avoid double taxation in the case of inheritance with the following countries:

France	Sweden
Germany	Switzerland
Hungary	United States (including donation)
Liechtenstein	

23. Taxes on Payrolls (Social Security)

In Austria, social security contributions include three types of insurance together with some other contributions to funds. All employees are compulsorily members of these insurances.

The basis of assessment for insurance contributions is the employee's monthly gross salary (or gross wage) up to AUS 30,000 in 1991. Any income in excess of these limits is irrelevant for the purpose of the assessment for contributions. The maximum basis of assessment is adjusted each year. The employer is required to withhold the employee's part and to pay this amount together with his own share.

Insurance	Employer's Share		Employee's Share	
	(%*)	(AUS max.)	(%*)	(AUS max.)
Health				
General	2.50	750.00	2.50	750.00
Accident	1.30	390.00	—	—
Old-age and long-term disability	12.55	3,765.00	10.25	3,075.00
Unemployment	2.20	660.00	2.20	660.00
Other social contributions	0.60	180.00	1.00	300.00
	19.15	5,745.00	15.95	4,785.00

*In percentage of gross salaries and contributions assessment ceilings.

The employer also has to pay a special health contribution on behalf of the workers up to a maximum amount of AUS 840.00 and other general health contributions. In addition, the employer must pay a payroll tax at the rate of 2% of the emloyee's wages and salaries to the local community and a contribution to the "family burdens equalization fund" at the rate of 4.9% of wages and salaries.

25. Other Taxes

Property Tax. Individuals and corporations subject to unlimited tax liability must pay capital tax on the net value of their entire property. Taxpayers subject to limited tax liability are taxed on the net value of those assets situated in Austria. The rate is 1.0% per year. Individuals are allowed a deduction of AUS 150,000 for themselves and each dependent. Corporations are subject to a surtax (equivalent to inheritance tax), which is collected in proportion to the value of shares of the corporation held by foreigners and non-individuals. This surtax amounts to 0.5% of the "net value" as stated above. Property tax is not deductible in determining the profit subject to income tax and trade income tax. Property tax is deductible from corporation taxable income.

Real Estate Tax. Real property is subject to a municipal tax on assessed value. Rates vary among the municipalities from 0.4 to 0.84%.

Land Transfer Tax. Real estate transactions are exempt from value added tax. On most transfers of land and buildings within Austria, the buyer is liable for a tax of 3.5% of the sales price.

Capital Transfer Tax. The most significant part of capital transfer tax is the *tax imposed on increases of capital*. Tax at 2% is levied on the issue of stock, on any increase of capital stock, and on other capital contributions to a corporation. If such issues prevent a reduction of the authorized capital, the tax rate is reduced to 1%.

The issue of bonds by an Austrian debtor and the first acquisition in Austria of bonds issued by a foreign debtor, or stock of a foreign corporation, are subject to *tax on the issue of securities other than stock* at a tax rate ranging from 1% to 2%. *Tax on the transfer of securities and shares* is imposed at rates which vary between 0.15% and 0.5%.

Stamp Duties. Documents subject to stamp duties are lease contract (1%), loan contract (0.8%), rent contract (1%), assignment of shares in a GmbH (2%), formation of a partnership (2%), etc.

COMPUTATION OF TAXABLE INCOME

26. Capital Gains
See items 3 and 11.

27. Depreciation and Depletion
Depreciation ("AfA") on buildings and other fixed assets such as machines, working plant, etc., purchased with the intention of profitable production, is usually based on cost. The prime cost (cost of acquisition) or the cost of production of

fixed assets must be spread over their useful lives. In general, depreciation is computed on the straight-line method. Extraordinary depreciation is allowed in cases of abnormal use and for impending obsolescence. Assets costing not more than AUS 5,000 each, may be written off in the year of acquisition.

For buildings, the following rates of depreciation apply:

Production buildings, warehouses, etc.	4%
Banks and insurance buildings	2.5%
Buildings listed above but with at least 80% consumer-designated space	4%
Other buildings	1.5% and 2%

In computing the taxable profit, the balance of depreciation of passenger cars are not deductible, in so far as the limits for income tax purposes are exceeded.

28.   Treatment of Dividends

Companies paying dividends domestically or to nonresidents must withhold 25% of the dividend, but the tax can be set off against corporation or personal income tax. Some double taxation treaty provisions reduce this rate (see item 17). Intercompany dividends are exempted from the requirement if the recipient is an Austrian corporation.

If a foreign corporation makes a distribution out of profits to a fully liable Austrian corporation that, during the entire business year, owned at least 25% of the stock in the distributing corporation, the distribution is not included in the taxable profit of the Austrian recipient corporation.

29.   Loss Carryovers

Losses resulting from agriculture and forestry, trade or business, or independent occupations, and determined in conformity with generally accepted accounting principles, may be carried forward for seven years. This applies to locally registered companies. For branches of foreign companies, losses may be carried forward in the same way if they have not been used in the foreign country or a nondiscrimination clause is included in the tax treaty.

Losses originating from or increased by the allocation to an investment allowance cannot be carried forward against, or deducted from, other income. Such losses are deductible from future profits of the same enterprise.

30.   Transactions between Related Parties

Royalties, interest, management fees and similar charges paid to foreign related companies are generally deductible if considered reasonable.

Any excessive payment or other monetary advantage given to an affiliated or parent company, whether in respect of sales or technical and managerial fees, may be considered by the tax authorities as a hidden distribution. This will be disallowed as a deduction and will be subject to withholding tax, trade tax, and corporation tax.

31. Consolidation of Income

A joint stock company or a private limited company that is fully liable to Austrian tax and that is in financial, economic, and legal reality a subsidiary of another parent company that is fully liable to tax may contract for a period of at least five years to transfer the whole of its profit/loss to the parent company. Profits and losses of the parent and its subsidiary are then added together or netted off against one another as appropriate (Vollorganschaft).

Financial dependence may be proved by a 75% to 100% direct ownership of the shares of the subsidiary.

Economic dependence is met if orders or supplies from the parent company to the subsidiary account for at least 50% of the total orders or supplies to the subsidiary.

Legal dependence is met if the managers of the parent company and the subsidiary are the same persons.

32. Tax Periods

The calendar year is the tax year. To file on a fiscal-year basis other than the calendar year, the permission of the tax authorities must be obtained.

RELATED CONSIDERATIONS

34. Incentives and Grants

In Austria, investments in industry are promoted to a very high degree and at different levels. Investment incentives can be subdivided into:

☐ Foreign trade incentives.
☐ Credit incentives.
☐ Fiscal incentives.

Fiscal incentives are mainly dealt with in the income tax law.

Reserve for Future Capital Expenditure. Austrian income tax law allows 10% of the taxable profit to be set aside as a reserve for future capital expenditure. This reserve can only be set aside if an investment allowance for the same period does not exceed 10% of taxable income. The reserve has to be credited against future capital expenditure equivalent to investment allowance (see below) within the following four years. If parts of this reserve remain four years after its creation, the amounts plus a surcharge become liable to income tax.

Investment Allowance. An investment allowance of up to 20% of the cost of movable or immovable fixed assets in the year of acquisition is deductible if a reserve for future capital expenditure has not been used. In addition, normal depreciation over the estimated useful life amounting to 100% can be applied. If fixed assets, for which this reserve has been made, are disposed of before the end of the following four years, the amount of the reserve relating to the assets disposed of must be credited to income. After four years, the investment reserve becomes a free reserve and may be withdrawn. The investment reserve set up for trucks is limited to 10% of the acquisition cost.

The investment allowance may not be set up in respect of sale and lease-back transactions or in the case of used fixed assets being transferred within related companies.

Profit from Realization of Appreciation of Assets. In certain cases, gains from the sale of fixed assets can be charged against the cost of other fixed assets acquired in the same or the next three fiscal years.

Research and Development. Under the condition of acceptance by the Ministry for Economics and Industry, an allowance in the amount of 12% or 18% of the expenditure for research and development is deductible from taxable income.

35. Exchange Controls

Prime responsibility for regulating currency rests with the Oesterreichische Nationalbank, which functions as a central bank. Effective February 1, 1989, the Austrian National Bank took a major step forward in liberalizing the movement of foreign capital. Effective November 4, 1991, all limitations to the free movement of capital have been abolished.

36. Investment Restrictions on Nonresidents

Any acquisition of real estate by nonresidents requires special permission of the local authorities.

SELECTION OF BUSINESS ENTITY BY NONRESIDENTS

A nonresident company can select between two basic forms of organization: it can set up a branch, which will operate as a division of the company, or it can establish a separate Austrian subsidiary. The registration procedure for a branch may be more complicated.

A local subsidiary is taxed on its worldwide income. Its income tax rate is 30%. Capital yields tax on distributions is 25% or less (see item 17).

A branch is taxed on its income earned in Austria. Interest and some other charges by foreign head offices to Austrian branches are not deductible. The corporation income tax rate for a branch is the normal rate of 30%; no withholding tax is imposed on profits transferred overseas.

SPECIMEN TAX COMPUTATION

Specimen example of the taxation of yearly employment income:

Facts: A man is married, the sole income earner, has one child, has a yearly gross salary of AUS 840,000 which was paid in 14 installments, and has a company car (acquisition cost of AUS 360,000).

	AUS
Gross salary (12 installments)	720,000
Gross salary (2 additional installments)	120,000
Total gross income	840,000
Total gross income	840,000
Social security contribution (1991)	(67,000)
Income tax (on 12 installments)	(201,500)
Income tax (on 2 installments)	(2,230)
Income tax (on company car)*	(32,400)
Net salaries	536,870
Subsidies for one child (below ten years)	15,600
Total net income	552,470

*The private use of a company car represents a taxable advantage in employment. The benefit in kind is assessed at 1.5% of the acquisition cost of the car, but with an upper limit of AUS 7,000 per month.

Taxable basis: 1.5% of AUS 360,000 × 12 = AUS 64,800.

BAHAMAS

1. Taxes

The Bahamas Government, aware of the importance to the economy of the continued development of The Bahamas as an offshore financial center, has given assurances that there is no intention to introduce income tax. Currently in The Bahamas there is no:

- [ ] Income tax,
- [ ] Corporate tax,
- [ ] Sales tax,
- [ ] Capital gains tax,
- [ ] Estate tax,
- [ ] Wealth tax,
- [ ] Gift or inheritance tax,
- [ ] Death duty, or
- [ ] Local withholding tax on interest payments or dividends.

The Bahamas has no double taxation treaties with other countries; consequently, interest and dividend income derived from sources in foreign countries are subjected to the full withholding tax deduction applicable in those countries.

The Bahamas has signed a mutual legal assistance treaty with the United States, which permits the exchange of information in cases considered criminal violations under Bahamian law, but the agreement specifically exempts investigations related to tax matters.

2. Tax Exemptions

Under various incentive legislation, foreign investors have been granted statutory exemption from direct taxes (which do not presently exist in The Bahamas) and from most forms of indirect taxes.

3. International Business Companies

International business companies (IBCs) are statutorily exempt from direct taxes and stamp duty for a period of 20 years from the date of incorporation.

The approximate minimum capital required to establish an IBC is $1,000. There is an annual government registration fee of $100 in addition to a professional management fee, which is approximately $1,000 per annum.

4. Indirect Taxes and Licence Fees

The principal revenue of the Government is derived from import duties on all goods arriving in The Bahamas, with the exception of certain basic food items and supplies. In addition, other revenue-raising taxes include the following:

☐ Business licence fee,
☐ Real property tax,
☐ Stamp tax,
☐ Insurance premium tax,
☐ Casino tax.

Business License Fee. The business license fee is assessable annually on all domestic business enterprises operating in The Bahamas, except banks, trust companies, and insurance companies. The fee is calculated on turnover (total sales or revenues), and the fee rate is dependent on the gross profit.

The rates range from 0.25% (low profit) of turnover for businesses with gross profit under 25%, to 1.50% (very high profit) of turnover for businesses with gross profit in excess of 75%. Businesses with turnover below $50,000 are exempt from the payment of a fee.

Companies designated as nonresident under the Exchange Control Regulations Act (companies that are foreign owned and do not trade in The Bahamas) pay a fee of $100 per annum.

Real Property Tax. Persons owning real property in The Bahamas are assessable annually to real property tax in respect of such holdings. The tax is payable on the assessed value of the property as determined by the Chief Valuation Officer of The Commonwealth of The Bahamas.

The rate of tax payable is as follows:

	Assessed Value		
	First $50,000	**Next $50,000**	**Balance**
Owner-occupied (residential)	exempt	.75%	.58%
Other property	.50%	—	1.00%

Stamp Tax. A nominal rate of stamp tax is levied on the execution of a variety of commercial documents. However, the highest incident of stamp tax is on property conveyances graded as follows:

Property Value	Rate of Tax
$0 – $100,000	.75% – 4.50%
Over $100,000	5.50%

In the case of property sales to non-Bahamians, the stamp tax is doubled.

Insurance Premium Tax. Registered insurers writing domestic risks pay a premium tax of 2% of gross premiums. Tax is not assessable on premiums relating to the writing of foreign risks.

Casino Tax. A casino is assessable to a tax on the gross gaming receipts of up to 25% on a graduated sale.

5. Currency

The currency is the Bahamian dollar (B$), which is on par with the U.S. dollar. U.S. dollars are accepted locally, and most nonresident users of The Bahamas as a tax haven conduct their business in U.S. dollars.

6. Exchange Controls

International business companies and those companies and individuals designated as nonresident under the Exchange Control Regulations Act are exempt from exchange control.

7. Banking Facilities and Secrecy Provisions

The Bahamas provides a sophisticated and a comprehensive range of banking services. There are some 400 financial institutions registered and licenced to carry on banking and trust business in or from within The Bahamas. Of these, approximately 300 hold unrestricted public licences. Under Bahamian legislation as well as common law, the principle of the client's fundamental right to privacy is protected, and there is a strict duty imposed on all bank and trust company personnel, as well as on such outside advisers as attorneys and accountants, against disclosure. Penalties for breaches of the secrecy provision include fine, imprisonment, or both.

BANGLADESH

INCOME TAXES ON CORPORATIONS

1. Rates

Companies are subject to tax on their total income at the following rates:

Publicly traded industrial companies	45%
Nonpublicly traded industrial companies	50%
All other companies (including banks, other financial institutions, and local authorities)	55%

A publicly traded company means a Public Limited Company under certain conditions.

A rebate of 10% of the tax is available for certain income brought into Bangladesh. Dividend income is subject to tax of 15%. Special provisions have been made for taxation of profits of insurance business company and mutual insurance associations.

Companies registered in Bangladesh are entitled to tax relief computed on the basis of the increase in the current year's production volume over that of the preceding year.

2. Local Income Taxes

No state or provincial taxes are levied.

3. Capital Gains Taxes

Capital gains are subject to tax at a flat rate of 25%. No other income tax or super-tax is imposed on the gain.

4. Branch Profits Taxes

Bangladesh branches of nonresident companies are subject to company income tax in the same manner as resident companies.

5. Foreign Tax Reliefs

Bangladesh grants a foreign tax credit with respect to foreign income of resident companies which is also subject to Bangladesh tax. The credit is allowed for income taxes imposed at the national level by any foreign country, but not for income taxes imposed at the state or provincial level in a foreign country. Certain limitations are applied so as to limit the credit to the portion of Bangladesh company tax that is imposed on foreign income.

INCOME TAXES ON INDIVIDUALS

9. Rates

The tax exemption limit for individuals is Tk. 40,000. Taxable income in excess of Tk. 40,000 is taxable at graduated rates varying from 10% to 45%.

Income in the form of bank interest and dividends is subject to deduction at source at specified rates.

Nonresident individuals are subject to tax at a maximum rate of 30% without deductions for the allowances granted to residents.

Income tax rates varying from 0.5% to 3% is deducted at source from payments to contractors and suppliers.

Self Assessment.   The income limit under the self-assessment scheme (self-employed professionals maintaining books of account) is TK. 1,000,000 for existing taxpayers and Tk. 125,000 for new taxpayers. New taxpayers are automatically allowed capital deductions of Tk. 200,000.

10. Local Income Taxes

None.

11. Capital Gains Taxes

Bangladesh has complex rules for taxing capital gains realized by individuals. In general, these gains are taxable at ordinary individual income tax rates. Partial relief is available depending on the holding period of the asset and which assets the gain is reinvested in. The following types of capital gain are exempt from tax:

☐   Gain on the transfer of land or buildings for stock of a new industrial company.

☐   Gain on the transfer of land or buildings which is invested in new issues of stock quoted on the stock exchange.

☐   Gain from the incorporation of a firm into a company.

☐   Gain on the transfer of shares by nonresident assessees.

12. Foreign Tax Reliefs

Individual citizens of Bangladesh residing outside of Bangladesh are exempt from Bangladesh tax on foreign income if they spend less than 180 days during the year in Bangladesh. Nonresident individuals are subject to tax on income arising outside of Bangladesh and remitted into Bangladesh only if the income is earned in connection with a business or profession or vocation maintained by the individual in Bangladesh.

13. Tax Period

The tax year ends on June 30. A different fiscal year may be adopted by a taxpayer at his own discretion. However, any change in a fiscal year requires the approval of the tax authorities. The tax period is the "income year." The last date for filing a return by individuals whose income year ends on June 30 is September 15.

INCOME TAXES ON NONRESIDENTS

15. Liability to Tax

A number of special rules are applied in determining whether a nonresident individual or company is subject to Bangladesh tax. Income subject to Bangladesh tax includes salary from work done in Bangladesh, income or capital gains from property in Bangladesh (including rents or royalties from patents or equipment used in Bangladesh), interest and dividends from Bangladesh residents or resident companies, and the profits of a business in Bangladesh. A nonresident person subject to Bangladesh tax may be taxed through an agent located in Bangladesh. Foreign technicians working in Bangladesh may be exempt from Bangladesh tax on their salary for a limited period. Foreign nationals who depart from Bangladesh are required to obtain tax clearance certificates from the Bangladesh tax authorities prior to their departure. The Finance Ordinance, 1984 has specifically excluded from total income various items of receipts and profits (with some limitations).

The tax rate and rules applicable to nonresident individuals are discussed in item 9.

19. Tax Treaties

Bangladesh has completed tax treaties with nine countries: Canada, France, Pakistan, Romania, Singapore, South Korea, Sri Lanka, Sweden, and the United Kingdom. At present, negotiations are being conducted with Belgium, the Federal Republic of Germany, the German Democratic Republic, India, Japan, Thailand, Turkey, and other countries.

Treaties for the promotion and protection of investment have already been concluded with Belgium, France, South Korea, West Germany, the United Kingdom, and the United States.

Bangladesh has invited foreign collaboration for industrial, commercial, economic, and financial development.

OTHER SIGNIFICANT TAXES

21. Sales (Value Added)

Through the recently introduced Value Added Tax Ordinance, 1991, effective July 1, 1991, VAT at the rate of 15% has been imposed on selected manufacturing and retail industries. Essential items, such as food, clothing, and transport, have been exempted from VAT. The VAT replaces the old Sales Tax and Excise Duty.

22. Inheritance and Gift Taxes

The Estate Duty Act, 1980 has been repealed with effect from July 1, 1982. Its provisions remain in force only for dealing with pending assessments relating to before that date.

The Gift Tax Act, 1963, has been reintroduced for the fiscal year 1990–1991.

23. Taxes on Payrolls (Social Security)

Social security tax provisions are minor and inadequate. Specific provisions provide exemptions and reliefs for pensions, gratuity, and Provident Funds. These welfare provisions apply to both employers and employees. There are special provisions as well for recognition of "Provident Fund and Super-Annuation Funds." By the Finance Act, 1987, Bangladesh employees of foreign missions or embassies have been allowed the benefit of Provident Funds.

24. Taxes on Natural Resources

Special rules are applied in computing the taxable income of companies engaged in petroleum operations and the mining of other resources.

25. Other Taxes

Land and Property. Taxes are imposed at varying rates by municipalities based on the value of land and buildings. Newly constructed houses may be exempt from tax in some cases. Tax at the rate of 5% is leviable by the registration authorities at the time of registration.

Stamp Duty. Stamp duty is imposed in connection with the registration of documents. A share transfer fee of 1.5%, which is levied on the value of shares transferred, does not apply to shares of public limited companies that are listed on the stock exchange.

Assignment of a copyright is exempt from stamp duty.

Wealth Tax. Wealth tax is imposed if the value of an individual's Hindu undivided family exceeds certain minimum levels and exemptions. Wealth tax is not levied on companies. Self-occupied residential houses are exempt from wealth tax up to valuation of Taka 5 million.

Import Duty on Capital Machinery.   Import duty at the rate of 10% is chargeable on capital machinery.

Other Taxes.   Other taxes in Bangladesh include excise and customs duties under the Customs Act, 1969 as amended; jute tax, turnover tax, foreign travel tax, and advertisement tax under the Finance Act, 1957; electric duty under the Electric Duty Act, 1935; betterment tax under the Finance Act, 1974; taxes on freight carried by inland vessels or by road; and others. There are specific provisions for imposition of the Land Development Tax.

COMPUTATION OF TAXABLE INCOME

26. Capital Gains

As indicated previously, companies are subject to capital gains tax at a 25% rate, while individuals are subject to tax at regular rates, subject to a reduction in tax depending on the period for which the asset was held.

27. Depreciation and Depletion

Depreciation rules in Bangladesh are quite liberal. New industrial undertakings approved by the National Board of Revenue may be eligible for 80% to 100% write-offs of depreciable property for the first and second year. Additional allowances of 50% and 100% of the normal deductions may be claimed where double and triple shifts are worked. Ships, other than those used on inland waterways, are eligible for special investment allowances. A specific schedule has been incorporated in the Income-Tax Ordinance, 1984 for computation of the depreciation allowance.

28. Treatment of Dividends

Under the provisions of Finance Act 1989, investment allowance at 25% is allowable on the amount invested on the new machinery set up in the industrial undertaking under BMR (balancing, modernization, and replacement of machinery) Scheme.

Dividends in excess of Taka 30,000 are taxed to individual shareholders, who forfeit the credit for the tax deducted at source on the exempt amount of dividends. This exemption does not apply to companies. Dividends received from tax-holiday companies are exempt under specific conditions. The dividend income of a public or private company is normally taxed at 15%. Bonus shares are not taxable. Dividends received from companies located in the Export Processing Zone are entirely exempt from tax in the hands of foreign shareholders.

29. Loss Carryovers

Operating losses from business activities may be carried forward for six years. Unutilized depreciation deductions may be carried forward for an indefinite period of time. Capital losses over Taka 5,000 may also be carried forward, but can only offset capital gains of the next six years. Other rules apply for losses of speculative businesses, unregistered firms, and companies that have received cash grants.

30. Transactions between Related Parties

The tax authorities have the power to increase the taxable income of any taxpayer subject to Bangladesh tax jurisdiction so as to prevent the transfer of profits to a nonresident person by means of transactions not conducted on an arm's-length basis.

Where assets are transferred between related parties at a price that does not reflect the fair market value of the assets, the tax authorities may impose capital gains tax on the basis of the full value of the assets as well as a penalty for undervaluation.

32. Tax Periods

June 30 is the tax year-end for all taxpayers, but there are legal provisions to use a different fiscal year.

33. Other Matters

Deductible Expenses.   In general, all expenses that are necessary to the operation of a business are permitted to be claimed as income tax deductions, providing they are not of a personal or of a capital nature. Special rules regarding income tax deductions are applied in computing taxable income from property, and from agricultural operations. A specific provision has been made by the Finance Act, 1990, for allowance of bad and doubtful debts up to 4.5% of certain banks and financial institutions.

RELATED CONSIDERATIONS

34. Incentives and Grants

Tax holidays may be granted for periods of from five to twelve years. In addition, resident taxpayers are granted a deduction for the investment of initial or additional share capital in approved private and public industrial companies, equal to one-third of the total income.

In general, profits from the export of local goods are tax-exempt within limits, except in the case of certain designated industries (including the tea and jute industries). Certain special concessions are also available to oil and gas companies and to mining companies. Three-year write-offs also are available for fishing trawlers and passenger vessels registered in Bangladesh.

Expenditures incurred for scientific research are allowed as current income tax deductions. Current deductions are also allowed for grants made to approved scientific research organizations. In order to encourage foreign investment tax concessions and reliefs are also available.

35. Exchange Controls

Although exchange controls are still quite stringent, certain relief has been made. Effective July 1, 1991, foreigners and nonresident Bangladeshis may buy securities on the Dhaka stockmarket; stock-market investors and most foreign companies may remit profits overseas without Central bank approval; state and privately owned manufacturing companies may borrow abroad; and resident and nonresident Bangladeshis may open foreign-currency bank accounts.

In an effort to attract increased foreign investment, foreign companies now are allowed to hold 100% equity, previously limited to companies operating in the Export Processing Zone only.

36. Investment Restrictions on Nonresidents

There are no investment restrictions. A law was passed in March 1980 that provides for the promotion and protection of foreign private investment in Bangladesh. Foreign investors have received aid and grants related to foreign participation in the textile, telephone and electric industries.

Board of Investment. A Board of Investment (BOI) was established in January 1990 to streamline foreign investment proposals.

BARBADOS

INCOME TAXES ON CORPORATIONS

1. Rates

The standard rate of corporation tax for resident and nonresident corporations is 35%. Building societies are taxed at 20%. Life insurance companies are subject to tax on gross investment income at the rate of 5%, and premium income is taxable at the rates of 3% and 5% for resident and nonresident companies, respectively. Nonresident corporations are taxed at 15% on local dividend, interest, royalty, and management fee income. Resident companies are taxable on income from all sources except on local dividends.

2. Local Income Taxes

None.

3. Capital Gains Taxes

None.

4. Branch Profits Taxes

In addition to corporation tax at 35%, branch profits are subject to a further 10% tax on remittances or deemed remittances.

5. Foreign Tax Reliefs

Resident corporations are granted relief on taxed foreign income. In addition to the Commonwealth Double Taxation Agreement, special agreements are in force with Canada, Denmark, Finland, Norway, Switzerland, the United Kingdom, the United States, and certain Caribbean countries. An agreement with Sweden is still to be ratified, and agreements with Japan and West Germany are currently being negotiated.

6. Classification of Corporations

The distinctions between corporations basically are not relevant for tax purposes. However, companies controlled by five or fewer persons are subject to special rules with respect to undistributed profits and loans to directors and shareholders.

7. Payment of Taxes

Corporations are required to pay tax by installments on a current-year basis. The dates on which the installments are due and the number of installments payable depend on the company's fiscal period.

Corporations with fiscal periods ending between January 1 and September 30 prepay 50% of the previous year's tax on September 15. The balance of tax due is payable on filing the return on the following March 15.

Corporations with fiscal periods ending between October 1 and December 31 prepay 50% of the previous year's tax on December 15 and a second installment of 50% of the previous year's tax on the following March 15. Any balance of tax due on the current year's profits must be paid when filing the return on June 15.

INCOME TAXES ON INDIVIDUALS

9. Rates

All persons resident for tax purposes qualify for a minimum personal allowance of $15,000 as a deduction from their assessable income. Any remaining taxable income is subject to tax at the following rates. The rates of tax payable by resident and nonresident persons are the same, except that nonresidents are taxed at 15% on local dividend, interest, royalty, and management fee income. Resident spouses file returns on an individual basis.

	Taxable Income	Rate	Tax	Total Tax
First $15,000:	$15,000	20%	$3,000	$ 3,000
Next 10,000:	25,000	30	3,000	6,000
Next 10,000:	35,000	40	4,000	10,000
Next 10,000:	55,000	45	9,000	19,000
Over	55,000	50		

Salaries and wages are taxed at source. Individuals in receipt of rental or business income prepay tax in installments by June 15, September 15, and December 15. The balance is payable on filing the return by the following April 30. Other individuals pay in two installments, half by April 30 on filing their return and half by the following September 30.

Effective from 1991 income year, individuals also are required to pay a stabilization tax of 1.5% on gross income from all sources, calculated in accordance with the Income Tax Act. However, pensions and certain sources of income presently exempt from income tax also are exempt from this tax, and the individuals in receipt of business and rental income are taxed on net profits. No personal allowances are to be deducted when calculating the tax.

Stabilization tax is deducted at source on salaries and wages. Individuals in receipt of rental or business income prepay stabilization tax by installments on the same dates as for income tax prepayments. Other individuals are required to pay the tax when filing their income tax returns.

10. Local Income Taxes

None.

11. Capital Gains Taxes

None.

12. Foreign Tax Reliefs

Same as item 5.

13. Tax Period

Individuals are required to file returns on a calendar-year basis. However, with the permission of the Revenue Authority, an individual who maintains accounts for his or her business or profession with a year-end other than December 31 may include in income the profit from the business or profession for the year ending in the calendar year. (See also item 32.)

INCOME TAXES ON NONRESIDENTS

15. Liability to Tax

A foreign entity that is a resident of a country with which Barbados has a tax treaty will be subject to Barbados tax only if it has a permanent establishment in Barbados, and on such income as is attributable to the permanent establishment. An entity that is resident in a non-treaty country will pay Barbados tax on all its Barbados-source income.

16. Rates

Nonresidents generally are taxed at the same rates as residents (see items 1 and 9), except that nonresidents are taxed at 15% on local dividend, interest, royalty, and management fee income.

17. Withholding Tax Rates

	Interest	Dividends (1)	Royalties	Rents (2)(3)	Management Fees
Nontreaty countries	15%	15%	15%	40%	15%
Treaty countries:					
Canada	15	15	0 (4)	40	15 (5)
Denmark	0	0	0	40	15
Finland	5	15 (6)	5	40	5
Norway	5	15 (6)	5	40	5
Switzerland	0	0	0	40	—
United Kingdom	15	0 (7)	0 (8)	40	15 (9)
United States	12.5	15 (6)	12.5	40	15 (9)

Notes:
  (1) Dividends on preferred stock issued prior to January 1, 1975 are taxed at the rate of 40%.
  (2) The withholding tax constitutes the final tax on all sources other than rental income. In the case of rental income, nonresident individuals may recover tax withheld in excess of the final personal tax liability on filing a return.
  (3) A person habitually filing returns of rental income may apply to the Commissioner for waiver of withholding tax.
  (4) Royalty payments on movie or television films are subject to withholding tax at 10% of gross royalty income.
  (5) The treaty provides that, if a lower rate is subsequently agreed with another country, the lower rate will apply. Therefore, 5% will be applicable.
  (6) If the beneficial owner of the dividends owns at least 10% of the voting stock, the rate will be 5% instead.
  (7) Dividends paid to a U.K. resident may be exempt from withholding tax if the dividend income is subject to tax in the United Kingdom.
  (8) Tax to be withheld on movie or television film royalties is restricted to 15% of the gross amount of the royalty.
  (9) This may be reduced to 0% in certain circumstances where no "permanent establishment" exists.

Withholding taxes are deducted under statutory legislation, but the Commissioner is favorably disposed to granting relief from payment if there are no infringements under double taxation relief agreements.

18. Special Withholding Provisions

Dividends paid to nonresidents out of special tax-exempted profits may be subject to withholding tax of 45%.

OTHER SIGNIFICANT TAXES

21. Sales (Value Added)

The sales tax levied on hotel income from rooms, food, and beverages, and sales in restaurants and proprietary clubs is 5%. There is also an 8% charge on income from the rental of premises (excluding business premises) and automobiles. A 20% tax is payable on airline tickets for journeys originating in Barbados.

22. Inheritance and Gift Taxes

None.

23. Taxes on Payrolls (Social Security)

All employers and employees contribute to the National Insurance Scheme at the rates of 9.00% and 9.75%, respectively. Contributions other than specific levies are tax deductible. Self-employed persons contribute at the rate of 13.25%. The earnings ceiling on contributions is $2,600 per month.

24. Taxes on Natural Resources

Annual license fees of $10,000 on sand quarries and $5,000 on stone quarries are charged. There is also a charge of $2.50 per cubic meter of sand and $1.00 per ton of clay.

25. Other Taxes

Property Transfer Tax. A special transfer tax is levied on the transfer of company shares (except shares listed on the Barbados Securities Exchange) and real estate and certain leasehold in such. The rates are:

Vendors (citizens or permanent residents)	5% — in excess of $25,000	
Nonnational purchasers	10%	
Nonnational vendors	8%	

Land and Property Tax. Tax is levied annually on each property owner based on the value of land and improvements thereon. The rates on unimproved land are 0.6% on the first $100,000 and 1.5% on the balance. The rates on land with improvements are 0.35% on values up to $300,000 and 0.95% over $300,000.

If property is owned by a foreign or foreign-controlled company, the rates are 3% for unimproved land and 2% for improved land. Banks and certain public companies actively engaged in business in Barbados are granted concessions in order to exempt them from the higher rate of tax.

Land Development Duty. If a person disposes of property situated in a specially designated development area within ten years of the date specified by statute, duty may be charged. This would be at rates of up to 50% on the excess of the proceeds over the value at the specified date.

Stamp Duty. Stamp duty is payable on various documents at the following rates:

Shares of listed companies	NIL
Real estate, leases, and other shares	1%
Mortgages	
first $500	$5
each additional $500	$3

No duty is charged on transfers of shares listed on the Barbados Securities Exchange.

Duty also is charged on every bill of entry or set of entries passed on the importation of goods or goods passed out of Bond for home consumption on the C.I.F. value. No duty is charged on goods imported from Caricom.

Machinery and equipment imported from extra-regional areas are subject to duty at 10% and 15%. Duty is 20% on other items. Raw materials and packaging materials imported from extra-regional sources are exempt from duty if the importer is a registered manufacturer.

Consumption Tax. Consumption tax ranges from 12% to 40% and is charged on goods and equipment imported or items manufactured in Barbados. Goods manufactured for export, whether to Caricom or non-Caricom areas, are exempt from consumption tax.

Machinery, equipment, and spare parts imported for use in the manufacturing or agricultural sector are exempt from tax. Other imports from extra-regional sources are taxable unless imported by enclave enterprises under the Fiscal Incentives Act or approved exporters of manufactured goods. Also, no tax is charged on computers and other related equipment or packaging materials in pharmaceutical and other manufacturing industries.

Customs Duty. Customs duty is levied on a range of imported goods at rates specified in Part I of the Customs Tariff. The duty is calculated on an ad valorem basis on most imports, and the duty payable can range from 5% to 50%.

Items listed in Part II of the Customs Tariff may be imported free of duty. For example, machinery, equipment, and spare parts for use in industry imports are exempted from customs duty.

COMPUTATION OF TAXABLE INCOME

26. Capital Gains

None.

27. Depreciation and Depletion

Annual allowances on fixed assets are calculated on the straight-line method. An additional "initial allowance" of 20% is given in the year that new equipment is acquired.

An allowance of 1% (10% for historic buildings) of the property tax value is provided for commercial buildings. Owners of properties qualifying as industrial buildings and hotels may not claim the commercial building allowance. Owners of properties qualifying as industrial buildings are entitled to a 40% initial allowance and an annual allowance of 4% of the cost of the building.

28. Treatment of Dividends

Resident corporations exclude ordinary dividend income in calculating assessable income. Nonresident persons are liable for tax at 15%. Individual resident shareholders and Pension Funds are eligible for a tax credit of 15% on the gross dividends.

29. Loss Carryovers

Effective the 1988 income year, losses may be carried forward nine years. Effective the 1990 income year, the restriction that the tax payable must not be reduced by more than 50% by the loss carryover is no longer applicable. Losses may not be carried back.

30. Transactions between Related Parties

Barbadian law and the various double taxation treaties contain provisions under which revenue transactions between related parties may be adjusted to the price that would have prevailed on an arm's-length basis.

31. Consolidation of Income

There is no provision for the filing of consolidated tax returns by related corporations.

32. Tax Periods

Fiscal periods must be approved by the Revenue Authority and cannot exceed 53 weeks. The Sugar Industry Act 1982 requires persons engaged in the sugar industry to adopt a June 30 year-end.

33. Other Matters

Deduction for Taxes Other than Income Taxes. In computing the liability for income tax, businesses may deduct land and property tax. Transfer tax and stamp duties are treated as part of the cost of the acquired assets.

Certain Payments to Nonresidents. Payments to a nonresident in respect of fees or charges arising under a contract for the provision of management or administrative skills are subject to tax at 15%. Payments for other services performed in Barbados are subject to tax at 25%. Royalty payments are also subject to tax at 15%.

RELATED CONSIDERATIONS

34. Incentives and Grants

The following incentives are available under the provisions of the Income Tax Act.

Fixed Assets. In lieu of initial allowance, a special deduction, known as "investment allowance," of 20% of the cost of new equipment or such that was imported into Barbados for the first time is allowed to basic industries, which generally are industries engaged in the manufacturing and processing of goods. An investment allowance of 40% is granted to businesses engaged in the manufacture of products from clay or limestone or in the manufacture of sugar. Effective from the 1985 income year, an investment allowance of 40% also is granted to manufacturing industries with export sales to areas other than the Caribbean Common Market. Agricultural operations receive rebates of 10% to 18% of the cost of equipment purchased for use in agriculture.

Agriculture. Incentives and subsidies are available for agricultural and farming activity, including spraying and irrigation facilities.

Manufacturing. Investors incurring expenditure on approved buildings will be eligible for an initial allowance of 40% and an annual allowance of 4% on the cost of the building.

Export Allowance. Persons manufacturing the product of an industry other than sugar and also those persons exporting data processing services or exporting products purchased wholesale from a local producer exclusively for export may be granted an export allowance. This allowance is in the form of a rebate on the amount of tax payable in relation to the amount of sales exported to countries outside of the Caribbean Common Market. These persons also may claim an allowance of 150% of market research and development expenses incurred to procure business in countries outside Caricom.

Foreign Currency Earnings. A special rebate of 50% of net foreign currency earnings is granted to persons receiving earnings from construction and professional services.

Construction Companies. The tax payable by a company on the income derived from the construction and sale in an income year of two or more dwelling houses, constructed of stone or other material that is permanently affixed to the land, is 20%.

The following incentives are available under the provisions of Fiscal Incentive Legislation:

Hotel Aids Act 1967. Hotels qualifying under this legislation are allowed to write off over ten years, including the year of expenditure, capital development cost (excluding land) against profits of the operation during that period. Expenditures for refurbishing or major improvements to hotels now qualify under this Act, which also provides for exemption from customs and other duties on such expenditures. Hotel owners can also claim an allowance of 150% of market research and development expenses incurred to encourage tourists to visit Barbados.

Fiscal Incentives Act 1974. This Act implements an agreement to which Barbados is a party between certain countries in the Caribbean region for the harmonization of fiscal incentives to industry. Foreign-owned enclave enterprises (which export their products to countries outside of Caricom) that reinvest their profits in Barbados will have the income from reinvestment taxed on the same basis as their income from exports. Under the Act, tax holidays of between six and ten years are granted to qualifying companies. Applications for this incentive are made to the responsible Minister who will seek to determine, among other things:

☐ The effect that approval would have on existing industries.
☐ Whether manufacture of the product would utilize raw materials or skills available in Barbados.
☐ The element of risk involved in establishing a successful manufacturing operation.
☐ The availability of trained personnel to carry on the industry.

International Business Companies. International business companies, which are granted several tax concessions, are corporations resident in Barbados that derive foreign-source income. Qualifying companies generally are taxed at the maximum rate of 2.5% on profits.

Off-Shore Banking. Such companies licensed to operate in Barbados pay tax at a maximum rate of 2.5% on profits.

Exempt Insurance Act 1983. Companies registered under this act pay a license fee, but there is no income or corporation tax on their profits or gains.

Shipping Incentives Act. Concessions are available to approved shipping companies engaged in specified shipping activities. These concessions include a ten-year tax exemption as well as freedom from customs duty on all materials connected with the company's shipping activities.

Barbados Foreign Sales Corporations Act 1984. This law permits the operation in Barbados of companies qualifying as FSCs in specified countries; for example, the United States. A Barbados FSC is totally exempt from Barbados taxation and exchange control regulations. An annual license fee of $2,000 is payable ($1,000 for a "small" FSC).

35. Exchange Controls

Exchange control is effective, and the movement of funds is monitored by the Central Bank. However, certain companies operating under the incentive legislation referred to in item 34 are permitted to operate external bank acounts.

36. Investment Restrictions on Nonresidents

Nonresidents acquiring property in Barbados require Central Bank approval and subsequent remittance of income or capital is subject to similar approval. Government policy is to encourage foreign investment in Barbados, and consequently, such approvals are usually readily obtained though they may be subject to conditions such as commitments to release a portion of shares in the local market or restrictions in the amount that the nonresident may borrow from local sources.

BELGIUM

INCOME TAXES ON CORPORATIONS

1. Rates

Companies which are domiciled or effectively have their management in Belgium are subject to taxation on their worldwide income. The basic rate is 39%, which is reduced as follows:

Taxable Income		Rate
Over	Not Over	
BEF 0	BEF 1,000,000	28%
1,000,000	3,600,000	BEF 280,000 plus 36% of the difference between the taxable income and BEF1,000,000.
3,600,000	13,000,000	BEF 1,216,000 plus 41% of the difference between the taxable income and BEF 3,600,000.

These reductions are not granted when at least 50% of the share capital is held by another company or other companies, Belgian or foreign, or when the company distributes a dividend exceeding 13% of its share capital or is classified as a holding company.

As a result of the above, subsidiaries of foreign corporations are subject to the flat rate of 39% on profit at all levels. For branches of foreign companies, the tax rate amounts to 43%. This rate is reduced in certain cases by the provisions of the tax treaties with foreign countries. If taxes are not prepaid during the year on an estimated basis, penalties on the unpaid tax are assessed.

2. Local Income Taxes

None.

3. Capital Gains Taxes

Gains realized on the sale of fixed assets or shares that have been held for less than five years are taxed as ordinary income. Gains realized on the sale of shares held for more than five years are taxed at a flat rate of 19.5%. Under certain conditions, such capital gains may be exempted if the proceeds of the sale are reinvested. Gains realized on the sale of fixed assets held for more than five years cannot benefit from the reduced rate of 19.5%, but under condition of reinvestment, the taxation can be deferred over the depreciation period of the asset acquired as reinvestment.

Capital losses are fully deductible and are offset against trading income.

It is anticipated that, effective the tax year 1992, gains realized on the sale of shares will be tax-exempt under certain conditions. Capital losses will no longer be tax deductible.

4. Branch Profits Taxes

If a nonresident company does not have a permanent establishment in Belgium, it is subject to tax only on income derived from property in Belgium, such as real property income, dividends, interest, and royalties. If a nonresident company has a permanent establishment in Belgium, it will be taxed as a branch of a foreign enterprise. All its Belgian real estate income must be included in the taxable income of the Belgian permanent establishment. Investment income will not be included, unless effectively connected with the permanent establishment.

To a large extent, a Belgian branch of a foreign company is subject to the same rules for determination of taxable income as a domestic Belgian corporation. However, no deduction is allowed for interest or royalties paid by a branch to its home office or to another branch or division of the same company. In addition, assessments to nonresidents tax (similar to corporation tax) are made on a notional basis if the branch cannot show that all transactions have been made on an arm's-length basis (see item 17).

5. Foreign Tax Reliefs

A 75% rate reduction applies to net income earned and taxed abroad, unless that income is exempt by application of a double tax treaty.

A system of tax credit is applicable to dividends received from non-permanent investments (see item 28) and to royalties. The tax credit amounts to 15/85 of the net amount received, must be added to the taxable basis, and is creditable against the corporate taxes. The tax credit is never reimbursed and cannot be carried forward.

A similar system applies to interest from a foreign source; however, depending on tax treaties, the credit amounts either to the foreign tax (limited to 15%) or to 15/85 of the net amount received. In addition, this tax credit is never available in case of channelling operations.

8. Other Matters

Withholding Taxes. Resident companies and Belgian branches are required to withhold tax payments at source on salaries, wages and other remuneration, dividend distributions, interest, royalties, and similar fees.

Payroll Withholding Tax. The employer is responsible for remitting payroll withholding taxes within two weeks following the month during which the remuneration was paid. Each year, before February 1, an annual return must be filed showing the total remuneration and relevant withholding tax for the preceding calendar year of each employee.

Dividend Withholding Tax. Belgian entities are subject to a 25% withholding tax on profits distributed in Belgium or abroad. This rate is generally reduced by treaty to 15% (see item 17).

Interest and Royalty Withholding Tax. Interest and royalties are in principle subject to a withholding tax of 10% on the amount distributed. This rate of tax may be reduced under tax treaties. The tax is generally calculated on 85% of the principal amount of the royalty.

Tax Implications of Mergers, Acquisitions, and Liquidations. A liquidating company still is subject to normal corporate taxation on its profits of liquidation. However, the reduced rate of 19.5% is applicable on capital gains realized during the liquidation period on the sale of fixed assets and shares.

Any payment to the shareholders in excess of the reimbursement of the revalued capital (the revaluation being made according to coefficients deemed to reflect currency devaluation) in principle is treated as a dividend, subject to the normal 25% withholding tax. The payment of this withholding tax, however, is not certain. Clarification is expected in the future.

The tax applies in principle when a corporation is liquidated in the course of a merger or split-up. However, a tax-free merger or split-up is permitted if the absorbing corporation has its seat or principal office in Belgium, the merger is performed solely through an exchange of stock in the other company, and there has not been a sale of the abolished corporation's fixed assets or financial investments.

Repurchase of a Company's Own Shares. Corporations repurchasing their own shares are deemed in certain circumstances to have distributed a dividend on the excess of purchase price over the amount originally paid in.

INCOME TAXES ON INDIVIDUALS

9. Rates

Residents of Belgium are subject to personal income tax on their total income from all sources. The incomes of a husband and wife are combined to determine the applicable tax rate, but this rule has two major exceptions: when husband and wife both have professional income, the professional income of the spouse who earns less is taxed separately; and, if only one spouse has professional income, 30% of the professional income is allocated to the other spouse (with a maximum of BEF 288,000) and taxed separately. Taxation on a sliding scale is applicable to the successive portions of the net taxable income at rates varying to 25% to 55% (plus municipal taxes). These portions of the net taxable income are automatically indexed every year. Reductions for family responsibilities become significant for taxpayers with more than three dependents.

The following examples illustrate the income tax in 1990 for an individual, married with two children.

Taxable Income	Tax	Average Rate
BEF 500,000	BEF 20,505	4.1%
1,000,000	201,873	20.2
1,500,000	421,520	28.1
3,000,000	1,193,425	39.8
5,000,000	2,293,429	45.9

10. Local Income Taxes

Item 9 does not include municipal and provincial taxes, which generally amount to 6% to 10% of the basic tax rates.

11. Capital Gains Taxes

Capital gains generated by an individual in his private capacity (e.g., on the sale of a private residence or privately owned securities) are not generally taxable, but capital gains from the sale of substantial holdings of shares in a Belgian company to foreign corporations are subject to tax at the rate of 16.5% (plus municipal taxes).

Capital gains of individuals who are not real estate dealers, arising from the sale of land, may be taxable if made within eight years of the acquisition of the property. The rate of tax is 33% or 16.5% (plus municipal taxes), depending on the period for which the property has been held.

12. Foreign Tax Reliefs

A 50% rate reduction applies to net income earned and taxed abroad, unless that income is exempt under a double tax treaty.

13. Tax Period

Personal income tax is always based on the calendar year. If an individual is resident in the country for only a part of a calendar year, his domestic income in that period is treated as if it were the income relating to the full calendar year; that is, there is no prorated restriction of allowances.

14. Other Matters

The taxable income of a resident individual can consist of real property income, personal property income, occupational income, and miscellaneous income. Taxable income is the net income from all sources. However, certain types of income may be taxed separately, such as certain capital gains and personal property income.

Real Property Income. The tax on income of individuals from real property situated in Belgium is based on an arbitrary net income (in principle, 60% of the 1975 gross normal rental income) fixed by the tax authorities and revised periodically.

Personal Property Income. Income from personal property includes such income as dividends, interest, and royalties from domestic or foreign sources. Personal property income received by Belgian individual residents is not globalized with other income; the withholding tax (either 25% or 10%) is considered the final tax. If Belgian withholding tax is not applied to the personal property income, the beneficiary has to report this income in his tax return but the rate of tax applicable will be limited to 25% or 10%.

Occupational Income. Occupational income consists of business income including sole trader and partnership profits, wages and salaries, and income from professions.

Miscellaneous Income. Miscellaneous income includes net revenues from casual services rendered to third parties, capital gains from disposition of certain land holdings or arising on substantial holdings of shares in a Belgian company (see item 11) or alimony, and lottery prizes on bonds.

INCOME TAXES ON NONRESIDENTS

15. Liability to Tax

Nonresident individuals are, in general terms, taxed on their total Belgian-source income, including income obtained from a permanent establishment in Belgium. A nonresident is any person whose domicile or principal residence is not located in Belgium.

16. Rates

The rates of taxation are the same as those for resident individuals. However, some tax reliefs (e.g., fixed abatement on real estate income, personal relief for spouse and children) may not be granted if the nonresident did not keep an abode in Belgium during the whole tax period. This exclusion may be overruled by the nondiscrimination clause of the treaties for avoidance of double taxation signed by Belgium.

Special Tax Regime. Special tax benefits may be available to foreign management personnel, foreign research personnel, and foreign personnel without managerial responsibilities but who are so highly specialized that their recruitment in Belgium is very difficult, if not impossible.

To benefit from the special regime, the foreign directors, executives, and employees must be *temporary* residents in Belgium and meet one of the following requirements:

☐ Is employed in a scientific research center or laboratory.

☐ Is transferred to or recruited by a business entity under foreign control or forming part of an international group.

☐ Is transferred to or recruited by a control and coordinating office.

To demonstrate the fact that the expatriate is temporarily posted to Belgium and, thus, considered as a nonresident from a tax point of view, it is necessary to prove either that:

☐ His family is located abroad.

☐ The location of the family fortune is not in Belgium. This is determined by the physical location of his tangible or intangible property, such as real estate, cash, bank accounts, shares and bonds, business interests, and debt claims.

All other evidence is taken into consideration, such as existence of life assurance contracts written abroad, continuation of affiliation to a foreign group pension scheme, and continuation of subscriptions abroad.

If the above-mentioned conditions are fulfilled, the persons concerned receive preferential tax treatment.

The salary package of a foreign executive must be divided into two parts: (1) a base salary, and (2) allowances that will be deductible for the employer and tax-free for the expatriate. Allowances may include those granted for cost of living and excess rents, home leave, tax equalization, moving expenses, school fees, exchange differences, and the like. A file must be submitted to the tax authorities initially to establish the nonresident status of the expatriate and annually to determine his tax-free allowances. The tax authorities consider as reasonable allowances whose amount does not exceed BEF 450,000 for expatriates employed by industrial and trading companies and BEF 1,200,000 for expatriates in headquarters companies. Only the base salary is subject to taxation. In addition, the expatriate is entitled to exclude from taxation that proportion of his total income represented by the percentage of working days spent outside Belgium for professional purposes.

Real Property Income. Nonresident corporations are taxable on the net rental income from rented properties at the normal rates of tax. Nonprofit organizations, whether resident or nonresident, are taxable on ratable value of property at applicable rates of property tax plus a flat rate of 20% on the excess of net rentals over the ratable value when let for professional use.

17. Withholding Tax Rates

The salient features of Belgium's tax treaties are as follows:

□ The withholding tax on dividends paid and received is generally reduced to 15%.

□ Royalties paid or received are frequently exempt from withholding tax.

□ A permanent establishment, defined as a fixed place of business of a foreign registered corporation in Belgium, is invariably subject to Belgian taxation unless:

—The activity relates to a construction site of less than 12 months' duration (with some exceptions).

—The activity is confined to purchase of goods, or storage and delivery of goods, or collection of orders without the authority to conclude contracts in the name of the enterprise.

Withholding taxes on outward remittances (and the tax rate on Belgian branches of foreign companies) are in the following table:

	Dividends	Interest	Royalties	Tax Rate on Branches
Nontreaty countries	25%	10%	10%	43%
Treaty countries:				
Australia	15	10	10	43
Austria	15	10 (1)	0 (2)	39
Brazil	15	10	10	39
Canada	15	10 (1)	10 (3)	43
China	10	10 (4)	10	39
Czechoslovakia	15	10	5 (3)	39
Denmark	15	10 (1)	0	39
Finland	15	10 (1)	5 (3)	42.05
France	15 (5)	10	0	43
Germany	15	10 (6)	0	39
Greece	15	10	5	39
Hungary	10	10	0	39
India	15	10	10	39
Indonesia	15	10	10	39
Ireland	15	10 (1)	0	43
Israel	15	10	10 (3)	39
Italy	15	10	5	39

	Dividends	Interest	Royalties	Tax Rate on Branches
Ivory Coast	15%	10%	10%	39%
Japan	15 (7)	10	10	39
Korea	15	10	10	39
Luxembourg	15 (8)	10 (6)	0	42.05
Malaysia	15	10	10	39
Malta	15	10	10 (3)	39
Morocco	15	10	10 (9)	39
Netherlands	15 (7)	10 (6)	0	42.05
New Zealand	15	10	10	43
Norway	15	10 (1)	0	39
Pakistan	15	10	10 (10)	39
Philippines	20 (11)	10	10	39
Poland	10	10	10	43
Portugal	15	10 (1)	5	39
Romania	10	10	10	39
Singapore	15	10	0	39
Soviet Union	15	10 (1)	0	39
Spain	15	10 (1)	5	39
Sri Lanka	15	10 (12)	10	43
Sweden	15 (7)	10	0	39
Switzerland	15 (5)	10 (1)	0	39
Thailand	20	10	10 (9)	39
Tunisia	15	10 (1)	10 (9)	43
United Kingdom	10 (7)	10	0	43
United States	15 (10)	10 (1)	0	39
Yugoslavia	15	10	10	43

Notes:
(1) Reduced to nil if arising from commercial credit resulting from deferred payments for goods or services.
(2) 10% if paid by a company to a person holding more than 50% of the capital.
(3) Reduced to nil on certain copyrights.
(4) 0% when interest paid to the State of China or to financial institutions whose capital is 100% held by the State of China.
(5) Further reduced to 10% if recipient is company which holds directly at least 10% of capital.
(6) Reduced to nil if paid to enterprises (generally no reduction in case of participation of 25% or more).
(7) Further reduced to 5% if recipient is a company which holds directly at least 25% of capital.
(8) Further reduced to 10% if recipient is a company which holds directly at least 25% of capital (participation of at least BF 250 million as to Luxembourg).

(9)   Reduced to 5% on certain copyrights.
(10) Reduced to 5% if recipient is a company that holds directly 10% of the voting stock.
(11) Reduced to 15% if the dividend is exempt from tax in the Philippines.
(12) Reduced to 0% if paid to the government or a government-owned organization.

Note that the EC Directive on dividends distribution will enter in force on January 1, 1992 at the latest: dividends distributed by a Belgian company to another company located in the EC will no longer be subject to withholding tax provided there is a shareholding of 25%.

OTHER SIGNIFICANT TAXES

21.   Sales (Value Added)

Value added tax is levied on goods, services, and imports but not on export sales. Goods subject to VAT are generally defined as being "moveable by nature." New buildings may be sold with VAT at the option of the builders; this allows recovery of VAT on construction costs. Companies that export more than 30%, 50%, 75%, or 90% of their sales in each year will, on application, receive in the following year a corresponding reduction on the total VAT payable on imports and local purchases that will be exported or used in production destined for export. This frees the exporter from financing refundable tax payments.

There are five rates of VAT: 25% (on luxury items); 33% (on selected luxury items); 6% (on basic necessities such as food and pharmaceuticals); 17% on energy and a few selected products; and the standard rate of 19% on other items not specifically designated.

22.   Inheritance and Gift Taxes

Gifts of real estate located in Belgium, or personal property wherever situated, made by a resident individual to another person are subject to a gift tax at the same rates as those applicable to inheritances. The tax is only payable if the gift is made by a notarial instrument (which will always be the case when real property is transferred), but there are provisions for including in the estate untaxed gifts made in anticipation of death.

The inheritance taxes payable by the heirs are based on the net amount inherited from the deceased by each heir, and not on the total value of the deceased's estate. The rates of tax payable by each heir vary according to the degree of relationship with the deceased, and increase progressively with the amount inherited. The tax rates vary from 3% to 30% for direct lineal inheritance, and from 30% to 80% in other situations. The higher rates apply to the upper "slice" of the amount inherited, not to the whole amount. There are minor statutory exemptions, the amounts depending on the relationship to the deceased, on which no tax is payable.

23. Taxes on Payrolls (Social Security)

Belgian social security benefits are as follows: unemployment relief, family allowances, sickness and disability payments, medical benefits, vacation allowances, and old-age pensions. All employees are compulsory members with the exception of temporary workers qualifying for exemption under reciprocal social security treaties. Contributions are payable in part by withholding from employees' remuneration and in part by the employer. The current monthly premiums are calculated as follows:

	Contributions	
	Employer	Employee
Manual workers	49.85%	12.07%
Salaried employees	34.60	12.07

For salaried employees, vacation pay equal to 85% of the monthly salary is paid directly to the employee once a year.

24. Taxes on Natural Resources

There are no special taxes on natural resources.

25. Other Taxes

Land and Property. A real property registration tax of 12.5% is generally applicable to sales or exchanges of real estate located in Belgium, whether made by a corporate entity or an individual. The tax is computed on the commercial value of the real property transferred, and the buyer is normally responsible for payment. Certain transactions may be exempt from the real property registration tax, generally when they are subject to some other form of taxation.

Capital. There are no wealth taxes in Belgium, although the 12.5% registration duty on the sale of real estate is frequently regarded as a form of wealth tax.

Registration and Stamp Taxes. All official documents require small stamp duties, as do bills of exchange. Registration tax is incurred on all capital issuance, whether original or increased. The rate is 0.5% of nominal value, but is abolished in the event of mergers if the resultant entity's center of operations remains within the EEC. Leases incur a registration tax of 0.2% on the rent and charges receivable under the contract. Mortgages are taxable at 0.2% of the principal amount.

COMPUTATION OF TAXABLE INCOME

26. Capital Gains

See item 3.

27.   Depreciation and Depletion

With the exception of land, most tangible and intangible fixed assets are depreciable. The depreciation methods permitted for tax purposes are the straight-line and the declining-balance methods. Original cost generally is the basis for depreciation, and the depreciation rate should be based on the normal useful life of the assets. Belgian tax law, however, provides only guidelines for depreciation rather than specific rates of depreciation.

The suggested depreciation rates under the straight-line method for the following fixed assets are:

Office buildings	3%
Industrial buildings	5%
Furniture	10%
Machinery and equipment	20%
Vehicles	20 or 25%

The annual depreciation rate under the declining-balance method cannot exceed twice the straight-line rate.

Patents and trademarks are amortized over their expected useful lives. Goodwill may be amortized only to the extent that it can be reasonably shown that its value has fallen below cost.

28.   Treatment of Dividends

Although dividends received are taxable, a 90% dividends-received exclusion applies in the case of a Belgian corporation or branch of a foreign corporation receiving dividends derived from permanent investments; an 85% exclusion applies to dividends received by a financial company.

Dividends received from Belgian sources are subject to the withholding tax of 25%. The net dividend to be declared must be increased by 1/3 in order to include the withholding tax. The tax withheld at source is creditable against the corporate tax and the excess is refundable. If the receiving company does not hold the investment during the entire year or if the dividend has been paid by a company not subject to corporation tax, no exemption of 90% or 85% may be granted, but the recipient will be allowed a tax credit equal to 46% (Belgian-source) and 15/85 (foreign-source) when subject to tax abroad of the net dividend received.

It is anticipated that, as of the 1992 tax year, the exclusion percentage will amount to 95%.

29.   Loss Carryovers

Losses realized in a tax year may be carried forward indefinitely. There are no carryback provisions. However, losses can be offset only up to half of the corporation's profit or BEF 20 million.

30. Transactions between Related Parties

If a company established in Belgium is directly or indirectly dependent on a foreign company, all abnormal transfers of profits to the latter company will be added to the net taxable income of the Belgian company. This rule also applies to abnormal transfers of profits granted to any other company, establishment, or individual when they are subject to significantly more favorable tax treatment than the Belgian company. Interest, royalties, and service fees paid to such companies are not deductible as business expenses unless shown to correspond to a normal business transaction at a reasonable amount. Certain antiavoidance measures are also in force. The names of the beneficiaries of the commissions and fees must be disclosed to the tax authorities; if not, the unidentified commissions are subject to a special tax of 200% (which is tax deductible, thus making an effective rate of 122%).

31. Consolidation of Income

There is no provision for the filing of consolidated tax returns by related corporations.

32. Tax Periods

Generally, the tax period is the calendar year and the tax assessment year is the following calendar year. However, corporations that maintain adequate accounting records may use their accounting year as their tax period. In such case, the tax on income of such year is assessed in the calendar year in which the accounting year ends.

RELATED CONSIDERATIONS

34. Incentives and Grants

The Belgian Government has sponsored legislation to foster industrial and economic development and national expansion. These laws enable the Government to grant aid to both Belgian and foreign investors. Three of these laws are currently in force. The Law of Economic Reorientation of August 4, 1978 introduced economic measures designed to stimulate small- and medium-sized businesses. The regional law of December 30, 1970 promoted activities which contribute directly to the formation of industrial undertakings in specified development areas. The law of July 17, 1959 enabled the Government to grant aid to investments outside the development areas.

Coordination Centers.   Royal Decree 187 has introduced fiscal incentives for a period of ten years to attract the establishment in Belgium of coordination centers. A coordination center:

☐   May be either a Belgian company or the Belgian branch of a foreign company.
☐   May not be part of a group which is a bank or insurance company.
☐   May not hold shares in other companies.

□ Must have as its *only* purpose the development and centralization of one or several activities for the *sole benefit* of all or part of the group of companies. The following activities are enumerated in the Decree: publicity; supply and gathering of information; insurance and reinsurance; scientific research; relations with international and national authorities; central accounting, administrative, and computer services; centralization of financial operations and covering risks of exchange rate fluctuations; and, in addition, all ancillary and preparatory activities.

□ Must be part of a group whose combined capital and reserves amount to a billion francs and whose turnover amounts to ten billion francs. For these purposes, a shareholding of only 20% is sufficient to constitute a group.

□ Must be part of a group with multinational character (e.g., the group must have subsidiaries in at least four different countries and a significant portion of its consolidated shareholders' equity and turnover outside its country of origin).

□ Must employ in Belgium at least ten persons within two years after the start of activities.

□ Must be recognized as a coordination center by a separate royal decree.

Coordination centers have been granted three tax benefits:

□ Coordination centers are taxed arbitrarily on the basis of their "operating costs," which includes all expenses except for personnel and financial costs. The rate which applies to the "operating cost" will be the same as the one the coordination center uses for charging out its costs to the group companies (except if the rate is considered to be abnormal). The tax payable will generally be minimal.

□ Dividends, interest, and royalties paid by a coordination center are also exempt from withholding tax. Buildings held by such centers are exempt from property taxes and no registration tax need be paid on the initial (or increase in) share capital.

□ Belgian companies that make loans to coordination centers will benefit from a notional withholding tax attributed to the interest paid by the coordination center if the proceeds are used by the center (or group companies) either for the purchase or construction of new fixed assets to be used in the Belgian business or for research and development in Belgium. This is important since banks retrocede this notional tax to the coordination center as a reduction of interest rate. Belgian companies receiving dividends from coordination centers will also benefit from the same notional withholding tax but with several restrictions.

Except in special circumstances, this notional tax will no longer be in force.

Distribution Centers.   A new tax regime has been introduced by the tax authorities for distribution centers.

Only the companies liable to corporate income taxes or to nonresidents corporate income taxes may qualify for this special regime, provided they limit themselves to carrying out exclusively any or part of the following activities:

☐ Purchase—in their name or in the name and on behalf of group companies—of raw materials and supplies intended for said companies.

☐ Storage, management, and packaging of these raw materials and supplies.

☐ Sale only to the group companies—as well as transport and supply—of these raw materials and supplies.

☐ Storage, management, and packaging, on behalf of the group companies, of goods and finished goods of such companies, which are the property of the latter companies.

☐ Transport and supply, on account of the group companies, of such goods and finished goods, with the exclusion of the sale itself; in this regard, it is specified that the distribution center can *in no way* intervene in the sale operation of the aforesaid goods and finished products.

The packaging can in no way give an added value to the goods stored, so that no processing operation, on the one hand, of raw materials and supplies, and on the other hand, of goods and finished goods can be made by the distribution center.

The taxable profit of a distribution center is determined in the same way as normal operating companies or Belgian branches of foreign companies. However, the tax authorities will accept that such a center does not grant any abnormal or gratuitous advantage to a foreign-related company when its turnover—exclusive of the amount corresponding to the purchase price of raw materials and supplies sold back—is not lower than 105% of its operating costs, being understood that this condition must be met for any group company considered separately.

By operating costs, it is meant the total amount of costs incurred, excluding:

☐ The purchase price of the raw materials and supplies.

☐ Some nondeductible expenses.

Scientific Research.   Scientific research is stimulated by granting an exemption from corporation tax equal to BEF 100,000 per additional person employed in qualifying work.

35.   Exchange Controls

Foreign payments are not subject to any restriction in Belgium. This means that external commercial and financial transactions do not require authorization and bank notes may be used freely in current transactions with foreign countries. Since 1990, there no longer is any difference in exchange rates due to the nature of the transaction, and there is no tie between the purchase of foreign currencies and foreign payments.

36. Investment Restrictions on Nonresidents

A public offer by a nonresident person or corporation to purchase the equity of a Belgian corporation listed on the stock exchange must receive prior approval by the Ministry of Finance. This restriction does not apply to offers made by nationals or registered corporations of one of the EEC countries. Government spokesmen have indicated that there is no intention of hindering foreign investment in general.

Any operation whereby at least ⅓ of the capital of any business in Belgium with a net worth of at least BEF 100,000,000 changes hands must be reported to the Ministry of Finance, the Ministry of Economic Affairs, and the Ministry of Regional Economy. This restriction also applies to Belgian investors.

37. Other Matters

Registration of Contractors. Any person who contracts as a principal or an entrepreneur with a nonregistered supplier of services belonging to the construction industry in the broadest sense is jointly liable for all taxes and social security contributions of his contractor for up to 85% of the price charged and is obliged to withhold as security 30% of the price charged. These measures do not apply to registered contractors. Branches of non-EEC residents cannot obtain such registration.

SELECTION OF BUSINESS ENTITY BY NONRESIDENTS

Nonresident investors can operate in Belgium either through a branch or a Belgian subsidiary. The tax consequences for a foreign entity operating in Belgium through a branch are:

☐ Branch profits are taxable at 43%. In most cases this rate is reduced by the provisions of the tax treaties with the foreign country concerned (see item 17).

☐ No additional tax is levied on remittances of branch profits.

☐ Withholding tax is imposed on foreign interest or foreign royalties charged to the branch.

☐ Interest and royalty payments from the Belgian branch to its foreign home office cannot be deducted, unless they represent the Belgian branch's share of payment due for use of a license paid for by the parent itself.

☐ If the branch is unable to show normal trading results on transactions made at an arm's-length basis and recorded in books of account, it will be taxed on a notional basis; that is, a percentage margin on gross sales determined by comparison with other enterprises, a fixed amount per employee occupied, or a percentage of expenses incurred (generally 10%). Headquarter branch offices of foreign companies may operate on a tax-free basis, provided that the Minister of Finance recognizes the nontrading character of its activity. If these offices are involved in marketing activities, they also are assessed on a percentage of expenses incurred.

The choice of a branch or a locally incorporated subsidiary will usually be determined by foreign, rather than Belgian, tax considerations and by considerations other than tax. Generally, there is a marked preference to use a branch where the operation is relatively small as there are fewer annual statutory formalities to complete. In many instances, the possibility of losses in the early years makes operation as a branch preferable as many tax treaties allow for immediate relief against the profits of the head office.

SPECIMEN TAX COMPUTATION

Information:

□ The resident corporation's operating profit for the year of BF 30,000,000 consists of the following:

	BEF '000's
Trading results in Belgium (including a capital gain on sale of shares of BF 5,000)	17,000
Trading results from a nontax treaty country—taxed in country of derivation	6,000
Trading results from a tax treaty country	1,000
Belgian dividend income	4,000
Foreign dividend income	2,000

□ All dividends are derived from permanent investments and have been taxed in the distributing company. The capital gain was realized on a sale of shares held for more than five years.

Computation:

	BEF '000's
Operating profit as per accounts	30,000
Less	
Trading results from tax treaty country	1,000
90% of Belgian dividend income (item 28)	3,600
90% of foreign dividend income	1,800
Taxable income	23,600

Capital gains taxes (BEF 5,000 at 19.5%) 975
Trading results from nontax treaty country
    (BEF 6,000 at 39% reduced to 1/4 or 9.75%) 585
Other
    23,600 less   5,000
                      6,000
                  11,000
    12,600 at 39% 4,914
Tax payable   BEF 6,474

BERMUDA

INCOME TAXES ON CORPORATIONS

None.

INCOME TAXES ON INDIVIDUALS

None.

INCOME TAXES ON NONRESIDENTS

15. Liability to Tax

None.

19. Tax Treaties

On July 11, 1986, Bermuda and the United States executed a Convention, which came into effect on December 2, 1988. From Bermuda's perspective, the Convention provides that:

☐ A Bermuda insurance enterprise is not subject to U.S. federal income taxes on its business profits, except to the extent that they are attributable to a permanent establishment in the United States through which the business of the enterprise is wholly or partly carried on.

☐ Premiums paid or credited on or after January 1, 1986 by a U.S. policyholder to a Bermuda insurance enterprise, which are allocable to insurance coverage for periods beginning before January 1, 1990, are not subject to U.S. federal excise taxes, if the enterprise is a controlled foreign corporation as defined by the U.S. Internal Revenue Code of 1986 and its income, or its related-person insurance income, is taxed to its U.S. shareholders, except (to prevent "treaty shopping") to the extent that the risks covered by such premiums are reinsured with a person not entitled to the benefits of this or any other convention that applies to these taxes. Premiums paid or credited after December 31, 1989 are subject to U.S. federal excise taxes.

☐ Also to prevent "treaty shopping," an insurance enterprise is not entitled to relief from taxation if it is owned 50% or less by Bermuda residents and U.S. citizens and residents, or if its income is used in substantial part to make certain distributions or payments to persons who are neither Bermuda residents nor U.S. citizens or residents. Such "distributions" are those that are made with respect to beneficial ownership interests but which are substantially disproportionate to such interests. Such "payments" include reinsurance premiums, but do not include payments of insurance claims. If an insurance company's principal class of shares is substantially and regularly traded on a recognized stock exchange or on the NASDAQ System, it is not subject to these limitations.

☐ The United States and Bermuda will provide assistance to each other in carrying out their respective domestic laws concerning taxes. There are provisions protecting confidentiality of information for persons not resident in the United States or Bermuda, protecting existing obligations to maintain confidentiality of information, and excluding assistance with respect to taxable years barred by a statute of limitations or beginning prior to January 1, 1977.

Except for the United States, Bermuda has no tax treaties or other arrangements with other countries, including the United Kingdom, and its courts will not enforce actions brought by the taxing authorities of those other countries.

20. Other Matters

There are no taxes on income, dividends, capital gains, sales or gifts. The Minister of Finance is empowered to give an exempted company or exempted partnership (see "SELECTION OF BUSINESS ENTITY BY NONRESIDENTS") a formal assurance that no tax computed on profits, income, or any capital asset, gain, or appreciation will apply prior to the year 2016 to it or to any of its operations, shares, debentures, or other obligations.

OTHER SIGNIFICANT TAXES

21. Sales (Value Added)

None.

22. Inheritance and Gift Taxes

Stamp duty is payable on an affidavit of the value of Bermuda property in a deceased's estate at a rate of 0% on the first $20,000, 5% on the next $80,000, and 10% thereafter.

Foreign currency assets situated in Bermuda, including shares in exempted companies and interests in exempted partnerships, are not Bermuda property.

23. Taxes on Payrolls (Social Security)

Employment tax is normally charged at a 5% rate on an employer's total payroll (including the value of fringe benefits). Exempted companies, exempted partnerships, registered charities, and public bodies are not subject to the tax, and exemptions are given to certain individuals and small employers. Hotels and restaurants are subject to reduced rates of tax.

A hospital levy is payable by all employers (other than for those employees engaged in domestic service) at a rate of 5% of payrolls. The employer may recover one half of the tax from employees. Tax paid by exempted companies and exempted partnerships is not assessed on actual payrolls but on a notional payroll of $48,060 per annum per employee. Exempted companies and exempted partnerships pay an additional hospital levy of 2% of the notional payroll in lieu of employment tax, and no part of this additional amount is recoverable from employees. It is intended to increase the rate of this additional levy by one percentage point annually until it reaches 5%.

Social insurance rates for contributory pensions are $33.82 per week for employed and self-employed persons over school leaving age and under the age of 65. One-half of the payment is recoverable from the employee.

24. Taxes on Natural Resources

None.

25. Other Taxes

Customs duties are calculated on an ad valorem basis on the value of imported goods. The normal rate is 20%, although many food items are exempt and lower rates apply for various essentials and materials used in local manufacturing. Certain luxury items are dutiable at higher rates. A surcharge of 10% is levied on duty payable.

Exempted companies and exempted partnerships are required to pay annual fees as follows:

Capital		Annual Fee
Over	Not Over	
	$ 12,000	$1,600
$ 12,000	120,000	3,200
120,000	1,200,000	4,800
1,200,000	12,000,000	6,400
12,000,000		8,000

Capital is defined as authorized share capital plus share premium account for exempted companies and as contributed capital for exempted partnerships.

In addition, insurance companies pay an annual license fee of $1,000. Permit companies pay an annual fee of $1,600, except for insurers, mutual funds, and public finance companies, which pay an annual fee of $3,200. A company that is a unit trust manager pays an additional fee of $2,250 for each unit trust it manages.

An instrument executed by an exempted company, permit company, exempted partnership or exempted unit trust scheme properly a party to the instrument, or person in respect of his or her interest in or property of such a company, partnership, or scheme is exempt from stamp duty.

Stamp duty on a trust or settlement inter vivos and subsequent additions thereto is payable at $250 plus:

In respect of Bermuda property	
on the first $20,000	nil
on the next $80,000	5%
over $100,000	10%
In respect of non-Bermuda property	
0.10% up to an aggregate of $40,000	

Additions of Bermuda property to a settlement, up to the point where duty paid equals $2,050 (i.e., $250 plus up to $1,800 at the 2.0% rate) are at 2.0% and 5.0% thereafter. Stamp duty is payable at the rate of 0.10% of the value of other (i.e., non-Bermuda) property.

Where a trustee in Bermuda is appointed trustee of a settlement originally created elsewhere, stamp duty on the instrument of appointment is limited to $250 where the settlement was created two years or more before the appointment of the trustee in Bermuda. Where the settlement is created less than two years before, stamp duty is payable at $250 plus 0%/5%/10% or at 0.10%, or $4,000, whichever is least.

There is an exemption for certain charitable trusts.

Stamp duty on conveyances or transfers of Bermuda land and local securities is at the following rates:

first $100,000	1%
next $400,000	2
next $500,000	3
greater than $1,000,000	4

Other taxes imposed include:

- □ Land tax. From 1.5% to 22.5% annually on increasing layers of assessed annual rental value of real property.
- □ Hotel occupancy tax. 6% on the daily "rack rate."
- □ Passenger tax. $15 per person ($5 for a child) on departures by air and $60 by sea.

☐ Vehicle license fees. Up to $694 per annum on private cars.

☐ Foreign currency purchase tax. A one-time tax of 10% on capital invested abroad (maximum of $25,000 per annum allowed) and on certain other payments. It applies to resident Bermudians, and to resident non-Bermudians employed by Bermudians to the extent of their Bermuda remuneration.

RELATED CONSIDERATIONS

34. Incentives and Grants

Customs duties have sometimes been deferred on imports necessary for the development of major capital projects.

35. Exchange Controls

Foreign-owned companies and foreign persons, except those employed by Bermudians or Bermudian-owned companies, are not subject to exchange controls and may maintain accounts and deal without limit in all major currencies. There are no restrictions on the remittance by such companies or persons of dividends, interest, and royalties, or on other transfers.

36. Investment Restrictions on Nonresidents

Investment in local companies is restricted to 40% ownership by non-Bermudians.

A non-Bermudian may be permitted to purchase a dwelling in Bermuda for his or her own use, and is liable on the purchase to tax of 20% of the purchase price. Permission for such purchases will only be granted for high value dwellings.

37. Other Matters

Banks. Bermuda's three local banks, all with close correspondent relationships with major banks worldwide, offer complete domestic and international banking, investment, and corporate and personal trust facilities (which include investment custody and management, registrar, transfer agent, and dividend paying services). The three local banks are connected to the worldwide telecommunications network operated by the Society for Worldwide Interbank Financial Telecommunications (SWIFT).

As in the United Kingdom, there is no law compelling secrecy. Under the Evidence Act, banks in Bermuda enjoy a favored position. Under general law, banks owe a duty of secrecy to their customers. All three banks in Bermuda observe a strict secrecy code, particularly with respect to the passing of confidential information to countries in which disclosure may be compelled. Disclosure of information to the United States is limited by the 1986 Convention (see item 19).

SELECTION OF BUSINESS ENTITY BY NONRESIDENTS

The most common entity available to non-Bermudians (resident or not) is the exempted company formed to conduct business outside of Bermuda, which generally is free of all exchange control restrictions. Incorporation is usually arranged through one of Bermuda's law firms at a cost, including fees and disbursements, of approximately $3,400 and is normally completed in approximately two weeks but may be completed sooner in some circumstances. Since at least two directors must be resident in Bermuda, secretarial and directors' services and the registered office are often provided by the company's legal firm and bank at approximately $2,500 to $4,200 per annum depending on the degree of services required.

The minimum authorized capital for an exempted company is $12,000, or its equivalent, which must be fully issued but need not be fully paid. For exempted insurance companies, the minimum capital is $120,000 to $370,000, depending on their business activities, which must be fully paid prior to commencement of underwriting.

Other entities include trusts and settlements, permit companies, and exempted partnerships (either general or limited) formed by non-Bermudians to conduct business outside Bermuda. These entities generally are free of all exchange control restrictions.

"Exempted companies" and "exempted partnerships" are exempted from certain restrictions on non-Bermudian shareholders, directors, and partners that are otherwise applicable to companies and partnerships.

"Permit companies" are companies incorporated outside Bermuda that have obtained a permit from the Minister of Finance to carry on a business outside Bermuda from a place of business in Bermuda.

BOLIVIA

INCOME TAXES ON CORPORATIONS

The new Bolivian tax law establishes a temporal system in which the net income is taxed, based on the assumption that the net income is equal to the net equity. The system might be interpreted as a tax on equity or capital, but it has been defined as a tax on income and is named as such: *Impuesto a la Renta Presunta de las Empresas*. For foreign businesses, this tax can be taken as a tax deduction on their home-country tax return, provided their tax laws allow it.

1. Rates

Taxable income of Bolivian corporations, limited liability companies, sole proprietorships, and branches of foreign corporations is taxed at the rate of 3% on the business's net worth at the closing day of its financial statements. However, investments in other companies subject to this tax are not taxed a second time.

Oil and electrical companies and nonprofit entities are exempt from the income tax.

Mining and smelting companies and mineral traders are subject to a 30% income tax rate, and they must make an advance payment of 2.5% on the value of their export shipments. If this amount is larger than the corresponding income tax, the difference benefits the tax authority.

2. Local Income Taxes

None.

3. Capital Gains Taxes

None.

4. Branch Profits Taxes

The income tax rate applying to branches and other permanent establishments of foreign companies also is 3%, except for international transportation or communications companies, which pay a 10% tax on 20% of their gross taxable income, which is 2% of their gross income.

5. Foreign Tax Reliefs

National corporations are not granted any relief from foreign income taxes paid.

6. Classification of Corporations

Corporations are classified for tax purposes as resident or nonresident and as commercial and services, industrial and construction, agricultural and agroindustry oriented, nonprofit cooperatives and mutuals, banks and financial institutions, and mining, petroleum, and public services.

7. Payment of Taxes

Corporations are not required to make advance payments toward their annual income tax liability but may do so if they prefer. The filing of financial statements with the IRS and the payment of taxes should be done together through a certified declaration no later than 120 days after the end of the fiscal year. The fiscal periods are as follows:

April 1–March 31	Industrial and construction companies
July 1–June 30	Agricultural and agroindustrial, and cattle farms
October 1–September 30	Mining and oil companies (for statistical purposes only)
January 1–December 31	Banking, insurance, commercial and services, and others not listed above

The following penalties apply if financial statements have not been filed and tax liabilities have not been paid by the required date:

☐ The tax due is indexed based on the exchange rate in force between U.S. dollars and Bolivian currency.

☐ 24% per annum interest is charged on the updated tax due.

☐ A fine of 10% on the interest is levied.

☐ A noncompliance fine for lack of filing of between US$ 50 and US$ 500 is levied.

These penalties are independent of the penalties for such violations of the tax law as fiscal evasion and fraud.

8. Other Matters

Oil Companies. The income tax on oil companies is determined on the basis of a payment equivalent to 30% of the price of a crude oil barrel at the well-hole.

INCOME TAXES ON INDIVIDUALS

9. Rates

Nonresidents and branches of foreign corporations earning income from Bolivian sources (from dividends, rents, utilities, royalties, technology transfers, etc.) are subject to the 10% tax on net income or receivables, with no exemptions.

10. Local Income Taxes

None.

11. Capital Gains Taxes

None.

12. Foreign Tax Reliefs

None.

13. Tax Period

Taxpayers must submit their tax returns and pay taxes quarterly, except for employees, who have their taxes withheld by their employers on a monthly basis.

INCOME TAXES ON NONRESIDENTS

15. Liability to Tax

None.

16. Rates

Nonresidents who earn income from Bolivian sources (from dividends, rents, utilities, royalties, technology transfers, etc.) are subject to the 10% tax on net income or receivables, with no exemptions.

OTHER SIGNIFICANT TAXES

21. Sales (Value Added)

The value-added tax has a very broad scope and is levied at all stages of production, trading, and retailing, as well as on a wide range of services and entertainment. The standard rate is 10%, and there are no exemptions.

Exports are not subject to VAT and may, in addition, recognize a tax credit for the VAT billed on the goods exported. Imports are subject to VAT at the general rate.

Tax payments are determined monthly by deducting from the fiscal debits the fiscal credits billed by suppliers.

22. Inheritance and Gift Taxes

Independent of the income taxes, inheritances and gifts are subject to a tax rate of 1%.

23. Taxes on Payrolls (Social Security)

The social security rates levied in Bolivia are as follows:

	Contributions Payable		
	Employer	Employee	Total
Health insurance	10%	—	10%
Pension fund	6	6%	12
National housing council	2	1	3
Workers education fund	1	—	1
	19%	7%	26%

Business enterprises that have a net profit from their operations during the calendar year must allocate 25% of such profits for bonuses to employees. Each bonus is limited to the equivalent of one month's salary.

One yearly bonus of one month's salary (*Aguinaldo*) must be paid as a Christmas bonus before December 25.

25. Other Taxes

Gross Income Tax. A 2% tax is charged on all business transactions and transfers of property, buildings, goods, and interest earned therein, even on free transactions.

Excise Duties. Excise duties are applied at the following rates:

Vehicles	10%
Beverages	20
Spirits, liquor, perfume, cosmetics	30
Beer	60
Cigarettes	50

Property Tax. The rates are as follows:

Rural property	1%–2% of estimated value of one hectare
Urban property (except property owned by the government, social institutions, and certain financial institutions)	0.35%–4% of its commercial value
Cars, trucks, other motor vehicles, planes, and boats	1%–5% of actual value

COMPUTATION OF TAXABLE INCOME

26. Capital Gains
None.

27. Depreciation and Depletion
None.

28. Treatment of Dividends
Dividends paid in cash are subject to a 10% complimentary value-added tax. Residents must include dividends received in their monthly tax return form. Taxes on dividends paid to nonresidents are withheld by the distributing company. Stock dividends are not taxed.

29. Loss Carryovers
None.

30. Transactions between Related Parties
For determining assets and liabilities for purposes of the equity tax (see item 1), certain balances of transactions between related parties are considered to be an asset or liability, and are treated like transactions with any third party.

33. Other Matters

Statute of Limitations. The statute runs for five years from the end of the calendar year in which the filing date falls.

Determination of Equity. Equity is the difference between computable assets and related liabilities. Investments in other companies that are subject to the equity tax are not computable. Debit or credit balances of owners or shareholders must also be excluded, unless they originate in transactions that could be made with any other third person.

Deductible expenses are only those incurred during the fiscal year necessary to increase or maintain the capital and profits of the company.

Determination of Assets. Computable assets include:

☐ Property and plant and equipment that technically are revalued at actual prices. Depreciation is based on the usable life of each asset.

☐ Inventory is valued at the lesser of replacement cost or market price.

☐ Accounts receivable denominated in a foreign currency are valued at their official rate at the closing date.

☐ All other items are valued at their actualized acquisition cost.

Determination of Liabilities.   Liabilities include:

□   All debts and provisions necessary to pay actual or accrued engagements.

□   Technical reserves of insurance companies.

□   Provisions for social benefits, bad debts, and obsolescence, as recognized by generally accepted accounting principles.

RELATED CONSIDERATIONS

34.   Incentives and Grants

Cash payments of taxes receive a 10% rebate.

35.   Exchange Controls

Bolivia has a free-money-exchange system, without exchange controls.

36.   Investment Restrictions on Nonresidents

Nonresidents and foreign companies may not acquire land along the international borders of Bolivia.

BOTSWANA

INCOME TAXES ON CORPORATIONS

1. Rates

Effective July 1, 1990, the corporate income tax rate is based on a two-tier system, with a basic company tax of 30% and an additional company tax of 10%. A withholding tax of 15% on dividends paid applies, but the withholding can be used to offset the 10% additional company tax due in that year.

If the 10% additional company tax due in any year is greater than the 15% withholding tax on dividends in that year, the excess may be carried forward to offset the 15% withholding tax due on dividends in succeeding years. If the 15% dividend withholding tax in any year exceeds the 10% additional company tax available for offsetting, however, the excess cannot be carried forward.

A judicious dividend distribution would ensure an effective tax rate of 40%.

If a company is accepted for listing on the Botswana Stock Exchange during a tax year and at least 25% of the paid-up capital is held by the general public throughout the relevant tax years, it will be entitled to a deduction from its chargeable income at the rate of 12.5% for the next five, successive tax years, resulting in a tax rate of 35%. This deduction also applies to a wholly owned subsidiary of such a company.

2. Local Income Taxes

None.

3. Capital Gains Taxes

A tax on capital gains became effective July 1, 1982. Effective July 1, 1990, chargeable net capital gains are taxed on the same two-tier system as other corporate income.

4. Branch Profits Taxes

The branch profits tax was abolished effective July 1, 1990. A branch of a foreign corporation now is subject to tax on the same basis as a resident corporation, and the effective rate of tax is 40%.

A "branch" has been defined as any factorship, agency, receivership, or management of a nonresident company.

5. Foreign Tax Reliefs

Income derived by residents from sources outside Botswana generally is not taxable in Botswana barring certain exceptions which are deemed to be from sources situated in Botswana. Double taxation agreements are in force with the United Kingdom and South Africa. Botswana residents are entitled to a foreign tax credit for the lesser of the foreign tax paid or the Botswana tax payable on taxable income derived from these countries.

INCOME TAXES ON INDIVIDUALS

9. Rates

The rates of individual income tax on taxable income from July 1, 1990, are listed in the following tables.

Resident Individuals

Taxable Income		Tax on	Percentage
Over	Not Over	Lower Amount	on Excess
P 9,000	P20,000	P 0	5%
20,000	30,000	550	10
30,000	40,000	1,550	20
40,000	50,000	3,550	30
50,000		6,550	40

Notes:

(1) A trust and estate of a deceased person is subject to tax under a separate table, ranging from 2.5% to 40% on the first P6,000 to P40,000 and 40% on the excess thereafter.

(2) A husband and wife are taxed separately.

10. Local Income Taxes

None.

11. Capital Gains Taxes

A tax on capital gains became effective July 1, 1982. Chargeable net capital gains arising from the disposal of certain immovable property and 50% of chargeable net capital gains from the sale of shares are taxed in the case of an individual on the basis of the following table.

Taxable Income		Tax on	Percentage
Over	Not Over	Lower Amount	on Excess
P 5,000	P15,000	P 0	5%
15,000	25,000	500	10
25,000	35,000	1,500	20
35,000	45,000	3,500	30
45,000		6,500	40

12. Foreign Tax Reliefs

Relief from Botswana tax is given on the same basis as for corporations (see item 5).

13. Tax Period

An individual is required to use June 30 as the tax year-end, but an accounting date other than the fiscal year may be used for the computation of business income.

INCOME TAXES ON NONRESIDENTS

15. Liability to Tax

Nonresidents are subject to tax on chargeable income accrued or deemed to accrue from sources in Botswana or deemed to be in Botswana. The tax rates are listed in the following table.

Taxable Income		Tax on	Percentage
Over	Not Over	Lower Amount	on Excess
P 0	P30,000	P 0	20%
30,000	42,000	6,000	30
42,000		9,600	40

17. Withholding Tax Rates

A 15% withholding tax is deductible from gross amounts of interest, commercial royalties, and management or consulting fees paid by any person to a nonresident. This is not refundable. The withholding tax is a final tax, and the income is not aggregated with other income. A 15% withholding tax also is deductible from dividends paid by a resident company to any shareholder, resident or nonresident, except in the case of dividends paid from one associated company to another associated company in the group. The definition of an associated company has been amended to mean that it is a resident company in which another resident company holds 20% or more of every class of equity shares. (See item 28.)

	Dividends	Interest	Royalties	Management and Consulting Fees
Nontreaty countries	15%	15%	15%	15%
Treaty countries:				
South Africa	15	15	15	*
United Kingdom	15	15	15	*

* See "Management or Consultancy Fee" below.

Commercial Royalty. For withholding purposes, commercial royalties are defined as any amounts payable for the use of (or the right to use) any copyright of a literary, artistic or scientific work (including cinematograph films, and films or tapes for radio or television broadcasting), any patent, trademark design or model, plan, secret formula or process, or for the use of (or the right to use) industrial, commercial, or scientific equipment, or for information concerning industrial, commercial or scientific know-how.

Management or Consultancy Fee. For withholding purposes, such fees are defined as any amount payable for administrative, managerial, technical or consultative services, whether such services are of a professional nature or not. When such fees are paid to residents of the United Kingdom or South Africa, whether they are taxable depends on the particular provisions of the double taxation agreements with these countries. It is advisable to seek clarification in such cases.

Construction. Payments on contracts with nonresidents relating to construction operations are subject to withholding tax if so directed by the Commissioner of Taxes. The amount to be deducted is usually 25% of the gross payment less the direct material costs or, alternatively, such lesser amount as the Commissioner may direct at his discretion, according to the circumstances. The tax withheld is allowed as a set off against assessed tax.

19. Tax Treaties

Tax treaties exist between Botswana and the Republic of South Africa and the United Kingdom.

OTHER SIGNIFICANT TAXES

21. Sales (Value Added)

A one-stage sales tax became effective September 6, 1982 on fuel (gasoline and diesel), beer, and spirits and wine at the point of importation or manufacture. The base has been broadened by the sales tax amendment regulations effective March 1, 1989. The rate on fuel is 10 Thebe per litre (100 Thebe = 1 Pula), and the rates on beer, wine, and spirits vary from 5 Thebe per litre to Pl.20 per litre. Cigarettes, cigars, etc., as well as electro-mechanical domestic appliances, microphones, turntables, video recorders, television receivers and cassettes, and record players, are taxed at 10%.

22. Inheritance and Gift Taxes

Succession and estate duties were levied at graduated rates on the value of the decedent's real and personal property located in Botswana. The Death Duties Act was repealed on May 31, 1985 and replaced by a capital transfer tax. The transfer of property by gift or death is subject to a progressive tax, which is based on the amount transferred and the relationship of the beneficiary to the deceased donor. The tax is imposed on the beneficiary.

23. Taxes on Payrolls (Social Security)

There are no payments for social security.

24. Taxes on Natural Resources

Royalties are charged on the exploitation of mineral resources.

25. Other Taxes

Land and Property Taxes.   Transfer duty is levied at 5% of the value of immovable freehold and leasehold property. The first P20,000 of such value is exempt from transfer duty on transfers to a Botswana citizen. In the case of agricultural property, transfer duty is levied at the rate of 30% for a non-citizen.

COMPUTATION OF TAXABLE INCOME

26. Capital Gains

Since July 1, 1982, capital gains realized on all moveable and immoveable property of a business carried on in Botswana and on investments in shares and debentures of a company have been taxable. Certain gains are exempt. Special rules apply to the valuation of immoveable property and to property acquired by gift or inheritance. These rules have now been further modified. For any tax year beginning July 1, 1988, any proportion of tax on capital gains on immoveable property used for business purposes may be postponed if the gain is reinvested in similar property within one year.

27. Depreciation and Depletion

Capital allowances on fixed assets other than land and buildings may be claimed at rates varying from 10% to 25% on a straight-line basis for expenditure incurred on or after July 1, 1982. On assets in use before that date, the previous rules apply under which up to 100% may be claimed in any tax year.

Effective July 1, 1982, an initial allowance of 25% is available on new industrial buildings in the year of first use, and an annual allowance of 2.5% may be claimed on the remaining balance of 75%. For industrial buildings that do not qualify for an initial allowance and for commercial buildings, an annual allowance of 2.5% applies from July 1, 1982 (residential buildings do not qualify).

28. Treatment of Dividends

Dividends are not taxable in the hands of shareholders. The 15% withholding tax on dividends can offset additional company tax. If any dividend is paid to a share-holder outside its group, the 15% withholding tax payable can be offset against the 10% additional company tax payable by that associated company or any other associated company in the group (see items 1 and 17). Group companies must be structured carefully to minimize the effect of dividend tax on dividends passing through the group structure.

29. Loss Carryovers

There is a five year carryforward (no carryback) of assessed losses. However, there is no time limitation on the carryforward of losses incurred in farming, mining, and prospecting activities. Farming losses of a person other than a company, which have been determined according to generally accepted accounting principles, may within three years be elected for set off against income from other sources in that tax year. A net capital loss (after setting off capital gains in that year) may be carried forward for set-off against capital gains in the next tax year only.

30. Transactions between Related Parties

If a transaction has created rights or obligations that would not normally be created between independent persons dealing at arm's length, the Commissioner of Taxes may determine the liability in such manner as he deems appropriate. This has been strengthened by the introduction of special clauses relating to "Close Companies."

31. Consolidation of Income

There are no provisions for group taxation of related corporations, except that special provisions apply to the Botswana Development Corporation and its subsidiaries.

32. Tax Periods

June 30 is the tax year-end, but the basis period for computing the tax liability of businesses is the particular accounting period, provided that this has been approved by the tax authorities.

33. Other Matters

Income Liable to Tax. Companies and individuals resident in Botswana generally are not liable to taxation on income other than that accruing in Botswana or on certain income deemed to be from sources situated in Botswana.

RELATED CONSIDERATIONS

34. Incentives and Grants

There are certain incentives for farmers and "pioneer" industries. Special development approval orders offering additional tax reliefs are granted for projects considered necessary for the development of the economy of Botswana. Provisions are also available for the negotiation of special tax agreements with the Government. Such agreements may, in respect of a person taxable in Botswana, vary the provisions of the Income Tax Act relating to that person.

Financial Assistance. A system of cash grants for new projects has been announced by the Government. This should be reviewed by potential investors as the assistance provided varies with the size of the project, the number of jobs created and other factors.

Special Deductions for Approved Training Expenditure. A company may deduct 200% of the cost of approved training of its citizen employees in arriving at its chargeable income. Approved training is described as:

- [ ] Approved education (not being primary or secondary education) or training, at an approved educational, professional, or vocational training establishment, of citizens of Botswana who are employed by or bonded to such person for the purpose of his business.
- [ ] The employment in Botswana of an approved training officer wholly engaged in approved vocational training of citizens of Botswana who are employed by or bonded to such person for the purpose of his business.

The required approval is obtainable from the Commissioner of Taxes upon application.

35. Exchange Controls

An Exchange Control Act is in force under which approval for foreign exchange transactions is required.

36. Investment Restrictions on Nonresidents

Direct foreign investment in Botswana in the form of share and loan capital is welcome, but specific permission for such investment is nevertheless required. Once permission has been obtained, payment of interest and dividends and repayment of current accounts are not normally restricted. Botswana companies wishing to borrow from nonresident sources or residents will normally be allowed to do so, provided the interest rate is 0.5% above the bank prime rate for pula loans, and 1% above the LIBOR rate for foreign currency loans. Repayment of loans cannot commence until at least three months of receipt of the loan.

Funds can be raised locally for working capital requirements by foreign controlled companies up to P300,000 without reference to the Bank of Botswana. Over this level, and for all fixed-investment requirements, specific approval is required. As a general rule, however, it is expected that nonresident shareholders' interest in a Botswana company (i.e., by way of equity, loan finance, and reserves) will be maintained at not less than one-fourth of local borrowings. This rule will be waived if the company's activities are judged to be highly beneficial to the economy of Botswana.

SELECTION OF BUSINESS ENTITY BY NONRESIDENTS

Nonresident investors can operate in Botswana either through a branch or by forming a local subsidiary company. Effective July 1, 1990, the effective tax rate for both entities is 40% (see item 1). The formulation of a group structure of companies in Botswana, however, should be carefully considered (see item 28).

BRAZIL

INCOME TAXES ON CORPORATIONS

1. Rates

The corporation income tax rate is 30%, except for agricultural-related companies, which are subject to a rate of 25%.

The portion of taxable income that exceeds Cr$30,000,000* is subject to an additional:

☐ 5% on Cr$30,000,000 to Cr$60,000,000.

☐ 10% on the portion exceeding Cr$60,000,000.

☐ On financial institutions, the rates applicable to the preceding are 10% and 15%, respectively.

In addition, the net profit of the corporation is subject to the withholding tax of 8%, exclusively at the source if the shareholder is an individual. If the beneficiary is a company, the withheld tax may be offset with its own profit.

*Note: Cr$1.00 is equivalent to approximately US$0.003 as of July 31, 1991.

2. Local Income Taxes

Profits and capital gains are subject to an additional state income tax of 5%, calculated on the federal income tax due.

3. Capital Gains Taxes

Capital gains realized by companies are added to operating profits and taxed at the regular rates.

4. Branch Profits Taxes

Branches of foreign corporations are subject to corporation tax at the full rate on the profits of the branch in addition to a 25% withholding tax on profits available for remittance abroad (whether or not actually remitted).

5. Foreign Tax Reliefs

Brazil has signed treaties for the avoidance of double taxation with several other countries. These treaties also provide for the reduction of withholding tax on income paid to business entities in treaty countries. Treaty countries are:

Austria	Finland	Norway
Argentina	France	Portugal
Belgium	Italy	Spain
Canada	Japan	Sweden
Denmark	Luxembourg	West Germany
Ecuador	Netherlands	

6. Classification of Corporations

Corporations can be civil corporations (in the case of service companies) or commercial corporations. Companies can be set up as corporations (Sociedades Anônimas) or companies with limited liability (Limitadas) or unlimited liability (partnerships). Foreign investors can also operate as a branch. There are no substantial differences for income tax purposes except that a branch may have certain disadvantages when compared to the other Brazilian entities.

7. Payment of Taxes

The basic taxable year is a calendar year. Companies must file their annual tax return in April.

INCOME TAXES ON INDIVIDUALS

9. Rates

Individuals resident in Brazil are subject to Brazilian tax on their worldwide income. Effective August 1991, new tax regulations provide that:

☐ Up to Cr$120,000 is exempt.

☐ From Cr$120,000 to Cr$288,000 is taxed at 10%.

☐ In excess of Cr$288,000, the rate is 25%.

During the year, income tax is withheld at source and estimated payments are calculated at the same rates and the same basis as above.

10. Local Income Taxes

The state charges an additional income tax of 5% based on the federal income tax due on capital profits, gains, or income.

11. Capital Gains Taxes

Gains on sales of real estate or sales of stock are determined by the difference between the disposal value and the acquisition cost, as monetarily corrected.

Profits on sales of real estate acquired before 1970 are tax-exempt. A 5% reduction of the taxable amount is granted for each year the property was held from that date onwards.

12. Foreign Tax Reliefs

Income tax paid by individuals to foreign countries may be credited against Brazilian income tax (within certain limits), provided that the foreign country grants reciprocal treatment for income arising in Brazil.

13. Tax Period

Individuals must pay tax on a current basis, monthly. The nature of the payor will determine the income taxation method, i.e., income paid by a Brazilian company will be taxed through withholdings at source, while income paid by an individual or received from a foreign source will be subject to taxation through estimated monthly payments made by the taxpayer.

A final calculation will then be made by those who have two or more sources of earnings to determine, on a monthly basis, the global tax due, and any tax liability resulting from this calculation will be payable either monthly or, monetarily corrected, when the yearly return is filed (the end of April of the following year).

INCOME TAXES ON NONRESIDENTS

15. Liability to Tax

Nonresidents are subject to tax on their Brazilian-source income. The tax is levied on any payment or credit to the nonresident. Holders of permanent visas are subject to tax on their worldwide income as of the date of their arrival in Brazil under this visa. Temporary visa holders are subject to a 25% withholding tax on their Brazilian-source income during the first 12 months of their stay in Brazil. During this 12-month period, the foreign person need not file an income tax return. Beginning with the earlier of residing in Brazil for more than 12 months (i.e., the 13th month) or the date of converting a temporary visa into a permanent visa, the foreign person must file a return and his or her worldwide income is subject to Brazilian tax.

16. Rates

Nonresidents of Brazil are subject to withholding tax of 25% on income paid or credited to them, except that tax relief may be provided by treaties designed to avoid double taxation (see item 5).

17. Withholding Tax Rates

Foreign investors are subject to a 25% withholding tax on dividends remitted by a Brazilian company. Dividends in excess of 12% per annum on a three-year moving average of the actual registered investment are also subject to "supplementary tax" at the rates of 40%, 50%, and 60% when the actual dividends distributed are between 12%–15% of foreign-registered capital, 15%–25% of foreign-registered capital, and over 25% of foreign-registered capital, respectively.

20. Other Matters

Exchange of Foreign Currency. Earnings in foreign currency paid, credited, remitted, received, or invested must be translated into national currency at the official rate of exchange in effect on the date of payment, credit, remittance, receipt or investment, or at the exchange rate by which the transactions were effectively made. On July 31, 1991, the official selling rate of US$1 was equal to Cr$348.00. Presently, the cruzeiro is being devalued at the approximate average rate of 0.2% per day.

OTHER SIGNIFICANT TAXES

21. Sales (Value Added)

Business transactions involving the circulation of merchandise are taxed at the rate of 18%, except for superfluous items, such as arms, ammunition, perfumes, etc., which are taxed at 25%. The rates for interstate transactions are 7% for the less-developed states and 12% for the more-developed states. The rate for export transactions is 13%, except for manufactured products, which are tax-exempt. This state tax is known as the ICMS.

This tax also covers service of intermunicipal and interstate transportation at the rate of 12% and communications such as telephone operations, satellites, etc., at the rate of 18%.

Under the new rules, the sales tax is levied also on minerals, fuel, electricity, and exported semi-manufactured goods.

23. Taxes on Payrolls (Social Security)

Monthly national insurance contributions on employees' salaries, up to the limit of ten minimum wages (which is determined monthly), are payable to the Social Security National Institute (INPS), as follows:

By the employee	8.0% to 10% (up to the limit above)
By the employer	27.2% (no limits)

The employer must also deposit monthly 8% of the employee's salary in a special bank account in the name of each employee. This payment is made pursuant to the rules regarding the Guarantee Fund for Length of Service (FGTS).

24. Taxes on Natural Resources
None.

25. Other Taxes

Excise Tax. Excise tax or IPI (Imposto sobre Produtos Industrializados) is imposed on sales and import transactions of any kind of manufactured products or goods. The tax rate varies by product, but generally ranges from 0% to 25%. As with value added taxes in Europe, products that pass through several manufacturing stages (i.e., from raw material to finished goods) are allowed offsetting adjustments to compensate for the required excise tax paid with each separate transaction. Excise tax is payable to the federal government.

Social Contribution Tax. Net profits, before income tax calculation, are subject to 10% social contribution (15% for financial institutions). This tax is deductible for income tax purposes.

Tax on Financial Operations. This tax is levied by the federal government on credit transactions and insurance contracts. Rates range from 0.0041% to 1.8% on credit operations, and from 0% to 25% for exchange contracts involving goods and services. On insurance contracts rates range from 0% to 4%.

Tax on Transfer of Property. A tax of 4% is imposed on the value of a sale, donation, or inheritance.

Service Tax. Professional services, entertainment and sporting events, use of local transportation, and transactions with brokers all incur a service tax. The tax is also imposed upon the income of advertising agencies and public relations firms.

The proceeds of the tax accrue to the levying municipality. The rates, which vary according to the municipality and the nature of the service rendered, average 5%. Professional firms and organizations are entitled to pay this tax on fixed amounts calculated according to the number of professional individuals in the company.

Social Integration Program. All companies must contribute to the Social Integration Program (Programa de Integração Social, or PIS) at the rate of 0.65% on monthly gross income.

Social Investment Fund. Effective January 1991, all companies must contribute to the Social Investment Fund (Fundo de Investimento Social, or FINSOCIAL) as follows:

Companies that sell merchandise	2% of invoices
Brokers, banks, finance, and leasing companies	2% of total operating and nonoperating revenue
Insurance companies and profitable private retirement and health insurance companies	2% of total operating income

COMPUTATION OF TAXABLE INCOME

26. Capital Gains

See item 3.

27. Depreciation and Depletion

Plant. Depreciation rates are generally determined by the tax authorities (administrative jurisprudence). Examples of depreciation rates are:

Machinery and equipment	10%
Installations	10%
Furniture and fixtures	10%
Vehicles	20%
Tools	15%
Computers	20%

Increased depreciation, at an index of 1.5 or 2.0, may be taken when two or three shifts are used, respectively. Depreciation must be calculated by the straight-line method.

Buildings. The rate of depreciation is 4% based on the straight-line method.

Mining. All expenditures incurred in prospecting, exploring, developing, and operating a mine are deductible. Machinery used in mining operations is depreciable at the annual rate of 20%.

Patent Amortization and Licensing Costs. The cost of purchased patents, when registered with the National Institute of Industrial Property (INPI), may be written off over the life of the patent. Royalties for the use of a patent registered in Brazil are deductible up to the limit of 5% of the net income from the manufacture or sale of the product, provided the licensing agreement is registered with INPI and remittances abroad are approved by the Central Bank of Brazil. The payment of royalties for the use of patents and trademarks by a branch or subsidiary of a company established in Brazil to its head office located abroad, or when the majority of capital of the company in Brazil belongs to the beneficiaries of the royalties abroad, is not permitted.

Technical Assistance. Technical, scientific, or administrative expenses are deductible as operating expenses to a maximum of 5% of the net income from the sale or manufacture of the product. The technical assistance fees paid by a branch or subsidiary company to its parent company abroad are not deductible.

Research and Development Expenses. The cost of scientific or technological research (including the testing or improvement of products, processes, formulas, and production) and administrative or sales techniques may be fully deducted when incurred or amortized over a minimum period of five years.

28. Treatment of Dividends

The net profit of a corporation, in addition to the corporate tax, is subject to withholding tax of 8% on the account of the shareholder. However, if the shareholder is a Brazilian resident individual, the tax is exclusively at the source. If it is a Brazilian-resident company, the withheld tax may be offset by its own profit.

When dividends are distributed to a foreign resident, corporate or individual, a withholding tax of 25% is applicable unless a treaty country is involved. The 25% withholding tax may be deducted by the 8% tax withheld from a resident company. This taxation does not exclude the supplementary income tax described in item 17.

29. Loss Carryovers

Normal taxable losses may be carried forward for four years but may not be carried back.

30. Transactions between Related Parties

All transactions must be carried out at fair market value. When property is transferred to a corporation at book value in exchange for shares, there are no tax implications. If the value of the property is later restated, the difference between this amount and the book value is taxable, but taxation may be deferred provided the difference is maintained in a revaluation reserve account until the difference is realized through disposition or depreciation.

When two or more corporations are amalgamated, the value of the assets of the absorbed entity may be restated and the tax on the increased value deferred until the reserve for revaluation is realized.

The transfer of assets between related parties must be made at fair market value to avoid the transfer being characterized as a disguised distribution of profits.

When a company is merged into another entity, the target's tax return must be filed up to the last working day of the month following the date of merger.

31. Consolidation of Income

No provisions exist for the filing of consolidated tax returns by related corporations.

33. Other Matters

Deductions for Taxes Other than Income Taxes. In computing income tax liability, the following taxes are deductible: payroll tax, including the 8% for the Guarantee Fund of Length of Service (severance tax), land and property taxes, sales tax, service tax, tax on financial operations, and social contribution.

Inventory Valuation. Inventories are valued at cost or market, whichever is lower. Average cost or FIFO are generally used, but the LIFO method is not permitted. Conformity is required between book and tax accounting.

Bad Debts. Provisions for doubtful accounts of up to 3% of outstanding debt are deductible.

Employee Benefit Provisions. Provisions for holidays, social security, and the 13th-month salary are deductible.

Management or Administration Fees. The deduction of these fees, for tax purposes, is limited to Cr$1,800,000 per month, effective August 1991, updated in accordance with inflation. The deduction is limited also to eight times the individual taxable income mentioned above, for up to eight administrators, and it cannot exceed 50% of the corporation's taxable profits. If the corporations operates at a loss or at a small profit, however, the individual deduction allowed is Cr$240,000 per month, effective August 1991.

RELATED CONSIDERATIONS

34. Incentives and Grants

Regional Incentives. Regional incentives have been designed to stimulate investment in specific geographical areas; for example, SUDAM (North Area), SUDENE (Northeast Area), Manaus Free Zone, and Grand Carajas Program.

SUDAM Incentives. New enterprises (those set up before December 31, 1993) that have been expanded, modernized, and diversified, and enterprises that come into operation before the aforementioned date are granted a full tax exemption for ten or 15 years. Other companies operating in the area enjoyed a 40% tax reduction until 1994.

SUDENE Incentives. New enterprises (those set up in the area before December 31, 1993) enjoy full tax exemption, provided that they are deemed important for economic development. The exemption can be extended for as long as 15 years. Until 1993, other companies in the area will enjoy a reduction of 40% in income tax.

Other Incentives.   Exemption from import duties and excise tax (IPI) may be granted for imports of machinery and equipment purchased by companies that are deemed important to the region's economic development.

Manaus Free Trade Zone.   The Manaus Free Trade Zone is comprised of 10,000 square kilometers near the junction of the Amazon and Negro Rivers, and includes the city of Manaus. Foreign products destined for consumption, processing, storage (for re-export), or use elsewhere in the territory enter the zone enjoying the benefit of suspended import duties and IPI (see item 25). The shipment of products from a domestic source for consumption or processing in the Manaus area results in import duties on the foreign-source components, which are reduced according to the percentage of value added locally. Goods manufactured in the Zone are exempt from IPI.

Grand Carajas Program.   This program is designed to develop priority projects in the area bounded by the 8th parallel and the Amazon, Xingu, and Parnaiba rivers. Projects include developing infrastructure services, agriculture, livestock, forestry, and exploration and exploitation of mineral resources. Participating companies are granted a 10-year exemption from income tax and exemptions (or reductions) from import tax and IPI tax with respect to imported machinery, equipment, and vehicles that have no Brazilian equivalent.

Export Incentives.   All export sales of manufactured products are exempt from ICM and IPI taxes and exporters may also keep the ICM and IPI tax credits resulting from the purchase of raw materials and intermediate or packaging materials used in the manufacture of export products.

Incentives Available under BEFIEX-Approved Export Programs.   Incentives for export programs approved by the BEFIEX, a Government agency, are increased depreciation and six years carryforward of taxable losses. The benefits are granted proportionally to the exports.

SELECTION OF BUSINESS ENTITY BY NONRESIDENTS

Investors in Brazil can operate through a variety of business entities, including corporations (Sociedades Anônimas), limited liability companies, joint ventures, consortiums, and partnerships.

Corporations.   Corporations are permitted to issue stock and/or debentures, and shares can be issued in either nominative or bearer form with different classes, rights, and privileges. The corporation's financial statements must be published annually in an official publication and a general circulation newspaper. Notices of stockholder meetings and general assemblies must also be published. Shareholder liability is limited to the amount of capital that is subscribed to. Corporations must appoint at least two directors.

Corporations are generally required to distribute annually to their shareholders at least 25% of their profits, after which management can participate in the corporation's profits. Rigid rules govern the distribution of corporate profits.

Limited Liability Companies. Limited liability companies cannot issue securities to the public and must have at least two partners (shareholders). Each partner is potentially liable to the extent of the company's total equity if all of the shares have been fully subscribed to and paid up. The transfer of shares is subject to the remaining shareholders' approval in accordance with the company's by-laws. The publication of minutes and financial statements and the holding of shareholder meetings are generally not required.

Limited liability companies are not subject to statutory minimum dividend requirements or restrictions as to profit distributions or legal reserves. A limited liability company is taxed at the company level, as is the case with corporations.

The management of a foreign-controlled limited liability company may consist of foreign residents, provided a local deputy manager is appointed.

Joint Ventures. A joint venture consists of an active partner and one or more silent partners. Legally, it is not structured as a corporation, but for tax purposes it is equal to a legal entity. All operations are carried out in the name of the active partner. The active partner verifies the joint venture's profits (losses) and pays the tax as if it were a corporation (see item 1).

Consortium. A consortium is a group of companies joining together to undertake specific activities. In Brazil, companies commonly join together to carry out large projects; for example, hydroelectric dams, and subways. The consortium is not considered to be a separate legal entity, and its primary features are:

☐ The consortium is not an incorporated firm and there is no corporate link among its members. The responsibilities, obligations, and participation in profits (losses) are determined by the bylaws of the consortium contract.

☐ The consortium is not required to file an income tax return or withhold tax when profits are paid to consortium members.

Professional Partnerships. Professional partnerships have the same tax obligations as other business firms, except with what relates to income tax. Accordingly, a 3% tax withheld at source is levied on payments for services rendered in legally regulated professions. Partnerships are not subject to the corporate tax, and the profits are taxed when earned by the partners (withholding tax on the same basis as described in item 9). The profits are verified at the partnership.

BRUNEI DARUSSALAM

INCOME TAXES ON CORPORATIONS

1. Rates

All corporations, whether incorporated overseas or locally or registered as a branch of a foreign company, are taxed at the rate of 30% on income accrued in, derived from, or received in Brunei Darussalam. Special tax concessions may be available (see item 34).

2. Local Income Taxes

None.

3. Capital Gains Taxes

There is no capital gains tax. Profits arising from the sale of capital assets are not taxable, and capital losses are not deductible. However, profits arising from the sale of assets acquired for the purpose of resale at a profit, rather than purchased for an entity's own use, are taxable as income.

4. Branch Profits Taxes

Brunei Darussalam branches of foreign corporations are taxed on the profits of the branch arising in Brunei Darussalam in the same manner and at the same rates as corporations. Accounts of the branch operations, which need not be audited, should be prepared to support the tax computations.

5. Foreign Tax Reliefs

A double taxation agreement with the United Kingdom provides proportionate relief from Brunei Darussalam income tax on any part of the income that has been or is liable to be charged with United Kingdom income tax. Both resident and nonresident companies may obtain unilateral relief on income arising from Commonwealth countries that provide reciprocal relief. The maximum relief cannot exceed half the Brunei Darussalam rate.

INCOME TAXES ON INDIVIDUALS

9. Rates

Individuals at present are not subject to income tax, and there are no payroll or employment taxes.

Partnership income is apportioned to the partners, so that individuals trading in partnerships at present are not subject to income tax. A corporate partner is taxed in the same way as a corporation on the share of profits relating to the corporate partner.

INCOME TAXES ON NONRESIDENTS

15. Liability to Tax

A nonresident individual is not taxed in Brunei Darussalam. A nonresident corporation is taxable on income accruing in, derived from, or received in Brunei Darussalam. The nonresident is assessable either directly or in the name of its agent, whether or not the agent has receipt of the income.

Where a nonresident corporation carries on business with a resident corporation and the business is so arranged as to provide the resident with profits smaller than might be expected to accrue to an independent concern, the business may be treated as being carried on in Brunei Darussalam by the nonresident through the resident as agent. Where the true profits of the nonresident corporation cannot be readily ascertained, they may be based on a fair percentage of the turnover between the nonresident and the resident.

16. Rates

Taxable income is taxed at the rate of 30%.

Income received by a nonresident corporation from shipping and airline operations is taxed on the basis of a ratio certificate issued by the Revenue Authority in the country of residence of the operator and agreed on by the Brunei Darussalam Collector of Taxes. By means of the ratio certificate, the Brunei Darussalam element of the worldwide income from the carriage of passengers, mails, livestock, and goods shipped is apportioned to the Brunei Darussalam operations. If a ratio certificate is not available, the Collector will tax the nonresident corporation on a fair percentage of the amounts received from the carriage of passengers, mails, livestock, and goods shipped, or loaded on an aircraft, in Brunei Darussalam.

17. Withholding Tax Rates

Withholding tax of 20% is payable to the Collector of Taxes in respect of interest paid under a charge, or debenture or loan interest by a person to a corporation not resident in Brunei Darussalam. There are no other withholding taxes.

OTHER SIGNIFICANT TAXES

21. Sales (Value Added)

None.

22. Inheritance and Gift Taxes

Estate duty is levied under the Stamp Act, Cap. 34 on all immovable property in Brunei Darussalam and movable property wherever situated for persons domiciled in Brunei Darussalam at the time of death, and on all property situated in Brunei Darussalam in respect of persons not domiciled in Brunei Darussalam at the time of death. There is double taxation relief for estate duty paid overseas on assets that are also charged to estate duty in Brunei Darussalam. The estate duties on the principal value of the estate excluding the value of any dwelling houses are:

Principal Value of the Estate

Over		Not Over		Rate
B$	3,000	B$	5,000	1%
	5,000		10,000	2
	10,000		25,000	3
	25,000		50,000	4
	50,000		100,000	5
	100,000		150,000	6
	150,000		200,000	7
	200,000		300,000	8
	300,000		400,000	9
	400,000		500,000	10
	500,000		750,000	11
	750,000		1,000,000	12
	1,000,000		1,250,000	13
	1,250,000		1,500,000	14
	1,500,000		2,000,000	15
	2,000,000		3,000,000	16
	3,000,000		5,000,000	17
	5,000,000		7,500,000	18
	7,500,000		10,000,000	19
	10,000,000			20

Estate duty is not payable in the case of a person dying on or after December 15, 1988 to the extent of B$2.0 million of the aggregate value of the deceased's interest in a dwelling house or dwelling houses, whether occupied by the deceased or not, and the amount thereof does not form part of the principal value of the estate chargeable with estate duty of any deceased person. If the value of the dwelling houses exceeds B$2.0 million, the estate duty payable on this part of the estate is 3% of the excess.

There is no gift duty. However, the value of the gifts made within one year prior to death of the donor will be brought into the estate for estate duty purposes.

23. Taxes on Payrolls (Social Security)

None.

24. Taxes on Natural Resources

Petroleum operations are subject to special legislation, and income from such operations is taxed under the Income Tax (Petroleum) Act, Cap. 119 as amended. The legislation follows the same general pattern as that of most major oil-producing countries in the Middle East.

25. Other Taxes

Customs Duties.   No duty is levied in Brunei Darussalam on food, building and construction materials, industrial machinery, or non-alcoholic beverages. Import duties are applied only to certain articles, and there are no export duties. An ad valorem duty of 10% is applied to clothing, jewelry, and watches; a 20% rate is applied to timber, tires, electrical equipment and appliances, photographic materials and equipment, motor vehicles and spare parts, and furniture; and 30% to cosmetics and perfumes. Duty also is charged on spirits, wines, and cigarettes.

Stamp Duty.   Stamp duty is imposed on documents. For certain types of documents, the duty is ad valorem. On others, the duty varies with the nature of the documents.

Land and Properties.   Property assessments are levied by the local authorities and are based on the annual valuation of the property. Land rent or rates are also payable. Ownership of property is restricted to Brunei Darussalam citizens.

COMPUTATION OF TAXABLE INCOME

26. Capital Gains

See item 3.

27. Depreciation and Depletion

Depreciation adopted in the accounts is added back for taxation purposes and is replaced by a system of capital allowances for qualifying capital expenditure. These allowances must be claimed and are deductible in computing taxable income, as follows:

Industrial Buildings. An initial allowance of 10% of the qualifying expenditure is given on industrial buildings in the year of expenditure, and an annual allowance of 2% of the qualifying expenditure is provided on a straight-line basis, until the total expenditure is written off.

Plant and Machinery. An initial allowance of 20% of the cost of plant or machinery is given in the year of expenditure, and a writing-down allowance is given annually on the reducing value of the asset. The rates are established by the Collector of Taxes and range from 3% to 25%.

Mining. All expenditure incurred in connection with the working of a mine or other source of mineral deposit of a wasting nature is considered qualifying mining expenditure. An initial allowance of 10% of the qualifying expenditure is given in the year of expenditure, and depletion allowances are deductible over the life of the mine. These are determined by multiplying the residue of the capital expenditure by the greater of 20% or the fraction of the output for the year divided by the output of the year plus the potential future output.

Disposal of Assets. When an asset is sold, scrapped, or destroyed, a balancing allowance or balancing charge is made, based on the difference between the disposal price and the tax written-down value on disposal. Any balancing charge is, however, limited to the actual allowances previously given. A balancing charge can be deferred where plant and machinery is replaced with similar plant and machinery.

Unabsorbed Capital Allowances. Unabsorbed capital allowances may be carried forward indefinitely to subsequent years of assessment, as long as the company continues to carry on the same trade or business.

28. Treatment of Dividends

Dividends accruing in, derived from, or received in Brunei Darussalam by a corporation are included in taxable income, except that dividends received from a corporation taxable in Brunei Darussalam are excluded. No tax is deducted at source on dividends paid by a Brunei Darussalam corporation.

Dividends received in Brunei Darussalam from Commonwealth countries or the United Kingdom are included gross in the tax computations, and credit is claimed against the Brunei Darussalam tax liability for tax suffered under the provision for Commonwealth tax relief or the double taxation treaty with the United Kingdom. Otherwise, dividends are included net in the tax computation, and no foreign tax credit is available. There is no withholding tax on dividends paid by Brunei Darussalam corporations.

29. Loss Carryovers

Losses for the year of assessment can be set off against all sources of income for that year, or may be carried back for one year of assessment and offset against taxable income of that year. The balance of unabsorbed losses may be carried forward to offset future profits within the five years following the year of assessment within which the loss was incurred. The loss is not restricted to the same trade, and there is no requirement involving continuity of ownership of the company.

30. Transactions between Related Parties

Transactions between related resident and nonresident persons must be on an arm's-length basis. The Collector of Taxes has the power to deem any nonresident as trading in Brunei Darussalam and raise an assessment in the name of a resident person as if he were the agent of the nonresident.

31. Consolidation of Income

There is no provision for the filing of consolidated tax returns by related corporations.

32. Tax Periods

Tax is assessed on the preceding-year basis. The calendar year ending December 31 is the basis period for assessment, except that corporations may adopt the corporation's financial year-end falling within the year preceding the year of assessment.

33. Other Significant Matters

Directors' Remuneration. As corporate tax but no personal income tax is levied in Brunei Darussalam, it has sometimes been the practice to pay large salaries to those directors who are also shareholders. The Collector is attempting to disallow payments that he considers excessive as being not wholly and exclusively incurred in the production of income.

Interest Expense. Interest paid on loans not used for acquiring income is not deductible.

Bad Debts. General provisions for doubtful debts are not deductible. A specific provision made for those debts proven to be irrecoverable is deductible. Recovery of any debt that has been written off or for which a specific provision has been claimed should be included in assessable income.

Employee Benefit Provisions. Provisions for employee benefits (pension, provident society, or fund) are only deductible if the scheme is approved by the Collector. The Collector will only approve schemes if they are set up as an entity separate from the company. If the scheme is not approved, deduction for such expenses is allowed only when payment is made to the employee.

Donations. Deductions are available for hospitals, benevolent institutions, and educational institutions that are not operated for profit and that provide funds for the relief of distress among members of the public. Total donations must not exceed 1/6 of the net income before the deduction for donations. No deduction is available if there is a loss.

Other Disallowable Items.   Other disallowable items include domestic or private expenditure, any sums not expended for the purpose of producing profits, and loss or withdrawal of capital or capital expenses.

RELATED CONSIDERATIONS

34. Incentives and Grants

Investment incentives in the form of tax concessions to approved enterprises or industries may be granted by the Economic Development Board under the Investment Incentives Act, Cap. 97, so as to encourage the development of business activities and investment in Brunei Darussalam. For an industry to qualify for investment incentives, either of the following conditions must be met:

☐   The industry is not previously carried on in Brunei Darussalam on a commercial scale suitable to the economic requirements of Brunei Darussalam, and there are good prospects of further developing the industry to provide for exports.

☐   There are insufficient facilities for the industry to operate on a suitable commercial scale, and it is in the public interest to encourage the development of the industry in Brunei Darussalam.

The main incentives are noted in the following paragraphs.

Pioneer Industries.   Complete exemption from income tax for up to five years, depending on the capital invested, is available to industries granted pioneer status, as follows:

	Capital Invested	
Tax Exemption	Over	Not Over
2 years	B$ 0	B$ 250,000
3 years	250,000	500,000
4 years	500,000	1,000,000
5 years	1,000,000	

The tax relief period may be extended to a maximum of five years under certain circumstances.

Expansion of Established Enterprises.   Partial tax exemption for up to five years, depending on increase in income from the expanded business.

Foreign Loans for Productive Equipment. The interest paid to nonresident lenders for an approved foreign loan is exempt from withholding tax.

Relief from Import Duties. A pioneer company may be exempted from customs duty on items to be installed in the pioneer factory.

Concessions from Income Tax. His Majesty The Sultan in Council can order a lower rate of tax than the rate in force to foster the development of business in Brunei Darussalam.

35. Exchange Controls
None.

36. Investment Restrictions on Nonresidents
There is no legal requirement for any of the shareholders of a company to be resident in or citizens of Brunei Darussalam. However, local (Bumiputra) participation in both share capital and management is encouraged by the Government, and does help (or in some cases may be a requisite) when tendering for contracts with the Government or Brunei Shell Petroleum Company Sendirian Berhad. There are requirements for at least half of the directors of a local company to be citizens of Brunei Darussalam.

SELECTION OF BUSINESS ENTITY BY NONRESIDENTS

The benefits of setting up a local company as compared to registering a branch are mainly that a local (Bumiputra) partner can be taken by the local company, while this is not advisable in the case of a branch, and because the local company is a separate entity the parent is not chargeable with its liabilities. As the Brunei Darussalam tax considerations are the same for both locally incorporated subsidiaries and branches, the selection of a business entity for Brunei Darussalam operations is generally governed either by considerations regarding taking a local (Bumiputra) partner or by considerations in the home country.

A foreign person or foreign persons may operate as a sole proprietor or partnership, respectively, provided the person or persons register with the Registrar of Business Names. Approval for registration of a business name may not be given to foreign-owned companies or to foreign individuals not possessing a Brunei Darussalam work permit.

Licenses are required for certain businesses such as banks, finance companies, money lenders, pawnshops, motor insurers, and some other businesses in which the public interest is directly affected.

CANADA

INCOME TAXES ON CORPORATIONS

1. Rates

Resident corporations currently pay federal tax on their worldwide income at the general rate of 38%. Nonresident corporations are subject to the same rates of tax on income earned in Canada. There are abatements of 10% for income earned in a province, and 5% for profits attributable to Canadian manufacturing and processing operations. A surtax of 3% of federal tax otherwise payable also is imposed. Thus, the maximum federal rate is 28.84%. Canadian-controlled private corporations receive an additional abatement (small business deduction), which reduces the federal income tax rate by 16%, on up to $200,000 of annual taxable income from an active business.

2. Local Income Taxes

Provincial taxes as a percentage of income are imposed at the following rates for 1991:

	General Rates	Corporation Eligible for Small Business Deduction
Alberta	15.5%	6%
British Columbia	15	9
Manitoba	17	10 (1)
New Brunswick	17	9
Newfoundland	17	10 (1)
Northwest Territories	12	5 (1)
Nova Scotia	16	10 (1)
Ontario	15.5 (2)	10 (1)
Prince Edward Island	15	10
Quebec	6.9 (3)	3.75 (1)
Saskatchewan	15	10 (1)
Yukon	10 (4)	5 (4)

Notes:
(1) If certain conditions are met this rate may be reduced to zero.
(2) A 1% reduction is allowed in respect of Canadian profits from manufacturing and processing, mining, farming, logging and fishing.
(3) Increased to 16.25% for non-active income.
(4) Reduced to 2.5% for manufacturing and processing income earned in the territory.

3. Capital Gains Taxes

There are no capital gains taxes as such, but three-quarters of realized post-1971 gains are included in income subject to tax at the general rates. Rules exist to exempt capital gains accrued to December 31, 1971.

4. Branch Profits Tax

In addition to tax at the general corporate rates, a tax of 25% (subject to bilateral tax agreements) is imposed upon branches of nonresident corporations carrying on business in Canada. This tax is based upon after-tax profits minus an investment allowance. No withholding tax is levied on distributions of branch profits.

5. Foreign Tax Reliefs

A foreign tax credit is provided on a per-country basis equal to the foreign tax paid or the Canadian tax on the net foreign-source income, whichever is the lesser. A separate computation is required for each country for business income tax and nonbusiness income tax. Unused foreign tax credits in respect of business income may be carried back three and forward seven years.

Special rules apply to dividend income from affiliated foreign corporations. In such cases a foreign tax credit is not allowed but the underlying foreign income tax is taken into account in determining the taxable portion of the dividend.

6. Classification of Corporations

Corporations are classified for Canadian tax purposes as:

☐ Resident or nonresident corporations.
☐ Public or private corporations.

A resident corporation is one whose central management and control is in Canada, but a corporation is deemed to be resident if:

☐ It was incorporated in Canada after April 26, 1965.
☐ It was incorporated in Canada at an earlier date and at any time after April 26, 1965 was resident or carried on business in Canada.

The distinction between resident and nonresident corporations is important in that resident corporations are subject to tax on their worldwide income whereas non-resident corporations are subject to tax only on their Canadian-source income.

Resident corporations are classified as either public or private corporations. Public corporations are those whose shares are listed on a Canadian stock exchange and the subsidiaries of such corporations. Other corporations, including subsidiaries of foreign public corporations, are private.

Private corporations that are at least 50% controlled by Canadians may be eligible for the small business deduction (see items 1 and 2).

Various corporations are subject to special refundable tax rules. All private corporations, and public corporations under the control of an individual or related group of individuals, are eligible for the refund of the full amount of a 25% tax imposed on dividends received from other Canadian corporations. Exempt from this 25% tax are most dividends received from controlled corporations or from other corporations in which there is a 10% or greater holding. In addition, Canadian-controlled private corporations add to their refundable tax account the portion of federal tax imposed on investment income. Refundable tax is recovered by corporations on the basis of $1 for every $4 of taxable dividends paid to shareholders.

7. Payment of Taxes

Corporations generally are required to pay monthly installments towards their current year's income tax liability based on the previous year's actual taxes payable. The balance of the tax liability is due two months after the corporation's year-end (three months in the case of certain corporations eligible for the small business deduction). The 25% refundable tax on certain dividends (see item 6) is not payable by installments, but must be paid not later than the date on which the balance of the corporation's tax liability is due. Canada imposes no restriction on what date a new corporation may choose for its year-end, but a change in that date requires permission from the taxation authorities.

INCOME TAXES ON INDIVIDUALS

9. Federal Rates

Tax is imposed at graduated rates upon the taxable income of individuals. Residents of Canada must include their worldwide income, whereas nonresidents include only their income from carrying on a business or from providing personal services in Canada, plus certain capital gains on the disposal of Canadian property. The tax brackets are indexed annually. The 1991 Federal rates of tax are as follows:

Taxable Income		Tax on Lower Amount	Percentage on Excess
Over	Not Over		
$ 0	$28,784	—	17%
28,784	56,568	$ 4,893	26
56,568	—	12,377	29

Residents of Quebec receive a tax reduction of 16.5% of the basic federal tax payable and all individuals are subject to a surtax of 5% of tax otherwise payable plus an additional 5% on tax otherwise payable that exceeds $12,500.

Individual taxpayers are entitled to a Federal tax credit equal to $13^{1/3}\%$ of the amount of grossed-up dividends received (see item 28). The dividend credit may be applied against other tax payable, but may not give rise to a cash refund.

In addition, personal tax credits can be utilized to reduce Federal taxes. These include a credit of $1,068 for the individual taxpayer, $890 for a dependent spouse, $69 for each of the first two dependent children, and $138 for each additional child. Tax credits also apply for charitable donations, medical expenses, and required contributions to the Canada/Quebec pension plans and for unemployment insurance (see item 23). In computing taxable income, individuals may deduct contributions to employers' Registered Pension Plans (RPP) and individual Registered Retirement Savings Plans (RRSP). Other deductions include interest on money borrowed to earn income, professional and union dues, and moving expenses.

An alternative minimum tax (AMT) in lieu of regular income tax is imposed if the use of tax preference items reduces regular federal tax to less than the AMT. Federal AMT is computed as 17% of taxable income plus specific tax preference items and less a basic $40,000 AMT exemption.

Salaries and wages are subject to federal and provincial tax deductions at source. Quarterly tax installments are payable where sources of income not subject to deductions at source exceed 25% of net income. Any balance of tax owing is due no later than April 30 of the following year when individual tax returns must be filed.

10. Local Income Taxes

Provincial and territorial income taxes are imposed in addition to the federal tax and, except in Quebec, are computed as a percentage of the basic federal tax payable (after deducting personal tax credits and the dividend tax credit). For ease of computation, all individuals are treated as being resident for the entire year in the province where they reside on December 31. The 1991 rates are as follows:

Residents of	Percentage of Federal Tax	Maximum Federal and Provincial Marginal Tax Rate (1)
Alberta	46.5%	46.96%
British Columbia	51.5	48.33
Manitoba	52.0	50.98
New Brunswick	60.0	50.69
Newfoundland	62.0	49.88
Northwest Territories	44.0	44.66
Nova Scotia	59.5	50.88
Ontario	53.0	49.11
Prince Edward Island	58.0	50.40

Residents of	Percentage of Federal Tax	Maximum Federal and Provincial Marginal Tax Rate (1)
Saskatchewan	50.0%	50.88%
Yukon Territory	45.0	44.95

Note:
(1) Includes federal and provincial surtaxes.

In lieu of provincial taxes, income not earned in a province, such as foreign income or income earned in Canada by nonresidents, is subject to a federal surtax of 52%. Quebec income taxes are imposed on taxable income as computed under the Quebec Taxation Act and range from 16% on the first $7,000 of taxable income to 24% on taxable income in excess of $50,000. A dividend tax credit of 8.87% is provided. The combined federal and Quebec tax may be approximated by adding 61% to the federal tax as calculated before the 16.5% Quebec abatement.

11. Capital Gains Taxes

The information in item 3 also applies here, but resident individuals are allowed a cumulative exemption from tax on capital gains up to a lifetime limit of $100,000. There are special provisions to have this limit increased to $500,000 for individuals who have capital gains from the disposition of a "qualified farm property" or "qualified small business corporation shares." In all cases, the limit may be reduced to the extent an individual has any "cumulative net investment losses" (in general, the amount by which the aggregate of investment expenses for the year and prior years ending after 1987 exceed the aggregate of the individual's investment income for such years).

12. Foreign Tax Reliefs

A foreign tax credit is provided on a per-country basis equal to the foreign tax paid or the Canadian tax on the net foreign source income, whichever is the lesser. A separate computation is required for each country for business income tax and non-business income tax. Unused foreign tax credits in respect of business income may be carried back three and forward seven years. Foreign taxes in excess of 15% on property income (other than real estate) may not be claimed as a credit, but may be deducted as an expense.

13. Tax Period

The tax year for individuals is the calendar year. However, a different fiscal period may be chosen for an unincorporated business carried on by an individual, in which case the individual's taxable income must include the income of the business for any fiscal periods ending in the calendar year. The tax year ends when an individual ceases to be resident in Canada or commences when the individual becomes resident in Canada. Those who "sojourn" in Canada for 183 days or more in a calendar year are deemed to be resident for the entire year, unless they specifically establish residence or nonresidence at some point in the year.

INCOME TAXES ON NONRESIDENTS

15. Liability to Tax

Where a nonresident individual is employed in Canada or where a nonresident individual or corporation carries on business in Canada or disposes of taxable Canadian property, the income reasonably attributable to that activity is subject to tax. In the case of an entity resident in a country with which Canada has a tax treaty, the right to tax is generally modified so that Canadian tax may be levied on profits only if the nonresident is carrying on a trade or business through a permanent establishment in Canada. Certain treaties also provide a limited exemption for income of a nonresident individual from employment or personal services performed in Canada.

16. Rates

Nonresident individuals and corporations are taxed on their Canadian-source income at the same rates as resident individuals or corporations. However, nonresident corporations are subject to the branch profits tax (see item 4), which may bring the effective corporate tax rate to between 53% and 59%, depending upon the province of operation before any tax treaty reduction in the branch tax rate.

17. Withholding Tax Rates

The general rate of withholding tax is 25% for virtually all payments to residents of non-treaty countries other than for the purchase of goods. Depending on the type of payment and the country with which Canada has a treaty, the rate can drop to 15% or 10%. Withholding tax rates under Canada's tax treaties are as follows:

Withholding Taxes on Outward Remittances

	Dividends	Interest	Royalties(1)
Nontreaty countries	25%	25%	25%
Treaty countries:			
Australia	15	15	10, 25
Austria	15	15, 25	10, 25
Bangladesh	15	15	10, 25
Barbados	15	15	10, 25
Belgium	15	15	10, 25
Brazil	15, 25	10, 15, 25	15, 25
Cameroon	15	15	15, 25
China	10, 15	10	10, 25
Cyprus	15	15	10, 25

Withholding Taxes on Outward Remittances

	Dividends	Interest	Royalties(1)
Czechoslovakia (2)	10%, 15%	10%	10%, 25%
Denmark (3)	15	15	15
Dominican Republic	18	18	18, 25
Egypt	15	15	15, 25
Finland (2)	10, 15	10	10
France	10, 15	10	10, 25
Germany	15, 25	15, 25	10, 25
Guyana	15	15	10, 25
India	15, 25	15	25
Indonesia	15	15, 25	15, 25
Ireland	15	15	15
Israel	15	15	15, 25
Italy	15	15	10, 25
Ivory Coast	15	15	10, 25
Jamaica	15	15, 25	10, 25
Japan	10, 15	10, 15	10, 25
Kenya	15, 25	15, 25	15, 25
Korea	15	15	15, 25
Liberia (2)	15	15, 20	10, 15, 20, 25
Luxembourg (2)	10, 15	15	10, 25
Malaysia	15	15	15, 25
Malta	15	15	10
Mexico (2)	10, 15	15	15, 25
Morocco	15	15	10, 25
Netherlands	10, 15	15	10, 25
New Zealand	15	15	15, 25
Norway	15	15	10, 15, 25
Pakistan	15	15	15, 25
Papua New Guinea	15	10	10, 25
Philippines	15	15	10, 25
Poland	15	15	10
Romania	15	15, 25	15, 25
Singapore	15	15, 25	15, 25
Spain	15	15, 25	10, 25
Sri Lanka	15	15, 25	10, 25
Sweden	15	15	10
Switzerland	15	15, 0	10, 5
Thailand	15	15	5, 15, 25
Trinidad & Tobago	15	15	15, 25
Tunisia	15	15, 25	15, 20, 25
Union of Soviet Socialist Republics	15	15	10, 25

Withholding Taxes on Outward Remittances

	Dividends	Interest	Royalties(1)
United Kingdom	15%, 10%	10%	10%, 25%
United States	15, 10	15	10, 25
Zambia	15	15, 25	15, 25

Notes:

(1) A 25% withholding tax is generally only required in respect of resource royalties.

(2) Signed but not yet in force (including any protocol).

18. Special Withholding Provisions

There is a full exemption from withholding tax on interest payable to arm's-length parties in respect of certain long-term debts incurred after June 1975, interest payable on most government obligations, interest payable on arm's length foreign currency deposits with a bank, and interest payable to qualifying tax-exempt organizations.

19. Tax Treaties

Canada has concluded an extensive range of double taxation agreements with numerous countries throughout the world (see item 17). These agreements may reduce the liability of nonresidents.

OTHER SIGNIFICANT TAXES

21. Sales (Value Added)

The goods and services tax (GST), a form of value-added tax, has been imposed at the rate of 7% on most goods and services supplied in Canada after 1990. Under this tax system, a business collects tax from its customers on the basis of the sale price of taxable goods or services multiplied by the 7% GST rate. Each registered business is entitled, however, to claim a credit or refund for any GST paid on the purchase of goods or services used in its taxable commercial activities. This credit (referred to as an input tax credit) is available to each person in the production and distribution chain except the final non-business consumer of the good or service.

Certain goods, such as basic groceries and health care and financial services, are exempt from the tax.

The total amount of tax collected by a business on sales in a given period, less the input tax credit for that period, must be remitted to the Government. If in any given period the input tax credit exceeds the tax collected on sales, the business is entitled to a refund equal to the difference.

Foreign business concerns that make supplies of goods or services in Canada are required to register and charge GST under the same rules as a domestic business. Foreign business concerns that incur GST on business costs but make no taxable supplies in Canada may apply to reclaim the GST that a Canadian business could recover.

Other commodity taxes are levied as follows:

☐ Excise duties are levied on alcohol, tobacco, jewelry, gasoline, and a few other minor items.

☐ Customs duties are applied to a wide range of goods imported into Canada.

☐ Special dumping duties can also be imposed.

In all provinces except Alberta, provincial sales taxes ranging up to 12% are imposed on most purchases of goods. The provinces of Quebec and Saskatchewan are moving to harmonize their provincial sales taxes with the GST effective January 1992.

22. Inheritance and Gift Taxes

No gift taxes are imposed. However, there is a deemed realization of capital property on death or emigration, and income from property transferred to a spouse or minor child may be attributed back to the transferor.

23. Taxes on Payrolls (Social Security)

Employees are required to contribute 2.3% (maximum $633) of annual pensionable earnings to the Canada or Quebec Pension Plan. Equal amounts are required from an employer. Employees must also contribute 2.25% (maximum $796) of annual insurable earnings for unemployment insurance. The employer's contribution is 1.4 times that of the employee's. Self-employed individuals must contribute to the Canada or Quebec Pension Plan (maximum $1,265), but not to unemployment insurance.

24. Taxes on Natural Resources

Most provinces impose a tax on forestry operations. Provinces also impose a royalty upon petroleum and natural gas or a tax on mineral production, which is not deductible as an expense for federal tax purposes, but is partially offset by a 25% resource allowance deduction. The allowance is equal to 25% of "resource profits" after deducting operating costs and capital cost allowance from gross revenues, but before deducting Canadian exploration expenses, Canadian development expenses, and interest.

25. Other Taxes

Land and Property.   All municipalities levy tax on real property to finance local expenditures. The provinces levy a tax on real property outside municipal boundaries. Certain provinces and cities impose a modest tax upon the transfer of immovable property. The provinces of Quebec and Ontario levy a substantial tax upon the transfer of some types of land to nonresidents or corporations controlled by nonresidents. There are, however, a number of exemptions from these land transfer taxes.

Capital Tax. Manitoba, Ontario, Quebec and Saskatchewan levy a tax on the capital (both paid-in and retained) of all corporations, while Alberta, British Columbia, Newfoundland, New Brunswick, Nova Scotia, and Prince Edward Island impose a capital tax only on banks and trust and loan companies. The tax rate is generally a fraction of 1%. An annual Federal "large corporations tax" at a rate of 0.2% is imposed on taxable capital employed in Canada in excess of $10 million. This tax is creditable against the 3% corporate surtax, with any unused portion available for a three-year carryback and a seven-year carryforward. The Federal government also imposes a 1.25% capital tax on the capital of banks and trust and loan companies with capital in excess of $200 million employed in Canada. This financial institution capital tax is creditable against any Federal income tax liability.

COMPUTATION OF TAXABLE INCOME

26. Capital Gains

Three-quarters of gains accrued and realized after 1971 must be included in income. Three-quarters of losses may be carried back three years and forward indefinitely to be applied against gains included in income. Additionally, three-quarters of capital losses on the shares of arm's-length Canadian-controlled private corporations may be treated as noncapital losses deductible from any sources of income in the current, the three preceding, or the seven succeeding years. Capital gains and losses are deemed to be realized on death or emigration. Capital gains realized by nonresidents on the sale of taxable Canadian property are subject to Canadian tax unless they are exempt as a result of bilateral tax agreements.

27. Depreciation and Depletion

Capital cost allowances are generally provided on the diminishing balance basis at favorable rates on an optional basis. The recapture of depreciation is treated as ordinary income. Numerous special rates, grants, and investment allowances are available. Incentives include a 100% deduction for capital property (except buildings acquired after 1987) used in scientific research.

28. Treatment of Dividends

Individuals. Dividends received from Canadian corporations by resident individuals are subject to a gross-up and tax credit mechanism, the effect of which is to reduce the taxation on dividends and thus minimize the impact of double taxation on the distribution of corporate earnings. The result of this mechanism is that Canadian dividends will generally be subject to a maximum rate of tax of about 33%. Similar rules apply in Quebec.

Dividends received from nonresident corporations do not receive the gross-up and credit treatment.

Corporations. Dividends received by one Canadian corporation from another are generally exempt from tax unless the recipient is a private corporation and is subject to paying refundable tax thereon (see item 6). Special rules may apply to dividends paid on preferred shares, if such shares are in substance merely debt substitutes. Dividends received from nonaffiliated foreign corporations are subject to normal rates of tax with a credit for foreign taxes withheld. Dividends from affiliated foreign corporations may or may not be taxable, depending on the surplus from which the dividend was paid.

Special Rules. Canadian taxpayers generally must include in income their participating percentage of the passive income of a controlled foreign affiliate, whether or not distributed.

29. Loss Carryovers

Noncapital (business or property) losses may be carried back three years and forward seven years. Where control of a company changes, losses may be carried forward only for application against income from the business that incurred the loss or a similar business. Net capital losses may be carried back three years and forward indefinitely to be used against capital gains, but will expire where there is a change of control. If a corporation has been formed by an amalgamation, the noncapital and net capital loss carryovers of the predecessor corporations may be utilized by the new corporation. The same principle applies to loss carryovers of a subsidiary owned 90% or more and which is wound-up into its parent. If the amalgamation or the wind-up is preceded by a change of control of the corporation with the loss carryover, the business losses will only be deductible by the amalgamated company or the parent company against income from the business that incurred the loss or a similar business. The net capital losses acquired will be forfeited.

30. Transactions between Related Parties

Revenue transactions must always be carried out at fair market value. Capital transactions must always be carried out at fair market value unless specific rollover provisions apply. Special provisions exist where property is transferred to a corporation in exchange for shares and other consideration, where shares are exchanged only for shares of another corporation in an arm's length transaction, where two or more corporations are amalgamated and where a subsidiary owned 90% or more is liquidated. Other rollover provisions apply with respect to certain capital reorganizations and transfers into or out of partnerships.

31. Consolidation of Income

No provisions exist for the filing of consolidated tax returns by related corporations.

32. Tax Periods

Individuals must use the calendar year as their taxation year. Corporations, partnerships and business enterprises use their fiscal period (which may not exceed 53 weeks) as the taxation year. Proprietors and partners of unincorporated businesses must therefore include in income the profits of their businesses for all fiscal periods ending in the calendar year. To change the fiscal year of a business, permission must be obtained from the taxation authorities. When changes in tax rates become effective within a particular fiscal period, the increase or decrease is prorated, based upon the number of days before and after the change.

33. Other Matters

Management or Administration Fees. These fees, when paid to related nonresident parties, are subject to withholding tax at normal rates. If, however, the charge is for a specific cost, service or indirect expenses for services rendered that can reasonably be considered as having been incurred on behalf of the Canadian company, there is no withholding tax. The purpose of this tax is to prevent the repatriation of profits by means of management fees, and the tax authorities will seek to disallow any excessive charges as well as imposing the withholding tax. This general treatment of management fees paid to related nonresidents can differ under some of Canada's tax treaties.

Inventory Valuation. The LIFO method of valuation is not acceptable for income tax purposes.

Thin Capitalization. Interest expense is not deductible on debt owing to nonresidents who own more than 25% of any class of shares of the corporation to the extent that the debt is greater than three times the equity attributed to the nonresidents.

Reserves. Reasonable reserves for sales proceeds not due at year-end may be deducted. The reserve provisions allow for a reserve over a maximum period of three years for dispositions of property that give rise to ordinary income and five years for capital property, other than certain farming and small business capital property disposed of to a child, in which case the maximum period is ten years.

RELATED CONSIDERATIONS

34. Incentives and Grants

Investment Tax Credit. Current tax credit rates range from 15% to 30%, depending upon the type of expenditure and the region of the country in which it is made. In rare cases, a 45% credit may apply. Qualified expenditures include purchases of new buildings, machinery and equipment to be used in manufacturing, processing, mining, logging, farming or fishing, and current and capital scientific research expenditures. The tax credit reduces capital cost for depreciation purposes or the amount of scientific expenditures which may be deducted. Credits earned may be claimed up to the amount of three-quarters of Federal income taxes otherwise payable for the year, the three preceding years, and the ten succeeding years. A portion of qualifying unused credits earned after April 19, 1983 can be refunded in cash. For individuals, the refund will be 40% of unused credits, while some corporations can claim a 20% refund. Some Canadian-controlled private corporations are eligible for a 100% refund of unused credits earned as a result of certain scientific research expenditures.

Grants. Grants and other incentives are offered to manufacturers and processors, to those engaged in industries which are important to a particular province, and to those establishing almost any type of industry in less-developed regions. These usually relate to capital expenditures and are provided by both the Federal and provincial governments. A number of programs are designed to defray the cost of scientific research. Financial services and assistance are available for exporters.

Royalty Rebates. Alberta, British Columbia, Manitoba, and Saskatchewan have royalty or mineral tax rebate or credit programs, which offset, to a degree, the additional Federal or provincial taxes resulting from the disallowance of Crown resource royalties or lease rentals as a deduction and from the deemed income resulting from the sale of production to a Crown agency at less than market value.

35. Exchange Controls

None.

36. Investment Restrictions on Nonresidents

There are various provincial and Federal laws or regulations restricting nonresident ownership of certain Canadian businesses and real property or imposing special purchase taxes. Nonresidents are advised to consult a lawyer in the province where they propose to purchase Canadian property.

SELECTION OF BUSINESS ENTITY BY NONRESIDENTS

A nonresident individual or corporation resident in a treaty country can do a certain amount of business in Canada without becoming subject to Canadian tax. Generally, if no office is maintained in Canada, no person in Canada is authorized to sign contracts, and no stock of goods is held in Canada for sale, no Canadian permanent establishment will be considered to exist and the nonresident will therefore be protected under Canada's treaties from the payment of Canadian tax. Where the nonresident individual or corporation is located in a nontreaty country, virtually any business activity in Canada will result in a liability for Canadian taxes.

Where a nonresident entity carries on business in Canada through a branch, the tax consequences are:

☐ The branch profits are taxable at ordinary rates plus a branch profits tax (see items 1 to 4). In the case of the Canada-Switzerland tax treaty, the branch profits tax is not imposed if the business of a Swiss company is not carried on principally in Canada. Other treaties impose limits on the accumulated income subject to the branch tax.

☐ No additional tax is levied on remittances of branch profits.

☐ Withholding tax is imposed on foreign interest and certain other foreign expenses charged against the branch.

Because of the branch profits tax (see item 4), the branch form of organization is not often used.

A Canadian corporation is the form of organization used by most nonresident investors. Special tax provisions to be considered are:

☐ Reduced rates are available to Canadian-controlled private corporations (see item 1). A corporation is Canadian-controlled, for these purposes, if 50% of its voting shares, regardless of class, are beneficially owned by Canadian residents.

☐ Dividends are subject to a withholding tax of 25% unless the investor is in a treaty country, in which event the rate is generally reduced to 15% or, in many cases, 10%.

☐ Interest on non-arm's-length indebtedness to nonresidents in excess of three times shareholders' equity is not deductible in computing taxable income (see item 33). All interest on non-arm's-length indebtedness is subject to a 25% (or treaty-reduced) rate of withholding tax.

☐ Interest on arm's-length indebtedness that is not repayable within five years is exempt from withholding tax (see item 18).

☐ The full Canadian tax on Canadian dividend income is potentially refundable (see item 6).

☐ A foreign investor is subject to Canadian tax on a capital gain realized on the sale of the shares of the Canadian subsidiary. This tax often is removed by treaty.

SPECIMEN TAX COMPUTATION

Information:

☐ The corporation's net income for the year, before the provision for income taxes of $600,000, is $1,600,000 and consists of the following:

	$'000's
Income from manufacturing and processing operations	1,145
Dividends from other taxable Canadian corporations:	
Portfolio dividends	60
Dividends from subsidiaries	75

Dividends from foreign affiliate (nontreaty country)	20
Gain on disposal of capital assets	260
Unrealized gain on conversion of foreign currency balances	40
	$1,600

☐ Depreciation and amortization charged against income was $685,000. Allowable tax depreciation consists of $990,000 in capital cost allowance.

☐ Expenditures on scientific research totalled $100,000.

☐ The corporation has $700,000 of noncapital loss carryovers from the previous three years.

☐ The unrealized foreign exchange gain included in income relates to long-term debt denominated in foreign currency.

☐ The underlying foreign taxes attributable to the dividend paid from the foreign affiliate were equivalent to Canadian Federal rates.

☐ Of the capital gain reported, $60,000 was accrued before 1972.

Computation:

	$'000's	$'000's
Net income per financial statement		1,000
Add (per financial statements)		
Provision for income taxes	600	
Depreciation and amortization	685	1,285
		2,285
Less (per financial statements)		
Dividends from other taxable Canadian corporations		
Portfolio dividends	60	
Dividends from subsidiary	75	
Gain on disposal of capital assets	260	
Unrealized gain on conversion of foreign currency balances	40	435
		1,850
Adjustments not reflected in financial statements:		
Add		
Taxable capital gain ($\frac{3}{4} \times (260,000 - 60,000)$)	150	
Investment tax credit on scientific research expenditures deducted in computing income	20	170
		2,020

Less

Capital cost allowance	990	
Allowance for underlying foreign taxes relating to dividend from foreign affiliate	20	
Losses of previous years	700	1,710
Taxable income		310

Tax computation assuming the corporation is a foreign controlled corporation.

	$'000's	$'000's
Taxable income		310
Federal income tax		
Basic tax at 38%	118	
Less		
Abatement for provincial tax at 10%	31	
Manufacturing and processing credit	15	
Investment tax credit		
On scientific research expenditures	20	
	66	52*
Temporary surtax		3
Federal refundable dividend tax		
(25% of Canadian portfolio dividends of $60,000)		15
Provincial income tax		
Basic (Ontario) tax at 15.5%	48	
Less		
Manufacturing and processing credit	3	45
Provincial capital tax (Ontario)		
(³⁄₁₀ of 1% of paid-up capital and long-term debt of $1,000,000)		3
		118
Refundable portion of Federal tax		
Refundable tax on dividends		15

*The Federal large corporations capital tax also may apply (see item 25).

Tax computation assuming the corporation operates in Canada through a branch and is resident in a country whose treaty with Canada permits a maximum branch tax of 15%

	$'000's	$'000's
Taxable income		310
Federal income tax		
Basic tax at 38%	118	
Less		
Abatement for provincial tax at 10%	31	
Manufacturing and processing credit	15	
Investment tax credit		
On scientific research expenditures	20	
	66	52
Temporary surtax		3
Branch tax		55
Taxable income	310	
Dividends from Canadian corporations		
deducted in calculating taxable income	60	
	370	
Less		
Federal income tax	55*	
Provincial income tax	45	
Reinvestment allowance	131	
	231	
	139	
Branch tax at 15%		21
Provincial income tax		
Basic (Ontario) tax at 15.5%	48	
Less		
Manufacturing and processing credit	3	45
Provincial capital tax (Ontario)		
(³/₁₀ of 1% of $3,875,000) (taxable capital		
deemed to be 12.5 times taxable income)		12
		136

*The Federal large corporations capital tax also may apply (see item 25).

CAYMAN ISLANDS

1. Taxes

There are no taxes on income, profits, wealth, capital gains, sales, estates, or inheritances. The major revenue producer is an excise tax levied on most imports together with license fees. Moreover, by incorporating as an exempted company or exempted trust, it is possible to obtain a guaranteed exemption from any possible future income, capital, and capital gains taxes for 20 years, as well as other benefits. An exempted company is one that declares it will not engage in trade within the Cayman Islands. Most foreign companies incorporate as exempted companies. The Islands have no tax treaties or arrangements with other countries, including the United Kingdom.

2. Exchange Controls

There are no exchange controls in Grand Cayman, and all foreign currencies are freely convertible.

3. Banking Facilities and Secrecy Provisions

The growing tourist industry, as well as trust, insurance, and mutual fund activities, require a sophisticated banking system to handle the inflow of offshore money. This is supplied by over 500 banks doing business in the Cayman Islands, including branches of many of the world's largest banks. The bank secrecy laws are as comprehensive as would be expected in a tax haven, and current legislation includes strict penalties for any breach of secrecy relating to confidential information of a business nature.

4. Approximate Costs

The establishment of an exempt company costs approximately US$2,600. The annual government fees are US$580, and the minimum annual charge for management ranges from US$850 to US$1,600. The fees for servicing a trust depend on the extent of the activity.

5. Insurance Industry

In 1980, the Cayman Islands Government passed an insurance law and regulations with a view to attracting the business of captive insurance companies to the Islands, but with a minimum of legislation. To date, over 450 companies have obtained licenses under the new law. The absence of taxation in the Cayman Islands often makes the formation of a captive insurance company an attractive proposition, particularly in respect of the management of the company's assets and investment portfolio.

6. Offshore Mutual Funds

It is anticipated that the number of mutual funds formed in the Cayman Islands will continue to increase due to minimal legislation, the absence of taxation, and straightforward incorporation procedures.

CHANNEL ISLANDS, GUERNSEY

Editor's Note: This chapter includes Alderney. See also Channel Islands, Jersey.

INCOME TAXES ON CORPORATIONS

1. Rates

Companies resident in Guernsey are subject to income tax on their worldwide profits at the standard rate of 20%. Nonresident companies are taxable only on income arising in Guernsey (with the exception of bank deposit account interest).

All companies incorporated in Guernsey are treated as resident for tax purposes unless they are exempt as defined and thus liable only for an exempt-company fee of £500 per annum (see item 6).

Offshore insurance companies may elect to pay tax on chargeable income by reference to a sliding scale rate after £250,000 of income has been charged at the standard rate of 20% (see item 8).

2. Local Income Taxes

None.

3. Capital Gains Taxes

None.

4. Branch Profits Taxes

Guernsey branches of overseas companies pay income tax on the profits of the Guernsey branch at the standard rate of 20%.

5. Foreign Tax Reliefs

Guernsey has double taxation agreements only with the United Kingdom and Jersey. Both of these agreements provide that industrial or commercial profits of an enterprise of one country shall not be subject to tax in the other country unless the enterprise is engaged in trade or business in that other country through a permanent establishment. These agreements also allow double taxation relief for Guernsey residents with respect to tax incurred in either Jersey or the United Kingdom on all income derived from those territories (other than dividends or debenture interest payable by U.K. companies). Claims for unilateral relief from Guernsey tax paid on U.K. debenture interest may be made to the U.K. Revenue.

Guernsey resident companies that receive income subject to foreign tax from sources other than the United Kingdom or Jersey receive a credit against their Guernsey tax liability as follows:

☐ Income taxed at source at rates exceeding three-quarters of the "effective rate." Relief from foreign taxes paid is given in part by way of a credit against Guernsey tax and the balance by a deduction from taxable income. The amount of the foreign tax credit is computed by grossing up the income net of foreign tax at three-quarters of the effective rate, which is the average rate of Guernsey tax suffered by the Guernsey resident. Thus, the income incurs Guernsey tax of up to 5% in addition to the foreign tax.

☐ Income taxed at source at rates equivalent to three-quarters of the "effective rate" or less. Guernsey tax at 20% is imposed less a foreign tax credit for the full foreign tax.

6. Classification of Corporations

All companies registered in Guernsey are liable for income tax unless they are "exempt companies." The location of management and control is of relevance only to companies incorporated outside Guernsey, and such companies with management and control in Guernsey will still be liable for Guernsey income tax unless they elect for exempt status and pay the same fee.

Exempt Companies. A company may claim to be an exempt company and be treated as nonresident if it is in the beneficial ownership of nonresidents. The exempt company fee is £500 per annum.

Exempt companies that are trading companies are not liable for income tax on their trading profits unless under normal circumstances they would be treated as trading in Guernsey without reference to the holding of directors' meetings in Guernsey or the execution of contracts in Guernsey.

An offshore insurance company managed in Guernsey may claim treatment as an exempt company (see item 8).

A collective investment fund may also claim to be treated as an exempt company. An exempt company that is a collective investment fund must deduct tax from the payment of dividends to any Guernsey resident shareholders.

7. Payment of Taxes

Income tax normally is payable in two installments on June 30 and December 31 in the year of assessment. When an assessment is issued after the normal payment dates for that year, the tax due is payable within 21 days of the date of issue of the assessment.

8. Other Matters

Offshore Insurance Companies. Insurance companies may be established in Guernsey if the requirements of the insurance legislation are satisfied. Offshore insurance companies may elect that:

☐ Exempt status be granted for an annual fee of £500 (see item 6).

☐ All income arising from the insurance underwriting activities, including investment income, should be exempted from income tax.

☐ Income tax should be charged on the other income of the company, by reference to a sliding scale rate.

If an election is not made, the company will be liable to income tax on all of its income. It is possible to postpone payment of the tax assessed. The amount available for postponement is related to the level of insurance reserves.

INCOME TAXES ON INDIVIDUALS

9. Rates

An individual's taxable income is taxed at a standard rate of 20%. A wife's income is normally aggregated with her husband's for tax purposes.

Employers carrying on business in Guernsey must deduct and remit tax from payments to employees at rates up to a maximum of 20%. The tax deducted counts as an installment of the employee's normal income tax liability.

Individuals resident and solely or principally resident in Guernsey are taxable on worldwide income on an arising basis after deducting personal and other allowances, and relief for interest paid.

Individuals resident but not solely or principally resident in Guernsey are liable to tax on income arising in the Island plus any income from outside the Island remitted to the Island in the year of assessment. Such residents are entitled to the reliefs and allowances described above. The rules for determining an individual's residence status are contained within the tax law. Individuals who have an abode in Guernsey but do not spend more than three months per year in the Island are considered to be nonresidents (see item 17).

10. Local Income Taxes

None.

11. Capital Gains Taxes

None.

12. Foreign Tax Reliefs

Treatment is the same as in item 5. However, claims to unilateral relief from the United Kingdom will extend to Guernsey tax paid on U.K. dividends in some circumstances.

13. Tax Period

The income tax year coincides with the calendar year, and tax generally is assessed on the income of the year preceding the year of assessment. Tax is payable in June and December of each year of assessment.

14. Other Matters

Income Taxes on Trustees. Trusts can be formed in Guernsey by any person, resident or nonresident in Guernsey. The most popular form of settlement is the discretionary settlement. By using this type of settlement, settlors, trustees, and beneficiaries enjoy maximum flexibility from a tax perspective.

If the trust is resident in the Island for tax purposes (i.e., the administration of the trust is carried out in the Island and a majority of the trustees is resident in the Island) and if neither the settlor nor any of the beneficiaries are resident in the Island, then the Income Tax Authority will, by concession, assess only the trustee to local income tax on income arising in the Island, with the exception of bank interest. The effect of this for practical purposes is that the income of the trustee will be free of local income tax. Guernsey trustees are liable to the normal withholding taxes deducted from dividends paid by companies throughout the world, and the trustees themselves cannot make a claim for repayment of such withholding taxes. In certain circumstances, if income is distributed by trustees to beneficiaries resident in a particular country, those beneficiaries may make claims under double taxation agreements existing between their country of residence and the country from which the dividend income arose.

INCOME TAXES ON NONRESIDENTS

15. Liability to Tax

Nonresident companies and individuals are liable to Guernsey income tax on income arising from within the Island. Interest on bank deposits in Guernsey is not subject to tax, except if an individual makes a claim for proportional relief. A claim to proportional relief may be made by a British subject not resident in Guernsey or by any other individual resident in the United Kingdom or Jersey. A proportion of the allowances normally due to residents would be allowed by reference to the proportion that the Guernsey income bears to worldwide income.

16. Rates

Tax is charged at the rate of 20%.

17.   Withholding Tax Rates

There are no separate withhholding taxes in Guernsey. However, dividends paid by a Guernsey company are paid from taxed profits and, in the hands of shareholders, are treated as gross dividends from which Guernsey tax was deducted at source. Loan interest (including that on a bank loan) paid by a Guernsey resident is not subject to withholding tax if the recipient is another Guernsey resident. Payments of interest to a nonresident are taxed at the rate of 20% at source. This requirement may be relaxed if the recipient is able to claim that the provisions of the double taxation agreements with Jersey or the United Kingdom apply to exempt the interest from tax.

18.   Special Withholding Provisions

None.

OTHER SIGNIFICANT TAXES

21.   Sales (Value Added)

The Channel Islands enjoy a special status within the European Economic Community whereby they are included in the EC for purposes of the free movement of goods and must apply the common external tariff, but they are not subject to value added tax. The provisions of the Treaty of Rome as to harmonization of taxes and social policies do not apply to the Islands.

22.   Inheritance and Gift Taxes

There are no inheritance or gift taxes in Guernsey. Probate duty is payable on death at varying scale rates, which should not exceed 0.5% of the estate's value.

23.   Taxes on Payrolls (Social Security)

Contributions are levied on employers, employees, and self-employed and nonemployed individuals. Provided earnings exceed £110.50 per month, an employee pays a contribution of 3.9% up to a maximum earnings limit of £1,495.00 per month. The employer pays 4.8%. The maximum monthly contribution of an employee is then £58.30. The maximum monthly contribution for the self-employed is £115.11, although a claim for reduced contributions can be made if details of relevant earnings are disclosed. The nonemployed rate of contribution is £69.07 per month, although an exemption may be claimed in some circumstances.

24.   Taxes on Natural Resources

None.

25.   Other Taxes

Land and Property.   Rates are charged annually on both owners and occupiers according to the value of the land and property.

Dwellings Profits Tax.   An anti-speculation tax on dwelling properties is charged at the rate of 100%. An exemption for owner-occupied dwellings is given after one year's occupation by the owner. In most other cases, the dwelling must be owned for five years before an exemption can be claimed.

COMPUTATION OF TAXABLE INCOME

26.   Capital Gains

Capital gains are exempt from tax.

27.   Depreciation and Depletion

Depreciation charged in the accounts is ignored for tax purposes, and the following allowances are applied instead:

☐   Annual Allowances.   An allowance is granted on plant and machinery used for trade purposes. A "pooling" system is operated for most plant and machinery, and the allowance for such assets is 20% based on the reducing-balance method. The straight-line method is used for certain assets, including greenhouses, new aircraft, new ships, computers, and certain other items.

☐   Balancing Allowances and Charges.   If an asset is sold at an amount other than its net tax written-down value, a balancing allowance (or charge) is calculated to increase (or reduce) the assessable trading profit. Balancing allowances and charges are not calculated for "pooled" assets. The sales proceeds or original cost, whichever is lower, is deducted from the written-down value of the asset. Balancing charges will not exceed the allowances previously given, and balancing allowances are not provided when assets are acquired in the same basis period as that of the sale.

☐   Replacement Allowances.   As an alternative to capital allowances, the cost of renewals may by concession be claimed in certain circumstances.

28.   Treatment of Dividends

For dividends from Guernsey income tax companies paid out of taxed profits, the normal practice is for the company to pay an amount equal to the tax "deducted" from the dividend, and this amount is treated as an advance payment of the company's normal tax liability. Dividends paid from reserves that have not been taxed can be paid gross. No further Guernsey tax is payable by the shareholders, and repayment may be claimed if the tax deducted at source exceeds the shareholder's liability to tax.

Exempt companies generally pay dividends gross. However, exempt companies that are collective investment funds must deduct tax when paying dividends to Guernsey resident shareholders.

Foreign-source dividends are subject to Guernsey income tax in the hands of resident companies or individuals (see item 5 for details of relief for foreign tax).

29. Loss Carryovers

Individuals and companies may offset trading losses against total income of the year of assessment. Any unrelieved loss may, subject to certain conditions, offset the income of the year of assessment in which the accounting year ends. Losses still unrelieved may be carried forward indefinitely against other profits from the same trade.

Annual allowances may be added to a loss or create a loss where the adjusted profit is less than the allowances for the relevant year. Unused annual allowances may be carried forward and added to allowances of future years and, thus, can offset total income of future years of assessment.

30. Transactions between Related Parties

There are no specific provisions that require arm's-length pricing for goods or services, but a provision against legal avoidance generally restricts any such schemes.

31. Consolidation of Income

There are no provisions that enable income from companies within a group to be consolidated. However, in practice, the income tax authority permits reasonable charges to be levied by one member of a group against another.

32. Tax Periods

The Guernsey year of assessment is the calendar year. With the exception of investment companies (see item 33) income generally is assessed on a preceding-year basis. Trading income is assessed on the basis of the accounting year ending in the previous calendar year. There are special rules in the case of the commencement or cessation of a business.

33. Other Matters

Investment Companies.   Investment companies resident in Guernsey are assessable on the investment income arising during the year of assessment, and an allowance is granted for management expenses incurred.

Partnerships.   Partners are assessed individually on their respective share of partnership profits.

RELATED CONSIDERATIONS

34. Incentives and Grants

None.

35. Exchange Controls

There have been no exchange controls within the Island since 1979.

36. Investment Restrictions on Nonresidents

There are no investment restrictions on nonresidents, but see "Selection of Business Entity by Nonresidents" with regard to the consents required by nonresidents when setting up a business in Guernsey.

37. Other Matters

Becoming resident in Guernsey. Controls operate in Guernsey and may be divided into three main categories:

- ☐ Open Market. Dwellings may be acquired from a fixed pool of "open market houses," and there are no income restrictions.
- ☐ Essentially Employed Persons. Application may be made to employ persons for a particular profession or trade if such person cannot be recruited locally. Such persons would be permitted to own and occupy property on the "local market." Such property is, however, normally reserved for the indigenous population, and stringent controls are applied by the States of Guernsey Housing Authority.
- ☐ Persons with the right to live in Guernsey.

SELECTION OF BUSINESS ENTITY BY NONRESIDENTS

A nonresident company may trade in Guernsey either through a locally incorporated subsidiary or through a local branch. The trading profits of the local company or branch will be subject to income tax (normally on a preceding-year basis) at the standard rate of 20%.

A nonresident individual may trade through a local branch, and the profits will be liable to income tax (on a preceding-year basis) at the standard rate of 20%. The nonresident individual may be entitled to claim proportionate allowances (see item 15). A nonresident individual may incorporate a local company to trade in Guernsey, and the profits of such a company will be taxable (on a preceding-year basis) at the standard rate of 20%.

A nonresident individual or company may be a partner in a Guernsey partnership, which would be of interest to a nonresident professional person who wishes to operate in a low-tax area but is unable, for professional reasons, to operate through a limited liability company.

Nonresidents may also operate through an exempt company (see item 6).

No specific consents are required prior to setting up a business in Guernsey. However, the Advisory and Finance Committee are able to control the establishment and operation of various parts of the finance industry, and persons contemplating a new business venture in the Island are advised to seek advice on the Committee's current position.

SPECIMEN TAX COMPUTATION

Information:

□ A long-established trading company resident in Guernsey had the following results for the year ended September 30:

Net profit		£500,000
After charging		
Depreciation	£50,000	
Bank interest paid to Guernsey bank	30,000	
Loan interest paid to nonresident	20,000	
Loss on sale of machinery	5,000	
Capital gain on sale of building		100,000
		£600,000

□ Capital allowances—the pool's written-down value brought forward amounted to £220,000. The proceeds of the sale of machinery amounted to £20,000 (each item was sold for less than cost), and there were no acquisitions in the basis period.

□ A dividend of £300,000 (net) was declared.

Computation:

Net profit per accounts		£500,000
Add		
Depreciation	£50,000	
Loss on sale of machinery	5,000	
		55,000
Adjusted profits		£555,000
Less		
Annual allowance (220,000 − 20,000) × 20%		40,000
		£515,000
Income tax (£515,000 × 20%)		£103,000
Income tax payable as agent for nonresident		
(£20,000 × 20%)		£ 4,000

The shareholders will be treated as receiving a gross dividend of £375,000 with £75,000 tax paid. The company pays to the Income Tax Authority the £75,000, which will offset its normal tax liability.

CHANNEL ISLANDS, JERSEY

Editor's Note: See also Channel Islands, Guernsey.

INCOME TAXES ON CORPORATIONS

1. Rates

Companies resident in Jersey are subject to income tax on their worldwide profits at the standard rate of 20%. Nonresident companies are taxable only on income arising in Jersey (with the exception of bank deposit account interest).

Effective January 1, 1989, all companies incorporated in Jersey are treated as resident for tax purposes unless they are exempt as defined and thus liable only for an exempt-company fee of £500 per annum (see item 6). Corporation tax, which previously applied to companies incorporated but not resident in Jersey, was abolished after December 31, 1988.

2. Local Income Taxes

None.

3. Capital Gains Taxes

None.

4. Branch Profits Taxes

Jersey branches of overseas companies pay income tax on the profits of the Jersey branch at the standard rate of 20%.

5. Foreign Tax Reliefs

With the exception of an arrangement with France, which is limited to the exemption of shipping and air transport concerns, Jersey has double taxation agreements only with the United Kingdom and Guernsey. Both of these agreements provide that industrial or commercial profits of an enterprise of one country shall not be subject to tax in the other country, unless the enterprise is engaged in trade or business in that other country through a permanent establishment. These agreements also allow double taxation relief for Jersey residents with respect to tax incurred in either Guernsey or the United Kingdom on all income derived from those territories (other than dividends or debenture interest payable by U.K. companies). Jersey tax paid on U.K. debenture interest may be the subject of claims to unilateral relief from the United Kingdom. In the case of income arising from all other countries outside Jersey, the Jersey resident is assessed tax on the net amount of income arising from the foreign source after deducting any foreign tax payable in the source country.

6. Classification of Corporations

Effective January 1, 1989, all companies registered in Jersey are liable for income tax unless they are "exempt companies." Previously, companies incorporated in Jersey were only liable for income tax if managed and controlled from Jersey and were otherwise liable for Jersey corporation tax. The location of management and control is now of relevance only to companies incorporated outside Jersey, and such companies with management and control in Jersey are liable for Jersey income tax unless they elect for exempt status and pay the same fee.

Exempt Companies. A company may claim to be an exempt company and be treated as nonresident if it is in the beneficial ownership of nonresidents. The exempt company fee is £500 per annum and is payable at the same time as the submission of the claim. Normally this will be by March 31 each year, although the authorities have discretion to accept late claims and during 1990 claims will be accepted up to June 30. Newly incorporated companies have three months from the date of incorporation to make the necessary claim if later.

Exempt companies have certain additional reporting requirements with regard to ownership of companies, and notification of such changes is made to the company registration authorities rather than to the revenue authorities.

Exempt trading companies are not liable for income tax on their trading profits unless under normal circumstances they would be treated as trading in Jersey without reference to the holding of directors meetings in Jersey or the execution of contracts in Jersey.

Collective Investment Schemes. A collective investment scheme also may claim to be treated as an exempt company. Any exempt company that is a collective investment scheme must deduct tax from the payment of dividends to any Jersey resident shareholders. It must also provide the income tax authorities with names, addresses, and shareholdings of any persons resident on the island. An informal clearance procedure exists for persons having Jersey addresses, but not resident on the island.

7. Payment of Taxes

The income tax law simply states that the tax is payable the day following the issue of an assessment, which, in practice, is issued between February and April in the year following the year of assessment. Investment income is assessed on a current year basis and trading income on a preceding year basis.

8. Other Matters

Captive Insurance Companies. Captive insurance companies may be set up in Jersey and generally are not taxable on their underwriting profits (but are subject to tax on other income).

INCOME TAXES ON INDIVIDUALS

9. Rates

An individual's taxable income is subject to income tax at the standard rate of 20%. A wife's income is normally aggregated with her husband's for tax purposes, although, by concession, wives may be assessed separately.

Individuals resident and ordinarily resident in Jersey are taxable on their world-wide income on an arising basis after deducting earned income relief, personal and other allowances, and relief for bank interest paid. For other annual interest, the tax is deducted and retained by the individual provided the individual has sufficient taxable income to cover the interest paid.

Individuals resident but not ordinarily resident in Jersey are assessed to tax on income arising in the Island plus any income from outside the Island remitted to the Island in the year of assessment. These individuals are entitled to the reliefs and allowances described above. Individuals who fall into this category include those who have an abode in the Island but do not spend more than three months per year in the Island and whose main centers of interest are outside the Island.

10. Local Income Taxes

None.

11. Capital Gains Taxes

None.

12. Foreign Tax Reliefs

Treatment is the same as in item 5. However, claims to unilateral relief from the United Kingdom will extend to Jersey tax paid on U.K. dividends in some instances. Individuals who receive pensions subject to income tax imposed by the laws of any Commonwealth country are subject to Jersey income tax on such pensions at half the appropriate rate of tax.

13. Tax Period

The income tax year coincides with the calendar year, and except for profits from trades, professions, and businesses tax is assessed on the income of the year of assessment. Tax is generally assessed about nine months after the year of assessment and tax is payable when assessed. There is no compulsory "pay-as-you-earn" system in Jersey.

14. Other Matters

Income Taxes on Trustees. Trustees resident in Jersey are strictly liable to income tax on all sources of income, but where there are no beneficiaries resident in the Island no tax is assessed by concession on the trustees except on income arising in the Island from sources other than bank deposits.

Jersey trustees are liable to the normal withholding taxes deducted from dividends paid by companies throughout the world and the trustees themselves cannot make a claim for repayment of such withholding taxes. In certain circumstances, where income is distributed by trustees to beneficiaries resident in a particular country, those beneficiaries may make claims under double taxation agreements existing between their country of residence and the country from which the dividend income arose.

INCOME TAXES ON NONRESIDENTS

15. Liability to Tax

Nonresident companies and individuals are liable to Jersey income tax on Jersey-source income. By concession, interest on bank deposit accounts in Jersey is not subject to tax unless an individual makes a claim for proportional reliefs. A claim to proportional reliefs may be made by a British subject not resident in Jersey. A proportion of the allowances normally due to a resident would be allowed in proportion to the ratio that Jersey income bears to worldwide income.

16. Rates

Tax is charged at the rate of 20%.

17. Withholding Tax Rates

There are no separate withholding taxes in Jersey. However, annual interest (except bank interest) paid by a Jersey resident is subject to the standard tax of 20% whether paid to a resident or nonresident. Dividends paid by Jersey companies are paid out of taxed profits and, in the hands of shareholders, are treated as gross dividends which have incurred Jersey tax by deduction at source. The United Kingdom provides unilateral relief to parent companies in receipt of dividends from Jersey subsidiaries.

18. Special Withholding Provisions

None.

OTHER SIGNIFICANT TAXES

21. Sales (Value Added)

The Channel Islands enjoy a special status within the European Economic Community. They are included in the Community for purposes of the free movement of goods and must apply the common external tariff, but they are not subject to value-added tax.

22. Inheritance and Gift Taxes

There are no inheritance or gift taxes in Jersey. Probate duty is payable on death and is calculated at £50 for the first £10,000 and 0.5% thereafter.

23. Taxes on Payrolls (Social Security)

Contributions are levied from employers, employees, and self-employed and unemployed individuals. An employee pays a contribution of 4% of earnings up to a maximum earnings limit of £1,318 per month. The employer pays 5.5%. The maximum monthly contribution is £125.21 per month, which is the same as the flat rate contribution for the self-employed or unemployed individual. In some circumstances, the self-employed or unemployed individuals may pay contributions related to their earnings or may be exempt.

24. Taxes on Natural Resources

None.

25. Other Taxes

Land and Property. Rates are charged annually on both owners and occupiers according to the value of the land and property.

COMPUTATION OF TAXABLE INCOME

26. Capital Gains

Capital gains are exempt from tax.

27. Depreciation and Depletion

Depreciation charged in the accounts is ignored for tax purposes, but capital allowances for expenditure on plant and machinery used for trade purposes are granted instead.

The cost of plant and machinery is incorporated into a pool of expenditures adjusted each year for the cost of new acquisitions and sale proceeds of assets sold. Capital allowances are granted at a single rate of 25% on the written-down value of the pool after taking into account acquisitions and dispositions during the basis period. If the sales proceeds during a year exceed the written-down value of the pool, a balancing charge will arise and this will be taxed as income of the trade. On cessation of trading the balance of the pool less sales proceeds will be allowed as a balancing allowance. There are special rules for expensive motor cars and glasshouses.

28. Treatment of Dividends

Dividends from Jersey resident (income tax) companies are paid out of taxed profits, and the payment of a dividend does not advance any liability by the company with respect to the income tax due on its taxable profits, i.e., dividends are paid net and no payment of tax has to be made to the Revenue authority at that time. No further Jersey tax is payable by the shareholders and repayment may be claimed if the tax deducted at source exceeds the shareholder's tax liability.

Exempt companies generally pay dividends gross. However, exempt companies that are collective investment funds must deduct tax when paying dividends to Jersey resident shareholders.

Dividends received from companies other than Jersey income tax companies or collective investment funds are liable to assessment to Jersey income tax in the hands of resident companies or individuals.

29. Loss Carryovers

Individuals and companies may offset trading losses against other income of that year of assessment. Except in years for which opening or closing rules of assessment apply, by concession the loss of an accounting year may be treated as the loss of the calendar year in which the accounting year ends. Any loss not so relieved may be carried forward against other profits from the same trade indefinitely. By concession capital allowances may be used to increase or create a loss. Any unused allowances may be carried forward and added to allowances of future years.

30. Transactions between Related Parties

No specific provisions prohibit the movement of business profits by means of artificially adjusting the price of goods or services, but a general provision against legal avoidance limits such schemes.

31. Consolidation of Income

There are no provisions that enable income from companies within a group to be consolidated. However, in practice, the Revenue authorities permit management charges to be levied by one member of a group against another.

32. Tax Periods

The Jersey year of assessment is the calendar year. Income is assessed on a current year basis except for trading income, which is assessed on the basis of the accounting year ending in the previous calendar year. There are special rules in the case of the commencement or termination of a business.

33. Other Matters

Investment Companies. Investment companies resident in Jersey are taxed on their investment income arising during the year of assessment and an allowance is granted for management expenses incurred.

Partnerships. A partnership is taxed as a separate entity, but the respective shares of the partners in the partnership profits are included in their taxable income for the purpose of obtaining deductions for personal allowances and reliefs.

RELATED CONSIDERATIONS

34. Incentives and Grants

None.

35. Exchange Controls

There have been no exchange controls within the Island since 1979.

36. Investment Restrictions on Nonresidents

There are no investment restrictions on nonresidents, but see "Selection of Business Entity by Nonresidents" with regard to the consents that are required by nonresidents setting up a business in Jersey.

37. Other Matters

Becoming Resident in Jersey. Jersey strictly controls how persons become resident in Jersey and these measures may be divided into three main categories.

☐ Wealthy Immigrants. Application to become resident may be made on economic or social grounds. The former involves, inter alia, an individual substantiating to the satisfaction of the Island's Economic Adviser, acting on behalf of the Housing Committee, that a substantial income liable to Jersey tax will arise. Approval is presently limited to five persons per annum. The number of applications for places normally exceeds the number available, and although there are no formal financial limits, currently applicants whose income-yielding assets are not significantly in excess of £5 million are likely to prove unsuccessful.

☐ Essential Employment. The authorities may permit individuals to become resident on grounds of essential employment if there is no suitable local candidate for a position, the qualifications and experience required are not to be readily obtained through local recruitment and training, and the position is "essential" to the Island. With few exceptions, permission is granted to the employer to lease or purchase accommodation for the employee's occupation. For the most part consent is granted for a limited period, normally for two to five years.

□ Temporary or Seasonal Employment.   Those not classified as essential employees for housing purposes, such as seasonal workers in the agricultural and tourism sectors, may occupy licensed lodging premises, or other accommodation the occupation of which is not subject to the control of the Housing Committee. Such employees do not acquire the right to lease or purchase accommodation through the completion of a period of residence in the Island.

Control of Business Undertakings.   Under the Regulation of Undertakings and Development Law, a license has to be obtained to commence any undertaking in the Island (i.e., any trade, business or profession) or to increase the number of employees.

SELECTION OF BUSINESS ENTITY BY NONRESIDENTS

A nonresident company may trade in Jersey either through a locally incorporated subsidiary or a local branch. The trading profits of the local company or branch will be liable to income tax (normally on a preceding year basis) at the standard rate of 20%.

A nonresident individual may trade through a local branch and the profits will be subject to income tax (on a preceding year basis) at the standard rate of 20%. The nonresident individual may be entitled to claim proportionate allowances (see item 15). A nonresident individual may incorporate a local company to trade in Jersey and the profits of such company will be taxable (on a preceding year basis) at the standard rate of 20%.

A nonresident individual or company may be a partner in a Jersey partnership. A partnership arrangement is likely to be of interest to a nonresident professional person who wishes to operate in a low tax area, but is unable, for professional reasons, to operate through a limited liability company.

Nonresidents may also operate through an exempt company. (See item 6.)

A nonresident starting a business in Jersey will require the consent of the Island's Finance and Economic Committee if separate premises or Jersey resident employees are needed. The granting of such consent will be influenced by the advantages which are likely to accrue to the Island from the establishment of the business.

SPECIMEN TAX COMPUTATION

Information:

□ A long-established trading company resident in Jersey had the following results for the year ended September 30, 1991:

Net profit		£500,000
After charging		
Depreciation	£50,000	
Bank interest	30,000	
Loan interest (gross)	20,000	
Loss on sale of machinery	5,000	
Capital gain on sale of building		100,000
		£600,000

□ The written-down value of the capital allowance pool after deducting allowances for the previous year amounted to £151,000. During the year a machine which had cost £15,000 with a book value of £12,000 was sold for £7,000. The replacement cost is £20,000.

□ A dividend of £300,000 (net) was declared.

Computation:

Net profit per accounts		£500,000
Add		
Depreciation	50,000	
Loan interest (paid under deduction of tax)	20,000	
Loss on sale of machinery	5,000	
		75,000
Taxable profits (assessable 1992)		£575,000
Less		
Capital allowances (2)		41,000
		£534,000
Income tax (£534,000 × 20%)		£106,800

Notes:

(1) The declared dividend has no tax significance for the company. The shareholders will be treated as receiving a gross dividend of £375,000 with £75,000 tax paid.

(2) (£151,000 − £7,000 + £20,000) × 25%.

CHILE

INCOME TAXES ON CORPORATIONS

1. Rates

The income of corporations, limited partnerships, and branches of foreign corporations is taxed in two stages: first, when income is accrued by the company; second, when profits are distributed to shareholders (or partners) or remitted abroad in the case of a branch.

The income tax rate on accrued but undistributed income is 10%. This rate has been raised temporarily to 15% for income earned between 1991 and 1993.

When income is withdrawn or distributed to nonresident partners or shareholders or when remitted abroad, the income is subject to a 35% additional tax. The taxpayer liable to the additional tax is entitled to a tax credit equivalent to the first category tax rate assessed on the income withdrawn, distributed, or remitted abroad. This credit must be added to the basis upon which the additional tax is calculated.

The overall approximate effective tax rate resulting from the above rules, assuming no income is retained, is

Taxable income	$100
Taxation on accrued income	
15% first category tax	15
Distributable income	$ 85
Additional tax on distributed income	
Distribution	$ 85
Plus credit	15
	$100
35% tax	35
Less credit	15
Additional tax payable	$ 20
Overall tax burden	$ 35

A foreign investor can elect to apply a standard income tax of 49.5% instead of the above normal rates, or, alternatively, a 40% rate plus a surtax in case of excessive remittances. These rates are guaranteed to remain unchanged for ten years, but the investor may waive this special regime at any time and become subject to the general tax regime. If so, the investor will be subject to changes in the general tax legislation with the same rights, options, and obligations pertaining to domestic investors. The waiver of the special regime is irrevocable. Due to certain technicalities when calculating income taxes, the effective tax burden of the foreign investor, in the case of the standard 49.5% rate, is approximately 44.33%, 15% of which is paid annually and the balance when profits are distributed, withdrawn, or remitted abroad. In the case of the 40% plus surtax regime, the effective tax burden depends on the surtax. Under normal remittance conditions, the tax burden is less than 45%.

2. Local Income Taxes

None.

3. Capital Gains Taxes

There is no specific tax dealing with capital gains. Under certain conditions, however, capital gains arising from the sale of shares, mining property, debentures, and certain other assets are subject to the first category tax. There is no taxation upon the distribution or remittance abroad of the corresponding profits.

4. Branch Profits Taxes

As indicated above, branches are subject to the 15% first category tax on accrued income as are limited partnerships and stock corporations. Income from the business activities of the branch, plus all other Chilean-source income, is subject to the 35% additional tax when remitted abroad. The branch is entitled to the credit against the additional tax, which is equivalent to the rate of the first category tax assessed on the remitted income. This credit must be added to the basis upon which the said tax is calculated.

5. Foreign Tax Reliefs

Foreign income taxes incurred in business transactions are allowed as a deductible expense.

7. Payment of Taxes

Income taxes are paid annually, but estimated partial payments must be paid monthly. The excess, if any, of estimated advanced payments over the corporation's final tax liability is reimbursed within the month subsequent to the filing of income tax returns.

8. Other Matters

General Considerations. As a general rule, profits subject to the first category tax reflect a system of accrual basis accounting. In general, worldwide income is subject to tax. However, this rule does not apply to branches or to foreigners during their first three years of Chilean domicile or residence. The profits shown in financial statements are usually subject to additions and deductions pursuant to the income tax law.

Businesses must keep their accounting records in Chilean currency; however, regional tax commissioners are empowered to authorize accounting in foreign currency if all or most of the capital contributed or business performed is in such a currency.

The assessment of taxable income begins with gross revenue, which includes all revenue received or accrued during the tax period. Direct prime cost (materials and wages) is deductible from gross revenue and factory overhead is generally treated as an expense. All expenses other than cost paid or due during the period are deductible when necessary for the production of income. Provisions for bad debts or contingencies that have not been incurred are not allowed, except in the case of banks and financial institutions according to special rules; for example, a deduction for bad debts is allowed only when the debt is in fact non-recoverable and written off. Organizational and start-up expenditures may be deferred and deducted over a period of up to six years, which begin when income is generated.

Inflation Accounting. To offset the effects of inflation, the Income Tax Law has established a comprehensive system of monetary adjustments (corrección monetaria) by which all balance sheet items are expressed in units of constant purchasing power. The procedure is to adjust all non-monetary assets and liabilities existing as of the end of the fiscal year, and the networth as of the beginning of the year, as well as increases and decreases in networth, in accordance with a method that restates historical balance sheet items at units of constant purchasing power with offsetting debits or credits to income.

To achieve the above, non-monetary assets and decreases in networth are adjusted with credit to profit and loss. Non-monetary liabilities, initial networth, and increases in networth are adjusted with debit to profit and loss. As a consequence, the balance of monetary adjustments is shown as a profit or a loss, whichever is the case. These monetary adjustments do not apply to companies authorized to keep their accounting records in foreign currency (see above).

INCOME TAXES ON INDIVIDUALS

9. Rates

The income of individuals is subject to progressive tax according to a schedule which is based on an indexed unit called the Annual Tax Unit (ATU). In August 1991, one ATU was equivalent to approximately US$461.

Annual Income		Tax
Over	Not Over	Rate
ATU 0	ATU 10	—
10	30	5%
30	50	15
50	70	25
70	100	35
100		50

10. Local Income Taxes

None.

11. Capital Gains Taxes

In general, the capital gains of individuals are subject to the same rules that apply to business entities. However, gains derived from the occasional sale of real estate by an individual are not taxable.

12. Foreign Tax Reliefs

During their first three years in Chile, domiciled or resident foreigners are taxed only on Chilean-source income.

INCOME TAXES ON NONRESIDENTS

15. Liability to Tax

Chilean-source income of foreign entities with a permanent establishment in Chile is subject to tax as indicated in item 4. Nonresident partners of a Chilean partnership are subject to the 35% additional tax on their participation in profits less the corresponding credit; the resulting effective tax rate is indicated in item 1.

17. Withholding Tax Rates

Cash dividends paid by a Chilean corporation to nondomiciled shareholders are subject, in principle, to a 35% withholding tax, against which an amount equivalent to the first category tax, if assessed on the corporation, may be credited. The basis to calculate the referred additional tax must include this credit.

As a general rule, a 40% tax on gross revenue is levied on payments to nondomiciled persons or entities as listed below:

☐ Remuneration for the use of trademarks, patents, formulas, technical assistance, and other similar services.

☐ Interest (except when paid to foreign banks or financial institutions, in which case the rate is 4%).

☐ Remuneration for services rendered abroad, except for payments for freight, shipping and clearance, weighting, sampling and analysis of products, insurance (other than those expressly taxed as mentioned below), international telecommunications, smelting, refining, and the application of other special processes to Chilean products. However, payments for engineering services or technical assistance rendered abroad are subject to the same tax at a 20% rate.

☐ Payments to insurance companies not established in Chile for insuring equipment or other goods in Chile or for life or medical insurance of persons resident or domiciled in Chile. The tax rate is 22% in the case of insurance and 2% in the case of reinsurance.

☐ Remuneration for maritime transportation from and to Chilean ports and for related services to vessels and freight in Chilean (or foreign) ports is subject to a 5% tax. The tax may be waived on the basis of reciprocity.

☐ Lease, sublease, charter, usufruct, or any other legal form of transference of the use of foreign vessels is subject to a 20% tax rate, with some exceptions.

☐ Remunerations paid by the lessee in lease or leasing agreements of imported fixed assets, which may qualify for the customs payment deferral system, are subject to a 2% rate.

19. Tax Treaties

Only a general double taxation agreement with Argentina is currently in force. Special double taxation agreements on transportation have been entered into with Brazil, Colombia, France, Germany, Spain, and the United States.

OTHER SIGNIFICANT TAXES

21. Sales (Value Added)

An 18% value added tax (VAT) is levied on imports, local sales, and payments for services rendered. Although the seller of goods or services is subject to the tax, the tax can be transferred to the buyer. On the other hand, the seller can credit the payment of the monthly tax in the amount of VAT that he has had to pay as a buyer of goods or services. If the credit in a given month is greater than the tax due, the difference can be carried forward and credited against future payments after being adjusted according to the Chilean Price Indexes.

Nonbusiness sales and the occasional sale of fixed assets are not taxable. However, the sales tax incurred in purchasing fixed assets may be credited against future payments or recovered in cash if the VAT credit has been accumulated for at least six months. Exports are exempt from VAT. Exporters may apply for reimbursement of the tax charged on the purchase of national goods, services, or imports used in exporting activities.

The tax borne by the buyer is not an expense or cost, except when it cannot be applied to future payments.

Interest paid to and received by banks or financial institutions is not taxable.

22. Inheritance and Gift Taxes

Gifts made during the donor's lifetime and transfers of property upon his death are subject to a progressive tax. The rate varies with the amount involved and the degree of decedent's relationship with the beneficiary.

23. Taxes on Payrolls (Social Security)

Social security is financed by employee and employer contributions, which total approximately 23% of the first 60 UF of monthly remuneration. In certain cases, it is possible to obtain an exemption from social security payments for foreign technicians or professionals. As of August 1990, the UF corresponds to approximately US$21.

24. Taxes on Natural Resources

As a general rule, the mining activity is subject to the general taxation regime. Exceptionally small mining producers are assessed tax on a presumptive basis (assumed income). Special legal provisions regulate the exploitation of oil and atomic materials. The President of Chile is authorized to determine whether a contractor in these areas may be subject to a special tax regime.

25. Other Taxes

Land and Property. Real estate is subject to an annual tax of approximately 20% of the fiscal assessment and is payable annually in four installments.

Stamp Tax. Due to a recent amendment, this tax applies to both local and foreign borrowing. The following transactions and documents are subject to stamp tax:

☐ Bills of exchange, promissory notes, and, in general, any other document containing a money credit agreement. The rate is 0.10% of the par value of the document for each month of the loan's term up to a maximum of 1.2%. If the document is payable on sight, the rate is a fixed 0.5%. Loans obtained to finance imports and imports with deferred payments also are subject to the same taxation.

☐ Checks, protest of bills, and promissory notes are subject to various stamp taxes.

COMPUTATION OF TAXABLE INCOME

27. Depreciation and Depletion

In general, the straight-line method of depreciation is accepted. The tax authorities have established a general time schedule for depreciation based on the asset's average useful life. If warranted by production conditions, a faster period of depreciation can be granted in certain cases. In addition, newly acquired or imported assets are entitled to an accelerated depreciation method, which uses the straight-line basis but reduces the period to one-third of the normal useful life.

The normal rates of depreciation for new assets used under normal working conditions are:

Trucks	7 years
Factory buildings	25 to 40 years
Heavy machinery	20 years

28. Treatment of Dividends

If a shareholder is a Chilean limited partnership or corporation, no taxes are applied to the dividend. However, when income reaches Chilean individuals, it will be taxed at the rates described in item 9, but the shareholder will have the corresponding credit. Stock dividends are not taxable.

29. Loss Carryovers

Losses can be carried indefinitely. Losses from any given year must first offset accumulated earnings, and the balance is carried forward.

30. Transactions between Related Parties

For transactions between related parties, the following items must be added to net income: use or conveyance of goods at no charge or under cost; debt remissions; excess interest paid; shares subscribed to at special prices; and other similar benefits. Moreover, in the case of exporters and importers, the IRS may question prices that differ from those currently applied in the domestic or foreign market.

31. Consolidation of Income

There is no provision for the filing of consolidated tax returns by related corporations.

32. Tax Periods

The calendar year is the tax period.

33. Other Matters

Certain economic activities that are regarded as essential to the development of the Chilean economy are granted rebates; for example, the forestry and shipping industries, and businesses located in the extreme northern and southern regions of the country. Certain mining, agricultural, and transportation activities carried on by a person or entity other than a corporation may be taxable on an imputed basis.

RELATED CONSIDERATIONS

34. Incentives and Grants

In general, there is no discrimination in taxation between Chilean and non-Chilean investors.

Various capital goods imported by foreign investors are exempt from VAT when listed by the Ministry of Economy.

35. Exchange Controls

As a general rule, foreign exchange may be freely traded at the exchange rate agreed upon by the parties. Transactions in which the Central Bank takes part must be carried out at an exchange unilaterally established by the bank. This mechanism may be used by the Central Bank to maintain the exchange rate within desired limits.

Certain transactions involving foreign exchange must be conducted only through the banking system. Such is the case with foreign trade, foreign investment, foreign loans, and in general the flow of capital. Specific operations need the prior approval of the Central Bank, such as foreign investment operations. The proceeds from exports must be repatriated and converted into pesos through the banking system within certain terms.

Recently, a new Central Bank regulation has been enforced, which provides that a 20% special reserve of the credits entering the country be deposited without interest at the Central Bank during a variable term that goes from 90 days if the credit is granted for less than 90 days, up to a year if the said term is greater than one year. The deposit may be substituted in some cases by the acquisition and sale on reversion of promissory notes issued by the Central Bank at a discount rate equivalent to the LIBOR rate in dollars, 180 days.

36. Investment Restrictions on Nonresidents

In general, there are no investment restrictions on nonresidents.

SELECTION OF BUSINESS ENTITY BY NONRESIDENTS

In broad terms, business may be carried on in Chile through a Chilean limited liability partnership association, corporation, or branch. Both limited partnerships and corporations are legal entities separate and distinct from their owners, and they are subject to a similar tax regime with some differences, which bring some interesting consequences depending on the type of business.

CHINA
PEOPLE'S REPUBLIC OF

INCOME TAXES ON CORPORATIONS

1. Rates

Effective July 1, 1991, the corporation tax rate applicable to enterprises with foreign investment (FIE) and foreign enterprise (FE) is 30%.

Concessionary Tax Rate. The following income qualifies for the concessionary tax rates:

☐ Income obtained by FIE and FE located in Special Economic Zones (SEZ) in Shenzhen, Zhuhai, Shantou and Xiamen, Hainan SEZ, and Economic and Technological Development Zones (ETDZ) in the coastal port cities and engaged in production or business operations is subject to tax at 15%.

☐ Income obtained by FIE and FE located in coastal economic open zones, in the old urban districts of cities where the SEZ are located, or in the ETDZ and engaged in production operations is subject to tax at 24%.

☐ Income obtained by FIE and FE located in coastal economic open zones, in the old urban districts of cities where the SEZ are located, in the ETDZ, or in other regions defined by the State Council and engaged within the scope of energy, communications, harbor, wharf, or other projects encouraged by the State may be subject to tax at 15%. This specific rule is regulated by the State Council.

☐ Income obtained by FIE and FE located in the old urban districts of cities where the SEZ are located and in the Coastal Open Economic Zones and engaged in the following projects is subject to tax at 15%:

—technology-intensive or knowledge-intensive projects;

—projects requiring a long period for recovery of capital with foreign investment not less than US$30 million; or

—energy, communications, or port development projects.

☐ Income obtained by FIE and FE located in Shanghai Pudong New Area and engaged in production operations, energy, and transportation construction projects is subject to tax at 15%.

2. Local Income Taxes

The tax rate is 10% levied on the assessed income tax. Exemption or reduction in local income tax may be granted to FIE located in SEZ, in the ETDZ, and in the old urban districts of cities where the SEZ are located, if the local tax authorities so decide.

3. Capital Gains Taxes

Gains on sale of fixed assets are taxable as ordinary income.

4. Branch Profits Taxes

There is no distinction between branch profits tax and corporation profits tax.

5. Foreign Tax Reliefs

The Chinese taxation system provides for avoidance of double taxation and prevention of evasion for taxes incurred in territories outside China under double taxation agreements.

Tax treaties exist with Belgium, Canada, Czechoslovakia, Denmark, Finland, France, Germany, Italy, Japan, Kuwait, Malaysia, The Netherlands, New Zealand, Norway, Pakistan, Poland, Romania, Singapore, Sweden, Switzerland, Thailand, United Kingdom, United States, and Yugoslavia.

An FIE may deduct from the amount of tax payable the foreign income tax already paid abroad in respect of the income derived from sources outside China. However, the deductible amount may not exceed the amount of income tax otherwise payable in China in respect of the income derived from sources outside China.

6. Classification of Corporations

Corporations are classified, for China tax purposes, in two ways:

□ as a resident or nonresident corporation; and
□ as an FIE and FE.

A resident corporation is one having its head office within the territory of China. The distinction between resident and nonresident corporations is important. Resident corporations are subject to tax on their worldwide income, whereas nonresidents with their head office outside China are subject to tax on their China-sourced income. Resident corporations are divided into FIE and FE with establishment in China. Nonresident corporations are FE without establishment in China. FIE includes Chinese-foreign equity joint ventures, Chinese-foreign contractual joint ventures, and wholly foreign-owned enterprises established in China. FE means foreign companies, enterprises, and other economic organizations having establishments or places in China and engaged in product or business operations. Establishments or places refers to management organizations (head office), business organizations, representative offices, and factories (places where natural resources are exploited, places where contracted projects of construction, installation, assembly, and exploration are operated, places where labor services are provided, and business agents).

7. Payment of Taxes

Income tax is levied on an annual basis and paid in four quarterly estimated installments. Provisional payments are due within 15 days after the end of each quarter. A final settlement is due within five months after the end of a year.

8. Other Matter

Permanent Representative Offices of Foreign Enterprises. The following proceeds and income of permanent representative offices are taxable:

☐ Commissions, rebates, and fees received by permanent representative offices for performing liaison, negotiation, and middleman services within Chinese territory on behalf of their home offices for engaging in agency business which are entrusted by other enterprises outside the territory of the PRC (People's Republic of China).

☐ Payments by scheduled installments or by reference to the volume of services provided, made to permanent representative offices by their clients for engaging on behalf of their clients (including the clients of their home offices) in such activities as conducting market surveys, providing liaison and consultation services, and collecting commercial information within the territory of the PRC.

☐ Commissions, rebates, and fees received by permanent representative offices for engaging in business within Chinese territory, as the agents of other enterprises or for liaison, negotiation, or middleman services for economic and trade transactions between other enterprises.

If it is not possible to ascertain the exact income or to produce accurate vouchers of costs and expenses of a permanent representative office, the gross income is determined either on the deemed commission basis or the expense grossing-up basis. The prevailing deemed profit rate is 10%.

Exempt Situations. Permanent representative offices engaged in certain activities (e.g., conducting market surveys, providing business information and business liaison, consultation, and other services) on behalf of their home offices are exempt from the industrial and commercial consolidated tax and foreign enterprise income tax, provided they do not receive proceeds for their operations or services.

Tax exemption for liaison services provided by a representative office to its home office is limited to its "immediate head office." Liaison services to affiliates within a group are considered to be taxable activities, unless all of the following criteria can be met:

□ the subsidiaries are 100% owned by the parent company;

□ both the parent company and the subsidiaries are incorporated in the same country;

□ all the business activities of the subsidiaries are under the control of the parent company; and

□ the group is allowed by the tax authorities in its home country to consolidate its profits and losses by filing consolidated income tax returns.

If the above criteria are met and appropriate documents are furnished, the entire group will be treated as a single "economic entity," and the liaison services provided by the representative office to the group will be exempt from tax.

Permanent representative offices appointed by enterprises within Chinese territory to act as agents mainly outside the territory of the PRC are exempt from taxes on the income derived thereof.

INCOME TAXES ON INDIVIDUALS

9. Rates

Income from wages and salaries is taxed according to a progressive seven-scale rate, ranging from 5% to 45% as follows:

Monthly Taxable Income		Tax on Lower Amount	Percentage On Excess
Over	Not Over		
RMB 800	RMB 1,500	RMB 0	5%
1,500	3,000	35	10
3,000	6,000	185	20
6,000	9,000	785	30
9,000	12,000	1,685	40
12,000		2,885	45

Only 50% of the tax computed is payable.

Employees of foreign employers can apportion their tax liabilities by the actual number of days resided in the PRC each month if certain criteria are met.

Income from compensation for personal services, royalties, leases on property, and other kind of income specified as taxable by the Ministry of Finance, such as interest, dividends, and bonuses, are taxed at a flat rate of 20%, payable in full.

Allowable Deductions. On income from wages and salaries, a monthly deduction of 800 yuan is allowed.

On income from compensation for personal services, royalties, leases on property, or other kind of income specified as taxable by the Ministry of Finance, a deduction of 800 yuan is allowed if the income received in a single payment is less than 4,000 yuan. If the income received in a single payment is more than 4,000 yuan, a 20% deduction is allowed.

No deduction is allowed for income from interest, dividends, or bonuses.

10. Local Income Taxes

None.

11. Capital Gains Taxes

None.

13. Tax Period

December 31 is the standard tax year end.

INCOME TAXES ON NON-RESIDENTS

15. Liability to tax.

Foreign individuals residing in the PRC for less than one year are subject to income tax only on China-source income derived during the period of residence in the PRC. An individual resident in the PRC for the entire tax year (but not for the previous five years) is taxed on all China-source income and all non-China-source income remitted to the PRC. Any individual who resides in the PRC for a period of five or more years is taxed on his or her worldwide income. Individuals who do not intend to reside permanently in the PRC need not pay any tax on their foreign-source income even if they have resided in the PRC for five years or more. Remuneration from foreign employers to individuals working in the PRC is exempt from tax if the individual resides in the PRC for less than 90 days within a calendar year. This 90-day period may be extended to 183 days if the individual is a citizen of a country which has signed a tax treaty with China.

The individual income tax may be collected through withholding at source. Taxpayers not covered by this withholding process are required to personally file a declaration of their income to the tax office and pay the tax due within the first seven days of the month following that in which the income was earned.

Those who earn income outside of the PRC should, within 30 days after the end of the year, pay the tax to the State Treasury and send the form in to the local tax bureau.

For foreign enterprises without establishment in China but that derive profit (dividends), interest, rental, royalty, and other China-sourced income, such income is deemed to be income derived in China and liable to tax.

Specific exemptions from income tax include:

☐ Profit derived by a foreign investor from FIE.

☐ Interest on loans provided by international monetary organization.

☐ Interest earned on money lent to China at preferential rates by banks.

- ☐ Interest income of foreign banks from loans at preferential rates to China's State banks.
- ☐ Interest paid at the international interbank rate on loans by oveseas banks and banks located in the Hong Kong–Macao region to foreign banks in the SEZs.
- ☐ Interest earned on deposits with SEZ's foreign banks by overseas and Hong Kong–Macao depositors before the end of 1995.

17. Withholding Tax Rates

A withholding tax of 20% shall be withheld for each gross China-sourced payment to a foreign enterprise and must be paid by the withholding unit to the local tax bureau within five days of each withholding.

Concessionary Tax Rate: The following income qualifies for the concessionary tax rates:

- ☐ Fees arising from the transfer of proprietary technology may, under certain conditions, be exempted from tax or be taxed at a preferential rate of 10%.
- ☐ Interest from loans, advances, and deferred payments obtained under credit contracts or trade contracts signed before the end of 1995 by foreign companies with Chinese concerns may be taxed, during the effective period of the contract, at a reduced rate of 10%.
- ☐ Leasing fees obtained by foreign leasing companies by way of the lease-sale method before the end of 1995 may also be taxed at a reduced rate of 10%.
- ☐ Dividends, interest, rentals, and royalties sourced in SEZ, ETDZ, or Shanghai Pudong New Area are taxed at a reduced rate of 10%. Where the terms are favorable and the technology transferred is advanced, royalty income may be exempted from tax.

19. Tax Treaties

China has concluded an extensive range of double taxation agreements with over 25 countries throughout the world. These agreements may reduce the liability of tax paid/payable.

OTHER SIGNIFICANT TAXES

25. Other Taxes

The Industrial and Commercial Consolidated Tax. This tax is in the nature of a tax on gross receipts or sales. All units or individuals engaged in industrial production, purchasing farm produce, importing foreign goods, retailing, communication and transport, and service trades must pay the industrial and commercial consolidated tax, which is levied on the turnover of industrial and agricultural products and the service trades.

☐ *Rates*. The taxable items of the industrial and commercial consolidated tax are classified according to the products or business operations of the taxable entities. Tax rates are fixed for different lines of business and products. For example, the maximum rates are 69% for cigarettes and 55% for cigars. The low rates are 5% for machines and equipment, 2% for gas, and 1.5% for cotton greys. The tax rates for most items are below 20%.

Four tax rates are defined for the retail sector, transport and communication, and service trades. The tax rates are 2.5% for transport and communication, 3% for retail sector and design and installation services, 5% for hotels and advertising agencies, and 7% for commissions and brokerage. For permanent representative offices of foreign enterprises, the rate is 5%. In addition, a local surtax is levied at the rate of 1% on the amount of industrial and commercial consolidated tax payable.

☐ *Payment of Tax*. Based on dates and amounts of tax as fixed by the local tax bureau, the taxpayer should calculate the amount of tax and pay it to the State Treasury. Imported industrial and agricultural products are to be taxed by customs at the time of importation.

☐ *Tax Exemptions*. Fixed-period or temporary reductions or exemptions may be applied for by those enterprises that experience difficulties in production or operations. Exemption from or reduction of industrial and commercial consolidated tax is granted to:

—all export products manufactured by FIE except a few items;

—import of building materials, production equipment, business equipment, spare parts, components, means of transport, and office supplies for own use and as investment or additional investment by FIE;

—import of raw materials, spare parts, accessories, components, and packaging materials for the manufacturing of export products;

—all building materials and ancillary equipment, indoor electrical appliances, and other goods and materials required by foreign contractors for the construction and renovation of hotels or guest houses in the PRC.

Stamp Tax. Both the Provisional Regulations and the Implementing Rules on Stamp Duty came into effect on October 1, 1988. All units and individuals who execute or receive "specified documentation" are subject to duty.

☐ *Rates*. Duty rates vary between 0.03% for property insurance contracts and 0.1% for property leasing contracts. A flat amount of 5 yuan applies to certification evidencing rights and licenses.

☐ *Tax Exemptions*. Foreign-funded enterprises that pay the Industrial and Commercial Consolidated Tax are exempt from stamp duty.

Housing Property Tax. The housing property tax is a tax on houses and buildings. It is imposed on the owners, users, or custodians of houses and buildings on the basis of the cost or rental value.

□ *Rates*. The tax rate is 1.2% of the cost or 18% on the rental value of the houses and buildings concerned.

□ *Payment of Tax*. The tax is levied once every quarter or half year. The payer should report in detail on a fixed date to the local tax office about the estate's location, structure, area, and number of rooms. After looking into the matter, the local tax bureau office will direct the payer to pay tax to the State Treasury on a fixed date.

Tax on Vehicles and Ships.   A tax is levied on all vehicles and ships used in districts within the PRC.

□ *Rates and Payment of Tax*. According to the Provisional Regulations for the Tax on Vehicles and Ships, a fixed amount of tax is to be levied on a yearly or quarterly basis.

Foreign ships are taxed according to tonnages. Domestic vehicles and ships are taxed on a fixed amount according to deadweight tonnage. Passenger cars and buses are taxed on a fixed unit amount.

COMPUTATION OF TAXABLE INCOME

26. Capital Gains

The net capital gain is the difference between the original value and the selling price. The original value is the purchase price plus relevant expenses incurred before they are put into use.

27. Depreciation and Depletion

Wear and tear allowances are granted on fixed assets and other capital assets used in the production of income. Only straight-line method of depreciation is allowed. In computing the depreciation on fixed assets, the residual value is assessed and deducted from the original value. The residual value cannot be less than 10% of the original value. Depreciation on fixed assets is computed beginning with the month following that in which the assets are put into use and ceasing the month following that in which the fixed assets are no longer used.

The minimum depreciation periods for different kinds of fixed assets are as follows:

Premises, buildings and structures	20 years
Trains, ships, machinery and other production equipment	10 years
Electronic equipment and others	5 years

Intangible assets can be amoritzed by the straight-line method over a period of not less than ten years or the stipulated time limit set out in an agreement where the intangible asset is put in as an investment in a FIE.

Pre-operating expenses are to be amortized over a period of not less than five years.

28. Treatment of Dividends

Dividends are to be included in taxable income, but dividends received from another FIE in China are not taxable. For dividends received by FE without establishment in China, see item 17.

29. Loss Carryovers

Net losses incurred by corporations engaged in production or business operations generally may be carried forward over a period not exceeding five years.

30. Transactions between Related Parties

All FIE are required to conduct revenue and capital transactions between related parties on an arm's-length basis; otherwise the tax authorities have the right to disregard, vary, or make adjustments to certain arrangements that are carried out for the purpose of tax avoidance and not for bona fide commercial reasons.

31. Consolidation of Income

Corporations having two or more business establishments set up in China may elect one establishment for consolidated tax filing and payment. However, that establishment shall meet the following requirements:

□ It assumes the supervisory and management responsibility over the business of other establishments.

□ It keeps complete accounting records and vouchers that correctly reflect the income costs, expenses, profits, and losses of other business establishments.

32. Tax Periods

The tax year is the Gregorian Calendar year starting from 1 January and ending on 31 December. A foreign enterprise may use its own 12-month fiscal year as the tax year if local tax authorities approve.

33. Other Matters

Inventory Valuation. Inventory of commodities, finished products, products-in-progress, semi-finished products, and raw materials of a FIE shall be priced according to the cost prices. For computation of the actual cost prices for delivery and acceptance of inventory, FIE may choose one of the following methods, first-in first-out, moving average, weighted average, and last-in first-out.

Bad Debts. Corporations engaged in the credit and leasing business may, according to their actual needs and after the approval of the local tax authorities, provide year by year for doubtful debts at not exceeding 3% of the year-end balances of their loans (not including interbank loans) or of their accounts receivable, bills receivable, and other receipts, and they may deduct the provision from the taxable income of that year.

Bad debt expenses incurred by an enterprise shall be reported to the local tax authorities for examination and confirmation.

Accounts receivable can be written off as bad under the following circumstances:

- [ ] bankruptcy of the debtor;
- [ ] death of the debtor; and
- [ ] the debtor has failed to repay the debts for over two years.

Entertainment. Entertainment expenses incurred in relation to the production and business operation of an FIE must be backed up by reliable records or vouchers, and are deductible within the following respective limits:

- [ ] Where the annual net sales is RMB15 million yuan or less, the entertainment expenses shall not exceed 0.5% of the net sales; for the portion above RMB15 million yuan, the entertainment expenses shall not exceed 0.3% of the said portion.
- [ ] Where the annual total business income is RMB5 million yuan or less, the entertainment expenses shall not exceed 1% of the total business income; for the portion above the limit of RMB5 million yuan, the entertainment expenses shall not exceed 0.5% of the said portion.

Wages, Benefits, and Allowances. Wages, benefits, and allowances paid to employees can be listed as expenses, but not foreign social insurance premiums paid for employees working inside China.

Currency. Income tax payable shall be computed in terms of Renminbi (RMB). Income in foreign currency shall be converted into RMB according to the exchange rate quoted by the state exchange control authorities for purposes of tax payment.

RELATED CONSIDERATIONS

34. Incentives and Grants

China provides a comprehensive program of tax incentives and concessions based primarily on such considerations as total investment, technical output, export potential, economic management and development, technology, and general conduciveness to China's economic activities.

China's open investment zones can be categorized into the following four groups:

- [ ] Special Economic Zones—Shenzhen, Zhuhai, Shantou in Guangdong province, Xiemen (Amoy) in Fujian province and Hainan Island.

- □ Economic and Technical Development Zones (ETDZ) in 14 coastal cities, namely Dalian, Qinhuangdao, Tianjin, Yantai, Qingdao, Lianyuangang, Nantong, Shanghai, Ninglo, Wenzhou, Fuzhou, Guangzhou, Zhanjiang and Beihai.
- □ Old City Districts of the 14 coastal cities and Coastal Open Economic Zones.
- □ Shanghai Pudong New Area.

Tax incentives that provide complete or partial exemption are outlined below.

Production. Businesses are eligible for two years exemption of income tax starting with the first profit-making year and a 50% reduction in income tax during the subsequent three years for those corporations with an operating term of not less than ten years.

Petroleum, Natural Gas, Rare Metals, and Precious Metals. Exemption from a reduction in income tax for those corporations is regulated separately by the State Council.

Agriculture, Forestry, or Animal Husbandry. FIE located in remote underdeveloped areas with an operating term of not less than ten years may apply for 15% to 30% reductions in their income tax for an additional ten years following the expiration of two-year tax exemption and three-year 50% reduction in income tax. Technically advanced enterprises may apply for a three-year 50% reduction in income tax. Technically advanced enterprises may apply for a three-year extension of the 50% tax reduction, and enterprises that export 70% or more of their products in a given year are eligible for a 50% reduction in that year. The minimum reduced tax rate is 10%.

Industry, Communication, Transportation, Agriculture, Forestry, and Animal Husbandry. Corporations located in an SEZ and with an operating life of ten years or longer, are qualified for a two-year income tax exemption starting from the first profit-making year, followed by a 50% tax reduction in the subsequent three years.

Service Industry. Corporations located in an SEZ with foreign investment exceeding US $5 million and a contract life of ten years or longer are exempted from income tax in the first profit-making year and permitted a 50% tax reduction in the following two years.

Agriculture or the Development and Operation of Infrastructural Facilities. Corporations located in Hainan Island and with a contract life of 15 years or longer are qualified for a five-year income tax exemption starting from the first profit-making year, followed by a 50% tax reduction in the following five years.

Production, Energy, and Transportation Construction Projects or Construction Projects of Infrastructure Facilities Together with Other Projects on Large Tracts of Land. Those FEI located in Shanghai Pudong New Area are eligible for a two-year income tax exemption starting from the first profit-making year, and a 50% tax reduction in the subsequent three years.

Financial Institutions. Financial institutions with foreign investment exceeding US $10 million and an operating life of ten years or longer located in Shanghai Pudong New Area are eligible for a one-year income tax exemption, starting with the first profit-making year, and a 50% tax reduction in the subsequent two years.

Tax Rebates on Reinvestment. A foreign investor of an FIE that reinvests its share of profit in China for a period of not less than five years may obtain a tax rebate of 40% of the income tax paid on the amount of reinvestment. If the reinvestment is made in establishing or expanding an export-oriented enterprise or a technologically advanced enterprise in China, the tax rebate is 100%.

A foreign investor of an FIE established in Hainan Island that reinvests its share of profit in Hainan's construction of infrastructural facilities or agricultural development may obtain a 100% tax rebate on the reinvested profit.

No Tax on Profit Remitted Abroad. No income tax will be imposed on profits remitted abroad by foreign investors of FIE.

Retrospective Application. The above pertaining to corporation income tax is in accordance with a new income tax law that came into effect July 1, 1991. However, the new law stipulates that the tax system will not be applied in such a way as to increase the tax rates of existing enterprises during their approved terms of operation or within five years from the effective date of the new tax law, should an enterprise not have a term of operation. However, the retrospective application applies only to FIE.

35. Foreign Exchange Control

Foreign currency transactions including cash, securities and bonds, deposits, and remittances are centralized and controlled by the State Administration of Exchange Control (SAEC) and its branch offices. The specialized foreign exchange bank of the PRC is the Bank of China. No other financial institutions shall engage in foreign exchange business unless approved by the SAEC. The major features of the exchange control in the PRC that may concern foreign investors are summarized as follows:

☐ A foreign currency borrowing by FIE is required to be registered with the SAEC or its branch offices.

☐ Export proceeds of FIE or receipts from sources outside China are required to be transferred into China. No foreign exchange receipts shall be kept with or lent to anyone outside China without the approval of the SAEC or its branch office.

□ FIE may, through the local foreign exchange adjustment center, sell their surplus foreign exchange at the market price or buy with Renminbi the foreign currency they need, subject to availability.

□ Repatriation of profit after tax, dividend, and capital in foreign currency is permitted if the FIE has sufficient foreign currency deposits with the Bank of China.

□ The foreign personnel of FIE may remit their after-tax salaries and other legitimate income abroad.

□ FIE may, with the approval of the SAEC or its branch offices, open a foreign exchange account with a bank abroad.

36. Investment Restrictions on Nonresidents

In the promotion of foreign investment, the PRC Government puts major emphasis on productive enterprises, i.e., capital-intensive and technology-intensive manufacturing industries, and those for the development of infrastructure facilities.

Foreign companies, enterprises, or individuals may, subject to the approvals from the Ministry of Foreign Economic Relations and Trade or other relevant ministries and the State Administration for Industry and Commerce, establish equity joint ventures, cooperative joint ventures, or wholly owned enterprises in the People's Republic of China. For equity joint ventures, the proportion of investment contributed by the foreign participants should not be less than 25%.

The required ratio of registered capital to the total investment of FIE is as follows:

Amount of Total Investment	Minimum Registered Capital
Less than US $3 million	7/10 of total investment
US $3–10 million	1/2 of total investment
US $10–30 million	2/5 of total investment
US $30 million or above	1/3 of total investment

Wholly foreign owned enterprises are prohibited or restricted to invest in the following areas:

□ Prohibited areas: news media, publishing, movie production, insurance, radio or television broadcasting, and post and telecommunication operations.

□ Restricted areas: public utilities, transportation and shipping, real estate, leasing, and trust and investment.

COLOMBIA

Editor's Note: As part of the economic opening and foreign investment policies of the new Colombian government, changes to the foreign exchange and income tax regulations are expected to be enacted soon.

INCOME TAXES ON CORPORATIONS

1. Rates

The rate of corporate income tax is 30%.

Presumed Income. For tax purposes, it is presumed that a taxpayer's taxable income is not lower than 7% of the net taxable assets on the last day of the preceding tax year or period. This rate will be reduced to 6% for the tax year 1992, to 5% for the tax year 1993, and to 4% for 1994 and subsequent tax years. This presumption may be overcome only if the company has been adversely affected by an unusual occurrence such as a natural disaster or similar event.

2. Local Income Taxes

There are no state or provincial income taxes. Municipalities levy a tax based on gross income, which affects commercial, industrial, and services activities. The rate varies from 0.2% to 1%, depending on the types of activity and revenue.

3. Capital Gains Taxes

In general terms, capital gains are considered to be ordinary income, taxed at the normal rate of 30%. However, the following transactions are taxed under the concept of "occasional gains and losses."

☐ The excess of capital contributed or invested in a company when realized upon the liquidation of the company.

☐ Gains from the disposition of any assets that have been part of fixed assets for two or more years. In computing such gain, asset cost may be increased annually by a percentage corresponding to the annual increase in the cost of living. This adjustment applies only to reduce the amount of occasional gain in the case of land or to reduce the depreciation recovered.

☐ Donations received.

Occasional gains are offset only against occasional losses. The tax rate is 30%.

4. Branch Profits Taxes

Branches of foreign corporations are subject to a 30% tax rate. In addition, a 19% remittance tax is imposed. This tax is levied in the income tax return and paid as stated under item 7 below; however, its payment may be deferred if commercial profits are reinvested or retained in branch's surplus through the increase of the net assets owned in Colombia.

The remittance tax rate will be reduced to 15% for tax years 1993 to 1995, and to 12% for 1996 and subsequent tax years.

In the case of new foreign investments made from 1991 and on, the remittance tax for their profits will be 12%.

However, if the profits are reinvested in Colombia, the remittance tax payment will be deferred while the reinvestment exists. If the reinvestment is kept for ten or more years, no remittance tax will be levied. All effective net Colombian assets increase is defined as the profit reinvestment.

5. Foreign Tax Reliefs

Taxpayers receiving income from foreign sources are entitled to deduct from Colombian tax the foreign taxes paid on such income. The deduction is limited to the Colombian tax on such income.

6. Classification of Corporations

The tax authorities have created the ''largest taxpayers'' category. Entities included in this category receive special treatment regarding the filing and paying of tax returns.

7. Payment of Taxes

Income tax is payable in two equal installments, after deducting advances already paid for such tax year, in May and July, with the exception of the ''largest taxpayers,'' who will pay in three equal installments in April, June, and August. The advance tax payments for the next tax year are generally the lower of:

☐ 75% of currently imputed taxes less taxes withheld at source.
☐ 75% of the average imputed taxes during the two prior years, less taxes withheld at source.

8. Other Matters.

Dividends. Dividends received by corporations are nontaxable, except if derived from untaxed profits.

Income by Comparison of Patrimonies (Net Worth). If the net worth for a tax year exceeds that of the preceding year, the difference is considered income, unless the taxpayer demonstrates that the increase was not caused by the realization of taxable income.

Withholding Tax Rates. Almost all payments made by entities are subject to a withholding tax that fluctuates between 1% and 30% of the gross payment.

INCOME TAXES ON INDIVIDUALS

9. Rates

The individual tax rates for natives or residents are progressive and range from 0.05% to 30%. Resident means living in the country for six continuous or discontinuous months within two consecutive calendar years. Only after foreigners have maintained residence in Colombia for five years will their foreign-source income and patrimony become subject to tax.

An individual is not required to file an income tax return if his or her (1) income is derived only from salary, (2) gross worth (wealth) is less than Col. Ps. 19,500,000, and (3) annual revenues do not exceed Col. Ps. 15,600,000. The employee must not have obtained during the respective tax year gross receipts exceeding Col. Ps. 9.4 million.

Presumed Income. As in the case of corporations, individuals are subject to a presumptive income tax if their taxable income is below a defined level (see item 1).

10. Local Income Taxes

The information in item 2 also applies to individuals.

11. Capital Gains Taxes

The information in item 3 also applies to individuals, adding the following transactions:

☐ Inheritances, legacies, donations, life insurance, and lotteries, raffles, and wagering.

☐ A partner's pro rata share of the excess of invested capital, net of prior years' undistributed profits when terminating a partnership if such excess is not related to undistributed profits and the partnership existed for two or more years.

12. Foreign Tax Reliefs

The information in item 5 also applies to individuals.

13. Tax Period

The tax year is the calendar year.

14. Other Matters

Dividends. The information in item 8 also applies to individuals.

Income by Comparison of Patrimonies (Net Worth). The information in item 8 also applies to individuals.

Patrimony (Net Worth) Tax. Patrimony consists of the total sum of the rights having a money value that a taxpayer possessed within Colombia on the last day of the tax year or period, after deducting the related liabilities. The rates range from 0.26 to 18 per thousand, depending on the amount of the individual's patrimony.

Withholding Tax Rates. Almost all revenues received from corporations are subject to a withholding tax that fluctuates between 1% and 30% of the gross payment.

INCOME TAXES ON NONRESIDENTS

15. Liability to Tax

Foreigners are subject to individual income tax on their income earned in Colombia.

16. Rates

The tax rate generally is 30%.

17. Withholding Tax Rates

Dividends, Partnership Profits, and Undivided Estates of Foreign Descendants. When credited or paid to nonresidents, these are subject to a 19% withholding on the total amount credited or paid. This rate will be reduced to 15% for tax years 1993 to 1995, and to 12% for 1996 and on. If they are generated by new foreign investments made from 1991 and on, a 12% tax rate will be levied as of the year the investment is made.

If dividends are capitalized in the generating company, and the reinvestment is kept for longer than ten years, the tax rate will be 0%.

Dividends from profits not taxed in the generating company as a result of any preferential treatment are subject to a 30% tax when credited to the shareholders.

Other Taxable Income. Credits or payments regarding taxable income in Colombia generally are subject to a 30% withholding when such credits or payments are made to nonresidents.

Remittances Abroad. Withholding tax at a general rate of 12% is levied on remittances of certain kinds of income to nonresidents. Remittances are considered to occur when payments or credits made on account imply resources situated abroad, such as those made through bank accounts abroad or compensation payments, or financing entities. Interest on short-term loans for financing importations and other special kinds of interest, duly registered with the Central Bank, as well as dividends, are exempt from this tax.

19. Tax Treaties

The Colombian government has signed tax agreements with other governments to eliminate the double taxation in the transportation industry.

OTHER SIGNIFICANT TAXES

23. Sales (Value Added)

The sale or import of goods and the rendering of certain services are subject to sales tax. The sale of real estate as well as of intangible or incorporeal goods is not subject to this tax. The general tax rate is 12%, but higher rates of 20% and 35% are applied to specific items, services, and products. Regulations provide exemptions for export sales and the selling of specific exempt goods. Those responsible for paying the tax are required:

- ☐ To register at the National Tax Offices.
- ☐ To issue invoices.
- ☐ To keep special records for sales, purchases, and sales tax liabilities.
- ☐ To file a sales tax return on a bimonthly basis.

23. Taxes on Payrolls (Social Security)

Social security tax is paid on a monthly basis and is approximately 13% of gross salaries. Two-thirds of the tax is paid by the employer, and one-third is paid by the employee.

SENA and Family Subsidy. To provide training for apprentices and family subsidies, this tax is levied on a monthly basis at the rate of 6% of gross salaries, including vacations.

Instituto Colombiano de Bienestar Familiar (ICBF). To provide aid for young children, this tax is levied on a monthly basis at the rate of 3% of gross salaries, including vacations.

25.   Other Taxes

Stamp Tax. All documents that contain evidence of opening, existence, modifications, and/or ending an obligation (i.e., currency or other legal entailments), as well as those evidencing extensions and/or payment of same, are subject to the stamp tax. The normal rate is .5%.

Land and Property Tax.   An annual tax is levied on all real estate properties. The tax is based on values fixed by the municipal authorities.

COMPUTATION OF TAXABLE INCOME

26.   Capital Gains
See items 3 and 11.

27.   Depreciation and Depletion
Normal depreciation rates are computed based on the straight-line method and on the total cost of the asset (no salvage value). The standard rates are:

	Estimated Life	Annual Rate
Buildings	20 years	5%
Machinery, furniture, and fixtures	10 years	10%
Vehicles	5 years	20%

Increased depreciation rates can be obtained if assets are used for more than one shift. Variable rates to a maximum of 40% per year may be used. Proof of additional shifts may be provided which would bring the maximum rate up to 60% per year (25% over the normal shift rate per additional shift). The use of variable rates is limited to new fixed assets acquired after 1975 and, in the case of imported assets, not used in Colombia before acquisition.

For tax purposes only, this depreciation system can be used until the 1991 tax year, after which the inflationary component adjustment system will be effective, allowing depreciation of fixed assets to be increased by the inflationary component. Other depreciation systems also may be used, provided they are justifiable from a technical standpoint and prior approval is obtained from the tax authorities.

Depletion generally is made in a five-year period, except that it can be shortened due to the nature or the lifetime of the business.

29.   Loss Carryovers
Corporations, branches, and partnerships may deduct the tax losses suffered in a taxable year or period from the income of the following five years. There is no loss carryback.

30. Transactions between Related Parties

The following are not deductible: direct or non-direct payments to foreign parent companies, of commissions, fees, administrative or directors' expenses, royalties, technical assistance fees, and payments for the exploitation of any type of intangible.

31. Consolidation of Income

There is no provision for the filing of consolidated tax returns by related corporations.

32. Tax Periods

The tax year is the calendar year.

33. Other Matters

Limitation of Expenses Incurred Abroad.　Expenses incurred abroad related to income generated in Colombia cannot exceed 10% of the taxable income computed before the deduction of such expenses, with the exception of expenses where a withholding tax is paid.

Integral Inflationary Adjustment, Inflationary Component, and Regulatory Sanctions.

□　Integral inflationary adjustment. As of 1992, business- and trade-related activities must adjust non-monetary assets and liabilities, as well as the preceding year's liquid patrimony, at the percentage that will be known as "PAAG" (for the initials of the Spanish words "tax year's adjustment percentage"), and which will be made public by the National Government.

Inflationary adjustments must be reflected in the financial statements and will be effective to determine commercial profits and the taxable basis for income tax.

Inflationary adjustments of assets and liabilities must be reflected on a profit and loss account, known as "monetary correction."

As of 1989, business- or trade-related activities may adjust new fixed assets acquired as of 1989 on the inflationary index, and depreciation on the adjusted asset may be requested.

Examples: Cost—1,000; inflation—20%; useful life—five years.

Year:	First	Second	Third	Fourth	Fifth
Adjusted Cost	1,200	1,440	1,728	2,074	2,489
Depreciation	240	288	346	415	498
Adjusted Depreciation	0	48	115	207	332
Acrued Depreciation	240	576	1,037	1,659	2,489

□ Inflationary component. The inflationary component of financial revenues and costs is not taxable income and not a deductible expense. The Government annually sets forth the corresponding percentages.

□ Tax regulatory sanctions. A great variety of sanctions exist, which may be classified as three types:

—Those purely monetary.

—Those of social or moral type, which aim to provide a severe public lesson.

—Those of a civil nature.

RELATED CONSIDERATIONS

34. Incentives and Grants

Free Zones. These are establishments whose object is the promotion of exportations, to generate employment and/or foreign currency, and to serve as an industrial development pole.

Users of free zones are those companies that obtain approval to operate in them.

Entities using the free zones are income-tax-exempt on those revenues obtained in the free zone. They also have free exchange legislation and enjoy free repatriation of profits.

35. Exchange Controls

The Colombian Government has established controls over currency remittances to foreign countries. Under these controls, stockholders of companies are required to register their capital investment with the exchange authorities in order to be able to convert dividends/profits into another currency. Foreign stockholders are allowed to receive dividends of up to 100% of their foreign investment base. Investments made in mining and oil activities must remit net profits at the rate resulting from adding 25 points to the annual average of the New York prime rate for the year during which the profits were made.

SELECTION OF BUSINESS ENTITY BY NONRESIDENTS

Foreign companies may open activities in all sectors of the economy, except the following, which are restricted to national investors:

□ defense and national security, and

□ disposal of toxic garbage, and dangerous and radioactive substances not produced in Colombia.

New foreign investments must be approved by the responsible authorities. Such approval generally is accompanied by a request that the operation be in the form of a branch.

The following do not require approval by the National Planning Department:

☐ Oil and natural gas exploration and exploitation, which require the approval of the Ministry of Mines and Energy.

☐ Companies located in the industrial free zones.

SPECIMEN TAX COMPUTATION

Individuals (Residents)

Compensation:

Salaries	16,000,000
Termination benefits and interest thereon	3,000,000
Gross income	19,000,000
Interest on home loans (limited)	2,300,000
Net income	16,700,000
Nontaxable income (as identified by tax law)	(1,800,000)
Net taxable income	14,900,000
Income tax (per tables)	2,972,000

Patrimony (Net Worth) Tax:

Cash and cash equivalents	1,000,000
House	12,000,000
Vehicle	10,000,000
Total gross assets	23,000,000
Liabilities	(6,000,000)
Excluded assets (as identified by tax law)	(8,869,000)
Net taxable assets	8,131,000
Tax on patrimony (per tables)	45,000
Total Taxes	3,017,000

Corporations

Net income	40,000,000	
Financial income	6,000,000	
Dividends	3,000,000	
Total income		49,000,000
Nontaxable income (as identified by tax law):		
Inflationary component of financial income (6,000,000 × 19.18)	1,151,000	
Dividends	3,000,000	(4,151,000)
Revenues		44,849,000

Less deductions:

Cost of sales	15,000,000	
Personnel expenses	3,000,000	
Depreciation	4,000,000	
Financial interest and expenses (7,000,000 − (7,000,000 × 15.42%))	5,884,000	
Exchange difference (4,000,000 − (4,000,000 × 14.23%))	3,377,000	
Other	7,000,000	
Total costs and deductions		(38,261,000)
Net taxable income		6,588,000
Income tax (30%)		1,976,000
Occasional gains (capital gains):		
Income from sale of fixed assets	10,000,000	
Cost of assets sold	(6,000,000)	
Taxable occasional gains		4,000,000
Tax on net occasional gains (30%)		1,200,000
Total tax		3,176,000

COSTA RICA

INCOME TAXES ON CORPORATIONS

1. Rates

All corporations pay income tax at 30% on net profits. Small companies, defined as enterprises having gross income up to ₡7,300,000, pay the following rates:

Up to ₡3,675,000 gross income: 10%
Up to ₡7,300,000 gross income: 20%

For tax purposes, the term "corporation" broadly covers stock companies, limited partnerships, general partnerships, joint stock companies, trust companies, foreign branches, and, in addition, undivided inheritances under probate and temporary associations, whether legalized or not.

2. Local Income Taxes

Different rates exist for each county.

3. Capital Gains Taxes

None.

4. Branch Profits Taxes

Branches of foreign companies are subject to the same income tax rates as corporations on their local net profits. In addition, the net profit after income tax is subject to an automatic withholding tax of 15%.

5. Foreign Tax Reliefs

Residents of Costa Rica are not taxed on foreign-source income and no foreign tax relief is provided.

7. Payment of Taxes

The tax year runs from October 1 to September 30 of the following year, and tax returns are due two months following the tax year-end. The tax is payable during the 30 days following the return filing; there are regulations concerning withholdings and partial payments.

The tax year can be changed if the holding company has a different year-end or the company activity requires it (banks, rice industry, etc.).

INCOME TAXES ON INDIVIDUALS

9. Rates

There is a tax on monthly salaries and other personal income, as follows:

Taxable Income		Tax on Lower Amount	Percentage on Excess
Over	Not Over		
₡55,000	₡83,000	₡ 0	10%
83,000		2,800	15

Tax credits are allowed for:

☐ Spouse—₡200 per month.
☐ Child—₡150 per month.

If income exceeds ₡144,750, a flat rate of 8.334% is applied, and tax credits are not applicable. Other payments, such as a bonus or gift, are taxed at the rate of 10%.

Tax Rates for Self-Employed Persons. All those individuals doing business in their personal names are subject to the following annual rates:

Taxable Income		Tax on Lower Amount	Percentage on Excess
Over	Not Over		
₡ 245,000	₡ 367,000	₡ 0	10%
367,000	612,000	12,200	15
612,000	1,225,000	48,950	20
1,225,000		171,550	25

10. Local Income Taxes

None.

11. Capital Gains Taxes

See item 3.

12. Foreign Tax Reliefs

Individuals are not taxed on foreign-source income and no foreign tax relief is provided.

13. Tax Period

Tax on monthly salaries and other personal income is paid on a monthly basis. The tax period for self-employed individuals ends on September 30 of each year.

INCOME TAXES ON NONRESIDENTS

15. Liability to Tax

Tax is required to be withheld by the payor on payments or credits to individuals or companies domiciled abroad, covering certain services rendered from abroad to individuals or companies domiciled in Costa Rica.

17. Withholding Tax Rates

The withholding rates vary with the nature of the payment or credit. The most important withholding taxes are those imposed on the following payments or credits:

Transport and communications	8.5%
Pensions, salaries, and all other personal remuneration	10.0%
Fees, commissions, and other payments made to members or directors	15.0%
Reinsurances	5.5%
Pictures and records	20.0%
Dividends	15.0% or 5.0%
Leasings	15.0%
Interest and commissions	15.0%
Technical, financial, administrative, or other advisory services; patents privileges, royalties, franchises	25.0%
All other remittances	30.0%

18. Special Withholding Provisions

Interest that is payable to a foreign lender is exempt from withholding tax if the foreign lender is an official banking or lending institution that is duly recognized as such by the Central Bank of Costa Rica. There is withholding on payments made for the lease of capital goods to be used only in agricultural, cattle, or manufacturing operations. For several payments abroad, the Income Tax Office is authorized to fully or partially exempt from the obligation to withhold whenever the withholding agent (person or company) proves that no foreign tax credit or reduction is granted to the recipients of such income in their countries of residence.

OTHER SIGNIFICANT TAXES

21. Sales (Value Added)

Except for basic necessities, sales of goods and services are taxable, generally at the rate of 13%. In addition, a consumption tax is levied on goods deemed nonessential in an official list at rates of 10% to 100% of the sales price.

22. Inheritance and Gift Taxes

None.

23. Taxes on Payrolls (Social Security)

The following rates of contributions apply to gross payroll, with no maximum limits on earnings:

	Employers' Contribution	Employees' Contribution
Social Security		
Illness and maternity	9.25%	5.50%
Disability, old age and death	4.75	2.50
Subtotal	14.00	8.00
I.N.A. (Trade Schools)	2.00	
I.M.A.S. (Institute of Social Aid)	0.50	
Banco Popular (Obligatory Savings)	0.50	1.00
Asignaciones Familiares (Family and Community Development)	5.00	
Work Accident Insurance (Average)	2.75	
Totals	24.75%	9.00%

24. Taxes on Natural Resources

By law, all surface and subsurface mineral resources belong to the State, which imposes annual rentals for exploration permits, and rentals and royalties when the leased properties enter the production stage.

25. Other Taxes

Land and Property. On a quarterly basis, land and property owners must pay the tax arising from the application of the following scale:

| Property Value | | Tax |
Over	Not Over	(per annum)
₡ 0	₡ 250,000	0.36%
250,000	500,000	0.63
500,000	3,000,000	0.90
3,000,000		1.17

Land and Property Transfer Tax. Real estate transfers are subject to taxes of 1.5% to 4.5% on amounts ranging from ₡400,000 to ₡1,000,000.

Stamp Taxes. Practically all legal and official documents covering contracts, permits, loans, certifications, court cases, wills, etc., must be drawn on stamped paper issued by the Government. Documents may also be subject to attachment and cancelation of fiscal stamps, whose value is calculated under various scaled rates, depending on the type and value of the document.

COMPUTATION OF TAXABLE INCOME

27. Depreciation and Depletion

For income tax purposes, assets may be depreciated over the useful lives assigned by the fiscal authorities to each asset. The allowable methods are generally the straight line and sum-of-the years' digits. The following are examples of depreciation rates in common use:

Buildings	2% to 8%
Machinery and equipment	5% to 20%
Vehicles	10% to 20%
Office furnishings and equipment	10%
Tools	10% to 25%

Mining operations are granted a depletion allowance, which is limited to 5% of net profits before this deduction. Exploration and preoperating expenses may be amortized during the first five years of operations.

28. Treatment of Dividends

Withholding taxes on dividends are taxed at the rate of 15% when paid to individuals domiciled in the country or when paid to nonresident shareholders (either individuals or companies). If shares are traded in a local stock exchange, the withholding tax amounts to 5%. Dividends paid to resident corporations and stock dividends are exempt from withholding taxes.

29. Loss Carryovers

Only agricultural and industrial enterprises may carry over losses. The loss is deductible in the following five years (agriculture) and three years (manufacturing) independent of earnings to absorb accumulated losses.

30. Transactions between Related Parties

No restrictions exist for transactions between related parties.

32. Tax Periods

In general, September 30 is the mandatory fiscal year-end for all taxpayers, and tax returns must be filed not later than November 30; however, there exist other tax year-ends (see item 7).

33. Other Matters

Deductions for Taxes Other than Income Tax. In computing the liability for income tax, businesses may deduct payroll taxes, land and property taxes, natural resources royalties and rentals, and fiscal stamp taxes and stamped paper. Sales and consumption taxes paid and customs duties paid are treated as part of the cost of the goods acquired.

Inventory Valuation. For tax purposes, inventories may be valued at cost or market whichever is lower, on the basis of purchase cost, average cost or LIFO, depending on the type of business. Industrial factory articles produced by the taxpayer are usually valued by the full absorption method, which includes raw materials, labor and other direct costs, plus a reasonable allocation of manufacturing overhead.

Agricultural products may be valued at market value less selling expenses, except when sales prices are determined by governmental decree, in which cases such prices must be used for valuation. However, if the taxpayer keeps an adequate cost system which includes all costs and expenses incurred for the agricultural products, the taxpayer (or the corporation) may use either method. Any change in the method requires prior authorization by the tax authorities. Real estate and livestock inventories are subject to special regulations.

Bad Debts. General provisions for doubtful accounts are not deductible. Specific bad debts may be deducted only if reasonable proof of their uncollectibility exists, in the judgement of the tax authorities. Any recovery after a debt has been written off must be included in taxable income.

Employee Benefits Provisions. Provisions for employee benefits such as annual vacation and Christmas bonus are deductible in the proportion that they are payable during the tax year in accordance with the law. Other provisions, such as contingencies for severance pay and termination notice, are not deductible; only those benefits actually paid to the employees during the tax year may be deducted.

RELATED CONSIDERATIONS

34. Incentives and Grants

Under the Central American Industrial Incentives Agreement, the Costa Rican Government may grant certain incentives to develop industrial activities. Examples of such incentives are an exemption of duties for raw materials, machinery and equipment, and income tax exemption on earnings reinvested during the fiscal year.

Tax certificates amounting to 15% of the FOB value of exports of nontraditional products to countries outside of the Central American Common Market are granted by the Government. These certificates, denominated "CAT'S," may be applied against payment of any taxes or duties due one year after date of issue and are freely negotiable. Traditional products include such items as coffee, bananas, and cattle. However, should these products be industrially processed (e.g., powdered coffee, baby's food, and canned meat products), their exportation is entitled to "CAT'S."

Other incentives exist for manufacturing companies producing nontraditional goods to be exported to third markets, such as tax deductions for taxpayers investing in capital stock of these companies and other benefits.

35. Exchange Controls

Since August 10, 1982, the law requires that all foreign exchange transactions must be carried out through banks authorized by the Central Bank of Costa Rica. Three foreign exchange markets are recognized: (1) the official market for limited types of transactions, (2) the interbank rate which must handle transactions classified in a preferential category, and (3) the free market in which transactions are carried out at the free rate of exchange. Foreign currency originating from exports must be liquidated at the interbank rate within 24 hours after receipt. Foreign currency from transactions other than exports need not be exchanged into colons but, when exchanged, the free market rate (also established by the Central Bank) must be used. The exchange rates in force on July 31, 1991 were:

Official rate	₡20 for US $1
Free rate	₡127.25 for US $1

36. Investment Restrictions on Nonresidents

Generally, there are no restrictions on foreign investment in Costa Rica.

37. Other Matters

Statutory Reports. For the tax year, enterprises may elect to present their tax returns, financial statements, and other pertaining information together with an auditor's report (issued by a certified public accountant).

Accounting for Income Tax. Beginning with the 1989 tax year, companies must account for timing differences on memorandum accounts.

SELECTION OF BUSINESS ENTITY BY NONRESIDENTS

Nonresident investors can operate in Costa Rica either through a branch or by forming a local subsidiary corporation. The tax consequences for such entities are:

☐ Both are subject to the same income tax rates.

☐ Branches are subject to a 15% automatic withholding tax on net profits after income tax, whether credited or paid to the home office.

☐ Dividends paid or credited to nonresident stockholders are subject to a 15% or 5% withholding tax, except if paid as a stock dividend.

☐ Withholding taxes are generally imposed on foreign interest (but see items 17 and 18) and on certain other foreign expenses charged to the branch or subsidiary (see item 17).

SPECIMEN TAX COMPUTATION

Information:

☐ The corporation's profit for the year of ₡10,000,000 (local currency) consists of:

	000's Colons
Local net operating profit	7,000
Dividend income from investments in local corporations	1,000
Dividend income from investment in foreign corporations	1,000
Capital gain from sale of land	1,000
	10,000

☐ The local net operating profit includes the following items:

Provision for employees' severance compensation charged to expense	500
Actual severance payments charged to liabilities' provision account	250
Provision for doubtful accounts charged to expense	500
Actual bad debts deducted	250

□ During the year, the corporation invested 5,000 in new industrial plant machinery, thus qualifying for reinvestment incentives under its contract with the government.

Computation:

	For Financial Purposes	For Income Tax Purposes
	(in 000's colons)	
Income		
Local net operating profit	7,000	7,000
Dividends from local corporations	1,000	
Dividends from foreign corporations	1,000	
Capital gain from sale of land	1,000	
Total income	10,000	7,000
Add		
Difference between provision and actual payments for employees' severance compensation		250
Difference between provision and actual bad debts write-off		250
		7,500
Less		
Reinvestment of profits in new industrial plant machinery		(5,000)
Taxable income		2,500
Tax payable		750
Provision for income tax	2,100	
Retained earnings	7,900	

CYPRUS

INCOME TAXES ON CORPORATIONS

1. Rates

The corporate tax rates are as follows:

Chargeable Income	Tax Rates
Up to C£100,000	20%
Over 100,000	25%

A minimum tax of 10% is imposed on all income that is tax exempt as a result of various incentives.

☐ 100% foreign-controlled companies incorporated in the Republic, irrespective of the place of their control and management, or 100% foreign-controlled companies registered in the Republic under section 347 of the Companies Law as "overseas" companies and having their control and management in the Republic and, in either case, earning their income from sources outside the Republic from any business, investment, royalty, or immovable property, pay income tax at the reduced rate of 4.25%. Dividends paid from such income are not subject to additional taxes. The provisions of this law are in force until December 31, 1996, and can be extended for any additional period at the option of the Council of Ministers.

☐ Effective from January 1, 1988 offshore banks (both companies and branches) are allowed, after obtaining the relevant permit, to lend money to local businesses. This income however, will be taxed at the normal rate of 20%–25%. In cases where it is considered that the interests of the Republic are best served, the Minister of Finance, at his discretion, may exempt from tax any interest received.

Tax Holiday For Businesses Manufacturing New Products. Manufacturing businesses producing new products (i.e., not previously produced in Cyprus) that commenced operations by April 6, 1990 are exempt from tax during the first ten years of their operation. Furthermore, dividends declared by these companies during the first ten years are also tax-exempt in the hand of the recipient.

Free Industrial Zone Operations. Effective January 1, 1983, and for a period of ten years, dividends paid to foreign shareholders of companies that operate from the Free Industrial Zone of Larnaca are liable to tax in Cyprus at the lower of the tax rate payable on the profit out of which the dividend is declared or the tax rate payable by the shareholder on this same dividend. The effect of this provision is that dividends declared out of profits that have not been taxed remain untaxed in the hands of the foreign recipient. Expatriate employees of companies operating from the Free Industrial Zone of Larnaca are subject to tax at half the normal tax rates (i.e., at rates ranging from zero to 20%).

2.   Local Income Taxes

Municipal authorities impose what is called "professional tax" on all business entities (including offshore entities) operating within their municipal boundaries. The tax payable is insignificant and varies among the different municipalities.

3.   Capital Gains Taxes

Tax is levied at the rate of 20% on gains arising from dispositions of immovable property and shares in companies that own immovable property.

4.   Branch Profits Taxes

Branch profits are taxed at the same rates that apply to corporations and the same provisions govern the computation of their chargeable income.

5.   Foreign Tax Reliefs

Cyprus provides unilateral relief for tax paid in another country with which no double taxation treaty exists. The foreign tax paid abroad is allowable as a tax credit against the tax payable in Cyprus. The maximum tax credit allowed is the tax payable on the foreign income taxable in Cyprus.

Cyprus has a number of tax treaties with other countries (see item 19). The purpose of these treaties is the avoidance of double taxation of income earned in any of these countries. Under these agreements, a credit is usually allowed against the tax levied by the country in which the taxpayer resides. The effect of these arrangements is that the taxpayer pays no more tax than the higher of the two rates. All of the treaties follow the more or less accepted pattern of similar double taxation treaties and contain provisions as to permanent establishments, royalties, interest, tax credits, and pensions.

INCOME TAXES ON INDIVIDUALS

9. Rates

The individual income tax rates since January 1, 1991 are:

Taxable Income		Tax on	Percentage
Over	Not Over	Lower Amount	on Excess
C£ 2,000	C£ 4,000	C£ 0	20%
4,000	8,000	400	30
8,000		1,600	40

Main Allowances and Deductions. The main allowances deductible in arriving at taxable income are:

Earned income relief	7%
Rent allowance (when joint income of spouses and dependent children does not exceed C£10,000 p.a)	Max. C£1,500
Transportation allowance (for taxpayers living in rural areas)	Cost of the bus fare

Life insurance premiums and contributions to approved pension funds (limited to 7% of the insurance amount and one-sixth of taxable income)

Life policies issued after January 1, 1988 that are surrendered before their expiration are subject to a 30% adjustment to income on the premiums previously allowed if surrendered within a three-year period. If a policy is surrendered between the fourth and sixth year, the adjustment is 20%.

Allowances on Investment Income. The following amounts of investment income are exempt from tax:

	Limited to
Government bonds	—
Interest from bank deposits and public company debentures	C£600
Dividend from public companies	C£1,200
Interest received by individuals from deposits with the Housing Finance Corporation	—
Interest received from certain government savings certificates	—

Other Allowances. Thirty percent of the amount invested by individuals and companies to acquire first-issue shares of a public company is tax deductible, provided the shares are kept at least until the end of the year following the year of acquisition and the amount deducted is not more than one-quarter of the individual's income before the deduction of personal allowances. Individual shareholders of a private company, which is converted into a public company, can also claim this allowance. Furthermore, the shareholder can carry forward for four years any unrelieved amount arising out of the last restriction above. For the purposes of this section, wholly owned subsidiaries of public companies are not classified as public companies. In addition, 40% of the amount deposited under the save-as-you-earn scheme of the Housing Finance Corporation is tax deductible under certain conditions.

Tax Credits. Effective January 1, 1991, individuals are entitled to the following tax credits:

	Credit
For married person living with spouse	C£200
For children under sixteen not attending secondary education	100
For children attending secondary education in Cyprus	150
For children attending an approved college or university outside Cyprus	500
40% of fees for children over the age of 16 studying abroad	Max. 1,500
For children attending higher education in Cyprus	300
For children serving in the National Guard	200
For disabled children	400
Children under the age of 6 attending nurseries or kindergarten	50
Dependent relatives whose income is less than C£600	100
Widow(er) when receiving tax credits for children	200
Elderly (over 65)	200
Blind individuals	200
Displaced individuals	200

The above tax credits are not given to alien employees of offshore companies or to other aliens who are subject to income tax at specially reduced rates. However, these employees may elect to be taxed at full tax rates, in which case they will be entitled to the tax credits.

No children tax credits are given in cases where the income of the child is over C£2,000 or, in the case of the child studying abroad, over C£4,000.

10. Local Income Taxes

Municipal authorities impose what is called "professional tax" on all salaried or self-employed individuals working within their municipal boundaries. The tax payable is insignificant and varies among the different municipalities.

11. Capital Gains Taxes

Tax is levied at the rate of 20% on gains in excess of:

☐ C£50,000 from the disposal of the taxpayer's own house.
☐ C£15,000 from the disposal of agricultural land.
☐ C£10,000 from the disposal of any immovable property.

12. Foreign Tax Reliefs

Special provisions in the Cyprus tax law provide unilateral relief for tax paid in any other country with which no double taxation treaty exists. The foreign tax paid abroad in respect of income brought to charge in Cyprus is allowed as a tax credit against the tax payable in Cyprus. The tax credit is restricted to a maximum of the tax payable on the foreign income taxable in Cyprus.

13. Tax Period

The tax period begins January 1 and ends on December 31 each year. However, both corporate and unincorporated businesses are allowed to prepare accounts at any other date provided they continue to draw up their accounts on the same date in the future. Profit in these cases is time apportioned to coincide with the fiscal year.

INCOME TAXES ON NONRESIDENTS

15. Liability to Tax

Any "body of persons," corporate or unincorporated, who carries on business in Cyprus is liable to Cyprus income tax at the rates described in items 1 and 9. The unilateral relief as well as the provisions of the double taxation treaties as described in item 5 are also applicable.

16. Rates

Foreign professionals and entertainers earning income in Cyprus are taxed at the flat rate of 15%. Gross royalties for copyrights, patents, know-how, or technical assistance are taxed at the rate of 10%. Foreigners employed outside Cyprus by a 100% foreign-controlled Cyprus company and who receive their remuneration from

Cyprus are exempt from taxation. Where the remuneration is not paid through Cyprus, it is taxed at one-tenth the normal rates (to a maximum rate of 4%). These individuals are only entitled to the allowance for earned income relief under item 9. If their services are performed in Cyprus, they are taxed at half the normal rates (to a maximum rate of 20%). For persons partly employed in Cyprus and partly abroad, tax is apportioned on a strict time basis and they are entitled to all of the allowances under item 9.

Foreign investment income remitted to Cyprus or pensions received from abroad by an individual who is not a permanent resident is taxed at zero per cent on the first C£2,000 and at 5% thereafter.

Persons that pay income to a nonresident must deduct tax (in the absence of a double tax treaty) at the standard rate of 20%–25%. The nonresident has the option of filing a tax return for his total income and, if warranted, any overwithholding will be refunded. The tax withheld on dividends (see item 28) is credited against the final tax liability and any excess is refunded. Taxation of payments to treaty country residents is determined by the provisions of the relevant treaty.

Capital Gains Taxes.   There is no capital gains tax upon the disposition of foreign-situs property by an alien residing in Cyprus or a Cyprus offshore company. In addition, no capital gains tax liability arises on the disposition of property held in Cyprus and acquired with foreign currency between August 1, 1980 and July 13, 1990 by a nonresident individual.

Immovable property acquired in Cyprus at any other time is subject to capital gains tax.

17.   Withholding Tax Rates

The treaties in force as of July 31, 1991, provided for the following withholding taxes:

	Received in Cyprus			Paid from Cyprus		
	Dividends	Royalties	Interest	Dividends	Royalties	Interest
Non-treaty countries				nil (1)	10% (2)	20% (3)
Treaty countries						
Austria	10%	nil	nil	nil (4)	nil	nil
Bulgaria	nil	nil (5)	nil	nil	nil	nil
Canada	15	10% (6)	15% (7)	nil	10 (6)	15 (7)
Czecho-						
slovakia	10	5 (8)	10 (9)	nil	5 (10)	10 (9)
Denmark	15 (11)	nil	10 (9)	nil	nil	10 (9)
Germany	15 (12)	nil (2)	10 (9)	nil	nil (2)	10 (9)
France	15 (13)	nil (2)	10 (14)	nil	nil (2)	10 (14)
Greece	25	nil (15)	10	25 (16)	nil (15)	10
Hungary (17)	15 (18)	nil	10 (9)	nil	nil	10 (9)
Ireland	nil	nil (15)	nil	nil	nil (15)	nil

	Received in Cyprus			Paid from Cyprus		
	Dividends	Royalties	Interest	Dividends	Royalties	Interest
Italy	15%	nil	10%	nil	nil	10%
Kuwait	10	5% (10)	10 (9)	nil	5% (10)	10 (9)
Norway	5 (19)	nil	nil	nil	nil	20 (3)
Romania	10	5 (8)	10 (9)	10% (18)	5 (10)	10 (9)
Sweden	15 (18)	nil	10 (9)	nil	nil	10 (9)
United Kingdom	15 (20)	nil (2)	10	nil	nil (2)	10
United States	15 (21)	nil	10 (14)	nil	nil	10 (14)
USSR	nil	nil	nil	nil	nil	nil
Yugoslavia	10	10	10	nil	10	10

Notes:
(1) 30% for nonresident individuals.
(2) 5% on film and TV royalties.
(3) 25% for any chargeable income in excess of C£100,000.
(4) 10% on dividends received by individuals, which may be refundable.
(5) 5% on patent royalties.
(6) Nil on literary, dramatic, musical or artistic work.
(7) Nil if paid to a government or for export guarantee.
(8) For literary, artistic or scientific work, film, and TV royalties.
(9) Nil if paid to the Government of the other state.
(10) 10% on literary, artistic or scientific work, film, and TV royalties.
(11) 10% if received by a company controlling 25% or more of the voting power.
(12) 25% if controlling less than 25% of the voting power.
(13) 10% if received by a company controlling 10% or more of the voting power.
(14) Nil if paid to a Government, bank or financial institution.
(15) 5% on film royalties.
(16) This is the maximum rate of tax to be deducted, where the effective rate of the underlying tax is less.
(17) The treaty provides for withholding taxes, but Hungary does not impose any in accordance with its legislation.
(18) 5% if received by a company controlling 25% or more of the voting power.
(19) Nil if received by a company controlling 50% or more of the voting power.
(20) Nil if received by a company controlling 10% or more of the voting power.
(21) 5% if received by a company controlling 10% or more of the voting power.

19. Tax Treaties

Cyprus has concluded a number of double tax treaties. Treaties ratified so far are those with Austria, Bulgaria, Canada, Czechoslovakia, Denmark, France, Germany,

Greece, Hungary, Ireland, Italy, Kuwait, Norway, Romania, Sweden, United Kingdom, United States, USSR, and Yugoslavia. Treaties with China, Egypt, Finland,
Japan, Malta, and Poland are under negotiation. The treaty with Belgium has been
signed and is pending ratification.

OTHER SIGNIFICANT TAXES

21.   Sales (Value Added)

There is no value added tax (VAT) as such in Cyprus at present. However, at
present, the services offered by the Cyprus Telecommunications Authority (CYTA)
are subject to a form of VAT at the following rates:

Value of Monthly Bill	Rate
Up to C£5	nil
C£5 to C£15	10% (on total bill)
Over C£15	20% (on total bill)

Furthermore, VAT legislation has been enacted and is expected to come into operation
in July 1992. The standard rate of VAT on goods and services is 5%. There also
is a zero rate as well as specific exemptions from VAT.

22.   Inheritance and Gift Taxes

An estate duty is levied on the value of the deceased's estate at rates varying from
0% to 45%, depending on the value of the estate. There is no gift tax.

23.   Taxes on Payrolls (Social Security)

Social Security contributions of 6% are payable by employees on a maximum gross
salary of C£923 per month. The same amount is payable by employers. Foreign
employees of offshore entities are exempt.

24.   Taxes on Natural Resources

None.

25.   Other Taxes

Tax on Immovable Property.   Subject to the exemption noted below and certain
other minor ones, immovable property is subject to property tax in Cyprus. The
tax is levied on the market value of the property on January 1, 1980, is payable
by the end of September each year, and is calculated in accordance with the rates
shown in the table below:

Value of Property

Over	Not Over	Rate
	C£ 35,000	0.15%
C£ 35,000	100,000	0.25
100,000	200,000	0.30
200,000		0.35

Property held by individuals up to a value of C£35,000 is tax exempt as is agricultural land used as such by its owner.

Special Contribution for Refugees.   Business profits and all other income (except from salaries) are subject to a temporary tax, the proceeds of which are deposited in a special fund for refugee relief. This additional form of taxation is imposed on the quarterly taxable profits of an entity. The rates are progressive and differ for companies and individuals. The maximum rate is currently fixed at 8% for quarterly profits exceeding C£1,800 for companies and C£2,900 for individuals. The contribution is deductible in computing taxable income for income tax purposes. Offshore entities are excluded from this tax.

Special Contribution for Defense.   Business profits (including dividend, interest, and rental income) are subject to a 3% special contribution for the Republic's defense, but it is not an allowable deduction for income tax purposes. Offshore entities are not subject to the tax. Salaries, wages, and other income of self-employed persons are subject to a 2% special contribution.

COMPUTATION OF TAXABLE INCOME

26.   Capital Gains

The tax is computed separately and does not come under the computation of the trading income.

27.   Depreciation and Depletion

Depreciation as included in the accounts of business entities is a disallowable expense for taxation purposes. Depreciation is replaced in the computation of chargeable income by depreciation allowances based on rates specified by the Commissioner of Inland Revenue. These are known as wear and tear allowances. Annual wear and tear allowances are calculated on the straight-line method of depreciation and are based on the cost of construction of buildings or the cost of acquisition of plant and machinery, which includes furniture used for business purposes but excludes private motor vehicles. The rates of depreciation are:

Plant and machinery	10%
Furniture and fittings	10%
Commercial vehicles, computer hardware, and operating software	20%
Industrial buildings	4%
Hotel buildings	4%
Commercial buildings	3%

Higher rates can be negotiated depending on the use of the asset.

Investment Allowances. An additional allowance (not available to offshore companies for assets held abroad) is granted on certain new or imported used depreciable asset when first employed in the business. This allowance is in addition to the normal wear and tear allowance and is granted at the following rates:

Category of Asset	Investment Allowance
New plant and machinery used in the production by manufacturing, mining, farming, and fishing businesses	20%
New plant and machinery used in the production by manufacturing joint ventures	40
New robots, computers, and computer programs	40
Bus Companies:	
—Existing companies for new buses acquired by December 31, 1991	45
—New companies for new buses acquired within five years from the formation of the company	45
—Businesses merged into a new bus company for used buses	45
Buildings:	
—Tourist village	25
—Auxiliary tourist project	25
—Mountain tourist village, hotel, or apartments	25
—New three- to five-star hotel or extension or improvement of an existing one in Nicosia	25

"Manufacturing joint ventures" require at least five manufacturing businesses that independently carry on their business and are cooperating only for the design of new products or for the setting up of common exhibition grounds.

"Auxiliary tourist project" includes only golf courses, marinas, camping sites, theme parks, and health clubs. "Mountain buildings" means buildings found at an altitude of at least 2,000 feet above sea-level.

Balancing Allowance or Charge. When business fixed assets previously depreciated for tax purposes are sold, discarded, or destroyed, the excess of sales proceeds over the tax written down value of the asset is brought into charge to the extent of the wear and tear allowances previously granted. If the tax written down value exceeds the sales proceeds, the difference is given as an allowance. No balancing allowance or charge is necessary when the disposed asset is a building owned by individuals and was used for the production of rental income.

28. Treatment of Dividends

There is a 30% withholding tax on dividends. The withholding tax is credited, and may be refundable, to the individual shareholders. The corporation tax is not credited to the individual shareholders. The dividends received by a company are not subject to corporation tax. However, the tax withheld on such dividends is returned to the recipient company only when it issues dividends. Tax withheld on dividends payable to a foreign company is returned unconditionally.

There is a transitional provision applicable until December 31, 1995 according to which, for dividends issued out of profits taxed under the previous system (which existed up to December 31, 1990), no tax will be withheld. For such dividends, the provisions of the previous system will apply. There is no tax withheld on dividends issued by offshore companies.

The provisions of the previous system, which are applicable for dividends issued until December 31, 1995 out of chargeable profits arising from periods up to December 31, 1990, are as follows.

The dividends are taxed only once, in the hands of the recipient, who can use as a tax credit the tax paid by the company on the profit out of which the dividend was paid. Dividends are declared net (after deducting the tax paid by the company). A dividend certificate is issued by the company in which the net dividend is grossed up, using the effective rate of tax paid by the company. Thus, the certificate shows the gross dividend, the tax credit, and the net dividend received by the recipient. The recipient declares the gross dividend in his tax return and utilizes the tax credit against his tax otherwise payable. The effect of this is: a recipient whose tax rate is higher than the company's rate will pay additional tax; a recipient whose tax rate is lower than the company's rate will get a refund; and if the two rates are equal no additional tax will be due or refundable.

In the case of a company paying tax at 4.25%, no further tax is imposed on dividends that emanate directly or indirectly from the income subject to the reduced rate of 4.25%.

29. Loss Carryovers

Losses incurred during the year in any trade or business carried on or controlled from Cyprus first offset income from other sources. Any unrelieved balance is carried forward to offset income of future years, until it is extinguished. Certain restrictions, however, apply: (1) if within any period of three years there is both a "change" in the beneficial ownership of a company and a "major change in the nature of a trade" carried on by a company; or (2) at any time after, the scale of activities in a trade carried on by a company has become small or negligible and before any considerable revival of the trade there is a change in the ownership of the company; then no trading losses incurred before the change of ownership can be carried forward to offset future profits of a period or year after such change. For these purposes, a "change" in the ownership of the shares of a company occurs if a single person acquires more than half the ordinary share capital, or if two or more persons each acquire a holding of 5% or more of the ordinary share capital and their combined holdings amount to more than half the ordinary share capital of the company. Effective January 1, 1988, the donation of shares between spouses as well as donations to second degree relatives, or to a family company in which the shareholders are members of the same family for a five-year period after the donation, do not constitute a change of ownership. A "major change in the nature of a trade" includes:

□   A major change in the type of property dealt in or services or facilities provided in the trade.
□   A major change in customers, outlets, or markets of the trade.

Effective January 1, 1988, loss carryovers will be allowed only when the relevant financial statements are submitted to the tax authorities on time. The time limit has been set to six years from the date the accounts are due.

Effective January 1, 1990, losses arising from exports may not offset income from other sources but should be carried forward to offset profits from subsequent exports.

In accordance with a recent change in the legislation, tax losses may not be carried forward to future years after January 1, 1996. Any losses not utilized by then will be lost.

30.   Transactions between Related Parties

Both revenue and capital transactions between related parties are treated in the normal way, provided they are made on an arm's-length basis.

The Commissioner of Income Tax may consider any loans made by a company controlled by up to five people to its directors, shareholders or up to second degree relatives as bearing interest at 9% per annum.

31.   Consolidation of Income

Effective January 1, 1988, group relief provisions have been introduced.

Regulations determining the conditions under which losses can be transferred between companies of the same group will be issued in due course.

Individuals are taxed on their aggregate income from various sources, thus enabling losses from one source to offset profits from another. There are restrictions regarding losses from agriculture.

A Cyprus corporation is taxed on its worldwide income; however, double taxation is avoided by means of foreign tax credits if a bilateral tax agreement is in existence with the country where the income is derived. If there is no agreement, then the foreign tax is deducted in accordance with the income tax law (see item 5).

32.   Tax Periods

The calendar year is the tax period. However, corporations and unincorporated businesses may choose any fiscal year provided they continue to use the same fiscal year. Profit in these cases is time apportioned to coincide with the fiscal year.

33.   Other Matters

Mining Operations.   The profit of an entity engaged in mineral exploration or extraction is calculated after the following deductions:

☐   130% of exploration expenditures.
☐   Initial allowances (including the cost of site acquisition).

Plant and machinery	25%
Any other expenditure	10%

☐   An annual allowance for any capital expenditure, varying with mine production.
☐   A depletion allowance that varies with the profitability of the mine and is in lieu of both initial and annual allowances.

Liquidation.   In the case of liquidation of a company, its chargeable income for the last five accounting periods may be deemed as distributable by way of a dividend.

Capital Reduction.   Any amounts paid to the shareholders by way of a capital reduction out of chargeable income will be deemed as dividends. For the purposes of this provision, the chargeable income is determined before the deduction of specific incentives or losses brought forward.

RELATED CONSIDERATIONS

34.   Incentives and Grants

The Government of Cyprus encourages foreign investment by offering liberal tax, exchange control, and other incentives for offshore companies established in Cyprus. The following tax exemptions are available:

☐   Manufacturing businesses producing new products (i.e., not previously produced in Cyprus) that commenced operations by April 6, 1990, are exempt from tax during the first ten years of their operation. Furthermore, dividends declared by these companies during the first ten years also are tax exempt in the hands of the recipient.
☐   Effective January 1, 1983, and for a period of ten years, dividends paid to foreign shareholders of companies which operate from the Free Industrial Zone of Larnaca are liable to tax in Cyprus at the lower of the tax rate payable on

the profit out of which the dividend is declared, or the tax rate payable by the shareholder on this same dividend. The effect of this provision is that dividends declared out of profits that have not been taxed, remain also untaxed in the hands of the foreign recipient.

☐ Expatriate employees of companies operating from the Free Industrial Zone of Larnaca are subject to tax at half the normal tax rates (i.e., at rates ranging from nil to 20%).

☐ Profits of a Cyprus ship from operations in international waters (this is in effect until 1993 and may be extended by the Council of Ministers).

☐ 90% of the profits and dividends imported from abroad by Cypriots residing in Cyprus are tax-free provided their interest in such businesses is not lower than 15%. The allowance is granted after the deduction of any losses incurred in the Republic.

☐ 100% of the profits of offshore partnerships irrespective of where managed and controlled.

☐ 100% of the profits of offshore branches managed and controlled outside Cyprus.

☐ Profits arising from exports of locally produced and manufactured products, excluding petroleum products are taxed at 50% of normal rates.

☐ 100% of foreign exchange imported to Cyprus from the rendering of services outside Cyprus of salaried services to private businesses.

☐ 60% of the profits imported to Cyprus from the rendering of professional services outside Cyprus are tax-exempt.

☐ Bank interest earned in Cyprus from foreign capital imported into Cyprus (this exemption is also available to interest earned on foreign loans to approved projects).

☐ Foreign residents or Cypriot subjects previously residing abroad remitting investment or pension income to Cyprus are subject to tax as follows:

C£	Rate of Tax
0–2,000	nil
Over 2,000	5%

☐ An additional allowance, known as "investment allowance," is granted for certain new or imported used depreciable assets when first used in a business (see item 27).

35. Exchange Controls

Resident individuals and companies are subject to restrictive exchange controls. No restrictions apply to nonresident individuals and companies provided prior approval of the Central Bank has been obtained. No restrictions apply to dividend remittances provided Central Bank permission, a mere formality, is obtained before the dividends are repatriated.

36. Investment Restrictions on Nonresidents

The approval of the Central Bank and the Ministry of Commerce and Industry is required before a nonresident may invest in Cyprus. Such approval is easily obtainable if the investment is not in a trade already saturated.

SELECTION OF BUSINESS ENTITY BY NONRESIDENTS

Nonresident investors who register companies or branches of overseas companies in Cyprus and whose income is derived from sources outside Cyprus enjoy the following important tax benefits.

□ Offshore companies irrespective of where managed and controlled, and offshore branches managed and controlled in Cyprus, pay tax at 4.25%.

□ Offshore branches managed and controlled abroad, and offshore partnerships irrespective of management and control, pay no tax at all.

Furthermore, foreign employees working for offshore entities in Cyprus pay tax at half the normal rates (i.e., at a maximum of 20%), whereas foreign employees working for offshore entities abroad are completely tax-exempt if they are paid through Cyprus. If the salaries are not paid through Cyprus, the tax is paid at one-tenth of the normal rate (i.e., at a maximum of 4%). Cyprus has very advantageous withholding tax provisions as seen in item 17 whereby no tax is withheld on dividends paid from Cyprus. This, coupled with the low tax paid by offshore companies, makes Cyprus an attractive business center for companies operating in the Middle East, South East Europe, and North Africa from high tax countries.

Of particular importance are the treaties with Eastern block countries since they are probably the only treaties of eastern countries with a country such as Cyprus, which provides substantial tax advantages for offshore companies. Cyprus offshore companies with management and control in Cyprus operating in high tax treaty countries in which they have no permanent establishment can extract untaxed profits from these countries taking advantage of the treaty article referring to business profits. This also applies to shipping profits. In addition, treaty companies can trade with other countries through a Cyprus offshore company in which case the profits would be taxed at only 4.25%. Any distribution of these profits would attract no withholding tax and, in addition, the recipient company would be able to avail itself of the benefits of the treaty and pay no additional, or very low tax depending on the country of registration. Cyprus' treaty system is advantageous to the following business operations:

□ Construction companies with Middle East operations.
□ Captive insurance companies.
□ Holding and investment companies.
□ Royalty companies to receive income from treaty countries.

Although the tax position in Cyprus of offshore companies and offshore branches (managed in Cyprus) is the same, experience has shown that a company is the preferred form of entity because:

□ Companies usually enjoy a more favorable tax treatment under the double tax treaties.

□ Other nontax reasons make companies more attractive because of their distinct legal identity.

SPECIMEN TAX COMPUTATION

Information:

□ The company's trading results for the year are as follows:

	C£
Profit for the year before tax	430,000
The results are arrived at after charging the following:	
Depreciation	25,000
Loss on sale of fixed assets	3,000
Unrealized loss on exchange	7,000
General provision for bad debts	2,000

□ Wear and tear allowance and investment allowance amounted to C£55,000 and C£22,000, respectively.

□ Taxes amounting to C£16,000 have been paid in other countries.

Computation:	C£	C£
Profit per accounts before tax		430,000
Add		
Depreciation	25,000	
Loss on sale of fixed assets	3,000	
Unrealized loss on exchange	7,000	
General provision for bad debts	2,000	37,000
		467,000

Computation:	C£	C£
Less		
Wear and tear allowance	55,000	
Investment allowance (1)	22,000	77,000
		390,000
Tax payable		
100,000 at 20%	20,000	
290,000 at 25%	72,500	
	92,500	
Minimum tax payable (3)		
22,000 at 10%	2,200	
		94,700
Less		
Taxes paid in other countries (4)		(16,000)
		78,700

Notes:
(1) Not allowed for offshore companies if fixed assets are outside of Cyprus.
(2) The rate of corporation tax for offshore companies is 4.25%.
(3) There is a minimum tax of 10% imposed on investment allowances.
(4) In the case of an offshore company and in the absence of a double taxation treaty, taxes paid abroad are not treated as a tax credit but as a business expense.

CZECH AND SLOVAK FEDERATIVE REPUBLIC

INCOME TAXES ON CORPORATIONS

1. Rates

The corporation tax comprises two components: (1) tax on income of legal persons, and (2) tax on total wages. The rates of tax range from 20% to 65% and differ according to activity. Foreign-owned (i.e., the degree of foreign ownership exceeds 30%) enterprises generally will be taxed on Czechoslovak income at 20% up to 200,000 KCs and 40% on income above that amount. A 50% wage tax is imposed on corporations and comprises the social security contribution. The amount of the wage tax is deductible from taxable income. In 1991, state-owned enterprises contribute 55% (65% in 1990) of their profits to the state budget, 65% (75% in 1990) by state financial institutions.

A new tax system will be introduced on January 1, 1993.

2. Local Income Taxes

There are various local fees but no local income tax.

3. Capital Gains Taxes

There is no provision for special treatment of gains realized on the sale of property.

4. Branch Profits Taxes

Foreign legal entities headquartered abroad are subject to a tax at the rate of 40% on Czechoslovak-source profit. Imported goods are not subject to the tax. A foreign legal entity may have a permanent establishment in the Czech and Slovak Federative Republic (CSFR)—either the trade representative office or a construction site existing up to six months. The trade representative office may not carry on business activities; it may only support the business of the parent company by advertising and signing contracts on behalf of the parent company.

A portion of the income derived from activities in the CSFR must be allocated to the representative office, which is taxable at the 40% rate. The tax authorities will compare the tax base of the representative office with that of a local company of a similar size and carrying on similar activities. Based on this comparison, the tax authorities may increase the representative office's tax base and then assess additional taxes (up to the amount paid by the comparable local company).

If the foreign legal entity's construction site exists six months or longer, the entity becomes resident and is taxable at the 40% rate. Advances on this tax are withheld by the local payors of invoices at the rate of 5%. These withholdings are considered a final tax unless the foreign company declares its actual tax liability, according to the Czechoslovak regulations, at the end of the calendar year.

5. Foreign Tax Reliefs

Relief is provided for foreign taxes paid both under double taxation treaties and under Czechoslovak law. If a Czechoslovak organization derives income from abroad, it may deduct from the amount subject to profits tax any amounts assessed under a similar tax paid abroad. The maximum deductible amount is the amount of Czechoslovak tax due on this foreign-source income. Under certain tax treaties, taxes paid in the Czech and Slovak Federative Republic can be credited against the taxpayer's total foreign tax liability, and taxes paid in foreign countries can be credited against Czechoslovak tax liability.

6. Classification of Corporations

Among the types of business enterprises liable for tax are: state enterprises, foreign trade companies and enterprises (joint ventures), joint stock companies, associates, state economic entities, and state banking and insurance enterprises.

Under other recently enacted laws, the following types of entities may now exist: company limited by shares, association, private company limited by shares, partnership limited by shares, general commercial partnership, and silent partnership.

7. Payment of Taxes

Taxes are due within 15 days from the date of final assessment. Financial authorities under the supervision of the Ministry of Finance conduct proceedings to determine tax liability. Taxpayers are required to submit any requested information to assist in the determination of liability. In certain cases, withholding is required when income is first received. In addition, taxpayers may be required to make partial advance payments of tax liability prior to assessment in monthly, quarterly, or other fixed installments. Refunds are provided if advance payments exceed final tax liability.

Taxpayers are required to use the calendar year for tax purposes.

INCOME TAX ON INDIVIDUALS

9. Rates

Individuals working in Czechoslovakia are subject to tax rates determined by source of income. Wage tax, ranging from 5% to 20%, subject to withholding by the enterprise, are applied to monthly taxable income, as shown below.

Taxable Income		Tax on	Percentage
Over	Not Over	Lower Amount	on Excess
1 KCs.	300 KCs.	0 KCs.	5%
300	400	0	8
400	600	32	10
600	800	52	11
800	1,000	74	12
1,000	1,200	98	13
1,200	1,400	124	14
1,400	1,600	152	15
1,600	1,800	182	16
1,800	2,000	214	17
2,000	2,400	248	18
2,400		320	20

This basic tax, which applies when the taxpayer has two dependents, may be increased by up to 60% or decreased by up to 70% according to the taxpayer's age, sex, and number of dependents.

Certain earnings are exempt from tax, including sick benefit, certain social security benefits, rewards for innovation, scholarships, certain agricultural payments, and interest on savings in banks. Tax rates on income from literary and artistic earnings range from 3% to 33% on earnings above 50,000 KCs annually. In addition, a separate tax rate scale up to 80% applies to other sources of individual income.

Effective January 1, 1991, the government instituted a new individual income tax. Primarily, this tax applies to income derived by owners of private companies not registered in the Company Register that have fewer than 25 employees and annual profits of less than 540,000 Kcs. Resident expatriates also are liable to this tax, although under certain conditions it may be possible to offset the liability against overseas tax liabilities.

The tax rate varies between 15% and 55%, depending on the amount of income.

This tax does not cover income from the following sources:

wages,	inheritances and gifts,
copyrights,	insurance benefits,
social security benefits,	alimony,
interest paid on bank accounts,	certain sales of movable and immovable properties

10. Local Income Taxes

There are no local income taxes.

11. Capital Gains Taxes

There is no provision for special treatment of gains on the sale of property.

12. Foreign Tax Reliefs

See item 5.

13. Tax Period

Individuals are assessed on a calendar year.

INCOME TAXES ON NONRESIDENTS

15. Liability to Tax

A foreign national becomes taxable as an exchange national after 183 days within a calendar year of his or her arrival in the country. Exchange nationals and Czechoslovak nationals who go abroad temporarily are subject to the same taxes as residents. Certain foreign nationals such as diplomats, staff of international organizations, and those remaining temporarily and exclusively for a certain project or task (such as students or technical consultants) are not regarded as exchange nationals.

Exchange Foreigners. Amounts paid to exchange foreigners (those who are not exchange nationals as defined above) are subject to withholding tax on Czechoslovak-source income generated by royalties, fees, rights, interest, and rental payments.

The tax is withheld by the payor of the remittance and transferred to Czechoslovak financial authorities. The withheld amount discharges any further tax liability, although, subject to treaty provisions, the rate may be reduced.

The Czechoslovak entity paying income (other than dividends, interest, or royalties) to a foreign recipient must withhold a prepayment of tax of 5% and transfer this amount to Czechoslovak financial authorities. Prepayments are credited against final tax liability.

Under current tax reform proposals, nonresidents will be subject to tax on all income from sources in Czechoslovakia.

16. Rates

Foreign nationals resident in the CSFR and employed by a foreign entity's representative office are taxed at the rate of 17% on their salaries (payable in abroad or locally) that results from employment in the Czech and Slovak Federative Republic. Salaries of foreign nationals employed by Czechoslovak companies are taxable at rates ranging from 0% to 32%. Also see items 5 and 17.

17. Withholding Tax Rates

Withholding on outward remittances, unless reduced by tax treaty, are:

	Withholding Rate
Dividends	25%
Interest	25
Industry royalties	30
Technical services	30
Rental fees	25
Leasing installments	25

In certain cases, the Federal Ministry may grant tax relief for leasing installments.

Czechoslovak tax treaties with the countries listed in item 19 provide, depending on the treaty provisions, reduced dividends withholding rates of 15% to 5%, interest withholding rates of 15% to 0%, and industrial royalties withholding rates of 15% to 5%.

19. Tax Treaties

Czechoslovakia has entered into a number of bilateral tax treaties based on the OECD Draft Convention for the Avoidance of Double Taxation with respect to taxes on income and capital. Treaties under negotiation include: Australia, Canada, Indonesia, Malaysia, Nigeria, Switzerland, Thailand, the United Kingdom, and the United States.

Tax treaties have been concluded between Hungary and the following countries to reduce the withholding on dividends, interest, and industrial royalties:

Austria	Italy
Belgium	Japan
China, Peoples Rep. of	Netherlands
Cyprus	Nigeria
Denmark	Norway
Finland	Spain
France	Sri Lanka
Germany	Sweden
Greece	Yugoslavia
India	

OTHER SIGNIFICANT TAXES

21. Sales (Value-Added)

A turnover tax is imposed on the sale of goods imported or manufactured domestically. Effective January 1, 1991, the tax rates have been reduced from over 1,500 to 4 primary rates: 0%, 11%, 20%, and 29%. Certain items, for example, alcohol, coffee and tea, tobacco, jewelry, and fuel, are taxed at special rates.

The charter of turnover tax rates defines which goods sold are liable to the tax. Goods defined as not liable to turnover tax are sold only to consumers registered in the Company Register. Exports are exempted.

Under the new system, goods are taxed once—compared to a value-added tax, in which the added value of the item is taxed until sold to the ultimate consumer. It is expected that, effective 1993, a value-added tax will replace the turnover tax.

22. Inheritance and Gift Taxes

An inheritance fee or tax is imposed on the acquirer of property received either by inheritance at death or by gift from the deceased in the last three months before death. The amount of tax depends on the value of the property transferred and the degree of relationship between the parties of the transfer.

Degree of Relationship	Inheritance Fee
Spouse, child, grandchild, parent	1%
Sibling, adult offspring (if sharing a household with parent for at least one year)	5%
Other	20%

Note that the Czechoslovakian Government recently announced a program of tax reform that includes new inheritance and gift taxes.

23. Taxes on Payrolls (Social Security)

Pension and health contributions are made through a tax on total wages. The rate of tax is 50%, and the amount is deductible from taxable income. The rate of 20% applies to certain types of services, such as repairs, maintenance, and public catering.

25. Other Taxes

Agricultural Tax. The agricultural tax is a land tax and a profits tax imposed on proceeds received from agricultural production. The land tax rate can be as high as 3,000 KCs per hectare of land. The profits tax is imposed on a sliding scale from 10% to 60% for individuals and on a flat rate of 50% for companies.

COMPUTATION OF TAXABLE INCOME

27. Depreciation and Depletion

Effective January 1, 1991, depreciation is calculated in accordance with tax and accounting regulations and is a deductible item for both purposes. Depreciation is computed at flat rates established by the legislation. Newly established companies may use accelerated depreciation for machinery (50% of the cost within the first three years, and a flat rate thereafter), and buildings (6% within the first five years, 4% within the following five years, and a flat rate thereafter).

29. Loss Carryovers

It is expected that a three-year carryforward of net operating losses will be allowed. Up to 33⅓% of the loss would be carried forward each of the three years.

RELATED CONSIDERATIONS

35. Exchange Controls

Effective January 1, 1991, the internal convertibility of the crown has been in force. Enterprises must deposit all hard currency earnings with the State Bank, which then exchanges it into crowns. If the enterprise requires hard currency, the State bank exchanges the crowns into the hard currency required in the local bank account and make the necessary payment. The State Bank also can permit an enterprise to open a hard currency account.

36. Investment Restrictions on Nonresidents

As noted below, "Selection of Business Entity by Nonresidents," nonresidents can invest in Czechoslovakia through joint ventures provided there is Government approval. Until recent law changes, at least one Czechoslovak partner was needed. This is no longer required. The recent law change permits private Czechoslovak citizens to take part in joint ventures. It is expected that companies with foreign participation generally will be taxed in the same way as domestically owned companies.

SELECTION OF BUSINESS ENTITY BY NONRESIDENTS

Joint Ventures. Joint ventures (enterprises with foreign private investment) are subject to a 40% profits tax (20% if profits do not exceed 200,000 KCs) and a deductible social security contribution of 50% of total payroll costs. Joint ventures are provided a tax holiday of up to two years with the permission of the Ministry of Finance.

The Government recently announced a major tax reform program that could establish appropriate tax incentives or tax holidays for foreign investments in Czechoslovakia.

Joint ventures with up to 100% foreign ownership may operate in Czechoslovakia. Joint ventures may operate in any field except those related to national security, if approved by a Government authority. Note that the State Bank of Czechoslovakia governs banking operations.

Joint ventures are required to establish a reserve fund in local currency to cover possible losses. Five percent of net profits is allocated to the reserve fund each year until the fund reaches an amount initially established by the joint venture agreement, which cannot be less than 10% of subscribed capital. Net profits, after taxes and fund contributions, may be distributed to shareholders.

Joint ventures are taxed on their profits and also on the amount of their wages. Tax rates on their profits are:

☐   20% up to 200,000 KCs.

☐   40% on profits above 200,000 KCs (55% from January 1, 1991 if foreign participation does not exceed 30%).

In addition there is a 50% tax on the total amount of wages.

The annual balance sheet and profit and loss statements of joint ventures must be audited annually by two independent auditors, one of which may be foreign. Rules governing auditing are supervised by the Ministry of Finance.

Joint ventures are required to establish a system of social and economic information in accordance with the provisions of Czechoslovak law applicable to Czechoslovak organizations. Bookkeeping and accounts must be kept in Czechoslovak currency under binding Czechoslovak legal provisions. Accounting and statistical data must be provided to Government authorities.

A tax return must be filed by February 15 for the preceding calendar year.

DENMARK

INCOME TAXES ON CORPORATIONS

1. Rates

The rate of corporation tax is 38%. Denmark taxes income on a worldwide basis.

2. Local Income Taxes

None.

3. Capital Gains Taxes

Most capital gains are added to taxable income and taxed at the regular corporate tax rate (see item 26).

4. Branch Profits Taxes

Branches of foreign corporations are subject to corporation tax of 38% on the taxable income of the branch.

5. Foreign Tax Reliefs

Relief for taxes incurred outside Denmark is granted in accordance with treaties for the avoidance of double taxation. If a treaty does not exist, credit for income taxes is given according to an internal provision.

Dividends from foreign subsidiaries are tax-exempt if the Danish parent company holds at least 25% of the share capital of the subsidiary and the subsidiary is taxed according to rules not substantially different from Danish tax rules.

According to domestic legislation, a Danish company that proves that part of its taxable income is derived from active business abroad is eligible for relief amounting to 50% of the tax relating to the foreign income.

6. Classification of Corporations

Joint-Stock Company (Aktieselskab—A/S).   The minimum share capital is DKK 300,000.

Private Company (Anpartsselskab—ApS). The minimum capital is DKK 80,000.

Employees' representation. Joint stock companies as well as private companies that have employed more than an average of 35 persons over three years must elect a board of directors, and the employees are entitled to be represented on the boards of directors.

Branch Office. Foreign joint stock companies may carry out business in Denmark through a registered branch office if it is in compliance with international agreement or with the permission of the Ministry of Industry.

7. Payment of Taxes

Computation of a company's taxable income is based on the company's own accounting year. The tax falls due in the fiscal year (April 1st to March 31st) subsequent to the end of the company's accounting year. Payment is due on November 1st in the fiscal year.

8. Other Matters

Mergers. Two or more companies can merge without either company realizing taxes. This applies also to parent companies and subsidiaries. If a tax-free merger is established, the continuing company acquires the status of the discontinuing company with regard to tax values as well as the dates and purposes of acquisition (trade, speculation, capital investments) of the assets. A tax-free merger of a Danish and a foreign company, with the Danish company as the continuing company is also possible.

INCOME TAXES ON INDIVIDUALS

9. Rates

Four types of income must be calculated:

□ Ordinary taxable income
□ Personal income
□ Capital income.
□ Dividend income.

The ordinary taxable income comprises all elements of taxable income less all tax allowances. Dividend income is taxed separately (see item 28).

1991 State Income Tax Rates

Taxable income	22%
Personal income, exceeding DKK 227,200	12%
Personal income + positive net capital income less basic deduction of DKK 155,100	6%
Maximum state income tax percentage	40%

10. Local Income Taxes

In addition to State income tax, municipal and church taxes are levied on the taxable income. These taxes vary, but the average rate is 28% of the taxable income. The sum of state, municipal, and church taxes is reduced by the tax value of a personal allowance, which varies with the municipal tax rate. The average allowance for 1991 is DKK 13,765.

11. Capital Gains Taxes

Tax on certain capital gains is charged at 50% of the gain (see also item 26).

12. Foreign Tax Reliefs

Relief from double taxation is granted either in accordance with tax treaties or on the basis of domestic credit rules.

13. Tax Period

The tax year is normally the calendar year.

14. Other Matters

Payment of Taxes. Ordinary income tax and capital tax (see item 25) are paid currently on a basis estimated by the individual. Capital gains tax is computed on the basis of the tax return and is collected in three installments in the year following the acquisition of the income.

The Act on Taxation of Firms. Individuals—fully as well as limited tax liable—carrying on independent business activities may choose to have income from these activities taxed according to the special rules of the Act on Taxation of Firms. By applying these rules, the individual obtains a higher tax value of interest expenses as well as income equalization to some degree from year to year. Profits not drawn from the firm are taxed temporarily at 38%, whereas profits drawn from the firm are taxed as personal income at up to 68%.

INCOME TAXES ON NONRESIDENTS

15. Liability to Tax

Nonresident individuals generally are subject to tax only on income from Danish sources. If an individual stays in Denmark for a continuous period of more than six months (apart from a sojourn for purposes of vacation or study), the individual becomes fully taxable on worldwide income. The elements of income listed below are comprised by the limited tax liability:

☐ Salaries/wages for work performed in Denmark and paid by an employer having venue in Denmark.

☐ Certain other types of personal income inclusive of directors' fee and pension distributions.

☐ Remuneration comprised by the special rules on labor demise.

☐ Income arising from business enterprises having a permanent establishment in Denmark.

☐ Any kind of remuneration from a business having a permanent establishment in Denmark.

☐ Income from real property located in Denmark.

☐ Dividends from Danish companies.

☐ Royalty income from Denmark.

☐ Under certain circumstances, remuneration for advisory assistance and interest from Danish sources.

Nonresident companies are companies not registered in Denmark. They are taxed only on income derived from business activities in Denmark or on dividends and royalties from Danish sources.

16. Rates

Nonresident individuals pay state income tax at the maximum 40% rate (see item 9) and an average of the local taxes for 1991 equal to 28% of their taxable income.

Individuals subject to limited taxation of income from employment and certain pension incomes are entitled to an annual personal allowance (see item 10) which is granted against these taxes.

Special rules apply to nonresident individuals who are hired out by a foreign employer to work for a Danish assignor (see item 17).

Nonresident companies are taxed in conformity with the rates applicable to domiciled companies, but only on income from Danish sources.

17. Withholding Tax Rates

Withholding tax applies to wage income, remuneration for labor demise, dividends, and some royalties.

Wage Income.   Withholding tax on wages applies to remuneration paid by Danish employers to residents as well as to nonresident employees who perform personal services in Denmark. This withholding tax is not a final tax.

Foreign artists, musicians, athletes, etc. are normally not regarded as employees and are, therefore, not considered to be subject to limited tax liability, if their stay in Denmark lasts for less than six months.

If a nonresident individual employed by a foreign employer is placed at the disposal of a Danish assignor to perform work in Denmark for a period of less than six months, the Danish assignor must withhold tax amounting to 30% of the employee's remuneration. This withholding tax is a final tax.

Royalty.   A coupon tax of 30% is withheld from some royalty payments from Danish sources to nonresident companies and individuals. The rate may be reduced according to a tax treaty.

Dividends.   A coupon tax of 30% is withheld from dividends distributed by resident companies to their shareholders, whether resident or nonresident. For nonresident companies and individuals, the 30% withheld constitutes a final tax, but according to a treaty the coupon tax may be entirely or partially reduced.

	Royalty	Dividends	
		Ordinary Shareholder	Parent Company (1)
Nontreaty countries	30%	30%	30%
Treaty countries:			
Australia	10	15	15
Austria	0, 10 (2)	10	10
Belgium	0	15	15
Brazil	15, 25 (3)	25	25
Bulgaria	0	15	5
Canada	15	15	15
China	10	10	10
Cyprus	0	15	10
Czechoslovakia	5	15	15
Egypt	20	20	15
Faroe Islands	0	15	0
Finland (4)	0	15	0
France	0	0	0
Germany	0	15	10
Greenland	10	30	30
Hungary	0	15	5
Iceland (4)	0	15	0

| | Royalty | Dividends | |
		Ordinary Shareholder	Parent Company (1)
India	20%	25%	15%
Indonesia	15	20	10
Ireland (5)	0	0	0
Israel	10	15	5
Italy	5	15	15
Japan	10	15	10
Kenya	20	30	20
Korea	15, 10 (6)	15	15
Luxembourg	0	15	5
Malaysia	30, 0 (7)	0	0
Malta	0	15	5
Netherlands	0	15	0
New Zealand	10	15	15
Norway (5)	0	15	0
Pakistan	12	30	15
Philippines	30	30	30
Poland	10	15	5
Portugal	10	15	10
Rumania	10	15	10
Singapore	15	10	5
Soviet Union	0	15	15
Spain	6	15	10
Sri Lanka	10	15	15
Sweden (4)	0	15	0
Switzerland	0	0	0
Tanzania	20	15	15
Thailand	15	30	20
Trinidad and Tobago	15	20	10
Tunisia	15	15	15
United Kingdom	0	15	0
United States	0	15	5
Yugoslavia	10	15	5
Zambia	15	15	15

Notes:

(1) The treaties define a parent company according to its shareholding in the Danish subsidiary, generally as follows:

Bulgaria, Cyprus, Egypt, Faroe Islands, Germany, Hungary, India, Indonesia, Luxembourg, Malta, Netherlands, the Nordic	At least 25% (directly)

countries, Poland, Portugal, Rumania, Singapore, Thailand, the United Kingdom, and Yugoslavia

Israel (directly or indirectly), Spain (directly)	At least 50%
Japan	At least 25% (minimum 12-month holding period)
Kenya	At least 25% (minimum six-month holding period)
Trinidad and Tobago (directly or indirectly)	At least 25%
United States (less than 25% of the Danish controlled-corporation's gross income can be derived from dividends and interest other than from its own subsidiaries)	At least 95%

(2) 10% if the recipient owns more than 50% of the capital of the paying company.
(3) 25% is applicable to royalties for the use of or the right to use trade marks.
(4) The Nordic multilateral tax treaty between Denmark, the Faroe Islands, Finland, Iceland, Norway, and Sweden.
(5) New treaty expected to take effect January 1, 1992.
(6) 10% in case of industrial investments.
(7) Nil if the royalty is accepted by the government in the country of source.

OTHER SIGNIFICANT TAXES

21. Sales (Value Added)

A 22% value-added tax (VAT) is levied on any sale of goods or services carried out by a business registered in Denmark. The VAT payments are normally settled quarterly with the customs authorities. VAT is paid on purchased goods and services, and VAT on imports are deductible from the VAT accruing to the State. Foreign enterprises having no registered office, residence, or the like, in Denmark, may, on application, obtain reimbursement of VAT paid on goods and taxable services purchased or imported for the commercial purposes of such enterprise in Denmark. However, travel agencies, insurance, banking, finance and passenger transport enterprises are not within the scope of enterprises that can obtain such reimbursement.

22. Inheritance and Gift Taxes

The basis for inheritance tax is the relationship between the heir and the decedent. The inheritance tax is charged if the decedent was resident in Denmark, or the inheritance consists of real property in Denmark or property rights.

The gift tax is charged on gifts and advances on inheritances to a spouse, children, stepchildren, and their issue, surviving spouse of a deceased child or stepchild, parents, stepparents, and grandparents, when the donor or donee is resident in Denmark or the gift consists of real property in Denmark or property rights.

Both inheritances and gifts are taxed at the same tax rate depending on the degree of relationship and on the value of the inheritance or the gift.

Gifts between unrelated individuals are taxable as ordinary personal income for the recipient if the recipient is fully tax liable in Denmark.

24. Taxes on Natural Resources

Personal income tax or corporation tax, calculated on a special basis, is levied on income from hydrocarbon extraction activities. A special hydrocarbon tax of 70% is also payable, but the personal income tax or corporation tax is an allowable deduction for hydrocarbon tax purposes.

25. Other Taxes

Labor Market Tax (arbejdsmarkedsbidrag). Employers must pay a special labor market tax. The tax amounts to 2.5% of the total sale of the enterprise, exclusive of exports, and with the deduction of the total purchases of the enterprises, exclusive of imports.

For certain enterprises (such as insurance companies, banks, etc.), the taxable base is the wage bill plus 90%.

Payroll Tax. Insurance companies, banks, etc., must pay a payroll tax amounting to 2.0%. The taxable base is the payroll plus 90%. The tax will not be payable if the payroll plus 90% does not exceed DKK 80,000.

Tax on Capital. In 1991, capital held by married individuals is subject to tax at a rate of 1.0% after an exemption of DKK 2,499,200 (DKK 1,452,700 if unmarried). In computing this tax, some business assets are stated at a lower value than market value. Private furniture and other movable property, including pieces of art, antiques and jewelry, are not included in the taxable capital. Debts may be deducted, however, only by an amount corresponding to the commercial value of the equivalent claim.

Land and Property Tax. The assessment value of real property is based on the authorities' cash valuation. The tax on land varies from 0.6% up to 3.4% in different parts of the country (the most expensive is Copenhagen). Furthermore, the rental value of a private dwelling is considered capital income. The rental value is 2.5% of the part of the value of the dwelling that does not exceed DKK 1,363,200 and 7.5% of the excess value.

Duty on Sale of Shares. A duty of 1% must be paid on sale of Danish and foreign shares and similar securities, calculated on the total market value of the sold shares, etc., provided the seller is resident in Denmark.

Capital Transfer Tax.   On transfer of capital or other funds to companies, a tax of 1% on the capital contributions must be paid provided either place of management of the company is situated in Denmark or provided its legal domicile is in Denmark but its place of management is situated in a country outside the EEC.

Other Indirect Taxes.   Indirect taxes are levied on tobacco, wine and spirits, gasoline, and motor vehicles. Other indirect taxes include stamp duties, registration duties, and motor vehicle registration duties.

COMPUTATION OF TAXABLE INCOME

26.   Capital Gains

Some capital gains are taxed at a flat rate of 50% according to the Special Income Tax Act. The following is regarded as special income:

☐ Retrieved depreciations on sale of buildings, depreciated for tax purposes.

☐ Profit or loss on relinquishment of patents, etc., time-limited rights, rights according to a profits agreement, tenancy and lease contracts.

☐ Profit from the sale of real property is taxable at 50% if the sale takes place within three years after acquisition. On sales after three years, the taxable profit is reduced by 20% for each additional year of possession; thus, a profit is tax-free after seven years of possession. Profit from family homes is tax-free if the owner has occupied the home. Losses are never deductible.

☐ Certain specified compensations granted to an employee by his employer. The payments must be nonrecurring and not connected with any particular period of employment.

☐ Gifts of respect paid out of public resources, foundations, or cultural funds.

☐ Profit or loss on sale of shares in some cases.

The taxable amount generally is the difference between sales and cost price (net of depreciation). In some cases indexed values are applied. No taxes of any kind are levied on profits from the sale of private furniture and other moveables, including works of art, carpets and antiques.

27.   Depreciation and Depletion

Machinery, Plant, and Similar Production Equipment.   All production equipment may be depreciated on the diminishing-balance method.

Each year, the taxpayer may write off from 0% to 30% of the balance value.

Ships and Machinery, Ship Equipment, and Other Plant.   Depreciation is collective and made according to the diminishing-balance method. The same rules apply here as for machinery, plant, etc., above.

Buildings.   Only buildings with industrial activities, cinemas, restaurants, garages, warehouses, etc. or buildings which are closely affiliated with such buildings, qualify for depreciation allowances. Generally, office and residential buildings, hospitals, and clinics do not qualify for depreciation allowances. Buildings and special facilities are depreciated individually on the straight-line basis; no depreciation is allowable on land. The basis of depreciation is the cash value of the acquisition price. The taxpayer chooses the depreciation percentage each year, up to a maximum, which is 4%, 6%, and 8%, respectively, for different categories of buildings and facilities. The taxpayer may continue to apply the initial (maximum) percentages until the accumulated depreciation amounts to 40%, 60%, or 80%, respectively. For subsequent years, 1%, 2%, and 4%, respectively, are the maximums.

Advance Depreciation.   Advance depreciation is allowed upon the signing of a binding contract or contemplated manufacture of machinery, buildings, and ships by any percentage up to 30% of the construction price. Advance depreciation in any single investment year cannot exceed 15%. For ships, the stipulated or agreed price must exceed Dkr. 200,000. For machinery and buildings, the purchase price must exceed Dkr. 700,000.

Leasehold Improvements.   These may be depreciated on a straight-line basis during the lease period.

Stock-in-Trade.   Stock-in-trade can be depreciated by an annual rate of 30%. The annual depreciation must be entered into the books as income for the following year.

28.   Treatment of Dividends

Individuals.   The dividend income consists mainly of dividends from Danish companies. Dividend from foreign companies does not form part of the ''dividend income,'' but is taxed as part of the capital income (see item 9).

Dividend income not in excess of DKK 30,000 (DKK 60,000 for a married couple) is taxed at the rate of 30%. Dividend income in excess of DKK 30,000 (60,000) is taxed at the rate of 45%.

Companies.   Danish resident companies owning at least 25% of the share capital in a Danish subsidiary are tax-exempt on dividends from the subsidiary. If dividends from Danish companies are not tax-exempt, 66% of the dividend actually received is taxable and thus taxable at the ordinary corporation tax rate.

Dividends from foreign subsidiaries in which a Danish parent company owns at least 25% of the share capital may also be exempt from tax if the subsidiary is taxed according to rules that do not differ essentially from Danish corporation tax rules. Otherwise, the full amount of such dividends is included in taxable income.

29. Loss Carryovers

A negative taxable income sustained in any year may be carried forward to the succeeding five years. However, the loss has to offset profits as soon as possible. No carryback is permitted.

Loss carryover may be restricted in certain situations, e.g., in case of remission of debt and compositions.

30. Transactions between Related Parties

According to provisions as well as court rulings, transactions for tax purposes between related parties may be disregarded if the transactions deviate from those which might be carried out on an arm's-length basis and the deviations were made for tax purposes. Such transactions will be subject to the taxation applicable to transactions made on an arm's-length basis.

31. Consolidation of Income

Group Taxation of Companies Domiciled in Denmark. If a parent company (alone or with other companies included in the joint taxation) possesses 100% of the subsidiary's shares, permission to compute taxes on a joint taxable income basis may be granted on certain terms and conditions. An advantage of joint taxation of Danish companies is the possibility of offsetting profits and losses in the individual companies. The access to offset net losses in a parent company against profits of a subsidiary may, however, under certain circumstances be restricted within the first seven years after acquiring the subsidiary.

Group Taxation of Danish Parent Company with Foreign Subsidiary. In order to obtain permission for joint taxation, the parent company must be domiciled in Denmark. In addition, the total share capital in a subsidiary (or that part of the share capital that may be possessed by foreign investors according to national legislation) must be owned by the parent company and/or one of the other jointly taxed companies. The joint taxation income is the sum of the taxable incomes of the individual Danish and foreign companies as computed according to Danish tax laws, including double taxation treaties. The joint taxation scheme is not required to comprise all subsidiaries in the group.

32. Tax Periods

See items 7 and 13.

RELATED CONSIDERATIONS

34. Incentives and Grants

Exempt Income. An individual subject to full tax liability is, under certain circumstances, exempt from taxation in Denmark of income from employment earned during stays in foreign countries of at least six months.

Special Grants or Allowances.

□ Expenses for basic research are tax deductible.

□ Companies may deduct expenses by 125% for participation in Eureka, Esprit, Brite, or Race research programs.

□ Companies may deduct certain donations for research.

□ Transfers to investment funds may be spent on research and experiments and on marketing relating to sale outside Denmark.

35. Exchange Controls

Denmark has very liberal exchange regulations based on the Foreign Exchange Act. The main features are:

□ Transactions of a commercial nature between residents and nonresidents, as well as investments into and from Denmark, can be made without permission from the Central Bank. The bank, however, must be notified of all payments exceeding DKK 60,000.

□ Certain transactions are always conditioned on preparation of a notification to the Central Bank. This applies to residents for exchange purposes who
—Open/retain accounts in foreign financial institutions, etc.
—Acquire foreign securities and Danish bonds issued outside Denmark.
—Take out of life insurance and pension plans with foreign insurance companies.
—Donate gifts exceeding DKK 60,000 to nonresidents.

SELECTION OF BUSINESS ENTITY BY NONRESIDENTS

Nonresident investors can operate in Denmark either through a branch or by forming a company. The tax consequences for a foreign entity that carries on business in Denmark are the same as for Danish companies except that the tax liability of a foreign corporation's branch is based only on Danish-source income, while a subsidiary is taxed on its worldwide income.

Danish branch profits may be repatriated on a current basis, but a subsidiary makes only annual dividend distributions.

SPECIMEN TAX COMPUTATION

Information:

□ Corporate tax computation of a Danish corporation and its foreign branch:

Computation:

Profit in Denmark		DKK 2,000
Less		
Trading expenses	200	
Interest payable	200	
Depreciation	100	500
Taxable income		1,500
Taxable income of foreign branch		2,000
Total taxable income		3,500
Corporation tax (at 38%)		1,330
Less		
Internal relief for active business performed abroad $(1,330 \times \dfrac{2,000}{3,500} \times 0.5)$	380	380
		950
Tax credit/Exemption (1) $\dfrac{2,000 \times 950}{3,500}$		543
Income tax payable		DKK 407

Notes:

(1) Foreign taxes paid by the branch total DKK 600. In this example, relief is given according to an exemption rule in a tax treaty.

DOMINICA
(COMMONWEALTH OF)

INCOME TAXES ON CORPORATIONS

1. Rates

The standard rate of income tax on corporations is 35%.

2. Local Income Taxes

There are no state or provincial income taxes in Dominica.

3. Capital Gains Tax

There is no capital gains tax in Dominica except for the land value appreciation tax (see item 26).

4. Branch Profits Tax

Branches of foreign corporations are subject to income tax at full rates on the profits of the branch. In addition, there is a 15% withholding tax on profits accruing to the nonresident company after deduction of income tax thereon and such part of the taxable income as has been reinvested in Dominica under certain conditions laid down in the Act. The withholding tax is payable when the profits are remitted.

5. Foreign Tax Reliefs

Dominica has tax treaties with a number of countries which provide relief from double taxation (see item 19). The relief provided depends on the terms of the agreement. The tax credit allowed for income from a foreign country with which there is no double taxation agreement is, generally, the lesser of the tax payable in the foreign country or the tax chargeable in Dominica.

6. Classification of Corporations

Corporations are classified for Dominican tax purposes as either resident or non-resident corporations. A resident corporation is one which is incorporated in Dominica, or is managed and controlled in Dominica. The distinction between resident and nonresident corporations is important in that Dominican residents are subject to tax on their worldwide income whereas nonresidents are subject to tax only on their Dominican-source income.

7. Payment of Taxes

Companies are required to pay tax by installments on a current year basis. The installments are based on either the total tax payable for the preceding income year or the total tax payable on the expected income for the current year. Penalties are charged where the prepayments are based on substantially underestimated income; that is, less than 75% correct.

Tax owned by companies with December 31 year-ends is payable as follows:

☐ On or before March 31st, any balance due with respect to the preceding income year and a first installment of 25% of the tax payable for the current year.

☐ On or before June 30th, a second installment of 35% of the tax payable for the current year.

☐ On or before September 30th, a third installment of 40% of the tax payable for the current year.

Taxpayers with fiscal year-ends other than December 31 pay installments at the end of the third, sixth, and ninth month following the beginning of their fiscal year, and any balance of tax due in respect of that fiscal year is payable upon filing their income tax returns.

INCOME TAXES ON INDIVIDUALS

9. Rates

Tax is imposed at graduated rates upon taxable income of individuals. Residents of Dominica must include their worldwide income, except that an individual who is resident but not ordinarily resident is taxed on income arising from outside of Dominica only to the extent it is received in Dominica. Nonresidents include only their income from carrying on a business or from providing personal services in Dominica.

The rates of taxes for a residential individual are as follows:

On the first $12,000	0%
On the next $18,000	20%
On the next $30,000	30%
For every dollar over $60,000	40%

Mortgage interest of up to $15,000 in respect of owner-occupied dwelling houses is allowed as a deduction in arriving at taxable income.

10. Local Income Taxes

None.

11. Capital Gains Tax

Same as item 3.

12. Foreign Tax Reliefs

The foreign tax reliefs are the same as for corporations (see item 5).

13. Tax Period

Normally, tax is levied on chargeable income for the year ended December 31. However, with the permission of the Comptroller, a taxpayer who keeps accounts for his business or profession with a year-end other than December 31 may include in his income for the calendar year the profit from the business or profession for the year ending in the calendar year.

INCOME TAXES ON NONRESIDENTS

15. Liability to Tax

Nonresidents are subject to tax on Dominican source income only. Income received by nonresidents from sources in Dominica is subject to withholding taxes only, except where a nonresident is carrying on a business or providing personal services in Dominica. Income arising from sources outside Dominica to retired persons who were not resident in Dominica prior to retirement is exempt from income tax. A nonresident's income chargeable to tax includes income arising directly or indirectly through an agency or branch.

16. Rates

Nonresident individuals and corporations subject to income tax are taxed on their Dominican-source income at the same rates as resident individuals or corporations (see items 1 and 9).

17. Withholding Tax Rates

Unless reduced by treaty, withholding tax rates are:

Dividends	15%
Rental of immovable property	10%
Rental of movable property	20%
Fees paid to public entertainers	30%
Interest, royalties, management charges, and other payments of an income nature	25%

19. Tax Treaties

Dominica has tax treaties with Barbados, Denmark, Guyana, Jamaica, Norway, Sweden, Switzerland, Trinidad and Tobago, and the United States.

OTHER SIGNIFICANT TAXES

22. Inheritance and Gift Taxes

None.

23. Taxes on Payrolls (Social Security)

Social security taxes are payable by all employees between 16 and 60 years. Contributions are payable at the rate of 10% of an employee's earnings (3% by the employee and 7% by the employer) up to a maximum of $300.00 per month. Self-employed persons are required to contribute 7% of their previous year's earnings.

25. Other Taxes

A gross receipts tax is payable at the rate of 3% on all retail sales.

COMPUTATION OF TAXABLE INCOME

26. Capital Gains

There is no capital gains tax in Dominica except for the land value appreciation tax.

Land Value Appreciation Tax. A gain on the sale of land is taxable at 10% if sold to the government or 5% if sold to a private person. The gain is computed as the proceeds from the sale less the original cost of the land.

27. Depreciation and Depletion

A taxpayer is allowed to deduct a reasonable amount for wear and tear on industrial buildings and plant and machinery (including furniture and equipment) used in carrying on a business. Typical annual allowances applied on the reducing balance method are:

Industrial buildings	4%
Furniture	15%
Machinery and equipment	15%
Motor vehicles	25%

A balancing allowance is given on the sale of an asset equal to the excess of the written-down value over the sales proceeds. A balancing charge is made if the sales proceeds exceed the written-down value.

Where a taxpayer incurs capital expenditure on residential accommodation, either by constructing a new dwelling or substantially reconstructing an existing one, a deduction is allowed over a ten-year period of the lower of 5% of such expenditure or EC $2,500 per year.

28. Treatment of Dividends

Where a resident company receives a dividend from another resident company, a tax credit is allowed to the receiving company equal to the amount by which its tax has been increased by the inclusion of the dividend in its assessable income. In a loss year, the increase in tax is based on the rate of tax that would have applied had there been sufficient taxable income. Any unused credit may be carried forward to future years until it is fully utilized.

Where a resident individual receives a dividend from a resident company, the individual receives a tax credit of the lower of 30% of the dividend received or the rate of tax applicable resulting from including the dividend in assessable income.

29. Loss Carryovers

Losses may be carried forward for off-set in full against future profits over a three-year period.

30. Transactions between Related Parties

The Comptroller may adjust the tax liability on any transaction which he determines was mainly designed to reduce or eliminate taxes.

31. Consolidation of Income

There is no provision for the filing of consolidated tax returns by related corporations.

32. Tax Periods

Tax normally is levied on chargeable income for the year ended December 31. However, with the permission of the Comptroller, tax may be levied based on the accounts year ending in the year preceding the year of assessment.

33. Other Matters

Company's Undistributed Income.   Where effective control of a company is exercised by, or the greater part of the issued share capital is held by, or more than 50% of the income effectively belongs to not more than five connected or related persons, the following provisions apply. Where such a company fails to make a sufficient distribution (in the opinion of the Comptroller) in relation to any year of assessment, it is liable to tax at the rate of 15% on such portion of the amount considered a sufficient distribution by the Comptroller as remains undistributed. The company has until December 31st in the year of assessment to make a sufficient distribution, as determined by the Comptroller, to avoid the tax. Distributions in later years do not qualify for relief from this tax.

Partnerships.   A partnership is required to make a return of partnership income, but each partner is assessable individually in respect of his share of the income.

RELATED CONSIDERATIONS

34.   Incentives and Grants

Exemption of Approved Enterprises.   A company incorporated in Dominica and engaged in any construction or manufacturing process which is or may be beneficial to the economy of Dominica may qualify for a complete or partial exemption from income tax for up to a maximum of 15 years.

Hotels.   Profits from a hotel are exempt from income tax for up to the first ten years after approval is granted by the Government.

Housing Loans.   Income derived by companies from Government approved housing finance loans are exempt from income tax. In addition, interest income up to 10% from mortgages up to EC $150,000 is exempt from income tax. Where a company or building society issues debentures for the purpose of financing such mortgages, the Minister of Finance may exempt such interest from income tax in the hands of the debenture holder.

Agricultural Income.   Income from agricultural operations carried out in Dominica is exempt from income tax.

Rental Income—Industrial Buildings.   Rental income from leasing an industrial building of not less than 5,000 square feet is exempt from income tax for ten years commencing with the date of occupation by the first tenant.

Income from Residential Accommodations.   Income from the sale or rental of residential accommodations undertaken in pursuance with an agreement with the Government is exempt from income tax for the first ten years.

Equity Investment.   Equity investment up to $5,000 per annum in public companies engaged in enterprises approved by the cabinet is tax deductible.

Investment Tax Credit.   An investment tax credit of 10% capital investments will be allowed for new investment or expansion on an existing enterprise, but will not be allowed for replacement of existing plant or equipment.

General.   Losses incurred by the above industries and corporations cannot be set off against taxable profits from other operations. Income distributed to shareholders from exempt income is also exempt in the hands of shareholders.

35. Exchange Controls

Exchange control regulations allow for the transfer of funds out of Dominica up to the equivalent of EC $100 without permission. Permission will be granted for higher amounts depending on the purpose for which the funds are needed and upon production of supporting documents. Such permission is usually not unreasonably withheld.

Foreign investors are allowed to repatriate the profits of their businesses.

36. Investment Restrictions on Nonresidents

There are no significant investment restrictions on nonresidents. Foreign investors may commence operations provided the necessary licenses and permits have been obtained, including work permits for nonresident staff in cases where local expertise is not available.

DOMINICAN REPUBLIC

INCOME TAXES ON CORPORATIONS

1. Rates

The rate of corporation tax is progressive according to the following scale:

Taxable Income		Tax on Lower Amount	Percentage on Excess
Over	Not Over		
RD$ 0	RD$ 5,000	RD$ 0	10%
5,000	10,000	500	13
10,000	20,000	1,150	16
20,000	30,000	2,750	19
30,000	40,000	4,650	22
40,000	50,000	6,850	27
50,000	60,000	9,550	31
60,000	100,000	12,650	36
100,000	250,000	27,050	41
250,000		88,550	46

Surtax. There is a surtax of 3% of the regular income tax. In addition, there is a surtax of 2% on corporate taxable income. This 2% surtax is computed on taxable income and is not subject to the 3% surtax.

For tax purposes, the term ''corporation'' broadly covers stock companies, limited partnerships, general partnerships, joint stock companies, and joint enterprises. All of these taxpayers are subject to the above income tax rates.

2. Local Income Taxes

There are no municipal or provincial income taxes for corporations in the Dominican Republic.

3. Capital Gains Taxes

In principle, capital gains are not subject to income tax, except that those derived from the sale of assets used in the business are part of ordinary taxable income.

4. Branch Profits Taxes

Profits of branches of foreign corporations are subject to the corporate income tax. Net profits of branches are subject also to a 20% remittance tax.

5. Foreign Tax Reliefs

Since income from foreign sources is not taxed in the Dominican Republic, there is no relief to corporations for taxes paid in territories outside the Dominican Republic.

6. Classification of Corporations

There are no differences in the tax treatment of corporations. Both domestic and foreign corporations are subject to the income taxes indicated above.

7. Payment of Taxes

Corporations are required to make two prepayments towards their annual tax liabilities and to pay the balance upon filing their income tax returns. The prepayments fall due on the seventh and eleventh months following the closing date, and are equivalent to 80% (40% each) of the previous year's income tax liability. The balance should be paid within a period of 120 days after the closing date, except for partnerships for which the period is limited to 60 days.

INCOME TAXES ON INDIVIDUALS

9. Rates

The rates of individual income tax on the five categories of taxable income are:

Leasehold income and property leasing	6%
Investment income	12%
Business, industrial, mining, agriculture, livestock, and forestry income	8%
Income from professions and other personal services	4%
Income of employees (subject to withholding)	2%

A "complementary" tax is also imposed on the total income of individuals at graduated rates, after deducting allowable personal and family expenses as shown in the following table:

| Taxable Income | | Tax on | Percentage |
Over	Not Over	Lower Amount	on Excess
RD$ 0	RD$ 2,000	RD$ 0	3%
2,000	4,000	60	5
4,000	6,000	160	7
6,000	8,000	300	9
8,000	12,000	480	12
12,000	16,000	960	15
16,000	20,000	1,560	18
20,000	25,000	2,280	25
25,000	30,000	3,530	30
30,000	40,000	5,030	35
40,000	100,000	8,530	40
100,000	200,000	32,530	45
200,000	400,000	77,530	50
400,000	600,000	177,530	55
600,000	900,000	287,530	60
900,000		467,530	70

In addition, a surtax of 3% of the related tax is payable with regard to the payment of all income taxes, including income tax withheld at the source and the complementary tax. Finally, an additional tax of 1% is imposed on net taxable income of RD$6,000 or more.

10. Local Income Taxes

There are no municipal or provincial income taxes for individuals in the Dominican Republic.

11. Capital Gains Taxes

Capital gains are not subject to income tax, except when the individual is regularly engaged in activities producing capital gains.

12. Foreign Tax Reliefs

Since income from foreign sources is not taxed in the Dominican Republic, there is no relief to individuals for tax paid in territories outside the country.

13. Tax Period

Individuals are taxed on a calendar-year basis. Tax returns must be filed no later than March 31 of the following year. Tax payment schedules are the same as those for corporations.

INCOME TAXES ON NONRESIDENTS

15. Liability to Tax

Nonresidents of the Dominican Republic are subject to tax on income derived from property situated or utilized in the Dominican Republic; or derived from any trade, industrial, agricultural, cattle, mining or similar activity carried on in the Dominican Republic. Income from services performed in the Dominican Republic as well as Dominican-source interest income and leasing payments are also subject to tax.

16. Rates

Corporations. Corporations doing business in the Dominican Republic having no permanent establishment in the country must pay tax at a 35% rate subject to withholding, as required by law No. 78-87 of November 1987. However, a only remittance tax of 20% (plus surtaxes noted in item 1) is imposed to those corporations that are beneficiaries of interest, dividends, royalties, and other income from investments and loans.

Individuals. Nonresidents' income from professions and other personal services and income of employees in the Dominican Republic are subject to the same income taxes as resident individuals, but personal expenses of these individuals and their families are specifically excluded. A nonresident is defined as a person that has not resided more than six months in the Dominican Republic during a calendar year.

A remittance tax exists for the following categories of income (complementary tax is not levied):

Income from rentals and leasing of urban real estate	15%
Income from rentals of rural real estate	50%
Interest, dividends, royalties, and other income from investments and loans	20%

18. Special Withholding Provisions

Remittance taxes must be withheld by the payor if the payee does not have at least an administrator or someone acting for the payee with power of attorney in the country.

Withholding of income tax is required on the income of persons temporarily in the Dominican Republic. No remittance tax is applicable.

OTHER SIGNIFICANT TAXES

21. Sales (Value Added)

A law imposing a 6% tax on transfers within the national territory and on imports of industrial goods became effective on November 24, 1983. Certain consumer goods, such as food and medicine, are not affected. Other goods taxed individually, such as beer and cigarettes, also are not affected by this tax, which is called a "Tax on Transfers of Industrialized Goods."

The scope of this tax was extended in 1985, 1986, and 1987 to include such services as telephone, telex, cable television, hotels, leasing operations, and car rentals.

22. Inheritance and Gift Taxes

The transfer of property by gift or at death is subject to a progressive tax, according to the amount transferred and the relationship of the beneficiary to the deceased or donor.

23. Taxes on Payrolls (Social Security)

National social insurance contributions are payable with respect to employed persons earning up to RD$466.00 per week; 2.5% is payable by the employee and 7% by the employer.

Instituto de Formacion Tecnico-Profesionan (INFOTEP). To finance technical and professional training of workers, employers must pay a monthly tax of 1% of the regular payroll. Employees contribute by payment of an annual tax of 0.5% of income derived from profit sharing and bonuses.

24. Taxes on Natural Resources

Mineral law No. 146, dated June 4, 1971, establishes that the right to explore, exploit or process mineral substances is originally acquired from the State through concessions or other contracts granted in conformity with such law. The State's taxation of the mining industry consists of:

☐ The annual mining patent.

☐ The royalty or minimum tax (5%) on the exportation of mineral substances in their natural state or in the form of concentrates of metaliferous minerals. This royalty on export may be credited against the payment of the income tax of the same fiscal year.

☐ Forty percent of the net profit each year, irrespective of the tax on the personal income of the owners or stockholders of the concessionary corporations.

Reduction or exoneration of taxes or duties apply to the importation of mining-metalurgical machinery and equipment, fuel (except gasoline), and other means of production required in the judgement of the Secretariat of State for Industry and Commerce.

25. Other Taxes

Import Duties. Custom duties together with a number of internal taxes are collected upon the introduction of goods into the country. Special incentives (e.g., exoneration of part of the corresponding duties) contemplated in various development incentive laws were revoked by the new customs duties law that went into effect pursuant to Decree No. 339-90 of September 12, 1990. Jointly with these customs duties, a selective tax on consumer goods was approved, pursuant to Decree No. 340-90 of September 12, 1990, which was further modified by Decree No. 222-91 of June 7, 1991. Since December 1983, ad-valorem import duties are applied by converting into RD$ the FOB price (in US $) of the imported goods at the current exchange rate established and reviewed periodically by government authorities (at present, minimum ad-valorem is RD$3.36 for US$1).

In addition, an "exchange commission" of 15% on FOB value of imports converted to RD$ using the prevailing exchange rate was established by Resolution of the Monetary Board in November, 1987, modified by the Tenth Resolution of December 13, 1990.

Tax on Dwellings.   An annual tax on the value of luxurious dwellings (RD$500,000 or more) and undeveloped urban land (regardless of its value) was imposed by Law 18-88 in February, 1988. Undeveloped urban land is considered to exist in cases where construction on the land covers less than 30% of its total area. The tax rate ranges from 1/4 to 1/2 of 1% of the value of the related property based on criteria established by the law.

COMPUTATION OF TAXABLE INCOME

26. Capital Gains

Only in exceptional cases are capital gains included in the determination of taxable income.

27. Depreciation and Depletion

For income tax purposes, depreciation deductions are allowed according to the nature of the particular assets and the depreciation rates established in Third Regulation on Income Tax Law. Accelerated depreciation is allowed only if special concessions are granted. Deductions resulting from mining depletion are not permitted. The amount and percentages of amortization of previous exploration expenses must be approved by the Secretariat of State for Industry and Commerce in conjunction with the Central Bank at the time the concession or contract is executed.

28. Treatment of Dividends

There is a 12% withholding tax on dividends paid to individuals, which is credited against the complementary tax. Dividends received by a Dominican corporation from another Dominican corporation also are taxed at a 12% rate, subject to withholding, as required by Decree No. 460-89 of November 1989. Dividends paid to a nonresident shareholder are subject to withholding tax of 20%. Stock dividends are not subject to tax.

Additional taxes based on the regular income tax and the taxable income also are applied (see items 1 and 9).

29. Loss Carryovers

Corporate losses may be carried forward for three years.

30. Transactions between Related Parties

Transactions between related parties, particularly inventory transfers, may be adjusted to the price that would have prevailed on an arm's-length transaction.

31. Consolidation of Income

An ''economic unit'' exists when a person or enterprise or group of persons conducts its business through companies taxable in Category 3 and their operations are related and are controlled or financed by those companies. This does not apply to entities that establish new industrial entities. Where such an economic unit exists, as defined by income tax law, the income of the various enterprises shall be combined in a single income tax return.

32. Tax Periods

Each corporation may determine its own fiscal period.

33. Other Matters

Expenses Incurred Abroad.   No deductions are allowed for wages or remuneration paid to directors or to other management or administrative authorities acting outside the country, nor can fees and remuneration paid for technical, financial or any other kind of services rendered abroad be deducted from taxable income.

RELATED CONSIDERATIONS

34. Incentives and Grants

Laws on investment protection and incentives have been enacted in order to promote investment in areas such as:

□   Industry and tourism.
□   Agriculture and livestock.
□   National merchant marine.
□   Mortgage banks.
□   Finance companies engaged in economic development activities.
□   Export of nontraditional products.
□   Agroindustry.

☐   Forestry.

☐   Frontier development.

☐   Privatization of electric energy.

☐   Free-zone development.

Benefits include partial or total tax exemption on income derived from some of those activities, tax-exempt reinvestment of profits made by natural or legal persons, and exoneration from import duties.

Law No. 71-86-30 of December 22, 1987 limited to 50% of net taxable income the exemptions for reinvestment of earnings established under the various incentive laws.

35. Exchange Controls

The inflow and outflow of foreign exchange must be conducted through the Central Bank in accordance with Law No. 251, which regulates the international transfer of funds. The RD$ is legally at par with the U.S. dollar, but pursuant to a Monetary Board resolution in April 1984, the Central Bank limited the conversion of foreign exchange at the legal rate to payments for certain foreign operations.

In January 1985, the Monetary Board resolved that all foreign exchange transactions may be realized based on the exchange rate in effect in the currency market. Effective June 17, 1987, the currency exchange system was restructured in order to exercise more control on international operations, including the establishment of priorities on delivery of foreign exchange. Subsequently, the exchange system was subject to modifications revolving mainly around a greater or lesser control from the Central Bank over the international operations. Effective August 1, 1988, a new regime (Foreign Currency Reintegration System) was adopted, whereby all transactions are controlled by the Central Bank though commercial banks and the exchange rate for these transactions is set by the Central Bank using the supply and demand of dollars as the basis. This rate for each US$1 was RD$7.30 and RD$7.60 for sale and purchase, respectively. At April 1, 1990, these rates were set at RD$10.20 and RD$10.50, respectively.

Recently, a new exchange system went into effect, pursuant to the Seventeenth Resolution of the Monetary Board of January 21, 1991, with the following principal characteristics:

☐   Control by the Central Bank of all foreign exchange; and

☐   An official market rate to be reviewed in accordance with private market (bank market) reactions and fluctuations. The current official rate is RD$12.50 is equal to US$1.00.

36. Investment Restrictions on Nonresidents

Foreign capital investment is permitted and guaranteed in areas in which the foreign capital and technology are deemed important to the economic development of the country in accordance with Foreign Investment Law No. 861. Such law requires investors to apply for registration with the Central Bank with respect to direct foreign investment, new foreign investment and foreign reinvestment (as defined in the law). Registration grants investors the right to exchange local currency for freely convertible foreign exchange for transfers abroad equal to the value of the registered investment and the profits generated thereby (limited to 25% of the registered foreign investment).

SELECTION OF BUSINESS ENTITY BY NONRESIDENTS

A foreign investor can either form a Dominican subsidiary corporation or register a branch office of the foreign parent company. Dominican subsidiaries and branches are subject to the same income tax on corporations (see items 1, 4, 6, and 28).

EGYPT

INCOME TAXES ON CORPORATIONS

1. Rates

The tax on annual net profits is 42%, except for oil exploration and producing companies, where the rate is 42.55%, and industrial and export activities, where the rate is 34%. In all cases, profits less than LE. 18,000 per annum are subject to a 2% exemption. Several activities are tax-exempt (see item 34).

2. Local Income Taxes

None.

3. Capital Gains Taxes

Capital gains are treated as part of ordinary business income and are taxed accordingly.

4. Branch Profits Taxes

Branches of foreign corporations and entities operating in Egypt are taxed at 42% on their annual net profits earned in Egypt, except for oil exploration and production companies, which are taxed at 42.55% (see item 1).

5. Foreign Tax Reliefs

Branches of foreign banks and corporations and other entities operating in Egypt are liable only for corporate tax on the profits arising from carrying out their activities in Egypt. Consequently, relief for foreign taxes is not relevant. However, entities with a permanent establishment in Egypt are subject to corporate tax at 42% on net profits. Interest earned outside Egypt net of foreign taxes is subject to the 34% rate. (See item 1.)

Countries with double taxation agreements with Egypt (see item 19) are treated in accordance with the provisions of these agreements.

7. Payment of Taxes

Corporate tax based on audited financial statements must be paid within one month of the shareholders' annual meeting approving the accounts or within a month of the date in the company's articles on which the annual meeting must approve the accounts. Branches of foreign companies must submit their tax returns within six months of their financial year-end date. The payment of tax must be accompanied by:

- ☐ Audited tax declaration.
- ☐ A copy of the audited financial statements and several other schedules.
- ☐ An extract of the resolution at the annual meeting approving the profit distributions.

In addition, any board of directors' resolution relating to profit distributions must be sent to the Tax Administration within one month of the board meeting.

8. Other Matters

Workers Participation in Profits. Ten percent of the distributable profits of branches of foreign companies operating in Egypt and of the distributable profits of Egyptian corporations must be set aside for distribution to labor working for the branch or corporation, not to exceed annual payroll; however, there is no limit if the entity is subject to Investment Law 230.

Tax Cards. Every entity operating in Egypt must have a tax card issued by the Tax Administration as evidence of having a tax file, and must keep proper books of account (some in Arabic) as specified by law. Entities operating in Egypt may only deal with other entities in possession of a tax card which states that tax returns have been filed annually, and report to the Tax Administration on a quarterly basis all payments and contracts entered into with individuals or companies.

Tax Administration. Any business operating in Egypt must advise the Tax Administration of any payments made to any contractor or supplier of goods or services and of any contract entered into with any of the above, and must withhold the following percentages from all payments over LE.10, and pay the tax deducted quarterly to the Tax Administration for the account of such persons (rates subject to change):

Contracting and supplying	1%
Services	3%
Commissions (with certain exceptions)	10%
Professional fees over LE.499	15%
Professional fees less than LE.499	10%

Corporate entities, branches of foreign corporations and several other named enterprises that lease property or sell goods for the purpose of trading or manufacturing must add a percentage, ranging from 1% to 5%, to the amounts collected on account of the payee's tax liability.

Every entity starting or terminating operations in Egypt must advise the Tax Administration accordingly within one month of the start or termination of their activities.

INCOME TAXES ON INDIVIDUALS

9. Rates

Income tax is first levied on the various sources of individual income (see below), which is then subject to the general tax on income (also below), with credit being given against income for the taxes already suffered.

Tax on Salaries.   This tax is withheld at source, from payments to those working in Egypt for more than six months in any calendar year, and for foreigners working less than six months (see item 16). Payments include salaries, overtime, bonuses, fringe benefits, and allowances and all other payments and benefits. This tax is also levied on the first LE.5,000 of amounts paid to executive directors of corporations for executive duties, who own no more than a nominal share in the equity of the corporation (only four named persons can be subject to this tax for amounts over LE.5,000, see Tax on Movable Funds, below).

Annual incomes up to LE.3,840 are taxed at escalating rates and, thereafter, at 22%. In addition, salaries in excess of LE.18,000 per annum are subject to a levy of 2% on the excess ''to support the financial resources of the state.'' The following annual allowances are usually granted:

- [ ] Family allowance:
  —LE.720 for single persons.
  —LE.840 for married persons without children or a widower with children.
  —LE.960 for married persons with a child or children.
- [ ] Social insurance contributions (under certain conditions).
- [ ] Punitive and unpaid sick leave deductions.
- [ ] Life assurance and pension fund premiums not exceeding LE.1,000 or 15% of income, whichever is less.
- [ ] Productivity incentives with a maximum of LE.3,000 or the salary, whichever is less, and LE.240 hardship allowance (under certain conditions).
- [ ] Representation allowance with a maximum of LE.3,000 (under certain conditions). Productivity allowance and representation allowance and the hardship allowance may not exceed the lesser of LE.4,000 per annum or the basic salary.
- [ ] Amounts paid to the representatives of regional offices of foreign companies and establishments in Egypt are taxed only on the portion of their income attributable to their activities in Egypt.
- [ ] Accommodation allowances for foreign experts, provided their employment in Egypt is for a period of more than six months.

□ 10% of the total income (after certain allowances) as an allowance for earning the income.

Nontrading Professions Tax. The net profits and nontrading income from professions earned in Egypt are taxed at escalating rates from 18% on the first LE.1,000 to 30% on profits in excess of LE.4,500. (For special rates see item 16). In addition, a "levy to support the financial resources of the state" of 2% is levied on profits in excess of LE.18,000 per annum.

Allowable expenses include: social insurance payments, 10% of net profit earning fee allowance, life insurance premiums to the extent of the lesser of LE.1,000 or 15% of net profit, and certain donations.

Losses may normally be carried forward for five years. Certain allowances are deductible if not claimed elsewhere. Tax returns must be filed by March 31 of the following year, when the tax payment is due. Amounts paid to nonresident foreign professionals are subject to tax at a flat rate of 20%. Such amounts are not subject to any other tax. Individuals subject to this tax must file a wealth declaration with the Tax Administration at the beginning of the activity and every five years thereafter.

Tax on Movable Funds. This tax is usually withheld at source at the rate of 32%. Otherwise, it is due within 15 days of receipt of income. The tax is levied on:

□ Interest payments (except for certain interest paid by banks in Egypt).

□ Most income received by Egyptians or non-Egyptians normally resident in Egypt, from sources outside Egypt, net of foreign taxes.

□ Interest payments to nonresidents.

□ All amounts paid and benefits given to nonexecutive members of corporate boards.

□ Remunerations and allowances over LE.5,000 per annum paid and benefits given to executive members of corporate boards for executive duties that are in excess of amounts paid to other nonexecutive directors. The first LE.5,000 is subject to the Tax on Salaries (see above).

□ Representation allowances paid to chairmen and executive directors in excess of LE.3,000 per annum. In addition, payments in excess of LE.18,000 per annum to chairmen and members of the boards of directors of joint stock companies that are subject to the tax on movable funds will be subject to a 2% levy "to support the financial resources of the state."

Tax on Commercial and Industrial Profits. This tax is levied at rates escalating from 20% on the first LE.1,000 to 40% on profits over LE.13,500 on commissions, letting commercial and furnished premises or plant, selling assets, building or dealing in real estate, exploitation of natural resources, poultry farms, animal husbandry, and land reclamation. Industrial and export activities are taxed at rates escalating to 32%. In addition, a "levy to support the financial resources of the state" of 2% is levied on profits in excess of LE.18,000 per annum. The tax is on annual net profits after deducting expenses, particularly those stated in item 33. The family allowances noted for the Tax on Salaries are deductible if not claimed elsewhere. Individuals subject to this tax must file a wealth declaration with the Tax Administration every five years.

General Tax on Income. Income earned by individuals subject to any of the above taxes and dividends received constitute taxable income for purposes of the general tax on income. Taxes previously paid on such income are creditable and certain deductions are also allowed, including:

☐ Interest not deductible under a specific tax.

☐ Insurance premiums (the lesser of 15% of net income or LE.2,000, if not allowed under another specific tax).

☐ Specific investments to a maximum of LE.3,000 (this and the deduction for insurance premiums should not exceed LE.4,000).

☐ Pensions received.

☐ All donations to the Government and up to 7% of the net profits to specified charities in Egypt.

Fifty percent of dividends distributed by Law 159 joint stock companies registered with Stock Exchange are exempt from income tax if the dividends are received from Investment Law 230/1989 companies, provided that they do not exceed 10% of the original value of the shares following the expiration of the tax holiday. This exemption is doubled for shares of joint stock companies having at least 40% of their share capital offered for public subscription.

The first LE.2,000 is exempt. Thereafter, the tax rate escalates from 8% on the next LE.1,000 to 65% on incomes over LE.200,000.

Foreign technicians and experts, living and employed in Egypt, are exempt from the general tax on income on their income arising from sources outside Egypt, and on income subject to salary tax received from corporations registered under Investment Law 230 for 1989, including free zones if their work in Egypt is for a period of less than one year.

Individuals subject to this tax must file a wealth declaration with the Tax Administration every five years.

Taxable Income		Tax on	Percentage
Over	Not Over	Lower Amount	on Excess
LE. 30,000	LE. 35,000	LE. 5,020	26%
35,000	40,000	6,320	28
40,000	45,000	7,720	30
45,000	50,000	9,220	32

| Taxable Income | | Tax on | Percentage |
Over	Not Over	Lower Amount	on Excess
LE. 50,000	LE. 60,000	LE.10,820	35%
60,000	65,000	14,320	40
65,000	70,000	16,320	45
70,000	75,000	18,570	50
75,000	100,000	21,070	55
100,000	200,000	34,820	60
200,000		94,820	65

10. Local Income Taxes

None.

11. Capital Gains Taxes

Individuals are not subject to capital gains tax, except for sales of real estate or building sites within the boundaries of Egyptian cities. These are subject to tax at a flat rate of 5% of the total value and are not subject to the general tax on income.

12. Foreign Tax Reliefs

Dividends and interest received from abroad by Egyptian residents, net of foreign taxes paid, are subject to the tax on movable funds at 32% (see item 9). Citizens from countries having double tax agreements with Egypt (see item 19) are treated in accordance with the provisions of these agreements. In general, these agreements provide that persons resident in Egypt for less than six months in any year are taxed in their country of origin and not in Egypt (under certain conditions).

13. Tax Period

The fiscal period for individuals is the calendar year.

14. Other Matters

Sole Proprietors and Partners.   Sole traders and partnerships are taxed according to the type of income. The tax burdens falls on the individual partners.

INCOME TAXES ON NONRESIDENTS

15. Liability to Tax

Nonresidents are taxed only on income earned in Egypt.

16. Rates

The tax rates vary with the type of income and are withheld at source.

☐ A flat tax of 10%, not subject to any relief, is levied on amounts (including rent) paid to foreign experts working in Egypt provided their stay does not exceed six months in any one year.

☐ A flat rate of 20%, not subject to any relief, is withheld at source from amounts paid to foreign nonresidents carrying out professional work in Egypt; such amounts are not subject to any other tax.

☐ Countries with which Egypt has double tax avoidance treaties are usually subject to tax at 15% of the gross amounts of the royalties.

19. Tax Treaties

Egypt has double taxation agreements with the following countries:

Austria	Japan
Canada	Norway
Denmark	Romania
Finland	Sweden
France	Switzerland
Germany	Tunis
India	United Kingdom
Iraq	United States
Italy	

20. Other Matters

Director's Remuneration.   The remuneration of directors is taxable at 34%, which is the tax on movable funds, except for Egyptian directors of companies registered under Investment Laws 43 and 230, where only their remuneration is subject to half the tax for the duration of the company's tax holiday. If they are investors, the non-Egyptian directors are exempted from the tax on movable funds for the duration of the company's tax holiday, provided that the payments are out of profits; otherwise, their remunerations, allowances, and fees will be taxable. In addition, payments in excess of LE.18,000 per annum to chairmen and members of the boards of directors of joint stock companies that are subject to the tax on movable funds will be subject to a 2% levy "to support the financial resources of the state."

OTHER SIGNIFICANT TAXES

21. Sales (Value Added)

A sales (value added) tax replaces the consumption tax, effective May 3, 1992. The rates range from 5% to 30%. On certain products, a fixed amount is taxed; for example iron bars for construction are taxed at LE.5.00 per imported ton.

22. Inheritance and Gift Taxes

Estate duty on inheritance is taxed at various rates, depending on the degree of parenthood with the deceased. The rate escalates from 3% on the first LE.10,000 to 15% on an inheritance in excess of LE.30,000.

A recipient is not taxed on an inheritance of less than LE.15,000 to LE.30,000, depending on the degree of parenthood. If the heir is still a minor, the exemption is double these amounts.

23. Taxes on Payrolls (Social Security)

Monthly combined social insurance contributions of up to LE.625 are paid to a central organization. These contributions cover medical care, old age, industrial accidents, and unemployment. The first LE.250 of the basic wage are subject to a 40% contribution of which 14% is borne by the employee and 26% by the employer. The second LE.375 of any other remuneration is subject to a 35% contribution of which 11% is borne by the employee and 24% by the employer.

Contractors are subject to social security on the estimated labor element of the contract value.

Foreigners are not subject to social insurance regulations if their country of origin offers reciprocal treatment to Egyptians.

24. Taxes on Natural Resources

Net profits from the exploitation of natural resources are taxed at 40%, except oil exploration and producing companies which are taxed at 40.55% (see item 1). In addition, governmental concession levies and fees are payable.

25. Other Taxes

Stamp Duty.   Stamp duty is charged on contracts, payments from government agencies, bank loans, documents, receipts, cheques, certificates, bank accounts, salaries, advertisements, annually at 0.8% on the issued capital of corporate entities for recording stock on the stock exchange if there are frequent dealings, and at 0.12% for shares not recorded and not dealt with on the stock exchange, and insurance premiums. The duty ranges from 8 per thousand to 20%.

COMPUTATION OF TAXABLE INCOME

26. Capital Gains

Capital gains are treated as ordinary business profits and are taxed accordingly. In some cases, where assets are replaced, the tax paid on profits realized from the sale of the assets may be recovered within three years.

27. Depreciation and Depletion

Depreciation is computed on the straight-line method and the rates are negotiated with the Tax Administration. The rates are based on the different types of assets and the number of hours worked. The following rates are common:

Buildings	2%– 5%
Furniture and fixtures	6%–15%
Plant and machinery	10%–15%
Office and accounting machines	12.5%–20%
Motor vehicles	20%–25%

The above allowances are for tax purposes only and replace the depreciation provided in the accounts. An additional allowance of 25% of the cost of new plant is given in the year production starts, which affects the cost basis of the assets for purposes of future depreciation.

28. Treatment of Dividends

There is no withholding tax; dividends are paid either out of corporate profits taxes at 40% (see item 1) or out of exempt profits (see item 34). Dividends paid to individuals, whether resident or not, are subject only to the general tax on income which is payable by the recipient at rates escalating from 8% on the first LE.1,000, after deducting allowances and the first LE.2,000, to 65% on incomes over LE.200,000 (see item 9).

Dividends net of foreign tax received by individuals from abroad are subject to tax on movable funds at 32%.

Ninety percent of dividends received by corporate entities in Egypt are deducted from their taxable profits. Dividends received from abroad are subject to the tax on movable funds at 32%, after allowing for foreign taxes as a deduction from income.

29. Loss Carryovers

Corporate losses may be carried forward for a maximum of five years; individuals may also carry forward losses for five years; provided they are not offset against profits from other sources.

30. Transactions between Related Parties

Revenue transactions are treated as ordinary transactions, except that transactions between a man and wife and a father and minor children are treated as one party.

Capital transactions are treated as ordinary transactions except that gifts or donations to individuals are considered as part of the benefactor's income for five years.

31. Consolidation of Income

Specific taxes are levied on each source of income, as far as individuals are concerned, which is followed by a general tax on income. Related corporations may not file consolidated tax returns.

32. Tax Periods

The calendar year ending December 31st is the fiscal period, unless otherwise specified in the company's articles. Special provisions exist for new businesses and for winding up.

33. Other Matters

Other Deductible Items. In addition to normal expenses, the following may be allowed as expenses for tax purposes:

☐ Amounts in lieu of rent for property owned by the establishment and used for its business.

☐ 25% of the cost of new machinery used in its business.

☐ Taxes paid other than commercial and industrial tax.

☐ All donations to government agencies and donations to approved agencies within 7% of the annual net profit.

☐ Provisions not exceeding 5% of the annual net profit.

☐ Amounts set aside for employee pension or welfare funds, not exceeding 20% of the total payroll.

☐ 90% of profits and dividends received from investments, agricultural land, and other real estate in Egypt.

RELATED CONSIDERATIONS

34. Incentives and Grants

Tax and other benefits are available for the following:

☐ Approved projects registered under Investment Law 230/1989 are exempt from corporate tax normally for five years from the year following the start of production or activities. A five-year tax holiday is granted for any approved expansion of activities, and a five-year tax holiday applies for any increase in funds used to rectify the financial structure of a project; the last exemption is valid until July 20, 1992.

☐ Free-zone companies under Law 230/1989 are exempt from corporate tax. A charge of 1% on all commodities entering or exiting the free-zone is levied. If there are no commodities entering or exiting, a charge of 1% is levied on the free-zone company's revenue.

☐ American entities operating in Egypt and financed by USAID normally are exempt from corporate tax, customs duties, and personal tax on U.S. citizens.

☐ Certain government agencies, if allowed by their incorporation charter, may exempt expatriates from taxes and sometimes agree to the insertion of a tax reimbursement clause in contracts with foreign corporations.

☐ Industrial projects set up after 1981 employing over 50 workers are tax-exempt for five years.

☐ Projects set up in new community areas (e.g., Tenth of Ramadan) are tax-exempt for ten years.

☐ Approved projects relating to the economic development plans for five years. This does not extend to workers participation in the profits (see item 8) nor to social security taxes (see item 23).

The profits of the following activities are tax-exempt:

☐ Land reclamation and cultivation corporations if formed and producing continue to be exempted for a period of ten years, starting with the first year in which the land was considered to be productive. New projects and those not currently productive are tax exempt for ten years.

☐ Poultry farming, animal husbandry, and fisheries for three to ten years.

☐ Honey producers.

☐ Tourism activities subject to Law 1/1973 for five years.

The tax law also provides the following tax exemptions and benefits for corporations:

☐ Amounts in lieu of rent for property owned by the corporation and used for its business.

☐ Amortization of depleting assets.

☐ An amount equal to the Central Bank of Egypt's declared interest rate calculated on the paid up capital of listed private or public corporations under certain conditions.

☐ Profits realized on amalgamations under certain conditions.

☐ Profits or dividends received by a corporation from a corporate entity in which it has participated in its equity on formation.

☐ Dividends paid by investment corporations employing at least 90% of their equity and loans in investments.

☐ All entities exempt from taxes in Egypt must present their books of accounts and records if so requested by the Tax Administration.

☐ 25% of the cost of new machinery.

☐ Taxes paid other than corporate tax.

☐ 90% of profits and dividends received from investments, agricultural land, bank interest, and other real estate in Egypt.

☐ Remuneration paid to and benefits given to directors.

☐ Profits declared and payable to employees.

☐ Provisions not exceeding 5% of the annual net profit.

☐ All donations to government agencies and approved agencies within 7% of the annual net profit.

35. Exchange Controls

Any individual or corporation may freely open and operate a bank account in foreign currencies. Dealing in foreign bank notes is not allowed.

36. Investment Restrictions on Nonresidents

None.

SELECTION OF BUSINESS ENTITY BY NONRESIDENTS

Nonresidents not intending to trade or do business may operate as a representation office (on certain conditions). Such an office needs registration, must be financed by transfers from abroad, must not generate income, and is not subject to tax.

Nonresidents intending to trade or do business in Egypt could operate as a branch of a foreign corporation, which requires registration and a commercial agent and is subject to tax as set out in item 4.

Alternately, a nonresident may choose to incorporate in Egypt in which case Egyptian equity participation is expected and the incentives and grants noted in item 34 are made available.

SPECIMEN TAX COMPUTATION

Information:

☐ The following computations are for a married employee with children resident in Egypt and employed by a corporation registered under the Companies Law 159 of 1981.

Computation:

Salary Tax

Annual salary		LE.60,000.00
Less		
10% cost of earning income	LE.6,000.00	
Family relief	960.00	6,960.00
Taxable salary		LE.53,040.00
Salary tax due		LE.11,270.40

Levy to Support the Financial Resources of the State

Taxable salary	LE.53,040.00
Less	
Basic exempted amount	18,000.00
Taxable amount	LE.35,040.00
Levy due	LE. 700.80

General Income Tax

Annual salary		LE.60,000.00
Less		
10% cost of earning income	LE. 6,000.00	
Salary tax	11,270.40	
Family relief	960.00	
2% levy*	700.80	18,931.20
Taxable general income		LE.41,068.80
General income tax due		LE. 8,040.70

*Levy to support the financial resources of the State.

Net Income

Annual salary		LE.60,000.00
Less		
Salary tax	LE.11,270.40	
General income tax	8,040.70	
2% levy	700.80	LE.20,011.90
Net income		LE.39,988.10

FIJI

INCOME TAXES ON CORPORATIONS

1. Rates

Income tax is levied in Fiji in the forms of basic and normal taxes. Basic tax is payable by all entities at the flat rate of 2.5% on total income and normal tax in the case of resident corporations at 35% on the taxable income. As the total income and taxable income of corporations are the same, the two taxes combined effectively tax resident corporations at 37.5%.

2. Local Income Taxes

None.

3. Capital Gains Taxes

Land sales tax is levied on the profit arising from the sale of undeveloped land within twelve years of purchase at a graduated rate up to a maximum of 30% where the profit exceeds $9,500. There are no other capital gains taxes as such, but income tax is levied on a gain resulting from property acquired for the purpose of selling or otherwise disposing of the ownership.

4. Branch Profits Taxes

A branch of a foreign corporation is taxed on its Fiji sourced income at the combined rate of 47.5%, the same as for nonresident corporations.

5. Foreign Tax Reliefs

Fiji residents are taxable on their worldwide income although:

☐ Relief is given with respect to income derived from countries with which Fiji has entered into double taxation agreements (i.e., Australia, Japan, New Zealand, and United Kingdom) in accordance with those agreements. The double taxation agreement with Korea is being negotiated; it is not known when the agreement will be ratified.

☐ Income derived from a country with which Fiji has not entered into a double taxation agreement is exempt from tax in Fiji to the extent that the income is subject to income tax in that other country.

6. Classification of Corporations

Corporations are classified for tax purposes as resident or nonresident, and as private or public.

A resident corporation is defined as one which is incorporated in Fiji or, if not incorporated in Fiji, carries on business in Fiji and has either its central management and control in Fiji or its voting power controlled by resident shareholders. Resident corporations are liable for tax on incomes sourced both in and outside Fiji at 37.5% whereas nonresident corporations are taxed only on Fiji sourced income at the combined rate (basic plus normal taxes) of 47.5%.

Whether a corporation is public or private is of importance only where resident corporations are concerned. In broad terms, a public corporation is one whose shares are listed on a recognized stock exchange or is a subsidiary of such a listed corporation. Bonus shares may be issued paid up from a corporation's unappropriated profits exempt from tax, but only issues by public corporations (listed on the Suva Stock Exchange) will remain tax-free when the bonus shares are subsequently sold. In the case of issue by other corporations, proceeds of the sale representing the nominal value of those shares will be treated as dividend income.

The tax legislation also isolates corporations under the control of not more than five persons for whom the deemed distribution provisions apply. These corporations are required to distribute up to 60% of the after-tax trading income including dividends and 100% in the case of investment corporations or where the main business is the provision of personal services.

7. Payments of Taxes

Twenty-five percent of a corporation's estimated income tax liability for a fiscal year is payable on the last day of the fiscal year, and a further amount to make up the equivalent of 50% of the actual tax liability is due within three months of that date. The balance is due upon issue of a notice of assessment.

INCOME TAXES ON INDIVIDUALS

9. Rates

Income tax is payable at the rate of 2.5% on total income (basic tax) and on a graduated scale on taxable income (normal tax) of up to 40% (previously 50%), which rate applies to the income in excess of $40,000. Taxable income in the case of individuals is arrived at after deducting personal allowances (see below) from total income. The rates are the same for residents and nonresidents, but residents are allowed a rebate of $255 on the aggregate of basic and normal tax and nonresidents a proportion, based on Fiji-source income over world income. An employee's income includes the imputed value of benefits provided by the employer, such as housing, a motor vehicle, electricity, telephone, and school fees. The following is an abbreviated summary of the rates of normal tax payable on taxable income:

| Taxable Income | | Tax on | Percentage |
Over	Not Over	Lower Amount	on Excess
$ 0	$ 1,500	$ 0	4.0%
1,500	3,000	60	8.0
3,000	4,000	180	14.4
4,000	5,500	324	22.0
5,500	7,000	654	26.0
7,000	9,000	1,044	30.0
9,000	15,000	1,644	34.0
15,000	25,000	3,684	36.0
25,000	40,000	7,284	38.0
40,000		12,984	40.0

Salary and wages incomes are subject to tax deductions at source (P.A.Y.E.). Provisional tax is payable on all other income not subject to tax deductions at source based on the estimated tax payable thereon and is paid in three equal installments in April, August, and November.

These rates are likely to be revised on introduction of the proposed value-added tax (see item 21).

Deductions for Individuals. In calculating the chargeable income of resident individuals, the following personal allowances may be deducted from total income:

Wife (separate income less than $750)	$ 750
Legally separated couple with custody of one or more children	750
Children:	
1st, 2nd, and 3rd	200 per child
4th to a maximum of 5	130 per child
Widow(er):	
Widower with dependent child	750
Widow with dependent child	950
Widow	750
Dependent brother/sister	130
Other dependent relatives	100
*Education	800
Superannuation and/or life insurance	1,000 (maximum)
Age	750
Professional subscriptions	100
Interest on loan for own residence	500

*Not available for overseas students up to and including sixth form level.

For nonresident individuals, only the wife and widow(er) allowances are available and apportionment is required on the basis of Fiji income to total worldwide income.

10. Local Income Taxes

None.

11. Capital Gains Taxes

The information in item 3 also applies here.

12. Foreign Tax Reliefs

See item 5.

13. Tax Period

Fiji's tax year is the calendar year ending December 31. Partnerships and businesses may adopt a fiscal year other than a calendar year by applying to the Revenue Authorities. Where the fiscal year is accepted as other than December 31, income for the year is taxed in the calendar year in which more than half of the fiscal year falls.

INCOME TAXES ON NONRESIDENTS

15. Liability to Tax

All Fiji-source income derived by residents of treaty and nontreaty countries is subject to Fiji income tax. The only exception is industrial or commercial profits derived by residents of countries with which Fiji has double tax agreements and these are liable to income tax only if derived through a permanent establishment in Fiji.

Dividends, royalties, know-how/management fees, and film hire or purchase payments are subject to withholding tax deductions at source (see item 17), which amounts offset the final tax payable. Only in the case of dividends is the withholding tax a final tax.

16. Rates

Most nonresident corporations pay tax at the combined rate of 47.5% (basic tax 2.5% and normal tax 45%). The only exceptions are certain insurance and shipping corporations which pay normal tax at lower rates.

The rates of tax applicable to nonresident individuals are the same as for resident individuals (see item 9).

17. Withholding Tax Rates

Rates of withholding tax are virtually the same for both treaty and nontreaty countries, except for dividends, interest, and royalties. The tax is payable on outward remittances or when amounts are credited.

	Rates
Dividends	
Nontreaty countries	30%
Treaty countries	15/20
Interest	
Nontreaty countries	15
Treaty countries	10
Royalties	
Nontreaty countries	25
Treaty countries	15
Know-how payments and management fees (on profit element only)	15
Film hire or purchase	15
Rents premiums, franchise fees, license fees	
Nontreaty countries	25
Treaty countries	15

18. Special Withholding Provisions

Exemptions from the interest withholding tax are allowable in some instances, including interest accruing from the Government, any local authority, or statutory corporation, interest required to be paid in Fiji to a nonresident having a permanent place of business in Fiji, interest in respect of agreements entered into on or before the 30th November 1973 or where such interest arises from a loan made for the economic development of Fiji.

Contract payments to nonresidents in respect of work to be carried out in Fiji are liable for up to a 15% deduction at source as payment of provisional tax.

20. Other Matters

Sale of Land.   Nonresidents who engage in the sale of any land in Fiji are deemed to be carrying on business in Fiji and any profits arising therefrom will be treated as income and taxed at rates applicable to nonresident individuals or corporations, as the case may be.

OTHER SIGNIFICANT TAXES

21. Sales (Value Added)

Introduction of a value-added tax on goods and services is proposed from July 1, 1992 at the probable rate of 10%. VAT will replace the customs duty, excise duty (presently levied at ad valorem rates on the sale of specified goods manufactured in Fiji and not exported), hotel turnover tax, and miscellaneous services turnover tax.

22. Inheritance and Gift Taxes

No estate or gift duty is payable in Fiji.

23. Taxes on Payrolls (Social Security)

Fiji has a national provident fund scheme (Social Security) to which all employers are required to contribute a minimum of 7% of their employees' salary, except for expatriate employees who are already contributing to an existing superannuation scheme. The same contribution is due from employees. A levy of 1% of the total payroll is payable to the Fiji National Training Council.

24. Taxes on Natural Resources

Fiji imposes a tax in the form of a royalty on timber, mineral, and oil recovered from a licensed area. The royalty on all petroleum recovered is between 10% to 12¹/₂%. The rate for timber varies according to species and location.

25. Other Taxes

Land and Property. An annual tax is imposed based on land owned or leased within urban district boundaries.

Stamp Tax. Fiji imposes duties on documents. Many of these are at ad valorem rates.

Land Sales Tax. See item 3.

Dividends Tax. A 5% dividend tax is required to be deducted at source and paid to the Inland Revenue on all dividends paid to resident individuals.

Hotel Turnover Tax. Tax is levied at the rate of 10% on the turnover of a hotel. Turnover is defined as amounts received or receivable for accommodation, refreshment, and all other charges to guests. Hotel guests are liable for the tax, which is collected by the hotel proprietor and paid to the Inland Revenue. However, see item 21.

Miscellaneous Services Turnover Tax. A tax of 10% is imposed on expenditures for bar (cash) sales, food and beverages in hotels and restaurants, cover charges to nightclubs, videotape rentals, rental cars, betting, live entertainment, overseas sea and air tickets, commercial advertising, certain liquor sales, recreational yacht charters, and lottery tickets. However, see item 21.

COMPUTATION OF TAXABLE INCOME

26. Capital Gains

Taxable capital gains are calculated on the excess of selling price over cost. In the case of undeveloped land, an adjustment for cost in respect of interest at 5% on the purchase price compounded from the time of purchase is allowable together with all other expenses incurred in respect to the land.

27. Depreciation and Depletion

Buildings, Plant, and Equipment. An initial allowance of 10% for buildings and 30% for plant and equipment is given in the year the expenditure is incurred. The allowance is not available to buildings not newly constructed or where used only for residential purposes and most light motor vehicles not used in the goods or passenger transport industry.

The annual allowance is given at specified rates which begin in the year the asset is first used for the production of income. In the case of buildings, the allowance is applied to the prime cost (total cost of construction excluding the cost of land) and, for plant and equipment, on cost less the initial allowance and any balancing charge calculated on the straight-line basis.

Agricultural Improvements. Capital expenditures incurred in improving agricultural land may be written off in full in the year incurred or spread over five years commencing with the year incurred.

Mining. All expenditures incurred in prospecting, including the cost of acquisition of any mining lease or tenement, are deductible either in the year incurred or over a number of years as directed by the Taxation Commissioner.

Capital mining expenditures may be written off over any five out of eight years commencing either in the year incurred or the immediately following year.

28. Treatment of Dividends

Dividends received by resident individuals are included in total income, however a deduction of between 100% and 33.33% in respect of the dividends is allowable—depending on the individual's total income including dividends—commencing at 100% where the total income does not exceed $7,200 and reduced to a minimum of 33.33% where total income exceeds $9,600.

Dividends received by a resident corporation from another resident corporation are treated as exempt income.

29. Loss Carryovers

Losses incurred in any trade or business may be offset against income from other sources for the same year. Any amount unrelieved may be carried forward and set off against total income for the next six years in succession provided there is continuity of ownership and trade. Losses in agricultural or other pastoral pursuits may be carried forward indefinitely.

Exemption from the six year carryover period and the same shareholding rule may be granted where the same operations are likely to be continued and these are considered necessary for the economic development of Fiji.

In respect of corporations or persons also entitled to an investment allowance under the Hotels Aid Act (see item 35), the investment allowance must in the first instance be exhausted against any taxable income within a five-year period after the year in which trading commenced. If the investment allowance has not been exhausted within this five-year period, any losses accumulated during this period can be carried forward for another five years.

30. Transactions between Related Parties

The tax laws provide that in a transfer of fixed assets between related parties, no additional claims by way of depreciation or loss on disposal can arise as a result of the transaction.

Other provisions give the Authorities discretion to make adjustments over certain transactions, mainly transfers of stock, remuneration for services rendered and gratuity payments to ensure as far as possible that an arm's-length position prevails.

31. Consolidation of Income

There is no provision for group consolidation of income of companies for tax purposes; however, losses incurred by a company engaged in specified agricultural pursuits for which a tax-free concession period has been granted may offset the losses incurred during the concession period against profits of the holding company or an associate company.

A husband and wife will be assessed on their combined income unless the wife is in receipt of independent personal exertion income, including income she has derived from inheritance (e.g., estate income), her own savings (e.g., bank interest), or assets acquired from her own earnings (e.g., rental income), in which case she can elect to be separately assessed on such income.

32. Tax Periods

See item 13.

33. Other Matters

The following matters in the 1990 budget became effective January 1, 1990:

☐ The income threshold free from tax is raised to $3,000 from $2,500.

☐ Any pension received by an individual is not subject to the basic and normal taxes to the extent of $3,000.

□ An averge 20% reduction of normal tax rates for individuals, estates of deceased persons, trusts, and settlements.

□ An increase in the nonresident dividend withholding tax from 15% to 30% on dividends paid to nontreaty countries.

RELATED CONSIDERATIONS

34. Incentives and Grants

Export Incentives. The Minister of Finance may specify any trade or product to be an approved trade and product qualifying for an export incentive. To be approved, the Minister of Finance must be satisfied that the trade or product is expedient for the economic development of Fiji.

Depending on the local content in the product's manufacturing cost, the incentive is the following percentage rebate of the tax payable on the export profit.

Local Content of Product		Percentage of Tax on Export Profit
Over	Not Over	
0%	30%	0%
30	39	50
40	49	75
50		100

The incentive is for eight years commencing with the fiscal year in which it is first granted.

Export Promotion Incentive. An export promotion incentive provides a tax deduction equal to 150% of the amount of any expenditure approved by the Fiji Trade and Investment Board incurred towards the promotion and marketing of export goods eligible for export incentives.

Hotels Aid. Assistance is given to companies and individuals who invest in the building of new hotels in Fiji. The assistance given under the Hotels Aid Act takes the form of an investment allowance, whereby a deduction from the total chargeable income, for income tax purposes, of 55% of the total capital expenditure (less the cost of any land for the project) can be claimed. This allowance can be carried forward indefinitely.

A recent amendment, applying retroactively to January 1, 1989, allows deductions on the costs of renovations and refurbishments.

Agriculture. The Government provides the following incentives to encourage individuals and companies to engage in agriculture. For individuals, farming income (defined as income from coconut growing, rice farming, and dairy or goat farming) will be wholly exempt from normal tax at the average rate of normal tax applicable to the individual for the year of assessment until December 31, 1990. Income from other farming activities (including fishing, forestry, and cane farming) will also be exempt until December 31, 1990.

Companies in specified agricultural pursuits may apply for a special concession. If granted, the company will enjoy a tax-free period of any five out of the 10 years commencing with the year commercial production begins.

Companies in cane farming will be treated the same as individuals.

Mining and Film Making. The Government is giving priority to these industries, and tax-free periods or lower tax rates may be granted on application.

Energy. An investment allowance of up to 40% or depreciation at accelerated rates may be obtained for expenditures on plant and machinery whose energy source is an alternative to electricity or fuel oil or its derivatives, or which generates energy from a source indigenous to and produced in Fiji.

Cyclone Reserve. Exemption is granted from basic tax and normal tax on amounts deposited in a bank account approved by the Commissioner for the purpose of providing a reserve against destruction of or damage to a building situated in Fiji caused by windstorm, tidal wave, landslide, or a similar catastrophe. The exemption is granted only in the year of deposit and is restricted to:

Buildings for commercial, individual, or agricultural purposes	1.5% of replacement cost
Buildings for residential purposes	The lesser of $500 or 1.5% of replacement cost

Amounts withdrawn, together with interest, if not applied towards the repairs of a damaged building will be taxable.

Accelerated Depreciation. 20% of write-off of expenditure in five out of eight years is available as an alternative to initial and ordinary depreciation, in respect of:

☐ Buildings, other than for hotels, effected between July 1, 1990 and March 31, 1992 for commercial, industrial, or agricultural purposes. Application for this concession is required to be furnished to the Commissioner on or before October 31, 1991.

Expenditure is limited to the lesser of the cost (excluding cost of land) or $2,000,000. Further erection of buildings could also qualify provided they are erected not less than 16 kilometers away by the most direct road route.

☐ Buildings, plant, and machinery for which a company proposes to incur substantial expenditure could also qualify provided the Minister is satisfied that it is expedient for the economic development of Fiji.

Purchase price of any land or any expenditure incurred on site preparation, or the purchase of any existing business premises or equipment or of any goodwill will not qualify.

35. Exchange Controls

All transactions involving foreign exchange are under the control of the Reserve Bank of Fiji. Strict limits are set on Fiji residents for the outward remittance of funds for nonbusiness purposes or investment; however, remittances in payment of goods, services, interest, and dividends or the repatriation of capital and earnings are generally allowable.

36. Investment Restrictions on Nonresidents

Approval from the Government is required before a nonresident can set up a trade or business in Fiji. In general, the Government is trying to attract foreign investment into Fiji and approval will only be refused where there is sufficient local expertise and capital to set up such a trade or business, such as the retail trade in which native Fijians hold less than 50% of the equity.

Restrictions are imposed on local borrowing where businesses are controlled by nonresidents. The ratio of locally borrowed funds to total loan funds employed in Fiji must not be greater than the ratio that locally held equity bears to total equity.

37. Other Matters

Tax-Free Zones/Tax-Free Factories. The Government has implemented the establishment of Tax-Free Zones and Tax-Free Factories (TFZ/TFF) covering enterprises involved in manufacturing, mixing, blending, packaging, assembling, and exporting professional services as approved by the Minister.

The criteria for qualifying for TFZ/TFF is that 95% of an enterprise's output/ activities is exported, re-exported, or supplied to an enterprise with a TFF designation. No minimum value added criteria applies.

The incentives available to TFF include:

☐ Total waiver from licencing controls and customs duty of all imports whether of a capital nature or for production.

☐ Exemption from excise duty.

☐ Remission of excise and customs duties on purchases.

☐ Exemption from corporate income tax for 13 years.

☐ Exemption from withholding tax on interest, dividends, and royalties paid or credited.

☐ Five percent final dividend tax for resident shareholders.

SELECTION OF BUSINESS ENTITY BY NONRESIDENTS

Nonresidents can operate in Fiji either as a branch or through a locally formed subsidiary.

A branch pays tax on Fiji sourced income at the nonresident rate of 47.5%. No further tax is payable on remittance of branch profits. A locally formed subsidiary pays tax at 37.5% and a further 15%/30% dividend withholding tax is payable when dividends are paid or credited.

While it would appear that a branch has a tax rate advantage over a locally formed subsidiary, there is no requirement for a subsidiary of a public corporation to declare dividends. The subsidiary is therefore able to retain profits in the business in addition to delaying payment of the dividend withholding tax.

FINLAND

INCOME TAXES ON CORPORATIONS

1. Rates

Finnish corporations are taxable on their global income (unlimited tax liability). The state income tax is levied at a flat rate of 23%. A lower rate is levied on taxable income up to FIM 100,000. The determination of taxable income is based on the Business Income Tax Act of 1968, under which the expenses of acquiring and maintaining income are deductible. Taxes are collected through a prepayment system during the tax year and tax returns are filed during the following year (assessment year). See item 2 for further information on effective tax rates.

2. Local Income Taxes

Municipalities levy income tax at a flat rate in each community, with an average rate of about 16%. Church tax is levied at a rate of approximately 1%, varying in different municipalities. Thus, the total tax maximum rate for a corporation is about 40%.

3. Capital Gains Taxes

According to the Business Income Tax Act, in principle all capital gains are taxed as ordinary income. However, gains on the sale of real estate and securities classified as fixed assets are taxed only to a limited extent if held for more than 10 and 5 years, respectively. Sixty percent of the sales proceeds for such real estate and securities is considered to be taxable income. From this amount the total book value of the asset sold may be deducted. If the book value of the asset sold is at least 60% of the selling price, no taxable capital gain is realized.

4. Branch Profits Taxes

A branch of a foreign corporation is taxed on branch profits as though it were a resident corporation (see item 16).

5. Foreign Tax Reliefs

Treaties between Finland and foreign countries on the avoidance of double taxation limit Finland's right of taxation. These treaties are based either on the exemption method or on the credit method. In the case of nontreaty countries, a unilateral tax credit is allowed for State income tax purposes.

6. Classification of Corporations

The main forms of incorporation are general partnership, limited partnership, limited liability company, and economic societies (e.g., cooperatives). The limited liability company is the most common form of business establishment in Finland and also the most important for foreign-controlled enterprises.

INCOME TAXES ON INDIVIDUALS

9. Rates

Individuals may deduct expenses incurred in acquiring or maintaining taxable income, as well as some other deductions. The remainder is taxable income, which is charged on a progressive scale. The state tax rates for 1991 are:

Taxable Income		Tax on	Percentage
Over	Not Over	Lower Amount	on Excess
FIM 40,000	FIM 56,000	FIM 50	7%
56,000	70,000	1,170	17
70,000	98,000	3,550	21
98,000	154,000	9,430	27
154,000	275,000	24,550	33
275,000		64,480	39

10. Local Income Taxes

Individuals are also liable to local income tax at rates from 14% to 18.5% of the income, varying with the municipality. The church tax is generally 1%. Both taxes are levied on the same taxable income. Individuals also are liable to social security contributions (see item 23).

11. Capital Gains Taxes

Capital gains generally are taxed as ordinary income. Gain on the sale of immovable property held for more than ten years and gain on movable property (including shares) held for more than five years is only partially taxed. Forty percent of the aggregate of the otherwise untaxed gains from the sale of such immovable and movable property is taxed as ordinary income to the extent the aggregate exceeds FIM 220,000. When calculating the amount of capital gain, the purchase price or

50% of the sales price is deducted from the sales price of each asset sold. If the property is owned less than two years, the purchase price or 25% of the sales price is deductible. Thus, if the total annual sales price of assets held for over ten or five years, respectively, does not exceed FIM 440,000 for the calendar year, no tax on capital gains is applied.

Special provisions apply to the tax-exempt capital gains on the sale of a permanent home.

12. Foreign Tax Reliefs

Double tax relief is given for taxes incurred outside Finland under double taxation treaties and under unilateral provisions of Finnish law.

13. Tax Period

The tax period is the calendar year.

INCOME TAXES ON NONRESIDENTS

15. Liability to Tax

Nonresident persons and corporations domiciled in another country are taxable in Finland on income derived from Finnish sources, from assets situated in Finland, from businesses or professions carried on in Finland, on salaries and wages paid from Finnish sources, on dividends from Finnish corporations, and on royalties from Finnish entities. Interest paid to nonresidents is usually tax-exempt.

16. Rates

The income of a foreign branch in Finland is subject to State income tax of 25%, local income tax of 15% (in Helsinki), and 1% church tax.

A final tax of 35% is levied on the salary or wages and on pensions of nonresident individuals.

17. Withholding Tax Rates

Dividends and royalties paid by Finnish corporations to nonresidents are subject to withholding taxes as set out in the following table. Under domestic law, interest paid to nonresidents is tax-exempt in almost all cases.

Recipient	Dividends (1)	Royalties (2)
Nontreaty countries	25%	30%
Treaty countries		
Australia	15	10
Austria	10	0 (3)
Belgium	15, 10	0, 5
Brazil	25	10, 25

Recipient	Dividends (1)	Royalties (2)
Treaty countries		
Bulgaria	10%	0%, 5%
Canada	15	0, 15
China	10	10
Czechoslovakia	15, 5	0, 5
Denmark	15,0	0
Egypt	10	25
France	0	0
Germany	15, 10 (4)	0, 5
Greece	13	0, 10
Hungary	15, 5	0, 5
Iceland	15, 0	0
India	25, 15	30
Ireland	0	0
Israel	15, 5	10
Italy	15, 10	0, 5
Japan	15, 10	10
Korea	15, 10	10
Luxembourg (5)	15, 5	0, 5
Malaysia	15, 5	5
Malta	15, 5	0, 10
Morocco	15	10
Netherlands	15, 0	0
New Zealand	15	10
Norway	15, 0	0
Philippines	25, 15	15, 25
Poland	15, 5	0, 10
Portugal	15, 10	10
Romania	10	10
Singapore	15, 5	0, 10
Spain	15, 10	5
Sri Lanka	15	10
Sweden	15, 0	0
Switzerland	10, 5	0
Tanzania	20	20
Thailand	20, 15	15
United Kingdom	5	0
United States	15, 5	0, 5
U.S.S.R.	0	0
Yugoslavia	15, 5	10
Zambia	15, 5	5, 15

Notes:

(1) The relevant treaty should be consulted to see if the reduced rate for dividends applies in the case of payments to corporate recipients.

(2) In many treaties, a 5% withholding tax is levied on industrial royalties.

(3) A 10% withholding tax is levied when the recipient owns more than 50% of the paying company's shares.

(4) A 25% withholding tax is levied when the recipient is a "stiller Gesellschaft."

(5) The treaty is not applicable to Luxembourg holding companies.

OTHER SIGNIFICANT TAXES

21. Sales (Value Added)

In Finland, an all-stage sales tax system is applied, which has several features of the value-added tax. It differs from the value-added tax in the sense that persons liable to pay taxes are entitled to deduct only the sales tax charged on purchase prices of inventories and such fixed assets that are used at the most three years. Fixed assets used more than three years are deductible only if these assets are used in manufacturing goods, i.e., the machinery and equipment of industrial enterprises are deductible.

A sales tax is levied on nearly all goods. In general, services are not subject to the sales tax. However, leasing of goods and services in connection with the installation and repair of goods are taxable. In the case of imported goods, the tax is based on the customs value. The tax rate is 22% of the price excluding tax.

22. Inheritance and Gift Taxes

These taxes are levied at progressive rates that vary with the amount received by each beneficiary and the recipient's relationship to the decedent or donor.

23. Taxes on Payrolls (Social Security)

Both employers and employees contribute a percentage of gross salaries to social security, in accordance with law and agreement. The average rates for employers are:

Pensions	average 17.2%
Unemployment insurance	0.6%
Accident insurance	0.32%–10.87% (average 1.1%)
Social security	2.85%
Group life insurance	0.18%

The employee's contribution to social security is about 3.25% plus 1% of the income in excess of FIM 80,000. These contribution rates change frequently.

24. Taxes on Natural Resources

No special taxes are levied on the exploitation of natural resources.

25. Other Taxes

Capital Tax.   This tax is imposed annually on the net wealth of the preceding year-end. In computing net wealth, the taxpayer's liabilities are deducted from gross assets. Only individuals, partnerships, and nonresident companies (including branches of foreign companies) are liable to this tax. The 1990 rates for individuals are as follows:

Amount of Property Over	Tax on Lower Amount	Percentage on Excess
FIM 1,100,000	FIM 500	0.9%

Nonresident companies, including branches of foreign companies, are liable to an annual tax of 1% on all property in Finland.

Excise Duties.   The main excise duties are those on liquid fuels and tobacco. In addition, excise tax is payable on electricity, sweets, beer, alcohol, certain foodstuffs, fertilizers, margarine, mineral water, soft drinks and sugar products.

Indirect Taxes.   A special tax is levied on cars and motorcycles. Stamp duty is payable on certain documents, trade register notifications, and transfers of certain assets.

COMPUTATION OF TAXABLE INCOME

26. Capital Gains

The capital gain is the difference between the sales price and any portion of the original cost not already depreciated.

27. Depreciation and Depletion

Machinery and Equipment.   Acquisition costs of machinery and equipment must be written off on the declining balance method. The maximum amount of depreciation is 30%. A corporation may use a lower rate.

Buildings and Other Construction.   Buildings and other construction are depreciated on the declining balance method at maximum rates of 5% to 20%. Special temporary rules on accelerated depreciation and free depreciation are applied in certain areas of Finland.

28. Treatment of Dividends

In early 1990, a new imputation system came into force. According to this system, when a Finnish company pays a dividends, the company pays tax, which is at least two-thirds of the dividends paid. The tax is credited against the shareholder's tax liability. Under this system, it is assumed that the company is liable to tax at the same rate as the tax credit attached to the dividend. If the distributing company has not paid at the rate of 40%, a supplementary tax is payable. If the receiving company pays a lower tax, it receives a refund (for example if it is in a loss position).

Tax credit is not given to nonresident shareholders until existing tax treaties are amended to allow shareholders who are resident in tax treaty countries to claim the tax credit. A tax credit will be given only on a reciprocal basis.

29. Loss Carryovers

A loss sustained in any income year may be carried forward and deducted from taxable income during any of the next five years. Losses arising in the first five years of a new business are deductible until the end of the tenth year of business. When over 50% of the ownership of shares changes, previous losses may no longer be carried forward.

30. Transactions between Related Parties

Finnish tax rules state that arm's-length principles should be applied to transactions between related parties. In practice, the burden of proof is on the company.

31. Consolidation of Income

There is no provision for the filing of consolidated returns by related corporations. A group subsidy may be given by one domestic company to another domestic company belonging to the same group. At least 90% ownership is required. The group subsidy is deductible for the company giving the subsidy and is taxable income for the recipient company. The provisions are applicable for state and municipal income tax purposes.

32. Tax Periods

The basis period for computing the liability to corporation tax is the company's own accounting period.

33. Other Matters

Reserves. For Finnish tax purposes, a corporation is allowed to claim various tax deductions, principally by charging income for adjustments to untaxed reserves and accumulating these charges in a balance sheet account "Reserves." The major reserves are the following:

☐ Inventory Reserve. The maximum inventory reserve that may be deducted is 25% of year-end inventory, after excluding all obsolete or unsaleable goods. If the inventories include securities, other than shares in housing companies or comparable real estate companies, then the maximum amount of inventory reserve is 10%.

☐ Operating Reserve. The maximum appropriation that may be made to the operating reserve is 30% of wage and salary payments during the previous 12 months.

☐ Reserve for Future Investments. Corporations are permitted to appropriate to this reserve 20% of profits for the financial period before the transfer to the reserve and before the deduction of direct taxes. The minimum investment reserve is FIM 30,000. Fifty percent of this appropriation must be deposited in an interest-bearing, restricted account with the Bank of Finland. Deposits can be withdrawn, when the investment reserve has been used, or will be used, for approved purposes during the fiscal year. The reserve may be used for such purposes as the construction of buildings used in the business, acquisition of machinery or equipment, product development, training, and promotion of exports.

RELATED CONSIDERATIONS

34. Incentives and Grants

Private investment in certain development areas is promoted by several financial incentives. These may consist of direct subsidies (loans or grants) as well as tax reliefs. Grants and loans may be obtained for the following main purposes: investments, employment, exporting, product development, and others.

35. Exchange Controls

The foreign exchange control system is administered by the Bank of Finland. It is permitted to make direct foreign investments in Finland without the permission of the Bank of Finland, with the exceptions of direct investments from countries with which Finland maintains payment agreements and direct investments in the financial and insurance sector. A foreign company belonging to a group may grant credit in the form of a direct investment to a Finnish subsidiary or associate.

Direct investments from countries with which Finland maintains payment agreements are subject to the permission of the Bank of Finland. Applications must be made in writing and submitted even when no capital is transferred.

No prior permit from the Bank of Finland is required for the remittance of dividends, interest, and royalties. Relevant documents are presented to the commercial currency bank that transfers the payment, which then notifies the Bank of Finland. A permit from the Bank of Finland is required for the repatriation of capital, which is usually granted.

36.   Investment Restrictions on Nonresidents

Foreign individuals and corporations may not, without special permission, establish a company in Finland, acquire real property or, in certain circumstances, acquire or carry on a business. These permits are usually granted.

SELECTION OF BUSINESS ENTITY BY NONRESIDENTS

In Finland, the common types of business entities are the general partnership, limited partnership, and limited company (joint-stock company). Few branches of foreign companies are in existence. Profits of general partnerships and limited partnerships are allocated to the individual partners for tax purposes. However, if the partnership is registered by the Trade Registrar and is considered to carry on business activities, half of the income will be taxed as corporate income and half as income of the partners. Additionally, foreigners need prior approval from the Ministry of Commerce and Industry to join a Finnish partnership. A branch of a foreign corporation is taxed on branch profits as though it were a resident corporation. Most foreign enterprises organize as a limited company. Income taxes on corporations have been described in items 1 and 2, and the computation of taxable income in items 26 to 33.

FRANCE

INCOME TAXES ON CORPORATIONS

1. Rates

Legal entities are subject to corporation tax by reason of:

- [ ] Legal Form. Limited companies (Societes Anonymes, Societe a Responsabilite Limitee, and Societes en commandite par actions for part of the profits).
- [ ] Profitable Activity (Civil law associations engaged in profitable activities).
- [ ] Choice (Partnerships electing to be liable to corporation tax).

The standard rate of corporation tax levied was 42% in 1988, 39% in 1989, 37% in 1990, and now is reduced to 34% for financial years beginning January 1, 1991. On distributions, this rate is increased 42% by application of a surtax. This surtax is equal to 3/58ths, 5/58ths, or 8/58ths of the net amount to be distributed if the distribution offsets profits respectively earned during financial years beginning January 1, 1989, 1990, and 1991.

The corporation tax is assessed only on the profits of companies engaged in business in France and those allocated to France by various treaty provisions.

Except for the surtax mentioned above, there is no tax payable by companies liable to corporation tax on distributions to French residents (either companies or individuals) when the distributed profits are from previously taxed profits (at the standard rate) and which were realized not more than five years before the distribution. Dividends distributed from profits that are not subject to corporation tax (at the rate of 34%; e.g., dividends received from subsidiary companies and profits earned in non-French establishments) are subject to a tax (so-called précompte) at the rate of 33.33% of the gross amount to be distributed so that the recipient could be entitled to a relevant "avoir fiscal" representing 50% of the net amount received in cash. Précompte applies also to dividends paid out of profits realized more than five years before the distribution. Précompte is reimbursed to shareholders residing in a country with which France has a tax treaty, if these shareholders are not entitled to an avoir fiscal.

Précompte does not apply to dividends paid out of foreign-source income if the French distributing company is a pure holding company that has assets constituting at least 66.66% of the foreign stocks. Correlatively, the French holding company shareholders are not entitled to an avoir fiscal, but foreign tax credits of the holding company are transferred to them.

2. Local Income Taxes

Only the State levies income taxes in France. The towns ("communes") and counties ("departements") levy rates that are not assessed on income.

3. Capital Gains Taxes

Gains on fixed assets are included in income. They are divided into short-term and long-term gains. Short-term gains are taxed at 34% with an option to extend the payment of the tax over three years for companies that are not subject to corporate tax. Long-term gains are taxed at three reduced rates:

15%—industrial property rights;
19%—standard rate; and
25%—construction land, portfolio securities;

but only if the net balance, i.e., 85%, 81%, 75%, respectively, is allocated to a "special long-term gain reserve."

Distributions offsetting this reserve are subject to the so-called précompte (see item 1) in order to bring the total burden on the gain from the original reduced rate to 42%.

Short-term gains are gains on fixed assets held for less than two years and also that part of the gain on depreciable fixed assets held for at least two years which corresponds to depreciation charged on these assets. Long-term gains are gains on sales of assets held for at least two years.

Long-term losses are losses on the disposal of nondepreciable assets held for more than two years. Short-term losses are losses on the disposal of any other fixed assets. Unrealized losses in investments in shares of other companies may, under certain conditions, be considered a deductible long-term loss.

Gains on disposals of investments in shares are treated as long-term or short-term gains.

4. Branch Profits Taxes

A branch or, more generally, any form of permanent establishment of a foreign company is taxed as though it were a resident company. Branch profits are deemed to be distributed to non-French residents. They, therefore, are subject to corporation surtax (as described in item 1). However, the 34% income tax rate will be applied if the branch can prove that the profits resulting from its activity in France are retained in the French establishment.

Moreover, the net after-corporation-tax profits of such French establishments are subject to a branch tax at 25% (lower rates may be provided by tax treaty) when realized and whether or not they are remitted outside France. However, if the foreign company has shareholders resident in France, does not distribute dividends within 12 months following the end of the tax year, or distributes dividends for an amount less than the net after-corporation-tax profits of its French permanent establishment, the whole or part of the branch tax is refundable.

5. Foreign Tax Reliefs

Income either earned in non-French establishments or derived from a complete cycle of operations carried out outside France is not subject to French corporation tax.

Dividends received from a non-French subsidiary are subject to corporation tax on the net amount received in France after payment of all foreign taxes. However, if the subsidiary is located in a tax treaty country, the amount subject to corporation tax is the gross dividend before foreign withholding tax and the foreign withholding tax is creditable against both the corporation tax and the précompte (see item 1).

A French parent company, or the French permanent establishment of a foreign company, owning at least 10% of the shares of a company or a stake exceeding F150 million may deduct from taxable income 95% of the dividends received from French or foreign subsidiaries; the parent company then pays tax on 5% of the dividends received including the avoir fiscal or tax credits. No credit is generally allowed for foreign taxes. However, if the dividends come from a tax treaty country, the credit offsets withholding taxes and the "précompte" (see item 1) but not corporation tax.

Fees, royalties, and interest income received from abroad are taxable in France. If derived from a nontax treaty country, the assessable amount is the net received after all foreign taxes. Tax treaties may provide for a credit for foreign withholding taxes, in which case the taxable amount is the gross amount before foreign withholding tax.

6. Classification of Corporations

There are three types of entities: limited companies, unlimited liability companies (U.L.C.), and partnerships.

Unlimited Liability Companies (Societe en nom collectif, societe civile, groupement d'interet economique, societe en commandite simple. Taxable income is determined at the company level. Income tax (personal income tax at a progressive rate if the partner is an individual or at a 34% rate if the partner is a corporation) is assessed on each partner according to his share in the U.L.C. profits. These U.L.C.s may become liable to the corporation tax by special election (see item 1).

Limited Companies (Societe anonyme, societe a responsabilite limitee and societe en commandite par actions). These limited companies are liable to corporation tax.

Partnerships (Association en participation) are taxed as described above for U.L.C.

7. Payment of Taxes

Corporation tax in four installments, which represent 38% of the taxable profits of the previous financial year, must be paid during the relevant financial year. The balance due, if any, must be paid not later than the fifteenth of the fourth month after the close of the relevant financial year. The overpayment, if any, will be offset against the next corporation tax installment due. Newly created companies are exempt from paying the first four installments. Under certain conditions, newly created companies may benefit from a total or partial exemption of corporation tax during the first five years following their creation.

8. Other Matters

Remuneration of Licenses for Patents and Know-How. Sums received by a company for licensing patents or know-how usually benefit from the special fiscal regime applicable to long-term capital gains (see item 3) and from the reduced 15% tax rate.

French Legislation on Group Relief. As of January 1, 1988, a group of French companies can consolidate the taxable income of its French subsidiaries with that of the parent. This group relief is optional and valid for five years, but some conditions are required. The parent company must own directly or indirectly at least 95% of voting and dividends rights of the subsidiaries it wishes to include in its consolidation without being itself owned by another French company in the same way. If a subsidiary leaves the consolidated group before the end of the five years, penalties may be required.

The taxable income of the group is derived by adding the profits and losses realized by each company after some adjustments such as those listed below:

☐ Waivers of the debts granted between two consolidated companies must be taken into account without tax impact at the group level.

☐ Gains and losses released by transfers of assets occurring inside the consolidated group are not taken into account.

☐ Reserves for bad debts owned inside the consolidated group are not deductible at the consolidated level.

☐ Director fees paid by one company are not tax deductible at the group level.

The parent company is liable for payment of tax and, if a consolidated loss occurs, may choose between carrying it forward for five years or carrying it back.

If one of the companies included in the group acquires shares of a company that is to become a tax-consolidated company from entities that have control (either direct or indirect, de jure or de facto) over the acquiring company or from companies directly or indirectly controlled by these entities, total financial charges borne by the companies of the group are deductible every year within the following limit, whether or not the acquisition is financed through loans:

$$\frac{\text{Price of Acquisition of the Target Shares}}{\text{Total Debts of the Consolidated Group}}$$

This limitation applies during the 15 years following the purchase.

INCOME TAXES ON INDIVIDUALS

9. Rates

Individuals resident in France for tax purposes are subject to tax on their worldwide income. A husband and wife are jointly and severally liable for income tax on their respective income and that of any dependent children. The tax due is calculated in the following manner. First, the net taxable income is divided by a certain number of shares ("parts") as follows: one for a bachelor, two for married persons, plus half a share for each of the first two dependent children and one full share for the third and each subsequent child.

Second, the tax on one share is determined from the following table (1990 income):

Taxable Income		Percentage on Excess
Over	Not Over	
FF 18,140	FF 18,960	5.0%
18,960	22,470	9.6
22,470	35,520	14.4
35,520	45,660	19.2
45,660	57,320	24.0
57,320	69,370	28.8
69,370	80,030	33.6
80,030	133,340	38.4
133,340	183,400	43.2
183,400	216,940	49.0
216,940	246,770	53.9
246,770		56.8

However, the reduction resulting from an additional half share for taxpayers' dependents is limited to FF12,180 per half share after two for married taxpayers and after the first share for widowed taxpayers. In addition, various tax deductions ranging from 11% to 3% are granted for taxpayers if the net income per share does not exceed FF322,670.

The 1991 Finance Act established a generalized social contribution to be withheld from income at the rate of 1.1%. All individuals deemed to be domiciled in France for the purpose of income tax are liable to this new tax. The generalized social contribution basis consists mainly of gross salaries and benefits in-kind paid after

January 31, 1991. A standard deduction of 5% for professional expenses applies to the remuneration.

The registration and the payment are the responsibility of the French employer. Employees who are assigned by a foreign employer to work in France are responsible for the registration and payment of this tax.

Effective January 1, 1990, the generalized social contribution also is levied at the rate of 1.1% on French-source passive income.

10. Local Income Taxes

None.

11. Capital Gains Taxes

Gains on the disposal of shares and bonds are taxed as follows:

□ At 18.1% if the total sales of shares and bonds quoted on an exchange during the relevant calendar year exceed FF307,600.

□ Gain on the disposition of unlisted shares is taxed at 18.1% if the seller or the seller's family held more than 25% of the share capital of the company at any time during the preceding five years.

□ If the seller holds directly or indirectly less than 25% of unlisted shares, the capital gain will be taxed at the flat rate of 18.1% if the annual proceeds of sales of all types of shares exceed FF307,600.

The same provisions apply to individuals nonresident in France. Exceptions are provided by tax treaties.

12. Foreign Tax Reliefs

Under the general law, individuals are taxed on their worldwide income. Foreign taxes are treated as a deduction and not as a credit. However, there are exceptions provided by tax treaties.

13. Tax Periods

All individuals are taxed on the basis of a calendar year. At the end of each February, every taxpayer subject to income tax must file a return for income earned or received in the preceding calendar year.

INCOME TAXES ON NONRESIDENTS

15. Liability to Tax

Nonresidents are subject to French personal income tax computed on the total of their French-source taxable income. However, their total income tax may never be less than 25% of their income from Metropolitan France and Corsica and less than 18% of their income from French Departments overseas. Income tax is withheld at source on income paid to nonresidents. The rate of withholding tax varies according to the type of income. Salaries are subject to a withholding tax after deduction of employee social security contributions and after application of a 10% allowance (up to FF66,950 for 1990) and 20% allowance (up to FF121,400 for 1990). For salaries paid during 1991, the withholding tax is computed as follows:

Annual Taxable Salary

Over	Not Over	Rate
FF 53,870	FF156,370	15%
156,370		25

Taxable salary above FF156,370 is subject to the progressive tax schedule, and the difference between the withholding tax of 25% and the tax calculated according to the schedule is due.

17. Withholding Tax Rates

Loan Interest. Interest paid in consideration of a loan contracted abroad by a French company is except from withholding tax in France if both of the following conditions apply:

☐ The loan contract is concluded prior to the interest payment.
☐ The loan contract is authorized by the French Ministry of Finance. No individual authorization is requested since a general authorization has been granted by the French Ministry of Finance.

Should one of these conditions not be fulfilled, interest payments would be subject to withholding tax, the rates of which are reported in the following table.

Bond Interest. Interest from bonds issued as of January 1, 1987 is exempt from withholding tax in France.

A withholding tax is levied at the rate of 12% for bonds issued before January 1, 1965, and at the rate of 10% for bonds issued after this date and before January 1, 1987. These rates apply to bond interest paid to any treaty country unless the treaty provides for a lower rate.

Interest paid on bonds issued on or after October 1, 1984 generally is exempt from withholding tax if the recipient is not a French resident. A 10% withholding tax applies to bonds issued by private entities.

| Countries | Dividends (1) Without Avoir Fiscal | Interest On | | Royalties (1,2) |
		Loans	Bonds and Securities	
Nontreaty countries	25%	35%	25%	33.33%
Treaty countries:				
Algeria	0	35	0/10/12	33.33
Argentina	15	20	0/10/12	18
Australia	15	10	0/10	10
Austria	15	0	0	0 (3)
Bangladesh	10/15 (4)	10	0/10/12	10
Belgium	10/15 (4)	15	0/10/12	0
Benin	25	35	0/10/12	0
Brazil	15	15	0/10/12	15 (5)
Bulgaria	5/15 (4)	0	0	5
Burkina Faso	15 (6)	35	0/10/12	0
Cameroon	25	35	0/10/12	15 (7)
Canada	10/15 (4)	10	0/10	10 (8)
Central African Rep.	25	35	0/10/12	0
Comores	15 (6)	0	0	0
Congo	15/20 (4)	0	0	15
China	10	10/0	10/0	10
Cyprus	15 (4)	10/0	0/10	0 (9)
Czechoslovakia	10	0	0	5 (10)
Denmark	0	0	0	0
Egypt	15 (4)	25	0/10/12	15 (11)
Finland	0	10/0	0/10/12	0
Gabon	15 (6)	35	0/10/12	10 (3)
Germany	0	0	0	0
Greece	25	0	0/10/12	5
Hungary	15 (4)	0	0	0
India	25	35	0/10/12	33.33
Indonesia	15 (4)	15 (12)	0/10/12	10
Iran	20 (4)	15	0/10/12	10 (10)
Ireland	10/15 (4)	0	0	0
Israel	15 (4)	15	0/10/12	10 (10)
Italy	15	15	0/10/12	0
Ivory Coast	25	35	0/10/12	10 (13)
Japan	15 (4)	10/0	0/10	10
Jordan	15 (4)	15/0	0/10/12 (15)	5/15/25
Korea (South)	15 (4)	15	0/10/12	15 (14)
Kuwait	0 (4)	5/0	0	0
Lebanon	0	0	0	33.33
Luxembourg	15 (4)(15)	10	0/10/12	0
Madagascar	25 (4)	15	0/10/12	10/15

Countries	Dividends (1) Without Avoir Fiscal	Interest On Loans	Interest On Bonds and Securities	Royalties (1,2)
Malawi	25%	35%	0%/10%/12%	33.33%
Malaysia	15 (4)	15	0/10/12	10 (16)
Mali	15 (6)	35	0/10/12	0
Malta	15 (4)	10	10/0	10 (10)
Mauritania	25	35	0/10/12	33.33
Mauritius	15 (4)	35 (17)	0/10/12 (17)	15 (10)
Monaco	25	35	0/10/25	33.33
Morocco	0 (18)	10	0/15	10 (19)
Netherlands	15 (4)	10/0	0/10/12	0
New Caledonia	5/15	0	0	10 (10)
New Zealand	15	10/0	0/10/12	10
Niger	15 (6)	35	0/10/12	0
Norway	15 (4)	10 (17)	0/10/12	0
Oman	0 (4)	0	0	0
Pakistan	25 (4)	12	0/10/12	0
Philippines	25 (4)	15	0/10/12	25
Poland	15 (4)	0	0	10 (10)
French Polynesia	25	0	0/10/12	33.33
Portugal	15	12	0/10/12	5
Romania	10	10/0	10/0	10
Saint-Pierre et Miquelon	5/15	0	0	0/10
Saudi Arabia (20)	0 (21)	0 (22)	0 (22)	0
Senegal	15 (6)	35	0/10/12	15 (10)
Singapore	15 (4)	10/0	10/0	0 (16)
Spain	15 (4)	10	0/10/12	6
Sri Lanka	25	10 (17)	0/10 (17)	10 (10)
Sweden	15/0 (23)	0	0	0
Switzerland (24)	5/15 (4)	10	0/10/12	5
Thailand	15/20 (4)	35 (25)	0/10/12 (25)	15 (26)
Togo	15 (6)	35	0/10/12	0
Trinidad and Tobago	10/15 (4)	0/10	0/10	0/10
Tunisia	25	12	0/10/12	15 (27)
Turkey	15/20 (4)	15	0/10/12	10
United Arab Emirates	0(4)	0/5	0	0
United Kingdom	5/15 (4)	0	0	0
United States	5/15 (4)	0	0	5 (10)
U.S.S.R.	15	0/10	0/10	0
Yugoslavia	15 (4)	0	0	0
Zambia	25	35	0/10/12	0 (28)

Notes:

(1) These rates may be modified according to the participation of the beneficiaries in the share capital of the paying company or the structure of the beneficiary entity.

(2) These rates may be modified according to the nature of the royalties paid.

(3) 10% on royalties paid to a company holding 50% or more of the capital of the paying companies.

(4) Special rates on dividends from important shareholding.

(5) 10% on copyrights and 25% on royalties for licensing of trademarks.

(6) 25% if dividends are not included in the beneficiary's personal income tax.

(7) 33% on royalties (which cannot be deducted from the debtor's taxable results).

(8) No withholding tax on literary copyrights except for television broadcasting.

(9) 5% on copyrights for films and television broadcasting.

(10) No withholding tax on literary copyrights.

(11) 25% on royalties for the use of trademarks.

(12) 10% on interest paid by a bank or agricultural or industrial enterprise to another bank or enterprise.

(13) No withholding tax on literary copyrights for television or record broadcasting when the beneficiary is a public enterprise.

(14) 10% on royalties for the use of patents and "know-how."

(15) 25% on dividends paid to Luxembourg holding companies exempted from income tax.

(16) 33.33% on copyrights for movies or records for broadcasting.

(17) No withholding tax on interest paid to a bank.

(18) 25% on dividends nontaxable in Morocco.

(19) 5% on copyrights except for movies.

(20) The treaty applies only to individuals.

(21) 5% on dividends paid to individuals holding more than 20% of the share capital of the French paying company.

(22) No withholding tax on interest on transferable bonds or on interest paid by a bank or linked with industrial or commercial operations.

(23) No withholding tax on dividends paid to a company holding less than 25% of the share capital of the French company.

(24) In some cases, Swiss companies under the control of residents of other countries cannot benefit from the treaty.

(25) Reduced to 10% on interest paid to a bank or financial institution.

(26) 5% on copyrights.

(27) 5% on copyrights except for movies; 20% on royalties for licensing of trademarks and copyrights for movies.

(28) Only if a tax has to be paid in Zambia.

18. Special Withholding Provisions

Dividends. Distributions of dividends made as of January 1, 1992 by a French company to an EC company that holds more than 25% of the distributing company will be exempt from withholding tax (EC directive, July 23, 1990).

Foreign parent companies are entitled to special withholding tax rates if they own a specified percentage of the French company's share capital or voting rights.

Countries	Minimum Shareholding (1)	Rate
Bangladesh	10%	10%
Belgium	10	10
Bulgaria	15	5
Canada	10	10
Congo	10	15
Cyprus	10	10
Egypt	10	5
Hungary	25	5
Indonesia	25	10
Iran	25	15
Ireland	50	10
Israel	50	10
Japan	15%	10%
Jordan	10	5
Korea (South)	25	10
Kuwait	20	5
Luxembourg	25	5
Madagascar	25	15
Malaysia	10	5
Malta	10	5
Mauritius	10	5
Netherlands	25	5
Norway	10	5
Oman	25	5
Pakistan	50	15
Philippines	10	15
Poland	10	5
Singapore	10	10
Spain	25	10
Switzerland	20	5 (2)
Thailand	25	15 (3)
Trinidad and Tobago	10	10
Turkey	10	15
United Arab Emirates	25	5
United Kingdom	10	5
United States	10	5
Yugoslavia	25	5

Notes:
(1) In some cases, the minimum shareholding has to be held for a minimum period.

(2) If the Swiss beneficiary company is not under the control of non-Swiss residents.

(3) If the paying company has an industrial activity.

OTHER SIGNIFICANT TAXES

21. Sales (Value Added)

VAT applies to all activities except salaried employment; that is, to all sales made under terms of delivery of goods in France, and to all services, as a general rule, if the entity providing the service is located in France. Some exceptions are transports, services rendered on real estate, software, banking activities, and rent or sale of trademarks. VAT also applies to imports, but exports are zero rated. The rates of VAT are:

☐ 5.5% on most food products, books, water, and other listed products.

☐ 22% on cars and motorcycles over 240cc and on listed "luxury" items including tape recorders and cameras.

☐ 18.6% when the above rates do not apply.

The tax must be invoiced to customers and paid to the tax collector. VAT invoiced by suppliers is deductible from VAT owed, and any excess may be reimbursible. The following activities are not subject to VAT: insurance, medicines and medical activities, teaching, some professions, banking, real estate rentals except furnished premises, and nonprofitable activities under certain conditions.

22. Inheritance and Gift Taxes

Inheritance and gift tax applies to the worldwide estate of residents and to nonresidents' estates located in France. France has signed tax treaties relating to inheritance taxes with many countries.

Gift and estate tax rates are as follows:

Between Direct Parents and Children
(after an allowance of F275,000*)

Over	Not Over	
FF 0	FF 50,000	5%
50,000	75,000	10
75,000	100,000	15
100,000	3,400,000	20
3,400,000	5,600,000	30
5,600,000	11,200,000	35
11,200,000		40

*Effective January 1, 1992, the allowance will be FF300,000.

Between Spouses
(after an allowance of F275,000*)

Over	Not Over	
FF 0	FF 50,000	5%
50,000	100,000	10
100,000	200,000	15
200,000	3,400,000	20
3,400,000	5,600,000	30
5,600,000	11,200,000	35
11,200,000		40

*Effective January 1, 1992, the allowance will be FF 330,000.

Between Brothers and Sisters
(after an allowance of F10,000 for inheritance)

Over	Not Over	
FF 0	FF 150,000	35%
150,000		45

Between relatives (until 4th degree): 55%
(after an allowance of FF10,000 granted only for inheritance)
Between other persons: 60%
(after an allowance of FF10,000 granted only for inheritance)

23. Taxes on Payrolls (Social Security)

Social Security includes insurance against sickness, disability, accidents, pensions, unemployment, and family allowances. All employees must contribute to Social Security. Contributions are levied on both the employer and the employee. Additional pension schemes are also compulsory. The cost varies with the options exercised by the employer. Contributions are approximately 35% to 45% for employers and 15% to 18% for employees.

24. Taxes on Natural Resources

Annual royalties are paid to the municipalities for the exploitation of natural resources. The rates are fixed by ton and vary according to the nature of goods extracted and the location of the exploitation.

25. Other Taxes

Business License Tax (Taxe Professionnelle). All persons or entities carrying out industrial, commercial or professional activities are subject to this tax. The rate varies according to the place where the activity is exercized. The tax is assessed on the basis of special schedules, which take account of the rental value of the assets used and the salaries paid.

Property Taxes (Taxes Foncieres).   These taxes are paid both on developed and undeveloped land. The tax is assessed against the owner and based on the rental value.

Personal Dwelling Tax (Taxe d'Habitation).   Personal dwelling tax is levied on any individual who occupies a dwelling as of January 1, even if the individual is not the owner. The tax is based on the rental value (effective January 1, 1992, part of the tax will be based also on the income of the individual); special deductions are granted according to the number of dependent children.

Compulsory Construction Investment.   All firms that employ ten employees or more must allocate to a construction program an amount equal to 0.65% of the salaries paid.

Apprenticeship and Training Taxes.   These taxes are levied on the basis of salaries. Apprenticeship tax is levied at the rate of 0.6%. The training tax is levied only on businesses employing at least ten persons and at the rate of 1.2%.

Payroll Tax.   Entities not subject to VAT on at least 90% of their turnover are subject to a payroll tax, as follows:

Annual Salaries

Over	Not Over	Rate
FF 0	FF35,900	4.25%
35,900	71,770	8.50
71,770		13.60

Registration Duties.   The main registration duties are:

□   Assessed on the purchase price or the fair market value, whichever is the higher.

　—On the sale of goodwill and leasehold rights, the rate of transfer duty is computed on a progressive basis: 0% on the first FF100,000, 7% between FF100,000 and FF300,000, and 14.2% on the excess.

　—On the sale of buildings used for commercial purposes: 16.6% plus local rates amounting to 1.6% (except for the Paris areas: 1.5%).

　—On the transfer of shares in companies: 4.8% (transfer of shares in an S.A. may be exempted or liable to 1% with maximum duties of FF20,000 if there is a deed).

□ Assessed on the amount contributed.

   —On capital contributions to companies: 1%; this rate is increased to 11.4% plus local rates when capital contributions of land, buildings, goodwill, and leasehold rights are made to a company liable to corporation tax by a person who is not; if the capital contributor commits to hold the shares received, the rate is reduced to 1.5%. Cash contributions are subject to a fixed registration fee of FF430.

New French Net Wealth Tax (ISF). Individuals are liable for the net wealth tax only if the net value of their assets exceeds FF4,260,000 as of January 1 of each year. French tax residents are liable for the tax on their assets located either in France or outside France (except if foreign internal rules or a tax treaty provides otherwise). Non-French tax residents are taxable only on their assets located in France, except financial assets and if provided otherwise by tax treaties. Business assets, including company shares, are exempt from taxation under certain conditions.

<table>
<tr><td colspan="2">**Taxable Net Wealth**</td><td></td></tr>
<tr><td>**Over**</td><td>**Not Over**</td><td>**Rate**</td></tr>
<tr><td>FF 4,260,000</td><td>FF 6,920,000</td><td>0.5%</td></tr>
<tr><td>6,920,000</td><td>13,740,000</td><td>0.7</td></tr>
<tr><td>13,740,000</td><td>21,320,000</td><td>0.9</td></tr>
<tr><td>21,320,000</td><td>41,280,000</td><td>1.2</td></tr>
<tr><td>41,280,000</td><td></td><td>1.5</td></tr>
</table>

COMPUTATION OF TAXABLE INCOME

26. Capital Gains

See item 3.

27. Depreciation and Depletion

Business enterprises apply one of the three following methods:

Straight-Line Method. All depreciable fixed assets can be depreciated under this method. The depreciation rate is obtained by dividing 100 by the number of normal useful life years for such assets.

Declining-Balance Method. This method is applicable to some new machinery, equipment, and tools. Depreciation is computed by multiplying the rate that corresponds to the straight-line method by a special coefficient (depending on the useful life of the asset).

Exceptional Depreciation. Business enterprises that invest for energy-saving purposes are entitled to deduct, under restrictive conditions, a depreciation allowance of 100% of the cost of the materials for the first 12 months. A depreciation rate of 100% can be used in the year of construction or purchase of buildings used for anti-pollution purposes. Software equipment purchased by a company can be depreciated in one year.

Tax Credit for Research Expenses. For research expenses up to 1992, the "increase" tax credit equals 50% of the difference between the amount of the research expenses for the year in question and the average of those incurred in the two previous years. A reduction in research expenses does not entail a repayment of any prior credits, but a portion equal to 50% of the negative variation of expenses must be offset against the tax credit obtained for the subsequent years. The tax credit is limited to FF40,000,000 annually. If the company is not liable to corporate income tax, the tax credit can be refunded.

Tax Credit for Increases in Expenses Incurred for Training Personnel. Through 1991, the credit is equal to 25% of the increase in expenses incurred for the training of personnel over the preceding year (eligible expenses are those above minimum legal requirements, presently 1.20% of gross salaries paid each year). The maximum annual tax credit is FF1,000,000.

If eligible expenses fall below the level of the preceding year, the previous tax credit must not be repaid but a portion equal to 25% of the negative variation of expenses will be offset against the tax credit obtained for the subsequent years.

A 40% increase of the training expenses is allowed for expenses incurred for the benefit of employees holding less qualified positions, or are older than 45 years, or for expenses incurred by companies with fewer than 50 employees. For these expenses, the maximum tax credit is increased to FF5,000,000.

28. Treatment of Dividends

Taxes payable by companies liable to corporation tax on their dividend distributions have been discussed in item 1. Recipients are subject to tax as noted below.

French Individual Shareholders. French individual shareholders are granted a tax credit (avoir fiscal) equal to 50% of the dividend received. This avoir fiscal, which is credited against their personal income tax, constitutes taxable income. Should the avoir fiscal exceed the income tax liability, the excess is refunded in cash by the authorities.

French Corporate Shareholders

□ Parent companies (i.e., which hold at least 10% of the distributing company and other conditions described in item 5) are entitled to an avoir fiscal equal to 50% of the net dividends paid by the subsidiary company. This avoir fiscal is not creditable against the corporation tax liability of the parent company. It is creditable during five years against précompte, but it is not creditable against withholding taxes payable by the parent company on its own distribution of dividends to foreign shareholders. It is not refundable in cash by the Treasury. Dividends received from subsidiary companies are exempted from French corporation tax, except for a quota corresponding to the expenses connected with the holding of the subsidiary shares. These expenses are deemed to be equal to 5% of the dividends received increased by the amount of the avoir fiscal or by tax credit related thereto.

☐ Corporate shareholders that do not qualify as parent companies are entitled to an avoir fiscal equal to 50% of the net dividends received. They are taxed on the net dividend received increased by the amount of the avoir fiscal. The avoir fiscal is credited against the corporation tax liability. If the avoir fiscal is higher than the corporation tax liability for the year during which the dividends were received, the excess cannot be carried forward and is not refundable in cash.

Non-French Shareholders

☐ Corporate and individual shareholders resident in a country having no tax treaty with France are liable for a withholding tax at the rate of 25% paid on the gross amount of the dividend paid. Précompte on amounts distributed is never reimbursed.

☐ Corporate and individual shareholders resident in a country having concluded a tax treaty with France are reimbursed for the ''précompte'' when it has been paid by the company. Avoir fiscal is granted under certain conditions to the shareholders. (When it is granted, the précompte if any, is not reimbursed). The rate of withholding tax is determined by the tax treaty. It is either the standard rate of 25% or a reduced rate.

29. Loss Carryovers

For tax purposes, net operating losses may be carried forward for five years. Operating losses resulting from depreciation can be carried forward indefinitely.

Companies subject to corporation tax may elect a form of loss carryback allowing them to offset the existing tax loss at the end of a financial year against the undistributed net profits (i.e., after corporation tax) of the three preceding years. Thus, the company is entitled to a credit from the French Treasury equal to 34% of the amount of losses carried back. This credit may be used to pay the corporate tax due for the following five years. At the end of this period the remainder may be reimbursed in cash by the Treasury.

30. Transactions between Related Parties

France has a tax provision (Article 57 of the Code General des Impots (C.G.I.)) which is roughly similar to Section 482 of the U.S. Internal Revenue Code. There is no important literature on how this article must be applied. *The key word in the matter is ''reasonableness.''* In fact, this article is used as a weapon against French branches or subsidiary companies that are permanently in a loss position. The French tax authorities consider that such business enterprises would not continue if the owners did not draw an advantage from their survival, which might be only having a presence in France. In their opinion, this deserves some remuneration. Article 57 is applied when the level of prices paid to foreign affiliates is more than what a French independent supplier would charge for supplying an identical product or service. For instance, engineering services rendered in the United States to the benefit of a French affiliate could be disallowed even if they were charged at cost, should such a cost be in excess of what a French firm would charge for the same services. Article 57 is also applied to sales by French taxpayers to related parties if the sale price is lower than the fair market price.

Royalties.   Royalty agreements between a French company and a foreign affiliate must be deposited with the French Ministry of Industry. This requirement has three goals:

☐   It allows the authorities to keep statistics.

☐   When the agreement is filed it receives a registration number. This is for statistical purposes only since exchange control regulations no longer require this registration number to allow the banks to make payments.

☐   A copy of the agreement is passed over to the tax authorities who can form an opinion on the "reasonableness" of the royalty agreed. There is no precise rule determining the reasonableness of royalties for tax purposes.

Management Fees.   Here again, there is not much literature on this point. Experience shows that management fees should preferably meet all the following conditions in order to be accepted:

☐   There should be a written contract.

☐   The management fee should be computed from the costs incurred by the company rendering the services rather than as a percentage of profits or sales.

☐   The invoice should state the specific services rendered and should be itemized, giving as many details as possible.

☐   The services rendered should be for the exclusive benefit of the payer.

☐   Evidence of the cost incurred by the company rendering the services should be readily available in case of a tax inspection.

☐   The profit margin should not exceed 10% of costs.

☐   When costs are allocated between several affiliates, the criterion used should be realistic; for example, the number of employees for payroll services.

☐   The amount of the management fees plus the overhead expenses of the receiving company should not be in excess of what independent companies pay as overhead (expressed as a percentage of their sales).

32. Tax Periods

The tax period is the financial year as defined in the articles of association of the company. It does not necessarily coincide with the calendar year.

If the financial year exceeds 12 months, the company must issue provisional financial statements as of December 31.

33. Other Matters

Taxable Income in General. Taxable income is the difference between the net book values of the company at the beginning and end of the tax period, plus and minus the following adjustments:

☐ The following adjustments increase taxable income:

—Charges that are not deductible such as certain taxes (mainly corporation tax), fines and penalties.

—"Sumptuary expenses" (expenses deducted in the financial statements of a luxury nature which are not deductible for tax purposes, usually because they lack a direct business purpose).

—Provisions for charges and losses that cannot be determined precisely, and/or are unlikely to materialize due to events that have taken place during the tax period.

—Excess interest charged on direct intercompany loans (by reference to the rate and/or the loan amount).

☐ The following adjustments decrease taxable income:

—Dividend income from subsidiaries.

—Profits earned by establishments located outside of France or resulting from a complete cycle of operations outside of France.

RELATED CONSIDERATIONS

34. Incentives and Grants

Most business incentives offered by the French government or by local municipalities relate to their wish to locate, or relocate, industry in the less industrialized areas of the country, where jobs are most needed. For this purpose, there are three main subsidies:

☐ For regional development, to develop jobs in certain areas of France. Buildings and equipment purchased by a business enterprise with a regional grant from public authorities also qualify for special depreciation based on cost plus 50% of the grant.

☐ For relocation of tertiary activity, which consists of the reimbursement by the government of part of an investment made by a company creating, expanding or transferring its general activities (administration, marketing, etc.) outside the Paris urban area.

□ For relocation of research activities, which may be granted to a company creating or expanding research activities in regions entitled to a subsidy for the relocation of tertiary activities.

A number of tax exemptions and reductions are granted for companies that set up or acquire plants:

□ The registration tax on transfer of property can be reduced from 16.6% to 4.8%.

□ The business license tax may be postponed for up to five years.

□ Enterprises may use exceptional depreciation (see item 27).

New or increased industrial activities anywhere in France are entitled to the following benefits:

□ Dividends distributed in respect of shares issued as of January 1, 1990 for cash contributions are deductible (up to 53.4% of their amount) for corporation tax purpose for six years. This period is restricted to ten years for cash contributions between January 1, 1983 and December 31, 1988 and to eight years for cash contributions in 1989. However, the new provisions do not allow a deduction for dividends distributed to a parent company holding 10% or more of the share capital of the distributing company. The same restriction is applicable to group distributions.

□ Effective October 1, 1988, newly created enterprises with an industrial, commercial, or artisan purpose may under restricted conditions benefit from a total exemption from income tax during their first 24 months of existence and from a partial exemption during the following 36 months.

   Those enterprises that do not benefit from the exemption are enterprises that were created to further a merger or a group restructuring, enterprises that took over a preexisting activity, or enterprises where at least 50% of the share capital is held directly or indirectly by corporate shareholders.

□ Effective October 1, 1988, companies created to acquire enterprises with financial difficulties and to carry out an industrial, commercial, or artisan purpose may under restricted conditions benefit from a total corporation tax exemption during their first 24 months of existence.

   These companies or enterprises may benefit also from real estate or business license tax exemption for the two years following their creation.

□ Since July 1987, the French government created "tax-free zones." They are Dunkerque, Aubagne-La Ciota, and La Seyne-Toulon. Up to 1992, industrial concerns setting up a new corporation with an industrial activity in these zones can be granted a ten-year corporation tax holiday. They do not qualify for any subsidy.

Through December 31, 1992, newly created enterprises in Corsica that are in the industry, hotels, or public works sector can benefit under certain conditions from a total corporation tax exemption for eight years.

35. Exchange Controls

Capital movements and payments of all kinds between France and another country, or between a French resident and a nonresident, must be carried out through approved intermediaries (i.e., almost all banks).

In practice, all currency transactions by importers and exporters must be conducted through approved banks.

36. Investment Restrictions on Nonresidents

Direct investment in French enterprises (i.e., investments giving a de facto or legal control of a French enterprise) usually requires a prior declaration, and sometimes a prior authorization, from the Ministry of Finance.

However, the creation or expansion of a branch in France or the participation in newly created companies does not require prior authorization or declaration but remains subject to a report within 20 days following the investment.

SELECTION OF BUSINESS ENTITY BY NONRESIDENTS

Nonresident investors can operate in France either through a branch or a subsidiary. Corporation tax, VAT, and registration duties are the same for a foreign company operating in France in the form of a branch or a corporate entity. However, a branch suffers two specific drawbacks:

- [ ] Profits realized in France by a branch suffer, in addition to corporation tax, a branch tax, whether or not the profits are remitted abroad. This withholding tax is 25% unless a tax treaty provides otherwise.
- [ ] Hidden reserves can be taxed at the rate of 34% if a branch is converted into a French corporate entity.

On the other hand, the profits realized in France by a subsidiary are taxed as follows:

- [ ] If the entity is a French limited liability company (e.g., a societe anonyme or a societe a responsabilite limitee), the profits are liable to corporation tax at the rate of 34% and, when distributed abroad, in addition to the surtax referred to in item 1, suffer a withholding tax at the rate of 25% unless a tax treaty provides otherwise.
- [ ] If the entity is a French unlimited liability company (e.g., a societe en nom collectif), profits are taxed in the hands of the beneficiary (at 34% if the beneficiary is a foreign company). If they are remitted abroad, they do not suffer any withholding tax.

FRENCH POLYNESIA

INCOME TAXES ON CORPORATIONS

1. Rates

The income tax rates range from 25% to 45%, with an additional 5% if the taxable income is greater than 50 million FCFP. The rate varies according to a ratio, computed as follows:

$$\text{Ratio} = \frac{\text{Net value of certain assets} + \text{Deductible personnel expenses}}{\text{Taxable income}}$$

Ratio	Rate
Greater than 10.5	25%
Less than 1	45%

The tax rate increases by 1 percentage point each time the ratio lowers 0.5 point.

The net value of assets includes those depreciable fixed assets held within French Polynesia and included in the balance sheet.

To determine taxable income, the accrual method of accounting must be used.

Minimum Tax.   A minimum tax, levied on a lump-sum basis, is equal to 0.5% of the turnover of 100,000 FCFP minimum and 2,000,000 FCFP maximum. Minimum tax paid can be deducted from the regular income tax due over the following three financial years.

New companies are exempt from the minimum tax for the first two financial years.

Deductions.   Expenses incurred to carry on business may be deducted from taxable income. Nondeductible expenses include:

☐ Penalties and fines

☐ Costs of houses, yachts, planes

☐ Expenses incurred on the windward islands to provide personnel accommodations (except hotels)

☐ Salaries received by persons not subject to the social security regime

2. Local Income Taxes

Minor taxes are levied by the municipalities, such as a tax on real property (see item 25) and taxes based on the trade tax (see item 25).

3. Capital Gains Taxes

Capital gains usually are included in taxable income. There are exceptions, however, for certain types of capital gains, according to when the assets were owned and, under special conditions, how the capital gains were used.

Real Property Capital Gains. Gains on sales of real property and shares of real property companies are determined after deducting costs incurred for the sale, the purchase costs (except interest), and expenses incurred to increase the value of the property. Historical costs may be converted to a present value by an official index, if the property was owned longer than three years.

Real property capital gains exceeding 200,000 FCFP are taxed at rates determined by the length of possession:

Ownership	Tax Rate
Not more than 3 years	30%
3 to 6 years	20
6 to 10 years	10
10 years or longer	0

Exemptions from real property capital gains tax are granted for:

☐ Capital gains taxable under other tax laws in French Polynesia, which includes capital gains received by companies subject to income tax.

☐ Capital gains realized in the case of expropriation.

☐ Capital gains realized by an individual on the sale of his or her personal residence.

7. Payment of Taxes

An annual tax return (declaration) must be filed indicating taxable income or loss of the preceding financial year. The return must be filed within three months after the end of the financial year or, if the financial year does not end within a calendar year, before April 1 of the following year.

OTHER SIGNIFICANT TAXES

23. Taxes on Payrolls (Social Security)

Apprenticeship Duty. An annual apprenticeship duty, based on a taxable entity's number of employees or workers, is levied at the rate of 5,000 FCFP per individual.

25. Other Taxes

Moveable Property Income Tax. A withholding tax at the rate of 10% (12% on premiums) is levied on the following:

☐ Dividends and any type of profit distribution.
☐ Interest paid to shareholders.
☐ Profit shares, attendance fees, etc.
☐ Premiums paid to creditors and bondholders.
☐ Redemptions and repayments of business capital.

Certain exemptions from this tax are provided by law.

Real Property Tax. Owners of certain buildings and land (see below) must file a declaration every five years on the rental value of their properties, as determined by a specialized commission. The tax is levied on an annual basis at the rate of 10%; municipalities may levy an additional surtax of up to 50%, resulting in a maximum tax burden of 15%.
  The tax is levied on the following real property:

☐ Buildings located in Tahiti.
☐ Land used for industrial or commercial purposes.
☐ Any industrial or commercial installations that represent a construction site.
☐ Boats situated at a fixed place.

The law provides several permanent and temporary exemptions. A five-year temporary exemption applies to new construction and reconstructions or additions. This temporary exemption does not apply to land used for commercial or industrial purposes.

Trade Tax. A trade tax applies to commercial or industrial activities and the exercise of a profession. Exemptions apply to certain professional activities.
  The trade tax generally is composed of two major elements:

☐ A fixed tax (droit fixe), which is determined by the type of activity and other issues, of which the number of employees is the most important.
☐ A proportional tax (droit proportionnel), which is based on the rental value of any professional premises.

The tax rates vary according to type of activity and the location of the activity. For example, a hotel in Papeete is liable to a 200,000 FCFP fixed tax and a 2% proportional tax.

Municipalities and the Chamber of Commerce may levy additional taxes based on the trade tax paid by a company. The maximum tax rates are 80% for municipalities and 22% for the Chamber of Commerce. Municipalities may levy another tax at the rate of 10% of the rental value used in the calculation of the proportional tax.

Beverage License Duty. Individuals and legal entities possessing a license to deal commercially with beverages are liable to an annual beverage license duty, regardless of any activity.

The amount of duty is determined by the level of the beverage license and its location. For example, a first-class license in Tahiti costs 70,000 FCFP per year.

COMPUTATION OF TAXABLE INCOME

27. Depreciation and Depletion

Depreciation on fixed assets is allowed as a deductible expense for purposes of computing taxable income. Straight-line method may be applied to all depreciable assets.

The declining-balance method may be applied to equipment with a useful life of at least three years and to industrial buildings with a useful life not exceeding 15 years. The rate of depreciation is determined by applying the following coefficient to the straight-line rate:

Useful Life	Coefficient
3 to 5 years	1.5
5 to 6 years	2.0
Longer than 6 years	2.5

29. Loss Carryovers

An enterprise may deduct a loss incurred during a financial year from the profits of the following year. Unused losses may be carried forward for the five years following the year in which incurred.

Unused depreciation may be carried forward indefinitely.

33. Other Matters

Reserve. The creation of reserves is recognized as a deductible expense if the following conditions are met:

□ An occurrence may result in a loss or decrease in value of an asset that normally should fall into the financial year in question.

☐ The event is probable, not merely possible.
☐ The reason or origin of the event occurred within the financial year in question.
☐ The loss or decrease in value is sufficiently concrete.
☐ The loss or decrease in value is explained in a separate statement.

Management Fees.   Day-to-day management fees in Tahiti are deductible from taxable income. Fees for other management services provided from abroad are deductible up to an amount linked to the ratio calculated as follows:

$$\text{Local turnover} \times \frac{\text{General management costs of company}}{\text{General turnover of the company}}$$

Only those fees corresponding to effective work are deductible.

Royalties.   Royalties are deductible in computing taxable income.

Interest.   Interest paid to banks or other financial institutions is deductible.

Interest paid to shareholders for loans is deductible up to a rate fixed annually by the territorial authorities. In 1988, the rate was 9%. Deductible interest cannot exceed two times the share capital amount (this limitation does not apply to loans granted by a parent company to a subsidiary).

Reservation Fees.   Reservation fees made by nonresidents for hotel rooms are deductible if the rates are comparable to those generally used.

RELATED CONSIDERATIONS

34. Incentives and Grants

Tax Benefits Program for Investments in the DOM-TOM Lois PONS.   Certain investments in French Polynesia's DOM (overseas departments) or TOM (overseas territories, such as Tahiti) are eligible for this program.

For corporations, the qualifying amount may be deducted in full from taxable income during the accounting year, applying before all other deductions, such as loss carryovers. Any amount not used in the current accounting year may be carried forward (see item 29).

For individuals, the tax benefit may be applied as a deduction to income tax payable. The deduction may be applied in the year the investment is made and in the following four years. The percentage of the total investment that is deductible is limited to:

Year	Investment Percentage per Year
1986–1989	10%
1990–1996	5%

Beneficiaries must be liable to French tax laws, in other words they must be residents of metropolitan France or the DOM. Beneficiaries may be corporations (liable to the corporate tax or the actual profits tax) or individuals (liable to the individual tax on revenue).

The investments must have a productive capacity and either create or extend business in the following areas:

Industry	Agriculture
Fisheries	Building
Hostels	Public Works
Tourism	Transportation
New energy sources	Cottage industries

Investments in maintenance activities, even if they relate to a productive activity, are not eligible for the tax benefits.

Qualified investments by individuals also include investments to acquire or construct buildings for primarily residential use, whether for owners or leaseholders.

The form of investment may be direct or through subscriptions in corporations with their registered offices in the DOM-TOM:

☐ Investments by individuals must be through share subscription, except for investments in the construction of residences.

☐ Share subscription investments must be made at the time of the company's incorporation or during a registered capital increase.

☐ Share subscription investments must be made in cash.

Purchasing existing shares or participations does not entitle the purchaser to the tax benefits.

Corporations receiving share subscription investments should comply with the following conditions:

☐ Carry on activities exclusively in the DOM-TOM;

☐ Exercise those activities listed above;

☐ Commit 90% of their assets to the qualifying business; and

☐ Be liable to corporate tax.

A direct investment is considered realized on the date of delivery or the date of completion. For share subscription investments, the investment is considered realized on the date the total amount is paid up.

To be eligible for benefits, investments in excess of 30 million FCFP must be declared to the Budget Minister prior to realization and should have not received any objections from the minister within the following 90 days.

The Investment Code.   Investments in excess of stated amounts to certain activities located in specified areas that have been approved by the Council of Ministers of the Territories are eligible for tax and monetary advantages. The following activities are eligible:

Tourism	Renewable energy
Agriculture	Inter-island communications
Cattle farming	Production and processing
Agro-industries	Manufacturing of which over 50%
Marine activities	is for export

Benefits include:

☐   Under certain conditions, exemptions for a maximum period of five years from
  —entry duty on the importation of new or second-hand primary equipment;
  —registration duty;
  —trade tax (except for the additional tax levied by municipalities or the Chamber of Commerce);
  —income tax on movable property;
  —real property tax; and
  —corporate income tax.

☐   An investment premium ranging from 5% to 16% for specific tourism activities and a maximum of 15% for other activities.

☐   A partial reimbursement of employers' social charges for three years.

☐   Guaranteed stability of the tax regime for the approved enterprise for a maximum of ten years.

☐   Temporary protective measures for the domestic market.

The total benefits granted may not exceed 30% of the total investment, less eventual costs for acquiring property and buildings and the amount of duties levied. In calculating the threshold for eligibility and benefits, projections for three years must be taken into account.

  The benefits granted under the Investment Code are subject to a convention that delimits the obligations of the Territory and the beneficiary.

GERMANY
FEDERAL REPUBLIC OF

OVERVIEW

A main feature of the German tax system is that individuals and companies operating a business are subject to two different taxes on income and two different taxes on capital. All income is subject either to income tax (Einkommensteuer) or to corporation income tax (Koerperschaftsteuer), depending on whether the income is earned by an individual or by a company. Furthermore, all business income is subject to municipal trade income tax (Gewerbeertragsteuer). All property owned by individuals or companies is subject to property tax (Vermoegensteuer). Furthermore, capital used for business purposes is subject to municipal trade capital tax (Gewerbekapitalsteuer).

For the purpose of income tax, corporation income tax, and property tax assessment, it is necessary to distinguish between resident and nonresident taxpayers; i.e., between taxpayers who are subject to unlimited tax liability and those who are subject to limited tax liability, respectively.

German law does not use the expressions "resident" and "nonresident," but instead distinguishes between:

☐ Taxpayers with unlimited tax liability (unbeschraenkte Steuerpflicht), who are subject to income tax on their worldwide income and to property tax with respect to their domestic and foreign property.

☐ Taxpayers with limited tax liability (beschraenkte Steuerpflicht), who are subject to income tax on various types of German-source income and to property tax only with respect to their domestic property.

A company is considered to be resident in Germany (i.e., subject to unlimited tax liability) if either its seat (Sitz) or place of management (Ort der Geschaeftsleitung) is located in the Federal Republic of Germany. Since a company organized under German law is required to specify in its articles a "seat" located in Germany, all German companies are resident taxpayers. If a nonresident company (i.e., a company having its seat and place of management abroad) conducts business in Germany through a branch, the nonresident company itself will be subject to tax on branch profits and on the net value of branch property.

East Germany. With the merger of the former German Democratic Republic into the Federal Republic, the tax system of the Federal Republic has been adopted with some minor exceptions, which aim at encouraging investment in Eastern Germany. The following special rules apply:

☐ Trade tax on capital (Gewerbekapitalsteuer) and net assets tax (Vermögensteuer) is not levied.

☐ Special depreciation of up to 50% for both movable and immovable property (except aircraft and vessels in international trade) are available.

☐ Various investment subsidies are granted.

INCOME TAXES ON CORPORATIONS

1. Rates

The normal tax rate for corporations subject to unlimited tax liability is 50%. The tax rate is reduced to 36% for distributed profits. In addition, shareholders subject to unlimited tax liability (i.e., resident shareholders) may claim a tax credit against their personal income tax (or corporation profits tax) liability equal to the amount of corporation income tax paid by the company on the distributed profits.

A "solidarity" surcharge of 3.75% on corporate income tax liability is imposed for 1992. Thus, the effective rates are 51.875% (retained earnings) and 37.350% (distributed profits).

2. Local Income Taxes

There are no state or provincial income taxes. However, the municipal authorities impose a trade tax based on the capital employed and on the business income (see Overview). Though this business income is based on profits, the profit figure is subject to a few specific adjustments for the purposes of trade tax. Every municipal authority determines its own tax rate valid for its area. The trade tax burden may thus be anywhere from approximately 15% to 25% of the business income and from approximately 0.6% to 1% of the trade capital. The trade taxes are deductible from taxable income.

3. Capital Gains Taxes

There is no special provision for taxing capital gains of a German corporation with unlimited tax liability. Profits from the sale of goods and services of all kinds are generally taxed at the normal rate. Under certain circumstances, the profit obtained from the sale of land, buildings, fixed assets with a long useful life, ships, and shares in corporations can be offset fully or partly against the purchase price or the manufacturing costs of new goods.

Foreign corporations with limited tax liability in Germany are liable (in certain circumstances)—if no double taxation convention is applicable—for corporation income tax on profits from the sale of shares in German corporations and real property.

4. Branch Profits Taxes

Foreign corporations maintaining a permanent establishment in Germany are subject to limited tax liability on the income received from the permanent establishment. The corporation tax rate is 46% in these cases. Due to the solidarity surcharge, the 1992 effective rate will be 47.725%. Additionally, trade income tax is payable.

5. Foreign Tax Reliefs

The double taxation conventions concluded by Germany provide in many cases for foreign income to be exempt from German taxation; in other cases, income taxes paid abroad can be credited against German tax.

There are also tax credit provisions in national tax law; for example, a corporation is entitled to tax credit for foreign taxes that correspond to the German corporation income tax against German corporation income tax liability on income from the foreign country (per-country limitation). In the event that such credit is not possible, foreign tax may be deducted in determining income; such deduction may be substituted for offsetting on application.

If the foreign income is a dividend paid by a foreign company of which the domestic corporation has held at least 10% of the capital for the 12 months preceding the balance sheet date, income taxes paid by the foreign corporation with respect to the dividend can upon application be creditable, provided the income of the foreign corporation falls within certain categories, which may be broadly defined as an active trade or business (international affiliation privilege).

There are further tax reliefs; e.g., for investment abroad, a lump-sum payment of German corporation income tax on foreign income is possible if certain prerequisites are met.

7. Payment of Taxes

Income tax returns must be filed on completion of a tax year (calendar year), and the due date generally is May 31 of the following calendar year. After the return has been reviewed by the tax authorities, a notice of assessment is issued (which is usually provisional and subject to tax audit). The assessed tax generally is payable within one month after the issue of the assessment.

Quarterly prepayments are required against anticipated tax liability, which generally are based on the last assessment.

INCOME TAXES ON INDIVIDUALS

9. Rates

All resident individuals are taxed on their worldwide income (i.e., unlimited liability). Generally, an individual is treated as resident in Germany if he or she is physically present in Germany for more than six months in any one calendar year or for at least six consecutive months over a year-end.

Income tax is levied on taxable income above DM 5,616. The tax rate increases progressively up to a maximum of 53%. The following income tax table is an abbreviated summary of the tax rates. It does not reflect the solidarity surcharge of 3.75% on the tax liability. Technically, a surcharge of 7.5% will be levied on the income tax prepayments for the first two quarters of 1992.

Taxable Income		Amount of Tax		Percent of Income	Marginal Tax Rate on Next DM 1,000
DM	10,000	DM	836	8.4%	19.2%
	20,000		2,943	14.7	22.1
	30,000		5,354	17.8	26.4
	40,000		8,067	20.2	29.6
	50,000		11,084	22.2	32.7
	60,000		14,423	24.0	33.9
	70,000		18,048	25.8	36.9
	80,000		21,977	27.5	42.0
	90,000		26,208	29.1	45.2
	100,000		30,743	30.7	48.3
	120,000		40,751	34.0	51.5

Married couples may elect to pay tax on their combined income (joint filing). In computing the tax liability, the tax payable on half the combined income is doubled.

Profits earned by individuals through the sale of a business, an interest in a partnership, or shareholdings of more than 25% qualify for reduced tax rates up to a total capital gain of DM 30,000,000.

10. Local Income Taxes

Income from a business establishment in Germany is subject to trade income tax (see item 2). There are no other state or provincial income taxes. However, there is a so-called church tax imposed by the major religious communities. Members of such communities, subject to unlimited tax liability (including foreigners), are required to pay this tax at a rate of up to 9% of their income tax payable. The tax is collected by the tax authorities.

11. Capital Gains Taxes

Profits from the sale of capital assets of a business are in principle liable to tax (see item 3). However, in principle, profits from the sale of privately owned capital assets are exempt from tax. Gains derived from the sale of property are deemed to be speculative gains if the period of ownership is less than two years (land) or six months (other assets). Capital gains resulting from the sale of shares in a corporation are taxable (outside the speculative term) only if the seller has a "substantial interest'' (i.e., more than 25% shareholding) in the company. Such a gain is eligible for reduced tax rates.

12. Foreign Tax Reliefs

See item 5 (except for the international affiliation privilege). Where income is exempt from German tax as a result of double taxation conventions, the remaining income taxable in Germany will be taxed at the rate applicable to the sum of the income earned both in Germany and abroad (progression clause). This principle applies equally to foreign-source income and losses.

13. Tax Period

The period for the income tax assessment is the calendar year. See item 32 for information on fiscal years ending on dates other than December 31st.

INCOME TAXES ON NONRESIDENTS

15. Liability to Tax

Persons having neither residence nor customary place of abode in the Federal Republic of Germany are subject to limited tax liability. The limited tax liability encompasses income from a trade or a business for the purpose of which a permanent establishment is maintained in Germany or a permanent agent is appointed, income from the practice of a profession and income from employment that is performed or the benefits of which arise in Germany, income from letting property situated in Germany, and income from German shares and securities. Profits from the sale of interests in excess of 25% of the share capital of German companies are also subject to taxes. The limited tax liability also includes rent paid for the use of movable property in Germany (e.g., on the basis of a lease contract) or any license fees paid for the use of know-how in Germany.

Corporations having neither their seat nor their place of management in Germany are subject to limited tax liability on their German-source income as described above.

16. Rates

The tax rate for individuals is basically the same as that for taxpayers subject to unlimited tax liability, the only difference being that the minimum tax rate is 25%. For corporations subject to limited tax liability, a uniform tax rate of 46% applies.

For 1992, a solidarity surcharge of 3.75% on the tax payable is levied, resulting in an effective corporate rate of 47.725% and a minimum individual rate of 25.9375%.

Neither nonresident individuals nor corporations are basically entitled to credit the withholding tax on dividends (rate 25%) or the underlying corporate tax of 36% on the gross dividends. An exception is made if the dividends are income of a German permanent establishment of the nonresident.

The domestic withholding rate of 25% is reduced under most treaties.

In addition, the EC parent-subsidiary directive sets a 5% limit on withholding tax if the parent holds at least 25% of the shares in the subsidiary.

17. Withholding Tax Rates

Wages, salaries, and dividends (including income from participation rights, stocks, shares in a GmbH, and a silent partnership) are subject to withholding tax. The tax rate for wages and salaries is graduated according to the progressive income tax rate. The rate for dividends is 25%. In case of unlimited tax liability, those taxes that are deducted at source are creditable to the income tax as assessed at the end of the year.

The a.m. withholding tax on dividends often is reduced by double tax treaties. However, the German debtor is obliged to withhold the tax at the nominal rate of 25%, and non-German creditors must claim refund of excess tax withheld from the German Federal Finance Authority "Bundesamt für Finanzen." The following table is an abbreviated summary of the withholding rates applied in double taxation conventions in connection with domestic tax law.

	Dividends (1)	Interest (2)	Royalties
Nontreaty countries	25% (3)	25%	25% (4)
Treaty countries:			
Argentina	15	10/15 (5)	15
Australia	15	10	10
Austria	25	25	—
Belgium (6)	15	15 (7)	—
Brazil	15	10/15 (8)	15/25 (9)
Canada	15	15	10
Cyprus	10/15	10	0/5 (10)
Denmark (6)	10/15	—	—
Egypt	15	15	—
Finland	10/15 (11)	—	0/5 (12)
France (6)	5/15	—	—
Greece	25	10	—
Hungary	5/15	—	—
Iceland	5/15	—	—
India	15	10/15	20
Indonesia	10/15	10	10
Iran	15/20	15	10
Irish Republic (6)	15	—	—
Israel	25	15	0/5 (14)
Italy (6)(13)	10/15	10	5
Ivory Coast	15	15	10
Jamaica	10/15	10/12.5 (15)	10

	Dividends (1)	Interest (2)	Royalties
Japan	15%	10%	10%
Kenya	15	15	15
Korea	10/15	10/15 (16)	10/15 (17)
Liberia	10/15	10/20 (18)	10/20 (19)
Luxembourg (6)(20)	10/15	—	5
Malaysia	5/15	15	10/25 (21)
Malta	5/15	10	0/10 (22)
Morocco	5/15	10	10
Mauritius	5/15	25	15
Netherlands (6)	15	—	—
New Zealand	15	10	10
Norway	25/15	—	—
Pakistan	15/25 (23)	20	—
Poland	5/15	—	—
Portugal (6)	15	10/15 (24)	10
Romania	10/15	10	10
Singapore	10/15	10	0/25 (21)
South Africa	15	10	—
Spain (6)	15	10	5
Sri Lanka	15 (25)	10	10
Sweden	5/15	—	—
Switzerland (26)	10/15	—	—
Thailand	15/20	10/25 (27)	5/15 (28)
Trinidad & Tobago	10/20	10/15 (15)	0/10 (29)
Tunisia	10/15	10	10/15 (30)
Turkey (6)	15/20	15	10
United Kingdom	15	—	—
United States	5/15	—	—
U.S.S.R.	15	5	—
Zambia	5/15	10	10

Notes:

(1) In the case of two rates given, the second rate generally applies to minority shareholders (i.e., less than 25%), except that a reduced tax rate applies in cases of Canada and Pakistan where the nonresident's interest exceeds 25% and 33.33%, respectively. Generally, income from a "silent partnership" is treated as dividend income. The preferential treatment for companies that control at least 25% of the voting power does not extend to silent partnerships.

(2) Following domestic law, no withholding tax is levied on interest payments to foreign creditors. Interest to foreign creditors on debts secured by mortgages on real estate is subject to normal income tax (levied by assessment).

(3) The rate of 25% increases to 33.33% if the debtor of the dividends takes over the withholding tax.

(4) The rate of 25% decreases to 15% for artistic and professional sports activities practiced in Germany.

(5) 10% in cases involving credits for equipment sales, bank loans, and financing of public works.

(6) EC parent-subsidiary directive limits the withholding rate for dividends to 5%.

(7) Reduced to nil if paid to enterprises (generally no reduction in cases of participation of 25% or more).

(8) 10% if the recipient is a bank and the loan is granted for a period of at least seven years in connection with the purchase of industrial equipment, with the study, the purchase, and the installation of industrial or scientific units, as well as with the financing of public works.

(9) 25% on royalties for trademarks.

(10) 5% if such payments are made for the use of any cinematographic films, including films and video tapes for television.

(11) 25% if the recipient is a silent partner.

(12) 5% if such payments are made as consideration for the use of patents, designs, plans, secret processes, formulas, and trademarks.

(13) Rates stated according to the new treaty. However, the new treaty has not yet been ratified. In case the treaty is not in force at publication date, the applicable rates will be 10/15 (dividends), 5 (interest), and 0 (royalties).

(14) 5% if such payments are made as consideration for the use of patents, trademarks, designs or models, plans, etc.

(15) 10% if the recipient is a bank.

(16) 10% if the recipient is a bank and the loan is made for a period of more than seven years.

(17) 10% in the case of industrial investment.

(18) 10% if the recipient is a bank.

(19) 20% if such payments are made as consideration for the use of copyrights, excluding cinematographic films or tapes for television or broadcasting or trademarks.

(20) Luxembourg holding companies are excluded from the treaty.

(21) 25% on payments made as consideration for the use of copyrights of literary, artistic, or scientific work, and films or tapes for television or broadcasting.

(22) 10% if such payments are made as consideration for the use of patents, equipment, or information concerning industrial, commercial, or scientific experience, etc.

(23) The lower rate applies on dividends to a Pakistani company owning at least one third of the voting rights of the German company.

(24) 10% in general if the recipient is a bank.

(25) Except that earned profits and dividends of companies are tax-free if the

earned profits and dividends derive from Sri Lanka or from the Federal Republic of Germany.

(26) A special clause that applies to German residents moving to Switzerland is still applicable for five years after the move. The treaty is not applicable to Swiss companies not fulfilling the prerequisites of article 23 of the treaty.

(27) 10% if the recipient is a bank company or an insurance company, if the enterprise paying the interest engages in an industrial undertaking in the meaning of article 10 of the treaty.

(28) 15% if such payments are made as consideration for the use of patents, secret formulas or processes, etc.

(29) Payments made as consideration for the use of copyrights (excluding cinematographic films or tapes for television or broadcasting) are tax-free.

(30) 15% if such payments are made as consideration for the use of patents, designs or models, plans, secret formulas or processes, trademarks, or films.

OTHER SIGNIFICANT TAXES

21. Sales (Value Added)

The system for collecting turnover tax is identical in all EC countries. The German tax rate is 14%. In special cases, the rate is reduced to 7%. Exempt from VAT are, among others, most transactions by banks and insurance companies, sales of land and buildings, and leases and rents received for the letting of land, buildings, and lodgings.

Imported items are subject to import turnover tax at the same rates as turnover tax. The company may deduct from its turnover tax liability both turnover tax invoiced to the company and import turnover tax paid by the company; where the balance is in the company's favor, a rebate is made. Companies that have no turnover in Germany may also, on application, recover invoiced turnover tax and import turnover tax paid. The application must be filed no later than six months after the year-end.

22. Inheritance and Gift Taxes

A federal tax is imposed on estates and gifts. As a rule, both kinds of transactions are treated alike. The applicable tax rates vary from 3% to 70% and are determined by two factors: they increase with the increasing value of the relevant asset as well as with decreasing kinship between beneficiary and bequeather/donor.

23. Taxes on Payrolls (Social Security)

In Germany, social security is not financed by taxes. Social security is a comprehensive insurance scheme that includes three types of insurance. Old age or long-term disability as well as unemployment insurance are institutions under public law, and all employees are compulsory members. Health insurance, the third type, is organized partly under public law and partly under private law; membership is only compulsory up to a certain wage/salary level (in 1991, DM 4,875 per month).

The basis of assessment for insurance contributions is the gross income of the insured employee up to DM 6,500 (in 1991). Any income in excess of this limit is irrelevant for the purpose of the assessment for contributions to old age or long-term disability insurance and unemployment insurance. For the purposes of health insurance, any income in excess of DM 4,875 per month (equal to the compulsory insurance limit) will be disregarded. These contribution assessment limits are adjusted on a yearly basis.

Both the employee and employer pay equal amounts of contributions, and the employer withholds the employee's portion from his or her compensation.

Insurance	Employer's Share		Employee's Share	
	(%)	(DM max.)	(%)	(DM max.)
Health	appr. 6.20	302	appr. 6.20	302
Old age and long-term disability	9.35	608	9.35	608
Unemployment	2.15	140		140
		1,050		1,050

All employers are obliged to insure their employees against industrial accident or illness. These contributions are borne solely by the employers.

24. Taxes on Natural Resources

No special taxes are levied on the exploitation of natural resources.

25. Other Taxes

Property Tax. A federal property tax is imposed on the owner, whether an individual or a corporation, of movable and immovable property. The tax rate is 0.5% for individuals and 0.6% for corporations, based in each case on the value of the property. In the case of land, however, the tax is not based on the market value but on a so-called unit value which is ascertained for tax purposes by a special method. This value is usually less than one-half of the market value. At present, the tax is based on a sum equivalent to 140% of this unit value.

Municipal authorities impose a land tax on the unit value of land. The tax rates vary with the location of the land.

COMPUTATION OF TAXABLE INCOME

26. Capital Gains

For the basis for determining profit, see item 3.

27. Depreciation and Depletion

The annual depreciation rate for buildings (for straight-line depreciation) is 4% of the purchase price or the cost of construction if the construction permit was applied for after March 31, 1985 and the building is an operating asset not used for residential purposes. The taxpayer may elect to write off 10% during the first four years, 5% during the next three years, and 2.5% during the subsequent eighteen years if the taxpayer erected the building or purchased it before the end of the calendar year of construction.

The straight-line depreciation for other buildings completed after December 31, 1924 is 2%. If the period of economic use can be shown to be shorter than 50 years, the depreciation can be adjusted accordingly.

One alternative to straight-line depreciation for such a building if newly purchased or newly constructed or purchased within the year construction has been completed.

During the first 4 years	10.0%
During the next 3 years	5.5%
During the subsequent 18 years	2.5%

And, if such a building is destined to be let for residential purposes, a second alternative is:

During the first 4 years	7.00%
During the next 6 years	5.00%
During the next 6 years	2.00%
During the subsequent 24 years	1.25%

In the case of movable goods and business assets, the taxpayer has the option to write off the purchase price or the cost of construction either in equal yearly amounts during their customary useful life (straight-line method), or at a fixed percentage of the balance of the book value (declining-balance method). This procedure is subject to the restriction that the applicable rate may not exceed three times the rate of straight-line depreciation, and in no case may it exceed 30%. As a third method, depreciation may also be based on the economic performance of the asset. Other goods such as immovable or immaterial assets may be depreciated only by the straight-line method. In addition, extraordinary technical or economic wear and tear are taken into account for depreciation purposes.

The tax authorities have published tables giving the "economic useful life" and AfA (depreciation for wear and tear allowed by tax regulations) rates for a wide range of goods. Deviation from these rates by the person or body liable for tax is permissible if it can be justified. There are various possibilities for so-called special depreciation. This is not based on wear and tear, but is granted as an investment incentive in certain industries.

28. Treatment of Dividends

The distributing company is required to deduct a 25% withholding tax from the amount of dividends payable to shareholders. A shareholder subject to unlimited tax liability can then offset the tax withheld against his or her liability for income or corporation tax.

The same procedure applies to the 36% corporation tax on the company's distributed profits. The total amount of tax liability is accordingly calculated as follows:

	DM
Income after trade income tax	100
Less corporation income tax	(36)
Income after taxes	64
Less 25% withholding tax	(16)
Income after withholding tax	48
Total tax liability	52

In some double taxation treaties, the withholding tax rate is limited to 5% or 15% (see item 17). In such a case, the tax withheld in excess of 15% is refunded to the foreign shareholder on application.

29. Loss Carryovers

The first DM 10 million of losses must first be carried back for two years. Any loss remaining out of the DM 10 million as well as any excess loss can be carried forward without any time limitation. Any loss carryover requires that the losses be connected with earnings in Germany and documented by records kept in Germany.

30. Transactions between Related Parties

Revenue transactions between related parties, in particular international transactions, have to be at arm's length.

The profit resulting from the liquidation of a corporation is taxed as if it had been earned in the ordinary course of business (see item 1). Generally, this rule also applies if the assets of a corporation are transferred to another legal entity without a liquidation (merger, change of legal status due to a take-over). These reorganizations are, however, governed by a number of special rules that provide for significant tax relief. These special rules also provide for relief in case of the reorganization of partnerships and the takeover of sole proprietorships and independent divisions of an enterprise by another corporation or a partnership.

31. Consolidation of Income

If a corporation is financially, economically, and organizationally controlled by another German enterprise (which may be the permanent establishment of a nonresident corporation), and if an agreement on the transfer of profits and losses has been entered into, the income of the subordinate corporation will be attributed directly to the dominant enterprise (so-called Organschaft—fiscal unity). Only a corporation that has its registered seat in Germany can be a subsidiary corporation within these rules.

32. Tax Periods

The period for income tax assessment is always the calendar year or, whenever the tax liability begins or ends during the year, the appropriate part thereof. Those who carry on a trade or business (both individuals and companies of any kind) can have fiscal periods that differ from the calendar year, but which in no case may exceed a period of 12 months. The fiscal year is that period for which financial statements are regularly prepared. The profit of one fiscal year together with all other income is assessed in that calendar year in which the fiscal year ended.

RELATED CONSIDERATIONS

34. Incentives and Grants

The federal government and the governments of all 16 states (Laender) offer an assortment of financial incentives to promote private investment. These consist of direct subsidies (loans or grants) as well as tax reliefs given as depreciation allowances. Both kinds of aid are restricted either as to the region where they apply or as to the type of purchased goods, or the industry concerned. The most important measures are:

- [ ] Grants, credits, and investment guarantees in specific industries (shipping, mining, steel, fishing, and building industries).
- [ ] Regionally restricted special depreciation allowances; e.g., in a corridor along the former eastern border of West Germany.
- [ ] Special depreciation allowances restricted to certain items; e.g., for ships, planes, investments in the mining industry, research plants, systems for the reduction of noise, water, and air pollution.
- [ ] Investment in West Berlin is promoted by financial grants, special depreciation allowances, turnover tax relief, and other incentives.
- [ ] A range of incentives is available for investment in Eastern Germany (see "Overview, East Germany").

Exempt Income. Specifically exempt from taxes are benevolent trusts and charitable organizations (provided they do not engage in business activity) and a number of pension funds.

35. Exchange Controls

Residents (corporations and individuals) must prepare an annual report if:

□ They hold 25% or more of the shares or of the votes of a corporation that has its registered office abroad, provided the total balance figure of that corporation is in excess of DM 500,000.

□ They operate a branch or a factory abroad with a gross working capital in excess of DM 500,000.

Reports also must be prepared by:

□ German corporations with a total balance figure in excess of DM 500,000, if a nonresident or a group of nonresidents operating in concert holds 25% or more shares or votes in the corporation.

□ German branches or permanent establishments with a gross operating capital in excess of DM 500,000, if they are run by nonresidents.

Residents, excluding banks, must report their accounts payable and their accounts receivable to and from nonresidents after every month during which they exceed DM 500,000.

In individual cases, notification is required of payments arising out of international transactions where these exceed DM 2,000 and of investments of residents abroad and nonresidents in West Germany. Investments here include, among others, the establishment or acquisition of companies, branches, and holdings and the provision of capital and loans for these.

36. Investment Restrictions on Nonresidents

None.

SELECTION OF BUSINESS ENTITY BY NONRESIDENTS

When a company intends to do business in, rather than with, Germany, it can choose between two basic forms of organization. It can set up a branch, which is only a division of the company, or it can establish a subsidiary as a separate entity. Some of the important factors that enter into the selection are:

□ A foreign corporation is exposed to liability for the debts of its branch, while a subsidiary corporation does not expose its parent to such liability.

□ A local subsidiary is taxed on its worldwide income, while a branch is taxed on its income in Germany.

□ The rate of corporation income tax for a subsidiary is 50% on retained earnings, and 36% where profits are distributed as a dividend. Capital yields tax on distributed dividends is generally levied at 25%, resulting in a charge (excluding trade income tax) of 52% on distributed profits (see item 28). However, if a double taxation treaty limits the capital yields tax to 15% (see item 28), the total tax burden on distributed profits of a subsidiary is only 45.6% (excluding trade income tax).

SPECIMEN TAX COMPUTATION

	No Distribution (DM)	Full Distribution (DM)
Income before taxes	120,000	120,000
Trade income tax (assumed municipal multiplier: 400	20,000	20,000
Income after trade income tax	100,000	100,000
Corporation income tax (at 50% and 36%, respectively)	50,000	36,000
Income after taxes	50,000	64,000
Capital yields tax (25% of amount distributed)		16,000
Income after withholding tax		48,000
Total income tax as percent of income before taxes	58.3%	60.0%

The corporation income tax rate for a branch is 46%, irrespective of appropriation of profit; no withholding tax is charged.

The above computation does not reflect the solidarity surcharge levied for 1992.

GHANA

INCOME TAXES ON CORPORATIONS

1. Rates

The following companies are taxed at 35%.

- [ ] Companies engaged in agriculture after the end of their period of exemption.
- [ ] Companies manufacturing excisable goods and registered under the Ghana Customs and Excise Decree 1972 (NRCD 114).
- [ ] Companies engaged in real estate development.
- [ ] Companies engaged in construction.
- [ ] Companies that provide services.

Companies engaged in mining operations (other than those taxed under Petroleum Income Tax Law—see item 24) are taxed at the rate of 45%.

All other companies, including those engaged in banking, insurance, commerce, and printing, are taxed at the rate of 50%.

2. Local Income Taxes

None.

3. Capital Gains Taxes

A capital gains tax is levied on capital gains derived by a person or a company, whether resident or not, from the realization of the following chargeable assets after August 22, 1975: permanent or temporary buildings, land (other than agricultural land), shares and businesses, and business assets (including goodwill).

Exemptions exist for the following:

- [ ] Capital gains arising during mergers, amalgamation, and reorganization of companies.
- [ ] Capital gains arising out of disposal of securities of companies listed on the Ghana Stock Exchange for the first five years of the Exchange's existence.

The capital gains tax rate varies with the number of years the asset was owned and is based on when the chargeable asset was realized, as follows:

Years Since Acquisition	Tax Rate
1	50.0%
2	47.5
3	45.0
4	42.5
5	40.0
6	37.5
7	35.0
8	32.5
9	30.0
10	27.5
11	25.0
12	22.5
13	20.0
14	17.5
15	15.0
16	12.5
17	10.0
18	7.5
19	5.0
over 19	2.5

Special rules apply if the sale proceeds were used partially or wholly to acquire a similar chargeable asset.

4. Branch Profits Taxes

A branch of a foreign company is taxed on its profits on the same basis and at the same tax rates as a resident corporation. The Commissioner of Internal Revenue has discretionary power to assess the branch by reference to the consolidated profits of the whole group of companies, both resident and nonresident, of which the branch is a part. However, where the Commissioner is satisfied with the results of the branch operating in Ghana, the chargeable income of the branch is computed without reference to the total consolidated profits of the whole group.

5. Foreign Tax Reliefs

A Ghanaian resident company may obtain relief under double taxation treaties. The reliefs may consist of tax credits, reduced rates, or exemptions.

INCOME TAXES ON INDIVIDUALS

9. Rates

Individuals resident in Ghana are liable to tax on their income accrued in or derived from, brought into, or received in Ghana. The incomes of a husband and wife are taxed separately. An individual's chargeable income includes all fixed cash allowances for housing in excess of 20% of his basic annual salary and entertainment (excluding reimbursed expenses incurred solely for the benefit of the employer), as well as prescribed amounts for accommodations or the use of a private car provided by the employer. An individual's income for a year of assessment is the income for that year of assessment. In the rate tables below, the first column applies to total income. Pensions are no longer taxable.

Chargeable Income		
Over	Not Over	Rate
¢ 0	¢ 84,000	5%
84,000	336,000	10
336,000	840,000	20
840,000	1,350,000	30
1,350,000	2,040,000	40
2,040,000		50

Each taxpayer is entitled to a tax-free allowance of ¢60,000 and may deduct personal reliefs up to an aggregate maximum of ¢210,000 for the following:

☐ Contributions to approved pension or provident funds.
☐ Social Security contributions (currently 5% of basic salary).
☐ Life insurance premiums paid in Ghana currency and not in excess of 10% of taxpayer's income and 10% of the sum assured.

In addition, the following reliefs are granted:

☐ Children's education relief of ¢30,000 (maximum three children) in respect of the education of a child or ward in any registered first- or second-cycle educational institutions designated educational institutions or registered secondary schools in Ghana.
☐ Marital and dependent relief of ¢10,000.
☐ Disability relief equal to 25% of the self-employment income of the disabled.
☐ Old age relief of ¢80,000 to self-employed individuals above the age of 60.
☐ Aged dependent relative relief of ¢12,000 up to a maximum of two such relatives.

10. Local Income Taxes

None.

11. Capital Gains Taxes

Capital gains tax is levied on assets sold after August 22, 1975. See items 3 and 26.

12. Foreign Tax Reliefs

Residents may obtain relief under double taxation treaties.

13. Tax Period

The fiscal year, which was July 1 to June 30, has been changed to a calendar year effective in 1983 fiscal year. The period July 1 to December 31, 1982 is deemed to form part of the 1981/1982 fiscal year.

14. Other Matters

Withholding Tax.   Tax is withheld from these payments:

Contract payments for personal services	5%
Fees payable to directors, part-time teachers, and commission agents	15
Dividends	15
Interest other than that earned by individuals	30

For dividends, the 15% withholding tax is also the final tax.

INCOME TAXES ON NONRESIDENTS

15. Liability to Tax

Nonresident individuals are liable to tax on their income accrued in or derived from Ghana. They are not liable on income brought into or received in Ghana from sources outside of Ghana.

Nonresidents who derive income from Ghana must pay a minimum tax of 35% of total income earned in or derived from Ghana, or at the individual rates for residents, whichever is the greater. Thus, the effective rates of tax for a nonresident are 35% on the first ¢3,272,000 and 50% on any excess.

16. Rates

Income derived by a nonresident company carrying on business in Ghana is taxed at the same rates as that of a resident company (see item 1). If a nonresident company does not carry on business in Ghana, such income is subject to a 50%

withholding tax. Interest and dividend income derived by a nonresident individual is treated as that earned by a resident, whereas royalty income derived by a nonresident individual is taxed at the rates noted in item 15. Under certain double taxation treaties, dividends, and a fair and reasonable amount of royalty are exempt from Ghana tax. A nonresident company or individual is not subject to tax on:

☐ Interest on bonds issued by the Ghana Government, a cooperative society, or a statutory corporation.

☐ Service fees received from Ghana for services provided outside Ghana.

Profits and similar distributions deemed to be remitted out of Ghana from chargeable income earned after July 1, 1970, are exempt from withholding tax. Such distributions deemed to be remitted out of chargeable income earned prior to July 1, 1970, are subject to tax on varying portions of such income at the rates applicable to the year of assessment, which were:

Fiscal year ended June 30, 1970	7.5%
Fiscal year ended June 30, 1969	12.5
Fiscal years ended June 1968 and 1967	20.0

19. Tax Treaties

Double taxation treaties exist between Ghana and the United Kingdom, Sweden, Gambia, Sierra Leone, and Nigeria. Except for the United Kingdom, an individual who is a resident of any of these countries is exempt from Ghana tax on any profit or remuneration for personal and professional services if, for the year of assessment:

☐ The individual's presence in Ghana does not exceed 183 days during that fiscal year.

☐ The services are performed on behalf of a person resident in any of the countries with which Ghana has a tax treaty.

☐ The remuneration or profits is subject to tax in the treaty country.

Income from professional services or other activities derived from Ghana by a U.K. resident is subject to tax in Ghana. Remuneration derived from employment in Ghana (other than aboard a ship or aircraft) by a U.K. resident is not taxable if:

☐ The individual's presence in Ghana does not exceed 183 days during that fiscal year.

☐ The remuneration is paid by (or on behalf of) an employer who is not resident in Ghana.

☐ The remuneration is not borne by a permanent establishment or a fixed base of the employer in Ghana.

The industrial or commercial profits of an entity from a tax treaty country is not taxed unless the entity is doing business through a permanent establishment in Ghana. If it is, only the profits attributable to that permanent establishment are taxed (see item 4).

OTHER SIGNIFICANT TAXES

21. Sales (Value Added)

If a loss results or if the chargeable income of a trade, vocation, or profession is lower than a "minimum chargeable income," which is 5% of the annual turnover, then tax is charged on the minimum income at the appropriate income tax rate (see item 1). Excepted from this rule are mining and farming concerns, businesses in their first five years of assessment, businesses granted a tax holiday under the Investment Code, and businesses that have for a minimum period of ten consecutive years of assessment, or lesser period for new businesses, maintained to the satisfaction of the Commissioner adequate books of account and have submitted reliable accounts for all those years.

22. Inheritance and Gift Taxes

No inheritance tax is levied. Gift tax is levied on the transfer of a chargeable asset whose value exceeds ¢50,000 and is paid by the donee. Where aggregate gifts in any year of assessment are less than ¢50,000, no tax is levied unless the aggregate value of gifts received over any period within five consecutive years exceeds ¢50,000. The chargeable assets are land, buildings, any means of transportation (land, air, or sea), goods and chattel not included above, money, and stocks, shares, bonds, and other securities.

	Gift's Value	
Over	**Not Over**	**Rate**
¢ 0	¢ 50,000	0%
50,000	250,000	5
250,000	500,000	7.5
500,000	750,000	10
750,000	1,000,000	12.5
1,000,000		15

Gift tax is not levied on chargeable assets transferred:

□ Under a will or upon intestacy.
□ By one spouse to the other.
□ By a parent to a child or vice versa.
□ By a parent's brother or sister to the parent's child or vice versa.

□ By a child to a parent's child.
□ To a religious body which uses the gift for a public purpose.
□ For charitable or educational purposes.

23. Taxes on Payrolls (Social Security)

Social security contributions are based on gross monthly salaries at the following rates:

Paid by employer	12.5%
Paid by employee	5.0%

Selective Alien Employment Tax. An annual tax of ¢500,000 is levied for each non-Ghanian employed under an immigrant quota. The tax is levied on the employer and is not deductible in arriving at chargeable profits. Certain exemptions from this tax are granted, including the managing director or other chief executive of an organization. Additionally, the Commissioner for Finance may, with prior approval of the Government, exempt any alien from payment of the tax.

24. Taxes on Natural Resources

Income from mineral oil operations is taxable under the Petroleum Income Tax Law, 1987, which has replaced the Mineral Oil Taxation Act. Regular income tax is not charged in respect of any income to which this petroleum oil tax applies; the tax is charged at 50% on the chargeable income.

A sub-contractor for any work or services in connection with a Petroleum Agreement will be subject to a withholding tax at a rate specified in the Petroleum Agreement and, as far as income from that source is concerned, will not be liable to tax under the provisions of any other law in force in Ghana.

25. Other Taxes

Land and Property Taxes. No property taxes are levied. Municipalities levy general rates on the rateable value of properties.

Wealth Tax. Any individual with a net wealth exceeding ¢500,000 with respect to certain assets may pay this tax.

Additional Profit Tax. This tax, which replaces the Minerals Duty, is payable yearly by every person engaged in mining operations in addition to the normal income tax payable under the Income Tax Decree 1975 (SMCD 5). It is calculated at the rate of 25% on the carry-forward cash balance existing on the last day of each year of assessment.

Stamp Duty. Stamp duties are imposed on the registration of documents. Most duties are ad valorem.

Standard Assessments. Certain classes of persons, as specified in the income tax law, are required to pay a standard assessment of income tax each year. This assessment is fixed by the tax law for each such class and must be paid before a tax clearance certificate, license, or permit to carry on a business will be issued. These standard assessments are regarded as tax credits and are set off against the actual income tax payable by such persons. This assessment is now referred to as the Quarterly Advance Tax Payment.

Commercial Passenger Vehicle Tax. Separate rates of tax on owners of commercial passenger vehicles:

Type of Vehicle	Rate of Tax
Taxi and cars on hire within town	¢100 per day
"One pound One pound" cars	¢30 per ¢1,000 fare per trip
Mini Buses	¢30 per ¢1,000 fare per trip
Long distance passenger buses	¢30 per ¢1,000 fare per trip
"Trotro" vehicles up to 44 seater	¢120 per day
"Trotro" vehicles 45 seater and above	¢150 per day
Container trucks in Accra-Tema	¢50 per ¢1,000 per trip
Light dry cargo service (Market service)	¢200 per day
Long distance cargo trucks and articulated vehicles	¢50 per ¢1,000 charge per trip
Wet cargo vehicles	¢50 per ¢1,000 charge per trip

Casino Revenue Tax. The gross revenue of a casino is taxed at the rate of 2.5%. In addition, a ¢10,000 tax is imposed on each casino table in the Greater Accra Administrative Area, and a ¢5,000 tax in any other area.

Entertainment Tax. A 25% entertainment tax is levied on the gross revenue from boxing tournaments, cinematograph or video exhibition, and horse-racing; 10% on theaters, dramas, concerts, and similar performances in cities and urban areas, dances, football matches, and night club entertainments.

Hotel and Restaurant Tax. A 10% tax is levied on bills for accommodations and food consumed at a hotel or restaurant, as well as snacks or snacks with drinks consumed in a snack bar. Persons on diplomatic passports are exempted. Customers of hotels and restaurants managed by the State Hotels Corporation or by the Ghana Government are exempt from the food portion of this tax. Bills under ¢200.00 are exempt from tax.

Purchase Tax, Etc. Imports of vehicles with petrol-operated engines exceeding 1600cc and diesel-operated engines exceeding 1800cc are subject to purchase tax of 10%, in addition to import and sales taxes of 5% to 25% and 7.5% to 35%, respectively. Other capital goods are subject to import duty of 10%.

COMPUTATION OF TAXABLE INCOME

26. Capital Gains

Capital gain tax is chargeable on the difference between the sum received or receivable and/or any receipt in kind, and the cost of acquiring the assets, increased by alterations and improvements and any expenditures incidental to the realization of the asset. No tax is levied if the capital gain is ¢50,000 or less.

27. Depreciation and Depletion

In place of ordinary depreciation, the tax system provides "capital allowances" which are deductible in computing taxable income. The current rates are:

| | Allowances | |
Assets	Initial	Annual
Buildings	10%	3%
Plant and machinery	20	5–20
Furniture and fixtures	20	7.5–12.5
Mining and timber expenditure	25	15
Airplanes and helicopters	20	7.5–10
Ships, trawlers, barges	20	5
Plantation	10	5

The initial allowance is based on the initial cost of the assets; the annual allowance is on the reducing balance basis. An additional investment allowance of 5% of the initial cost is granted for qualifying plant and machinery used in an industrial establishment.

Special rates are applicable to specified cases as follows:

☐ Mining. Qualifying mining expenditure attracts capital allowance of 75% in the year of investment and 50% in subsequent years. The residue of qualifying expenditure on which the annual allowance is computed is, in this case, adjusted by the exchange rate factor in the event of an adjustment of the exchange rate during the year of assessment. In this connection, the exchange rate factor is the exchange rate at the end of the year divided by the exchange rate at the end of the preceding year.

☐ Petroleum Operations. In the case of petroleum operations, the capital allowance for the year of commencement is one-fifth of the total qualifying petroleum capital expenditure for the years up to and including that year, the remaining four-fifths being deducted equally in the immediately succeeding four years.

For any year after the year of commencement, annual capital allowance is related to the total petroleum capital expenditure and deducted equally in five successive years.

After the year of commencement, the deduction of the capital allowances shall proceed concurrently.

28. Treatment of Dividends

Dividends paid in Ghana to residents or nonresidents are now taxable. Stock dividends are not considered distributions for tax purposes.

29. Loss Carryovers

Except for petroleum operations, farming enterprises, and real estate development operations, losses are not carried forward or back. However, capital allowances (item 27) that cannot be absorbed by available assessable income may be carried forward until fully utilized. Companies engaged in the insurance business may be allowed to carry forward losses.

30. Transactions between Related Parties

No special provisions apply to revenue transactions between related parties.

For tax purposes, the sales price of an asset constitutes its value at the time of disposal. An asset disposed of other than by sale is valued at its open market price at the time of disposal.

31. Consolidation of Income

Income tax is assessed on income from all sources.

There is no provision for the filing of consolidated tax returns by related corporations.

32. Tax Periods

Effective January 1, 1982, the fiscal year of assessment that ended June 30 has been changed to December 31. The period July 1, 1982, to December 31, 1982, is deemed to form part of the 1981/82 fiscal year. With effect from January 1, 1983, the assessable income of a company for a year of assessment is the income for that year of assessment. By way of modification, with effect from the year of assessment 1988, the assessable income of any person whose accounting year ends on a date other than December 31 will be the income for his or her accounting year ending within the year of assessment. Any change in a person's accounting year will be subject to the approval of the Commissioner of Internal Revenue.

RELATED CONSIDERATIONS

34. Incentives and Grants

A number of incentives and grants are available to stimulate production in certain priority areas of the economy; that is, agriculture, mining and manufacturing industries, exports, tourism, construction and building industries and non-metropolitan industries. The incentives include:

□ Manufacturing companies not engaged in woodworking or metal processing are entitled to export rebates ranging from 30% to 75% of their tax liabilities if they export between 5% and 25% or more of production during their basis period.

□ Persons engaged in the export of specific agricultural produce are entitled to export rebates ranging from 40% to 75% of their tax liabilities if they export between 5% and 25% or more of such agricultural produce during their basis periods.

□ Persons, other than companies engaged in real estate development, i.e., construction and sale or leasing of residential premises, who invest not less than 20% of their business profits in the construction of residential premises for sale or leasing will be entitled to offset 50% of such investment against their tax liabilities for the year following the year of investment. (For tax purposes, the maximum investment allowed is 50% of the business profits of each person.)

□ The Ghana Investment Center may under the Investment Code 1985 grant to approved projects:

—Income tax rebates spread over a three-year period at the rates of 75%, 50%, and 25%, respectively, to enterprises engaged in forestry and agriculture. An income tax rebate is available for specified enterprises that use Ghanaian labor rather than imported machinery.

—Complete exemption from selective alien employment tax.

—Complete exemption from the payment of customs duties on machinery, plant, equipment, and accessories imported especially and exclusively for the establishment of the approved enterprise. Guaranteed immigration and personal remittance quotas for expatriate personnel and exemption from any tax with respect to the transfer of foreign currency out of Ghana.

—A reduction of 15%–40% in income tax payable with respect to approved nonmetropolitan industries.

—Special capital allowances in addition to those provided under the Income Tax law.

—Full deduction of capital expenditures with respect to scientific research.

—Reduction or deferment of income tax payable by rural enterprises undertaking infrastructural works.

35. Exchange Controls

Comprehensive exchange control regulations are embodied in the Exchange Control Act of 1961 (Act 71). These restrict the transfer of money outside Ghana for all purposes. In addition, the transfer of shares to nonresidents requires the prior approval of the Minister of Finance through the Exchange Control Department of the Bank of Ghana.

36. Investment Restrictions on Nonresidents

Only a Ghanaian is permitted to carry on certain businesses in Ghana:

☐ Where a wholesale or retail business is carried on in a supermarket, a business representation for foreign companies, or a product brokerage, foreign participation is permitted if the employed capital is not less than US$500,000.

☐ Minor trading operations in markets, kiosks, and the like.

☐ Other specified enterprises unless a nonresident alien is exempted.

Other enterprises can be operated by aliens, but require specified degrees of Ghanaian and/or State participation, as follows:

☐ Forty per cent Ghanaian participation is required for banking

☐ Insurance enterprises require 60% State and/or Ghanaian participation.

☐ For mineral enterprises and enterprises engaged in the production of mineral oil or natural gas, the degree of State participation is based on the terms agreed between the Centre and the foreign investor.

☐ The degree of Ghanaian participation in other enterprises will be determined by the terms agreed between the Ghanaian and foreign investor and approved by the Centre.

The implementation of these provisions is the responsibility of the Ghana Investment Centre.

SELECTION OF BUSINESS ENTITY BY NONRESIDENTS

Nonresident investors can operate a business in Ghana through either a locally-incorporated company or a branch. Nonresidents must register an incorporated company under the Companies Code, 1963 (Act 179) before they can begin operations in Ghana.

Branch profits are computed by reference to the total consolidated profits of the affiliated group (including both resident and nonresident companies) and taking into account the proportion which the turnover of the branch bears to the group's total turnover. The Commissioner, however, may compute the branch's profits without reference to the total consolidated profits of the whole group. The accounts of the branch and group are needed for tax assessments, and where the accounts are not in English, a certified translation is required. A nonresident company operating in Ghana through a branch can distribute all of its after-tax profits without the payment of any additional tax, but locally-incorporated companies suffer withholding tax on dividend distributions. The withholding tax on dividends and interest is 15% and 30%, respectively. In the case of dividends, it is the final tax.

Tax incentives generally depend upon where the nonresident is operating and not the form of business entity.

SPECIMEN TAX COMPUTATION

Information:

☐ Lagoon Salt Limited is a manufacturer which qualifies as an industrial establishment for investment allowance purposes.

☐ The accounts are for the year ended December 31, 1984.

☐ Turnover consists of:

Export sales	¢1,000,000
Local sales	9,000,000
Sale of fixed assets	50,000

☐ Profits for the year ended December 31, 1984 are ¢2,500,000.

☐ Charged to profits are the following disallowable items:

Depreciation	¢ 50,000
Selective Alien Employment Tax	20,000
Provision for gratuity	40,000
General provision for bad debt	30,000
Management expenses	
Customs purification rite	5,000
Funeral grant	10,000

☐ Capital allowances available for use:

Investment allowance	¢ 10,000
Initial allowance	50,000
Balancing charge	40,000
Capital allowances carried	
forward from 1983	100,000

☐ Company's tax rate is 50%.

☐ Applicable export rebate rate is 25%.

☐ The company paid an advance tax of ¢40,000 with respect to the 5% contract deductions made by the Treasury.

☐ The asset sold was a vehicle with an adjusted cost base of ¢10,000.

☐ The applicable capital gains tax rate is 45%.

Computation:

Net profits		¢2,500,000
Add		
Depreciation	¢50,000	
Selective Alien Employment Tax	20,000	
Provision for gratuity	40,000	
General provision for bad debt	30,000	
Customs purification rite	5,000	
Funeral grant	10,000	155,000
		¢2,655,000
Less		
Profit on sale of fixed assets	50,000	50,000
Adjusted Profit		¢2,605,000
Less		
1983 capital allowances	¢100,000	
Investment allowances	10,000	
Initial allowance	50,000	
Balancing charge	(40,000)	120,000
Chargeable income		2,485,000
Tax payable at 50%		¢1,242,500
Less		
Advance tax	¢40,000	
Export rebates	250,000	290,000
Net tax payable		¢ 952,500

Notes:
(1) The capital gains tax is computed as follows:

Amount realized	¢50,000
Less	
Adjusted cost base	10,000
Chargeable gains	¢40,000
Tax on ¢40,000 @ 45%	¢18,000

GIBRALTAR

INCOME TAXES ON CORPORATIONS

1. Rates

The income tax rates for corporations are:

Other companies	35%
Qualifying companies	2% to 18% (negotiable)
Exempt companies	Nil

2. Local Income Taxes

None.

3. Capital Gains Taxes

There is no separate capital gains tax in Gibraltar, but gains from the disposition of business assets are taxed at the regular corporate rate (see item 1).

4. Branch Profits Taxes

Any foreign registered company earning income in Gibraltar is taxed at the rates set out in item 1.

5. Foreign Tax Reliefs

Gibraltar has not concluded any tax treaties with other countries. Relief is allowed for U.K. tax on income which is also taxed in Gibraltar. Partial relief is given for taxes imposed by other Commonwealth countries if reciprocal arrangements apply.

6. Classification of Corporations

Three distinct types of companies are recognized under Gibraltar tax law, each of which is treated differently for tax purposes:

☐ Exempt Companies and Qualifying Companies. "Exempt companies" pay an annual tax not exceeding £300 regardless of the amount of profits and are exempt from all other taxes and duties (except for the 0.05% duty on nominal share capital). Exempt status is granted to companies that comply with certain requirements, particularly that no Gibraltarian or resident of Gibraltar may hold a beneficial interest in any of the company's stock and that the company may not trade with a Gibraltarian or resident of Gibraltar. Such requirements do not restrict the ability of residents of Gibraltar to hold shares as nominees or trustees or to act as directors of such companies. Therefore, management and control of an exempt company can take place in Gibraltar without jeopardizing its exempt status.

A "qualifying company" pays tax at a rate between 2% and 18% of taxable profits, such rate being determined by negotiations with the Tax Authorities. A qualifying company may be useful in those situations where a jurisdiction will not levy further taxes on receipts of income by residents if such income has borne tax at source.

It is not necessary for a company to be incorporated in Gibraltar in order to gain exempt or qualifying status.

☐ Other Companies. All other resident companies are classified as "other companies" and are taxed at the rate of 35%. The income of both qualifying and other companies is taxable if it accrues in, is derived from, or is received in Gibraltar. Dividends and interest arising outside Gibraltar are exempt if the amounts are taxed at source and not received in Gibraltar. A company is treated as resident in Gibraltar if it is either managed and controlled in Gibraltar or by persons ordinarily resident there.

7.   Payment of Taxes

Assessments are made on the basis of annual audited accounts filed with the Income Tax Office. Assessments are payable in two installments: 50% of the tax not later than three months from the date of service of the notice of assessment, and the balance not later than six months from that date.

INCOME TAXES ON INDIVIDUALS

9.   Rates

Individuals resident in Gibraltar are subject to Gibraltar tax, but a number of reliefs are available depending on the status of each individual. An individual is treated as resident in Gibraltar if the individual spends more than 183 days in Gibraltar in any one year. A resident's worldwide income is taxable except for earnings taxed at source and not remitted to Gibraltar. Relief is allowed for U.K. tax on income which would also be taxable in Gibraltar.

The tax rates for the 1991/92 year are as follows:

Taxable Income

Over	Not Over	Rate
£ 0	£ 1,500	20%
1,500	7,000	30
7,000	12,500	35
12,500	16,000	40
16,000	19,500	45
19,500		50

Personal deductions range from £1,450 for a single taxpayer to £3,300 for a married taxpayer with one child. Other deductions include interest on housing loans (i.e., to purchase a residence in Gibraltar) and pension contributions and life insurance premiums, both of which are allowable up to designated amounts.

Salaries and wages have Gibraltar tax deducted at source. Married persons are individually assessed except for unearned income, which is taxed to the husband only. Partners are individually assessed on their portion of the partnership's income.

10. Local Income Taxes
None.

11. Capital Gains Taxes
None.

12. Foreign Tax Reliefs
See item 5.

13. Tax Period
The tax year ends on June 30. However, a different fiscal period may be chosen by any person where the accounts of his or her trade, profession, business, or vocation are made up to a different date in the year.

Income tax is charged for each year of assessment on the basis of the income of the preceding year, except for income from employment or pensions which is charged on the basis of the income for the current year.

Commencement provisions are applied to "other companies" and self-employed individuals, which effectively means that the first year's profits are taxed twice. On cessation of business only two of the last three years' profits are subject to tax.

INCOME TAXES ON NONRESIDENTS

15. Liability to Tax
Nonresidents are subject to income tax on all income arising in Gibraltar, except interest earned on Bank and Building Society deposits. All gains or profits derived

from any employment exercised in Gibraltar are deemed to arise in Gibraltar whether or not received in Gibraltar.

16. Rates

Nonresident individuals and corporations are taxed on their Gibraltar-source income at the same rates as resident individuals (except for the first £1,500, which also is taxed at 30%) or corporations.

17. Withholding Tax Rates

In general, dividend and interest payments by "other companies" incur withholding tax at the rate of 35%. However, interest paid to a resident or nonresident individual is taxed at the rate of 30%. Payments to nonresidents exceeding £7,000 will be taxed at higher rates (see item 9). Substantially reduced withholding rates apply to payments by "qualifying companies" (see item 18), while payments by exempt companies are not subject to withholding taxes of any kind.

18. Special Withholding Provisions

Special withholding tax provisions apply to payments of interest or dividends by both other and qualifying companies under the Gibraltar Income Tax Ordinance:

- [ ] **Interest.** In the case of payments of mortgage, debenture, or capital loan interest by other companies to either residents or nonresidents, tax is withheld at the rate of 30% if paid to an individual (or possibly more in the case of nonresidents, see item 17) and 35% if paid to a company. In certain circumstances, the Commissioner may grant relief from these requirements. Such interest payments by qualifying companies normally do not suffer withholding tax; however, the Financial and Development Secretary may impose withholding tax under certain circumstances.

- [ ] **Dividends.** In the case of dividends paid by other companies to either residents or nonresidents, tax must be withheld at the company rate of 35%. This tax may be credited by the shareholder against his or her own income tax liability. Qualifying companies must withhold tax from dividend payments at the rate at which the company is taxable (see item 1). The tax deducted by the company must not be paid over to the Commissioner unless and to the extent that the tax deducted is higher than the company tax to be paid on its income.

- [ ] **Other Payments.** Management or consulting service fees and royalties paid to nonresidents are subject to 35% withholding tax if paid to a company and 30% if paid to an individual. The requirement to make these deductions may be waived by the Commissioner if he is satisfied that the services were performed outside Gibraltar and the payment will subject to income tax in the country in which the services were performed. Such payments by qualifying companies have tax withheld at a rate negotiated with the Commissioner. Tax may also be withheld from payments to construction subcontractors. Directors fees have tax withheld under the normal PAYE provisions at the appropriate rate (see item 9).

☐ Exempt companies are not subject to withholding taxes of any kind.

OTHER SIGNIFICANT TAXES

21. Sales (Value Added)

None.

22. Inheritance and Gift Taxes

Estate duties are levied at rates ranging from 5% (£20,000 to £40,000) to 25% (over £100,000). Certain relief is available where assets are taxed in other jurisdictions. Deposits in Gibraltar banks and building societies are not part of the taxable estate of a nonresident deceased person.

There is no gift tax as such, but gifts made within three years of the decedent's death are included in the estate for estate duty purposes.

23. Taxes on Payrolls (Social Security)

Social security is required to be paid for each employee by both the employer and the employee at approximately £12 per week each. There are no other taxes on payrolls.

24. Taxes on Natural Resources

None.

25. Other Taxes

Import duties are levied on most imported goods. Excise duties are levied on alcohol, wine, and tobacco. Certain stamp duties are also levied.

COMPUTATION OF TAXABLE INCOME

26. Capital Gains

There is no separate capital gains tax in Gibraltar, but gains on the disposition of business assets are taxed at the appropriate corporate rate.

27. Depreciation and Depletion

Various rates of depreciation are prescribed by the taxing authority. These vary from 15% to 25%. Building depreciation is not normally an allowable deduction.

28. Treatment of Dividends

Dividends received are included in assessable income, but any Gibraltar tax withheld at source from that dividend offsets any tax chargeable on that dividend.

29. Loss Carryovers

Tax losses may be carried forward indefinitely.

30. Transactions between Related Parties

There is no specific tax legislation covering such transactions, but the Commissioner does have general powers to disregard any transaction which, while reducing the amount of tax payable, is artificial or fictitious.

31. Consolidation of Income

There is no provision for the filing of consolidated tax returns by related corporations.

32. Tax Periods

Tax is normally levied on taxable income for the year ending June 30.

RELATED CONSIDERATIONS

34. Incentives and Grants

Tax incentives are available under the Develoment Aid Ordinance. If a development aid license can be obtained, the company will be exempt from income tax with respect to any gains or profits arising from the development program until aggregate gains exceed the allocated percentage of capital expenditures on the project. Shareholders are exempt from tax on the distributed profits up to the amount granted under the license. Interest income of lenders to a project granted Development Aid status is also exempt from Gibraltar tax.

To obtain a Development Aid license, the project normally must create local housing, and it must result in a minimum level of expenditure (usually £500,000).

35. Exchange Controls

None.

36. Investment Restrictions on Nonresidents

There are no investment restrictions on nonresidents. Foreign investors may commence operations provided the usual licenses and permits have been obtained.

37. Other Matters

Trusts. Gibraltar law recognizes and gives full legal effect to the concept of a trust. The non-Gibraltar income (together with Gibraltar-source bank and building society interest income) of a trust created by a nonresident of Gibraltar is exempt from Gibraltar tax even if the trustees are resident in Gibraltar. This concession requires that, under the provisions of the trust deed, no Gibraltarian or resident of Gibraltar is or may be a beneficiary of the trust.

Gibraltar trustees are subject to the normal withholding taxes deducted from dividends paid by companies throughout the world, and the trustees themselves cannot make a claim for repayment of such withholding taxes. In certain circumstances, if income is distributed by trustees to beneficiaries resident in a particular country, those beneficiaries may make claims under double taxation agreements existing between their country of residence and the country from which the dividend income arose.

Incorporation Costs. Total professional costs involved in the incorporation and registration of a Gibraltar exempt company usually do not exceed £700. A company ordinarily can be set up within three to four days assuming there is no objection from the Registrar as to the name chosen. For an exempt or qualifying company, the application for the granting of a certificate can take a further 7 to 60 days depending on the circumstances and nature of the case but can be granted retrospectively if the relevant criteria were met during this time. Annual costs include the annual tax (not exceeding £300) and, where applicable, secretarial fees, director fees, and registered office fees (none of which normally exceeds £150). An annual certificate is required to be signed by both the secretary and the director confirming the company's compliance with the exemption requirements.

SELECTION OF BUSINESS ENTITY BY NONRESIDENTS

A company (whether incorporated in Gibraltar or elsewhere) may be able to obtain tax-exempt status and establish operations in Gibraltar without being subject to any Gibraltar taxes. The principal criteria for obtaining tax-exempt status are set out in item 6. Such companies may be particularly useful for investment holding and international trading activities.

GREECE

INCOME TAXES ON CORPORATIONS

1. Rates

Undistributed profits of corporations are generally taxed at an effective rate of 46%.

However, reduced rates are applicable on undistributed profits of the following corporations:

☐ Manufacturing, handicraft, and mining   40%
☐ If the corporations above are quoted in the Athens Stock
    Exchange or make approved investments   35%
☐ Trading and other corporations making approved investments   40%

In calculating taxable undistributed profits, dividends are deducted and subject to withholding tax as explained in item 28.

2. Local Income Taxes

There are no state or provincial income taxes in Greece.

3. Capital Gains Taxes

Capital gains are taxable when derived from:

☐ The sale of any right pertaining to the operation of an enterprise or to a profession.
☐ The sale of a commercial or other enterprise in its entirety or of the firm's name, trademark or goodwill, etc.

Gains referred to above are taxable at a flat rate of 20% or 30%. Similarly, gains resulting from the sale of fixed assets of an enterprise (except for real estate and ships) are considered as income derived from commercial activity. Such income is not taxable, provided it is utilized for the purchase of other existing machinery and industrial plant, or new machinery and plant to be installed by the enterprise within the following year, or the year after that. Alternatively, such income is not taxable if it is transferred to a reserve. Capital gains resulting from the sale of securities (bonds and shares) are exempt from income tax. In the case of businesses keeping double entry books of account, such gains are to be credited to a special reserve fund intended to offset possible losses from the future sale of other securities. Should these gains ever be distributed, they are subject to taxation upon distribution.

4. Branch Profits Taxes

Foreign business organizations trading in Greece are subject to Greek corporate tax (46%) on their total net income derived from Greek sources and/or from their permanent establishment in Greece.

5. Foreign Tax Reliefs

Agreements for the avoidance of double taxation exist between Greece and the following countries: Austria, Belgium, Czechoslovakia, Cyprus, Finland, France, Germany, Holland, Hungary, India, Italy, Sweden, Switzerland, United Kingdom, and the United States.

6. Classification of Corporations

The following types of entities exist in Greece:

☐ Corporation (Societe Anonyme).
☐ Limited liability partnership (E.P.E.).
☐ Partnerships (O.E. or E.E.).
☐ Branch of a foreign company.
☐ Offshore company (Law 89 company).
☐ Joint venture.

The Greek corporation is similar to a U.S. corporation and a U.K. limited liability company.

7. Payment of Taxes

Corporations are required to pay income tax in seven monthly installments, with the first one payable within 130 days after the year-end. In addition, 50% is payable in advance in seven monthly installments. The computation of these installments is illustrated in the specimen tax computation at the end of this summary.

INCOME TAXES ON INDIVIDUALS

9. Rates

The following tax rate table is applicable as of January 1, 1990. This is adjusted annually for inflation.

| Taxable Income | | Tax on | Percentage |
Over	Not Over	Lower Amount	on Excess
Drs.1,200,000	Drs.3,000,000	Drs. 216,000	30%
3,000,000	7,500,000	756,000	43
7,500,000		2,691,000	50

The tax is calculated using the table above as follows:

(a) Tax is calculated on the total income (without allowances).
(b) Tax is calculated on the tax allowances, which depend on family status, nature of the income, and certain expenses.

The tax calculated under (b) is deducted from the tax calculated under (a), and the net figure is the tax payable.

Income is classified according to its source:

☐ Income from leasing or use of buildings and land.
☐ Income from securities, interest, dividends, and directors' fees (as distinct from directors' salaries).
☐ Profits of industrial and commercial business organizations.
☐ Income from agricultural enterprises.
☐ Income from salaries, wages, pensions and other forms of remuneration.
☐ Income from professional fees and other sources.

Different rules apply and different deductions are made in the computation of net income of each category.

Income Liable to Tax. Individuals domiciled in Greece are liable to tax on their total net income from all sources, regardless of their nationality. Partnerships and limited liability partnerships are not subject to company tax, the partners or members being finally taxed as individuals on their share of the profits.

A wife's income is generally assessed separately, unless it consists of business profits derived from an undertaking economically dependent on the husband.

Interest earned from funds deposited with banks operating in Greece and interest from government and certain other bonds are free of tax.

Imputed Income. Individuals may be taxed according to deemed or imputed income in cases where this income is higher than the actual income declared and the taxpayer cannot substantiate the difference. The following give rise to imputed income:

□ Acquisition of cars.
□ Main and secondary residences.
□ Private cars.
□ Expenses for more than one household servant.
□ Private boats.
□ Company owned cars.
□ Loans to businesses.

Company-owned automobiles may be included in the calculation of the imputed income of directors and partners. In cases where the difference between declared and imputed income does not exceed 20% of the earned income, the tax is assessed on the earned income. This difference is reduced by:

□ Amounts which are not considered as taxable income.
□ Capital spending which has already been taxed.
□ Foreign currency imported.
□ Loans.
□ Proceeds from sales of property.

10. Local Income Taxes
None.

11. Capital Gains Taxes
Capital gains realized by an individual are normally taxed at the rates referred to in item 3.

Effective January 1, 1991, capital gains derived from the sale of property are taxed at the following rates, on the basis of the difference between selling price and cost, which will be adjusted annually for inflation.

Years of Ownership	Tax on Difference
up to 5	25%
6–10	20
11–20	15
over 20	10

12. Foreign Tax Reliefs
In the absence of a double taxation agreement, unilateral relief is given by way of a credit for foreign taxes. This credit may not exceed the amount of Greek tax which would have been payable had the income been earned in Greece.

13. Tax Period

Personal income tax is always based on the calendar year. Income of individuals who are resident in Greece for a part of a calendar year is treated as income relating to the complete year. There are no prorated reductions of allowances. Certain of the double taxation agreements entered into by Greece provide that income earned by foreigners resident in Greece for a period less than six months is exempt from tax.

INCOME TAXES ON NONRESIDENTS

15. Liability to Tax

Nonresident individuals are, in general terms, taxed on their total Greek source income, including income obtained from a permanent establishment in Greece. A nonresident is any person whose domicile or principal residence is not located in Greece. Nonresidents are not entitled to tax abatements.

Business organizations which are considered as having a permanent establishment in Greece are liable to tax on their income from all sources.

16. Rates

Income of nonresidents is taxed at rates similar to those for residents (see item 9).

17. Withholding Tax Rates

Royalties paid to foreign enterprises and organizations, which do not have permanent establishments in Greece, are generally subject to a 25% withholding tax.

Net profits derived by foreign enterprises and organizations that prepare studies and plans or conduct research of a technical, scientific, or general nature are subject to a 20% income tax (which is calculated on the gross fee) whether or not the work is performed in Greece.

Foreign enterprises undertaking construction or similar work in Greece will be taxed on a deemed profit basis at the following income tax rates on the gross value of the contracts:

☐ 5% on contracts with the federal government, municipalities, or state-owned companies.

☐ 6% on private-sector contracts.

☐ 12% on contracts where the contractor does not use his own materials.

The above taxes should be withheld when the royalties are paid or credited. The taxes must be deposited (together with the relevant declaration) by the end of the month following that in which the withholding occurs.

If the recipient of royalties does not have a permanent establishment in Greece, the withholding is limited to the rate specified in the double tax treaty between

Greece and the country in which the recipient is resident, provided that such a treaty exists and a residency certificate can be obtained.

19. Tax Treaties

See item 5.

20. Other Matters

Foreign nationals wishing to work in Greece must first obtain a work permit from the Ministry of Labor and a residence permit from the Aliens Bureau. Renewable work permits are granted sparingly unless the employee has a special skill. Personal and household effects may be imported duty-free but must be taken out of the country upon leaving. Similarly, foreign-registered cars can be imported for personal use by foreign nationals for a limited period. For E.E.C. nationals, only a residence permit is required.

OTHER SIGNIFICANT TAXES

21. Sales (Value Added)

A value-added tax on imports, sales, and services took effect on January 1, 1987. Effective April 28, 1990, the basic VAT rates are 8%, 18%, or 36% depending on the nature of the goods or services. Certain transactions are exempt from VAT, such as most banking, insurance, and services of state-owned organizations.

Sales of goods for export are not liable to tax, and the exporter is given a refund of the tax paid on raw materials incorporated in the exported products.

22. Inheritance and Gift Taxes

Inheritances.   All persons, except foreigners covered by a double taxation agreement, who inherit property situated in Greece are liable to inheritance tax. There are six categories of heirs or legatees, according to their degree of relationship with the deceased, with different rates of tax and allowances for each category.

Gifts.   The tax rates and rules are the same as for inheritances, with certain additional exemptions.

Dowries.   These are taxed at half the rates applied to inheritances and gifts and are accorded greater allowances.

23. Taxes on Payrolls (Social Security)

Social Security Contributions.   Social security coverage is compulsory for all employees (foreigners may be exempted in certain cases). On the average, the employee pays 14.25% and the employer 24.35% of the employee's remuneration up to a maximum of approximately Drs. 298,250 per month.

Stamp Duty on Salaries and Wages. Stamp duty of 1.2% is levied on gross salaries and wages, and is payable half by the employer and half by the employee.

25. Other Taxes

Transfer Tax on Immovable Property. The usual tax rate for property transferred is 9%. This is increased by 2% in urban areas to cover the cost of fire protection. In addition, there is a surtax of 3% on the assessed tax. Lower taxes may be levied in certain cases; e.g., merger of companies. On compulsory exchange of one piece of land for another, the rate is 4% or 5%. The division of land between co-proprietors is taxed at 2%.

Tax on Movements of Funds. Transactions relating to funds for share capital increase or working capital injection from foreign (non-EEC) head offices to local branches are subject to 1% tax.

Luxury and Consumption Tax. Certain goods that are considered luxury items are subject to luxury or consumption tax in addition to turnover tax. This tax is levied at varying rates on a wide variety of locally produced and imported goods.

Shipping Taxation. Profits from shipping are subject to a shipping tax in place of income or company tax. The tax applies only to ships operating under the Greek flag. These are divided into two categories: Category I includes freighters, tankers and refrigerated ships of gross tonnage of 3,000 koros (8,460 tons) or more, and passenger vessels plying from Greece to foreign ports or between foreign ports. Category II includes other power-driven vessels, sailing vessels and small craft. There are various exemptions for each category. With some exemptions, ships in Category I are taxed quarterly at the following rates payable in U.S. dollars:

Number of Years		Rate per Ton
Over	Not Over	
10	20	Drs.0.20
20	25	0.30
25		0.40

Ships in Category II, again with some exemptions, are taxed annually at the following annual rates payable in Greek drachmae:

Gross Tonnage		Annual Rate of
Over	Not Over	Tax per Koros
K 0	K 10	Drs. 10
10	20	15
20	40	20
40	70	25
70	100	30
100		35

COMPUTATION OF TAXABLE INCOME

26. Capital Gains

See item 3.

27. Depreciation and Depletion

All business organizations are allowed to depreciate their fixed assets on the straight-line method at predetermined rates as laid down in Law 88/1973. Depreciation is based on the value of the assets at the date of acquisition, plus expenditure on improvements, and can only be claimed as a deduction for taxation purposes if it is recorded in the books of account. Depreciation cannot be claimed either retrospectively or cumulatively in subsequent years. Depreciation rates may vary with regions and usage. The basic rates are:

Description of Asset	Annual Depreciation Rate
Industrial buildings	8%
Other buildings	5
Machinery	10–20
Computers	20
Furniture and similar items	20
Office equipment	15
Trucks	20
Other vehicles	12
Software	25

28. Treatment of Dividends

Dividends may be included in the taxable income of shareholders. A withholding tax is deducted at source at the following rates:

	Shares Quoted on the Athens Stock Exchange	Shares Not Quoted on the Athens Stock Exchange
Bearer shares	45%	50%
Registered shares	42	47

Dividends received by a shareholder from companies quoted on the Athens Stock Exchange are exempt from income tax for amounts up to Drs. 50,000 received from each company, with a maximum exemption of Drs. 200,000. In the case of dividends received from companies quoted on the Athens Stock Exchange, or dividends on registered shares, the shareholder may elect to declare this income together with his income from all other sources, and be taxed at the general rates set out in item 9. Any excess of withheld tax may either be offset against taxes due from other sources or refunded.

Companies must distribute annually dividends equal to 6% of their share capital or 35% of their net profit, whichever is the higher. Exemption from this rule can only be obtained with the approval of shareholders representing 80% or 95% of the paid-up capital. If an exemption is obtained, such nondistributed profits must be capitalized by issuing bonus shares. Only if the approval of shareholders representing 100% of the paid-up capital is obtained can both the distribution and capitalization of profit be waived.

29. Loss Carryovers

Operating losses under certain conditions may be carried forward for five years.

30. Transactions between Related Parties

Transactions between companies resident in Greece and companies not resident in Greece which are not carried out on an arm's-length basis may be subject to tax on the basis that would have obtained had the transactions been carried out on an arm's-length basis.

31. Consolidation of Income

Group taxation is not permitted.

32. Tax Periods

The tax year is normally the calendar year. Business organizations keeping double entry books may end their accounting periods at June 30 or December 31. Branches and subsidiaries of foreign companies may adopt their parent's year-end under certain conditions.

RELATED CONSIDERATIONS

34. Incentives and Grants

In order to encourage the decentralization of industry away from the Athens-Piraeus area, various regional tax incentives have been adopted. These are somewhat complex and Law 1892/1990 has substantially amended them. The legislation provides grants of up to 55% of the total investment (excluding land and working capital), interest rate subsidies up to 55%, extra depreciation allowances to a maximum of 150%, and fixed corporate tax rates. Tax-free deductions from profits are available only as an alternative to the other incentives (except they may be combined with extra depreciation allowances), but they can rise to 100% of the annual profit.

The incentives vary by region and the importance attached to the investment. Five basic regions are defined but the regions applicable to tourism investments differ from those for manufacturing and mining.

Investments deemed ''special'' enjoy even higher incentives; such designation may be due to the type of investment, the characteristics of the investor, or the precise location of the investment.

Under certain conditions, trading companies may transfer to tax-free reserves up to 25% of their undistributed profits, provided capital investments amounting to 200% of the reserve will be made over a period specified by the law.

Export Incentives.   Raw materials, fuel and, in some cases, packing materials to be used for the production of export products may be imported free of import duties and taxes. Other incentives for export are:

☐   Exporters are entitled to a deduction from their taxable profits of a proportion of their export sales at the rate of 1%–3%.

☐   Export companies are entitled to reduced rates of bank interest.

To qualify for the various export incentives, businesses must obtain a certificate of export activity after each export permit (see item 35) has been settled. The certificate is based on the F.O.B. value of exports paid in free foreign exchange; settlements through bilateral clearing accounts are not eligible for certificates unless they are for mining exports.

Protection of Foreign Capital.   The importation of foreign capital, represented by joint stock or loans, is free; but when the investor wishes to repatriate his capital in the future, or remit profits abroad, then the investment must first be approved according to the provisions of item 35 below. Approval of the importation of foreign capital under the terms of Law 2687/1953 can be obtained from the Ministry of National Economy. The agreed terms, formalized in a ministerial decree, are published in the Government Gazette. A foreign investor will be granted the following advantages from an agreement concluded under Law 2687/1953:

☐ Business assets are not subject to compulsory expropriation. Government requisition with appropriate compensation is only permitted in times of war.

☐ The Government cannot unilaterally alter terms of the agreement; disputes are referred to arbitration.

☐ By agreement, income tax may be fixed at the current or a lower rate for a period of up to ten years.

☐ Repatriation of imported capital is permitted at the rate of 15% annually commencing one year after the start of operations. Repatriation of loan capital may be permitted at certain rates if the loan is less than twice the capital stock.

Various other concessions and advantages are granted to foreign investments, primarily in the following areas:

☐ Remittance of profits abroad; up to 20% of the imported share capital remaining in Greece (also see item 35).

☐ Maximum rates of interest on imported loan capital.

☐ Foreign exchange remittances for rent, royalties, etc.

☐ Preferential tax treatment for export mining or quarrying companies which save foreign exchange.

☐ Subsequent increases in income tax not applying to companies established under the above-mentioned laws.

35. Exchange Controls

The foreign exchange environment had been tightly regulated by the Bank of Greece in order to discourage capital outflows and encourage capital inflows. Beginning in May 1986, capital movement between Greece and EEC member states has been partially liberalized. However, approval by the Bank of Greece or the Minister of National Economy is still required depending on the transaction.

Investments from EEC Countries. In accordance with Presidential Decree 207/ 87, prior approval is required for capital, interest, and profits expatriation rights. This necessitates an application to the Ministry of National Economy, which examines only the authenticity and origin of the investment. The application should include:

☐ Certificate of investor's residency.

☐ Standardized questionnaire.

The time required for the approval normally does not exceed two to four weeks.

Investments from Non-EEC Countries. These are governed by Decision No. 825/86 of the Bank of Greece, where the relevant applications should be filed for approval prior to the importation of the funds. The application should describe the nature of the investment and the parties involved, and should be accompanied by a certificate of the investor's residency.

The time required for the approval normally does not exceed two to four weeks.

Imports. Import permits are still required for the importation of certain categories of goods in Greece. These permits must be obtained from authorized banks and are generally valid for a period of six months. The system in force is in a state of flux as a result of entry to EEC.

Exports. Licenses are no longer required for exports with the exception of all exports to State-trading countries which require a permit of the Ministry of Commerce. Exporters are subject to invoice control by the commercial banks for all invoices over $30,000. Approval is normally given automatically if prices are up to 20% higher on an annual basis than the previous prices. Where invoice prices have fallen, or have risen by more than 20% or where no earlier comparable invoices are available, the banks' approval may be delayed by the need to consult with the Bank of Greece.

The approvals of the commercial banks for the payment of foreign exchange for invoiced exports normally have a validity of six months and may be extended to twelve months.

Nontrading Greek Branches of Foreign Companies—Law 89/67. Law 89 of 1967 provides special benefits to offices established by foreign commercial, industrial and shipping companies exclusively to conduct business outside Greece. Permission is granted by Ministerial Authority.

Offices established under Law 89/67 are allowed to operate foreign currency accounts for remittances outside Greece and conversion into drachmae.

The Greek expenditure of these offices must be financed by the importation of foreign exchange which should be equivalent to $12,000 per annum per employee with a minimum total requirement of $50,000.

Companies operating under this law may obtain work and residence permits for foreign personnel for periods of two years, renewable for like periods. They may import essential equipment free of import duties, tax, revenue stamp duties, turnover tax and other import charges. Alien personnel may also under certain conditions import cars and household effects duty-free.

Although a company set up under Law 89/67 cannot do business in Greece, the rules offer generous tax incentives, which essentially exempt all the office's overseas income from income tax as well as turnover taxes, import duties and all other charges on imported equipment for the operation of the management branch.

36. Investment Restrictions on Nonresidents

There are no investment restrictions on nonresidents. A nonresident may do business in Greece either by establishing a branch of an organization formed under the laws of a foreign country, or by setting up an organization permitted under Greek law (see item 6). Foreigners cannot acquire property in border areas.

SELECTION OF BUSINESS ENTITY BY NONRESIDENTS

Most nonresident investors prefer to operate in Greece by establishing either a branch, a corporation (Societe Anonyme), or a limited liability partnership.

Branch of a Foreign Company. Branch profits derived from Greek sources and/ or from the permanent establishment in Greece are taxable at 46%.

Corporation. Assuming a trading company is not listed on the Athens Stock Exchange, profits are taxable at 46%, after deducting dividends, directors' fees, and transfers to tax-free reserves. Dividends are taxable in the hands of shareholders at 47% or 50% (see item 28), but this tax is deductible at source. Dividend tax rates may be lower if the shareholder is a resident of certain treaty countries (Belgium, Cyprus, Germany, Holland, and Italy).

The main characteristic of the corporate income tax is that profits are taxed only once, either as retained earnings or as dividends.

Limited Liability Partnership. The tax is ultimately levied on the partners and not on the entity, which pays only an advance tax of 15%.

SPECIMEN TAX COMPUTATION

Computation:

Profits for the year ended December 31, 1989, per official books of account	Drs. 2,000,000
Add	
Nondeductible items (e.g., car expenses, fines)	200,000
	2,200,000
Less	
Dividend	700,000
Tax-free income (e.g., bank interest)	100,000
Directors' fees	250,000
Transfers to tax-free reserves	110,000
Losses brought forward	40,000
	1,200,000
Taxable undistributed profit	1,000,000

□ Assume a corporation is not listed on the Athens Stock Exchange and dividends are paid to:

German shareholders   500,000
Local shareholder   200,000

Basic corporate income tax (Drs. 1,000,000 × 46%) (1)		460,000

Tax advance
  Tax withheld on dividends

German shareholders (Drs. 500,000 x 25%)	125,000		
Local shareholder (Drs. 200,000 x 50%)	100,000		
	225,000		
Basic corporate tax as in (1) above	460,000		
	685,000 × 50%	342,500	
Total taxes payable (2)		802,500	

□ In the case of a branch, there are no distributions and the taxable profit would be:

Profit per official books of account	2,000,000
Plus items not deductible for tax purposes	200,000
Less	
Tax-free income	(100,000)
Losses brought forward	(40,000)
Total taxable profit	2,060,000
Basic income tax (Drs. 2,060,000 x 46%)	947,600
Tax advance (Drs. 947,600 x 50%)	473,800
Total taxes payable	1,421,400

Notes:

(1) Payable in seven monthly installments beginning on May 10, 1990.
(2) A 10% tax reduction is available if the total tax due is paid by May 10, 1990.

GRENADA

INCOME TAXES ON CORPORATIONS

1. Rates

A business levy is payable on net profits at the following rates:

First $50,000	30%
Remainder	40%

2. Local Income Taxes

There are no local taxes in Grenada.

3. Capital Gains Taxes

There are no capital gains taxes.

4. Branch Profits Taxes

A branch of a foreign corporation is taxed on the activities of the branch as though it were a resident corporation.

5. Foreign Tax Reliefs

None.

6. Payment of Taxes

The business levy is payable in 12 equal monthly installments in the year in which the profit is made. The amount payable is based on the previous year's profit until the results of the current year become available.

INCOME TAXES ON INDIVIDUALS

9. Rates

A debt service levy is payable on salaries over $12,000 per annum at the rate of 10%.

INCOME TAXES ON NONRESIDENTS

There are no income taxes on nonresidents.

OTHER SIGNIFICANT TAXES

21. Sales (Value Added)

A value-added tax is payable as follows:

Locally manufactured products	15%
Hotels, guest houses, apartment buildings, and restaurants	8% of gross sales
Services	5% of gross billings

25. Other Taxes

There are no other taxes payable by companies or individuals.

GUATEMALA

INCOME TAXES ON CORPORATIONS

1. Rates

Corporate income is subject to the following tax rates:

Annual Taxable Income		Tax on	Percentage
Over	Not Over	Lower Amount	on Excess
Q 0	Q30,000	Q 0	12%
30,000	60,000	3,600	22
60,000		10,200	34

2. Local Income Taxes

None.

3. Capital Gains Taxes

The profit on sale of fixed assets, securities or any other asset for more than its net book value is treated as part of taxable income of the year. Income tax derived from capital gains can be paid over three years without any charge.

4. Branch Profits Taxes

Branches of foreign companies are subject to the same income tax rates as corporations on their local net profits. An additional 12.5% tax is withheld on transfers of profits to the parent company.

5. Foreign Tax Reliefs

Foreign-source income is not taxable.

6. Classification of Corporations

Guatemalan business law recognizes the following entities:

☐ Corporations.
☐ Limited liability partnerships.
☐ General partnerships.

7. Payment of Taxes

Income tax is payable annually within 90 days after the close of the tax period.

INCOME TAXES ON INDIVIDUALS

9. Rates

Individual income is subject to tax as follows (only selected taxable incomes are shown):

Annual Taxable Income

Over	Not Over	Tax Rate
Q 0	Q 5,000	4%
20,000	30,000	12
50,000	60,000	18
70,000	80,000	22
90,000	100,000	26
120,000	130,000	32
130,000		34

10. Local Income Taxes

None.

11. Capital Gains Taxes

See item 3.

12. Foreign Tax Reliefs

Individuals are not taxed on foreign-source income.

13. Tax Period

The tax period ends on June 30 of each year.

INCOME TAXES ON NONRESIDENTS

15. Liability to Tax

Tax is required to be withheld by the payor on payments or credits to individuals or companies domiciled abroad for certain services rendered from abroad to individuals or companies domiciled in Guatemala.

17. Withholding Tax Rates

Withholding taxes vary with the nature of the payment or credit. The most important withholding taxes are those imposed on the following payments or credits:

Dividends or other participations in capital	12.5%
Interest, fees, commissions, salaries	25.0%
Patents, privileges, royalties, franchises, technical or financial advisory services, and any other Guatemalan-source income	34.0%

19. Tax Treaties

Guatemala has not entered into tax treaties with other countries for the avoidance of double taxation.

OTHER SIGNIFICANT TAXES

21. Sales (Value Added)

A 7% value-added tax is levied on imports, sales, and services. The tax is borne by the buyer, but it is not an expense, except when it cannot be applied to future payments. The seller can credit the amount of tax that he has paid on his own purchases of goods. If the credit in a given month is greater than the tax due, it can be carried forward and credited against future payments. The following are exempt from VAT: exports, inland transportation, the construction and engineering industry, funeral services, medicines, chemicals, and services provided by banks, other financial institutions, and insurance and reinsurance companies.

22. Inheritance and Gift Taxes

Gifts made during the donor's lifetime and property transferred on his death are subject to a progressive tax. The rate varies with the amount involved and the degree of relationship.

23. Taxes on Payrolls (Social Security)

Social security is financed by employers' and employees' contributions of 11.3% and 4.5%, respectively, of total compensation with no maximum limits.

24. Taxes on Natural Resources

All surface and subsurface mineral resources belong to the State, which imposes annual rentals for exploration permits, and rentals and royalties when the leased properties enter the production stage.

25. Other Taxes

Land and Property. Land and property is subject to property tax based on an official valuation and is paid quarterly at the following annual rates:

Property Value

Over	Not Over	Rate
Q 0	Q 2,000	0%
2,000	20,000	0.20
20,000	70,000	0.60
70,000		0.90

Stamp Tax.   A 3% stamp tax is levied on the following services and contracts:

☐ Contracts and all documents in which obligations are contracted and that result in the payment, collection, transfer, or cancellation.

☐ Professional services rendered by individuals.

☐ Insurance policies.

☐ Dividends or profits distribution.

☐ Funeral services.

Registration and Annual Fees. Profit-making companies or partnerships incorporated abroad and authorized to establish branch offices or agencies in Guatemala, pay 0.10% of their net assets (maximum Q10,000).

COMPUTATION OF TAXABLE INCOME

26. Capital Gains

A capital gain is measured by the difference between cost (tax basis of depreciable assets) and selling price.

27. Depreciation and Depletion

Depreciation is calculated on the straight-line basis at the following maximum rates:

Buildings	5%
Machinery, equipment, vehicles	20%
Office furnishings and equipment	10%
Tools	25%

Tax authorities may allow other depreciation methods, upon request, for special cases.

Mining operations are granted a depletion allowance, subject to specific authorization by the tax authorities. Exploration costs can be absorbed in the first fiscal year or in the next five consecutive years.

28. Treatment of Dividends

Dividends paid to residents are tax-exempt. Dividends paid to nonresidents are subject to withholding tax of 12.5%.

29. Loss Carryovers

Operating losses cannot be deducted in the following taxable profit years, except for farm losses resulting from uncontrollable events.

30. Transactions between Related Parties

The tax authorities do not concern themselves with transactions between related parties and transactions between a foreign parent company and a Guatemalan subsidiary or branch are not normally scrutinized carefully.

31. Consolidation of Income

Each legal entity must pay its own taxes.

32. Tax Periods

In general, the tax period begins July 1st and ends on the following June 30th. Upon request, the Income Tax Bureau may establish different tax periods.

33. Other Matters

Inventory Valuation. For tax purposes, inventories may be valued at cost or market, whichever is lower, on the basis of FIFO, average cost, LIFO, or last purchase. Industrial articles produced are usually valued by the absorption method, which includes raw materials, direct labor, and manufacturing overhead. Direct cost (variable) is also allowed for tax purposes.

Bad Debts. A taxpayer may either provide a general reserve for doubtful accounts of no more than 2% of the accounts receivable or deduct specific bad debts.

Employee Benefits Provisions. Provisions for employee benefits such as annual vacation and Christmas bonus are deductible. Provision for severance compensation is deductible to a maximum of 5% of salaries paid during the tax year. If the provision method is not used, actual severance payments are fully deductible.

Royalties. Royalties are deductible if the taxpayer obtains authorization from the Ministry of Economics. The maximum deduction is 10% of the net sales.

Income. Taxpayers must report their income on the accrual basis. Cash basis can be used in agricultural activities or upon request.

Nontaxable Income. Interest income from deposits in Guatemalan banks is not taxable.

Investment Deduction. The increase in social security paid by the employer in respect to the previous year, due to an increase in workers making less than Q500 a month, can be deducted directly from the income tax. A 50% deduction is permitted if the company is located in the state of Guatemala; 100% for other areas.

Investment in new machinery or equipment incorporated in the production process can be deducted from the taxable income. A 10% deduction is permitted if the company has total assets of more than Q200,000, and 20% if less.

RELATED CONSIDERATIONS

34. Incentives and Grants

Companies whose only activity is exporting goods out of the Central American Market (which excludes Panama and Belize) are exempt from income tax and from import duties on machinery and raw material for ten years. Companies that export but also have other activities are exempt only on import duties related to exports.

There is a free zone (ZOLIC) where industries and commercial operations can be performed fully tax-exempt for 12 years. Goods sold to the local market must pay duties.

Industrial companies establishing operations in certain regions outside the Central area are granted income tax exemption up to 90% for 10 years.

35. Exchange Controls

The following markets are established for the purchase and sale of foreign currency:

□ Official Market. The official market concerns only payments for obligations and debts contracted by the Guatemalan Central Bank at the exchange rate of Q1 to US$1.

□ Bank Market. Foreign currency can be obtained on the bank market to pay for imports, loans, interest, tourist and business trips, medical care, and dividend remittances. The rate of exchange on the bank market changes every day and is established by the monetary board according to supply and demand.

Foreign currency must be sold to the Central Bank or any other authorized bank.

36. Investment Restrictions on Nonresidents

In general, there are no investment restrictions on nonresidents.

SELECTION OF BUSINESS ENTITY BY NONRESIDENTS

A foreign company can operate in Guatemala through a branch or agency, or as a local corporation. The foreign company may be a shareholder in the local corporation, but at least two individuals, of any nationality, must also be shareholders.

SPECIMEN TAX COMPUTATION

Information:

□ The corporation's profits for the year of Q600,000 (local currency) consists of:

Local net operating profit	Q300,000
Dividend income from local corporations	100,000
Dividend income from foreign corporations	100,000
Capital gain from sale of assets	100,000
	Q600,000

□ During the year, the corporation invested Q200,000 in new industrial machinery, thus qualifying for investment incentives.

Computation:

	For Financial Purposes	For Income Tax Purposes
Income		
Local net operating profit	Q300,000	Q300,000
Dividends from local corporations	100,000	—
Dividends from foreign corporations	100,000	—
Capital gain	100,000	100,000
Total income	Q600,000	Q400,000
Less investment deduction		
10% new machinery	Q200,000	(20,000)
Taxable income		Q380,000
Income tax (34% rate) (1)	(129,200)	Q(129,200)
Net profit	Q470,800	

Notes:
(1) Tax on capital gains may be paid optionally in three years without any charge. (Q100,000 × 34% = Q34,000)

HONG KONG

INCOME TAXES ON CORPORATIONS

Persons, including corporations, partnerships, trustees, and bodies of persons carrying on any trade, business or profession in Hong Kong are subject to tax on all profits arising in or derived from Hong Kong from such trade, business, or profession. Income derived from outside Hong Kong is exempt from tax.

No distinction is made between residents and nonresidents. A resident may, therefore, receive profits from abroad without being liable to tax, while a nonresident may be liable to tax on profits arising in Hong Kong.

1. Rates

Corporations are taxed at the rate of 16.5%, while individuals and partnerships of individuals are taxed at 15%. Partners that are corporations are taxed at the rate of 16.5%.

3. Capital Gains Taxes

None.

4. Branch Profits Taxes

There is no distinction between branch profits tax and corporation profits tax. Branch profits are also taxed at the rate of 16.5% on Hong Kong-source profits.

5. Foreign Tax Reliefs

Hong Kong does not have any double taxation agreements (other than the agreement with the United States on shipping income), but legislation provides relief when profits chargeable to tax in Hong Kong have borne tax in another Commonwealth territory (apart from the United Kingdom). In practice, the legislation rarely applies.

7. Payment of Taxes

Corporations are required to pay provisional tax for the current year based on profits of the preceding year. The provisional tax is payable in two installments. The payment dates differ according to the accounting dates of corporations. The normal due dates for payment are as follows:

Accounting Date	First Installment	Second Installment
April to November	October of following year (total tax due)	None
December	November of following year (75%)	Three months after the first installment (25%)
January to March	January of following year (75%)	Three months after the first installment (25%)

If the first installment is not paid by the due date, the second installment becomes automatically payable on the due date of the first installment. Any under- or over-payment of the actual profits tax of the preceding year, when results are known, is adjusted in the first installment of provisional tax payable.

The year of assessment ends on March 31.

INCOME TAXES ON INDIVIDUALS

A salaries tax is imposed on all income of individuals arising in or derived from Hong Kong, from any office or employment or pension, including income derived from services rendered in Hong Kong. Special provisions apply to seamen, airmen, and other persons who do not spend more than 60 days in Hong Kong in any tax year, the effect of which is to exclude from tax income arising from services rendered in Hong Kong during such periods. The 60-day rule does not apply to income derived from an office or pension.

Income includes the rental value of accommodation provided rent-free by an employer or the excess of this rental value over the rent actually paid by the employee to his employer for the accommodation; the rental value is deemed to be 10% of the employee's total income from the employer.

Married couples will be taxed separately unless an election is made for joint assessment.

Individuals with non-Hong Kong employment will pay Hong Kong tax on the proportion (ascertained on a time-apportionment basis) of their income arising in Hong Kong. In general, employment will be regarded as a non-Hong Kong employment if it meets three criteria:

☐ the contract of employment is negotiated and entered into, and is enforceable outside Hong Kong;

☐ the employer is resident outside Hong Kong; and

☐ the employee's remuneration is paid to him outside Hong Kong.

9. Rates

Taxable Income		Tax Rate
On the first	HK$20,000	2%
On the next	20,000	9
On the next	20,000	17
On the remainder		25

The total salaries tax payable by an individual is not to exceed 15% of total assessable income before the deduction of any allowances.

Allowable Deductions.   Apart from the deduction for expenses incurred wholly, exclusively, and necessarily in the production of income, the following allowances are applied in reduction of assessable income:

Personal allowance:	
—for single person	HK$41,000
—for married couple	82,000
Child allowance:	
—1st child	14,000 (1)
—2nd child	10,000
—3rd child	3,000
—4th, 5th, and 6th child, each	2,000
—7th, 8th, and 9th	1,000
Dependent parent allowance, each	12,000 (2)
Additional dependent allowance, each	3,000 (2)
Single parent allowance	20,000 (3)

Notes:
(1) Relief only applies to an individual maintaining an unmarried child who is either under 18 years of age in the year of assessment, or is over 18 but under 25 and receiving full-time education, or over 18 but incapacitated for work by reason of physical or mental disability.
(2) Relief only applies to an individual maintaining a dependent parent who is a permanent Hong Kong resident and over 60 years of age. The individual must either live with the parent for a continuous period of at least six months during the year of assessment or contribute not less than HK$1,200 towards the maintenance of the parent. The additional dependent parent allowance is granted to an individual who resides with the parent throughout the tax year.
(3) Relief only applies to a single parent who is solely or primarily responsible for the care of a child.

10. Local Income Taxes

None.

11. Capital Gains Taxes

None.

12. Foreign Tax Reliefs

Any income that a person derives from services rendered outside Hong Kong will be excluded from Hong Kong salaries tax if the income is liable to a similar tax in the territory in which it is earned.

13. Tax Period

March 31 is the standard tax year-end. An individual rarely obtains permission to adopt a different year-end.

The provisional tax system as described in item 7 also applies to individuals. Due dates for payment of the provisional tax are January and April of the calendar year.

INCOME TAXES ON NONRESIDENTS

15. Liability to Tax

A nonresident is assessable, either directly or in the name of the nonresident's agent, on all profits arising in Hong Kong whether or not the agent has receipt of the profits. Tax may be recovered out of the assets of the nonresident or from the agent, who is required to retain sufficient money to pay the tax. A person making a payment to a nonresident entertainer or sportsperson for a commercial occasion or event performed in Hong Kong is required to withhold tax from the payment.

When a resident carries on a business with a nonresident and the business is so arranged as to provide to the resident smaller profits than would be expected to accrue to an independent concern, the business may be treated as being carried on in Hong Kong by the nonresident through the resident as agent.

Where the true profits of a nonresident cannot be readily ascertained, they may be computed on a fair percentage of the turnover in Hong Kong, but where head offices are outside Hong Kong and the accounts do not identify true profits of a Hong Kong permanent establishment, the amount taxable in Hong Kong is arrived at by apportioning the overall profit in the ratio of the turnover of the various branches.

Offshore Income. Profits arising in or derived from outside Hong Kong are not subject to profits tax in Hong Kong. The question of whether a business is carried on in Hong Kong and whether profits are derived from Hong Kong is largely one of fact. The present Hong Kong tax laws governing the determination of offshore income play an important part in the planning of clients' tax affairs and it is, therefore, imperative that this subject be examined in depth before any action is taken or advice given.

16. Rates

Nonresidents are taxed at the same rates as residents. Resident consignees are required to submit quarterly returns showing the gross proceeds from local sales on behalf of their nonresident consignor and to pay the Inland Revenue a tax at 1% of such proceeds, or such lesser sums as may have been agreed. At present, the rate is 0.5%. This tax is recoverable from the consignor.

Royalties received by nonresidents, not trading in Hong Kong, from the exhibition or use in Hong Kong of films, tapes or recordings or for use in Hong Kong of a patent, design, trademark, copyright material, etc. are taxable on the gross receipts at an effective rate of 1.65% for a corporation and 1.5% for an individual or a partnership.

The legislation does not specify a rate of withholding to be applied to payments to entertainers and sportspersons. The tax withheld, however, should be sufficient to discharge the performer's Hong Kong tax liability.

18. Special Withholding Provisions

There is no withholding tax on dividends or repatriation of profits. Withholding tax may apply, however, to certain payments to nonresidents (see item 15).

20. Other Matters

Specific legislation deals with the following entities:

- [ ] Partnerships.
- [ ] Insurance corporations.
- [ ] Shipowners and aircraft-owners (both resident and nonresident).
- [ ] Clubs and trade associations.
- [ ] Financial institutions.

Interest Tax. Interest tax was abolished on April 1, 1989. However, interest sourced in Hong Kong that accrues to corporations or individuals carrying on business in Hong Kong will continue to be liable to profits tax.

Property Tax. With the exception of land and buildings occupied by the owner as his residence, this tax is charged on the net assessable value of any land or buildings in Hong Kong.

Property tax is charged at the standard rate of 15% on the property's net assessable value. The assessable value is the consideration (in money or money's worth) payable to the owner for the right to use the land or building, after deducting any unpaid rent. The net assessable value is arrived at by deducting from the assessable value the amount of rates (government imposed charges on property by reference to its specified "ratable value") paid by the owner and a statutory allowance for repairs and other expenses equal to 20% of the assessable value after deducting the rates.

The provisional tax system also applies to the owner of the property. Provisional tax is paid in one installment, and the due date for payment falls on any date commencing from November of the calendar year. Any overpayment or underpayment of the actual property tax of the preceding year is adjusted in the provisional tax payment.

If the individual's income from property is subject to profits tax, the amount of property tax paid may be deducted from the amount of profits tax assessed. Corporations carrying on a trade, profession, or business in Hong Kong are exempt from property tax as income from property is aggregated with other income and assessed to profits tax.

OTHER SIGNIFICANT TAXES

21. Sales (Value Added)

None.

24. Land and Property

See items 16 to 18.

22. Inheritance and Gift Taxes

Estate duties are imposed at graduated rates (up to 18%) on the value of an individual's Hong Kong property passing on death. The exemption limit for estate duty is HK$4,000,000. There is no gift tax. However, gifts made within three years before death are included in the deceased's estate. The matrimonial home of a deceased is exempt from estate duty.

23. Taxes on Payrolls

None.

25. Other Taxes

Stamp Duty. Stamp duty applies to four major types of transaction:

□ Contract notes on shares and marketable securities listed in Hong Kong.
□ Assignments of immovable property in Hong Kong.
□ Leases and assignment of leases relating to property in Hong Kong.
□ Issuance of bearer instruments.

Transactions in shares or marketable securities attract an ad valorem duty of HK$5 per HK$1,000 or part thereof, payable equally by the buyer and the seller. Stamp duty on assignment of immovable property is levied at the following rates (subject to marginal relief):

Property Value

Over	Not Over	Rate
HK$ 0	HK$ 250,000	HK$20
250,000	500,000	0.75% of value
500,000	1,000,000	1.50% of value
1,000,000	1,500,000	2% of value
1,500,000		2.75% of value

Stamp duty on the issue of bearer instruments is levied at HK$3 per HK$100, based on the market value upon issuance.

COMPUTATION OF TAXABLE INCOME

26. Capital Gains

Capital gains on the sale of fixed assets or long-term investments are not taxable.

27. Depreciation and Depletion

Industrial Buildings and Structures.   An initial allowance of 20% is granted for capital expenditure incurred in the construction of an industrial building or structure occupied for the purposes of a qualifying trade, and an additional allowance of 4% of the expenditure (on a straight-line basis) is given annually until the total expenditure is written off. If an industrial building or structure is acquired which was previously occupied for industrial purposes, no initial allowance is given. Instead, an annual allowance equal to the construction cost of the industrial building divided by the number of years remaining of its useful life for tax purposes (i.e., 25 years less number of years used by previous occupiers) is given until the purchase price is completely written off.

Commercial Buildings and Structures.   A building or structure not included above but nevertheless used for the purposes of a trade profession or business otherwise than as stock in trade can qualify for a Rebuilding Allowance; that is, an annual allowance of 2% of the capital expenditure incurred in the construction of the building.

Plant and Machinery.   An initial allowance of 60% of the cost of an item of plant is given, together with an annual allowance computed on the reducing value of a pool of plant and machinery falling under the same rate of depreciation as prescribed by the Government. The rates range from 10% to 30% according to the estimated useful life of the particular item of plant or machinery. When an asset is disposed of, the proceeds received (restricted to the original cost) will be deducted from the reducing value of the pool. The excess of proceeds over the original cost is not taxable.

28. Treatment of Dividends

Dividends received from a local or overseas corporation, whether the corporation is subject to tax in Hong Kong or not, are not taxable in the hands of the recipient.

29. Loss Carryovers

The amount of loss incurred in a trade, profession, or business in Hong Kong for any year of assessment is computed in the same manner and for such basis period as the assessable profits for that year would have been computed. Losses may be carried forward indefinitely and set off against future profits, and, in the case of corporations, are not limited to profits from the same trade. However, any change in the ownership of a corporation with the sole (or primary) purpose of utilizing the tax losses of the corporation may result in disallowance of the corporation's tax loss. There is no provision for relief of tax losses between affiliated companies. If an individual elects for personal assessment (see item 39), the losses incurred in that year can be first set off against the individual's other income arising in that year before being carried forward.

30. Transactions between Related Parties

Transactions between related resident and nonresident persons should be on an arm's-length basis. The Commissioner has power to deem any nonresident as trading in Hong Kong and raise assessments in the name of the resident person as if he were the agent of the nonresident.

31. Consolidation of Income

There is no provision for the filing of consolidated tax returns by related corporations and no group relief is available.

32. Tax Periods

Generally, March 31 is the year-end for all individual taxpayers. A corporation may adopt its own year-end.

33. Other Matters

Interest Income. Hong Kong source interest income received by or accruing to business enterprises carried on in Hong Kong is subject to profits tax. The source of interest income earned by business enterprises other than financial institutions is determined by the place where the provision of credit or funds is made available to the borrower.

Deductible Items. In arriving at assessable profits, deductions are allowed for revenue expenditures incurred in the production of the chargeable profits in the basis period, which include:

☐ Rents of buildings or land occupied for the purpose of producing the profits.

☐ Bad and doubtful debts.

☐ Depreciation allowances computed at the rates prescribed by the tax authority.

☐ Repairs of articles, premises, plant, and machinery used in producing the profits.

☐ Purchase and registration costs of a patent or trademark used in the production of such profits (subject to certain restrictions).

☐ Expenditure for scientific research and payments for technical education subject to certain rules.

☐ Employers' annual contributions or premiums paid to approved retirement scheme funds, limited in respect of any one employee to 15% of his total emoluments for the relevant period.

☐ Interest expense if it falls within one of the following categories:

—Interest on money borrowed by a financial institution.

—Interest taxable in Hong Kong in the hands of the recipient.

—Interest on money borrowed from a financial institution, but not secured or guaranteed by a deposit with a financial institution made by the borrower (or a related person or corporation), the interest on which is not chargeable to Hong Kong tax.

—Interest on money borrowed wholly and exclusively for the provision of (a) plant and machinery that qualifies for tax depreciation allowances, or (b) trading stock used in the production of taxable profits. If the lender is a related person or corporation, however, this will make the interest disallowable even if conditions (a) and (b) are met.

—Interest paid on debentures.

—Interest paid to the holder of any instrument issued:

(i) In the course of carrying on a business, which is bona fide and marketable in either Hong Kong or a major foreign financial center approved by the Hong Kong tax authorities; or

(ii) Pursuant to any agreement or arrangement where public announcements that refer to or any documents which contain advertisements or invitations for such agreements or arrangements have been authorized by the Securities Commission under the Protection of Investors Ordinance.

—Interest on loans from a related corporation, where the creditor raised the borrowed amount entirely from the proceeds of an issue of debentures or any such instrument described above by the related corporation in an amount not exceeding the interest payable by the creditor to the holders of its debentures or other such instrument.

Nondeductible Items. The following expenditures do not qualify for relief:

☐ Domestic or private expenditures and any sums not expended for the purpose of producing profits.

☐ Any loss or withdrawal of capital, the cost of improvements and any expenditure of a capital nature.

☐ Any sums recoverable under insurance or contract of indemnity.

☐ Rent of, or expenses relating to, premises not occupied or used for the purpose of producing the profits.

☐ Taxes paid under the Inland Revenue Ordinance, apart from tax paid on behalf of employees.

☐ Any remuneration or interest on capital or loans payable to members of a partnership or a sole proprietor and his or her spouse.

RELATED CONSIDERATIONS

35.   Exchange Controls

None.

37.   Other Matters

Personal Assessment. An individual who is a permanent or temporary resident of Hong Kong may obtain relief from the flat rate of 15% tax on profits and income by electing to be assessed personally. As a result of such an election, the individual will be required to report total Hong Kong income subject to the separate taxes outlined previously, and will be granted similar allowances and charged to tax at the same rates as applied in salaries tax. Such an election will only be advantageous where the tax so computed is less than the tax at the standard rate on the individual's Hong Kong profits and income.

For these purposes a "temporary resident" is defined as an individual who stays in Hong Kong for more than 180 days in any year of assessment or for a period of 300 days in any two consecutive years of assessment, one of which is the year for which the election was made.

SELECTION OF BUSINESS ENTITY BY NONRESIDENTS

Nonresident investors can operate in Hong Kong either through a branch or by forming a local subsidiary corporation. They are subject to the same tax rates as resident partnerships or corporations. The choice depends on the requirements and circumstances of each case, though there seems to be a preference to use a local subsidiary.

SPECIMEN TAX COMPUTATION

Computation:

	HK$000's	HK$000's
Operating profit as per accounts		1,000
Add		
Book depreciation on fixed assets	300	
Loss on disposal of fixed assets	100	
General provision for bad and doubtful debts	200	
Amortization of goodwill	300	900
		1,900
Less		
Dividend received	100	
Offshore income net of attributable expenses	300	
Capital profit on sale of long-term investment	200	
Surplus on revaluation of investment	200	800
Adjusted profit		1,100
Less		
Depreciation allowances	300	300
Assessable profit		800
Corporation profits tax at 16.5%		132

HUNGARY

Editor's Note: During 1991, Hungary introduced sweeping changes to its system of accounting, which will have effect January 1, 1992. The tax system, which traditionally has relied heavily on the accounting system, also will require revision. As of October 1991, the government is considering such an overhaul, and draft tax provisions are currently being prepared by the Ministries concerned. These have not yet been considered by parliament, and a published version is unlikely to be available until 1992.

INCOME TAXES ON CORPORATIONS

1. Rates

All business organizations formed under the jurisdiction of Hungarian law pay the entrepreneurial profits tax at the rate of 40% of taxable income calculated according to prescribed rules. Presently, these rules are very detailed in nature. Special relief given by way of reduction of tax payable is given to corporations with at least 30% foreign participation. (see item 34).

2. Local Income Taxes

Regional authorities may levy local taxes within the parameters established by the national government, which are:

☐ Community tax—a fixed charge of up to HUF 2,000 per employee, or

☐ Local business tax—at rates of up to 0.3% of revenue. Temporary activities also may be taxed at this rate with an additional limit of HUF 5,000 per day.

3. Capital Gains Taxes

Capital gains derived from the sale of certain assets are taxed as normal business income and calculated as the difference between purchase and sale price. The tax may be reduced by 20% of the gain if the asset has been owned for longer than two years.

4. Branch Profits Taxes

Hungarian law does not recognize branches as such, but foreign corporations are subject to tax in Hungary if they conduct business of any sort for three consecutive months during the course of a year. Through 1991, subject to the provisions of double tax treaties, this has been levied as the business entity tax, which presently is being reviewed by the government with a view to reform.

The rate of business entity tax is 40% and, in the case of normal trading activity, is charged on gross margin rather than profit. If a business provides services, rather than products, or is engaged in construction-related activities, the 40% rate is applied on a notional margin of between 5.4% and 6% of total revenue.

Foreign corporations, with or without a permanent establishment, are liable to the business entity tax at the rate of 20% of revenue received from Hungary in respect of intangible property rights, such as royalties. The tax usually is levied by withholding at source.

5. Foreign Tax Reliefs

Hungarian tax law provides for relief by deduction (rather than by credit) for taxes paid abroad.

6. Classification of Corporations

A business organization may be structured as a limited liability company, a joint stock company (also with limited liability but subject to more stringent regulation and with the ability to sell shares to the public), or as a partnership (either limited and/or unlimited). Foreign investors may not join partnerships.

7. Payment of Taxes

Hungary operates a "self-taxation system," whereby taxpaying entities calculate their own tax liability and make advance payments throughout the year. At the end of the year, taxpayers must prepare tax returns for submission to tax authorities. Penalties and interest may be charged if tax payments are insufficient to cover tax liabilities.

INCOME TAXES ON INDIVIDUALS

9. Rates

Progressive rates apply to most types of income. In 1991, they are as follows:

Taxable Income		Tax on Lower	Percentage
Over	Not Over	Amount	on Excess
HUF 55,000	HUF 90,000	HUF 0	12%
90,000	120,000	4,200	18

Taxable Income		Tax on Lower	Percentage
Over	Not Over	Amount	on Excess
HUF 120,000	HUF 150,000	HUF 9,600	30%
150,000	300,000	18,600	32
300,000	500,000	66,600	40
500,000		146,600	50

All income of an individual is subject to income tax. Tax is charged on total income of any form, including benefits in-kind, as reduced by allowable deductions and expenses. Generally, persons domiciled or "usually resident" in Hungary will be taxed on their worldwide income, and temporary residents will be taxed only on that originating within Hungary. For these purposes, the customs-free zone is regarded as being within Hungary, and income of an individual arising there will not escape the charge to tax.

Specific categories of income are treated separately; details of these are given below.

10. Local Income Taxes

Regional authorities have the power to levy local taxes on individuals within parameters set by the national government. These may take the form of a property tax (maximum HUF 3,000 per property owned or rented from a public body) or a community tax (again property based).

11. Capital Gains Taxes

Although there is no capital gains tax per se, capital gain may be taxed either as a part of business income or where, for example, it falls to be included as personal income.

A transfer tax exists, which is levied where property is sold, inherited, gifted, or otherwise transferred. See item 22.

12. Foreign Tax Reliefs

Income arising abroad is considered to be a special category and is taxed at the flat rate of 20% (see item 15). Remuneration for duties carried out in Hungary but paid abroad (usually in hard currency) by a foreign company qualifies as income arising abroad and is taxed at the 20% rate.

In addition, foreign employees of operations either wholly or partly owned by foreign investors are taxed on only 55% of their personal income arising within Hungary.

13. Tax Period

Income is determined on the calendar-year basis, with annual filing required.

14. Other Matters

Tax credits, deducted once the tax charge has been calculated as above, are available in respect of particular types of expenditure. These include private pension contributions (the credit is 20% of the amount paid) and premiums on life assurance policies with a duration of more than ten years (again 20% to a maximum of HUF 7,200). In addition, 20% of amounts saved for the purpose of buying a building or dwelling (to a maximum of HUF 12,000 pa) are allowable as a credit.

Certain categories of income are subject to special rules.

Income on savings, shares, securities, and income derived from abroad are subject to a flat rate tax at 20% and excluded from normal taxable income. If paid within Hungary, a 20% withholding usually is levied. Income and exchange gains on foreign currency securities issued by the National Bank are exempt from tax.

Other categories of personal income, of less significance from an international point of view, include income derived from inventions, income from scientific and artistic activities, income from agricultural small-holdings, and rental income.

Income From Business Ventures.   An incorporated business or a partnership will be taxed as outlined under "Income Taxes on Corporations," above. A sole trader may elect for the business to be taxed under the entrepreneurial profits tax rules, otherwise income is taxed at the normal progressive rates. The accounting rules for determining profit in these circumstances are complex.

INCOME TAXES ON NONRESIDENTS

15. Liability to Tax

Foreign corporations with activities in Hungary will be subject to the business entity tax, and those without such activities may still be liable if they receive income from intangible property rights (see above).

In general, foreign individuals are subject to the same rules as Hungarians except where a double tax treaty provides otherwise.

Foreigners without a permanent domicile in Hungary who work for foreign businesses or Hungarian businesses with foreign participation pay tax on only 55% of their income. This 55% is treated as the total of taxable income subject to the general rules set out above.

Where the foreign business or the foreign participant in a Hungarian business provides additional remuneration outside Hungary (often in hard currency), this is treated as taxable income arising abroad and is subject to a flat rate of 20%.

16. Rates

See item 15.

17. Withholding Tax Rates

In general, a 20% withholding rate applies to dividends or interest paid to individuals.

19. Tax Treaties

Hungary has entered into tax treaties with the following countries:

Austria	Netherlands
Belgium	Norway
Cyprus	Poland
Denmark	Romania
Finland	Spain
France	Sweden
Germany	Switzerland
Greece	Thailand
India	United Kingdom
Italy	United States
Japan	Yugoslavia
Luxembourg	

In addition, Hungary has multilateral agreements with the following ex-Comecon countries:

Bulgaria	Poland
Czechoslovakia	Romania
Mongolia	Soviet Union

OTHER SIGNIFICANT TAXES

21. Sales (Value-Added)

A general turnover tax, similar to a value-added tax, is charged at the rate of 25% on most products and services, 15% or 0% on specified services, and 0% on specified products and exports.

With some exceptions, generally all imports, exports, and domestic sales are taxable. The customs-free zone is not considered a domestic territory for these purposes, and all activities within this area are exempt from the turnover tax.

22. Inheritance and Gift Taxes

Property duties are charged when property is transferred, inherited, or gifted. In simple situations, the tax applies as follows:

	Rate
Straightforward transfer (e.g., sale)	
Residential property	2%
All other property	5
Gift or inheritance to a	
Child, parent, spouse	5
Grandchild, grandparent, sibling	8
Other	10

Exemptions exist, for example, if property is acquired through a business reorganization (e.g., merger), a contribution in kind for the acquisition of share capital, the distribution of accumulated profits when a joint venture terminates, or the direct sale of a residential accommodation by the builder to an individual.

23.   Taxes on Payrolls (Social Security)

Various taxes on payroll exist and should be distinguished from the payroll tax that was repealed in 1989 and was levied as a penalty if a business's payroll exceeded a fixed proportion of the value-added of its production.

Social Security.   The Hungarian social security system is compulsory, and contributions are paid by both employers (at 43% of gross salaries) and employees (at 10% in respect of state pension rights). It does not apply to foreign employees of companies with foreign participation, but the Social Security Authority will negotiate policies for such individuals on a voluntary basis.

Unemployment Fund.   The Government levies contributions for an unemployment fund on both employers (at 1.5% of gross salaries and wages paid to Hungarian employees) and employees (at 0.5% of gross salaries). The employee's contribution for this fund is deductible for purposes of the personal income tax.

Vocational Fund.   A levy of 1.5% on total annual wages may apply to businesses to fund this program.

Rehabilitation Fund.   Businesses that fail to employ a stipulated minimum level of handicapped employees are liable to a tax intended to assist in the rehabilitation of persons with diminished working capabilities due to handicaps. Businesses exceeding the employment level receive a subsidy.

25.   Other Taxes

In addition to the previously mentioned taxes, businesses in Hungary may be subject to various, minor taxes, including:

Excise Tax and Subsidy.   The excise tax is a consumption tax paid in addition to the general turnover tax on certain, typically luxury products, such as branded fine porcelain and lead crystal, precious metals and jewelry, cosmetics, coffee, alcoholic beverages, tobacco, chocolate, and gasoline. It does not apply to goods sold second-hand.

Correspondingly, some products and services considered to be necessities are entitled to a consumer subsidy if sold or provided within the country. Essentially, a business may be entitled to receive a price subsidy, a sort of negative tax, on such products as milk and other dairy products, household energy, and the supply of drinking water.

Dividend on State Property. If state property is tied up in a business, the government makes a levy on the profits to correspond to a return on its "investment." If profits are nil, no levy is made.

COMPUTATION OF TAXABLE INCOME

26. Capital Gains

There is no capital gains tax as such. Taxable gains are subject to the normal income tax. In certain circumstances (essentially, if the asset has been owned for longer than two years), the tax arising is reduced by 20%. In addition, special rules apply to specific categories of assets, such as real estate.

27. Depreciation and Depletion

Effective January 1, 1992, new accounting rules apply. Historically, depreciation rates and the assets that are depreciated were rigidly fixed for accounting purposes, with the resulting figures used for tax purposes as well. Under the new accounting system, there is considerably more freedom, both regarding rates and the assets to be depreciated—for example, intangibles now may be depreciated. As a result, changes to the tax rules are anticipated in order to limit the tax relief that will be available.

28. Treatment of Dividends

At the time of publication, dividends received by businesses subject to the entrepreneurial profits tax or the business entity tax (in other words, all companies, domestic or foreign) are excluded from the calculation of taxable income.

Dividends paid in Hungary to individuals usually are subject to a 20% withholding tax, and no further taxes are payable. The 20% rate may be reduced if the provisions of a double tax treaty dictate otherwise.

29. Loss Carryovers

Businesses paying the entrepreneurial tax that realize a net operating loss (NOL) for the tax period may carry the NOL forward for up to two years but may not carry it back. Loss relief does not apply to the business entity tax or the personal income tax.

30. Transactions Between Related Parties

There are no special rules on transactions between related parties.

31. Consolidation of Income

There currently are no tax provisions for the consolidation of income, although the new accounting rules do include consolidation provisions.

32. Tax Periods

Enterprises must use the calendar year.

RELATED CONSIDERATIONS

34. Incentives and Grants

Special incentives are available to businesses with foreign participation. Changes to the rules came into effect in 1991; however, businesses that qualified for relief under the old rules may continue to claim relief according to the old statutes subject to certain limitations of time.

Under the new rules, a business with at least 30% foreign participation and capitalization of HUF 50 million will qualify for relief in the following circumstances:

☐ If at least 50% of its revenues is derived from manufacturing or operating a hotel either built or renovated by the business, the tax charge is reduced by 60% for five years and by 40% for a further five years.

☐ If at least 50% of its revenue is derived from specified activities of particular importance (see below), the tax charge is eliminated for the first five years and reduced by 60% for the following five years.

Activities of Particular Importance

Electronics
Production of vehicles and component parts
Production of machine tools
Production of equipment for agricultural, forestry, or food processing
Pharmaceuticals
Telecommunications
Tourism
Biotechnology

In addition, further tax relief is available if a foreign participant reinvests dividends paid by a Hungarian company in the same or any other Hungarian company. The company receiving the reinvested proceeds will qualify for a reduction of its tax charge calculated with reference to the value of the reinvested dividend.

35. Exchange Controls

Hungary operates exchange controls, and the forint is not yet freely convertible. Business profits, however, may be converted and repatriated in hard currency.

36. Investment Restrictions on Nonresidents

There are no investment restrictions on nonresidents.

ICELAND

INCOME TAXES ON CORPORATIONS

1. Rates

The rate of income tax on corporations for 1991 is 45% on net income.

2. Local Income Taxes

None.

3. Capital Gains Taxes

Capital gains are added to other taxable income and taxed at the regular corporate rate.

4. Branch Profits Taxes

Branches of foreign corporations are taxed at the regular corporate rate.

5. Foreign Tax Reliefs

Double taxation relief is given for taxes paid by a resident of Iceland in those countries with which Iceland has double taxation treaties (see item 19).

6. Classification of Corporations

There is no difference in tax rates based on classification of corporations.

7. Payment of Taxes

All taxes are paid in the assessment year, which is the year after the year of operations. The taxes are due in ten payments on the first day of each month except January and July.

Until the tax has been calculated, which is usually no later than July 31 each year, a corporation must pay a proportion of the taxes levied in the previous year. This proportion is assessed yearly in accordance with changes in the general price level (55% in 1991).

INCOME TAXES ON INDIVIDUALS

9. Rates

The state income tax rate for 1991 is 32.8%. The income tax is paid as the income is earned. A monthly deduction of kr. 23,922 is provided from the tax.

10. Local Income Taxes

The local income tax rate for 1991 is 6.99% and is paid as the income is earned.

11. Capital Gains Taxes

Capital gains from the sale of homes are not taxed if the homes were owned and used by the owners for more than five years. Gains on the sale of other personal property are not taxed.

12. Foreign Tax Reliefs

Double taxation relief is given for taxes paid by a resident of Iceland in those countries with which Iceland has tax treaties (see item 19).

13. Tax Period

The tax period for individuals is the calendar year.

INCOME TAXES ON NONRESIDENTS

15. Liability to Tax

Nonresident Individuals. Nonresident persons are subject to tax on income from Icelandic sources, including but not limited to salaries, wages, and pensions paid from Icelandic sources, and income derived from business carried out in Iceland and from real property.

Individuals staying in Iceland for longer than 183 days are subject to tax on their worldwide income. Individuals in Iceland for a temporary stay, i.e., less than 183 days, are taxed only on Icelandic-source income.

Tax rates and payments term can vary depending on the type of income concerned.

Exemptions from the above rules can be provided in double taxation agreements.

Nonresident Companies. Nonresident companies and other entities are subject to tax on their income from Icelandic sources. They are taxed in conformity with the rules applicable to companies domiciled in Iceland on income derived from business activities or participation in business activities with a permanent establishment in Iceland.

17. Withholding Tax Rates

The following table outlines the rules applying to payments from an Icelandic company to foreign corporations:

	Dividends (1)		Interest	Royalties
	To Parent	**Others**		
Nontreaty countries	20%	20%	0%	(2)
Treaty countries				
Denmark	0	15	0	0%
Faroe Islands	0	15	0	0
Finland	0	15	0	0
Germany	5	15	0	0
Norway	0	15	0	0
Sweden	0	15	0	0
Switzerland	5	15	0	0
United States	5	15	0	0

Notes:
(1) The parent company must own directly at least 25% of the share capital in the company that pays the dividend. The treaty with the United States provides a 10% or more ownership requirement. On the part of the dividends allowed as a deduction from income of the Icelandic corporation (15% of the share capital), the rate is 15% instead of 5%. This does not apply to the United States.
(2) The tax rate depends on whether the recipient is a person or a corporation.

19. Tax Treaties

Iceland has concluded double taxation treaties with Denmark, the Faroe Islands, Finland, Germany, Norway, Sweden, Switzerland, and the United States.

OTHER SIGNIFICANT TAXES

21. Sales (Value Added)

A 24.5% value-added tax is levied on any sale of goods, power, or services with various exceptions including the following:

- ☐ All export sales.
- ☐ Public health-care services.
- ☐ Schools and other educational institutions.
- ☐ Domestic and international passenger transportation and cargo transport between Iceland and foreign countries.
- ☐ Postal services.

☐   House rentals and sales and rentals of trade aircrafts and vessels.

☐   Insurance services.

☐   Banking and the operation of other financial institutions and sales of bonds.

Assessable are all corporations, individuals, and state and municipal entities that sell or grant any kind of taxable goods or services.

The VAT period is two months, and the tax is due within 35 days from the end of each period.

VAT must be paid with custom dues when customable goods are imported.

22.   Inheritance and Gift Taxes

Gifts are taxable to the donee on the same basis as normal income. Inheritances are taxed as follows:

Relationship to Decedent	Rate
Next of kin	up to 10%
Parents and children	up to 25
Others	up to 45

23.   Taxes on Payrolls (Social Security)

An insurance contribution is assessed on all salaries and wages on a monthly basis. This includes contribution to the Icelandic National Insurance Scheme as well as a salary tax. The rates are as following:

☐   2.5% for fishing, farming, and industrial activities.

☐   6.0% for all other activities.

25.   Other Taxes

Municipal Business Operating Expense Tax.   All municipalities have the right to levy a business operating expense tax on all business or professional activities carried on in the municipality by individuals, corporations, or other taxable entities. The tax base is all operating expenses allowed as deductions from gross income for state income tax purposes, though limited to gross income in the case of operating losses. The tax rate can vary from one municipality to another, with the minimum rate of 0.33% and the maximum rate of 1.3%.

Cemetery Charge.   This can be assessed by the municipalities as a surcharge on municipal income or business operating expense taxes. The rate varies from one municipality to another but generally ranges from 1.5% to 2.3%.

Industrial Loan Fund Contribution.   This is assessed on all industrial activities by individuals, corporations, and other taxable entities. The contribution rate is

0.18% on all operating expenses allowed to industrial concerns as deductions from gross income for state income tax purposes, though limited to gross income in the case of an operating loss.

Industrial Fee.   This is assessed on the same industrial activities as are subject to the industrial loan fund contribution. The rate is 0.1%.

Export Council Charge.   This charge is levied on the following activities:

□   Tax rate of 0.05% on industrial activities including fish-industry and building construction.
□   Tax rate of 0.03% on fishing.
□   Tax rate of 0.01% on sea and air transport. Domestic transport is exempted.

The tax base for the export council charge is the same as for the municipal business operating expense tax.

National Rate.   National rate is a tax levied on some governmental businesses, domestic oil companies, and banks. The benefits from this tax accrue to the municipalities.

Property Tax.   Land and property tax at nominal rates is paid to the municipal authorities; the rates vary between municipalities and also in regard to use. The principal taxes and rates are those on property, water use, fire insurance, and disaster insurance.

Capital Taxes.   Capital taxes are computed on net capital. The rates are:

	Amount	Rate	Amount in Excess of	Rate (1)
Individuals	kr. 3,219,300– 5,798,025	1.2%	kr. 9,017,325	1.95%
Married couples	6,438,600–11,596,050	1.2	18,034,650	1.95
Corporations	—	1.2		

Notes:
(1)   The tax rate will increase by 0.75% for those individuals who have net capital over kr. 9,017,325 (married couples, kr. 18,034,650), although proportionally if a person's income is under kr. 1,839,600 until the excess rate drops to zero when the income is lower than kr. 919,800.

Additional capital tax is calculated as follows (the tax base is the same as for the capital tax):

	Amount in Excess of	Rate
Individuals	kr. 4,653,750	0.25%
Married couples	9,307,500	0.25
Corporations	—	0.25

Persons who have reached the age of 67 in 1990 do not pay the additional capital tax.

Special Property Tax. Owners of commercial buildings must pay a tax of 1.5% assessed on the official value of buildings and land.

COMPUTATION OF TAXABLE INCOME

26. Capital Gains

Capital gains generally are treated as ordinary income, but gains from certain assets may not be subject to tax.

27. Depreciation and Depletion

Annual depreciation is calculated as a fixed percentage of the revalued acquisition cost.

Buildings	2%–10%
Ships and aircraft	8%
Production machinery and equipment	12%
Motor vehicles, machines, tools, and office equipment	8%–20%

Accelerated depreciation is allowed when a fixed asset is sold at a taxable profit and when the inflation adjustment in item 33 (4) exceeds that of item 33 (3).

28. Treatment of Dividends

A resident limited company is entitled to deduct from taxable income dividends paid to shareholders up to a maximum of 15% of the share's nominal value. The dividend is deductible in the year of operations it refers to.

Shareholders resident in Iceland obtain income tax relief for dividends received, which amounts to a maximum 15% of each share and a maximum amount of kr. 125,925 for a single person and kr. 251,850 for a married couple. These amounts are adjusted annually for inflation. For nonresident shareholders see item 17.

29. Loss Carryovers

Operating loss carryforwards are adjusted annually for the effects of inflation by applying the inflation rate, and such losses may be carried forward indefinitely. Carrybacks are not permitted.

30. Transactions between Related Parties

The tax authorities may substitute fair market value for such transactions.

31. Consolidation of Income

Each entity is taxed separately.

32. Tax Periods

The calendar year is mandatory for all taxpayers, but on application, a corporate taxpayer may be granted a different fiscal year if special reasons exist.

33. Other Matters

Accounting for Inflation for Tax Purposes.   The Income Tax and Capital Tax Act contains significant provisions with respect to financial income, expenses, and depreciation. The law stipulates that an inflation adjustment must be taken into account in the annual reporting of taxable income.

The purpose of these provisions is to redefine taxable income in a way that corresponds more closely with inflationary conditions. Under these provisions, the effects of general price level changes on corporate income and financial position are calculated and taken into account. The main provisions are as follows:

(1)   Buildings, machinery, and other depreciable assets and their accumulated depreciation are revalued annually by applying a price-adjustment factor which is based on an official price index. The increase in the book value of fixed assets resulting from this revaluation is not regarded as income for tax purposes.

(2)   Depreciation is based on the revalued cost of fixed assets.

(3)   The effect of inflation on monetary assets and inventories is calculated and reported as an expense in the profit and loss account.

(4)   The effect of inflation on all liabilities is calculated and added to taxable income in the profit and loss account.

The calculation base for (3) and (4) is the balance at the beginning of the year, which is then multiplied by the price adjustment factor.

All financial income and expenses accrued during the year must be reflected in the income tax report. This means that all forms of financial income and expenses are treated in the same way for tax purposes. Thus, the effects of exchange rate fluctuations and price index regulations will be fully shown in the income tax report.

Other Business Deductions.   Corporations and other business entities are allowed to deduct from their taxable income the following provisions, among others:

□ A special write-down of up to 5% of notes and accounts receivable less the prior year's write-down amount.

□ Corporation and other business entities are allowed to deduct up to 10% of their pretax profits in an investment fund. However, an amount equal to 50% of the reserve must be deposited in an Icelandic bank account not later than five months after the year end. When an amount is withdrawn from such a bank account, which is permitted six months after the deposit, an equal amount is taxable, but the taxpayer is allowed a special depreciation of fixed assets bought in the same year.

RELATED CONSIDERATIONS

34. Incentives and Grants

None.

35. Exchange Controls

There still are some restrictions on transactions of a capital nature, which generally will be abolished by the 1992 year-end.

The import and export of goods and services and the related foreign currency transactions to a large extent are not restricted.

36. Investment Restrictions on Nonresidents

Nonresidents may invest in a business enterprise in Iceland within some limitations, which are stipulated in the Act on Investment by Nonresidents in Business Enterprise or in special legislation and upon the fulfilment of other conditions and acquisition of licenses required by law, provided Icelandic parties enjoy at least equal rights to investment in the nonresident investor's home country.

The primary restrictions on investment by nonresidents are the following:

□ Only Icelandic citizens with legal domicile in Iceland, and legal persons with domicile in Iceland that are wholly owned by Icelandic citizens with legal domicile in Iceland, are permitted to conduct fishing operations within the Icelandic fisheries jurisdiction.

□ Only Icelandic citizens with legal domicile in Iceland, and legal persons with domicile in Iceland that are wholly owned by Icelandic citizens with legal domicile in Iceland, are permitted to run enterprises dealing with fish processing.

□ Only the Icelandic State, Icelandic local authorities, Icelandic citizens with legal domicile in Iceland, and legal persons with domicile in Iceland that are wholly owned by Icelandic citizens with legal domicile in Iceland are permitted to own energy exploitation rights as regards waterfalls and geothermal energy for other than domestic use. The same applies to enterprises that produce or distribute energy.

□   Total shares owned by nonresidents in Icelandic airline companies may not at any time exceed 49%.

□   Nonresidents are permitted to own 25% of the shares in an Icelandic commercial bank operated by a limited-liability company.

   From January 1, 1992, limited-liability banks registered abroad having their legal venue there are permitted to establish branches in Iceland upon the acquisition of a license from the Minister of Commerce.

□   Investment by foreign states or state-owned enterprises in enterprises in Iceland is prohibited except with special permission from the Minister of Commerce.

SELECTION OF BUSINESS ENTITY BY NONRESIDENTS

Nonresident investors normally can operate in Iceland either through a branch or by forming a local limited company. In planning to establish a joint limited company in Iceland, the majority of the founders must have been domiciled in Iceland for at least one year, although no conditions are imposed with regard to the Icelandic nationality of the founders. The director and members of the board must be domiciled in Iceland, but the Minister of Commerce can provide an exemption from this particular condition. The right of foreigners, however, to direct or own shares in joint limited companies is limited by statutes which vary according to the economic activity engaged in by the company.

   A joint limited company domiciled abroad may be permitted to operate in Iceland if the following requirements are met:

□   The company meets all of the legal requirements in its country of domicile.

□   The company meets the main legal requirements for being considered an Icelandic joint limited company.

□   Icelandic joint limited companies enjoy the same right in the country of domicile of the foreign company.

□   The company meets the requirements of Icelandic legislation that relate specifically to its operations in Iceland.

□   The company has a branch office that is registered in Iceland.

The director(s) of the branch office must be domiciled in Iceland and generally must be Icelandic citizens, unless the Minister of Commerce exempts them from this condition.

   Both branches and foreign-owned companies are taxed in the same way as resident companies.

INDIA

INCOME TAXES ON CORPORATIONS

1. Rates

The tax rates on domestic companies for the 1991–1992 assessment year are:

Widely held Indian company	40%
Closely held Indian company	
Trading or investment company	50%
Other companies	45%

The amount of tax computed above is increased by a surcharge calculated at 15% of such tax where the total income exceeds Rs. 75,000. For the 1992–1993 assessment year, the rates will be 45%, 50%, and 50%, respectively, and the surcharge will remain unchanged at 15%.

The tax rates applicable to foreign companies are (except where Double Tax Treaties provide for lower rates):

Dividends and interest derived from sources in India (1)	25%
Royalties or technical services fees received from an Indian concern under a government-approved agreement:	
—made before April 1, 1976	50%
—made after March 31, 1976 (1)	30%
Income of offshore funds from units (dividends or capital gains) (1)	10%
Other income	65%

Notes:
(1)   Expenses incurred in earning such income are not deductible.

2. Local Income Taxes

Taxation on income other than agricultural income is the province of the central government. Taxation of agricultural income is determined by the states and different rates are levied on such income by different states. Sixty percent of income from growing and manufacturing tea is treated as agricultural income.

3. Capital Gains Taxes

Profits or gains arising on the ''transfer'' of nondepreciable capital assets held for more than three years (more than one year in the case of a share in a company) are called long-term capital gains, while profits or gains arising on the transfer of nondepreciable assets held for not more than three years (not more than one year in the case of a share in a company) are called short-term capital gains. However, any profit arising on transfer of depreciable capital assets is treated as short-term capital gains, irrespective of the period for which the assets have been held (see item 27).

The transfer of a capital asset includes the sale, exchange, or relinquishment of the asset; the extinguishment of any rights therein; the compulsory acquisition thereof under any law; any transaction involving the allowance of the possession of any immovable property to be taken or retained in part performance of a contract of the nature referred to in Section 53A of the Transfer of Property Act, 1882, or any transaction that has the effect of transferring, or enabling the enjoyment of, any immovable property or, in a case where the asset is converted into or is treated as stock-in-trade of a business, such conversion or treatment. The notional profit arising from the transfer by way of conversion of the capital asset into stock-in-trade will be chargeable in the year in which the stock-in-trade is sold or otherwise transferred. If the net consideration received (value received less transfer expenses) on the transfer of a capital asset held for more than three years (or one year, as the case may be) is invested in specified assets within six months from the date of transfer, no loan or advance is secured by these assets within three years of their acquisition, and the assets are retained for at least three years, the capital gains are exempt from tax.

Capital gains are computed by deducting from sale proceeds the aggregate of expenditures incurred wholly and exclusively in connection with the transfer, the cost of acquisition of the capital asset, and the cost of any improvement thereto. In computing long-term capital gains for assets acquired prior to April 1, 1974, the fair market value on that date may be substituted for the actual cost of acquisition. A further deduction is allowed of a sum of Rs. 10,000 plus 10% of the amount by which the capital gain exceeds Rs. 10,000 where the asset sold is building or land (or rights therein) or gold, bullion, or jewelry. For other assets, the deduction from capital gains over Rs. 10,000 is 30%. (Deduction is raised to Rs. 15,000 effective the 1992–1993 assessment year.)

From assessment year 1992–1993 in the case of capital gains arising to a venture capital company from the sale of equity shares of a venture capital undertaking, the amount of further deduction will be Rs. 15,000 plus 60% of the balance. A venture capital company is a company engaged in providing finance to venture capital undertakings, mainly by acquiring equity shares of the venture capital undertaking. Venture capital undertakings means a company approved as such.

Capital gains so computed are taxed at the general rate applicable to the taxpayer. Long-term capital losses, if any, are scaled down in the same manner as profits. Losses under the head ''capital gains,'' whether short-term or long-term, will be permitted to be adjusted only against positive income under that head and not against income under any other head, effective the 1992–1993 assessment year. Unabsorbed losses may be carried forward for a maximum of eight years and set off against only taxable capital gains.

4. Branch Profits Taxes

Profits of the Indian branches of a nonresident company are taxed at 65%.

5. Foreign Tax Reliefs

An Indian company is taxed on income accruing or arising either in India or outside India and on income deemed to accrue or arise in India. A nonresident company is taxed only on income accruing or arising in India or deemed to accrue or arise in India. Actual receipt of income in India is taxable in either case. Double taxation of foreign income of either entity is avoided by means of double taxation treaties which also provide for tax relief in appropriate situations. Where no such treaty exists, relief is allowed to an Indian company on the double-taxed income at the lower of the Indian or foreign tax rate.

Double taxation relief treaties exist with the following countries:

Afghanistan (international transport only), Australia (international air transport only), Austria, Belgium, Brazil, Bulgaria (merchant shipping only), Canada, Czechoslovakia, Denmark, Ethiopia (operation of aircraft only), the Federal Republic of Germany, Finland, France, the German Democratic Republic, Greece, Hungary, Indonesia, Iran (international transport only), Italy, Japan, Kenya, Kuwait (international air transport only), Lebanon (international transport only), Libya, Malaysia, Mauritius, Nepal, Netherlands, New Zealand, Norway, Oman (international air transport only), Pakistan (international air transport only), Poland, Republic of Korea, Romania, Singapore, Sri Lanka, Sweden, Switzerland (international transport only), Syrian Arab Republic, Tanzania, Thailand, the United Arab Republic, the United Kingdom and Northern Ireland, the United Arab Emirates (international air transport only), the United States, the Union of Soviet Socialist Republics, the Yemen Arab Republic and the Peoples' Democratic Republic of Yemen (international air transport only), and Zambia. See item 12 for unilateral relief available to Indian residents.

7. Payment of Taxes

Taxpayers are required to pay advance tax in three installments in the financial year preceding the assessment year. Any further tax on the basis of the returned income is required to be paid before the return is filed. For short or delayed payments of advance tax or delay in filing the return, interest is payable before filing the return.

8. Other Matters

India-Source Income. The following categories of income are deemed to accrue or arise in India for which taxpayers in all categories (including corporations) are liable to Indian tax:

□ All income accruing or arising, whether directly or indirectly, through or from any business connection, property, asset or source of income in India, or through the transfer of a capital asset situated in India.

□ Dividends paid by an Indian company outside India.

□ Income by way of interest payable by the government or in respect of any debt incurred, or monies loaned and used, for the purposes of a business or a profession carried on in India.

□ Income by way of royalty payable by the government or in respect of any right, property, or information used or services utilized for the purposes of a business or profession carried on in India except lump-sum payments for computer software supplied with a computer or computer-based equipment.

□ Income by way of fees payable in respect of technical services by the government or utilized in a business or profession carried on in India.

The normal methods of computing income do not apply with respect to income from shipping operations or operation of aircraft, income from services rendered in connection with the exploration of mineral oils derived by all nonresidents, and income from royalties, technical service fees, and turn-key power projects derived by nonresident corporations. Income tax liability in these cases is computed on a notional basis as follows:

□ Royalties or Fees. The gross amount of royalties or fees received by a nonresident corporation is treated as taxable income if the agreement under which the receipts arise was made after March 31, 1976. However, if the taxes on such income are paid by the Indian company or the Government under the terms of an agreement approved by the central government, then the tax paid will not be included in computing the total income of the foreign company.

Remuneration received by a nonresident consultant or an employee of such consultant will be exempt from tax provided (1) the agreement for rendering of services has been entered into between the Government of India and an international organization, (2) the consultant is engaged by the international organization and the agreement relating to the engagement is approved by the specified authority, (3) funds are made available to the international organization under a technical assistance grant agreement between such organization and the government of a foreign state, and (4) the remuneration to the consultant or the consultant's employees is paid out of such funds.

For earlier agreements, the maximum amount deductible on account of expenditure is 20% of the gross amount of the royalty or the fees.

□ Shipping Business. Income from a shipping business operated by a nonresident is 7.5% of the total of the following:

—The amount paid or payable (whether in or out of India) for carrying passengers, livestock, mail or goods shipped at any port in India.

—The amount received or deemed to be received in India for carrying passengers, livestock, mail, or goods shipped at any port outside India.

□ Business of operation of Aircraft. Income derived from the business of operation of aircraft by a nonresident is 5% of the total of the following:

—The amount paid or payable (whether in or out of India) for carrying passengers, livestock, mail, or goods from any place in India.

—The amount received or deemed to be received in India for carrying passengers, livestock, mail, or goods from any place outside India.

□ Services toward exploration of mineral oil. Income of a nonresident from the business of providing services or facilities in connection with, or supplying leased plant and machinery used or to be used in the prospecting for or extraction or production of mineral oil is 10% of the aggregate of the following:

—The amount paid or payable (whether in or out of India) for the provision of services and facilities as above for prospecting for or extraction or production of mineral oil in India.

—The amount received or deemed to be received in India for the provision of services or facilities as above in the prospecting for or extraction or production of mineral oil outside of India.

□ Turnkey power projects. Income of a foreign corporation from the business of civil construction, erection of plant and machinery or testing or commissioning thereof, in connection with an approved turnkey power project financed under any international aid program, is 10% of the amount paid or payable (whether in India or outside of India.)

INCOME TAXES ON INDIVIDUALS

9. Rates

An individual's total income for the assessment year 1991–1992 and 1992–1993 is subject to tax at the following graduated rates:

| Total Income | | Tax on | Percentage |
Over	Not Over	Lower Amount	on Excess
Rs. 22,000	Rs. 30,000	Rs. 0	20%
30,000	50,000	1,600	30
50,000	100,000	7,600	40
100,000		27,600	50

Income tax computed above is reduced by 20% of savings in the form of payments of life insurance premiums, contributions to the Provident Fund, Superannuation Fund, Deferred Annuity Scheme, etc. The maximum admissible deduction generally is limited to Rs. 10,000. Investment in the purchase of equity shares forming part of an "eligible issue of capital" or in the purchase of units of specified mutual funds entitles the investor to a 20% tax deduction, subject to a maximum of Rs. 5,000, provided the investment is held for at least three years.

The amount of tax computed above in the case of resident individuals will be increased by a surcharge calculated at 12% of such tax if the total income exceeds Rs. 75,000.

10. Local Income Taxes

See item 2.

11. Capital Gains Taxes

Profits or gains arising on the "transfer" of capital assets, depreciable or non-depreciable, are treated as long-term capital gains or short-term capital gains in the same manner as for corporate assessees (see item 3). The provisions in force for companies as regards computation of capital gains (see item 3) apply also to noncorporate taxpayers except for the amount of further deductions admissible.

Long-term capital gains exceeding Rs. 10,000 are subjected to tax after allowing deduction of Rs. 10,000 plus 50% of the excess over Rs. 10,000 of such gains derived from transfer of building or land (or rights therein) or gold, bullion, or jewelry, and Rs. 10,000 plus 60% of the amount exceeding Rs. 10,000 for other assets. The net gain so determined and also short-term capital gains are taxed at the rate applicable (see item 9). (Basic deduction raised to Rs. 15,000 effective the 1992–1993 assessment year.)

Long-term capital losses are scaled down in the same manner as profits. Losses under the head "capital gains," whether short-term or long-term, will be permitted to be adjusted only against positive income under that head and not against income under any other head, effective the 1992–1993 assessment year. Unabsorbed losses may be carried forward for a maximum of eight years and set off only against taxable capital gains.

Subject to certain conditions, long-term capital gains arising on the transfer of a residential house will be exempt from tax if the consideration for transfer does not exceed Rs. 200,000.

As in the case of corporate assessees, no tax is payable on long-term capital gains if the net consideration (value received less transfer expenses) for transfer of the long-term capital asset is invested in specified assets within six months after the date of transfer and the specified assets are retained for three years.

12. Foreign Tax Reliefs

Tax treaties exist with the countries noted in item 5. Unilateral relief is available to persons resident in India with respect to double taxation of income in countries with which there is no treaty arrangement.

13. Tax Period

Income of both corporate and noncorporate taxpayers for the period commencing April 1 (for new businesses, from the date of starting up the business) and ending

March 31 (called the previous year) is taxed in the following assessment year commencing April 1 every year.

INCOME TAXES ON NONRESIDENTS

15. Liability to Tax

An individual ordinarily resident in India is subject to tax on his or her worldwide income. Nonresidents are subject to tax on Indian-source income (i.e., received, accrued or deemed so in India). A person not ordinarily resident is generally taxed like a nonresident and is also liable to tax on any income accruing abroad if it is derived from a business controlled in or profession set up in India.

A person is resident in India during a fiscal year if present in India for: (1) at least 182 days in a year, or (2) 60 days in a year and 365 days or more during the preceding four years. Individuals fulfilling neither of these conditions are nonresidents. An individual who was not present in India for 730 days during the preceding seven years or who was nonresident in nine of ten preceding years is not ordinarily resident. In effect, a newcomer to India remains not ordinarily resident for the first nine years of his or her stay in India.

An Indian citizen leaving India in any fiscal year (previous year) for employment outside India will become a nonresident if he or she is in India for less than 182 days in that year. An Indian citizen or person of Indian origin who resides outside of India may stay in India for a maximum of 149 days without affecting his or her nonresident status.

Certain classes of income received by foreign employees and foreign companies are not taxable in India:

☐ Leave passage for the employee and his or her family (subject to certain restrictions).

☐ Remuneration received for being the official representative of a foreign government.

☐ Remuneration received as an employee of a foreign enterprise for services rendered in India if not present in India for more than 90 days (provided the employer is not engaged in any trade or business in India and such remuneration is not deductible in computing the employer's taxable income in India).

☐ Salaries received, up to certain limits and subject to certain conditions, for services rendered as a technician (in the fields of construction, manufacturing, mining, agriculture, ship building, etc.) in the employment of the government or of any corporation engaged in business in India where such services commenced before April 1, 1988. Where such services commenced after March 31, 1988, the salary received by the foreign technician is not exempt, but income tax on the salary paid by the employer to the government is exempt.

☐ Remuneration for teaching or pursuing research in India (subject to certain conditions).

☐ Tax paid by the government or by an Indian concern on income (not salary, royalty, or fees for technical services) derived by a nonresident or a foreign company from the government or an Indian concern in pursuance of an agreement between the central government and the government of a foreign state or an international organization.

☐ Tax paid by the government or an Indian concern on royalty or fees for technical services received by a foreign company from the government or the Indian concern under an approved agreement.

☐ Remuneration received by a nonresident consultant or an employee of such consultant will be exempt from tax provided (1) the agreement for rendering of services has been entered into between the Government of India and an international organization, (2) the consultant is engaged by the international organization and the agreement relating to the engagement is approved by the specified authority, (3) funds are made available to the international organization under a technical assistance grant agreement between such organization and the Government of a foreign State, and (4) the remuneration to the consultant or the consultant's employees is paid out of such funds.

☐ Lump-sum royalty payments from a resident for the transfer of rights, including grant of a licence, in respect of computer software supplied by a nonresident manufacturer along with a computer or computer-based equipment under a scheme approved by the Government of India.

☐ Fees for technical services received by specified foreign companies for providing services in or outside India for projects connected with the security of India.

16. Rates

The same rates of tax apply to nonresidents as to residents (see item 9) except that a surcharge is not payable by nonresidents.

18. Special Withholding Rates

See item 1 for foreign companies. There are special withholding rates for certain incomes of resident and nonresident individuals.

19. Tax Treaties

See items 5 and 12.

20. Other Matters

Foreign Exchange Assets. In the case of "nonresident Indians," income derived from any "foreign exchange asset" and long-term capital gains relating to foreign exchange capital assets will be subject to tax at the flat rate of 20%. A foreign exchange asset means any "specified asset" acquired, purchased, or subscribed to by the nonresident Indian in convertible foreign exchange as defined in the Foreign

Exchange Regulation Act, 1973 and any rules made thereunder. The "specified assets" are:

☐ Shares in an Indian company.

☐ Debentures issued by a public limited Indian company.

☐ Deposits with a public limited Indian company.

☐ Securities of the central Government.

☐ Any other asset specified by the central Government in the Official Gazette.

There are certain special provisions for computing capital gains on the sale of shares or debentures of Indian companies that were purchased by a nonresident Indian using foreign currency.

OTHER SIGNIFICANT TAXES

21. Sales (Value Added)

Taxes are payable at varying rates on sales within the States of India and also on inter-state transactions.

22. Inheritance and Gift Taxes

The Gift Tax Act 1958 provides for a levy of gift tax on the donor at a flat rate of 30% on the value of gifts exceeding Rs. 20,000.

23. Taxes on Payrolls (Social Security)

Under the Employees' State Insurance Scheme, employees pay 2.25% and employers 5% of the wages of workers receiving over 1 Indian rupee per day. The insurance covers factories using power and employing 20 or more persons whose wages or salaries do not exceed 1,600 Indian rupees monthly. Social security under the Provident Fund amounts to 10% paid by the employer and employees. Twenty percent of employee contributions to an approved Provident Fund may be deducted from the tax payable. Employers must contribute 0.5% of gross payroll of employees whose salaries do not exceed 2,500 Indian rupees monthly to a Government insurance fund, with the Government contributing 0.25%. Total fringe benefits average from 30 to 40% of salaries or wages paid by employers.

Under the 1971 family pension and life insurance scheme, employees who contribute 10% of their earnings to the Provident Fund are entitled to make a contribution, which is matched by the employer, to a separate fund, plus a Government contribution so that 3.5% of earnings are credited to the fund.

24. Taxes on Natural Resources

No special taxes are levied on natural resources.

25. Other Taxes

Land and Property. Taxes are levied at varying rates by municipalities on the value of land and property situated within their local limits.

Tax on Capital. Capital is not taxed as such, but tax is payable under the Wealth Tax Act, 1957, on the "net wealth"; that is, the aggregate value of all the assets in excess of all the debts owed by the taxpayer on the valuation date (which is the last day of the fiscal year).

In addition, wealth tax is payable in respect of certain assets by closely held companies.

Banking companies, including cooperative societies engaged in the banking business, public financial institutions, State financial corporations, and other financial companies, will be subject to a 3% interest tax under the Interest Tax Act 1974, effective October 1, 1991. The interest tax will be allowable as a deduction in computing taxable business profits.

COMPUTATION OF TAXABLE INCOME

26. Capital Gains
See items 3 and 11.

27. Depreciation and Depletion

Depreciation. A deduction is allowed for depreciation on assets owned and used by the taxpayer for the purposes of any business or profession, such assets being classified under buildings, furniture and fittings, machinery and plant, and ships. Under each classification, assets are grouped into blocks, and depreciation is allowed at rates varying from 5% to 100% for buildings, 10% to 15% for furniture and fittings, 25% to 100% for machinery and plant, and 10% to 20% for ships.

Where any asset forming part of a block is transferred, the excess of the sale proceeds over (a) the aggregate of the opening written down value of the block, (b) transfer expenses, and (c) the cost of any asset falling within the block that is purchased during the year is taxed as short-term capital gains at the applicable tax rate (see item 1 and 9).

Amortization. Amortization of certain preliminary expenses is allowed in the case of an Indian company or a person (other than a company) who is resident in India. The allowance is spread over a period of ten years. No such deduction is available to a non-Indian company.

28. Treatment of Dividends
Dividends received by different classes of taxpayers are given different tax treatment as follows:

Non-Indian Companies. The gross amount of the dividend (without any deduction for expenses incurred in earning the dividend) is taxed at 25% as indicated in item 1.

Indian Companies. Net dividend income received by an Indian company from any other Indian company is allowed to be deducted in computing the taxpayer's taxable income, to the extent the dividend is distributed by the recipient company, and the balance is taxed at the rate applicable to the company.

Other Taxpayers. For individuals, no tax is payable on dividend income up to Rs. 10,000. A further exemption of Rs. 3,000 is available for dividends on units of the Unit Trust of India or units of specified mutual funds.

29. Loss Carryovers

Subject to certain conditions, losses incurred in any business carried on by taxpayers are allowed to be carried forward for eight years and set off against the income from the same business or any other business, provided the business in which the loss was incurred was carried on in the year of such set-off. However, so much of the business loss as represents unabsorbed depreciation is allowed to be carried forward indefinitely and set off against any income, provided there is some income from business in the year of set-off. Losses, other than those computed under the headings "Profits and Gains of Business or Profession" and "Capital Gains," are not allowed to be carried forward and set off against future income.

30. Transactions between Related Parties

Expenditure incurred on revenue transactions between related parties may be disallowed in full or in part if the expenditure is considered to be excessive or unreasonable with regard to the fair market value of the goods, services or facilities for which the payment is made or the legitimate needs of the business or profession of the taxpayer or the benefit derived by, or accruing to, him therefrom.

31. Consolidation of Income

Except in specified cases, the income of each taxpayer is computed separately and classified under different headings and the aggregate amount of the income so computed is charged to tax at the rate applicable to the taxpayer. (See items 3 and 11 for exception for capital gains.) It is not possible for the income of a company to be aggregated with the income of its subsidiary or any other company for the purpose of determination of the tax payable by the company.

32. Tax Periods

See item 13.

33.   Other Matters

Deductions.   In computing the total income of a taxpayer, certain deductions are generally allowed, including:

☐ Profits and gains from newly established industrial undertakings (including hotels and ships) for ten successive assessment years, beginning with the year in which operations or manufacturing commences, up to a certain extent.

☐ Expenditures incurred in connection with income tax proceedings by an assessee carrying on a business or profession, subject to a maximum of Rs. 10,000.

☐ Profits and gains of a newly established industrial undertaking are exempt from tax for five successive assessment years, provided the undertaking is established in a Free Trade Zone (i.e., the Kandla Free Trade Zone, Santacruz Electronics Export Processing Zone, Falta Export Processing Zone, West Bengal, Madras Export Processing Zone, Tamilnadu, Noida Export Processing Zone, Uttar Pradesh and Cochin Export Processing Zone, Kerala, and any other zone the Government may specify) and it begins to produce articles during the accounting year relevant to assessment year commencing on or after April 1, 1981.

☐ Profits and gains derived by an assessee from an approved, 100% export-oriented undertaking that manufactures (including processing, assembly, recording of programs on disc, tape, etc.) or produces any article are exempt from tax for five consecutive assessment years.

The following amounts are not deductible in computing the taxpayer's total income:

☐ Entertaining and traveling expenses in excess of specified limits.

☐ Expenses incurred by the head office of a foreign company for managing Indian branches that exceed specified amounts.

☐ Any sum paid on account of wealth tax and gift tax.

☐ Subject to certain conditions, interest, royalties, fees for technical services paid or payable outside India if tax has not been deducted at source.

☐ Salaries payable outside India if the tax has not been deducted at source.

☐ Certain cash payments exceeding Rs. 10,000.

☐ Certain liabilities deductible only if paid.

RELATED CONSIDERATIONS

34.   Incentives and Grants

Taxpayers are encouraged to set up new industrial undertakings through exempting from tax the profits of such undertakings, including hotels, up to a specified limit.
Income derived by an Indian company or a resident Indian from the export of

any goods or merchandise (other than mineral oil, minerals, or ores) is wholly exempt, subject to certain conditions.

Savings are encouraged by granting individuals certain deductions in respect of life insurance premiums, provident fund contributions, etc.

Subject to certain conditions, 1/14th of the capital expenditure to acquire patent rights or copyrights may be deducted in each of fourteen years.

Businesses (with certain exceptions) may deduct up to 20% of their profits if an equal amount is either deposited with the Development Bank or used to purchase plant and machinery within a specified period of time. (This incentive has been withdrawn effective the 1991–1992 assessment year, except for tea companies.)

35. Exchange Controls

Transactions involving foreign exchange are regulated by the Foreign Exchange Regulation Act, 1973, and the Foreign Exchange Regulation Rules, 1974. Imports and exports are controlled by the Imports & Exports Control Act, 1947, and the Imports (Control) Order 1955.

36. Investment Restrictions on Nonresidents

A person who is not a citizen of India or a company (other than a banking company) which is not incorporated under Indian law or in which the nonresident interest is more than 40% cannot, except with the prior permission of the Reserve Bank of India, acquire, hold, transfer or dispose of by sale, mortgage, lease, gift, settlement or otherwise any immovable property situated in India.

A nonresident of India (whether a citizen of India or not) or a person who is not a citizen, but is a resident of India, or a company (other than a banking company) which is not incorporated under Indian law or in which the nonresident interest is more than 40%, or any branch of such company, cannot, except with the permission of the Reserve Bank of India, carry on any business in India or acquire the whole or any part of any undertaking in India.

37. Other Matters

No person resident in India can, except with the permission of the Reserve Bank of India, make any payment to or for the credit of any person resident outside India or receive, otherwise than through an authorized dealer, any payment by order or on behalf of any person resident outside India.

No person resident in India can, without the previous permission of the Central Government, associate himself with, or participate in, whether as promoter or otherwise, any concern outside India (whether incorporated or not) engaged in any trading, commercial or industrial activities.

A nonresident, whether a citizen of India or not, or a citizen of India who is not a resident of India, or a company (other than a banking company) which is not incorporated in India or in which the nonresident interest is more than 40%, or any branch of such company cannot, without the permission of the Reserve Bank of India:

☐ Act, or accept appointment, as agent in India of any person or company in the trading or commercial transactions of such person or company.

☐ Act, or accept appointment, as technical or management adviser in India of any person or company.

☐ For any direct or indirect consideration, permit the use of any trademark by another person or company which does not have the exclusive right to use the mark.

A national of a foreign country cannot, without the prior permission of the Reserve Bank of India, take up employment in India, practice any profession, or carry on any occupation, trade or business in India where such national desires to make use of any foreign exchange for remittance outside of India of any monies received by him in India from such employment, etc.

SELECTION OF BUSINESS ENTITY BY NONRESIDENTS

Foreign companies may engage in business in India by entering into collaboration agreements with Indian concerns, or by setting up their own business or branch, but the approval of the Reserve Bank of India is required in all cases. Income tax is payable at the rates noted in item 1. No additional tax is levied on the remittance of profits or income, but approval of the Reserve Bank of India is necessary for such remittance.

INDONESIA

INCOME TAXES ON CORPORATIONS

1. Rates

Corporation income tax is levied as follows:

General (excluding corporations classified below).

On the first Rp. 10,000,000	15%
On the next Rp. 40,000,000	25%
Thereafter	35%

Oil and Gas Companies Operating Under Production-Sharing Contracts.

Companies operating under contracts entered into prior to January 1, 1984	45%
Companies operating under contracts entered into after January 1, 1984	35%

Withholding tax at the rate of 20% is further applied on income after tax, resulting in an effective tax of 56% for contracts prior to January 1, 1984 and 48% for subsequent contracts.

Mining Companies Operating Under a Contract of Work.

☐ For companies operating under contracts entered into prior to February 28, 1985:

On the first five years of operation	35%
On the next five years	40%
Thereafter	45%

Some contracts also provide for a 60% rate on income exceeding a 15% rate of return.

☐ For companies operating under contracts entered into thereafter: 35%.

2. Local Income Taxes

None.

3. Capital Gains Taxes

Capital gains are considered ordinary income and are taxed at the regular corporate tax rates. If assets have been depreciated (or amortized) for tax purposes, the disposal is treated as follows:

- [ ] Buildings and Extraordinary Disposals (i.e., disposals of major significance): The difference between proceeds and tax value is included in the computation of taxable income.
- [ ] Other Disposals: The proceeds are included as an adjustment in the calculation of tax depreciation (or amortization).

4. Branch Profits Taxes

Branches and "permanent establishments" of foreign corporations operating in Indonesia are subject to corporate tax at normal rates on their income attributable directly to their Indonesian operations. The after-tax income of such branches and permanent establishments is subject to a further 20% withholding tax irrespective of whether the profit is declared and remitted as dividend or retained in Indonesia.

5. Foreign Tax Reliefs

Income derived from outside Indonesia is fully taxable at normal corporate tax rates. Credits for foreign tax paid or due in the same tax period on that income is allowed against the tax imposed. The credit should not exceed the total tax due on foreign income under Indonesian tax law, applied on a country-by-country basis.

6. Classification of Corporations

For tax purposes, no distinction is made between corporations. However, oil and gas and mining contractors are subject to the tax regulations established by their contract. In general, these are those to which either the current tax laws or the old pre-1984 tax laws apply.

7. Payment of Taxes

Monthly installments of tax payments are required to be paid during the year, the amount of which is one-twelfth of the total corporate tax due for the preceding year less income tax withheld by third parties in the same year. Further, withholding of tax by other parties is required on certain transactions such as dividends, interest, rent, royalties, etc. Any balance of tax outstanding must be paid before the corporate tax return is filed. Corporate tax returns should be filed within three months after the company's balance sheet date. Late payments of taxes are penalized at the rate of 2% per month with a maximum of penalty of 48% (unless considered as tax evasion, in which case the penalty can be materially higher).

8.   Other Matters

Income Determination.   With respect to certain industries, the normal method of income computation does not apply. In such industries, income tax liability is determined on a notional basis, such as:

☐   Oil drilling: Income of permanent establishments of foreign entities is determined using a norm, presently 15% of gross drilling revenue on which the normal tax rates are imposed. Effective 1991, Indonesian companies no longer may use the aforementioned method and must use their actual results to compute taxable income.

☐   Shipping and airlines: Taxable income of foreign shipping and airline companies is calculated at a deemed percentage of income, on which no deductions are allowed.

In certain industries, regulated deductions from income are allowable, e.g.:

☐   Banking: An allowance for uncollectible accounts not exceeding a certain percentage (6% for state-owned banks and 3% for other banks and non-bank financial institutions) of the average balance of opening and closing receivables is tax-deductible.

☐   Insurance: Premium reserve is to be computed at the following deferral rates:

Marine	30%
Aviation and hull	50
Others	40

☐   Leasing: From 1991, lessors may no longer capitalize finance-type leases as fixed assets for tax purposes and tax depreciation claimed. For new finance leases, revenue will include only the interest component of lease installments. In addition, an allowance for uncollectable amounts not exceeding 2.5% of average opening and closing lease receivables is tax deductible. Implementing regulations are awaited to define the treatment for pre-existing leases.

☐   Contractors: The percentage of completion method should be used in income determination, including short-term contracts.

Interest Earned From Time Deposits.   Interest earned from time deposits, which should not be less than one month, in on-shore banks is subject to an at-source final withholding tax of 15%.

Tax Administration and Procedures.   The Indonesian tax law is based on the self-assessment method; monthly installments of taxes for the current year (i.e., one-twelfth of the final tax payment of the preceding year for income tax) are generally obligatory and can be decreased or exempted only for specific reasons and after approval from the authorities. The 2%-per-month penalty applies on negligence to pay these prepayments. Overpayments by the end of the year should be followed by a request for refund. Applications for refund, however, are generally processed only after a tax audit has been performed.

Books and records must be maintained in Indonesian language, although approval can be obtained to maintain records in English. No other language is permissible.

Tax Audits. Broad authority has been granted to the tax authorities to perform tax audits, which are generally a lengthy and vigorous process. Selection for audit may arise from the following:

- [ ] Application for refund.
- [ ] Decrease of taxes payable relative to the preceding year.
- [ ] Suspicious conduct of or report to tax authorities by other parties of tax evasion measures.
- [ ] Random sampling.
- [ ] Value-added tax audits are performed periodically (e.g., quarterly basis) on entities liable for VAT. VAT audits are, in general, less rigorous compared to income tax audits.

Investment and Venture Capital Funds. Pending legislation will exempt investment income from income and withholding taxes provided certain conditions are fulfilled.

INCOME TAX ON INDIVIDUALS

9. Rates

Normal Rates. Income not attributable to more than one tax period is taxed at the same rate as for corporations (see item 1). Married couple's income is normally aggregated, and a joint return should be filed. Allowable deductions are:

- [ ] Occupational support computed on the basis of 5% of gross salaries and wages earned during the year, not exceeding Rp. 540,000.
- [ ] Contributions to government-approved pension funds, 5% of gross salaries and wages earned during the year.
- [ ] The above deductions are applicable only to salaries and wages earned on a regular basis, excluding bonuses, directors' remuneration, and other irregular employee earnings.
- [ ] Annual tax-free allowances: Rp. 1,440,000 for each taxpayer, Rp. 720,000 for the spouse, and Rp. 720,000 for each dependent, with a maximum of three dependents.

Average Effective Rate. Net income (gross less allowable deductions) attributable to more than one tax period, such as severance pay, pensions, rents, and capital gains, are taxed at the average effective rate, which is determined as follows:

☐ The sum of the portion of income attributable to the period (depending on the type of income, e.g., 10% on pensions, total gain divided by the length of time between the purchase and sale of the asset on capital gains, etc.) is added to normal income.

☐ Normal tax rates are applied against this amount, and a tax percentage rate is derived, which becomes the average effective rate.

This rate is applied to all current-year income and income during the current year that accrued from prior years.

10. Local Income Taxes

There are no state or provincial income taxes in Indonesia.

11. Capital Gains Taxes

Capital gains on land and buildings are taxed at the average effective rate (see item 9) after deduction of an inflation adjustment factor. Other capital gains are taxed at nominal rates.

12. Foreign Tax Reliefs

Individuals are subject to income tax on their worldwide income. A credit for foreign tax paid or due on total income is allowed against the Indonesian tax imposed on a limited basis (see item 5).

13. Tax Period

December 31 is the standard tax year-end. It is unusual for an individual to obtain permission to adopt a different year-end.

14. Other Matters

Income Distribution From Partnerships. Partnerships are taxed at normal tax rates; income distribution to partners is not subject to further tax.

Deductions Against Income. Deductions against income, e.g., mortgage payments, hospitalization, etc. (other than those set forth in item 9), are not allowable.

Benefits In Kind. Benefits in kind (e.g., housing, use of motor vehicles) are not assessable to the individual nor are they deductible to the employer. Conversely, allowances paid in cash are assessable and deductible, respectively.

Bank Deposit Interest. Interest on certain bank deposits is exempt from tax for deposits that in the aggregate do not exceed Rp. 5 million. In addition, interest on time deposits of more than a one-month period with on-shore banks is subject to an at-source final tax of 15%.

INCOME TAXES ON NONRESIDENTS

15. Liability to Tax

A nonresident corporation is subject only to a final withholding tax on certain types of income derived from Indonesian sources. However, a permanent establishment is treated as a separate resident taxpayer and, thus, is liable to the regular Indonesian corporate tax on profits directly or indirectly attributable to the permanent establishment in Indonesia, including withholding tax (see item 17).

A nonresident corporation from a tax treaty country is deemed to have a permanent establishment should its employee(s) be present in Indonesia for business purposes for more than 183 days in a 12-month period. For non-treaty countries, this test does not apply; they are considered to have a permanent establishment from the time their employee(s) arrives in Indonesia for business purposes. Further, the first three types of income referred to in item 17 may be included in the profit of the permanent establishment if related to the permanent establishment's operations.

An individual will be regarded as a nonresident if he or she is neither present in Indonesia for more than 183 days in any 12-month period nor present in Indonesia during a calendar year with the intention of residing in Indonesia. However, an individual who had previously been a resident taxpayer will only be treated as a nonresident taxpayer if he or she either is leaving Indonesia permanently or has not been residing in Indonesia for two consecutive years.

16. Rates

Permanent establishments are subject to corporate tax at the same rates as resident corporations. Nonresident individuals are assessed at 20%.

17. Withholding Tax Rates

Withholding tax of 20% is levied on the gross amount of the following:

☐ Interest and like costs on overseas borrowings.
☐ Dividends, rents, royalties, and other income for the use of property.
☐ Compensation for technical, management, or other services entirely or partly performed in Indonesia.
☐ After-tax profits of a permanent establishment in Indonesia.

If the recipient is a resident of one of the following countries with which Indonesia has a tax treaty, the following rates apply:

	Dividends (1)	Royalties (2)	Interest (3)	Branch Profits (4)
Austria	15%, 10% (5)	10%	10%, 0% (6)	20%, 12% (7)
Belgium (8)	15	10	15, 10 (9)	15
Canada (8)	15	15	15,0 (6)	15
Denmark	20, 10 (5)	15	10, 0 (6)	15
France (8)	15, 10 (5)	10	15, 10, 0 (6) (9)	10
Germany (8)	15, 10 (5)	10	10, 5, 0 (6) (10)	10
India	15, 10 (5)	15	10, 0 (6)	10
Japan	20, 15, 10 (11)	10	10, 0 (6)	10
Korea	15, 10 (5)	15	10, 0 (6)	10
Netherlands (8)	20, 10 (5)	20, 10, 5 (12)	20, 10 (9)	10
New Zealand	15	15	10, 0 (6)	15
Norway	15	15, 10 (13)	10, 0 (6)	15
Philippines	20, 15 (5)	15	15, 10, 0 (14)	20
Singapore (15)	15, 10 (5)	15	10, 0 (6)	15
Sweden	15, 10 (5)	15, 10 (13)	10, 0 (6)	—
Thailand	15	15, 10 (16)	15, 0	20
United Kingdom (8)	15, 10	10	15, 10	0
United States	15	15, 10 (17)	15, 0 (6)	15

Notes:

(1) With the exception of Belgium, Germany, Netherlands, Thailand, and United Kingdom these rates are applicable only if the shareholder is the beneficial owner.

(2) For Denmark, France, India, Japan, Korea, New Zealand, Norway, Singapore, and the United States, these rates are applicable only in cases of beneficial ownership.

(3) Beneficial ownership is necessary (for Denmark, France, India, Japan, Korea, New Zealand, Norway, the Philippines, Singapore, and the United States) for these rates to be applicable.

(4) Only on amounts actually remitted for Belgium, Netherlands, Philippines, and West Germany; levied on total after-tax profit for other countries.

(5) The lower rate applies if the recipient controls 25% or more of the voting shares.

(6) If amounts are paid to the government or an approved bank or financial institution, no withholding tax is required to be deducted.

(7) 20% on deemed dividends of oil and gas sector production-sharing contractors.

(8) Treaties with these countries are under renegotiation, the result of which cannot be determined at this time.

(9) The lower rate applies only to interest owed by certain industries (banks and financial institutions, agriculture, plantation, forestry, fishery, livestock, mining, manufacturing, transportation, inexpensive housing projects, tourism, infrastructure, or other manufacturing industries) to banks, financial institutions, or other corporations.

(10) 5% for interest arising in Indonesia paid to Deutsche Gesellschaft fur Wirtschaftliche Zusammen-arbeit.

(11)   20% on deemed dividends of oil and gas sector production-sharing contractors; 10% if the recipient owns at least 25% of the voting stock of the payor for the whole year in which dividends are distributed; 15% on other dividends.

(12)   The 10% rate applies to royalties on copyrights and scientific work use or the rights to use industrial, commercial, and scientific equipment, and information concerning scientific experience. The 5% rate applies to royalties on patents, trademarks, designs, models, plans, secret formulas, processes, and production/ marketing-related information.

(13)   The 10% rate applies to royalties for use of industrial equipment, commercial or scientific knowledge, and information concerning industrial, commercial, or scientific experience. The 15% rate applies to all other royalties.

(14)   0% for interest on government bonds, government debentures, loans to/guaranteed by/insured by either the Indonesian or Philippines Central Bank; 10% for interest on listed bonds, notes payable or related debts; 15% for interest on other types of debt.

(15)   The Singapore Indonesia tax treaty is effective as of January 1, 1992.

(16)   The 10% rate applies to royalties on copyrights for literary, artistic, or scientific work; the 15% rate applies to all other royalties.

(17)   The 10% rate applies to royalties for use of industrial, commercial, and scientific equipment and for rights to use such equipment; the 15% rate applies to other royalties.

18.   Special Withholding Provisions

Withholding taxes are considered due and payable on an accrual basis, whether or not actual remittance has been made; for example, on interest credited or dividends declared.

19.   Tax Treaties

Treaties with certain countries have been signed and ratified, and Indonesia is currently negotiating/proposing to negotiate tax treaties (which generally follow the principles of the OECD model Taxation Convention on Income and Capital) with other countries, including Australia, Finland, Hungary, Italy, Malaysia, Pakistan, Romania, Saudi Arabia, Sri Lanka, and Yugoslavia.

20.   Other Matters

☐   Expatriates working in Indonesia for more than 183 days in a 12-month period are considered as resident taxpayers and are taxed on their worldwide income. Minimum deemed salary levels based on country of origin and qualifications apply to expatriates for salary withholding tax purposes.

☐   Withholding taxes borne by the payor are not tax deductible for income determination under the Indonesian tax laws.

☐   Indonesian tax is not imposed on gains on disposal of listed shares by nonresidents (provided the shares are not connected with a permanent establishment).

OTHER SIGNIFICANT TAXES

21. Sales (Value Added)

Value-added tax is levied on supplies of goods and services within the customs area of Indonesia and imports into the customs area. In addition, VAT applies to services performed abroad relating to assets or property used, or located, in Indonesia. The tax rates of value-added tax are

Export of goods	0%
Other goods and services	10%

Input VAT can be credited against output VAT except for:

☐ Purchases not directly for business purposes.

☐ Purchases before registration as a business liable to VAT.

☐ Purchases and costs of certain vehicles.

☐ Costs for staff welfare, business trips, and entertainment.

☐ Goods where the VAT is borne by the Government.

☐ Purchases with an incomplete VAT invoice.

☐ Purchases relating to activities exempt from VAT.

The principal exempt activities are as follows:

☐ Retail sales.

☐ Sales of unprocessed goods, e.g., agricultural produce.

☐ Banking, insurance, and leasing services.

☐ Manpower services

☐ Social, health, and educational services

☐ Land and ship transport

☐ Hotel and catering services

☐ Services performed abroad (unless relating to assets or property located in Indonesia).

The principal reliefs relate to:

☐ Capital equipment, spares, and a limited amount of raw materials imported for approved investment projects.

☐ Capital equipment for manufacturing activities.

☐ Purchases of goods and services used for exports.

☐ Imports used for aid-funded projects.

☐ Temporary imports of equipment for the oil and gas industry.

Sales Tax on Luxury Goods. This tax is collected in the event of either import or sale of certain goods. This tax currently is levied at the rates of 10%, 20%, or 30%, depending on the type of goods, as determined by the Government. Exported luxury goods carry a zero rate.

Collection of VAT. A taxable supplier is obliged to account for all output VAT, and to pay the net amount monthly to the State Treasury. If the customer is a Government entity, an oil and gas contractor, or a mining company, however, the VAT is to be paid by these customers directly to the State Treasury. This output VAT cannot be utilized by the supplier for credit of input VAT.

22. Inheritance and Gift Taxes

None.

23. Taxes on Payrolls (Social Security)

None.

24. Taxes on Natural Resources

Mining companies will be subject to royalties and deadrent as set forth in the contract of work.

25. Other Taxes

Land and Building Tax. This tax is imposed at the rate of 0.5% of the market value of land and buildings as determined by the government. Utilization of appraisal companies is presently under consideration. Certain market-value determination methods are applicable for specific uses, such as forestry rights.

Stamp Duty. A two-rate stamp duty imposing a tax of either Rp. 500 or Rp. 1,000 on certain documents such as receipts, checks, agreements, powers of attorney, etc., is applied.

Exit Tax. Residents leaving the country by air are subjects to an Rp. 250,000 exit tax, the total amount of which during the tax year constitutes prepaid income tax. A similar tax of Rp. 150,000 applies to residents leaving by ship.

Excise Duties. Excise duties are levied by the government on certain products, such as cigarettes, cigars, pipe tobacco, and alcohol.

Other Taxes. Other taxes such as entertainment tax, radio and television tax, road tax, dog tax, motor vehicle tax, bicycle tax, advertisement tax, foreigners tax, and development tax (on restaurant and hotel sales) are levied by regional governments.

COMPUTATION OF TAXABLE INCOME

26. Capital Gains

See items 3 and 11.

27. Depreciation and Depletion

Fixed assets other than buildings are depreciated on a pooled reducing-balance method at a 10%, 25%, or 50% rate, depending on the asset category and useful life as determined by the government. As such, depreciation is applied on the year-end book value of the specific pooled balance. Sales proceeds are deducted and purchases added to this balance (see item 3).

Buildings are depreciated on a 20-year straight-line basis.

Depletion of oil and gas or mining costs incurred prior to the commercial production is allowed for contracts not specifically subject to the old pre-1984 tax law at the rate of 25% per year on the reducing-balance method.

28. Treatment of Dividends

Dividends are fully assessable at normal personal income and corporate tax rates except when received by a resident corporation having an economic relationship with and owning at least 25% of the value of the issued shares of the resident payor. In this case, dividends are exempt from tax. Pending legislation will extend this exemption to all domestic dividends received by resident companies.

29. Loss Carryovers

Fiscal losses can be carried over for five consecutive years or, in the case of certain agricultural, mining businesses, and certain new projects in the eastern provinces of Indonesia, eight years. No loss carrybacks are permitted.

30. Transactions between Related Parties

The tax authorities pay particular attention to related party transactions to ascertain whether these are reflective of an arm's-length relationship and, based on their findings, might affect certain adjustments. The term "special relationship" is widely used by the Directorate General of Taxation and is defined as either direct/indirect common ownership/control or ownership of 25% of more in another taxpaying entity.

31. Consolidation of Income

There is no provision for consolidation of income or losses by related corporations for tax purposes.

32. Tax Periods

The basis period for assessment is the company's accounting year.

33. Other Matters

Inventory Valuation. All taxpayers are required to value inventories at full historical cost on a consistent basis, using either the average cost or the FIFO basis.

Amortization. Intangible assets used in the business can be amortized. Amortization is determined through the declining balance method at 50%, 25%, and 10% of ending book value based on the asset's useful life; organization and share issue costs are amortized using the 50% rate.

Bad Debts. Except for certain industries (see item 8), allowances for doubtful accounts are not deductible for tax purposes. Write-offs are permitted only on an actual basis.

Employee Benefits in Kind. Benefits received in kind by employees (e.g., free housing, annual leave, personal use of cars, club memberships, etc.) are not tax deductible for the employer. Allowances to employees are tax deductible and are treated as employee income.

Revaluation of Assets. Revaluation of assets, for purposes of taxation, is not allowed unless granted by special decree of the Minister of Finance, such as in 1971, 1979, and 1986 in which all tangible assets used in the business except land (considered as intangible, as freehold ownership is legally unavailable for corporations) must be revalued according to government index rates that are based on the acquisition year.

Exchange Gains and Losses. Exchange gains and losses arising from normal fluctuations should be included in the taxable income of the period. In the event that prior to January 1, 1984 the company had chosen the historical exchange rate method, gains and losses are taken into account at realization.

Exchange gains and losses arising from the 1986 devaluation are taken into account only at the time of realization.

Entertainment Expenses. For entertainment expenses to be tax deductible, sufficient evidence and details should be submitted, for example: name, position, company, and type of business of those entertained, date and exact place of the activity, a description of and the total amount spent for the entertainment.

Donations. Contributions and donations to any organization are not tax deductible.

Pension Fund Contributions. Contributions to an employees' pension fund are deductible only if the fund is approved by the Minister of Finance.

Foreign Aid Related Income. Tax and value added tax on the income of direct contractors, consultants, and suppliers attributable to foreign aid funded government development projects (e.g., World Bank, Asian Development Bank, OECD) are borne by the government. In the event of the taxpayer performing several contracts, the "foreign aid portion" of income is determined as the proportion of foreign-aid-related gross revenue to total gross revenue.

Practical Considerations. The "self-assessment" method of tax determination implies that no finalization of taxes occurs except in cases where verification by the tax authorities is available. Tax returns may be corrected at the taxpayer's discretion provided that an investigation by the tax authorities has not commenced. A penalty of 2% per month, not exceeding 24 months, is applicable on back taxes. Tax offenses or negligence, whether intentional or unintentional, may be considered criminal and carry maximum penal implication of three years and/or 400% of balances due. Statutes of limitation are five years for non-criminal offenses and ten years for criminal offenses.

RELATED CONSIDERATIONS

34. Incentives and Grants

Bonded Areas. A number of areas adjacent to seaports have been designated bonded areas and include industrial estates and bonded warehouses. Within these areas, customs concessions and special conditions apply for the import, export, and processing of goods.

Tax Incentives. Since the introduction of new taxation laws, January 1, 1984, previous tax incentives have been withdrawn. Current incentives still remaining include import duty exemption or concessionary rates on BKPM-approved capital goods and raw materials for investment projects. Facilities are available for companies exporting the majority of their production, whereby import duty may be refunded when the finished goods are exported.

Eastern Provinces. New projects and certain expansion projects are eligible for carryforward of tax losses for eight years (normally limited to five years) and a 50% reduction in land and buildings tax for eight years. In addition, import duties into East Timor are reduced by 25% compared to normal rates.

35. Exchange Controls

There are no exchange controls operating in Indonesia except that individuals may not physically take more than Rp. 50,000 in Rupiah banknotes abroad on any one trip.

36. Investment Restrictions on Nonresidents

Foreigners are, normally, permitted to invest only in joint venture companies operating in areas not listed in the annual foreign investment negative list (in which case the foreign shareholding should not exceed 80% and should be reduced to 49% within 15 years after the commencement of commercial production) or in existing Indonesian companies not operating in the listed industries. Investment in other industries and/or increase of shareholding up to 95% to be reduced to 49% within 15 years of the commencement of commercial production is permitted provided that:

☐ A minimum of 65% of the products is exported (85% for textiles);
☐ The investment is located in designated remote areas; or
☐ The initial investment exceeds US$10 million.

Maximum share acquisition by foreigners in existing Indonesian companies depends on the purpose of acquisition. A 25% limit is imposed if the acquisition purpose is to improve the company's financial position. On the other hand, if the acquisition purpose is to enable the partial or full export of the company's product, the limits are 49% and 80%, respectively.

Foreigners already owning shares in joint venture companies may increase their shareholding up to 95% provided that the Indonesian shareholders are unable to increase their shareholdings and a genuine urgent requirement for such additional capital exists to improve the joint venture's financial condition, and to enable the export of its products. However, such shareholdings should be reduced to the original level or, in cases where the Indonesian shareholding was less than 51%, to 49% within five years commencing from the time approval for the capital increase is granted.

Foreign investment companies are permitted to export other companies' products after obtaining the necessary export permit. Export credits at the subsidized rate of 9.5% per annum are available for up to 85% of working capital requirements.

SELECTION OF BUSINESS ENTITY BY NONRESIDENTS

As an alternative to operating in Indonesia through the methods described in item 36, a nonresident investor may operate in any of the methods discussed in the following paragraphs.

Establish a Representative Office. A representative office is usually established to promote imported products and to provide technical assistance to local importers and distributors. Such an office however may not engage directly in trading, including accepting orders, making sales, or collecting debts.

Establish a Branch. This is normally restricted to companies offering an expertise or service that is not adequately provided by Indonesians in specialized areas such as major infrastructure construction, the oil industry, engineering, financial consultants, and other specialized areas. To do business on this basis, it is necessary to obtain a license from the government ministry responsible for the area in which the work is to be carried out. To obtain this, it is usually necessary to show evidence of the intention to carry out the work by a signed contract or evidence of negotiations on a contract. Corporate tax is payable on the net income attributable to the branch together with withholding tax on the after-tax profit.

Petroleum and Mining Operations. Participation in oil, natural gas, and mining industries requires entrance into a contract of work with the appropriate government ministry concerned, as follows.

For oil and natural gas projects, this is accomplished through tendering for a production-sharing agreement with Pertamina, the state-owned oil company. Under this agreement, the contractor is required to finance all exploration, development, and production costs relating to the area specified in the agreement. In return, the contractor is entitled to recover all operating costs, including capital investment, out of crude oil production. The balance of oil production is then divided between Pertamina and the contractor, normally on an after-tax sharing ratio of 85% to Pertamina and 15% to the contractor. Production-sharing contracts are usually for a period of 30 years, although provision is included for the contract to expire after an unsuccessful six to ten years exploration period. The terms of contracts covering natural gas projects are similar to those for oil with the exception that the after-tax sharing ratio is 65% Pertamina and 35% to the contractor.

Mining operations are currently carried out in accordance with fourth generation contracts of work, which are basically a development of earlier generation contracts. Under these agreements, the operating company (including foreign operators, which must be incorporated in Indonesia unless special exemption is obtained) is granted control and management of all activities under the agreement. The agreement provides for a general prospecting period of three years, a one-year evaluation period, three years for construction, and a 20-year operating period. Transfer to Indonesians of at least 51% of the equity of the operating company is required within ten years from commencement of production.

IRAN

INCOME TAXES ON CORPORATIONS

1. Rates

Taxable income of private sector business entities in Iran from all sources is subject to graduated income tax rates ranging between 12% and 75%. In addition, a 3% municipality tax also is payable by most businesses during the Government's current five-year economic plan. The top rate of 75% applies to taxable income in excess of Rls. 25 million. A 10% tax, loosely entitled "corporation tax," is deducted from taxable income of Iranian-registered corporations before the graduated rates are applied.

Taxable income of Iranian-registered corporations will be deemed to be divided between registered shareholders or partners in proportion to their participation, with the share of each being subject separately to graduated rates. Therefore, in this context, it would be advantageous to have as many shareholders or partners in a company as possible.

Foreign corporations are subject to tax on their income generated in Iran or, for certain types of income, even if merely received from Iran.

Computation of Taxable Income. While maintenance of proper books of accounts is a legal necessity for almost all business operations, taxable income is not always determined by reference to book profits. Notable exceptions are as follows:

☐ Contracting operations (see "Contracting Operations," below).

☐ Income of foreign entities derived from granting of licenses and other concessions, or from technical assistance and training. Taxable income in these categories is deemed to be a fixed percentage of gross receipts, ranging between 20% and 90%.

Contracting Operations. Contracting operations within the meaning of the Tax Act include any type of construction work, technical installations, transportation (excluding shipping and aviation), design and planning of buildings and installations, drawing and topographical surveying, supervision, and technical calculations.

Tax authorities reserve the right to determine the taxable income of contracting operations by reference to their books of account. However, if they take up the deemed profit option, which is likely to be the case in practice, taxable income in any given fiscal year will be 10% of contract receipts for prime contractors and 8% of receipts for subcontractors, even if the books record a loss.

A 5% withholding is made at source from each payment to a contractor. The withholding is not a separate tax but merely an advance payment towards the overall tax liability of the contractor. Ongoing contracts proposed prior to April 1988 will be taxed on the basis of the Old Taxation Act. The amount of taxes imposed on a contractor under the old tax regime will be approximately 33% more than similar taxes under the current Act.

2.   Local Income Taxes

There are no provincial income taxes in Iran.

7.   Payment of Taxes

Taxes must be paid by business entities within four months from the end of a financial year, accompanied by an annual tax declaration, and receipts for taxes already paid, if any. The fiscal year of a nonregistered foreign entity is the Iranian calendar year, which commences on March 21 each year. Full taxes should be withheld at source from nonregistered entities.

INCOME TAXES ON INDIVIDUALS

9.   Rates

Earned income from employment, including cash and non-cash benefits, is subject to income tax at graduated rates and is deductible at source by employers on a monthly basis. Monthly net taxable earned income (after allowances and exemptions) of up to Rls. 60,000 is exempt from taxes, with the excess being taxable at rates ranging between 12% and 75%. The following are some examples:

Monthly Salary and Benefits	Amount of Tax
Rls. 180,000	Rls. 20,000
200,000	24,200
250,000	35,900
300,000	49,100
400,000	79,300
500,000	113,500

During the Government's current five-year economic plan, a surcharge of 23% is payable by foreign employees on their salaries and benefits. This is collected by the Labor Department at the time a work permit is issued or when an existing permit is being renewed.

14. Other Matters

Social Security. Social security contributions are payable for all persons employed in Iran on their employment income (salaries or wages) but only up to an income ceiling of Rls. 160,000 per month. Foreign individuals may seek exemption by proving that they have coverage outside Iran for the same hazards envisaged in the Social Security Act.

Contributions are currently 27%, with 20% being payable by employers and 7% being payable by employees. To ensure that contractors conform with social security regulations, the Act requires contract employers to retain 5% from each payment they make to their contractors, as well as the entire amount of their last invoice. Retentions may only be released when contractors produce a clearance certificate from the Social Security Organisation.

INCOME TAXES ON NONRESIDENTS

19. Tax Treaties

Iran has double taxation agreements in force with Germany and France. Some of the important provisions, for qualifying entities, are:

☐ It does not apply to income derived from the extraction and processing of crude oil and its derivatives in Iran.

☐ Income from aircraft and shipping operations are taxed only in the country from which management is exercised.

☐ Dividends paid directly, and not to another resident company, will be subject to a maximum withholding tax of 15% if at least 25% of the voting shares are held; otherwise, the withholding tax is limited to 20%.

☐ Royalties paid directly, and not to another resident company, are subject to a maximum withholding tax of 10%.

☐ Tax credit will be available to the extent that the taxes on income levied in one country do not exceed the taxes payable thereon in the other country: notional credit will be available in West Germany if the income arising in Iran has been subject to total or partial exemption. References to "permanent establishments" include branches registered in Iran; income arising from the activities of such a permanent establishment will be taxed in Iran but not in the home country.

RELATED CONSIDERATIONS

35. Exchange Controls

The Iranian rial is not a freely convertible currency. Although exchange control restrictions have been considerably relaxed over the past year, foreign nationals and entities still cannot officially repatriate funds at will. There remains a multi-exchange rate system in force; however, the recently introduced "floating rate," which values the rial against hard currencies at almost 20 times less than the official rate, now is available to almost all foreign individuals and entities.

SELECTION OF BUSINESS ENTITY BY NONRESIDENTS

To register a branch or a subsidiary, foreign corporations need a supporting letter from a government affiliate. Such letters normally are given only if a business relationship has already been established or is in the process of being established with the supporting body. In the absence of direct foreign investment in recent years, branch offices remain the most popular legal formation among foreign corporations.

IRELAND
REPUBLIC OF

INCOME TAXES ON CORPORATIONS

1. Rates

Companies resident in Ireland are liable to corporation tax at the rate of 40% on their worldwide income. A special tax rate of 10% applies to all manufacturing and qualifying services companies until December 31, 2010 and in areas designated for regional incentives until December 31, 2005 (see item 34).

2. Local Income Taxes

None.

3. Capital Gains Tax

Chargeable capital gains realized by companies are subject to corporation tax. The tax rate for gains realized depends on the period of ownership, as follows:

Holding Period	Rate
Up to three years	50%
Three to six years	35
More than six years	30

Relief for inflation is granted if the holding period is more than one year. Special rules apply to development land and to shares quoted on the Smaller Companies Market. In the absence of advance clearance by the Tax Authorities, purchasers must withhold tax of 15% of the consideration when acquiring certain Irish assets costing in excess of IR£100,000.

4. Branch Profits Taxes

A branch of a foreign corporation is subject to corporation tax on the profits of the branch at the same rate as would apply to an Irish company.

5. Foreign Tax Reliefs

Double taxation relief is provided for taxes imposed by territories outside Ireland, both under tax treaties and unilateral provisions of Irish law. Relief is given for direct withholding taxes on income received and, in the case of dividends received from foreign companies, for taxes on the profits out of which those dividends are paid. A foreign tax credit is given only to residents of Ireland, which term does not include branches of foreign corporations.

6. Classification of Corporations

Corporations are classified for Irish tax purposes as either resident or nonresident. A company is deemed to be resident where its central management and control are exercised.

Companies controlled by five or fewer persons are subject to special rules with respect to loans to shareholders and certain undistributed income.

7. Payment of Taxes

Corporation tax is payable in one installment seven months after the company's accounting year-end.

8. Other Matters

Tax-Exempt Government Securities. Irish resident subsidiaries or branches of foreign companies controlled from tax treaty countries may invest in certain short-term Irish Government securities that are exempt from Irish tax. The securities may be denominated in the major trading currencies.

INCOME TAXES ON INDIVIDUALS

9. Rates

The rates of individual income tax on taxable income from April 6, 1991, computed after deducting the individual's personal and other allowances, are as follows:

	Taxable Income		
	Married Couples	**Other Taxpayers**	**Rate**
The first	IR£13,400	IR£6,700	29%
The next	6,200	3,100	48
Over	19,600	9,800	52

The income of a married couple may be aggregated for tax purposes. There is no surcharge on investment income.

Income Liable to Tax. Individuals resident and ordinarily resident and domiciled in Ireland are liable to tax on their income from all sources (with certain exceptions).

Individuals who are resident but not domiciled in Ireland are liable to tax on income arising in, and income remitted to, Ireland, but not on income arising outside Ireland that is not remitted to Ireland. Income earned outside Ireland that is applied in satisfaction of certain loans may be considered as income remitted to Ireland. Income arising in the United Kingdom is taxable in Ireland whether remitted to Ireland or not.

Foreign nationals intending to take up residence or employment in Ireland are advised to obtain detailed advice before arrival.

10. Local Income Taxes

None.

11. Capital Gains Taxes

Chargeable capital gains realized by individuals are taxable under a capital gains tax and not under the normal income tax. The rules set out in item 3 also apply to individuals. No tax liability arises on dispositions between spouses.

12. Foreign Tax Reliefs

Relief is given for taxes imposed by territories outside Ireland in respect of income from sources outside Ireland, both under tax treaties and under unilateral provisions of Irish law.

13. Tax Period

The tax year is from April 6 to April 5. Most individuals in employment have tax deducted from their wages under the Pay-As-You-Earn (P.A.Y.E.) scheme. The date of payment for other individuals is November 1 in the tax year.

14. Other Matters

Dividends. Dividends paid by Irish companies qualifying for the 10% rate of tax may attract a reduced tax rate of 22% in the hands of an Irish resident shareholder.

INCOME TAXES ON NONRESIDENTS

15. Liability to Tax

Nonresidents of Ireland are liable to tax on income derived from property situated in Ireland or from any trade carried on in Ireland. A withholding tax (recoverable to the extent that it exceeds the liability) of 29% applies to payments made by State Authorities and certain public bodies in respect of professional services.

16. Rates

Interest payments on loans of more than one year, annuities, and patent and mineral royalties, are subject to a withholding tax of 29%. This tax may, however, be reduced or eliminated under the terms of a tax treaty (see item 17).

No withholding taxes are deducted from dividends paid by Irish companies. Nonresident shareholders of Irish companies may be entitled, under the terms of a tax treaty, to a tax credit similar to that applicable to Irish resident shareholders (see item 28).

17. Withholding Tax Rates

	Dividends	Interest	Royalties
Nontreaty countries	0%	29%	29%
Treaty countries:			
Australia	0 (1)	10	10
Austria	0	0	0
Belgium	0	15	0
Canada	0	29	29
Cyprus	0	0	0
Denmark	0	0	0
Finland	0	0	0
France	0	0	0
Germany (F.R.)	0	0	0
Italy	0	10	0
Japan	0	10	10
Luxembourg	0	0	0
Netherlands	0	0	0
New Zealand	0 (1)	10	10
Norway	0	0	0
Pakistan	0	0	0
Sweden	0 (1)	0	0
Switzerland	0 (2)	0	0
United Kingdom	0 (1)	0	0
United States	0	0 (3)	0
Zambia	0	0	0

Notes:
(1) There is no withholding tax on dividends paid. Recipients, other than a company that controls 10% or more of the voting power of the paying company, are entitled to the tax credit attributable to the dividend and may claim a refund of the tax credit which usually equals $^{25}/_{75}$ of the dividend. However, there is a withholding tax on this refund of 15% of the aggregate of the dividend plus the tax credit.
(2) There is no withholding tax on dividends paid. Recipients, other than a com-

pany that controls 25% or more of the voting power of the paying company, are entitled to the tax credit attributable to the dividend and may claim a refund of the tax credit which usually equals $^{25}/_{75}$ of the dividend. However, there is a withholding tax on this refund of 15% of the aggregate of the dividend plus the tax credit.

(3) 29% if it is paid by an Irish company to a U.S. corporation that controls more than 50% of the voting power of the Irish company.

There is no withholding tax on interest paid to nonresidents by companies carrying on activities that qualify for the 10% tax rate in the International Financial Services Centre in Dublin or the Shannon Customs Free Airport (see item 34).

OTHER SIGNIFICANT TAXES

21. Sales (Value Added)

VAT is chargeable on the supply of goods and services by a taxable person in the course of business. Registered traders are, in general, able to recover the VAT paid on business expenses, including capital expenditures, so that the tax is borne only by the ultimate consumer. VAT is charged at the following rates:

Food, books, exports, and children's clothing and footwear	0%
Construction services, immovable goods, most newspapers, and hotel and certain other holiday accommodations	10%
Fuel for heating and lighting, telecommunications services, repair and maintenance of vehicles and machinery, adult clothing and footwear, hotel and restaurant meals, and certain agricultural services	12.5%
Other goods and services	21%

Certain transactions are exempt from VAT, such as most insurance and banking services. Exempt traders may not recover VAT paid on business expenses.

22. Inheritance and Gift Taxes

Capital acquisitions tax consists of two taxes relating to the transmission of property other than for full consideration. The taxes are *donee*-based.

Gift Tax. Chargeable on the donee. A charge to gift tax may arise whenever a donee takes a right or an interest in property other than for full consideration.

Inheritance Tax. Inheritance tax may arise on each occasion a successor takes a taxable inheritance.

The relationship of the donee or successor to the donor or disponer is recognized by the provision of thresholds of exemption which must be breached before the donee or successor becomes liable to tax in respect of acquisitions, by gift or inheritance. If the gift or inheritance is received on or after January 1, 1990, the exemption thresholds may be adjusted for inflation. The current maximum exempt threshold is IR£161,400. The rate of inheritance tax rises on a scale from 20% to 40%. The rates of gift tax are 75% of the corresponding rates of inheritance tax. All gifts and inheritances received from all sources since June 2, 1982 by the same donee or successor are aggregated when computing the tax payable on a current gift or inheritance.

Inheritances between spouses on or after January 30, 1985 and gifts on or after January 31, 1990 are exempt.

23. Taxes on Payrolls (Social Security)

State insurance contributions and income levies are payable in respect of employed and self-employed persons.

For the employed person, part is payable by the employee and part by the employer. There are various contribution rates for different classes of employment. The most common are:

Employee's Salary	Employer	Employee
First IR£18,000	12.2%	7.75%
Next IR£ 1,300	12.2	2.25
Over IR£19,300	Nil	2.25

The rates of contribution for self-employed persons are

Self-Employed's Salary	Percentage of Income
First IR£18,000	7.25%
Over IR£18,000	2.25

24. Taxes on Natural Resources

No special taxes are levied on the exploitation of natural resources.

It is expected that special rules will be introduced for the taxation of profits arising from the exploitation of oil and gas resources.

Depreciation allowances are available for expenditures for scheduled minerals.

25.   Other Taxes

Land and Property.   Local authorities levy taxes known as rates on nonresidential property. The rates are normally paid by the occupier and are based on a notional rental value of the property. Charges are made for services supplied by local authorities to businesses in respect of water, refuse collection, and discharge of industrial effluent. Individual residents in certain local authority areas may also be charged for water and refuse collection. In addition, an annual residential property tax is payable by persons who own and occupy residential property whose market value exceeds a limit (currently IR£96,000) and where household income exceeds IR£28,500. The rate of tax is 1.5% on the excess of value over IR£96,000.

Stamp Duty.   A duty is levied, at varying rates, on certain instruments for the transfer of property, based on a percentage of the consideration for the transfer. The following are the main rates for the conveyance on sale of property:

☐ Stocks and other marketable securities.	1%
☐ Units in Irish Unit Trusts and UCITS	0%
☐ Other property	
—consideration between IR£25,000 and IR£50,000	4%
—consideration between IR£50,000 and IR£60,000	5%
—consideration in excess of IR£60,000	6%

Capital Duty.   The duty is chargeable on certain transactions relating to limited companies. The most common are the formation of a company and an increase in a company's issued share capital. The duty is charged at a rate of 1% of the actual value of the net assets contributed to a company in consideration for the issue of shares.

COMPUTATION OF TAXABLE INCOME

26.   Capital Gains

There is a comprehensive system of taxation of capital gains in Ireland, and any disposal of a capital asset may give rise to a liability to tax on capital gains. Disposals by way of gifts or in other circumstances that are not at arm's length are treated as disposals at market value. The chargeable gain is the difference between the cost of the asset plus certain allowable expenditure and sale proceeds. Account is taken of inflation to reduce the chargeable gain (see items 3 and 11).

27.   Depreciation and Depletion

Depreciation charged in arriving at an accounting profit is ignored for tax purposes. There is, instead, a system of tax depreciation allowances for qualifying capital expenditure. These allowances are given as deductions in computing taxable income. Qualifying expenditure normally is reduced by the amount of any grants received by the business for that expenditure. The basis of granting allowances is outlined below.

Allowances on Plant.   A depreciation allowance is granted on a reducing-balance basis in respect of plant and machinery used for the purposes of the business. The three basic rates are 10%, 12.5%, and 25%.

Industrial Buildings.   The basic depreciation allowance is 4%. No depreciation allowance is granted on offices, shops, and residential buildings except in certain designated areas, including the International Financial Services Centre in Dublin.

Accelerated Allowances.   Until March 31, 1992, the taxpayer may choose to accelerate the claim for allowances on plant and buildings by claiming up to 25% of the qualifying expenditure in the first year. Effective April 1, 1992, accelerated allowances will be available only in respect of expenditure in the International Financial Services Centre in Dublin and certain designated areas where up to 100% of qualifying expenditure may continue to be claimed in the first year.

Accelerated allowances of up to 100% also may be claimed in respect of industrial buildings and plant in Shannon.

28.   Treatment of Dividends

No withholding taxes are deducted from dividends or other distributions by Irish companies. With certain exceptions, the payment of dividends and other distributions will generate a liability to pay advance corporate tax (ACT) equal to the tax credit associated with the dividend or distribution. For most companies, this amounts to $^{25}/_{75}$ of dividends and other distributions and will be reduced if the company is entitled to a reduced tax rate as outlined in item 34.

ACT is payable six months after the end of the accounting period and is allowed as a credit against the company's corporation tax liability. ACT only offsets tax on the income of a company and is not available to cover tax on chargeable capital gains or sales of development land. If ACT paid exceeds the tax for the accounting period, the surplus ACT may be carried back to offset tax of accounting periods ended in the preceding 12 months. Any balance still not utilized can be carried forward and set off against future tax.

ACT does not apply to dividends and interest paid to 75% parent companies resident in tax treaty countries.

Irish resident noncorporate shareholders obtain a tax credit against their personal income tax liability equal to the tax credit attributable to dividends received.

Dividends passing between Irish resident companies are treated as having been fully taxed. Although dividends paid by an Irish resident company to foreign shareholders are assessable to Irish income tax, the Irish Government has indicated that such income tax will not be assessed.

29. Loss Carryovers

A trading loss is computed on the same principles as trading income. A trading loss of a company may be carried forward and set off against trading income of the same trade in succeeding accounting periods. Trading losses may be offset against the total profits (including capital gains) of the same accounting period or carried back and set off against the total profits of the accounting period, equal in length, immediately preceding the one in which the loss was incurred. In an Irish group of companies, losses incurred by member companies (other than life assurance companies) may be set off against profits earned (including capital gains) by other members of the group in the same accounting period. However, losses arising from activities that qualify for the 10% tax rate (see item 34) may be offset against only member company profits earned in similarly qualifying activities. In addition, it is not permissible to offset losses incurred in a trade carried on in the International Financial Services Centre against other income arising in Ireland. Anti-avoidance provisions apply when there are changes in the ownership of a company with unused losses. Capital losses may only offset capital gains arising in the same year or in the future.

An individual who incurs a trading loss may carry the loss forward and set it off against profits of the same trade, or set it off against total income for the year of assessment in which the loss was incurred.

30. Transactions between Related Parties

If a transaction between commonly controlled corporations does not take place at arm's length and one of the parties benefits from any of the reliefs outlined in item 34, various tax provisions may apply which treat the transaction as entered into at arm's length. Tax treaty provisions may also deem transactions to be on an arm's-length basis (e.g., transactions between a nonresident company and its Irish branch).

Transfers of assets during corporate reorganizations may give rise to income and capital gains tax liabilities. Such liabilities may be eliminated by virtue of relieving legislation dealing with reconstructions and amalgamations.

31. Consolidation of Income

There are no provisions for the filing of consolidated tax returns by related companies. In general, however, trading losses incurred by a group company may be offset against the profits of other members of the group for the same accounting period. For this purpose, a group is defined as a parent company together with its 75% subsidiaries that are resident in Ireland. Relief for losses also is available where a company's ordinary share capital is owned by a consortium of Irish resident companies none of which owns 75% or more of the ordinary share capital.

32. Tax Periods

The basis period for computing the liability to corporation tax is the company's own accounting period (which may not exceed 12 months).

33. Other Matters

Tax Returns. These should be submitted within nine months from the end of a tax period for companies and by January 31 following the end of a tax year for other taxpayers. A surcharge of 10% of the tax liability may be imposed for late submission.

RELATED CONSIDERATIONS

34. Incentives and Grants

Tax Reliefs. Companies engaged in manufacturing and qualifying service activities in Ireland are charged to Irish corporation tax at a reduced rate of 10%. This special, low rate of tax applies to manufacturing activities until December 31, 2010 and to international financial services until December 31, 2005.

The reduced 10% tax rate is available only to corporations. However, it is not necessary that a claimant company be incorporated or tax resident (managed and controlled) in Ireland.

Foreign corporations operating in Ireland and claiming the low tax rate may do so by using an Irish branch of a foreign resident company. The country of incorporation may accordingly be chosen by reference to optimization of worldwide tax benefits.

A wide range of activities carried out in Ireland are eligible for the 10% tax rate. The main items of international relevance are:

☐ Manufacture of goods in Ireland.

☐ Manufacturing services, where processing of customers' products is undertaken in return for a service fee;

☐ Computer services comprising data processing, software development, and related technical and consultancy services the work on which is carried out in Ireland in the course of a service undertaking that has received financial assistance through an employment grant;

☐ International financial services activities carried out in the International Financial Services Centre in Dublin;

☐ International trading operations undertaken in Shannon Airport;

☐ Certain repair and maintenance activities, including aircraft, ships, and computer equipment and subassemblies;

☐ Film production, either for cinema/television distribution or for training or documentary purposes;

☐ Engineering services, where design and planning activities are undertaken in Ireland for projects located outside the European Community;

☐ Organic production, including micropropagation, plant cloning, fish farming and mushroom production.

Companies locating in the International Financial Services Centre in Dublin also may obtain other reliefs, such as accelerated tax depreciation on plant and non-industrial buildings, a double rent allowance for tax purposes, and a holiday from municipal rates.

Authorized investment funds based in Ireland are subject only to a 29% withholding tax on distributions to resident unitholders and on undistributed fund income. The income and gains of such funds are otherwise exempt from Irish tax.

Income from stallion services and commercial forestry is tax-free, and there are grants available from Government agencies for investment in forestry.

Irish resident artists, composers, and writers may receive an exemption from tax on income derived from an original and creative work that has cultural or artistic merit.

Income from a patent received by an Irish resident will be exempt from tax if the work leading to the patent has been carried out in Ireland.

Special Grants. Government agencies such as the Industrial Development Authority may offer grants to new or existing industry for expenditure under the following headings

☐ Buildings and plant
☐ Training and employment
☐ Research and development
☐ Technology acquisition and feasibility studies

Interest subsidies may be available and the agencies have advance factories available for sale or lease, as well as greenfield sites in an existing landbank. Equity participation may be taken by Government agencies in some projects.

35. Exchange Controls

Ireland has exchange control regulations, which are mainly directed toward financial transactions between residents of Ireland and residents of other countries. Transactions of a capital nature above specified limits are controlled by the Central Bank of Ireland, and current payments of a revenue nature are supervised by authorized banks but are not normally restricted.

36. Investment Restrictions on Nonresidents

Foreign nationals who wish to make a direct investment in the Republic of Ireland in excess of IR£1M must obtain exchange control clearance from the Central Bank of Ireland, which is readily granted.

SELECTION OF BUSINESS ENTITY BY NONRESIDENTS

A nonresident who carries on business in Ireland through a branch or agency normally incurs a tax liability on Irish trading profits and on any capital gains on Irish assets used for trading purposes. A distinction is, however, drawn between trading *with* Ireland and trading *in* Ireland; in this connection, the place where contracts of sale are concluded is of fundamental importance. For a nonresident based in a country with which Ireland has a tax treaty, the alternative test of the permanent establishment is applied.

Foreign entities carrying on business in Ireland through a branch are taxed on their branch profits at the normal rate of corporation tax subject to the reliefs outlined in item 34. A foreign entity may choose to operate as a branch because passive investment income arising on profits generated and then unutilized by the branch may not be liable to Irish tax. No withholding taxes are levied on the repatriation of branch profits.

Although there may be tax or commercial reasons for setting up branch operations in Ireland, the normal form of organization is the limited company. In general, foreign-owned companies are taxed in exactly the same way as domestically owned ones. A point of special difficulty arises, however, with interest payments to nonresident parent companies and to other nonresident companies under 75% common control. With some exceptions, interest of this type is regarded as a distribution, which means that it is not tax deductible.

It is necessary to operate as an Irish company to benefit from the tax related low cost finance, which is available from Irish banks.

The profits of a European Economic Interest Grouping (EEIG) are taxable only in the hands of its members, and the EEIG itself is not subject to tax.

SPECIMEN TAX COMPUTATION

	Manufacturing Company		Nonmanufacturing Company
Accounting profits	IR£1,000		IR£1,000
Adjustments			
Book depreciation	200		200
Entertainment (other than staff)	10		10
Interest to nonresident parent company	200		200
Interest on tax-related low-cost finance (1)	180		—
Passenger vehicle running costs (2)	30		30
Tax depreciation	(400)		(250)
Tax adjusted profits	1,220		1,190
Corporation tax (3)	122	476	

	Manufacturing Company	Nonmanufacturing Company
Less		
ACT on low-cost finance (1) (10)	112 —	476
Advance Corporation Tax (1) —	10	—
Total tax	122	476
Profit after tax	878	524
Dividend to parent company (4)	878	524
Withholding tax	0	0
Net transfer	IR£878	IR£524

Notes:

(1) Advance Corporation Tax (ACT) is payable on interest paid for tax-related low-cost finance, normally at the rate of ⅟₁₈ of the interest. The ACT is creditable against corporation tax payable. Low-cost finance generally is available only to manufacturing companies.

(2) Passenger vehicle running costs are restricted in proportion to the excess of the cost of the vehicle over IR£7,000.

(3) The corporate tax rate is assumed to be 40% for the nonmanufacturing company.

(4) In both cases, the parent company is assumed to be resident in a tax treaty country.

ISLE OF MAN

INCOME TAXES ON CORPORATIONS

1. Rates

Both public and private resident companies pay tax at the rate of 20% on their taxable profits. Taxable profits are arrived at after deducting allowable expenses from worldwide income. Double taxation relief is granted in respect of all foreign taxes suffered. An Isle of Man exempt company (see item 6) is not liable to Isle of Man income tax. In general terms, an Isle of Man nonresident company is also exempt from Isle of Man income tax and instead pays a nonresident company duty at the standard rate of £450 per annum (see item 6).

2. Local Income Taxes

None.

3. Capital Gains Taxes

None.

4. Branch Profits Taxes

Manx branches of foreign companies pay income tax on the profits of the Manx branch at the normal rate of 20%.

5. Foreign Tax Reliefs

A resident company with income from sources outside the Isle of Man can claim double taxation relief where foreign tax has been incurred. The foreign tax must not be an underlying tax, such as value-added tax, but must be a withholding or direct profits tax.

The Isle of Man's only double taxation treaty is with the United Kingdom. The Isle of Man Taxes Acts, however, permit relief at the lower of the Manx rate or the foreign tax rate suffered.

The U.K. dividend income received by an Isle of Man company does not qualify for double taxation relief because a tax credit is not an attributable tax.

6. Classification of Corporations

There are various classes of companies that can be incorporated in the Isle of Man:

- [ ] A company limited by shares, limited by guarantee, or unlimited.
- [ ] A public or private company.
- [ ] A resident, nonresident, or exempt company.

A resident company is discussed in item 1.

A company incorporated in the Isle of Man will be considered nonresident of the Isle of Man only when it has filed a nonresident declaration with the registrar of companies and has paid the nonresident company duty of £450 per annum. It is not liable to Isle of Man tax on its profits except on Isle of Man-source income. Isle of Man-source income is liable to tax at 20% unless that income is interest from an approved bank or an approved investment company. A nonresident company may maintain its records and have its administration carried out in the Isle of Man without affecting its nonresident status. A nonresident company may be public or private.

An exempt company must be beneficially owned by persons not resident on the Island. Companies requiring a licence under the Banking Act 1975 (other than exempt schemes under the Financial Supervision Act 1988) and exempt insurance companies (see below) do not qualify as exempt companies. An exempt company is permitted, with prescribed exceptions, to carry on any activity in or outside the Isle of Man.

An exempt company is liable to a flat fee of £250 per fiscal year ended April 5. Application generally must be made between April 6 and June 30 in the relevant year or within 30 days of commencing business.

Exempt insurance companies may be licensed under the Exempt Insurance Companies Act of 1981. They are exempt from Isle of Man income tax on all of their profits. A fee of £2,000 per annum is payable to the Isle of Man Government for this category of insurance company.

An approved investment company issuing participating redeemable preference shares also has exemptions from Isle of Man income tax, provided certain conditions are fulfilled. This category of company is designed as a vehicle for a roll-up fund, which may be used in place of a unit trust.

7. Payment of Taxes

Income tax is payable on or before the January 1 for each fiscal year ended on the following April 5.

INCOME TAXES ON INDIVIDUALS

9. Rates

Resident individuals are charged an income tax at the standard rate of 15% on taxable income up to £8,000 single or £16,000 married couple and at a higher rate of 20% on income in excess of that figure. Taxable income is an individual's total income from all sources on a worldwide basis less any specific deductions and after deducting personal allowances due. Nonresident individuals face a nonresident or withholding tax on their Isle of Man-source income with the exception of interest from approved banks and dividends from approved investment companies. They are not entitled to personal allowances. An individual employed in the Isle of Man has income tax deducted from any remuneration paid to him or her under the Income Tax Instalments Payments system.

10. Local Income Taxes
None.

11. Capital Gains Taxes
None.

12. Foreign Tax Reliefs
Foreign tax paid is relieved at the lower of the foreign tax rate or the Manx rate.

13. Tax Period
April 5 is the standard tax year-end.

INCOME TAXES ON NONRESIDENTS

15. Liability to Tax
A foreign corporation with a branch in the Isle of Man is liable to Isle of Man income tax on its branch profits. An individual resident outside the Isle of Man with Isle of Man-source income generally incurs Isle of Man nonresident tax at a rate of 20%. This liability will not apply to interest paid by an approved bank or dividends from an approved investment company. Exempt and nonresident companies (see item 6) are not subject to nonresident tax.

16. Rates
All taxes are charged at the rate of 20%.

17. Withholding Tax Rates
Levied at the rate of 20% of the income arising.

18. Special Withholding Provisions
None.

OTHER SIGNIFICANT TAXES

21. Sales (Value Added)

Value added tax applies in the Isle of Man on an identical basis to that in the United Kingdom. It is charged on taxable goods and services at the rate of 17.5%.

22. Inheritance and Gift Taxes

None.

23. Taxes on Payrolls (Social Security)

A National Insurance Contribution system applies in the Isle of Man on an identical basis to that in the United Kingdom. The system is reciprocal with the United Kingdom system.

24. Taxes on Natural Resources

None.

25. Other Taxes

Land and Property.   An annual rates charge is made on the value of land and property owned.

Stamp Duty.   There is no stamp duty, but the filing of certain documents results in a duty charge.

COMPUTATION OF TAXABLE INCOME

26. Capital Gains

There is no capital gains tax as such, but the sale proceeds (restricted to cost) of a fixed asset that has been the subject of a depreciation claim is taxable at the rate of 20% after deducting the tax written-down value.

27. Depreciation and Depletion

Plant and Equipment.   An initial allowance of 100% of the purchase price is deductible from the trading profits of a taxpayer. If a lesser percentage is claimed in the year of acquisition, the maximum subsequent annual claim is restricted to 25% of the written-down value.

Industrial Buildings, Tourist Premises, and Agricultural Buildings.   An initial allowance of 100% of the cost is deductible from trading profits. If a lesser percentage is claimed, an allowance of 4% of the original cost (10% for tourist premises) is allowed per tax year until 100% of the cost has been deducted.

28. Treatment of Dividends

Residents must include all dividends, whether or not remitted to the Isle of Man, in their assessable income. Dividends paid by a Manx resident company to a nonresident are subject to nonresident tax. Isle of Man resident companies are not liable to income tax on that portion of their income that is distributed to shareholders.

29. Loss Carryovers

Income tax losses sustained by a company, person, or partnership in any trade can be offset against other income in the year of loss and/or the subsequent year and thereafter offset against profits from the same trade in future years. Individuals incurring losses in the first four years or the last year of a trade can carry the losses back. If a company pays a dividend in excess of its income for a particular year, the excess can be carried forward as a loss.

30. Transactions Between Related Parties

Provisions exist to counter the movement of business profits arising in the Isle of Man out of the Isle of Man by means of artificially adjusted pricing of goods or services.

31. Consolidation of Income

There are no provisions covering this.

32. Tax Period

The income tax year ends on April 5. There is no reason why a company cannot adopt a year-end different from April 5. The normal basis of assessment is the income arising in the financial year ending in the year immediately preceding the year of assessment.

33. Other Matters

Partnerships. The members of a partnership are taxable individually on their share of profits.

Trusts. A Manx trust created by a foreign settlor, which has Manx trustees and foreign beneficiaries, is not liable to Manx tax except on Manx-source income other than interest from approved banks and dividends from approved investment companies.

The law of the Isle of Man is based upon U.K. common law principles, and the

Isle of Man has comprehensive trust acts, with the most recent being the 1961 Trustee Act.

RELATED CONSIDERATIONS

34. Incentives and Grants

The Government offers industrial set-up grants of up to 40% of the capital costs. Working capital loans of up to 50% and rent rebate grants are available. As an alternative, all or part of the profits of an industrial undertaking may be exempted from tax for a period of five years.

35. Exchange Controls

None.

36. Investment Restrictions on Nonresidents

None.

SELECTION OF BUSINESS ENTITY BY NONRESIDENTS

A nonresident company may trade in the Isle of Man through a locally incorporated subsidiary company or through a locally registered branch. The trading profits of either entity will be taxed at the rate of 20%. Similar circumstances prevail for a nonresident individual trading in the Island.

SPECIMEN TAX COMPUTATION

Information:

☐ The company's trading results for the year are as follows:

Pretax profit of £150,000 after charging:

Depreciation	£15,000
Loss on sale of fixed assets	8,000
General provision for bad debts	1,000
Specific provision for bad debts	3,000
Legal fees (sale of property)	1,000

☐ A dividend of £50,000 is proposed.

☐ Plant and equipment amounting to £20,000 were purchased during year.

Computation:

Profit per accounts		£150,000
Add		
Depreciation	£15,000	
Loss on sale of fixed assets	8,000	
General provision for bad debts	1,000	
Legal fees	1,000	25,000
		£175,000
Less		
Dividend	£50,000	
Capital allowance (100% first-year allowance)	20,000	70,000
Taxable income		£105,000
Income tax (at 20%)		£21,000

ITALY

INCOME TAXES ON CORPORATIONS

1. Rates

The rate of corporation tax (IRPEG) is 36% and is levied on all Italian business entities, associations, nonresident enterprises, and branches deriving income in Italy. Resident businesses are subject to tax on worldwide income, while nonresident entities are taxable only on Italian-source income.

2. Local Income Taxes

Local income tax (ILOR) is levied at 16.2% and is a deductible expense at 75% for years ending after January 1, 1991 when calculating taxable income for the purposes of IRPEG.

3. Capital Gains Tax

Capital gains realized by companies are subject to IRPEG and ILOR. Capital gains form part of taxable income at the option of the taxpayer either for the entire amount in the tax period in which they have been realized, or in equal amounts over a maximum period of five years.

4. Branch Profits Taxes

A branch of a foreign corporation is taxed on its profits as though it were a resident corporation.

5. Foreign Tax Reliefs

Foreign taxes paid on income earned abroad are deductible from the taxes due in Italy on the same income, for an amount equal to that part of the Italian tax which is proportional to the ratio between foreign source income and aggregate income.

6. Classification of Corporations

There are two types of companies: partnerships and limited liability companies. Limited liability companies (*societa per azioni, societa a responsabilita limitata, societa in accomandita per azioni*, and branches of foreign companies) are subject to an overall tax rate of 47.826%, which includes the local tax (ILOR) and corporation tax (IRPEG).

In partnerships (*societa in nome colletivo, societa semplice, societa in accomandita semplice*), taxable income is determined at the company level, and local tax (ILOR) is paid by the partnership. Income tax (IRPEF—personal income tax at progressive rates for partners who are individuals) is assessed on each partner according to his share of the partnership profits.

7. Payment of Taxes

Each year, a payment on account must be calculated at the rate of 98% of the IRPEG and ILOR taxes due for the previous year; payment is in two installments: (1) 40% is due upon filing of the income tax return for the previous year, and (2) 60% is due by the end of the eleventh month of the tax year. The taxpayer can, however, elect to pay a lower amount if the estimated taxable profit for the current year will be lower than that declared for the previous year. The balance of IRPEG and ILOR taxes must be paid when filing the tax return. An off-setting between ILOR and IRPEG receivable or payable, or vice versa, is possible. It is possible to request for the refund of any accounts in excess (and tax receivables), as well as to record such excess as decreasing the tax of the subsequent tax period.

8. Other Matters

Minimum Capital Requirements of Limited Companies.   The minimum share capital of companies incorporated as S.p.A. (Societa Per Azioni) is Lit. 200,000,000 and the capital of companies incorporated as S.r.l. (Società a Responsabilità Limitata) is Lit. 20,000,000.

The following are Civil Code regulations, i.e., they are not prescribed by the tax laws, which are applicable in the event of losses incurred by limited liability companies (S.p.A., S.r.l.):

☐ If the loss of over one-third of the share capital results in the share capital falling below the legally required minimum, immediate action must be taken to cover the losses or reorganize the company.

☐ If the loss exceeds one-third of the share capital without the capital falling below the legal minimum, it is possible to defer the loss coverage or the reduction of the share capital for one year.

Authorization to Increase Share Capital and Issue Debentures.   The formation of limited liability companies (except for S.R.L.s) with a share capital exceeding Lit. 10,000,000,000, as well as increasing the share capital and issuing debentures for amounts exceeding this limit, are subject to authorization from the Ministry of Treasury.

Tax on Dividends. If a company distributes to its shareholders more than 64% of the income declared for purposes of computing the corporate income tax, an additional corporate income tax equal to 56.25% of the excess is imposed. Companies are subject to an additional corporate income tax equal to 56.25% of dividends distributed. If these dividends are paid from: (1) reserves consisting of premiums received upon the issue of shares and similar tax-free reserves, upon distribution, they are not subject to corporate income tax; and (2) reserves (other than the reserves described above) created before December 1, 1983, they are subject to an additional tax of 15% of the reserves distributed. This additional tax applies even if the reserves were created out of taxed profits.

INCOME TAXES ON INDIVIDUALS

9. Rates

The national income tax (IRPEF) is applied to the aggregate taxable income realized in Italy and abroad by residents after deducting individual personal and other allowances, as shown:

Taxable Income		Tax on	Percentage
Over	Not Over	Lower Amount	on Excess
Lit. 0	Lit. 6,800,000	Lit. 0	10%
6,800,000	13,500,000	680,000	22
13,500,000	33,700,000	2,970,000	26
33,700,000	67,600,000	8,762,000	33
67,600,000	168,800,000	22,308,000	40
168,800,000	337,700,000	67,520,000	45
337,700,000		151,965,000	50

10. Local Income Taxes

ILOR is due on income realized only in Italy by individuals, but is not levied on wages, salaries, professional fees, and dividend income. Taxable income subject to ILOR is essentially the same as for IRPEF, but the following exemptions and deductions from the business income should be noted:

Taxable Income		Deductions and
Over	Not Over	Exemptions
	Lit. 7,000,000	Exempt
Lit. 7,000,000	14,000,000	7,000,000
14,000,000	28,000,000	50% of taxable income
28,000,000		14,000,000

ILOR tax is deductible at 75% for the purpose of computing the net taxable income subject to IRPEF. A setting-off between ILOR or IRPEF receivable or payable or vice versa is possible. The income of a wife is taxed separately, both for the purpose of IRPEF and ILOR. Nonresidents are taxable only on income arising in Italy.

ILOR rate of tax is 16.2%.

11. Capital Gains Taxes

All capital gains—other than gains arising in carrying out commecial businesses—realized on sales of shares and relevant rights, are subject to a definitive tax, which may be calculated either analytically or on a lump-sum basis.

For nonresidents, relevant international tax treaties rules may apply.

Lump-sum Method. Tax is due at the rate of 15% and applies to the capital gain calculated according to specific percentages. Gains cannot be lower than 2% or higher than 7% in the case of sales of listed securities and cannot be higher than 7% in all other cases. Without prejudice to different options, the lump-sum method is applicable only in the case of sales lower than 2% of the share capital for listed shares, 5% for shares of companies not quoted on the Stock Exchange, and 15% for any other security. Higher sales are subject to the analytic method.

Analytic Method. The tax rate is increased to 25% and applies to the capital gain after the taxation of any losses. If the amount of the loss is higher than the amount of the gain, the difference can be deducted from income in the following five tax periods.

12. Foreign Tax Reliefs

See item 5.

13. Tax Period

The tax year is the calendar year. An annual payment on account must be made by the end of November of the tax year in an amount equal to 95% of the IRPEF and ILOR liability of the previous year. The payment on account is due twice; see item 7. The balance of the IRPEF and ILOR taxes is due by May 31, the date when tax returns must be submitted.

14. Other Matters

Withholding Tax. Withholding is required when certain amounts are paid by business entrepreneurs, partnerships, companies, the State (and other public entities), and self-employed individuals (under certain circumstances). These "tax substitutes" must pay, usually by the fifteenth of the following month, the amount withheld to the revenue authorities. The amount withheld can be considered either advance payments or definitive taxation. Amounts treated as advance payments are deducted from the IRPEF or IRPEG (but no ILOR) tax liability shown in the annual tax return by having the tax substitute attach a document that indicates the gross amount subject to withholding. Withheld amounts considered to be definitive taxation constitute a final settlement of tax liability with respect to the income subject to withholding. This income is not included on the tax return and is excluded from taxable income for ILOR purposes.

The following amounts are generally subject to withholding:

☐ Income from employment (the employee's tax bracket determines the amount withheld).

☐ Income from self-employment or coordinated collaboration (e.g., statutory auditors, company directors, and journalists). If the taxpayer is a resident, 19% is withheld and treated as an advance payment; if the taxpayer is a nonresident, the amount withheld is 20% and is treated as definitive taxation.

☐ Interest from banks (the amount withheld is 30% and considered an advance payment for IRPEG and IRPEF due by partnerships and definitive taxation for IRPEF due by individuals).

☐ Interest from debentures and similar securities (the withholding tax is 10.8% for securities issued prior to January 1, 1984, 12.5% for securities issued after that date, and 30% for securities issued after January 1, 1989, excluding securities issued by credit instititutions and S.p.A.'s with listed shares, for which the withholding tax is applicable at the rate of 12.5%). The tax is considered definitive taxation for IRPEF purposes on individuals and an advance payment for IRPEG and IRPEF purposes on partnerships.

☐ Interest received by nonresidents (this interest, both from loans and trade transactions, is subject to a withholding rate of 15% and is treated as definitive taxation).

☐ Dividends (dividends paid to Italian residents are subject to a withholding tax of 10%, which is considered a tax advance). Savings shares of quoted companies and shares of cooperative credit banks are subject to a withholding tax of 15% (treated as a final IRPEG and IRPEF tax payment; in the latter case, the shareholder can opt for the withholding tax of 10%). If the beneficiary is not an Italian resident, the withholding tax is due at the rate of 32.4% (which is treated as a final IRPEG and IRPEF tax payment).

☐ Interest income from government bonds issued during the period September 20, 1986 to August 24, 1987 is subject to a withholding tax of 6.25%, while interest income from government bonds issued after August 24, 1987 is subject to a withholding tax of 12.5%. The withholding tax is considered as definitive taxation for IRPEF purposes on individuals and an advance payment for IRPEG purposes on partnerships.

INCOME TAXES ON NONRESIDENTS

15. Liability to Tax

Nonresidents (persons who for the greater part of the tax period are not registered with the General Registry Office of the resident population or who do not have their domicile or residence in Italy) are subject only to tax on income earned in Italy. The following income is regarded as earned in Italy.

- ☐ Income from ownership of land and buildings located in Italy.
- ☐ Income from employment carried out in Italy and relevant old-age pensions and staff-departure indemnities.
- ☐ Trading income realized through a permanent establishment in Italy.
- ☐ Gains deriving from the sale of assets existing in Italy.
- ☐ Gains realized through the transfer of ownership interests in an S.R.L. and in partnerships.
- ☐ Interest income paid by a resident in Italy.
- ☐ Dividends paid by Italian companies.
- ☐ Royalties paid by Italian residents.

16. Rates

The same rates of taxation apply to nonresidents as to residents, except that the income deriving from royalties, interest, and dividends are subject to withholding tax equal to the tax due thereon.

17. Withholding Tax Rates

Withholding Rates on Outward Remittances
If the Payee Is Not an Individual

	Dividends	Interest	Royalties
Nontreaty countries	32.4%	15% (1)	21% (2)
Treaty countries:			
Argentina	15	20	10, 18 (3)
Australia	15	10	10
Austria	15	10	0, 10 (4)
Belgium	15	15	5
Brazil	15	15	15, 25 (5)
Bulgaria	10	—	5
Canada	15	15	10
China	10	10	10
Cyprus	15	10	—
Czechoslovakia	15	—	5
Denmark	15	15	5

Withholding Rates on Outward Remittances
If the Payee Is Not an Individual

	Dividends	Interest	Royalties
Ecuador	15%	10%	5%
Egypt	20, 32.4 (6)	25	15
Finland	10, 15 (7)	15	5
France	15	15	—
Germany	32.4	0, 15 (8)	—
Great Britain and Northern Ireland	5, 15 (9)	10	8
Greece	25	10	—
Hungary	10	—	—
India	32.4	15	21 (2)
Ireland	15	10	—
Israel	25	15	—
Ivory Coast	15	15	10
Japan	10, 15 (10)	10	10
Kenya	15, 20 (11)	15	15
Luxembourg	15	10	10
Malaysia	10	15	15
Malta	15	10	10
Morocco	10, 15 (12)	10	5, 10 (13)
Netherlands	0, 32.4 (14)	15	—
New Zealand	15	10	10
Norway	15	15	5
Pakistan	15, 25 (15)	30	30
Philippines	15	10, 15 (16)	15, 25 (17)
Poland	10	10	10
Portugal	15	15	12
Rumania	10	10	10
Singapore	10	12.5	15, 20 (18)
Spain	15	12	4, 8 (19)
Sri Lanka	15	10	10, 15 (20)
Sweden	10, 15 (21)	15	5
Switzerland	15	12.5	5
Tanzania	10	15	15
Thailand	15, 20 (22)	10, 15 (23)	5, 15 (24)
Trinidad and Tobago	10, 20 (25)	10	5
Tunisia	15	12	5,12,16 (26)
United States	5,10,15 (27)	15	5, 8, 10 (28)
U.S.S.R.	15	—	—
Yugoslavia	10	10	10
Zambia	5, 15 (29)	10	10

Notes:

(1) 25% if deriving from investment participation certificates.

(2) 30% on 70% of the amount.

(3) 10% in the case of royalties derived from the use of copyrights on literary, artistic, or scientific works.

(4) 10% if the beneficiary is a company owning at least 50% of the Italian company's stock.

(5) 25% in the case of royalties derived from the use of trademarks or trade names.

(6) 20% if the beneficiary is an Italian individual.

(7) 10% if the beneficiary is a corporation owning directly more than 50% of the capital of the company paying the dividends.

(8) 15% if the receivables are collateralized by real estate located in Italy.

(9) 5% if the beneficiary controls at least 10% of the voting shares of the company that distributes the dividends; 15% in all other cases. The double tax treaty provides a tax credit for both States. The tax credit is granted at the following rates:

—60% to U.K. companies controlling 10% or more of an Italian company;

—100% both to Italian companies controlling 10% or more of U.K. companies and to U.K./Italian individuals and companies controlling less than 10%.

(10) 10% if the beneficiary is a company that owned at least 25% of the voting shares of the Italian company during the six months preceding the end of the accounting period in respect of which there is distribution of income.

(11) 15% if the beneficiary is a company having owned at least 25% of the Italian company's voting shares during the six months preceding the payment date of the dividends.

(12) 10% if the beneficiary is a corporation owning directly at least 25% of the capital of the company paying the dividends.

(13) 5% on royalties derived from the use of copyrights on literary, artistic, or scientific works (except movie and television films).

(14) 0% if the beneficiary is a company with at least a 75% interest in the Italian company.

(15) 15% if the beneficiary owns at least 25% of the capital of the industrial company paying the dividends.

(16) 10% in the State of issue at the charge of beneficiary for interest on public issues.

(17) 15% if the Philippine company is registered with the Philippine investment committee and carries on activities in preferential sectors.

(18) 20% in the case of royalties derived from the use of copyrights on literary or scientific works, including movies and broadcasting television registrations.

(19) 4% for consideration of whatever nature paid for the use of copyrights on literary, dramatic, musical, or artistic works.

(20) 10% for consideration of whatever nature paid for the use of copyrights on literacy, dramatic, musical, or artistic works.

(21) 10% if the beneficiary is a corporation owning directly at least 51% of the Italian company's capital.

(22) 15% if the beneficiary is a company resident in Thailand owning at least 25% of the voting shares in the company paying the dividends.

(23) 10% if the beneficiary is a holding (finance) company.

(24) 5% for royalties derived from the use of copyrights on literary, artistic, or scientific works.

(25) 10% if the beneficiary is a corporation owning directly at least 25% of the Italian company's capital.

(26) 16% on royalties deriving from the use of trademarks and trade names, movie and television films, and industrial, commercial, and scientific equipment; 5% of the gross royalties deriving from the use of copyrights on literary, artistic, or scientific works; and 12% in other cases.

(27) 5% if the recipient company owns more than 50% of the voting stock of the payor company for a 12-month period ending on the date the dividend is declared, and 10% if the recipient company owns 10% or more of the voting stock of the payor company for a 12-month period, provided that not more than 25% of the gross income of the payor company in either situation is derived from interest and dividends. 15% in all other cases.

(28) 5% of the gross royalties derived from the use of, or the right to use, any copyright of literary, artistic, or scientific work; 8% of the gross royalties derived from the use of, or the right to use, motion pictures and films, tapes or other means of reproduction used for radio or television broadcasting; and 10% of the gross royalties in all other cases.

(29) 5% if the recipient corporation owns directly 25% of the capital of the payor company.

18. Special Withholding Provisions

Foreign parent companies are entitled to special withholding tax rates if they own a given percentage of the Italian company's share capital or voting rights.

	Minimum Shareholding (1)	Rate
Finland	50%	10%
Great Britain and Northern Ireland	10	5
Japan	25	10
Kenya	25	15
Morocco	25	10
Netherlands	75	0
Sweden	51	10

	Minimum Shareholding (1)	Rate
Thailand	25%	15%
United States	50,10	5,10
Zambia	25	5

Notes:

(1) In some cases the minimum shareholding must be held for a minimum period.

19. Tax Treaties

Italy has concluded an extensive range of double taxation agreements with the countries listed (showing only those entered into force) in item 17. Following the tax reform which became effective January 1, 1974, some treaties are being renegotiated. A major area of difficulty is ILOR tax which, according to the Italian tax authorities, is not covered by many double taxation agreements.

OTHER SIGNIFICANT TAXES

21. Sales (Value Added)

Value-added tax (I.V.A.) was introduced in Italy in 1973. The basic rate in effect is 19%. Reduced rates of 4%, 9%, and 12% are applicable to certain foods and goods. The rate of 38% is applicable to certain goods, such as cars over 2,000 C.C., furs, and photographic equipment. Exports are exempt from VAT.

22. Inheritance and Gift Taxes

Inheritance tax is levied generally on all items of capital passing from a deceased person to his heirs; the amount of capital passing is grossed up by 10% as a notional addition for jewelry, cash, and furniture. Assets transferred during the six months prior to death are, with certain exemptions, subject to tax.

Taxable Value (Lit. millions)		Tax on Total Value of the Net Inheritance	Tax on Portions of Inheritance and Gifts		
Over	Not Over		Relatives (1)	Relatives (2)	Other Parties
5	60	—	—	3%	6%
60	120	—	3%	5	8
120	200	3%	6	9	12
200	400	7	10	13	18
400	800	10	15	19	23

Taxable Value (Lit. millions)		Tax on Total Value of the Net Inheritance	Tax on Portions of Inheritance and Gifts		
Over	Not Over		Relatives (1)	Relatives (2)	Other Parties
800	1,500	15%	20%	24%	28%
1,500	3,000	22	24	26	31
3,000		27	25	27	33

(1) Brothers, sisters, and directly descending kin.
(2) Other relatives up to fourth cousins or kin up to third cousins.

Only the basic rate is due if the heirs are the parents or children of the deceased. Taxes are higher if the heirs were related to the deceased only distantly or not at all.

In addition, a registration tax amounting to 2% is applicable to transfers of land and buildings. INVIM tax is due on transfers of land and buildings (see item 25), and it is deductible from the inheritance tax. The tax is reduced by 50% for the heirs (parents or children) of the deceased.

23. Taxes on Payrolls (Social Security)

Social security contributions due by companies in respect of employees and manual workers are calculated on the basis of the gross salary at the following rates:

☐ 32.71% on all amounts received;
☐ 9.6% on fees between Lit. 0 and Lit. 40,000,000;
☐ 3.8% on fees between Lit. 40,000,000 and Lit. 100,000,000

In the case of "dirigenti" (executives), the first rate changes from 32.71% to 29.26%.

The employers' contribution for executives is about 38.86%, the employees' and the executives' contributions are about 8.79%. Self-employed professionals are required to pay a contribution for the national insurance scheme, equal to 5% on all income earned in Italy as declared on the income tax return, up to Lit. 40 million, and equal to 4.20% on the part that exceeds Lit. 40 million up to Lit. 100 million, if a tax return must be filed. If the self-employed individual need not file an income tax return in Italy but still would like to benefit from the national insurance scheme, such individual must contribute a fixed amount.

24. Taxes on Natural Resources

None.

25. Other Taxes

Land and Property. Taxable income is based upon land registry data, unless actual property income can be proved to be lower or higher by certain percentages than the income calculated from land registry data.

Registration Taxes. A registration tax ranging from 6% to 17% is levied on all transfers of real estate between individuals. Transfers between companies of land not destined for construction purposes is also subject to the registration tax. Share capital increases of corporations, or other shareholders' contributions, are subject to a registration tax of 1%. The constitution and increase of the working capital (''fondo di dotazione'') of a branch owned by a company that is not resident in a member country of the EEC is subject to a registration tax of 1%. The sale of business concerns are subject to a registration tax varying from 3% to 8% on the net equity in proportion to the assets recorded in the balance sheet. The transfer of a business concern in exchange for shares is subject to a proportional tax of 1% on the net assets transferred.

INVIM. This tax is due on the gain realized on the sale of land and buildings. In the case of companies that own property which is not directly used for their productive activity and that cannot be otherwise utilized unless substantial modifications are made, the tax is due every 10 years on the increase in value which is deemed to have taken place. Expenses for construction and improvement to buildings are deductible from the amount of the gain. Taxes are computed as shown below, taking into account the number of years elapsed since the date of purchase or the date of reference.

Up to 20% on the initial value	number of years
From 20% to 50%	every year
From 50% to 100%	every year
From 100% to 150%	every year
From 150% to 200%	every year
Over 200%	every year

Stamp duty. In respect of transfers of shares, a tax equal to 0.14% (0.05% for shares, quotas, and stakes in companies of any kind, which are not negotiated on the stock exchange) is due on the transfer price. This rate is reduced in case one of the parties involved in the transaction is a bank or a stockbroker. Transactions with nonresidents are exempt from the tax.

Corporate Franchise Tax (''Tassa di Concessione Governativa''). All companies resident in Italy must pay a corporate franchise tax, first upon incorporation in respect of the registration with the Registrar of Enterprises of the Tribunal and subsequently by June 30 of each year. The amounts due are as follows:

□ By partnerships: Lit.   500,000
□ By limited liability companies:
   —Società a responsabilità limitata (S.r.l.)   Lit. 3,500,000
   —Società per Azioni (S.p.A.)
     Società in Accomandita per Azioni (S.A.P.A.)   Lit. 12,000,000

Permanent establishments set up in Italy by foreign companies are subject to a tax of Lit. 118,000 upon formation, in respect of the registration with the Registrar of Enterprises of the Tribunal.

COMPUTATION OF TAXABLE INCOME

26. Capital Gains

For companies, the taxable gain is the difference between the cost (for corporations, cost less depreciation) of the capital assets and the sales proceeds obtained from the disposal. For individuals, see item 11.

27. Depreciation and Depletion

All fixed assets used in business, except land, are depreciable. Depreciation is deductible from the tax period during which the asset came into use by applying to the cost of the assets the rates published by the Ministry of Finance, reduced by 50% in the first tax period. Accelerated depreciation may be claimed, in addition to normal depreciation, as follows:

□ For certain industries in the case of intensive use of equipment, as for example when two or three workshifts are in operation.
□ For the first three years of depreciation. In such a case, the maximum depreciation which may be claimed in one year is equal to two times the rate of annual depreciation.

If the assets purchased have been used by a third party, the maximum depreciation in the first year is equal to the ordinary rate of annual depreciation.

Depreciation claimed for tax purposes must be entered in the books and disclosed in the financial statements.

28. Treatment of Dividends

A 10% withholding tax is levied on dividends payable to resident individuals and companies which may be credited against the national income tax. Nonresident individual and corporate shareholders are generally subject to a 32.4% withholding tax. The numerous tax treaties existing between Italy and other countries often reduce the withholding taxes (see item 17).

The dividends are subject to IRPEF in the case of individuals and IRPEG in the case of corporations, but are exempt from ILOR. With respect to dividends distributed by Italian companies, the Italian taxpayer (individual or company) obtains a tax credit equal to the amount of the IRPEG tax (calculated at the rate of 36%) paid by the distributing company and of the withholding tax on dividends (10%). Only 40% of the dividends paid by foreign subsidiaries are subject to IRPEG tax. Furthermore, with respect to the withholding taxes on dividends deducted by the foreign country, the Italian resident can claim the tax credit discussed in item 5.

29. Loss Carryovers

Losses derived from business operations may be carried forward for a maximum of five fiscal periods and can be utilized for the purpose of offsetting future taxable income only with respect to IRPEG and IRPEF taxes; therefore, ILOR is always payable on the taxable profits of an accounting period. No loss carrybacks are allowed. In the case of merger, the incorporator can set off its income against the fiscally allowable losses of the companies participating in the merger to the extent of the lowest amount of their net equity values that results from the comparison between the last financial statements (accounting values) and the balance sheet requested by the Civil Code regulations (current values) in the case of merger, without taking into account transfers, contributions, or payments effected in the preceding 24 months.

The loss carryover of the companies participating in the merger to the above-mentioned extent is subject to the following two conditions:

☐ The amount of income arising from the sales and the performances of services and the amount of the expenses for performances of subordinate employment and relevant payrolls (which result in the profit and loss account of the year prior that in which the merger is resolved) must exceed 40% of the respective amount resulting from the average of the two previous years.

☐ If the shares or quotas of one or more companies participating in the merger are held by another company participating in the merger, the loss cannot be carried forward up to the amount of (1) the depreciation of these shares or quotas that formed part of the taxable income of the participating company, and (2) the untaxed capital gains recorded in the financial statements of the company resulting from the merger (see item 33).

30. Transactions between Related Parties

The tax authorities may substitute a fair market value instead of the value used in the case of transactions between related parties. Transaction prices between resident and nonresident parties belonging to the same group must reflect the "normal value."

31. Consolidation of Income

Each company is taxed as a separate entity. However, a company may reduce the value at which the investment in a subsidiary is carried in its financial statements.

For tax purposes, a deduction can be taken equal to the proportion existing between the net asset value of the subsidiary (as shown in the latest financial statements approved by the shareholders) and the net asset value as shown in its financial statement prior to the acquisition of the subsidiary.

32. Tax Periods

The base period for computing the liability to corporation taxes is the company's own accounting period.

33. Other Matters

Revaluation. In the case of merger through incorporation, the incorporator can revalue the assets of the incorporated company to the extent of the difference between the value of the investment shown in the financial statements of the incorporator and the net equity of the incorporated company. The revalued value of the assets can be depreciated. The new value attributed to the assets of the incorporated company cannot exceed the market value.

Tax authorities may disclaim for tax purposes the part of cost incurred in respect of shareholdings as well as any tax advantages deriving from mergers, concentrations, transformations, spin-offs, and capital reductions carried out without any financial reason and for the sole purpose of obtaining tax savings in a deceitful manner.

RELATED CONSIDERATIONS

34. Incentives and Grants

Special Tax Rates. New industrial companies operating and having their legal premises in the south of Italy receive a 100% exemption for ten years from ILOR. Companies established after March 29, 1986 are entitled to a 100% exemption from IRPEG tax. The exemption from ILOR tax is also applicable to additional new investments made in the South. New industrial companies which are located in certain areas of Central and Northern Italy also enjoy exemptions for ten years from ILOR. Profits obtained by companies operating in Italy and reinvested in the South are exempt from ILOR on up to 70% of such profits.

Special Grants and Other Allowances. Grants of up to 40% are available for companies operating in the South of Italy; in addition, loans can be obtained from special institutions at reduced rates, and social security contributions are payable at reduced rates.

35. Exchange Controls

Exchange controls in Italy gradually are becoming less severe than in the past. They are generally performed by banks and mostly concern transfer prices, and the terms and conditions agreed for payments or collections of payables or receivables. Overseas investments by Italian residents generally are not subject to restrictions.

36. Investment Restrictions on Nonresidents

There are no investment restrictions on nonresidents.

SELECTION OF BUSINESS ENTITY BY NONRESIDENTS

Nonresident investors can operate in Italy either through a branch or by establishing a subsidiary corporation. Branches and foreign-owned corporations are taxed in the same way.

In general, the choice between a branch and a subsidiary is influenced by the following factors:

	Branch	Subsidiary
Applicable tax rate	47.826%	47.826%
Liability of the parent company	Liable	Not liable unless it is wholly owned by the parent company
Withholding tax on dividends	Not due	Reduction or exemption under a treaty
Withholding tax on royalties	Reduction or exemption under a treaty	Reduction or exemption under a treaty
Registration tax	Due in certain cases	Due
Inspections by exchange control authorities	Yes	Yes

If the branch is transferred to an independent company in a subsequent phase an appraisal of the net assets is required. The transfer is subject to a registration tax equal to 1% of the branch's net asset value. The registration tax is levied at a fixed amount of Lit. 100,000 if the company to which the branch is transferred has its registered office in another EC country.

The purchase by a foreign investor of an Italian company with existing operations can be carried out in two ways:

□ Purchasing the Italian company's shares. This is the most straightforward method.

□ Establishing a new company in Italy. The new company purchases the already existing and operating Italian company. Subsequently, the new company incorporates the already operating company through a merger. This transaction permits an allocation of the amount paid in excess of the net equity through the revaluation of the assets owned by the incorporator (see item 33), taking into account the limits indicated in item 33.

There are no specific rules regarding the ratio between net equity and liabilities. However, loans granted to Italian subsidiaries are subject to inspection by the exchange control authorities, particularly the conditions and terms of repayment and the interest rate.

SPECIMEN TAX COMPUTATION

Information:

□ The company's profits before taxes is equal to Lit. 1 billion and consists of:

	Lit. millions
Trading profits	600
Dividends from Italian companies	200
Capital gain from sales of holdings in S.P.A.s	100
Dividends from foreign subsidiaries	100

Computation:

□ ILOR

	Lit. millions
Profit before taxes	1,000
Dividends from Italian companies	(200)
Dividends from foreign subsidiaries	(100)
ILOR taxable income	700
ILOR (16.2%)	113.4

□ IRPEG

Profit before taxes	1,000
Dividends from foreign subsidiaries	(60)
ILOR (113.4 × 75%)	(85.05)
IRPEG taxable income	854
Tax credit (56.25% of Lit. 200,000,000)	112.5
	967

IRPEG (36%)	348.28
Tax credit	(112.5)
IRPEG payable	235.78

Notes:

(1) When computing taxes it is necessary to bear in mind the following:
   — Dividends are exempt from ILOR and give rise to a tax credit for IRPEG purposes equal to 56.25% of the gross dividend, which is added to the IRPEG taxable income and deducted from the IRPEG tax.
   — Dividends received from a foreign subsidiary are subject to IRPEG tax at a 40% rate.
   — ILOR is deductible from IRPEG for 75% of the tax.

IVORY COAST
(CÔTE D'IVOIRE)

INCOME TAXES ON CORPORATIONS

1. Rates

The corporation profits tax is known as B.I.C. The applicable rate is 35%. For assessment of this tax, taxable income is the difference between the net book values of the company at the end and at the beginning of the taxable period, less share capital contributions, plus amounts distributed to shareholders. Other specific adjustments are also made to arrive at the final taxable income. Net book value means assets, less amounts due to third parties, depreciation, and provisions for various charges and losses.

The 10% National Contribution Tax levied on top of the B.I.C. has been abolished by the Finance Bill of 1991.

Minimum Tax. After the first year's operations, a company is deemed to earn a minimum profit, and a minimum tax of F/CFA 1,000,000 is payable. For profits exceeding this amount, tax is payable thereon as above.

Special Relief for New Plants. Income derived from a newly installed factory is free from B.I.C. for five to seven years depending on the plant's location.

2. Local Income Taxes

None.

3. Capital Gains Taxes

Capital gains are normally incorporated and taxed with other profits. However, relief may be obtained if the company undertakes to reinvest within three years an amount at least equal to the capital gain and acquisition cost of the asset concerned.

4. Branch Profits Taxes

Profits of branches of foreign companies established in the Ivory Coast are taxed as in item 1. Total after-tax income is presumed to be paid as dividends to the parent company and, therefore, is subject to a 12% withholding tax of 50% of the amount forming the basis of corporation tax.

5. Foreign Tax Reliefs

Double taxation agreements exist with France, Belgium, Germany, Norway, Italy Canada, the United Kingdom, and those African countries that are members of the O.C.A.M. Agreement. When a double taxation treaty applies, foreign taxes paid are usually an allowable deduction.

6. Classification of Corporations

For Ivoirian tax purposes, there is no major distinction between the two forms of corporations generally registered: the "Societe Anonyme" and the "Societe a Responsabilite Limitee" which are both limited liability companies. They are both liable to the same rates of corporation income tax as specified in item 1.

7. Payment of Taxes

Corporations are required to pay tax in three equal installments after the end of the fiscal year. The first installment is due prior to January 1, the second prior to April 1, and the third prior to July 1. Heavy penalties can be imposed for late payments or underpayments.

8. Other Matters

Special Relief for Agreed Investment Programs.   Companies may deduct 40% to 60% of capital investments from the taxable income of the year of the investment and from the taxable income of the three following years, provided the annual deduction is limited to 50% of the yearly taxable income. However, that tax relief cannot be cumulative with others (see items 1 and 3).

INCOME TAXES ON INDIVIDUALS

9. Rates

Persons domiciled in the Ivory Coast are subject to three taxes on earned income, regardless of where the personal services are rendered. These taxes are the salary tax (IS), the national contribution (CN), and the solidarity contribution (CNS). CN and CNS are essentially surtaxes on IS. Persons domiciled outside the Ivory Coast are subject to the same taxes on earned income sourced within the country. Regardless of domicile, habitual residents of the Ivory Coast are subject to the general revenue tax (IGR) on their worldwide income.

Taxpayers are allowed deductions based on the numbers of parts to which they are entitled. One part each is allowed to the taxpayer and spouse and one-half part for each child. A maximum of five parts is permitted. A 20% relief is granted against the income tax liability.

□ A 1.5% wages and salary tax (IS); a solidarity contribution (CNS) of 1 % of the gross salary is also required.

□ National contribution (CN) at varying rates according to the amount of monthly income (after the 20% relief), as follows:

Monthly Income		Rate
Over	Not Over	
F/CFA 0	F/CFA 50,000	0%
50,000	130,000	1.5
130,000	200,000	5
200,000		10

□ General income tax (IGR).

B = taxable income tax before the 20% relief

$R = [(^{80}/_{100} \times B) - (IS + CN)] \times ^{85}/_{100}$

N = number of parts

R/N	IGR
0 to 300,000	None
300,000 to 547,000	R x (10/110) − 27,273 x N
548,000 to 979,000	R x (15/115) − 48,913 x N
980,000 to 1,519,000	R x (20/120) − 84,375 x N
1,520,000 to 2,644,000	R x (25/125) − 135,000 x N
2,645,000 to 4,669,000	R x (35/135) − 291,667 x N
4,670,000 to 10,106,000	R x (45/145) − 530,172 x N
More than 10,106,000	R x (60/160) − 1,183,594 x N

10. Local Income Taxes

None.

11. Capital Gains

Capital gains are taxed only in rare cases.

13. Tax Period

All individuals are taxed on the basis of a calendar year. At the end of each February, taxpayers receiving income other than salaries must file a return for income earned or received in the preceding calendar year. Taxpayers whose only income consists of salaries are not required to lodge an annual tax return; taxation on salaries being retained and remitted monthly by employers.

14. Other Matters

Benefits in Kind. Benefits in kind are taxable to the employee according to a schedule of deemed values (in F/CFA per month):

□ Living quarters.

No. of Rooms	Unfurnished	Additional for Furniture	Additional for Electricity (Except Air Conditioning)
1	F/CFA 40,000	F/CFA 6,000	F/CFA 10,000
2	60,000	9,000	12,000
3	80,000	12,000	15,000
4	100,000	15,000	18,000
5	120,000	18,000	20,000
6	150,000	24,000	25,000

□ Servants
 —Gardener   F/CFA 21,000
 —Houseboy   30,000
 —Cook   45,000
□ Air conditioning   (F/CFA 9,000 per room).
□ Water   (F/CFA 1,500 per person in the family).

INCOME TAXES ON NONRESIDENTS

15. Liability to Tax

Nonresidents are liable to Ivoirian income tax on income earned or received in Ivory Coast.

16. Rates

Income tax is withheld at the source on income paid to nonresidents. The rate of withholding tax varies according to the type of income. International tax treaties would apply where their application is beneficial to nonresidents.

17. Withholding Tax Rates

In the absence of international tax treaties, the following rates apply:

□ Salaries paid to nonresidents based on activities performed in Ivory Coast: same rates as residents (see item 9).

□ Royalties and technical or administrative assistance fees paid to nonresidents:

25% on 80% of the total income (this withholding tax is waived or reduced when a tax treaty applies).

☐ Dividends, "tantiemes," director's remuneration for attending board meetings: same rate as residents (see item 25).

☐ Debenture interest: same rate as residents (see item 25).

☐ Loan interest and deposits on accounts with a banker not established in Ivory Coast: applicable rate is 18% (9% for loan interest granted for more than three years by a foreign financial institution in order to finance investments).

OTHER SIGNIFICANT TAXES

21. Sales (Value Added)

Individuals engaged in the business (regularly or occasionally) in the Ivory Coast of buying for the purpose of selling, or engaged in any activities other than as a wage earner or in agriculture, are subject to turnover taxes. There are two turnover taxes:

☐ Value added tax (T.V.A.).
☐ Tax on services rendered (T.P.S.).

The rates for the two turnover taxes are identical.

☐ Normal Rate: 20% on the after-tax amount or 25% on the before-tax amount.
☐ Reduced Rate: 10% on the after-tax amount or 11.11% on the before-tax amount.
☐ Super Reduced Rate: 5% on the after-tax amount or 5.26% on the before-tax amount.
☐ Increased Rate: 26% on the after-tax amount or 35.13% on the before-tax amount.

Taxable and Exempt Businesses. Businesses involved in producing, selling, and importing goods are subject to T.V.A. All other business activities are subject to T.P.S. Numerous business sectors are exempted from the turnover taxes either by law or by agreement. The distribution business sector, which used to be exonerated from TVA, falls under the scope of this tax from January 1, 1988.

Service companies are normally liable for T.P.S. but can elect to be subject to T.V.A., except banks and companies involved in money and value business. The advantage of this election is that T.V.A. paid may be recovered from T.V.A. charged to customers, which is not the case with T.P.S. However, T.V.A. must be paid to the tax authorities on delivery of the merchandise (in practice, when invoicing) while T.P.S. is payable when payment is received from the customer.

Businesses subject to turnover taxes must file a declaration of the existence of the business within ten days after activities commence. Monthly declarations must be filed within 15 days of each month's end.

Installment on Various Taxes (ASDI). Businesses involved in the wholesaling of goods on the local market are subject to ASDI at the rate of 5%. ASDI paid by any business can be set off against ASDI charged or turnover taxes due (TVA and TPS) or salary taxes due. The balance remaining can be carried forward indefinitely.

10% Tax Credit. Any payment by a public entity to a permanent establishment located in the Ivory Coast is liable to a 10% withholding tax, which can constitute a 10% tax credit. This tax credit can be used to pay either turnover tax (TVA or TPS), salary taxes (employer and employee shares), or the National Solidarity Contribution.

23. Taxes on Payrolls (Social Security)

All employers are subject to a payroll tax ("Contribution Employeur") on salaries as follows:

On expatriates' remuneration	12%
On local employees' remuneration	6%

Social security includes insurance against accidents, pensions and family allowances. All employees are covered by social security. Contributions are levied on both the employer and the employee. Employer contributions are roughly 10% to 12% and employee contributions are 2%.

24. Taxes on Natural Resources

Annual royalties are paid for the exploitation of natural resources. The rates are fixed by ton and vary according to the nature of the goods extracted.

25. Other Taxes

Taxes on Dividends, Debenture Interest, and Loan Interest. Dividends, "tantiemes," and director's remuneration for attending board meetings, are subject to a withholding tax (I.R.V.M.) at a rate of 12%. The rate is raised to 18% on dividends from new plant exempt from income tax.

Debenture interest is subject to I.R.V.M. at the rate of 25%.

Loan interest is subject to a withholding tax (I.R.C.) at the rate of 18%. The rate is reduced for interest on deposits with a banker established in Ivory Coast to 13.5% for individuals and 16.5% for businesses.

Business License Tax. All persons or entities carrying on industrial, commercial or professional activities are subject to this tax. The rate varies according to where the activity is exercised and its nature. The tax is assessed on the basis of special schedules which take account of the rental value of the premises and the equipment used.

Property Taxes.   These taxes are paid both on improved and unimproved land. They are assessed against the owner and based on the rental value. The total of property taxes applicable to constructed real estate corresponds to approximately 35.5% of 50% of the property's rented value determined by the Property Tax Authorities. Fifteen percent of property rents paid periodically should be paid to the tax authorities on the property tax's account. All new buildings benefit from a partial exemption of property taxes over a period that may extend through ten years.

Registration Duties.   The main registration duties are:

☐   On sale of buildings, land, goodwill: 10% assessed on the higher of the agreed price or the fair market value.

☐   On capital contributions to companies or capital increases: 1.2%.

☐   On accumulated surpluses of companies converted into share capital: 6% assessed on the amounts so converted.

COMPUTATION OF TAXABLE INCOME

26. Capital Gains

Capital gains are determined, except in certain cases, by the excess of the sale proceeds over the book value of the asset concerned.

27. Depreciation and Depletion

Depreciation of fixed assets is based on the probable useful life. Depreciation must be calculated on the straight-line method. The tax authorities can approve the use of the declining balance method for equipment and tools with at least a three-year useful life and purchased after September 30, 1984. The following write-off periods can be used as a general guide:

	Years
Buildings	20
Major plant and equipment	10
Office furniture	10
Minor equipment	5
Office equipment	5
Vehicles	3

Start-up costs are written off in the year they are incurred unless they are exceptionally high, in which case they may be spread over a maximum of five years. These periods may be varied, but only after approval by the tax authorities. New plant and equipment may be depreciated at twice the normal rate in the first year of utilization. Depreciation charges may be deferred when losses are incurred and written off against profits in future years, without any time limitation.

28. Treatment of Dividends

All dividends paid by an Ivoirian company are subject to the withholding tax discussed at item 25. This withholding tax is deductible from the I.G.R. for individual taxpayers in Ivory Coast. In the case of nonresident persons, this tax is the only one levied on dividends.

For Ivoirian companies, dividends must be included in taxable income at 50% of the net amount received. This amount is reduced to 5% for parent companies; i.e., companies domiciled in Ivory Coast that own at least 10% of the subsidiary.

29. Loss Carryovers

Losses may be carried forward for three years against future profits. Special conditions are available for companies carrying out exploration for and exploitation of oil deposits in Ivory Coast. These companies may carry forward losses indefinitely for tax purposes. Losses arising from depreciation can be carried forward without time limit.

30. Transactions between Related Parties

Ivory Coast has a tax provision (Article 22 of the "Code General des Impots" (C.G.I.)) which might be used to assess Ivoirian branches or subsidiary companies which are permanently in a loss position. Article 22 may be applied by the Tax Authorities when the cost of services rendered to foreign affiliates (e.g., technical assistance fees) is in excess of what an Ivoirian firm might reasonably charge for the same services.

31. Consolidation of Income

There is no provision for group taxation of related companies.

32. Tax Period

In all cases, the fiscal year must end on September 30.

RELATED CONSIDERATIONS

34. Incentives and Grants

Tax incentives for new investments were introduced in 1959. The list of priority industries includes:

□ Certain housing construction.
□ Processing activities.
□ Research, extraction, or refining of mineral resources.
□ Power production.
□ Farming, fish, industrial breeding, and related processing activities.

Special tax advantages may also be granted to new investments in the Ivory Coast tourist industry. The tax benefits available include:

□ Exemption from income tax for 25 years on housing projects constructed and held for rental by the builder.
□ Exemption from income tax for five years for other industries (see item 1).
□ Exemption from business license tax for five years.
□ Exemption from import duties for ten years.
□ Beneficial export duty rates.

Small and medium-sized businesses are the primary beneficiaries of the 1984 Investment Code, which grants various tax exemptions and accelerated depreciation to qualifying investments.

35. Exchange Controls

Basic rules provide that the CFA Franc cannot be exported from Ivory Coast nor be exchanged for non-franc currencies without the approval of the Economic Affairs Department of the Ministry of Finance. An order dated December 23, 1968 sets down a number of operating rules and includes general authorization for payments for certain transactions to be made outside the franc zone. The list is extensive and includes, inter alia:

□ Purchases and related expenses.
□ Commissions.
□ Advertising.
□ Insurance.
□ Travel expenses.
□ Royalties on patents, trademarks, and licenses.
□ Interest, rent, and dividends.
□ Income of branches and other income from foreign capital invested in the country.
□ Repatriation of capital.

All payments must be made through an institution approved to handle such transactions, normally a bank, called "intermediaire agree." The law regulating banking and finance applies to all institutions doing business in the country, regardless of form and nationality.

36. Investment Restrictions on Nonresidents

All foreign investment or financing requires prior approval by the Government. Such approval is usually routinely granted.

SELECTION OF BUSINESS ENTITY BY NONRESIDENTS

Nonresident investors can operate in Ivory Coast either through a branch or a subsidiary. Corporation tax, VAT, and registration duties are the same for a foreign company operating in Ivory Coast in the form of a branch or a corporate entity. However, one specific drawback applies to a branch:

□ The withholding tax on dividends (I.R.V.M.) is to be paid with the annual tax return whether or not the profits are distributed.

On the other hand, the registration of a branch is less complex than that of a subsidiary company.

JAMAICA

INCOME TAXES ON CORPORATIONS

1. Rates

The company income tax rate is 33⅓% as of January 1, 1987.

In addition to any company profits tax, an "additional income tax" is levied at the rate of 10% of chargeable income on any bank (licensed under the Banking Act) and any company accepting deposits (licensed under the Protection of Depositors Act).

Life insurance companies subject also to an income tax at 7½% of chargeable income. Chargeable income is investment income less management expenses, which must be incurred in earning the income.

Life insurance companies also are subject to an income tax on their premium income of .5% for regionalized companies and 2% for nonregionalized companies.

The international finance company profits tax rate is 2.5%, which applies to a company primarily engaged in financial transactions and:

☐ At least 95% of the issued share capital is held by nonresidents of Jamaica.

☐ Not more than 5% of the assets on liquidation will be received by residents of Jamaica.

☐ Not more than 5% of the loan interest or dividends are received by residents of Jamaica.

Foreign Sales Corporations (FSC). Designated corporations under the Foreign Sales Corporations Act are exempt from:

☐ Income tax with respect to income arising from foreign trade transactions, interest on loans or deposits, and other approved investment activity.

☐ The Human Employment and Resource Training Act (H.E.A.R.T.) (see item 25).

☐ Provisions of the Exchange Control Act relating to foreign trade transactions, interest on loans or deposits, and other approved investment activity.

☐ Customs duty, stamp duty, and retail sales tax on equipment, machinery, or

J-1

materials imported to carry out foreign trade transactions, and such duties, consumption duty, or excise duty, that is paid or payable, are waived upon the purchase of Jamaican goods.

□ Filing of Accounts and the Declaration of Assets and the payment of asset fees under the Companies Act.

Directors and employees of designated corporations, who are not ordinarily resident in Jamaica, shall be exempt from the National Housing Trust Act, any law relating to the education tax, and the National Insurance Act.

Nonresident shareholders of designated corporations shall be exempt from income tax with respect to dividends paid from tax-exempt income and any withholding tax required under the Income Tax Act.

2. Local Income Taxes

None.

3. Capital Gains Taxes

None (but see item 25).

4. Branch Profits Taxes

For taxes on remittances of branch profits, see item 28.

5. Foreign Tax Reliefs

Jamaica has tax treaties with Canada, Denmark, Israel, Norway, Sweden, the United Kingdom, the United States, and West Germany.

By treaty, Jamaican tax on foreign income may be reduced by a credit for foreign tax on that income. Such credit is allowed only if the taxpayer is resident in Jamaica for the relevant year of assessment. Relief is allowed for income tax chargeable in other Commonwealth countries of one-half the rate of Jamaican tax, if the other country allows similar relief. This applies regardless of treaty. Aside from the reliefs noted, there is no other relief from double taxation.

6. Classification of Corporations

None.

7. Payment of Taxes

Corporations are required to pay tax in four equal quarterly installments on a current-year basis, whereby the tax payable is computed on the previous year's income. Quarterly payments are due on the fifteenth day of March, June, September, and December. The balance of the tax due is paid when filing the return on the following March 15.

Corporations that can establish that current profits are substantially less than the previous year may file a declaration of estimated income showing the reduced income and tax payable.

INCOME TAXES ON INDIVIDUALS

9. Rates

Individual income taxes are imposed at the rate of 33.33% on a resident individual's taxable income that exceeds J$10,400. Nonresident individuals are subject to a 33.33% income tax on their total income (except as described in item 16).

10. Local Income Taxes

None.

11. Capital Gains Taxes

None (but see item 25).

12. Foreign Tax Reliefs

See item 5.

13. Tax Period

If the individual's business or professional practice has a fiscal period that ends other than on December 31, the Commissioner may permit the profit to be reported in the calendar year in which the fiscal period ends (see item 32).

INCOME TAXES ON NONRESIDENTS

15. Liability to Tax

Nonresidents are subject to tax on all Jamaican-source income except interest earned on foreign currency "A" accounts, which is exempt from income tax (see item 35).

16. Rates

Nonresident corporations are taxed on their Jamaican-source income at the same rates as resident corporations. Nonresident individuals are taxed on their Jamaican-source income at the rate of 33.33%.

Income from interest, dividends, royalties, and certain rentals and technical or management fees is subject to income tax at 33.33%, except where rates under a double taxation treaty are less (see item 17 for applicable treaty rates) or interest is earned on foreign currency "A" accounts, which is exempt from income tax (see item 35).

17. Withholding Tax Rates

Withholding tax is deducted at source from payments to nonresidents except for payments of dividends out of franked income (see item 28). The rate applicable to nontreaty countries is 33.33%, whereas rates for treaty countries are:

	Interest	Dividends	Royalties and Certain Rentals	Technical or Management Fees
Treaty countries				
Canada	15%	15%	10%	12.5%
Denmark	12.5	33.33	0	15
Israel	15	15	10	33.33
Norway	12.5	33.33	0	15
Sweden	12.5	10	10	10
United Kingdom	12.5	15	10	12.5
United States	12.5	15	10	15
West Germany	12.5	10	10	10

18. Special Withholding Provisions

Withholding tax rates on dividends vary if the receiving corporation has a controlling interest in the Jamaican company, as follows:

	Controlling Interest	Withholding Tax Rate on Dividends
Treaty countries		
Canada	10%	22.5%
Israel	10	22.5
Sweden	10	22.5
United Kingdom	10	22.5
United States	10	10
West Germany	25	15

A corporation resident in West Germany is subject to a withholding tax rate of 10% on interest payments if the payments are received by a bank recognized as a banking institution under the laws of that country.

The withholding tax on royalties (see item 17) does not apply if the recipient corporation controls more than 50% of the payor company or has a permanent establishment in the other territory (i.e., Norway, Sweden, the United Kingdom, or the United States).

OTHER SIGNIFICANT TAXES

21. Sales (Value Added)

A sales tax is imposed at the retail level on, mainly, goods considered to be luxuries. The tax is paid by the purchaser and is levied only on goods not previously subject to this tax (see item 25, "General Consumption Tax").

22. Inheritance and Gift Taxes

No taxes are levied on gifts or on property passing on death except for real estate and securities. The transfer tax is 7.5% of value.

23. Taxes on Payrolls (Social Security)

National Insurance Scheme. Employers and employees are required to contribute; the maximum annual contributions are J$377 each for an employer and for an employee. Self-employed individuals contribute a weekly amount of J$30.

National Housing Trust. Contributions are required of employers (3% of payroll) and of employees (2% of wages). Self-employed individuals contribute 3% of their net earnings. Expatriate holders of valid work permits are entitled to a refund of their contributions at the expiration of their contract.

Human Employment and Resource Training Program (The H.E.A.R.T. Trust). Contributions are levied on employers at the rate of 3% of payrolls that exceed J$87,000 per year. The contributions are subject to certain tax exemptions.

Education Tax. Contributions are required from employers (3% of payroll) and employees (2% of wages). The employer's contribution is deductible. Self-employed individuals contribute 2% of their net earnings.

25. Other Taxes

General Consumption Tax. The General Consumption Tax (GCT) Act, 1991, was enacted in July 1991 to come into effect on October 22, 1991, whereby GCT will be levied at 10% on the supply and on the importation of goods and services.

   GCT, as a simpler form of taxation, replaces the folloiwng taxes (subject to exceptions below):

☐ Excise duty;
☐ Retail sales tax;
☐ Consumption duty;
☐ Other selective taxes, such as travel tax, hotel tax, stamp duties, entertainment

duty, tax on betting, gaming, and lotteries, motor vehicle licences, and other forms of licenses.

Instead of the GCT, excise duty and a special consumption tax will be payable on beer, cigarettes, motor spirits, diesel oil, and alcoholic beverages.

Certain goods and services are zero-rated, and others are exempt from GCT.

GCT is charged in the form of an output tax on supplies and accounted for monthly to the Collector of Taxes, GCT. Input tax paid is a tax credit against output tax, and the net balance monthly is payable or refundable, as appropriate. Simplified accounting methods will be introduced to account for the net tax by the taxpayer who will elect one of the options offered.

On the day the GCT comes into effect, a registered taxpayer is eligible to claim tax credits at certain prescribed rates on unused goods that are stock-in-trade, on which certain specified duties were paid and are included in the inventory as of that day.

Land and Property Tax.   Property tax is payable on all real property based on the unimproved value of the land as assessed by the government's valuation office. Rates are ad valorem and vary with usage; that is, commercial, agricultural, or housing.

Stamp Duty.   Duties are imposed on documents, usually ad valorem.

Customs Duty, Consumption Tax, and Excise.   For the protection of manufacturers, customs duties are imposed on certain imported raw materials and capital goods. Consumption tax is also levied on finished goods and certain components. Excise is payable on certain locally produced goods, but these are exempt when exported (see "GCT," above).

Transfer Tax.   A tax is levied on the transfer of real estate and securities equal to 7.5% of sales proceeds (but not in excess of 25% of the net gain).

Contractors Levy.   A 2% tax is deducted at source on gross payments made to a contractor or subcontractor (except for service contracts) for construction, tillage, or haulage. The Income Tax Act indicates that, from the 1985 year of assessment onwards, the levy qualifies as a tax credit for income tax liability purposes. Inland Revenue disagrees with this interpretation, and the Institute of Chartered Accountants is currently in discussion with them on this subject. The contractor or subcontractor must disclose the gross amount as income and the levy as an expense, but it is not a deductible expense for income tax purposes.

COMPUTATION OF TAXABLE INCOME

26.   Capital Gains

Not applicable.

27. Depreciation and Depletion

An initial allowance is deductible in the year in which expenditures are incurred for certain income-producing assets. This initial allowance reduces the basis of the asset for purposes of depreciation in subsequent years. Initial allowances and the subsequent annual allowances must be approved by the Minister of Finance. The following rates are normally approved:

	Allowances	
Asset	Initial	Annual
Buildings and structures		
Industrial	20%	2.5%–3%
Housing	0	5
Machinery and plant	20	7.5–10
Motor vehicles		
Business	12.5	12.5
Other	0	12.5 (1)
Scientific research	0	20
Ships	0	4

Notes:
(1) Limited to J$400 per annum.

28. Treatment of Dividends

Dividends are taxable to recipients by withholding at the rate of 33⅓%. Stock dividends are not taxable. Where tax is deducted at the source from a distribution of income of a corporation resident in the island, that income is referred to as "franked income."

On distribution of franked income to another corporation subject to income tax which is resident in the island, the deduction of tax in the first instance is treated as discharging the liability to tax of

☐ the corporation that received the franked income,

☐ any other corporation to which the original corporation may distribute franked income,

☐ any other corporation receiving the franked income from another corporation,

☐ any individual to whom the franked income may be distributed by corporations such as discussed above.

29. Loss Carryovers

Losses may be carried forward for six years if such losses were incurred during the 1986 year of assessment or earlier. Losses for the 1987 year of assessment and after may be carried forward indefinitely. Loss carrybacks are not allowed.

30.   Transactions between Related Parties

There are provisions to negate any tax advantages that might be obtainable from transactions between related parties.

32.   Tax Periods

In the normal case, income tax is chargeable for the calendar year ending December 31. Any other date must be specifically approved by the Commissioner of Income Tax.

RELATED CONSIDERATIONS

34.   Incentives and Grants

Capital Allowances.   A special allowance up to the normal amount of depreciation is allowed for businesses in "qualified industries," which includes a broad range of manufacturing and agricultural operations.

A special investment allowance of 40% of the capital expenditures incurred is granted for the purchase, alteration, or improvement of a ship. An annual allowance of 4% is also granted.

Qualified capital expenditures in basic industries are granted a special 20% investment allowance.

Investment allowances, which are not deductible in arriving at the basis for annual allowances, are given to encourage the following industries:

Basic industries (i.e., manufacturing and construction)	20%
Sugar industry	40
Ships	40
Agriculture	40
Livestock breeding	40
Motion picture industry	70

Industrial Incentives.   Approved incentive companies are relieved from income tax on profits earned from the manufacture of "incentive products" during the incentive period, which is usually a period of five to ten years. Accumulated incentive products may be distributed tax-free to the shareholders. Approved companies engaged in the hotel and motion-picture industries also are relieved from income tax on profits earned during periods ranging from five to ten years, and these profits also may be distributed tax-free to shareholders. Motion-picture companies may postpone claims for capital allowances for up to five years. Note that the tax relief to nonresident shareholders on dividends paid out of tax-free products is generally limited to the applicable foreign tax rate.

Export Incentives.   Approved companies manufacturing certain products for export only are granted a tax credit on their export profits. The credit is based on the proportion of export profits to total profits, and ranges from 10% to 50% of the income tax payable on export profits.

Agricultural Incentives. Corporations and individuals accredited as approved farmers are relieved from income tax on profits earned in the farming of approved agricultural products.

Free Zones. Certain designated areas in Kingston and Montego Bay are approved industrial free zones. These areas are considered to be transshipment ports for income tax purposes, and consequently, nonresident corporations operating in free zones are required to operate through a local company incorporated for this purpose. Company profits earned in free-zone operations are not subject to Jamaican income tax. Free-zone operations also are not constrained by local custom import and other duties unless products are transferred into Jamaica for local consumption. Free-zone corporations are exempt from the Central Bank regulations.

35. Exchange Controls

Holders of work permits who are not married to residents may remit each month up to 30% of their gross salary earned in Jamaica. Foreign nationals employed in diplomatic posts or by international health or similar international organizations are not subject to the 30% limit. Remittances of dividends or profits arising from investments by nonresidents that have been registered and approved by the Bank of Jamaica will be approved provided: (1) audited statements are presented to substantiate the remittances, and (2) the Commissioner of Income Tax certifies the tax withheld.

A formal auction system is operating that permits commercial banks to buy foreign exchange, on behalf of their customers, from the Central Bank in accordance with approval guidelines. There is also a forward foreign exchange market.

Effective July 1, 1990, the Bank of Jamaica has authorized commercial banks to operate foreign currency accounts within certain limits.

These are called foreign currency 'A' accounts and may be operated only by:

☐ Nonresident individuals, work permit holders, and nonresident corporate bodies not undertaking business in Jamaica.

☐ Resident individuals.

Interest earned on these accounts is exempt from income tax.

There are restrictions on the type of deposits permitted to be credited to these accounts.

The accounts may be debited to make any payment outside of Jamaica. Foreign currency cash limited a maximum of US$300 may be debited for travel purposes; amounts in excess of US$300 are given in traveler's checks.

JAPAN

INCOME TAXES ON CORPORATIONS

1. Rates

Japanese corporations are taxable on their worldwide income at the following corporate national tax rates and the corporate local income tax rates described in item 2, below:

Corporation with paid-in capital in excess of ¥100 million	37.5%
Corporation with paid-in capital of ¥100 million or less:	
First ¥8 million of annual taxable income	28.0
Remainder	37.5

To secure the source of revenue for expenditures incurred concerning the Gulf Area Peace Support Measures, the Temporary Special Surtax Law was enacted. A corporation with a national tax liability for an accounting year ending during the period April 1, 1991 to March 31, 1992 is subject to this surtax. The tax base of the surtax is the ordinary corporate national tax (excluding the additional tax of a family corporation and before application of withholding tax and foreign tax credits). The tax rate is 2.75%, thus increasing the effective corporate tax rate by approximately 1%.

2. Local Income Taxes

Corporate Enterprise Tax. A domestic corporation may be subject to a maximum corporate enterprise tax at the rate of 13.2% on its net income. The tax is payable to each prefecture in which a domestic corporation locates its business offices or factories, and is computed by allocating the net income on the basis of the number of employees, etc., in each prefecture. If a domestic corporation that does not have a business office, etc., in three or more prefectures or is capitalized at less than

¥ 10 million, the maximum tax rates are 6.6%, and 9.9% on the first ¥ 3.5 million and the second ¥ 3.5 million of income, respectively. For certain prefectures other than Osaka, Kyoto, or similar large prefectures, and for certain small businesses in any prefecture (defined by capital and annual income within certain amounts), tax rates of 6%, 9%, and 12% are applied instead of the 6.6%, 9.9%, and 13.2% rates, respectively. For Tokyo, corporate enterprise tax rates of 6.3%, 9.45%, and 12.6% are applied. Enterprise tax is not imposed on the income of a foreign branch of a domestic corporation. Enterprise tax is deductible from income in the accounting period in which it is paid.

As an exception to these general principles, gross receipts instead of net income is used as the taxable base, and different tax rates are applied for insurance and electric, power, or gas supply corporations.

Corporate Inhabitant Taxes. The corporate inhabitant taxes are payable to both prefectures and municipalities where a domestic corporation locates its business office, etc., at the maximum rates of 6% and 14.7%, respectively, of the national income tax liability, allocated on a basis similar to corporate enterprise tax by each prefecture or municipality. The rate in Tokyo, Osaka, Kyoto, or similar large prefectures is 20.7% (7.76% on net income), combining prefectural and municipal tax rates. For certain other localities, representative cities, or small businesses, lower rates of 5% and 12.3% apply. In addition to these rates, inhabitant per capita (equalization) taxes are payable regardless of net income or national tax liabilities. For example, in Tokyo, the combined prefectural and municipal tax per capita ranges from ¥ 50,000 to ¥ 3,750,000, depending on the size of the corporation.

3. Capital Gains Taxes

Generally, there are no capital gains taxes as such. Capital gains are subject to the normal corporate national and local tax rates in aggregation with other operating income. However, for the sale of land, right to land, or certain shares that, in substance, represent the land value (hereafter refer to as land, etc.) on or after January 1, 1992, after ownership of more than five years, additional taxes are imposed on the capital gain (long-term gain) at the rate of 10% for national tax purposes and at 2.07% for inhabitant tax purposes. For the gain from sale of land, etc., after the ownership of five years or less but more than two years (short-term gain), additional national and inhabitant tax rates are 20% and 4.14%, respectively. Further, for gains from sale of land, etc., after the ownership of two years or less (super short-term gains), national tax is imposed as the separate taxation at 67.5% from January 1, 1992. Enterprise tax and inhabitant tax are imposed on this gain at 12.6% and 13.96% (7.76% plus additional inhabitants tax of 6.2%), respectively. The ownership years of five or two years is computed from the acquisition date of land, etc., to January 1 of the year of sale.

4. Branch Profits Taxes

A Japanese branch of a foreign corporation is taxed on its income earned from sources in Japan in the same manner and at the same tax rates as a domestic corporation. A foreign corporation with a branch in Japan is required to pay corporate income taxes on its entire Japan-source income whether or not the income is earned through the Japanese branch (entire base taxation concept). However, for a corporation from a country that has an OECD-type tax treaty with Japan, only income attributable to its Japan branch operations is taxable (attributable concept). The repatriation of branch profits to a foreign head office is not subject to further taxation.

5. Foreign Tax Reliefs

A foreign tax credit is allowed against national and inhabitant taxes for foreign income taxes paid on income derived from abroad by a domestic corporation. Alternatively, a deduction from taxable income may be taken in lieu of the tax credit. The tax credit is determined by source on an overall basis as opposed to a per-country or per-nature-of-income basis. Excess foreign taxes over the limitation, or the limitation in excess of the foreign taxes, may be carried forward for three years. On dividends received from a first-tier affiliated foreign corporation whose voting shares are 25% or more owned by a domestic corporation (10% or more for an Australian corporation or 10% or more of voting shares for a U.S. or Brazilian corporation), foreign corporate taxes paid with respect to the profit out of which dividends are paid are included as foreign taxes paid. Under tax treaties with certain developing countries, the original tax rates under the foreign tax law are deemed as foreign taxes paid instead of the actual reduced or exempt taxes due to special economic or political arrangements (tax-sparing system).

For income from investment in foreign countries by a Japanese branch of a foreign corporation, foreign tax is not creditable against Japanese tax. However, such income may be treated as exempt income, provided that income tax is imposed on such income in the foreign country.

6. Classification of Corporations

For tax purposes, corporations are classified as: (1) domestic or foreign, and (2) family or nonfamily. A foreign corporation that does not have a branch or permanent establishment in Japan is subject to corporate national tax on Japan-source income earned from the sale or lease of Japanese real properties or similar income.

A family corporation is defined as one whose shares are 50% or more owned by three or fewer shareholders, including their relatives. The undistributed earnings of a domestic family corporation are subject to an additional tax of 10%, 15%, or 20%, depending on the amount of taxable undistributed earnings.

A wholly owned subsidiary is not subject to the tax on undistributed earnings if the parent corporation is not a family corporation, but the tax authorities still have the power to reallocate income between the entities.

7. Payment of Taxes

A corporation is, as a rule, required to file final income tax returns and pay taxes within two months after the end of an accounting period. The due date for filing may be extended for an additional month for a domestic corporation (longer for a foreign corporation) when an application for extension has been approved by the tax office. Interest charged on taxes paid during an extension period is deductible. Also an interim tax return must be filed within two months after the end of the first six months in any fiscal year or any short year longer than six months. Interim taxes are computed on either one-half of the previous year's annual taxes or the net income for the preceding six-month accounting period.

INCOME TAXES ON INDIVIDUALS

9. Rates

National individual income tax is payable on income less various deductions at the following rates:

Taxable Income*		Tax on Lower Amount	Percentage on Excess
Over	Not Over		
¥ 0	¥ 3,000,000	¥ —	10%
3,000,000	6,000,000	300,000	20
6,000,000	10,000,000	900,000	30
10,000,000	20,000,000	2,100,000	40
20,000,000		6,100,000	50

10. Local Income Taxes

Inhabitant Income Tax. Inhabitant income tax is payable on income less the employment income deduction, personal deductions, etc., at the following rates, which combine prefectural and municipal taxes.

For 1990 income

Taxable Income*		Tax on Lower Amount	Percentage on Excess
Over	Not Over		
¥ 0	¥ 1,600,000	¥ —	5%
1,600,000	5,500,000	80,000	10
5,500,000		470,000	15

*In addition, a per capita tax of ¥3,200 is payable.

The most common deductions from gross income to arrive at taxable income (to which the tax rates in items 9 and 10 are applied) are:

☐ The employment income deduction is deductible from employment income for national and inhabitant tax purposes in the following amounts:

Salary Allowance, etc. (Column 1)		Multiply Column 1 by (Column 2)	Amount Added to the Product of Column 2
Over	Not Over		
¥ 0	¥ 1,650,000	40% (minimum ¥570,000)	—
1,650,000	3,300,000	30	¥ 165,000
3,300,000	6,000,000	20	495,000
6,000,000	10,000,000	10	1,095,000
10,000,000		5	1,595,000

☐ The personal basic deduction is deducted from income in the amount of ¥350,000 for national tax purposes and ¥310,000 for local tax purposes. These amounts are for the taxpayer and each dependent family member. The deduction increases for aged taxpayers, etc. Furthermore, a spouse special deduction amounting to ¥350,000 for national tax purposes and ¥310,000 (maximum) for local tax purposes is added to the personal deduction provided the total income of the taxpayer is less than ¥10,000,000.

Enterprise Tax. Enterprise tax is imposed by the prefectural office on an individual who is engaged in business as a sole proprietor. The tax ranges from 3% to 5%, depending on the nature of business (5% for an attorney or CPA), of net income after a deduction of ¥2.4 million. Enterprise tax is deductible from income when paid.

11. Capital Gains Taxes

Capital gains on the sale of certain listed securities may be taxed in either of two ways, depending on the election of the taxpayer.

First, the taxpayer may elect that national withholding tax of 20% of the deemed gain on the securities be applied. The deemed gain is 5% of the sales proceeds of stock and 2.5% of the sale proceeds of convertible bonds or warrants. No local withholding tax applies.

Should the taxpayer not elect the above withholding, the taxpayer is taxed at a rate of 20% nationally and 6% locally on capital gains. For securities that are not listed, the 20% and 6% taxes are mandatory.

Special rules apply to capital gains from sales of real property by individuals. Gain from sales of real estate is classified as long-term or short-term for national income tax purposes. The classification of gains is similar to that of corporate income taxes. However, there is no super-short-term gain category—it is classified as a short-term gain for individual tax purposes. Long-term gain is taxed at a flat 30% (20% and 25% phased taxes for sales before January 1, 1992). Short-term gain is taxed at the greater of (1) a flat 40%, or (2) 110% of the graduated tax on the gain for national tax purposes. The inhabitant tax rate on the long-term gain is a flat 9% (previously 6% and 7.5% phased rates). The inhabitant tax rate for short-term gain is 12%. Up to ¥30 million of gain from the first sale of a principal residence in any three-year period beginning on the date of such first sale is not subject to national and inhabitant income taxes. If the principal residence is sold after ownership of ten years or more, the gains in excess of ¥30 million will be taxed at reduced rates as follows:

	National Tax	Local Tax
For the first ¥60 million	10%	4%
Over ¥60 million	15	5

If the principal residence, which was succeeded from a parent or grandparent after their ownership of ten or more years and had been used for residence by the individual (successor) for 30 years or more, is sold and the sale proceeds are reinvested in another principal residence, the gain from the sale will be exempt from income taxes.

12. Foreign Tax Reliefs

Taxpayers may credit income taxes paid to foreign governments on foreign-source income against their Japanese tax liability to the extent that Japanese income tax applies to such income. Foreign tax credits are applied against the national tax liability first; any excess up to 30% of the creditable limitation for national tax purposes may then be applied as a credit against the inhabitants tax. Alternatively, the taxpayer may take foreign tax payments as a deduction from gross income for national income tax purposes.

13. Tax Period

The tax year for individuals is the calendar year, and taxpayers generally must file a national tax return by March 15 of the following year.

INCOME TAXES ON NONRESIDENTS

15. Liability to Tax

An individual whose employment requires that he or she remain in Japan for less than one year usually qualifies as a nonresident taxpayer. As such, the individual is subject to tax on his or her salary, wherever paid, at a flat 20% rate. If such individual is subject to tax as a resident in his or her home country, he or she may be exempt from this 20% tax, provided the home country and Japan have a tax treaty, his or her stay in Japan was not more than 183 days during the tax (calendar) year, his or her employer is a nonresident or foreign corporation, and his or her salary is not charged to a permanent establishment in Japan. A nonresident who fails to meet any of these tests is subject to the 20% tax. A nonresident's Japanese-source business income attributable to a permanent establishment in Japan, income for services, or the sale or rental of real property, etc., located in Japan is taxed at the same graduated national income tax rates as resident persons.

Inhabitant and enterprise taxes are levied on nonresidents who have permanent establishments in Japan to which their business-related individual income is attributable.

17. Withholding Tax Rates

Generally, dividends or interest paid to a domestic or foreign corporation, or to a resident or nonresident individual, in or from Japan, are subject to withholding tax. The tax rate on dividends is 20% for national tax purposes. The tax rate on interest is 15% for national tax purposes and 5% for inhabitant tax purposes. A foreign corporation and nonresident individual are not subject to the 5% withholding inhabitant tax. For an individual, both national and inhabitant taxation on interest are finalized with this withholding tax (separate taxation). The interest includes not only interest on bonds or bank deposits, but also revenue from similar finance products (e.g., mortgage securities and time deposit on foreign currency basis). National tax and inhabitant taxes withheld on dividends and interest are creditable against corporate national tax and corporate inhabitant tax, respectively. Interest and redemption income on foreign currency denominated bonds or Euroyen bonds (which are issued abroad with a four-year or more maturity date) paid to nonresident or foreign corporations are exempt from Japanese withholding income taxes. Royalties, rent, or interest on loans paid to a foreign corporation or a nonresident are subject to withholding tax of 20%; however, if a foreign corporation, etc., has a permanent establishment in Japan and corporate income taxes are imposed on these payments, withholding tax may be exempt if an application is filed with the tax office. Instead of the above tax rates, withholding tax rates are reduced under the tax treaties as summarized in the following table.

In addition to the above, if a nonresident or a foreign corporation sells real estate located in Japan, the seller must withhold 10% of gross revenue on the sale of that real estate. Note, however, that if the gross sales amount is ¥ 100 million or less and the buyer uses the real estate for his or her family's primary residence, then there is no withholding.

Withholding Taxes on Outward Remittances

Recipient	Dividends (portfolio)	Dividends (substantial holdings) (1)	Interest	Royalties
Nontreaty countries	20%	20%	20%	20%
Treaty countries:				
Australia	15	15	10	10
Austria	20	10	10	10
Belgium (2)	15	15	15	10

Withholding Taxes on Outward Remittances

Recipient	Dividends (portfolio)	Dividends (substantial holdings) (1)	Interest	Royalties
Brazil	12.5%	12.5%	12.5%	12.5%/25%
British Virgin Islands	15	10	10	10
Canada	15	10	10	10
China	10	10	10	10
Czechoslovakia	15	10	10	0/10
Denmark	15	10	10	10
Finland	15	10	10	10
France	15	10	10	10
Germany	15	10	10	10
Hungary	10	10	10	0/10
India	15	15	15	20
Indonesia	15	10	10	10
Ireland	15	10	10	10
Italy	15	10	10	10
Korea	12	12	12	12
Malaysia	15	10	10	10
Netherlands	15	10	10	10
New Zealand	15	15	20	20
Norway	15	10	10	10
Pakistan	20	15	0/30	0
Philippines	25	10	10/15	10/25
Poland	10	10	10	0/10
Romania	10	10	10	10/15
Singapore	15	10	15	10
Soviet Union	15	15	10	10
Spain	15	10	10	10
Sri Lanka	20	20	0/20	0/10
Sweden	15	10	10	10
Switzerland	15	10	10	10
Thailand	20/25	15	0/10/20	15
United Arab Republic	15	15	20	15
United Kingdom	15	10	10	10
United States	15	10	10	10
Zambia	0	0	10	10

Notes:

(1) Substantial holding rates vary depending on the tax treaty provision; e.g., 10% or more for the United States, 25% or more for the United Kingdom, Canada, and the Netherlands, and 50% or more for Austria.

(2) Treaty soon to be modified.

OTHER SIGNIFICANT TAXES

21. Sales (Value Added)

Goods and services supplied for use in Japan are subject to a 3% consumption tax. Exports are zero-rated transactions; imported products are subject to the 3% tax.

A taxpayer with sales subject to the consumption tax that are not more than ¥ 30 million has no tax liability; a taxpayer with sales subject to the consumption tax of less than ¥ 50 million can pay a reduced tax liability.

The final consumption tax return is due when the corporate tax return is originally due, unless the taxpayer elects to file on a quarterly basis. A quarterly election would be made when the taxpayer expects to be in a refund position. Taxpayers who paid more than ¥ 5 million consumption tax must file on a quarterly basis.

22. Inheritance and Gift Taxes

An individual who acquires property by gift from another individual is subject to gift tax. The gift tax is imposed on a calendar year basis. The rates range from 10% on the first ¥ 1,000,000 to 70% on gifts over ¥ 70 million, after deducting an allowance of ¥ 600,000.

An individual who acquires property through inheritance is subject to inheritance tax. The inheritance tax is computed on the value of inherited property as computed under the inheritance tax rules less basic deductions of ¥ 40 million plus ¥ 8 million multiplied by the number of statutory heirs. The total inheritance taxes computed on this basis are allocated to the inheritors in proportion to the value of the assets actually distributed to them. Rates range from 10% on the first ¥ 4 million to 70% on the taxable net amount over ¥ 500 million. Generally, a surviving spouse is exempt from the inheritance tax on property received to the extent of his or her statutory share of succession or ¥ 80 million, whichever is larger.

23. Taxes on Payrolls (Social Security)

Health, welfare pension, unemployment and workmen's accident compensation insurance are government sponsored and participation is compulsory, as a rule, for both employers and employees. Except for workmen's accident compensation insurance, the premiums are generally paid equally by the employer and employee. The combined monthly health insurance premium approximates 8.4% of monthly compensation up to ¥ 710,000 and remains the same thereafter. The combined monthly welfare pension contribution approximates 14.15% and 14.5% for female and male employees, respectively, of their monthly compensation up to ¥ 530,000. The combined monthly unemployment and worker's accident compensation insurance premium approximates 2.05% of monthly compensation, with 1.5% borne by the employer and 0.55% borne by the employee.

25. Other Taxes

Taxes on Land and Property. Annual taxes are generally imposed on land and buildings at 1.7% and on other depreciable fixed assets used in businesses at 1.4% of their taxable value. Purchasers of land and other real property pay an acquisition tax of 3% or 4% of the taxable value of real estate at the time of acquisition.

Business office tax is imposed at the rate of ¥600 per square meter of the floor space used for business and 0.25% of the annual payroll. This tax is exempt for a corporation or an individual enterprise with the floor space of 1,000 or less square meters or 100 or fewer staff members.

Effective January 1, 1992, a new land value tax is imposed. The tax rate is 0.2% in 1992 and 0.3% thereafter. The tax base will be the assessed value less an exemption amount of ¥1.5 billion for individuals and corporations with capital stock not exceeding 100 million, and an exemption of ¥1 billion for all other corporations.

Stamp Tax. An individual or corporation that prepares certain documents (e.g., contracts, power of attorney, promissory or exchange notes, receipts) is subject to stamp tax. Rates depend on the nature of documents and the amounts contained in them.

COMPUTATION OF TAXABLE INCOME

26. Capital Gains

Corporation. Taxable capital gains are, as a rule, measured by the difference between the net proceeds and the cost of the asset sold or otherwise transferred. If capital assets are transferred at a price substantially lower than an arm's-length price, such transfer may be deemed for tax purposes to have occurred at a fair market price, with a resultant capital gain and donation expense for the transferor. Since the deduction for a donation is allowed on a limited basis, the transferor may be taxed on a substantial portion of the imputed capital gain. In addition, the transferee will be taxable on donation income based on the fair market value of the transferred asset.

Individual. When capital assets are transferred by one individual to another, deemed capital gain will not generally be taxed to the seller. However, the individual who acquires the assets at a substantially lower price or without consideration may be charged gift tax on the benefit received.

27. Depreciation and Depletion

Unless recorded in the books, depreciation and depletion are not deductible for tax purposes. Estimated useful lives of depreciable assets are prescribed by tax law and unless prior approval of the tax authorities is obtained, these prescribed useful lives must be used. Several methods of depreciation are allowable. However, the declining balance and straight-line methods are commonly used, at the taxpayer's option. The salvage value of depreciable assets is 10% of acquisition cost. Assets, however, may be depreciated to 5% of cost.

Special Depreciation. In addition to ordinary depreciation based on the statutory useful lives, additional depreciation ranging from 7% to 30% (up to 50% in Okinawa) is allowed in the first year for designated depreciable assets. Newly constructed residential rental properties have allowances of 24% or 40% of ordinary depreciation in addition to ordinary depreciation for the first five years.

28. Treatment of Dividends

For Japanese corporations owning 25% or more of the outstanding shares of a dividend-paying Japanese corporation, 100% of the dividend is deductible from income.

For Japanese corporations owning less than 25% of the outstanding shares of a dividend-paying Japanese corporation, 80% of the dividend is deductible.

29. Loss Carryovers

Only corporations qualified to file "blue returns" may elect either to carry forward losses for five years or to first carry back losses for one year and then carry forward the remaining losses for five years. Casualty losses may be treated in the same way as net operating losses, even if a corporation is not on the blue return filing status. Individual taxpayers qualified to file "blue returns" may elect to carry forward losses for three years or carry back losses for one year.

30. Transactions between Related Parties

Revenue transactions between related parties that are not carried out on an arm's-length basis may be challenged by the tax examiners. They can assess taxes as if the transactions were between unrelated parties.

For an accounting period which begins on or after April 1, 1986, intercompany transfer pricing rules apply to a company's overseas transactions with its foreign related company. The corporation will be required to demonstrate comparable arms-length prices upon request by the Japanese tax authorities. If the company or its affiliate has had tax adjusted in a country with which Japan has entered into an appropriate tax treaty, either company may request competent authority assistance for a correlative adjustment.

31. Consolidation of Income

No provisions exist for combining the profits and losses of affiliated corporations for tax purposes or for eliminating intercompany transactions.

32. Tax Periods

The taxable period for computing the liability for corporation tax is the corporation's own accounting period.

33. Other Matters

Deduction for Tax Other than Income Taxes. In computing taxable income, businesses may deduct payroll tax, fixed assets tax, business premises tax, and automobile tax. Liquor tax, etc., is treated as part of the cost of the goods acquired.

Inventory Valuation. For tax purposes, inventories may be valued at cost or at the lower of cost or market. For this purpose market value means repurchase price. For computation of cost, average, FIFO, LIFO, latest purchase price, retail price, or individual identification methods are allowed.

Bad Debts. A provision for doubtful accounts may be deductible to the extent determined by the nature of the business as shown below and as a percent of the outstanding receivables at the end of an accounting period.

Retail or wholesale trades	1.0%
Manufacturing	0.8
Financial or insurance institutions	0.3
Installment sales	1.3
Others	0.6

For a corporation capitalized at ¥100 million or less, 116% of the above rates are allowed. In addition, 50% to 100% of receivables from certain insolvent debtors may be deductible, depending on the circumstances.

Reserve for Retirement Allowance. The amount credited to a reserve for retirement allowance may be deducted, depending on the applicable circumstances, up to the lowest of the following amounts:

☐ Up to the increase in the total retirement allowances claimable if all employees remaining at the end of the accounting period had terminated their employment on a voluntary basis, computed according to the retirement allowance policy established by the corporation.

☐ Up to 6% of the salaries, bonuses, and allowances paid in the accounting period if the retirement allowance policy is not based on a labor union agreement. If the company reports to the tax office that it has notified every employee of the retirement allowance regulations, this test is not applied.

☐ Up to 40% of the total retirement allowances claimable by all employees remaining at the end of the accounting period had all employees terminated their employment then on a voluntary basis, less the related allowances claimable by all such employees in the preceding accounting period.

RELATED CONSIDERATIONS

34. Incentives and Grants

Tax Credit for Incremental Research and Development Expenses. If research and development expenses for an accounting period exceed the largest annual research and development expenses of any year since 1966, 20% of such excess may be credited against corporate national tax to the extent of 10% of the national tax until March 31, 1993. Further, if a corporation acquires and places in service certain depreciable assets which are designated by the Ministry of Finance as facilities for researching and developing fundamental high technologies, the corporation may credit against the corporate national tax the lower of: (1) 20% of the increment in research and development expenses plus 7% of the acquisition costs described above, or (2) 15% of the corporate national tax. In the case of a small or medium-sized corporation (i.e., the share capital of the corporation and the parent corporation do not exceed ¥ 100 million), 6% of research and development expenses of the current year may be used in lieu of 20% of the increment in research and expenses computed above.

Import Incentives. If a manufacturing, wholesale, or retail company imports an amount of specified goods in the current accounting period that exceeds by at least 10% the largest annual amount of such imports for the preceding year, the company may claim an incentive benefit as follows.

□ **Manufacturing company**
— an additional 10% or 20% (depending on the acquisition date) of the current year's depreciation deduction, or
— a tax credit for 5% of the amount of such increase in imports.

□ **Wholesale or retail company**—a deductible allowance equal to 20% of the amount of such increase in imports.

This incentive applies to accounting periods that include any day between April 1, 1990 and March 31, 1993.

Tax Incentives for Capital Expenditure which Contribute to the Efficient Use of Basic Energy Resources. A corporation which acquires qualifying machinery, equipment, and other depreciable assets may use special depreciation rates based on 30% or 15% of the assets' acquisition costs or elect an investment tax credit at 7% or 3.5% of the acquisition costs to the extent of 20% of corporation tax when they are put into business use.

35. Exchange Controls

Under the foreign exchange and trade control law that went into effect on December 1, 1980, all external economic transactions are free of restrictions in principle, unless specified as restricted. The change represents a complete reversal from the earlier legal system that banned all such transactions except those specified to be free. Restrictions of external transactions in trade, foreign exchange and capital will be imposed only in exceptional situations to cope with an economic emergency such as an unusually massive transfer of funds, unusually wild fluctuation in the foreign exchange market, etc. Investments in Japanese companies by foreign companies are also free from restrictions except for certain regulated industries. A timely filing of foreign exchange forms with the Bank of Japan is required for investments by foreign companies in shares of Japanese companies, extensions of loans by foreign companies, conclusions of license agreements, and certain other transactions prior to investment.

SELECTION OF BUSINESS ENTITY BY NONRESIDENTS

Nonresident investors can operate in Japan through either a branch or a local subsidiary corporation. The tax consequences of operating in Japan through a branch are:

- [ ] Branch profits are taxable at the same rate as a domestic corporation.
- [ ] No additional or withholding tax is levied on remittances of branch profits.
- [ ] No income tax is levied on branches engaged solely in auxiliary or preparatory operations for their head or other foreign offices (of the same corporation), such as purchasing, research, or liaising.
- [ ] An employee can be assigned as the general manager of the Japanese branch. Unless the general manager is concurrently assigned as an officer, his or her remuneration may be deductible and the taxable house benefit is a nominal amount (e.g., 5% to 10% of rent).
- [ ] If the capital stock of the foreign corporation is high, certain tax benefits available to smaller corporations are lost.

A local incorporated company is commonly used by foreign investors, with the following tax consequences:

- [ ] Withholding tax is levied on remittances of corporate earnings at 10% to 20%, depending on the relevant tax treaties. Bonuses and other irregularly paid compensation to full-time officers are not deductible. The taxable portion of an officer's housing benefit is, as a minimum, 35% of the actual rent paid by the domestic corporation while, for employees, the taxable portion is only about 5% to 10% of rent.
- [ ] Certain tax benefits (e.g., reduced tax rates and deductibility of entertainment expenses within a maximum of ¥4 million) are available to local companies with small capitalization; this can be achieved by establishing a small-size foreign subsidiary with all de facto operations conducted through a Japanese branch.

☐ Officers' compensation paid by a domestic subsidiary is treated as Japan-source income, even when considered to be earned outside of Japan, and will be subject to Japanese tax, with exceptions under certain tax treaties.

Whether a branch or a local corporation is optimum for Japanese tax purposes depends on the nature and scope of the activities in Japan as well as on the foreign tax considerations.

SPECIMEN TAX COMPUTATION

Information:

☐ Assumptions for a corporation (for tax years beginning after March 31, 1990 and before April 1, 1991):

Taxable income of ¥1,000
Paid-in capital of ¥200 million
Business offices in Tokyo

Computation:

	Domestic Corporation	Foreign Corporation
Corporate national tax:		
¥1,000 at 37.5%	¥375.0	¥375.0
Corporate enterprise tax:		
¥1,000 at 12.6%	126.0	126.0
Corporate inhabitant tax:		
¥375 at 20.7%	78.0	78.0
	¥579.0	¥579.0

Notes:
(1) Inhabitant per capita tax is not included in the above computation.
(2) Enterprise tax and inhabitant tax are based on the total of prefectures and municipalities.
(3) Effective tax rates are computed as follows:

Corporate national tax	37.5 %
Corporate enterprise tax	12.6
Corporate inhabitants tax	7.8
	57.9 %
Less effect of corporate enterprise tax, as it is deductible when paid (12.6% at 51.4%)	(6.5)
	51.4 %

For computation of deferred tax, a 51.4% effective tax rate is usually used. The special one-time surtax for a corporation tax year ending between April 1, 1991 and March 31, 1992 would increase the effective tax rate by 1%.

Information:

□ Assumptions for an individual:

Resident individual
Married with one child
Salary and allowance
Deductions other than the personal deduction are not considered

Computation:

National Income Tax

Salary and allowances	¥10,000,000
Employment income deduction	
(5% of ¥10,000,000 + ¥1,595,000)	(2,095,000)
Employment income	7,905,000
Personal deductions	
(¥350,000 × 3 + ¥350,000)	(1,400,000)
	¥ 6,505,000
National income tax	
(¥900,000 + [¥6,505,000 − ¥6,000,000] × 30%)	¥1,051,500

Local Inhabitants Income Tax

Employment income	¥7,905,000
Personal deductions	
(¥310,000 × 3 + ¥310,000)	(1,240,000)
	¥6,665,000
Local inhabitant income tax	
(¥470,000 + [¥6,665,000 − ¥5,500,000] × 15%)	
+ equalization tax of ¥3,200	¥644,700

KENYA

INCOME TAXES ON CORPORATIONS

1. Rates

Corporation income tax is imposed at the following rates:

Locally incorporated companies	40.0%
Mining companies (mining specific minerals)	
First five profit-making years	27.5
Thereafter	42.5
Resident life insurance companies	40.0

Effective as of the year of income commencing January 1, 1992, corporation income tax will be charged at the following rates.

Locally incorporated companies	37.5%
Mining companies (mining specific minerals)	
First five profit-making years	27.5%
Thereafter	40.0%
Resident life insurance companies	40.0%

2. Local Income Taxes

None.

3. Capital Gains Taxes

The capital gains tax imposed on property transfers has been suspended effective June 14, 1985.

4. Branch Profits Taxes

Branches or permanent establishments of nonresident companies are taxed on their profits at a rate of 47.5%. The calculation of the taxable profit of a branch is the same as for a resident company except that no deduction is allowed for any interest, royalties, and management or professional fees and foreign exchange differences paid by the branch to its nonresident parent company. Special provisions apply to shipowners, charterers, and air transport operators.

Effective as of the year of income commencing January 1, 1992, branches or permanent establishments of nonresident companies will be taxed on their profits at a rate of 45%.

5. Foreign Tax Reliefs

Income derived from sources outside Kenya is not liable to tax in Kenya, whether the income is remitted to Kenya or not. Therefore, no relief for foreign taxes is necessary. In the case of a resident corporation which carries on business partly inside and partly outside Kenya, *all* the business income is deemed to have been derived from Kenya. Foreign taxes suffered on such income will be allowed as a deduction in calculating the profit liable for Kenya tax.

7. Payment of Taxes

Tax on estimated results is payable within three months of the end of the company's financial accounting year. An income tax return must be filed within nine months of the end of the company's financial accounting year following which an assessment will be raised as soon as the computation is agreed. The assessment gives credit for the estimated tax paid and the balance of tax is payable within one month of the date of the assessment but not earlier than September 30 of the year following the year of income. If, by reason of an underestimate of tax payable, the final balance payable is greater than 10% of the estimated tax paid, interest is charged at the rate of 1% per month on the difference between the tax assessed and the tax estimated.

Businesses, including individuals whose income, other than income from emoluments, is more than 50% of those emoluments, are required to complete an installment tax return and pay installment tax at the end of the ninth month of their financial year. The installment tax payable for any year of income will be the lesser of:

☐ The amount equal to the tax that would be payable by that person if his or her total income for the current year was an amount equal to his or her installment income; or

☐ The amount specified in the preceding year's assessment.

The installment tax will be phased in over a period, and the tax payable will be as follows:

Financial Year Commencing On or After	Tax Payable
January 1, 1991	30% of estimated tax
January 1, 1992	45% of estimated tax
January 1, 1993	60% of estimated tax
January 1, 1994	75% of estimated tax

A nonresident company, not having a permanent establishment in Kenya, which receives from Kenya income of the type set out in item 17, suffers withholding tax deducted at source by the payer of the income at the rates set out in item 17. Consequently, its tax liability is automatically discharged.

INCOME TAXES ON INDIVIDUALS

9. Rates

Individuals are taxed at the following rates.

□ Income year 1991:

Taxable Income		Tax on	Percentage
Over	Not Over	Lower Amount	on Excess
K£. 0	K£. 2,100	—	10%
2,100	4,200	K£. 210	15
4,200	6,300	525	25
6,300	8,400	1,050	35
8,400		1,785	45

Family relief	K£.132
Single relief	K£. 53
Single person supporting a child	K£. 66
Life insurance relief	10% of the premiums paid to a maximum of K£. 60.

□ Income year 1992:

Taxable Income		Tax on	Percentage
Over	Not Over	Lower Amount	on Excess
K£. 0	K£. 2,300	—	10%
2,300	4,600	K£. 230	15
4,600	6,900	575	25
6,900	9,200	1,150	35
9,200		1,955	45

Family relief	K£.132
Single relief (including married women)	K£. 66
Single person supporting a child	NIL
Life insurance relief	10% of the premiums paid to a maximum of K£.60.

An individual is considered to be resident if he has a permanent home in Kenya and was present in Kenya, even for one day, in any year of income. If he does not have a permanent home in Kenya but was present in Kenya for 183 days or more in any year of income, or an average of 122 days in three years of income, he is also considered a resident. A resident individual is liable to tax on all income from his employment, regardless of where paid or where the services were rendered. Thus, a resident representative of a foreign company, paid in that foreign country, is liable to Kenya tax on his employment income even if his duties cover other countries as well as Kenya.

Special provisions relate to an individual working in the Kenya regional office of a nonresident employer. If certain conditions are satisfied, only two-thirds of the worker's employment income is liable to Kenya tax.

10. Local Income Taxes

None.

11. Capital Gains Taxes

The capital gains tax on transfers of property located in Kenya has been suspended effective June 14, 1985.

12. Foreign Tax Reliefs

The information in item 5 also applies to resident individuals.

13. Tax Period

The tax "year of income" is the calendar year. However, any business income will be based on the financial accounting year of the business ending within the calendar year. Other income, such as dividends, will be that arising during the calendar year. For instance, if an individual has several sources of income, including a business which makes up accounts to June 30 each year, his taxable income for any year of income will be:

☐ Business—taxable profits as disclosed by the accounts to June 30 in that year.
☐ Dividends—amounts received during the year ended December 31.
☐ Rental income—profits arising during the year ended December 31.
☐ Employment—income earned during the year ended December 31.

14. Other Matters

Benefits Included in Taxable Income. Effective January 1, 1991, the taxable annual value of fringe benefits are:

☐ Free car—K£.2,160 to K£.8,640 (depending on the type of vehicle and engine size).

- ☐ Free house servant—K£.900.
- ☐ Free light, water, electricity, and telephone—K£.1,320.
- ☐ Free security personnel and alarm systems—K£.1,860.
- ☐ Free school fees—actual amounts paid.
- ☐ Free housing—15% of employment income (including the above).
- ☐ Free use of furniture—K£.240.

Effective June 13, 1991, the taxable annual value of the benefits are:

- ☐ Free car—K£.2,160 to K£.8,640 (depending on the type of vehicle and engine size).
- ☐ Free use of furniture—K£.240.
- ☐ Free telephone—K£.180.
- ☐ All other benefits—Actual amounts paid.

The following fringe benefits are *not* taxable:

- ☐ Expenditure on passages for an expatriate between Kenya and another country, including leave passages.
- ☐ The value of medical services provided by the employer.
- ☐ Contributions to a pension or registered provident fund made by the employer.

Payment of Tax. Employment income is taxed at source by the deduction of P.A.Y.E. If the individual has income which has not suffered P.A.Y.E., he must file a return within four months of the end of the year of income. When the assessment is raised, the tax is payable within one month of the date of assessment but not earlier than September 30 in the year following the year of income. (See item 7 regarding installment tax.)

INCOME TAXES ON NONRESIDENTS

15. Liability to Tax

In determining its tax liability, a nonresident corporation is defined as other than a resident corporation. A resident corporation is incorporated in Kenya, managed and controlled in Kenya, or declared resident in Kenya by the Minister. A "permanent establishment" is defined as a fixed place of business. It includes a construction site that was in existence for six months or more.

17. Withholding Tax Rates

A nonresident person, including a corporation, not having a permanent establishment in Kenya, is taxable on the following gross amounts of income derived from Kenya at the following rates:

	Management or Professional Fees	Royalties
Nontreaty countries	20%	20%
Treaty countries		
Canada	15	15
Denmark	20	20
Germany	15%	15%
India	17.5	20
Norway	20	20
Sweden	20	20
United Kingdom	12.5	15
Zambia	20	20

The following rates are applicable for payments both to nontreaty and treaty countries:

Rents	30%
Dividends	15
Interest	12.5
Pensions and retirement annuities	5
Appearances as an entertainer, instructor, or athlete	20

If a nonresident petroleum company operates in Kenya through a permanent establishment and incurs management or professional fees outside Kenya, the withholding tax is limited to 12.5% of the gross sum payable. Similarly, where interest is paid which can be fairly and reasonably allocated to the permanent establishment, the withholding tax is limited to 10% of the gross sum payable to the nonresident person.

Other income derived from Kenya by a nonresident corporation would be taxed at 42.5% if collection were possible. The withholding rates, it is emphasized, apply only to income accrued in or derived from Kenya. A nonresident individual who receives the types of income subject to withholding would have the same withholding rates deducted at the source by the payer. As with a company, the tax withheld automatically discharges the tax liability.

19. Tax Treaties

Kenya has tax treaties for the relief from double taxation on income arising in Kenya with Canada, Denmark, Germany, India, Norway, Sweden, the United Kingdom, and Zambia. These treaties may reduce withholding rates (see item 17).

Treaties with Italy and the United States are being negotiated.

OTHER SIGNIFICANT TAXES

21. Sales (Value Added)

A value-added tax (VAT) is payable by resident and nonresident persons on the value of specified goods and services supplied in the course of carrying on a business in Kenya and on goods and services imported into Kenya.

Registered persons can recover the VAT paid on business expenses, including certain capital expenditures but excluding motor vehicle fuels and entertainment. Business with taxable turnover exceeding K£.12,500 per annum are required to register for VAT. Exports of goods and taxable services are zero-rated.

22. Inheritance and Gift Taxes

There is no gift tax as such. Estate duty is not levied on the property of a person who died on or after January 1, 1982.

23. Taxes on Payrolls (Social Security)

Monthly contributions to the National Social Security Fund are required. The rate is 5% of salaries with a maximum of K£.4 per month contributed by both the employer and employee, for a total of K£.8 per month per person.

Subject to certain limitations, contributions by employers and employees to registered pension and provident funds will be allowable deductions against chargeable income. (See Specimen Tax Computation.)

24. Taxes on Natural Resources

The Income Tax (Amendment) Act 1984 introduced new legislation covering the taxation of petroleum companies and service subcontractors. Profits of companies and branches of nonresident companies are taxed at the rates of 40% and 47.5%, respectively. Nonresident petroleum service subcontractors, however, are taxed on "deemed profits" of 15% of the service fees received at the branch rate of 47.5%. Service fees do not include payments for mobilization (or demobilization) and reimbursement of expenses. The petroleum company withholds tax from the payment, which constitutes the service subcontractor's final tax.

The branch rate of tax will be 45% effective January 1, 1992.

25. Other Taxes

Land and Property. No annual value tax is payable to the Government, other than land rent in the case of leasehold property. However, taxes on property values are levied as rates by local authorities. The rates are normally fixed annually. There is no tax on capital or net wealth.

Presumptive Income Tax. A presumptive income tax is deducted from the proceeds of specified agricultural produce payable by an authorized agent to an individual.

The rate of deduction is 5% of the gross amount of payment, and no further tax will be charged on the gains or profits from the sale of that specified produce.

COMPUTATION OF TAXABLE INCOME

26. Capital Gains

See item 3.

27. Depreciation and Depletion

Depreciation provided in the accounts is ignored for tax purposes, and specified capital allowances are granted instead.

Heavy machinery and earth-moving equipment	37.5% (1)
Cars, trucks, and aircraft	25.0% (1)
All other machinery, including ships (2)	12.5% (1) (3)
Industrial buildings	2.5% (4)(5)(6)
Hotels	4.0% (4)(5)
Farming operations	33.33%
Mining operations	40% in the year the expense is incurred and 10% annually for the next six years; 100% in the year the expense is incurred for specified minerals

Notes:

(1) Capital allowances are calculated on a reducing-balance basis (from which sales proceeds and previous allowances were deducted).

(2) An investment allowance of 40% is available on new ships (in addition to any other allowances).

(3) Effective January 1, 1992, computers and peripheral computer hardware, calculators, copies, and duplicating machines will attract a capital allowance of 30% per annum.

(4) Capital allowances are computed on a straight-line basis of original construction cost, which may not be the building's purchase price.

(5) An investment allowance at the rate of 85% if construction occurs outside the municipalities of Nairobi and Mombasa and 35% if construction occurs within the municipalities of Nairobi and Mombasa is also available on new industrial buildings and hotels (and any new machinery installed therein). This allowance is not in addition to other capital allowances. It is deducted in arriving at the capital cost available for calculating other capital allowances.

Effective January 1, 1992, the investment allowance also can be claimed on construction of a building used for manufacture even if the machinery installed in it is not new and on the purchase and installation of machinery even if this is installed in an old building used for manufacture.

(6) If capital expenditure is incurred for the construction of a building and the purchase and installation therein of new machinery and the owner uses both the machinery and the building for the purpose of manufacture under bond, then such person is entitled to an investment deduction on the capital expenditure of 65% (within the municipalities of Nairobi and Mombasa) and 15% (outside the municipalities of Nairobi and Mombasa) if the year of first use is a year of income commencing on or after January 1, 1990. This deduction is in addition to any deduction available under (4) above. Provisions exist whereby, if manufacturing under bond ceases within three years of the expenditure being incurred, the amount of the additional relief will be recaptured.

Effective January 1, 1992, an investment allowance of 100% can be claimed on the construction of a building or on the purchase and installation of machinery by or for an export-processing-zone enterprise within the first 20 years of becoming such an enterprise.

28. Treatment of Dividends

Dividends paid by Kenya companies are liable to tax if:

☐ The recipient resident company controls less than 12.5% of the voting power of the payor.

☐ The dividend forms part of the investment income of the life fund of a resident insurance company.

When taxable, a 15% withholding tax is deducted at source from dividend payments to resident and nonresident persons of Kenya.

Withholding tax at the rate of 15% on taxable dividends paid to residents constitutes final tax liability.

Special provisions relate to profits distributed in a voluntary liquidation, to the issue of debentures or redeemable preference shares at a discount, and to the avoidance of tax by nondistribution of dividends.

29. Loss Carryovers

Income and losses are divided into categories (i.e., rental, employment, and farming), and although losses may be carried forward indefinitely they may only offset future profits from the same category of income.

30. Transactions between Related Parties

Where one related party is resident and the other nonresident, revenue transactions between them may be adjusted for tax purposes to achieve the same results as if the revenue transaction had been carried out by independent persons dealing at arm's length.

Where any asset subject to "wear and tear allowances" (see item 27) is sold from one such party to another, the price may be adjusted to an open market price. If both parties elect, the asset may be transferred for tax purposes at the tax written-down value.

31. Consolidation of Income

There are no provisions for consolidating the results of related corporations, and no subvention payments are allowed.

32. Tax Periods

The term "year of income" is a calendar year. Business income will be based on the accounts year ended within the year of income. There is no preceding year basis. Individuals and companies are alike in this respect.

RELATED CONSIDERATIONS

34. Incentives and Grants

Exporters of goods originating in Kenya are entitled to an export compensation payment based on the FOB value of certain specified goods. Export processing zones (EPZs) were established effective June 7, 1990. Investors in EPZs will be offered a competitive package of incentives. Other investment allowances are discussed in item 27.

35. Exchange Controls

Extensive rules and regulations are in force under authority of the Exchange Control Act. Persons resident in Kenya may not transfer funds outside Kenya without Central Bank permission. In broad outline, the following paragraph applies but, as regulations change constantly, prior advice is necessary.

Imports may be paid in foreign currency on production of specified documents. Profits, other than capital profits, may be remitted subject to approval and availability of foreign exchange. Individual savings of "expatriates" may be remitted subject to certain limits. Protection may be sought for foreign investment under the Foreign Investments Protection Act. This gives protection for repatriation of both profits and capital. Severe restrictions on local borrowing by a company are imposed if any of the shareholders are nonresident, but the Central Bank now permits foreign investors to borrow from local banks to cover the cost of import duties on capital equipment.

Exchange control approval is required for the purchase of airline tickets if payment is to be made in Kenya currency. A fee of 10% of the ticket cost is payable to the Central Bank.

SELECTION OF BUSINESS ENTITY BY NONRESIDENTS

The advantages of operating as a branch are: registration is easily and cheaply accomplished, a proportion of the head office expenses may be claimed by agreement with the Tax Department, no audit is required by law and the scope of any audit required for the parent company can be agreed on, the filing requirements for the Registrar of Companies are minor although the accounts of the company as a whole may have to be filed, and offshore funds earned by the branch but received by the nonresident company may be retained abroad. The disadvantages are that no deductions are allowed for payments by the branch to its parent for management fees, royalties, interest, or foreign exchange differences and that a higher rate of income tax applies (see item 4). Only if most of a company's profits were to be declared as dividends would the company tax rate be higher [(40% + (60% × 15%)) = 49%].

The advantages of operating as a company include its lower rate of tax (assuming minor dividend distributions), its limited liability, the possibility of attracting local participation in its share capital, and the ability to charge management fees, royalties, interest, and foreign exchange differences (although subject to exchange control approval to remit these payments). The disadvantages include that a company is more costly to incorporate and operate, a company secretary must file the necessary returns to the Registrar of Companies, a full audit is required, head office expenses cannot be charged, and any earned offshore income must be remitted to Kenya.

SPECIMEN TAX COMPUTATION

Information:

☐ The company is resident in Kenya and its year-end is June 30, 199X.
☐ The company's operating profit for the year consists of:

	K£.
Trading results in Kenya	300,000
Trading results of a Tanzanian branch	40,000
Dividends from a wholly owned subsidiary	100,000

Dividends from investments (share holdings are less than 12.5%)	30,000
Overseas dividend income (net of overseas tax)	10,000
	480,000

☐ The operating profit is after the following charges:

Depreciation	50,000
Pension contributions to non-registered fund (1)	10,000

☐ Movement on fixed assets:

Tax written down value of plant brought forward from previous year	500,000
Additions during the year	50,000
Sales proceeds of plant	10,000

☐ The following tax has been deducted at source:

Withholding tax on investment dividends (15% of K£.30,000)	4,500

Computation:

	K£.	K£.
Profit per accounts		480,000
Dividends from subsidiary	100,000	
Overseas dividend income	10,000	
Depreciation		50,000
Pension contributions		10,000
Capital allowance (2)	67,500	
Tanzania tax paid (55% × K£.40,000)	22,000	
Adjusted tax business profit	340,500	
	540,000	540,000
Tax thereon (£340,500 at 40%)		136,200
Less tax suffered at source (on dividends)		4,500
Tax liability		131,700

Notes:
(1) The following maximum contributions to *registered* funds are tax deductible.

□ Pension funds:
  From January 1, 1991: employees K£.480, employers K£.480
  From January 1, 1992: employees K£.528, employers K£.528
□ Provident Funds:
  From January 1, 1991: employees K£.120, employers K£.120
  From January 1, 1992: employees K£.528, employers K£.528

(2) The capital allowance for "wear and tear" is calculated as follows:

Written down value brought forward	K£.500,000
Additions	50,000
Sale proceeds	(10,000)
	540,000
12.5% wear and tear deduction	(67,500)
W.D.V. carried forward to next year	K£.472,500

KOREA
REPUBLIC OF

INCOME TAXES ON CORPORATIONS

1. Rates

Tax Base	Tax Rate
W100,000,000 or less	20%
Over W100,000,000	W20,000,000 + 34% of the tax base in excess of W100,000,000

The previous tax rates that varied depending on the type of corporation (such as general corporations, including listed corporation, unlisted large-scale corporations, and nonprofit domestic corporation) were abolished by the 1990 tax revision.

The above, single tax rate is applied to all types of corporations. In addition, the defense surtax, which had been levied on the corporation tax under the previous law, was repealed effective January 1, 1991.

2. Local Income Taxes

A 7.5% resident surtax is levied by local governments on the corporation tax.

3. Capital Gains Taxes

Capital gains and losses are treated in the same manner as ordinary income and loss, except that gains from the sale of land, buildings, or real estate rights, stocks, or investment shares are subject to an additional special surtax (see item 26):

	Surtax Rate (before resident taxes)
If the acquisition of the property was registered with the Court	25%
If the acquisition of the property was not registered with the Court	40%

4. Branch Profits Taxes

A branch of a foreign corporation is subject to corporation taxes on its income generated from Korean sources at the same rates as Korean corporations. Allocation of expenses from the head office may or may not be allowed as deductible expenses of the branch, depending on the reasonableness of the charges and the provisions of tax treaties.

However, a foreign corporation carrying on its business through a branch in Korea is not required to pay taxes on the repatriation of after-tax income.

5. Foreign Tax Reliefs

A tax credit is allowed to the extent of foreign taxes paid on the foreign-source income. The credit, however, cannot exceed the amount of Korean taxes attributable to the foreign-source income.

If a resident or a domestic corporation receives foreign-source income, the taxpayer can elect either of the following methods. A different method can be elected each tax year.

☐ Method of deducting total amount of foreign taxes paid from gross income when calculating the income amount for the respective tax year.
☐ Method of crediting foreign taxes paid.

If the income from foreign sources of a resident or a domestic corporation is exempted from income tax by the provision of laws in a foreign country with which Korea has concluded a tax treaty, the exempted tax amount shall be deemed to have been actually paid to the foreign country and, thus, shall be eligible for the above election, subject to the provision of the tax treaty.

6. Classification of Corporations

Corporations are classified for Korean tax purposes primarily as domestic or foreign. A domestic corporation is one whose head office or main office is in Korea. Domestic corporations are taxed on their worldwide income, whereas foreign corporations are subject to tax only on Korean-source income.

A foreign corporation, which has a fixed place of business (permanent establishment) in Korea, is subject to tax on its Korean-source income attributable to the permanent establishment, applying the same tax rates and the same taxation method as a domestic corporation. On the other hand, a foreign corporation without a permanent establishment in Korea or one without Korean-source income attributable to its permanent establishment in Korea, is subject only to stipulated withholding taxes on its Korean-source income.

A permanent establishment includes, but is not limited to, a branch, subbranch, store and any other fixed sales place, workshop, factory, warehouse, site of construction or installation or assembly, or place for furnishing the directions or supervision or engineering services of such works, and any mine or quarry or place for prospecting and gathering natural resources and any other resources.

7. Payment of Taxes

In general, corporations are required to pay tax when filing their tax returns. Corporations whose fiscal periods exceed six months are required to pay an interim tax for the first six-month period no later than 30 days after the end of that period, and the tax is based on either 50% of the prior year's tax or the actual operating results for the six-month period. The taxpayer can elect either of these interim payment calculation methods unless no taxes were due in the previous year, in which case the actual operating results method must be used.

8. Other Matters

Revision of Tax Returns. Revised corporation tax returns may be filed within six months after the due dates for the return. However, revisions requiring entries in the books of account are not allowed.

Determination of Assessments. Corporate tax returns are not necessarily subject to examination by the tax authorities to determine the final tax assessment. The corporation's income tax liability will be accepted as filed unless the tax authorities deem an examination necessary.

Accumulated Earnings Tax. An unlisted large-scale corporation or an unlisted domestic corporation belonging to a large-scale conglomerate (excluding non-profit corporations) that has accumulated distributable income in excess of a prescribed level is subject to an accumulated earnings tax at the rate of 25% on such excess. In this case, an unlisted large-scale corporation is defined as an unlisted domestic company having paid-in capital in excess of five billion Won or equity (including retained earnings but excluding net income or loss) of over ten billion Won.

INCOME TAXES ON INDIVIDUALS

9. Rates

The taxes on an individual's taxable income (computed after deducting the individual's personal and other basic deductions) are as follows (all amounts are in thousand won):

Tax Base		Tax on	Percentage
Over	Not Over	Lower Amount	on Excess
W 0	W 4,000	—	5%
4,000	10,000	W 200	16
10,000	25,000	1,160	27
25,000	50,000	5,210	38
50,000		14,710	50

Expatriates employed in Korea may exclude overseas service allowances (e.g., cost-of-living allowance, hardship differential, education allowance, and tax reimbursement) within the limit of 20% of the expatriate's base salary. However, if the amount of the overseas service allowance is unidentifiable, $^{20}\!/_{120}$ of total salary, including the taxable allowance, may be deductible as an overseas service allowance.

	Annual Deduction
Basic deduction	W480,000
Spousal deduction	W540,000
Dependents deduction	W480,000 each (generally up to two dependents)
Deduction for a handicapped person	W480,000 each
Deduction for age 65 or older	W480,000 each
Deduction for a female household	W540,000
Wage and salary deduction	100% of the first W2,300,000 of wage and salary income plus 30% of the excess over W2,300,000, not to exceed a deduction of W4,900,000.

Also, for a resident who has earned wage and salary income not exceeding W36,000,000 a year, a wage and salary income tax credit of 20% of the income tax for the year is available up to a maximum of W500,000.

Individuals who receive their compensation in foreign currency from sources outside Korea are entitled to a 20% tax credit for such compensation voluntarily declared and subjected to monthly withholding through a taxpayers' association. However, the 20% tax credit may be granted only if the compensation in foreign currency from sources outside Korea is not included in the deductible expenses in computing the taxable income of a foreign corporation's permanent establishment in Korea to which the individual receiving such compensation is employed.

10. Local Income Taxes

A 7.5% resident surtax is levied by local governments on the income tax.

11. Capital Gains Taxes

Gain from the sale of land, buildings, real estate rights, or unlisted stocks is taxed separately on the basis of a special capital gains tax as follows (also see item 26):

	Capital Gains Tax Rate (before resident taxes)
Registered acquisitions	
Real estate held for more than two years	
—Small houses	30%

	Capital Gains Tax Rate (before resident taxes)
—Others	40%–60% (progressive)
Real estate held for less than two years	60
Nonregistered acquisitions	75
Unlisted stocks	20

12. Foreign Tax Reliefs

See item 5.

13. Tax Period

An individual must use the calendar year as the tax period.

14. Other Matters

Limitation on Tax. Certain dividend and interest income is not included in the individual income tax base, but is subject to withholding tax, which represents the final tax on that income. The rate of withholding of income tax and surcharges is limited to approximately 21.5% in the following cases:

☐ On dividends received from a listed company by a minority shareholder (i.e., a shareholder who owns less than 1% of the total issued shares or W100 million par value of shares, whichever is the lower).

☐ On interest received from commercial banks and/or short-term finance companies.

INCOME TAXES ON NONRESIDENTS

15. Liability to Tax

A nonresident having no permanent establishment in Korea is subject to tax only on Korean-source income. The tax is collected through withholding. However, a nonresident having a permanent establishment in Korea is subject to tax on its Korean-source income in the same manner as a resident.

17. Withholding Tax Rates

The normal withholding tax rates on the Korean-source income of nonresidents are as follows:

Korean-source Income	Withholding Tax
Gross revenue from business	2%
Compensation for personal services	20%

Korean-source Income	Withholding Tax
Gain from sale of stock in Korean corporations	10% of the sales price or 25% of the difference between the sales price and the seller's original cost, whichever is less
Dividend, interest, and royalties	25%

In addition, the 7.5% resident surtax is assessed on these withholding taxes. For residents of countries with which Korea has a tax treaty there are various limitations on these withholding taxes. For dividends, interest, and royalties the withholding tax rates are limited as follows:

	Withholding Rates on Outward Remittances		
	Dividends	Interest	Royalties
Australia	15%	15%	15%
Austria	10/15	10	10
Bangladesh	10/15	10	10
Belgium	15	15	10/15
Canada	15	15	15
Denmark	15	15	10/15
Finland	10/15	10	10
France	10/15	15	10/15
Hungary	5/10	0	0
India	15/20	10/15	15
Indonesia	10/15	10	15
Japan	12	12	12
Luxembourg	10/15	10	10/15
Malaysia	10/15	15	10/15
Netherlands	10/15	10/15	10/15
New Zealand	15	10	10
Norway	15	15	10/15
Pakistan	10/12.5	12.5	10
Philippines	10/15	10/15	15
Singapore	10/15	10	15
Sri Lanka	10/15	10	10
Sweden	10/15	10/15	10/15
Switzerland	10/15	10	10
Thailand	10/20	10	15
Tunisia	15	12	15
Turkey	15/20	10/15	10

Withholding Rates on Outward Remittances

	Dividends	Interest	Royalties
United Kingdom	10%/15%	10%/15%	10%/15%
United States	10/15	12	10/15
West Germany	10/15	10/15	10/15

OTHER SIGNIFICANT TAXES

21. Sales (Value Added)

VAT is computed without determining value added, but by applying the rate, 10%, to outputs (sales) and crediting against this amount any tax paid on inputs (purchases). Certain goods and services prescribed by the law are exempted from VAT; therefore, corporations dealing in those goods and services are treated as if they were ultimate consumers. A zero tax rate applies to exports and certain other goods and services that earn foreign currency. A corporation that exports its whole product will obtain refunds of the tax paid on its purchases. In the situation where both exemption and zero rating are applicable, the zero tax rate can be applied by giving up VAT exemption status.

22. Inheritance and Gift Taxes

Inheritance and gift taxes are levied on all property, wherever located, when the beneficiary is domiciled in Korea. When domiciled outside Korea, these taxes are applied only to property located in Korea.

The inheritance tax rates are:

Tax Base		Tax on Lower Amount	Percentage on Excess
Over	Not Over		
W 0	W 20,000,000	—	10%
20,000,000	200,000,000	W 2,000,000	20
200,000,000	500,000,000	38,000,000	30
500,000,000	1,000,000,000	128,000,000	40
1,000,000,000		328,000,000	55

The gift tax rates are as follows:

Tax Base		Tax on Lower	Percentage
Over	Not Over	Amount	on Excess
W 0	W 10,000,000	—	15%
10,000,000	90,000,000	W 1,500,000	25
90,000,000	250,000,000	21,500,000	35
250,000,000	500,000,000	77,500,000	45
500,000,000		190,000,000	60

25. Other Taxes

Special Consumption Tax. Certain commodities are subject to a special consumption tax as follows:

	Rate
Gasoline	100%
Vehicles (by size)	10% to 25%
Television sets color (by size)	15% to 20%
Refrigerators (by size)	15% to 20%
Other	10% to 100%

Property Tax. Annual property taxes at rates between 0.3% and 10% are levied by the local authorities. Property tax rates on new factories or expansions of existing factories in the "major cities" are five times the normal rate.

Limit of Housing Land Ownership (LHLO). A person possessing a housing lot exceeding a limit prescribed by law for each region is subject to a charge at rates ranging from 4% to 11% on the value of the land in excess of the limit, depending on the period of possession.

Aggregate Land Tax (ALT). The ALT, newly enacted to replace the existing property tax on land and the excess land ownership tax, is intended to discourage speculative investment in land in a more efficient and positive manner. A registered owner as of the date of assessment (June 1 of each year) is liable to pay ALT at rates between 0.2% and 5%, depending on the category of land.

Tax on Excessive Increased Value of Land (TIVL). The TIVL is imposed on the value of idle land that increased in value during a tax period in excess of the normal increased value.

Government Redemption of Profit Earned Privately from Land Development Project. A person who has carried out a land development project, obtained from the Government, that excessively exceeds the normal rate of increased land value is subject to an assessment equivalent to 50% of the excessively increased value.

Assets Revaluation Tax. Tangible fixed assets directly used for operating purposes, except land, may be revalued. Such increase of asset bases is subject to a 3% asset revaluation tax (see item 33).

Defense Tax. The defense tax was repealed effective December 31, 1990.

Minimum Tax System. Under the former tax laws, a taxpayer must have paid at least the defense surtax at a rate ranging from 6 to 12% of the tax base, even if wholly exempt from the corporate or individual income tax. However, since the defense surtax was repealed effective January 1, 1991, a taxpayer granted an income tax exemption may bear no tax burden. This is against the spirit of tax equality and may adversely affect the Government's tax revenue. In order to solve this problem, the Government introduced a minimum tax system, while repealing the previous general tax privilege ceiling system.

Before Reform (Ceiling)	After Reform (Minimum Tax)
The tax incentives granted under the former Tax Exemption and Reduction Control Law should be available within the limits listed below. — Deduction of special depreciation or reserve: 50% of taxable income before deducting these items. — Income deduction: 50% of taxable income before this income deduction. — Tax credit: 30% of tax amount before credit	Minimum tax will be imposed. — Corporate income tax: 12% of tax base before deduction of tax preferential items or the tax amount reflecting such items, whichever is larger. — Individual income tax: 30% of tax base before considering tax preferential items or the tax amount reflecting such items, whichever is larger. — Capital gains tax: The exemption and reduction of capital gains tax per person for the year shall not exceed W300,000,000.

Acquisition Tax. A 2% acquisition tax is levied primarily on the acquisition of property such as land, buildings, motor vehicles, ships, heavy equipment, forests, and membership in a golf club or condominium. However, a 10% acquisition tax is levied on the acquisition of such properties when used for the construction of plant facilities in "major cities." A 15% acquisition tax is levied on golf courses, residences, motor vehicles or ships of a high standard, and land owned by a corporation but not used for business purposes.

Business Place Tax. Business entities with over 50 permanent employees are subject to a tax of 0.5% of monthly employee compensation.

Registration Tax. A 0.1% to 5% registration tax is levied on the public registration of an acquisition, transfer, change, or abolition of title to property and other rights, or the public registration of an incorporation and a capital increase of a company. However, in case of a company located in "major cities," the registration tax rates for the acquisition of land and buildings, the incorporation, and the capital increase will be five times the normal rates.

Education Tax. Effective January 1, 1991, an education tax is levied as follows:

Tax Basis	Rate
Liquor tax	10.0%
Revenue of banks, banking corporations, and insurance companies	0.5
Special excise and automobile taxes	30.0
Property, registration, aggregate land, and horse taxes	20.0

COMPUTATION OF TAXABLE INCOME

26. Capital Gains

Taxable gain, for special surtax purposes, from the sale of land, buildings, real estate rights, stocks, or investment shares is determined by deducting the adjusted acquisition cost and any selling costs from the sales proceeds. The acquisition cost is increased by the actual rate of increase in the wholesale price index for each year the asset was owned. For special surtax purposes, past depreciation is not taken into account. If acquisition cost and sales proceeds are not documented, the Government-determined market price at the time of transfer is applied.

27. Depreciation and Depletion

Classes of depreciable assets and their useful lives are described in the tax laws. The straight-line, fixed-percentage-of-declining-balance, or production-output methods can be applied. It is required that a 10% salvage value always remain. Additional depreciation, ranging from 20% to 90% of allowed depreciation, can be deducted in certain situations, such as by exporting industries and for machines used longer than 12 hours per day. When assets are revalued (see item 33), depreciation may be deducted on the increase in value.

28. Treatment of Dividends

A dividend tax credit is not available to corporate shareholders. Individual shareholders are entitled to a tax credit for their dividend income as follows:

Individual income tax amount to be paid = [(income amount other than dividend income + dividend income + (dividend income × 17/99) − various income deductions or personal exemptions) × income tax rate]

− [tax credits other than dividend income tax credit + (dividend income × 17/99)].

29. Loss Carryovers

Operating losses may be carried forward for five years. Loss carryback is not allowed.

30. Transactions between Related Parties

Tax liability is computed by the taxing authority without regard to the actual terms of a transaction between related parties if it is determined that the transaction was made to reduce the tax burden unreasonably.

If the transfer price established between a domestic corporation and its foreign affiliated company is regarded as unreasonably reducing tax liability, the Government may adjust the domestic corporation's taxable income based on an arm's-length price as determined by using one of the methods enumerated below. In this case, the application of the methods should be made in the order listed.

☐ Comparable uncontrolled price method
☐ Resale method
☐ Cost plus method
☐ Other reasonable methods

31. Consolidation of Income

Consolidation of income for tax purposes by a parent company and its subsidiaries is not allowed.

32. Tax Periods

A corporation may use its fiscal period as its tax period provided the fiscal period does not exceed one year. An individual must use the calendar year.

33. Other Matters

Unsupported and Entertainment Expenses. Expenses that are unsupported (paid in accordance with prescribed policy) are deductible to an annual maximum of 0.05% of revenue plus 1% of paid-in capital. Entertainment expenses, including unsupported expenses, are deductible to an annual limit of W6 million plus 0.1% (0.2% for small and medium companies, 0.05% for transactions with related parties) of revenue plus 2% of paid-in capital. For purposes of this computation, paid-in capital may not exceed W5 billion.

Bad Debts. An entity may deduct a provision for doubtful accounts to the extent of 1% of the eligible accounts receivable outstanding at the fiscal year-end.

Severance Pay. Generally, a provision for severance pay is deductible to the extent of the lower of (a) 10% of total salaries and bonuses paid in each fiscal year, or (b) 50% of the total severance liability accrued at the end of that year minus the provision for severance pay carried over from the previous fiscal year.

Exchange Gains and Losses. Realized exchange gains and losses resulting from actual payment or collection of foreign currency assets and liabilities are chargeable currently. Translation gains and losses from ''short-term'' foreign currency assets or liabilities are chargeable currently. Translation gains and losses from ''long-term'' foreign currency assets or liabilities, which are due more than one year from the fiscal year-end, must be deferred and amortized over the period remaining until their maturity.

Interest Expense. Normal interest expense incurred on bank loans is deductible. However, interest incurred on construction must be capitalized and charged against future income through depreciation of the related asset. In cases where it is not obvious whether the interest expense relates to construction in progress or to normal operations, the interest expense related to construction must be calculated by the following formula:

$$\text{Construction interest} = \text{total interest} \times \frac{\text{construction in progress}}{\text{receivables} + \text{inventory} + \text{construction in progress}}$$

However, the interest for the construction period resulting from this formula cannot exceed the theoretical interest expense obtained by applying the bank overdraft interest rate to the weighted average balance of the construction in progress account.

In any year in which a corporation acquires equity in another corporation, the deductibility of interest on the acquiror's total outstanding indebtedness becomes subject to a limitation, not only in that year but as long as the equity is held. The limitation is computed by a formula that applies when the average balance of the acquiror corporation's outstanding loans is more than two times the total shareholders' equity in that corporation.

Asset Revaluation. As an inflation relief measure, corporations may revalue their tangible fixed assets (except for land) and compute depreciation on the basis of the appraised values. The increase due to revaluation, net of the assets revaluation tax (see item 25), may be transferred to paid-in capital by declaring a stock dividend, which does not constitute taxable income to the shareholder recipient.

RELATED CONSIDERATIONS

34. Incentives and Grants

Income tax on income derived from a business eligible for tax incentives by a foreign-invested enterprise is 100% exempt for the first tax year and the three subsequent years, and is reduced by 50% for a further two years, in reference to the ratio of stock or shares owned by the foreign investor under the Foreign Capital Inducement Law (FCIL). In addition, acquisition tax, property tax, and aggregate land tax is 50% reduced throughout the period for which the income tax is exempt or reduced. Examples of such exempted businesses include those engaged in high technology. In addition, the related dividend income of the foreign investor is 50% exempt from income tax for five years.

A foreign lender's interest income accruing from a public loan may be tax exempt or reduced in accordance with the provisions of the public loan.

Royalties paid under a technical inducement agreement accepted by the Government in accordance with the FCIL may be exempt from income taxes for five years from the date of acceptance if an application for the tax exemption is approved by the MOF, given that the technology induced under the agreement is one of the high technologies as designated by the Government.

Furthermore, the compensation received by a foreigner working in Korea under such a technology inducement agreement is exempt from income taxes for five years from the date of acceptance. Under the Tax Exemption and Reduction Control Law (TERCL), the compensation of eligible foreign technicians employed by domestic entities in specified businesses is also exempt from income tax for five years from the date of their entrance into Korea.

Various tax incentives are granted under TERCL. Some of the examples are:

A resident or a domestic corporation (including a foreign-invested enterprise) investing in productivity-promotion facilities, energy-saving facilities, antipollution facilities, industrial-hazard-prevention facilities, etc., or investing in business assets to operate a new business using such new technology as prescribed by Presidential Decree, may enjoy one of the following tax incentives under the TERCL:

☐ Tax credit of an amount equivalent to 3%–5% (10%–15% in the case of investment using domestically produced materials) of the amount invested in the business year in which the investment is complete.

☐ Income deduction of an amount equivalent to 30% (50% in the case of investments using domestically produced materials) of the value of business assets is deducted in calculating the income amount for the business year in which the business assets are acquired.

A resident or a domestic corporation engaging in a business earning foreign currency may set aside reserves for export losses within the limit of an amount equivalent to 1% of foreign currency revenue from export business or tourist industry for the concerned business year or 50% of the income thereof, whichever is lower. The amount so reserved shall be added back to the gains in three annual installments beginning from the second year after the year in which the reserves were set aside to the extent that the reserves were not offset against actual export losses incurred.

If a domestic enterprise (including a foreign-invested enterprise) qualifies as a Newly Organized Small-Medium Enterprise (NOSME), then the income tax and resident surtax on its taxable income will be exempt for the period of the first four years and will be reduced by 50% for the subsequent two years. In addition to this, various reductions of local taxes such as the acquisition tax, registration tax, and property tax are also granted to a NOSME. In this case, the NOSME means a newly organized enterprise whose objective is to engage in a manufacturing or mining project in an Agricultural or Fishery Area as designated by the Government or whose objective is to carry on a technology-intensive manufacturing or mining project. To qualify for the Small-Medium Enterprise, the number of employees of the concerned enterprise should be no more than 300, and the total assets of the enterprise should not exceed a certain limit, ranging between 8 and 30 billion Korean Won depending on the industrial sector.

35. Exchange Controls

Virtually all transactions between residents of Korea and nonresidents, and transactions by residents involving foreign currency or assets situated outside Korea, require the approval of the Bank of Korea or foreign exchange banks. Approval is based on policy guidelines laid down from time to time by the Government. It is important to note that Government policy in this area is constantly changing, and therefore investors should obtain detailed advice prior to entering into transactions that may involve Korea's exchange control rules.

A branch in Korea of a foreign enterprise is required to register with the Bank of Korea and to report to the Bank of Korea on the funds received from its overseas parent. Overseas remittance of operating income is possible without the Bank of Korea's approval if it is confirmed by the head of the designated foreign exchange bank.

36. Investment Restrictions on Nonresidents

Shares in domestic corporations may not be owned by a nonresident, except with Government approval.

SELECTION OF BUSINESS ENTITY BY NONRESIDENTS

Foreign investors can operate in Korea through a branch or by establishing a local subsidiary or joint venture corporation. Establishment of a branch in Korea requires the approval of the Bank of Korea. Applications for investment for establishing a local subsidiary or joint venture corporation will be reported to and accepted by the Bank of Korea without requiring further review by the Minister of Finance or other ministers if all of the following conditions are met:

☐ The industry is not on the list of industries specifically restricted or prohibited (negative list).

☐ The foreign ownership is not limited by other laws excepting the Foreign Exchange Control Law or the Securities Exchange Law.

☐ The industry does not fall under the categories of the industries inherent to small- or medium-sized enterprises designated by the Government.

☐ The industry does not fall under the categories of the designated industrial systematization industries prescribed by the Small- and Medium-Sized Enterprise Adjustment Law.

☐ In case of investing in a manufacturing industry in which the foreign ownership is restricted by the Ministry of Finance, the foreign ownership shall not exceed the restricted level.

☐ The industry does not fall under the categories of the nonmanufacturing industries, such as the service industry announced by the Minister of Finance.

☐ The foreign investor has not violated labor laws.

All other investment applications will be submitted to the Minister of Finance for approval and subject to individual review and consultation with other relevant ministers or the Foreign Capital Inducement Deliberation Committee, as appropriate.

Government policy regarding foreign investment is constantly changing in the direction of liberalization, but the considerations in general are related to the improvement of Korea's international balance of payments, advancement of domestic technology, and protection of domestic industry.

SPECIMEN TAX COMPUTATION

Information:

☐ The specimen tax computation compares the tax consequences of a foreign corporation operating in Korea through: (1) a Korean subsidiary corporation which is exempt from tax for three years under the FCIL; (2) a Korean subsidiary corporation or a Korean joint venture; and (3) a Korean branch.

Computation:

	Cases		
	1	**2**	**3**
Profits before corporation taxes	W200,000,000	W200,000,000	W200,000,000
Corporation tax (1)	0	54,000,000	54,000,000
Resident tax	0	4,050,000	4,050,000
Profit after taxes	W200,000,000	W141,950,000	W141,950,000
Dividend (2)	200,000,000	141,950,000	0
Korean withholding tax (3)	0	38,149,000	0
Net proceeds after tax	W200,000,000	W103,801,000	W141,950,000

Notes:

(1) (W100,000,000 × 20%) plus (W100,000,000 × 34%).

(2) Assuming no compulsory or optional reserves.

(3) The withholding tax rate is 26.875% (25% of corporation tax plus 7.5% resident surtax). Many treaties, however, provide for withholding rates as low as 10%.

Information:

☐ Assumptions for an individual:
   —Expatriate deemed to be resident in Korea.
   —Married with one child.

Computation:

Base salary		W20,000,000
Overseas service allowances		7,000,000
Gross income		27,000,000
Less		
Overseas allowances exclusion		
(⅙ of W27,000,000)	4,500,000	4,500,000
Adjusted gross income		22,500,000
Less		
Basic deduction	480,000	
Spousal deduction	540,000	
Dependents deduction	480,000	
Wage and salary deduction	4,900,000	6,400,000
Taxable income		W16,100,000
Income tax (1)		2,307,000
Resident surtax (7.5% of income tax)		173,025
Total tax (2)		W2,480,025

Notes:

(1) W1,160,000 plus (W6,100,000 × 27%) less earned income credit of W500,000.

(2) If the individual elects to pay taxes through a licensed taxpayers' association on a monthly basis, the amount of income tax payable would be reduced by a credit equal to 20% of the tax payable.

KUWAIT

Editor's Note: This summary contains information available as of the spring of 1991, based (unless otherwise stated) primarily on Kuwait law and practices prior to the invasion of August 1990. Although every effort has been made to recognize the effects of the invasion and the war that followed, it should be noted that the state of business affairs in Kuwait will remain subject to substantial change during the period of martial law and thereafter. Action should not be taken based on the information in this summary without professional advice on recent changes and developments.

INCOME TAXES ON CORPORATIONS

1. Rates

Income tax was imposed by Law No. 3 of 1955, which has seen little amendment since enactment but has been subject to a series of interpretations and amplifications by the Minister of Finance and Economy, who is the Director of Income Taxes. In 1989–1990, a new draft law codifying and amending income tax practices was under discussion. This process was interupted by the August 1990 invasion. For the time being, it must be assumed that the original law and its subsequent amendments and interpretations remain in force.

There is no tax liability on 100% Kuwaiti-owned businesses in Kuwait. Only the profits and capital gains of foreign "corporate bodies" conducting business and trade in Kuwait, directly or through an agent, or carrying on a business or trade in Kuwait as an agent of others are liable to income tax (see item 15).

INCOME TAXES ON INDIVIDUALS

9. Rates

There is no tax liability on individuals.

INCOME TAXES ON NONRESIDENTS

15. Liability to Tax

Only the profits and capital gains of foreign corporate bodies ("taxpayer") conducting business and trade in Kuwait, directly or through an agent, or carrying on a business or trade in Kuwait as an agent of others are liable to income tax.

A corporate body is defined as an association that has a legal existence completely separate from that of its constituent members and registered as such under the jurisdiction of any country in the world. Foreign partnerships, such as firms of lawyers or engineering or management consultants, fall within this definition even if they are not recognized as having a separate legal personality in their own countries.

Conducting a trade or business is defined to include:

☐ Purchases and sales in Kuwait *and* keeping a permanent place of business in Kuwait in which place contracts for such purchases and sales are executed (it does not include the mere purchase of properties, goods, or services in Kuwait);

☐ The operation of any industrial and commercial project in Kuwait;

☐ The rental of properties in Kuwait;

☐ The provision of services in Kuwait.

For this purpose, Kuwait does not include the Divided Zone between Kuwait and Saudi Arabia, or certain small islands and their territorial waters.

In general, the following types of income are subject to Kuwaiti income tax:

☐ The net profits of a taxpayer operating within or outside Kuwait to the extent that profits are connected with, or related to, operations within Kuwait (profits, in this case, do not include dividends, royalties, interest payments, or branch remittances);

☐ The proportion of the net profit of a Kuwait corporate entity attributable to the taxpayer;

☐ The proportion of the net profit of a Kuwaiti partnership or joint venture attributable to the taxpayer.

In respect of the last two classifications, the taxpayer's profit includes amounts receivable for royalties, management fees, technical services, or interest.

Normally, income arising from activities outside Kuwait are not taxable, provided it is not connected with operations within Kuwait. Supply and installation contracts, however, present a special difficulty. In principle, the taxpayer must account for the full amount received under the contract, including the offshore supply element, unless it is specifically exempted under a double taxation treaty. This difficulty can be overcome by having a separate contract for the supply of goods with no reference linking it to other parts of the main or other pertinent contracts.

In the past, foreign companies could escape tax liability if their interest in a Kuwaiti corporate entity or joint venture was registered in the names of individual nominees. However, it is understood that the tax authorities have moved in the last three to four years to close this loophole.

Deductions. Income tax is imposed on the profit of the business in Kuwait as calculated by the normal commercial criteria, using generally accepted accounting principles including the accrual basis. In calculating profit, the following items can be deducted from income:

☐ All expenses, other than capital, incurred in the conduct of a business or trade, wherever incurred, provided the expenditure is supported by full documentation;

☐ Depreciation on fixed assets at specified rates (see item 27);

☐ Head office overhead at the following rates

—for contractors and consultants working through an agent: 3.5% of revenues less payments to subcontractors,

—for foreign minority shareholders in a Kuwaiti company or foreign partners in a Kuwaiti joint venture: 2% of revenues of the Kuwaiti company or joint venture less payments to subcontractors,

—for insurance companies: 3.5% of net premiums, i.e., gross premiums less reinsurance premiums and related commissions.

☐ Up to 3% of the income as a commission to an agent in Kuwait whatever the amount actually paid.

16. Rates

Income tax in Kuwait is not progressive. Instead, it is levied on the "slap" principle, which means that the whole amount of profit is taxed at the highest rate. There is some marginal relief on movement into a new tax band.

Taxable Profit		Rate	Marginal Relief
Over	Not Over	of Tax	Ceases at
KD 0	KD 5,250	0%	KD 0
5,250	18,750	5	5,526
18,750	37,500	10	19,780
37,500	56,250	15	39,765
56,250	75,000	20	59,765
75,000	112,500	25	80,000
112,500	150,000	30	120,535
150,000	225,000	35	161,538
225,000	300,000	40	243,750
300,000	375,000	45	327,272
375,000		53	458,333

Tax is calculated as the lower of (1) the full taxable profit at the highest applicable tax rate, or (2) the profit up to the upper limit of the previous tax band at the rate applicable to that band *plus* the excess of profit over that upper limit. For example:

	Taxpayer A	Taxpayer B
Taxable profit	KD 39,000	KD 50,000
Method 1	KD 39,000 at 15%	KD 50,000 at 15%
	KD 5,850	KD 7,500
Method 2	KD 37,500 at 10%	KD 37,500 at 10%
	KD 3,750	KD 3,750
plus excess profit	1,500	12,500
	KD 5,250	KD 16,250

Therefore, the tax payable for Taxpayer A is KD 5,250 (under Method 2) and for Taxpayer B is KD 7,500 (under Method 1).

19. Tax Treaties

Kuwait has double taxation treaties with Canada, Cyprus, France, Germany, and Italy. It is believed that the United Kingdom and the United States tax authorities would allow a measure of unilateral relief in respect of income tax paid in Kuwait.

20. Other Matters

Accouting Records. The taxpayer must keep in Kuwait certain accounting records, which are subject to inspection by the Tax Department's officials. Accounting records may be in English and may be in a computerized system used to prepare financial statements, provided that the system includes the required records and the Tax Department is first informed.

Tax Returns Records. The tax return should be supported by:

☐ Audited balance sheet and profit and loss account for the period;
☐ Detailed list of fixed assets—additions, disposals, etc.;
☐ List of subcontractors and the latest payments to them;
☐ Copies of current contracts and a statement of income and expenditure on each;
☐ Trial balance forming the basis of the accounts;
☐ Last payment certificate from the client.

OTHER SIGNIFICANT TAXES

25. Other Taxes

Customs Duties. The standard customs duty is 4% on the c.i.f. value of goods. A higher duty, normally 15%, sometimes is imposed to protect local industry.

No liability to income tax arises on foriegners whose activity is confined to exporting goods to Kuwait.

Export Tax. An export tax of 4% is levied on all goods that have not been subject to import duty.

27. Depreciation and Depletion

Depreciation rates are set out in Law No. 3 of 1955 and apply to the original cost of assets, i.e., depreciation is calculated on a straight-line basis. The rates of depreciation are:

Asset	Rate
Such buildings as offices, dwellings, stores, hospitals, clubs	4%
Roads and bridges	4
Tanks, pipelines, jetties, wharfs	5
Office furniture and equipment	15
Plant, machinery, equipment, other than that mentioned below	10
Motorcars and motorcycles	33.33
Trucks and trailers	25
Marine craft	7.5
Airplanes	25
Drilling tools	33.33
Service replacement plant (e.g., construction and road-making equipment, workshops and equipment, handling equipment, and sundry others)	25
Service station buildings and driveways	10
Carts	20
Refining plants, pipelines (within refineries) and small tanks	10

COMPUTATION OF TAXABLE INCOME

32. Tax Periods

Tax is imposed on profits arising in a taxable period, which is defined as the accounting period of the taxpayer and further assumed to be the calendar year. However, the Director of Income Taxes may agree to a written request from the taxpayer to change the year-end to a date other than December 31. Also, at the taxpayer's request, the Director of Income Taxes may agree to prolong the accounting period, provided it does not exceed 18 months.

The taxpayer must submit a tax return, based on the taxpayer's books of account within 3½ months of the end of the taxable period. On application, the Director of Income Taxes can extend the filing period by a maximum of 75 days.

The tax is payable in four equal installments falling on the fifteenth day of the fourth, sixth, and ninth, and twelfth months following the end of the tax period. If an extension is approved by the Director of Taxes, the whole tax is payable on the expiration of the extension. Failure to timely file or pay the tax attracts a penalty of 1% of the tax liability for every 30 days of delay or part thereof.

RELATED CONSIDERATIONS

35. Exchange Controls

Normally there are no foreign exchange regulations in Kuwait other than the prohibition on dealing with Israel and South Africa. For the duration of the emergency period, however, the Kuwait authorities have imposed limits on the amounts of local currency that may be withdrawn from Kuwaiti banks and the amounts that can be remitted abroad each month by residents and nationals. There is reported to be no limit on remittances to settle expenses and operating costs of business entities.

36. Investment Restrictions on Nonresidents

As a general rule, all the capital of a joint stock company must be Kuwaiti owned. Companies other than banks and insurance companies, however, may have up to 49% foreign ownership if there is a need for foreign capital or experience and provided that authorization is obtained from the Ministry of Commerce and Industry.

Kuwaitis are required to constitute at least 25% of the work force, although this requirement may be waived if sufficient numbers of qualified Kuwaitis are not available.

Commercial Registration. Every enterprise doing business in Kuwait, with the exception of joint ventures, is required to be entered into the Commercial Register at the Ministry of Commerce and Industry. Registration is necessary in each area in which the enterprise has a branch or agency and whenever the enterprise changes its capacity, location, or business. The application for registration must be made within 30 days of establishing the enterprise. For a company or partnership, the application must include details of the paid-up and nominal capital, the members and managers, and the registration numbers of trade marks and patents registered in the company's name.

All commercial, industrial, and trading enterprises must register at the Chamber of Commerce and Industry. Certain businesses are subject to certain additional conditions or requirements to protect general security and public health: companies dealing in foodstuffs must register with the Ministry of Health, and industrial enterprises must register with the Industry Department at the Ministry of Commerce and Industry.

When applying for commercial registration, entities in which a foreign company participates are required to supply the following additional information about the foreign company:

☐ Last two audited balance sheets translated into Arabic;

☐ Memorandum and Articles of Association translated into Arabic.

Industrial enterprises are required to supply the Ministry of Commerce and Industry with their annual accounts, to keep records of goods imported duty-free, and to allow Ministry officials to inspect warehouses to check the latter records.

Real Estate. Foreigners generally are not permitted to own real estate in Kuwait. Leases of real estate, however, may be granted under the Investment Law.

37. Other Matters

Expatriate Employment. Foreigners going to work in Kuwait require an entry visa and work permit prior to arrival in the country. On arrival, the foreigner is required to apply for a residence permit.

Work permits must be obtained for employees, professionals, and non-Kuwaiti members of Kuwaiti companies or partnerships. To apply for a permit to employ a foreigner, the employer must have a need for the employee, and the Ministry of Labor is entitled to carry out an inquiry to ensure that this condition is fulfilled. Permits are issued for renewable two-year periods. Once the permit has been issued, the employer must confirm the employment within one month of the foreigner entering the country, otherwise the Ministry may refuse to issue new work permits for a period of three months.

Expatriate employees may change employers provided their first employer agrees and an application of transfer is made to the Ministry. Transfers generally may not be made during the first year of employment.

In general, the issue of work permits for expatriates is limited to the following sectors and types of business:

Contractors carrying out Government contracts	Clubs and associations of public interest
Companies wholly or partially owned by the Government	Airline companies
	Travel and tourism offices
Hospitals and private clinics	New cooperative societies
Hotels	Farms
Private schools	Industrial projects

There are no restrictions on the number of foreign nationals employed by a Kuwaiti business.

LEBANON

INCOME TAXES ON CORPORATIONS

1. Rates

Income taxes in Lebanon are independently applied on the type of profit generated. In general, the following classifications of profit are independently taxed:

- ☐ Real profits.
- ☐ Salaries and wages.
- ☐ Income from moveable assets (e.g., interest income and share dividends).

Rates on Profits. In general, corporations or joint stock companies pay tax on net real profits derived in Lebanon at a flat rate of 26%. Taxes on profits resulting from certain real estate operations are reduced by 50% to a rate of 13%. An additional tax at the rate of 15% is imposed on the regular tax for municipalities. Consequently the overall tax rate on profits is 29.9%.

Holding companies, which are exempt from this tax, pay other specified taxes. Offshore companies are also tax-exempt on profit; they pay a flat tax of LL 10,000 annually (see item 31).

Rates on Dividends. Except for holding companies and offshore companies, distributions of corporate profits are taxed at the flat rate of 12% in all cases even though a corporation may be tax-exempt on real profits. Redistributable dividends received by a parent company are also taxed unless such a company operates under the statutes of a holding company. Additionally, 3% reconstruction tax is imposed thereon if the tax so determined is in excess of LL 1,000. See item 31 for holding companies and offshore companies.

2. Local Income Taxes

None.

3. Capital Gains Taxes

Lebanese income tax law recognizes as capital gains those gains derived from revaluation appreciation or sale of fixed assets and long-term investments. Capital gains in this context include gains from intangible assets (key money and goodwill). Gains derived from appreciation of fixed assets and long-term investments on re-valuation will be tax-exempt if the appreciation value is dealt with as memo accounts in the balance sheet, or the appreciation value is utilized to offset losses appearing in the balance sheet to the extent that such gains are used. Otherwise this profit is taxed at 15%, in which case depreciation may be charged and applied on the new revalued amount. Gains derived from partial or total sale of fixed assets and long-term investments are taxed at 15% unless the gains realized are reinvested in total or in part, within a period of two years, for the construction of permanent residential units for the taxpayer's employees.

4. Branch Profits Taxes

Branches of foreign corporations are subject to the standard tax rates under item 1 on profits derived in Lebanon. Such profits are assumed to have been distributed and hence are also subject to the dividend tax. If the entity is a branch of a foreign bank, then 10% of the profits, which are required for the compulsory statutory reserve, are exempt from the distribution or dividends tax.

5. Foreign Tax Reliefs

Lebanese income tax is due on profits derived from activity or effort expended in Lebanon, regardless of the nationality or domicile of the taxpayer. On the other hand, except for income derived from moveable assets (dividends and interest), residents in Lebanon, regardless of nationality, are exempt from Lebanese income tax on profits realized abroad. Besides foreign taxes normally deducted, movable assets income is taxed at 12% plus 3% thereon for reconstruction if the base tax exceeds LL 1,000 per annum.

Tax treaties have been drawn up between Lebanon and France, India, Italy, Japan, Norway, and Pakistan. Treaties with the latter five countries exempt sea and air transport companies from tax. The treaty with France governs the framework of income and inheritance taxes. Generally, double taxation between Lebanon and France is avoided by the application of tax at source for corporeal or specific taxes and on the basis of residence for personal taxes.

6. Classification of Corporations

Special tax laws were recently decreed for holding companies and offshore companies. Otherwise, no distinction is made between resident, nonresident, and private or public corporations. Profits derived in Lebanon by branches of foreign corporations are treated as profits of resident Lebanese corporations for income tax purposes.

7. Payment of Taxes

Corporations are required to pay taxes when filing their tax returns, normally within five months after the standard tax year-end, which has been set at December 31 of each year, except in certain cases where special permits are granted for a different year-end. On examination of the returns, the income tax authorities may discover understatements or overstatements of taxes. Field examinations and assessments may be made within four or five years from the financial year-end.

INCOME TAXES ON INDIVIDUALS

9. Rates

The Lebanese tax system is based on the imposition of graduated taxes on real profits, salaries, and real estate income. Other sources of income, mainly from movable capital (dividends and interest) are taxed at a flat rate. The tax rates on real profits are:

Taxable Income		Tax on	Percentage
Over	Not Over	Lower Amount	on Excess
LL 0	LL 2,250,000	LL 0	6%
2,250,000	3,750,000	135,000	9
3,750,000	5,625,000	270,000	12
5,625,000	7,500,000	495,000	15
7,500,000	11,250,000	776,250	19
11,250,000	15,000,000	1,488,750	23
15,000,000	37,500,000	2,351,250	27
37,500,000	60,000,000	8,426,250	31
60,000,000	82,500,000	15,401,250	35
82,500,000	112,500,000	23,276,250	40
112,500,000	150,000,000	35,276,250	45
150,000,000		52,151,250	50

An additional tax of 15% on the foregoing taxes is imposed for municipalities, and a reconstruction tax of 3% is applied on all taxes if they exceed LL 1,000. Personal exemptions are based on the minimum salary decreed (LL 75,000 for 1991) for the private sector. An additional 50% of this exemption is allowed for a dependent wife and 10% for every legitimate dependent child up to five children.

Tax Rates on Salaries. Salaries and wages are taxed at source and withheld by the employers, institutions, associations, or companies that pay pensions or annuities. Personal exemptions are the same as those for real profits. Those earning wages on a daily basis are exempt from the first LL 2,500 per day. The rates applicable are the following:

| Taxable Income | | Tax on | Percentage |
Over	Not Over	Lower Amount	on Excess
LL 0	LL 450,000	LL 0	2%
450,000	1,200,000	9,000	3
1,200,000	2,250,000	31,500	4
2,250,000	3,600,000	73,500	6
3,600,000	5,250,000	154,500	8
5,250,000	7,200,000	286,500	10
7,200,000	9,450,000	481,500	13
9,450,000	12,150,000	774,000	16
12,150,000	15,300,000	1,206,000	19
15,300,000	19,050,000	1,804,500	22
19,050,000	23,550,000	2,629,500	25
23,550,000	28,000,000	3,754,500	28
28,000,000		5,224,500	32

A surtax of 3% for reconstruction is applied on all taxes that are in excess of LL 1,000. Annual salary returns are filed by employers as follows:

Individuals or partnerships	Before April 1
Corporations	Before June 1

10. Local Income Taxes
None.

11. Capital Gains Taxes
See item 3.

12. Foreign Tax Reliefs
See item 5.

13. Tax Period
December 31 is the standard tax year-end. It is unusual for an individual to obtain permission to adopt a different year-end.

14. Other Matters
Salaries to partners in private partnerships, limited partnerships, or sole proprietorships are treated as shares in profits and hence are not deductible for income tax purposes. Directors' salaries in joint stock companies or corporations are taxed as salaries and are deductible by these entities.

INCOME TAXES ON NONRESIDENTS

15. Liability to Tax

Whether residents or nonresidents are liable to Lebanese tax depends on the place in which effort or activity is expended to generate profits, regardless of the nationality or residence of the taxpayer. Consequently, it is the activity in Lebanon and not the presence of the entity or taxpayer that decides the tax liability. On the other hand, residents in Lebanon are not liable to pay income tax on profits realized abroad except for income derived from moveable assets. Nonresidents, however, whether individuals, companies, or institutions, who have no business registration or address in Lebanon are liable for income tax on taxable remuneration, and on profits, revenues, and proceeds in Lebanon.

17. Withholding Tax Rates

The net taxable amount for nonresident taxpayers is assessed as follows:

- [ ] 50% of the proceeds if such proceeds are in lieu of services rendered.
- [ ] 10% of the proceeds in other cases.

Tax is due on this assessed income at the rate of 15%. Additionally, another 15% thereon for municipality and 3% thereon for reconstruction are levied. These taxes are to be withheld at source and declared (and paid in the case of corporations) on the deadlines set for filing the tax returns.

OTHER SIGNIFICANT TAXES

21. Sales (Value Added)

None.

22. Inheritance and Gift Taxes

Duty is imposed on all real, movable, and fixed assets transferred to third parties, except the state and municipalities, in the way of inheritance, will, or gift or otherwise without compensation. Progressive duties are applied on the real value, varying with the relationship of the beneficiary, with minor exemptions. A fixed amount of LL 5,000 is also imposed on all sums transferred in excess of LL 100,000.

23. Taxes on Payrolls (Social Security)

Three schemes are operational in the Lebanese social security system: family allowance, medical, and end-of-service schemes. The employer contributes for all three schemes with a minor contribution by the employee for the medical scheme as follows:

	Annual Ceiling	Rate	
		Employer	**Employee**
Family allowance	LL 2,700,000*	7.5%	—
Medical	1,800,000	11	2%
End-of-service	Total remuneration	8.5	—

*For family allowance, three times the legal minimum (LL 225,000 per month). For medical scheme, twice the legal minimum (LL 150,000 per month).

Under certain conditions, the employer will have to pay the difference between the actual severance indemnity, based on the last monthly salary multiplied by the number of years of service, and the total contributions made.

24. Taxes on Natural Resources

None.

25. Other Taxes

Built Property Tax. A proportionate flat tax and a graduated tax are imposed on built property. Exemptions generally are allowed for public buildings and nonprofit organizations. The proportionate flat tax is 8% plus 3% for municipalities (total 11%) of gross proceeds. The graduated tax is on net proceeds in excess of LL 350,000 after deducting maintenance costs. Presently, this tax is being revised to cover past and future periods.

Real estate profits of corporations are exempt from the graduated tax and pay the higher of either the proportionate real estate tax or the corporate tax.

Amusement Tax. An amusement tax, payable by the public, is levied on night clubs and theatres, as well as on revenues of beaches, swimming pools, betting institutions, etc. The rates are:

Night clubs (on revenues)	15%
Theatres (on tickets)	17
Beaches (on entrance fees not exceeding LL 10)	10
Beaches (on other entrance fees, subscriptions, chalet, or cabin rentals)	20
Betting institutions (on entrance tickets and bets)	50

Stamp Duty. Stamp duty in Lebanon may be a proportionate duty of 3 per mil, usually applied to documents with specified sums, such as contracts, paid-up capital, and drafts. A fixed stamp duty varies with the type of document and is usually applied to licenses, certificates, applications to public offices, receipts, and invoices.

COMPUTATION OF TAXABLE INCOME

26. Capital Gains

See item 3.

27. Depreciation and Depletion

Plant. Ranges of upper and lower rates of depreciation are laid down by the tax authorities. Any of these rates or ranges may be adopted provided the tax authorities are notified of the rates; otherwise, it will be assumed that the lower rates have been adopted. Depreciation must be calculated on the straight-line method.

Buildings. Similarly, ranges of upper and lower rates of depreciation are laid down for buildings; these depend on the purpose or use of the building.

Intangible Assets. Key money and goodwill are not depreciable, whereas patents and licensing costs may be depreciated over their useful lives.

28. Treatment of Dividends

See items 1 and 4.

29. Loss Carryovers

Normally, real trading losses may be carried forward for three years but may not be carried back.

Losses sustained by taxpayers who are assessed on a lump-sum or estimated basis (see item 33) cannot be carried over. Individuals who own several entities or are partners in more than one partnership may apply their share of real losses from one entity against their share of real profits from another during a given year. Loss balances, if any, may be carried forward for three years. Such losses may not be transferred on the sale of a partnership to new partners or to heirs of deceased partners.

A new law allows losses from 1989 and 1990 to be carried forward for eight years and applied against 100% of the profits of the first four years and 50% of the profits of the remaining four years. The balance of profits earned during the second four years remains subject to current law.

30. Transactions between Related Parties

If local institutions which are either subsidiaries of or control institutions abroad transfer part of their profits by increasing or decreasing sales or purchase prices or by any other means, such transferred profits are added back to the book profits or, alternatively, the profits may be reassessed.

31. Consolidation of Income

Holding companies and offshore companies are exempt from income tax on real profits as well as from tax on distributions of dividends. Holding companies, however, are subject to:

☐ Tax on interest earned from companies operating in Lebanon.

☐ Tax on capital gains on fixed assets and investments in Lebanon (see item 3), but capital gain on foreign fixed assets and investments is not subject to this tax.

☐ A 12% tax on administrative charges billed to subsidiaries and similar services, provided such charges are not in excess of limitations to be set by the Minister of Finance.

☐ A 25% tax on charges for allowing the use of trademarks or other rights to establishments in Lebanon.

☐ An annual tax on capital and reserves of LL 1.5 per mil if such does not exceed 20 million pounds and LL 1 per mil for the portion between 20 and 50 million pounds and LL 0.5 per mil for the portion in excess of 50 million pounds provided that such tax does not exceed LL 100,000.

Offshore companies pay a flat tax of LL 10,000 annually besides capital gains tax on their Lebanese assets. Foreign employees of offshore companies working in Lebanon are allowed exemptions up to 30% of their basic salary. Other corporations that consolidate accounts are exempt from corporate taxes on income already taxed. They are not allowed a credit, however, for dividend taxes on dividends earned.

32. Tax Periods

Generally, December 31 is the mandatory year-end for all taxpayers (both individual and corporate) except where a reasonable cause can be shown for the adoption of an alternative date.

33. Other Matters

Interest Charges.   Interest charged by sole proprietors and partners in partnerships is not deductible from income.

Bad Debts.   Only banks are allowed to set up provisions for bad debts before exhausting all means of collection, provided that approval is obtained from the Control Commission of the Central Bank. Write offs and provisions can be made after exhausting all means of collection for other taxpayers.

Donations and Contributions.   Allowable up to 10% of annual net profits.

Inventory Valuation.   For tax purposes, inventories must be valued at cost.

Taxation on the Basis of Lump-sum Profits. Classified taxpayers, usually individual shopkeepers, artisans, and small traders, are assessed on a lump-sum basis by applying a fixed rate on the income from each trade or industry. Except for these specified trades, taxpayers assessed on a lump-sum basis may elect to be taxed on the basis of real profits. Other taxpayers whose profits are compulsorily assessed on a lump-sum basis are:

☐ Insurance and savings institutions (different rates are applied to insurance categories to determine profits).
☐ Air and sea transport associations that are subject to tax.
☐ Refineries.
☐ Public contractors (to the extent of their collections from government agencies for work performed).

RELATED CONSIDERATIONS

34. Incentives and Grants

Permanent tax exemptions are granted to educational, medical, and other institutions that operate in the public interest. Ten-year tax exemptions are granted to industrial companies offering new products and operating in development areas, to the extent of their investment. Industrial companies that invest a part of their annual profits to buy new equipment or to build employee housing are exempt for up to 50% of their profits for up to four years, provided such exemptions do not exceed the investment. A seven-year tax holiday is granted to specialized intermediate and long-term banks.

35. Exchange Controls

None.

36. Investment Restrictions on Nonresidents

One-third of the capital of corporations whose objectives are public concessions and utilities must have nominal shares in the name of Lebanese shareholders. Other restrictions applying to non-Lebanese, whether individuals or corporations, are in relation to the acquisition of property rights in Lebanon. Special conditions and regulations govern ownership of property by non-Lebanese; these are detailed in a special decree. Newspapers and periodicals are subject to similar restrictions.

SELECTION OF BUSINESS ENTITY BY NONRESIDENTS

Considering that a branch of a foreign corporation is viewed as a resident corporation for tax purposes, the selection of the type of statutory registration becomes an organizational and financial decision. As regards foreign-sourced income, however, a recent decree allows the establishment of offshore companies which are exempt from income tax on profits and only pay a flat tax of LL 10,000 annually.

SPECIMEN TAX COMPUTATION

Information:

□ A corporation's profits for the year is LL 1,000,000 and consists of the following:

	LL '000's
Trading results in Lebanon	500
Dividend income, local	100
Dividend income, overseas	100
Capital gains	200
Interest income, local	50
Interest income, overseas	50
	LL 1,000

□ The Lebanese trading results are arrived at after charging depreciation of LL 200, whereas allowable tax depreciation is LL 100.

□ The company has installed plant during the year at a cost of LL 250,000, which qualifies for investment allowance.

Computation:

Operating profits as per accounts		LL 1,000,000
Add		
Accounts depreciation		200,000
		1,200,000
Less		
Tax depreciation	100,000	
Dividend income, local	100,000	
Dividend income, overseas	100,000	
Capital gains	200,000	
Interest income, local	50,000	
Interest income, overseas	50,000	
Investment allowances	250,000	850,000
Taxable income (real profits)		350,000
Tax (at 26%)		91,000
Municipality tax (15% thereof)		13,650
		104,650

Total real profit tax

Tax on capital gains (at 15%)	30,000	
Reconstruction tax (3% thereof)	900	30,900
Total tax liability		135,550

Notes:
(1) Taxes on dividends to be distributed are calculated at 12% plus 3% thereof for reconstruction if the tax is in excess of LL 1,000.
(2) It is assumed that dividend income (local and overseas) and interest income (local and overseas) are taxed at source at the rate of 12% plus 3% thereof for reconstruction on all taxes in excess of LL 1,000. If such taxes are not deducted at source, as the case may be in relation to foreign-sourced income, then the Lebanese beneficiary will subject the related income to the foregoing rates and duly pay the taxes.
(3) For taxable income of holding companies, see item 31.

LIBERIA

Editor's Note: Note that due to civil unrest, there have been no changes to the tax system.

INCOME TAXES ON CORPORATIONS

1. Rates

Taxable Income		Tax on	Percentage
Over	Not Over	Lower Amount	on Excess
L$ 0	L$ 10,000	—	20%
10,000	50,000	L$ 2,000	30
50,000	100,000	14,000	40
100,000		34,000	50

Corporations whose majority of stock is held by nonresidents of Liberia and which derive their income from sources outside of Liberia are not subject to tax.

2. Local Income Taxes

None.

3. Capital Gains Taxes

Gains or losses derived from dealing in real and/or personal property attributable to ownership, use of, or interest in real or personal property (including securities) are charged to or allowed against corporation income tax.

4. Branch Profits Taxes

A branch of a foreign corporation is taxed on the profits of the branch as though it were a resident corporation, at the rates in item 1.

5. Foreign Tax Reliefs

The Government of Liberia does not have an extensive range of double taxation treaties. A foreign corporation may, however, apply for relief where it can satisfy the Minister of Finance that no relief, or only partial relief, from Liberian tax is available in the country of residence.

6. Classification of Corporations

The distinctions between corporations and between a corporation and a branch are basically not relevant for corporation income tax purposes.

7. Payment of Taxes

Corporations must pay tax in installments on a current basis. Based on income, 40% of the tax liability is payable within seven months after the commencement of the fiscal year, another 40% within one month after the end of the fiscal year and the balance upon filing the corporation income tax return, which is due by the first day of the fourth month after the year-end.

INCOME TAXES ON INDIVIDUALS

9. Rates

Income Tax. The rates of individual income tax on taxable income, computed after deducting the individual's personal and other allowances, are:

Taxable Income		Tax on	Percentage
Over	Not Over	Lower Amount	on Excess
L$ 0	L$ 2,000	—	11%
2,000	3,000	L$ 220	13
3,000	4,000	350	16
4,000	6,500	510	20
6,500	9,000	1,010	24
9,000	14,000	1,610	26
14,000	19,000	2,910	31
19,000	49,000	4,460	36
49,000	74,000	15,260	45
74,000	99,000	26,510	50
99,000		39,010	65

The above rates also apply to partnerships.

Noncash benefits (e.g., the provision by the employer of free housing and utilities) are subject to taxation in the hands of the employee as follows:

□ Employees of a company which has a concession agreement with the Government of Liberia are exempt, except for car benefits that are taxed by adding a notional 10% to the employees' gross taxable salary.

☐ Employees other than those above are taxed on the actual value of all noncash benefits received up to a maximum of 20% of the gross taxable salary. A notional 20% is usually added to the employee's gross taxable salary. The burden of proof that the actual value is less than 20% lies with the taxpayer.

Personal Allowance for Individuals. An individual is allowed a personal allowance of L$83.33 as a deduction from income subject to income tax for each month or part thereof during which such individual is present in Liberia.

National Reconstruction Tax. This flat rate tax, which is in addition to income tax, is levied on the gross salary or earnings of all individuals, excluding the 20% noncash benefits uplift and before any personal or other allowances. The rates which apply to each month's salary or earnings are as follows:

Monthly Earnings		
Over	Not Over	Rates
L$ 0	L$ 200	1.0%
200	500	4.5
500	1,000	7.5
1,000		8.0

Filing and Payment. Amounts deducted for income tax and national reconstruction tax are filed and paid on or before the 15th of the following month.

10. Local Income Taxes

Several counties levy additional payroll taxes, but these are generally not significant when compared to other personal taxes.

11. Capital Gains Taxes

Gains or losses derived from dealing in real and/or personal property attributable to ownership, use of, or interest in real or personal property (including securities) are charged to or allowed against an individual's taxable income for income tax purposes.

12. Foreign Tax Reliefs

The information in item 5 applies.

13. Tax Period

In general, the tax year is the calendar year. However, a taxpayer, with the approval of the Minister of Finance, may use any period of 12 months.

14.   Other Matters

Taxation of Income of Resident Foreign Nationals.   Income of resident foreign nationals that is not derived from Liberia is taxable only at such time as the income is remitted to Liberia.

INCOME TAXES ON NONRESIDENTS

15.   Liability to Tax

Interest, dividends, royalties, rents, compensation, or other fixed or determinable income paid by resident corporations, sole traders, and partnerships to nonresidents are taxable to the extent that such payments constitute gross income in the hands of the nonresident arising, occurring, or derived from the Republic of Liberia.

17.   Withholding Tax Rates

Withholding tax at the following rates is imposed on the payments noted in item 15. In all cases, the payor is deemed to be the withholding agent.

☐   Interest paid to a nonresident bank or other financial institution—15%

☐   Dividends paid by a corporation which is a resident of Liberia to a nonresident corporation or person—15%

☐   All other payments—30%

Nonresident companies, which are registered in Liberia but not doing business in Liberia, need not withhold tax.

The withholding tax should be deducted at source at the time of payment by the withholding agent and filed and paid to the Revenue authorities by the 15th of the following month.

18.   Special Withholding Provisions

The Government of Liberia has not concluded an extensive range of double taxation treaties. Accordingly, the Minister of Finance is authorized to grant appropriate relief from nonresident withholding taxes in those cases where such taxes would impose an inequitable tax burden on the nonresidents.

OTHER SIGNIFICANT TAXES

21.   Sales (Value Added)

A sales tax, the Business Trade Levy, is charged when obtaining an annual license to operate a business in Liberia. The type of business determines the applicable rates (0.5% to 2%). The levy is calculated on the prior year's gross sales and is payable on or before April 1 each year.

22.   Inheritance and Gift Taxes

The value of property acquired by gift, bequest, devise or inheritance is exempt from taxation.

23.   Taxes on Payrolls (Social Security)

An employment injury scheme was introduced in February 1980 to provide medical care and cash benefits for injuries arising out of or in the course of employment. The cost is borne by employers. Monthly payments are set at 1.75% of gross taxable salaries (excluding any taxable non-cash benefits).

A national pension scheme has been established by the National Social Security and Welfare Corporation and goes into effect September 1, 1988. The scheme covers all employers with five or more employees. The rate of contribution is 6% (employer 3%, employee 3%). The contribution for one month should be paid to the National Social Security and Welfare Corporation by the end of the following month. Under certain conditions, contributions by alien employees can be reimbursed upon their leaving Liberia.

24.   Taxes on Natural Resources

Taxes are imposed upon the exploitation of natural resources. The taxes generally depend upon the terms of the concession agreement negotiated with the Government of Liberia but usually take the forms of royalties and stumpage taxes.

25.   Other Taxes

Real Property Tax.   A real property tax is levied on the assessed value of real property (which is not necessarily the fair market value). Rates vary depending on the location and use of the property. The tax is payable on or before July 1st each year.

Realty Lease Tax.   Realty lease tax at the rate of 10% is levied on rentals paid under a lease agreement. The tax is assessed on the lessor, but is frequently passed on to the tenant in lease agreements. The tax is payable on or before the 15th day of the month following that in which the rent is paid.

Capital.   No annual wealth or capital worth taxes are imposed by the Government of Liberia.

COMPUTATION OF TAXABLE INCOME

26.   Capital Gains

Capital gain is measured by the difference between the adjusted cost of the capital asset and its sale proceeds. The principal adjustment to cost is the depreciation previously allowed for income tax purposes.

27. Depreciation and Depletion

Various rates of depreciation are laid down by the taxing authority. Assets costing L$100,000 or more are subject to individual rulings by the income tax division regarding the rate of depreciation.

Where a lease agreement includes an option to extend the lease for a specified number of years at a specified rental, this option period must form part of the period over which the cost of the leasehold may be written off unless the aggregate combined period exceeds 40 years, in which case 40 years is used as the depreciable period.

28. Treatment of Dividends

Dividends are considered to be part of taxable income, and are taxed on the same basis as other taxable income.

29. Loss Carryovers

Losses can be carried forward for a maximum period of five years. There are no carryback provisions.

30. Transactions between Related Parties

Where two enterprises are deemed not to be dealing at "arm's length" and conditions are made or imposed between them in their commercial or financial relations which differ from those which would occur between independent enterprises, then any revenues which the taxing authorities consider would have accrued to one of the enterprises but, by reason of those conditions, have not so accrued, will be included in the profits of that enterprise and taxed accordingly.

31. Consolidation of Income

Liberian corporations are liable to corporation income taxes on their income from all sources. Related corporations are permitted to file consolidated tax returns only if the Minister of Finance permits or requires it.

32. Tax Periods

See item 13.

33. Other Matters

Other Allowances. A deduction is allowed, whether or not paid or received in connection with an activity carried on for gain or profit, for any contribution or gift for public purposes made to the Government of Liberia or a political subdivision thereof or to a charitable, religious or educational organization which has been accredited by the Minister of Finance. However, in no event shall the deduction for contributions or gifts made in a tax year exceed 15% of the taxpayer's taxable income for that year.

RELATED CONSIDERATIONS

34. Incentives and Grants

Exempt Income. In the case of individuals, the following are exempt from taxation: the value of property acquired by gift, bequest, devise or inheritance; and compensation for personal injuries or sickness. In the case of foreign corporations, generally only income derived from or connected with operations carried on in Liberia is taxable.

Special Tax Rates or Concessions. Investors are able to negotiate concession agreements with the Government of Liberia for the exploitation of natural resources. These agreements usually provide tax holiday periods and other favorable tax concessions. Apart from this, there are no special grants or allowances.

35. Exchange Controls

Businesses that export goods for sale out of Liberia are required to surrender 25% of their foreign currency proceeds to the government of Liberia in exchange for Liberian dollars. The regulations covering such transactions are still evolving. It is strongly recommended that up-to-date information is obtained before making any decisions that may be affected by this issue.

36. Investment Restrictions on Nonresidents

Neither nonresidents nor corporations with any nonresident equity ownership may buy any freehold land in Liberia. There are no other apparent restrictions; however, there are possibilities that local equity participation may be required in certain classes of business.

37. Other Matters

Importation of Goods. Goods imported into Liberia are subject to a mandatory preshipment inspection by Societe Generale de Surveillance (supervised by the Ministry of Commerce, Industry, and Transportation) to ensure that quality and quantity conform to contracts and that prices invoiced correspond to the export prices generally prevailing in the country of origin of the goods. A nonrefundable fee of 1.5% of the CIF value of the goods is payable for this inspection.

SELECTION OF BUSINESS ENTITY BY NONRESIDENTS

The circumstances surrounding proposed business ventures usually are unique to each venture, and normally are negotiated on an individual basis covering such matters as exemption from and imposition of special rules for a number of taxes. The existing general practices that might affect the selection of a particular type of entity are largely not in written form. Accordingly, it is useful to consider each investment proposal on its own merits as a separate case.

SPECIMEN TAX COMPUTATION

Information:

□ The company's profits before tax for the financial year-ended December 31, 1989 are L$250,000 after charging/(crediting):

Foreign exchange gains (unrealized)	(L$27,000)
Provision for doubtful debts	L$15,000
Depreciation	L$75,000

The depreciation charge is based on the depreciation rates allowable for tax purposes, which are reasonable estimates of the assets' useful lives and are commonly used for both accounting and tax purposes.

□ The company recorded sales during the year of L$6,250,000, of which L$500,000 represented cash sales and L$750,000 were sales on credit to the Government of Liberia or a division thereof.

Computation:

Profit per financial statements (before tax)	L$250,000
Less	
Foreign exchange gains (not taxable until realized)	(27,000)
Add	
Provision for doubtful debts	15,000
Less	
Allowance for bad debts (1)	(25,000)
Taxable income	L$213,000
Corporate income tax	
First L$10,000 at 20%	L$ 2,000
Next L$40,000 at 30%	12,000
Next L$50,000 at 40%	20,000
Balance of L$113,000 at 50%	56,500
Income tax (2)	L$90,500

Notes:
(1) For purposes of its income tax computation, the company has elected to account for bad debts by creating a general reserve. The reserve is calculated as 0.5%

of total sales excluding sales to the government of Liberia ("GOL") or divisions thereof, associated companies, and cash sales. The net tax balance sheet provision after the write-off of debts considered irrecoverable is restricted to 5% of non-GOL debts at the balance sheet date, and any excess is added back to taxable income. The alternative exists whereby specific debts written off will be allowed; however, the conditions that each write-off must satisfy are onerous, so usually the reserve method is used.

(2) The tax would normally be paid in three installments: two estimated payments of 40% each, seven and 13 months after the previous year-end, and the final 20% based on the actual computation, which is due by the first day of the fourth month following the year-end.

LIBYA

INCOME TAXES ON CORPORATION

1. Rates

The current tax rates on all private and public limited companies, whether resident or nonresident, on their net income derived from their activities in Libya or abroad (as long as the foreign operations are related to the Libyan activities) are as follows:

Net Income		Tax on Lower Amount	Percentage on Excess
Over	Not Over		
L.D. 0	L.D. 10,000	L.D. 0	20%
10,000	30,000	2,000	25
30,000	60,000	7,000	30
60,000	100,000	16,000	40
100,000	150,000	32,000	45
150,000		54,500	60

A deduction of 30% from tax due is allowed to Libyan public companies on the condition that they fulfill their obligations established by the Income Tax Law No. 64 of 1973.

2. Local Income Taxes

None

3. Capital Gain Taxes

There are no capital gain taxes as such. Capital gains are subject to the normal companies tax rates in aggregation with their other operating income.

4. Branch Profits Taxes

A Libyan branch of a foreign corporation is taxed on its income earned in the same manner and at the same tax rates as domestic corporations. A foreign corporation with a branch in Libya is required to pay the company's income tax on its entire income derived from Libyan activities, whether or not the income is earned from sources within or outside Libya.

☐ Foreign corporations or a foreign corporation's branch in Libya is not entitled to the 30% special deduction from tax due, which is usually granted to Libyan corporations.

☐ For foreign corporate branch tax calculation purposes, charges from the head office for general overhead, services, interest, and commission will be considered to the extent deemed necessary by the tax authorities to achieve the branch's purposes.

☐ Tax authorities may estimate net income earned by a foreign corporation as a percentage of the total income of the foreign corporation proportionate to the branch's activities.

☐ Tax authorities may estimate net income of foreign corporations or a branch thereof as a percentage of its gross income (usually 15% of the contract value for construction companies).

☐ General People's Congress Decision Number 5 of 1981 authorizes the General People's Committee to issue decisions to exempt foreign contractors from payment of income tax as well as other taxes. The decision will be issued on justifiable request of the national contracting party.

☐ The income of a foreign corporation's branch arising from telecommunication and transportation activities is subject to tax in Libya.

5. Foreign Tax Reliefs

None

6. Classification of Corporations

Corporations are classified according to the origin of their capital as national, mixed, or foreign. The 30% deduction described in item 1 is available only to a national corporation.

7. Payment of Taxes

The tax year is a calendar year. Income tax is payable by installments, which are due on the tenth day of March, June, September, and December. Failure to pay any installments on or before the due date makes the other installments due too, in addition to the penalties established by the tax law.

8. Other Matters

Income Taxes on Partnerships.   Income taxes on partnership companies are based on the individual partner's share of net income. However, the company is responsible for filing the returns and paying the tax due on the partners' income from its operations.

INCOME TAXES ON INDIVIDUALS

9. Rates

Tax rates on individuals are levied on sources of income and after personal deductions and other allowances as follows.

Real Estate Income. Taxable income is estimated on the basis of gross income less 20% thereof for depreciation and maintenance expenses. The tax rates are as follows:

Taxable Income		Tax Rate
First	L.D. 6,000	15%
Next	4,000	20
Over	10,000	25

Agricultural Income. The tax rate on income from agricultural activities is 5% with an exemption from payment of tax for ten years, starting in 1973.

Commerce, Industry, and Crafts Income. The taxable income arising from these occupations is assessed on the net income from operations after considering some nonallowable expenses. The tax rates are as follows:

Taxable Income		Tax Rate
First	L.D. 4,000	15%
Next	4,000	20
Next	4,000	25
Over	12,000	30

Independent Professions Income. Income from free occupations and fees earned by professional persons are subject to the independent profession income tax. The taxpayer is exempt from tax for the first two years from the beginning of the activities, and the taxpayer's activities abroad shall be accounted for in determining the exemption period. Taxable income is assessed on the result of net operations of the professional, and the tax rates are:

Taxable Income		Tax on	Percentage
Over	Not Over	Lower Amount	on Excess
L.D. 0	L.D. 4,000	L.D. 0	15%
4,000	8,000	600	18
8,000	12,000	1,320	20
12,000	16,000	2,120	25
16,000		3,120	35

Wages and Salaries. The wages and salaries income tax is levied on all income and benefits arising from occupations and services rendered, whether or not the work or service is rendered in Libya or abroad, with certain exemptions. In determining the income of all wages, salaries, allowances, commissions, and benefits, whether cash or in kind, shall be considered as the gross income of the individual. Taxable income is determined after deducting personal allowances and any other justifiable expenses incurred in performing the job or rendering the services. The tax due is deducted at the source of income, and the source is responsible for payment of the tax.

Taxable Income		Tax on Lower Amount	Percentage on Excess
Over	Not Over		
L.D. 0	L.D. 1,800	L.D. 0	8%
1,800	3,000	144	10
3,000	4,800	264	15
4,800	6,600	534	20
6,600	8,400	894	25
8,400		1,344	35

Foreign Income of Residents. All individuals resident in Libya, whether Libyan citizens or noncitizens, are subject to tax on income from foreign sources except for compensation for labor or personal services performed abroad. Foreign-source income of non-Libyan individuals, their spouse, and their children is also exempt from tax if their residency in Libya is required because of a contract with an entity in Libya. This tax is 15% of the individual's taxable income.

Interest on Deposits with Banks. Income consisting of interest on bank deposits or on saving accounts in excess of 5,000 L.D. are subject to a 15% tax, regardless of the duration of the deposit.

10. Local Income Tax

None

11. Capital Gains Tax

None

12. Foreign Tax Reliefs

None

13. Tax Period

Individual taxpayers must file their return on a calendar year basis, except for taxes on wages and salaries that are deducted at source and paid monthly.

INCOME TAXES ON NONRESIDENTS

15. Liability to Tax

A foreign nonresident corporation is subject to Libyan companies' tax on the profit directly or indirectly attributable to its permanent establishment in Libya. An individual will be regarded as a nonresident of Libya and, thus, not liable for personal income tax, only if he can demonstrate that he has not resided in Libya for more than 30 days and his entry visa is for a business visit. However, if his residency is for more than 30 days and his salary is subject to the personal or corporate income tax, then such individual's income will be subject to personal tax as indicated in item 9.

16. Rates

The repatriated profits of a branch of a foreign corporation are subject only to the taxes indicated in item 4 as well as the other taxes generally levied on resident corporations and individuals.

19. Tax Treaties

Libya has tax treaties with India, Italy, Malta, Morocco, Pakistan, and Tunisia. Air and sea transportation companies are exempt from corporate tax on income derived from their business activities.

OTHER SIGNIFICANT TAXES

21. Sales (Value Added)

None

22. Inheritance and Gift Taxes

None

23. Taxes on Payrolls (Social Security)

Employee	3.75%
Employer	11.25%
Total	15.00%

24. Taxes on Natural Resources

A royalty of 16.667% is imposed on petroleum production, which is generally deductible as an expense. A petroleum profit tax of 65% is imposed on companies engaged in the search for, or the extraction and transportation of, petroleum oil or gas. A petroleum company first becomes liable to the petroleum profit tax when it makes its first bulk sale of crude oil or natural gas.

25. Other Taxes

Stamp Duty. This tax is imposed at varying rates on certain documents and transactions as specified in the Stamp Duty Law No. 65 of 1973. The main stamp duties may be categorized as follows:

	Rate
Bills and promissory notes	0.002%
Shares and bonds	0.002
Receipt and invoices	0.002
Advertisement	5
Actions in-lieu-of right	5–15 annually
Mortgages	0.008
Property rentals	0.005
Contracts of supply and con-struction	1
Mines and quarries use	4
Corporate and partnership contracts	0.004
Letters of credit contracts	0.005
Agency contracts	0.005
Salaries and wages	0.002
Transportation insurance contracts	1
Subcontracts	0.001

Documents evidencing an action or agreement that are written in a foreign country are subject to the stamp duty in Libya prior to their utilization before they can become enforceable in Libya.

General Income Tax. The General Income Tax is levied on the annual income of individuals, whether Libyans or foreigners, and is payable on January 1st for income realized in the preceding year. However, quarterly payments are allowed. The tax is assessed on all of the income realized by the individual from the various branches, occupations, or activities indicated in items 1 and 9 after deducting the personal income tax. Foreigners are required to pay the General Income Tax and show evidence of payment before their final departure. The tax rates are as follows:

Taxable Income		Tax on Lower Amount	Percentage on Excess
Over	Not Over		
L.D. 4,000	L.D. 7,000	L.D. 0	15%
7,000	12,000	450	25

| Taxable Income | | Tax on | Percentage |
Over	Not Over	Lower Amount	on Excess
L.D. 12,000	L.D. 20,000	L.D. 1,700	35%
20,000	35,000	4,500	45
35,000	60,000	11,250	55
60,000	100,000	25,000	65
100,000		51,000	90

Jihad Tax. The Jihad tax for individuals is imposed on income arising from salaries and wages as follows:

| Monthly Salary | | Rate |
Over	Not Over	
L.D. 0	L.D. 50	1%
50	100	2
100		3

A Jihad tax of 4% is assessed on a corporation's taxable income.

Great Man-Made River Tax. This special tax is imposed at the following rates:

Item	Rate
Gasoline	L.D. 0.020 per litre
Diesel	L.D. 0.50 per litre
Cigarettes	L.D. 0.010 per cigarette
Airline tickets	10% of value
Foreign currency transfers by individuals	10% of value
Foreign currency transfers made by general public companies	15% of value
Certain letters of credit	5% of value

COMPUTATION OF TAXABLE INCOME

26. Capital Gains

Taxable capital gains of a corporation are, as a rule, measured by the difference between the net proceeds and the net book value of the asset sold. Gains are treated as any other income from the corporation's normal activities.

There is no capital gain tax to an individual from the sale of his property.

27. Depreciation and Depletion

Depreciation and depletion expenses are annually deductible from income according to the following rates:

	Rate
Buildings with fixed machinery	5%
Buildings without fixed machinery	3
Transport equipment (passenger)	20
Transport equipment (goods)	15
Vessels	12.5
Airplanes	10
Office, shops, and house furniture	10
Hotel, restaurant, and camp furniture	20
Office equipment	10
Generator equipment	20
Other equipment	20
Petroleum (tangible assets)	10
Petroleum (nontangible assets)	5

28. Treatment of Dividends

Dividends received by a corporation are treated as income, and the tax rate applicable to other corporate income applies to the dividends.

Dividends received by an individual from an investment in corporations or partnership companies are subject to the general income tax.

29. Loss Carryovers

Losses are carried forward against taxable profits for the subsequent five years. There are no loss carrybacks.

30. Transactions between Related Parties

Notional losses incurred by a company on a transaction may be regarded by the tax authorities as hidden profit distributions and added back to trading income.

31. Consolidation of Income

An individual's income from all sources is consolidated only for the purpose of assessing the general income tax.

32. Tax Periods

Companies are assessed tax on the basis of their financial statements terminating during the taxable year—January 1st to December 31st. The accounting period of the company may not exceed 12 months and the balance sheet date may only be changed pursuant to an agreement with the tax authorities.

33. Other Matters

Disallowable Items. Taxable income is determined after disallowing the following charges:

☐ Any depreciation or depletion amounts in excess of the rates established by the tax authorities.

☐ Any amount spent on enlargement or enhancement of an asset. However, the taxpayer is entitled to the depreciation on this expenditure based on the normal depreciation rates.

☐ Personal or family expenses of the taxpayer.

☐ Salaries of the taxpayer, his spouse, and underage children.

☐ Any amount deducted from the taxpayer's income as reserve for bad debts, reduction in prices, losses, suspended obligations, and other reserves.

LIECHTENSTEIN

INCOME TAXES ON CORPORATIONS

1. Rates

Income tax is based on the ratio of earnings to taxable net worth and applies to domestic operating companies (see item 6) and to permanent establishments of nonresident companies. The income tax rate is one-half of that ratio, expressed as a percentage (between 7.5%, minimum, and 15%, maximum) of net earnings.

Business expenses and all taxes paid except the coupon tax (see item 17) are deductible from gross earnings. Gross income of a domestic operating company includes worldwide earnings except dividends from substantial participations and income from foreign, unincorporated permanent establishments or foreign real estate.

If dividend distributions exceed 8% of the entity's taxable net worth, the tax rate increases 1% for the first 2% of dividends in excess of 8% and 0.5% for each additional 2%. The maximum increase is 5% for dividends in excess of 24% of taxable net worth, for a combined, maximum income tax rate of 20%.

Domiciliary and holding companies (registered entities not conducting any trade or business within Liechtenstein, see item 6) are not taxable on their profits or income. They are liable to the annual capital tax at the reduced rate of 0.1% of taxable capital (see item 25) and, if a company limited by shares, the 4% coupon (withholding) tax (see item 17).

2. Local Income Taxes

There are no local income taxes.

3. Capital Gains Taxes

Capital gains realized from the sale of real property located in Liechtenstein are subject to a real estate profits tax. Long-term gains (for property held longer than ten years) are subject to real estate profits tax rates ranging from 3.6% to 17.82%. The rates for short-term gains (held for three years or less) range from 7.2% to 35.64%.

Capital gains realized from the sale of other corporate or personal assets are taxed as ordinary income.

4. Branch Profits Taxes

Both subsidiaries and branches of foreign companies are liable to income tax at rates between 7.5% and 20%. A domiciliary (see item 6) subsidiary or branch, however, is exempt from income tax on its business income earned outside of Liechtenstein.

A 4% coupon tax (see item 17) is levied on dividends distributed by a subsidiary, including domiciliary companies, if its capital is divided into shares. No coupon tax applies to payments of a branch.

6. Classification of Corporations

Companies are classified as "domiciliary and holding companies" or "domestic operating companies." Domiciliary and holding companies are registered, legal entities domiciled in Liechtenstein, which do not conduct any trade or business in the country. These companies do not require a local office but must have a permanent director and legal representative in Liechtenstein. The representative may be a corporate entity or an individual.

A company is classified as a domestic operating company in order to conduct trade or commercial activities within the country. The company must receive specific permission from the Government and meet complex requirements to obtain a business license. Foreign investors will find it difficult to obtain the business license.

A company becomes resident in Liechtenstein by registering with the country's commercial register. The company's board of directors must include one Liechtenstein citizen or permanent resident who meets Government criteria as a qualified director.

Liechtenstein recognizes most internationally recognized corporate forms. The most frequently used forms, however, are as follows:

☐   Limited company—this form of legal entity has basically the same characteristics as limited companies elsewhere. It is most often used when the capital structure is complex and the business purpose is international trade or commerce. The minimum legal share capital is SF 50,000.

☐   Private establishment—this form of business is unique to Liechtenstein; it is an autonomous fund with legal personality. Its capital is not divided into shares, and the economic benefits usually are vested in the holder of the "founder's rights." The private establishment often is used for asset management or for facilitating intercompany transactions. The minimum legal capital is SF 30,000.

☐   Trust enterprise—it is frequently referred to as a business trust, yet can be formed as a separate legal entity for business purposes similar to those carried on by limited companies and establishments. The trust enterprise often is used to operate family businesses or partnerships (e.g., a holding function). The minimum legal fund is SF 30,000.

☐   Trust—contrary to the trust enterprise, the trust has no legal personality. It is similar to the common law trust used elsewhere, but is legally more flexible than similar trusts in other jurisdictions. The Liechtenstein trust frequently is used to manage family assets through a trustee. There is no minimum legal fund required.

□ Foundation—this is a legal endowment fund for a specified purpose. It is used for charitable purposes as well as to manage assets or economic interests of families, individuals, or legal entities. The foundation cannot carry on commercial or trading activities. The minimum endowment capital is SF 30,000.

Domestic operating companies usually are organized as limited companies, establishments, or trust enterprises. Domiciliary and holding companies may be organized in any of the above forms.

A company is liable only to the exent of its net assets. Shareholders are liable only to the extent of their share subscription and founders only to the extent of their donation to or equity in the fund.

7. Payment of Taxes

The tax year-end is December 31 for taxes assessed on the accounting year ending within the tax year. Tax returns are due by June 30 of the year following the tax year-end. Payment is due within 30 days of receipt of the tax assessment. Subject to prepayment of 80% of the previous year's tax assessment, a filing extension may be granted for up to five months.

INCOME TAXES ON INDIVIDUALS

9. Rates

The rate of tax payable by individuals is determined annually by the Parliament. It is a percentage of the basic tax rate, which is 2%. Since 1984 the rate has been 60% of the basic rate, for an effective rate of 1.2% of taxable income (up to 5.94% including surcharges and excluding local taxes—see item 10).

Married couples are taxed on their combined earnings. A tax credit of one-third of the lesser of the combined income tax or SF 4,000 may be taken if the married couple shares the same residence.

Deductions from gross income are:

Personal Allowances

Individual maintaining a household	SF 4,800
Married couple living together	6,000
Other individual	2,400

Other deductions include a per-child deduction and deductions for educational costs, medical expenses, and insurance premiums (including social security).

Salaries and wages are subject to withholding of between 4% and 9% of gross earnings from Liechtenstein employers. The employer withholds the amount from pay and remits it to the tax authorities quarterly. Withholdings are deductible from tax due; any excess is refunded to the individual.

10. Local Income Taxes

The municipalities add a surcharge of up to 200% to the state income tax (see item 9), bringing the maximum tax on income to a rate of 17.82%.

11. Capital Gains Taxes

Capital gains realized from the sale of personal assets other than real estate are taxed as ordinary income. Individuals are entitled to a capital gains deduction of SF 3,000 per year.

Capital gains realized from the sale of real property located in Liechtenstein are subject to a real estate profits tax. Long-term gains (for property held longer than ten years) are subject to real estate profits tax rates ranging from 3.6% to 17.82%. The rates for short-term gains (held for three years or less) range from 7.2% to 35.64%. The capital gains deduction is SF 1,500 per transaction.

13. Tax Period

The tax year for individuals is the calendar year. Tax returns are due by April 15, and the tax payable is due within 30 days of receipt of the assessment notice. Extensions of up to five months may be granted provided an installment of 80% of the previous year's tax liability has been paid.

INCOME TAXES ON NONRESIDENTS

15. Liability to Tax

Nonresident companies and individuals are liable to tax only on income derived from a permanent establishment in Liechtenstein.

16. Rates

Branches and subsidiaries of foreign companies are subject to the same taxes as resident companies (see item 1).

17. Withholding Tax Rates

Coupon Tax. The 4% coupon or withholding tax applies to

☐ Dividends, other distributions, or liquidation proceeds from companies whose capital is divided into shares (usually a limited company).

☐ Benefits paid by a trust enterprise where the beneficial interest is in the form of a security instrument.

☐ Interest payments on loans exceeding SF 50,000 with a term exceeding two years.

☐ Interest from bank deposits having a term exceeding one year.

The coupon tax does not apply to royalties or rents.

There are no other withholding taxes on payments to nonresidents.

19. Tax Treaties

Liechtenstein has a double taxation treaty with Austria covering domestic operating companies and individuals. Also, to regulate the taxation of border commuters, Liechtenstein and the adjacent Swiss cantons of Graubuenden and St. Gallen have double taxation treaties.

Other tax treaties have not been concluded, and foreign taxes paid are nonrecoverable in Liechtenstein.

OTHER SIGNIFICANT TAXES

21. Sales (Value Added)

The Swiss federal turnover tax applies in Liechtenstein. It is a sales tax imposed on sales and imports of goods and merchandise, but not on services. The rates are as follows:

Retail level	6.2%
Wholesale level	9.3%

The tax is collected by the Swiss tax authorities and redistributed to Liechtenstein on a per capita basis. There are no other sales or value-added taxes in Liechtenstein.

22. Inheritance and Gift Taxes

Estate, succession, and gift taxes apply to Liechtenstein residents only. The estate tax is levied at graduated rates of: up to 2.5% if the heir is a child, spouse, or parent of the deceased; and up to 5% on others. Succession and gift tax rates range from 0.5% to 27% depending on the relationship—the highest rate applying to unrelated persons.

23. Taxes on Payrolls (Social Security)

Old Age, Disability, and Survivors Insurance. A national social security tax is assessed on all compensation received by residents under the age of 65 (males) or 62 (females) for work performed, including salaries, wages, bonuses, director's fees, etc., without upper limits.

	Contribution
Employee	4.18%
Employer	7.0058%
Total	11.1858%
Self-employed Person	11.1858%

Foreign nationals generally are not eligible for a refund of contributions made, but they may claim, under certain circumstances, benefits on a pro rata basis of their contributions.

Unemployment Insurance.   A compulsory contribution to the national unemployment insurance plan is levied on wages up to SF 8,100 monthly. The rate is 0.25% on the employer and 0.25% on the employee, up to a maximum total contribution of SF 468 per year.

25.   Other Taxes

Capital Tax.   Domestic operating companies are liable to an annual capital tax at the rate of 0.2% of the taxable capital, which includes paid-in capital, reserves, and unappropriated retained earnings.

Domiciliary and holding companies are liable to a reduced annual capital tax rate of 0.1% of the company's taxable capital. Foundations may request a reduced rate of 0.075% on their net equity in excess of SF 2 million and 0.05% on their net equity in excess of SF 10 million. The minimum capital tax is, in all cases, SF 1,000 per year.

Net Worth Tax.   Individuals resident or having an unincorporated, permanent establishment in Liechtenstein are liable to a net worth tax. Nonresidents without a permanent establishment in Liechtenstein are liable to a net worth tax only on their real property located in Liechtenstein. State and municipal surcharges bring this tax to a maximum rate of 0.891%.

Stamp Duty.   Stamp duty of 3% is levied once on the paid-in capital of entities limited by shares. Trust enterprises and establishments may request a reduced stamp duty of 1.5% if their start-up capital exceeds SF 5 million or 1% if their start-up capital exceeds SF 10 million. Family and religious or charitable foundations usually receive, on application, a reduced rate of 0.2%.

Stamp duty also is levied on any capital increases on disposition of a shell company holding only liquid assets.

Businesses dealing in securities or classified by the tax authorities as dealers of securities are liable to stamp duty based on the Swiss laws, at rates ranging from 0.1% to 0.3% on the transaction value.

Other rules apply to the issue of mutual funds, the registration of a nonresident company, the transfer of a nonresident company to Liechtenstein, etc.

Customs Duties.   Customs duties are levied on the transfer of goods across the border. The rate varies on the category of tariff and is based on the weight of the goods.

COMPUTATION OF TAXABLE INCOME

26.   Capital Gains

See items 3 and 11.

27.   Depreciation and Depletion

Liechtenstein law provides for depreciation under the declining-balance method at the following maximum rates (the straight-line method may be used with maximum rates of one-half of the following):

Commercial buildings	2%
Industrial buildings	2%–5%
Technical installations	15%
Office equipment	20%
Patents, licenses, goodwill	25%
Machinery	30%
Vehicles	35%
Tools and dies	50%–100%

28.   Treatment of Dividends

Domestic- and foreign-source dividends (except on substantial participations greater than 20%), net of any foreign or Liechtenstein withholding or coupon taxes paid, received by a domestic operating company or a permanent establishment are treated as ordinary income.

Domestic- and foreign-source dividends and other passive income received by individuals are tax-exempt. Likewise, there are no deductions for expenses incurred (e.g., interest) or depreciation of property by individuals.

29.   Loss Carryovers

Companies may carry forward losses not absorbed by income of the same year for two succeeding years. Losses may not be carried back.

Individuals may offset losses against the income from the same source for the current or two following years.

31.   Consolidation of Income

There is no consolidation of income, and there are no provisions in the law for one company to offset losses against the income of another company of the same group. Each company is taxed separately.

33. Other Matters

Inventories. Inventory is valued at the lesser of cost or market value. One-third of the value is allowed as a tax reserve.

RELATED CONSIDERATIONS

34. Incentives and Grants

The major advantage to establishing operations in Liechtenstein is the favorable tax treatment of domiciliary and holding companies. Restrictive Government policies exist concerning the granting of work permits and business licenses.

LUXEMBOURG

INCOME TAXES ON CORPORATIONS

1. Rates

Income. Luxembourg-registered companies are liable to Luxembourg taxation on their worldwide income. The basic rate of corporate income tax is 33% from 1991 on. The following reduced rates apply, however, to lower incomes:

Taxable Income		Tax On	Percentage
Over	Not Over	Lower Amount	on Excess
LF 0	LF 400,000	20%	
400,000	600,000	LF 80,000	50 %
600,000	1,000,000	30%	
1,000,000	1,313,000	LF300,000	42.6%
1,313,000		33%	

The total tax is presently subject to a surcharge of 1% of the tax to support the funding of unemployment relief. The maximum effective rate of the state income is therefore 33.33%.

Net Worth. Companies are subject to an annual net worth tax (impôt sur la fortune) of 0.5%. Net worth is determined from the disclosed net assets of the company, although investments in affiliates (see item 5) and the value of foreign immovable property situated in treaty countries are excluded from the computation. The official value of real property (see item 2) situated in Luxembourg and the market values of securities are substituted for book values.

Capital. The capital tax—taxe d'abonnement—has been suppressed for all commercial companies effective January 1, 1991. Only holding companies and investment funds will be liable for the tax (0.20% of the estimated value of issued capital for holding companies, 0.06% of the net asset value for investment funds).

2. Local Income Taxes

Income. An additional tax on income is levied in favor of the municipalities. The effective tax rate varies according to location. In Luxembourg City the rate is 10%. The tax is assessed upon the net income of the year as determined for income tax purposes subject to computation adjustments (see item 33) and after deduction of municipal taxes. Thus, the rate of 10% becomes, effectively, 9.09%. The municipal tax is deductible from net income for computation of state income tax. There is an abatement of LF700,000 for companies. The effective rate of the combined rate of state and municipal income tax with the surcharge is 39.39%.

Net Worth. An additional net worth tax on net assets is levied in favor of the municipalities. There is an abatement of LF1,800,000 for companies. The effective tax rate varies according to location. In Luxembourg City, the rate is 0.5%.

Property. Freehold property is subject to a ground tax. The tax is levied at rates varying from 0.7% to 1% fixed by the law on the official value of the property. The official value is in general less than 10% of actual value. The tax is calculated on this value and multiplied by local coefficients generally varying between 100% and 500%.

Summary of Corporate Taxation. The effective combined rates of state and municipal taxes assessed upon income, net worth, and capital are as follows.

	Rate	Comments
Profits	39.39% (1)	Reduced rates for Luxembourg companies with profits below LF1,313,000.
Net Worth	1.0% (2)	Minimum tax LF2,500.
Capital		Holding companies 0.20% (minimum LF2,000)

Notes:
(1) With the 1% surcharge.
(2) State and local combined.

3. Capital Gains Taxes

The taxable profit of a company is based upon the difference between net assets at the beginning and end of the financial year. Capital gains arising during the year are, therefore, included in corporate profit and taxed at corporate income tax rates. However, the following exceptions apply:

☐ Profits on the sale of property and nonamortizable assets forming part of a permanent establishment in Luxembourg that have been owned for at least five years, may be taken to a replacement reserve and consequently exempted from income tax, provided that the proceeds of sale are reinvested within two years of the end of the financial year in which the sale has taken place. On application to the tax authorities, this period of two years can be extended in appropriate cases.

☐ Profits arising on the destruction or expropriation of any asset (i.e., when compensation exceeds net book value) also may be taken to a replacement reserve and are exempted from income tax, provided reinvestment of the proceeds in economically and technically similar assets takes place within two years of the end of the financial year (this period may also be extended as above).

☐ As concerns the specific tax regime of capital gains for corporations benefitting from the affiliation privilege, see item 5 and, in particular for the SOPARFI, see item 6.

4. Branch Profits Taxes

Branches of foreign corporations are subject to the taxes outlined in items 1 and 2 based upon the income, net worth, and capital of the Luxembourg branch. The reduced rates of income tax applicable to lower incomes (see item 1) apply only to branches of corporations whose worldwide income does not exceed the lower income limits.

5. Foreign Tax Reliefs

Treaty Countries. Countries with which double taxation treaties have been concluded are listed in item 17. Dividend and interest income of Luxembourg resident companies received net from any of the treaty countries is grossed up for Luxembourg tax purposes, and credit for foreign withholding tax is allowed against the resulting tax liability.

Dividend income received from affiliated companies (i.e., companies in which a 10% or 25% share interest has been held for a complete fiscal year) registered in treaty countries is subject to reduced rates of withholding tax in the treaty country and is exempted from tax in Luxembourg.

Income of a branch of a Luxembourg resident company situated in a treaty country normally is exempted from Luxembourg tax. The tax treaty with the United States provides, however, that the tax credit method of taxation applies to branch income.

Nontreaty Countries. Several Grand-Ducal decrees were issued in May 1979 to implement the law of November 30, 1978 concerning credit for foreign taxes. The main features of the law and its enabling decrees are as follows:

☐ In principle, credit for foreign taxes levied by countries with which Luxembourg has no tax treaty is granted on income from agriculture, from business, from independent activity, from employment, from pensions, from letting and leasing, and from capital assets.

☐ The benefit of the law is extended to permanent establishments of nonresident taxpayers.

☐ As a rule, the credit is calculated on a country-by-country basis. However, upon application to be made every year by the taxpayer, foreign dividend, interest and royalty income can be globalized.

Several limitations were introduced by the decrees. The lowest of the tax credits arrived at by the application of the limitation rules are the effective tax credits. The balance of foreign tax is a deductible item in the calculation of the Luxembourg tax.

Affiliation Privilege.   It is frequently necessary today for undertakings to be organized in groups. Luxembourg has developed a special tax regime for parent companies and their affiliates, known as the "Schachtelprivileg" or "affiliation privilege."

Where a company *resident* in Luxembourg, which is fully subject to tax, has held uninterruptedly from the beginning of the financial year (and in any case for 12 months preceding the year-end) either a direct holding in the capital of another company of at least 10% of total capital or a direct holding of which the acquisition cost is at least LF50,000,000 income receivable from the holding (*dividends*) is exempt from tax on condition that the distributing company is a fully taxable company resident in Luxembourg or a *nonresident* company fully subject to an equivalent *corporation tax* abroad.

With regard to holdings in *nonresident* companies, an indirect holding will also qualify for exemption if the aggregate holdings of two or more companies *resident* in the Grand-Duchy obtain the same thresholds of 10% of LF50,000,000, but with the supplementary condition that one of the *resident* companies holds a participation of more than 50% in each of the other companies *resident* in Luxembourg.

From the viewpoint of distributions from the Luxembourg source, a provision of the tax reform promulgated on December 6, 1990 and in force since January 1, 1991 (article 147 LIR) authorizes exemption from *withholding tax* on *dividends* and other income from shareholdings when they are distributed by a fully taxable Luxembourg company to a fully taxable company *resident* in a member State of the European Community. In this case, it is necessary for this *foreign parent* of the Luxembourg company to prove that it has held title to a direct participation of at least 25% during an uninterrupted period of at least two years at the time of distribution.

As for *capital gains* arising from disposal of a substantial holding, they also qualify for exemption under the *affiliation privilege* in a manner similar to that applicable to *dividends* except that the threshold of participation here is raised to LF250,000,000 or 25% of total capital (compared with LF50,000,000 or 10% for *dividend* exemption) and that the uninterrupted period of holding must have existed throughout the 12 months preceding the commencement of the financial year in which disposal took place (compared with 12 months preceding the close of the financial year in respect of *dividend* exemption).

6. Classification of Corporations

Holding Companies and Investment Funds.   The Luxembourg holding company is regulated by the law of July 31, 1929 and is defined as a company whose sole object is the holding of investments. The holding company may not, therefore, have any commercial activity, hold real estate (except as is necessary for its investment business), or earn fees or commissions. Investment funds are companies (or unit trusts) whose shares (or units) are offered to the public, and the collected funds are invested in a variety of securities. These entities, which previously were categorized as holding companies, were granted special status by the law of August 25, 1983, including additional tax exemptions and reductions (see below). It has been replaced since by the law of March 30, 1988, but the fiscal provisions remain identical.

□   Taxation.   Luxembourg holding companies (law of July 1929) are exempted from taxes on income and capital gains, and withholding taxes do not apply to distributions. Similarly, they may not recover foreign taxes withheld from foreign-source income. The only annual tax payable is that of 0.20% on the estimated value of the capital (see item 1). In the absence of a stock exchange quotation, the tax is assessed on the paid-in capital (retained earnings being disregarded unless they reach a substantial level compared to share capital), but the estimated value is never less than ten times any dividend paid by the company, if such amount exceeds par value. Holding companies whose capital (shares only or shares and issued debenture bonds) exceeds the equivalent of LF1 billion may claim "billionaire status," in which case a tax on distributions is levied subject to a minimum of LF2 million, which replaces the annual tax.

   The law of August 25, 1983 has significantly reduced the costs of Investment Funds by: (1) abolishing the 1% registration duty on issues of share capital and replacing it by a fixed duty of LF50,000, irrespective of the value of the capital and future increases; and (2) reducing the annual capital tax from 0.20% to 0.06% for both unit trusts ("fonds commun de placement") and fixed or variable capital investment companies.

□   Income.   The income of a holding company may comprise dividend income from its investments, interest income from loans to companies in which it has an interest, patent income, and capital gains arising from the sale of investments. The holding company may be financed by liabilities of up to three times its subscribed capital and may issue bonds to the equivalent of ten times its paid-up capital.

□   The Financial Holding Company.   The financial holding company may lend monies to companies within the group of companies to which it belongs without maintaining a direct investment in the recipient. The conditions for this concession are that the shares of the financial holding company must be shown to be held by member companies of the group, and at least 10% of its subscribed capital (minimum capital is 50 million francs) must be represented by investments in group companies.

☐ Tax Treaties.   Both Luxembourg holding companies and investment funds are excluded from the benefits of the provisions of the tax treaties concluded by Luxembourg with other countries.

☐ Reinsurance Companies.   Captive reinsurance companies are required to take the form of a limited liability company. The shareholders' equity must be appropriate to the level of commitments with a minimum paid-up capital of LF50 million. These companies may qualify for a privileged tax status based on the creation of tax-deductible catastrophe provisions. The effect of these provisions can be to defer taxation of such companies for many years.

☐ Coordination Centers and Financing Companies.   The Luxembourg tax administration has recognized these two types of companies as centers of multinational activity and grants a simplified tax regime reducing the tax base to a low percentage of costs.

Holding Companies Constituted Under General Company Law, or SOPARFI.   The tax reform of December 6, 1990 and the subsequent Grand-Ducal regulations have laid the foundation for a system that, in some cases, will provide an extremely valid alternative to the traditional holding company.

The affiliation privilege of parent and affiliated company applies henceforth by virtue of general law (subject to certain conditions) to dividends and the related withholding tax and to capital gains on disposal of shares. This application of general law allows, in principle, for the tax treaties to take effect. The exemptions combined with the benefits of the tax treaties can be most advantageous for an international group of companies. Thus, a normally taxable commercial company, which by its by-laws limits its objects to holding shares, can usurp one of the important functions of the traditional holding company while remaining within the general law and the scope of the terms of the classic tax treaties. Such companies are known as SOPARFI (sociétés de participation financière) in the tax jargon of the Grand Duchy.

7.   Payment of Taxes

Corporations are required to pay tax in advance during the year of income in four quarterly installments (March 10, June 10, September 10, and December 10). The amount of each installment is fixed by the tax authorities on the basis of tax paid in the previous year. On assessment in the following year the balance is paid or recovered.

8.   Other Matters

Withholding Taxes.   Companies are required to withhold taxes on salaries and wages, directors' and commissaire fees, dividends, and royalties. The rates of withholding taxes to be applied are as follows:

☐ Payroll.   Amounts due by the employees are based on their income and family status (item 9).

□ Fees Paid to Commissaires and Nonexecutive Directors. Deductions of 20% of payments to Luxembourg residents and 20% plus 8.40% (advance income tax) of payments to nonresidents. The 20% tax cannot be imputed against the final tax liability, which is calculated on 80% of the gross fees.

□ Dividends, Bond Interest, and Royalties. Dividends paid are subject to a withholding tax of 15%. Bond interest (except on profit sharing bonds) is free of withholding tax. No withholding tax is required from dividends paid by holding companies and investment funds, or from dividends paid to a Luxembourg-resident commercial company by another Luxembourg commercial company in respect of a single shareholding of at least 10% of the share capital or of a minimum acquisition cost of at least LF50 million, at the condition that the distributing company is a fully taxable company resident in Luxembourg or a nonresident company fully subject to an equivalent corporation tax abroad. Royalties paid to nonresidents are subject to withholding tax of 10% or 12%.

Mergers and Liquidations. A company is liable for income tax at normal rates on gains arising on liquidation. If, however, a company is merged with another resident company under a share exchange scheme, no tax liability will arise for the absorbed company if the assets acquired are brought into account post merger at their previous net book values.

INCOME TAXES ON INDIVIDUALS

9. Rates

Luxembourg residents are liable to Luxembourg income tax on their worldwide income. Nonresidents are liable to Luxembourg tax on earned income arising in Luxembourg. The income of a husband and wife is combined to determine the basis of taxation, but an abatement of LF180,000 for a working couple has been introduced in 1991. Taxation on a sliding scale applies to successive portions of the net taxable income at rates varying from 0% to 50%, plus a surcharge of 2.5% of the tax, for a total of 51.25%. The maximum rate of 51.25% applies to the bracket of income exceeding LF1,269,000 in 1991 for a single person.

Employers must deduct income tax at source on salaries and wages in accordance with published tax tables, which take into account child allowances and standard expense deductions. In addition, a number of specified expenses can be deducted to arrive at net taxable income of which the most generally applied items are:

□ Total of social security contributions.

□ Insurance premiums (subject to conditions and ceilings).

□ Gifts to authorized charities (subject to limitation).

□ Interest on loans (subject to conditions and ceilings).

□ Shares subscribed in a resident Luxembourg company (the deduction increases according to the number of dependents).

☐ A special expense deduction for foreign managerial staff of banks established in Luxembourg.

The following example illustrates the income tax on salaries in 1989 on taxpayers with two dependent children.

Taxable Income	Tax (1)	Average Rate
LF 600,000	LF 0	0 %
1,200,000	18,462	0.02
1,800,000	186,246	10.34
2,500,000	484,448	19.38
4,000,000	1,250,807	31.27

Notes:
(1) With the 2.5% surcharge.

10. Local Income Taxes

The same additional taxes for companies are levied by the municipalities (see item 2) on trading income, net worth affected by trading, and freehold property except that the standard deductions are LF900,000 for trading income and LF2,500,000 for net worth affected by trading.

11. Capital Gains Taxes

The following profits are treated as speculative gains and are included in taxable income:

☐ Gains on real property disposed of within two years of acquisition.
☐ If the real property is disposed of after two years of ownership, the profit derived from the sale is taxable, but the amount benefits from a certain number of abatements and adjustments with the effect of significantly reducing the taxable amounts.
☐ Gains on other assets disposed of within six months of acquisition.

Profits on the disposition of a shareholding or interest in any business in the G.-D. Luxembourg in which a resident taxpayer has a total interest of more than 25% are subject to capital gains tax at half of the corresponding rate of tax applicable to total income, with a maximum rate of 25.625%.

12. Foreign Tax Reliefs

The same foreign tax reliefs are available to Luxembourg resident individuals as are available to Luxembourg companies (see item 5).

13. Tax Period

Individuals are assessed to income tax on the basis of the trading income disclosed by accounts terminating during the tax year (January 1 to December 31). The accounting period may not exceed 12 months, and the balance sheet date may be changed only with the agreement of the fiscal authorities.

14. Other Matters

Wealth Tax.   Luxembourg residents are subject to a wealth tax of 0.5% per annum on their declared net wealth. For the purposes of computing net wealth, real property is valued at its official value (see item 2). Liabilities are, however, allowable in full. The taxpayer is also entitled to a deduction from net wealth of LF100,000, LF100,000 for his/her spouse (living or dead), and LF100,000 for each dependent.

An abatement of LF1,400,000 is available for money in bank accounts and other deposits in LF as well as for investments in shares and other securities of resident joint stock companies quoted on the stock exchange.

INCOME TAXES ON NONRESIDENTS

15. Liability to Tax

Nonresidents are subject to tax in Luxembourg on income derived from activities in Luxembourg. Nonresidents are taxed at the same rate as a married person without children or at a minimum rate of 15% plus a 2.5% surcharge (i.e., 15.375%), whichever is greater. Income subject to withholding tax at source is generally not included in an assessment, and such tax is the nonresident individual's final tax liability. An individual is deemed to be resident for tax purposes if he either has his permanent home in Luxembourg, or if he has been living in Luxembourg continuously for more than six months. Nonresidents receiving a salary in Luxembourg are only granted the tax deductions for social security contributions and special travel costs. For this group, the minimum rate of 15% is not applicable, and the family situation is taken into consideration.

17. Withholding Tax Rates

Dividends and profit sharing bond interest paid to nonresidents are subject to withholding tax of 15%. Dividends paid by a Luxembourg holding company are not subject to withholding tax. There is no withholding tax on interest.

Royalties paid to nonresidents are subject to withholding tax of 10% or 12%. They are further subject to value added tax, usually at a rate of 12%, and the licensors are assessable to the net worth tax.

The rates of withholding taxes on dividends and royalties paid to nonresident individuals and corporations under the double taxation treaties concluded by Luxembourg are set out below.

Country	Dividends		Royalties (2)
	To Affiliates (1)	Others	
Austria	5%	15%	— (3)
Belgium	10	15	—
Brazil	15	15	10% or 12%
Denmark	5	15	—
Finland	5	15	5 (4)
France	5	15	—
Germany	10	15	5
Ireland	5	15	—
Italy (4)	15	15	10
Morocco	10	15	10
Netherlands	2.5	15	—
Norway	5	15	—
South Korea	10	15	10 or 12
Spain	5	15	10
Sweden	5	15	—
United Kingdom	5	15	5
United States	5	7.5	—

Notes:
(1) The definition of an affiliate is not identical in each treaty.
(2) Royalty payments in Luxembourg are subject to value added tax at 12% (10% for royalties on films or tapes for radio or television broadcasting).
(3) Rate is 10% if payment is to company with over 50% shareholding, otherwise nil.
(4) No withholding tax on payments for the use or the privilege of using a copyright, artistic or scientific work, motion picture films, or film or tape for radio or television broadcasting.

No withholding tax is levied on interest (bonds, loans, and bank accounts) except on profit sharing bonds and except that interest on mortgage loans secured by property situated in Luxembourg is subject to income tax.

OTHER SIGNIFICANT TAXES

21. Sales (Value Added)

The rates of value added tax applied in Luxembourg to sales of goods and services are as follows:

☐   Standard rate—12%.

□ Essential goods and services (e.g., most food, hotels, and professional fees)—6%.

□ Certain special categories (e.g., meat, drugs, and milk products)—3%.

□ Exports—zero rated.

□ Works of art—6%.

22. Inheritance and Gift Taxes

There is no duty on an estate passing to resident direct descendants. Nonresidents are assessable only on real estate located in Luxembourg. An estate passing to brothers or sisters attracts duty at rates between 6.0% and 19.2%, according to the value of the transfer. An estate passing to other persons is subject to duty at rates from 9.0% to a maximum of 48% at LF70,000,000.

23. Taxes on Payrolls (Social Security)

Social security is administered through state funds. Contribution is obligatory in respect of all employees. Contributions are applied at fixed rates on gross salary. The monthly payments in respect of office staff are:

	Percent of Gross Salary		Salary Computation Ceiling (Index: May 1991)
	Employer	Employee	
Pension	8 %	8 %	LF138,349
Health	2.425	2.425	172,936
Family allowance	1.70	—	138,349
Work accidents	0.50 to 6	—	138,349

Contributions for industrial manual workers are higher than for office staff and depend upon the degree of risk involved in the occupation. Family allowances are linked to the cost of living, and currently are LF1,940 for one child, LF5,914 for two children, LF13,012 for three children, and LF5,820 for each additional child. These amounts are slightly increased for children over six years old (+ LF189) and over 12 years old (+ LF618).

24. Taxes on Natural Resources

None.

25. Other Taxes

Property Transfer Tax.   The sale or transfer of property is subject to a registration duty of 6% on the value of the property. Property situated in Luxembourg City is subject to a surcharge of 3%, making a total of 9%.

Capital Tax. A registration duty of 1% is levied on the paid-up amount of share capital subscriptions.

COMPUTATION OF TAXABLE INCOME

26. Capital Gains

Capital and speculative gains are included in taxable income. However, profits on sales of buildings or nondepreciable assets to be replaced may be offset against the cost of the new asset under certain circumstances (see item 3).

27. Depreciation and Depletion

Depreciation is required on all depreciable assets costing in excess of LF35,000. Assets costing less than LF35,000 or with a life of less than one year may be written off immediately. Depreciation is normally calculated on a straight-line basis at rates related to the estimated life of the asset. If the straight-line basis does not accurately reflect the reduction in value of the asset during its lifetime, then the declining-balance basis may be used. The taxpayer may switch from the declining balance method to the straight-line basis when this provides a higher tax deduction. The rate applied on the declining-balance basis may not exceed three times the rate normally applicable on the straight-line basis or 30%. On equipment for scientific and technical research, this rate may not exceeed 40% or four times the straight-line rates. Investments in environmental protection and energy-saving assets qualify for accelerated depreciation in the year of acquisition at the rate of 60%. Accelerated depreciation may be exercised in the year of acquisition or in any of the four following years, or spread equally over five years.

In special circumstances and subject to justification, the fiscal authorities will also accept depreciation on the basis of utilization, and also extraordinary depreciation to reflect exceptional loss in value of the asset concerned.

The straight-line rates of depreciation commonly used are:

Asset	Rate
Office buildings	2.5% to 3.5%
Industrial buildings	2% to 4%
Equipment and machinery	20%
Vehicles	20% to 25%
Office furniture	10% to 15%

28. Treatment of Dividends

Dividend income is included in taxable income, except for dividends received from affiliated companies resident in Luxembourg or not resident if at least 10% held for a full year and which have been subject to corporate income tax in their country of residence. When dividend income is included in taxable profit, it qualifies for the unilateral tax relief as described in item 5.

Withholding taxes which are not allowable as foreign tax credits under the double tax treaties are allowed as a deduction from profits, except for the part thereof relating to exempted income.

29. Loss Carryovers

Losses are available for offset against taxable profits arising during the following years (unlimited). There is no loss carryback.

30. Transactions between Related Parties

Notional losses incurred by a company on transactions with its shareholders for other than an "arms-length" consideration may be regarded by the tax authorities as hidden profit distributions and added back to trading income. Interest paid on monies borrowed to acquire a shareholding in an affiliated company is only allowable as a deduction from trading income to the extent that it exceeds the amount of any dividends received in respect of the shareholding.

31. Consolidation of Income

Group taxation for affiliated resident companies is possible if the parent company holds directly or indirectly at least 99% of each affiliate or, under certain circumstances, 75%.

32. Tax Periods

Companies are assessed to tax on the basis of their financial statements terminating during the tax year (January 1 to December 31). The accounting period of the company may not exceed 12 months, and the balance sheet date may only be changed by agreement with the fiscal authorities.

33. Other Matters

Taxable trading income for state income tax is arrived at after disallowance of the following charges:

□ Charges for state income and state net worth tax, and the annual capital tax.
□ Nonexecutive directors' fees.
□ Profit distributions, including hidden distributions.

RELATED CONSIDERATIONS

34. Incentives and Grants

The following fiscal incentives are currently available in respect of new investment:

□ A tax credit of 12% of supplementary investment in new tangible assets located in Luxembourg and subject to depreciation is granted. Supplementary investment is the difference between the total qualifying assets at the accounting year end and the average value of qualifying assets at each of the five previous years. Intangible assets, buildings, and second-hand assets are the most common assets not qualifying for the tax credit.

□ A tax credit of 6% on the acquisition price of qualifying assets with a life of over four years up to LF6 million and a 2% credit on any excess. An additional exclusion is made for cars for this second tax credit.

□ On the proposal of the tax authorities and by formal decision of the government, the Minister of Finance may fix a standard rate of tax for persons from abroad who establish their fiscal domicile in Luxembourg; this rate remains in effect for a maximum of ten years from commencement of such domicile.

□ Twenty-five percent of profits arising from investment in industries or techniques not previously exploited in Luxembourg may be exempted from tax during the first eight years of operations by the Minister of Economic Affairs.

□ Investment for trade and industrial purposes in immovable property can benefit from a capital subsidy up to 15%. For investment in movable property, the capital subsidy can amount up to 25%.

35. Exchange Controls

The Luxembourg franc has parity with the Belgian franc and is tied to certain other European currencies through the E.M.S. There are no restrictions on the transfer of funds into or out of Luxembourg.

36. Investment Restrictions on Nonresidents

None.

SELECTION OF BUSINESS ENTITY BY NONRESIDENTS

Nonresident investors can operate in Luxembourg through a branch or a local subsidiary corporation.

Branch. Branches of foreign corporations are subject to the same basic taxation as corporations (see item 4). No additional tax is levied when branch profits are remitted overseas. Note, however, that the branch profit is aggregated with the profit of its head office to determine the tax rate applicable (see item 1).

Local Corporation. Unless losses are anticipated by foreign investors in the early years of operations (in which case operating as a branch may have some clear advantages), their usual preference is to form a locally incorporated company even though profit distributions of corporations are subject to dividend withholding tax of 15%, or a lower treaty rate. Although a corporate entity suffers a higher aggregate level of Luxembourg taxation when profits are distributed, the choice of a business entity is usually influenced by the tax laws in the home country of the investor. Note that the corporation benefits from the graduated rate of tax (see item 1).

SPECIMEN TAX COMPUTATION

Information:

□ A Luxembourg corporation's net profit of LF 28,400,000 is determined from the following basic data:

	LF '000
Trading result in Luxembourg before taxes	20,000
Net trading result in non-tax treaty country N	12,000
Income tax paid in country N	5,000
Trading result from tax treaty country T	4,000
Luxembourg dividend income (substantial holding)	1,000
Net dividend income from tax treaty country (substantial holding)	1,650
Withholding tax on foreign dividends (nondeductible)	730
Net worth tax paid	450
Provision for corporate income tax	9,800

Computation of net profit:

Trading result in Luxembourg	20,000
Trading result from country N	12,000
Trading result from country T	4,000
Luxembourg dividend income	1,000
Foreign dividend income	1,650
Net worth tax	(450)
Provision for corporate income tax	(9,800)
Profit per accounts	28,400

Computation of taxable income:

Profit per accounts		28,400
Add		
Net worth tax paid	450	
Provision for income tax	9,800	
Income tax in country N	5,000	
Withholding tax on foreign income	730	15,980
		44,380

	LF '000
Less	
Trading result from country T	4,000
Luxembourg dividend income	1,000
Foreign dividend income (see item 5)	1,650
Non creditable portion of income tax on foreign dividend	730 7,380
Taxable income	37,000
Computation of income tax payable:	
Income tax (33%)	12,210
Contribution to unemployment fund (1% of LF12,210)	122
Total income tax	12,332
Less	
Income tax paid on country N (actual tax paid less than ceiling) (1)	(5,000)
Income tax payable	7,332

Notes:

(1) Computation of the ceiling for the creditable portion of income tax paid in a non-tax treaty country:

$$i = \frac{rt}{1 - t}$$

$i =$ creditable portion of income tax

$r =$ foreign income net from nontax-treaty-country tax

$t =$ income tax rate

Ceiling for creditable portion of tax paid in country N:

$$i = \frac{rt}{1 - t} = \frac{12,000 \times 0.33}{1 - 0.33} = 5,910$$

MALAWI

INCOME TAXES ON CORPORATIONS

1. Rates

Effective April 1, 1991, companies incorporated within Malawi are taxed at a flat rate of 40% on taxable income arising from a source within, or deemed to be within, Malawi. Branches or permanent establishments of externally incorporated companies are taxed at a flat rate of 45%.

Dividends declared by companies incorporated in Malawi are payable from after-tax profits and are therefore deemed to be declared net of income tax.

Dividends received by a Malawi incorporated company from another company resident in Malawi are not taxable. Only individuals are taxable on dividend income arising in Malawi.

Dividends payable to nonresident shareholders will be subject to a final tax of 15% of the amount declared. However, this would not apply if the dividend is exempt from tax under a double taxation agreement between Malawi and the country of residence of the recipient.

The 15% tax should be deducted by the payer and forwarded to the Commissioner of Taxes prior to obtaining exchange control approval for the remittance of the balance payable.

Minimum Income Tax. Effective April 1, 1990, minimum tax based on income is payable by companies where:

☐ A taxable loss is sustained,
☐ The minimum tax is greater than the tax payable on a taxable profit, or
☐ A taxable profit is offset by tax losses (see item 29).

The rates of applicable tax are:

Annual Income		Minimum Income Tax
Over	**Not Over**	
K 0	K 100,000	K 500
100,000	300,000	1,000
300,000	500,000	2,500
500,000	1,000,000	5,000
1,000,000		10,000

2. Local Income Taxes

None.

3. Capital Gains Tax

There is no tax on capital gains in Malawi. However, where an asset on which capital allowances have been claimed is sold for more than its tax written down value, the profit on the sale is taxable but only to the extent of the capital allowances previously claimed and granted on that asset.

4. Branch Profits Tax

Very few companies in Malawi operate external branches. For those who do, all revenue and expenses of the external branch are excluded from the computation of taxable income since they have accrued externally. Externally incorporated companies that operate branches in Malawi are subject to tax at a rate of 45% on taxable income. Such branches are ordinarily allowed to repatriate all or any portion of their after-tax profits.

Income arising from services or work performed for a permanent establishment (e.g., branch) in Malawi and claimed by the permanent establishment as a deductible expense is subject to tax in Malawi, irrespective of where the work or service was performed, the place of residence of the recipient, or the place of payment. In these circumstances the recipient would be required to submit a return of such income to the Malawi tax authorities.

5. Foreign Tax Reliefs

Since Malawi tax is based on income arising from a source within, or deemed to be within Malawi, the question of foreign tax reliefs does not arise.

6. Classification of Corporations

There are basically two classes of corporations:

□ Statutory bodies (some of which are exempt from tax by legislation).
□ Limited liability companies (most of which are private or family companies and are subject to tax).

7. Payment of Tax

Provisional income tax (other than PAYE) must be paid in advance by selecting either of the following two methods as a basis of payment.

Method 1: Tax payable under this method is based on the income tax actually paid for the previous year of assessment and is to be paid in four equal installments paid quarterly in arrears. Each taxpayer's quarter is determined by the business year-end.

Method 2: Under this method, the provisional tax payable is based on the taxpayer's own estimate of the current year's taxable income and is to be paid in four quarterly installments as follows:

— The first quarter's installment should not be less than 20% of the total estimated provisional tax payable.

— The amount of the second or subsequent installments may be varied in accordance with latest taxable income details available to the taxpayer.

— There is provision for charging a penalty for underestimating the tax liability.

Transitional Arrangements for Payments of Tax.   In order to ease the tax burden on the taxpayers, The Commissioner of Taxes has made transitional arrangements regarding the payment of tax during the first four years of assessment commencing April 1, 1988 and ending on March 31, 1992.

Under these arrangements, the total amount of provisional tax payable for the year of assessment shall be equal to the percentage specified for that year of assessment and shall depend upon whether or not provisional tax payable is based on method 1 or method 2 above.

Below is a table giving details of provisional tax payable during the first four transitional years.

Year of Assessment	Method 1 (% of actual tax paid for the previous year)	Method 2 (% of estimated current tax liability)
First Year	25%	20%
Second Year	50	40
Third Year	75	60
Fourth Year	100	80

It should be noted that the balance of tax payable, between the actual tax liability as reflected by the accounts and tax computations and the provisional tax paid in advance, must be paid at the time of forwarding the accounts, tax returns and tax computations to The Department of Taxes, which is 180 days after the end of the financial year of the particular business.

Provision for Interest and Penalty.   Any taxpayer who fails to forward to The Department of Taxes the quarter's installment of provisional tax payable either under method 1 or method 2, or any taxpayer who, at the time of submitting to The Department of Taxes the tax returns, accounts and tax computations, fails to pay the difference of tax between the actual tax as computed and disclosed in the tax returns and accounts and any provisional tax forwarded or any PAYE or with-holding tax deducted shall be liable for:

☐   Interest equal to 15% of the unpaid tax; and
☐   A penalty at the rate of 5% of the unpaid tax for each month or part thereof up to maximum period of four months during which the tax remains unpaid.

Neither the penalty nor the interest charge is an allowable deduction for tax purposes.

Mode of Payment.   Tax is normally paid by check or cash. However, legislation exists that empowers The Commissioner of Taxes to distrain the goods and chattels of a taxpayer who is unable to pay his or her tax liability. These could be sold by public auction, and the proceeds applied to off-set the tax liability. Any surplus funds realized from the sale would be refunded to the taxpayer.

INCOME TAXES ON INDIVIDUALS

9.   Rates

Graduated Tax.   All employees whose annual earnings do not exceed K2,400 are subject to a graduated tax. The tax deducted is payable to the Commissioner of Taxes or, in the case of a business employing fewer than five persons, used to purchase tax stamps, which are affixed to the employees' tax cards.
   The tax rates effective from April 1, 1990 are:

Annual Earnings	Rate of Graduated Tax
Not exceeding K1,200	2%
Over K1,200 but less than K2,400	3%

Other Taxpayers.   The tax rates effective from April 1, 1991 are:

Taxable Income		Tax on	Percentage
Over	Not Over	Lower Amount	on Excess
K 0	K 2,400	K 0	3%
2,400	8,400	72	12
8,400	18,000	792	22
18,000	36,000	2,904	32
36,000		8,664	40

Minimum Income Tax.   Effective April 1, 1990, minimum tax based on income is payable by individuals engaged in business activities where:

☐   A taxable loss is sustained,
☐   The minimum tax is greater than the tax payable on a taxable profit, or
☐   A taxable profit is offset by tax losses (see item 29).

The rates of applicable tax are:

Annual Income		
Over	Not Over	Minimum Income Tax
K 0	K 500	K 0
500	2,500	25
2,500	5,000	50
5,000	10,000	75
10,000		100

Currently, no child or personal allowances are granted, and there is no relief for life assurance premiums. Employee contributions to an approved pension scheme are deductible, subject to a maximum of the lower of 8% of earnings or K3,000 per year.

Payment of Provisional Tax.   Every individual who is liable to pay income tax under the Taxation Act shall, at the beginning of every year of assessment, estimate the total amount of provisional tax payable in respect of that year of assessment and shall pay such tax in quarterly installments within 30 days after the end of each quarter of that year of assessment.

Exemption From Provisional Tax.   The following classes of individuals are exempt from payment of provisional tax:

☐   Any individual whose income for the year of assessment does not exceed K6,000.00.

□   Any individual whose income, although exceeding K6,000.00, is wholly from employment or pension or from both employment and pension and from which PAYE tax is being deducted.

However, all the above taxpayers at the time of submitting returns of income to The Department of Taxes are required to pay the difference in tax between the actual tax as disclosed in the tax returns and the amount of any PAYE tax paid or withholding tax deducted from their income.

Interest and Penalty.   Any taxpayer who fails to forward to The Department of Taxes the quarter's installment of provisional tax payable either under method 1 or method 2, or any taxpayer who, at the time of submitting to The Department of Taxes the tax returns, accounts and tax computations, fails to pay the difference in tax between the acutal tax as computed and disclosed in the tax returns and accounts and PAYE tax or withholding tax deducted from income is liable to:

□   Interest equal to 15% of the unpaid tax; and

□   A penalty at the rate of 5% of the unpaid tax for each month or part thereof up to the maximum period of four months during which the tax remains unpaid.

Income of Minor Children.   For income tax purposes, a minor is one who is under 21 and unmarried. Minor children who work or run a business, and are living independently of their parents, are subject to tax in their own right. The practice regarding dependent minors is to assess their income in the hands of their parents. However, for minimum tax purposes the effective age is 18.

Income of Married Women.   The income of a married woman is deemed to be the income of her husband and is taxed accordingly. However, if separate taxation of the wife's and husband's earned income would result in a lower tax liability, a tax credit will be granted against the tax produced by combined assessments.

10. Local Income Taxes

None

11. Capital Gains Taxes

None, but the same treatment as for companies applies to the sale of assets on which capital allowances have been claimed and granted (see item 3).

12. Foreign Tax Reliefs

These are not applicable as Malawi taxes are based on income from a source within, or deemed to be within, Malawi.

13. Tax Period

The government financial year runs from April 1 to March 31. A business year may end on March 31 or, subject to approval of The Commissioner of Taxes, any other date that is suited to the nature of trading. A rough working rule is used by the tax authorities to determine the year of assessment of businesses whose year-end falls on dates other than March 31. Businesses with year-ends in April or May are assessed to tax in the prior year ended March 31, while businesses whose year-ends are after May are assessed in the subsequent year that ends March 31.

INCOME TAXES ON NONRESIDENTS

15. Liability to Tax

Unless specifically exempt from tax under an agreement, a double taxation agreement or under tax law, income of a nonresident arising or deemed to arise from a source within Malawi will be subject to tax.

16. Rates

Branch Profits Tax. A nonresident company (i.e., a company not incorporated in Malawi) having a permanent establishment in Malawi (i.e., a branch, office, or other place of business through which business activity is carried on) will be subject to tax at a rate of 45%.

Nonresident Tax. Any income paid, remitted, credited, or accruing to a nonresident arising from a source within Malawi is liable to a nonresident tax of 15% of the gross amount remittable. Exceptions arise in the following circumstances:

☐ Where there is in force a double taxation agreement between Malawi and the country in which the nonresident resides and the provisions of the agreement exempt from Malawi tax the income payable to the nonresident.

☐ The income is specifically exempt from Malawi tax under Schedule 1 of the Taxation Act.

☐ The income is in the nature of a pension or annuity payment.

☐ The payment relates to the importation of tangible goods.

☐ The income arises from the rendering of international transport services by a resident of a country that also exempts from tax any payments to residents of Malawi for rendering similar services.

☐ Payments for education, medical services, gifts, life assurance and pension premiums, maintenance of property abroad, repair charges, navigation charges, recruitment expenses, and principal loan repayments.

☐ Income receivable by a nonresident from his or her business or for services performed for a permanent establishment in Malawi that would result in the nonresident person being treated as a resident of Malawi and therefore subject to Malawi income tax.

Interest. Interest received by a nonresident from a debtor in Malawi is subject to the nonresident tax of 15%, with the following exceptions:

☐ If the interest is from local registered stocks on which interest has been specifically exempted from tax by the Minister of Finance.

☐ If the interest is specifically exempt from tax under agreement or tax law or is covered under a double taxation agreement (see item 19).

Royalties, Etc. Royalties, know-how payments, management fees, machine rentals, etc., payable to nonresidents are subject to the 15% nonresident tax except where such payments are exempt from Malawi tax under the provisions contained in double taxation agreements.

19. Tax Treaties

Malawi has entered into double taxation agreements with Denmark, France, Kenya, Netherlands, Norway, South Africa, Sweden, Switzerland, and the United Kingdom.

OTHER SIGNIFICANT TAXES

21. Sales (Value Added)

Surtax is levied on a wide range of imported and locally manufactured goods and, effective July 1, 1991, on certain services provided locally. It is collected by the Department of Customs and Excise from the importer, manufacturers, or service provider.

The surtax tariff has been restructured into the following tariff categories: exempt, 0%, 5%, 10%, 30%, 50%, 75%, and 100%. The higher rates apply to "nonessential" items.

Manufacturing for surtax purposes means the conversion, by manual, mechanical, or other means, of organic or inorganic materials into a new product by changing the size, shape, or nature of the materials, and includes assembly, cooking, mixing, packaging, bottling, mining, refining, and purifying.

Persons affected by the new surtax legislation are all persons who make or import taxable goods. Taxable goods means goods that are wholly or partially made in Malawi or goods imported into Malawi that are specified in the surtax tariff as being liable to surtax.

The type of goods that are liable to surtax have been specified in the Customs (Tariff) Order.

The following services are subject to surtax at a rate of 5%.

☐ Auditors, accountants, and consultants.
☐ Architects, planners, draftsmen, and engineers.
☐ Legal practitioners.
☐ Auctioneers and estate agents.

□   Mail or parcel couriers.

□   Advertising, both audio and visual.

□   Hairdressing, laundry, or dry cleaning.

□   Security guard services.

□   Vehicle maintenance and engine reconditioning.

□   Telecommunications (telephone, telex, fax) and electricity suppliers to commercial and industrial users.

Any person engaged in the provision of taxable goods or services whose gross value exceeds K50,000 in any 12 consecutive months must apply to the Controller of Customs and Excise for registration for surtax within 30 days of exceeding the prescribed value or turn-over limit.

Value for surtax purposes is the selling price that would be charged to an independent third party. This is called the normal selling price. The effect of this definition is that any transfers, sales, or gifts of goods to staff, branches, associated parties, or anyone at a price other than the "normal selling price" must be calculated for surtax purposes at the arm's-length price applicable to an independent buyer.

Once a person is registered for surtax, that person must submit monthly surtax returns to the Department of Customs and Excise before the twentieth day of the following month.

The surtax returns contain details of sales tax (or output tax) and tax on purchases (or input tax). If the value of output tax is greater than the value of input tax, the excess is payable to the Department of Customs and Excise. If input tax exceeds output tax, the excess is carried forward to the next month.

Providers of services cannot offset input tax on imported or manufactured goods against output tax, while manufactures cannot offset input tax on services against output tax on manufactured goods. To ensure compliance with the surtax legislation, provision has been made for the charging of penalties by way of an additional surtax levy if persons delay or default in the rendering of the monthly returns.

Some registered persons for surtax are wholly or partially exempt from payment of surtax in the following circumstances.

□   If a person makes goods that are wholly for export, no surtax is charged on the goods exported and the person reclaims any surtax paid on the materials from which the exported goods were made. In these circumstances, the person is always in a net refund situation and is considered to be wholly exempt.

□   If a person makes sales from goods of which some are exempt and others are not, then the person is partially exempt. The effect of this is that the person cannot take credit on the tax that is borne on the raw materials used to manufacture/supply the exempt goods.

22.   Inheritance and Gift Taxes

Estate duty is payable on all estates over K30,000 at the following rates:

Principal Value of Estate

Over	Not Over	Rate
K 30,000	K 40,000	4%
40,000	80,000	5
80,000	140,000	6
140,000	200,000	7
200,000	400,000	8
400,000	600,000	9
600,000		10

No gift taxes are levied in Malawi.

23. Taxes on Payrolls (Social Security)

There are no social security taxes. Contributions by employers and employees to approved pension funds and annuity schemes operated by insurance companies are allowable deductions, as are premiums paid for workmen's compensation insurance policies.

24. Taxes on Natural Resources

None.

25. Other Taxes

Land and Property Transfers. Land and property are subject to transfer duties that approximate 3% of the value of the property, plus a registration fee of K15.

Donation Tax. Only donations between K20 and K10,000 to charitable organizations approved by the Minister of Finance normally are deductible.

Withholding Tax. Certain payments for supplies and services are subject to a withholding tax. The tax is deducted by the payor and remitted to the Department of Taxes on a monthly basis (by the 14th of following month). The payee will treat the deduction for bookkeeping purposes as an advance payment of tax which will be offset against the income tax subsequently assessed. The Commissioner may exempt from withholding tax the receipts of certain persons or organizations. Withholding tax exemption certificates will normally be issued to taxpayers whose tax affairs are up to date.

Most fees and commissions	10%
Royalties	10%
Most rents	10%
Payments of over K500 for supplies to traders and institutions (e.g., Government	

Departments) under tender or any similar
arrangements:

Foodstuffs	5%
Other	10%
Transportation	5%
Payments to all contractors and subcontractors (of whatever category)	5%
Payments of over K500 for tobacco and other farm produce	5%
Payments over K500 for personal services	5%
Payments for public entertainment	5%
Bank interest exceeding K100	10%

Life Assurance. The investment income derived by life assurance companies (excluding pensions, provident, and annuity funds) is taxed on the basis of a formula, which is gross taxable investment income (including income from properties) less expenses relating to taxable investment income (but not to exceed 70% of gross taxable income). Taxable income is taxed at a rate of 30%.

Fringe Benefits Tax. The Taxation (Amendment) Act, 1991, contained provisions for the introduction of a fringe benefits tax. The regulations governing the introduction, administration, and payment of the tax were included in a Government Gazette Extraordinary dated May 16, 1991.

The fringe benefits tax is applicable to fringe benefits provided by an employer to an employee. Fringe benefits include payments made by an employer directly to third parties in respect of goods and services provided to an employee. Fringe benefits do not include payments made by an employer directly to an employee. Payments of allowances, rentals, and expenses made directly to an employee are termed cash benefits and form part of an employee's assessable income.

Effective April 1, 1991, all employers, other than the Government, are liable to pay fringe benefits tax on all fringe benefits provided to employees whose annual taxable income exceeds K3,000. A fringe benefit is defined as any asset, service or other benefit provided by or on behalf of an employer to an employee where the benefit includes an element of personal benefit to the employee. The term employee includes a company director.

☐ Rate and Calculation of Fringe Benefits Tax. Fringe benefit tax is payable at a rate of 40% calculated on the taxable value of fringe benefits provided by an employer. The taxable values of fringe benefits are to be calculated as follows:

Accommodation	Tax
Furnished accommodation	12% of an employee's basic salary
Unfurnished accommodation	10% of an employee's basic salary

The benefit is subject to a maximum taxable value of K15,000 per employee per annum. Where the accommodation is situated within the business premises, the taxable value of the benefit may be reduced by 30%. Business premises include the entire area of land on which the premises are situated. Agricultural estates are classified as business premises.

The payment of rent to an employee occupying his own property renders the employer liable to the tax. The employee is liable to income tax on the rental income. However, the employee may claim expenditure incurred on the property and building society interest as allowable deductions.

Motor vehicles	Annual Taxable Value
Not exceeding 1600 cc	K4,800
Exceeding 1600 cc but not exceeding 2000 cc	6,000
Exceeding 2000 cc	9,600

□ School Fees. The taxable value is calculated on the basis of 50% of the cost of school fees and related expenses paid by an employer directly to institutions.

□ Other Fringe Benefits. The taxable value is the total cost to the employer. Other fringe benefits include charges for telephone, electricity, water, security guards and watchmen, household items, gardeners and house servants, and any other benefits provided.

Fringe benefits tax is payable quarterly in arrears. The initial quarter ran from April 1, 1991 to June 30, 1991. The tax is payable within 14 days of the quarter end. Any delay in the payment of the tax renders an employer liable to a penalty of 20% of the tax due. A completed fringe benefit tax return FBT2 must accompany the remittance.

Employers are required to maintain records showing: (a) the nature of fringe benefits provided; (b) the names of employees receiving fringe benefits; and (c) the taxable values of fringe benefits.

Employers already providing fringe benefits were required to register by May 31, 1991. New employers or employers not already providing fringe benefits are required to register within the month in which fringe benefits are first provided to employees. Registration is to be effected by submitting a completed Form FBT1 to the Commissioner of Taxes. Failure to register or any delay in registration renders an employer liable to a penalty of 20% of the tax due.

Allowances and other cash benefits paid to employees (e.g., housing, car, and educational allowances) are not subject to fringe benefits tax. Unless an allowance has been approved by the Commissioner of Taxes as being payable free of income tax, the allowance forms part of an employee's taxable income and is therefore subject to PAYE.

Effective April 1, 1991, any sum payable by an employer to an employee in respect of expenses shall be treated as a perquisite of employment and included as assessable income on an employee's Form P9. However, an employee may claim as a deduction any sum expended by him wholly and exclusively in performing his duties. An employee includes a company director.

COMPUTATION OF TAXABLE INCOME

26. Capital Gains

See item 3.

27. Depreciation and Depletion

Depreciation as recorded in the accounts is disregarded and capital allowances are granted as follows:

	Initial Allowances	Annual Allowances	
		1st Year	Thereafter
Industrial buildings	10%	5%	5%
Trucks and heavy lorries	20	25–33.33	25–33.33
Saloons and pick-ups	20	20	20
Plant and machinery	20	10–15	10–15
Furniture and fittings	20	10	10
Motorcycles and bicycles	20	20–25	20–25

The initial and first year allowances are normally based on cost and the annual allowances thereafter are normally based on the reduced balance of undepreciated cost. In addition, certain businesses such as manufacturing and farming are granted an investment allowance on new and unused assets brought into use during the year of assessment. The investment allowance is 40% of cost and is deductible from cost of the asset in the capital allowances computation.

No initial allowance is due in respect of assets upon which investment allowance has been claimed.

Capital allowances may be claimed on the cost of qualifying fixed assets acquired under finance leases. Finance charges incurred represent an allowable expense.

28. Treatment of Dividends

Dividends received by resident individuals from external sources are not subject to tax as it is not income from a source within, or deemed to be within, Malawi.

Dividends received by resident individuals from Malawi companies which have been declared out of taxed profits are grossed-up by the attributable tax paid by the company. The gross dividend is taxable but a tax credit equal to the grossing-up element is given in the assessment. Dividends declared from untaxed profits, such as profit on the sale of assets, are not taxable.

Dividends received by taxpayers other than individuals are exempt from income tax.

29. Loss Carryovers

Taxpayers can carry losses forward indefinitely for set off against future income; there is no loss carryback. In the case of individuals, losses from one source of income may be offset against profits from another source in the same year of assessment with any losses not fully utilized being carried forward.

Provisions exist which do not permit bankrupt or insolvent persons, or those who have made deeds of arrangement with creditors, to carryover losses. Also, new companies cannot be formed for the specific purpose of taking over the assessed losses of other companies.

30. Transactions between Related Parties

All transactions between related parties are deemed to be at open market values and at arm's length. Where this is not the case, the Department of Taxes may place arbitrary values on such transactions.

31. Consolidation of Income

Related corporations are not permitted to file a consolidated tax return, but branches or unincorporated divisions of the same organization are taxed on a consolidated basis.

32. Tax Periods

The year of assessment does not coincide with the government financial year, which runs from April 1 to March 31. The year of assessment means any 12-month period with respect to which the tax leviable under the Malawi Taxation Act is chargeable.

The income tax forms are issued throughout the year depending on the taxpayer's financial year-end. Tax, based on actual income, should be paid within 180 days after the closing of the financial year-end. Extensions of time are available if reasonable grounds exist.

After the assessor examines the tax return and agrees with the information provided, an assessment is issued to the taxpayer who has 45 days from the issue date of the assessment to pay the outstanding tax liability. After the 45-day period, a 14-day grace period is allowed before interest is charged for late payment.

33. Other Matters

Assessable Income Defined. Assessable income is the total amount, in cash or otherwise, received by or accrued to the taxpayers in any year of assessment from a source within or deemed to be within Malawi, but excluding:

☐ Any amount so received or accrued which is proved by the taxpayer to be of a capital nature.

☐ Any amount exempt from tax under the Act (e.g., foreign-source income).

"Taxable income" is defined as assessable income less any expenditure and losses wholly and exclusively incurred by the taxpayer for the purposes of his trade or in the production of income—such expenditures or losses should not be of a capital nature.

RELATED CONSIDERATIONS

34. Incentives and Grants

As a developing nation, Malawi seeks to promote farming and industry through the following incentives and grants:

☐ Investment allowance of 40% of the cost of new and unused plant or machinery or industrial buildings which are brought into use during the year of assessment. This is deductible from the cost of the asset for capital allowances purposes.

☐ Taxpayers engaged in pastoral, agricultural, or other farming are allowed to deduct in full, in the year of assessment, the cost incurred for:
—Stumping, leveling, and clearing of land.
—The prevention of soil erosion.
—Boreholes or wells.
—Aerial or geophysical surveys.
—Any "water control work" connected with the cultivation of rice, sugar cane, or any other crop designated by the Minister.

☐ The proposed introduction of an export allowance enabling exporters to obtain relief in respect of exports made during the year of assessment would be based on a relief of 4% of the F.O.B. value of the export sales.

35. Exchange Controls

A company (or branch) may apply to remit dividends (or profits) abroad provided it does not have a local overdraft facility. Currently, to obtain approval to remit dividends or profits, a taxpayer must furnish the Reserve Bank with:

☐ A tax clearance certificate from the Commissioner of Taxes certifying that the tax for the year has been paid or that satisfactory arrangements have been made.

☐ Proof of the income tax assessment and, where necessary, receipt for tax payment.

☐ A copy of the audited accounts showing the dividend payable and a copy of the minutes of the annual general meeting at which the dividend was declared.

☐ A receipt or exemption certificate in respect of remittances subject to the 15% nonresident tax.

36. Investment Restrictions on Nonresidents

There are no apparent restrictions on foreign investors. Investment that is vital to the economy is welcomed. However, there are possibilities that local participation on an almost equal basis will be required. All investments require prior exchange control approval.

The government appears to encourage operations that are labor intensive and geared toward import substitution. Most businesses require government trading licenses.

SELECTION OF BUSINESS ENTITY BY NONRESIDENTS

Nonresident investors can operate in Malawi either through a branch or by forming a local company. Branches of externally incorporated companies are liable to tax at 45%; whereas locally incorporated companies are taxed at 40%. However, unless exempted under double taxation agreements, dividends remitted abroad by a local company will attract a 15% nonresident tax. Profits remitted by a local company by way of dividend will therefore suffer tax at an effective rate of 49%.

Although the use of a branch rather than a limited company prima facie seems advantageous, it should be remembered that income arising from services or work performed for a branch (permanent establishment) could render the recipient liable to Malawi income tax. In these circumstances, a decision would need to be based on matters such as the nature of the business and its mode of operations.

If expatriate staff are required by a business operation in Malawi, then work permits must be obtained from the Department of Immigration before they can commence work.

SPECIMEN TAX COMPUTATION

Information:

☐ Company incorporated in Malawi and based on the accounts for the year ended August 31, 1991.

Computation:

Profit per accounts		K21,000
Add		
Depreciation	K 1,500	
Donations to nonapproved bodies	150	

Exchange loss on foreign loan	100	
General expenses	50	
Doubtful debts (general provision)	200	
Provision for claims (general provision)	100	
Income tax interest (per accounts)	275	
Legal expenses (non-trade debt collection)	40	
Loss (capital) on sale of fixed assets	125	
Rent and rates (undeveloped property)	55	2,595
		K23,595
Passage and gratuity provisions carried forward	15,000	
Less		
Passage and gratuity provisions brought forward		1,000
	14,000	K24,595
Less		
Passages and gratuities paid		12,000
		K12,595
Less		
Capital allowances		
Investment at 40% of cost (1)	3,000	
Annual	750	
Balancing allowance (2)	150	
	3,900	
Less		
Balancing charge (3)	200	
	3,700	
Profit on sale of fixed assets	150	3,850
Taxable income		K 8,745
Income tax (at 40%)		K 3,498

Notes
(1) No initial allowance is available for assets qualifying for investment allowance.
(2) Where written-down value for tax purposes exceeds sales proceeds.
(3) Where written-down value for tax purposes is less than sales proceeds.

MALAYSIA

INCOME TAXES ON CORPORATIONS

1. Rates

The scope of the Malaysian Income Tax Act 1967 is territorial, i.e., tax is charged on income accruing in or derived from Malaysia or received in Malaysia from outside Malaysia.

All corporations are subject to income tax at a flat rate of 35% on Malaysian-source income or foreign-source income received by corporations resident in Malaysia. An additional income tax, the "development tax," is imposed at the rate of 3% on "development income," which is defined as income from any trade or business and from rental income of property situated in Malaysia after deducting unabsorbed business and property losses.

Effective from the 1988 year of assessment, the definition of the term "Malaysia" means: ". . .the territories of the Federation of Malaysia, the territorial waters of Malaysia and the sea-bed and subsoil of the territorial waters, and includes any area extending beyond the limits of the territorial waters of Malaysia, and the sea-bed and subsoil of any such area, which has been or may hereafter be designated under the laws of Malaysia as an area over which Malaysia has sovereign rights for the purposes of exploring and exploiting the natural resources, whether living or non-living."

With the wider definition of "Malaysia," activities carried on outside the territorial waters but within the exclusive economic zone of Malaysia are deemed to be carried on in Malaysia, and any income derived therefrom would be subject to Malaysian income tax.

Income of the following would be taxed:

☐ persons engaged in exploration activities off the coast of Malaysia;
☐ persons engaged in sea transport undertaking; and
☐ persons working off-shore and not residing in Malaysia.

2. Local Income Taxes

None.

3. Capital Gains Taxes

There is no comprehensive capital gains tax. However, gain from the sale of ''any land situated in Malaysia and any interest, option, or other right in or over such land'' is subject to a real property gains tax. The rate of tax on the gains depends on the period the property was held prior to the date of disposition, as follows:

Asset's Holding Period	Rate of Tax
Less than two years after acquisition of the asset	20%
In the third year	15
In the fourth year	10
In the fifth year	5
In the sixth year or thereafter	Nil

In the case of a corporation, the rate of tax will be 5% with respect to dispositions of real property in the fifth year or thereafter, effective October 24, 1986.

There is no real property gains tax on dispositions after October 22, 1981 as a result of a compulsory acquisition under the law. A real property gains tax exemption is provided for gains on the transfer of assets under a scheme approved by the Director General of Inland Revenue for the reconstruction of corporations, or for gains arising from the distribution of assets on the liquidation of assets or of a company with similar approval. A transferor corporation qualifies for the exemption only if the transferee corporation is restructured under the plan.

Gains from the disposal of shares in real property companies are subject to real property gains tax at the above rates. A real property company (RPC) is a controlled company (i.e., a company having not more than 50 shareholders and controlled by not more than five persons which holds real property or shares owned in a real property company (chargeable asset), the market value of which is not less than 75% of the value of its total tangible assets as of October 21, 1988 or a subsequent date. If the RPC acquires additional real property or shares in an RPC the market value of which is equivalent to or exceeds 50% of the market value of the real property or shares in an RPC it already owns, then the date of acquisition of the chargeable asset is the date of acquisition of the additional real property or shares in the RPC or both.

4. Branch Profits Taxes

Branch profits of a nonresident corporation in Malaysia are taxed at the regular corporate rates (see items 1 and 16).

5. Foreign Tax Reliefs

Corporations resident in Malaysia can claim a credit against Malaysian tax with respect to foreign taxes paid on foreign-source income either under a double tax treaty or by unilateral relief.

□ Double Taxation Relief. The credit allowed a taxpayer shall not exceed a sum equal to so much of the Malaysian tax payable for that year as bears to the whole of that Malaysian tax the same proportion as that foreign income bears to total income for that year. However, the total credit allowed for a year of assessment shall not exceed the total Malaysian tax payable on the taxpayer's chargeable income for that year before the allowance of any credit.

□ Unilateral Relief. Unilateral relief shall not exceed one-half the foreign tax payable on that income for that year.

6. Classification of Corporations

Corporations are classified for Malaysian tax purposes as resident corporations or nonresident corporations. A corporation carrying on business is resident in Malaysia for the basis year for a year of assessment if at any time during that basis year the management and control of its business are exercised in Malaysia. Any other corporation is resident in Malaysia for the basis year for a year of assessment if at any time during that basis year the management and control of its affairs are exercised in Malaysia by its directors or other controlling authority. A resident corporation is liable to Malaysian tax on the income accruing in or derived from Malaysia or received in Malaysia from outside Malaysia. A nonresident corporation is not liable to Malaysian tax on income arising from sources outside Malaysia and received in Malaysia. The distinction between resident and nonresident corporations has a bearing on the amount of income tax payable and the treatment of dividends paid.

7. Payment of Taxes

The tax for a year of assessment is due and payable upon the service of the notice of assessment. However, the Director General of Inland Revenue allows the tax to be paid by five monthly installments beginning in January or February; January for tax reference numbers ending in odd numbers and February for even numbers. All earlier assessments must be settled as arranged or within 30 days of the service of the relevant notices of assessment.

A penalty of 10% is imposed on any tax that is not paid within 30 days after service of the assessment notice. Any balance remaining unpaid on the expiration of 60 days from the date of such increase is increased by a further 5% of the balance unpaid.

Effective January 1, 1989, every taxpayer (individuals and businesses) subject to tax must make payments by installments, as the Director General may direct whether the tax has been assessed. A penalty of 10% will be imposed if:

□ the taxpayer underestimates his tax liability by more than 30% compared with the actual assessment made by the Director General, or

□ the taxpayer fails to settle the tax installment within 30 days from the date stipulated by the Director General.

INCOME TAXES ON INDIVIDUALS

9. Rates

Individuals resident in Malaysia are subject to tax at graduated rates on taxable income after deducting personal allowances. The rates of tax applicable to the various brackets of taxable income beginning at M$2,500 are:

Taxable Income		Tax on Lower Amount	Percentage on Excess
Over	Not Over		
M$ 0	M$ 2,500	M$ 0	4%
2,500	5,000	100	7
5,000	10,000	275	10
10,000	20,000	775	12
20,000	35,000	1,975	17
35,000	50,000	4,525	22
50,000	70,000	7,825	27
70,000	100,000	13,225	32
100,000		22,825	35

A nonresident individual is taxed at a flat rate of 35% on gross income.

Individuals, whether or not resident, are also liable to development tax if they have development income (see item 1). Where an individual derives income from a business (whether as a sole proprietor or a partner), the tax is imposed at the rate of 3% of his development income in excess of M$5,000. Individuals resident in Malaysia are entitled to the following personal reliefs:

Self	M$4,000
Dependent (automatically given with self relief)	M$1,000
Wife	M$3,000
Children	
First to fifth child	M$800 (each)
Physically or mentally disabled children	M$1,000 (each)
Insurance premiums and contributions to approved pension funds	M$3,500 maximum

If any child is over the age of 16 and receiving full-time instruction at a university, college or other establishment (similar to a university or college) in a place outside Malaysia and Singapore, the relief is up to four times the usual deduction.

A tax rebate of M$90 is given to a resident married man supporting a nonworking wife or whose wife's income is aggregated with his income for tax assessment. A wife is assessed separately on all of her income unless she elects a combined assessment. In this case, she is allowed a tax rebate of M$30, while her husband is entitled to a rebate of M$60. To every other resident individual, a tax rebate of M$60 is allowed.

However, the income tax rebates of M$60 and M$30 for a resident individual and his wife, respectively, is given only for taxable income not exceeding M$10,000.

A tax deduction scheme applies to employees who are liable to tax of M$1,000 or more. For expatriate employees, the deduction scheme would include advance collection of tax for several years of assessment.

The tax for a year of assessment is due and payable upon the service of the notice of assessment. However, arrangements may be made beginning each calendar year for settlement of the tax in monthly installments. Failure to do so would result in the imposition of a late payment penalty of 10% of the tax so unpaid after 30 days as well as 5% of the unpaid balance after a further 60 days.

10. Local Income Taxes

None.

11. Capital Gains Taxes

There is no capital gains tax other than the tax on real property gains. An individual is assessed on net chargeable gains in the year of assessment after a deduction equal to the greater of M$5,000 or 10% of the gain. The rate of tax is inversely proportional to the duration of ownership (see item 3).

12. Foreign Tax Reliefs

Same as item 5.

13. Tax Period

December 31 is the standard tax year-end. For Malaysian tax purposes, the calendar year immediately preceding a year of assessment constitutes the basis year for that year of assessment. For individual employees, the basis of assessment for any year is the income of the preceding year. In the case of individuals deriving income from a business or profession, the basis will depend on the accounting or financial year of the business or profession.

INCOME TAXES ON NONRESIDENTS

15. Liability to Tax

A nonresident is liable to Malaysian tax on all income accruing in or derived from Malaysia. Income arising from foreign sources and received in Malaysia by a nonresident is not subject to Malaysian tax. In the case of a person (including a corporation) resident in a country which has a double taxation treaty with Malaysia, such person is not liable to Malaysian tax on the income from business carried on in Malaysia unless the person has a permanent establishment in Malaysia. The liability is on the income or profits attributable to that permanent establishment. However, Malaysian tax is nevertheless imposed on other income accruing in or derived from Malaysia whether or not there is a permanent establishment.

16. Rates

Nonresident corporations are liable to income tax on their Malaysian sourced business income at the rate of 35%. This rate also applies to other Malaysian sourced income such as dividends and rents. However, interest and royalty derived from Malaysia by nonresident corporations are subject to tax on the gross amount (see item 17). Development tax of 3% is also imposed on nonresident corporations with development income (see item 1). A resident of a treaty country deriving interest and royalties from Malaysia may not be liable to excess profit tax on such income.

17. Withholding Tax Rates

There is no dividend withholding tax in Malaysia (see item 19, note 1). A withholding tax is imposed on the gross amount of interest or royalties derived from Malaysia and paid to a person not known to be resident in or have a place of business in Malaysia. Certain tax treaties reduce the rate to zero. In the case of loans or credit to the Malaysian Government, state governments, local authorities, or a statutory body by a nonresident person, there is no tax withheld on interest payments to nonresidents. Interest paid to nonresidents by a commercial or merchant bank operating in Malaysia is also exempt from tax.

Subject to double taxation treaties (see item 19), withholding tax at the rate specified is required to be deducted in the case of payments made to nonresidents:

Interest	20%
Rent or other payments for the use of movable property	15%
Royalties	15%
Services in connection with the use of property or the installation or operation of plant or machinery purchased from nonresidents	15%
Technical advice, assistance, or services in connection with technical management or administration	15%

Interest paid to resident individuals on fixed loans and savings deposits by financial institutions are subject to a withholding tax of 5%, which is a final tax.

18. Special Withholding Provisions

Payments of interest and royalties derived or deemed to be derived from Malaysia and paid or credited to a nonresident person not having a place of business in

Malaysia are subject to 20% and 15% withholding tax, respectively, which may be reduced under a double taxation agreement (see item 17). Since January 1, 1983, a person making or crediting payments to a nonresident contractor for services under a contract must deduct tax at the rate of:

☐ Fifteen percent of the contract payment on account of tax that is or may be payable by the nonresident contractor for any year of assessment.

☐ Five percent of the contract payment on account of tax that is or may be payable by employees of that nonresident contractor for any year of assessment.

Effective October 23, 1983, a person who makes or is liable to make payments to a nonresident for services in connection with the use of property, for technical advice, assistance or services in connection with technical management or administration of any scientific, industrial, or commercial undertaking, venture, project, or scheme, or for rent or other payments that are not payments for film rentals made under any agreement, or arrangements for the use of any movable property shall be liable to deduct 15% tax on the gross amount. Development tax and excess profit tax are not imposed on income from such services or rent.

There are penal provisions for failure to withhold tax on payments of interest, royalties, or other payments.

Agents of nonresident shipping operations are required to withhold tax at the rate of 1.9% of the principal's gross Malaysian freight earnings in respect of each voyage.

19. Tax Treaties

Withholding Taxes

	Interest	Royalties and Certain Rentals	Dividends (1)
Nontreaty countries	0%, 20%	15%	0%
Treaty countries:			
Australia	0, 15	0, 15	0
Austria	0, 15	10, 15	0
Bangladesh	0, 15	0, 15	0
Belgium	0, 10, 20	0, 10	0
Canada	0, 15	0, 15	0
China	0, 10	0, 10, 15	0
Denmark	0, 20	0, 15	0
Finland	0, 15	0, 5, 15	0
France	0, 15	0, 10, 15	0
Germany (East) (2)	0, 10	0, 15	0

Withholding Taxes

	Interest	Royalties and Certain Rentals	Dividends (1)
Germany (West) (2)	0, 15%	0, 10%	0%
Hungary	0, 15	15	0
India	0, 20	0, 15	0
Italy	0, 15	0, 15	0
Japan	0, 10, 20	0, 10	0
Korea	0, 15	0, 10, 15	0
Netherlands	15	10, 15	0
New Zealand	0, 15	0, 15	0
Norway	0, 20	0, 15	0
Pakistan	0, 15	0, 15	0
Philippines	0, 15	0, 15	0
Poland	0, 15	0, 15	0
Romania	0, 15, 20	0, 12	0
Singapore	0, 20	0, 15	0
Soviet Union	0, 15	0, 10, 15	0
Sri Lanka	0, 20	7.5, 15	0
Sweden (3)	0, 20	0, 15	0
Switzerland	0, 10	0, 10	0
Thailand	0, 10, 15, 25	0, 15	0
United Kingdom	0, 15	0, 15	0
U.S.S.R.	0, 15	0, 10, 15	0
Yugoslavia	0, 15	10	0

Notes:

(1) Malaysia does not levy a separate withholding tax on dividends in addition to the 35% corporate income tax. Upon paying a dividend, a corporation resident in Malaysia is required to deduct tax at the rate of 35%. Where no deduction of tax is made, the tax is deemed to be withheld on the dividend as an advance tax by the payor corporation. The tax so deducted or deemed to be deducted is creditable against the income tax liability of the payor company on its income. At the end of each year of assessment, two total amounts must be calculated for each corporation resident in Malaysia. One figure represents the tax paid or payable by the corporation on its income. The other total represents the tax deducted or deemed to be deducted from dividends paid to its shareholders. Where the former total exceeds the latter, the difference is carried forward for franking future dividends. Where the latter exceeds the former, the excess becomes a debt due to the Director General of Inland Revenue.

(2) East and West Germany were reunited, and a new treaty will be negotiated.

(3) A new tax treaty has been initiated with Sweden; details were not available at the time of publication.

There also is an agreement with the United States limited to mutual tax exemption of income from shipping and air transport operations.

OTHER SIGNIFICANT TAXES

21. Sales (Value Added)

Sales tax at 10% is levied on goods (other than beer, wine, vermouth, other fermented beverages, ethyl alcohol, manufactured tobacco, tobacco extracts, and essences, which are taxed at 15%) imported by any person for domestic consumption and on the sales value of goods manufactured and sold or disposed of (otherwise than to another licensed manufacturer who is authorized to acquire such goods without payment of tax). Where the tax has been paid and the goods are exported, there is provision for drawback for sales tax paid. A wide range of goods are exempt from sales tax.

Manufacturers of exempt goods and persons exempt from licensing are prohibited from obtaining their raw materials and components tax-free. However, manufacturers of controlled items and products that are not subject to sales tax need not pay sales tax on raw materials used in the production of these goods if written exemption is obtained from the Customs and Excise Department. Also, manufacturers that cater to the export market can apply for sales tax exemption.

22. Inheritance and Gift Taxes

Estate duty is levied at graduated scales on the estate of the deceased. In the case of any person dying on or after October 19, 1984 who was domiciled in any part of Malaysia, the rate of estate duty payable is as follows:

Taxable Estate		Duty on Lower Amount	Percentage on Excess
Over	Not Over		
M$2,000,000	M$4,000,000	M$ 0	5%
4,000,000		100,000	10

In the case of any person dying on or after October 19, 1984 who is domiciled outside Malaysia, the rates of estate duty payable are as follows:

There is no gift duty in Malaysia. However, effective October 19, 1984, the value of gifts made within the seven-year period prior to the death of the donor will be brought into his estate for estate duty purposes.

23. Taxes on Payrolls (Social Security)

Employers with five or more employees whose individual wages are less than M$1,000 a month are liable for a monthly contribution of between M$0.40 and M$16.65 per employee for invalidity and employment injury schemes, under the Employees' Social Security Act 1969. Employers who are not required to contribute under this Act are required to insure with a locally registered insurance company against any liability which they may incur under the Workmen's Compensation Act, 1952, which covers all manual workers regardless of their wages and nonmanual workers whose earnings do not exceed M$500 a month.

24. Taxes on Natural Resources

Petroleum Income Tax Act.   Persons engaged in petroleum operations are liable to income tax under the Petroleum Income Tax Act, 1967. "Petroleum operations" is defined as searching for and winning or obtaining of petroleum in Malaysia by or on behalf of any person for his own account or on a joint account with any other person by drilling, mining, extracting or other like operations or process, in the course of a business carried on by that person engaged in such operations, and all operations incidental thereto, and any sale or disposal by or on behalf of that person of petroleum so won or obtained, and includes the transportation within Malaysia by or on behalf of that person of petroleum so won or obtained to any point of sale or delivery or export, but does not include:

☐   Any transportation of petroleum outside Malaysia.
☐   Any process of refining or liquefying of petroleum.
☐   Any dealings in petroleum products, refined or liquefied.
☐   Service involving the supplying and use of rigs, derricks, ocean tankers, and barges.

The assessment year is the calendar year and the rate of tax is 45%.

25. Other Taxes

Land and Property.   Property assessments are levied by the local authorities and are based on the annual valuation of the property. Land tax or quit rent is also payable to the State Government.

Stamp Tax.   Stamp duty is imposed on documents. For certain types of documents, the duty is ad valorem. For others, the duty is a fixed fee. For real property and shares, the stamp duty is as follows.

□ Real property. 1% on the first $100,000 and 2% on the balance based on the market value or money value of the consideration, whichever is greater.

□ Shares. 0.3% of the consideration.

Film-Hire Duty. A film-hire duty is payable in respect of proceeds derived from the renting of motion picture films in Malaysia. The duty is 15% of the gross receipts and is payable in quarterly installments.

Custom Duties. Custom duties include import duty, export duty, surtax, and surcharge or cess imposed under the Customs Act, 1967. These duties are levied on goods imported or exported, and are fixed by the Minister of Finance from time to time.

Import Duties. Import duties are levied on the importer and are normally at ad valorem rates ranging from 0–200% of the CIF value. Most dutiable goods are subject to duty within the 15–25% range. Most raw materials, machinery and equipment required for manufacturing and export industries are exempted from this duty, on a case-by-case basis, on written application to the customs authorities. Where duty has been paid, claims may be filed for the refund of the duty.

Surtax. This tax generally is imposed at 5% on imports except for certain goods and essential commodities. The surtax on imported raw materials that are not available locally has been abolished or integrated into the import duty. Full exemption is given on machinery and equipment not produced locally and used in manufacturing. Exemption is allowed on imports of ships exceeding 26 tons.

Export Duty and Surcharge. Export duties and surcharge are levied on exports of primary commodities which include rubber, tin, palm oil and timber. The rates normally increase in proportion to the increase in the prices of the commodities concerned.

Excise Duties. Manufactured goods, such as liquor, tobacco, petroleum products and electrical appliances are subject to excise duties. The methods according to which such duties are to be levied are prescribed by the Minister of Finance. Such duties are payable by the manufacturer upon the sale of the products.

Exemption may be given to a certain class of goods or persons from the payment of the whole or any part of any excise duty which may be payable. But any goods in respect of which an exemption from the payment of excise duties has been granted are deemed dutiable goods until the conditions, if any, subject to which the exemption from duty was granted are fulfilled.

Service Tax. A 5% tax is payable on taxable goods and services sold or provided by prescribed establishments (including hotels, restaurants, private clubs, night clubs, health centers, and public beer houses) in Malaysia (excluding Langkawi and Labuan). Restaurants and private clubs with annual turnover of less than M$500,000 are not regarded as prescribed establishments.

COMPUTATION OF TAXABLE INCOME

26. Capital Gains

Taxable capital gains (see item 3) are calculated on the excess of the sales price over the acquisition price.

27. Depreciation and Depletion

Depreciation adopted in the accounts is ignored for taxation purposes. Instead, there is a system of capital allowances for qualifying capital expenditure. These allowances are given as deductions in computing taxable income, as follows:

Plant. An initial allowance of 20% is given on all qualifying plant expenditure in the year of acquisition. An annual allowance, ranging from 6% to 20% of qualifying plant expenditure is also given the year of acquisition and subsequent years.

Buildings. No capital allowance is allowed on buildings except where used for the purposes of a business and used as a factory, dock, wharf, jetty or warehouse. Initial allowance is allowed at 10% of the qualifying building expenditure and annual allowance on a straight-line basis at an annual rate of 2%.

Buildings used for the purposes of approved research or industrial training or for the storage of imported goods that are to be processed and reexported qualify for industrial building allowances.

Mining. All expenditure incurred in connection with the working of a mine or in preparation for the working of a mine or the acquisition of the mine or rights in or over the mine, in very broad terms, is considered qualifying mining expenditure. Depletion allowances granted to persons incurring such expenditure are deductible over the life of the mine, by dividing the residue of capital expenditure at the end of that period by the residual life of the mine at the beginning of that period.

Effective October 19, 1984, expenditures incurred with respect to exploration for minerals shall be allowed as deduction from aggregate income as and when it is incurred. However, the entire exploration expenditure will then be added to the aggregate income when the prospecting is successful and the mining allowance will be allowed instead. No mining allowance will be allowed if the exploration expenditure is not added back to the aggregate income of the mine. The miner is given the option not to elect for the new treatment.

Other Depletion Allowances. Other allowances are available for capital expenditure incurred by certain businesses. These include a forest allowance, an agricultural allowance and an allowance for abortive prospecting expenditure.

28. Treatment of Dividends

Dividends paid, credited, or distributed by a Malaysian corporation are subject to a deduction of 35% tax at source. Dividends are included at gross in computing the income tax of the recipient. A tax credit of the tax deducted at source on the dividend (at 35%) is allowed in arriving at the net tax payable. Dividends received from overseas are also taxed on the gross amount. The tax credit allowable for the foreign tax imposed on the dividends depends on whether Malaysia has a double tax agreement with the source country. A unilateral tax credit is also granted for the tax imposed on the dividends from countries with which Malaysia has no tax treaty. There is no withholding tax on dividends.

29. Loss Carryovers

Trading losses of the basis year can be offset against income from other sources of that basis year. The balance of the unabsorbed trading losses may be carried forward indefinitely, but may only be offset against business income.

30. Transactions between Related Parties

Transactions between related parties should be at arm's length. The Revenue can disregard certain transactions between related parties and treat such transactions as if they had been on an arm's-length basis. Related corporations shall be deemed to take over capital assets at the net tax written down value of the assets.

31. Consolidation of Income

There is no provision for the filing of consolidated tax returns by related corporations. Each corporation files its own tax return and is taxed on all its income accruing in or derived from Malaysia or received in Malaysia from outside Malaysia.

32. Tax Periods

Tax is assessed on the preceding year basis; that is, for the year of assessment 1992, the basis year is 1991. The calendar year ending December 31 is the basis period for assessment, except in the case of businesses and corporations where a financial year other than December 31 may be allowed.

33. Other Matters

Deductions for Taxes Other than Income Taxes. In computing the liability for income tax, businesses may deduct quit rent and assessments of land and buildings used for the businesses, royalties tax, and service tax. Import duty, surtax, sales tax, and stamp duty are treated as part of the cost of goods acquired. No deduction is available for estate duty, real property gains tax, and development tax.

Inventory Valuation. For tax purposes, inventories may be valued at cost or market value. The method of valuation adopted must be consistently followed in subsequent years.

Bad Debts. General provisions for doubtful debts are not deductible. However, provisions for specific debts are allowable. Bad debts not provided for are deductible when they are actually written off. Any recovery after a debt has been written off is includable in assessable income.

Employee Benefit Provisions. Provisions for employee benefits are not deductible. Deductions for these expenses are allowable only when payments are made to the employee.

Expenses on leave passages, entertainment, and entertainment allowances are not deductible by the employer, effective from the year of assessment 1989.

Entertainment Expenses and Entertainment Allowances. Effective as of the basis period for the year of assessment 1989, an employer may not claim a tax deduction for expenses incurred in providing entertainment, including entertainment allowances paid to employees.

This restriction does not, however, apply to:

- □ Entertainment to employees, except if it is incidental to the provision of entertainment to others.
- □ Entertainment to clients or customers for payment, if the person in question is carrying on the business of providing entertainment.
- □ Expense incurred for promotional gifts at trade fairs or industrial exhibitions held outside of Malaysia for the promotion of exports.
- □ Promotional samples of products of the business of that person.
- □ Entertainment expenses for public, cultural, or sporting events that are incurred wholly to promote the business of that person.

An employee's deduction for entertainment expenses incurred is restricted to a maximum of any entertainment allowance he or she received as part of the employee's gross employment income.

Patent Amortization and Licensing Costs. No allowance is given for such expenditures.

Research Expenses. A double deduction is given if expenses are incurred by the taxpayer on research approved by the Minister. Buildings used for such research will qualify for the industrial building allowances. A double deduction also can be claimed from the gross business income for revenue expenses for

- □ Cash contribution to an approved research institute; and
- □ Payment for services of an approved research institute or an approved research company.

Interest Expenses. Interest paid on loans not used for business purposes is not deductible. If loans were taken for making investments, interest will be allowed against investment income on a source-by-source basis.

Lease Rentals. Lease rentals are deductible unless paid on leases not deemed to be a lease in accordance with the Income Tax Leasing Regulations 1986. Lease rentals on certain motor vehicles in excess of M$50,000 in total per vehicle are not deductible.

RELATED CONSIDERATIONS

34. Incentives and Grants

Tax Rebate on Loans to Small Businesses. A rebate against income tax charged will be given to a person who gives any loan to a small business, where such loan conforms to specific guidelines and the loan is approved before March 30, 1985. The rebate is calculated at 2% pro-rated annually on the outstanding balance, and before any set offs for tax deducted at source, double tax relief, and unilateral relief. Where the rebate exceeds the tax charged, it must be carried forward to set off any income tax chargeable in future years of assessment.

Double Deduction of Expenses. Double deduction of expenses against the adjusted business income is available for:

☐ Export promotion expenses incurred by a resident corporation other than a pioneer corporation.

☐ Freight charges incurred by manufacturers in exporting rattan and wood-based products (excluding sawn timber and veneer).

☐ Insurance premiums on imported cargo paid to Malaysian insurance corporations.

☐ Expenses incurred on training construction workers for three months for approved on-site training.

☐ Interest paid under special loan plan for small businesses.

☐ Export credit insurance with the Malaysia Export Credit Insurance Berhad.

☐ Approved research expenses.

☐ Revenue expenditure for use of facilities and services of approved research companies or institutions.

☐ Cash contributions to approved research institutions.

☐ Remuneration payable to each physically or mentally disabled employee where the employee is not able to perform the work of a normal person.

☐ Expenses for training of handicapped persons, who are not employees, to enhance their employment prospects.

☐ Approved training given by a manufacturing corporation.

☐ Expenses incurred to train workers in small-scale industries with the National Productivity Centre, SIRIM, Mara Institute of Technology, and MARDI.

☐ Specified overseas promotion expenses incurred by hotel and tour operators.

☐ Expenses incurred on approved training for tourist industry.

Investment Incentives. A comprehensive program of tax and investment incentives is available to local and foreign investors in Malaysia. These include:

☐ Tax-free period (pioneer status) for approved hotel and industrial and commercial undertakings; the relief is fixed at five years from the production date; the tax-free period for specified, promoted products may be extended, however, up to ten years.

☐ New corporations that are established by existing pioneer corporations would be given pioneer status/investment tax allowance to manufacture the same products, subject to certain conditions.

☐ The income that is exempt from tax for pioneer corporations is the gross income net of allowable expenses. Losses incurred during the pioneer period are carried forward to the post-pioneer period. Capital allowances are claimed only after the pioneer period.

☐ For applications received on or after January 1, 1991 from corporations that apply for pioneer status, the incentives will be restricted as follows:

—Capital allowances must be utilized during the pioneer period. All capital allowances not utilized will not be allowed to be carried forward.

—Losses unabsorbed during the pioneer period will not be allowed to be carried forward to the post-pioneer period.

☐ For a nonpioneer corporation participating in a promoted activity or product, an investment tax allowance of up to 100% of qualifying capital expenses incurred within a specified five-year period is given as a deduction from adjusted income.

☐ Abatement of adjusted income for resident manufacturing corporations located in promoted industrial areas.

☐ 5% abatement of adjusted income for resident small-scale manufacturing corporations.

☐ Small-scale manufacturing resident corporations would be granted pioneer status, effective as of the year of assessment 1990. Alternatively, reinvestment allowance of 50% of qualifying capital expenditure will be given. Also, full exemption from import duties will be granted on machinery and raw materials and preference given to government procurement. Small-scale corporations must not have shareholders' funds exceeding M$500,000.

☐ 5% abatement of adjusted income or 5% of total value of components purchased, whichever is lower, for resident manufacturing corporations that purchase components under subcontract exchange program registered with the Ministry of International Trade and Industry.

☐ Abatement of adjusted income for exports manufactured by resident corporations. The abated amounts can be used to distribute tax exempt dividends.

☐ An export allowance for agricultural products produced by a resident corporation, agro-based cooperative society, farmer's association, fishermen's association, sole proprietorship, partnership, or association solely engaged in agriculture.

☐ Export allowance for resident trading corporations which export any product manufactured in Malaysia.

☐ Accelerated depreciation allowances of 40% annually.

☐ Tariff protection for certain local industries.

☐ Exemption from import duties on raw materials and machinery for pioneer corporations and for certain industries.

☐ Exemptions or drawbacks from import and excise or other duties for certain goods exported.

☐ Preferential government buying of locally manufactured products.

☐ Approved Operational Headquarters (OHQ) set up by foreign-owned multinationals operating in Malaysia and carrying out activities for subsidiaries and associates in the region will be subject to concessionary income tax of 10% on management fees, interest, and royalty income. Dividends received from investments by OHQs will be exempt from tax.

☐ Gains accruing to an approved venture capital corporation from the disposal of shares in a venture corporation and dividends distributed out of those gains are eligible for tax exemption.

☐ Pioneer status/investment tax allowance/export allowance for a corporation or noncorporate business engaged in approved agricultural projects may claim a deduction of captial expenditure against aggregate income, subject to a timeframe and minimum hectarage of production.

Industrial Adjustment Allowance (IAA). A manufacturing corporation that undertakes an approved industrial adjustment program can apply for an IAA based on capital expenditures incurred. Industrial adjustment means any approved activity proposed to be undertaken by a particular sector in the manufacturing industry to restructure by way of reorganization, reconstruction or amalgamation with that particular sector with a view to strengthen the basis for industrial self-sufficiency, improving industrial technology, increasing productivity, enhancing the efficient use of natural resources, and the efficient management of manpower.

Double Deduction for Manufacturing Sector Training Expenses. A corporation in the manufacturing sector that has obtained approval from the Ministry of Human Resources to participate in a training program for full-time employees who are Malaysian citizens is allowed a double deduction of certain specified training expenses. To qualify for approved status, training programs proposed by the manufacturing sector should be directed toward developing and upgrading skills required to:

□ Manufacture new or improved products.

□ Improve manufacturing process in line with new technologies adopted.

Double Deduction for Construction Industry Training Expenses. A person who has registered to participate in a scheme for the training of employees in the construction industry is allowed a double deduction not exceeding the first three months' remuneration payable to those employees.

Effective October 21, 1988 to December 31, 1993, income earned by Malaysian construction corporations from overseas projects and remitted to Malaysia will be abated by 50% and the amount abated will be exempt from income tax and development tax. Dividends paid from the exempt income also will be exempt in the hands of the recipient. The overseas income must be remitted to Malaysia within five years of the project commencement.

Unit Trusts. Effective as of the year of assessment 1990, a special deduction of one-tenth of the qualifying capital expenditure would be given to a unit trust on machinery and plan installed to derive rental income from the leasing of the real property. A minimum of 10% and a maximum of 25% of certain expenses, which normally would not be allowable for tax purposes, would be allowed. However, any unabsorbed allowances or unabsorbed expenses could not be carried forward to a subsequent year. Gains from realization of investments by unit/property trusts will not be subject to income tax and development tax. However, gains from the sales of real property and shares in real property companies will be subject to real property gains tax.

Insurance Businesses. An insurer carrying on inward reinsurance business whether or not with other general business or life insurance, would be subject to income tax at the rate of 5% and development tax at 4% on the profits from such inward reinsurance business. The balance of the chargeable income from such inward reinsurance business less 5% income tax can be paid as tax-exempt dividends to shareholders. Similar incentives are given to an insurer engaged in offshore insurance.

Reinvestment Allowance. A corporation resident in Malaysia may obtain a reinvestment allowance on capital expenditure incurred on a factory or on plant and machinery or other apparatus for the purpose of a qualifying project. Expenditure incurred from January 1, 1988 to December 31, 1995 qualifies for reinvestment allowance of 40% of qualifying capital expenditure. The reinvestment allowance will be 50% of qualifying capital expenditure for small-scale industries.

A qualifying project is one for manufacturing or processing undertaken by a corporation in expanding or modernizing its existing business or diversifying into related products.

The reinvestment allowance is deducted from the adjusted income of that year of assessment. Where the reinvestment allowance is not allowed in full, the balance is carried forward to subsequent years until the corporation has received the full allowance. The reinvestment allowance can be paid as tax-exempt dividends to shareholders.

Tax Relief for Shipping Corporations.   The statutory income of a resident person from the business of transporting passengers or cargo aboard certain Malaysian ships registered under the Merchant Shipping Ordinance, 1952, is exempt from tax. Any amount of income of the Malaysian ship is exempted from tax, and such amount is available for paying tax-free dividends.

Tax Haven Status for Labuan Island.   Labuan Island, off the coast of Sabah in East Malaysia, has been established as a tax haven. The principal tax provisions are contained in the Labuan Offshore Business Activity Tax Act, 1990. The Act takes effect as of the assessment year 1991. In summary, the provisions of the Act are as follows.

☐   Tax will not be charged under the Income Tax Act of 1967 on the income of an offshore corporation on income from its offshore business activity.

☐   The applicable tax rate will be 3% of the chargeable profits of an offshore corporation from banking, insurance, trading, management, licensing, or any other activity that is not an offshore non-trading activity.

☐   An offshore corporation means an offshore corporation incorporated under the Offshore Companies Act of 1990 and includes a foreign offshore corporation registered under that Act and an offshore trust.

☐   An offshore corporation carrying on an offshore non-trading activity, i.e., investment holding on its own behalf, is not subject to tax under the Act.

☐   An offshore corporation carrying on both offshore trading and non-trading activities is deemed to be carrying on an offshore trading activity.

☐   The tax must be paid at the time of filing the statutory declaration or returns.

35. Exchange Controls

There is only minimal control on all payments, including the repatriation of capital and the remittance of profits or technical assistance fees. No exchange control permission is required for a nonresident to undertake direct or portfolio investment in Malaysia. No permission need be sought nor form filed for all payments of M$10,000 or less. Where a single payment in foreign currency exceeds M$10,000, an Exchange Control Form P must be completed and approved by an authorized bank before the payment can be effected. An authorized bank may approve any Form P without reference to the Controller of Foreign Exchange, provided that, if the payment is for the purchase of shares or immovable property (whether in or outside Malaysia), the payment is not financed with funds borrowed in ringgit in Malaysia.

36. Investment Restrictions on Nonresidents

There are generally no investment restrictions on nonresidents, but the New Economic Policy of the Government must be followed. Guidelines have been issued to regulate the acquisition of assets, mergers, and takeovers by foreign or Malaysian interests. These guidelines apply to the following transactions:

☐ Proposed acquisitions of ''substantial'' fixed assets in Malaysia.

☐ Proposed asset acquisitions, mergers, or takeovers of Malaysian corporations that will result in ownership or control passing to the foreign investor.

☐ Proposed acquisitions of at least 15% or 30% (in the aggregate) of the voting power of a Malaysian corporation by a single interest (or associated group) or foreign interests, respectively.

☐ Obtaining control of a Malaysian corporation under a joint venture, management, or technical assistance agreement.

☐ Any merger or takeover of a Malaysian corporation by Malaysian or foreign investors.

☐ Proposed acquisitions of assets or interests exceeeding M $5 million in value by Malaysian or foreign investors.

The guidelines do not apply to specific projects approved by the Government. Some modifications will be made to the guidelines by October 1991.

SELECTION OF BUSINESS ENTITY BY NONRESIDENTS

Nonresident investors can operate in Malaysia through a branch or a local subsidiary corporation. The tax consequences for a foreign entity that carries on business in Malaysia through a branch are:

☐ Branch profits are liable to income tax and development tax (see item 16).

☐ Repatriation of branch profits is not subject to tax.

☐ Subject to an agreement for the avoidance of double taxation, interest and royalties derived or deemed to be derived from Malaysia are subject to tax at 20% and 15%, respectively.

Foreign investors are encouraged to incorporate local corporations with equity participation by Malaysians. Dividends paid by such resident corporations are deemed to be derived from Malaysia and a tax credit of the tax deducted at source is allowed (see item 28). Thus, the question of whether a branch or a locally incorporated corporation is optimum for Malaysian tax purposes does not arise, except in certain cases where the registration of a Malaysian branch is permitted.

SPECIMEN TAX COMPUTATION

Information:

□ The corporation's operating profit for the year ended December 31, 1991 of M$2 million consists of the following:

	M$ '000's
Trading results in Malaysia	1,600
Trading results from overseas—taxed in country of derivation and remitted to Malaysia	100
Malaysian dividend income (gross)	100
Overseas dividend income (remitted to Malaysia)	100
Profit on sale of land	100
	M$ 2,000

□ The Malaysian trading results are arrived at after charging the following items:

Accounts depreciation	500
Transfer to provision for employee benefits	200

□ Allowable tax depreciation for the year is M$200,000 and payments debited to the employee benefits provisions are M$100,000.

□ The vacant land, acquired on January 1, 1981 at a cost of M$400,000, was sold for M$500,000 on September 30, 1991.

□ The overseas dividend income is from a nontreaty country and has suffered tax at 40%.

□ The trading profit from a treaty country has suffered foreign tax at 40%.

Computation:

	Resident Corporation		Nonresident Corporation	
	(M$ '000's)	(M$ '000's)	(M$ '000's)	(M$ '000's)
Calculation of Taxable Income:				
Business operating profit as per accounts		2,000		2,000
Add				
Accounts depreciation	500		500	
Transfer to provision for employee benefits	200	700	200	700
		2,700		2,700

Less				
Tax depreciation	200		200	
Payment debited to provision for employee benefits	100		100	
Profit on sale of land	100		100	
Overseas dividend income (assessed separately)	100		100	
Trading results from overseas	—		100	
Malaysian dividends (assessed separately)	100	600	100	700
		2,100		2,000
Dividends				
Malaysian	100		100	
Overseas	100	200	—	100
Taxable income		M$ 2,300		M$ 2,100
Calculation of Tax Liability:				
Income and other taxes:				
Income tax at 35%		805		735
Development tax at 3% on business income only		63		60
		868		795
Less				
Tax deducted at source	35		35	
Unilateral credit	20		—	
Bilateral credit	39	94	—	35
		774		760
Real Property Gains Tax:				
Disposal price	500		500	
Less Acquisition price	400		400	
Chargeable gain	100		100	
Tax at 5%		5		5
Total tax liability		M $779		M $765

MALTA

INCOME TAXES ON CORPORATIONS

1. Rates

Effective January 1, 1991 (i.e., for any financial year ending in or after 1990), the corporate income tax rate has been increased to 35% from 32.5%.

2. Local Income Taxes

None.

3. Capital Gains Taxes

None.

4. Branch Profits Taxes

A branch of a foreign corporation is taxed on the profits of the branch as though it were a resident corporation.

5. Foreign Tax Reliefs

The Malta income tax system provides the following reliefs for foreign taxes imposed on income which is liable to Malta tax:

☐ Treaty relief.
☐ Relief for income taxes levied by Commonwealth countries.

Treaty relief exists for taxes on income levied in the countries listed in item 19. Relief is also available in respect of countries within the British Commonwealth with which no treaty is in force and provided the other commonwealth country has relief provisions similar to Malta's in respect of the incidence of Malta tax and its own tax on the same income. In the absence of treaty or commonwealth relief, foreign tax is allowed as an expense by concession.

6. Classification of Corporations

All partnerships with limited liability of all or some of their members and whose capital is divided into shares fall under the general definition of "company" and are subject to the same rate of tax (see item 1). But while companies that are both incorporated and resident in Malta are subject to tax on their world income, other companies are taxed only on income arising in or remitted to Malta. A resident company is one whose management and control are exercised in Malta.

The profits of partnerships with unlimited liability of their members, or whose capital is not divided into shares, are apportioned and taxed directly in the partners' hands.

All classes of corporations are subject to the same rate of tax unless they qualify for special incentives (see item 34).

7. Payment of Taxes

Corporations are required to pay provisional tax every four months during the basis year equal to one-third of the tax liability in the last assessment. These provisional tax payments are regarded as advance payments of the tax liability.

Corporations are also required to make a further advance payment by June 30th of each year. The amount payable (if any) will be the excess of the tax chargeable in accordance with the corporation's own tax computation over the sum of the tax paid in advance, any tax deducted at source, and any double taxation relief. Any balance of tax liability resulting from assessment is payable within one month of receipt of the claim.

INCOME TAXES ON INDIVIDUALS

9. Rates

Individuals ordinarily resident and domiciled in Malta are liable to tax on their income from all sources. Individuals not domiciled or not ordinarily resident in Malta are liable to tax on income arising in Malta and on any foreign income remitted to Malta.

Resident individuals may qualify for certain personal deductions (e.g., social security contributions), which may be applied against total income to arrive at the taxable income.

The following are the rates of tax on the taxable income of individuals (effective as of the assessment year 1991, i.e., on income earned during or after 1990).

	Taxable Income		Tax on Lower Amount	Percentage on Excess
	Over	Not Over		
Married	Lm 0	Lm 350	Lm 0	10%
Resident	350	1,400	35	20
Individuals	1,400	3,300	245	25
	3,300	5,000	720	30
	5,000		1,230	35

	Taxable Income		Tax on	Percentage
	Over	Not Over	Lower Amount	on Excess
Single	Lm 0	Lm1,500	Lm 0	18%
Resident	1,500	2,100	270	20
Individuals	2,100	2,900	390	25
	2,900	4,100	590	30
	4,100		950	35

The tax assessed at the above rates is then reduced by the following rebates.

Resident married individuals	Lm 440
Other resident individuals	275
Nonresident individuals	12

Certain other rebates may apply to resident individuals.

The wife's income is added to that of her husband's, but if both spouses receive earned income (income from dependent or independent personal services), they may elect to calculate the wife's earned income separately from their other income. In this situation, the single individual tax rates apply and rebates are granted as if the spouses were single residents, but only one assessment is raised.

Foreign nationals taking up permanent residence in Malta under a residence permit and persons born in Malta who return after an absence of at least 20 years qualify for special tax rates (see item 34).

10. Local Income Taxes

None.

11. Capital Gains Taxes

None.

12. Foreign Tax Reliefs

See item 5.

13. Tax Period

See item 32.

INCOME TAXES ON NONRESIDENTS

16. Rates

Nonresidents (married or unmarried) are liable to tax on income arising in Malta at the same rates as married residents (see item 9). They are not entitled to any personal deductions.

17. Withholding Tax Rates

All income arising in Malta and paid to nonresidents is subject to withholding tax at 35% if the payment is made to a corporation or if it consists of a dividend, and 25% in other cases. Withheld tax is not final and is credited against the tax liability resulting on assessment. Any difference is payable within one month or refunded, as the case may be.

A lower rate may be authorized if it is shown that the statutory rate would result in a refund or if a lower maximum rate is provided for in the relative double taxation treaty.

The treaties in force provide for the following maximum rates:

	Dividends (1)		Interest	Royalties
Austria	35%	(2)	5%	10%
Australia	35	(3)	15	10
Belgium	35	(2)	10 (4a)	10
Bulgaria	30	(3)	—	10
Canada	35	(2)	15 (4b)	10
Denmark	35	(2)	10 (4c)	10
Finland	35	(2)	10 (4d)	10
France	35	(2)	10	10
Germany	35	(2)	10 (4d)	10
Italy	35	(2)	10	10
Libya	—	(5)	—	—
Netherlands	35	(2)	10 (4e)	10
Norway	35	(2)	10 (4f)	10
Pakistan	35		10 (4g)	10
Sweden	35	(2)	10 (4h)	10
United Kingdom	35	(3)	—	0
United States	35		12.5	12.5

Notes:

(1) 35% is the current rate of tax on corporate income effective as of the 1991 assessment year.

(2) Reduced to 15% if dividends are paid out of gains or profits earned by certain tax-incentive companies.

(3) Where dividends are paid out of company profits which are taxed at a reduced rate under special provisions designed to promote investments necessary for the economic development of Malta, the rate of Malta tax on dividends shall not exceed such reduced rate.

(4) Interest paid to the following entities is exempt:

(a) The Government of Belgium, the National Bank of Belgium, or any other institution the capital of which is owned by the Government of Belgium.

(b) The Government of Canada, the Central Bank of Canada, and the Export Development Corporation.

(c) The Government of Denmark, the National Bank of Denmark, or the Industrialization Fund for Developing Countries of Denmark.

(d) The Government of Finland or the Bank of Finland.

(e) The Netherlands Government, the Central Bank of the Netherlands, the Netherlands finance company for developing countries, and the Netherlands Bank of developing countries.

(f) The Government of Norway or the Norges Bank.

(g) The Government of Pakistan or the State Bank of Pakistan.

(h) The Government of Sweden, the Central Bank of Sweden, or the Swedish National Debt Office.

(5) Taxable only in the source country.

19. Tax Treaties

Comprehensive treaties are in force with Austria, Australia, Belgium, Bulgaria, Canada, Denmark, Finland, France, Germany, Italy, Libya, Netherlands, Norway, Pakistan, Sweden, the United Kingdom, and the United States. A treaty with Switzerland provides for the elimination of double taxation on shipping and air transport profits. Treaties with various other countries are in the process of negotiation.

20. Other Matters

Exemption for Interest Income. The interest accruing to any individual not resident in Malta on any deposit held in a bank in Malta is exempt from tax, except that the exemption does not apply:

☐ For any year in which the individual is engaged in trade or business in Malta through a permanent establishment situated therein.

☐ Unless the Commissioner is satisfied that the individual to whom the interest accrues is the beneficial owner thereof.

Other Exempt Income. Interest on fixed deposits with commercial banks is exempt from tax as to the first Lm 18 per year per taxpayer and per dependent person. Provisions exist for the exemption from tax of income derived by approved pension or provident funds, philanthropic institutions, trusts or foundations of a 'public' character, members of the diplomatic corps of foreign countries, trade unions and clubs, and similar institutions. A nonresident shipowner is also exempt from Malta tax provided the law of the country of residence of the shipowner allows a reciprocal exemption.

OTHER SIGNIFICANT TAXES

21. Sales (Value Added)

An expenditure levy of 10% was introduced in 1990 on the value of prescribed restaurant and travel services and on the acquisition or transfer of foreign investments.

22. Inheritance and Gift Taxes

The rates of estate and gift duty vary from 6% to 54%, depending on the value of the property and the degree of consanguinity of the heir or donee.

23. Taxes on Payrolls (Social Security)

The weekly rates of social security contribution payable by an employed person are based on a proportion of the employee's *basic* pay. This proportion is fixed at one-twelfth of the basic pay, but:

☐ The minimum contribution is Lm 2.84 a week.
☐ The highest contribution is Lm 9.16 a week.

The employer's contribution is the same as that paid by the employee.
Contributions of self-employed persons are:

Annual Income		Contribution (Weekly)
Over	Not Over	
	Lm 1,796	Lm 4.46
Lm 1,796	Lm 2,326	5.76
2,326	2,856	7.06
2,856	3,386	8.36
3,386	3,916	9.61
3,916	4,656	11.41
4,656		13.76

The payment of these contributions is incorporated with the P.A.Y.E. for employees and with the provisional tax payments for self-employed persons.

24. Taxes on Natural Resources

A petroleum profits tax is levied as an income tax. The production-sharing contracts entered into between the licensee and the Government provide for the licensee to carry out oil exploration at his expense and to receive reimbursement of expenses only if oil is struck. These contracts also stipulate that the Government and the contractor will share the oil in agreed proportions. Income tax payable on the sale or disposal of the oil produced in Malta is at the rate of 50%.

25. Other Taxes

Land and Property.   There are no taxes on land and property.

Stamp Tax.   Stamp duty is imposed on various documents executed in Malta. These include checks, insurance policies, transfers of immovable property, cars, ships, aircraft, and securities, allotments and transfers of shares, auction sales, and valuations. In the case of documents executed outside Malta, these become subject to duty when use thereof is made in Malta.

COMPUTATION OF TAXABLE INCOME

26. Capital Gains

Not applicable.

27. Depreciation and Depletion

Depreciation charged in the accounts is ignored for taxation purposes. There is, instead, a system of capital allowances. These allowances fall under three main headings:

- ☐ Initial deduction.
- ☐ Wear and tear.
- ☐ Balancing allowances and charges.

Initial Deduction.   The initial deduction is fixed by law at 20% of cost with respect to plant and machinery and 10% of cost for an industrial building or structure.

Wear and Tear.   The wear and tear allowance for industrial buildings and structures is 1% (of cost) per year. For plant and machinery, the ''Deduction (Wear and Tear of Plant and Machinery) Rules 1965'' apply. These rules set out the prescribed rates for various items and state that the Commissioner of Inland Revenue is to determine a reasonable rate for items not so listed. These rates are applied on a reducing balance basis. The initial and wear and tear allowances in the aggregate cannot exceed the cost of the asset.

Balancing Allowances and Charges.   Balancing allowances and charges are made on the disposal of premises and plant and machinery. The balancing allowance is the amount by which the wear and tear allowances and the proceeds of sale or disposal fall short of the original cost of the asset. Where the allowances and the receipts on disposal together exceed the original cost of the asset, a balancing charge is made. Where an asset is sold for more than its purchase price, the balancing charge is limited to the total of the allowances made.

28. Treatment of Dividends

The tax paid by a resident company on distributed profits is added to the net dividend, and the shareholders are taxed on the gross amount. The company tax then is credited in full to the shareholders. This, in practice, means that no tax is payable on dividends in addition to company tax, except for distributions out of pre-1990 profits and distributions out of untaxed profits (e.g., capital gains). Any excess credit is refundable to the shareholders.

Distributions on liquidation are treated as dividends to the extent they are made out of undistributed income.

29. Loss Carryovers

Trading losses may be set off against profits in subsequent years until they are all absorbed. The losses which are admitted are those losses which, if they had been profits, would have been chargeable with the tax. Losses cannot be carried back.

30. Transactions between Related Parties

Transactions between related parties are accepted by the authorities provided these transactions are not artificial or fictitious, in which case they are disregarded.

31. Consolidation of Income

There are no provisions for consolidation of income for taxation purposes.

32. Tax Periods

Tax liability arises in the calendar year (year of assessment) following the year (basis year) in which the income arises.

Permission may be obtained from the Commissioner of Inland Revenue for companies and certain other entities (but not individuals) to adopt a basis year other than the calendar year, but the basis year must always be a 12-month period ending in the calendar year immediately preceding the year of assessment.

RELATED CONSIDERATIONS

34. Incentives and Grants

Incentives for Industrial Development. Special legislation was introduced in 1988 offering tax and other incentives to corporations registered in Malta and engaged in the manufacturing and related industries. The tax incentives include a ten-year tax holiday to companies satisfying prescribed thresholds of exports, exemption on profits derived from increased exports of companies not qualifying for a tax holiday, reduced rate of tax on profits used for approved projects, enhanced capital allowances, and inflated deductions in respect of costs on training, export promotion, and research and development. Beneficial tax treatment is also available to shareholders and expatriate employees of qualifying companies. Other incentives include relief from customs duty, soft loans, subsidized rents on factories, and grants.

Permanent Residents. Foreign nationals taking up permanent residence in Malta are subject to reduced rates of tax. Income derived by foreign nationals who are granted a permanent residence permit on or after January 1, 1988, is taxed at the rate of 15% subject to a minimum liability, after double taxation relief, if any, of Lm 1,000 per fiscal year.

On the death of a permit holder, property situated outside Malta and inherited by the spouse is exempt from death duty.

Special Concessions to Shipping Companies. A body corporate registered under Maltese Law and having a place of business in Malta, and which satisfies the Minister that the laws of Malta relating to merchant shipping will be observed, is exempted from income tax, succession and donation duties, and stamp duties related to gains or profits derived from the ownership or operation of an exempted ship.

Offshore Legislation. Comprehensive legislation was enacted in 1988 to regulate the setting up of and the control over offshore companies and trusts. These laws grant substantial tax and other fiscal benefits. An offshore company may be a trading company (e.g., a bank, a unit trust, an insurance or captive insurance company, or a general trading company) which is taxed at 5%, or a non-trading company (e.g., an investment or management company) which is exempt from tax, unless it elects to become liable to tax. Dividends, interest, and other income paid by any offshore company are exempt from tax. Annual fees ranging from Lm 500 to Lm 25,000 are payable depending on the type of company. An offshore trust is subject to a tax of Lm 200 per year.

Freeport. The Malta Freeports Act, 1989, designates certain zones in Malta as freeport areas. A company licenced to carry out operations in a freeport (e.g., storage, labelling, packing, stevedoring) is exempt from tax on profits thereon and is entitled to other benefits, subject to an annual fee of Lm1,000. Depending on the value added as a result of operations in Malta, a certificate of Maltese origin may be issued in respect of goods treated in a freeport.

35.   Exchange Controls

Malta has comprehensive exchange control regulations, which are embodied in the Exchange Control Act 1972. The Act controls the movement of gold, currency and securities in and out of Malta.

36.   Investment Restrictions on Nonresidents

There are no restrictions on investment in Malta by nonresidents. However, an investment project of an industrial nature would require acceptance from the exchange control division at the Central Bank, the Malta Development Corporation and other ministries before formal approval is granted. The transfer of profits accruing to a foreign investor is guaranteed.

SELECTION OF BUSINESS ENTITY BY NONRESIDENTS

Nonresident investors can operate in Malta either through a branch or through a locally registered subsidiary company. The tax rates are the same for both entities.

Most nonresident investors operate through a locally registered and resident company, which is taxed on its worldwide income. A branch is taxed only on the profits arising on operations carried out in Malta and a proportion of certain expenses incurred overseas is allowed. Special provisions apply to nonresident insurance companies.

Foreign tax considerations are usually a determining factor in deciding to operate in Malta through a locally registered company.

SPECIMEN TAX COMPUTATION

Information:

The company, which is registered and resident in Malta, is a fully-owned subsidiary of a company resident in a treaty country. It does not qualify for any benefits under incentive legislation.

The company's profits for the year are:

—interest received from a company resident in a treaty country including 10% withholding tax	Lm 300,000
—trading profits	150,000
	Lm 450,000

The trading profits were adjusted for:

—depreciation	4,000
—provision for bad debts	5,000
—unrealized exchange loss	1,000
—nondeductible expenses	2,000

Computation of Company Tax:

Profits per accounts	Lm 450,000
Add depreciation, bad debts provision, unrealized exchange loss, and nondeductible expenses	12,000
	Lm 462,000

Less capital allowances	5,000
Chargeable income	Lm 457,000
Tax at 35%	159,950
Double taxation relief for foreign tax on interest	30,000
Net Malta tax	Lm 129,950

A dividend of Lm250,000 is distributed eventually out of the year's profits.

Computation of Tax on Dividend:

Net dividend	Lm 250,000
Add corresponding company tax (1,2)	134,615
Gross dividend	Lm 384,615
Tax at 35%	134,615
Credit for tax paid by company	134,615
Net Malta tax	NIL
Malta tax on dividend deemed paid by parent company for double taxation relief purposes	
	Lm 134,615

Notes:

(1) At 35% of gross dividend, taking the net dividend as representing 65%, but not to exceed the company tax, before double taxation relief, on the profits out of which the distribution is made.

(2) Different rates apply in the grossing up of distributions out of pre-1990 profits.

MEXICO

INCOME TAXES ON CORPORATIONS

1. Rates

Effective January 1, 1989, the full implementation of a new tax base began, which recognizes the effects of inflation (see item 8).

The new base has a fixed rate of 35%. Reduced tax rates have been granted to certain industries for economic or educational reasons. These are in the form of percentage reductions from the regular rates as follows:

Book publishers	50%
Agricultural, cattle, forestry, or fishing activities	25% to 50%

2. Local Income Taxes

None.

3. Capital Gains Taxes

Corporate capital gains normally are treated as ordinary income and taxed at the regular rates. However, to determine the gain on the sale or other disposition of land or structures, the acquisition cost can be subject to adjustment by taking into account the years elapsed between the acquisition and the sale. The adjustment consists of multiplying the acquisition cost by an inflation factor calculated using the Consumer Price Index published by the Banco de México (Central Bank).

To determine the gain on a sale of stock, a complicated formula that, in addition to the inflation factor, takes into account the taxable income or losses of the issuing company and the dividends paid during the period in which the taxpayer held the stock.

4. Branch Profits Taxes

Branches of foreign corporations are subject to the normal corporate income tax rate of 35%.

5. Foreign Tax Reliefs

A Mexican corporation is taxed on its worldwide income, but the taxpayer is entitled to credit foreign income taxes paid against its Mexican income tax. The amount creditable is subject to several limits. In general, the law attempts to avoid tax credits higher than the tax that would be effectively due in Mexico on the income received abroad.

In the case of dividends on profits distributed by nonresident corporations, the income tax paid by those corporations can also be credited in the proportional amount that corresponds to the dividend or profit, but whoever makes the credit must consider, in addition to the dividend income, the amount of the tax from that dividend of profit. The crediting is applicable if the resident in Mexico owns at least 10% of the capital of the nonresident corporation.

7. Payment of Taxes

Effective January 1, 1990, all companies must have a fiscal year for tax purposes equal to the calendar year. Companies are required to make monthly income tax advance payments, based on the total monthly income and the profit of the company for the previous tax year; in addition, two adjustments to those advances have to be made in the sixth and eleventh months to approximate the actual payment of income tax for the year. The final balance is paid together with the tax return filing.

8. Other Matters

The new base includes, in general, the same provisions as the traditional Income Tax Law. However, there are important modifications in the treatment of the following items:

☐ Interest
☐ Purchases and cost of sales
☐ Investments.

The new base attempts to reflect the effect of inflation on certain financial assets and liabilities.

Tax Treatment of Interest.   From the total interest accrued in the month in favor of the taxpayer, an inflationary component on monetary assets will be subtracted. The difference, if positive, will be taxable interest; if negative, it will be deductible as an inflationary loss.

From the interest accrued in the month, charged to the taxpayer, the inflationary component of debts will be subtracted. The difference, if positive, will be deductible interest; if negative, it will be included as an inflationary gain.

	Example 1	Example 2
Interest income for the month	P. 100	P. 100
Inflationary component of credits	(80)	(115)
Taxable interest (deductible inflationary loss)	20	(15)
Interest expense for the month	120	120
Inflationary component of debts	(110)	(150)
Deductible interest (inflationary gain)	10	(30)

Purchases and Cost of Sales.   In the new base, the following purchases—instead of the cost of goods sold—will be deductible:

☐ Goods.

☐ Raw materials and semi-finished and finished products, used by taxpayers to manufacture other goods.

In the case of imported goods, they are deductible only when the import duties have been paid.

The following items will not be deductible as purchases:

☐ Capital assets.

☐ Titulos valor (securities), except those representing ownership of goods.

☐ Land, except if the taxpayer's activity consists of trading in real estate.

Such assets are deductible under other income tax law provisions. This treatment breaks with the traditional rule that matches the cost of sales in the same period as related revenues.

Taxpayers should carefully plan for purchases, since taxes will depend largely on them under this new base.

Investments.   See item 27.

INCOME TAXES ON INDIVIDUALS

9.   Rates

Graduated rates of tax, ranging from 3% up to 35%, are applied to income of individuals. Mexican citizens and resident aliens are taxable on their income from all sources. Income determination is based on a schedular concept; after income is so determined, various deductions are allowed, such as medical, dental, hospital, and funeral expenses, and contributions made to Mexican charitable or educational institutions authorized by the Treasury Department. An exemption also is allowed for annual bonuses received of 30 days' minimum wage prevailing in the taxpayer's area, as are several other exemptions.

Taxable Income		Tax on	Percentage
Over	Not Over	Lower Amount	on Excess
P. 0	P. 1,118,926	P. 0	3%
1,118,926	9,496,855	33,568	10
9,496,855	16,689,756	871,361	17
16,689,756	19,401,257	2,094,154	25
19,401,257	23,228,398	2,772,029	32
23,228,398	73,839,500	3,996,714	34
73,839,500		21,204,489	35

A quarterly adjustment to the tax table will be published by the Treasury Department.

Taxpayers have a credit equal to 10% of the annual minimum wage against the tax payable. Additionally, in 1991 a subsidy to the tax is granted ranging from 40% of the tax in the lower bracket to around 1% in the higher bracket.

10. Local Income Taxes

Some states tax salaries (but generally not income); these taxes are payable by the employer.

11. Capital Gains Taxes

Individuals are subject to tax on capital gains derived from the transfer of real and personal property. In general, rules similar to those discussed in item 3 apply to dispositions of land, structures, and shares of stock.

It should be mentioned that if these properties constitute a normal transaction for the taxpayer, income tax must be paid as if a common business enterprise were being dealt with, since the activity is a commercial one.

Gain on the sale of widely held securities traded on an authorized securities exchange is not taxable.

12. Foreign Tax Reliefs

See item 5.

13. Tax Periods

The fiscal period for individuals is always the calendar year.

INCOME TAXES ON NONRESIDENT ALIENS

15. Liability to Tax

Resident individuals are subject to Mexican income tax on their worldwide income. Nonresident individuals, including citizens of Mexico, are taxed only on their Mexican-source income. An individual is considered to be resident in Mexico if he establishes his "home" in Mexico, unless the individual is outside of Mexico for more than 183 days (consecutive or not) in a calendar year and demonstrates residence in another country. If a nonresident individual performs activities in Mexico through a permanent establishment, however, the individual is subject to the regular individual income taxes on income attributable to the permanent establishment.

Resident corporations are taxed on their worldwide income. The Mexican branch or other permanent establishment of a foreign corporation, however, is generally subject to tax only on the income attributable to its business operations in Mexico from whatever source derived. Mexican-source income of a nonresident corporation not arising from a permanent establishment is usually taxed at a flat rate applied on a withholding basis to the gross amount.

17. Withholding Tax Rates

Income received by a nonresident alien from a Mexican corporation or individual is subject to withholding tax as follows:

Dividends. Effective in 1989, the finance authorities, with the purpose of encouraging the reinvestment of profits, established a new concept within the income tax law called the "net taxable income account." This account is formed by the annual "net taxable income," which is calculated from the taxable income minus the income tax and employee profit-sharing for the year as well as the nondeductible expenses for the year; to the balance of this account, the dividends received from other entities are added. The balance of this account is restated, through the Consumer Price Index published by the Central Bank, up to the time a dividend is paid. There will be no withholding tax. If the dividend is not paid from or is in excess of this account, there will be a withholding tax of 35%.

The tax payment should be made no later than the seventeenth day of the calendar month subsequent to the withholding.

Interest.

□ Interest paid to foreign banks and financial institutions registered with the Treasury Department	15%
□ Interest paid by Mexican financial institutions to foreign creditors other than those described above, and interest paid on bonds and other credit instruments	21%

☐	Interest paid to foreign suppliers of machinery and equipment that become part of the fixed assets of the buyer	21%
☐	Other interest	35%

Royalties.

☐	For the use of artistic, literary, and scientific works	15%
☐	For the use of patents, trade names, and advertising	35%
☐	Technical assistance fees	15%
☐	Leasing (in the case of capitalized leasing, it is possible to deduct the cost of the property, and only the balance is subject to withholding)	21%
☐	Construction, installation, maintenance, and inspection of real estate (on gross income)	30%
☐	Salaries and fees	30%

Where real property in Mexico or stock of Mexican companies is sold, the purchaser generally should withhold 20% of the gross proceeds. Nonresidents may elect to pay a withholding tax of 30% on the net profit if the nonresident has a representative in Mexico and certain other requirements are met.

In the case of a sale of credits with more than a six-month maturity or swap transactions for investment, the Mexican debtor should withhold 20% of the gross proceeds or elect the withholding of 30% on the net profit if the debtor has a representative in Mexico.

OTHER SIGNIFICANT TAXES

21. Sales (Value Added)

The tax is payable on the following activities:

- ☐ Sale or other disposition of property.
- ☐ Independent services (VAT does not apply to wages).
- ☐ Temporary use or enjoyment of property (leasing).
- ☐ Imports of goods or services.

General Provisions. The purchaser or user of the goods or services must accept the passing on of the tax. The taxpayer can credit the VAT that has been passed on expressly to him and pay only the difference; if the creditable tax exceeds the tax due, the difference can be offset later only against VAT or a refund obtained. The principal exempt transactions are sales of land, credit instruments, residential construction, banking services, medical services, certain types of public entertainment, and most activities of government agencies.

VAT is payable at a general rate of 15%. The rate in the border and free zones is 6%. Certain luxury items (including services) are taxed at a 20% rate. The zero percent VAT generally applies to certain agricultural goods, listed basic foodstuffs, and exports of goods and services. In 1991, medicines and food products are subject to the zero percentage rate; this rate will be subject to ratification during January 1992.

23. Taxes on Payrolls (Social Security)

The employer must contribute approximately 13.3% of its employees' salaries with a maximum of ten times the minimum wage in effect in Mexico City, as quotas for health and maternity insurance, as well as for disability, old age, unemployment, and death insurance; the employee also contributes 4.75% of his salary. The following insurance is paid entirely by the employer:

☐ Occupational risks (1.67% to 166.67% on the disability, old age, unemployment, and death quota of 4.9%), according to the employer's activities.

☐ Day care (1% of normal wages).

INFONAVIT (National Workers' Housing Fund Institute). Corporations are required to contribute 5% of their employees' salaries, up to a maximum of ten times the minimum wage in the respective geographic area. These contributions are used by the Institute to finance employees' acquisition or enlargement of homes or to liquidate prior housing loans. If an individual retires or dies, INFONAVIT will pay these employer contributions to the employee.

24. Taxes on Natural Resources

Mining activities are subject to an exploitation annual fee established by the Mexican Government.

25. Other Taxes

2% Tax on Assets. Starting in 1989, a 2% tax on assets was established. The base is the total assets minus liabilities with Mexican companies (no banks are considered). The value of the assets is determined as follows:

☐ Monetary assets: through the average for the year.

☐ Inventories: they should be restated using the National Consumer Price Index or their replacement cost.

☐ Fixed assets: the net depreciable value should be restated up the end of the previous year using the National Consumer Price Index.

☐ Other assets: they should be restated using the National Consumer Price Index.

The liabilities to be deducted are determined using the annual average.

The 2% tax on total assets payable is credited with the corporate income tax paid. If the corporate income tax paid is higher than the 2% tax, the income tax credit is limited to the amount of the 2% tax payable.

Companies should make monthly advances of the 2% tax equal to the proportion of tax paid in the previous year; the 2% tax advances to be made may be credited with the monthly income tax advances paid.

The 2% tax is not imposed during preoperating periods, the first year of activity and the *following*. The 2% tax paid in one year is collectible in the following three years if the income tax paid in those years exceeds the 2% tax.

Property Taxes.   Property taxes are levied by the states and the Federal District. The rates vary in each of the states and are highest on property located in the Federal District.

Tax on Real Estate Acquisition.   The states, in conjunction with the federal government for purposes of this tax, apply an 8% rate to the acquisition value of property during 1991. After 1991, the tax rate will decrease 2% every year to reach 2% in 1994.

Profit Sharing.   Employers are required to share profits with their employees. Subject to certain exceptions for new enterprises, the profit-sharing amount is 10% of the company's taxable income plus some items from the inflation adjustments deductible for income tax purposes, dividend income exempt from income tax, and amortization of losses. The director general or the general manager, depending on the company's structure, is not entitled to participate in profit sharing.

COMPUTATION OF TAXABLE INCOME

26.   Capital Gains

See item 3.

27.   Depreciation and Depletion

Fixed assets must be depreciated on the straight-line basis at maximum rates set by law. Taxpayers may adopt rates lower than the maximums, but will have only one opportunity to change.

Buildings and other structures	5%
Office furniture and equipment	10%
Automobiles and trucks	20%

Under the new base there are two depreciation procedures:

☐   Application of a fixed percentage over a number of fiscal years (straight line).

☐   The entire allowable depreciation is taken in one fiscal year. This applies to only new fixed assets (mainly machinery and equipment) and applies some percentage according to the type of asset.

The first procedure allows for the restatement of the depreciation through the application of inflation actualization factors.

29. Loss Carryovers

Tax losses incurred in a given fiscal year will be deducted only from taxable income in the ensuing five years (carryforward), thus eliminating the possibility of applying them against profits in prior-year taxable income (carryback). Subject to certain rules, losses carried forward may be extended another five years, for a total of ten years.

The amount of tax losses deducted in a fiscal year will be adjusted by the restatement factor corresponding to the period between the last month of the previous year to the one in which tax losses are deducted and the last month of the fiscal year in which the loss occurred.

30. Transactions between Related Parties

The Treasury Department is authorized to estimate buying and selling prices in any transaction carried out abroad (whether or not the company is related) and to estimate buying and selling prices in transactions between related companies resident in Mexico. The principal factor considered for purposes of the estimate is the current market price. In the case of interest paid to a related company abroad, under certain circumstances the Treasury Department can treat the interest as dividends.

31. Consolidation of Income

Holding companies may file consolidated income tax returns provided certain requirements are met. Each company involved in the consolidation must file an individual return; subsequently the holding company files the consolidated return and determines the consolidated tax due. If the consolidated tax is less than would be due on an individual return basis, the difference will benefit only the holding company. Under certain law provisions, in some cases the benefit of reducing the consolidated income tax does not apply.

32. Tax Periods

The tax year comprises the calendar year, except in the first year of operations, in the closing date, in which event a shorter period may apply.

RELATED CONSIDERATIONS

34. Incentives and Grants

Higher depreciation percentages for new assets used in certain activities in priority national economic zones have been abolished.

The income tax law provides a tax credit to companies that sell real estate in the Federal District (Mexico City) or nearby zones and invest the proceeds in fixed assets (except office and transportation equipment) for use in other zones. The credit is 50% of the tax on real estate acquisition imposed at the time of sale.

No other incentives apply to income taxes; however, for businesses along the border with the United States and exporters, several benefits exist.

35. Exchange Controls

A mixture of exchange controls has been in effect. Certain transactions are controlled by the Central Bank, and other transactions may take place in the free-exchange market. A minimum difference between both exchange rates exists.

36. Investment Restrictions on Nonresidents

The Constitution provides that nonresidents cannot own property in Mexico, except by authorization of the Federal Government, which is granted in special cases. In general, Mexico has been open to foreign investment. The Government continues to provide measures and conditions to increase it—just restricting foreign investment in some industries (such as banks, mining, and insurance) and reserving others to the Federal Government (such as oil extraction, electricity, nuclear power, railroad, and a few others).

SELECTION OF BUSINESS ENTITY BY NONRESIDENTS

Limited companies are the most common form of business entity in Mexico. Foreign-owned corporations are generally taxed in the same manner as domestic corporations. Nonresidents engaged in business in Mexico through a branch or agency are subject to the normal corporate income tax. In addition, all branch profits (i.e., after-tax and compulsory employee profit sharing) are deemed to be distributed to its foreign head office on the last day of the fiscal year, whether or not any remittances abroad are actually made.

THE NETHERLANDS

INCOME TAXES ON CORPORATIONS

1. Rates

Profits of corporations and other taxable entities are taxed at 40% on the first DFls 250,000 of taxable profits and 35% on taxable profits in excess of this amount.

2. Local Income Taxes

None.

3. Capital Gains Taxes

Capital gains or losses (excluding those realized under the participation exemption) are considered as normal income and taxed accordingly. There is no special tax rate for capital gains.

Taxation of capital gains on fixed assets can be deferred if the sales proceeds are reinvested in new, similar fixed assets. Taxation of capital gains on intangible assets also can be deferred, provided the intangible assets are not held as a portfolio investment. Reinvestment should usually occur within four years of the disposal date.

4. Branch Profits Taxes

Dutch-source income of nonresident corporations is taxed at the same rates as stated in item 1. There is no additional branch profits tax.

5. Foreign Tax Relief

A resident corporation is taxed on its worldwide income. Certain types of foreign source income (inter alia, income derived through a permanent establishment abroad, and income from foreign real estate) are exempt from tax, either unilaterally or pursuant to treaty provisions. The exemption is calculated as a pro rata reduction of the amount of tax computed on worldwide income. Foreign losses can reduce current taxation on domestic income. Other types of foreign income are normally fully taxable in The Netherlands, but a credit for foreign tax may be granted under various tax treaties or, unilaterally, with respect to dividends, royalties and interest derived from certain developing countries.

7. Payment of Taxes

Tax is payable upon receipt of assessments. Payments should be made after receipt of the assessment and within the period specified on the assessment (normally within one or two months). For corporate income tax, at least two preliminary assessments can be issued; one in January and one in August if the book year coincides with the calendar year.

The January assessment is based on the average taxable profit of the two preceding years. This assessment is payable in 11 monthly installments.

The August assessment is based on the company's estimate of the taxable profit for the year. This estimate may also lead to a refund. This additional assessment is payable in five monthly installments (September through January).

8. Other Matters

Participation Exemption. If a Dutch corporation owns 5% or more of the paid-up capital of another Dutch corporation and the shares are not held as inventory, dividends and capital gains on the shares are exempt from Dutch corporate tax. Capital losses, however, are deductible only upon liquidation of the participation (under certain conditions). These rules also apply to a participation in a foreign corporation if the following additional conditions are met:

☐ The foreign corporation in which the participation is held is subject to a profits tax in its country of residence.

☐ The shares in the foreign corporation are not held as a portfolio investment.

However, expenses connected with a foreign participation that qualifies for the participation exemption are not deductible for Dutch corporate income tax purposes.

INCOME TAXES ON INDIVIDUALS

9. Rates

Individuals resident in The Netherlands are taxed on their worldwide income.

Progressive rates apply to taxable income after deducting personal allowances (the tax base). Examples of personal allowances for 1991 are:

☐ Single taxpayers: DFls 4,660.
☐ Couples (married): DFls 9,320.
☐ Single taxpayer with children: DFls 4,660 to DFls 12,116.

Income tax and social security tax are included in a single tax. The combined tax is levied in the first bracket. The percentage in the first bracket consists in fact of two rates, being the social security tax rate of 22.75% and the income tax rate of 13%.

The 1991 tax rates for resident individuals are:

| Taxable Income | | Tax on | Percentage |
Over	Not Over	Lower Amount	on Excess
DFls 0	DFls 42,966	DFls 0	35.75%
42,966	85,930	15,360	50.00
85,930		36,842	60.00

For persons over 65, the personal income tax rate in the first bracket differs from the basic rate of 35.75% and amounts to 18.8%.

A special personal income tax rate applies to certain nonrecurring items of income, such as a golden handshake, or profit on the sale or liquidation of a business. This fixed special rate amounts to 45%. Further, a restricted number of specified items of income are taxed at a fixed special rate of 20% (e.g., the capital gain on the sale of a "substantial interest" in a company as mentioned in item 11).

Salaries and wages are subject to wage withholding tax. Provisional income tax assessments can be issued in the course of a fiscal year. If the wage withholding tax and/or provisional assessments are higher (lower) than the ultimate income tax liability, refund is made (or additional tax is payable) upon receipt of a final income tax assessment. In certain cases, the wage withholding tax is a final levy, and no further income tax assessments are issued.

10. Local Income Taxes

None.

11. Capital Gains Taxes

Capital gains (and losses) arising from the sale or exchange of private assets are exempt from taxation. If private assets are employed as capital of a business, the capital gains and losses form part of the individual's taxable income and are taxed at the normal progressive rates. Capital gains realized on the sale of shares are taxed at a special fixed rate of 20% if the seller has a "substantial interest" in a company.

12. Foreign Tax Relief

Foreign tax relief is available to resident individuals on the same basis as in item 5. Due to the progressive income tax rates, the pro rata exemption method has the result that the effective tax rate on the nonexempt income will be increased due to the inclusion of the exempt income ("exemption with progression method").

13. Tax Period

Individuals are taxed on a calendar-year basis, although exceptions are available for individuals who carry on a trade or business.

14. Other Matters

"35% Ruling." Foreign individuals who are transferred on a temporary basis within an international group to a Dutch group company can obtain a special ruling whereby they are entitled to a deduction equal to 35% of their employment income. The same applies if a foreign national is recruited abroad with the intention of being temporarily assigned to the Dutch group company as part of a career plan. If a Dutch company, not being part of an international group, recruits a foreign national from abroad because of the person's special skills and know-how, it is also possible—under certain conditions—to obtain the 35%-ruling.

Under this ruling, they are taxable only on their employment income (after deduction of 35% thereof) and on income from specific Dutch sources, including:

☐ Income from Dutch real estate.

☐ Dividend income (including capital gains) from shares in a Dutch company forming a "substantial interest".

This ruling is valid, in principle, for a maximum period of 60 months, if applied for within four months of arrival in The Netherlands.

INCOME TAXES ON NONRESIDENTS

15. Liability to Tax

Nonresident individuals are subject only to Dutch personal income tax on specific Dutch sources of income (e.g., employment income, income from Dutch real estate). These individuals are, in principle, entitled only to the basic personal allowance of DFls 4,660.

For nonresident individuals whose Dutch income is less than 90% of their total worldwide income and who are not subject to Dutch social security taxes, the personal income tax rate in the first bracket is 25%. Under certain conditions, the rate in the first bracket can differ from this tax rate of 25% and varies between 5.8% and 35.75%. The same income tax rates apply in the second and third bracket as for resident taxpayers (see item 9).

Nonresident corporations that derive income from certain sources within The Netherlands (e.g., permanent establishment and real estate) are taxed at the normal domestic corporate income tax rates (see item 1).

17. Withholding Tax Rates

Dividends (including income from certain profit sharing bonds) distributed by a Dutch corporation are subject to 25% withholding tax. Under tax treaties, this rate is normally reduced as shown in the following table. Interest and royalties paid by a Dutch corporation are not subject to withholding tax.

Withholding Tax Rates (%) on Dividend Remittances

	Ordinary (Treaty) Rate	Special Rates	
		Minimum Participation in Dividend-Paying Company	Special Rate
Nontreaty countries	25%	—	—
Treaty countries:			
Australia	15	—	—
Austria	15	25%	5%
Belgium	15	25	5 (2)
Brazil (1)	15	—	—
Bulgaria (1)	15	25	5
Canada	15	25	10
China (3)	10	—	—
Czechoslovakia	10	25	0
Denmark	15	25	0
Finland (4)	15	25	0
France (4)	15	25	5 (2)
Germany (4)	15	25 (voting stock)	10 (2)
Greece	15	25	5 (2)
Hungary	15	25	5
India	15	—	—
Indonesia	15	25	10
Ireland (4)	15	25 (voting stock)	0
Israel	15	25	5
Italy (5)	0	0	0
Japan	15	25 (voting stock)	5 (3)
Korea (South)	15	25	10
Luxembourg (6)	15	25	2.5 (2)
Malaysia	15	25	0
Malta	15	25	5
Morocco	25	25	10
Netherlands Antilles	15	25	5, 7.5
New Zealand	15	—	—
Norway	15	25	10 (3)
Pakistan	20	25	10
Philippines (1)	15	25	10
Poland	15	25	0
Romania	15	25	10
Singapore	15	25	0
South Africa	15	25 (voting stock)	5 (2)
Soviet Union	15	—	—

Withholding Rates (%) on Dividend Remittances

	Ordinary (Treaty) Rate	Special Rates	
		Minimum Participation in Dividend-Paying Company	Special Rate
Spain (4)	15%	50%, 25%, 25%	5% (2)
Sri Lanka	15	25	10
Surinam	20	25	7.5, 15
Sweden (5)	15	25	0
Switzerland (4)	15	25	0 (3)
Thailand	25	25	5
Turkey	20	25	5 (3)
United Kingdom	15	25 (voting stock)	5 (2)
United States (4)	15	25 (voting stock)	5 (3)
Venezuela (1)	10	25	0 (3)
Yugoslavia	15	25	5
Zambia	15	25	5
Zimbabwe	20	25	10

Notes:
(1) Treaties with Brazil, Bulgaria, the Philippines, and Venezuela have been negotiated but have not yet entered into force.
(2) Following the EC-Directive on parents and subsidiaries, dividends paid by a Dutch company to its qualifying EC-parent company will be exempt from Dutch dividend withholding tax as from January 1, 1992.
(3) Under certain circumstances.
(4) These tax treaties are currently being renegotiated or will be renegotiated shortly.
(5) These tax treaties have been renegotiated but have not yet entered into force. The rates of the old treaty are mentioned.
(6) The tax treaty does not apply to certain exempt Luxembourg holding companies.

OTHER SIGNIFICANT TAXES

21. Sales (Value Added)

The value-added tax (VAT or ''BTW'') is a general tax on consumption expenditures within The Netherlands. The tax is levied on the supply of goods and the performance of services within The Netherlands by registered businesses and on the importation of goods into The Netherlands.

Business transactions are taxed at 18.5%. Certain basic necessities are taxed at 6%. Exports are subject to a zero rate. Certain services are exempt, e.g., insurance and banking. Foreign business concerns (whose services are non-exempt) can apply for a refund of Dutch value-added tax charged even if they have no operations in The Netherlands.

22. Inheritance and Gift Taxes

Dutch inheritance and gift tax is imposed on the recipient of an inheritance or gift.

Gifts and receipts from estates are taxed after deduction of varying tax-free amounts. The rates (5% up to 68%) depend on the amounts received and the relationship of the beneficiary to the deceased or the donor. Receipts from the estate of a Dutch citizen who had been a resident of The Netherlands within a period of 10 years before death are taxed in The Netherlands at normal rates.

23. Taxes on Payrolls (Social Security and Social Insurance)

An extensive compulsory social security system is in effect in The Netherlands. This system includes a social security part, for which social security taxes are due, and a social insurance part, for which social insurance premiums are due. The social security part covers both employed and self-employed persons, with coverage under the social insurance only for employees.

Social security tax is included in the wage withholding tax and personal income tax (see item 9). Social security taxes are levied on employees. This is compensated by a compensation allowance, which is paid by the employer to the employee. The compensation allowance is restricted to an annual maximum of DFls 7,557 in 1991.

Social security and social insurance contributions are payable on the employee's salary, which includes vacation allowance, Christmas bonus, overtime, etc., and are restricted to an annual maximum. Contributions payable by the employer and employee are:

	Employer's Share		Employee's Share	
	Rate	Maximum	Rate	Maximum
Social Security Taxes:	—		—	22.75% DFls 9,773
Covering both employees and self-employed persons				
AOW, old age pension				
AWW, widows'/orphans' pension				
AKW, child allowance (1)				
AAW, general disability insurance				
AWBZ, special health insurance				
Social Insurance Premiums:				
Covering only employees				
WW, unemployment insurance (2)	1.44	1,030	1.04	744
ZW, health insurance (2)	6.20	4,434	1.20	858
WAO, disability insurance	—	—	12.00	5,606
ZFW, sickness fund (3) (4)	4.95	2,209	2.85	1,272
		DFls 7,673		DFls 18,253

Notes:

(1) An individual employed within The Netherlands is entitled to receive child allowances for dependent children.

(2) Premiums vary according to the industry. These are averages.

(3) An employee is not insured under ZFW if his or her fixed annual income as of November 1, 1990 exceeded DFls 52,300. In that case, private health insurance is required.

(4) Apart from this premium withheld on salary, a fixed contribution is payable by the employee to the sickness fund, varying from DFls 226 per year for a single person to DFls 677 per year for a family with two children or more.

24. Taxes on Natural Resources

In general, royalties are due upon the extraction of natural resources in The Netherlands. Special profit-sharing arrangements with the Dutch government exist for oil and gas exploitation activities in the Dutch continental shelf area. The Dutch tax jurisdiction also includes the Dutch part of the continental shelf. As a result oil and gas related activities which are carried out on the Dutch part of the continental shelf can be subject to Dutch corporate, income and/or wage withholding tax.

25. Other Taxes

Taxes on Capital. A 1% capital tax is levied on all capital contributed to a Dutch limited company. Exemption can be claimed in most cases of mergers and reorganizations. There are no wealth or net worth taxes for companies. Individuals are subject, however, to an annual net wealth tax (0.8% of net worth after deduction of certain exempt amounts).

Land and Property Tax. A small municipal tax applies to the ownership and use of immovable property.

Transfer Tax. The acquisition of immovable property or certain rights in immovable properties (e.g., buildings, houses, shares in real estate companies) is subject to a 6% transfer tax. Exemption can be claimed in certain cases of corporate restructurings.

COMPUTATION OF TAXABLE INCOME

26. Capital Gains

Capital gains are included in taxable income (for individuals, see item 11). An exception from capital gains on the disposal of certain participations in other corporations is discussed in item 8. Taxation of capital gains on the sale of tangible fixed (and most intangible) assets can be deferred if replacement is intended (see item 3).

27. Depreciation and Depletion

Depreciation must be taken on all fixed assets that have a limited useful life. Depreciation should be based on cost, economic life, and residual value. Various methods may be used, including the straight-line and declining balance methods. No detailed guidelines exist as to the depreciation percentages to be used. A declining-balance method of depreciation is only acceptable if the benefit of the asset follows a declining pattern throughout its life. Purchased intangible assets, including goodwill, can be amortized over their useful lives (usually five years).

28. Treatment of Dividends

Dividends are included in taxable income. An exception to this rule is referred to in item 8.

29. Loss Carryovers

Losses are offset against income of the three preceding years (starting with the oldest year) and the following eight years. Losses incurred during the first six years of operation are offset against future income without time limit. Loss carryovers may be subject to limitations when the ownership of the company changes.

30. Transactions between Related Parties

Transactions between related parties which are not concluded on an arm's length basis may be disregarded or may be adjusted appropriately. Special provisions exist for tax-free mergers between Dutch companies and for tax-free incorporation of a sole proprietorship.

Dutch legislation will be amended to implement the EC Merger Directive per January 1, 1992.

31. Consolidation of Income

If a Dutch resident company owns at least 99% of the shares of one or more other Dutch resident companies, these companies can apply for a fiscal unity. Companies included in a fiscal unity are taxed for the year as one entity. As a result, the year's losses of one of the companies may be offset against profits realized in the same year by the other company (or companies).

32. Tax Periods

The fiscal year of a Dutch company is the accounting year as stated in the company's articles of association. For Dutch branches of foreign companies, in principle, the calendar year must be the fiscal year.

33. Other Matters

Principles of Computing Profits. The main principle is that all profits generated during the lifetime of a business or trade are taxed. These lifetime profits are attributed to particular years on the basis of "sound business practice." The computation of profits for tax purposes need not follow commercial profits where law and jurisprudence provide otherwise. Examples of jurisprudence include:

☐ Inventories may be valued by using a base stock method or LIFO method.

☐ A provision may be established for unfunded pensions, including earned back-service.

☐ Insurance companies may establish a special reserve.

☐ Work in process may be valued excluding certain overheads (direct costing).

☐ Profit on work in progress of contractors, etc., may be deferred until the project is finished.

☐ Unrealized exchange profits on long-term loans may be deferred until realized (unless the difference between historical and actual exchange rates is substantial and permanent), while unrealized losses may be taken in the current book year.

In computing taxable profit for personal income tax or corporate income tax purposes, a number of mixed expenses is not (fully) deductible. These include food, beverages, canteen facilities, clothing, conference costs, business gifts, and business entertainment costs.

RELATED CONSIDERATIONS

34. Incentives and Grants

According to the Investment Credit Act, investments in qualifying fixed assets generated a credit (WIR) against corporate income tax. However, effective January 1, 1990, the Investment Credit Act has been abolished and replaced by an investment deduction.

The investment deduction applies to qualifying investments made in book years beginning on or after January 1, 1990. The investment deduction reduces the taxable profit. The higher the qualifying investments made during the year, the lower the rate of investment deduction. The investment deduction varies from 2% to 18% of qualifying investments. The investment deduction can be claimed if the total of qualifying investments made during the year is between DFls 3,100 and DFls 457,000.

Securities, goodwill, land, private houses, ships, automobiles, and a few other categories of fixed assets do not qualify for the investment deduction. Fixed assets with an investment amount lower than DFls 1,000 do not qualify for the investment deduction either.

The investment deduction is (partly) added back to the taxable profit if the assets, for which the investment deduction was granted, are disposed of within five years of the beginning of the book year in which the investment was made.

In certain areas of The Netherlands, an investment grant (IPR) can be obtained for commencing or expanding manufacturing establishments and other industrial projects. Further, various Government grants can be obtained if research and development activities are carried out in The Netherlands (e.g., PBTS and TOK).

35. Exchange Controls

There are no restrictive exchange controls.

36. Investment Restrictions on Nonresidents

None.

SELECTION OF BUSINESS ENTITY BY NONRESIDENTS

Nonresident investors can operate in The Netherlands either through a branch or by forming a local subsidiary corporation. A branch and a local corporation are taxed at the same rates. Principally, the same tax provisions apply to both entities. However, no withholding taxes are imposed on profit distributions by branches.

In the case of start-up losses, it could be advantageous to operate through a branch in The Netherlands in order to utilize such losses against possible profits of the foreign corporation. If desired, the branch may be converted at any time into a subsidiary corporation under a tax-free reorganization scheme.

Apart from the above considerations regarding initial (start-up) losses, foreign investors normally prefer to operate through a subsidiary corporation, largely for administrative and commercial reasons.

Dutch corporate law recognizes two types of limited liability companies, the "N.V." and the "B.V." Nonquoted companies are normally incorporated as a B.V.

SPECIMEN TAX COMPUTATION

Information:

☐ The corporation's operating profit for the year of DFls 1,000,000 consists of the following:

	DFls '000'
Trading result in The Netherlands	650
Trading results of a qualifying foreign branch	100
Dividend income received from participation	100
Gain on sale of shares in a qualifying participation	150
	1,000

□ For tax purposes, inventories are valued according to a basestock system as defined in Dutch jurisprudence resulting in a lower tax valuation in the year of DFls 300,000.

Computation:

		DFls '000'
Operating profit as per accounts		1,000
Less		
Differences in inventory valuations	300	
Exempt income (participation exemption):		
—Dividend	100	
—Gain on sale of shares in a qualifying participation	150	
		550
Taxable income		450
Corporation tax on worldwide income (at 40% for taxable profits up to DFls 250,000 and at 35% for excess taxable profits)		170
Less		
Foreign tax relief for income of foreign branch (100/450 × 170)		38
Tax payable		132

NETHERLANDS ANTILLES

INCOME TAXES ON CORPORATIONS

1. Rates

The tax rates may vary depending on whether a company is primarily engaged in business activities within the Netherlands Antilles (N.A.), the so-called on-shore companies, or outside the Netherlands Antilles—the so-called off-shore companies. An on-shore company also may qualify for special lower tax rates as may be provided for in the various N.A. tax investment incentive schemes. The various tax rates are listed below.

On-Shore Companies.

Taxable Income		Tax on	Percentage
Over	Not Over	Lower Amount	On Excess
NAfls 0	NAfls 40,000	NAfls 0	27%
40,000	50,000	10,800	30
50,000	60,000	13,800	33
60,000	70,000	17,100	36
70,000	80,000	20,700	39
80,000	90,000	24,600	41
90,000	100,000	28,700	43
100,000	1,000,000	33,000	33
1,000,000		330,000	34

Special rates apply to the taxable income of certain on-shore companies:

Free-zone companies	2%
Shipping and aviation companies (1)	
First NAfls 100,000	7.7%

Over NAfls 100,000	9.6%
Real estate companies (2)	0
Mutual funds	(3)
Insurance companies (4)	31.05% to 39.10%
New industries and hotels (5)	2%
Land development companies (6)	0

Notes:
(1) Or election tonnage taxation NAfls 0.40 per registered ton.
(2) Foreign real-estate-source income is tax-exempt. Dividends paid by a foreign (non-Dutch) real estate company to its N.A. parent company are also tax-exempt.
(3) Mutual funds may request to be taxed on a sliding scale, based on the funds' net asset value. The minimum annual tax is U.S.$1,000, and the maximum tax is U.S.$10,000.
(4) Insurance companies may request to be taxed at the above-mentioned rates on the basis of a fixed profit (e.g., 10% of their gross premiums received in a tax year) for a period of five years.
(5) Five- to 11-year tax holiday.
(6) Tax holiday for land development within the Netherlands Antilles.

Off-Shore Companies. Investment, holding, financial, and patent holding companies are subject to a 2.4% to 3% rate. The 2.4% rate applies to taxable profits up to NAfls 100,000, and the 3% rate is on the balance.

Subject to a specific tax ruling, a 4.8% to 6% rate may apply to N.A. off-shore trading and service companies.

Captive insurance companies may request to be taxed at (1) 2.4% to 3% (these low rates also apply to investment income), or (2) a fixed amount of tax of NAfls 2,400 per year.

The reduced rates for free-zone companies, shipping and aircraft companies, and "off-shore companies", as discussed under item 1, are guaranteed to be maximum tax rates; therefore, no other tax will be levied. The rates for free-zone and "off-shore companies" presently are guaranteed until 1999.

2. Local Income Taxes

In addition to the corporation tax, an island surcharge is levied at the rate of 15% of the corporation tax imposed. Consequently, the effective rate of corporation tax, including the 15% island surcharge, ranges from 31.05% to 39.1%.

The off-shore companies are not subject to the 15% island surcharge.

3. Capital Gains Taxes

For the on-shore companies, capital gains or losses are considered ordinary income and are subject to the standard corporate tax rates. Under the special tax regime for investment holding, finance, and patent holding companies, capital gains and losses are tax-free.

4. Branch Profits Taxes

N.A. branches of nonresident companies are subject to corporation tax in accordance with the rules applicable to on-shore companies. A deduction of a reasonable part of head office expenses normally is allowed.

5. Foreign Tax Reliefs

In principle, a resident on-shore company is taxed on its worldwide income. However, the tax on certain types of foreign income may be reduced either unilaterally or pursuant to treaty provisions. Depending on the country of source and type of income, among other things, either a full exemption or a reduced rate of N.A. tax may be obtained. Except as provided in treaty arrangements, there is no general provision in the tax law granting foreign tax credits.

7. Payment of Tax

Tax is payable upon receipt of assessments. A preliminary assessment also may be issued on a preliminary tax return filed or pending completion of the accounts.

8. Other Matters

Taxation of Foreign Branch Income.   Profits derived from a foreign branch of an on-shore N.A. company are subject to N.A. tax at one-tenth of the normal rate, provided these profits have been subject to an income tax in the foreign country. Subject to a ruling, profits derived from a foreign branch of an offshore N.A. company are subject to the 2.4% to 3% rates. Income received from a permanent establishment of an N.A. company within the Kingdom of the Netherlands is fully tax-exempt in the Netherlands Antilles.

INCOME TAXES ON INDIVIDUALS

9. Rates

Progressive rates are levied on taxable income. In addition, an island surcharge is levied on the amount of tax due. The rates for a married individual (including the island surcharge) may vary from approximately 8% on NAfls 20,000 annual income to 32% on an annual income of approximately NAfls 100,000. The maximum rate amounts to approximately 58%.

Special reduced rates of tax apply to certain nonrecurring items of income; for example, liquidation proceeds from a company, capital gains on sale of "substantial share interests."

Under certain conditions, a reduction in tax may be obtained if income includes dividend receipts from an N.A. on-shore company. Salaries and wages are subject to tax withholdings at source. Provisional assessments can be issued during a fiscal year. Incremental tax is payable upon receipt of an assessment.

11.   Capital Gains Taxes

Capital gains and losses arising from the sale or exchange of private assets are exempt from taxation. If private assets are employed as capital of a business, the capital gains and losses form part of the personal taxable income. Also, capital gains realized on the sale of shares are taxed if the seller has a "substantial interest," that is, at least a 25% shareholding in an N.A. on-shore company. The gain is subject to the reduced rate of tax applicable to non-recurring items of income.

12.   Foreign Tax Reliefs

Netherlands Antilles tax relief may be obtained for specific sources of foreign income.

13.   Tax Period

The tax year is the calendar year.

14.   Other Matters

Retiree Incentives.   Legislation has been enacted whereby (retired) individuals who meet certain requirements (have a residence permit, have no employment within the Netherlands Antilles, own and use a residence in the Netherlands Antilles with a value of at least US $135,000, employ at least one Netherlands Antillean, etc.) may opt to be taxed as follows on their non-N.A.-source income. The tax benefit offered is, at the option of the individual:

☐   A flat 5% tax rate, or
☐   The non-N.A.-source income is fixed at the amount of NAfl 150,000 and is taxed at the normal rates. The annual tax due will amount to approximately US $32,000.

Non-N.A.-source income includes inter alia, interest on N.A. bank accounts, and dividends from N.A. offshore corporations.

   The individual should not have been an N.A. resident during five years preceding taking up residence in the Netherlands Antilles and applying for this tax incentive.

Taxation of Expatriates.   Expatriates in the Netherlands Antilles are those individuals who are highly qualified, recruited from abroad, whose activities require special knowledge or involve particular responsibilities, and whose stay in the Netherlands Antilles is on a temporary basis. The regulations allow qualifying staff to elect a 35% deduction of certain defined fringe benefits. The provisions limit eligible fringe benefits to 40% of total wages with a maximum of NAFls 40,000.

   Allowances or expenses for travel, hotel room, refurnishing, etc., during the first two months of stay are specifically excluded from the definition of fringe benefits for this purpose.

   These regulations are retroactively effective as of January 1, 1987.

INCOME TAXES ON NONRESIDENTS

15. Liability to Tax

Individuals living in the Netherlands Antilles for more than one year generally are considered residents. Residents are taxed on their worldwide income. Nonresidents who derive income from certain sources within the Netherlands Antilles (e.g., permanent establishment, N.A. real estate, and employment) are taxed at normal domestic rates, except that not all individual allowances are granted. Nonresident individuals earning directors' fees from N.A. companies are, in general, liable also to income tax.

17. Withholding Tax Rates

There is no withholding tax on dividends, interest, and royalties paid by an N.A. company.

19. Tax Treaties

As part of the Kingdom of The Netherlands, the Netherlands Antilles is party to a Federal Tax Agreement with The Netherlands. Subject to this treaty, dividends, interest, and royalties paid out to an N.A. recipient may qualify for reduced or nil rates of withholding taxes in the subject countries. Under the renegotiated Federal Tax Agreement with The Netherlands, which is effective January 1, 1986, the Dutch withholding tax on dividends paid by a Dutch company to an N.A. company holding at least 25% of the Dutch subsidiary's shares is 7.5% (or 5% if the dividends are subject to N.A. profit tax of at least 5.5%).

On January 1, 1988, the treaty with the United States was terminated except for the interest provisions (article viii of the current treaty), which remains in force. This article among others allows U.S. corporations that (prior to mid-1984) issued Eurobonds through N.A. corporations to continue paying interest without deducting 30% U.S. withholding tax.

In November 1989, Norway and the Netherlands Antilles signed a new treaty. This treaty came into force January 1, 1991. The principal features of the new treaty are:

□ The new treaty provides for the following rates of withholding taxes: on dividends, 15% reduced to 5% for direct investment dividends; on royalties, 0%; and on interest 0%.

□ There is a "limitation on benefits" article denying the benefits of the treaty to certain N.A. companies (e.g., those controlled by nonresidents of the Netherlands Antilles).

Treaty Developments. Treaty negotiations with Austria, Belgium, and Italy are presently being held. Negotiations with Sweden may begin shortly.

OTHER SIGNIFICANT TAXES

21. Sales (Value Added)

No general sales tax is levied.

22. Inheritance and Gift Taxes

Gifts and receipts from an estate of a Dutch citizen are taxable to residents of the Netherlands Antilles. Nonresidents owning real estate in the Netherlands Antilles also are subject to these taxes.

Gifts and receipts from estates of a nonresident shareholder of an N.A. company are not subject to Antilles estate and gift taxes.

25. Other Taxes

Land and Property Taxes. The transfer of N.A.-located immovable property is subject to a 2.75% transfer duty. A land tax is levied on real estate located in the Netherlands Antilles at an annual rate of 0.5% on the value of undeveloped land and 0.6% of the value of built-up land. The 15% island surcharge also is levied.

On some of the N.A. islands, an annual 5% occupancy tax is levied on the rental value of buildings. Industrial buildings are exempt.

Taxes on Capital. No capital duties are levied in the Netherlands Antilles. There is no net wealth tax for individuals or companies.

COMPUTATION OF TAXABLE INCOME

26. Capital Gains

For on-shore companies, capital gains are included in taxable income (see item 3).

Capital gains of off-shore companies are tax-exempt (see item 3). (For individuals, see item 11.)

27. Depreciation and Depletion

There are no specific rules for methods of depreciation. Depreciation normally should be spread over the useful economic life of the asset. The method usually applied is the straight-line method, but the declining-balance method is, in some cases, also allowed.

In 1986 (applicable as from January 1, 1985), accelerated depreciation equal to one-third of the acquisition or manufacturing cost of assets used in the conduct of a business was introduced for all taxpayers receiving business income. The accelerated depreciation is in principle restricted to the year in which the asset is actually put into use. However, with regard to buildings, the depreciation is allowed as soon as commitments for the acquisition, improvement, or construction costs are made.

Purchased goodwill that is carried as an asset in the accounts is also depreciable.
In addition to the above-mentioned accelerated depreciation, shipping companies may depreciate a vessel at a further accelerated rate provided the vessel was purchased after December 31, 1980 and before January 1, 1996.

28. Treatment of Dividends

Dividends are included in taxable income. However, dividends received from resident companies are not subject to tax, provided the company paying the dividend is not an off-shore investment holding, finance, or patent holding company. However, this exemption would apply if the recipient company is also an off-shore company.

Dividends received from a foreign (non-Dutch) company are subject to N.A. corporation tax at one-tenth of the normal rate provided the N.A. company has at least a 10% share holding in the foreign company and the foreign company has been subject to an income tax in the latter country. The 15% island surcharge is then also levied. Dividend income of N.A. off-shore companies generally is subject to the reduced 2.4%–3% tax rate.

29. Loss Carryovers

In general, losses may be carried forward for five years, and by shipping and aircraft companies for six years. These companies may also offset losses incurred during the first six years against future income without time limitation.

30. Transactions between Related Parties

Transactions between related parties that are not on an arm's-length basis may be disregarded or may be adjusted appropriately.

31. Consolidation of Income

Antilles tax law does not provide for consolidation of income between related companies. However, under certain circumstances, tax rulings may be obtained allowing a consolidation.

32. Tax Periods

The fiscal year of a corporation need not be a calendar year, but is the official year as stated in the corporation's articles of association.

33. Other Matters

Reserves. An asset replacement reserve may be set up to defer taxation of capital gains on the sale of fixed assets, provided that replacement is intended. Subject to the specific tax facility provisions for N.A. shipping and aircraft companies, these companies may set up tax-deductible reserves for the equalization of business expenses, self-insurance, and replacement or repair in case of loss or damage to their ships or aircraft.

Inventory Valuation. There are no special rules concerning the valuation of inventories. Inventories generally are valued at the lower of cost or market and both LIFO and FIFO are allowed.

Other Deductions. In calculating taxable income of an N.A. company, all expenses incurred in connection with the business of the company will be allowed as a deduction. All taxes incurred by the company are deductible, except the N.A. corporation tax and the additional island surtax.

Royalties paid to third parties are deductible. Those paid to an individual or company controlling the N.A. company could be disallowed as a deduction in the Netherlands Antilles.

Interest normally is allowed as a deduction when paid to a recognized bank. In other cases, it is recommended to obtain a ruling from the tax authorities.

RELATED CONSIDERATIONS

34. Incentives and Grants

The following types of companies may qualify for a special reduced tax rate (see item 1) and/or tax treatment:

Manufacturing Companies.

☐ 2% tax rate for five or ten years, or up to the year 2000.

☐ Exemption from import duties for raw materials, semi-finished products, packing materials, and machinery related to the construction of a manufacturing facility.

☐ Exemption from land and/or occupancy tax for up to ten years, or up to the year 2000.

☐ Losses incurred during the first four years of operations may offset future income indefinitely.

Renovation Hotels.

☐ Exemption from import duties for up to two years on imported goods used to extend, improve, and/or renovate the building.

Free-Zone Companies.

☐ 2% corporation tax.

☐ No import or export duties.

☐ Formerly, free-zone incentives were limited to nonmanufacturing activities, such as assembling, (re)packaging, storing, and the subsequent export. As of December 15, 1986, it has become a full free processing zone and an international service center (e.g., repair and maintenance of machinery situated outside the Netherlands Antilles and other export services).

Shipping and Aircraft Companies.

□ 7.7–9.6% corporation tax.

□ Investment allowance, during two years of 8% of acquisition or improvement cost is tax deductible, subject to recapture if the vessel is disposed of within ten years after the investment date.

□ Accelerated depreciation (see item 27).

□ Certain reserves are tax deductible (see item 33).

□ Six years loss carryforward (see item 29).

□ Ships and aircraft should, in principle, be registered in the Netherlands; countries with comparable shipping or aviation legislation may also satisfy this requirement.

□ Company should be a N.A. company resident in the Antilles.

□ Annual charges range from U.S.$1,773 to U.S.$23,177. There is no initial registration fee.

□ In addition to the existing tax regime, a tonnage taxation (applicable as from January 1, 1987) has been introduced. Ships may opt for the above described profits taxation or for NAfl0.40 taxation per registered ton/GT with a minimum of U.S.$560 per ship per year.

Insurance Companies.

□ 31.05–39.10% corporate tax.

□ Companies may request to be taxed for five years on the basis of a fixed profit.

□ Profit is fixed at, for example, 10% of the life insurance premiums received in the tax year. This same low rate will apply to investment income.

□ Captive insurance companies may request to be taxed at the 2.4% to 3% rates at a fixed amount of NAfls 2,400 annually. The 2.4% to 3% rates also will apply to investment income. Prior approval from the Antilles Central Bank is required for forming a captive insurance company.

□ Legislation has been enacted providing for supervision of insurance companies by the Central Bank.

New Industries and Hotels.

□ Partial exemption from profit tax; a 2% tax rate for a period of five to eleven years.

□ Exemption from import duties on materials and goods necessary for construction and initial equipment.

☐ Exemption from land and occupancy tax.

☐ A minimum investment and/or number of new jobs is required.

☐ For new hotels, losses incurred during the first four years of operations may be offset against taxable income indefinitely.

Land Development Companies.

☐ Tax holiday.

☐ Exemption from import duties on materials and goods utilized in the development-construction activities.

☐ Exemption from tax on profits realized on the sale of the developed land.

☐ A minimum investment is required. Activities should be expected to expand the economic development of the Netherlands Antilles.

Investment Holding Companies.

☐ Tax rate 2.4%–3% on net investment income.

☐ No tax on capital gains.

☐ No island surcharge.

☐ Guarantee of above rates until 1999.

☐ Company should be resident in the Netherlands Antilles, and shareholders should be nonresidents.

☐ Object of company should be to invest in securities, such as stocks and bonds.

Mutal Funds.

☐ Subject to a ruling, the minimum annual tax is U.S.$1,000, and the maximum tax liability amounts to U.S.$10,000.

☐ Tax exemption on funds with a minimum capital of U.S.$50,000,000 and 50 or more shareholders (direct or indirect) provided the fund employs at least four resident individual nationals of the Netherlands Antilles. If, however, the mutual fund has a minimum capital of U.S.$300,000,000 and employs at least two national individual residents of the Netherlands Antilles, the tax exemption will also be applicable.

Finance Companies.

☐ Tax rate 2.4%–3% to be applied on a minimum taxable spread arranged in advance with N.A. tax authorities.

☐ No N.A. debt-equity requirements.

☐ Other main incentives/requirements are the same as those imposed for investment holding companies.

Patent Holding Companies.

☐ The object of the company should be to derive income from the sale or granting of licenses for copyrights and patents, the supply of technical assistance outside the Netherlands Antilles and royalties/rentals of motion pictures.

☐ Other main incentives and requirements are the same as those for investment holding companies.

Real Estate Companies.

☐ Foreign real-estate-source income, including dividends received by a N.A. company paid by a foreign (non-Dutch) subsidiary that holds real estate, are tax-exempt.

Other Companies.

☐ For offshore trading companies (i.e., companies engaged in any trade or business outside the Netherlands Antilles), tax rulings can be obtained which apply a special effective tax rate of approximately 6% on net income. These rulings can also be obtained for off-shore (management) service companies.

In 1986 an investment allowance was introduced (effective January 1, 1985) which allows 8% of the invested amount to be charged against taxable income during a two-year period. The investments should be made in certain qualifying business assets and exceed NAFls 5,000. The allowance should be claimed in the year investment commitments or construction costs are made. For buildings (new or improved) the allowance is increased to 12%. If assets for which the allowance is claimed are sold within six years (15 years for buildings) after the investment has been made, the amount deducted is added to the profit of the year in which the assets are sold.

35. Exchange Controls

In general, the exchange control regulations are very liberal for off-shore companies. Off-shore companies established in the Netherlands Antilles can obtain nonresident status for exchange control purposes, which basically provides for a total exemption from exchange control. On-shore companies are subject to slightly stricter rules.

36. Investment Restrictions on Nonresidents

No specific restrictions are imposed on nonresidents. As a formality, certain licenses are required for nonresidents carrying on business activities within the Netherlands Antilles.

37. Other Matters

Trust. Legislation has been proposed under which this legal entity could also perform commercial activities.

Transfer of a Company's Legal Seat. Legislation has been enacted under which an N.A. company is allowed to transfer its legal seat to another jurisdiction (if permitted) and vice versa.

Restricted and Non-Voting Shares. An N.A. company is allowed to issue non-voting shares and shares with restricted voting rights.

SELECTION OF BUSINESS ENTITY BY NONRESIDENTS

Nonresident investors can operate in the Netherlands Antilles either through a branch or by forming a local subsidiary company. Both entities however, generally are subject to the same tax provisions and are taxed at the same rates. However, since certain N.A. tax investment incentives are available only to N.A.-incorporated companies, this is the entity used by most foreign investors. The Naamloze Vennootschap (N.V.) is the only form of corporate entity in the Netherlands Antilles.

NEW CALEDONIA

INCOME TAXES ON CORPORATIONS

1. Rates

All corporations, whether public or private, pay tax at the rate of 30% on New Caledonia-source income only. Nickel-related industries are taxable at the rate of 35%. Corporations created in development zones as of May 1989 are eligible for a tax holiday for eight years; development zones are not yet defined.

Taxable income is defined as the difference between the net book values of the company at the beginning and at the end of the financial period, less share capital contributions plus distributions. Other specific adjustments are made to taxable income. Net book value includes intangible assets.

Dividend income received from nonresident companies is subject to tax as normal company income, for its net amount reduced from three times the withholding levied in the state of source.

Dividend income received from resident companies is exempt from tax.

2. Local Income Taxes

Only the Territory levies income taxes. Communes levy rates which are not assessed on income.

3. Capital Gains Taxes

There are no separate capital gains taxes as such. Such gains or losses are, however, considered as taxable income as a consequence of the definition of taxable income in item 1.

As an exception, companies were allowed to revalue their assets as of January 1, 1979, the surplus being carried to an asset revaluation account free of tax. This account is to be reintegrated into taxable income when the asset is retired; except if the company is wound up, the reserve is converted to capital or it is offset against operating losses carried forward.

Where companies file an undertaking to reinvest capital profits in the Territory within three years, the capital gain is excluded from taxable income.

4. Branch Profits Taxes

A branch of a foreign corporation is taxed on the profits of the branch as though it were a resident corporation. Further, all profits are deemed to be automatically distributed and subject to 13.25% (IRVM: 12.5% + CES: 0.75%) withholding tax.

5. Foreign Tax Reliefs

Except for dividends and royalties, only income from local sources is taxed. There is, therefore, no relief necessary for foreign taxes.

7. Payment of Taxes

Companies are required to pay tax in three installments. The first two installments are payable by the end of the seventh and eleventh month during the financial year, and are calculated on the basis of one-third of the tax paid for the previous year. The balance is payable four months after the balance sheet date.

INCOME TAXES ON INDIVIDUALS

9. Rates

All income from all family sources is accumulated (except dividends) since the family is the taxable entity, and the following deductions are allowed:

Interest on housing loan	Limit CFP 500,000 (Noumea)
	No limit (others)
Life assurance	Limit CFP 250,000
Retirement/superannuation	No limit
Alimony paid	No limit
Withholding taxes paid	No limit
Certain investment incentives	Limit CFP 1,000,000
Housemaids/child supervision	Limit CFP 300,000

The family income is then divided by the number of "parts." Each adult counts as one part and minor dependents are one-half each. After deductions, income tax on each part is calculated as follows:

Income		Rate
Over	**Not Over**	
CFP 0	CFP 1,000,000	0%
1,000,000	1,300,000	5
1,300,000	1,600,000	10
1,600,000	2,200,000	15

Income		
Over	Not Over	Rate
CFP 2,200,000	CFP 2,800,000	20%
2,800,000	4,500,000	30
4,500,000		40

The six classes of taxable income and the applicable rules are:

□ Rental income.   Actual income less actual expenses including interest, major repairs plus management expenses (excluding agent), insurance, and depreciation which are deemed to be 15% of income. Capital gains are not taxable.

□ Commercial and industrial income.   Computed under generally accepted accounting rules. However, taxpayers may elect a scheme under which taxable income is arbitrarily half of the gross profit less personnel and subcontracting costs. This option is not available if turnover exceeds CFP 25 million for commerce and 7.5 million for service industries. Turnover does not include exceptional items (sale of assets).

   Where capital gains are taxable, they may be claimed as a deduction subject to an undertaking to reinvest within three years.

□ Agriculture.   Taxable income is arbitrarily one-sixth of income, but a taxpayer may choose the generally accepted accounting rules scheme.

□ Salaries, wages, and pensions.   Taxable income is 80% of income net of social security contributions, grossed up for fringe benefits (excluding travel), and after a 10% arbitrary deduction for professional expenses limited to CFP 500,000. For this class of income, the tax year ends December 31 and there is no deduction at source.

□ Professional and other income.   Two-thirds of turnover where turnover is less than CFP 7.5 million; otherwise, on generally accepted accounting rules including capital gains.

□ Investment income.   Dividends received from foreign sources are taxed for the net amount except French dividends taxed for the gross amount (the French WH/T being considered as a tax credit). Dividends received from local sources are not taxable but subject to a WH/T of 13.25%.

   Capital gains are not taxable.

Losses in one category of income may be carried forward but may not be offset against profits in any other category.

10. Local Income Taxes

Only the Territory levies income taxes.

11. Capital Gains Taxes

Capital gains may be taxed as revenue depending on which category of income is the source (see item 9).

12. Foreign Tax Reliefs

On condition that taxpayers can prove that foreign earned income has been subjected to foreign income tax, such income is tax-free. There are no reliefs.

13. Tax Period

The tax year for employees and retired persons ends on December 31. The year-end for other sources of income is at the taxpayer's option.

All persons must pay one-third of the tax paid in the prior year on March 31 and July 31.

INCOME TAXES ON NONRESIDENTS

16. Rates

Income derived by a nonresident corporation carrying on business locally is taxed as though the corporation were a resident. Profits are deemed to be automatically distributed and are subject to 13.25% withholding.

Dividend income derived by a nonresident corporation not carrying on business locally, or derived by a nonresident individual, is subject to withholding tax of 13.25% on such dividends.

Nonresident individuals are taxed at the flat rate of 25% on income derived from the Territory.

19. Tax Treaties

The only tax treaty is with Metropolitan France, of which the country is a "Territorie." Under this treaty, dividends are taxable at source at the rates of 5% and 15%, depending on whether the taxpayers are corporations (other than a partnership) or individuals, respectively, and royalties at up to 10%. Interest is not subject to withholding.

OTHER SIGNIFICANT TAXES

21. Sales (Value Added)

There are no sales taxes.

22. Inheritance and Gift Taxes

Death duties are payable on the market value of an estate as at the date of death as shown below. Gift taxes between unrelated persons may be as high as 50%.

Bequeathed To	Up to CFP 1 Million	CFP 1 Million to CFP 3 Million	CFP 3 Million to CFP 10 Million	More than CFP 10 Million
Spouse or direct descendent or ascendent	5%	10%	15%	20%
Sibling	30	30	30	30
Relatives up to the fourth degree	40	40	40	40
Others	50	50	50	50

23. Taxes on Payrolls (Social Security)

All employers are obliged to pay to the local social security organization (C.A.F.A.T.) a tax based on employee remuneration. The rate of tax is variable according to the accident risk of the employment; however, the minimum rate is at present 29.94%. The ceiling to which this is applied varies according to the cost of living index and is currently F. 198,920 per month. An employee is defined as any person receiving a remuneration for services performed who is not a patente (see below) and who does not, either individually or with his fellow employees, own more than 50% of the enterprise, the latter not being a societe anonyme (public corporation).

Individual employees contribute to the social security fund at the rate of 7.11% of their earnings up to the same ceiling.

24. Taxes on Natural Resources

The Territory imposes a tax in the form of a rental or royalty on mineral and oil tenements, whether for exploration purposes or development and extraction.

25. Other Taxes

Land and Property. Each commune imposes an annual tax based on land owned.

Stamp Duties. The Territory imposes duties on documents that effectively transfer title in real property and private companies at the rate of 13% and 3%, respectively. Certain other documents must also be registered and are subject to duty at a nominal rate.

Patente. This is a business license tax divided into fixed and variable components. All businesses, whether commercial or professional, are subject to the license. The fixed component is calculated by various formulas, including area utilized and number of employees. The variable component is 1.6% of the C.I.F. value of imports.

Capital Tax. There are no taxes on capital.

Tax on Interest.   Interest on certain loans is subject to retention at source (called IRCOC) of 7%. Notable exclusions are loans between individuals, bank savings, and current accounts financing real estate operations.

Dividends.   Dividends are subject to retention at source of 13.25%. The definition of dividends includes all forms of distribution of unappropriated profits. If the retention has been effectively made, the dividends are not taxable in the hands of individuals.

COMPUTATION OF TAXABLE INCOME

26.   Capital Gains

There are no capital gains taxes as such (see item 3).

27.   Depreciation and Depletion

Depreciation is by the straight-line or reducing-balance method, at the option of the taxpayer. Reducing-balance method rates are automatically 50% higher than straight-line method rates.

28.   Treatment of Dividends

Dividends paid to companies or individuals are subject to a withholding tax at the rate of 13.25%. Dividends paid by a Caledonian company subject to corporate income tax to another Caledonian company subject to corporate income tax are not taxable. Dividends received from a foreign company are subject to tax as normal company income, for its net amount reduced from three times the WH/T levied in the state of source.

29.   Loss Carryovers

There is a five-year loss carryforward (no carryback), except for that part of the loss representing depreciation, which can be carried forward without time limit.

30.   Transactions between Related Parties

There are no special provisions for transactions of this nature.

31.   Consolidation of Income

There is no provision for group consolidation of income for tax purposes.

32.   Tax Periods

Generally, December 31 is the fiscal year-end for companies. However, the choice of tax year is up to the company.

33. Other Matters

Provisions for Price Increases.   Entities may calculate a tax deductible provision for price increases on items in stock. This is calculated by identifying unit price increases of more than 10% over a maximum of two years and multiplying the excess of 10% by the quantity of that article in stock. Charges to this provision must be added back to taxable income at the end of the sixth year following the provision being set up.

Import Duties.   Rates and definitions of import duties vary widely and are significant in the budget of the Territory. Consultation with a specialist is recommended. Being part of the E.E.C., penalty rates are imposed on imports from non-E.E.C. countries.

Deductions for Taxes.   In computing the liability for income tax, a deduction is available for amounts paid by way of social security taxes, and land and property taxes. Stamp duty would be deductible by way of depreciation or as part of the cost of inventory or if it were part of borrowing expense (deduction over five years).

No deduction is available in respect of tax fines.

RELATED CONSIDERATIONS

34. Incentives and Grants

Investments by companies and individuals in the sectors of tourism, hotels, industry, fishing, agriculture, construction, public works, transport, and energy are 100% tax deductible for the investor for the amount invested by it.

As of January 1, 1991, profit realized by a corporation in the sector of hostelry and tourism will be exempted of corporate income taxes during a 15- to 20-year period subject to a prior agreement.

Further incentives exist in the form of subsidies obtained by application to the Investment Code Authority. These may in certain cases be up to 40% of the total funds required for investment.

35. Exchange Controls

Since December 1989, exchange operations of all kinds with a foreign country or between a resident and a nonresident are free, but the physical transfer of funds that exceed CFP 900,000 must be declared to the Customs Administration and scriptural transfer must be carried out through approved intermediaries (i.e., almost all banks), except within the "Zone franc" (French franc finance zone).

36. Investment Restrictions on Nonresidents

Setting up of a branch or a company in New Caledonia by a nonresident is free. Investment in French existing enterprises (i.e., investments involving de facto or legal control of a French enterprise) is:

☐ Free, if the investor is resident from an EC country but is in principle subject to a declaration,

☐ Subject to a prior authorization from the Ministry of Finance based in Paris, if the investor is a non-EC resident.

Investments up to 20% are in fact automatically allowed.

SELECTION OF BUSINESS ENTITY BY NONRESIDENTS

Nonresident investors can operate in New Caledonia either through a branch or a locally incorporated company. The tax drawback of operating through a branch is that all profits are deemed to have been distributed and the distribution tax of 13.25% is payable immediately. Interest charged on loans to the subsidiary or branch are not subject in New Caledonia to the IRCDC (7%). There is no limit to the amount of the loan, but the deductible interest rate is limited to the interest rate of the ''Banque de France'' plus two points (i.e., 12.5%).

NEW ZEALAND

INCOME TAXES ON CORPORATIONS

1. Rates

Resident corporations and public authorities	33%
Life insurance companies	33%–38%
Insurance underwriters	38%
Nonresident corporations	38%
Nonresident mining operations	38%

Dividends received by resident companies before April 1, 1992 are generally exempt from tax. Although dividends received by resident companies from nonresident companies are exempt, the recipient company is liable for a 33% withholding payment on such dividends, reduced by a credit for foreign withholding tax. Life insurance companies are taxed in their own right and as proxies for policyholders. Foreign life insurers may elect to be taxed as residents.

2. Local Income Taxes

None, other than rates payable to local authorities, as a result of the ownership of land.

3. Capital Gains Taxes

There is presently no capital gains tax as such. The Income Tax Act, however, includes in assessable income certain capital gains derived from real property transactions. Liability is based on factors such as length of ownership, rezoning of property, and the other business activities of the taxpayer or persons associated with the taxpayer. Certain other rules abolish the capital/income distinction in respect of debt transactions.

4. Branch Profits Taxes

Nonresident corporations are subject to tax at 38% on New Zealand-source income, except where the withholding tax is deemed to be final (e.g., arm's-length interest, cultural royalties, or where a treaty provides for such limitation) and where a special tax rate applies (e.g., insurance premiums paid to overseas insurers, film rentals, and income derived from transportation by sea outside of New Zealand).

5. Foreign Tax Reliefs

Income derived by a resident corporation from outside New Zealand is taxable on the same basis as if it had a New Zealand source, including recalculation of the income according to New Zealand law. A foreign tax credit is allowed equal to the lesser of the foreign tax paid or the New Zealand tax payable on that income. Foreign dividends generally are not included in the income of a New Zealand corporation (except life insurance companies and certain dividends paid by overseas companies to resident corporations). The foreign tax credit must be utilized in the same fiscal period in which it is paid. There is no provision for carryover of excess credits.

6. Classification of Corporations

Corporations are classified for tax purposes as either resident or nonresident. A classification of "proprietary" (private) company exists for certain restrictive provisions of the Act, but this does not affect the rate of tax on the company's income, impose any special tax on distribution, or impose any obligation to distribute. From April 1, 1992, it is proposed that closely held resident companies may elect to be "qualifying companies," thus enabling tax treatment in a similar manner to partnerships.

A resident corporation is incorporated in New Zealand or has its head office, center of administrative management or director control in New Zealand. The distinction is important because nonresident corporations are subject to tax on only their New Zealand-source income. The distinction also affects the rate of tax (see item 4).

7. Payment of Taxes

Provisional Tax. Corporations are required to pay tax in three installments during the year in which the liability will arise, and to settle any adjustment after the end of the year. Provisional tax liabilities must be calculated with reference to estimated income tax if the corporation expects to pay more than NZ $300,000 in tax. The installments are payable in the fourth, eighth, and twelfth month of the corporation's financial year. Any adjustment required is payable by companies with early balance dates (October 1 to March 31, inclusive) in the eleventh month after the end of the financial year. Companies with late balance dates (April 1 to September 30, inclusive) are required to pay the adjustment the following February. Payment of all installments, and final adjustment, is required even if an assessment has not been issued.

Resident Withholding Tax. As of October 1, 1989, resident corporations that do not hold certificates of exemption are liable to have 24% (or 33%) of any interest payments made to them deducted and remitted to the Revenue authorities. A full credit for any resident withholding tax paid is allowed in respect of the corporation's ultimate liability to New Zealand tax. Certificates of exemption are issued by the Revenue authorities and normally are available only to banks and similar institutions and to corporations with gross annual incomes in excess of NZ$2 million.

Tax Period.   March 31 is the standard year-end. However, with the prior approval of the Revenue, an alternative date can be adopted.

8.   Other Matters

Controlled Foreign Corporations (CFCs) and Foreign Investment Funds (FIFs).   A CFC is a nonresident company controlled by five or fewer New Zealand residents. Effective April 1, 1988, CFC income is attributed to New Zealand residents with an income interest of 10% or greater subject to certain transitional provisions and exemptions for fifteenth schedule countries: Australia, Canada, France, Japan, the United Kingdom, the United States, and West Germany. The regime allows credits for foreign tax by jurisdiction, precludes the deduction of CFC losses from the resident's other income and involves recalculation of income applying New Zealand tax principles.

New Zealand holders of an interest in a FIF (a non-CFC entity located outside New Zealand and holding defined investments) are required to report FIF income each year, effective April 1, 1991. FIF income is calculated with reference to valuation changes and realized gains and losses each year.

Group Assessments.   See item 31.

INCOME TAXES ON INDIVIDUALS

9.   Rates

Income tax rates are the same for residents and nonresidents. There exists a low-income earner rebate only for New Zealand residents. Rebates also are allowed for housekeepers and charitable donations in certain circumstances.

Effective April 1, 1989, the following rates apply to the total of all forms of income:

Taxable Income		Tax on Lower Amount	Percentage on Excess
Over	Not Over		
NZ$ 0	NZ$30,875	NZ$ 0	24%
30,875		7,410	33

10. Local Income Taxes

See item 2.

11. Capital Gains Tax

See item 3.

12. Foreign Tax Reliefs

The basis of assessment of foreign income and the calculation of available tax credits is the same as for corporations, except that foreign dividends are included in the total income of an individual and the New Zealand tax payable is computed as the average rate applicable to total income.

Generally speaking, no credit is allowed for the underlying tax on a dividend received from a foreign corporation, but, in most cases, a special basis of assessment of United Kingdom dividends gives credit for a portion of the advance corporation tax paid.

13. Tax Period

March 31 is the standard year-end, but with the prior consent of the Revenue, an alternative date may be adopted with respect to business income only.

14. Other Matters

Payment of Tax. Salaries, wages, and certain types of contract or commission payments are subject to tax deductions at source. These deductions are credited against the final liability which is determined when a return is filed. If there are no other sources of income, a terminal adjustment is required the following November. Provisional installments are payable during the year on other types of income, including certain investment income and income from self-employment. The installments, including the terminal adjustment, are payable in the same way as for corporations (see item 7).

As of October 1, 1989, resident withholding tax is liable to be deducted from interest and dividends paid to individuals. Deductions are made at a rate of 24% (or 33%) for interest payments and at the rate of 33% for payments of dividends. Interest and dividends paid to an individual holding a certificate of exemption are not subject to resident withholding tax (see item 7), neither are dividends paid to the extent that imputations credits are attached (see item 28).

Controlled Foreign Corporations and Foreign Investment Funds. See item 8.

Accident Compensation Earner's Levy. From April 1, 1992, an accident compensation levy will be imposed on earners. The levy will be up to 1% of an employee's income from employment and generally will be deducted at source by employers.

INCOME TAXES ON NONRESIDENTS

15. Liability to Tax

Foreign entities are subject to New Zealand tax on all New Zealand-source income, except that an entity that is a resident of a country with which New Zealand has a tax treaty (see item 19) may be taxed on business profits only if it has a permanent establishment in New Zealand. Except for Australia, Fiji, India, Malaysia, the Philippines, and Singapore, a foreign entity having a permanent establishment in New Zealand will be taxed only on the profits attributable to the permanent establishment.

16. Rates

Nonresident corporations are taxed on their New Zealand-source income at the special nonresident corporation rate of 38%, except for those categories where a special basis applies or the withholding tax is the final tax (see items 4 and 17). The New Zealand-source income of a nonresident individual, other than an "insurance underwriter" or a "mining operator," is taxed at the same rates that apply to residents. Nonresident individuals, however, have restrictions on their eligibility for rebates (see item 9).

17. Withholding Tax Rates

New Zealand domestic law imposes nonresident withholding tax on designated income at the following rates:

Interest	15%
Royalties	15%
Dividends	30%

Such withholding tax is both a minimum and a final tax in the case of dividends, cultural royalties, and interest between parties at arm's length, where the payee does not have a permanent establishment in New Zealand. In the following cases, the withholding tax is the minimum tax only, and the income may be taxed at the rates noted in item 16 (unless the payee's liability is limited by a tax treaty):

☐ Interest between associated persons.
☐ Industrial royalties.
☐ Natural resources royalties.
☐ Know-how payments.

Effective August 1, 1991, withholding tax on payments of interest can be at the rate of 0% if the parties are not associated and the appropriate levy is paid (see item 25).

19. Tax Treaties

The following is a list of treaties in force:

Australia	Italy
Belgium	Japan
Canada	Malaysia
China	Netherlands
Denmark	Norway
Fiji	Philippines
Finland	Republic of Korea
France	Singapore
Germany	Sweden
India	Switzerland
Indonesia	United Kingdom
Ireland	United States

20. Other Matters

Nonresident Contractors Withholding Tax (NRCWT). NRCWT is deductible at the rate of 15% (or 30%) from contract payments made to nonresident contractors unless a certificate of exemption is obtained from the Inland Revenue Department. NRCWT is a payment on account of the nonresident's ultimate liability to New Zealand tax to be detemined from returns filed. Notwithstanding the fact that a tax treaty may apply to exempt the nonresident recipient from New Zealand tax, the payer is obliged to make deductions, thus obligating nonresident recipients to determine their liability or otherwise with the New Zealand Tax Authorities.

OTHER SIGNIFICANT TAXES

21. Sales (Value Added)

Goods and Services Tax (GST). GST, a broadly based consumption tax on goods and services supplied in New Zealand, is chargeable by registered persons on taxable supplies at the rate of 12.5%. Registered persons are able to deduct input tax in calculating tax payable. GST applies to all goods and services supplied in New Zealand other than exempt financial services and domestic rental accommodation. Exports of goods and certain services are zero-rated.

Sales tax was abolished effective October 1, 1986. However, in addition to GST, selective taxes continue to be levied on alcoholic beverages, tobacco products, and motor vehicles.

22. Inheritance and Gift Taxes

Gift duty at rates up to 25% is imposed on gifts during the donor's lifetime in excess of an annual exemption of NZ$27,000. Estate duty at the rate of 40% is imposed on the net value of all real and personal property in excess of a special exemption of NZ$450,000.

23. Taxes on Payrolls (Social Security)

Accident Compensation Levy. An accident compensation levy is imposed on all employers (whether or not resident in New Zealand) for all employee earnings liable to income tax in New Zealand. This is in addition to the levy on earners (see item 14). The rates vary according to the employer's industrial activity.

Fringe Benefit Tax (FBT). FBT is imposed on employers at a flat rate of 49% on the taxable value of fringe benefits provided to employees or their associates. FBT applies to non-cash fringe benefits such as employer-provided cars, low-interest loans, subsidized transport, certain retiring allowances and redundancy payments, discounted or free goods or services, and other benefits, subject to a limited range of exemptions. In addition, New Zealand resident corporations that provide non-cash dividends to their shareholders (except for a limited number of exempt shareholder types) are deemed to be employers of such shareholders for FBT purposes, and FBT is accordingly payable on the taxable value of the non-cash dividend. FBT is a deductible expense for income tax purposes only if an employee-employer relationship exists or is deemed to exist.

Specified Superannuation Contribution Withholding Tax (SSCWT). Employers who make contributions to superannuation funds for the benefit of employees are required to deduct and remit 33% by way of a withholding tax to the Revenue authorities. Employer superannuation contributions are fully deductible.

24. Taxes on Natural Resources
None.

25. Other Taxes

Land and Property. A land tax is imposed on the value of certain classes of land held on March 31. The rate for 1991 is 0.5%, and the tax is abolished thereafter.

Stamp Duty. Stamp duty is payable only on registration of documents relating to conveyances and leases of land excluding conveyances, and leases of dwellings and associated land. (The rates are up to 2%.)

Approved Issuer Levy. Where a New Zealand borrower pays a 2% levy, payments of interest to a nonresident can be made without deduction of withholding tax. However, parties must be at arm's length and interest must be in relation to money advanced on or after August 1, 1991.

COMPUTATION OF TAXABLE INCOME

26. Capital Gains

Except for the special case of assets purchased for the purpose of resale at a profit, defined categories of land transactions, and certain gains in respect of financial arrangements, capital gains are generally not taxable. In most cases, the gain is calculated as the excess of selling price over cost. There are limited exceptions in the case of land transactions relating to profits arising from rezoning, subdivision, or development of land. In these cases, allowances may be made for inflation or market value at the commencement of development or division schemes is the base from which taxable gains are calculated.

27. Depreciation and Depletion

Depreciation rates are fixed by the Commissioner of Inland Revenue pursuant to authority granted under the Income Tax Act. In general, the allowance relates to the asset's useful life. Straight-line methods apply to buildings, but plant and machinery (including motor vehicles) are depreciated on the reducing-balance method.

Mining. Special rules apply to the determination of income from the mining of specified minerals. These include accelerated deductions for exploration and development expenditures whether of a capital or revenue nature. A review announced in the 1986 budget, with the object of terminating tax concessions for the mining of specified minerals, has yet to be completed.

Most development costs of petroleum mining ventures must be capitalized, with deductions being allowed in full in the year in which an exploratory well is sealed and abandoned or over a ten-year period if the well enters commercial production.

Patents. The cost of purchasing patent rights or research and development leading to the grant of a patent may be written off over the life of the patent.

Research and Development. Scientific or industrial research expenditures are deductible in full in the year incurred. The cost of plant or buildings associated with such research must be capitalized and depreciated at the rate applicable to such assets purchased for other purposes.

Leases. For specified leases of personal property, deductions are allowed to the lessee for depreciation of the leased asset and the interest component of the lease payments (calculated on a reducing-balance basis). Where the leased asset is sold after the termination of the lease, the lessor is assessed tax on any excess not remitted to the lessee of the sales price of the leased asset over any guaranteed residual value.

Annual deductions proportional to the lease term are permitted for aggregate lease payments made under nonspecified leases of personal property.

28. Treatment of Dividends

Effective April 1, 1988, an imputation system applies to most dividends paid by resident corporations (i.e., dividends can carry a credit for New Zealand tax paid at 33% at the corporate level). Prior to payment of a benchmark dividend, corporations must determine the extent of the ratio between the imputation credits attached. The imputation ratio of subsequent dividends paid in the year must be made to the same extent unless a statutory declaration is lodged. If the tax credit carried by a dividend paid to resident shareholders (other than certain exempt categories of shareholders) is less than 33%, resident corporations are obliged to deduct withholding tax until the total imputation credits and withholding tax come to 33% and notify the shareholder of the amount of the dividend and the categories of credit attached. The gross amount of the dividend is assessable, while the credits may be applied against income tax payable.

All dividends received by resident individuals comprise assessable income. Dividends received by resident corporations from other resident corporations are to be assessable from April 1, 1992. Transitional rules apply from July 30, 1991 to March 31, 1994 for certain types of dividends. Previously all such dividends were exempt. To the extent dividends carry imputation credits, they are taken into account in determining the ability of the corporation to impute dividends paid to its own shareholders.

Dividends received by resident corporations from nonresident corporations are exempt subject to certain exceptions. However, the recipient corporation is liable to a 33% withholding payment on such dividends reduced by a credit for any foreign withholding dividend tax. In circumstances where the dividend is received from a CFC (see item 8), branch equivalent tax account credits may remove liability to the withholding payment. Tax loss corporations may avoid the payment by electing to reduce losses.

Nonresidents deriving dividends are subject to nonresident withholding tax (NRWT) at the rate of 30%, reduced to 15% by an applicable treaty. Imputation credits are not available to nonresidents and do not form a part of the taxable dividend. However, credits in respect of the 33% foreign dividend withholding payment can be imputed to dividends payable to nonresidents and will reduce or eliminate the NRWT liability.

29. Loss Carryovers

Losses may be carried forward indefinitely but, in the case of corporations, there must be a minimum level of continuity in the economic ownership of the corporation. Various amendments, effective from July 30, 1991, make the criteria for loss carryforward much more stringent and increase the continuity percentage from 40% to 66%. Transitional rules apply.

There is provision for set-offs or contributions towards losses by corporations within groups where the common holding is at least 66%.

30. Transactions between Related Parties

New Zealand law generally provides for the review of such transactions on an arm's-length basis, and this is reinforced in all tax treaties.

31. Consolidation of Income

Effective April 1, 1992, there will be provision for the filing of consolidated tax returns by corporations that have 100% common ownership. Intercompany dividends, interest payments, and asset transfers may be disregarded as a consequence. The group is assessed as if it were a single entity. Where the common shareholding of separate taxable entities (consolidated or corporate) is 100% (66% from April 1, 1992), losses may be transferred by a simple election, subject to certain restrictions. In other cases, it is necessary for a payment to be made with respect to the losses (see item 29).

32. Tax Periods

Generally, March 31 is the prescribed fiscal year-end. Application must be made for an alternative year-end and will generally be approved if there is a distinct seasonal element in trading, or there are other valid commercial reasons, and the date approved is unlikely to cause undue delay in the filing of the return or adverse effects on government revenue.

33. Other Matters

Accrual Expenditure. Subject to limited exceptions, expenditure in respect of goods (other than trading stock) and services must be deducted on an accrual basis over the period to which it relates.

Financial Arrangements. Income and expenditure in respect of financial arrangements (widely defined to include debt and similar instruments, forward exchange contracts, futures contracts, defeasance transactions, and deferred property settlements) must generally be calculated, and then expensed or treated as income over the life of the instrument on a yield-to-maturity basis, or an accounting approximation thereof unless a market value method is applicable.

Deductions for Taxes Other than Income Taxes. In computing income tax liability, deductions may be claimed for land taxes (including local government taxes), accident compensation levies, and fringe benefits tax. Goods and Services Tax paid generally will be recoverable by registered persons but, in circumstances where it is not, deductibility for income tax purposes will generally depend on the tax treatment of the underlying transaction. Customs duty and stamp duty are treated as part of the cost of the goods acquired. Approved issuer levies are deductible if the related interest payment is deductible. No deduction is available for estate or gift duties.

Inventory Valuation. Inventories may be valued at cost, market selling value, or replacement price at the taxpayer's option. Different valuation methods may be applied to items of the same general class. An alternative valuation to the above three may be adopted on the grounds of obsolescence, but only where prior notice of the proposed basis is filed with Revenue. LIFO is not permitted as a basis of valuation unless it approximates physical flows.

Bad Debts. Bad debts may be claimed as a deduction only when actually written off. General provisions for anticipated losses are not permitted. Any recovery of a debt previously written off is included in taxable income when received.

Employee Benefit Provisions. Deductions are allowed for contributions to approved pension, sickness, and other benefit plans under certain conditions. Deductions for pensions to former employees are also permitted, subject to approval of the amount (particularly with respect to directors and their relatives).

Payments to Nonresidents. The Revenue has a broad power to deny deductions in respect of payments to nonresidents in circumstances where information requisitions are not responded to within 90 days. Objection rights cease in respect of relevant expenditure.

RELATED CONSIDERATIONS

34. Incentives and Grants

None.

35. Exchange Controls

None.

36. Investment Restrictions on Nonresidents

New Zealand's policy on nonresident investment is administered by the Overseas Investment Commission, which receives direction from time to time from the Government as to the criteria to use for the approval of nonresident investment proposals. In general, the establishment or acquisition of a local enterprise involving less than 25% overseas ownership will be approved. Moreover, effective August 25, 1989, and with the exception of certain specified business activities, any investment not exceeding NZ$10 million in value will be exempted from the requirement to obtain OIC approval. However, for overseas participation above both the 25% level and the NZ$10 million level, it will be necessary for the applicant to demonstrate benefits to New Zealand in the form of "contributions to national development based on efficient specialization, exports, and advanced technology." Policy statements by Government Ministers have made it clear that, within this restrictive environment, overseas investment is to be encouraged where it will meet the criteria established for such investments, and the Overseas Investment Commission has been instructed accordingly. Although some local participation will be encouraged, approval for a substantial proportion of foreign equity will be given if the criteria are met.

SELECTION OF BUSINESS ENTITY BY NONRESIDENTS

Although a number of overseas investors conduct operations in New Zealand through branches, most substantial operations established in recent years are carried on through New Zealand registered subsidiaries. This preference is normally based on tax considerations and the disclosure of information requirements of the Registrar of Companies. A branch pays tax at the nonresident rate of 38%, and no further tax is imposed on remittance of the branch profits. Deductions are permitted for expenses incurred overseas with respect to the branch's operations.

A New Zealand registered subsidiary pays tax at the domestic corporation rate of 33%, but must withhold 30% from dividends remitted to overseas shareholders (unless the rate of dividend withholding tax is reduced by the provisions of an applicable tax treaty).

The following example compares the tax payable by a branch with that payable by a local subsidiary remitting all after-tax profit as a dividend:

	Nontreaty Corporation	Treaty Corporation	Branch
Profit before tax	NZ$100.00	NZ$100.00	NZ$100.00
Income tax	33.00	33.00	38.00
Profit after tax	NZ$ 67.00	NZ$ 67.00	NZ$ 62.00
Withholding	20.10 (30%)	10.05 (15%)	
Total tax payable	NZ$53.10	NZ$43.05	NZ$38.00

A New Zealand registered corporation with at least 25% foreign ownership is required to file audited accounts with the Registrar of Companies. A branch of an overseas corporation is required to file separate accounts for the business carried on in or from New Zealand and also to file accounts for the overseas corporation. Accounts filed with the Registrar of Companies are available for public inspection upon the payment of a nominal fee.

NIGERIA

INCOME TAXES ON CORPORATIONS

1. Rates

Companies income tax rate is 40%, which is chargeable on all profits of a company. See item 24 for the special tax rate on petroleum companies. A special levy of 15% has been imposed on excess profits earned by banks, in addition to the normal income tax. Excess profits are calculated on a formula contained in the law.

Payments to contractors and consultants, as well as commissions, are subject to a 2.5% (to 10%) withholding tax, which is deductible at source. Transactions exempted from withholding tax are contracts for the purchase and sale of property.

Interest on bank deposits is subject to a withholding tax of 15% at the time the interest is paid or credited. The deduction of tax at source is applicable to interest paid or credited by banks to the accounts of their depositors. In the case of pass-book savings accounts, tax deductions at source from interest are to be made only if the amount of deposit is greater than ₦50,000. Banks are required to promptly account for the tax deducted to the appropriate tax authorities.

A withholding tax of 15% applies to directors' fees, fees payable or paid for the use or hire of any equipment, chartered vessels, ships, or aircraft, including payments for the use or hire of movable or immovable property.

2. Local Income Taxes

None.

3. Capital Gains Taxes

A capital gains tax of 20% is payable on the total chargeable gains accruing to corporate bodies during any year of assessment.

4. Branch Profits Taxes

A branch of a foreign corporation is taxed on the profits of the branch in the same manner and at the same rates as Nigerian corporations.

5. Foreign Tax Reliefs

All prior tax treaties ceased to have effect after April 1, 1979. A new double taxation treaty between the Federal Republic of Nigeria and the United Kingdom and Northern Ireland took effect July 5, 1988. It is believed that new treaties are currently being negotiated with some countries.

7. Payment of Taxes

Every company is expected to pay its taxes within three months of the commencement of each tax year. If the accounts and tax computations are not yet prepared, the company is expected to pay provisionally the same tax that it paid for the preceding income tax year.

The Federal Board of Inland Revenue may permit a company to pay its taxes in up to six equal monthly installments.

Where the Board issues an assessment that is not in dispute, the company has the option of paying either the full amount or one-half the amount within two months of the service of assessment notice. The remaining half is payable on or before December 14 of the year of assessment.

8. Other Matters

Levy on Dormant Companies. Companies which fail to commence business operations within six months of incorporation in any year of assessment (but before submitting accounts for the first twelve or eighteen months of operation) must pay ₦500 for first year (or portion thereof) and ₦400 for every subsequent year during which the company remains dormant.

Deduction of Tax at Source. The Federal Board of Inland Revenue is empowered to recover income tax payable by any company from any person (or class of persons) indebted to the company, whether or not an assessment has been issued to the company. The order must be in writing and addressed to the person (or published in the gazette), and shall specify the nature of payments and the rate at which tax is to be deducted. The tax deducted at source can be offset against the tax liability of the company up to the amount of the assessment. In addition to paying the tax, a penalty of ₦5,000 plus interest (at the prevailing commercial rate) is now imposed on any person convicted of failing to deduct tax or to forward the tax deducted to the Board (or other relevant tax authority) within thirty days from the date the amount was deducted (or when the duty to deduct arose).

Collection of Taxes at Source. Effective January 1, 1990, interest will be charged at the going bank rate on amounts due to the Revenue from withholding tax deductions not paid over to the Revenue within the stipulated time, which is 30 days from the date it was withheld. Similarly, tax withholdings from payments made by companies to any person on all types of contracts, building and construction activities, commissions, and professional and technical services, that became effective after 1984 are now extended to all payment within and outside Nigeria by oil companies to any person, both resident and nonresident.

Penalty for Late Returns.   Any company that files its annual tax return late, or fails to submit its accounts on due dates, is subject to a penalty of ₦5,000, which is imposed by the Federal Board of Inland Revenue and cannot be challenged in any court of law. No decree has been promulgated by the federal military government to give this proposal the force of law.

Minimum Tax Payable by Corporations.   Effective January 1, 1990, corporations that commenced operations but have no taxable profits, or whose tax payable for a given assessment year is less than the minimum tax, will be assessed and taxed as follows:

☐ If the turnover is not more than ₦500,000 and the corporation has been in business for more than four years, the tax payable is the highest of
—0.5% of gross profits,
—0.5% of net assets,
—0.25% of paid-up capital,
—0.25% of turnover.

☐ If the turnover is higher than ₦500,000, the minimum tax will be the tax payable on a turnover of ₦500,000 as determined above plus the excess turnover (that over ₦500,000) will be taxed at 50% of the rate used for the first ₦500,000.

☐ The minimum tax will apply to partnerships and self-employed persons at the rate of 0.5% of the total income.

Payment of the minimum tax does not apply to the following companies:

☐ Companies that have been in business for less than four years.
☐ Enterprises engaged in agricultural trade or business.
☐ Companies with at lest 25% imported equity capital.

INCOME TAXES ON INDIVIDUALS

9.   Rates

All individuals are liable to personal income tax on the basis of a uniform system of reliefs, allowances, and rates of tax. Each state, however, administers the collection of personal tax from persons deemed resident in it for tax purposes. The most important factor in deciding to which state an individual is liable to pay personal income tax for any particular year of assessment is the location of his principal residence on January 1st of that assessment year.

In general, personal allowances are granted to both men and women if they are resident in Nigeria, in addition to child allowances and further reliefs in respect of dependent relatives, life insurance premiums, and contributions to approved pensions, provident and other retirement schemes.

Income tax is levied at graduated rates upon taxable income, which includes all assessable income of individuals resident in a state. The rates of income tax on the taxable income of an individual, computed after deducting the individual's personal and other allowances, are:

Taxable Income		Tax on Lower Amount	Percentage on Excess
Over	Not Over		
₦ 0	₦ 2,000	₦ 0	10%
2,000	4,000	200	15
4,000	6,000	500	20
6,000	8,000	900	25
8,000	10,000	1,400	30
10,000	15,000	2,000	35
15,000	20,000	3,750	40
20,000	30,000	5,750	45
30,000	40,000	10,250	50
40,000		15,250	55

The personal allowance for all individual taxpayers is ₦2,000 plus 15% of earned income. The wife's allowance has been increased from ₦300 to ₦500, while the child's allowance has also been increased from ₦250 to ₦400, up to a maximum of four children under 16 years of age (or children over 16 years of age who are full-time students or are undergoing a period of apprenticeship). The dependent relative allowance has been increased from ₦400 to ₦600.

Salaries and wages income are subject to tax deductions at source under the P.A.Y.E. system. A minimum amount of tax is payable by each chargeable individual. This has been fixed at 0.5% of total income before the deduction of personal allowances and other reliefs. Individuals earning no more than ₦3,000 per year are no longer required to file an income tax return for any assessment year.

Tax Exemption on Deposit Accounts of Nonresidents. Interest accruing on deposit accounts of nonresidents, corporate or noncorporate, will be tax-exempt provided that the deposits are made by transfer of funds to Nigeria after December 31, 1989 and the depositor does not become nonresident after making the deposit while in Nigeria. Similarly, interest on foreign currency domiciliary accounts are tax-exempt.

Income From Abroad. Effective January 1, 1990, all of an individual's income from abroad, without exception, will be tax-exempt if the amount is brought into Nigeria through authorized channels. This provision replaces the previous restriction that only investment income from abroad was tax-exempt and that other income was taxable when brought into Nigeria.

Employment Income and Residency Test. Effective January 1, 1990, the 183-day residency test for taxation of gains and employment income will be changed to a 12-month period, commencing in a calendar year and ending either within the calendar year or the following year. The test will no longer be limited to 183 days in an assessment year.

Persons liable to personal income tax in Nigeria are entitled to a personal allowance of ₦2,000 plus 15% of the earned income. Tax relief is granted on interest paid on mortgage loans used to finance owner-occupied houses in order to encourage home ownership. The tax relief is the interest paid in the immediately preceding financial year, and only one mortgage loan per individual is eligible at a time.

A disabled person who is a salaried employee and who uses special equipment and the services of an attendant is entitled to an additional personal allowance of ₦2,000 or 10% of his earned income, whichever is lower.

10. Local Income Taxes

None.

11. Capital Gains Taxes

Tax at 20% is payable on capital gains realized in any year of assessment by individuals and other noncorporate bodies.

12. Foreign Tax Reliefs

The information in item 5 also applies here.

13. Tax Period

The Government's fiscal year runs from January 1 to December 31.

14. Other Matters

Tax Clearance Certificates. Ministries, departments, government agencies, and commercial banks must receive from participants in specified transactions a tax clearance certificate with respect to the three years of assessment immediately preceding the current year of assessment.

An applicant for exchange control permission to remit funds to a nonresident recipient with respect to income accruing from rents, royalties, interest, or dividends is required to produce a tax clearance certificate confirming either that tax has been paid on the income to be repatriated or that no tax is payable thereon.

The Board may refuse to issue a tax clearance certificate to an applicant who fails to account to the Federal Board of Inland Revenue for tax deducted at source as provided in the Companies Income Tax Act (even if that person has fully discharged his own liability).

Transactions for which a tax clearance certificate is required include:

□ Applications for government loans.

□ Applications for foreign exchange or exchange control permission to remit funds outside Nigeria.

□ Applications for the award of contracts by the government, agencies, and registered companies.

□ Applications to approve building plans.

□ Applications for a trade license.

□ Applications for the transfer of real property.

□ Applications for import or export licenses.

□ Applications for registration as a contractor.

□ Applications for distributorships.

□ Applications to register a limited liability company or business name.

To facilitate the procurement of a tax clearance certificate, the Federal Board of Inland Revenue and the Joint Tax Board will appoint area ombudsmen to expedite complaints, while final recourse will be with the Chairman of the Board.

In addition to the existing penalties, any person or company obtaining a tax clearance certificate through misrepresentation, forgery, or falsification will be liable to a fine equal to twice the amount of evaded tax or imprisonment for three years, or both.

Investigative Powers of Tax Authorities. To discourage tax evasion, the Government strengthened the investigative powers of Revenue authorities to ensure effective tax investigations of individuals and corporations.

Effective January 1, 1990, the tax authorities are empowered to enter and search premises if they believe there is reasonable ground for suspecting that an offense involving any form of total or partial nondisclosure of information or any irregularity or offense in connection with or in relation to tax has been committed, and if they are of the opinion that evidence of the offense or irregularity is to be found on the premises of any other vocation, profession, or business, or in the residence of the principal officer, factor agent, or representative of the individual. On production of the warrant to enter and search the premises, the person whose premises is being searched is expected to cooperate fully with the investigators.

A penalty of ₦5,000 or three months imprisonment has been prescribed on conviction. In the case of a corporation, the fine is ₦10,000, imprisonment of not less than six months, or both.

Tax Identification Number. Effective January 1, 1990, every company will be required to display its incorporation number, which will serve as the identification number on all transactions and correspondence. For returns and correspondence with the Revenue authorities, companies must display both their tax reference numbers and their identification number.

INCOME TAXES ON NONRESIDENTS

15. Liability to Tax

The profits of a nonresident corporation are taxable to the extent they derive from operations in Nigeria.

16. Rates

The profits of a nonresident corporation are taxed as though derived by a resident corporation. Income derived by a nonresident corporation, such as management fees, interest, royalties, and service charges are taxed at source at 15%. Management and service charges will not be charged if they are proven to be strictly reimbursements of actual expenditure or the true costs of services rendered.

Tax is payable on income accruing in, derived from, brought into, or received in Nigeria from employment. Employment compensation is tax-exempt if the employer is in a country other than Nigeria, if the employee is not in Nigeria for a period or periods amounting to 183 days or more in any 12-month period commencing in a calendar year and ending either within that same year or the following year, and if the compensation is taxable in that other country. The remuneration is also exempt if the employer is in Nigeria provided the duties are wholly performed, and the remuneration paid, outside Nigeria.

Interest on foreign loans is exempt from tax on the following basis:

Repayment Period (including moratorium)	Grace Period	Tax Exemption Allowed
Above 7 years	Not less than 2 years	100%
5–7 years	Not less than 18 months	70
2–4 years	Not less than 12 months	40
Below 2 years	nil	nil

Tax concessions on interest on foreign loans for agricultural purposes are to be extended to manufacturing exporters.

OTHER SIGNIFICANT TAXES

21. Sales (Value Added)

Effective July 1, 1986, the Federal government introduced a sales tax of 5% on certain goods and services, such as hotels, catering services, tobacco and cigarettes, soft drinks, jewelry, perfume, and cosmetics and 10% on wine, liquor, and spirits. State governments will enforce payment of the tax.

22. Inheritance and Gift Taxes

None.

23. Taxes on Payrolls (Social Security)

National provident fund contributions are payable monthly for employed persons; part is payable by individual employees and part by employers. The maximum contribution by each party in respect of an employee is ₦4 per month.

24. Taxes on Natural Resources

The Federal government imposes a royalty upon petroleum production, which is generally deductible as an expense.

Only companies incorporated in Nigeria can participate in petroleum operations. The taxation of companies engaged in the prospecting for, or the extraction and transportation of, petroleum oil or natural gas is governed by the Petroleum Profits Tax Act, 1959 as amended by the Petroleum Profits Act (Amendment) Decrees 1967, 1970 and 1973. A petroleum company first becomes liable to petroleum profits tax when it makes its first bulk sale of crude oil. It is required to make up its first accounts from the date of commencement to December 31st and, thereafter, for a period of one year commencing on January 1st and ending on December 31st each year. It is assessed in respect of such accounting period.

Capital Allowances. Capital allowances are granted for qualifying capital expenditure. Capital allowances are, however, restricted, so that in any accounting period, the tax chargeable on a company should not be less than 15% of the tax that should have been chargeable had no capital allowances been granted to the company. Capital allowances unutilized because of this restriction are available for carryforward and to be relieved against future profits.

Annual capital allowances have been increased so as to permit oil companies to amortize their fixed assets in five equal annual installments. Such companies will be required to retain in their books 1% of the initial cost of the assets concerned, and this residue can only be written off on the authority of a certificate of asset disposal issued by the Federal Commissioner for Petroleum. A capital investment tax credit has been introduced for new investment in assets to be used in petroleum operations. The rates vary from 5% to 20%, depending on whether the company operates on-shore, off-shore, or both.

Losses. Losses can be carried forward in the normal way, but a company can elect to carry forward a loss to the next accounting period, even though profits are available in the current accounting period for relieving such losses.

Tax Rate. The assessable tax of a petroleum company is an amount equal to 85% of its chargeable profits of the period in respect of export sales, and at 65.75% of the chargeable profits from domestic sales. Deductions are made from the tax charge so arrived at in respect of royalties, duties, and taxes. If these deductions exceed the tax chargeable for the period, no tax is payable and the excess is carried forward to be deducted from the chargeable tax of the subsequent period.

Payment of Tax. Payments of tax in any accounting period of 12 months are in 12 installments, together with a final installment which is payable within 21 days of the date of service of the notice of an assessment. The final installment is for the amount of the assessment less the sum already paid. The first monthly installment is due on the last day of the third month of the accounting date.

25. Other Taxes

Land and Property Taxes. Land and property taxes are imposed by each state.

Capital Transfer Taxes. Capital assets transferred by one individual to another, whether inter vivos or at death, are subject to capital transfer tax. The first ₦ 100,000 of such transfers will be free of tax, the next ₦ 150,000 will attract tax at 10%, and so on up to a top rate of 60% on all transfers of ₦ 2,000,000 and above.

COMPUTATION OF TAXABLE INCOME

26. Capital Gains

The capital gain is the difference between the cost of a capital asset and its sale proceeds. Disposals that are not at arm's length are treated as disposals at market value (see item 29).

27. Depreciation and Depletion

Depreciation on fixed assets is not allowed as a deduction from profits, but initial allowances, based on costs, and annual allowances, calculated on the straight-line method, are granted in respect of all qualifying capital expenditures incurred, provided the asset in respect of which the expenditure was incurred was in use on the last day of the basis period of the relevant year of assessment. The rates of capital allowances on qualifying capital expenditures are:

	Initial	Annual
Corporations		
Industrial buildings	15%	10%
Nonindustrial buildings	5	10
Mining, housing estate	20	10
Plantations and ranching	25	15
Plant and machinery	20	10
Furniture and fixtures	15	10
Motor vehicles	25	20
Individuals		
Industrial buildings	15	10

	Initial	Annual
Individuals		
Other buildings	5%	10%
Mining, housing estate, plant and machinery	20	10
Furniture and fixtures	10	15
Plantations and ranching	25	15
Research and development	25	12.5
Motor vehicles	25	20
Plantation equipment	20	33.33

There is no restriction on the maximum capital allowances available to manufacturing companies and agro-allied industries.

For other companies, however, the maximum capital allowances remains 66.66% of the assessable income for each tax year. This restriction does not apply to businesses in the agro-allied industry.

All capital expenditure on plant and equipment incurred on agricultural production by companies and individuals enjoys a 10% investment allowance in addition to the normal capital allowances. Companies engaged in manufacturing, construction, and agricultural production including qualified ranching and plantation expenditure, and public transportation with a fleet of not fewer than three buses enjoy an additional initial capital allowance of 5% in respect of new qualifying expenditure on plant and machinery acquired for business use as of January 1, 1988.

A special reconstruction investment allowance of 25% is granted in respect of any qualifying expenditure incurred after April 1, 1969 on a new asset to replace a qualifying asset damaged or destroyed in any part of Nigeria at any time during the period July 16, 1967 to January 15, 1970 as a direct consequence of any military or other operations connected with the Nigerian civil war. For companies manufacturing export products, when claiming annual allowances taxpayers must retain ₦10 as the asset's value (for tax purposes) until the asset is sold or exchanged. Annual allowances are now computed on a straight-line basis (and not the reducing-balance method) after deducting the initial allowance, and special rules limit the amount of the annual allowance if the asset was placed in service before January 1, 1985.

Effective January 1, 1990, the 10% investment allowance on qualifying capital expenditures or new production machinery is deductible only from profits in the year of expenditure.

28. Treatment of Dividends

All dividends are generally subject to a 15% withholding tax which is deductible at source by the payor. If the recipient of the dividend is a nonresident shareholder, the 15% withholding tax constitutes a final tax. Both the corporation tax (at 40%) and dividend withholding tax must be paid before the dividends are distributed. If the dividend is paid out of profits which have not yet been taxed, whether or not the recipient is a Nigerian company, the payor is subject to the 40% tax as if the dividend represents the total profits of the company for the year of assessment which relates to accounts out of which the dividend is declared. The payor is not entitled to repayment of tax paid.

Franked Investment Income. The concept of "franked investment income," whereby a company receiving a dividend from a Nigerian company is not subject to further tax on the amount as part of its profits, was effective beginning January 1, 1985. Where such income is redistributed (and tax is to be accounted for on the gross amount of the distribution), the company may offset the withholding tax paid on the dividend received against the withholding tax on dividends distributed to its shareholders. Thus, a holding company both avoids being taxed twice on the dividend received from a subsidiary during an accounting period and obtains relief for the withholding tax on the dividend received from the subsidiary to the extent that the dividend income received from the subsidiary is utilized by the holding company in paying its own dividends.

Payment of Income Tax Prior to Payment of Dividend. Effective January 1, 1985, a company must pay tax at the regular rate before distributing dividends to its shareholders. The tax paid is regarded as a deposit against the tax due from the company on the profits out of which the dividend is paid, and the company is also entitled to deduct from such tax payable any "provisional tax" already paid by it. "Provisional tax" means the tax which every company is required to pay not later than three months after the commencement of each tax year on account of its tax liability for that year. The amount of such tax is the company's tax liability for the immediately preceding year of assessment, and is payable in a lump sum or no more than six monthly installments. Penalty for late payment of tax is to be calculated at the rate of 10% per annum on the tax outstanding.

29. Loss Carryovers

Losses from any trade or business can only be relieved against future profits arising from the same trade or business. Such losses must be relieved against future profits within four years of the end of the fiscal year in which they were incurred. Losses incurred by a company engaged in agriculture can be carried forward indefinitely and not just for four years as is the case with other companies.

A capital loss arising from one disposition cannot be set off against a capital gain arising from another disposition irrespective of whether or not the two dispositions took place in the same year of assessment. Such a capital loss can only be relieved against future capital gains of the same source.

30. Transactions between Related Parties

The various revenue authorities are empowered to disregard, for tax purposes, any disposition or transaction which is, in their opinion, artificial or fictitious. They can raise additional assessments to counteract any revenues lost by such a disposition or transaction.

31. Consolidation of Income

Companies operating in Nigeria are liable to income tax on their total assessable profits from all sources in Nigeria in a year of assessment. Group taxation of related companies is not permitted.

32. Tax Periods

The fiscal year is to be from January 1 to the following December 31. However, if a company makes up its accounts to a different date, the basis period for computing the liability to income tax is the company's own accounting period. Transitional arrangements have been announced following the change in the Government's fiscal year-end from March 31 to December 31 for the 1980 year of assessment only.

RELATED CONSIDERATIONS

34. Incentives and Grants

Exempt Income. The profits of a pioneer company may be exempt from income tax during an initial period varying from three to five years. A company may be granted pioneer status (upon application to the Federal Executive Council) where an industry is not being carried out in Nigeria on a scale suitable to the economic requirements of Nigeria, or where there are favorable prospects for further development of the industry. Dividends paid by a pioneer company are exempt from Nigerian tax in the hands of shareholders and are deemed to be paid out of income on which tax is not paid or payable. The payor, however, must deduct the 15% withholding tax from the dividend and account for the tax to the relevant tax authorities. In addition, irrespective of to whom such dividend is paid, the payor is liable to tax at the normal company rate of 40% on the gross amount of the dividend paid. The tax paid is not refundable to either the payor or the recipient.

Exemption from Income Tax. Tax exemption is granted in certain cases, including:

☐ Emoluments of certain government, diplomatic and military officials and the income of certain international and other organizations.

☐ Capital sums drawn by individuals, after five years' membership, on retirement from any pension or provident fund which has been approved by the Joint Tax Board.

☐ Investment income of any pension or provident fund which has been approved by the Joint Tax Board.

☐ Any sums received by way of death gratuities or as consolidated compensation for death or injuries.

☐ Any compensation for loss of employment (applicable to Lagos State only).

☐ Gratuities of not more than ₦100,000 paid by employers in the private sector to an employee in respect of services rendered by him under a contract of service with his employer and described as gratuities either in such contract, or some other document issued by, or on behalf of such employer in connection with such contract. To qualify for tax exemption, the period of service with the employer must not be less than ten years. Any excess over and above ₦100,000 shall be deemed to be income of the employee on the last day of his employment including any terminal leave arising therefrom.

☐ Dividends paid to any person by a Nigerian company where the equity participation of the investor in the company paying the dividends is either wholly paid for in foreign currency, or by assets brought into Nigeria between January 1, 1987 and December 31, 1992 and the investor owns not less than 10% of the equity share capital of the company. The tax-free dividend period is to commence from the year of assessment following that in which the new capital is brought into Nigeria for the purpose of the trade or business in Nigeria of the company paying the dividends for five years if the business of the company paying the dividends is that agricultural production within Nigeria or processing of Nigeria agricultural products produced within Nigeria or production of petro-chemicals or liquefied natural gas. In any other case, the tax-free period is to be restricted to three years.

☐ A new allowance for equity shareholdings in a company floated exclusively for the purposes of research and development up to 25% of the total income of the individual for the relevant year of assessment has been introduced by the Federal government.

☐ Small- and medium-size companies with turnover of ₦500,000 or less in the year of assessment that are engaged in either manufacturing, agricultural production, or mining of solid minerals are taxed at a lower rate of 20% for three years from the commencement of business. Existing companies in the same category enjoy the same concession effective January 1, 1988.

☐ Provision for research and development, subject to a limit of 10% of a company's total profit for the year under consideration, is now available as an allowable deduction from profits.

35. Exchange Controls

Nigeria has comprehensive exchange control regulations which are embodied in the Exchange Control Act 1962 and Exchange Control Anti-Sabotage Decree 1984. Broadly, the effect of the regulations is to prohibit the following, if necessary approvals have not been obtained:

☐ The issue of any security which is registered or is to be registered in Nigeria to a person resident outside Nigeria.

☐ The making, by a resident, of any payment to or for the credit of a person resident outside Nigeria, or the taking or acceptance by a resident of any loan, bank overdraft, or other credit facilities from a nonresident.

36.   Investment Restrictions on Nonresidents

The Nigerian Enterprises Promotion Decree 1977 has been amended to allow a company whose shares are quoted on the Nigerian Stock Exchange to issue, through the Exchange, non-voting paid-up shares of the company for the subscription of persons, regardless of Nigerian citizenship or residence within Nigeria.

Such shares may not have voting rights and they may not be taken into account in determining the proportions of shares held by Nigerians and non-Nigerians under the Nigerian Enterprises Promotion Act 1977 or under any other enactment. Such shares also may not exceed 20% of the existing nominal share capital of the company.

In recognition of the vital role of the manufacturing sector in the Nigerian economy, the Nigerian Enterprises Promotion Act 1977 has been amended substantially so that the schedules of businesses have been reduced from three to only one. Although the enterprises listed in the schedule are exclusive to Nigerians, all other unscheduled businesses, except banking, insurance, and petroleum prospecting and mining in which the federal government has and will continue to have varying levels of equity, are open for 100% Nigerian or foreign participation separately or in partnership.

Nonresidents who wish to invest in the scheduled businesses are allowed to do so subject to a minimum capitalization of ₦20,000,000 and the approval of the Industrial Development Coordination Committee.

NORWAY

Editor's Note: Recently, a comprehensive tax reform was enacted, which for most changes will take effect fiscal-year 1992. The following summary is based on how the tax system will operate effective fiscal-year 1992 unless otherwise noted. For information on the tax regulations valid for 1991, please refer to the 1991 edition of *International Tax Summaries*.

INCOME TAXES ON CORPORATIONS

1. Rates

The national income tax rate for corporations in principle is no longer applicable effective fiscal-year 1992.

2. Local Income Taxes

The municipal income tax rate (including contribution to the tax equalization fund) is 28%.

3. Capital Gains Taxes

Effective fiscal-year 1992, capital gains are fully included in taxable income, and are subject to municipal income taxes at the above rate.

4. Branch Profits Taxes

A branch of a foreign corporation is taxed on the profit of the branch as though it were a resident corporation.

5. Foreign Tax Reliefs

The Norwegian taxation system provides for double tax relief for taxes paid by a resident of Norway in territories outside Norway with which Norway has double taxation treaties. Taxes paid in territories not covered by tax treaties are deductible from taxable income. However, tax credit may be granted on application.

6. Classification of Corporations

Norwegian law provides for different entities, such as partnerships (limited and general), economic societies (e.g., cooperatives), mutual insurance companies, and joint stock companies. Partnerships are not taxed as separate entities, and their members are individually liable for income taxes. The others are taxed as separate entities.

7. Payment of Tax

Corporation taxes are payable in four installments in the year following the income tax year. The first two installments are payable on February and April 15, in accordance with a preliminary tax bill issued in December of the income tax year. The preliminary tax bill is normally based on the previous year's final assessment. The remaining two installments are payable on September and November 15 in accordance with a final tax bill that is issued in August of the following year.

INCOME TAXES ON INDIVIDUALS

9. Rates

Effective fiscal-year 1992, taxation will be based on two income concepts, that of ordinary income and that of personal income (tax rates and tax-exempt amounts will not be fixed until autumn 1991 by the Parliament):

☐ Ordinary income covers all types of taxable income from employment and capital. Deductions are given to certain costs and expenses, including full deduction for interest. The ordinary income is subject to local income taxes at a flat rate of 28% exceeding NOK 21,700 in tax class 1 (single persons with no dependents) and NOK 43,400 in tax class 2 (married couples and single persons with dependents).

☐ Personal income is the net income arising from business activity in which the taxpayer is actively involved, gross income derived from employment, and pensions. Personal income is the base for the calculation of a national super tax called the top tax (and social security contribution). The two-rate top tax is:
  —Tax class 1 (single persons without dependents): 9.5% exceeding NOK 200,000 and 13% exceeding NOK 225,000;
  —Tax class 2 (married couples and single persons with dependents): 9.5% exceeding NOK 242,000 and 13% exceeding NOK 252,000.

10. Local Income Taxes

See item 9.

11. Capital Gains Taxes

Effective fiscal-year 1992, all capital gains are fully included in ordinary income. Special rules apply, however, to gains from the sale of privately owned housing if the property was used as the owner's residence during the past two years.

12. Foreign Tax Reliefs

See item 5.

13. Tax Period

The calendar year is the mandatory tax year.

INCOME TAXES ON NONRESIDENTS

15. Liability to Tax

Nonresident individuals are subject to tax on income from Norwegian sources, including income from real property and movables in Norway, business carried on in Norway, and salaries and wages paid from Norwegian sources for services performed in Norway. Furthermore, director's fees from Norwegian companies are subject to Norwegian taxes.

Individuals staying in Norway for more than six months generally are treated as resident in Norway for tax purposes and are taxed on their worldwide income. Individuals staying in Norway for less than six months usually are taxed only on Norwegian-source income.

Individuals temporarily staying in Norway, i.e., less than four years, are entitled to a standard deduction of 15% on gross earnings. The standard deduction replaces tax-deductible expenses incurred.

Foreign corporations are taxable on income from real property and movables in Norway, on income from all sources to the extent that it is effectively connected with the conduct of a trade or business in Norway, and on gains arising outside the ordinary course of business on the disposal of real property, movables, or a business or parts thereof.

Up to and including 1991, foreign individuals and corporations may be taxable under certain circumstances on gains arising from the sale of shares in Norwegian companies. Whether this will be the case when the tax reform is effective from fiscal-year 1992 is uncertain.

16. Rates

Income derived by a nonresident corporation carrying on business in Norway, or by a nonresident individual, is taxed as though the nonresident were a resident.

17. Withholding Tax Rates

The withholding tax applies only to dividends. Unless a tax treaty provides otherwise, the withholding tax is 25% of dividends distributed.

The following is a list of the countries with which Norway has concluded treaties for the avoidance of double taxation and the treaty rates that apply to an ordinary shareholder and to a parent company, respectively. The rates are valid from January 1, 1991.

	Dividends	
	Ordinary Shareholder	Parent Company (1)
Nontreaty countries	25%	25%
Treaty countries:		
Australia	15	15
Austria	15	15
Belgium	15	15
Benin	20	20
Brazil	15	15
Canada	15	15
China	15	15
Czechoslovakia	15	5
Denmark	15	15
Egypt	15	15
Finland	15	15
France	15	5
Germany	15	0
Hungary	10	10
Iceland	15	15
India	25	25
Indonesia	15	15
Ireland	10	0
Israel	15	5
Italy	15	15
Ivory Coast	15	15
Japan	15	10
Kenya	25	15
Korea (South)	15	15
Luxembourg	15	15
Malaysia	0	0
Malta	15	15
Morocco	15	15
The Netherlands	15	15
Netherlands Antilles	15	15
New Zealand	15	15
Pakistan	15	15
Poland	15	5
Portugal	15	10
Rumania	10	10
Singapore	15	15
Soviet Union	20	20
Spain	15	10
Sri Lanka	5	5
Sweden	15	15

Dividends

	Ordinary Shareholder	Parent Company (1)
Switzerland	15%	15%
Tanzania	20	20
Thailand	25	20
Trinidad and Tobago	20	10
Tunisia	20	20
Turkey	25	20
United Kingdom	15	15
United States	15	15
Various present and previous British colonies	5	0
Yugoslavia	15	15
Zambia	15	15

Notes:

(1) The treaties define a parent company according to its shareholding in the Norwegian subsidiary, generally as follows:

Czechoslovakia, Germany, Ireland, the Netherlands, Poland, Portugal, Thailand, and Trinidad and Tobago	At least 25%
France	At least 10%
Israel and various present and previous British colonies	At least 50%
Japan	At least 50% (minimum 12-month holding period)
Kenya	At least 25% (minimum 6-month holding period)

Under certain treaties, Norway is entitled to apply a 15% withholding rate under the current Norwegian system where dividends are deductible for state tax purposes.

Some treaties in force provide for a 15% withholding tax on dividends to substantial shareholders as long as Norway maintains a split-rate system on dividends. The new tax reform introduces an imputation system, which under some treaties will reduce the withholding tax on dividends to foreign companies with a participating interest in Norwegian companies (e.g., France, Luxembourg, Switzerland, and the United Kingdom from 15% to 5%, Nordic countries and the Netherlands from 15% to 0%) for dividends received in 1993 and onwards.

OTHER SIGNIFICANT TAXES

21. Sales (Value Added)

Value added tax, introduced in Norway on January 1, 1970, is, on the whole, based on the same principles as those in the European Economic Community. A 20% tax is, in principle, levied on all domestic sales, imported goods, and specified services.

Special Sales Taxes.   In addition to the VAT, special sales taxes are levied on motor vehicles, gasoline, tobacco, cosmetics, spirits, liquor, wine, beer and chocolate.

Tax on Investments, Etc.   A special tax on investments, etc., was introduced on January 1, 1970, and is closely related to the VAT system. The rate is 7% on cost price, exclusive of VAT, with the exception of production plant, equipment, and supplies and maintenance in certain industries. This investment tax is imposed primarily on the procurement of, and work on, durable items of equipment for use in businesses that are liable for VAT. It is proposed that the rate be reduced to 5% effective 1992.

22. Inheritance and Gift Taxes

Inheritance tax is levied on nearly all items of capital passing from a deceased person to his heirs, including gifts made by the donor during his lifetime. Tax exemption for occasional gifts is kept within the customary limits such as gifts for educational purposes, for support of dependents and, to some extent, gifts for the benefit of the public. The rate scale is graduated from 8% to 30% of amounts exceeding NOK 100,000 depending on the value of the estate/gift and the relationship between the heir and the deceased or donor.

23. Taxes on Payrolls (Social Security)

Employer Contributions.   The employer's contribution is calculated on the basis of wages and other remunerations. The rates are stipulated by six geographical regions, depending on the taxation municipality of the employee. The rate in central parts of Norway is 16.7% and reduced to 0% in the Northern counties.

Employee and Other Individual Contributions.   Old-age pension contribution and health insurance contribution to the Norwegian National Scheme are combined into one contribution. The rates are supposed to be 7.8% for employees, 3% on pension income, and 10.7% for self-employed individuals.

24. Taxes on Natural Resources

Norway has special tax legislation concerning exploration for and exploitation of submarine petroleum deposits, etc. (including activities such as drilling-rig operations and work connected therewith at the Norwegian continental shelf in the North Sea and pipeline transport of extracted petroleum). The computation of taxable income for petroleum production and pipeline transport is based on price norms stipulated by the King for petroleum (not gas), which means, in practice, that the prices are determined quarterly by competent authorities. For 1991, the national income tax rate is 50.8%. No municipal income tax is levied on income derived from petroleum and gas production or from pipeline transportation of these products. In addition, a special national income tax is levied on such income at the rate of 30%. The basis for assessment of this special tax is taxable income for the purposes of the regular national income tax, with some adjustments—deduction is not allowed for dividends declared or for losses from other business activities. It is assumed, however, that the taxation of petroleum production and pipeline transport will be adapted to conform with the new tax legislation effective fiscal-year 1992.

25. Other Taxes

Land and Property Taxes.   Property tax on real estate is levied by the municipality at a maximum tax rate of 0.7%. The local authorities are free to decide whether to levy this tax. The tax is assessed on the basis of a special evaluation of the property.

Taxes on Capital.   Taxes on net taxable capital (net worth), including offshore capital, are levied on individuals and certain associations and institutions (excluding joint stock companies), as follows.

Taxable Associations/Institutions.   The capital tax is 0.3%.

Individuals.   A municipal capital tax is levied on individuals at the rate of 1% on capital exceeding NOK 120,000.

The national capital tax is levied at the following progressive rates:

Taxable Net Worth

Class 1*		Class 2**		
Over	Not Over	Over	Not Over	Rate
NOK 0	NOK 120,000	NOK 0	NOK 150,000	0%
120,000	235,000	150,000	260,000	0.1
235,000		260,000		0.3

* No dependents.
** With dependents.

COMPUTATION OF TAXABLE INCOME

26. Capital Gains

Under the existing rules, no gain will be recognized on sales of depreciable fixed assets and the remaining book value will not be adjusted. If a negative balance occurs in any asset group, it may be carried forward and credited against new acquisitions or credited against positive depreciation balances for fixed assets of the same or higher depreciation percentages, and any negative balance that has not been used within four years (eight years for ships, rigs, and aircraft) should be taxed as income by the end of the fourth (eighth) year.

Effective fiscal-year 1992, there is no possibility when disposing of a depreciable fixed asset, of establishing negative balances, which could previously be carried forward for reinvestment or write-down on other depreciation balances. Asset groups (a) through (c) (see item 27) normally include a large number of individual items. The disposal value of such assets will be deducted from the group's balance. If the balance becomes negative, this amount will be returned to income each year at a rate equivalent to that group's depreciation rate. This means that gain or loss will be taxed over time at the same rate as the depreciation rate for the asset (based on the reducing-balance method). Fixed assets for the asset groups (d) through (g) (see item 27) must be booked individually. Losses and gains must be calculated individually. Losses and gains are to be booked on a general gain and loss account. A positive account, i.e., net gains, is to be returned to income at the rate of 20% annually (based on the reducing-balance method). A negative account, i.e., net losses, is to be deducted at an equivalent rate. For assets in all groups, there will be the opportunity to take the whole or part of the sales price to income in the year of realization.

Under the existing rules, gains and losses are calculated on sales of nondepreciable fixed assets. The taxable gains may in certain cases be allocated to a tax-contingent reserve for later acquisition. Effective fiscal-year 1992, this regulation is to be repealed, and gains or losses will be booked on the general gain and loss account and treated in the same way as depreciable fixed assets.

Effective fiscal-year 1992, gains from the sale of shares, securities, and other financial assets are subject to tax as ordinary income in the year of realization. Losses from the sale of shares or securities are tax deductible in the year of realization.

Gains or losses on the sale of Norwegian shares are the difference between the realization amount and the acquisition cost of the shares, with deduction of purchase and sales costs and adjustment for changes to the company's taxed equity. To avoid double taxation, the acquisition costs must be adjusted up or down in conformity with movement in the company's taxed equity during the shareholder's period of ownership. When calculating gains or losses on sales of foreign shares, no such adjustments may be made.

Transition Arrangement. An alternative transition arrangement is allowed for existing negative balances established in 1990 or earlier.

(1) 40% of the negative balance is tax-exempt (60% if the taxpayer is resident in certain specified developing areas).

(2) Up to 60% of the negative balance can be used before the end of fiscal-year 1992 to acquire new shares or bonds issued by Norwegian commercial banks, savings banks, and bond-issuing credit institutions.

(3) Up to 30% of the negative balance can be used before the end of fiscal-year 1992 to acquire new stock-exchange-quoted shares in Norwegian companies that are engaged in onshore activities or make venture investments in onshore activities.

(4) An additional 30% can be used before the end of fiscal-year to acquire new shares in investment companies that make venture investments in onshore activities.

(5) Negative balances that are not tax-exempt or used according to these regulations should be transferred to a gain and loss account and be added to income at the rate of 20% annually, effective fiscal-year 1992.

The negative balances utilized to acquire new shares or bonds according to these provisions will reduce the cost price of the shares or bonds acquired. The negative balance then will be taxable only when the shares or bonds are sold. Negative balances utilized for the acquisition of shares mentioned in (2) above will not reduce the cost price of the shares acquired if the shares are sold after five years. The utilized negative balances are tax-exempt in these cases. Existing negative balances established in 1991 can be utilized as mentioned in (3) and (4) above.

Deferred gains from 1991 or before will be transferred to the general gain and loss account and added to income by 20% annually.

27. Depreciation and Depletion

The reducing-balance method of depreciation is mandatory. The reducing-balance system does not apply to assets used in oil extraction and pipeline activities; special depreciation rules are based on the straight-line method with a maximum annual depreciation rate of 16.66%.

According to the existing reducing-balance system, fixed assets are divided into groups, each with its maximum depreciation rate. Effective fiscal-year 1992, there are new asset groups as well as changes in certain depreciation rates. The new asset groups and rates are:

Asset Group	Rate
(a) Office equipment, etc., and purchased goodwill	30%
(b) Trucks, buses, and taxis	25%
(c) Cars, tractors and other transport items, other machines, equipment, instruments, furniture, etc.	20%
(d) Ships and rigs	20%

(e)	Airplanes and helicopters	12%
(f)	Buildings, hotels, restaurants, etc.	5%
(g)	Ordinary office buildings	2%

It is assumed that the depreciation rates for office buildings in certain areas and buildings with a short remaining useful life shall be increased to 4% and 10%, respectively.

With the change to new regulations for the depreciation of fixed assets, remaining balances of existing fixed assets are to be transferred to the new asset groups. Future depreciation will then be carried out in accordance with the new rates.

28. Treatment of Dividends

Under the existing legislation, dividends received by corporate or individual resident shareholders from domestic companies are subject to national income tax only. Dividends received from foreign companies are subject to normal rates of tax (except where relief is provided by double taxation treaties). Dividends distributed by domestic joint-stock companies from the current year's profits are deductible from taxable income for the purpose of national income tax (i.e., 27.8%).

Pursuant to the new tax legislation, an imputation system in connection with the taxation of company profits and dividends is introduced in order to avoid double taxation of companies and shareholders. The imputation system implies that the company will pay tax on the whole of its profits, irrespective of any distribution of profits. Norwegian shareholders will receive credit for the amount of tax paid by the domestic company on its profit that is distributed as dividends. Foreign resident shareholders will not be entitled to credit for corporate tax. Dividends received from foreign companies will be treated as ordinary income and subject to tax. Norwegian parent companies, however, that receive dividends from overseas subsidiaries are allowed a tax credit for foreign corporate tax. The credit will be limited to the Norwegian tax on the dividend.

According to the new regulations, for purposes of the calculation of the credit it will no longer be relevant whether the company distributes from the current year's or previous year's profit. The changes will be effective fiscal-year 1992 for companies and fiscal-year 1993 for shareholders. Dividends distributed in 1992 will be based on profits that have been taxed according to the 1991 regulations. To avoid company dividend policies influenced by the change to a new tax system, dividends received by individuals in 1992 are taxed at a flat tax rate of 19.5% (14.5% in the Northern counties), which is the same as the highest marginal tax rate for personal taxpayers in 1991. Dividends received by companies are to be taxed at the present state tax rate of 27.8%.

29. Loss Carryovers

There is a ten-year carryforward period for losses. Losses carryforward from the sale of shares outside the ordinary course of business before 1992 can be balanced only against gains from the sale of shares within four years after the year of losses.

Deductions for operating losses in connection with the exploration for and exploitation of submarine petroleum deposits, etc., may be claimed in the 15 subsequent years.

When a substantial part of the shares of a company is sold or a company merges with another company, the company will maintain its right to carry forward accumulated losses. However, if the ownership of a company has been wholly or partly changed, either by a merger or other transactions, and it is likely that the transactions in substance are motivated by achieving tax benefits for the parties concerned, the company will lose its right to carry forward accumulated losses and losses for the year in which the transactions take place. When a company is subject to the forgiveness of debts, losses carried forward are reduced by an amount equal to the forgiven debts.

If a business activity ceases or an enterprise goes into liquidation, the losses may be carried back for two years.

30. Transactions between Related Parties

Gross income, deductions, credits or allowances may be reallocated to clearly reflect income among organizations owned or controlled by the same interests. In the case of capital transactions, the taxing authorities may substitute fair market value for value applied.

31. Consolidation of Income

Companies are taxed individually. However, Norwegian group companies, where the parent company owns more than 90% of its subsidiary's shares, may be balanced by contributions between the companies. Group contributions between Norwegian subsidiaries of a foreign parent (provided more than 90% held) can be granted and received; the ownership should be substantiated when tax returns are filed. This would allow one group company to deduct from its taxable income a group contribution to another company within the group. Such contribution cannot exceed taxable income before the contribution and represents taxable income to the receiving company. The granting company will be entitled to deduct only the contribution for tax purposes to the extent that the contribution covers losses of the receiving company.

32. Tax Periods

The calendar year is the mandatory tax year. On application, a corporation taxpayer may be granted a different accounting year if special reasons justify this (normally, Norwegian subsidiaries of foreign parent companies having a different accounting year).

RELATED CONSIDERATIONS

34. Incentives and Grants

Exempt Income. No provisions exist to exempt income from tax, except for income received by charitable or nonprofit organizations. Effective fiscal-year 1992, cooperative organizations will be taxed as ordinary limited companies; certain rules apply, however, in respect of deductible item for tax purposes.

Special Grants or Allowances. The ability to allocate to the "District Development Fund" for future investment is repealed. The ability to allocate to the "Investment Fund" or investments for environmental protection is repealed. The ability to make allocation to the "Consolidation Fund" is abolished as of 1992. At this time, the previously built-up Consolidation Fund allocations may be resolved without taxation.

35. Exchange Controls

The majority of Norway's strict currency exchange rules have been abolished effective July 1, 1990. However, normally all the foreign exchange transactions will go through an authorized Norwegian bank.

36. Investment Restrictions on Nonresidents

Direct investment in Norway by nonresidents is welcomed. Effective July 1990, no specific permission by the Bank of Norway is required. Foreign exchange transactions will go through an authorized Norwegian bank. According to Norway's concession legislation, concession is necessary for the purchase and lease of waterfalls, mines and other real estate, lease of electric power in excess of 1,000 kw and, in certain cases, for the purchase of shares. Special legislation exists for exploration of underwater resources. The repatriation of investment is a matter of form only and presents no problem.

Dividend Restrictions. Dividends may be distributed only after a statutory allocation to a legal reserve, the Reserve Fund. Until the Reserve Fund equals 20% of the corporation's share capital and/or total share capital and Reserve Fund equals total liabilities, an annual application to the Reserve Fund must be made of:

☐ Ten percent of annual profit not used to cover losses of prior years.

☐ An additional amount at least equal to the excess of dividends distributed for the year over 10% of the total of share capital and Reserve Fund at the beginning of the financial year.

SELECTION OF BUSINESS ENTITY BY NONRESIDENTS

Nonresident investors can operate in Norway either through a branch or by forming a local subsidiary corporation. Both branches and foreign-owned corporations generally are taxed in the same way as domestic companies.

A withholding tax is imposed on dividends paid by a subsidiary to its overseas parent (see item 28). No withholding taxes are levied on the remittance of branch profits.

Many nontax considerations may influence the decision as to whether business in Norway should be carried on through a branch or through a subsidiary, including that an overseas corporation is exposed to liability for the debts of its branch while a subsidiary does not expose its parent to such liability.

SPECIMEN TAX COMPUTATION

Information:

☐ Company tax computation of a Norwegian company and its foreign branch.

Computation:

		NOK
Operating income (gross) in Norway		2,000
Less		
Operating expenses	500	
Interest payable	200	
Depreciation	100	(800)

	1992	1993
Add		
Dividends (gross) paid by a foreign company (1)	100	100
Foreign branch profits of NOK 300 (2)	—	—
Dividends paid by domestic companies (3)	—	138
Taxable income	1,300	1,438
1992: Corporation tax (28% of NOK 1,300)	364	
1993: Corporation tax (28% of NOK 1,438)		403
Less		
Tax credit for withholding tax on foreign dividends	(15)	(15)
Tax credit for foreign corporation tax (1)	(10)	(10)
1992		
Taxes on dividends paid by domestic companies (100 × 27.8%) (3)	28	
1993		
Less tax credit for domestic corporation tax (3)		(28)
Tax payable	367	350

Notes:
(1) Domestic parent companies may achieve credit for foreign corporation tax of foreign subsidiaries (see item 28).

(2)   In general, foreign branch profits are tax exempted according to the relevant tax treaty.

(3)   Dividends received in fiscal-year 1992 from domestic companies are subject to a flat tax rate of 27.8%. Effective fiscal-year 1993, the shareholder is given credit for the amount of tax paid by the company on its profits that are distributed as dividends. The computation of tax credit for corporation tax is based on a standardized 7/18 of dividends received.

OMAN

INCOME TAXES ON CORPORATIONS

1. Rates

Income tax on taxable income that has been realized or has arisen in the Sultanate of Oman (Oman) is payable by all corporations, whether or not registered in Oman. Corporations include companies, partnerships, joint ventures, and branches of foreign corporations. The tax rates for corporations are as follows:

Taxable Income		Rate
Over	**Not Over**	**Rate**
RO 0	RO 5,000	0%
5,000	18,000	5
18,000	35,000	10
35,000	55,000	15
55,000	75,000	20
75,000	100,000	25
100,000	200,000	30
200,000	300,000	35
300,000	400,000	40
400,000	500,000	45
500,000		50

Tax payable is computed by applying to the total taxable income the percentage rate in the above table for the band into which the taxable income falls. For taxable income marginally in excess of a particular rate band limit, the tax payable can be reduced by adding 100% of the excess to the maximum amount calculated in the next lower band. Income tax is assessed by and payable to the Director of Taxation Affairs, Ministry of Finance and Economy.

Exemptions from Tax.   The following exemptions are currently in force:

☐ Corporations wholly owned by Omani nationals are exempt from income tax until December 31, 1992.

☐ Corporations whose main object is industry, agriculture, or fishing are exempt from income tax for five years from the date of incorporation.

☐ Corporations that contribute to the development of the national economy and whose paid up capital exceeds one hundred thousand Rials Omani may be exempt from tax by a Ministerial Decision for five years from the date of incorporation; the exemption period may be extended for a further five years.

Reduced or Special Tax Rates.   Royal Decree 46/87, promulgated in June 1987, introduced the following rates on corporations with Omani shareholding of 35% or more for tax years ending after June 16, 1987:

Taxable Income		Omani Shareholding		
Over	Not Over	35% to less than 51%	51% or more	100% (1)
RO 0	RO 30,000	0%	0%	0%
30,000	200,000	25	20	5
200,000		30	25	7.5

Note:

(1) Royal Decree 77/89 introduced income tax for commercial and industrial establishments that are wholly owned by Omani citizens. Application of this law will not commence before January 1, 1993.

For corporations with Omani shareholding of 35% or more that are engaged in agriculture, fisheries, mining, and industry, Royal Decree 46/87 maintained the following rates of tax as initially applied by Royal Decree 65/77:

Taxable Income		Omani Shareholding	
Over	Not Over	35% to less than 51%	51% or more
RO 0	RO 20,000	0%	0%
20,000		20	15

Special rules apply to the taxation of income derived from the sale of petroleum. The tax rate on taxable income arising from the sale of petroleum since November 14, 1970 is 55%. It is considered that action should be taken only on the basis of specific advice.

Taxation Parity between AGCC and Omani Nationals. In accordance with the Ministerial Decision 18/89 issued in June 1989, the citizens of Arab Gulf Cooperation Council ("AGCC") States will be treated equally with Omani citizens in the matter of taxation when they carry out authorized economic activities. This decision became effective March 1, 1989.

Several Ministerial Decisions have been issued by the Ministry of Commerce and Industry and the Ministry of Finance and Economy permitting AGCC citizens to carry on certain economic activities; however, no firm decision has been taken as of July 31, 1991 as to which activities are covered within the provisions of Ministerial Decision 18/89. It is suggested that specific advice should be obtained in this respect before taking any action.

During July 1991, the Muscat Securities Market (MSM) introduced a regulation allowing foreign companies to participate in the trading of shares of the companies listed on the MSM. This regulation is likely to have a significant effect on the structure and taxable status of the listed companies, and the matter is under consideration as of July 31, 1991.

2.   Local Income Taxes

There are no local (e.g., state or district) income taxes.

3.   Capital Gains Taxes

Capital gains are treated as part of the taxable income.

4.   Branch Profits Taxes

A branch of a foreign corporation is taxed on its taxable income in the same manner as corporations (see item 1).

5.   Foreign Tax Reliefs

The Government of Oman has entered into a double taxation treaty with France (Royal Decree 45/90, May 15, 1990). There are no other double taxation treaties except for agreements with India, Jordan, Kuwait, and the Netherlands relating to air transportation income. There is no provision for relief from income tax in Oman as a result of foreign taxes paid.

Relief may be obtained in certain countries in respect of income tax paid by corporations in Oman, depending on the tax regulations in the individual countries concerned.

6.   Classification of Corporations

The following types of business enterprises may be utilized in Oman:

- □   Joint stock company.
- □   Limited liability company.

□ General partnership.
□ Limited partnership.
□ Joint venture.
□ Branches of foreign corporations.
□ Sole traders.

Business enterprises, except joint ventures, must register in the Commercial Register, and companies are required to register also with the Chamber of Commerce. Commercial registration, in some instances, is renewable annually, and approval by the Department of Taxation Affairs is one of the prerequisites for renewal. For Joint Ventures, the establishing contract must define the venture's objectives, rights, and obligations. The present view of the Department of Taxation Affairs is that, unless the joint venture is registered with the Ministry of Commerce and Industry and Omani nationals hold the specified proportion of the capital, the reduced rates of tax are not available. Foreign corporations desiring to own or participate in the capital of an Omani company require approval from the Ministry of Commerce and Industry. The Foreign Business and Investment Law requires that the paid-up capital of a company with a foreign participation will be determined by the Committee of Foreign Capital Investment, with a minimum paid up capital of RO 150,000. See also "Selection of Business Entity by Nonresidents."

7. Payment of Taxes

Every corporation is required to make a provisional declaration of its income chargeable to tax within three months from the date on which its accounting period ended. The final declaration is to be presented within six months following the end of the accounting period. Corporations with a capital in excess of RO 20,000 are required to file accounts of their Oman operations audited by a locally registered auditor with their final declaration. Tax payable in accordance with the declarations should be paid to the Director of Taxation Affairs at the time of filing each declaration.

Penalties. Failure to present a declaration of income to the Director of Taxation Affairs may lead to an arbitrary assessment made by the authorities on the corporation and penalties as prescribed by law. Delay in payment of income tax normally will result in additional tax calculated at 1% per month on the outstanding sum. The Director may also impose other penalties in the event of noncompliance with the law, including an additional assessment of up to half the value of the tax payable by the corporation. There is a right of appeal against decisions and assessments of the Director of Taxation Affairs.

INCOME TAXES ON INDIVIDUALS

9. Rates

No income taxes are levied on individuals, whether nationals or expatriates.

INCOME TAXES ON NONRESIDENTS

15. Liability to Tax

The income tax law does not distinguish between resident and nonresident corporations.

OTHER SIGNIFICANT TAXES

21. Sales (Value Added)

There are no sales taxes. Hotels and restaurants collect a municipal tax of 5% on the bill of each guest. Municipality tax also is levied at the rate of 2% on electricity bills in excess of RO 50 and at 3% on the annual rental of leased premises.

22. Inheritance and Gift Taxes

None.

23. Taxes on Payrolls (Social Security)

Corporations employing more than 19 people are subject to a training levy on the aggregate of expatriate salaries, wages, and certain related employment costs paid annually at the following rates:

Number of Employees		
Over	Not Over	Rate
19	50	2%
50	300	3
300	1,000	5
1,000		6

Employees may be aggregated if the same employer carries on separate activities in different businesses and under distinct commercial registrations.

Social Security. No social security contributions are payable by individuals or corporations. The 1973 Labor Law regulates the conditions of employment for persons outside government service. The Law covers the calculation of the statutory end of service gratuity, leave entitlements, hours of work, overtime pay, dismissal, and notice requirement. The end of service gratuity is calculated on the final basic salary at a rate of fifteen days for each of the first three years of continuous service and, thereafter, at a rate of thirty days for the years following the first three. The law further provides that the worker will not be entitled to any end-of-service benefit if he has served less than one year with an employer.

A Sultani Decree 72/91, promulgated on July 2, 1991, introduced the Social Security Law, which provides for various contributory pension schemes for Omani workers in the private sector.

24. Taxes on Natural Resources

Special rules apply to taxation on income derived from the sale of petroleum (see item 1).

COMPUTATION OF TAXABLE INCOME

26. Capital Gains

As stated in item 3, capital gains form part of taxable income. The capital gain is the excess of sale proceeds over the net book value of assets for taxation purposes.

27. Depreciation and Depletion

Capital assets owned and used by a corporation are permitted an annual deduction for depreciation when computing the income chargeable to tax. Amortization of intangible assets may also be an allowable deduction, at a rate that requires approval of the Director of Taxation Affairs. Annual depreciation on the cost of capital assets is calculated on the straight-line basis. The rates of depreciation for categories of assets are summarized below:

	Annual Percentage
Buildings (depending upon grade of construction)	4%–15%
Bridges, pipelines, and platforms	10
Tools, furnishings, and equipment:	
Heavy equipment	33.33
Other equipment	15
Light vehicles	33.33
Furnishings	33.33
Aircraft and ships	15
Hospital buildings, educational establishments, and scientific research equipment	100

Special rates of depreciation apply to:

☐ Buildings used for industrial purposes for which the stated rates of depreciation may be doubled.

☐ Tools and equipment used for three shifts of work per day, for which the depreciation rate stated above will be increased by a maximum of 50%; the additional depreciation will be computed by reference to the number of days the tools and equipment are used for three shifts in proportion to three hundred days.

28. Treatment of Dividends

Royal Decree 77/89 (mentioned in item 1) states that dividends received from an entity that has already settled any tax payable in Oman will not be taxable in the hands of the receiving company.

29. Loss Carryovers

A loss is set off against taxable income arising in each subsequent year, taken in order. However, the loss may not be carried forward for more than five years after the end of the year in which it was incurred.

30. Transactions between Related Parties

Transactions between related parties are subject to particular attention to confirm that prices are at arm's length and that expenses exclude any profit element.

31. Consolidation of Income

Corporations are taxed as separate entities. A separate income tax declaration is required for each taxable entity.

32. Tax Periods

The tax year ends on December 31, and corporations normally prepare their accounts for the year that corresponds to that date. An annual accounting date other than December 31 may be selected provided this date is followed consistently. The basis period for computing the liability to income tax is the corporation's own accounting period.

33. Other Matters

Accounting Methods. Taxable income is computed in accordance with generally accepted methods of commercial accounting, applied on a consistent basis subject to any adjustments considered necessary by the tax authorities. The accrual method is required unless the Director of Taxation Affairs approves the adoption of another method of accounting. The audited accounts are to be prepared in accordance with International Accounting Standards, as required by Royal Decrees 77/86 and 21/88, which govern the accounting and auditing profession in Oman.

Allowable Expenditure. Expenditure incurred wholly and exclusively for the business is, in principle, an allowable deduction from income. Certain types of expenditure are restricted or disallowed, particularly expenses incurred outside of Oman, amounts charged against profit, payable to related parties, and provisions.

Specific regulations relating to sponsor's or agent's fees and head office expenses charged to the accounts of branches of foreign companies have been introduced by Ministerial Decisions on October 14, 1984. These regulations apply to assessments for all accounting periods that were not at that date settled by the Department of Taxation Affairs.

□ Sponsors Fees. Allowance is restricted to 5% of taxable income.

□ Head Office Expenses. Should the head office incur expenses in providing specific services to the branch and if the Department of Taxation Affairs cannot quantify the actual expenses incurred from the documentation provided, the allowance shall be the lowest of:

—The expenses estimated by the branch.

—The average head office charge in the last three years.

—3% of the gross revenue of the branch.

The percentage applicable with respect to banking and insurance companies is 5%. In all instances where the activity of the head office is restricted to mere supervision of the branches, no amounts will be allowed as a deduction for tax purposes.

If the head office of a large industrial company provides technical or specialist assistance, the limiting percentage may be increased to 10%. The Deputy Prime Minister for Financial and Economic Affairs is empowered to increase the allowance to more than 10%.

Ministerial Decision 23/89, issued on July 6, 1989, regulates the allowance of commissions paid to authorized agents by foreign insurance companies. Under this decision, for purposes of computing the taxable income of foreign insurance companies operating through an authorized agent, no deduction in excess of 25% of the net premiums received will be allowable as agent's commission in respect of tax years commencing after August 1, 1989.

Gifts made to organizations specified by the Council for Financial Affairs will be allowable as deduction for tax purposes provided that the total value of such gifts do not exceed 1% of gross income.

Accounting Records. Accounting normally should be maintained in Rials Omani, but the records may be maintained in a foreign currency if approved by the tax authorities. It is anticipated that accounting records will be required to be maintained in Oman. Accounting records, including registers and documents, should be retained for at least ten years.

RELATED CONSIDERATIONS

34. Incentives and Grants

As stated in item 1 ("Exemptions from Tax"), corporations satisfying certain criteria are exempt from tax for specified periods.

35. Exchange Controls

None.

36. Investment Restrictions on Nonresidents

Non-Omanis may not participate in equity without government permission (see item 6).

SELECTION OF BUSINESS ENTITY BY NONRESIDENTS

Nonresidents may operate in the Sultanate of Oman through a branch or a corporation (which includes companies, partnerships, and joint ventures). The tax consequences are:

☐ Profits of branch operations with 100% foreign ownership are taxed according to the table shown in item 1.

☐ Profits of corporations are taxed at the rates according to the extent of Omani participation, as specified in item 1.

Branches are used normally by foreign entities that are permitted to operate through a permanent establishment in Oman without Omani participation. Registration of a branch normally is limited to those companies wishing to operate under the terms of a contract with the Government or quasi-Government organizations. Such branches are not permitted to seek other business or contracts with private sector parties. The majority of business activities are required by Law to have Omani participation of at least 35%. Most nonresidents, therefore, operate through companies, partnerships, or joint ventures. Dividends paid by a locally incorporated company are not subject to withholding tax.

SPECIMEN TAX COMPUTATION

Information:

Net profit as per accounts		RO 54,000
Adjustments to taxable profits as determined by tax authorities	2,000	2,000
Taxable income		RO 56,000

Computation:

	Corporations with Omani Participation		
	Nil	**35% to less than 51%**	**51% or more**
Adjusted income	RO 56,000	RO 56,000	RO 56,000
Basic exemption		30,000	30,000
Taxable income	RO 56,000	RO 26,000	RO 26,000
Tax rate	20%	25%	20%
Tax payable	RO 9,250	RO 6,500	RO 5,200

Notes:

(1) Relief is available if income is marginally in excess of a particular tax bracket (see item 1). For example, the tax payable by a foreign corporation would be RO 9,250 rather than RO 11,200 under the alternative computation:

Tax at 15% on RO 55,000	RO 8,250
100% of excess of income over RO 55,000	1,000
Tax payable	RO 9,250

PAKISTAN

INCOME TAXES ON CORPORATIONS

1. Rates

The current tax rate on all private and public limited companies, whether resident or nonresident, on their profits from business are:

	Banking Companies	Other Companies
Income tax	30%	30%
Super tax	30%	20%* (15% for public companies)

Notes:
*A public company is allowed a further super-tax rebate of 5%, making the effective super-tax rate 10%.

In the case of total income of Rs.100,000 or more, a surcharge is payable at the rate of 10% of the income tax and supertax payable for that year.

For the purposes of application of rate of tax and rebates of super tax a public company means:

☐ A company in which not less than 50% of the shares are held by the Government;

☐ A company whose shares were the subject of dealings in a registered stock exchange in Pakistan at any time during the income year and remain listed on the stock exchange until the close of that year; or

☐ A trust formed by or under any law in force at the time.

Minimum Tax. Companies resident in Pakistan are liable to a minimum tax of 0.5% of turnover. This applies even if the company shows a loss or has been otherwise exempted from tax.

Dividend Income. The tax rates on income from dividends from a company formed and registered under the Companies Ordinance, 1984 are:

Dividends received by a public company	5%
Dividends received by a body corporate or a foreign association declared to be a company	15%
In other cases (e.g., private limited companies)	20%

In the case of total income of Rs.100,000 or more, a surcharge is payable at the rate of 10% of the tax payable for that year.

2. Local Income Taxes

Taxation of agricultural income is determined by the provincial governments on the produce index basis. Capital gains tax on the sale of immovable properties has been repealed effective July 1, 1986.

3. Capital Gains Taxes

Capital gain arising on the transfer (sale, exchange, etc.) of shares of public companies is exempt until the assessment year ending on or before June 30, 1994. Capital gain arising on the transfer of capital assets (excluding immovable properties and assets on which tax depreciation is claimed) held for not more than 12 months is taxable at the normal rates shown in item 1. Capital gain arising on the sale of capital assets held for more than 12 months is taxable at 25%.

4. Branch Profits Taxes

Profits of the Pakistan branches of a nonresident company are taxed at the same rates as specified in item 1.

5. Foreign Tax Reliefs

Tax treaties (excluding treaties which only deal with airline and shipping income) exist with Austria, Bangladesh, Belgium, Canada, Denmark, France, Germany, Indonesia, Ireland, Japan, Korea, Libya, Malaysia, Malta, Netherlands, Northern Ireland, Norway, Philippines, Poland, Romania, Sri Lanka, Sweden, Switzerland, Thailand, Turkey, the United Kingdom, and the United States. The taxation of business profits in cases where tax treaties have been entered into with other countries essentially depends upon the existence of a permanent establishment.

See item 12 for unilateral relief which is also available to Pakistani companies.

6. Classification of Corporations

Corporations for Pakistan tax purposes are classified as resident and nonresident and as domestic and foreign. A resident corporation has been defined as a Pakistani company (i.e., formed and registered under the Companies Ordinance, 1984) or any other company the control and management of whose affairs is situated wholly in Pakistan in the income year. A company for tax purposes is defined as:

□ A company formed and registered under the Companies Ordinance, 1984.

□ A body corporate formed by or under any law for the time being in force.

□ A body corporate incorporated by or under the law of a country outside Pakistan relating to incorporation of companies.

□ The government of a province.

□ A foreign association, whether incorporated or not, which the Central Board of Revenue may, by general or special order, declare to be a company.

□ A trust formed by or under any law for the time being in force.

A nonresident company is defined negatively (any company which is not resident is classified as nonresident). The difference between resident and nonresident corporations is important because residents are taxed on their worldwide income whereas nonresidents are subject to tax on their Pakistan source income.

A domestic company means a Pakistani company formed and registered under the Companies Ordinance, 1984 whereas a foreign company is defined as a company which is not a domestic company. Rebates in supertax are available only to domestic companies (see item 1).

7. Payment of Taxes

A company is required to pay advance tax in four installments on September 15, December 15, March 15, and June 15 on the basis of the tax assessed for the latest assessment year. However, an assessee has the option to file his own estimate if in his opinion tax payable for the current year will be less than the amount assessed for the latest assessment year. A company whose income year ends between July 1 and December 1 must file a tax return by July 31 of the following year. A company whose income year ends between January 1 and June 30 must file by December 31. Any balance of tax due, after deducting the advance tax paid and the tax collected at source, must be paid along with the income tax return.

8. Other Matters

The following categories of income, inter alia, are deemed to accrue or arise in Pakistan and taxpayers in all categories (including corporations) are liable to Pakistan tax:

□ Any income accruing or arising, whether directly or indirectly, through or from any business connection in Pakistan or through or from any asset, property, or source of income in Pakistan, or through the transfer of a capital asset situated in Pakistan.

□ Income by way of interest payable in respect of any debt incurred, or monies borrowed and used, for the purposes of a business or profession carried on in Pakistan.

□ Income by way of royalty payable in respect of any right, property or information used or services utilized for the purposes of a business or profession carried on in Pakistan.

☐ Income by way of fees payable in respect of technical services utilized in a business or profession carried on in Pakistan.

The normal method of computation of income does not apply to the income of a foreign company arising by way of royalty or fees for technical services received from a Pakistani concern. The salient features of such computations are:

Royalties. The gross amount of royalty income is treated as income liable to tax if received in pursuance of any agreement made on or after March 8, 1980.

Fees for Technical Services. In case of agreements made on or after May 4, 1981, deductions from income are allowed for expenditures incurred outside Pakistan but only to the extent of up to 10% of the gross fees received. However, in the case of agreements made after June 30, 1987 tax is to be levied at 20% of the gross income, and this will be considered as the final tax liability of the nonresident.

INCOME TAXES ON INDIVIDUALS

9. Rates

A new simplified procedure has been introduced for the assessment of individuals whose total income is less than Rs.100,000. The rate of tax is 10% of total income, but in the case of an individual with more than 50% of total income chargeable under the head salary, the tax payable will be reduced by Rs.4,000. While in other cases, it will be reduced by Rs.3,000. There is no rebate on tax allowed for investment, donations, etc.

For non-salaried individuals whose total income is less than Rs.100,000, there is a surcharge of Rs.300.

If an individual's total income is Rs.100,000 or more, it is taxed at graduated rates, as follows:

Taxable Income		Tax on	Percentage
Over	Not Over	Lower Amount	on Excess
Rs.100,000	Rs.200,000	Rs. 7,000	20%
200,000	300,000	27,000	30
300,000		57,000	35

If the total income of any person is Rs.100,000 or more (Rs.200,000 or more for a salaried person), a surcharge is payable at the rate of 10% of the income tax.

11. Capital Gains Taxes

Capital gain arising on the sale of shares of public companies is exempt until the assessment year ending on or before June 30, 1994, but capital gain on the transfer (sale, exchange, etc.) of capital assets (excluding immovable properties and assets on which tax depreciation is claimed) held for not more than 12 months is taxable at the rates mentioned in item 9. Capital gain arising on the sale of capital assets held for more than 12 months is also taxable at the rates noted in item 9, but the taxable gain is reduced by the higher of Rs.5,000 or 60% of the gain.

12. Foreign Tax Reliefs

Tax treaties exist with the countries noted in item 5. Apart from these, unilateral relief is available to persons resident in Pakistan in respect of tax paid in foreign countries.

13. Tax Period

The tax year in Pakistan commences on July 1 and ends on June 30. All companies and individuals other than those deriving salary income are required to close their accounts on either June 30 or December 31. Special permission is required from the Central Board of Revenue to select any other accounting year-end. For salaried individuals, the tax year ends on June 30. In respect of certain industries, such as sugar and textile, the Central Board of Revenue has specified September 30 as their accounting year-end.

14. Other Matters

Residence.   An individual resident in Pakistan is generally taxed on his worldwide income. An individual not resident (i.e., a nonresident) in Pakistan pays tax only on income which accrues or arises in Pakistan or is deemed to accrue or arise in Pakistan or is received or deemed to be received in Pakistan. An individual is said to be resident in Pakistan in any income year if the individual either:

□   Is in Pakistan in that year for an aggregate of 182 days or more.

□   Is in Pakistan for a period or periods amounting in all to ninety days or more in that year and who, within the four years preceding that year, has been in Pakistan for 365 days or more.

The following classes of income are, inter alia, exempt from tax in the hands of an individual who is not a citizen of Pakistan:

□   Persons stationed in Pakistan, in acordance with an Aid Agreement entered into by the Government of Pakistan, whose salary is paid by a foreign government or out of funds or grants released as aid to Pakistan in pursuance of such agreement.

□   Remuneration for services in Pakistan as the official representative of the government of a foreign state.

□   Remuneration paid by the government of a foreign country to any employee of a recognized educational institution in Pakistan.

□   Remuneration received as an employee of a foreign enterprise not engaged in any trade or business in Pakistan for services rendered during his stay not exceeding ninety days in any income year in Pakistan.

☐ Subject to certain conditions, the salaries received for a period of two years commencing from the date of his arrival in Pakistan for service rendered as a professor or teacher at a recognized university, college, or other educational institution in Pakistan.

☐ Salary received by a person by virtue of his employment with the British Council.

☐ Any emoluments received in lieu of services rendered to the Pakistan Sports Board as a coach.

INCOME TAXES ON NONRESIDENTS

16. Rates

Nonresidents, other than corporations, are taxed on Pakistan-source income at 30% of their income or the regular income tax, whichever is greater. A nonresident individual may elect to be taxed with reference to his or her worldwide income. See item 14 regarding residency in Pakistan.

Companies, including branches of foreign companies not resident in Pakistan, are taxed at the same rates as resident companies (see item 1). A 15% tax is withheld from gross dividends paid to a foreign company unless a different rate is specified in a double tax treaty.

18. Special Withholding Provisions

Any person responsible for paying to a nonresident any sum chargeable under the provisions of the income tax law must withhold tax at the maximum rate (presently 50%) at the time of payment. A lower withholding rate would apply provided a certificate from the Income-Tax Officer is obtained by the assessee or a double tax agreement so specifies.

However, effective July 1, 1987 branches of foreign banks are exempt from deduction of tax on any payments made to them by way of return on finance.

It has also been made obligatory on a payor to deduct tax at 20% from all payments of "fees for technical services."

19. Tax Treaties

See item 5.

20. Other Matters

Interest Payable to Nonresidents.   Interest payments to nonresidents are exempt from withholding tax in the case of certain domestic and foreign loans approved by the Pakistan government provided the interest rate and repayment terms are reasonable. Qualifying loans include loans on approved projects which result in foreign exchange earnings or savings greater than the debt servicing costs, private loans for approved new industrial projects in Pakistan, and foreign loans to Pakistani industrial enterprises to purchase equipment manufactured abroad.

OTHER SIGNIFICANT TAXES

21. Sales (Value Added)

Sales tax is generally levied at 12.5% on manufactured goods and on the landed cost of imported goods. A total exemption is available on certain listed items.

Excise Duties. Excise duties are generally levied at 15% on specified goods manufactured in Pakistan and specified services provided or rendered in Pakistan. The Government has the power to declare any goods or class of goods exempt from such duty.

23. Taxes on Payrolls (Social Security)

There are a number of social laws, for example, Employees Old Age Benefits Act, Employees Social Security Ordinance, Workers Children (Education) Ordinance, and so forth. The payments under these laws are insignificant and generally apply to employees earning less than Rs.1,500 per month.

25. Other Taxes

Land and Property. Taxes are levied at varying rates by municipalities on the value of land and property situated within their boundaries.

Wealth Tax. Tax is payable under the Wealth Tax Act, 1963, on the "net wealth," (the aggregate value of all assets belonging to the assessee on the valuation date as reduced by the aggregate value of all debts owed by the taxpayer). Certain assets are specifically exempt as are assets on which Zakat (Islamic tax on assets) has been levied.

Zakat (Islamic Tax). Zakat is levied at 2.5% on certain specified assets with the object of assisting the needy and the poor but this tax applies only to a Muslim citizen of Pakistan and to a company in which the majority of shares are owned by such citizens.

COMPUTATION OF TAXABLE INCOME

26. Capital Gains

Chargeable capital gains (see items 3 and 10) are determined by deducting the following from the consideration received for transfer of the capital asset:

☐ Expenditure incurred wholly and exclusively in connection with such transfer.

☐ Cost of acquisition and of any improvements.

Any capital loss exceeding Rs.5,000, other than a loss incurred during the exemption period, may be carried forward to offset capital gains for six years.

27. Depreciation and Depletion

Depreciation recorded in the financial statements is not allowed for tax purposes. Instead, depreciation allowances are given on assets, such as buildings, plant and machinery, furniture, etc., owned by the assessee and used for business purposes. Hence, the assessee must use the assets purchased for business purposes during the assessment year if he wishes to obtain the depreciation allowance.

Depreciation is calculated on the reducing-balance method at the following rates:

Buildings	5%
Residential quarters for laborers	10%
Plant and machinery	10%

There are several specific types of plant and machinery for which different rates apply. Motor vehicles are depreciated on the reducing-balance method at the rate of 20% subject to the provision that the cost of vehicle is deemed to not exceed Rs.600,000. Depreciation also is available on plant and machinery given on lease by a scheduled bank, financial institution, or leasing company approved by the Central Board of Revenue.

28. Treatment of Dividends

Dividend income is included in the recipient's income tax return. The rates of tax on dividend income received by companies are in item 1. Effective July 1, 1991, dividends received by other taxpayers are taxed at 10%.

29. Loss Carryovers

Unabsorbed business losses are allowed to be carried forward and set off against future profits of the same business for a maximum period of six years. However, the element of unabsorbed depreciation included in the business loss is allowed to be carried forward indefinitely against future profits.

Each company is a separate entity for tax purposes. There are no provisions for filing consolidated returns and for group relief. It should, however, be noted that subject to certain conditions too numerous to enumerate, a quoted company is allowed to offset the current losses, excluding depreciation allowances, of its wholly owned subsidiary against its current profits for three years.

30. Transactions between Related Parties

Where a person acquires a capital asset from an assessee directly or indirectly connected to him, and the Income Tax Officer has reason to believe that the transfer was effected with the object of avoiding or reducing the liability of the assessee, the fair market value of the capital asset on the date of the transfer shall be deemed to be the consideration received by the assessee for its transfer.

31. Consolidation of Income

Except in special cases (see item 29), the income of each taxpayer is computed separately and classified under different headings and the aggregate amount of the income so computed is charged to tax at the rate applicable to the taxpayer.

32. Tax Periods

See item 13.

33. Other Matters

Nondeductible Items. The following amounts are, inter alia, not deductible in computing the taxpayer's (including corporations) total income:

☐ Any sum paid to a nonresident on account of interest, brokerage, or commission or any other sum chargeable under the provisions of Income Tax Ordinance, 1979, if the tax due thereon has not been paid or deducted at source.

☐ Expenditures incurred by an assessee in providing perquisites, allowances, or other benefits to any employee in excess of 50% of his salary before such perquisites.

☐ Head office expenditure of a nonresident assessee in excess of such limits as may be prescribed.

☐ Any sum paid on account of salaries unless tax thereon has been paid or deducted at source.

A ceiling is fixed for the deduction of salaries of directors of companies (other than public companies as defined in item 1) at the lower of the following:

☐ 40% of the total income of the company before charging the aggregate salaries of directors.

☐ Rs.30,000 per month per director.

RELATED CONSIDERATIONS

34. Incentives and Grants

The Government has given complete tax holidays for three, five, and eight years, depending on location, to companies engaged in industrial activities that are set up between December 1990 and June 1995.

Subject to certain conditions, where the total income of the taxpayer includes any income derived from the export of goods manufactured in Pakistan, rebate in respect of super tax and income tax is allowed at 50% of the tax attributable to export sales. Effective July 1, 1987 the Central Board of Revenue may specify varying rates of export rebate for goods manufactured in Pakistan.

Where a company registered in Pakistan and having its registered office in Pakistan repatriates to Pakistan any income chargeable to tax under the head "income from business or profession" which is derived from its construction work outside Pakistan, no supertax (as shown in item 1) is payable on such income.

Income derived by a taxpayer from the business of poultry farming, fishing, cattle or sheep breeding, and dairy farming is not subject to tax up to June 30, 1988. Thereafter, businesses established prior to June 30, 1988 can obtain exemption for a period of five years from the date of establishing the business.

35. Exchange Controls

Exchange control in Pakistan is administered under the provisions of the Foreign Exchange Regulation Act, 1947 and the notifications issued thereunder. Remittances of dividends by companies and profits by branches are allowed to the foreign shareholder and the head office, respectively, provided prior approval is obtained from the State Bank of Pakistan.

36. Investment Restrictions on Nonresidents

The Government has issued a list establishing the areas in which foreign investment is prohibited, e.g., agricultural land, forestry, insurance, health, etc.

For setting up industries, Government permission is required in all cases if projects cost over Rs.1,000 million. However for industries on the specified list, which covers arms and ammunition, security printing, currency and mint, high explosives, radioactive substances, alcohol and beverage industry based on imported concentrates, manufacturers of automobiles, tractors and farm machinery, and petroleum-blending plants, Government permission is required even if the investment is below Rs.1,000 million.

If an industry is set up that requires Government approval or a branch office is to be opened in Pakistan, permission must be obtained from the Investment Promotion Bureau (IPB). For this purpose, an application must be made to the IPB, which is then circulated to the various ministries and the State Bank of Pakistan for comments. If there is no objection from any of the agencies, the IPB issues a letter of sanction and approval.

37. Other Matters

No person resident in Pakistan can, except with the permission of the State Bank of Pakistan, make any payment to or for the credit of any person resident outside Pakistan, nor may he receive, other than through an authorized dealer, any payment by order, or on behalf of, any person resident outside Pakistan.

A national of a foreign country cannot work in Pakistan unless he holds a valid work permit issued by the Government.

Any agreement for the payment of interest, royalty, or a technical assistance fee by a Pakistan company to a foreign incorporated company is subject to the prior approval of the I.P.B. unless it meets certain standard terms and conditions specified by the State Bank of Pakistan.

SELECTION OF BUSINESS ENTITY BY NONRESIDENTS

Nonresidents can operate in Pakistan by forming a company or a branch. There is no difference in the tax levied on a company or a branch of a foreign company. However, at the time of remitting dividends to a foreign company, tax is withheld at the rate of 15% of the gross dividend unless a different rate is specified in the double tax treaty, while no tax is withheld from profits remitted by branches of a foreign company. On the other hand, rebates in supertax and reduced rates of tax on income from dividends are available to companies (see item 1).

PANAMA

INCOME TAXES ON CORPORATIONS

1. Rates

The corporation tax rates are as follows:

Taxable Income		Tax on	Percentage
Over	Not Over	Lower Amount	on Excess
US$ 0	US$ 30,000	US$ 0	20%
30,000	100,000	6,000	30
100,000	500,000	27,000	45
500,000		207,000	50

Preferential Income Tax for Companies. Companies operating in the Colon Free Zone are subject to special income tax rates. For tax purposes, the operating income is categorized as either local, foreign, or direct operations and the income tax is determined as follows:

Local Operation Rates. The rates for local operation are the standard rates for corporations as noted above.

Foreign Operation Rates (Colon Free Zone Only).

Taxable Income		Tax on	Percentage
Over	Not Over	Lower Amount	on Excess
US$ 0	US$ 15,000	US$ 0	2.5%
15,000	30,000	375	4.0
30,000	100,000	975	6.0
100,000		5,175	8.5

Direct Operations. This refers to transactions where the physical movement of goods takes place abroad without landing in Panamanian territory, but the billing is made in Panama. The profit generated from such direct operations is tax-exempt.

2. Local Income Taxes

There are no state or provincial income taxes in the Republic of Panama, but municipal taxes are in force for corporations operating in Panama. These taxes are based on the volume of sales.

3. Capital Gains Taxes

Capital gains on the sale of stock and other securities are exempt from tax if the securities are issued by companies registered with the National Securities Commission; otherwise, gains are taxed at normal rates.

Capital gains on the sale of real estate are subject to special treatment. Once the real estate profit has been established, it is divided into the number of complete years the property had been owned (the beginning and ending dates are the Public Register inscription dates). The result of this division is added to the taxable income from other sources of the year in which the real estate gain is being reported. Based on this total, a tax computation is made and, from this computation, an effective tax rate is obtained. This rate is applied to the profit generated from real estate operations only to obtain the actual tax liability.

Preceding this calculation, a minimum tax of 2% of the higher of the sales price or the registered value of the property in the Public Register must be paid. This 2% constitutes an advance tax and is credited to the actual tax computed as above.

4. Branch Profits Taxes

Branches of foreign corporations are taxed on the profits of the branch at the same rates as Panamanian corporations.

5. Foreign Tax Reliefs

There is no tax relief for taxes incurred in territories outside the Republic of Panama, but all income received from foreign countries is exempt from tax in Panama.

8. Other Matters

Interest Income. Interest income from loans to foreign borrowers (offshore loans) is tax-exempt provided the borrower does not invest the loan proceeds within Panamanian territory and does not receive taxable income in Panama (see also item 34).

Reinsurance. Reinsurance companies may have income from local sources as well as from offshore sources. The premiums generated from reinsurance activities of foreign risks are not subject to taxes. Profits generated from reinsurance of foreign risks are not subject to income tax. For the purpose of determining taxable income, the following are deductible:

□ Technical reserves legally admitted.

□ Reserves for losses incurred, claims pending, and payments being transacted.

□ Reserves for catastrophes or contingent risks, and other reserves, authorized by the National Reinsurance Commission.

International Maritime Commerce. Profits from international maritime commerce are not considered taxable income for companies registered as Panamanian.

INCOME TAXES ON INDIVIDUALS

9. Rates

Citizens and residents of Panama are taxed on income derived from sources in Panama, except dividends which are subject to only a 10% withholding tax. No tax is levied on the first US$1,000 of taxable income and the maximum rate is 56% which applies to taxable income over US$200,000. The tax rates in the following table are applied to income after deducting exemptions for a single person of US$600, US$1,000 for a married couple, and US$150 for each dependent.

| Taxable Income | | Tax on | Percentage |
Over	Not Over	Lower Amount	on Excess
US$ 1,000	US$ 2,000	US$ 25	3.5%
2,000	3,000	60	5.0
3,000	4,000	110	6.0
4,000	5,000	170	7.5
5,000	6,000	245	9.0
6,000	8,000	335	11.0
8,000	10,000	555	13.0
10,000	15,000	815	17.0
15,000	20,000	1,665	19.5
20,000	30,000	2,640	22.0
30,000	40,000	4,840	26.0
40,000	50,000	7,440	30.0
50,000	60,000	10,440	34.0
60,000	70,000	13,840	37.0
70,000	80,000	17,540	41.0
80,000	90,000	21,640	44.0
90,000	100,000	26,040	48.0
100,000	200,000	30,840	52.0
200,000		82,840	56.0

"In-kind" salaries (i.e., salaries assumed by companies on behalf of their executives, such as rent and living allowances) are included in taxable income.

10. Local Income Taxes

None.

11. Capital Gains Taxes

Those capital gains realized by individuals that are subject to tax are taxable at normal rates. Capital gains on real estate are subject to the special treatment described in item 3.

12. Foreign Tax Reliefs

There is no tax relief for taxes incurred in territories outside the Republic of Panama, as all income received from foreign countries is exempt from tax in the Republic of Panama.

INCOME TAXES ON NONRESIDENTS

15. Liability to Tax

For tax purposes, a person living in the Republic during a fiscal year for over 180 days, whether or not continuously, is considered a resident, and a nonresident is any person living in Panama for up to 180 days. Nonresidents are liable for tax on income derived from property situated in the Republic of Panama or from any trade carried on in the Republic of Panama. A nonresident individual is taxable on 80% of his gross revenue earned at the rate of 8% (effective rate of 6.4% of gross income). In addition, an educational tax is payable at the rate of 2.75% of the full gross income.

Income received by individuals having a "special temporary visitor's visa" is taxed at normal rates for individuals, prorated by the number of days worked in each fiscal year. This special visa is granted only to foreign executives hired by corporations to work in Panama for a specific term.

A nonresident whose stay in Panama exceeds 60 days will also be subject to social security withholding (see item 23).

All persons, individuals, and corporations who remit to or credit the accounts of persons abroad with any kind of taxable income are required to withhold, at the time of payment or crediting, taxes resulting from the application of tax rates. The amounts withheld must be paid to the Government within ten days following the payment or credit.

16. Rates

Taxable income for remittance abroad is determined as follows. Interest, commissions, and remuneration for personal services (salaries, wages, and fees) remitted abroad is 100% taxable. Royalties, rent, and other types of income not specified in the Fiscal Code or regulations are 50% taxable. Taxable income so determined is subject to the applicable corporate or individual tax rates.

19. Tax Treaties

None.

OTHER SIGNIFICANT TAXES

21. Sales (Value Added)

A 5% tax is levied on all sales, except those for medicine, food, gasoline, and services. Hotel accommodations are subject to a 10% tourism tax. A 5% tax is charged on all types of leasing agreements except for real estate properties and capital leases.

23. Taxes of Payrolls (Social Security)

Monthly national insurance contributions are payable by individual employees (withheld) and by employers, as follows:

Contribution	Individuals	Employers
Social Security	7.25%	10.75%
Educational	1.25	1.50
Professional risks		0.56 to 5.67

Payroll taxes are imposed on "in kind" salaries to the extent of 20% of the employee's cash compensation.

25. Other Taxes

Franchise Tax. National and foreign companies registered in the Public Register as a corporation (sociedad anonima) must pay an annual franchise tax of US $150. The tax is due within three months after the anniversary date of the articles of incorporation, and is deductible for income tax purposes.

Land and Property Taxes. Taxes on property are levied as rates by local authorities. The rates are normally paid by the owner and are based on the value of the property. Payment is made quarterly. New properties are exempt for the first ten years.

Property Value		
Over	Not Over	Tax
US$ 0	US$10,000	0%
10,000	20,000	1.40
20,000	50,000	1.75
50,000	75,000	1.95
75,000		2.10

License Tax. A 1% license tax is paid annually by all corporations and individuals engaged in a trade or business, except those exempted by specific laws (e.g., certain leasing activities, educational institutions, and professional activities). The tax is based on the individual's or corporation's annual net worth, and varies from a minimum of US$10 up to US$20,000. Payables to a home-office are considered net worth.

Banking Operations Tax. Banks are taxed depending on the type of license granted. Tax is nominal and payable within the first three months of each year. Taxes are as follows:

General License Banks	US$25,000
International License Banks	US$15,000
Exchange Houses	US$660

Insurance Operations Tax. Insurance companies are charged with an operation tax based on the total assets as of December 31st of each year. Taxes are as follows:

Assets	
US$5 million or less	US$10,000
US$5 million to US$9,999,999	US$20,000
US$10 million and more	US$25,000

Finance Companies Tax. Finance companies (involved in consumer loans operations) are taxed at 2.5% based on the paid-in capital as of December 31st of each year. Tax will not exceed US$12,500 and is payable during the first three months of the following year.

Shipping Agencies Tax. Shipping agencies are taxed at 6% on the total services rendered and billed to ships in Panamanian territory. Tax excludes reimbursable expenses and local shipping. Payment is due within the first 15 days of each month.

COMPUTATION OF TAXABLE INCOME

26. Capital Gains

The taxable gain is the difference between the cost of the asset and the proceeds of the sale. In the case of real estate, taxable gain is the difference between the sales price and basic cost (acquisition cost or assessed value or net book value of properties used for commercial purposes); less expenses incurred (such as realtor commissions and legal and notarial fees); less an allowance of 10% of the basic cost multiplied by the number of full years the property has been owned. This 10% allowance cannot exceed the profit on the sale. For tax purposes, when more than one transaction occurs during the same fiscal year, losses can be used to offset gains to determine the taxable gain on real estate.

27. Depreciation and Depletion

Depreciation is based on the estimated useful life of the asset, which cannot exceed the depreciation rates set forth in the income tax law. Depreciation can be computed, at the election of the taxpayer, using the following methods:

☐ The straight-line method.
☐ The declining balance method.
☐ The sum of the year's digits.

Accelerated depreciation may be granted upon request. The following are examples of the maximum depreciation rates allowed for tax purposes:

Buildings	
Concrete	2.5%
Wood	5%
Office equipment	
Metal	7%
Wood	10%
Transportation equipment	
Automobiles, buses, trucks, and trailers	15%
Motorcycles and bicycles	25%
Other vehicles	10%
Industrial machinery and equipment	
Used in food processing, plastic products, metallurgy, furniture and glass	7.5%
Used in refining sugar and oil, alcoholic beverages, tobacco, vegetable oil and grain processing	5%
Other industries	8.5%
Tools and minor equipment	25%

28. Treatment of Dividends

Withholding tax of 10% is deducted from dividends paid by any company in the Republic of Panama, except for bearer shares, which are subject to a 20% withholding rate.

If a Panamanian company does not declare a dividend at the end of the fiscal year, it should pay a 4% dividend tax in advance on the net profit after tax. This tax is recovered proportionately upon the next dividend distribution. Branches of foreign companies must pay the 10% tax even though the profits have not been repatriated to the home office. The fact that 10% is paid on 100% of the current year's profits makes possible automatic repatriation.

For companies established in the Colon Free Zone, dividends paid from profits earned from outside operations are exempt from any withholding requirement.

29. Loss Carryovers

Tax regulations in Panama require that each year be considered independent for income tax purposes. Therefore, operating losses cannot be carried over to other years, unless the right to carry losses forward has been granted in a special contract by government authorities.

30. Transactions between Related Parties

Transactions between related parties must take place as if they transpired between unrelated parties. The tax authorities will allocate income between related companies so as to reflect arm's length prices, if necessary.

31. Consolidation of Income

In the Republic of Panama, a consolidated tax return is not permitted for a group of related companies. Each member of the group is considered independent for income tax purposes.

32. Tax Periods

The normal accounting period is the calendar year. However, the right to use a different fiscal year may be granted upon request.

RELATED CONSIDERATIONS

34. Incentives and Grants

Exempt Income.   All income received from foreign countries is exempt from tax. Income received in the nature of interest on time deposits, savings accounts, and government securities is also exempt. Interest income from loans made to the government and governmental institutions and agencies is exempt from tax. Income generated from commercial tree operations is exempt from tax provided the sprouts have been sown during a seven-year period beginning in March 1986.

Farm producers with gross income of US$100,000 or less are exempt from tax. When gross income exceeds US$100,000, producers can deduct from net taxable income an amount equivalent to the average interest rate on time deposits (determined by the National Banking Commission) plus 3% of the capital invested in the activity.

Special Grants or Allowances.   There are no special incentives given to foreign investors that are not also available to Panamanian companies. However, the Colon Free Zone in the Republic of Panama allows a preferential income tax rate to all companies operating there (see item 1). Transactions between companies established in this zone are treated as part of the companies' foreign operations. This benefit was created by a transitory note which has been effective since 1984.

Banks may benefit from a preferential interest regime on certain mortgage loans. The regime provides that banks can obtain a fiscal credit for the first 10 years of the loan based upon the difference between the "reference rate" (indicated every three months by the National Banking Commission) and the interest rate assigned to each mortgage loan subject to the law. The credit is transferable, applicable to any national tax, and the proceeds are tax-exempt if sold or transferred.

Export Incentive. Exporters of non-traditional products (companies or individuals) may obtain on request to the Treasury Ministry a Certificate of Tax Credit (CAT) equivalent to 20% of the aggregate value of the goods exported. Such certificate can be used to pay any direct national tax or import duties. The certificates are nominative, transferable by endorsement, tax-exempt, and pay no interest.

Investment Incentives. Incentives are offered for investments in tourism and exports. Manufacturing and assembly operations (for export and re-export) both in the city of Panama and Colon, and in some specific districts in the interior, are covered by special incentive law.

The incentives include income tax exemption, accelerated depreciation, loss carry forwards, and exemption from import duties for machinery, equipment, raw materials, and spare parts. Companies qualifying for these incentives should be registered with the Ministry of Commerce and Industry. Exemptions are granted for a period of ten years and thereafter renewed annually.

35. Exchange Controls

None.

36. Investment Restrictions on Nonresidents

Nonresidents may not engage in retail businesses in Panama.

PAPUA NEW GUINEA

INCOME TAXES ON CORPORATIONS

1. Rates

The rate of income tax for corporations incorporated in Papua New Guinea for the year ended December 31, 1991 is 30%. Corporations that are not resident in Papua New Guinea will, for the year ended December 31, 1991, pay income tax at the rate of 48% on their Papua New Guinea-source income. Resident corporations deriving assessable income from mining operations are taxed at 35% (nonresidents at 48%) on the income. Resident and nonresident corporations deriving assessable income from petroleum operations are taxed at 50% on such income. Unit trusts are taxed at 41.9%, subject to certain requirements.

Normal corporation income includes dividend income, but resident corporations receive a rebate of income tax on dividend income (net of related expenses) from other corporations whether resident or nonresident in Papua New Guinea.

Property rental income from Papua New Guinea or overseas is subject to a surcharge of 10% of the income tax attributable to net property income.

2. Local Income Taxes

None.

3. Capital Gains Tax

The capital gains tax proposed in the 1988 Budget was not enacted and has been indefinitely deferred.

However, the existing law provides that the assessable income of a taxpayer includes any profit arising on sale of property, or any profit arising from the carrying out of a profit-making enterprise.

There is also a "specific gains" tax which applies to sales of shares by a shareholder who, with associated persons, owns or has owned 20% or more of the issued share capital of a company. The taxable gain is the lesser of:

☐ The sale consideration less the paid-up value of the shares.

☐ The dividend entitlement of the shares (assuming all revenue reserves are distributed).

The gain is taxed at 17%. The purchaser is obliged to notify the Chief Collector of Taxes and to withhold tax from the consideration payable.

4. Branch Profits Tax

Nonresident corporations are taxable on Papua New Guinea-source income at the rate of 48%. No withholding or remittance taxes are levied on branch profits which have suffered income tax.

5. Foreign Tax Reliefs

A resident corporation is entitled to a credit in respect of foreign tax paid on income other than dividends, but the credit allowable is not to exceed the average rate of Papua New Guinea tax payable on the foreign source income. There is no relief for underlying tax.

6. Classification of Corporations

Corporations are classified for Papua New Guinea tax purposes as resident or nonresident corporations, and as public or private corporations.

A resident corporation is one which is incorporated in Papua New Guinea or, if not incorporated in Papua New Guinea, carries on business in Papua New Guinea and has either:

☐ Its central management and control in Papua New Guinea.

☐ Its voting power controlled by shareholders who are residents of Papua New Guinea.

Resident corporations are taxable on worldwide income. Nonresident corporations are subject to tax only on their Papua New Guinea-source income.

A public corporation is, broadly, one in which either shares are listed on a stock exchange and the 20 largest shareholders have less than 50% of voting rights or dividend entitlement, or the corporation is ultimately controlled by such a public corporation or public corporations.

Private corporations are subject to the following provisions:

☐ A dividend may be deemed to have been paid on noncommercial loans, gifts, excessive remuneration, and other benefits provided to a director, shareholder, or other associated person of the company.

☐ Dividend withholding tax credits are recoverable only on payment of a dividend (see item 28).

☐ Superannuation fund distributions exceeding a prescribed scale are taxed at the full rates (see item 9).

7. Payment of Taxes

Corporate income tax is assessed and paid in the year following the income year. If notified by the Taxation Office, corporations pay "notional tax" based on income of the year preceding the income year but may elect to pay by three equal install-ments, on March 31, June 30, and September 30. The corporation may elect to reduce notional tax, but any underestimate of the final tax liability may be penalized. Any balance of income tax is due on the later of September 30 or 30 days after assessment. Notional tax for 1991 is, therefore, based on 1990 income; income tax is based on 1990 income; and both are payable in 1991.

INCOME TAXES ON INDIVIDUALS

9. Rates

Individuals resident in Papua New Guinea are taxed on their worldwide income. The resident individual income tax rates for the year ended December 31, 1991 are:

Taxable Income	Tax	Percentage on Excess
K 2,400	K 0	15%
4,000	240	20
6,000	640	25
8,000	1,140	30
10,000	1,740	35
12,000	2,440	40
15,000	3,640	45

Residents are entitled to concessional rebates in respect of up to six dependents, as follows:

☐ 1st dependent   15% of gross tax assessed with a minimum of K45 and a maximum of K375

☐ 2nd, 3rd, and 4th dependents 10% of gross tax assessed with a minimum of K30 and a maximum of K250 per dependent

☐ 5th and 6th dependents   10% of gross tax assessed with a minimum of K30 per dependent; available only to a taxpayer with taxable income less than K4,000 in the year

Withholding tax on dividend income is creditable against income tax for residents but is a final tax on nonresidents. Salary or wage income is taxed separately (see below) but is used to determine the income tax rates on other income.

Property rental income from Papua New Guinea or overseas is subject to a surcharge of 10% of the income tax attributable to net property income after de-ducting any dependents and salary or wages rebates.

A provisional tax is payable on all non-salary or wages income, based on the estimated tax payable on such income. The tax is payable no earlier than September

30th of the year of income and is credited in the assessment of that year's income which is issued in the following year.

Salary or wages tax applies to all salary or wage income of a resident and to such income of a nonresident for all services performed in Papua New Guinea, irrespective of the residence of the employer and the place of payment. This tax incorporates the following features:

☐ The tax is assessed by employer deductions from the fortnightly (two-weeks) equivalent of the annual salary.

☐ The tax tables incorporate a K200 annual expense deduction. Expenses in excess of K200 may be subject to a 30% rebate, to be claimed after the year-end.

☐ Deductions of tax are final and may not be adjusted by applying the income tax rates to salary or wage income for the year. Thus, taxpayers with only salary or wage income are not required to lodge tax returns.

☐ Salary or wages includes any payment substantially for personal services, such as to a freelance consultant.

☐ The fortnightly equivalent of the dependents' rebate is allowed to residents against their fortnightly tax.

☐ Salary or wages includes certain benefits paid by the employer at values determined by the Taxation Office, such as electricity, accommodations up to a fortnightly maximum of K126, and motor vehicles up to a fortnightly maximum of K60. Other benefits are tax-free, including school fees and annual leave fares.

☐ A special 2% tax rate applies to gratuities paid on the third anniversary of the employment contract or last gratuity payment, and on termination of employment. This 2% rate applies to gratuities of up to 25% of salary and wage income taxed at the full rates. On termination of employment, the 2% rate also applies to payments for accrued annual leave (provided the contract entitlement does not exceed six weeks a year), superannuation fund distributions not exceeding certain limits, long service leave accrued at not more than six months for 15 years of service (provided the employee has served at least six years), and court compensation.

Tax-efficient employment conditions, particularly for expatriate staff, are an important consideration for businesses operating in Papua New Guinea.

10. Local Income Taxes

None.

11. Capital Gains Tax

Same as item 3.

12. Foreign Tax Reliefs

Resident individuals are entitled to credits in respect of foreign tax deducted or paid by them in respect of foreign source dividend or other income. The credit is limited to the average rate of Papua New Guinea tax suffered in the year.

13. Tax Period

The financial year for all taxpayers is January 1 to December 31, unless otherwise permitted by the authorities.

INCOME TAXES ON NONRESIDENTS

15. Liability to Tax

A nonresident individual pays Papua New Guinea income tax on all Papua New Guinea-source income at the rates given in item 9.

Property rental income from Papua New Guinea or overseas is subject to a surcharge of 10% of the income tax attributable to net property income after deducting salary or wages rebates.

16. Rates

Nonresident corporations are taxed on their Papua New Guinea-source income at 48%, but note the exceptions in items 17 and 18. Nonresident corporations are not entitled to dividend rebates.

A nonresident individual pays income tax on all Papua New Guinea-source income. The nonresident individual tax rates for the year ended December 31, 1991 are:

Taxable Income	Tax	Percentage on Excess
K 0	K 0	15%
1,600	240	20
3,600	640	25
5,600	1,140	30
7,600	1,740	35
9,600	2,440	40
12,600	3,640	45

17. Withholding Tax Rates

Dividend withholding tax at 17% is a final tax on all dividends (other than dividends paid out of income derived from petroleum) paid or credited to nonresidents. Dividends paid to nonresidents by petroleum mining companies are exempt from income tax and dividend withholding tax to the extent they are paid out of income from petroleum.

Interest paid or credited by a corporation to a nonresident is taxable at the nonresident rates of 48% if it relates to:

☐ The use or lodgement at interest of money in Papua New Guinea.

☐ The acquisition of assets for use or disposal in Papua New Guinea.

The tax is assessed on and may be deducted by the payer. No tax is payable if the payee can enforce payment without tax deduction. However, the lender may still have an income tax liability if the interest income has a source in Papua New Guinea. If interest is paid to a nonresident in respect to borrowings secured by property in Papua New Guinea and the security document is issued in Papua New Guinea, the interest is subject to income tax in Papua New Guinea.

Royalties paid to a nonresident by a resident or by a nonresident with a permanent establishment in Papua New Guinea are taxable as follows:

☐ 30% of gross payments if paid to an associated person.

☐ The lesser of 10% of gross or 48% of net royalty income if paid to a nonassociated person.

The taxpayer also is subject to applicable double tax treaties (see item 19).

Royalties are widely defined to include payments for know how or forebearance from exercising a right. Permanent establishment includes a place of installation of machinery or equipment and a construction project. The payer must seek Taxation Office clearance before making a royalty payment to a nonresident or he may render himself liable for the tax. There also is a 5% withholding tax on mining, petroleum, timber, and fishing royalties to landowners.

Lease payments paid by a resident taxpayer to a nonresident associate for the lease of equipment may not be fully deductible. The deduction is limited to an amount equivalent to the depreciation on a diminishing value (from January 1, 1990 only) or, at the taxpayer's option, prime cost basis and an amount for notional interest based on the long-term bond rate on a loan equal to the cost of the equipment had the resident taxpayer purchased the asset. Similarly, the total deduction over the term of the lessee is limited to the cost of the leased asset and the notional interest.

A 17% withholding tax applies to management fees paid to nonresidents.

There is a system of tax collection for persons engaged in certain industries (business income payees) and for persons making eligible payments (paying authorities). The affected industries are:

Building and construction	Security
Road transport	Cleaning and maintenance
Motor vehicle repairs	Advertising
Joinery and cabinet making	Entertainment
Architecture	Consultancy
Engineering	Sign writing
Surveying	

A paying authority is required to deduct and remit to the Taxation Office 17% of the gross amount of the payment, and the business income payee furnishes a Business Income Declaration. Business income payees may obtain a Nil Deduction Authority, in which case this is presented to the paying authorities and payments may be made free of deductions. If there is no declaration, a paying authority is required to deduct and remit 20% of the gross payment.

18. Special Withholding Provisions

Special provisions apply to deem a Papua New Guinea source and notional taxable income and to impose clearance procedures on income derived by nonresidents in the following classes of business:

□ Foreign Contractors. All nonresident contractors (other than individuals operating in their own name) undertaking installation and construction projects or providing associated consultancy services in Papau New Guinea, as well as equipment lease and charter payments to nonresidents, are subject to tax. They are taxed on a deemed taxable income equal to 25% of gross contract income, which is taxed at 48%. The 48% rate applies to all foreign contractors, including non-corporate contractors.

Alternatively, the foreign contractor may elect to be taxed on actual taxable income. In this situation, the amount deductible for general administration and management expenses (other than expenses relating directly to the derivation of the Papua New Guinea income) shall not exceed the lesser of:

—5% of the gross income from the contract; or

—the same proportion of worldwide general administration and management expenses as gross income from the contract bears to worldwide income.

The Papua New Guinea contracting entity must provide the Taxation Office with a copy of a relevant contract within 14 days of its signature and ensure that satisfactory arrangements have been made to pay the foreign contractor's tax before making any payment to the foreign contractor.

□ Shipping. Deemed taxable income is 5% of gross receipts from carrying outbound freight and passengers.

□ Insurance and Reinsurance of Property in or Risks limited to Papua New Guinea. Deemed taxable income is 10% of gross premiums; alternatively, the payer may forego a tax deduction. A tax rate of either 48% or 30% would apply to this deemed taxable income depending on whether the nonresident insurer is an incorporated or unincorporated entity.

□ Film Business. Income derived by a nonresident from a film business in Papua New Guinea will in most cases be subject to the foreign contractor's withholding tax of 12%. Alternatively, the income may be subject to a royalties tax of 10%, or 30% if the recipient is an associated person.

☐ Unit Trusts. Distributions of income to unit trust holders will be subject to a 30% withholding tax.

In some cases it is possible to obtain exemption from the withholding provisions if the payee undertakes to lodge tax returns and pay tax on the normal basis.

19. Tax Treaties

The double taxation treaties with Australia and Canada have been in effect since January 1, 1990. Negotiations are currently in progress for treaties with Germany, New Zealand, Singapore, the United Kingdom, and the United States.

OTHER SIGNIFICANT TAXES

21. Sales (Value Added)

Sales taxes are imposed by all provincial governments on retail sales of various goods and services, including beer, spirits, tobacco products, gasoline and tires at rates of 2.5% to 7.5%.

22. Inheritance and Gift Taxes

There is no inheritance tax.

There is no gift tax as such but rates of stamp duty up to 5% are imposed on documents which constitute a deed of gift.

23. Taxes on Payrolls (Social Security)

An employer of 25 or more persons must register with the National Provident Fund, unless operating in an exempt industry (currently certain agricultural sectors) or the employer provides an equivalent superannuation scheme. Membership is compulsory for Papua New Guinea citizen employees working for 60 days in any period of up to three months. Non-citizens may join voluntarily. The rates, as a percentage of gross basic salary (excluding overtime, bonuses, and commissions), are 5% for employees and 7% for employers.

Training Levy. All businesses with an annual payroll exceeding K100,000 are subject to a 2% training levy, effective January 1, 1991, calculated on the taxable salary/wages, including benefits, of all personnel.

Qualifying expenses incurred in training citizen employees are creditable up to the actual amount of the levy.

24. Taxes on Natural Resources

Royalties are payable to the Papua New Guinea government of 1.25% of the export sales value or net smelter returns of mined products, or of net wellhead value of petroleum production. Larger mining corporations operating special mining leases and petroleum extraction corporations are liable to additional profits tax. Broadly, the tax applies to the positive cash flow on a tenement after recovery of initial net outgoings uplifted by interest and currency fluctuation factors. The current rates are 35% for mining operations and 50% for petroleum operations. This tax is in addition to income tax.

25. Other Taxes

Land and Property. The various provinces and municipalities impose an annual tax on the unimproved value of land. An annual rental is also payable to the Government for the occupation of leasehold land.

Stamp Duty. Stamp duties are levied on all deeds, share transfers, and a wide range of other documents. The rates range from 0.1% to 6.5%.

Customs Duties. These are imposed on the CIF value of most imports. There are six rate bands, subject to a few significant exceptions. The rates are nil for rice, tinned fish, medicines, and books; 5% for industrial, agricultural, and fisheries imports; 8% mainly for capital goods; 25% for commercial vehicle parts; 30% for items produced in Papua New Guinea, and 50% for luxury goods. Special higher rates apply for goods such as tobacco and liquor.

Import duty on imports for the manufacturing, agricultural, tourism, and fishing industries have a nil rate of duty, effective January 1, 1991.

Export Taxes. These apply to most exports of natural and primary products.

	Rate
Unprocessed timber:	
Rosewood, kwila, teak, blackbean	40%
Cedar, planchonella	35
Mersawa, tuan, walnut, calophyllum	22
Terminalia, buckela, hopea, glutea	12
Other	9
Fish:	
Prawn	15
Barramundi, crayfish	5
Other	10
Gold:	
Processed and unprocessed aluvial gold	5

Telephone Tax. This is a tax levied on non-citizen subscribers at K52 per line per year.

Manufacturers Excise Tax. Effective January 1, 1991, certain manufacturers are subject to a 3% excise tax. This tax does not apply to exports and is intended to apply to *all* manufacturers as of January 1, 1992.

Departure Tax. There is a tax of K15 levied on persons departing Papua New Guinea.

COMPUTATION OF TAXABLE INCOME

26. Capital Gains

See item 3.

27. Depreciation and Depletion

Plant. Rates of depreciation are based on the estimated lives of the assets, which are established by the tax authorities. Depreciation may be calculated by the reducing-balance or, optionally, the straight-line method. Reducing-balance method rates are automatically 50% higher than straight-line rates.

Buildings. Depreciation is allowed on buildings constructed in Papua New Guinea after December 31, 1960 and used in income earning activities.

The following are examples of straight-line rates:

	Rate
Buildings	2% or 3%
Construction plant	20%
Motor vehicles	20%
Office equipment	10%

Accelerated Depreciation. New plant or property (other than residential property with a cost exceeding K100,000) with a useful life exceeding five years that is used in Papua New Guinea for certain commercial activities qualify for accelerated depreciation at the rate of 20% in the first year of use in addition to the standard annual deduction. Accelerated depreciation is also available at 20% for improvements in fuel efficiency and at 30% for acquisition or conversion to a fuel source other than imported petroleum products. Total deductions for depreciation may not exceed cost. Solar heating equipment may be written off in full in the year of expenditure, with no recovery of the deduction on disposal.

Flexible Depreciation. Any industrial plant not previously used in Papua New Guinea is eligible for increased depreciation in the first year of use of up to 100% of cost, but the allowance may not create a loss for the year. To qualify, the plant must have a useful life exceeding five years and be used in the manufacturing process. Expenditures on buildings to house such plant or for the storage of raw materials or finished products also qualifies for the allowance.

Agriculture and Fishing. Expenditure on new plant or assets acquired after March 4, 1986 that are used in agricultural production or commercial fishing activities qualifies for a 100% initial depreciation deduction. Ships exceeding seven metres in length and their ancillary equipment are specifically excluded.

Mining, Petroleum, and Timber Operations. Expenditure on exploration and development of oils and minerals is amortizable over periods that vary with the circumstances, as are the infrastructural and reforestation costs of a timber operation.

Primary Production. A wide range of capital expenditure in the agricultural, plantation, animal husbandry, and fishing industries may be written off in full as incurred.

28. Treatment of Dividends

Dividend withholding tax of 17% is payable in respect of dividends and deemed dividends paid by resident corporations (see item 6). Dividend withholding tax is also payable in respect of dividends derived by resident corporations from sources outside Papua New Guinea.

Where a dividend is passed successively through a chain of corporations, withholding tax is payable only on the occasion of the first dividend giving rise to the liability, provided the resident corporation receiving the dividend records in its books the gross dividend and the withholding tax liability.

A resident public corporation is entitled to credit the withholding tax on dividend income against other tax liabilities or to obtain a refund after the year-end. Both public and private corporations may credit withholding tax against a withholding tax liability on payment of dividend.

Provincial and local government bodies and corporations wholly owned by these entities are exempt from the payment of dividend withholding tax, as are a wide range of non-commercial institutions. In effect, companies do not pay income tax on dividend income (see item 1). However, dividend income does absorb losses from other sources.

For individuals, the gross amount of the dividend is included in taxable income and a credit is given for the dividend withholding tax suffered.

In the case of unit trusts, if the gross amount of any distribution is included in the assessable income of a unit holder, a full credit is available for the tax deducted.

29. Loss Carryovers

Losses incurred in Papua New Guinea are deductible from total income (including exempt income). Losses incurred in deriving foreign-source income may only be deducted from overseas income. Losses by a corporation are not deductible unless the corporation satisfies the Chief Collector of Taxes that at all times during the year of income and the year in which the loss was incurred not less than 50% of its shares were beneficially owned by the same persons. If this test is not met, the company must show that it carried on the same business during the year of loss recoupment as it carried on immediately prior to the change of shareholding which prevented it meeting the 50% continuity of shareholding test.

Losses of a primary production business may be carried forward indefinitely; other losses expire after seven years.

30. Transactions between Related Parties

There are comprehensive provisions for transactions between related parties and for non-arm's-length international transactions, which may be adjusted to an arm's-length basis.

31. Consolidation of Income

There is no provision for the filing of consolidated tax returns or transfer of losses by related corporations.

32. Tax Periods

The financial year for all taxpayers is January 1 to December 31, unless otherwise permitted by the authorities.

33. Other Matters

Deduction for Taxes Other than Income Tax. In computing the liability for income tax, businesses may deduct land and property taxes and various royalties and rentals. Stamp duty is treated as part of the cost of the goods acquired.

Inventory Valuation. For tax purposes, inventories may be valued at cost, market selling value, or replacement price. A different valuation method may be used for different items of the same class of inventory, at the one-time election of the taxpayer. Provisions for obsolescence or other special circumstances may be allowed with the consent of the Chief Collector of Taxes. Average cost or FIFO is generally used to determine cost. Other methods are available, but the LIFO method is not permitted unless it approximates actual physical flows.

Management Fees. Management fees paid by taxpayers operating in Papua New Guinea are deductible only to the extent of the greater of A or B, where A is the lesser of 10% of assessable income derived from the relevant part of the business or the same proportion of worldwide expenses as Papua New Guinea-source income bears to worldwide income, and B is 15% of the total amount of allowable deductions attributable to the relevant part of the business, excluding management fees. The restriction on deductibility applies to payments by both residents and nonresidents. However, effective January 1, 1990, this restriction does not apply to payments between non-associated persons.

Bad Debts. General provisions for doubtful accounts are not deductible. Bad debts are deductible only in the year they are actually written off. Any recovery after a debt had been written off is included in assessable income.

Provisions.   Provisions for future liabilities (such as leave pay, staff gratuities, and warranties) are not deductible until the relative expenditure falls due for payment or is paid.

Club Fees and Leisure Facilities.   Expenditures for club fees of a recreational nature are not deductible. Monetary gifts with a value of K1,500 or more made by a company to certain sporting bodies are deductible.

South Pacific Games (1991) Foundation.   Gifts of money or property equal to K1,500 or more purchased by the taxpayer in the 12 months preceding the gifting are tax deductible by an amount equal to twice the eligible amount.

Foundation for Law, Order, and Justice.   Gifts of money or property purchased by the taxpayer in the 12 months preceding the gifting are tax deductible.

Prepaid Expenses.   Generally, prepaid expenses are deductible in the years in which the benefit thereof is obtained. Expenditure on goods is deductible when possession is taken.

Petroleum Extraction Companies—Interest Payable.   Interest incurred by a petroleum company after the issue of a development license is deductible only to the extent the company maintains no more than a 2:1 ratio of non-current debt to total shareholder funds.

Exchange Gains and Losses.   Realized business-related exchange losses arising from foreign currency debts or borrowings are deductible to the extent they relate to loans incurred or borrowings undertaken after November 10, 1986.

RELATED CONSIDERATIONS

34. Incentives and Grants

Export Incentives.   Taxpayers who begin to export certain qualifying goods after September 1, 1984, are entitled to treat as exempt income 100% of the net export income attributable to the first four years of export sales. For the following three years the net income relating to the excess of export sales over average export sales of the previous three years is exempt. Taxpayers who commenced exporting prior to September 1, 1984, are entitled to varying levels of exemption depending upon the year in which the exports began. For these provisions to apply the exported goods must have been manufactured by the taxpayer in Papua New Guinea and disposed of by the taxpayer while he was the owner of the goods. Losses on other activities are not reduced by exempt export income.

Wage Subsidy. Companies manufacturing new products may receive a subsidy payment for up to five years based on a percentage of the relevant minimum wage for each full-time employee who is an automatic citizen. The subsidy is itself taxable and constitutes a declining percentage of the relevant statutory minimum wage ranging from 40% in the first year to 10% in year five. To qualify the company must obtain a New Product Manufacturing Certificate from the Chief Collector of Taxes.

Additional Deduction for Export Market Development Costs. A double deduction is allowed for expenditures incurred after September 1, 1984, on export market development. The double deduction is not absorbed by any exempt export sales income. The qualifying expenditures include the costs associated with overseas publicity and advertising, market research, tender preparation, samples, trade fairs, overseas sales offices, and certain travel. The tax savings resulting from the double deduction is limited to 75% of the actual expenditures incurred.

Additional Deduction for Staff Training Costs. Employers are allowed a double deduction, limited to a tax saving of 75% of actual expenditure, for the salaries or wages of registered apprentices, full-time indigenous citizen students at a prescribed college or university, and full-time training officers exclusively engaged in training activities and not engaged directly in deriving the employer's income.

Exempt Interest Income. The first K500 (individuals) or K1,000 (corporations) of interest income received annually by residents from licensed financial institutions within Papua New Guinea is exempt from income tax where the interest is credited after January 1, 1986. This exemption expired on December 31, 1990.

Primary Production. Outright deductions are allowed for certain capital expenditures, including those incurred for clearing, preparing, or conserving land for agriculture, the eradication of pests, labourers' accommodations, and for the conservation and conveyance of water. An initial accelerated depreciation deduction is allowed for new agricultural plant with a life exceeding five years. Losses incurred by a primary production business can be carried forward indefinitely, unrestricted by the seven-year limitation.

Investment in Primary Production. A primary production company that has incurred primary production development expenditures (defined to include the cost of assets used for agricultural production) may surrender its available deduction in favor of its shareholders, in proportion to the amounts of their paid-up capital (paid on or after January 1, 1987.) The total deduction available to a shareholder may not exceed the total amount paid on his shares. A shareholder may waive his entitlement.

Rural Development Incentive. Qualifying new businesses started in certain specified under-developed areas will be exempt from income tax on their net income from carrying out a rural development industry for ten years following the year of commencement of business.

Losses arising from these newly exempt activities will be deductible against taxable income from other activities.

Businesses involved in exploitation of nonrenewable resources (mainly mining and petroleum companies) are specifically excluded from the exemption, and anti-avoidance measures have been introduced to ensure that the incentive is not abused.

Incentive to Pioneer Industries. A person undertaking a new economic activity considered to be of benefit to the country and meeting certain specific criteria may apply for certification as a pioneer industry.

The income of a qualifying activity is exempt from income tax for a period ending on the last day of the fifth year the qualifying activity commenced.

Where a qualifying entity incurs a tax loss in any year during the period of exemption, the loss is carried forward to offset profits subsequent to the period of exemption but not against other profits arising during the period of exemption.

The entity may carry on only the activity for which a certificate of exemption has been issued unless an exemption from this requirement has been granted.

35. Exchange Controls

Exchange controls are administered by the Bank of Papua New Guinea. Routine current account transactions (such as for imports and exports, management fees, and royalties) are often approved by the commercial banks under their delegated authority so long as certain specified conditions are complied with. Investment proposals, transactions on capital account, substantial revenue items, and formal agreements involving foreign exchange may require direct Bank of Papua New Guinea approval, which is readily granted for most transactions. Exports are expected to be at full value and the proceeds to be remitted to Papua New Guinea. Resident businesses borrowing overseas are expected to maintain a 3 to 1 ratio of loans to shareholders' funds, and there is a one-year moratorium on principal repayments; these restrictions do not apply to mineral exploration companies, citizen-owned entities, and export credit funded purchases of capital goods.

Resident corporations will usually be permitted to invest overseas if there will be direct benefits to Papua New Guinea. A permanent resident individual may, with the Bank's permission, remit overseas up to K15,000 a year for portfolio investments in real estate or marketable securities from which any income must be repatriated. Noncitizens resident for up to five years, with no significant business interests and no real estate worth more than K50,000 in Papua New Guinea may remit their own funds overseas without restriction.

36. Investment Restrictions on Nonresidents

All foreign businesses operating in Papua New Guinea were required to be registered with N.I.D.A., a statutory authority set up under the National Investment and

Development Act. In the appraisal of the application for registration consideration was given to many aspects of the proposed new venture including the investor's past record both in Papua New Guinea and overseas, the employment and training opportunities for Papua New Guineans, and the generation of additional Government revenue. Certain activities were exempt from all or part of the registration requirements, for example, minerals and hydrocarbons exploration and enterprises exclusively supplying goods and services to the State or Statutory Bodies. Prior approval by NIDA also was required for a large range of agreements involving foreign exchange to which a foreign-owned enterprise was a party. This requirement was in addition to exchange control approval.

In May of 1991, the N.I.D.A. authority was abolished, and the Investment Promotion Authority was created to replace it. The IPA will adopt a more flexible and incentive-oriented approach. The legislation has been passed to enact this new authority; however, the governing regulations have not yet been announced.

37. Other Matters

Tax Clearance Certificates. Exchange control approval for a wide range of remittances overseas involving funds in excess of K10,000 per-year is dependent on production of a tax clearance certificate issued by the Chief Collector of Taxes. Transactions with a scheduled tax haven require a tax clearance certificate for all such remittances.

SELECTION OF BUSINESS ENTITY BY NONRESIDENTS

Almost all nonresident investors operate in Papua New Guinea either through a branch or by forming a local subsidiary corporation. The tax consequences for a foreign entity that carries on business in Papua New Guinea through a branch are:

☐ Branch profits are taxed at the nonresident rate of 48%.
☐ No additional tax is levied on remittance of branch profits.
☐ The branch will not be entitled to dividend rebates on any PNG-source dividend income, which will therefore be fully taxable.

Most foreign investors, except those undertaking short-term projects, operate through a locally incorporated corporation. Indeed, a locally incorporated corporation may prove more acceptable to Papua New Guinea authorities. The following major tax considerations apply to locally incorporated corporations:

☐ Income tax is payable on the worldwide income of the corporation, including dividends, which are however rebateable (see item 1).

□ Dividend income will have suffered 17% dividend withholding tax and any foreign tax on overseas dividends. The PNG withholding tax is creditable (see item 28), but there is no credit for foreign tax.

□ In practice, there will usually be no tax on interest payments overseas (see item 17).

Even if a locally incorporated corporation distributes all its after-tax profits, its effective rate of tax (income tax and dividend withholding tax) is only 41.9% compared with 48% for a branch operation. There is no requirement for a locally incorporated corporation to pay dividends, but because of exchange control requirements, there may be no other alternative available than to remit surplus funds overseas. If the locally incorporated corporation is private for income tax purposes, loans to its shareholders or related entities may be deemed to be dividends. A shareholder who sells the shares of a locally incorporated corporation with accumulated profits may be required to pay 17% specific gains tax (see item 3).

SPECIMEN TAX COMPUTATION

Information:

□ The corporation's operating profit for the year of K100,000 consists of the following:

Trading results in Papua New Guinea	60,000
Trading results from overseas—taxed in country of derivation (tax paid K3,000)	10,000
Papua New Guinea dividend income—effectively connected with Papua New Guinea operations	10,000
Overseas dividend income	10,000
Capital profit on the sale of a long-term investment	10,000
	K100,000

□ The Papua New Guinea trading results are arrived at after charging the following items:

Accounts depreciation	30,000
Transfer to provisions for employee benefits	20,000

□ Allowable tax depreciation for the year is 20,000.
□ Payments debited to the employee benefits provisions are 10,000.
□ The company has installed plant during the year, which qualifies for the accelerated depreciation allowance, at a cost of 50,000.

Computation:

	Resident Corporation		Nonresident Corporation	
Operating profit as per accounts		K100,000		K100,000
Add				
Accounts depreciation	K30,000		K30,000	
Transfer to provisions for employee benefits	20,000	50,000	20,000	50,000
		K150,000		K150,000
Less				
Tax depreciation	K20,000		K20,000	
Payments debited to provision for employee benefits	10,000		10,000	
Nontaxable capital profit	10,000		10,000	
Exempt income				
Resident				
Nonresident (total overseas income)			20,000	
Accelerated depreciation	10,000	50,000	10,000	70,000
Taxable income		K100,000		K80,000
Primary tax at				
30% (resident)		K 30,000		
48% (nonresident)				K38,400
Less				
Credit for overseas tax paid		3,000		
		K 27,000		K38,400
Less				
Dividend rebate				
(K20,000 at 30%—resident)		6,000		
(K10,000 at 48%—nonresident)				4,800
Tax payable		K21,000		K33,600

PARAGUAY

INCOME TAXES ON CORPORATIONS

1. Rates

Income tax is computed at the following rates:

Taxable Income		Tax on	Percentage
Over	Not Over	Lower Amount	on Excess
₲ 0	₲ 500,000	₲ 0	25%
500,000	1,000,000	125,000	26
1,000,000	2,000,000	255,000	27
2,000,000	3,500,000	525,000	28
3,500,000	5,000,000	945,000	29
5,000,000		1,380,000	30

2. Local Income Taxes

None.

3. Capital Gains Tax

There are no capital gains taxes in Paraguay. Capital gains are treated as ordinary income, except profits arising from the occasional sale of real estate that are taxed at the rate of 5%.

4. Branch Profits Taxes

Branches of foreign corporations are subject to income tax at the rates shown in item 1. In addition, the remittance of profits to the head office is subject to a 10% income tax withholding.

5. Foreign Tax Reliefs

There are no provisions for foreign tax relief. Foreign-source income is not taxable in Paraguay.

INCOME TAXES ON INDIVIDUALS

9. Rates

Individuals are taxed at the following rates:

Taxable Income		Tax on	Percentage
Over	Not Over	Lower Amount	on Excess
₲ 0	₲ 50,000	₲ 0	5%
50,000	100,000	2,500	9
100,000	150,000	7,000	16
150,000	200,000	15,000	22
200,000	250,000	26,000	28
250,000	300,000	40,000	32
300,000	400,000	57,000	31
400,000	500,000	88,000	37
500,000	1,000,000	125,000	26
1,000,000	2,000,000	255,000	27
2,000,000	3,500,000	525,000	28
3,500,000	5,000,000	945,000	29
5,000,000		1,380,000	30

Exemptions. The following items are exempt from income tax in Paraguay:

□ Income from farming.
□ Earned income of employees.
□ Earned income of professionals (unless classified as executive remuneration).

The so-called executive has the alternative of deducting from taxable income the maximum remuneration allowed by law and paying no tax (since the employer covers the tax by taking only a partial deduction for remuneration) or treating all of the remuneration as a deductible expense of the employer (and taxed at the above rates).

Personal Allowances:

□ Personal Allowance	360 Minimum daily salaries
□ Spouse	180 Minimum daily salaries
□ Children and other dependents (each)	60 Minimum daily salaries

Note: Minimum daily salary is equivalent to ₲ 8,165

10. Local Income Taxes

None.

11. Capital Gains Taxes

Profits arising from the occasional sale of real estate are taxed at the rate of 5%.

12. Foreign Tax Reliefs

None.

13. Tax Period

The tax period coincides with the calendar year in most cases, except insurance companies whose period ends June 30.

INCOME TAXES ON NONRESIDENTS

15. Liability to Tax

Only income from Paraguayan sources is taxable.

16. Rates

The remittance of dividends and company (or branch) profits to nonresidents is subject to 10% withholding tax. Fees, commissions, interest, royalties, rents, annuities, partnership profits, directors' emoluments and other items are subject to a 30% withholding tax. This withholding tax is considered a final tax.

19. Tax Treaties

None.

OTHER SIGNIFICANT TAXES

21. Sales (Value Added)

A sales tax is levied on sales at the following rates:

Goods produced in Paraguay	4%
Imported necessities	8%
Imported luxury goods	14%
Services (professional, technical, and others)	4%

Agricultural produce and most food products are exempt from sales tax.

22. Inheritance and Gift Taxes

All transfers of property because of death or as gifts are subject to the following inheritance and gift taxes:

□ Inheritances over G 4,000,000

Between parents, sons, and spouses	15%
Between collaterals up to 2nd grade of consanguinity	25%
Between others	36%

□ Gifts over G 500,000

Between parents, sons, and spouses	10%
Between collaterals up to 2nd grade of consanguinity	12%
Between others	20%

23. Taxes on Payrolls (Social Security)

Employers must contribute 16.5% of gross salaries for social security benefits, and employees are subject to 9.5% withholding for the same purpose. There is no maximum for purposes of these contributions.

Employee Benefits. Various social laws provide for a compulsory legal bonus (equivalent to an additional month's salary each year), payment of a family allowance for each child under 16 (5% of the employee's salary per child, provided such salary is not more than double the minimum salary, which is currently G 244,950 per month), paid vacations ranging from six working days after one year of service to 30 working days after 12 years of service, and indemnities in the event of dismissal.

24. Taxes on Natural Resources

There are no taxes on natural resources except in the case of the forest industry, which is taxed on the basis of the quantity of wood produced.

25. Other Taxes

Capital Tax. Capital tax is levied at 0.5% on the paid up capital and accumulated reserves of corporations, stock issuing partnerships, mixed companies and branches of foreign companies. The latter are also taxed on home office credit balances. Deductions are allowed for shares held in other companies subject to capital tax, current losses, and current income tax.

Corporation Inspection Tax. This tax is determined according to the following sliding scale:

Paid-Up Capital		
Over	Not Over	Annual Tax
₲ 0	₲ 500,000	₲ 1,300
500,000	1,000,000	2,500
1,000,000	5,000,000	4,800
5,000,000	10,000,000	8,000
10,000,000	15,000,000	12,000
15,000,000	20,000,000	17,000
20,000,000	30,000,000	21,000
30,000,000	50,000,000	25,000
50,000,000	70,000,000	32,000
70,000,000	1,000,000,000	45,000
1,000,000,000	1,500,000,000	60,000
1,500,000,000	2,000,000,000	75,000
2,000,000,000		100,000

Stamp Tax. A stamp duty is payable on all commercial documents. The rates vary with the document and are between 0.5% and 2%.

COMPUTATION OF TAXABLE INCOME

26. Capital Gains

Profits derived from the occasional sale of real estate are taxed at the rate of 5%. The taxable profit is determined by deducting from the contract sale price or the fiscal value of the property in the year of the sale, the greater of:

☐ The greater of the property's original cost, revalued value, or the fiscal value two years before the year of the sale.

☐ Five percent of the sales price as a single expense deduction (which is not required to be substantiated by vouchers).

27. Depreciation and Depletion

Depreciation is computed on the straight-line method at maximum annual rates that are fairly conservative. Higher depreciation rates require the specific approval of the Income Tax Bureau. Depreciation is computed on cost plus revaluation increments for inflation, if any.

28. Treatment of Dividends

Corporations must pay a 1.7% tax on dividends to be distributed.

29. Loss Carryovers

Loss carryovers and carrybacks are not allowed.

30. Transactions between Related Parties

There are no provisions covering such transactions.

31. Consolidation of Income

There are no provisions for the filing of a consolidated tax return by related corporations.

32. Tax Periods

The tax period coincides with the calendar year in most cases, except insurance companies whose period ends June 30.

33. Other Matters

Income Liable to Tax. Income tax is levied on income of Paraguayan source obtained by individuals or juridical persons conducting a gainful business within the country. The following are exempt: farming income; earned income of employees; and earned income of professionals, except when it is classified by the Executive Power as being of a commercial nature.

Statute of Limitations. Five years.

RELATED CONSIDERATIONS

34. Incentives and Grants

Incentives are available under Law 60/90, which approves a system of incentives for the economic development. The incentives are granted on a case-by-case basis after an official analysis of all factors involved.

Law 60/90 approves, with amendments, Decree-Law 27/89. The purpose of Law 60/90 is to promote the investment of domestic and foreign capital by means of granting special benefits for furthering the production of goods and services, the creation of jobs, increased exporting, and the substitution of imports, the incorporation of know-how that would improve production efficiency, and make possible higher and better use of raw materials, manpower, and domestic energy resources, thus, the investment of profits in capital goods and the performance of services in the activities established by the Executive, in conformity with the economic and social policy of the National Government. This Law introduces incentives to the capital goods introduced into the country under leasing contracts. Benefits range from complete exemption from many taxes, including a 95% reduction of income tax in proportion to the gross sales generated by the investment performed and carried out for the period of five years as of commissioning the project, according to the schedule of the approved investment.

36. Investment Restrictions on Nonresidents
None.

SELECTION OF BUSINESS ENTITY BY NONRESIDENTS

Nonresident investors can operate in Paraguay through a branch or a local subsidiary company, which may be either a corporation or a limited partnership. The repatriation of profits to nonresidents by either entity is subject to 10% withholding.

PERU

INCOME TAXES ON CORPORATIONS

1. Rates

The tax rate applicable to a corporation's taxable income is 30%. For income tax purposes, a corporation is a broad term including stock companies, joint-stock companies, cooperative enterprises, state-owned companies, foundations, associations, among others, which are incorporated in the country. This term does not include partnerships, civil partnerships, limited-liability companies, or joint ventures.

Taxable income is determined including all income, both earned locally and abroad.

2. Local Income Taxes

None.

3. Capital Gains Taxes

Capital gains are treated as ordinary income and are taxed accordingly.

4. Branch Profits Taxes

Branches of companies incorporated abroad are considered juridical persons (corporations) for income tax purposes, and are subject to the tax rate of 30%, referred to in item 1. Taxable income is determined including only income earned locally. The resulting amount is increased by adding tax-exempt interests and dividends earned during the period, and then is levied with an additional 10% rate.

Branches of companies incorporated locally are not taxed separately, but together with their parent company.

5. Foreign Tax Reliefs

Foreign tax reliefs apply only to companies incorporated locally, since only they are taxed on their worldwide income. In such cases, taxes paid to foreign countries, at tax rates not higher than the local tax rate, are deductible from income tax payable in Peru.

6. Classification of Corporations

Stock companies are classified as: (1) ordinary stock companies; and (2) transparent stock companies. The first are taxed like ordinary corporations, as stated in item 1. The second are a hybrid business entity, which operates as a corporation but whose corporate income, loss, deductions, and credits pass through to the shareholders on a pro rata basis. Shareholders are taxed on such corporate income whether distributed or not.

Only close corporations may choose the transparent status and, once chosen, may not change it at least for five years.

7. Payment of Taxes

Income tax is payable within three months after the business year-end; however, estimated tax payments must be made monthly during the year.

8. Other Matters

Tax-Stability Contracts. Under special circumstances, the government may sign tax-stability contracts with corporations. In such cases, the corporation is not subject to any further change in the tax law, during the period stated in the contract.

Bookkeeping. Companies investing locally in foreign currency, doing business with the government or state-owned corporations are allowed to keep their books in the corresponding currency and consequently use said currency to determine their tax basis and tax liability, as well as to make their tax payments.

INCOME TAXES ON INDIVIDUALS

9. Rates

An individual's income is calculated separately for each category of income. The consolidated taxable income is then subject to tax at the rates stated in each of the following income brackets (see item 14 for explanation of U.I.T.):

Taxable Income		
Over	Not Over	Rate
0 U.I.T.	15 U.I.T.	8%
15	20	10
20	25	12
25	33	16
33	41	20
41	50	25
50	60	31
60		37

10. Local Income Taxes

None.

11. Capital Gains Taxes

Capital gains of individuals are treated as ordinary income if the taxpayer is a regular buyer and seller of goods. The status of regular buyer and seller is determined for stock or real estate by the number of transactions during one fiscal year.

12. Foreign Tax Reliefs

See item 5.

13. Tax Period

The tax period for individuals is the calendar year.

14. Other Matters

Applicable Taxable Unit (U.I.T.). The U.I.T. is an official index used to calculate individuals' liability to income tax. Due to the regular adjustment of its value to the inflation, it is also used to determine tax liability for other taxes, as well as to set limits to deductions accepted by the tax administration regarding a corporation's income tax.

The U.I.T. is established at the beginning of the year and adjusted monthly according to the official inflation rate. Each month, the tax administration publishes the monthly U.I.T. and the monthly average U.I.T., the latter being the average of all monthly U.I.T.s published during the calendar year. Said average U.I.T. is used for calculating each month's partial income tax payment or withholding tax, and the year's average U.I.T. is used to determine the year-end income tax liability of individuals, both applying the income brackets shown in item 9.

Special Deduction. Individuals earning a salary or professional fees may deduct from taxable income 70% (during 1991, the deduction is of 35%) of their expenses for goods and services, provided such expenses are backed by properly issued invoices.

INCOME TAXES ON NONRESIDENTS

15. Liability to Tax

Nonresidents are taxed only on income from Peruvian sources.

16. Rates

Nonresidents are taxed at the highest rate applicable to residents, which currently is 37%. If income has been taxed formerly (e.g., on branch's income, which is subject to 30%), the nonresident partner corporation is taxed at 10%, to achieve a final income tax burden of 37%.

17. Withholding Tax Rates

The following withholding taxes apply to the income of nonresidents; corporations, and individuals:

Dividends	10%
Earnings from branches	10%
Royalties	28%
Services rendered locally	37% (1)
Salaries and pensions	37%
Interests	1% (2)
Other sources	37%

Note:
(1) Services rendered abroad to locally incorporated companies are not subject to tax.
(2) Interests may be exempt, if certain requirements are met. If there is no bank or customs evidence of the loan (for cash loans or financed acquisitions, respectively), or if the interest rate is higher than the prime rate prevailing in the lender's market plus 3%, the applicable tax rate is 37%. At both rates (1% or 37%), withholding tax on interests may be assumed and deducted as expense by the local company.

18. Special Withholding Provisions

Fees paid to nonresidents for services, where the source of income is partially local and partially foreign, are subject to withholding tax, applying the tax rate of 37% on the following percentages of the proceeds:

Air transport	1%
Marine transport	2
Communications	5
Film distribution	20
Technical services	40
Other professional services	90
Oilfield exploration	25

19. Tax Treaties

Peru has signed double taxation treaties with the Andean Pact Countries (Bolivia, Colombia, Ecuador, and Venezuela) and with Sweden.

OTHER SIGNIFICANT TAXES

21. Sales (Value Added)

A multiple stage, nonaccumulative or "value added" system applies to construction, production, and commerce as well as to services not rendered by professional individuals or partnerships. In the case of production and commerce, the tax is applied on the transfer of merchandise at any stage in the distribution process, including imports into the country. In this case, the tax is applied on the sales value. For services and construction, the tax is applied on the resulting income. For imports, it applies on the CIF value plus taxes and import duties. For real estate sales, it applies only to the first transfer made by the constructor: on the sales proceeds less the value of the land.

The tax rate is 14%, and it is applied through the fiscal credit system, which entitles the buyer to deduct the tax paid on merchandise purchases when selling any merchandise.

Exports are exempt from sales tax and the employer's FONAVI contribution. Taxes paid to acquire local and imported goods and services used in production of export goods may be applied as a tax credit for income tax or enterprises' net worth tax. Any reminder credit may be transferred to other taxpayers.

On transactions subject to Selective Consumption Tax, the basis for computing value added tax includes that tax.

No tax is levied on the value of goods sold as a consequence of the reorganization or transfer of an enterprise.

Municipal Promotion Tax. The tax rate is 2% and is applied on sales together with the sales tax. Hence, the effective tax rate applied on sales is 14%.

Selective Consumption (Excise) Tax. This tax is applied on the sales amounts at the production or import stage of certain products specified by law, and on the provision of certain services. The rates for goods vary between 10% and 134%, depending on whether the goods are considered luxury items or not, and for services between 10% and 70%, depending on the type of services rendered.

Traditional Export Tax. This tax is imposed on the FOB value of traditional export goods (mainly raw materials) at the rate of 5%, at the time the goods are shipped. In the case of copper, silver, zinc, and lead, the rate may be increased to 10% or reduced to 0%, depending on their monthly average international price.

22. Inheritance and Gift Taxes

No tax is levied on the transfer of property at death. Donations and other transfers of real estate are taxed at 3% of real value, payable by the receiver.

23. Taxes on Payrolls (Social Security)

The mandatory contributions are:

National Pensions System (retirement, disability and survivorship). Six percent of the total salary is paid by the employer, and 3% is paid by the employee.

National Health Assistance System. For employees' illness or maternity, the same rates apply as for the national pension system.

FONAVI Contribution. This is a mandatory contribution which is used to finance a housing program. The employer must pay 4% of the total monthly remunerations and each employee pays 1% of monthly compensation. The contribution applies to remuneration up to eight U.I.T., established for the month the salary is accrued (see item 1).

Labor Accidents and Occupational Disease Contribution. The rates are regulated in accordance with the nature and frequency of risks, percentages of accidents, and occupational diseases at the place of work. These payments are made by the employer.

SENATI Contribution. Companies employing industrial workers pay 1.5% of their payroll as a contribution to the Industrial Technological School.

24. Taxes on Natural Resources

Taxes on natural resources are called "canones" and are levied on wood, water, oil, among others.

25. Other Taxes

Tax on Vacant Land. A tax is levied on vacant urban land until at least two-thirds of the construction is completed, with rates of 1% or 0.5%, depending on whether the owner is engaged in real estate activities.

Tax on Enterprise's Net Worth. This tax is applied on the net worth, at the end of the fiscal period, of all undertakings currently in business, at the rate of 2%. During 1991, the tax basis is increased by adding 50% of all liabilities sourced in accounts payable.

Tax on Personal Assets. This tax is levied on the added value of personal real estate, cars, aircrafts, yachts, insuranced jewelry, and accounts receivable from non-corporations that exceeds 10 U.I.T. The applicable tax rate is 1% (during 1991, the rate is 1.5%). Municipal taxes paid on real estate, cars, aircrafts, and yachts are allowed as tax credits.

Tax on Real Estate Property Value. This tax is imposed on all real estate held by individuals and corporations. The tax is applied on the total value of all real estate owned by a taxpayer within each district.

The property value is updated each year by local regulators on the basis of certain indicators. The amounts paid by corporations are deductible to establish the basis for the tax on the enterprise's net worth.

Municipal Tax. This tax is paid on a monthly basis and is computed as a percentage of the electricity bills. The revenues are used by the district councils.

COMPUTATION OF TAXABLE INCOME

26. Capital Gains

Capital gain or loss is measured by the difference between the book value (cost with adjustments for revaluation and depreciation) of capital assets and its sales proceeds.

27. Depreciation and Depletion

The usual method of depreciation allowed is the straight-line method, which is based on the useful life of the asset as established by the tax authorities. At the request of the taxpayer, other depreciation methods may be used; i.e., sum-of-the-years-digit, machine hours, or production unit. The taxpayer, at his election, may write-off the undepreciated portion of an asset's cost when such asset becomes obsolete and/or is scrapped.

Buildings	3%
Mining equipment and machinery	20%
Other fixed assets	10% (1)
Vehicles	20%

Note:
(1) Fixed assets acquired after 1990 may be depreciated at the annual rate of 20%.

28. Treatment of Dividends

Resident individuals and corporations are not subject to dividend withholding. Tax withheld on payments of dividends is only applicable to nonresident individuals and entities.

Dividends received from Peruvian corporations by resident individuals are subject to a gross-up and tax credit mechanism, the effect of which is to reduce the taxation on dividends and thus minimize the impact of double taxation on the distribution of corporate earnings. The result of this mechanism is that dividends earned by residents are taxed only when the individual taxpayer is levied on a rate higher than 30%.

29. Loss Carryovers

Resident taxpayers are allowed to offset net losses against the profits obtained in the four years following the year in which a profit is made. Any remainder, which has not been offset in this period, cannot be used later. For activities in which larger investments and long production consolidation periods are required, losses can be carried forward for periods longer than four years. No carrybacks are allowed.

30. Transactions between Related Parties

Revenue and capital transactions between related parties are always considered to be carried out at fair market value.

31. Consolidation of Income

Each corporation is taxed as an individual entity. Neither consolidated nor combined tax returns are accepted.

32. Tax Periods

The fiscal period is the calendar year.

33. Other Matters

Revaluation of Fixed Assets. Annual revaluation of fixed assets is mandatory (quarterly revaluations are also allowed)—except for petroleum and mining companies, where it is optional—applying the official fixed-asset-price-level index published by the tax administration, based on the inflation rate of the previous year (for quarterly revaluations, the index is based on the inflation of the previous three months). Such revaluation is computed on the historical cost basis and on the accumulated depreciation and, hence, affects the period's depreciation and the sales cost of capital assets. For 1990, the published index was 6,678.6% for buildings and 5,711.1% for other fixed assets.

Special Adjustment for Real Estate. Companies' real estate, not considered as fixed asset and therefore not subject to revaluation, may be adjusted applying a special index, published by the National Statistics Institute (INE), to the historical cost.

RELATED CONSIDERATIONS

34. Incentives and Grants

Even though many companies still profit from such tax benefits as tax reductions and exemptions due to tax stability contracts, all major benefits have been revoked in order to achieve a more even tax system and to increase Government revenue.

35. Exchange Controls

A new exchange control policy is in force, since April 1991. Accordingly, the official exchange rate is fixed by market forces at the banking system.

Besides the official rate, there is the free-market exchange rate, which also is fixed by market forces at independent agencies, where foreign currency also may be bought or sold.

Currently, the official exchange rate is of I/.0.82 per US$1. The free-market exchange rate is about 1% higher.

36. Investment Restrictions on Nonresidents

Peru is one of the five signatories of the Andean Pact. According to the Decision 291 of said pact, enforced April 4, 1991, the previously existing restrictions have been abolished, and, other than a registration requirement granting foreign investors similar rights as any local investor plus the right to remit abroad their profits, capital reductions, stock sales proceeds, etc., there is no outstanding restriction.

SELECTION OF BUSINESS ENTITY BY NONRESIDENTS

Nondomiciled individuals may operate in Peru as a branch, as a corporation (with local participation in capital regulated by Decision 291 to enjoy the benefits of the Andean Pact), and as an association in participation (i.e., a joint venture) with registered corporations. Occasional technical services may be provided directly, without establishing a branch or corporation. The selection of entity often depends on the nature of the planned activities.

PHILIPPINES

INCOME TAXES ON CORPORATIONS

1. Rates

For domestic corporations the rate is 35% on net taxable income from all sources. The 35% rate generally became effective January 1, 1986.

2. Local Income Taxes

None.

3. Capital Gains Taxes

Capital gains are generally treated as ordinary income. However, gains from the sale of shares of stock that are not listed on or traded through a stock exchange are taxed at 10% on gains not over P100,000 and at 20% on the excess. The sale of shares listed on and traded through a stock exchange is taxed at ¼ of 1% of the gross selling price. These rates also apply to individuals.

4. Branch Profits Taxes

Branches of foreign corporations (resident foreign corporations) are taxed at the same rates as domestic corporations but only on their net taxable income from Philippine sources. In addition, any after-tax branch profits remitted to the head office abroad are subject to a tax of 15%, except that branches authorized to engage in petroleum operations in the Philippines are subject to a 7.5% rate. However, certain foreign corporations are taxed at special rates as follows:

- ☐ International carriers are taxed at 2½% of gross Philippine billings.
- ☐ Offshore banking units are only subject to a 10% final withholding tax on interest income derived from foreign currency loans to residents other than offshore banking units or local commercial banks.
- ☐ Foreign mutual life insurance companies are subject to a tax of 10% on their gross investment income.

5. Foreign Tax Reliefs

The Philippine taxation system provides for comprehensive double taxation relief for taxes incurred in territories outside the Philippines both under unilateral provisions of Philippine tax laws and under double taxation agreements. Under the Philippine Tax Code, a taxpayer may elect to take a credit or deduction for foreign income tax. The amount of foreign tax credit is subject to the per country and overall limitations. The Philippines has tax treaties with Australia, Austria, Belgium, Canada, Denmark, Finland, France, Germany, Indonesia, Italy, Japan, Korea, Malaysia, New Zealand, Pakistan, Singapore, Sweden, Thailand, the United Kingdom, and the United States.

INCOME TAXES ON INDIVIDUALS

9. Rates

Taxable compensation income, business income, and other income of an individual derived from all sources (except for certain passive income which is subject to final withholding taxes) is subject to graduated rates ranging from 0 to 35%. In computing taxable income, a taxpayer deriving compensation income is entitled only to deductions for personal exemptions, while a taxpayer receiving compensation income and income from other sources (or solely from the latter) is taxed after deducting personal exemptions and other deductions. The rates are as follows:

Taxable Income		Tax on	Percentage
Over	Not Over	Lower Amount	on Excess
P 0	P 2,500	P 0	0%
2,500	5,000	0	1
5,000	10,000	25	3
10,000	20,000	175	7
20,000	40,000	875	11
40,000	60,000	3,075	15
60,000	100,000	6,075	19
100,000	250,000	13,675	24
250,000	500,000	49,675	29
500,000		122,175	35

The above rates apply to Philippine citizens and resident aliens.

However, income of a nonresident citizen from foreign sources, computed after deducting the personal exemption and allowance for foreign income taxes paid, is subject to the following rates:

Taxable Income		Tax on	Percentage
Over	Not Over	Lower Amount	on Excess
US$ 0	US$ 6,000	US$ 0	1%
6,000	20,000	60	2
20,000		340	3

A nonresident citizen is one who establishes to the satisfaction of the Commissioner of Internal Revenue the fact of his physical presence abroad with a definite intention to reside there.

Married individuals with separate incomes can elect either to consolidate their taxable incomes or compute their respective incomes separately.

10. Local Income Taxes

None.

11. Capital Gains Taxes

Capital gains on capital assets are taxed at the same rates as ordinary income, except for gains from sales of real property and stock. Capital gain from dispositions of real property by individuals is subject to final income tax equal to 5% of the gross selling price or the fair market value prevailing at the time of sale, whichever is higher. Net capital gains from sales of shares are taxed at the same rates as imposed on corporations (see item 3).

12. Foreign Tax Reliefs

See item 5.

13. Tax Period

Individual taxpayers must file their returns on a calendar year basis.

INCOME TAXES ON NONRESIDENTS

15. Liability to Tax

Nonresident foreign corporations (not engaged in trade or business in the Philippines) and nonresident alien individuals are taxed only on their Philippine source income.

16. Rates

Nonresident foreign corporations are taxed at the rate of 35% (subject to withholding) based on gross Philippine income, except that capital gain realized from the disposition of stock in any domestic corporation is taxed as follows:

□ Net capital gain from the sale of stock that is not listed on nor traded through a stock exchange is taxed at 10% if not over P100,000 and 20% on the excess.

□ The sale of stock listed and traded through a local stock exchange is taxed at ¼ of 1% of the gross selling price.

Nonresident alien individuals not engaged in trade or business in the Philippines are subject to a 30% withholding tax on their gross Philippine-source income. Nonresident aliens engaged in trade or business in the Philippines are taxed on their net taxable Philippine-source income at the same rates as resident aliens.

A nonresident alien is presumed to be engaged in trade or business in the Philippines if his aggregate stay in the Philippines during any one calendar year exceeds 180 days. If the stay is 180 days or less, he is deemed as not engaged in trade or business in the Philippines.

Alien individuals employed by regional headquarters established under Presidential Decree No. 218 or by Offshore Banking Units under Presidential Decree No. 1034 or by Petroleum Service Contractors and Subcontractors under Presidential Decree No. 87 are taxed at 15% of their gross income from salaries, wages, compensation, emoluments, etc. from such entities.

17. Withholding Tax Rates

There are special withholding tax rates for certain types of income as follows:

Type of Income	Rate
Interest	20%
Dividends if the country of domicile of recipient:	
Does not tax Philippine-source dividends	
Allows a tax credit with the Philippines tax ''spared'' or relieved of 20% as a tax credit	
Allows as tax credit equivalent to at least 20% of the dividend taxes deemed to have been paid in the Philippines	15
Gross income of cinematographic film owners, lessors, or distributors	25
Rentals and charter fees paid to nonresident owners of vessels by Philippines nationals	4.5
Rentals, charter, and other fees payable to nonresident lessors of aircraft, machinery, and other equipment	7.5

OTHER SIGNIFICANT TAXES

21. Sales (Value Added)

A value added tax (VAT) is imposed on any person who in the course of trade or business (a) sells, barters or exchanges goods, (b) renders services or engages in a similar transaction, or (c) imports goods. The tax is levied on each sale or service rendered starting from the beginning of production/manufacture down to the distribution, and culminating with the sale to the final customer.

The rate is 10% and is levied on the gross selling price of goods sold in the case of sales, barters, or exchanges of goods, or on the gross receipts by persons engaged in the sale of services, or on the total value used by the Bureau of Customs in determining tariff and customs duties, plus customs durties, excise taxes if any, and other charges, in the case of importation of goods. Export sales and sales to persons or entities exempt under special laws or international agreements to which the Philippines is a signatory are zero rated.

Persons engaged in the sale of goods or services subject to the tax whose aggregate gross annual sales and/or receipts exceed P200,000 are required to register with the Bureau of Internal Revenue. Persons not covered by the tax may register with the Bureau of Internal Revenue as a VAT registered enterprise. Such application requires prior approval.

22. Inheritance and Gift Taxes

An estate tax is levied upon transfers of property by reason of death and is based upon the value of the net estate of the decedent. The tax rates, which are paid by the executor, administrator or any of the legal heirs, vary from 3% to 60%.

Gift tax is imposed on the total net gifts made during the calendar year. However, gifts made in different years are not accumulated. The gift tax rates vary from 1.5% to 40% and are payable by the donor.

23. Taxes on Payrolls (Social Security)

The various social and labor laws of the Philippines have been consolidated into the Labor Code of the Philippines. Social security and medical care benefits are granted to employees. Private employees are compelled to register under the Social Security System, which is financed by monthly contributions from both employers and employees. The rates effective January 1, 1992 through December 31, 1991 are:

		Monthly Salary	Monthly Contribution	
Over	Not Over	Credit	Employer	Employee
P 1	P 150	P 125	P 9.20	P 5.65
150	200	175	12.95	7.90
200	250	225	16.45	10.30
250	350	300	21.95	13.75
350	500	425	31.20	19.45
500	700	600	43.90	27.50
700	900	800	58.50	36.70
900	1,100	1,000	73.20	45.80
1,100	1,400	1,250	88.95	57.35

Over	Not Over	Monthly Salary Credit	Monthly Contribution	
			Employer	Employee
1,400	1,750	1,500	104.75	68.75
1,750	2,250	2,000	136.30	91.70
2,250	2,750	2,500	167.95	114.55
2,750	3,250	3,000	193.25	131.25
3,250	3,750	3,500	218.55	147.95
3,750	4,250	4,000	243.95	164.55
4,250	4,750	4,500	269.25	181.25
4,750		5,000	294.55	197.95

24. Taxes on Natural Resources

Minerals, mineral products, and quarry resources extracted or produced from mineral lands are subject to royalty taxes at the rates of 3%–5% of market value of the gross output of minerals. These royalty taxes are payable to the Bureau of Internal Revenue.

Forest charges at varying rates are imposed on each cubic meter of timber and firewood cut in any forest land. A charge of 10% is also imposed on any person removing certain forest products, such as gums, resins, and rattan. These forest charges are payable to the Forest Management Bureau. Entities operating under a gratuitous license of the Bureau of Forest Development may be exempt from paying these forest charges.

Indigenous petroleum is subject to a 15% tax based on the fair international market price on the first taxable sale, payable by the purchaser to the Bureau of Internal Revenue.

25. Additional Significant Taxes

Customs Duties. Customs duties on imports range from 10% to 100% ad valorem. The dutiable base is generally the home consumption value plus 10% thereof. In addition, a 5% import levy is imposed.

Land and Property Tax. Owners of land (and improvements thereon) and buildings are required to pay real estate taxes to the province or city in which the property is located. The rate (maximum 2%) is based on the assessed value of the property and varies slightly with the locality.

Excise Tax. Excise tax is imposed on certain specific articles enumerated in the Tax Code. The commodities subject to excise tax are distilled spirits, wines, fermented liquors, manufactured tobacco, cigars, cigarettes, fireworks, manufactured oils and motor fuels, coal and coke, bunker fuel oil, diesel fuel oil, cinematographic films, and saccharine. Excise tax is levied on these articles whether they are produced locally for domestic sale or imported.

Gross Receipts Tax. On specific business activities, a percentage or miscellaneous tax is imposed based on the gross receipts of the business. The following are illustrative examples of percentage or miscellaneous taxes:

Type of Business	Tax Rates
Banks and finance companies	From 1% to 5% of gross receipts, varying with terms of instruments from which income is derived
Mining companies*	3% of market value of the gross output of nonmetallic minerals and quarry resources 5% of market value of the annual gross output of all metallic minerals 15% of the fair international market price of indigenous petroleum products
Common carriers (air, sea, or land)	3% of gross receipts
Brokers (stock, real estate, commercial, customs)	10% of value-added tax
Contractors, business agents, service businesses	10% of value-added tax
Dealers in securities and lending investors	6% of gross income

*The tax on mining companies is no longer collectible by the Bureau of Internal Revenue but by the municipality where the mining claim is located.

COMPUTATION OF TAXABLE INCOME

26. Capital Gains

The net capital gain is the difference between the adjusted cost basis of the property sold and the selling price. In the case of an individual, only 50% of long-term capital gains is taken into account, except gains from sale of real properties and shares of stock. Capital losses can be offset only against capital gains. There is generally no capital loss carryforward or carryback except for individuals, who may carry a net capital loss only to the succeeding year.

27. Depreciation and Depletion

Any method of depreciation is allowed as long as it is reasonable and consistent. Once a particular method is adopted, subsequent changes require the prior approval of the Commissioner of Internal Revenue. "Depreciation Guidelines and Rules" published by the U.S. Internal Revenue Service (Revenue Procedure No. 62-21,

Publication No. 456, August 1964) prescribing the estimated useful life of depreciable assets has persuasive effect in the Philippines. A written agreement may be entered into between the taxpayer and the Commissioner of Internal Revenue as to the useful life of the property subject to depreciation.

Only cost depletion is allowed.

28. Treatment of Dividends

Gross dividends received by a domestic corporation or a resident foreign corporation from another domestic corporation are not taxed. For dividends received by a nonresident foreign corporation from a domestic corporation, see item 17.

Dividends from all sources received by citizens of the Philippines and resident aliens are not subject to a final withholding tax. Dividends from foreign sources received by nonresident citizens constitute taxable income subject to the 1%, 2% and 3% rates (see item 9).

Dividends from Philippine sources received by nonresident aliens engaged in trade or business in the Philippines are subject to a tax of 30%. Dividends from Philippine sources received by nonresident aliens not engaged in trade or business in the Philippines are subject to a 30% withholding tax.

Royalties (except payments to mining claim owners or lessees of mining rights) received by individuals and domestic and resident foreign corporations are subject to a 20% final withholding tax. Interest on bank deposits and yields from deposit substitutes are subject to a final withholding tax of 20%.

Income distributed to beneficiaries of estates and trusts is subject to a 15% creditable withholding tax. Income from all other trusts and similar arrangements are subject to a 20% final withholding tax.

29. Loss Carryovers

No operating loss carryovers or carrybacks are allowed except for registered tourism enterprises under Presidential Decree No. 535, which are allowed to carry a net operating loss incurred in any of the first ten years of operation to the following six years.

30. Transactions between Related Parties

The Commissioner of Internal Revenue is authorized to allocate gross income or deductions between or among organizations or businesses owned or controlled directly or indirectly by the same interests, if he determines that such allocation is necessary to prevent evasion of taxes or to clearly reflect income.

31. Consolidation of Income

Philippine law does not provide for reporting income on a consolidated basis for tax purposes.

32. Tax Periods

The base period for computing the liability to corporation tax is the company's own accounting period. Unless it chooses a different fiscal year, a corporation's accounting period is the calendar year. Individuals are required to use the calendar year for reporting income.

RELATED CONSIDERATIONS

34. Incentives and Grants

The Omnibus Investments Code of 1987 through the Board of Investments consolidated all of the investment incentive laws and grants preferential tax and other benefits to registered enterprises, export producers, export traders, and service producers in preferred investment areas, which are divided into two categories: nonpioneer and pioneer. To be entitled to register, the applicant must be a Philippine corporation whose foreign equity must not exceed that provided under the Negative List of the Foreign Investment Act of 1991. One-hundred percent foreign ownership is allowed in areas outside the Negative List.

Some of the incentives grant full exemption from corporate income tax, contractors tax, taxes and duties on imported capital equipment, spare parts, and raw materials, and export tax, duty and wharfage fees on outbound shipment; full deduction from taxable income of the cost of major infrastructure; additional deduction for labor expenses; tax credits for taxes and duties on supplies and raw materials used in the manufacture of exported products and on the purchase of domestic capital equipment equivalent to the value of taxes and duties that would have been waived on such capital equipment if imported; unrestricted use of consigned equipment; and the employment of foreign nationals.

Export Processing Zones have been designated by the Government. Full foreign ownership is allowed in enterprises established in these Zones. Generally, foreign and domestic merchandise, raw materials, equipment and machinery brought into the Zone are exempt from customs duties and national and local taxes.

The Omnibus Investments Code of 1987, which repealed Presidential Decree No. 218, prescribes certain incentives for the establishment of regional or area headquarters of multinationals having affiliates, subsidiaries, and branches in the Asia-Pacific Region. These incentives are exemption from travel tax, tax and duty-free importation of personal and household effects and training materials, and enjoyment by foreign personnel of the regional headquarters, as well as their spouses and unmarried children under 21 years of age, of multiple entry visas and exemption from immigration fees and charges. These headquarters should, however, act merely as supervisory, communications, and coordinating center for their affiliates, subsidiaries, or branches of such multinational corporations. A regional office executive is taxed only at 15% of his gross compensation received from the regional office.

Presidential Decree No. 1034 authorizes, with incentives, a foreign banking corporation to set up a branch, subsidiary or affiliate to engage in offshore banking in the Philippines with the approval of the Central Bank of the Philippines (CB).

Other laws grant incentives to foreign investors engaging in specific areas of investments; e.g., the Oil Exploration and Development Act of 1972 and the Coal Development Act of 1976 (which were revoked in 1984 but restored in 1985).

35. Exchange Controls

Foreign Investments. Foreign borrowings and foreign equity investments require prior Central Bank (CB) approval. All foreign investments must be registered with the CB to be entitled to capital repatriation and profit remittance rights. Remittance of after-tax profits and dividends to nonresidents will be allowed as long as the investments have been registered with the CB.

Remittance of Royalties. Royalty or technical service contracts must be registered with the Technology Transfer Board. Such contracts must also be registered with the CB to be able to remit the fees. For actual transfers of know-how and processes, the fee should not be more than 5% of the wholesale price of the manufactured commodity and 1% for the use of trademarks, etc.

36. Investment Restrictions on Nonresidents

Generally, there are no restrictions on the extent of foreign ownership of export enterprises. In domestic-market enterprises, foreign investment may be high as 100% of the equity except in areas covered in the Foreign Investments Negative List (FINL) provided by the Foreign Investments Act of 1991. The FINL lists the areas of economic activity where foreign ownership is limited to 40%.

Foreign investment, upon registration with the Securities and Exchange Commission (SEC), or with the Bureau of Trade Regulation and Consumer Protection (BTRCP) of the Department of Trade in the case of a sole proprietorship, may do business or invest in a domestic corporation up to 100% unless prohibited or limited by existing laws or the FINL. Any enterprise seeking to benefit from incentives under the Omnibus Investments Code of 1987 must register with the Board of Investments (BOI). Export enterprises that are not Philippine national are required to register with the BOI.

SELECTION OF BUSINESS ENTITY BY NONRESIDENTS

Nonresident investors can operate in the Philippines by directly entering into transactions with residents, or by establishing either a branch office or a subsidiary corporation. For other purposes, a representative office or a regional or area headquarters may also be established. However, representative offices and regional headquarters of multinationals are limited to acting as supervisory, communications and coordinating centers for their affiliates and cannot carry on business in the Philippines.

The tax consequences for a foreign entity that carries on business in the Philippines are:

☐ A branch is subject to income tax at 35% (see item 4).

☐ Branch profits remitted are generally subject to a 15% tax (see item 4).

☐ A foreign subsidiary is subject to income tax at 35% (see item 1).

☐ Dividends paid to a foreign parent company are subject to a 35% withholding tax unless reduced by a tax treaty.

The formation of a local company provides more tax advantages to foreign investors because of the tax incentives allowed (see item 34). However, foreign participation in a local company is subject to certain restrictions and the repatriation of capital invested is also subject to Central Bank regulations.

POLAND

INCOME TAXES ON CORPORATIONS

1. Rates

The tax rate on net profit of a Polish enterprise is 40%. Net profits are defined as gross profits less allowable expenses, including labor costs and social security contributions (see item 23). Note that tax holidays and incentives are provided to foreign joint ventures (see item 34).

2. Local Income Taxes

There are various local taxes applying to real property and to the ownership of vehicles. In addition, other administrative fees can be imposed by local authorities.

3. Capital Gains Taxes

There are no special capital gains taxes.

4. Branch Profits Taxes

Foreign enterprises doing business in Poland are taxable if there is a permanent establishment in Poland, if there is direct economic activity, or if they participate in a joint venture.

In general, foreign companies are treated for tax purposes under the same rules that apply to foreign individuals. Foreign companies are subject to a maximum overall tax rate of 40%. Companies that are legal persons are taxed on net profits. Costs then are deductible under rules similar to those that apply to foreign individuals (see item 34).

Representative offices (as distinguished from foreign enterprises) are subject to a tax of 2% of the contract amount for any foreign trade activity.

Dividends paid by Polish companies abroad are subject to tax at a rate of 20% (or lower rate provided by tax treaty) to be withheld by the distributing company.

5. Foreign Tax Reliefs

Income derived from abroad generally is exempt from income tax provided that the income is subject to tax in the foreign country and the foreign country respects the principle of reciprocity for similar income derived in Poland.

6. Classifications of Corporations

Among the types of taxpayers liable for the corporate income tax are a limited liability company or a joint stock company (referred to in Polish law as "companies"), other legal persons established under Polish law, natural persons domiciled in Poland, and foreign enterprises enjoying legal personality.

7. Payment of Taxes

Tax procedures involve verification of tax liability through the forwarding of tax returns or declarations, tax assessment made by competent tax authorities, tax audit and accounting under the direction of the Minister of Finance, and tax payment within the period fixed by law.

Appeals can be lodged with tax authorities and are decided in various state courts.

INCOME TAXES ON INDIVIDUALS

9. Rates

Effective January 1, 1992, individuals who reside in Poland for a period longer than 183 days in a given tax year must pay personal income taxes on income from whatever source. This tax obligation, however, does not apply to foreign individuals employed by joint ventures (see item 15). Individuals who are not residents of Poland and who reside in Poland for less than 183 days are liable for personal tax only on all employment salary and any income arising in Poland.

Pursuant to recent regulations, new tax rates and rules are effective January 1, 1992. The law assumes allowable costs in respect of employment income of 3% 64,800,000 zloties (i.e., 1,944,000 zl) per annum. The tax rates for 1992 are:

Tax Base (zloties)		Tax (zloties)	Percentage
Over	Not Over	on Lower Amount	on Excess
0	64,800,000		20% less 864,000 zloties
64,800,000	129,600,000	12,096,000	30%
129,600,000*		31,536,000	40%

* An additional tax band, with a 50% tax rate for income over 194,400,000, is proposed but not yet enacted.

A 20% flat tax rate applies to dividend, interest, and royalty income. Pursuant to the recent regulations, additional changes to the tax rules are expected to come into effect January 1, 1992.

10. Local Income Taxes

There are no local income taxes.

11. Capital Gains Taxes

There are no special capital gains taxes.

12. Foreign Tax Reliefs

Individuals who reside in Poland for longer than 183 days in a calendar year are subject to tax on their worldwide income. Income derived from sources located abroad is exempt from tax provided that such income is subject to tax in a foreign country and the foreign country provides reciprocity for similar income derived from Polish sources.

Foreign employees of companies established under the Foreign Investment Law are subject to tax on salaries and wages at 20%, subject to relief under double taxation treaties.

13. Tax Period

In general, individuals must file annual tax returns based on the calendar year.

INCOME TAXES ON NONRESIDENTS

15. Liability to Tax

A foreign corporation or foreign individual with a Polish residence or who stays in Poland for at least six months is taxed on income on the same principles as Polish companies or Polish residents. Nonresidents—defined as individuals who do not have a Polish residence, stay in Poland for less than six months, or are diplomatic representatives—who earn income are subject to tax in Poland solely on Polish-source income.

16. Rates

Nonresidents liable for tax are required to pay the same tax rate as Polish individuals or corporations.

17. Withholding Tax Rates

Dividends, interest, and royalties paid abroad by Polish companies are subject to tax at a rate of 20% (subject to reduction by tax treaty) to be withheld by the distributing company. Polish tax treaties with the countries listed in item 19 provide, depending on the treaty provisions, reduced dividends withholding rates of 15% to 0%, interest withholding rates of 15% to 0%, and royalties withholding rates of 10% to 0%.

19. Tax Treaties

Poland has tax treaties with the following countries for the avoidance of double taxation (* indicates under negotiations, signed but not yet enacted):

Australia*	Israel*	Singapore*
Austria	Italy	South Korea*
Belgium	Japan	Soviet Union*
Canada	Kuwait*	Spain
China	Libya*	Sri Lanka
Cyprus*	Malaysia	Sweden
Czechoslovakia	Mongolia	Switzerland*
Denmark	Netherlands	Thailand
Finland	Nigeria*	Turkey*
France	Norway	United Kingdom
Germany	Pakistan	United States
Greece	Philippines*	Uruguay*
Hungary	Portugal	Venezuela*
India	Romania	Yugoslavia
Indonesia*		Zimbabwe*

OTHER SIGNIFICANT TAXES

21. Sales (Value Added)

A turnover tax is levied on any activity in which goods and services are supplied with a view to earning a profit. The tax is levied on the amount of consideration that will be received for the supply of the goods and services. In general, the tax is imposed on 100 separate groups of goods and services, with rates ranging from 5% on some services, 20% on industrial products, to 100% on some alcohol products.

The Minister of Finance has the authority to establish special rates for specific goods and services. Advance payment of the tax is required and, depending on the type of tax, is made monthly, quarterly, or annually.

The transformation of the turnover tax to a European-style VAT system is planned effective May 1992, whereby two tax rates would be applied: 5% on food and 18% on most other goods and services. There would be limited exemptions for certain goods and services, health care, finance, and insurance. The excise tax would remain on certain alcohol, tobacco, petroleum, and jewelry products.

22. Inheritance and Gift Taxes

The inheritance or gift tax varies according to the relationship with the deceased or donor.

Relationship	Exemption (zloties)	Rate
Spouse, child, parent	26,400,000	5–19%
Sibling	19,800,000	11–32
Other	13,200,000	17–45

The highest marginal rate cannot exceed 40%.

23. Taxes on Payrolls (Social Security)

Payroll taxes paid by employers are intended to stimulate enterprises to improve labor conditions as well as finance the cost of public benefits. The tax rate is 43% (plus 2% unemployment) of all salaries paid to workers (including money and the value of goods received).

24. Taxes on Natural Resources

Among the different types of taxes on natural resources are the following:

- [ ] An agricultural tax imposed on land used for crops or special purposes.
- [ ] Water duties.
- [ ] Environmental duties payable by persons who cause air, land, or water pollution, or by those who cut down trees.

COMPUTATION OF TAXABLE INCOME

26. Capital Gains

There are no special capital gains taxes.

27. Depreciation and Depletion

The system of depreciation is determined by the Minister of Finance. Revised depreciation regulations that permit faster asset recovery were introduced in 1991. Depreciation is permitted for tangible assets (in 60 separate groups, ranging from 1.5% for buildings, 17% annual depreciation for autos, to 100% for certain assets) as well as for leases on land and buildings and other fixed assets attached to land, and other intangible assets and rights.

The recent amendments, combined with revaluation of book assets to account for inflation, increase depreciation expenses. Accelerated depreciation is permitted for certain assets.

29. Loss Carryovers

Deductions exceeding income during the tax year may be carried forward with one-third of the loss allowed in each of three subsequent years. The loss carryforward rules apply to individuals and corporations.

30. Transactions Between Related Parties

There are no specific tax guidelines on transactions between related parties.

31. Consolidation of Income

The consolidation of entities' production income and loss may be permitted. Ownership eligibility for consolidation is not clearly established.

32. Tax Periods

In general, individuals and enterprises report on the calendar year for tax purposes.

33. Other Matters

Companies generally use the accrual method of accounting for revenue and expense recognition.

Under the general corporate tax law, the tax base is defined as the enterprise's annual income reduced by expenditures for construction or modernization of buildings, environmental protection, one half of the cost of machinery and equipment relating to food stuffs, manufacturing equipment, and 10% of charitable contributions. LIFO inventories, consistently applied from year to year, and financial statements are permitted for tax purposes. Research and development expenditures are currently deductible for tax purposes.

During periods of significant inflation, reevaluations of inventories and plant and equipment have been permitted.

RELATED CONSIDERATIONS

34. Incentives and Grants

Foreign investment is encouraged through joint venture legislation. Investment can come in a variety of forms.

☐ Establishment of a limited liability company 100%-owned by foreign capital.

☐ Participation with Polish or other foreign partners through a joint venture or where shares are sold publicly.

☐ Purchase of shares in an existing Polish limited liability or joint stock company.

Foreign investors can contribute to a company's equity both in cash and in kind, including tangible assets and intangible assets such as know-how. Cash contributions must be made from the zloty proceeds of the sale or foreign currency converted at the official exchange rate.

Foreign Enterprises. Poland encourages foreign enterprises to engage in economic activity through either direct investment or participation in joint ventures. Foreign enterprises doing business in Poland in any other form generally are not subject to tax if they do not generate Polish-source income or have a permanent establishment in Poland.

Foreign Companies. The new Law On Foreign-Owned Companies (June 14, 1991) does not require a permit for the establishment of a company except for selected business, such as the operation of sea- and air-ports, dealing in real estate or acting as an intermediary in real estate transactions, defense industry not covered by licensing, wholesale trade with imported consumer goods, and rendition of legal services. A permit is also required where shares in a company are acquired by a state-owned legal entity, apart from wholly owned by the State Treasury, and where a state entity's in-kind contributions are in the form of a separate enterprise, real estate, or a part of an enterprise. A permit also is required for the following transactions:

☐ purchase of shares in existing Polish company if the company's business:
    —covers those selected business exceptions above,
    —requires a license or a permit pursuant to separate regulations;
☐ extension of a company's business into at least one of the selected business exceptions above;
☐ a company entering into a contract for the use of state-owned enterprise or part of it, real estate for at least six months.

A permit is given by the Minister of Privatization.

Tax Holiday. A foreign-owned company or the founders of a company before its establishment may apply through the Minister of Privatization to the Minister of Finance for the exemption from corporate income tax. The following preliminary conditions must be met to start the negotiations:

☐ the contribution of the foreign parties to the company's initial share capital exceeds the equivalent of two million ECU's in zlotys according to the purchase rate of exchange set by the National Bank of Poland on the date of the Articles of Association signing or on the date of taking over shares by the foreign party in existing company; and
☐ the company will *in particular*:
    —establish its business in the regions with high structural unemployment, or
    —ensure the implementation of the new technology to the national economy, or
    —enable the export of goods and services 20% of the company's total sales worth.

The above conditions are examples. The State may at its discretion apply other criteria and nominate preferential treatment industrial sectors. The possible tax exemption is available to companies in which the foreign parties acquire or take over shares till December 31, 1993. It also applies where the foreign party acquires the shares held by the State Treasury on secondary market.

In addition to tax-exemption conditions which can be imposed at the discretion of the Minister, the Law defines the circumstances that automatically trigger the loss of the tax exemption: the commencement of the liquidation proceedings of the company during the exemption or within two years of the exemption expiration;

and the reduction of the initial share capital of the company within the aforementioned period.

The new Law does not provide for any time limit of tax credit. The amount of tax credit is determined in each case with the value of the shares acquired or taken over and the average annual rate of ECU exchange to the zloty. Thus, the income tax credit cannot exceed the value of the transaction. The tax credit utilized each year is computed according to the average annual rate of ECU exchange to the zloty.

35. Exchange Controls

Foreign shareholders have the right to repatriate 100% of their share of the previous year's taxed profit. The Law also guarantees the full repatriation of the amounts due upon the liquidation of a company, redemption, and sale of shares, and any form of compensation for expropriation.

Exchange Regulations. The Foreign Exchange Law (February 15, 1989) has eliminated the former state monopoly on foreign exchange. The amendment of the Law has introduced so-called "internal convertibility" of Polish currency, zloty (PZL), as of January 1, 1990. Internal convertibility is based on the general obligation to resell foreign currency revenues to foreign exchange banks and, conversely, on the general right to buy hard currency to cover liabilities due. The system of internal convertibility has given all domestic entities equal access to foreign exchange and has introduced the rule of uniform zloty exchange rate application.

Foreign exchange rates to the zloty are fixed daily by the National Bank of Poland (NBP) using a basket of currencies and daily world-market quotations. The basket contains five currencies in the following ratios: U.S. dollar (45%), German mark (35%), sterling pound (10%), swiss franc (5%) and french franc (5%). The sale and purchase foreign exchange rates set by the NBP, must be applied by business entities excluding natural persons and foreign exchange offices.

The objective of the Foreign Exchange Law is to regulate any foreign exchange transaction carried out either exclusively within Poland or overseas. Domestic and foreign persons who carry out foreign exchange operations must observe certain limitations, duties, and prohibitions. The scope of foreign exchange control can be relaxed by the Minister of Finance with general exchange permits. All transactions not falling within the scope of these general permits require individual exchange permits, which are available by application to the relevant branch of the NBP. If a permit is refused, an appeal can be made to the President of the NBP; if the appeal is rejected, a further appeal to the Supreme Administrative Court can be lodged.

It is also possible for foreign partners to receive royalty payments in respect of licensed patents and know-how.

Enterprises are required to convert all foreign exchange earnings into zloties through the banks. It will no longer be possible to hold foreign currency earnings in special hard currency accounts.

PORTUGAL

INCOME TAXES ON CORPORATIONS

1. Rates

Corporation tax is levied on taxable profits (accounting profits adjusted to comply with tax law) at a rate of 36%.

Corporations in which income from agricultural activities exceeds 60% of total income are subject to income tax at the following reduced rates:

Year	Tax Rate
1991	20.0%
1992	25.0%
1993	31.0%
1994	36.5%

2. Local Income Taxes

A municipality tax (derrama) up to 10% of the corporation tax may be levied by local authorities.

3. Capital Gains Tax

Gains on the sale of tangible fixed assets and investments in securities are exempt from corporation tax if the proceeds are reinvested to acquire tangible fixed assets, shares in Portuguese companies, or treasury bonds up to the end of the second calendar year following the sale.

4. Branch Profits Tax

Branches of companies duly constituted in accordance with Portuguese law, but operating outside Portugal, are not liable for any direct taxation except to the extent that branch profits must be consolidated into the head office accounts and will be taxed as part of the whole.

Branches of foreign companies are liable for tax on profits obtained in Portugal in exactly the same way as Portuguese companies. Furthermore, remittances of profits to a foreign head office is not subject to withholding tax.

5.   Foreign Tax Reliefs

Relief from double taxation is governed by tax treaties that Portugal has concluded with other countries. In addition, a foreign tax credit may be allowed for foreign-source income included on the Portuguese tax return, computed as the lesser of:

☐   The foreign tax paid on the foreign-source income, or
☐   The Portuguese tax attributable to the foreign-source income.

7.   Payment of Taxes

An advance payment in respect of current year's corporation tax should be made as follows:

☐   25% of the previous year's tax is due in July, September, and December.
☐   The balance of the tax is paid during May of the year following that in which the income is earned.

INCOME TAXES ON INDIVIDUALS

9.   Rates

Individuals are liable for income tax on family worldwide income if they are considered resident in Portugal for tax purposes and otherwise on income earned in Portugal. A resident is an individual who is in Portugal for more than 183 days during a calendar year or who owns a residence in Portugal that can be assumed to be the individual's habitual residence.

Income tax is levied on income from virtually all sources, including: salary and fringe benefits, income as independent professionals (lawyers, accountants, etc.), income from business activities, income from agricultural activities, income from investment in securities, etc., income from leasing or renting real estate, income from the sale of real estate or securities, retirement pensions, as well as income from other sources.

Allowances.   Portugal has a tradition of minimum allowances that can be deducted from gross income. Under the tax law, the major allowances are:

☐   65% of salaries earned, but limited to the higher of Esc. 340,000 or social security contributions paid by the individual.
☐   50% of the profit from the sale of real estate.
☐   Expenses incurred in the normal course of business as independent professionals, individuals, entrepreneurs, and farmers.
☐   The value of a pension received up to Esc. 560,000 and 50% of the excess. The total allowance is limited to Esc. 1,400,000.
☐   100% of expenses for health care, if properly documented.

□ The following allowances for interest, school fees, and insurance premiums:

Married	minimum Esc. 120,000	maximum Esc. 260,000
Unmarried	minimum Esc. 60,000	maximum Esc. 140,000

□ Pensions paid.

□ Donations. 100% if the beneficiary is a state or local authority, but limited to 15% of gross income if beneficiary is a church, museum, library, etc.

Splitting. Family taxable income is split to determine the tax rate applicable as follows:

If one member earns more than 95% of the family's gross income

$$\frac{\text{taxable income}}{1.9}$$

Other situations

$$\frac{\text{taxable income}}{2}$$

The following tax rates apply to the split income of Portuguese nationals or residents:

Taxable Income		Tax Rate	Amount Deductible
Over	Not Over		
Esc. 0	Esc. 750,000	15%	Esc. 0
750,000	1,750,000	25	75,000
1,750,000	4,500,000	35	250,000
4,500,000		40	425,000

The amount of tax due is calculated by multiplying the split amount by the tax rate and then doubling the result to arrive at the gross amount of tax due. From the gross tax due, the following amounts are deducted:

Single person	
Alone	Esc. 25,500
Each child	Esc. 14,000
Married couple	
Husband and wife	Esc. 38,000
Each child	Esc. 14,000

If dividends are included in gross income, a tax credit of 35% of the corporation income tax paid by the corporation declaring the dividend is offset against the tax due.

Special Tax Rates. The taxpayer, in relation to earnings from the following sources, has the option either to pay the taxes referred to below or to include the earnings as income on his tax declaration and pay the normal tax rate.

Interest from bank deposits	20%
Income from securities (dividends, interest, etc.)	25%
Profit from the sale of shares	10%

11. Capital Gains Taxes

A special tax rate of 10% is imposed on net capital gains on securities obtained in the tax period. Any capital gains on securities owned for more than one year are excluded from taxation.

Capital gains on the sale of a personal residence are tax exempt if the proceeds are reinvested in another residence.

12. Foreign Tax Reliefs

See item 5.

13. Tax Periods

The calendar year is the mandatory tax year.

INCOME TAXES ON NONRESIDENTS

15. Liability to Tax

Nonresidents are taxed only on income arising in Portugal. Payments to nonresidents are closely monitored by the Bank of Portugal, which allows transfers abroad only when the taxes on such income have been paid and proof of the payments is furnished. In most cases, payments to nonresident individuals or companies for services or goods should be authorized by the Bank of Portugal in advance to ensure that payment can be made.

16. Rates

The applicable rate is 25%, except for types of income listed in item 17.

17. Withholding Tax Rates

The following types of income are subject to tax, which should be withheld at source, on earned or unearned income received in Portugal at the following rates:

	Rate
Salaries	25%
Pensions	25
Interest	20
Dividends (also see item 22)	25
Royalties	15

Leasing of equipment	15%
Profit on sale of securities	
issued by Portuguese companies	10
Other income	25

When tax is withheld at source, there is no further liability.

19. Tax Treaties

Portugal has treaties to avoid double taxation with Austria, Belgium, Brazil, Denmark, Finland, France, Germany, Italy, Norway, Spain, Switzerland, and the United Kingdom.

Country	Dividend	Interest	Royalties
Austria	15%	10%	10%/15%
Belgium	15	15	5
Brazil	15	15	10/15
Denmark	10/15	15	10
Finland	10/15	15	10
France	15	10/12	5
Germany	15	10/15	10
Italy	15	15	12
Norway	10/15	15	10
Spain	10/15	15	5
Switzerland	10/15	10	5
United Kingdom	10/15	10	5

Higher rates generally apply to minority holdings.

It should be noted that Portugal has not yet signed any treaty agreement with Canada, Holland, Japan, Sweden, or the United States.

OTHER SIGNIFICANT TAXES

21. Sales (Value Added)

VAT is payable on the value of goods and services supplied in the course of carrying on a business in Portugal and on goods and certain services imported into Portugal. Generally, goods and services will be taxed at the rate of 17%. A registered VAT taxpayer is entitled to recover VAT paid on purchases of goods and services by deducting it from the VAT calculated in its sale of goods and services. VAT is payable to the tax authorities within two months of each monthly invoice period.

□ Zero-rated items.

   —Exports.

   —Agricultural equipment and supplies.

—Agricultural products without any transformation (e.g., vegetables, bread, rice, fish, and meat).

—Pharmaceutical products.

—Doctors.

—Books and educational material.

☐ 8%-rated items.

—Hotel bills.

—Telephone, gas, electricity, telex, etc.

—Gasoline and other fuels.

—Lawyers.

—Certain food, wines, and services.

☐ 30% rate on luxury products.

22. Inheritance and Gift Taxes

Bequests by a decedent are taxed when the value of a beneficiary's share exceeds certain limits. The tax rates are progressive, from 4% to 50%, varying with the degree of relationship and the amount involved.

A 5% inheritance and gift tax is imposed on dividends paid by shareholding companies (sociedades anónimas).

23. Taxes on Payrolls (Social Security)

Social security contributions, which provide unemployment, sick, and pension benefits, are payable as follows:

		Percentage of Salary
Employer		24.5%
Employee		11.0%
	Total	35.5%

25. Other Taxes

Stamp Duty. Stamp duty is applied to a range of acts and documents. The rate payable varies according to the type of article or document and to the amount involved.

Tax on the Transfer of Real Estate (SISA). This tax is levied on the transfer of real estate and buildings at a 10% rate, and on the transfer of farm land at an 8% rate.

Tax on Sale of Vehicles. This tax is payable on the sale of new vehicles. The rates of this tax are based on the motor capacity of the vehicle.

Capital Property Tax. This tax is levied on the registered value of land and buildings. The tax rate is 0.8% for land and between 1.1% and 1.3% for buildings.

COMPUTATION OF TAXABLE INCOME

26. Capital Gains

Gains on the disposal of tangible and financial property forming part of the assets of a corporation are taxed in the same way as the income of the corporation (see item 3).

27. Depreciation and Depletion

Fixed assets can be depreciated under the straight-line or declining-balance methods. The tax law allows the use of a variation of rates of depreciation between the maximum specified in the tax law and 50% of the maximum.

28. Treatment of Dividends

Treatment of dividends received by a Portuguese company with investments in share capital or other companies are treated as part of operating income of the parent company, but to avoid double taxation, 95% of dividends received by the parent company are deductible from taxable income if the investment has been held for at least two years or from the date of incorporation of the subsidiary and interest exceeds 25% of the share capital. Other dividends received are included in the taxable income of the recipient, but 35% of the corporation tax paid by the company declaring the dividend is credited against the corporation tax payable.

29. Loss Carryovers

Tax losses (operating losses adjusted to comply with tax law) can be offset against taxable profits arising in the following five years, but losses cannot be carried back.

30. Transactions between Related Parties

Transactions between related parties should be carried at arm's length. By a tax ruling, interest rates and royalties paid to companies domiciled outside Portugal are restricted to certain limits and are subject to administrative control of the Bank of Portugal and of the Portuguese Foreign Trade Institute (ICEP).

31. Consolidation of Income

A corporation domiciled in Portugal may request to be taxed on group profits, including all subsidiaries, if the following conditions are met:

□ A holding company owns directly or indirectly more than 90% of the capital of the subsidiaries.

□ All companies are resident and managed in Portugal.

□ Approval is granted by the tax authorities after application is made.

32. Tax Periods

As a rule, the tax period coincides with the calendar year. A branch may elect to be taxed on a different closing date as well as any company, providing authorization is granted by the Ministry of Finance.

33. Other Matters.

Leasing. Under the current interpretation of the tax law, all leasing contracts are regarded, for tax purposes, as operating leases, and lease payments are allowed as a tax expense at the time of payment, with certain restrictions for land, buildings, and private cars.

Provision for Doubtful Debt. Companies may create specific provisions for doubtful debts that are allowed as a tax expense, on the following basis:

100% if the debt claim is in court.

100% if the debtor is under bankruptcy process or in a similar situation.

The following rates if the debt is outstanding for longer than six months:

6–12 months	25%
12–18 months	50%
18–24 months	75%
Over 24 months	100%

No provision is allowed if the debtor is the state, a municipality, a local government office, or group company.

Provision for Stocks. Companies may create specific provisions for stocks if the market value is lower than cost. Provision should be calculated on the difference between cost and the net sales price or replacement cost.

No general provision is allowed for tax purposes.

Other Provisions. Portuguese tax law provides for the setting up of a provision for contingent liabilities arising from litigations in courts of law. Any other provisions that may be required for the fair presentation of the accounts are not accepted, and the charge is allowed only as a tax expense when the actual liabilities arise or are paid.

National Chart of Accounts.   Companies must use the national chart of accounts, which requires the production of standard financial statements and the disclosure of certain financial information in notes to the accounts, in accordance with EC 4th Directive.

Consolidation.   Groups of companies are required to file consolidated financial statements in accordance with the provisions of the EC Seventh Directive.

RELATED CONSIDERATIONS

34. Incentives and Grants

Several regulations and programs have been created to stimulate the Portuguese economy, reorganize industries, create jobs, and provide training. These are supported by EEC grants as follows:

Agriculture	PEDAP
Industry	PEDIP, SIBR
Job creation and training	E. SOCIAL FUND
Tourism	SIFIT

Special incentives can be negotiated with the Government for very large investment projects. These are subject to European Commission approval.

35. Exchange Controls

Permission from the Bank of Portugal is required for all major transfers of funds, and such transfers require proper documentation. The transfer of dividends is controlled by Decree 197-D/86 of July 18, 1986, which governs foreign investment in Portugal.

The transfer abroad of dividends and profits is guaranteed after deduction of withholding taxes, taking into account the participation of nonresidents in the company's capital, and always is authorized provided that the legal conditions governing the investment have been fulfilled.

36. Investment Restrictions on Nonresidents

Foreign investment is authorized by the Portuguese Foreign Trade Institute (ICEP). Prior authorization is not required for direct initial investment in Portugal from the present members of the European Economic Community. However, a previous declaration of investment must be filed with the above-named institute, and only after its indication of registration can the foreign investment be made.

Foreign investment can be carried through the establishment of a branch, the constitution of a subsidiary company, or by acquisition of shares or quotas in already existing companies. There are no specific advantages or disadvantages in forming a subsidiary or buying shares or quotas except that in the latter case there are no formation costs.

No minimum capital for a subsidiary or branch is established under the Foreign Investment Law. In these circumstances, the amount of share capital may require the agreement of the ICEP, namely in respect of debt/equity ratio.

Tax and financial benefits available for Portuguese are also available for foreign investors.

SELECTION OF BUSINESS ENTITY BY NONRESIDENTS

It should be appreciated that the translation of the terms of the various forms of association allowed under Portuguese law are only approximate. Company law of 1986 provides for partnerships, limited partnerships, and joint-stock or public companies. Brief particulars of the various forms of association and their respective tax treatments are given in the following paragraphs.

Joint-Stock or Public Companies (SA). In this type of limited liability company, the capital is created by the purchase of shares (acções), which are freely transferable. There must not be fewer than five shareholders, except if the state directly or through public or nationalized enterprises is the largest shareholder, for under these circumstances a special provision has been laid down according to which the corporation may be constituted and/or carry on its activities irrespective of the number of shareholders. The company's affairs are managed by a board of directors, which is to be composed of an odd number of members (not necessarily shareholders) and which is responsible to an Assembly of Shareholders.

Limited Liability or Private Companies (LOA). Each member of this type of company provides a definite and stated amount (his quota) of the total capital. Quota holdings are not supported by share certificates and can be transferred only by deed.

Limited Partnerships. This form of association, used infrequently, provides for one or more general partners with unlimited liability and one or more special partners with limited liability.

Partnerships. This form of association, also used infrequently, provides for the joint and unlimited liability of all partners. However, arising from the fact that under Portuguese law partnerships are incorporated (i.e., endowed with personality) its partners only suffer judicial dispossession of personal wealth after insufficiency of social net worth has been recognized in a proper hearing.

Foreign Companies. These may operate in Portugal through branches or by way of a Portuguese subsidiary, normally in the form of a limited liability company.

Branches or any company with foreign investment must be registered with the Commercial Register and with the Portuguese Foreign Trade Institute (ICEP). See item 4 for the taxation of branches.

SPECIMEN TAX COMPUTATION

The following is an example of the tax liability on the net profit received by foreign owners.

	LDA (Esc. 000's)	SA (Esc. 000's)	Branch (Esc. 000's)
Net profit before tax from normal operations	800	800	950
Net profits of sale of fixed assets	50	50	50
Dividends received			
From subsidiaries	100	100	—
From short-term investments	50	50	—
	1,000	1,000	1,000
Adjustments:			
Reduction from net gain on sale of fixed assets	(50)	(50)	(50)
95% of dividends received from subsidiaries	(95)	(95)	—
Tax paid on other dividends that will be offset against corporation tax due (78 × 36%) × 35%	10	10	—
Taxable income	865	865	950
Corporation tax rate (without Derrama)	36%	36%	36%
Gross corporation tax	311	311	342
Less			
Tax credit on dividends received	(10)	(10)	
Corporation tax due	301	301	342
Net profit before tax	1,000	1,000	1,000
Taxation	301	301	342
Net profit after tax	699	699	658
5% allocated to legal reserve	(35)	(35)	—
Net profit available for dividends	664	664	658

	LDA (Esc. 000's)	SA (Esc. 000's)	(Esc. 000's)
Withholding tax rate	25%	25%	N/A
Withholding tax	(166)	(166)	N/A
Withholding inheritance tax 5%	—	(33)	—
Net amount receivable by foreign owners	498	465	658

PUERTO RICO

INCOME TAXES ON CORPORATIONS

1. Rates

There is a flat 22% normal tax on net taxable income of a corporation or partnership plus a progressive surtax on net taxable income in excess of the $25,000 "surtax exemption." The resulting effective rates are applicable to tax years beginning after December 31, 1988 and before January 1, 1992 as follows:

Corporate Tax Rate—Short Method
(Surtax Exemption Available)

Net Taxable Income		Corporate Tax
Over	Not Over	(normal tax plus surtax)
$ 0	$ 25,000	22%
25,000	100,000	28% less $ 1,500
100,000	150,000	38% less 11,500
150,000	200,000	39% less 13,000
200,000	250,000	40% less 15,000
250,000	300,000	41% less 17,500
300,000	500,000	42% less 20,500
500,000	910,000	47% less 45,500
910,000		42%

A controlled or affiliated group of corporations is limited to just one surtax exemption that may be allocated unevenly among the members of the group, if so desired. If two or more corporations in a group use up the $25,000 surtax exemption, the remaining member corporations may not use any exemption and would calculate their tax liability on the basis of the following effective rates:

Corporate Tax Rate—Short Method
(Surtax Exemption Available)

| Net Taxable Income | | Corporate Tax |
Over	Not Over	(normal tax plus surtax)
$ 0	$ 75,000	28%
75,000	125,000	38% less $ 7,500
125,000	175,000	39% less 8,750
175,000	225,000	40% less 10,500
225,000	275,000	41% less 12,750
275,000	500,000	42% less 15,500
500,000	810,000	47% less 40,500
810,000		42%

The above rates are applicable only to corporations not enjoying Puerto Rico grants of industrial tax exemption (see item 34).

The applicable rates for corporations enjoying a grant of tax exemption are as follows:

Corporate Tax Rate—Short Method
(Surtax Exemption Available)

| Net Taxable Income | | Corporate Tax |
Over	Not Over	(normal tax plus surtax)
$ 0	$ 25,000	22%
25,000	100,000	31% less $ 2,250
100,000	150,000	41% less 12,750
150,000	200,000	42% less 13,750
200,000	250,000	43% less 15,750
250,000	300,000	44% less 18,250
300,000		45% less 21,250

Foreign corporations engaged in trade or business within Puerto Rico are taxed on their Puerto Rico-source income and on income effectively connected with a trade or business within Puerto Rico at the same rates as Puerto Rican corporations. Foreign corporations not engaged in trade or business within Puerto Rico are subject to a flat withholding tax on their Puerto Rico-source income at the following rates:

Dividends and partnership profits derived from manufacturing, hotel, or shipping activities or industrial development income (reduced rates and a

special 100% withholding tax credit on dividends are
available if certain investment and repatriation
requirements are met)   10%

Dividends and partnership profits derived from nonmanufacturing activities   25%

Interest, royalties, and other fixed or determinable,
annual or periodical income   29%

Corporate Alternative Minimum Tax. For the years beginning after December 31, 1986, domestic and foreign corporations may be subject to a 22% alternative minimum tax (AMT). The AMT is imposed on taxable income increased by tax preference items and certain adjustments. Some significant preference items include: accelerated depreciation, certain accounting methods for installment sales and long-term contracts, and 50% of the excess of financial accounting income over alternative minimum net income.

Subject to certain limitations, the AMT paid in one year may be credited against the regular tax liability in a future year. The credit may not be used to offset the future AMT.

The AMT is not applicable to corporations enjoying Puerto Rico grants of industrial tax exemption (see item 34).

2. Local Income Taxes

There are no local income taxes.

3. Capital Gains Taxes

The taxation of capital gains varies according to the holding period of the property. Capital assets held for more than six months are treated as long term, and those held for less than six months are considered short term. Net capital losses are not deductible from the corporation's ordinary income, but can only offset future capital gains. Such losses must be carried forward for five taxable years, and are treated as short-term capital losses. A loss resulting from the sale of depreciable property or from land used in a business is generally an ordinary deduction from income.

Short-term Gains. Corporations and partnerships are subject to tax on 100% of net short-term capital gains. No alternative tax is available.

Long-term Gains. Corporations and partnerships are subject to tax on 100% of net long-term capital gains, but an alternative tax is available of 25% of the gain.

4. Branch Profits Taxes

A branch operating in Puerto Rico is taxed at the same rates as a corporation and is entitled to the same deductions and credits. Branches of foreign corporations are subject to income tax only on their Puerto Rico-source income and on income effectively connected with a trade or business within Puerto Rico and also may be subject to a 25% branch profits tax on deemed payments made to their home office since they are "engaged in a trade or business within Puerto Rico."

5. Foreign Tax Reliefs

Domestic corporations and partnerships are entitled to credit foreign income taxes against the Puerto Rican income tax, subject to a per country limitation and an overall limitation. As an alternative, foreign taxes may be deducted from gross income. Foreign branch operations are allowed a deduction for foreign taxes paid, subject to limitations.

7. Payment of Taxes

Corporations are required to make four quarterly estimated tax payments towards their annual tax liability and pay any balance due upon filing their income tax return. The installment payments are due on or before the 15th day of the 4th, 6th, 9th, and 12th months of the taxable year, and each payment is equivalent to 25% of the current year's estimated income tax liability.

INCOME TAXES ON INDIVIDUALS

9. Rates

Individual income is taxed at progressive rates. The following tax rates apply to taxable years beginning after December 31, 1990 but before January 1, 1992.

Taxable Income (1)		Tax on	Percentage
Over	Not Over	Lower Amount	on Excess
$ 0	$ 2,000	$ 0	9%
2,000	17,000	180	15
17,000	30,000	2,430	25
30,000	-	5,680	36

(1) These rates apply to married persons living with their spouse, single persons, or heads of household.

Taxable Income (2)		Tax on	Percentage
Over	Not Over	Lower Amount	on Excess
$ 0	$ 1,000	$ 0	9%
1,000	8,500	90	15
8,500	15,000	1,215	25
15,000	-	2,840	36

(2) These rates apply to married persons living with their spouse and filing separate returns.

Gradual Adjustments of Tax Rates.   In addition, the normal tax mentioned above will be increased by 5% of the excess of the net taxable income over $75,000 or $37,500 for married individuals living with spouse and filing separately. This increase in tax will be limited to $5,120 plus 36% of the amount of the personal exemption and the credit for dependents allowed to the taxpayer.

Alternative Basic Tax.   In addition, individuals may be subject to an alternative basic tax in lieu of the regular tax, if the alternative basic tax is greater than the regular tax.

The alternative basic tax is determined pursuant to the following table:

Adjusted Gross Income

Over	Not Over	Tax
$ 75,000	$125,000	10%
125,000	175,000	15
175,000	-	20

A flat tax of 17% is imposed on interest income (in excess of $2,000) earned by individuals in interest-bearing accounts held in commercial banks, savings associations, cooperatives, and any other banking organization in Puerto Rico. The first $2,000 of interest income is tax exempt. Taxpayers have until April 15th of each taxable year to authorize the financial institution to withhold the tax.

In addition, resident or nonresident individuals are subject to a maximum 20% tax on dividends received from a domestic corporation or partnership or a foreign corporation or partnership whose gross income from Puerto Rico sources has been at least 80% for each of the prior three years.

10. Local Income Taxes

None.

11. Capital Gains Taxes

The taxation of capital gains for individuals is similar, but not identical, to that of corporations (see item 3).

Individuals may pay a maximum 20% tax on the excess of net long-term capital gains over net short-term capital losses, or they may opt to include the net gain as part of gross income and pay the tax in accordance with the normal tax rates.

12. Foreign Tax Reliefs

Puerto Ricans and other U.S. citizens who are residents of Puerto Rico are allowed a credit for foreign income taxes. Resident aliens are allowed this credit only if their home country allows a similar credit to U.S. citizens. The credit allowed is noted in item 5. U.S. citizens who have been bona-fide residents of Puerto Rico for an entire taxable year may exclude their Puerto Rico-source income for U.S.

tax purposes. If a U.S. citizen transfers from Puerto Rico and was a resident of Puerto Rico for at least two years prior to the date of change in residence, his Puerto Rico-source income derived prior to the date of transfer may also be excluded.

13. Tax Period

The tax period for individuals is normally the calendar year. An individual may adopt a different tax period when first subject to income taxation or if permission is obtained for such a change; in both cases, however, the taxpayer's books also must be maintained on the non-calendar year basis.

INCOME TAXES ON NONRESIDENTS

15. Liability to Tax

Nonresident alien individuals that are engaged in trade or business within Puerto Rico are taxed on the same basis as residents; however, gross income includes only Puerto Rico-source income. Nonresident alien individuals that are not engaged in trade or business within Puerto Rico are subject to tax only on items of a "fixed or determinable annual or periodical nature" (i.e., interest, dividends, partnership profits, rents, salaries, wages, premiums, annuities, compensations, remunerations, emoluments, etc.) and upon net capital gains from sources within Puerto Rico. Nonresident U.S. citizens are not considered nonresident aliens; consequently, they are taxed on the same basis as a resident, but only upon income from Puerto Rican sources.

16. Rates

The tax on nonresident aliens not engaged in trade or business within Puerto Rico is satisfied through withholding at source and depends on their total annual income. If total taxable income does not exceed $22,200, the tax is withheld at a flat rate of 29%. If total taxable income exceeds $22,200, the nonresident alien is taxed on the same basis as a resident, with the following exceptions:

- [ ] The tax rate cannot be less than 29%.
- [ ] Gross income consists only of fixed or determinable annual or periodical income, plus net capital gains, from sources within Puerto Rico.
- [ ] The only deductions allowed are those properly allocable to the gross income noted above.
- [ ] The standard deduction, personal exemptions, and credits for dependents are not allowed.

The tax on nonresident U.S. citizens not engaged in a trade or business within Puerto Rico is also withheld at source but at a rate of only 20%.

19. Tax Treaties

The Commonwealth of Puerto Rico has not entered into tax treaties with the U.S. or foreign countries. U.S. tax treaties do not literally extend to Puerto Rico; however, the Supreme Court of Puerto Rico has ruled that U.S. tax treaties are binding on the Puerto Rican Treasury.

OTHER SIGNIFICANT TAXES

21. Sales (Value Added)

None.

22. Inheritance and Gift Taxes

Aggregate gifts by residents of property located in Puerto Rico are generally exempt from the gift tax. If the property is located outside of Puerto Rico, it is subject to gift tax after an annual exclusion of $10,000 per donee and a lifetime unified exemption of $400,000. Gifts by nonresidents are subject to tax (but only on property located within Puerto Rico), and the $10,000 per donee annual exclusion and the $400,000 lifetime unified exemption are available. Estate tax is imposed only on property owned by residents which is located outside of Puerto Rico. Nonresidents are subject to estate tax only on property which is located in Puerto Rico. If the gross estate of a U.S. citizen resident in Puerto Rico is included in the gross estate for federal estate tax purposes, the Puerto Rico tax on the portion of the estate is an amount equal to the allowable credit under the U.S. Internal Revenue Code for tax paid to Puerto Rico. If the gross estate, wherever located, of such U.S. citizen is not included in the federal gross estate, the estate in Puerto Rico is taxable as a resident estate. A U.S. citizen's gross estate in Puerto Rico, if the individual is not a resident of Puerto Rico at the time of death and the gross estate is not included in the federal gross estate, is taxable in Puerto Rico as a nonresident estate. For both residents and nonresidents, the gross estate excludes the value of property passing to the surviving spouse. In computing the taxable estate, the aforementioned lifetime unified exemption of $400,000 is available on the unused portion of said exemption. Foreign estate taxes paid on property includable in the Puerto Rican estate are creditable by residents and are proportionally deductible by nonresidents in determining their taxable estate.

23. Taxes on Payrolls (Social Security)

The social security tax of the U.S. is in force in Puerto Rico with the same wage bases and tax rates. Consequently, the information in the U.S. Tax Summary on social security is applicable here.

25. Other Taxes

Property Tax. Property tax is imposed jointly by the Commonwealth and municipalities on the assessed value of real property (generally lower than market value) and on the book value of certain personal property. The tax rates vary between municipalities and range from 3.07% to 4.83%.

Tax on Unreasonable Accumulation of Earnings.   Domestic corporations and partnerships and foreign resident corporations and partnerships are subject to an additional surtax if they permit their earnings to accumulate beyond the reasonable needs of the business instead of distributing them. The tax is 50% of the income accumulated during the taxable year, after certain adjustments. Tax-exempt income earned under an incentive or other grant is not subject to this surtax.

Taxes on Capital.   None.

Municipal License Taxes.   Municipalities levy license taxes based on the gross receipts of designated types of businesses. The tax rates are set by each municipality, and cannot exceed approximately 1% for financial businesses and approximately 0.3% for all other businesses.

COMPUTATION OF TAXABLE INCOME

26. Capital Gains

The gain upon the sale or exchange of a capital asset is the difference between the "adjusted basis" of the asset and the "amount realized" from its sale or exchange. The adjusted basis is generally the cost of the asset net of depreciation and other adjustments. The amount realized is the money and/or fair market value of property received in exchange for the capital asset.

27. Depreciation and Depletion

Depreciation is normally computed on the straight-line basis. Accelerated depreciation methods and the special optional "flexible depreciation" (deduction of any portion of the qualifying asset's basis) may require prior approval from the Puerto Rican Treasury. The following are examples of acceptable useful lives of some assets:

Asset	Number of Years
Concrete building	40 or 50
Steel frame factory	33
Rental housing (constructed between 3/31/80 and 1/1/83)	
Wood	10
Concrete	15
Machinery and equipment	10 to 20 (depends upon type and taxpayer's experience)

28. Treatment of Dividends

A resident corporation may deduct from gross income 85% of the dividends received from another domestic resident corporation that is subject to Puerto Rican income tax. In the case a distribution of dividends or partnership profits made during any tax year from industrial development income, the credit for the tax year will not exceed 82.7% for tax years commenced after December 31, 1990 and before January 1, 1992. The deduction may not exceed 85% or 82.7% (in the case of industrial development income) of the taxpayer's net income. Industrial development income includes the net income of a grantee from the manufacturing or other activities described in its grant of industrial tax exemption as well as specified investment income (see item 34). A credit against net income equal to 100% of the amount received by corporations as dividends consisting of principal derived from industrial development income may be obtained if certain investment requirements are satisfied.

Dividends paid by a corporation to residents of Puerto Rico are taxable. However, dividends paid by a corporation which enjoys a grant of industrial tax exemption to residents of Puerto Rico may be wholly or partially tax exempt.

29. Loss Carryovers

Net operating losses (i.e., the loss computed for tax purposes, with certain adjustments) must be carried forward seven years to offset ordinary income. Capital losses are treated differently than operating losses and are subject to special rules that vary with the classification of the taxpayer (see items 3 and 11).

30. Transactions between Related Parties

The Puerto Rican Treasury has broad powers to reallocate gross income, deductions, credits, or allowances to clearly reflect income of organizations owned or controlled by the same interests.

The income tax law authorizes a number of tax-free transactions such as the organization of a corporation, the exchange of property for corporate stock, corporate reorganizations (such as mergers, consolidations, and exchange of shares for other shares or assets). For tax years beginning after December 31, 1986, a ruling is no longer needed before a plan of corporate reorganization is carried out and one of the parties to the reorganization is a foreign corporation. In the past, a ruling from the Secretary of Treasury was a prerequisite to the reorganization if it was going to be treated as a tax-free transaction. With the 1987 tax reform legislation, the corporate reorganization would be considered tax-free if, within 183 days after the reorganization took place, all the necessary evidence is submitted to the Secretary of Treasury to establish that it was not intended to evade taxes.

31. Consolidation of Income

Puerto Rican law does not provide for consolidated income tax returns by related corporations.

32. Tax Periods

A corporation's tax period is its own accounting period. Estimated tax must be paid during the year. Tax returns are due by the fifteenth day of the fourth month after the end of the taxable year. Any tax due must be paid in full with the return. Extensions of time for filing may be requested for up to 90 days. However, interest will be assessed from the original due date if there is any unpaid balance due.

RELATED CONSIDERATIONS

34. Incentives and Grants

Puerto Rico enacted in 1987 a comprehensive incentive program whereby certain activities (e.g., manufacturing, export, maritime freight transportation activities, and some designated service units) may be partially exempt from income and property taxes and 60% exempt from municipal license taxes for varying periods. Exempt businesses are partially exempt from income taxes on their industrial development income, to the extent and for the periods indicated in the following table. For this purpose, all of Puerto Rico has been classified into four industrial zones.

	Periods and Rates of Exemption				
Industrial Zones	1–5 Years	6–10 Years	11–15 Years	16–20 Years	21–25 Years
(1) High Industrial Development	90%	90%	None	None	None
(2) Intermediate Industrial Development	90	90	90%	None	None
(3) Low Industrial Development	90	90	90	90%	None
(4) Vieques and Culebra	90	90	90	90	90%

The taxable portion of industrial development income will be subject to the income tax rates in effect on the date the decree is issued. Hotels and guest houses may also be entitled to partial tax exemptions. Other benefits available to investors include lines of credit, the availability of plant facilities on a rental basis, allowances for training employees, etc.

In addition, the two principal harbors in Puerto Rico have been classified as foreign-trade zones and foreign or domestic goods may be entered without a formal U.S. Customs inspection and without the payment of any duties or excise taxes.

35. Exchange Controls

Puerto Rico is part of the U.S. dollar area, and there are no exchange controls in this area. In rare cases, reporting requirements mandated by U.S. laws apply to Puerto Rico.

36. Investment Restrictions on Nonresidents

Puerto Rico does not restrict investments by nonresident aliens or foreign corporations. Dividends from exempt companies paid to nonresident corporate shareholders may be subject to a toll gate tax.

SELECTION OF BUSINESS ENTITY BY NONRESIDENTS

Any form of business entity may be utilized for Puerto Rican operations (e.g., corporation, partnership, joint venture, or sole proprietorship). Furthermore, any form of entity may repatriate earnings without restriction provided the applicable Puerto Rican taxes have been paid. However, the selection of the form of entity in which to do business requires considerable study. Factors that enter into the selection process are:

☐ U.S. corporations should give due consideration to Section 936 of the U.S. Internal Revenue Code, which provides special treatment to U.S. companies operating in Puerto Rico.

☐ A local subsidiary is taxed at regular rates on its worldwide income while a foreign subsidiary or foreign branch is taxed at regular rates only on its Puerto Rico-source income and income that is effectively connected with a trade or business within Puerto Rico.

☐ The tax benefits from a grant of industrial tax exemption are potentially more favorable for a subsidiary than for a branch.

SPECIMEN TAX COMPUTATION

Information:

The tax consequences of the following cases are compared with and without a Puerto Rico (P.R.) grant of an industrial tax exemption:

☐ Case 1. A foreign individual (i.e., a non-P.R./U.S. citizen or resident) owns a P.R. corporation.

☐ Case 2. A foreign individual (i.e., a non-P.R./U.S. citizen or resident) owns a P.R. corporation through a foreign parent corporation.

☐ Case 3. A foreign individual (i.e., a non-P.R./U.S. citizen or resident) owns a foreign corporation with a P.R. branch.

Industrial Tax Exemption Granted

	(1)	(2)	(3)
Profit before exemption and tax	$500	$500	$500
Exempt profits (90%)	(450)	(450)	(450)
Profit before tax	$ 50	$ 50	$ 50
Income tax	(23)	(23)	(23)
Profit (including exempt profit) after tax	$477	$477	$477
Distribution (dividend)	$477	$477	$477
Withholding tax *	(48)	(48)	___
Net distribution (dividend)	$429	$429	$477

Notes:

* Puerto Rican withholding tax rates are 10%, 10%, and none in cases 1, 2, and 3, respectively. The withholding tax rates may be reduced provided certain investment and repatriation requirements are satisfied.

Industrial Tax Exemption Denied

	(1)	(2)	(3)
Profit before tax	$500	$500	$500
Income tax	(210)	(210)	(210)
Profit after tax	$290	$290	$290
Distribution (dividend)	$290	$290	$290
Withholding tax *	(84)	(73)	(73)
Net distribution	$206	$217	$217

Notes:

* Puerto Rican withholding tax rates are 29% and 25% in cases 1 and 2, respectively. In case 3, a 25% branch profit tax may be imposed. If the distribution is from a hotel, manufacturing, or shipping activity, the branch profit tax in (3) would be 10%.

ROMANIA

Editor's Note: The tax system in Romania is undergoing a transformation to adapt to the changing business environment. New systems of corporate and personal taxation have been introduced, as well as a new turnover tax. The laws governing foreign investment, as well as the incentives, also reflect the changing environment.

INCOME TAXES ON CORPORATIONS

1. Rates

A profits tax is levied on all enterprises (public and private), including those with foreign participation. Profits of companies with foreign participation are taxed according to a progressive scale that varies between 7.5% for annual profits of 100,000 Lei to 57.37% for annual profits greater than 955,000,000 Lei.

Profits are defined as revenue less expenses incurred, such as costs of goods and promotion.

INCOME TAX ON INDIVIDUALS

9. RATES

A progressive individual income tax system applies, with rates ranging from 6% for monthly income of up to 900 Lei to 45% for monthly income exceeding 37,500 Lei.

INCOME TAXES ON NONRESIDENTS

15. Liability to Tax

Foreign personnel residing in Romania are subject to income tax on the portion of their salary received in Romania. There is no tax on any portion of income deposited directly into an account outside of Romania.

17. Withholding Tax Rates

Corporations must pay a withholding tax of 10% of profits transferred out of Romania.

OTHER SIGNIFICANT TAXES

21. Sales (Value Added)

An expanded turnover tax was introduced in November 1990. Taxable items include all products made in Romania, imported products, and services provided within the country. Certain products are exempt from tax, such as those from extractive industry, electric and thermal energy, and agricultural products.

23. Taxes on Payrolls (Social Security)

Corporations must pay contributions for social insurance for unemployment. Social insurance contributions are 25% of the employer's payroll. Contributions to the unemployment fund amount to 4% of payroll.

RELATED CONSIDERATIONS

34. Incentives and Grants

Foreign investments receive specific guarantees against nationalization, expropriation, confiscation, and other such items. Depending on the investment, foreign investors are granted tax exemptions for a specified number of years:

Business Activity	Years
Industry, agriculture, construction	5
Natural resources, communications, transportion	3
Trade, tourism, banking, other services	2

Additional reductions in taxation can be obtained, including a 50% reduction if profits are reinvested in a Romanian company engaged in technology-related activities or if the investment concerns environmental protection. A 25% tax reduction is available if the following criteria are met:

□ at least 50% of the necessary raw materials, energy, and fuel are imported,

□ at least 50% of the products and services are exported,

□ more than 10% of the expenditures are made for scientific research and development of new technology and for professional training,

□ at least 50 new jobs are created through a new investment or expansion of an existing investment.

35. Exchange Controls

Foreign investors may transfer abroad all profits earned in convertible currencies as well as a portion of the annual profit in Lei, equivalent to 8% to 15% of their contribution in kind or in cash to the registered capital. Recent amendments would enable investors to remit abroad a sum equal to 100% of their paid contribution in cash or in kind.

36. Investment Restrictions on Nonresidents

The latest version of Romania's foreign investment law compares favorably with legislation in other Eastern European countries. Investment can take the form of a wholly owned company, participation in an existing Romanian entity, or a joint venture with a Romanian partner.

The minimum level of investment is set at US$10,000 in cash or in kind. A foreign partner's contribution may be provided in hard currency, machinery or equipment, other goods or services, rights, or expertise. Investments by foreign individuals must be approved by the Romanian Development Agency (approval is presumed to be granted if the agency does not reply within 30 days). Companies must register with the local chamber of commerce and fiscal authority.

Foreign investment can take the form of a partnership, partnership limited by shares, joint-stock company, or limited liability company.

Foreign persons cannot own land, although they can purchase production facilities and buildings.

ST. LUCIA

INCOME TAXES ON CORPORATIONS

1. Rates

Corporations ordinarily resident (both public and private) pay tax at a flat rate of 33⅓% on income accruing in St. Lucia or elsewhere, whether received in St. Lucia or not.

Normal company income includes dividends, interest, rents, and royalties.

General insurance companies are taxed at 33⅓% on their chargeable income. The increase in the reserve for unexpired risk will be treated as a deduction from net income.

Associations of underwriters pay tax at 10% on the gross premiums arising in St. Lucia.

Life insurance companies are subject to tax at 10% on the gross investment income arising in St. Lucia.

2. Local Income Taxes

None.

3. Capital Gains Taxes

There are no capital gains taxes. If a person is deemed to be trading, the gain is treated as income and is taxed at the existing rate of income tax.

4. Branch Profits Taxes

None.

5. Foreign Tax Reliefs

Income derived by residents from sources outside of St. Lucia will be eligible for double taxation relief as follows:

☐ If a double taxation agreement exists, the full amount of the tax payable in the other country or as governed by the agreement.

☐ If there is no agreement, the relief will be the lesser of the tax payable in the other country or the tax charged in St. Lucia on the said income.

7. Payment of Taxes

In each year of income (defined as the period of 12 months commencing on January 1 in each year or where the financial year does not begin in January, the financial year shall be deemed to be the income year) the tax for that year of income is paid as follows:

☐ Three equal installments, March, June, and September based on the estimated liability for the year. If the liability is determined by the taxpayer, the balance of tax payable is paid by March 31 in the succeeding year, or if, in the case of a company, its financial year does not commence in January, within three months of the end of its financial year.

Transitional arrangements exist for the payment of tax under the previous act, which relate to the 1988 year of income.

Tax in respect of income from emoluments (excluding any salary and income from self-employed individuals) is payable by deduction at source in accordance with the prescribed rates. If the employer fails to deduct the tax as prescribed, he will be liable to that tax plus penalties.

Persons leaving the country require a tax exit certificate. This will be granted if the taxpayer is in good standing. Otherwise the Comptroller may require that the taxpayer give security for the outstanding tax.

Any person making payments to a contractor for the supply of labor or labor and materials or for the hiring of equipment shall deduct tax from the gross amount of such payment at the rate of 10%.

INCOME TAXES ON INDIVIDUALS

9. Rates

The income of a married woman is taxable in her own name.

A partnership is required to make a return of partnership income, but each partner is assessable individually on his share of the partnership income.

Income tax is charged at the following graduated rates:

Taxable Income		Rate
Over	Not Over	
$ 0	$10,000	10%
$10,000	20,000	15%
20,000	30,000	20%
30,000		30%

These rates apply to income after deducting the following personal reliefs:

- ☐ Personal allowance. A general deduction of $10,000.
- ☐ Allowance for spouse. If the taxpayer had his or her spouse living with him or her or maintained by and not separated from him or her a deduction of $1,500 may be claimed. This allowance is reduced by $1.00 for every dollar earned by the spouse in excess of $1,500.
- ☐ Alimony allowance. Allowed in full by court order.
- ☐ Child allowance. If less than 16 years, or a student child, or an invalid child $1,000.
- ☐ Education allowance. Over ten years if a student child residing outside of St. Lucia—$2,000.
- ☐ Higher education allowance—$5,000.
- ☐ Dependent relative allowance. Maximum of $350.
- ☐ Housekeeper allowance. $200.
- ☐ Life insurance relief. Maximum of $8,000.
- ☐ Medical expenses. $400 without support, unlimited if bills provided.
- ☐ Bank interest income is not subject to tax.
- ☐ Payments under deed of covenant for specified purposes are deductible.
- ☐ Subscription for shares in a building society or cooperative society. Maximum of $3,600. (Shares must be held for at least five years.)
- ☐ Age allowance—60 years and older. $6,000.
- ☐ Overseas pensions. Earned prior to taking up residence—allowed in full. Local pensions allowable up to $6,000.
- ☐ Owner-occupied residence—allowable deductions:
  —Mortgage interest. Maximum of $15,000.
  —Rates and taxes.
  —Insurance premiums.
  —Reasonable expenses for upkeep and maintenance.
- ☐ Gratuities. Up to 25% of gross income during the period of contract are allowed tax-free.
- ☐ Pension contributions. Allowed in full with restrictions if the fund is not constituted in St. Lucia.

10. Local Income Taxes
None.

11. Capital Gains Taxes
Same as item 3.

12. Foreign Tax Reliefs

Same as item 5.

13. Tax Period

Same as item 7.

INCOME TAXES ON NONRESIDENTS

15. Liability to Tax

Where a nonresident individual is employed in St. Lucia or where a nonresident corporation carries on business in St. Lucia, the income received is subject to tax. A nonresident's income includes income arising directly or indirectly through an agency or branch.

16. Rates

Nonresident individuals and corporations are taxed on their St. Lucia-source income at the same rates as resident individuals or corporations.

17. Withholding Tax Rates

The following payments to nonresidents are subject to the following rates of withholding tax:

Royalty	25%
Management charges	25%
Commissions or fees (not for employment)	25%
Distribution of income of a trust	25%
Premiums, including insurance premiums but excluding reinsurance premiums	25%
All payments other than amounts derived from a business and excluding dividends, interest or discounts, lease premiums or licenses, or annuities or other periodic payments	25%

OTHER SIGNIFICANT TAXES

22. Inheritance and Gift Taxes

There are no inheritance or gift taxes.

23. Taxes on Payrolls (Social Security)

National Insurance Contributions are required from each employee at 5% of the gross monthly salary up to a maximum contribution of $125.00 per month. The employer's contribution is equal to that of the employee.

25. Other Taxes

Stamp Duty. Stamp duty is levied on the registration of documents and on imported goods.

Customs Duties. Customs duties are applied to almost all goods imported into St. Lucia.

Foreign Currency Export Tax. A 1% tax is levied on all foreign export transactions.

Travel Tax. A tax is levied on the cost of airline tickets purchased locally as follows:

Destinations within the Caricom area	2.5%
Destinations outside of the Caricom area	5%

Insurance Premiums Tax. Insurance companies are subject to tax on their premiums as follows:

Resident companies	
Life insurance	1.5% of premium income
General insurance	3% of gross premiums
Nonresident companies	
Life insurance	3% of premium income
General insurance	5% of gross premiums

Property Transfer Tax. Stamp duty is payable on the conveyance, transfer, or sale of any immovable property as follows:

On the purchaser	2% ad Valorem
On the vendor	
Where the vendor is not a citizen of St. Lucia or is a company not registered in St. Lucia	10% ad Valorem
Where the vendor is a citizen of or is a company registered in St. Lucia	2.5% ad Valorem: $50,000–$75,000 3.5% from $75,001 to $150,000 5% over $150,000

Alien Land Holding License. A license to hold land as an owner is imposed on non-nationals of St. Lucia at the rate of 7.5% of the consideration or purchase price. Where a non-national wishes to hold shares in a company which holds land, or wishes to lease land, the license fee is 5% of the consideration.

COMPUTATION OF TAXABLE INCOME

26. Capital Gains

Taxable capital gains are calculated on the excess of selling price over cost (see item 3).

27. Depreciation and Depletion

Machinery and Other Plant. There is an initial allowance of 20% on all capital items that qualify for capital allowance. In addition, an annual allowance is calculated as a percentage of the residual value of the asset. A balancing charge or allowance may arise on disposal.

Industrial Buildings. There is an initial allowance of 20%. An annual allowance of 5% of the written-down value of the building is deductible. Should the building be sold or cease to be an industrial building, an adjustment will be made to the allowances claimed.

Agricultural Works. This can be written off over five years on the straight-line basis.

28. Treatment of Dividends

Distributions from companies are exempt from tax for both residents and nonresidents.

29. Loss Carryovers

A loss incurred in any trade, business, profession or vocation, to the extent that it cannot be set off against the taxpayer's other income for the year of income may be carried forward and deducted in the following years. The unexhausted balance deductible in each subsequent year is restricted so as to ensure that the tax payable for that year is not reduced to less than one-half of the amount which, but for the set off, would have been payable for that year. The loss may be carried forward for six years.

30. Transactions between Related Parties

These must always be carried out at fair market value.

31. Consolidation of Income

There is no provision for the filing of consolidated tax returns by related corporations.

32. Tax Periods

Income tax is levied for the year of income ending on December 31 upon the taxable income for that year. Trade or business profits may, with the permission of the Comptroller of Inland Revenue, be computed on the basis of the accounting year ending in the year of income.

33. Other Matters

Loans to Directors, Shareholders, or Higher Paid Employees. If a controlled company loans or advances any money to a director, shareholder, associate of a shareholder, or higher-paid employee, the amount of such loan or advance shall be deemed to be income accrued to them in the period in which it is received, unless the director, shareholder, or higher-paid employee can prove that:

- ☐ The loan or advance is repaid within one year after the end of the period in which it is received and that the repayment was not made as part of a series of loans or advances and repayments.
- ☐ The loan or advance was made by a company in the ordinary course of its operations, where such operation includes the lending of money.

When loans or advances were included in the chargeable income of a director, shareholder, or higher-paid employee and the loan or advance is subsequently repaid, the director, shareholder, or higher-paid employee shall be entitled to relief in the year of assessment in which the amount was received. A tax credit of so much of the tax payable for that year of assessment will be credited against the current year's tax liability.

A higher paid employee is considered to be a person whose remuneration exceeds $24,000.

Accommodations. A taxpayer will be liable to tax on any allowance, or the actual rent paid by the company on his behalf less any rent paid by the taxpayer. Where the accommodation is owned by the company, the taxpayer will be taxed on the annual rental value, which is expected to be the rental value that could be obtained in the market place. A taxpayer will not be subject to tax on accommodations provided by the employer when the employee is required by the employer to reside in those particular premises, and either (1) the occupation of the premises enables the employee to better perform the duties of his/her employment to a material degree, or (2) there is a special threat to the employee's security, special security arrangements are in force and the employee resides in the accommodation as part of those arrangements. However, the Comptroller has indicated that these exemptions will be granted in very rare circumstances.

In addition, if the company pays for the taxpayer's maid, gardener, electricity, water, and provide furniture for their accommodation, these benefits will also be taxable.

Entertainment. Where a taxpayer receives an entertainment allowance, the whole amount is chargeable to tax. Entertainment expenses will only be allowed if the taxpayer can provide the following:

☐ Bills and invoices of the expenses.
☐ A list of the persons entertained.
☐ Reasons for entertaining the persons concerned.
☐ Proof that income was derived as a result of the entertainment.

Car Allowances. If a taxpayer owns his own car and uses it in the performance of his duties, any allowance paid by the employer up to a maximum of $300 a month will not be taxed. Where the employer provides the taxpayer with a car, the benefit that will be taxed in the taxpayer's hand will be calculated as follows:

☐ Where the employee owns a second car: 30% × (running expenses + 20% of capital cost of car).
☐ Where the employee does not own a second car: 40% × (running expenses + 20% of capital cost of car).

RELATED CONSIDERATIONS

34. Incentives and Grants

Exemption from Tax. Under the Fiscal Incentives Act 1974, certain companies incorporated in St. Lucia and engaged in manufacturing or processing a product approved by the Cabinet may be granted a tax-exemption status for a period not exceeding 15 years. Tax losses arising during the exempt period may be carried forward and offset against profits arising after the tax-exempt period.

Under the Income Tax Ordinance 1989, hotels constructed after January 1, 1988 will be exempt from tax for 15 years. Extensions to existing hotels will give rise to exemption from tax for ten years on a proportion of the income.

Export Allowance. The Fiscal Incentives Act of 1974 provides relief for exporting companies. A company that exports to another country that is not a member of the Caribbean Common Market may receive an export allowance in the form of the following tax credits:

Export Sales as a Percentage of Total Sales	Tax Rebate as a Percentage of Income Tax on Export Profits
Between 10% and 21%	25%
Between 21 and 41	35
Between 41 and 61	45
Over 61	50

35. Exchange Controls

An exchange control act is in force, which generally requires approval for foreign exchange transactions as follows:

☐ Loans made by a nonresident company to a resident company can be repatriated if the funds are registered with the Ministry of Finance at the time the proceeds are transferred to St. Lucia.

☐ Invoices for services rendered by a nonresident company require approval.

☐ Approval will be given for the payment of dividends to a nonresident shareholder, once the company's income taxes have been settled.

☐ Any other payments to a nonresident company will require approval from the Exchange Control Authority.

ST. VINCENT AND THE GRENADINES

INCOME TAXES ON CORPORATIONS

1. Rates

The basic corporate rate of tax is 45% of taxable income. A reduced rate is applicable to companies that manufacture goods for export. The rates are as follows:

- [ ] On the chargeable income from exports to the Organization of Eastern Caribbean States (O.E.C.S.) market—35%.
- [ ] On the chargeable income from exports to the non-O.E.C.S. Caricom markets—30%.
- [ ] On the chargeable income from exports to the extra-Caricom market—25%.

International companies are required to pay only a small fixed registration fee and fixed annual charges in lieu of income taxes, and to pay tax on dividend distributions to nonresidents.

Normal company income includes dividend income, but resident corporations receive a rebate of tax on dividends received from other resident corporations so that, effectively, no tax is paid.

2. Local Income Taxes

None.

3. Capital Gains Taxes

None.

4. Branch Profits Taxes

Branches of foreign corporations are subject to corporation tax at full rates on the profits of the branch. The after-tax profits of a nonresident company carrying on business through a branch or agency are deemed to be remitted in full and, therefore, are liable to withholding tax (see item 17), except to the extent that the profits have been reinvested in St. Vincent, other than in the replacement of fixed assets or in short-term bank notes.

5. Foreign Tax Reliefs

St. Vincent residents receiving income from foreign sources are entitled to a foreign tax credit calculated in accordance with the provisions of any existing treaties. Where income has accrued to a resident on which income tax has been paid under the laws of another country with which no treaty exists or, where treaties do exist, if the income received has not been specifically provided for, relief is granted to the extent of the lesser of the tax payable in the other country or the tax payable in St. Vincent.

6. Classification of Corporations

Corporations are classified for St. Vincent tax purposes as a resident or nonresident corporation, and as a public or private corporation. A resident corporation is one which is incorporated in St. Vincent; or carries on business in St. Vincent and has either:

□ its central management and control in St. Vincent
□ its voting power controlled by shareholders who are residents of St. Vincent.

The distinction between resident and nonresident corporations is important in that St. Vincent residents are subject to tax on their worldwide income whereas non-residents are only subject to tax on their St. Vincent source income. The distinction also has a bearing on the treatment of dividend income (see item 1).

Resident and nonresident corporations are divided into public and private corporations. Generally, public corporations are those whose shares are listed on a stock exchange or are subsidiaries of listed corporations. All other corporations are private. Currently, both public and private corporations pay income tax at 45%, except for international business companies. Companies formed in St. Vincent qualify as 'international' companies if they do not engage in buying or selling goods or providing services in St. Vincent and if no resident of St. Vincent receives directly more than one-tenth of the total assets, issued share capital, issued loan capital or interest, dividends or other consideration payable in respect of any loan or preference shares.

7. Payment of Tax

Corporations are required to pay tax in installments that are based on the preceding year's chargeable income or the latest year for which an assessment has been raised. In the case of a corporation not previously assessed to tax, the tax payable is based on the estimated income for the current year. The installments are payable as follows:

□ The first two installments by September 30 and December 31 of the income year forming the basis period for the year of assessment.

□ The third installment by March 31 in the year of assessment immediately following the basis period for that year of assessment. The third installment is an amount equal to one-third of the previous year's charge if the return is not filed by March 31, or the balance of the tax payable based on the tax return for the year of assessment for which the return is furnished.

INCOME TAXES ON INDIVIDUALS

9. Rates

Tax is charged at the following rates:

Taxable Income		Tax on Lower Amount	Percentage on Excess
Over	Not Over		
$ 0	$ 2,000	$ 0	10%
2,000	4,000	200	15
4,000	6,000	500	20
6,000	10,000	900	25
10,000	15,000	1,900	30
15,000	25,000	3,400	35
25,000	35,000	6,900	40
35,000	45,000	10,900	50
45,000		15,900	55

The income on all pensions (including social security payments), whether earned locally or abroad, are exempt from income tax up to a maximum of $20,000.

Salaries and wages are subject to tax deductions at source. The tax is payable within fifteen days after the end of the month during which that tax was deducted or deductible.

10. Local Income Taxes

None.

11. Capital Gains Taxes

None, except for dividends received of a capital nature (see item 28).

12. Foreign Tax Reliefs

Same as item 5.

13. Tax Period

Income tax is levied for the year ended December 31, termed a year of assessment. However, with the permission of the Comptroller, a taxpayer may include in his income for the calendar year the profit from a business or profession whose year-end falls within the calendar year. Individuals are required to pay all tax due based on a self-assessment system by March 31 in the year of assessment.

INCOME TAXES ON NONRESIDENTS

15. Liability to Tax

Nonresident individuals and corporations are subject to tax on St. Vincent source income. A nonresident's chargeable income includes any income arising directly or indirectly through an agency or branch.

16. Rates

Nonresident individuals and corporations are taxed on their St. Vincent source income at the same rates as resident corporations. However, nonresident corporations are subject to withholding tax on unremitted branch or agency profits (see item 17) except to the extent that the profits have been reinvested in St. Vincent, other than to replace fixed assets or in short-term bank notes.

17. Withholding Tax Rates

Withholding tax applies when remittances are made or when amounts accrue to nonresidents with respect to royalties, management fees, interest, branch profits (net of income tax and investments), insurance premiums, mortgage interest, and any other payment of an income nature (at 20%), dividends (at 15%), and real estate rentals (at 10%).

	Dividends	Interest	Royalties
Nontreaty countries	15%	20%	20%
Treaty countries:			
Barbados	(1)	25	25
Guyana	(1)	25	25
Jamaica	(1)	25	25
Trinidad & Tobago	(1)	25	25
Antigua	(1)	25	25
Belize	(1)	25	25
Dominica	(1)	25	25
Grenada	(1)	25	25
Montserrat	(1)	25	25
St. Lucia	(1)	25	25
St. Kitts, Nevis, and Anguilla	(1)	25	25

Notes:

(1) The lesser of 15% or the rate of tax chargeable in respect of the profits of the company paying the dividend.

OTHER SIGNIFICANT TAXES

22. Inheritance and Gift Taxes

Succession duties at graduated rates are levied on the value of a deceased person's real and personal property (except the family home) situated in St. Vincent. There are no gift taxes but, for the purpose of assessing estate duties, gifts made within a certain period prior to the date of death are includable.

23. Taxes on Payrolls (Social Security)

National Insurance Contributions are required from each employee at 2.5% of gross salary up to a maximum monthly contribution of $41.75.

25. Other Taxes

Stamp Duty. Stamp duty is levied on the registration of documents on imported goods.

Customs Duties. Almost all imported goods are subject to customs duties.

COMPUTATION OF TAXABLE INCOME

26. Capital Gains

See item 28.

27. Depreciation and Depletion

Buildings. An initial allowance of 10% is deductible for expenditures incurred in the construction or purchase of any building used for business purposes, except for buildings used for residential purposes or as a retail shop, showroom, or office. Annual deductions of 4% of the written-down value of the building at the end of the immediately preceding year are permitted.

Plant and Machinery. In addition to an initial allowance of 20%, annual deductions equal to the following percentages are permitted:

□ Office furniture and equipment, electrical appliances, light plant and machinery, professional instruments and equipment, electrical wiring, plumbing fixtures, air conditioning plant and ducting, and machinery not specified below	15%
□ Air conditioning units, computers, lifts, elevators, escalators, ships, boats, tugs, barges and other vessels	20%
□ Motor vehicles other than heavy vehicles	25%

□ Heavy motor vehicles, heavy plant and machinery and earth
    moving equipment   33.33%
□ Aircraft and equipment   50%

Where allowances have been granted for previous years and any such asset is
disposed of, a balancing allowance or charge may result.

Agricultural Expenditures. Capital expenditures on any agricultural works are
deductible on a straight-line basis over five years.

28. Treatment of Dividends

Residents and nonresidents carrying on business in St. Vincent include all dividends
received in their assessable income. However, resident corporations receive a rebate
from their tax payable on dividend income. Dividends received by nonresidents not
carrying on business in St. Vincent are not included in assessable income but are
subject to withholding tax (see item 17).

Where a controlled company (meaning a company controlled by not more than
five shareholders excluding the government) does not distribute to its shareholders
as dividends a reasonable proportion of its total income, the company is liable to
pay tax of 15% on its undistributed profits of that year of assessment. The time
allowed for making a sufficient distribution is the period ending December 31 in
the year of assessment; however, where any controlled company proves to the
satisfaction of the Comptroller that distribution by such date would be detrimental
to the business, the Comptroller may waive the requirement to make a distribution.
Where excess distributions are made in a year of assessment, the amount of such
excess is deemed to be a distribution in relation to the next year of assessment. A
controlled company is considered to have made a sufficient distribution if its dividend
payments are a proportion of its after-tax income that the Comptroller deems reasonable.

A dividend is defined as any distribution of the assets of a company, whether
in cash or otherwise, to its shareholders, and includes:

□ Any profit distributed (whether or not of a capital nature).
□ Any amount by which the paid-up value of the shares is reduced.
□ In a reorganization, any distribution in excess of the paid-up value of the
    shares.
□ In a winding-up, any distribution in excess of the paid-up capital of the company.

29. Loss Carryovers

Losses may be carried forward indefinitely; however, the maximum amount that
may be applied to any subsequent year is an amount that would cause the tax for
the subsequent year to be one-half of what it would have been without the loss
carryforward.

30. Transactions between Related Parties

These must always be carried out at fair market value.

31. Consolidation of Income

There is no provision for the filing of consolidated tax returns by related corporations.

32. Tax Periods

Income tax is levied for the year ended December 31. Corporations may, with the permission of the Comptroller, compute business profits for a period of 12 months ending in the calendar year.

RELATED CONSIDERATIONS

34. Incentives and Grants

Where any company has been approved as a pioneer enterprise for the manufacture of pioneer products or as a hotel development enterprise, such company shall be exempt from tax to the extent provided under the Fiscal Incentives Act, 1982 and Hotels Aid Act.

Entrepreneurs who are granted "Approved Enterprise" status by the Cabinet are entitled to fiscal incentives, which vary with the following classifications of Approved Enterprises:

- [ ] Group 1 Enterprise. Fifteen-year tax holiday to an enterprise that adds local value of 50% or more of the total sales of the approved product.
- [ ] Group 2 Enterprise. Twelve-year tax holiday for adding local value of between 25% and 50% of total sales of the approved product.
- [ ] Group 3 Enterprise. Ten-year tax holiday for adding local content of 10% to 25% of the total sales of the approved product.
- [ ] Enclave Enterprise. An enterprise that exports 100% of its production outside the CARICOM area may be granted a tax holiday of 15 years.
- [ ] Capital Intensive Industry. An approved enterprise that is a highly capital intensive industry, and whose initial capital investment is not less than 25 million EC dollars or its equivalent may be granted a tax holiday of 15 years.
- [ ] Hotels. A ten-year tax holiday is granted to a new hotel enterprise, and in accordance with the Hotels' Aid Act of 1988, if a hotel constructs an extension of five or more rooms, a ten-year tax holiday is granted on the net earnings from those rooms.

On the expiration of a tax holiday period under the Fiscal Incentives Act, 1982, the net losses incurred during the period may be carried forward and offset profits for a five year period following the tax holiday period. The Act defines net losses as the excess of all losses over all profits earned during the period it was an approved enterprise.

Under the 1979 Income Tax Act, if during the last year of a hotel's tax holiday period an assessed loss (calculated under the provisions of that act) is incurred, such loss may be carried forward in accordance with item 29.

35. Exchange Controls

Permission must be obtained from the Ministry of Finance for the remittance of all funds to nonresidents. A 2% tax is levied on the remittance.

SAUDI ARABIA

INCOME TAXES ON CORPORATIONS

1. Rates

Income taxes on profits are payable by all business enterprises (including branches of foreign corporations, partnerships, and individuals trading for their own account), except to the extent that entities formed or registered in Saudi Arabia are Saudi-owned. Citizens of the Gulf Cooperation Council countries (GCC) (i.e., Kuwait, Saudi Arabia, Bahrain, Qatar, United Arab Emirates and Oman) who are resident in Saudi Arabia are treated as Saudis for this purpose. The portion of entities owned by GCC nationals, formed under the regulations of a GCC state and registered to do business in Saudi Arabia, are subject to Zakat (an Islamic direct tax on property and income). The results of enterprises formed or registered in Saudi Arabia and owned jointly by Saudis and non-Saudis are divided and the non-Saudi owners are taxed on their portions. Saudis who hold shares in business entities formed or registered outside Saudi Arabia are treated like other aliens when these entities do business in Saudi Arabia. Corporations and limited partnerships are treated as companies for tax purposes. The tax rates for foreign companies operating in Saudi Arabia are as follows:

Taxable Income		Tax on	Percentage
Over	Not Over	Lower Amount	on Excess
SR 0	SR 100,000	SR 0	25%
100,000	500,000	25,000	35
500,000	1,000,000	165,000	40
1,000,000		365,000	45

Saudi-owned enterprises, and the Saudi-owned portion of joint enterprises incorporated or registered in Saudi Arabia, are not liable to income tax on profits but are subject to a religious tax known as Zakat. This is calculated, subject to certain detailed adjustments, at 2.50% of owner's funds invested minus net fixed assets. Zakat is due after the new business has passed through a full annual cycle.

These taxes are assessed by, and payable to, the Directorate of Zakat and Income (DZIT) of the Ministry of Finance. This is a central Government organization.

2. Local Income Taxes

There are no local (i.e., state or district) taxes.

3. Capital Gains Taxes

Capital gains (either made by a commercial enterprise, or made as a result of selling an interest in a commercial enterprise) are taxed as though they were revenue profits.

5. Foreign Tax Reliefs

The Saudi-Arabian tax authorities have only ratified one double tax treaty, which is with France and applies only to income and inheritance tax of individuals; the term of this treaty has expired, but it is expected to be extended. There is no provision for relief from Saudi-Arabian income tax as a result of foreign taxes paid. There are arrangements (see item 1) whereby citizens of certain neighboring Arab countries are treated as Saudis for some purposes.

Relief may be obtained in certain other countries in respect of Saudi income taxes, depending on the tax regulations in the individual countries concerned. However, there is sometimes difficulty in establishing that the Saudi income taxes are computed on net profits, particularly where arbitrary assessments have been made (see item 17) based on turnover. Relief in respect of penalties is generally not obtainable.

6. Classification of Corporations

The following methods of commencing business operations in Saudi Arabia establish taxability and, thus, necessitate the filing of annual accounts:

☐ Entering the Kingdom by invitation from a government department or agency to carry out a contract (the contractor to leave the Kingdom when the contract is completed), or to carry out a subcontract for a prime contractor who, in turn, is working for a governmental body (the subcontractor to leave the Kingdom when the subcontract is completed), the venture obtaining temporary registration.

☐ Establishing a commercial venture jointly with one or more Saudis (the venture obtaining a Foreign Capital Investment License and Commercial Registration).

☐ Registering a wholly owned branch of a foreign company to trade in Saudi Arabia (with permission from the Foreign Capital Investment Committee and the Ministry of Commerce).

In other cases, infrequently and with considerable difficulties in registration, a wholly owned foreign enterprise can establish a branch in the Kingdom and secure its registration as a technical representation office; in this event, a small number of personnel will be granted the necessary residence and work permits by the Saudi-

Arabian authorities. The technical representation office may look after the technical (or client relations, quality control, general promotion, etc.) affairs of the firm, but may not trade in the Kingdom. Since no sales are made nor income earned through the activities of a technical representation office, there are no tax implications in this type of operation. It must be pointed out, however, that the prohibition against such a technical representation office earning income is strictly enforced.

Since November, 1979, as pointed out above, the Ministry of Commerce has commenced allowing registration of subcontractors on Government projects, even though the prime contractors on such projects may be private companies, without requiring such subcontractors to join with Saudi partners in their registered enterprises in Saudi-Arabia, and without requiring them to appoint Saudi agents. The registration formalities for such subcontractors, as for contractors engaged in direct Government projects, lead to the grant of a temporary Commercial Registration, which is valid for the term of the contract which the enterprise is performing.

7. Payment of Taxes

Income tax, withholding taxes, Zakat, and penalties (if applicable) are payable at the DZIT only by certified check or banker's draft in Saudi Riyals payable in Riyad. The instrument (check or draft) should be made payable to "Director General of Zakat and Income." Banking procedures in Saudi Arabia are often slow and undependable, and payment arrangements should be made early.

8. Other Matters

Tax Holidays. Taxpayers wishing to enjoy permanent residence must apply for registration under the Foreign Capital Investment Code (FCIC), which is another way to obtain a tax holiday. Registration is dependent on the project or business being deemed to relate to the economic development of the Kingdom. If registration is granted, and the enterprise is Saudi-owned to the extent of at least 25%, a tax holiday is generally granted for five years (ten years for industrial and agricultural enterprises) covering the share of profits of the foreign owners (the Saudi shareowners remain liable for the Zakat). Profits from contracts signed before the inception date of the tax holiday continue to be taxable for their duration, even if it extends into the tax holiday. Therefore, only new contracts signed after the inception of the tax holiday qualify for the tax exemption of the foreign owners' share of profits therefrom. During the tax holiday, the enterprise remains obliged to file tax returns, and must account for Zakat on the Saudi-owned shares, as well as withholding taxes, and Zakat on Saudi subcontractors.

Allowable Expenditures. All expenditure incurred wholly and exclusively for business is, in theory, an allowable deduction from income. However, restrictions are placed on certain types of expenditure and these are detailed in the items that follow. In computing the expenditure incurred in a particular year, it is necessary to employ ordinary principles of commercial accountancy, as interpreted by the

DZIT. In practice, income and expenditure are dealt with by the DZIT along the following lines:

☐ Income can be checked with information obtained from the customer (often another Government department or agency).

☐ Expenditure is allowable if it can be demonstrated that it goes toward another Saudi taxpayer's or potential taxpayer's taxable income. Evidence is often required that this criterion is met.

☐ Imports of goods from unrelated enterprises are normally allowable, provided they are supported by original invoices and customs manifests. If the goods are imported from the head office, the taxpayer should also provide a certificate from the head office's auditors stating that the goods are priced at international market levels at the date of dispatch.

☐ Depreciation is computed on the straight-line method after deducting from the original cost the estimated residual value of the assets (normally 10%). Certain types of assets, such as loose tools and containers, can be depreciated on an annual revaluation basis. Rates of depreciation are laid down by the DZIT.

☐ Payments to enterprises outside Saudi Arabia for equipment rental, insurance premiums, interest, services, and most subcontract work are accepted, provided the DZIT receives the tax due thereon.

☐ Normal revenue payments of a minor nature to unrelated enterprises outside Saudi Arabia (e.g., hotel bills, travel) are allowable, and are not subject to withholding.

☐ Social insurance contributions paid outside Saudi Arabia for employees working in Saudi Arabia are not allowable deductions in the accounts of the local enterprise.

☐ A deduction from profits may be made in respect of bad debts, provided the taxpayer can show that legal action has been taken against the defaulting debtor and his auditor certifies that the amount has been removed from the books. A general provision for bad debts, such as on a percentage basis, is regarded as an appropriation of profit and is therefore not allowable.

☐ Preoperational costs which can be allocated properly to capital expenditure can be amortized for tax purposes with other capital costs. Other preoperational costs which cannot be attributed to capital expenditure can be written off in equal instalments over a period of up to five years from the date of commencement of operations, or over the life of a project if it is less than three years.

Allocation of Expenditures.   Head office overhead and similar general expenses allocated to the Saudi Arabian operations from abroad are not allowable deductions from income. However, direct expenses incurred exclusively for the execution of engineering, chemical, geological, industrial and research work are allowable deductions provided the DZIT is furnished with the following information:

- □ Name of engineer.
- □ Nationality.
- □ Number of hours worked.
- □ Rate per hour (include only salary and directly related employment costs).
- □ Type of work performed.
- □ Name of project in Saudi Arabia for which the work was performed.

The above information should be listed on a statement and certified by the auditors of the enterprise abroad, stating that they have examined the overall costs that have been incurred and that the basis of allocation is proper. However, problems may still arise in getting such costs allowed.

In practice, this is the most difficult aspect of agreement of tax. A non-Saudi engineering or construction contractor will often incur substantial selling, preparation, design, engineering and administrative costs outside the Kingdom. If such costs are disallowed, the Saudi tax payable on the profit, after disallowing these items, can exceed 100% of the profit after deducting them. This may be partly, but often not wholly, offset in the home country by way of double tax relief. There is no wholly satisfactory solution to this problem; however, if the amounts involved are likely to be material, the difficulty may be avoided or mitigated by adopting one or more of the following procedures:

- □ Maximizing the engineering effort to be carried out in the Kingdom. This has the disadvantage that direct payroll costs and associated expenditure are significantly increased.
- □ Negotiating separate contracts for services inside and outside the Kingdom for separate companies to perform so that the "outside" company is not in the position of doing business inside and outside the Kingdom at the same time. Subject to commercial constraints, the price for the 'outside' portion can take into account any tax liability which may arise.

A firm with activities both in and out of Saudi Arabia at the same time is clearly taxable under the Saudi Arabian income tax regulations. For a company not to be subject to Saudi Arabian tax, it must be able to show that it carries out its activities wholly outside Saudi Arabia and has no presence or "derived" income in Saudi Arabia. In the case of companies that obtain Saudi Arabian business, this is usually difficult to achieve, as an element of local work is inevitable in most instances and this may be enough to jeopardize the tax status of the whole contract. Negotiating separate contracts for services inside and outside the Kingdom can help to minimize the risk of offshore business being assessed to tax. It should be noted that certain customers in Saudi Arabia would be opposed to the idea of separate contracts, for administrative and other reasons, although the idea has been accepted and put into practice by some organizations and government bodies.

Supply of Services. Particular difficulties arise where an enterprise purchases services supplied from outside the Kingdom, often from related parties. The expenditure might be considered by the DZIT as one or more of the following, all of which have disadvantages:

- Payments to nonresidents (see item 5).
- Head office costs (see item 8).
- Payments to related parties (see item 8).

Contractor's Income. The income of a contractor from a long-term contract is usually computed using a simple form of the percentage of completion basis. The work performed during the year is generally calculated in accordance with engineers' certificates.

INCOME TAXES ON INDIVIDUALS

9. Rates

The basis of assessment of Saudi income taxes on profits is almost identical for corporations and individuals trading on their own account. However, the tax rates for such self-employed individuals are lower than those set out in item 1, as follows:

Annual Profits

Over	Not Over	Rate
SR 0	SR 6,000	0% (if resident for full year)
6,000	16,000	5
16,000	36,000	10
36,000	66,000	20
66,000		30

In practice, non-Saudi individuals trading on their own account are rare due to the difficulty encountered in obtaining commercial or professional registration, and are confined to a small number of professional practitioners (e.g., doctors, architects, and auditors).

Non-Saudi employees, similarly to Saudi citizens, are currently not liable to Saudi income taxes on their earnings from salaries and wages.

INCOME TAXES ON NONRESIDENTS

15. Liability to Tax

The tax regulations do not explicitly differentiate between residents and nonresidents, but between nationals and aliens (i.e., between Saudis and non-Saudis). All profits arising or "derived" from the Kingdom (which term is interpreted extremely broadly) are assessable to tax, and all enterprises carrying on business in the Kingdom are required to file accounts with the DZIT in order to establish the liability.

17. Withholding Tax Rates

It is recognized by the DZIT that they have no effective direct power to compel the filing of accounts and payment of tax by certain categories of nonresidents (e.g., subcontractors, insurance companies, and lessors of plant), and in these instances the taxpayer who has employed the services of the nonresident is required to withhold from the payment for the service, and pay over to the DZIT with its own income tax, income tax on behalf of the nonresident based on an estimate of the profits made. Customarily, this estimate has been that profits amount to 15% of turnover (i.e., profit is estimated at 15% of the price of the services and income tax is computed and paid accordingly). However, the assumed profit rate may be increased by the DZIT for certain classes of business (e.g., engineering consultancy). Other types of payments, such as royalties, may be construed as containing 100% profit.

If the withholding is not recovered from the nonresident, the tax should be calculated on the grossed-up income of the nonresident; that is, including the amount of the tax to be paid on behalf of the nonresident as additional compensation to the nonresident from the withholding taxpayer.

Government ministries, departments, and agencies must retain certain amounts, including the last payment of the contract price, until the contractor produces an appropriate, valid tax clearance certificate from the DZIT. Contractors employing 100% Saudi subcontractors not registered with DZIT must withhold Zakat of 0.375% of gross payments to such subcontractors, which is then forwarded to the DZIT with the employer's annual tax return.

OTHER SIGNIFICANT TAXES

23. Taxes on Payrolls (Social Security)

Social security taxes are payable by the employer at 13% of total emoluments, in cash or in kind, earned by Saudi nationals. A share of 8% is to be borne by the employer (10% if the employer has been advised that he is subject to the Occupational Hazards Branch) and 5% by the Saudi national. The salary is sometimes adjusted to take the payment into account so that the whole 13% (or 15%) amount is effectively borne by the employer. In such cases the 5% employee share is disallowed as an expense of the employer. Beginning March 1987, foreign employees are not subject to social security. However, the employer is still subject to 2% (Occupational Hazards) of the total emoluments of foreign employees.

24. Taxes on Natural Resources

Levies are imposed upon the exploitation of natural resources. The levy depends upon the terms of the concession agreement negotiated with the government of

Saudi Arabia, but usually takes the form of royalties. A special tax rate applies to petroleum-producing concessionary companies.

25. Other Matters

Import Duties. Import duties are payable at 12% to 20% on the CIF value of most imports. There is a 20% protection tariff rate applying to certain commodities, mostly manufactured items, which are in competition with similar locally manu-factured goods. Only a few items of foodstuffs, medicine and medical products, military equipment, books, machinery, and raw materials imported by companies licensed under the FCIC are exempt from customs duty.

COMPUTATION OF TAXABLE INCOME

26. Capital Gains

As noted in item 3, capital gains form part of assessable profits and are taxed as ordinary profits. The capital gain is the difference between the cost, less any applicable depreciation or amortization of the capital asset, and the proceeds from its disposal.

28. Treatment of Dividends

No taxes are payable on distributions, whether as dividends from profits already taxed or from capital in a winding-up.

29. Loss Carryovers

Tax losses are not allowed to be carried back or forward. Consequently, certain options available to the taxpayer (e.g., spreading of preoperating costs) should be carefully considered.

30. Transactions between Related Parties

In cases where work is carried out in the Kingdom by companies under common control, the DZIT requires that each such corporation, limited partnership, or con-sortium pay the tax due from the foreign partners therein; it is not permissible to offset losses suffered in one such venture against profits from another in the same year. The main purpose of this aggregation is to prevent the duplication of use of lower tax brackets by the component members of a group of enterprises.

Expenses charged in the accounts that represent payments to related parties may be the subject of particular attention by the DZIT to determine whether (a) they represent nondeductible allocations of overhead from abroad, or (b) their prices are at arm's length. Although a transaction with a party whose relationship is not obvious (e.g., another company with a dissimilar name) may not come to the attention of the DZIT, the accounts that must be filed with the DZIT, in order to "present the actual financial position and results of operations in accordance with generally accepted accounting principles as modified by the tax regulations of the Kingdom of Saudi Arabia'' (the normal form of words in the audit opinion (''certificate'')

32. Tax Periods

Corporations are required to file tax returns and audited accounts and pay the tax due before the fifteenth of the third month following their year-end. Self-employed professional individuals are required to submit their accounts and pay the tax due within 15 days following their year-end. The accounts are required to be certified by a licensed auditor registered to practice in Saudi Arabia. Fines are imposed for late filing of tax returns or for late payment.

The time limit for filing the tax returns and accounts may be extended for up to six months, provided a provisional return is filed and the estimated tax due is paid to the DZIT within the unextended time limit. Where a filing extension has been granted and a tax payment made on account, the rules must be followed carefully.

The agreement of tax assessments can be a lengthy and difficult procedure and can take up substantial management time. All detailed information requested by the DZIT should be supplied, however onerous, and it is essential to ensure that the estimated income tax is paid on time, and is sufficient to avoid penalties.

Basis of Assessment. The basis of assessment is the actual profit disclosed by audited accounts as adjusted for tax purposes. It is generally presumed by DZIT that the taxpayer follows a predetermined financial year. In the case of foreign taxpayers, this should be the financial year adopted in their accounts abroad, and in the case of a company registered in Saudi Arabia the financial year should be as specified in the registration documents. Initially, income should be computed for a twelve-month period starting from the date the taxpayer commenced business. Long and short first accounting periods may be applied for and are subject to special rules. In particular, a long accounting period cannot exceed eighteen months in duration. The purpose of the long or short initial period is to allow the taxpayer to file accounts for the taxpayer's regular financial year thereafter. A change of year-end can involve complications in agreement of tax liabilities for the lengthened or shortened periods, and is very difficult to obtain.

Requests to the DZIT for the approval of the first accounting period should be submitted shortly after the start of operations and, at the latest, within two and one-half months from the end of the (first) annual or short period (or 14½ months from the start of the long period). If this is not done, request for long accounting periods may be refused, giving rise to the risk of the imposition of fines for nonpayment of tax by the due date. When a long period is used, the taxpayer must make a payment of estimated tax within 14½ months from the commencement of activities (or inception), which payment will be credited against the eventual amounts which are due for payment two and one-half months after the end of the long period. Upon filing the long-period return, the results are then prorated to test whether the interim payment was sufficient, that is, that it did not fall short by more than 10% of the pro rata amount due. If the shortfall exceeds 10%, a fine of 25% of the entire shortfall will be levied. The tax brackets are ''annualized'' for a long or short year.

33. Other Matters

Accounting Records. Taxpayers are required to keep Arabic books of account and documentary support in Saudi Arabia that record their income, expenditures, sales, purchases, receipts, and payments. In cases where the DZIT is not satisfied that proper books of accounts are kept, arbitrary assessments may be made. The authorities require that the journal book, general ledger, and inventory book be maintained. The licensed auditor is also required to mention in his report whether the taxpayer has kept these books in the Arabic language.

Arbitrary Assessments. In certain cases, and particularly when the returns submitted by the taxpayer are inadequate or when the taxpayer is unable to produce or does not keep proper accounts, DZIT has the power to impose an arbitrary assessment of tax. This is done by applying a percentage estimate of deemed profit (not less than 15% of gross income or turnover), and subjecting the result to the graduated tax rates. As pointed out earlier, this may be deemed a turnover tax in some countries, and the taxpayer may be unable to obtain credit or double tax relief for amounts thus assessed and paid. Penalties can be added to the arbitrary tax amounts.

Termination of Business. The DZIT must be advised within 60 days of termination of a business, within which period any returns due must be filed and any taxes outstanding must be paid; otherwise, additional tax for a further year and/or penalties can be assessed. Extensions of time for filing final returns are not available.

Authorization and Undertaking Letter. In order to enable a registered auditor to make submissions to DZIT on behalf of a client, DZIT requires that an "Authorization and Undertaking" letter be filed with it in Arabic, signed and stamped (or sealed) by both the client and the accountant. The language of this letter is as laid down by DZIT. An English translation follows:

(Client Letterhead)
(Date)

DELEGATION AND UNDERTAKING

From: (Name and position of signatory)
       (Client name and address)
       PARTY OF THE FIRST PART
To Auditor: (Name)
       (Address)
       PARTY OF THE SECOND PART

The first Party hereby delegates unto the Second Party the representation of the

First Party before the Directorate-General of Zakat and Income in the Kingdom of Saudi-Arabia, and its Divisions and Branches, and to submit and receive all correspondence including the temporary and final certificates and receipts, as well as delegating to the Second Party the reply to all objections of the Directorate and its Branches, and the acceptance of adjustments and assessments which the Directorate may make in the accounts and statements of the First Party.

The Second Party agrees hereby that he accepts the above delegation and undertakes to represent the First Party and present and argue his case for him, before the Directorate-General of Zakat and Income on behalf of the First Party, and he avers hereby that his responsibility to do so is an absolute and unconditional responsibility towards the said Directorate.

This Delegation and Undertaking has been made up to witness the above.

PARTY OF THE FIRST PART

Official Stamp:

PARTY OF THE SECOND PART

Official Stamp:

RELATED CONSIDERATIONS

37. Other Matters

Ministerial Decree No. 124. Foreign companies and enterprises must obtain certificates from their customers certifying their compliance with the terms of Decree No. 124. Failure to present this certificate will delay the issuance of their final tax clearance certificates.

The Decree requires all non-Saudi contractors (foreign individuals or companies, mixed companies with F.C.I.C. licenses where foreign ownership is more than 49%, and joint ventures) to subcontract to wholly owned Saudi contractors (individuals or companies registered in Saudi Arabia and wholly owned by Saudis) not less than 30% of the work specified in their contracts. The Decree covers public work contracts which require general construction, repairs, and maintenance work. The 30% requirement can be satisfied by either performing services or providing materials, and the percentage can be divided between various Saudi contractors.

Bidders should be notified of the Decree and its requirements. The customer must condition awarding the contract on the foreign contractor fulfilling the 30% participation clause and providing to the customer the Saudi contractor's legal documents—for example, his Commercial Registration, Zakat clearance certificate, and Chamber of Commerce membership certificate. No advance payment (or payment against the first progress invoice) will be made until the foreign contractor provides proof that he has contracted with one or more Saudi enterprises to execute not less than 30% of the contract's value. If the foreign contractor wishes to postpone Saudi participation until the final phases of the project, the customer's payments should generally not exceed 50% of the billings until the requirements are met.

The Decree also obligates all contractors (whether Saudi or non-Saudi) to purchase machinery and equipment from Saudi agents and to use local Saudi establishments for transportation (unless the contractor uses his own equipment and personnel), insurance, banking, and real estate transactions.

SENEGAL

INCOME TAXES ON CORPORATIONS

1. Rates

In Senegal, corporations (limited companies, profitable activities of legal entities) and profits made by partnership electing to be liable to corporation tax are subject to corporation tax (C.T.). The rate of this tax is equal to 35%.

The taxable profit is equal to the net profit minus the total of: other taxes, the loss from the last three years, and reduction of income tax for investments. The net profit is obtained by using the following formula:

Net profit = gross receipts (gross operating profit + miscellaneous earnings + capital gains) minus costs (expenses and losses)

Exemptions. The following legal entities are not subject to the C.T. tax:

☐ Consumer cooperatives.

☐ Economic housing offices (EHO).

☐ Mutual farm credit banks and mutual benefit societies.

☐ Agricultural cooperative and pre-cooperative agencies.

Temporary exemptions are also prescribed by the Investment Code (Act No. 87-25 of August 18, 1987). However, in the area of tax advantages, the Senegalese legislators opted for a method based on digressive exemptions.

Fixed Rate Minimum Tax (Articles 24 to 26 of the new General Tax Code of Senegal). It is levied on companies and other corporate bodies subject to the I.S. tax with the following exceptions:

☐ Companies that benefit from a deduction for investments if said deduction for the year in question is equal to or greater than F.CFA 750,000.

☐ Companies which began operations in the year prior to the year in which assessment began, and companies that filed their first balance sheet either during or at the end of said year, as long as the fiscal period lasted no more than twelve months.

☐ Companies whose major objective is the publication, printing or sale of periodicals.

☐ Airlines or maritime shipping companies.

☐ Companies that ceased all professional activities prior to January 1st of the year of assessment and are not subject to payment of the trade tax on the previous year's books.

The amount per annum of the minimum tax is now calculated with regard to the turnover exclusive of tax realized by the company in the year prior to the year in which assessment began.

Turnover		Amount of Tax
Over	Not Over	
F.CFA 0 500,000,000	F.CFA 500,000,000	F.CFA 500,000 1,000,000

2. Local Income Taxes

None.

3. Capital Gains Taxes

Capital gains generally appear as part of the income and are taxed in the same manner as other taxable profits. However, capital gains arising from the disposition of fixed assets are not included in taxable profits for the fiscal period during which they were realized as long as the taxpayer decides to reinvest an amount in a business he owns in Senegal prior to the end of a three-year period beginning with the close of that fiscal period. The amount of the investment must equal the amount of the capital gains plus the cost of the fixed assets sold.

The amount of the re-investment must come from:

☐ undistributed profits realized before the re-investment period, or

☐ profits earned during the re-investment period.

4. Branch Profits Taxes

Generally, any form of permanent establishment is taxed as if it were a resident company.

Partnership and stock companies with a head office located out of Senegal must pay the I.S. levied on the profits earned by their main branch in Senegal on the base of transactions realized in the country.

5. Foreign Tax Reliefs

Senegal has signed bilateral income tax treaties with a number of countries, including France and the African member nations of the Common African and Mauritian

Organization (OCAM). These treaties resolve problems of double taxation by providing the right to a deduction for foreign taxes paid.

6. Classification of Corporations

Senegalese tax law makes relatively few distinctions between stock companies and limited liability companies, which are liable for the C.T. (corporation tax) at the same rate.

7. Payment of Taxes

Corporation tax is paid annually in two installments before February 15 and April 15 on income earned during the previous year.

The balance of the tax must be paid before June 15. Each installment is equal to one-third of the tax due based on the taxpayer's liability from the previous year.

8. Other Matters

Exemptions for Approved Investments. (Articles 161 to 173 of the General Tax Code of Senegal)   Corporations liable for the C.T. and that reinvest all or a portion of their taxable profits in Senegal may, under certain conditions and at their request, deduct from their taxable profit an amount equal to no more than half of the expenses they incurred during the year for approved investments, and 50% of the taxable profit earned during the year in question. This benefit applies during an eight-year period beginning with the year in which the investment program was approved.

INCOME TAXES ON INDIVIDUALS

9. Rates

Individuals established in Senegal are subject to tax on their worldwide income taking into account each category of income (real estate, salaries and wages, profits from commercial, noncommercial or industrial activities, deposits, securities and movable assets, etc.).

Income tax on wages and salaries (progressive rates—see below), movable assets (16% rate), deposits and securities (16% rate) is a withholding tax.

The income tax on individuals is based on the total net annual income of each taxpayer. The net income is determined by taking into consideration the property and capital that each taxpayer owns, the profession he practices, the salaries, wages, pensions, and life annuity he enjoys, as well as the earnings from all profitable transactions in which he engages. Taxable income is distinguished by category and by member of the household.

A husband and wife are separately liable for income tax on their respective income. However, they can choose to be jointly liable on their income and that of any dependent children.

Abatements and standard deductions are possible. Abatements are possible for dependent persons (wife who has no income and dependent children), but these are limited to five persons.

The rates applicable to an individual's taxable income are set progressively as follows:

Taxable Income				Tax on Lower Amount		Percentage on Excess
Over		Not Over				
FCFA	400,000	FCFA	800,000	FCFA	0	14%
	800,000		2,000,000		56,000	32
	2,000,000		4,000,000		464,000	36
	4,000,000		7,000,000		1,184,000	42
	7,000,000				2,444,000	48

10. Local Income Taxes

None.

11. Capital Gains Taxes

None.

13. Tax Period

Income taxes are payable annually in installments on the profits or income earned the previous year. The installments are due within the first 15 days of March and June and must be paid to the General Treasurer cashier or to the agent at the place of taxation. The amount of each installment is equal to one-third of the tax owed on the results of the most recent fiscal period for the previous year. For taxpayers who receive wages only, the employer withholds at source from the employee's paycheck.

Benefits In Kind. Benefits-in-kind are taxable to the taxpayer and are included in the GIT. The system for establishing the value of benefits-in-kind is as follows:

Type of Benefit	Monthly Value
Housing	
per room of primary residence	
Dakar	F.CFA15,000
Other county towns	9,000
Other parts of Senegal	6,000
Services	
Guard, gardener	20,000
Cook, maitre d'hotel	30,000
Other household employees	25,000

Type of Benefit	Monthly Value
Water	5,000
Electricity	
per room of primary residence	5,000
Company car	10,000
Food	Actual value
Telephone	20,000

INCOME TAXES ON NONRESIDENTS

15. Liability to Tax

Nonresidents are subject to tax on their earned and unearned income in Senegal.

16. Rates

The tax is withheld in advance for income paid to nonresidents. The withholding rate varies according to the type of income. Tax treaties may be applied where they are advantageous to nonresidents.

17. Withholding Tax Rates

Pursuant to tax treaties signed by Senegal:

- ☐ Remuneration to technical advisors from a foreign nation or an international organization is not subject to the tax on salaries and wages. The same is true for emoluments paid to diplomatic and consular agents as long as the nations they represent grant similar benefits to Senegalese diplomats.
- ☐ Dividends, percentages of profits, and payments made to directors of businesses are subject to the same rate as are residents (see item 28).
- ☐ Receipts from bonds are subject to the same rate as are residents (see item 28).
- ☐ Income from interest on debts and current accounts is taxable in Senegal only if the creditor is domiciled in Senegal.
- ☐ Companies and individuals established outside Senegal are taxed on noncommercial profits derived from services performed in Senegal if the remuneration is not connected to another type of profit (or income).

OTHER SIGNIFICANT TAXES

21. Sales (Value Added)

Value-added tax applies to all activities (services, production, sales, etc.) except salaried employment and exports. The rates of VAT are:

Normal rate	20%
Reduced rate	7%
Increased rate	30%
Special rate (oil products)	34%

There is a long list of transactions and products that are exempt from VAT. The VAT must be invoiced to customers and paid to the tax collector. VAT invoiced by suppliers is deductible from VAT owned, and any excess can be reimbursed under certain conditions.

23. Taxes on Payrolls (Social Security)

All employers established in Senegal must pay an annual fixed tax. According to the terms of Law 87-10 of February 21, 1987, the tax rates are 3% for wages and salaries paid to Senegalese workers and 6% for wages and salaries paid to workers of any other nationality.

24. Taxes on Natural Resources

There are no specific taxes on the exploitation of natural resources in Senegal. In general, a start-up agreement signed by the Senegalese Government and the company sets the rights and duties of each party. Furthermore, a Petroleum Code, which was established by a government order, determines the fiscal and legal framework for the research, exploitation, and transportation of hydrocarbons.

25. Other Taxes

Banking Activities Tax. Banking activities are liable for a special tax called the tax on banking activities (T.B.O.) with two rates:

| Normal rate | 17% |
| Reduced rate | 7% |

Equalizing Tax. Commercial activities of tradespersons (with local suppliers) and importers are subject to this special tax, which serves as a substitute for the value-added tax (see item 21). The taxpayer elects to be liable to the equalizing tax in place of the VAT. Their suppliers are responsible for calculating and paying the tax to the Government. The rates are as follows:

| | Equalizing Tax Rate | |
VAT Rate Applicable	Local Purchase	Imports
7%	1%	2%
20%	2%	4%
30%	3%	6%

Trade Tax. The trade tax is levied on any person who operates a business, industry, or profession in Senegal which is not exempt from tax under the General Tax Code.

The rates vary according to the place and nature of the activity. Effective 1990, there is a standard rate for certain activities.

Recording Taxes. This tax is paid on all alterations in registrations, with certain exceptions. These taxes are paid by notaries, clerks, government secretaries, private parties, heirs, legatees, donees, and executors of wills. The recording taxes are fixed, proportional, progressive or regressive according to the nature of the documents and alterations to which they correspond.

Equipment Budget Levy. The levy was a compulsory loan (rather than a tax) based on commercial and noncommercial profits and property income. It was repealed by Act No. 90-08 of June 26, 1990.

COMPUTATION OF TAXABLE INCOME

26. Capital Gains

A capital gain arises when the real value of an asset exceeds its book value. Realized capital gains are taxable and included in the gross receipts for the fiscal period in which it was realized (even if it is totally or partially acquired during the prior fiscal period).

27. Depreciation and Depletion

There are several depreciation systems, but straight-line depreciation is the most widely used system in Senegal. A general rule for straight-line depreciation is that the depreciation must be equal to the actual decline in value:

$$\text{Depreciation} = \frac{\text{Cost of the article}}{\text{Probable useful life}}$$

The typical rates used in Senegal are as follows:

Asset	Depreciation Rate
Buildings	3% to 5%
Furnishings	10
Equipment	10 to 15
Rolling stock operated in urban areas	20 to 25
Rolling stock operated in rural areas	33

Special System for Accelerated Depreciation. Equipment and machinery that meet the following conditions may take advantage of accelerated depreciation:

□ Must be used solely for manufacturing, operations, transportation or farming.

□ Must have a useful life of more than five years.

The depreciation rate is twice the normal rate in the first year, after which the regular deduction is taken.

New Decreasing Method of Depreciation (Article 7 BIS GTC). The decreasing method of depreciation can be used for new capital goods of professional use.

□ Exceptions
—premises, building yards and real estate

□ Rates
—straight-line depreciation rate × 2 when the probable useful life is five years or less
—straight-line depreciation rate × 2.5 when the probable useful life is more than five years.

28. Treatment of Dividends

Dividends paid by Senegalese companies are subject to a withholding tax on income from negotiable securities (TINS). Senegalese corporations may deduct this tax from the corporation tax (C.T.). Nonresident payees are subject to the withholding tax unless exempted by a tax treaty or a specific agreement with the Senegalese government. The tax on income from negotiable securities (TINS) is as follows:

Dividends, income from securities, and shares in limited
   partnerships   16%

29. Loss Carryovers

Operating losses may be carried forward to offset profits earned in three years; carryback of losses is not permitted. However, operating losses resulting from depreciation may be carried forward indefinitely.

31. Consolidation of Income

None.

RELATED CONSIDERATIONS

34. Incentives and Grants

A number of incentives are provided to encourage the economic development of Senegal.

Large companies as well as small and medium sized corporations can benefit from investment advantages under the investment code (Act No. 87-25 of August 18, 1987) if engaged in one of the following sectors:

☐ Manufacturing
☐ Agriculture, fishing, breeding, and connected activities of stocking and packaging of vegetable, animal, or sea products
☐ Research, extraction, and transforming of minerals
☐ Tourism
☐ Cinematic industries run by small and medium sized companies
☐ Services run by small and medium sized companies in one of the following sectors in health, education, industrial equipment, or maintenance of industrial equipment.

Conditions of qualification for the investment incentives:

☐ Small and medium sized firms
  —investment of F.CFA 5,000,000 minimum and F.CFA 200,000,000 maximum
  —three jobs at least must be created for Senegalese
  —the accounting must be in accordance with the Senegalese accounting plan
☐ Firms valorizing local resources
  —intermediate consumption of local goods over 65% of the total cost of the intermediate consumption of products made by the firm in one fiscal year
☐ Firms developing technological innovation
  —investment of a percentage of turnover in research, by contracting with a Senegalese research institution.
  —present an investment project based on the results of research made by a Senegalese institution (s) or individual (s).
☐ Decentralizing firms
  —firms employing 90% of the staff away from Dakar and other large towns

The available incentives including exemptions from various import taxes, duties, and other assessed taxes (e.g., turnover tax, ICP) are automatically granted to all firms complying with these conditions for a period of five to 12 years depending on the location of the premises. The granted advantages are decreasing during the last three years.

Industrial Free Zone of Dakar. (IFZD) Exporting Industrial companies located in IFZD are granted tax and duties exemptions with respect to their activities in the zone.

35. Exchange Controls
The new Investment Code provides that, other than exchange control regulations, there are no restrictions on the repatriation of capital and earnings.

36.   Investment Restrictions on Nonresidents

Foreign investors are generally treated as nationals and must simply comply with the requirements of the local legislation on business activities and obtain from the appropriate authorities all licenses that could be required.

SELECTION OF BUSINESS ENTITY BY NONRESIDENTS

Foreign investors may operate in Senegal as either a branch or a subsidiary. Business taxes, the VAT, and recording taxes are the same whether the foreign company operates in Senegal as a branch or a subsidiary.

SINGAPORE

INCOME TAXES ON CORPORATIONS

1. Rates

Generally, all entities, whether locally incorporated or registered as a branch, pay tax at the rate of 31% on income accruing in or derived from Singapore, or received in Singapore from outside Singapore.

Concessionary Tax Rate. The following income qualifies for the concessionary tax rates:

☐ The income of Asian Currency Units of financial institutions arising from syndicated offshore loans is exempt from tax where the syndication work is carried out in Singapore.

☐ The income of an approved financial institution derived from the operation of its Asian Currency Unit (Asian Currency is the equivalent of the Eurodollar) is subject to tax at 10%.

☐ The income earned by finance and treasury centers from trading in foreign exchange, offshore investments, and provision of financial services to related companies is subject to tax at 10%.

☐ The income from approved offshore transactions of members of the Singapore International Monetary Exchange (SIMEX) is subject to tax at 10%.

☐ The income of an insurance company derived from carrying on the business (other than the business of life insurance) of insuring and reinsuring offshore risks is subject to tax at 10%.

☐ The offshore investment income of a life insurance company is subject to tax at 10%.

☐ The net income from offshore leasing of machinery or plant is subject to tax at 10%.

☐ The income of approved fund managers for providing fund management services is subject to tax at 10%.

☐ The income earned by nonresident investors from funds managed by approved fund managers is exempt from tax. The income earned by unit trusts owned by nonresidents but managed by fund managers in Singapore is exempt from tax.

☐ Certain income of an approved operational headquarters company derived from providing approved services in Singapore and income from trading in foreign exchange and foreign investments on its own account are subject to tax at a 10% rate for up to ten years (plus extension).

☐ The income of approved securities companies from trading in non-Singapore dollar securities and transacting in non-Singapore dollar securities on behalf of nonresidents is subject to tax at 10%.

☐ Trading income and broking commission of approved oil trading companies that is derived from prescribed transactions in petroleum, petroleum products, and petroleum futures with nonresidents or other approved oil traders is subject to tax at 10%.

☐ Trading income and brokerage commission of approved international trading companies that is derived from trading in approved commodities with nonresidents and other approved international trading companies is subject to tax at 10%.

☐ Companies qualifying for relief under the Economic Expansion Incentives (Relief from Income Tax) Act are subject to special tax concessions (see item 34).

☐ Companies owning and operating sea-going Singapore registered vessels deriving income from the transportation of passengers, mails, livestock or goods or income from the charter of such ships are exempt from tax.

☐ The taxable income on royalties and other payments received by any author or composer from local publishers for the assignment of or the right to use the copyright in any literary, dramatic, musical, or artistic work is deemed to be an amount not exceeding 10% of the gross royalties or payments. The deemed 10% taxable income also is available for royalties and other payments received by a local inventor or author in respect of approved invention and product innovation.

Shareholders receiving dividends out of these profits (except the last item) are not subject to further taxation.

In the 1991 Budget, it was announced that the qualifying income of an approved international shipping enterprise will be exempt from tax. This is to encourage international shipping conglomerates to locate their base of operations in Singapore. In addition, it was announced that the concessionary rate of 10% will apply to the qualifying income of approved trust companies (ACUs) and to income derived by ACUs and approved securities companies from arranging, underwriting, managing, and placing of international securities from Singapore. These incentives will be effective from the year of assessment 1992.

2. Local Income Taxes

None.

3. Capital Gains Taxes

Capital gains are not taxed and capital losses are not deductible. However, the distinction between capital transactions and ordinary gain and loss is not always clear. Generally, a gain on a fixed asset purchased by a corporation for its use, and later sold at a profit, is a capital gain. However, if the same asset was purchased with intent to make a profit, and later sold, the profit would be treated as income and taxed at the rate of 32%.

Effective April 1, 1988, unit trusts and investment holding companies may elect to have their profits taxed according to a sliding scale based on their holding period of the securities. For securities held for less than 18 months, the profits will be subject to tax that ranges from 3.3% for 18 months to 33% for holdings less than six months. Gains on stocks held for more than 18 months are tax-free.

Effective July 1, 1989, approved Singapore-based unit trusts are taxed on 10% of the gains arising from the sale of shares and securities at the prevailing corporate tax rate. The distribution of the remaining 90% will be exempt from tax in the hands of individual and foreign unit holders but taxed in all other cases.

4. Branch Profits Taxes

Branch profits are taxed at the rate of 31%.

5. Foreign Tax Reliefs

Foreign-source income derived by corporations resident in Singapore is subject to tax when remitted to Singapore. Treaty relief is available through foreign tax credits granted under the relevant tax treaty. Unilateral relief is granted to residents on income derived from professional, consultancy, and other specified services and sourced to certain countries with which Singapore has no double taxation agreements. A unilateral tax credit is extended to approved operational headquarter activities in nontreaty countries. A restricted form of unilateral relief is granted on income arising in Commonwealth countries which provide reciprocal relief.

6. Classification of Corporations

Corporations are classified, for Singapore tax purposes, as either resident or nonresident. A resident corporation is one which is incorporated in Singapore or carries on business in Singapore and has its control and management exercised in Singapore. Generally, the control and management of a company is vested in its directors and a company is usually regarded as resident in Singapore if its directors' meetings are mainly held in Singapore. The main differences in taxation between resident and nonresident corporations are related to the payment of dividends and the entitlement to double taxation relief. A resident company must deduct tax at the rate of 31% from dividends paid to shareholders (see item 8). Only resident corporations are entitled to double taxation relief in respect of foreign tax suffered.

7. Payment of Taxes

On the submission of an income tax return, or in the instance of a corporation carrying on a trade or business with an accounting year ended on a date other than December 31, on the submission of estimates, the Inland Revenue Department issues a Notice of Assessment. Unless arrangement is made to settle the tax liability by installment payments, the tax stated in the Notice of Assessment must be paid within one month from the date of service of the assessment, notwithstanding any objection lodged. A penalty of 5% is imposed if the tax is not paid within the stipulated period. Furthermore, if the tax is not paid within 60 days of the imposition of the first penalty, an additional penalty of 1% of the outstanding tax is payable for each completed month the tax remains unpaid, up to a maximum of 12% of the tax outstanding. The number of installment payments allowed by the Inland Revenue Department depends on when the first installment is paid. The maximum number of installments allowed is ten.

8. Other Matters

Payment of Dividends. A resident corporation may distribute its accumulated profits by declaration of dividends. Although there is no withholding tax applied to such dividends, tax at the rate of 31% is deemed to have been deducted at source. The tax deducted from the dividends is franked by the tax paid (''tax credit'') by the corporation on its profits. If there is insufficient tax credit to frank the dividend distribution, the corporation would have to create it by paying the shortfall to the Inland Revenue Department, which can be offset against future tax liabilities of the corporation. Dividends paid out of profits which are exempt or subject to a concessionary rate of tax are generally not subject to any further tax.

In the 1991 Budget, it was announced that dividends paid out of foreign-sourced income for which there is insufficient franking credit due to foreign tax credit claimed will be exempt from tax. The exemption will apply to dividends paid out of foreign income assessable to tax from the year of assessment 1992.

INCOME TAXES ON INDIVIDUALS

9. Rates

A resident individual is eligible for personal reliefs in arriving at his taxable income. Taxable income is taxed at the following rates subject to a rebate of 15% of tax payable on the first S$10,000 of taxable income. Tax payable is shown net of this rebate. In addition, a straight 5% rebate will be granted against the income tax payable for the 1991 tax year.

| Taxable Income | | Tax on | Percentage |
Over	Not Over	Lower Amount	on Excess
S$ 0	S$ 5,000	S$ 0	3.5%
5,000	7,500	149	6
7,500	10,000	276	8
10,000	15,000	446	8
15,000	20,000	846	9
20,000	25,000	1,296	12
25,000	35,000	1,896	14
35,000	50,000	3,296	17
50,000	75,000	5,846	21
75,000	100,000	11,096	24
100,000	150,000	17,096	26
150,000	200,000	30,096	28
200,000	400,000	44,096	31
400,000		106,096	33

10.   Local Income Taxes
None.

11.   Capital Gains Taxes
See item 3.

12.   Foreign Tax Reliefs
See item 5.

13.   Tax Period
The tax year is the calendar year, which is generally referred to as the year of assessment. Income tax is assessed based on the income earned, received, or derived during the preceding calendar year. The tax assessed is payable within 30 days of the date of the assessment, whether or not the taxpayer has filed a notice of objection. Note, however, that a company's tax year is governed by its own financial year which ends in the calendar year preceding the relevant tax year.

INCOME TAXES ON NONRESIDENTS

15.   Liability to Tax
An individual is generally resident in Singapore if he or she resides in Singapore. If an individual is physically present or employed (other than as a company's director) in Singapore for at least 183 days during the year preceding the year of

assessment, the individual is treated as resident for that year of assessment. A company's residence is determined by where its control and management is exercised, which generally is the place where the director's meetings are held.

Generally, any income accruing in, derived from, or received in Singapore (from foreign sources) is subject to Singapore income tax. When a nonresident person carries on a trade or business of which only part of the operations is carried on in Singapore, the gains or profits of the trade or business are deemed to be derived from Singapore to the extent to which such gains or profits are not directly attributable to that part of the operations carried on outside Singapore.

When a nonresident person is engaged in the shipping, chartering, or aviation business, the profits accruing in Singapore are generally deemed to be equal to 5% of the gross receipts from outward shipments from Singapore.

The following items of income are deemed to be derived from Singapore where the payments are borne directly or indirectly by a person resident in Singapore or a permanent establishment in Singapore, or where the payments are deductible against any income accruing in or derived from Singapore:

- □ Interest, commission, fees or any other payments in connection with any loan or indebtedness.
- □ Royalties, technical fees, and management fees.
- □ Rents or other payments for the use of any movable property.

Additionally, any income derived from loans is also deemed to be derived from Singapore where the funds provided by such loans are brought into or used in Singapore.

However, a foreign person who is a resident of a country with which Singapore has concluded a tax treaty (see item 19) may claim an exemption or a measure of relief, whichever the treaty provides.

Specific exemptions from income tax include:

- □ Interest earned on deposits in an approved bank and interest from Asian Dollar Bonds received by nonresident individuals and other nonresident persons who do not carry on a business in Singapore. However, nonresident individuals who carry on business in Singapore can qualify for tax exemption on interest from Asian Dollar Bonds provided the funds used for investing in such bonds are not from their Singapore operations and the proceeds from the issue of the bonds are used only outside Singapore.
- □ Any payment in the nature of income referred to in the above prior listing where an application for exemption is made, and the Minister of Finance is of the opinion that the payment is made for a purpose which will promote or enhance the economic or technological development of Singapore.
- □ Gains or profits from an employment exercised in Singapore for not more than 60 days in any calendar year by a nonresident employee (other than a director).
- □ Income arising from sources outside Singapore and remitted therein by a nonresident individual.

16. Rates

The chargeable income of every person not resident in Singapore is taxed at the rate of 31%, subject to the provisions of tax treaties where applicable and the special and concessionary rate below.

Concessionary Tax Rate. This 10% rate applies on the same basis as in item 1.

Special Rates. Employment income earned by a nonresident individual (excluding a director of a Singapore corporation) who is present in Singapore for more than 60 days but less than 183 days in any calendar year is subject to tax at the rate of 15%, or at the graduated rates (after personal reliefs), whichever yields the greater tax. However, should such individual reside in Singapore for the duration of three consecutive years of assessment, he will be regarded as resident from the date of his arrival.

17. Withholding Tax Rates

Interest, loan fees, royalties, management fees that incorporate a mark-up, technical assistance fees in respect of assistance rendered in Singapore, rents for the use of movable property, and taxable director's remuneration are generally subject to withholding tax at the rate of 31% when paid to nonresidents, although the withholding tax may be reduced or nullified in accordance with the provisions of tax treaties where applicable.

18. Special Withholding Provisions

Concessionary rates apply to charter fees, as follows:

Recipient of Charter Fees Resident in	Time Charter	Bare Boat Charter
Country with double taxation agreement with Singapore providing full exemption of shipping and aircraft profits	0%	2%
Country with double taxation agreement with Singapore providing for 50% exemption of shipping and aircraft profits	1	2
Country which has no double taxation agreement with Singapore and is not a tax haven country	2	2
Country regarded by Singapore as a tax haven country	3	3

For this purpose, Singapore regards the following countries as tax havens: the Bahamas, Bermuda, British Virgin Islands, Cayman Islands, Gibraltar, Hong Kong, Isle of Man, Jersey, Liberia, Liechtenstein, Luxembourg, Netherlands Antilles, New Hebrides, Norfolk Island and Panama.

19. Tax Treaties

Tax treaties have been concluded by Singapore with the following countries:

	Dividends (1)	Interest	Royalties
Nontreaty countries	31% (imputed)	31%	31%
Treaty countries:			
Australia	15	10	10
Bangladesh	15	10	10
Belgium	15	15	Exempt
Canada	15	15	15
China, People's Republic of	7,12	7,10	10
Denmark	5,10	15	15
Finland	5,15	10	10
France	10,15	10	Exempt
Germany (2)	10,15	10	Exempt
India	31	31	31
Indonesia	10,15	10	15
Israel	Exempt	15	Exempt
Italy	10	12.5	15,20
Japan	10,15	15	10
Korea, Republic of	10,15	10	15
Malaysia	31	31	31
Netherlands	Exempt,15	10	Exempt
New Zealand	15	15	15
Norway	15	15	15
Pakistan (3)	—	—	—
Papua New Guinea (3)	—	—	—
Philippines	15,25	15	25
Sri Lanka	15	Exempt,10	15
Sweden	10,15	10,15	Exempt
Switzerland	10,15	10	5
Taiwan	31	31	15
Thailand	20	10,25	15
United Kingdom	15	15	15
United States (4)	—	—	—

Notes:

(1) Except for the Malaysia-Singapore treaty, dividends paid by a company resident in Singapore to a resident of a treaty country are exempt from any

Singapore tax imposed on dividends in addition to the company tax. Therefore, the rates shown in this column reflect the position of the other treaty country.

(2) Negotiations are currently being held to agree on the date on which the double tax treaty between West Germany and Singapore is to apply to the former East Germany.

(3) Double tax agreement has been signed but not ratified.

(4) Double tax agreement under negotiation.

Singapore has concluded a limited tax treaty with the Saudi Arabia, the United Arab Emirates, and the United States on the avoidance of double taxation on income derived from international operation of ships and aircrafts.

OTHER SIGNIFICANT TAXES

21. Sales (Value Added)

None, except for a 3% tax levied on food and beverages.

22. Inheritance and Gift Taxes

There is no gift tax.

Estate duty is levied on the value of the decedent's real and personal property situated in Singapore at the following rates:

Principal Value of Estate	Duty	Rate
First	S$10,000,000	5%
Above	10,000,000	10

If a person is domiciled in Singapore at his or her date of death, estate tax is also levied on movable property wherever situated.

Residential properties (up to S$3 million) owned at death are exempt from estate tax, as is S$500,000 for all other property. The amount of the decedent's interest in the Central Provident Fund (and in any designated pension or provident fund) is generally exempt from estate tax to the extent that it is more than S$500,000. A special exemption from estate tax is granted to individuals who were neither resident nor domiciled in Singapore at the time of their death with respect to Asian Currency Unit bonds, gold deposits and certificates held in Singapore, and certain other investments.

23. Taxes on Payrolls (Social Security)

Payroll Tax. The payroll tax was suspended effective April 1, 1985.

Skills Development Levy. This is a levy on employers only. The current rate is 1% of the salary of employees earning not more than S$750 per month.

Central Provident Fund (CPF). The CPF is essentially a savings scheme to provide for employees in their old age. The required contributions, as a percentage of each employee's earnings, effective from July 1, 1991, are:

	Ordinary Wages (1)	Additional Wages (2) (Periodic Bonus, Commission, etc.)
Employers	17.5%	17.5%
Employees	22.5%	22.5%

Notes:
(1) CPF contributions (employer's and employee's) are due on monthly wages of up to $6,000 per month.
(2) CPF contributions (employer's and employee's) may be restricted if total wages (ordinary plus additional wages) exceed $100,000 a year.

Under certain conditions, employers and their expatriate employees can contract out of CPF.

Foreign Worker Levy. An employer of foreign workers is required to pay a monthly levy for each foreign worker. The applicable levies are:

	Rate per Month
Domestic servants	$250
Manufacturing and service sector	$300
Construction industry	
Skilled worker	$250
Unskilled worker	$350
Shipbuilding and shiprepair industry	$350

24. Taxes on Natural Resources

None.

25. Other Taxes

Land and Property. Property tax is imposed at the rate of 16%, effective July 1, 1990, of the property's annual value.

Stamp Tax. Stamp tax is imposed at varying ad valorem rates on a variety of legal documents. Certain duties have been removed altogether and others rationalized at a single rate.

COMPUTATION OF TAXABLE INCOME

26. Capital Gains

Not applicable (see item 3).

27. Depreciation and Depletion

Depreciation is not an allowable deduction for tax purposes. In its place, the following capital allowances on qualifying capital expenditure are deductible from the adjusted income:

Industrial buildings	Initial allowance	25%
	Annual allowance	3%
Accelerated allowance	Per annum for three years on qualifying expenditure	33.33%
Plant and machinery	Initial allowance	20%
	Annual allowances (on a straight-line basis at prescribed rates)	
Approved know-how and patent rights	Writing down allowance on a straight-line basis	20%
Computer and prescribed automation equipment		100%

Carryover of Unabsorbed Capital Allowances.   A continuity of ownership test, similar to that applicable to losses, must be met before a carryover is allowed. The beneficial ownership of the company on the last day of the year of assessment in which the allowances arose and the first day of the year of assessment in which such allowances are to be utilized, must not have changed by more than 50%. In addition, the company must continue to carry on the trade in respect of which the allowances were given.

28. Treatment of Dividends

Dividends are includible in taxable income. Singapore dividends are received gross and the 31% deducted at source is offset against the tax liability. The treatment of foreign dividends remitted into Singapore depends on whether or not they are derived from a Commonwealth or tax treaty country. If they are received from such countries, the gross dividends are includible in the tax computation and a credit is claimed for the foreign tax suffered against the Singapore tax liability (see item 5). Otherwise, the dividends are included net in the tax computation as no foreign tax credit is available.

Dividends paid by a Singapore resident company out of profits which are exempt or subject to a concessionary rate of tax are generally not subject to tax in the hands of the shareholders.

29. Loss Carryovers

Generally, any unabsorbed trading loss can be carried forward indefinitely and set off against all sources of income. However, in the case of a company, the continuity of ownership test must be met before such a claim can be admitted (i.e., the beneficial ownership of the company on the last day of the year in which the loss is incurred and the first day of the assessment year in which the loss is to be relieved, must not have changed by more than 50%). The Minister can exercise his discretion to waive the continuity of ownership test if he is satisfied that the substantial change in the shareholders of the company is not for the purpose of deriving any tax benefit or obtaining any tax advantage. Upon such waiver, the loss can be set off only against profits from the same trade or business.

30. Transactions between Related Parties

Singapore revenue law and the various double tax treaties contain provisions under which revenue and capital transactions between related parties are required to be at the value which would have prevailed on an arm's-length basis. The Tax Comptroller is empowered to disregard, vary, or make adjustments to certain arrangements that are carried out for the purpose of tax avoidance and not for bona fide commercial reasons.

31. Consolidation of Income

There is no provision for the filing of consolidated tax returns by related corporations.

32. Tax Periods

An assessment is raised on the business/trading income of a corporation in respect of its accounting year ended during the preceding calendar year. Nonbusiness/ nontrading income, however, is taxed on the preceding calendar-year basis.

33. Other Matters

Deductions for Taxes Other than Income Taxes. In computing the liability for income tax, a deduction may be taken in respect of any taxes which are incurred wholly and exclusively in the production of assessable income.

Inventory Valuation. For tax purposes, inventories may be valued at cost or net realizable value. Average cost or FIFO is generally used to determine cost. However, in the case of specialized industries a different method of valuation may be used, except for the LIFO method which is not acceptable.

Bad Debts. General provisions for doubtful debts are not deductible. A specific provision made in respect of debts which are proven to be irrecoverable is deductible. Recovery of any debt which has been written off for which a specific provision has been claimed is included as assessable income.

Bank Provisions. It was announced in the 1991 Budget that, with effect from the year of assessment 1992, banks and merchant banks in Singapore will be allowed limited deductions for general provisions made by them. This is to encourage banks and merchant banks to build up adequate reserves.

Employee Benefit Provisions. General provisions for employee benefits (annual leave, sick leave, retirement, etc.) are not deductible. A deduction for such expenses is allowed only when payment is made to the employee.

Interest Paid. Payments of interest on loans not used for acquiring income are not deductible.

Head-Office Expenses Recharged. Foreign central overhead expenses charged to a Singapore entity are subject to detailed examination by the Inland Revenue and must pass stringent local laws to be tax deductible in Singapore.

RELATED CONSIDERATIONS

34. Incentives and Grants

Singapore provides a comprehensive program of tax incentives and concessions based primarily on considerations such as total investment involved, technical output, export potential, employment opportunities and general conduciveness to Singapore's economic activity. Tax incentives which provide complete or partial exemption are outlined below.

Pioneer Industries (including certain service companies). Complete exemption for periods of from five to ten years.

Post-Pioneer Companies. The income is subject to tax at a rate as low as 10% for up to ten years.

Expansion of Established Enterprise (including certain service companies). Partial exemption dependent on increase in income from expanded business for a period up to five years.

Operational Headquarters (OHQ). The income arising from the provision of approved services to related entities and the income earned by OHQs from trading in foreign exchange and offshore investments on their own account are subject to tax at 10%. Qualifying foreign dividend income remitted to Singapore may be exempt from tax. The relief period is up to ten years with provision for extension.

Export of Services. Partial exemption equivalent to 90% of the incremental income for a period of five years.

Production for Export.   Partial exemption equivalent to 90% of qualifying export profits for periods of from three to 15 years.

International Trade Incentives.   One-half of export income is exempt from tax for a period of five years.

Foreign Loans for Productive Equipment.   The interest received by nonresident lenders in respect of an approved foreign loan is exempt from tax.

Approved Royalties, Fees, and Development Contributions.   These are taxed at reduced rates.

Investment Allowances.   Up to 50% of the fixed investment in plant, machinery, and factory buildings (excluding land) incurred by the corporation on an approved project for the manufacture of any product, provision of specialized engineering or technical services, research and development, construction operations, or the promotion of the tourist industry (other than hotels) is given as an additional deduction against chargeable income.

Industrial Building Allowance.   Industrial building allowances have been extended to approved tourist promotion projects, except hotels. It is proposed that this incentive be extended to service companies engaged in agrotechnology, horticulture, and other approved services that require specialized structures for the purpose of their activities.

Warehousing and Servicing Incentives.   One-half of profits from export sales or export services in excess of a fixed base are exempt from tax for a period of five years.

International Consultancy Services.   One-half of profits in excess of a fixed base are exempt from tax for a period of five years.

Research and Development.   Double deduction for R&D expenditure (other than on buildings and equipment) for manufacturing and service companies involved in computer software and information services, agrotechnology services, medical research, and laboratory and testing services; investment allowance of up to 50% of the capital investment in an R&D project; and extension of the initial allowance of 25% and annual allowance of 3% to R&D buildings.

New Technology Companies.   Losses and unabsorbed capital allowances incurred by an approved technology company at the end of three years from the commencement of its trade are deductible to the holding company in the proportion of the percentage of shares held in the technology company. The maximum deduction available to the holding company is not to exceed 50% (or such lower percentage as may be specified in the certificate issued to the technology company) of the paid-up capital of the technology company held by the holding company.

Venture Capital. Losses incurred from the sale of approved stock (up to 100% of the equity invested) within eight years from the date of approval of such stock are deductible against the investor's other taxable income. This incentive is also available for losses from the sale of shares in or liquidation of approved overseas investment.

35. Exchange Controls
None.

36. Investment Restrictions on Nonresidents
None.

SELECTION OF BUSINESS ENTITY BY NONRESIDENTS

The Singapore tax considerations are the same for both branches and locally incorporated subsidiaries. Therefore, the question of which type of entity is optimum for foreign investors depends on the preferences of the investor as well as other considerations not germane to taxation in Singapore.

SPECIMEN TAX COMPUTATION

Information:

☐ The corporation's operating profits of S$1,300,000 consists of:

Local trading profits	S$1,100,000
Foreign-source trading profits	80,000
Singapore dividend income (gross)	20,000
Foreign-source dividend income (gross)	20,000
Foreign-source interest income (gross)	10,000
Profit on sale of property	70,000

☐ The local trading profits are arrived at after charging:

Accounts depreciation	S$150,000
Transfer to general provision for bad debts	400,000
Transfer to provision for leave passage	100,000

☐ The foreign-source dividend income is from a nontreaty country and was subject to a 50% withholding tax.

□ The interest income is from a tax treaty country and incurred a 10% withholding tax.
□ The trading profit from a treaty country was subject to foreign tax at source of 45%.
□ Profit on sale of property is a capital gain.
□ Allowable tax depreciation is S$300,000 and payments debited to leave passage are S$150,000.

Computation (for year of assessment 1991):

	Resident Corporation		Nonresident Corporation	
Profit per accounts	S$1,300,000		S$1,300,000	
Add				
Accounts depreciation	150,000		150,000	
Transfer to provision for leave passage	100,000		100,000	
Transfer to general provision for bad debts	400,000	650,000	400,000	650,000
		1,950,000		1,950,000
Less				
Capital gain	70,000		70,000	
Singapore dividend (gross) (assessed separately)	20,000		20,000	
Foreign-source dividends (gross) (assessed separately)	20,000		20,000	
Foreign-source interest (gross) (assessed separately)	10,000		10,000	
Foreign-source trading income	80,000		80,000	
Leave passage paid	150,000	350,000	150,000	350,000
Adjusted profit		1,600,000		1,600,000
Less				
Tax depreciation		300,000		300,000
Singapore trade income		1,300,000		1,300,000

	Resident Corporation		Nonresident Corporation	
Add				
Singapore dividend	20,000		20,000	
Remittances to Singapore				
Overseas dividend (net)	10,000		10,000	
Overseas interest	10,000		9,000 (net)	
Overseas trade income	80,000	120,000	44,000 (net)	83,000
Taxable income		1,420,000		1,383,000
Income tax (at 31%)		440,200		428,730
Less				
Tax deducted at source				
on Singapore dividend	6,200		6,200	
Foreign tax credit				
Interest	1,000			
Trade (1)	24,800	32,000		6,200
Net tax payable		S$408,200		S$422,530

Notes:

(1) Restricted to 31% × S$80,000.

SOLOMON ISLANDS

INCOME TAXES ON CORPORATIONS

1. Rates

The corporation tax rates are:

For resident corporations incorporated locally	35%
For corporations incorporated overseas	50%

2. Local Income Taxes

None.

3. Capital Gains Tax

There is no capital gains tax in the Solomon Islands. However, the capital gain arising on the sale of any business assets on which depreciation (wear and tear deduction) has been allowed is subject to tax at normal rates. (Applies to plant, machinery, vehicles, vessels, and business premises.)

4. Branch Profits Taxes

Nonresident corporations are subject to tax at 50% on Solomon Islands source income, except where withholding tax is deemed to be final as in the case of dividends, arm's-length interest, royalties, professional services, insurance premiums paid to overseas insurers, film rentals, professional services, payments to overseas contractors and fishermen, or where a treaty provides for such limitations.

The Minister has the power to amend, by order, the rate of tax to be deducted from nonresident income.

5. Foreign Tax Reliefs

Income derived by a resident corporation from sources outside the Solomon Islands is taxable on the same basis as if it had a Solomon Islands source only when the funds are received in the Solomon Islands. Foreign income is ascertained according to the income tax legislation of the country in which it was derived. A foreign tax credit is allowed equal to the lesser of the foreign tax paid or the Solomon Islands tax payable on that income. The foreign tax credit must be utilized in the same fiscal period in respect of which it is paid.

6. Classification of Corporations

Corporations are classified for tax purposes as either resident or nonresident. Under the Companies Act a classification of private company exists, but for income tax purposes this distinction is not recognized. A resident corporation is one which is incorporated in the Solomon Islands or either has its central management and control in the Solomon Islands or its voting power controlled by shareholders who are resident in the Solomon Islands. The distinction between resident and nonresident corporations is important in that nonresident corporations are subject to tax only on their Solomon Islands income. The distinction also effects the rate of tax (see item 4). A company incorporated outside the Solomon Islands, even though it may be carrying on business only in the Solomons is also liable to tax at 50%.

Corporations may be classified as prescribed companies under the Investment Act if the investment is likely to provide significant benefits to the Solomon Islands economy. Such companies are granted a tax holiday. (See item 34.)

7. Payment of Taxes

Corporations are required to pay tax in four installments during the year for which the tax liability will arise, and to settle any adjustment after the end of the year. Installments are payable in the third, sixth, ninth, and twelfth months of the calendar year and any adjustment required is payable nine months after the end of the corporation's financial year. Payment of all installments is required even where an assessment has not been issued, unless prior approval is obtained from the Commissioner of Inland Revenue to amend or dispense with installments.

8. Other Matters

Turnover Tax. The Income Tax Act was amended in July 1990 to introduce a turnover tax on loss companies and low-profit companies. The tax will apply to income derived after January 1, 1991 and has the following features:

☐ The tax is an income tax and is charged at the rate of 0.5% (to a maximum tax of $10,000 per fiscal year) on gross income if
—gross income less allowable deductions (chargeable income) is nil or a loss;
—the normal corporate tax on chargeable income (35% resident, 50% nonresident) is the lesser of 0.5% of gross income or $10,000.

☐ The tax does not reduce the total of carried forward losses.

☐ The tax is final and is not offset against normal corporate tax levied after losses are recouped.

☐ The tax does not apply to companies receiving tax incentives (e.g., pioneer companies).

INCOME TAXES ON INDIVIDUALS

9. Rates

Resident individuals are subject to tax only on taxable income accruing in, derived from, or received in the Solomon Islands. Income tax rates are the same for residents and nonresidents, but residents are entitled to a basic exemption from income ($2,700 for a single taxpayer, $5,100 for a married taxpayer whose spouse is not working) and to deductions from income for certain medical, education, insurance and superannuation payments.

Most benefits in kind are taxable, including the value of free or subsidized housing and vehicles supplied by employers and education allowances paid by employers. A PAYE system of taxation applies to all income from employment or services rendered.

The tax payable on total income *less* personal exemptions and deductions is:

☐ Married Person (spouse not working). 14 cents per dollar for the first $2,500, increasing by 4 cents per dollar for each successive $2,500 until a maximum rate of 42 cents per dollar is reached (at $17,500 taxable income).

☐ Single Taxpayer. 14 cents per dollar for the first $2,100, increasing by 4 cents per dollar for each successive $2,100 until the maximum of 42 cents per dollar (at $14,700 taxable income).

10. Local Income Taxes

None, but local Councils are permitted to charge a head tax on individuals, which is known as the basic rate. Employers are required to withhold this tax from employees' salaries and wages and to account to the Council by June 30.

11. Capital Gains Tax

Same as item 3.

12. Foreign Tax Reliefs

The basis of assessment of foreign income and the calculation of available tax credits is the same as for corporations (see item 5). The Solomon Islands tax payable is computed as the average rate applicable to total income.

13. Tax Period

December 31 is the standard year-end, but an alternative date may be adopted by business taxpayers.

14. Other Matters

Residents' Withholding Tax. See item 25.

INCOME TAXES ON NONRESIDENTS

15. Liability to Tax

Nonresident corporations are taxed as described in item 4. For nonresident individuals, Solomon Islands source income, other than income subject to withholding tax, is taxed at the same rates that apply to single residents. Nonresident individuals, however, are not eligible for exemptions or deductions (see item 9).

17. Withholding Tax Rates

Certain gross income payments to nonresidents are liable to withholding tax in lieu of individual and corporation taxes. Effective July 1, 1990, the rates of deductions are:

Interest	15%
Royalties	15
Income from contracting	7.5
Outward income from ships and aircrafts	2.5
Insurance premiums	5
Professional services	7.5
Pole and line fishermen	10
Purse seiner fishermen	15

19. Tax Treaties

The Solomon Islands has a tax treaty in force with the United Kingdom.

20. Other Matters

Dividend Withholding Tax. Resident companies are required to deduct withholding tax at the rate of 35% on dividends paid to nonresidents and 20% on dividends paid to residents. The gross dividends are a deductible expense of the paying company when calculating assessable income. In some cases, this tax is a final tax (see item 28).

OTHER SIGNIFICANT TAXES

21. Sales (Value Added)

A comprehensive Sales Tax Act was introduced, effective August 1990. The tax is currently applied to telephone services, cooked food supplied by licensed restaurants, and tickets purchased for overseas travel. The Minister has the power to add to the schedule of taxable items. Customs and excise duties are applied at various scheduled rates.

22. Inheritance and Gift Taxes

None.

23. Taxes on Payrolls (Social Security)

A National Provident Fund provides social security benefits to residents on retirement. Employers are required to contribute 7½% of employees' salaries or wages; employees are required to contribute 5% (minimum). Income tax deductions apply to these contributions (within limits), and proceeds on retirement are tax-free. Expatriate employees are required to contribute unless approval to contribute to a nonresident scheme has been granted. Benefits withdrawn on final departure from the Solomon Islands are tax-free.

25. Other Taxes

Bonus Issue Tax.   Bonus issues are subject to tax when the amount capitalized is distributed. The rate of tax on such a distribution is 20%. The tax is separate and distinct and is credited against dividends paid on wind up.

Stamp Duty.   Stamp duties are payable on registration of certain documents, either as a flat rate per document or as a percentage of the value of property defined in the document. Stamp duty also is charged on increases in nominal share capital.

Resident Withholding Tax.   Effective July 1, 1990, a new resident withholding tax has been introduced that applies to gross payments made to persons (including corporations) as listed in the following table. The tax is a prepayment of tax assessed on lodgement of an annual income tax return, except for a body of persons other than a corporation (e.g., a village group) and resident individuals whose total income is less than $10,000.

The payor is responsible for deduction of the tax and monthly remittance to the Tax Office. Provisions exist for exemption certificates for "good taxpayers."

Income Subject to Withholding	Rate
Contracting and subcontracting	7.5%
Royalties (timber and material resources removal/exploration)	10
Fishing operations	10
Leases of property (including sub-leasing)	10
Sales of copra	nil
Sales of cocoa	nil
Marine products (beche-demer, shells, shark fin)	10

The Minister has the power to vary the rates.

COMPUTATION OF TAXABLE INCOME

26. Capital Gains

The revenue arising upon the sale of any capital asset subject to the wear and tear deduction, which is in excess of its written down value for tax purposes, is subject to tax at normal rates. Capital gains on sales of shares, private dwellings, etc. are not subject to tax (see item 3).

27. Depreciation and Depletion

The Income Tax Act provides for a capital allowance deduction (wear and tear deduction) in lieu of depreciation. The allowance is calculated using the reducing-balance method. The current rates are:

Buildings, building fixtures and fittings, bridges, wharves, slipways, boilers and oil storage tanks	5% d.v.
Assets used by a timber concessionaire for cutting, extracting and processing timber from a timber concession and low cost housing for employees	35% d.v.
Cost of purchasing and planting coconuts, oil palms and cocoa; provision of yards, fences, and water supplies for livestock; prevention of soil erosion; experimentation, scientific or other research expenditure	100%
Capital expenditure on mining	20% p.a.
Vehicles, vessels, aircraft and all plant not otherwise specified	25% d.v.
Special development assets used by a business (deemed by the Minister as likely to benefit the national interest)	100%

28. Treatment of Dividends

All dividends received in or remitted to the Solomon Islands by residents form a part of their assessable income. The withholding tax deducted on local dividends (see item 20) is the final tax in the case of all nonresidents, including corporations and resident individuals with income (including gross dividends) of less than $10,000.

29. Loss Carryovers

A deficit for any year may be set off against the profits of a future year if the shareholders are substantially the same (51%). There are no time restrictions.

30. Transactions Between Related Parties

Solomon Islands law provides for the review of such transactions on an arm's-length basis.

31. Consolidation of Income

There is no provision for the filing of consolidated tax returns by related corporations. Provisions do exist to aggregate the income of married individuals in certain circumstances.

32. Tax Periods

Same as item 13.

33. Other Matters

Interest Received. The first $5,000 received from Solomon Island banks is exempt from income tax.

Business License Fees. License fees paid to a council under the Local Government Act are treated as a prepayment of income tax.

Bad Debts. Bad debts may be claimed as a deduction only when actually written off. General provisions for anticipated losses are not permitted.

Entertainment. Business entertainment is currently tax deductible.

RELATED CONSIDERATIONS

34. Incentives and Grants

When the Investment Board approves an investment proposal, the following forms of Government assistance are available:

☐ Assistance with siting of proposal and security of land.
☐ Tax relief.
☐ Drawback of duty on re-exports.
☐ Import duty-free concession on capital goods used in the capital construction of new projects.
☐ Assistance with training, employment, counselling, and staff selection, and a double tax deduction for training apprentices and other professional staff at SICHE or other approved institutions.
☐ Contracts to purchase output.

The new legislation granting tax concessions is targeted at the following investments:

☐ Manufacturing that has local value-added of greater than 25% of ex-factory sales of approved products (three- to six-year tax holiday depending on percentage of LVA).

- [ ] Export-orientated manufacture with greater than 25% LVA (three- to six-year tax holiday).
- [ ] Investments over SBD$10million attract a five- to ten-year tax holiday.
- [ ] Investments fostering tourism may alternatively apply for a five-year holiday plus a two-year writeoff of depreciable assets constructed or purchased and 150% deduction for approved overseas promotion costs.
- [ ] Export businesses involved in agricultural produce, manufactured or processed goods, or fresh seafood may alternatively apply for a three- to six-year holiday irrespective of LVA and 150% tax deduction for export promotion.
- [ ] Businesses involved in agricultural or export agricultural produce, dairy or goat farming, beef production, reforestation or fisheries, or off-shore deep-sea fishing, may apply alternatively for a tax holiday on the profits of such activities for five years out of any ten years from commencement of commercial production.
- [ ] Any business approved by the Investment Board can claim special addition incentives for writeoff of new or expanded factories and training expenses and a 150% deduction for the interprovince transport of raw materials and qualifying products.

35. Exchange Controls

There are comprehensive controls on foreign currency transactions both to and from the Solomon Islands. In most cases, approval must be obtained prior to making the commitment. A $3.00 duty is imposed on foreign currency remittances greater than $3,000.

36. Investment Restrictions on Nonresidents

Solomon Islands policy on nonresident investment has been eased during 1991 and is presently administered by the Ministry of Commerce and Primary Industry, which receives direction from time to time from the government as to the criteria to use for the approval of nonresident investment proposals. Any investment by a non-Solomon Islands citizen which acquires equity or ownership in a company or organization or substantial capital asset investment in the Solomon Islands requires the approval of the Investment Board. An application for approval of the foreign investment should be made to the Foreign Investment Division of the Ministry of Commerce and Primary Industry.

SELECTION OF BUSINESS ENTITY BY NONRESIDENTS

While some overseas investors conduct operations in the Solomon Islands through branches, the current trend is to establish a Solomon Islands registered subsidiary corporation. This preference is generally based on tax considerations. The following compares the tax payable by a branch with that payable by a local subsidiary remitting all profits as a dividend.

	Local Subsidiary	Branch
Operating profit	$100	$100
Dividend	100	
Profit before tax		$100
Tax payable	—	50
Profit after tax		$ 50
35% dividend withholding tax	$ 35	
Total tax payable	$ 35	$ 50

Thin capitalization rules are not formalized in the Income Tax Act, although the Commissioner has broad powers to review non-arm's-length interest charges. An anti-avoidance provision (modeled very closely on the New Zealand Income Tax Act Provision) has been adopted by the Tax Act.

SOUTH AFRICA

INCOME TAXES ON CORPORATIONS

1. Rates

Taxable income, other than from mining operations and long-term insurance business, of all companies derived from a source within or deemed to be within South Africa is subject to a flat rate tax of 48%.

On taxable income from diamond and other mining operations, the rate is 50.88% (basic 48% plus 6% surcharge). On taxable income from gold mining operations, a formula is applied which reduces or increases the rate according to the relationship between mining taxable income and gross mining revenue. The tax rate applicable to taxable income from oil mining operations is 68.8%.

Dividends received by a company are not taxable in its hands.

2. Local Income Taxes

Most regions impose a regional services levy of 0.25% to 0.345% of payroll and a regional establishment levy of 0.1% to 0.138% of turnover. The rates vary according to region.

3. Capital Gains Taxes

None.

4. Branch Profits Taxes

A branch of a foreign corporation is taxed on the profits derived in South Africa as though it were a resident corporation.

5. Foreign Tax Reliefs

As South African income tax is levied only on taxable income derived or deemed to be derived in South Africa, the question of foreign tax relief does not normally arise. Relief will generally only be granted if provided for in a tax treaty with the foreign state.

6. Classification of Companies

Companies are basically classified for tax purposes in two ways: South African companies and other companies; and private and public companies. There are also close corporations which are classified as private companies. A South African company is a company incorporated, formed, or established in South Africa. An external company is not a South African company. Some consequences of the classification are:

☐ Dividend payments to a non-South African company are subject to nonresident shareholders tax on dividends (see items 16 and 17).

☐ Royalty and know-how payments to a non-South African company are subject to withholding tax (see items 16 and 17).

A public company is, broadly, a company which has all classes of its equity shares listed on a stock exchange or has the general public interested throughout the year in more than 50% of all classes of its equity. Insurance and gold and diamond mining companies are also classified as public companies. Other companies (and close corporations) are, for tax purposes, private companies. Public companies are exempt from donations tax (see item 22).

Close Corporations. The Close Corporation Act permits the incorporation of up to ten persons (restricted to natural persons and testamentary trusts) as a close corporation (CC). The CC has a separate corporate identity and, subject to certain conditions, the liability of its members is limited to their "members contributions." A CC is taxed as a company. Effective financial years ending in 1991, dividends received by a CC are exempt from tax.

Distributions by a CC to its members are exempt income in their hands for normal tax purposes (but distributions by a CC to members who are nonresidents are subject to withholding taxes; see items 16 and 17).

On conversion of a company to a CC or vice versa the company and the CC are deemed to be the same company for tax purposes. Thus, the CC "inherits" the assessed loss, if any, and the tax values of fixed assets, etc., of the company or vice versa.

7. Payment of Taxes

A system of provisional tax payments applies to companies. Three provisional payments may be made: the first (half the estimated tax liability for the year) within six months of the commencement of the year of assessment is compulsory; the second (the balance of the estimated tax liability) before the end of the year of assessment is also compulsory; and the third (to pay the difference between the estimated and actual tax liability) within six months after the end of the year of assessment is not compulsory but is made to avoid a nondeductible interest charge. Balancing payments are made upon final assessment for the year by the revenue authorities.

INCOME TAXES ON INDIVIDUALS

9. Rates

Income tax is calculated on the taxable income of individuals who are divided into three categories, as follows:

□ Married woman. A woman married in the ordinary sense of the word but *excluding* a married woman who is

—living apart from her husband in circumstances indicating a permanent separation.

—a party to a polygamous marriage and who is not the wife in the longest subsisting marriage, or

—the sole bread-earner.

□ Married person

—a male who, during any period of assessment, was married and not living apart from his wife in circumstances indicating a permanent separation.

—a person who, during any period of assessment, was a widow or widower, or

—a person who, during any period of assessment, was entitled to a child rebate.

□ Person who is not a married person

—a male or female who has never married and who is not entitled to a child rebate.

—a divorced person who is not entitled to a child rebate.

—a woman who is the second or subsequent wife in a polygamous marriage and who is not entitled to a child rebate, or

—a married male or female who is living apart from his or her spouse in circumstances indicating a permanent separation and who is not entitled to a child rebate.

The tax payable on the taxable income of each category of person is calculated according to the following tables.

Married Women

Taxable Income		Tax on	Percentage
Over	Not Over	Lower Amount	on Excess
R 0	R 4,000	R 0	15%
4,000	8,000	600	18
8,000	12,000	1,320	21
12,000	16,000	2,160	24

Taxable Income		Tax on	Percentage
Over	Not Over	Lower Amount	on Excess
R16,000	R20,000	R 3,120	27%
20,000	24,000	4,200	30
24,000	28,000	5,400	32
28,000	32,000	6,680	34
32,000	36,000	8,040	35
36,000	40,000	9,480	37
40,000		10,960	38

Rebates

Primary	R 800
Over 65 years (additional)	2,100

Married Persons

Taxable Income		Tax on	Percentage
Over	Not Over	Lower Amount	on Excess
R 0	R 5,000	R 0	15%
5,000	10,000	750	17
10,000	15,000	1,600	19
15,000	20,000	2,550	21
20,000	25,000	3,600	23
25,000	30,000	4,750	26
30,000	35,000	6,050	29
35,000	40,000	7,500	32
40,000	45,000	9,100	35
45,000	50,000	10,850	38
50,000	55,000	12,750	39
55,000	60,000	14,700	40
60,000	70,000	16,700	41
70,000	80,000	20,800	42
80,000		25,000	43

Rebates

Primary	R2,000
Over 62 years (additional)	120
Over 65 years (additional)	1,980
Each child	100
Each sixth and successive child (additional)	50

Persons Who Are Not Married

Taxable Income		Tax on	Percentage
Over	Not Over	Lower Amount	on Excess
R 0	R 5,000	R 0	14%
5,000	10,000	700	17
10,000	15,000	1,550	21
15,000	20,000	2,600	25
20,000	25,000	3,850	29
25,000	30,000	5,300	33
30,000	35,000	6,950	36
35,000	40,000	8,750	39
40,000	45,000	10,700	40
45,000	50,000	12,700	41
50,000	56,000	14,750	42
56,000		17,270	43

Rebates

Primary	R1,800
Over 62 years (additional)	120
Over 65 years (additional)	1,980
Each child	100
Each sixth and successive child (additional)	50

10. Local Income Taxes

In most regions, a regional services levy of 0.25% to 0.345% of payroll and a regional establishment levy of 0.1% to 0.138% of turnover are imposed on individuals conducting businesses. The rates vary according to region.

11. Capital Gains Taxes

None.

12. Foreign Tax Reliefs

As income tax is levied only on taxable income derived or deemed to be derived in South Africa, the question of foreign tax relief does not normally arise. Relief will generally only be granted if provided for in a tax treaty with the foreign state.

13. Tax Period

The tax year for individuals runs from March 1 to February 28.

14. Other Matters

Taxable Income. Taxable income no longer includes dividend income. Medical expenditure is allowed as a deduction in arriving at taxable income in full in the case of taxpayers over the age of 65. In all other cases, the amount of medical expenditures deductible is the expenditure less the greater of R1,000 or 5% of the taxpayer's taxable income.

Standard Income Tax on Employees (SITE). SITE is a final deduction tax. The system ensures that an employee's tax liability on certain of his or her remuneration is finally determined by SITE deductions. SITE applies to all the net remuneration from employment of persons earning less than R50,000 per annum.

SITE deductions are not refundable.

Husband and wife are taxed separately.

INCOME TAXES ON NONRESIDENTS

15. Liability to Tax

In South Africa, the general income tax is called "normal tax." Generally, all companies and individuals, whether or not resident in South Africa, that receive income from a source within or deemed to be within South Africa will be subject to normal tax on such income. Dividends received by nonresident individuals not carrying on business in South Africa, by resident individuals, and by all companies are exempt from normal tax. Nonresident individuals are entitled to the rebates and deductions referred to in items 9 and 14.

16. Rates

The rates of normal tax for nonresident companies and for individuals are the same as for residents. Further tax relief is provided for in tax treaties. The following payments are subject to withholding taxes:

- □ Dividends paid by a company to a non-South African company (item 6) or an individual not ordinarily resident nor carrying on business in South Africa, or by a close corporation to a nonresident member not carrying on business in South Africa.

- □ Royalty and know-how payments to a non-South African company or a company not managed and controlled in South Africa or to an individual not ordinarily resident in South Africa.

17. Withholding Tax Rates

Withholding tax at the following rates is imposed on outward remittances:

Dividends	15%
Royalties and know-how payments	14.4%

Tax treaties with other countries abate or preclude these withholding taxes in some circumstances.

	Dividends	Royalties
All countries other than those specifically noted below:	15%	14.4%
Sweden	15(1)	7.2(2)
Zambia, Zimbabwe, South West Africa, and Malawi	15	14.4(3)
Lesotho	15	14.4(4)
Switzerland	7.5	
United Kingdom	5, 15(5)	14.4(3)
Netherlands	5, 15(5)	
Germany	7.5, 15(6)	14.4(3)
Swaziland	15	14.4(3)
Israel	15	(7)

Notes:

(1) Dividends paid to a company are exempt from the tax.

(2) Royalties paid for copyright are exempt; other royalties are taxed at 7.2%.

(3) Royalties are exempt from the tax if taxable in the recipient country.

(4) Royalties payable for the operation of a mine or quarry or for the extraction of natural resources are exempt.

(5) The rate is 5% if the recipient is a company which controls at least 25% of the voting power in the paying company, and 15% in all other cases.

(6) The rate is 7.5% if the recipient is a company which controls at least 25% of the voting power in the paying company, and 15% in all other cases.

(7) As in (3) except that tax at the rate of 7.2% is imposed on royalties for cinematograph or television films.

OTHER SIGNIFICANT TAXES

21. Sales Tax (Value Added)

Value-added tax is levied at the rate of 10% on the value of imported goods, imported services, and taxable supplies of goods and services made by registered vendors in the course of business. Certain supplies are zero rated or exempt from VAT.

22. Inheritance and Gift Taxes

Donations tax is payable by a donor at a flat rate of 15% of the value of gratuitous dispositions of property. This does not apply to donations:

□ between spouses.

□ to universities, schools, churches, certain charities, and approved public institutions.

□ of property outside South Africa acquired by the donor other than from funds or assets remitted from South Africa.

□ by companies which are public companies for tax purposes.

□ up to R20,000 per individual per tax year.

Estate duty is payable at a flat rate of 15% of the dutiable amount of an estate in South Africa (irrespective of where the deceased was resident). Dutiable amount is determined after allowing certain deductions, the principal one being a general deduction of R1,000,000. The dutiable amount is also reduced by any amount inherited by the decedent's spouse.

23. Taxes on Payrolls (Social Security)

There are no social security taxes as such. Employers are obliged to pay workmen's compensation insurance premiums. Both employers and employees are obliged to contribute to a State Unemployment Insurance Fund where the employee's annual remuneration does not exceed R42,000. For payroll taxes see items 2 and 10.

24. Taxes on Natural Resources

Rights to diamonds, gold and other precious metals vest in the State (i.e., Central Government) and it is necessary for a new mining venture in respect of such minerals to obtain a mining lease. Such leases usually provide for a lease consideration payable to the State, which is allowable as a deduction in arriving at taxable income.

25. Other Taxes

Land and Property. Transfers of immovable property not subject to VAT (see item 21) are subject to a transfer duty at the following rates on the purchase price or fair market value (whichever is the greater):

Into the name of a company	5%
Into the name of an individual:	
—on first R30,000	1%
—on excess over R30,000	3%
—on building stands which do not exceed R12,000	Nil
—on dwellings costing not more than R30,000	Nil

Annual rates are payable to local authorities on the local authority valuation of immovable property.

Interest. Interest received by banks, building societies, and certain other financial institutions is subject to a nondeductible financial services levy of 0.75%, in lieu of VAT (see item 21).

Taxes on Capital. It has been announced that a capital transfer tax will be introduced, but the date of introduction is uncertain.

Stamp Duties. Stamp duties are payable on numerous documents. In particular, the transfer of listed and unlisted shares attracts stamp duty of 1% on the purchase price or the value of the shares (whichever is greater) and of 3% if the transfer is delayed more than six months.

Company Duties. The following duties are payable by companies:

☐ Upon the formation of a company, and upon an increase in authorized share capital, a share capital duty of R5 per R1,000, or part thereof, of the nominal value of authorized share capital.

☐ Upon the registration of an external company, a registration fee of R170.

☐ Upon the issue of shares, a stamp duty of 5 cents per R20, or part thereof, of the nominal value plus share premium in respect of such issue.

COMPUTATION OF TAXABLE INCOME

26. Capital Gains

Capital gains are excluded from taxable income and there are no capital gains taxes.

27. Depreciation and Depletion

Wear and tear and depreciation allowances are granted on plant, machinery, implements, utensils and other articles used for the purpose of trade. Rates allowed vary according to the type of asset, life expectancy and intensity of use. Both the straight-line and reducing-balance methods are permitted. There is a scrapping allowance (or taxable recoupment) on disposal or scrapping of assets eligible for the wear and tear allowance. (For special grants and allowances on capital assets, see item 34.) No allowances are granted for expenditure on goodwill, mineral rights, land or buildings (other than factory and hotel buildings and certain housing projects which are eligible for an annual allowance of 5% or 2% p.a. on the cost).

Most mining capital expenditures (other than the cost of land and mineral rights) are deductible in full in the year in which they are incurred to the extent of mining income for that year. Any excess may be carried forward to offset future mining income. In the case of a new mine, the capital expenditure (including preproduction expenditure) is first allowed in the year in which the mine comes into production.

Research and Development Cost. Capital expenditure (including the cost of buildings) in respect of scientific research and development is deductible over four years at 25% per annum. Other expenses in respect of scientific research and development are deductible in the year incurred.

Patents and Trademarks. The cost of devising, developing, obtaining or acquiring any patent, trademark or property of a similar nature is deductible equally over the period of probable use or 25 years, whichever is less.

28. Treatment of Dividends

Dividends paid to:

☐ Companies, close corporations (CCs), and resident individuals are exempt from normal tax in the companies' hands.

☐ Non-South African companies are subject to a withholding tax of 15% but this rate is abated under the terms of certain tax treaties (see item 17).

☐ Individuals not ordinarily resident nor carrying on business in South Africa are subject to a withholding tax of 15% on dividends and on distributions by a CC, but this rate is abated in terms of certain tax treaties.

29. Loss Carryovers

Where permissible deductions exceed the income in a year of assessment, an "assessed loss" results. An assessed loss is carried forward indefinitely and set off against the income of subsequent years until the loss is recouped, so long as the taxpayer (if a corporation) continues to carry on business. An assessed loss cannot be carried back.

30. Transactions between Related Parties

The Commissioner for Inland Revenue is entitled to disregard transactions that are not on normal and arm's-length terms and that result in avoidance, diminution, or deferment of tax. In practice, the Commissioner seldom interferes with trading relationships between taxpayers in South Africa unless special circumstances (e.g., an assessed loss) suggest that tax avoidance may be the motive for the transaction(s). Various tax treaties contain provisions under which revenue transactions are adjusted to terms that would have prevailed on an arm's-length basis.

In the case of capital transactions, as there is no capital gains tax, the Commissioner will be primarily concerned with:

☐ Dispositions for insufficient considerations, which might constitute donations (see item 22).

☐ The implications as to wear and tear and other allowances on eligible capital expenditure.

31. Consolidation of Income

In South Africa, each company and each individual is a separate legal entity for tax purposes. Subject to certain exceptions, subvention of losses and the consolidation or combining of income or expenditure between group companies are not permitted.

32. Tax Periods

For companies, the year of assessment for each company corresponds with the company's financial year (i.e., its accounting year). The fiscal year (for tax rate purposes) runs from April 1 to March 31 and applies to companies whose years of assessment end within that period. For individuals, the year of assessment runs from March 1 to February 28.

33. Other Matters

Taxable Income. Taxable income can be expressed very broadly as all income (other than certain specified exempt income) of a revenue nature from a source within or deemed to be within South Africa less expenditures of a revenue nature incurred in the production of that income and less specific allowances for capital expenditure and certain allowances designed to encourage development in certain areas. Income includes amounts received or accrued whether in cash or in kind. The value of benefits in kind granted to an employee by an employer is included in the employee's taxable income, generally at the cost to the employer.

RELATED CONSIDERATIONS

34. Incentives and Grants

Government Policy. The Income Tax Act is used to further Government fiscal and economic policy. This is in the process of being changed, and greater use is to be made in future subsidies.

Exempt Income. To encourage investment in particular directions, notably certain Government bonds and shares in building societies, exemption is granted in respect of income derived therefrom. Nonresident investors in stocks issued by the Government and by local authorities are also exempt from tax on the income subject to meeting certain requirements. Amounts received by way of export rebates or subsidies are exempt from tax.

Special Grants or Allowances. In lieu of deductions for wear and tear and depreciation (see item 27), the cost of the items listed below may be deducted from income tax over five years at 20% per annum.

☐ Machinery or plant (other than for mining and farming) used directly in a process of manufacture or a similar process.

☐ Machinery or plant used by an agricultural cooperative for storing or packing pastoral, agricultural, or other farm products.

☐ Machinery, implements, utensils, or articles brought into use in a hotel.

Machinery, implements, utensils, or articles (other than livestock) brought into use by a farmer may be written off over three years: 50% in the first year used, 30% in the second, and 20% in the third.

Certain of the above allowances for plant, machinery, and buildings used in a beneficiation process of minerals and products for export may be claimed sooner or at enhanced rates.

For certain housing projects (of at least five residential units), there is a 10% (of cost) initial allowance. The initial allowance represents accelerated depreciation and is deducted from the cost for the purposes of the annual allowance (see item 27).

Special inducements are provided for operations in selected industrial development areas.

Mining taxpayers are permitted to deduct mining capital expenditures (other than on land and mineral rights for which there is no deduction, and on residential housing for employees, hospitals, schools, railway lines, and motor vehicles for private or semi-private use, the cost of which is deductible over a period of five or ten years) in the year in which they are incurred to the extent of mining income for that year. Any excess may be carried forward to offset future mining income. In the case of a new mine, the preproduction and capital expenditure is first allowed in the year in which the mine comes into production.

Exporters are granted incentives in the form of:

☐ An additional deduction in respect of certain export marketing expenditure.

☐ Tax-free subsidies under a general export incentive scheme.

☐ Low interest loans from the Industrial Development Corporation towards the financing of export capacity.

Donations to universities and other approved educational institutions are deductible by corporations in amounts up to 5% of taxable income (before such deductions), and the greater of R500 or 2% of taxable income (before such deductions) in the case of individuals.

35. Exchange Controls

Policies.   Strict exchange control regulations are enforced. The severity of their application by the Reserve Bank tends to vary according to the state and trend of the foreign exchange reserves.

Imports.   There are generally no restrictions on the purchase of foreign exchange to pay for goods imported, provided that import permits have been obtained when applicable. The Republic of South Africa is a member of GATT and as such is required to abide by GATT regulations and requirements. Up until 1972, a wide-ranging import control existed but since then there has been a systematic reduction in the types of imports which require permits. Nevertheless, there remain categories of imports requiring permits. The permits serve for customs purposes and for the granting of foreign exchange facilities by the Reserve Bank.

Residents. Residents, other than new immigrants, are obliged to declare their foreign assets and may be required to repatriate them to South Africa. Reserve Bank consent is required before a resident can enter into any obligation to a non-resident but the above paragraph must be taken into account in this context. Residents traveling abroad are restricted to an annual foreign exchange allowance of R15,000 each for adults and R7,500 each for children. Businessmen are allowed an additional R1,200 per day up to a maximum of R22,500 p.a. for business visits. Fares may be paid beforehand and do not form part of these allowances. Residents leaving South Africa permanently are permitted to take:

☐ The normal annual travel allowance (R15,000 per adult and R7,500 per child), which may be remitted in commercial rands.

☐ Motor vehicles up to R50,000 and personal belongings and effects to the value of R50,000 per family.

☐ Up to R200,000 per family (R100,000 for a single person), which may only be remitted in financial rands.

Assets in excess of the above are required to be left in South Africa and any realization from them will be dealt with as "blocked Rands." Income (up to R300,000) earned on such assets can be remitted through normal banking channels in commercial rands.

Remittance of Profits/Dividends to Foreign Investors. Remittances of profits and dividends to overseas shareholders and foreign investors in commercial rands are permitted provided: the permitted local borrowing limit is not exceeded; and profits earned prior to January 1, 1984 and capital profits, whenever earned, can be remitted (whether directly or as dividends) in financial rands only after receiving special permission from the Reserve Bank.

Restriction on Permitted Local Borrowings. Restrictions are imposed on the local borrowings of businesses which are more than 25% foreign owned. Where foreign ownership is 100%, the permitted local borrowings are limited to 50% of the effective foreign investment. The application of a formula increases the permitted local borrowings percentage as local ownership increases and foreign ownership decreases.

36. Investment Restrictions on Nonresidents

There are no restrictions on nonresidents making investments in quoted or unquoted securities or other equity investments. The making and repatriation of loans made by nonresidents to residents requires the permission of the Reserve Bank. Payments of foreign loans outstanding on August 28, 1985 are currently blocked but are subject to the repayment agreements.

The gain on the disposition of stock may only be paid and remitted to nonresidents in financial rands or through stock exchange arbitrage deals. Arbitrage permits rapid repatriation but is usually subject to a substantial discount. "Financial rands" can be bought and sold by nonresidents on markets in Johannesburg and London and generally are quoted at a significant discount (20%–40%) against the official rate for the rand.

Nonresidents investing in South African-listed securities (and in other investments, subject to Reserve Bank approval) can do so at the discount afforded by "financial rand." In special cases, particularly where there are strategic considerations, it may be possible to negotiate in advance with the Reserve Bank to obtain consent for future repatriation of capital to be invested in South Africa.

SELECTION OF BUSINESS ENTITY BY NONRESIDENTS

External Company. Upon establishing a place of business in South Africa, a company is obliged to register as an "external company." The significant implications of such registration are:

☐ The profits of the external company can be remitted without the imposition of withholding taxes.

☐ The taxable income attributable to the external company will be taxed at normal company rates (see item 1).

☐ The annual accounts of the foreign company (in addition to audited annual financial statements of the South African operations) must be lodged with the Registrar of Companies in whose office they will be available for public inspection. Exemption can be obtained from this provision on the grounds that such disclosure would not be in the public interest, would be harmful to the company, or would be of no real benefit in view of the insignificant amounts involved.

Local Subsidiary. The alternative to an external company is a locally incorporated subsidiary. The significant implications of such an entity are:

☐ The South Africa source taxable income will be subject to tax at normal company rates (see item 1).

☐ Dividend payments to the holding company will be subject to nonresident shareholders' tax (see items 15 and 17).

☐ Audited annual financial statements are obligatory but need only be lodged if the subsidiary is a public company under company law.

Withholding taxes on royalty remittances (items 16 and 17) apply equally to both external companies and local subsidiaries. Exchange control regulations apply to both types of entity.

SPECIMEN TAX COMPUTATION

Information:

☐ Total receipts and accruals of company for the year aggregate R1,000,000 as follows:

Trading income from South Africa sources	R600,000
Trading income from foreign sources	100,000
Dividend income	200,000
Sale of capital asset	100,000

☐ Expenditure incurred during the year amounted to R300,000, of which R75,000 was attributable to foreign-source trading income and R80,000 attributable to dividend income.

☐ During the year, new plant eligible for the 20% annual initial allowance and costing R100,000 was purchased and brought into operation.

☐ On the sale of the capital asset, previous wear and tear allowances amounting to R50,000 were recouped.

Computation:

Total receipts and accruals		R1,000,000
Less		
Foreign-source income	R100,000	
Capital receipts	100,000	200,000
Gross income		800,000
Add		
Recoupment of wear and tear allowances		50,000
		850,000
Less		
Exempt income (dividends)		200,000
Income		R650,000
Less		
Expenditure incurred in the production of income (1)	145,000	
Capital allowances on new plant: Allowance (20%)	20,000	
		165,000
Taxable income		R485,000
Tax payable (at 50%)		R242,500

Notes:
(1) Expenditure incurred in the production of foreign-source income and dividend income is not deductible. Thus, the deduction is R145,000 (R300,000 − (R75,000 + R80,000)).

SPAIN

INCOME TAXES ON CORPORATIONS

1. Rates
The corporate income tax rate is fixed at 35%. There are tax incentives for investment and the creation of new jobs.

☐ Investment. A 5% tax credit based on the value of new fixed assets purchased in 1991 is available in addition to a 15% tax credit on expenses incurred in the acquisition of intangible fixed assets and a 30% tax credit based on the value of fixed assets applied to the research and development of new products. However, these credits cannot exceed 25% of the net tax payable for the year. Excess credits may be carried forward for five years.

☐ New Jobs Creation. A tax credit of Ptas.500,000 is given for each man-year increase in the average payroll numbers. The credit is computed by comparing the average payroll in the current tax period with that of the preceding tax period, but takes into account only full-time employees with indefinite employment contracts. There is no limit for this tax credit and the excess may be carried forward for five years.

Certain advertising expenses incurred abroad are also eligible for tax credits.

2. Local Income Taxes
The Chamber of Commerce and Industry collects a surcharge of 1.5% of the corporate income tax payable before the application of tax incentives.

3. Capital Gains Taxes
There is no special tax on capital gains. Capital gains arising from dispositions of real estate or other assets forming part of the corporation's property are included with the company's other taxable income and taxed at the corporate income tax rate. For Spanish companies, these gains may escape taxation by reinvesting them in specific ways for certain periods.

4. Branch Profits Taxes

A branch of a foreign corporation is taxed at the standard corporate rate of 35% on Spanish-source income. The incentives stated in item 1 are also available. However, the following differences exist:

□ Certain exchange control formalities are imposed.

□ A branch may claim a percentage of the parent company's expenses.

□ No withholding tax is imposed on the transfer of branch after-tax profits to its parent company. However, when the parent company distributes a dividend, it may be required to withhold Spanish tax on the proportion of the dividend attributed to the Spanish branch.

5. Foreign Tax Reliefs

Relief from double taxation is governed by tax treaties that Spain has concluded with other countries. In addition, a foreign tax credit may be allowed for foreign-source income included on the Spanish tax return, computed as the lesser of:

□ the foreign tax paid on the foreign-source income, or

□ the Spanish tax attributable to the foreign-source income.

6. Classification of Corporations

Entities lacking legal capacity, such as joint ownership and unsettled estates, are not subject to corporate income tax. In these cases, the income tax is assessed on each joint owner in accordance with his or her share of the profits.

Some companies (i.e., professional corporations and certain holding companies) are subject to "tax transparency," in which case they are not liable to corporate income tax. Under this system, each shareholder is liable to income tax on the shareholder's portion of the profits.

7. Payment of Taxes

A corporation tax return must be filed within 25 days after the date of the general shareholders meeting when the annual financial statements are approved, or within six months following the year-end when a branch is involved or if no approval is obtained during this period.

During the first 20 calendar days of April, October, and December 1991, Spanish-resident companies and nonresident companies operating in Spain through a permanent establishment must make three advance corporate income tax payments. The amounts, which correspond to the accounting period in progress on the first day of each of the aforementioned months, total 20% each time, of the tax paid over the prior year, the returns of which had to be filed within those dates.

Nonresident companies without a permanent establishment in Spain must file a return within 25 days after the transaction which generated the revenue.

INCOME TAXES ON INDIVIDUALS

9. Rates

An individual who is present more than 183 days in Spain is considered a resident for Spanish tax purposes and is subject to tax on worldwide income according to the following schedule applicable for 1991:

Income		Tax on	Percentage
Over	Not Over	Lower Amount	on Excess
Ptas. 681,300	Ptas.1,135,500	Ptas. 0	25.0%
1,135,500	1,703,250	113,550	26.0
1,703,250	2,271,000	261,165	27.0
2,271,000	2,838,750	414,458	28.0
2,838,750	3,406,500	573,428	30.0
3,406,500	3,974,250	743,753	32.0
3,974,250	4,542,000	925,433	34.0
4,542,000	5,109,750	1,118,468	36.0
5,109,750	5,677,500	1,322,858	38.5
5,677,500	6,245,250	1,541,441	41.0
6,245,250	6,813,750	1,774,219	43.5
6,813,750	7,380,750	2,021,190	46.0
7,380,750	7,948,500	2,282,355	48.5
7,948,500	8,516,250	2,557,714	51.0
8,516,250	9,084,000	2,847,266	53.5
9,084,000		3,151,013	56.0

There is a maximum effective tax rate of 70% when combined with the wealth tax (see wealth tax rates, item 25).

The Spanish tax return is filed on the basis of the family unit, which generally includes husband, wife, and children under 18 years of age. The entire family unit is considered resident of Spain if either spouse is resident. Nevertheless, the members of the family unit may choose to pay the tax individually, in accordance with the changes introduced by Law 20/1989 of July 28, by filing separate tax returns.

Several deductions are allowed against the gross tax payable (e.g., children, variable deduction when both spouses work, purchase of a home, or certain securities, and an earned income deduction).

10. Local Income Taxes

Autonomous regional governments may impose surcharges on income tax payable.

11. Capital Gains Taxes

Although there is no special capital gains tax, capital gains are included in taxable income as explained in item 26. Capital gain from dispositions of real estate are subject to a special municipal tax. Capital gains arising from the sale of a principal residence may be deferred if the proceeds are reinvested within two years (there is no limit on the amount).

12. Foreign Tax Relief

The information in item 5 also applies to individuals.

13. Tax Period

The fiscal period for individuals is the calendar year.

14. Other Matters

Tax is withheld on salaries according to a rate table, on the basis of marital status and number of children. Fifteen percent is withheld on payments to professionals, and the applicable rate is 25% for unearned income (e.g., dividends and interest). All of the aforementioned taxes withheld are credited against the final tax payable upon filing the income tax return.

INCOME TAXES ON NONRESIDENTS

15. Liability to Tax

Nonresidents are subject to tax on their Spanish-source gross income without allowance for deductions or tax credits. An individual is considered nonresident when present within Spanish territory for 183 days or less during the calendar year.

Effective January 1, 1991, individuals resident in other EC countries who do not have a permanent establishment in Spain generally are not subject to Spanish tax on interest and capital gains derived from assets other than real property. This rule also applies to interest or capital gains derived from investments in public debt (deuda publica) regardless of the investor's residence, except for tax havens.

See item 16 for the taxation of nonresident corporations operating in Spain.

16. Rates

Individuals. Nonresidents are subject to tax at a flat rate of 25%. Spanish-source capital gains of nonresidents are taxed at the 35% rate.

Corporations without a Permanent Establishment. The general tax rate is 25%. For services rendered, technical assistance and, in general, trading operations in Spain, taxable income is calculated on the basis of the difference between total revenues and the sum of personnel costs incurred in Spain and all supplies.

Payments for a share of parent company's expenses are subject to withholding tax of 14%.

Revenue from film rentals has a 10% tax rate.

Capital gains are subject to a 35% tax rate. Taxable income is determined by valuing the contribution or initial cost at the exchange rate prevailing at the time of the transaction. In general, when capital gain is received by an individual or company resident in a tax treaty country it is taxed in Spain only when it relates to real property located in Spain or personal property which is part of a permanent establishment located in Spain.

The exemption mentioned in item 15 for interest and capital gains obtained in Spain by individuals also applies to corporations.

Revenue from reinsurance operations is subject to taxation at 4%. Taxable income is calculated as the difference between the gross reinsurance premium and the commissions and indemnities paid by the foreign insurance company.

Since January 1, 1990, income assigned to nonresident shareholders of transparent companies is subject to taxation at 25%.

Corporations with a Permanent Establishment. These entities are taxed as indicated below unless there is a tax treaty with the foreign company's home country providing more favorable treatment. Foreign companies that are not residents of a country having a tax treaty with Spain are generally taxed under the following systems:

☐ With Continuous Activity. Branches, head offices, offices, agencies or representatives empowered to enter into contracts, workshops, locations, mines, quarries, and agricultural, forestry and cattle operations, as well as continuous or habitual professional or artistic activities, are taxed as explained in item 4.

☐ With Sporadic Activity. Construction on installation projects lasting more than 12 months, the rendering of services without a branch during a period of more than 183 days in a given year, as well as the activities listed above carried out or to be carried out during a period of no more than three years, may choose to be taxed as a permanent establishment with continuous activity or as a company without a permanent establishment.

☐ Establishments Which Do Not Close the Business Cycle. Installations or locations in Spain whose products or services are for their own use and are reimbursed only by covering expenses. The general corporate income tax (35%) is levied on 15% of the expenses incurred. Capital gains are subject to the general tax rate.

17. Withholding Tax Rates

Spanish-source income of nonresidents is subject to withholding tax (see item 16) which in principle constitutes a final tax. Spain's income tax treaties provide advantageous treatment for revenue obtained by nonresidents without a permanent establishment, ranging from complete exemption from Spanish taxes (in the case of performing services and trading) to reduced rates as shown in item 19. Most treaties are based on the OECD model income tax treaty.

18. Special Withholding Provisions

Nonresidents operating in Spain without a permanent establishment are entitled to remit abroad Spanish-source income after paying the relevant withholding tax indicated in item 16.

In the case of a branch remitting profits prior to year-end, a withholding tax of 25% applies. The amount withheld is deducted from the corporate income tax payable by the branch for the relevant tax period.

No clearance from the exchange control authorities is required in case of profit remittances made by branches and interim dividends paid by subsidiaries.

19. Tax Treaties

Country	Dividends (General)	Dividends to Parent Company		Interest	Royalty
		Percent Capital	Withholding Tax		
Austria	15%	50%	10%	5%	5%
Belgium	15	—	15	15	5
Brazil	15	—	15	15, 10(1)	10, 15(1)
Bulgaria	15	25(1)	5	0	0
Canada	15	—	15	15	10
Czechoslovakia	15	25	5	0	5
Denmark	15	50	10	10	6
Finland	15	25	10	10	5
France	15	25	10	10	6
Hungary	15	25	5	0	0
Italy	15	—	15	12	4, 8(1)
Japan	15	25	10	10	10
Luxembourg	15	25	10	10	10
Morocco	15	25	10	10	5
Netherlands	15	50(1)	10, 5(1)	10	6(1)
Norway	15	50	10	10	5
Poland	15	25	5	0	10
Portugal	15	50	10	15	5
Rumania	15	25	10	10	10
Sweden	15	50	10	15	10
Switzerland	15	25	10	10(1)	5
Tunisia	15	50	5	10, 5(1)	10
United Kingdom	15	10	10	12(1)	10
United States	15	25	10	10	5, 8, 10(1)
U.S.S.R.	18	—	18	—	5
West Germany	15	25	10	10(1)	5

Note:

(1) See treaty for special rules.

OTHER SIGNIFICANT TAXES

21. Sales (Value Added)

A value-added tax was introduced in 1986. The rates are:

Regular goods and services	12% (general rate)
Luxury goods and services	33%
Basic necessities	6%

Nonresidents operating in Spain through a permanent establishment must charge VAT ("output VAT") on all their invoices relating to Spanish operations. VAT paid on business expenses and capital expenditures ("input VAT") generally can offset "output VAT" when filing monthly or quarterly VAT returns. VAT paid on certain items cannot be offset; for example, cars, hotels, restaurants, and travel.

Nonresidents operating in Spain without a permanent establishment may claim a refund of VAT paid on operations in Spain. In the case of a nonresident belonging to a non-EEC member state, however, reciprocity must be provided. A special procedure must be followed to obtain this refund.

Certain transactions are exempt from VAT, including:

☐ Most banking activities.

☐ Exports and related services.

☐ Insurance.

☐ Certain consulting services and transactions related to industrial property when rendered to companies not established in Spain or to individuals not resident in EEC-member countries.

22. Inheritance and Gift Taxes

As of January 1, 1988, a new tax regulation came into effect by which property transfers between individuals, at death or inter vivos, are taxed at market value. For tax purposes, place of residence, rather than nationality, is taken into account, without affecting the provisions of double taxation treaties regarding inheritance. Spain has signed agreements of this kind only with France, Greece, and Sweden. The amount of tax depends on the value of the estate of the decedent, the degree of kinship, and the preexisting estate of the inheritor. The rates, both for inheritance and donations, are the following.

Inheritance or Donation		Tax on Lower Amount	Percentage on Excess
Over	Not Over		
Ptas. 0	Ptas. 1,135,500	Ptas. 0	7.65%
1,135,500	2,271,150	86,871	8.50
2,271,150	3,406,725	186,395	9.35

Inheritance or Donation			Tax on Lower Amount	Percentage on Excess
Over		Not Over		
Ptas. 3,406,725	Ptas.	4,542,300	Ptas. 289,672	10.20%
4,542,300		5,677,875	405,400	11.05
5,677,875		6,813,450	530,881	11.90
6,813,450		7,949,025	660,015	12.75
7,949,025		9,084,600	810,801	13.60
9,084,600		10,220,175	965,239	14.45
10,220,175		11,355,750	1,129,329	15.30
11,355,750		17,033,625	1,303,072	16.15
17,033,625		22,711,250	2,220,049	18.70
22,711,250		34,067,250	3,281,812	21.25
34,067,250		56,778,750	5,694,909	25.50
56,778,750		113,557,500	11,486,341	29.75
113,557,500			28,378,019	34.00

23. Taxes on Payrolls (Social Security)

Social security costs in Spain are financed by employers' and workers' contributions and by budget allocations. For this purpose, the contributors are classed into 11 earning groups, and the contributions are based on the legal salary (24% of it is payable by the employer and 4.8% by the worker) for each group. These percentages are supplemented by others provided to cover unemployment and occupational training (6.2% payable by the employer and 1.2% by the worker).

Employers must also provide insurance coverage for accidents occurring at work. This may be arranged with a private insurance company, a mutual association of employers, or one of the social security agencies established for this purpose. In addition, some larger enterprises provide, generally as part of the labor agreements, other benefits for their workers and employees, including canteens, medical and hospital care, subsidized holiday resorts, company stores, and recreational facilities.

24. Taxes on Natural Resources

There are no specific tax regulations covering natural resources except for the research and exploitation of hydrocarbons and mining resources and to promote energy conservation. The most important tax regulations in each of these areas are listed below:

☐ Hydrocarbon Companies.
—Corporation tax is levied at 40%.
—Amounts fulfilling one of the following conditions and credited to a reserve account called "depletion factor" are deductible from the taxable base:
Up to 25% of sales
Up to 40% of the assessable base

—This reserve account can only be used for future development and research expenditure.

—Amortization of tangible assets is governed by special rates.

—Intangible investments and expenses are considered as deferred costs and the annual amortization rates may not exceed 25%.

—Operating losses may be offset against future profits in the years following that in which they are incurred without the usual limitation of five years, and with an upper limit of 25% per annum.

—Entities engaged in prospecting for and development of hydrocarbons are exempt from the following taxes:

  Land and urban taxes

  Sales tax on sales to the state-owned hydrocarbon company

  Local taxes

  Customs duties on imported goods

□ Mining Companies. The tax relief which these companies may claim varies significantly with the mineral involved. In general, the tax benefits are:

—Freedom of depreciation during the first ten years after the start of exploitation of the mining assets.

—Possibility of appropriating up to 30% of the taxable base to the depletion factor reserve. In some cases, the ceiling may be 15% of the value of the mineral sold. This reserve may be used in a manner similar to that indicated for hydrocarbons.

—Other tax relief measures, usually with a five-year limit, entail exemptions of up to 95% for certain taxes, such as custom duties on imported equipment not manufactured in Spain.

□ Energy Saving Programs. Several kinds of relief may also be claimed by companies that adopt energy-saving programs. The more important of these are freedom of depreciation and reduction of up to 95% of custom duties on imported equipment.

25. Other Taxes

Tax on Property Transfers. In general, this tax is applied to transactions not subject to VAT. Transfers of assets are taxed at the following rates applied to their true property value: 6% on real estate and 4% on personal property. The incorporation and increase in capital of corporations and non-incorporated companies and the merger and demerger of these companies are also taxed at a 1% rate (payable on the nominal value of the capital contributed in the cases of incorporations, capital increases, and mergers). Decreases in capital and the dissolution of corporations are subject to a 1% tax on the capital decreased or on the net amount paid to the partners. Documented legal proceedings are also subject to tax.

Whenever an investor acquires more than 50% of the share capital of companies where at least 50% of assets consist of property in Spain, the operation is subject to 6% Property Transfer Tax.

Wealth Tax. This tax became effective December 31, 1977 at the following rates:

Taxable Base		Rate
Over	Not Over	
Ptas. 0 million	Ptas. 25 million	.20%
25	50	.30
50	100	.45
100	250	.65
250	500	.85
500	1,000	1.10
1,000	1,500	1.35
1,500	2,500	1.70
2,500		2.00

In the case of personal liability, there is a Ptas.10,000,000 minimum exemption.
The double taxation treaties are also applicable for the purposes of this tax.

Local Taxes. Law 39/1988, dated December 28, provides for a new system of local taxation. However, not all of the new taxes came into effect in 1991. As a result, some of the old taxes are still in force.

The most important taxes in effect during 1991 are as follows:

☐ Professional and Industrial Activity Fiscal License. An annual tax at fixed amounts in the Tax Code is based on the practice of professionals and industrial activities of individuals and companies.

☐ New Property Tax. The basis of assessment is determined using the official values set by each municipality and is based on the market value of the property. Urban property is subject to 0.4% tax, and rural property is taxed at the rate of 0.3%. However, depending on the size of the municipality, these rates may be approximately 1%.

☐ New Municipal Capital Gains Tax. This tax is levied on the capital gain on the sale of urban land. The basis of assessment is calculated by each municipality and varies between 2% and 3% of the ratable value of the land (depending on the number of years since last sold). The rate of taxation is established every year by each municipality between a maximum and a minimum rate, depending on population (e.g., for municipalities with populations exceeding 100,000, the maximum rate is 30% and the minimum rate is 20%).

Special Taxes. The manufacturing, processing, or importing of the following products is subject to special taxes:

☐ Alcohol, spirits, and beverages.
☐ Beer.
☐ Hydrocarbons.
☐ Tobacco.

COMPUTATION OF TAXABLE INCOME

26. Capital Gains

Gains on the disposal of property forming part of the assets of a corporation are taxed in the same way as the income of that corporation (see item 1). Companies may avoid paying taxes on dispositions of property if the total amount received is reinvested in capital assets.

Capital gains realized by individuals are taxed as follows: The gain is calculated as the difference between the selling price and (a) the cost or (b) the market value at December 31, 1978, whichever is greater. Coefficients for updating the cost or market value at December 31, 1978 vary from 1.050 to 2.559, depending on the year of acquisition. The gain is divided by the number of years of ownership or, if the period is unknown, five years. This quotient is included in general income and taxed accordingly. The remainder of the gain is taxed separately at the average rate for general income. Capital losses are calculated similarly, but may only be used to offset capital gains. Unused losses may be carried over for five years.

The taxation of capital gains of nonresidents operating in Spain without a permanent establishment is explained in item 16.

27. Depreciation and Depletion

Depreciation in the value of operating assets is regarded as deductible for tax purposes if the depreciation is effective and is reflected in the accounts. Depreciation is considered effective if it is calculated by one of the established methods, which are:

Straight-Line Method. The tax authorities have issued publications that give straight-line rates by type of asset. These rates may not be exceeded unless it can be shown that higher rates correspond to the actual depreciation. Some examples of these rates are:

	Rate	Maximum Years
Industrial buildings	3%	50
Personal property	10	15
Tools and utensils	20	8
Machinery (in general)	8	18
Computer equipment	25	6

Declining-Balance Method. This method may be used only for industrial machinery and installations and vehicles which, when new, are assigned a useful life of three years or more. Two permissible variants of this method are the constant percentage method and the sum-of-the-years-digits method.

Plans. In general, companies may depreciate their fixed assets according to depreciation plans designed by them if the plans are first approved by the tax authorities. Fixed assets are considered to depreciate at a rate at least sufficient to recover their value during their useful lives according to the method used.

28. Treatment of Dividends

Dividend payments are subject to a 25% withholding tax at source. Corporations may deduct from their income tax payable the amount withheld plus 50% of the tax actually payable on the dividend received (100% if the recipient owns more than 25% of the payor's capital).

Individuals can deduct 10% of the dividends received from his or her income tax.

29. Loss Carryovers

A loss may be offset against profits earned in the five years following the year in which the loss was incurred; there is no loss carryback.

30. Transactions between Related Parties

Transactions between related parties are treated as arm's-length transactions. Companies are considered to be related when one's participation, directly or indirectly, in the other's capital exceeds 25%.

In the case of related party loans, the tax law prescribes a notional minimum interest rate and such interest is subject to withholding tax.

31. Consolidation of Income

Groups of companies can elect to be assessed for corporate income tax on their consolidated income. Consolidation may be required in certain instances. The percentge ownership must be more than 90% and must have been acquired at least two years prior to requesting consolidation. Nonresident companies may not consolidate their returns with resident companies in Spain.

32. Tax Periods

A corporation's fiscal year coincides with its accounting year. The fiscal period may never exceed 12 months. Foreign companies that trade in Spain without a permanent establishment must pay corporate income tax transaction by transaction.

33.   Other Matters

Deferral of Income.   For deferred payments whose final due dates are more than one year away, the profit may be deferred proportionately to collections.

Adjustment of Asset Values.   Every few years, a budget law allows the value of fixed assets to be increased on the basis of rates set by the Ministry of the Treasury without exceeding market value. Depreciation is then allowed on the basis of the increased values.

Tax Fraud.   Tax fraud in an amount exceeding Ptas. 5 million is considered a criminal offense.

Access to Bank Records.   Tax authorities are empowered to investigate bank accounts.

RELATED CONSIDERATIONS

34.   Incentives and Grants

Many regulations and programs have been created to stimulate the Spanish economy. The most important types are listed below:

Regional Incentives.   Regional incentives are applied by government-specified geographical areas, according to their degree of development. The incentives that may be granted in each case are:

☐   Outright grant of 20% to 75% of the approved investment.
☐   Subsidized interest and loan repayment.
☐   Reduction of up to 50% of the employer's Social Security contribution.

These incentives are processed by the regional authorities and granted by the government.

Research Investments.   Five-year depreciation (seven years for buildings) is available for investments in machinery, equipment, and intangibles to be used in research and development.

In addition, 15% of expenses for intangibles and 30% of the cost of fixed assets for research and development may be deducted from the corporate income tax payable for the year in which they are incurred.

Special Incentives.   The following tax incentives are available for national or foreign individuals or companies collaborating with the committees managing the

Barcelona 1992 Olympic Games, the Fifth Centennial of the Discovery of America, or the Seville World Expo.

□ Individual and corporate donations to these committees are tax deductible.
□ There is a 15% tax credit on investments in new assets and renovation work.
□ There is a 95% reduction of transfer taxes for these events.
□ A VAT exemption is available for work performed for these events.

Groups of Companies, Joint Ventures, and Partial Transfer of Projects. Although they are legal nonentities, these groups are taxed as follows:

□ Groups of companies formed for the joint promotion or development of the members' business activities are eligible for a 99% rebate on the transfer tax on the formation, modification or liquidation of the entity, as is the partial transfer of projects.
□ Instead of paying corporate income tax as a separate entity, groups of companies and joint ventures may elect for their members to add their share of the entities' income to their other income for corporate income tax purposes.

Mergers. The Ministry of Finance may grant the following benefits to mergers and separations of companies regarded as beneficial to the domestic economy:

□ Revaluation of assets to their market value with a rebate of up to 99% of the corporate income tax on the capital gain.
□ Rebate of up to 99% of the property transfer tax on merger or separation operations.
□ Rebate of up to 99% of the local taxes on transfers of property.

35. Exchange Controls

The regulations governing foreign investment have been greatly relaxed, and the protectionist barriers have largely disappeared. This deregulation process has accelerated considerably following Spain's entry into the European Economic Community.

Responsibility for foreign exchange operations is shared by the Bank of Spain, which handles movements in foreign currencies and clears foreign loans to Spanish borrowers (only loans exceeding 1,500 million pesetas require clearance), and the Directorate-General of Foreign Transactions (DGTE), whose administrative functions include clearing inward and outward remittances and foreign investments in Spain. (See item 36.)

Foreign-owned Spanish companies and the Spanish branches and establishments of foreign companies have access to domestic credit in the same conditions as Spanish companies.

36. Investment Restrictions on Nonresidents

The new regulations virtually deregulate foreign investment. Foreign investments can be classified according to the degree of administrative control involved, as explained below:

☐ "Liberalized investments" require no prior notification to the authorities.

☐ "Deregulated investments" are effectively free but require advance notification to the Spanish authorities on a standard form. The authorities must reply within 30 days; otherwise, the proposal is considered approved. Most investments are included in this category.

☐ "Investments subject to authorization" are those made in the following areas:

— Defense
— Television
— Radio
— Gambling
— Air transport

Except for the defense area, this rule does not apply if the investor is resident in an EEC country.

Investments made by foreign-owned Spanish companies or by branches and permanent establishments of nonresident foreign individuals or companies are also considered as foreign investments. In this case, the investment would be liberalized if the foreign holding does not exceed 50% or, in any case, if its amount does not exceed Ptas. 25,000,000. Otherwise, the investment would be classified as deregulated.

Investments in real estate for purposes other than business are liberalized, except the acquisition of rural property, undeveloped urban lots, commercial property, and real estate located in strategic areas.

SELECTION OF BUSINESS ENTITY BY NONRESIDENTS

Nonresidents can operate in Spain either through a branch or a subsidiary. Both types of entities have basically the same tax treatment, but branches may claim a certain percentage of the parent company's expenses (see item 4), are not subject to withholding taxes on after-tax profits remitted to the parent company, and may not use foreign tax credits.

Direct operations (those not carried out through a branch or permanent establishment) are subject to the taxes mentioned in item 16. Trading income obtained in Spain by nonresidents without a permanent establishment is not taxed when a tax treaty is applicable.

SPECIMEN TAX COMPUTATION

Information:

□ The computation compares the taxation of a subsidiary, branch, and nonresident corporation without a permanent establishment in Spain. The operating results for the 1991 calendar year are:

Operating profits	Ptas. 4,000,000
Dividends received in Spain from minority-held companies (less than 25%)	2,000,000
Foreign-source net income (Ptas. 500,000 in foreign taxes paid)	1,000,000
Capital gain from fixed assets (net book value is the Ptas. 100,000 equivalent to $1,000) (1)	200,000
Total profit	Ptas. 7,200,000

□ The subsidiary and the branch invest Ptas. 10,000,000 in new fixed assets, of which Ptas. 300,000 were reinvested from sales of fixed assets.

□ The subsidiary and the branch distribute a Ptas. 500,000 dividend from current earnings and profits. See note 2.

Computation:

	Subsidiary (Ptas.)	Branch (Ptas.)	Nonresident Company (3)		
			Operating Income (Ptas.)	Capital Gain (4) (Ptas.)	Dividend (Ptas.)
Profits for the year	7,200,000	7,200,000	4,000,000	166,000	2,000,000
Reinvestment of capital gains	(200,000)	(200,000)			
Taxable base	7,000,000	7,000,000	4,000,000	166,000	2,000,000
Tax rate	35%	35%	25%	35%	25% (6)
Tax payable	2,450,000	2,450,000	1,000,000	58,100	500,000
Deduction for inter-company double taxation (50% × 35% × Ptas. 2,000,000)	(350,000)	(350,000)			

	Subsidiary (Ptas.)	Branch (Ptas.)	Nonresident Company (3)		
			Operating Income (Ptas.)	Capital Gain (4) (Ptas.)	Dividends (Ptas.)
Deduction for international double taxation (35% × Ptas. 1,000,000)	(350,000)				
Net tax payable	1,750,000	2,100,000			
Deduction for investments (to a maximum of 25% of net tax payable) (5)	(437,500)	(485,000)			
Withholding tax (25% × Ptas. 2,000,000) (2)	(500,000)	(500,000)			
Tax payable	812,500	1,115,000			
Profit after taxes	6,387,500	6,085,000			
Withholding tax on dividends (25%) (6)	125,000				
Tax credit not applied for investments (to be carried forward for five years)	47,500				

Notes:
(1) The sales price was Ptas. 300,000, which is $2,239 at Ptas. 134 per US$1.
(2) Dividend payments by subsidiaries are subject to an 25% withholding tax.
(3) Foreign companies operating in Spain without a permanent establishment must pay corporate income tax on a transaction-by-transaction basis.
(4) In the case of a nonresident company operating without a permanent establishment in Spain, capital gain is computed by applying the exchange rate prevailing at the date of the sale; i.e., Ptas. 300,000 − 134,000 = 166,000.
(5) 5% × (Ptas. 10,000,000 − 300,000) = Ptas. 485,000.
(6) Reduced rates apply to treaty countries (see item 19).

SRI LANKA

INCOME TAXES ON CORPORATIONS

1. Rates

Resident companies (both public and private), in general, pay tax at the rate of 50% on their worldwide income. A resident public company whose shares are quoted by the Colombo Stock Exchange (equivalent to a quoted or listed company) is taxed at 40%. A quoted public company will be required not only to have more than 200 shareholders but also to ensure that no five persons will hold directly or through nominees more than 60% of the total issued share capital. If these additional requirements are not fulfilled by March 31, 1992, a quoted public company will be taxed at 50% for tax years 1990/91, 1991/92. The tax rate of 50% will also apply for any subsequent tax year if these additional requirements are not satisfied at March 31, the tax year-end. The concessionary rate of 40% also applies to "peoples companies." Peoples companies, among other things, are required to:

- ☐ Have a minimum of 101 shareholders.
- ☐ Limit the shares held by any one person and his immediate family to 5% of the issued capital.
- ☐ Prohibit issue of its shares to any other company.

A resident company whose issued share capital is Rs 500,000 or less and the taxable income of which is not more than Rs 333,333 is referred to as a small company. The company will be taxed as follows:

Taxable Income		Rate of Tax
Over	**Not Over**	
Rs 0	Rs 250,000	33⅓%
250,000	333,333	Rs 83,333 plus the amount of the excess of taxable income over Rs 250,000

Nonresident companies pay tax as follows:

□ 50% on taxable income.
□ A tax amounting to one-third of its remittances abroad in the tax year or 11.11% of its taxable income, whichever is lower. Careful tax planning and timing can minimize this tax.

Dividends paid by a resident company will not form part of taxable income in the hands of the receiving company (resident or nonresident).

Resident companies are required to withhold 15% of the aggregate amount of the gross dividends distributed out of taxable income. Quoted public companies are not required to withhold tax on dividends paid to resident shareholders. Further, a resident company that pays a dividend to a nonresident out of a dividend (which is not exempt) received from a quoted public company directly or through one or more intermediary companies is required to withhold 15% of the dividend. The tax withheld should be paid by the company to the Inland Revenue within 30 days of distribution of the dividends.

Effective from the 1988/1989 tax year, every resident company is required to pay an advance company tax (ACT) concurrently with the payment of every dividend out of profits made on or after April 1, 1988, which are liable to tax. Such ACT is creditable against the company's income tax due on taxable income up to a limit of 50% of such tax. Any unrelieved balance of ACT can be carried forward to future tax years for credit against income tax due.

ACT is payable at a prescribed percentage of every qualifying dividend:

Class of Resident Company	ACT Rate
Small company	25%
Quoted public company	33⅓%
People's company	33⅓%
Others	50%

A surcharge on income tax of 15% of the tax chargeable on a company has been imposed for tax years 1989/1990, 1990/1991, and 1991/1992. However, the surcharge will not apply to:

□ The dividend tax payable by a resident company (see item 6).
□ The tax on remittances (see above) payable by a nonresident company.

2. Local Income Taxes

None.

3. Capital Gains Taxes

Capital gains resulting from the transactions described below are treated like normal income.

□ Change of ownership of property.

□ Redemption of shares or debentures.

□ Formation of a company.

□ Dissolution of a business or the liquidation of a company.

□ Any transaction to which a taxpayer is not a party but in the promotion of which he is engaged for commission or reward.

The income tax rate on a capital gain is not more than 25%, but this limitation does not apply to the capital gain from a change of ownership of property (other than a share in a quoted public company) occurring within two years of its acquisition.

A capital gain resulting from the change of ownership of a share in a quoted public company, which occurs within one year of its acquisition, is taxed at no more than 20%, and, if the change of ownership occurs after one year, the capital gain is tax-exempt. If there is a change of ownership of property after two years of its acquisition, the income tax rates on the capital gain are subject to ceilings, depending on the taxpayer's period of ownership as shown below:

Period of Ownership	Tax Ceiling on Capital Gain
More than 2 years but not more than 5 years	25.0%
More than 5 years but not more than 15 years	17.5
More than 15 years but not more than 20 years	12.5
More than 20 years but not more than 25 years	5.0
More than 25 years	exempt

Exemption from capital gains tax is accorded to the following categories of transaction:

□ The sale of non-business personal assets, the proceeds from which are invested in full within a year of sale, but on or before April 1, 1992, in the purchase of ordinary shares in a pioneering industry, industrial expansion, a unit trust, a mutual fund, or a venture capital company.

□ The sale of investments in shares or stocks by a unit trust, a mutual fund, or a venture capital company.

□ The sale, after one year of acquisition, by a unit holder of units in a unit trust or mutual fund.

To calculate capital gain, first reduce the sales price (if the property is sold) or the adjusted market value (if it is exchanged) by the following deductions:

□ Market value at April 1, 1977 or the price at purchase (if later).

□ Cost of improvements.

□ Acquisition expenses.

In the case of immovable property acquired by gift or inheritance, the "period of ownership" is deemed to include the period of ownership of the person from whom the property was acquired.

4. Branch Profits Taxes

A foreign incorporated company having a place of business in Sri Lanka will be taxed in the same manner as a nonresident company (see item 1).

5. Foreign Tax Reliefs

Tax treaties have been entered into with Bangladesh, Belgium, Canada, Czecho-slovakia, Denmark, East Germany, Finland, France, Germany, India, Italy, Japan, Malaysia, Netherlands, Norway, Pakistan, Poland, Rumania, Singapore, South Korea, Sweden, Switzerland, Thailand, United Kingdom, and Yugoslavia.

A company not resident in Sri Lanka but resident in a Commonwealth country that has no treaty with Sri Lanka may deduct from Sri Lanka income tax half of either the Sri Lanka tax or the tax charged in that country on doubly taxed income, whichever is lower.

A company resident in a country not in the Commonwealth nor having a treaty with Sri Lanka may deduct, in computing profits for Sri Lanka tax purposes, the income tax charged in the other country on doubly taxed income.

6. Classification of Corporations

Corporations (companies) are classified for Sri Lanka tax purposes as:

☐ A resident or nonresident company.

☐ A quoted public company, peoples company, small company or other (private or public) company.

☐ An offshore company.

A resident company is one which is incorporated in Sri Lanka or is controlled or managed from Sri Lanka. The distinction between a resident and nonresident company is important in that:

☐ A resident company is subject to tax on worldwide income whereas a nonresident company is subject to tax only on Sri Lanka income.

☐ A resident company is taxed a prescribed percentage of taxable income plus 15% of dividends distributed, whereas a nonresident company is taxed at 50% plus either one-third of the profits remitted or one-ninth of taxable income, whichever is lower. Dividends distributed by a resident quoted public company among resident shareholders will not be taxed at 15%.

For rates of tax on resident companies, see item 1.

The distinction between a quoted public company, peoples company, small company and other companies, and the application of different tax rates for income and dividends are set out in item 1.

Offshore Companies. Companies not carrying on business in Sri Lanka can have a physical base in Sri Lanka registered as an offshore company. Registration is granted on payment of a fee of Rs 11,000, remittance to Sri Lanka of not less than US$25,000 to defray the costs of the Sri Lanka office, and meeting other routine filing and legal requirements (see item 34).

7. Payment of Taxes

Companies and individuals are required to pay income tax in installments on a self-assessment basis as follows:

Installment	Payment Due By
First	August 15 of the tax year
Second	November 15 of the tax year
Third	February 15 of the tax year
Fourth	May 15 of the following year
Final	November 30 of the following year

If each of the first four payments is on an estimated basis of not less than one-quarter of the income tax for the tax year immediately preceding, the balance of income tax due may be paid as the final installment without incurring penalties (see item 33). However, if exemption of income from a particular source ended in the tax year immediately preceding, the estimated quarterly installments of income tax will be computed on the income of such year, including the exempt income.

In the case of a resident company, any payment of ACT (see item 1) or such unrelieved part of the ACT brought forward from the previous tax year is treated as an advance payment of the next quarterly installments due for the current tax year.

The tax return for the year is also due by November 30 following the end of the tax year.

INCOME TAXES ON INDIVIDUALS

9. Rates

Income tax rates are the same for residents and nonresidents (except for expatriates, see below) but residents are given an allowance (tax-free) of Rs 27,000 per annum before arriving at taxable income.

| Taxable Income | | Tax on | Percentage |
Over	Not Over	Lower Amount	on Excess
Rs 0	Rs 21,000	Rs 0	10%
21,000	45,000	2,100	20
45,000	69,000	6,900	30
69,000		14,100	40

Expatriate employees (i.e., noncitizens of Sri Lanka) will be treated as nonresidents for a period of three years from the date of commencement of employment in Sri Lanka. During this period they will be liable to tax at a concessionary flat rate of 25% on income arising in or derived from Sri Lanka even if payment is made overseas for services rendered in Sri Lanka.

A surcharge on income tax of 15% of the tax chargeable on an individual has been imposed for the tax years 1989/1990, 1990/1991, and 1991/1992. However, the surcharge will not apply to:

□ The income tax payable by a resident employee on the terminal benefits drawn by him at retirement.

□ The tax payable at 25% (see above) by an expatriate.

10. Local Income Taxes

None.

11. Capital Gains Taxes

The information in item 3 applies here.

12. Foreign Tax Reliefs

Same as item 5.

13. Tax Period

The tax year is April 1 to March 31 and the income assessable is the income of that year.

INCOME TAXES ON NONRESIDENTS

15. Liability to Tax

A nonresident person (including a company) is liable to income tax only on profits and income arising in or derived from Sri Lanka. A nonresident is now liable to Sri Lanka income tax on profits derived from the insurance business and sales or other disposals of property even when effected overseas if such transactions are brought about through the instrumentality of a person in Sri Lanka acting on behalf of the nonresident person. For this reason, before a nonresident person appoints a resident as a liaison representative to foster business relations in Sri Lanka, it is important to determine carefully the scope of his duties and responsibilities in Sri Lanka so as to exclude acts that may be construed as being instrumental in bringing about the overseas contracts of the nonresident person.

There are antiavoidance measures designed to tax the arm's-length profits attributable to a nonresident person who attempts to reduce his actual profits by so arranging his transactions in association with closely connected persons in Sri Lanka (see item 30).

Special treatment is accorded to business profits from Sri Lanka of residents in countries that have double tax treaties with Sri Lanka. Tax is charged in general only if the profits can be attributed to the permanent establishment in Sri Lanka of the nonresident person. In some cases, profits of shipowners and operators of aircraft are wholly exempt from Sri Lanka income tax while in others the tax is reduced by 50% of the normal tax.

16. Rates

Nonresident corporation tax rates are given in item 1. Nonresident individual tax rates are given in item 9.

17. Withholding Tax Rates

Payments to nonresidents of interest, rent, royalties or annuities attract a withholding tax of 33.33%. The actual tax liability will however be much higher; for example, 61.11% of taxable income for a nonresident company.

Dividends, interest, and royalties remitted to certain countries with which Sri Lanka has double tax treaties qualify for exemption or a lower withholding rate of 10% to 15%.

19. Tax Treaties

	Dividends	Interest	Royalties
Treaty countries:			
Bangladesh	15%	15%	15%
Belgium	15	10	10
Canada	15	15	10
Czechoslovakia	15	10	10
Denmark	15	10	10
Germany (East)	15	10	10
Germany (West)	15	10	10
Finland	15	10	10
France	15	10	10, 0(1)
India	15	10	10
Italy	15	10	10
Japan	—	—	(2), 0(1)

	Dividends	Interest	Royalties
Malaysia	—	—	(2)
Netherlands	15%, 10%	15%, 10%	10%
Norway	—	—	10, 0(01)
Pakistan	15	10	20
Poland	—	10	10
Rumania	12.5	10	10
Singapore	15	10	15
South Korea	15, 10	10	10
Sweden	15	10	10
Switzerland	15, 10	10	10
Thailand	15	10	15
United Kingdom	15	10	10
Yugoslavia	12.5	10	10

Notes:

(1) 0% for copyright royalties.
(2) 50% of normal tax.

OTHER SIGNIFICANT TAXES

21. Sales (Value Added)

There is no sales tax or value added tax (VAT), but a turnover tax (TT) is levied on the sales of every business that has a turnover of Rs 25,000 or more for a quarter and either:

☐ Carries on business in Sri Lanka.
☐ Renders services outside Sri Lanka for which payment is made from Sri Lanka.

Turnover tax is also payable on all imports and this is recovered as a customs levy. The turnover tax paid by a manufacturer on imports of inputs for the manufacture of his products is deductible from the turnover tax payable on sales. Where the cost of input of a manufactured article includes an element of turnover tax, such tax is deductible from the turnover tax payable at the time of sale. Payment of tax is on a self-assessment basis, quarterly, at rates that vary from 1% to 40%. Some of the rates are: 3, 5, 6, 10, 12½, 15, 20, and 40% for manufactured or imported articles, 3% for construction contracts, 5% for professions, and 1% for merchants (nonmanufacturers) and hoteliers.

22. Inheritance and Gift Taxes

These taxes were abolished effective November 13, 1985.

23. Taxes on Payrolls (Social Security)

There is no payroll tax as such but all employers are required to contribute a minimum of 12% of wages or salaries to an Employees Provident Fund (EPF) and a further 3% to an Employees Trust Fund. Employers are required to pay statutorily determined gratuities to employees who complete more than five years of service at the time of their termination of service.

24. Taxes on Natural Resources

None.

25. Other Taxes

Land and Property Taxes. Except for municipal taxes, there are no land or property taxes. There is, however, a property transfer tax of 100% of value of the property, chargeable from the transferee, when the transfer is from a resident to a nonresident company or a nonresident individual who is not a citizen.

However, the transfer tax is not chargeable on the transfer of shares in a Sri Lanka company that is either a GCEC company (see item 34) or one in which the total holding of shares by nonresidents (other than nonresident citizens), including current transfers to them, is not more than 40% of the total issued capital of the company.

Tax on Capital. Capital is not taxed as such, but tax is payable on the net wealth. The rates of wealth tax for individuals are:

	Taxable Wealth	
Over	Not Over	Rate of Tax
Rs 0	Rs 500,000	0.5%
500,000	1,500,000	0.75
1,500,000	3,000,000	1.0
3,000,000		2.0

A deduction of Rs 500,000 from the net wealth is allowed in arriving at taxable wealth. Wealth tax is not payable by resident companies.

For a nonresident company that has immovable property in Sri Lanka, its taxable wealth is five times its taxable income derived from that property, and wealth tax is charged at 1% of taxable wealth.

A surcharge on wealth tax of 15% of the tax chargeable has been imposed for the tax years 1989/1990 and 1990/1991.

Stamp Tax. Stamp duties, usually ad valorem, are levied on documents which include share certificates, receipts for acknowledgement of payments, title deeds, registered agreements, and memorandum of association.

COMPUTATION OF TAXABLE INCOME

26. Capital Gains

See item 3 for the calculation of capital gains.

27. Depreciation and Depletion

The annual depreciation rates allowed for tax purposes, on a straight-line basis, are:

Motor vehicles and office furniture	25%
Plant, machinery, and fixtures	33.33%
Industrial and commercial buildings	10%

The allowances for depreciation begin in the year of assessment in which the asset is first used, although it may have been acquired in a prior year.

28. Treatment of Dividends

Effective April 1, 1985 through March 31, 1989, dividend income of up to Rs 12,000 per annum will not be taxed in the hands of an individual. Tax is payable on the gross dividends (received by individuals) and the dividend tax deducted at source as well as the ACT are deductible from the total tax payable. The amount of the gross dividend of a resident shareholder of a resident company that is liable to tax is the total of the net dividend received, the amount of the withholding tax (see item 1) retained by the company, and the amount of the ACT paid by the company in respect of such dividend. Both resident companies and nonresident companies receiving dividends which have suffered tax (deducted at source) are not required to add such dividend received to income, and any dividend distributed by the second company out of the dividend received is exempt from a further deduction of tax at source.

Subject to certain conditions, an individual shareholder of a resident company is exempt from income tax on dividends received that are paid out of exempt profits of the company or out of exempt dividends received by that company from two or more intermediate companies.

29. Loss Carryovers

Losses can be carried forward for any period of time to be set off from taxable profits in the future. For a going concern, there is no provision to carry back losses but, on cessation of a business, losses can be carried back for three years.

A capital loss cannot be deducted from other income but is deductible from capital gains or can be carried forward for deduction from future capital gains. However, any capital loss left unabsorbed at the time of liquidation of a company or the death of a person can be carried back for deduction from the total income of any of the three tax years immediately preceding the last tax year.

If more than one-third of a company's share capital changes ownership, business losses can only be carried forward to offset future profits of that particular business. This limitation does not apply to the change in the composition of share ownership in a company that is caused by the transfer of shares to the heirs of a deceased shareholder.

30. Transactions between Related Parties

Expenditure incurred on revenue transactions between related parties may be disallowed in full or in part if the expenditure is considered to be excessive or unreasonable in regard to the fair market value of the goods, services, or facilities for which the payment is made, or the legitimate needs of the business or profession of the taxpayer or the benefit derived by, or accruing to, him therefrom.

If property is sold and the tax authority is satisfied that the sale price is not reasonably adequate, the tax authority is empowered to substitute the market value of the property on the date of sale (if that is higher) in computing the capital gain from the sale.

31. Consolidation of Income

Each company is assessed separately. There is no provision for special treatment of companies in a group.

In the case of individuals, husbands and wives are treated separately for tax purposes. The income of a child under 18 is aggregated with the father's income. However, if marriage between the parents does not subsist in the tax year, the child's income is aggregated with that of the parent who maintains the child and with whom the child lives in that year. Aggregation does not apply if the child is married, is illegitimate, or is adopted without legal sanction.

32. Tax Periods

March 31 is the standard tax year-end. Subsidiaries of foreign companies may obtain approval from the Commissioner General of Inland Revenue to adopt a different group accounting period for tax purposes. If such approval is obtained, the Inland Revenue may further direct that income be computed on the profits of the accounting year that ends in the tax year. If the taxpayer subsequently fails to keep accounts to such date as is approved, income will be computed for the tax year in which such failure occurs and for the two years immediately following, on such basis as the Inland Revenue considers just and equitable. The turnover tax is charged on the turnover of each quarter in the calendar year.

33. Other Matters

Deductions for Taxes. In computing the taxable profits, turnover tax (TT), duty on non-capital items of expenditure, contributions to the employees provident and trust funds, and municipal property taxes are deductible. No deduction is available for income tax or wealth tax. Company formation expenses are allowed as deductions.

A business employing not less than ten individuals, which commences operations with the approval of the Minister of Finance in an area of high unemployment, is permitted to deduct in computing taxable profits twice the expense incurred on contributions to the EPF and ETF (see item 23).

Under special incentive legislation, the following deductions are allowed in the computation of business profits:

☐ One-tenth of the payment (over ten years) made as consideration for using a licensed manufacturing process in the production of goods.

☐ Twice the amount of expenditure incurred before April 1, 1995 by an exporter of nontraditional products on participation in overseas fairs or exhibitions, the maintenance of an overseas trade office, advertisement in overseas publications, and the publication of catalogues, brochures, commercial literature, or such other publication meant to promote the sale of the exported goods.

☐ Twice the amount of expenditure incurred before April 1, 1995 by any manufacturing business on scientific, industrial, or agricultural research or the local training of employees for upgrading the manufacturing process or the quality of the product.

Bad Debts.   Specific provisions for trade or staff debtor balances are deductible. Any recovery of a written-off or provided debt is included in taxable profits.

Disallowed Expenditure.   In computing the total income of an individual or company, the following expenditures are, among others, not deductible:

☐ Entertainment expenses are disallowed. If an employee is reimbursed for entertainment expenses by the employer, the employee is not liable for tax but the employer is not allowed to deduct such expense from total income liable for tax.

☐ One quarter of the cost of advertising in Sri Lanka. The cost of advertising outside Sri Lanka for the export of goods or services is deductible.

☐ Any prescribed tax or levy (see above).

☐ Payments to any pension or provident fund not approved by the Commissioner of Inland Revenue.

Specific Deductions—Qualifying Payments.   Deductions in respect of the following payments, among others, are allowed in arriving at taxable profit. The total deductions in respect of qualifying payments are limited to one-third of the assessable income in the case of a company, and one third of assessable income or Rs 50,000, whichever is lower, for other taxpayers. Gifts or donations to the Government are deductible without limit.

☐ The cost of investment in the purchase of ordinary shares (other than existing shares) in an approved undertaking.

□ The amount spent by an individual on the construction of a house at a cost of not more than Rs 1 million, except such portion of expenditure met from a loan referred to just below.

□ The amount spent by an individual on the purchase, at a price of not more than Rs 1 million, of either the first house or the first housing site.

□ An amount paid to a banking or other approved credit institution in settlement of a loan obtained for the construction of a house by an individual at a cost of not more than Rs 1 million.

□ Life assurance premiums paid by an individual.

□ Contributions by an individual to an approved pension or provident fund.

□ Donations and gifts to "approved charities" or to the Government.

□ Under special incentive legislation, if a person sells his or her personal non-business assets and invests the full proceeds of sale in the purchase of ordinary shares in a pioneering industry, an industrial expansion, a unit trust, a mutual fund, or a venture capital company, such investment will qualify for deduction provided the person has not claimed exemption of the capital gain derived from such sale (see item 3). The seller will be entitled to deduct the full amount of the investment up to an upper limit equal to one-third of assessable income, which is *in addition* to the limit fixed for deduction of other qualifying payments referred to above. Any unabsorbed excess of such investment can be carried forward for deduction from the assessable income of subsequent years.

Penalties.   Taxes not paid when due attract penalties which accrue over time to a maximum of 50%.

RELATED CONSIDERATIONS

34.   Incentives and Grants

Greater Colombo Economic Commission (GCEC).   The GCEC is an autonomous entity created by act of Parliament. It is the authority for the Sri Lankan Investment Promotion Zones (IPZ) as well as for the approval of all foreign investment in Sri Lanka and functions directly under the President of Sri Lanka. Its objectives are to promote export-oriented foreign investment, create employment opportunities, increase export earnings and induce technology transfers. The GCEC can grant exemption from, or modify the application of certain laws of the country, in order to offer investors a suitable and attractive investment package. It may offer an exemption from income tax for not more than 15 years depending on the number of people employed, net foreign exchange earned, introduction of new technology, and magnitude of fixed capital investment. Thereafter, for a period of not more than 15 years, a tax based on turnover of not less than 2% will apply in place of the income or corporate tax. A GCEC venture will also enjoy exemptions from import duties on machinery, equipment, construction material, and raw materials.

In addition, dividends to nonresident shareholders are exempt from taxes and exchange control.

GCEC operations usually require 100% export and, as such, are exempt from turnover tax (TT). In the rare instance of a GCEC company having turnover other than exports, TT will apply to the nonexport turnover. Dividends paid by a company which has entered into an agreement with the GCEC will not be taxed if the recipient is a nonresident. A resident individual will also enjoy exemptions from tax on dividends received from a GCEC company during the period the company is exempt from tax and one year thereafter.

Noncitizen employees of GCEC companies are exempt from income tax during the period the company is exempt from tax. During the period within which the GCEC company is exempt from income tax, no tax is levied on royalties paid.

Property Development.   Any person carrying on an undertaking for the construction and sale of houses, on obtaining approval from the Commissioner of National Housing shall be exempt from tax on the profit arising from the sale (being the first sale of that house) of houses subject to certain restrictions on the floor area.

Other Tax Exemptions.   Tax exemptions are also available for:

☐   Profits from the export of gems.

☐   Profits earned abroad in foreign currency by residents (companies or individuals) from services rendered abroad are exempt from income tax if such profits are remitted to Sri Lanka net of expenses.

☐   Fees and emoluments earned in foreign currency by a resident individual or partnership from professional or vocational services rendered in Sri Lanka for a person outside Sri Lanka are exempted if the earnings are remitted to Sri Lanka through a bank.

☐   Profit (of companies) from the manufacture and export of nontraditional products for a period of five years reckoned from the tax year in which each company begins to make profits from transactions in the year.

☐   Profits (of companies) for five years, from the provision for payment in foreign currency, of the services of ship repairs, ship breaking, repair and refurbishment of marine cargo containers, and the provision of computer (other than hardware) services. The period of five years begins with the tax year in which each company begins to make profits from transactions in the year.

☐   Profits for five years of companies engaged in animal husbandry, cultivation of sugar cane, marine or inland fisheries, and processing of agricultural produce of Sri Lanka.

☐   Profits from exports and services rendered for payment in foreign currency not covered by the above exemptions will qualify for a tax exemption up to March 31, 1991. However, exports of traditional products will not qualify and the services that qualify are limited to ship repairs, repair and refurbishment of marine cargo containers, and computer (other than hardware) services.

□ Profits from exports that enjoy a five-year tax holiday will be granted an abatement of half the normal tax on export profits for a further period of five years provided the net foreign exchange earnings are at least 25% of the FOB value of the exports.

□ Profits from the export of precious stones or metals not mined in Sri Lanka, and petroleum products.

□ The profits of a producer or manufacturer from the supply of articles to an exporter or a GCEC company are exempted, subject to certain conditions being fulfilled.

□ Under special incentive legislation, the following incentives are provided:

—a ten-year exemption of business profits for a venture capital company;

—a five-year exemption of profits for a unit trust or a mutual fund;

—a five-year exemption of profits for a company engaged only in a pioneering industry, in the training in manufacturing processes, industrial design, or in the training in computer software and computer-related development;

—a five-year exemption of profits for purchasing centers that are to be set up country-wide to promote the distribution of village-level production of non-traditional goods or commodities;

—a five-year exemption of profits for a company engaged only in providing infrastructure facilities with floor area of not less than 2,000 square feet for each of not fewer than 20 enterprises engaged in the production or manufacture of articles;

—a five-year exemption of profits for a unit of industrial expansion of a company, such expansion being recognized only if new capital investment of not less than Rs 5 million is spent on the purchase of equipment designed to increase the productive capacity and the provision of employment for not less than 25 additional persons;

—a three-year exemption of profits for a person who operates a new omnibus with a seating capacity for not less than 30 passengers.

Offshore Companies. Offshore shipping companies are not liable for income tax except on income arising on the carrying of passengers and cargo from Sri Lanka.

Offshore companies may, with approval of the Registrar of Companies, carry on value adding operations within Sri Lanka provided there are no sales in, nor income realized from, Sri Lanka. In such case, the offshore company will be required to supply foreign currency to defray all local expenses. The value adding operation will be liable to Sri Lanka income tax at the rate applied to a nonresident company— 61.11% (see item 1).

The Commissioner General of Inland Revenue may allow the computation of Sri Lanka income on a fair percentage of value added so that, viewed as an incentive, the tax chargeable at 61.11% will compare favorably with taxes payable in other countries where the company operates (see item 6).

The offshore company is an attractive business entity for entrepot trading as it may not attract any tax in Sri Lanka. The institutional arrangements and business operations should be carefully planned to avoid tax pitfalls.

Under special incentive legislation, profits of off-shore companies engaged on-shore in off-shore insurance, aviation, underwriting of loans, syndication of loans, or international consultancy are exempt for five years if the profits are remitted to Sri Lanka.

35. Exchange Controls

A noncitizen seeking to invest in shares in a Sri Lanka company is required to obtain approval of the exchange control authorities; similar approval is required prior to granting any finance to either a Sri Lanka company or citizen. A resident who pays monies to a nonresident should also obtain exchange control approval.

Approval is not required for nonresidents who purchase shares traded on the Colombo Stock Exchange provided the total foreign investment in the share capital of the company is not more than 40% of the issued capital.

36. Investment Restrictions on Nonresidents

An enterprise outside the GCEC, in general, will not be permitted 100% foreign ownership. The GCEC usually insists on a 51% local ownership except where the enterprise is:

□ A five-star hotel with over 200 rooms.
□ A construction project with a government institution.
□ A project which results in significant transfer of technology and generation of employment.

The tax statute applies to all companies other than those governed by agreements with the GCEC under Law No. 4 of 1978.

SELECTION OF BUSINESS ENTITY BY NONRESIDENTS

All projects seeking GCEC (see item 34) tax exemptions are required to operate through a Sri Lankan company—usually a private company, which limits the number of shareholders to 50 and imposes restrictions on transferability of shares. A GCEC company can be 100% foreign owned.

Foreign investors seeking approval (see item 36) are required to operate through a Sri Lankan company in which local collaborators are usually required to have a 51% interest. Operating as a quoted public company attracts less tax.

Offshore companies can be 100% foreign owned (see items 6 and 34).

Construction companies and consultants may find it more convenient to operate as a foreign incorporated company having a place of business in Sri Lanka. Foreign contractors should obtain professional tax advice prior to drafting agreements because the liability for business turnover tax and income tax may be minimized by an appropriate agreement. Where the Sri Lanka party (usually a Government agency) is prepared to reimburse the foreign contractor for Sri Lanka income tax arising from the contract, the possibility of obtaining tax credit in the home country should be explored, provided a double tax treaty is in effect.

Tax planning may also be very advantageous for foreign investors in GCEC companies and, also, for investors from countries which have tax treaties with Sri Lanka.

SPECIMEN TAX COMPUTATION

	Resident Company Not Quoted	Resident Quoted or Peoples Company	Nonresident Company
Adjusted profit before tax	Rs18,000	Rs18,000	Rs18,000
Corporate tax	50% (9,000)	40% (7,200)	50% (9,000)
Profits available for distribution	9,000	10,800	9,000
Dividend tax of 15%	(1,350)	(1,620)	
Remittance tax (11.11% of taxable profit)	----	----	(2,000)
Net remaining for shareholders outside Sri Lanka	7,650	9,180	7,000

Note:

Nonresident company profits distributed in the form of dividends are not liable for tax in the hands of the recipients unless they are residents. Resident company profits distributed in the form of dividends will be treated as follows:

— Where the recipient is a company, the dividends received will not form part of taxable income.

— Where the recipient is an individual (resident or nonresident), the gross dividend is liable for income tax. The dividend tax deducted at source will be deductible from his total tax liability. In the case of a nonresident individual shareholder, the gross dividend will not include the amount of the ACT (see item 28).

SUDAN

INCOME TAXES ON CORPORATIONS

1. Rates

The tax rates on all limited companies including banks and insurance companies are:

Taxable Income		Rate
Over	Not Over	
Ls. 0	Ls. 5,000	25%
5,000	20,000	35
20,000	75,000	40
75,000		45

The tax rates on professionals are:

Taxable Income		Rate
Over	Not Over	
Ls. 0	Ls. 3,000	0%
3,000	4,500	10
4,500	6,500	15
6,500	9,500	20
9,500	18,500	25
18,500	50,000	35
50,000		45

2. Local Income Taxes

No local taxes are levied on corporations. Corporations that own a building are subject to municipal rates that are calculated at the ratable value of the building.

3. Capital Gains Taxes

If land or buildings are sold at a profit exceeding net book value, the profit is taxable. A building that is sold at a profit is subject to property gains tax. The rates of capital gains tax vary with the period of ownership as follows:

☐ If property is sold within three years of its purchase, the capital gain is added to other profits of that year and assessed accordingly.

☐ If property is sold after three years of its purchase, the tax rates are:

First Ls.5,000 profit	5%
Next Ls.5,000 profit	10%
Next Ls.10,000 profit	15%
Next Ls.10,000 profit	20%
Balance	25%
Limited companies: all profits at	40%

4. Branch Profits Taxes

See Selection of Business Entity by Nonresidents.

5. Foreign Tax Reliefs

Double taxation relief is provided by treaties between Sudan and Egypt, Rumania, and the United Kingdom.

8. Other Matters

Tax Period. Tax is levied on income derived in the base year, which is the prior calendar year for the following types of income:

☐ Business profits.
☐ Rent income from property.
☐ Personal income (salaries and wages).
☐ Capital gains.
☐ Development.

However, for business profits, the base year may be any period selected by the enterprise provided it is followed systematically. If an enterprise wishes to change its year-end, it must inform the Director of Taxation. Base year income includes:

☐ Any income derived from Sudan, whether or not the person is resident in Sudan.

☐ Any income derived outside of Sudan, even if not transferred to Sudan in the case of a resident person. However, the Minister of Finance can exempt any

Sudanese, or any foreigner domiciled in Sudan, if the income was taxed outside the Sudan.

INCOME TAXES ON INDIVIDUALS

9. Rates

Individuals are subject to a personal income tax that is levied on employment income, including fees, commissions, bonuses, living allowances, entertainment allowances, and any other allowance received in consideration of the individual's employment. However, if the Director of Taxation is satisfied that an allowance is a repayment of expenditure wholly used for the production of the income received, such allowance is not subject to assessment. In general, any benefit or advantage received by an employee is subject to personal income tax, except the following:

☐ Traveling expenses between the Sudan and any other country, provided the employee is not a relative or a director of the company.

☐ Employer contributions for social security, pension funds, saving or post-service benefit funds, etc., on behalf of an employee, or to his dependents when the employee dies or retires.

☐ Medical and dental care provided to employees.

☐ Entertainment allowance of less than Ls.20 per month.

☐ A reasonable allowance for transportation (between Ls.30 and Ls.60 per month).

The Director of Taxation has issued a directive on the taxable amounts of the following benefits in kind furnished to employees:

Automobile	Ls.50 per month
Furnished house with food	35% of basic salary
Furnished house without food	30% of basic salary
Unfurnished house without food	25% of basic salary

The personal income tax rates for residents and nonresidents are:

Income	Rate
Ls. 3,000	0%
Next Ls. 1,500	10
Next Ls. 2,000	15
Next Ls. 3,000	20
Next Ls. 9,000	25
Next Ls. 31,500	35
Over Ls. 50,000	45

Business Profits Tax. Business profits earned by individuals, as well as land rent income, are subject to the business profits tax instead of the personal income tax. For this purpose, the determination of profit follows normal accounting rules. The general principle is that any expense incurred wholly and exclusively to earn assessable income is allowable. Nevertheless, the amounts deductible for proprietors' salaries and directors' compensation are subject to limitations; personal expenses are not deductible; payments of income tax and business profits tax are not deductible; and certain types of interest payments may not be deductible.

In the case of a contracting business, if the profit cannot be ascertained until a project is completed, the Director of Taxation may treat the final profit as though a proportionate part had been earned each day. In the case of foreign contractors, a proportion of head office overhead expenses may be set off against income arising in Sudan. The percentage of allowable expenses is subject to negotiation with the Director of Taxation. The rates of business profit tax are:

Business Profits Tax (Excluding Banks and Insurance Companies)

Income		Rate
First Ls.	5,00	25%
Next Ls.	20,000	35
Next Ls.	75,000	40
Over Ls.	100,000	45

Business Profits Tax Banks and Insurance Companies

Income		Rate
First Ls.	5,000	25%
Next Ls.	20,000	35
Next Ls.	75,000	45
Over Ls.	100,000	50

10. Local Income Taxes

None.

11. Capital Gains Taxes

Capital gains realized by an individual on the sale of land or buildings are subject to property tax, which is applied as follows.

Sale within three years of purchase is taxable under business profit tax rates (item 9). If sold after three years of purchase, the following rates apply:

Capital Gain	Rate
On the first Ls.5,000	5%
On the next Ls.5,000	10
On the next Ls.10,000	15
On the next Ls.10,000	20
On the balance	25
Limited companies: tax rate	40

14. Other Matters

Development Tax. Nil.

INCOME TAXES ON NONRESIDENTS

15. Liability to Tax

The discussion of personal income tax at item 9 also applies to nonresidents.

16. Rates

The personal income tax rates for nonresidents are the same as for residents.

17. Withholding Tax Rates

None.

19. Tax Treaties

See item 5.

OTHER SIGNIFICANT TAXES

21. Sales (Value Added)

A sales tax is levied on hotels, lodging houses, night clubs, restaurants, travel agents, and ordinary clubs. The rate is 10% of the invoice, which is paid to the tax authorities, who have the right to inspect the invoices and books of the subject enterprises.

23. Taxes on Payrolls (Social Security)

The Social Security Act of 1974 applies to all private companies employing 30 or more workers. The weekly contributions vary with the employee's aggregate weekly salary, and are payable by both employers and employees.

24. Taxes on Natural Resources

Prior to exploration for natural resources, agreements covering rights, concessions, and exemptions must be concluded with the Department of Geological Survey of the Ministry of Industry.

COMPUTATION OF TAXABLE INCOME

26. Capital Gains

Profit from the sale of land or buildings is measured by the difference between the original cost plus improvements and expenses of selling and any other expenses incurred by the taxpayer.

27. Depreciation and Depletion

Depreciation is allowed for buildings, machinery, plant, trucks, motor cars, furniture, and other assets. The annual depreciation allowed, as a percentage of cost, for typical assets is:

Permanent brick buildings	2.5%
Wooden buildings	10%
Computers	15%
Air conditioning apparatus	5%
General rate on machinery	5%
Automobiles and station wagons	20%
Trucks	25%
Aircraft	20%

28. Treatment of Dividends

Dividends paid by limited companies that have been subject to business profits tax are not taxable when paid to shareholders, either individuals or other limited companies (franked investment).

29. Loss Carryovers

Provided audited accounts are presented, net losses can be carried forward and offset against the profits of the following five years. The accounts must be audited by a member of either:

- [ ] The Institute of Chartered Accountants in England and Wales.
- [ ] The Institute of Chartered Accountants in Scotland or Ireland.
- [ ] The Association of Certified and Corporate Accountants.
- [ ] Any other body approved by the Director of Taxation.

32. Tax Periods

See item 8.

RELATED CONSIDERATIONS

34. Incentives and Grants

Although the following explanation of available incentives and grants is presented under the title of the original Act, these Acts are now consolidated into one Act.

The Encouragement of Investment Act 1980. The Act's purpose is to encourage investment in projects that foster the objectives of the Development Plan of the Sudan. These include: increase in national income, removal of development bottlenecks, provision of services necessary to consolidate economic and social development, use of local raw materials, assist in achieving self sufficiency and exports, improve the balance of payments, create jobs, foster economic ties with Arab and African countries, and have defense or strategic importance. Investments that meet these criteria may obtain the incentives set forth in the Act, such as partial or full exemption from business profits tax for five years. The Minister (the person appointed by the President of the Republic as secretary general for investment) may extend this exemption for up to five more years for integrated projects that contribute to infrastructure, such as roads, in addition to production.

The Minister may allow any loss occurring during the period of whole or partial exemption to be deemed incurred during the last year of such period. The Act also exempts the project wholly or partially from customs duties on imported raw materials, intermediary materials which are not available locally in the required quality or quantity, and customs duties on imported machinery, equipment, appliances or apparatus and spare parts necessary for the project. Full or partial exemption is also available for export duties on the project's semiprocessed goods as well as other fees or taxes imposed on the project.

The Minister may allot the land necessary to establish the project and may reduce the cost of such land or permit payment in installments. He may reduce the cost of electric power as well as the rates for incoming and outgoing freight. The Minister may increase, for a specific period, the custom duties on imports that compete with, or are substitutes for, the project's output.

No local fees or taxes may be imposed on any project that has been granted an exemption. The project may not be nationalized unless the public good so requires, and the investor shall receive fair compensation based on an evaluation of the project at prices current at the date of nationalization. The transfer abroad of profits, interest, and capital is guaranteed.

35. Exchange Controls

The transfer of foreign currency from Sudan to other countries requires authorization of the Bank of Sudan, which is the Central Bank. Such authorization is usually granted on the bases outlined as follows:

☐ Foreign capital, loans, dividends, and interest are transferable in foreign currency if the capital or loans are registered in the Central Bank's Register of Capital and Loans.

☐ A reasonable percentage of foreign directors' remuneration and expatriates' salaries is transferable in the currency of the employee's home country.

☐ Technical fees and fees for know-how and management are transferable, provided the related agreements are approved by the Central Bank. Up to 80%, but usually 40%, of the gross fee is considered as an expense of earning the fee, and the remaining 20% or 60% is taxed as follows:

	Rate
First Ls. 1,000	25%
Next Ls. 9,000	40
Ls. 10,000	50
Over Ls. 20,000	60

It is advisable to arrange that taxes on these fees be borne by the Sudanese payer and not by the recipient, although this may entail grossing the fee.

36. Investment Restrictions on Nonresidents

There are no restrictions on foreign investment in agricultural or industrial projects. However, the purchase of land requires special permission. Trading activities are restricted to Sudanese nationals.

SELECTION OF BUSINESS ENTITY BY NONRESIDENTS

Nonresident investors can operate in Sudan either through a branch or by forming a local subsidiary limited company. Both are subject to local tax unless exempted. For tax purposes, both are treated as public or private limited companies.

Dividends and profits can be repatriated in full after payment of tax.

SWAZILAND

INCOME TAXES ON CORPORATIONS

1. Rates

Companies, other than mining companies, are subject to a flat rate of 37.5% of taxable income from a source within or deemed to be within Swaziland. For mining companies, the rate is 27% of taxable income up to E20,000 and 37.5% of taxable income in excess of E20,000. Dividends received by a company are exempt from income tax.

2. Local Income Taxes

None.

3. Capital Gains Taxes

There are no capital gains taxes.

4. Branch Profits Taxes

A branch of a foreign company is taxed on the profits derived in Swaziland as though it were a resident company.

5. Foreign Tax Reliefs

As Swaziland income tax is levied only on taxable income derived or deemed to be derived in Swaziland, the question of foreign tax relief does not normally arise. Relief will only be granted if provided for in a tax treaty with the particular foreign country.

INCOME TAXES ON INDIVIDUALS

9. Rates

Income tax is payable at graduated rates, with a maximum rate of 40% which applies to the taxable income in excess of E40,000 per annum. The following examples illustrate the tax rates:

Taxable Income		Tax on	Percentage
Over	Not Over	Lower Amount	on Excess
E 0	E12,000	E 0	12%
16,000	18,000	880	20
20,000	22,000	1,680	24
30,000	32,000	4,560	36
40,000		8,320	40

All benefits-in-kind must be included in taxable income:

Benefit	Addition to Annual Taxable Income
Free housing	E100 to E2,400 depending on size and location of house
Free use of a car	E1,440 to E4,300 depending on cubic capacity of engine and determined value of the vehicle
Utilities	E120 per service
Domestic servants	E600 per household servant (cooks, maids, etc.)
Tuition payments	80% of payments

10. Local Income Taxes

None.

11. Capital Gains Taxes

There are no capital gains taxes.

12. Foreign Tax Reliefs

See item 5.

13. Tax Period

The tax year runs from July 1 to June 30.

14. Other Matters

Computation of Taxable Income. Taxable income includes basic wages, commissions, fees, annual value of benefits, bonuses, and dividend income in excess of E2,000 from a Swaziland source (except in the case of nonresidents not carrying on business in Swaziland), and such excess is taxable at 20% unless received by a company listed with the Swaziland Stock Exchange, in which case it is taxed at 10%. Any gratuity or bonus received by or accrued to an employee under the terms of a written agreement on bona fide termination of employment is exempt from tax to the extent that it does not exceed 25% of the total of actual salary received for the period of employment provided the period of the agreement of employment is not less than two years, or, if the period of the agreement is less than two years, the employee shall not enter into another agreement of employment with the same employer.

In determining the taxable income of any person, the following deductions are allowed:

Current contributions to a pension fund	
Funds established by law	Actual contributions
Other pension funds approved by the Commissioner	Maximum of E1,750
Current contributions to any retirement annuity fund approved by the Commissioner	The greatest of: —15% of the taxable income in respect of a trade carried out, provided the maximum allowable deduction shall not exceed E5,000; or —An amount of E3,500 less current contributions made to a pension fund; or —An amount of E1,750.
Interest on property loans	200% of interest paid if gross income does not exceed E10,000 for the assessemnt year 100% of interest paid if gross income exceeds E10,000 but does not exceed E40,000 for the assessment year 50% of interest paid if gross income exceeds E40,000 for the assessment year

INCOME TAXES ON NONRESIDENTS

15. Liability to Tax

A nonresident corporation carrying on business in Swaziland is subject to normal tax in the same way as a resident company on income other than dividends from a source within or deemed to be within Swaziland. Royalties and know-how payments to a nonresident licensor are subject to tax in Swaziland if the income is from a source within Swaziland. Tax treaties with the United Kingdom and Republic of South Africa exempt such royalties from Swaziland tax.

17. Withholding Tax Rates

Dividends paid by Swaziland companies to a company which is nonresident and not carrying on business in Swaziland or to a nonresident individual are subject to a withholding tax of 15%. If the dividend is paid to a company registered in Botswana, Lesotho, or the Republic of South Africa, and such a company is not a subsidiary or branch of a corporation registered outside any of such countries, then the withholding tax is reduced to 12.5%.

Interest paid by a debtor in Swaziland to a company not registered in Swaziland or to a nonresident individual is subject to a withholding tax of 10%. If the interest is also from a source within Swaziland, it is included in taxable income and is subject to normal tax but credit is then given for the 10% already withheld.

Any person entering into an agreement relating to construction operations or professional services which are to be performed in Swaziland, under which payments will be made to a nonresident, may be required by the Commissioner of Taxes to withhold 10% from such payments on account of the liability to tax of the nonresident person with respect to the profits derived from such agreement.

A nonresident individual (apart from entertainers or sportsmen) is taxed on income (other than dividends) derived from a source in Swaziland in the same way as a resident individual, and is entitled to the same rebates, but the minimum tax payable is 3% of taxable income consisting of a pension and 10% of other taxable income. Dividends from Swaziland are subject to the withholding tax of 15% or 12.5%. The remuneration of nonresident public entertainers and sportsmen is subject to a nonresident tax of 15%.

19. Tax Treaties

General tax treaties exist between Swaziland and the United Kingdom and South Africa.

OTHER SIGNIFICANT TAXES

21. Sales (Value Added)

A one-stage sales tax at rates varying between 5% and 20% is imposed on goods at the point of importation or manufacture, local services, hotel accommodations, and restaurant meals. The 20% rate is applied only to alcohol and tobacco.

22. Inheritance and Gift Taxes

None.

23. Taxes on Payrolls (Social Security)

There are no social security taxes as such. Employers must pay workmen's compensation insurance premiums. Organizations and their Swazi-National employees each must contribute 5% of monthly earnings to a National Provident Fund, with a maximum total contribution of E20 per employee per month.

A graduated tax ranging from E4 to E18 per annum is payable by every individual (except women earning less than E15 per month) who is resident or domiciled in Swaziland. Employers are obliged to deduct graded tax from earnings of employees.

24. Taxes on Natural Resources

An annual mineral rights tax is payable by the holder of any mineral right in Swaziland. The tax is payable in advance on July 1st of each year at the following rates:

For the first five tax years from the date on which the holder has been granted a mineral right	E10 per hectare, or part thereof, over which the mineral right is held
Thereafter	E50 per hectare or part

Any reasonable expenditure (excluding general administration and management expenditure) actually incurred by the holder in respect of bona fide mining operations or prospecting or development work carried out in the said area during the preceding tax year is allowed as a deduction from the amount of the mineral rights tax. No mineral rights tax is levied for the first tax year in which the mineral rights are granted.

25. Other Taxes

Land and Property.   Transfers of immovable property are subject to transfer duty at the rate of 2% on the first E40,000, 4% on the next E20,000, and 6% on the excess over E60,000 of the purchase consideration. The duty is payable by the transferee. Annual rates on property are payable to the Town Councils, based on the Council valuation of the property.

Capital Taxes.   No annual wealth or capital worth taxes are levied except for the tax on mineral rights (see item 24).

Stamp Duties.   Stamp duties are payable on numerous documents. The transfer of marketable securities attracts a stamp duty of 1% which is payable by the purchaser.

COMPUTATION OF TAXABLE INCOME

26. Capital Gains

There are no capital gains taxes.

27. Depreciation and Depletion

Wear and tear allowances are granted on plant and machinery and other capital assets used in the production of income. The rates vary according to the type of asset, life expectancy, and intensity of use and are based on the reducing-balance method. The straight-line method is only permitted if the prior consent of the Commissioner of Taxes is obtained. There is a scrapping allowance (or taxable recoupment) on disposal or scrapping of assets eligible for the wear and tear allowance. An annual allowance of 4% of the cost of any industrial building and any improvements thereto is granted. No allowances are granted for expenditure on goodwill, mineral rights, or lands.

In respect of mining operations, capital expenditure incurred (which includes preproduction expenditures but excludes expenditures on land and mineral rights) less any recoupments may be deducted from income in full in the year of assessment in which the expenditure was incurred.

28. Treatment of Dividends

Dividends received by companies are exempt from income tax. Dividends in excess of E2,000 received from a Swaziland source by resident individuals are included in taxable income and are taxable at 20% unless received from a company listed with the Swaziland Stock Exchange, in which case they are taxed at 10%. Dividends received by nonresident shareholders are subject to withholding tax of 15% or 12.5%.

29. Loss Carryovers

Where permissible deductions exceed the income in a year of assessment, an "assessed loss" results. An assessed loss is carried forward indefinitely and set off against the income of subsequent years until the loss is recouped, as long as the taxpayer continues to carry on business and derive income. Special provisions discourage dealing in assessed loss companies.

30. Transactions between Related Parties

The Commissioner of Taxes is entitled to disregard transactions which are not on normal and arm's length terms and which result in avoidance, diminution or deferment of tax. The Commissioner of Taxes has discretion as to what deduction he will allow to a Swaziland taxpayer claiming expenditure incurred outside Swaziland in the production of taxable income.

The prior paragraph also applies to capital transactions between related parties. However, as there is no capital gains tax other than on mineral rights, the Commissioner of Taxes is primarily concerned with the implications as to wear and tear and other allowances on eligible capital expenditure.

31. Consolidation of Income

In Swaziland, each company and/or individual is a separate legal entity for tax purposes. It is not permissible to consolidate, combine, or subvent income or expenditure between group companies.

32. Tax Periods

For both individuals and companies, the year of assessment runs from July 1 to June 30, and the applicable tax rate is fixed by a King's Order-in-Council each year. If the income cannot be conveniently determined for that period, the Commissioner may accept returns ending on a date other than June 30.

33. Other Matters

Concept of Taxable Income. Taxable income can be expressed, very broadly, as all income (other than certain specified exempt income) of a revenue nature from a source within or deemed to be within Swaziland, less expenditure of a revenue nature incurred in the production of that income, and less specific allowances in respect of capital expenditure and training expenditure.

RELATED CONSIDERATIONS

34. Incentives and Grants

Exempt Income. Investment is encouraged in particular areas, notably, deposits in the Swaziland Development and Savings Bank and certain shares in building societies. Income derived therefrom is wholly or partially exempted from tax. Exemption is also granted in respect of interest receivable by nonresidents on loans made to the King in trust for the Swazi Nation. Nonresident investors in stocks issued by the Government or any local authority or approved statutory or parastatal corporations are also exempt from tax on the income, if the investor is not carrying on business in Swaziland.

Special Grants or Allowances. Inducements to invest in additional productive capacity are given by way of special deductions allowed in respect of the cost of new industrial buildings and of new plant and machinery brought into use in a process of manufacture, any other similar process, or the hotel industry. The deductions also apply in respect of secondhand plant and machinery which has not previously been used in Swaziland and to leased plant and machinery. The deductions are as follows:

Initial allowance on new plant and machinery brought into use	50% of cost
Initial allowance on new industrial buildings placed in service that house machinery qualifying for the initial allowance	50% of cost
Initial allowance on used machinery housed in a building which qualifies for initial allowance, used in Swaziland for first time, and not replacing other machinery	50% of depreciated value

The initial allowances represent accelerated depreciation in the first year and are deducted from the cost basis for wear and tear or annual allowances. The following allowances are granted in respect of capital expenditure incurred in connection with:

□ The erection of housing (excluding the cost of land) for employees, excluding management and supervisory employees, engaged in a process of manufacture:

For the first year in which such expenditure was incurred	20% of expenditure with a maximum allowance of E4,000 for any one house
In each of the next 8 years	10% of expenditure with a maximum allowance of E2,000 for any one house

□ The erection of a new hotel or improvements to an existing hotel:

For each of the first 5 years after such expenditure was incurred	10% of cost
For each succeeding year	5% of cost

Tax Holiday. The taxable income of a new business engaged in a manufacturing operation that is not already in existence or any business that is predominantly involved in the export of goods from Swaziland is exempt from tax for five years, provided that the cumulative taxable income less cumulative remuneration paid to Swaziland employees does not exceed 150% of the value of the assets of the business. Any excess is taxed at normal rates.

Training Schemes. A special deduction is granted for training expenses incurred in connection with an approved training scheme. The deduction is 100% of the training expenses incurred in the year of assessment and may include the remuneration of the trainees and the instructors; expenditure in respect of training premises or equipment including rent, repairs and maintenance, property assessment rates, insurance or finance costs; cost of materials, fuel or power; travelling expenses; and training fees. This deduction is in addition to any other deductions which may have been allowed in determining taxable income and effectively gives the taxpayer an allowance of up to 200% in respect of approved training expenditure.

The Minister for Finance and Economic Planning may issue regulations for the designation of specific areas as development areas, and of specific industries as pioneer industries, and for the granting of special additional tax concessions to persons setting up in the designated areas or the designated industries.

35. Exchange Controls

Common Monetary Area. Swaziland, Lesotho, and South Africa are the member countries of the Common Monetary Area. There is no restriction on the transfer of current or capital funds within this area. There is a restriction on financial institutions in Swaziland, which are required to maintain certain funds within Swaziland in accordance with the Financial Institution Order, 1973. Exchange control regulations therefore apply only to the transfer of funds between Swaziland and areas outside the Common Monetary Area.

Temporary Residents. Temporary residents are persons who are domiciled abroad and have resided for less than six years in Swaziland. After living in Swaziland for six years, they may apply to the Central Bank of Swaziland for permission to continue to be treated as temporary residents for exchange control purposes. They are allowed to transfer funds from Swaziland to areas outside the Common Monetary Area as follows:

☐ Up to one-third of locally earned income before tax or, if the temporary resident's family lives outside the Common Monetary Area, up to one-half of such income.

☐ Amounts to cover medical and educational expenses incurred abroad.

☐ End of contract gratuities up to a maximum of 25% of salary earned during the employment period; also, in addition to the first item above, on savings which have been deposited or otherwise invested in Swaziland, up to one-third of locally earned income.

Residents. Residents are obliged to declare their foreign assets and may be required to repatriate them to Swaziland. The consent of the Central Bank of Swaziland is required before a resident may enter into any obligation to a nonresident. This does not apply to purchases of goods in the ordinary course of trade (provided that import permits have been obtained when required).

Residents travelling abroad are restricted to an annual allowance of E15,000 in foreign exchange, but fares may be paid beforehand in addition to the E15,000. Residents travelling in the neighboring states of Botswana, Indian Ocean Islands, Malawi, Mozambique, Zambia, and Zimbabwe are entitled to an additional allowance of E7,500. Individuals are entitled to a business allowance of up to a maximum of E22,500 per year for business travel to countries outside Swaziland. Residents leaving Swaziland are permitted to take the greater of E20,000 or half their total personal assets, up to a maximum of E200,000 for a family unit or E100,000 for a single person. Amounts in excess of E200,000 are subject to the consent of the Central Bank. The remaining assets are placed in a "blocked account," and only income thereon may be remitted.

Nonresidents. Consent is generally given for the repatriation of capital imported from outside the Common Monetary Area for investment in Swaziland with the approval of the Central Bank. Income receivable by nonresidents in the form of dividends or interest is normally freely remittable, after deduction of the withholding taxes. Payment for directors' fees, travelling expenses, royalties, and technical services and management fees are subject to prior Exchange Control approval. Permission is normally given for reasonable requests.

36. Investment Restrictions on Nonresidents

Transfer of Investment Funds into Swaziland. All capital transfers to Swaziland from outside the Common Monetary Area require the prior approval of the Central Bank of Swaziland. In practice, this approval is routinely granted where required for genuine investment activity.

Capital Issues. The raising of capital in Swaziland by issues of shares, bonds, etc., in aggregate amounts of more than E100,000 during any period of 12 months requires the prior approval of the Central Bank.

Local Borrowings. Companies with more than 25% of their capital (including equity, shareholders' loans and retained earnings) owned directly or indirectly by nonresidents require the permission of the Central Bank of Swaziland to raise loans or use bank overdrafts or advances within the Common Monetary Area.

SELECTION OF BUSINESS ENTITY BY NONRESIDENTS

Nonresident investors can operate in Swaziland either through a branch or by forming a local subsidiary company. Both entities are treated alike in the following matters:

☐ Capital and other incentive allowances.
☐ Withholding tax on foreign interest and certain other foreign expenses.
☐ Corporation tax of 37.5%.

The only difference is that a locally incorporated company is subject to a 15% nonrefundable withholding tax on dividends remitted to a nonresident shareholder whereas the remittance of branch profits is not subject to tax in Swaziland. To illustrate:

	Resident Corporation	Branch of Nonresident Corporation
Taxable income	E100,000	E100,000
Corporation tax	37,500	37,500
After-tax profit	62,500	62,500
Tax on dividend remittance	9,375	0
Effective tax rate	46.875%	37.5%

Also important in the choice of entity are the tax considerations in the home country of the nonresident corporation. For example, if the corporation tax in the home country were 50%, and branch profits were also taxed at that rate with a rebate for the 37.5% Swaziland tax, whereas divided income from Swaziland is not taxable, it would be advantageous to operate as a locally incorporated subsidiary with an effective tax rate of 46.875% as compared to 50% for a branch.

SWEDEN

INCOME TAXES ON CORPORATIONS

1. Rates

Swedish corporations (joint stock companies) are liable to national income tax on their income from all sources. Income tax is levied on net taxable income.

The corporate tax rate is 30%. All income of the corporation is taxed as business income and as income from one source. The possibility to offset income to untaxed reserves has been abolished. However, a tax equalization reserve has been introduced in its place (see item 33).

2. Local Income Taxes

Corporations do not pay local income taxes.

3. Capital Gains Taxes

All income of a corporation is taxed as business income, including gains realized on the sale of stock, real property, or other capital assets, whether held inside or outside the ordinary course of business. Thus, capital gains are not subject to any special taxation treatment. However, losses realized on the disposition of capital assets (primarily securities) outside the ordinary course of business can be offset only against gains on the same kind of assets. Losses that cannot be offset the same year may be carried forward. Losses on the disposition of assets held within the ordinary course of business are fully deductible against other income.

4. Branch Profits Taxes

A branch of a foreign corporation is taxed on the profits of the branch as though it were a resident corporation.

5. Foreign Tax Reliefs

The Swedish tax system provides comprehensive double tax relief for taxes incurred in territories outside Sweden, both under double taxation treaties and under unilateral provisions of Swedish law. The credit given for foreign taxation under both tax treaties and internal law is subject to certain limitations.

6. Classification of Corporations

Swedish law provides for different entities, such as partnerships (limited and general), economic societies (e.g., cooperatives), mutual insurance companies and joint stock companies. Of these associations, partnerships of all types (e.g., joint ventures) are not taxed as separate entities, their members being individually liable to state tax. The other forms are taxed as separate entities.

INCOME TAXES ON INDIVIDUALS

9. Rates

The income of individuals is classified into three kinds of income: earned income, income from capital, and business income.

On earned income and business income of amounts up to approximately SEK 180,000 only local tax of approximately 31% is levied. On income above this level a national tax of 20% is added. The top marginal rate is, thus, 51% on these kinds of income.

Income from capital, i.e., interest, dividends, and capital gains, is taxed only with a national tax at the flat rate of 30%. Deficits from this type of income entitle the taxpayer to a tax reduction of 30% of the deficit.

There is a personal allowance of SEK 10,000 against the assessed income. On assessed income between SEK 58,000 and SEK 175,000, the personal allowance is raised. At the most it amounts to SEK 18,000 on an assessed income of SEK 90,000 to SEK 95,000. The personal allowance is allowed, however, only against earned income and business income.

	Less than SEK 180,000	Greater than SEK 180,000
Tax on Earned and Business Income:		
Local income tax	Approx. 31%	Approx. 31%
National income tax	—	20%
Total	Approx. 31%	Approx. 51%
Tax on Income from Capital:		
National tax	30%	30%

11. Capital Gains Taxes

See item 9.

12. Foreign Tax Reliefs

Double tax relief is given for taxes incurred outside Sweden, both under double taxation treaties and under unilateral provisions of Swedish law. Under Swedish domestic law, and in the absence of a tax treaty, a nonresident individual who performs services in Sweden and who receives compensation for those services from a Swedish source is subject to Swedish income tax on that compensation. For temporary visitors, however, there is usually a special provision in Sweden's tax treaties: a person who is not a resident of Sweden is not taxable in Sweden on compensation for services rendered in Sweden if he performed those services during a temporary visit.

13. Tax Period

The fiscal period is identical with the calendar year.

INCOME TAXES ON NONRESIDENTS

15. Liability to Tax

Nonresident individuals are subject to tax on income from Swedish sources, including income from real property in Sweden, business carried on in Sweden, and salaries, wages, and pensions paid from Swedish sources for services performed in Sweden. Furthermore, director's fees from Swedish companies are subject to Swedish tax. All income taxes are withheld at source. Individuals staying in Sweden for more than six months are generally treated as resident in Sweden for tax purposes, and are taxed on their worldwide income. Individuals present in Sweden for less than six months are usually taxed only on Swedish-source income.

Foreign corporations are liable to taxation on income from real property in Sweden, on income from all sources to the extent that it is effectively connected with the conduct of a trade or business in Sweden, and on gains arising outside the ordinary course of business on the disposition of real property or a business or parts thereof.

Exemption from the above rules can be provided for in double taxation agreements.

16. Rates

If a nonresident individual or foreign corporation is liable to taxes in Sweden, under the rules in item 15, the taxable income, in principle, is computed and taxed in the same manner as for a resident. The total income tax rate for an individual is, however, only 25%.

17. Withholding Tax Rates

Dividends paid by Swedish corporations are subject to withholding taxes as set out in the following table. Unless a tax treaty provides otherwise, royalties are taxed as Swedish source income at ordinary income tax rates. Interest, unless treated as ordinary business income, is not subject to withholding tax.

Recipient	Interest	Cash Dividends (1)	Royalties and Certain Rentals (2)
Resident corporations	Nil	Nil	Nil
Resident individuals	Nil	Nil, 30%	Nil
Nonresident corporations and individuals:			
Nontreaty	Nil	30%	(3)
Treaty			
Argentina	Nil	30	15%
Australia	Nil	15	10
Austria	Nil	Nil	10, Nil
Bangladesh	Nil	15, 10	10
Belgium (4)	Nil	15, 5	Nil
Brazil	Nil	25, 15	25, 15
Bulgaria	Nil	10	5
Canada	Nil	15	10, Nil
Cyprus	Nil	15, 5	
Czechoslovakia	Nil	10, Nil	5
Denmark	Nil	15, 0	Nil
Egypt	Nil	Nil	Nil
Faroe Islands	Nil	15, 0	Nil
Finland	Nil	15, 0	Nil
France	Nil	Nil	Nil
Germany	Nil	15, 5	Nil
Greece	Nil	Nil	5
Hungary	Nil	15, 5	Nil
Iceland	Nil	15, 0	Nil
India	Nil	25, 15	20
Indonesia	Nil	15, 0	
Iran (5)	—	—	—
Iraq (5)	—	—	—
Ireland	Nil	15, 5	Nil
Israel	Nil	15, 5	(3)
Italy	Nil	15, 10	(4)
Jamaica	Nil	22.5, 10	10
Japan	Nil	15, 10	10
Kenya	Nil	25, 15	20
Korea (South)	Nil	15, 10	15, 10
Kuwait (5)	—	—	—
Lebanon (6)	—	—	—
Luxembourg	Nil	15, 5	Nil
Malaysia	Nil	Nil	Nil
Malta	Nil	15, 5	10, Nil

Recipient	Interest	Cash Dividends (1)	Royalties and Certain Rentals (2)
Morocco	Nil	Nil	Nil
Netherlands	Nil	15, 0	Nil
New Zealand	Nil	15	10
Norway	Nil	15, 0	Nil
Pakistan	Nil	30, 15	10
People's Republic of China	Nil	10	10
Peru	Nil	30	20
Philippines	Nil	25, 15	25, 15
Poland	Nil	15, 5	10
Rumania	Nil	10	10
Singapore	Nil	15, 10	Nil
South Africa	Nil	30	26
Soviet Union	Nil	15	Nil
Spain	Nil	15, 10	10
Sri Lanka	Nil	15	10
Switzerland	Nil	5	Nil
Tanzania	Nil	25, 15	20
Thailand	Nil	20, 15	15
Trinidad and Tobago	Nil	20, 10	20
Tunisia	Nil	20, 15	15, 5
Turkey	Nil	20, 15	10
United Kingdom (7)	Nil	5, Nil	Nil
United States	Nil	15, 5	30, 0
Uruguay (5)	—	—	—
Yugoslavia	Nil	15, 5	Nil
Zambia	Nil	15, 5	10

Notes:

(1) The relevant treaty should be consulted to see if the reduced rate for dividends applies in the case of payments to corporations having requisite control.

(2) Royalties paid by Swedish licensees are treated as ordinary taxable income earned by licensors. Taxes are not withheld at source.

(3) Treated (partly or wholly) as earned taxable income in Sweden and taxed at full rates (treaty should be consulted).

(4) Treaty expected to apply effective January 1, 1991.

(5) Applies only to income from aviation.

(6) Applies only to income from aviation and shipping.

(7) Old U.K. treaties that have applied to some former British territories have been terminated from January 1, 1988.

OTHER SIGNIFICANT TAXES

21. Sales (Value Added)

Business enterprises selling goods or services within Sweden (including importers) are subject to this tax. The tax is based on the amount received for sales of goods and certain services rendered in relation to goods. In the case of imported goods, the tax is based on the value of the goods for purposes of customs duty, including the customs duty itself. In computing final tax liability, the tax paid on purchases of goods and services may be deducted so that, in effect, only the value added is taxed. The rate of tax is 19% of the price including tax (effective rate of 23.46%). However, the tax rate is temporarily raised to 20% (effective rate of 25%) until December 31, 1991. There are two types of exemptions: full exemptions with a refund of the tax paid on purchases, and limited exemptions without such refund.

22. Inheritance and Gift Taxes

The rates of the gift and estate taxes are high and progressive, and the scope of liability is broad. The estate tax is a legacy tax levied separately on each beneficiary's share in the estate. Its rates are progressive and vary both with the value of the property received and with the legatee's relationship to the benefactor. For the most favored group (includes spouse and children), there is an exemption of SEK 280,000 for legacies to the surviving spouse and SEK 70,000 for each child. If the child has not reached the age of 18, SEK 10,000 is deducted for each year or part thereof remaining until the age of 18 is reached. Legacies above the exemption levels are taxed at rates which start at 10% on the first SEK 140,000 and progress to a maximum of 60% on the portion of a legacy in excess of SEK 11,200,000. There are certain relief provisions for family corporations. Gifts made within the ten-year period ending on the date of the decedent's death are included for estate tax purposes.

23. Taxes on Payrolls (Social Security)

All types of earned or business income form the basis for liability to pay taxes on payroll (social security), i.e., either full social security charges or a special wage tax amounting to 22.2%.

An employer is liable for the payment of social security charges, in accordance with law and agreement, as a percentage of gross salaries. The rate is 37.5% according to law and an additional amount according to collective agreement, which varies from 5% to 10%.

24. Taxes on Natural Resources

No special tax is levied on the exploitation of natural resources.

25. Other Taxes

Land and Property Tax. The assessment value of real property is based on 75% of the estimated sales value. The owner of real property designed for housing or office use pays an annual property tax amounting to 1.5% for private homes and 2.5% for apartment houses and office buildings.

Tax on Capital. The net wealth tax is an annual tax on individuals' (including nonresidents') net wealth, at the following rates:

Net Wealth		Tax on	Percentage
Over	Not Over	Lower Amount	on Excess
SEK 800,000	SEK 1,600,000	—	1.5%
1,600,000	3,600,000	SEK 12,000	2.5
3,600,000		62,000	3.0

Swedish corporations do not pay net wealth tax.

Undistributed Profits Tax. This tax (rarely applied) is levied only upon those Swedish holding companies which fail to make adequate distributions of profits giving tax advantages to individuals ultimately entitled to the profits. The taxable base is the amount of profits deemed to be unreasonably withheld, and the rate is 25%.

Turnover Tax. A tax of 1% of the price is imposed on sales of shares, convertible debentures, and certain other securities. The tax is apportioned between the seller and the buyer so that each pays 0.5%. A nonresident is taxed only if a Swedish broker is acting on his or her behalf.

Excise Duties. Confectionery and certain chemical products are subject to a special excise tax. This tax will be abolished January 1, 1993.

Other Indirect Taxes. Other indirect taxes are levied, such as taxes on tobacco, wine and spirits, registration duties, stamp duties, and annual vehicle tax. Outbound travelers by charter have to pay an extra tax of SEK 300 per person.

COMPUTATION OF TAXABLE INCOME

26.   Capital Gains
See item 3.

27.   Depreciation and Depletion
Corporate taxpayers may depreciate machinery and equipment according to either of two methods: book depreciation or remaining value depreciation. Both methods apply to machinery, equipment, and certain intangible assets.

Book Depreciation. Under book depreciation, a corporation may deduct for tax purposes in any income year whatever amount of depreciation it chooses to take on its books for that year, provided, however, that the deduction does not exceed the highest figure computed using either of two alternative provisions prescribed in the tax law (declining-balance or straight-line methods). The deduction for depreciation on the declining-balance method in any one year may amount to 30% of the total of (1) the book value of the corporation's entire stock of machinery and equipment at the beginning of the year, increased by (2) the cost of items acquired during the year and still in the possession of the corporation, and reduced by (3) sums received for items acquired in earlier years and sold or disposed of during the year. The amount of the deduction is optional; the corporation may, in any year, take less than the maximum of 30%, as it deems appropriate.

The straight-line method is based on a 20% per year deduction. Regardless of the ceiling imposed by the 30% declining-balance method, the corporation may deduct depreciation in any year of whatever amount is necessary to reduce the book value of all of its machinery and equipment to its total acquisition cost reduced by 20% yearly depreciation on a straight-line basis since acquisition.

Remaining Value Depreciation. This method allows corporations to deduct for tax purposes a maximum of 25% in any income year of the total of (1) the remaining value for tax purposes of the corporation's entire stock of machinery and equipment at the end of the preceding year, increased by (2) the costs of items acquired during the year and still in the possession of the corporation, and reduced by (3) sums received for items acquired in earlier years and sold or disposed of during the year.

Regardless of the maximum depreciation deductions permitted by these alternatives, a corporation may always take a sufficient depreciation deduction to reduce the remaining value of its machinery and equipment to actual value. The cost of machinery and equipment whose useful life may be expected to be only three years or less may be written off in full in the year of acquisition.

Depreciation for land and buildings is less liberal. Allowances for industrial buildings are 4% straight-line and for office and commercial buildings 2% straight-line. Depreciation is allowed on the value of the building but not on the land. Allowances are available for depreciation of improvements to land, such as access roads, sewage pipes, parking, etc.

28. Treatment of Dividends

Dividends on business-related holdings and holdings greater than 25% are tax-free for corporations. Otherwise dividends received by companies and individuals are considered as normal taxable income. Special regulations exist for investment companies.

According to the so-called Annell-legislation, a deduction is allowed for dividends paid up to an annual maximum of 10% of qualifying capital (paid in after January 1, 1979), if the dividend is paid to certain qualifying shareholders such as individuals, foreign corporations subject to Swedish withholding tax, etc. This means that over a maximum of twenty years, dividends to the amount of the increase of the share capital are tax deductible.

29. Loss Carryovers

A loss sustained in any income year may be carried forward and deducted from taxable income during the next year. If the next year also shows a loss, the accumulated losses will be deducted the following year. No carryback is permitted. Special rules will apply when ownership of a closely held corporation changes during the period.

30. Transactions between Related Parties

Swedish tax rules state that normal commercial customs should be applied on transactions between related parties, i.e., the same prices/conditions that would have been used if the transactions were made between independent parties. Although the burden of proof lies on the tax authorities, the company must be prepared to give all necessary information to enable the authorities to judge the prices/conditions applied.

31. Consolidation of Income

The filing of consolidated tax returns by related corporations is not permitted. It is, however, possible to transfer income between the companies of a group by way of group contributions.

32. Tax Periods

The liability to corporate income tax is based on the company's accounting period.

33. Other Matters

Tax Equalization Reserve (SURV). Corporations have been granted the right to allocate funds to a special tax equalization reserve, based on the corporation's equity capital, to a maximum of 30%. The SURV will, in principle, be based on the tax accounting values of various assets, less deductions for corporate liabilities in accordance with closing balance sheets. Alternatively, a SURV may be based on payroll.

Inventory Valuation. For tax purposes, the true value of inventory is the procurement (cost) or real value (net sales value), whichever is lower, based on an inventory or other reliable method of valuation. Procurement value is reckoned on the FIFO method. The real value is net sales value or, under special conditions, reprocurement value less 3% for unsalable goods.

The ability to create untaxed reserves by the previously allowed write-down of the value of inventories with 50% has been abolished as part of the tax reform. Previous write-downs will be released to taxable income at the 1992–1995 assessments and taxed at the new rate of 30%.

Salary Reserves. The salary reserves and investment reserves also have been abolished as part of the tax reform.

RELATED CONSIDERATIONS

34. Incentives and Grants

The tax reform, effective January 1, 1991, will drastically lower the tax rates. This will partly be financed through a broadening of the tax base. Thus, most incentives and grants have been discontinued apart from the tax-equalization reserves (SURV) (see item 33), which are part of the tax reform.

35. Exchange Controls

Sweden has for many years had exchange control regulations. During 1989, the regulations have been changed radically. Permission is no longer needed to transfer capital for inbound or outbound investments.

36. Investment Restrictions on Nonresidents

Foreign individuals and corporations may not, without special permission, acquire real property or, in certain circumstances, acquire or carry on a business or buy shares of a joint stock company.

SELECTION OF BUSINESS ENTITY BY NONRESIDENTS

Nonresident investors normally operate in Sweden through a branch or by forming a local subsidiary company. The trading partnership and limited partnership are available but are rarely used. The limited company is by far the most frequently used entity. In general, the same tax rules apply to limited companies and branches, and there are few practical differences.

SWITZERLAND

INCOME TAXES ON CORPORATIONS

1. Rates

The federal direct tax on worldwide net profits is imposed at graduated rates. Between the minimum tax rate of 3.63% and the maximum of 9.8%, the rate varies in three brackets according to the yield (i.e., the proportion of taxable profits to equity capital) as follows:

Yield (%)	Applicable Tax Rate (%)
4 and less	3.63
5	4.356
10	6.776
15	8.55
23.15 and above	9.8

2. Local Income Taxes

The majority of the cantons and municipalities impose a tax on worldwide net profits in a manner similar to the federal direct tax which is in addition to the federal tax. Between the minimum and the maximum basic tax rate specifically laid down in the tax laws the applicable basic tax rate is determined according to the yield. A few cantonal tax laws, even though prescribing graduated rates, do not rely on the yield for determining the basic tax rate. Normally the basic tax rate is multiplied by a certain percentage fixed annually or periodically. The result gives the effective tax rate.

The total (federal, cantonal, and municipal) tax burden in five Swiss cities as a percentage of the net profits of a corporation is indicated below. In order to give a comprehensive picture, the annual tax on capital has been included. It is assumed that the corporation is operating in Switzerland and has a capital of SFr.100,000 and net profit (before deduction of paid taxes) of (a) SFr.12,000, (b) SFr.20,000, and (c) SFr.50,000:

Cities	Total Tax Burden		
	(a)	(b)	(c)
Basel	23.73%	26.82%	27.83%
Berne	16.45	18.31	19.88
Geneva			
(without business tax)	21.98	27.20	31.67
Lausanne	17.51	20.54	26.81
Zurich	22.88	31.62	31.40
Zug	15.73	18.52	18.32

These figures reflect the situation during the calendar year 1990 and are subject to change for any subsequent year. Special provisions apply to corporations that are in liquidation.

For the tax reliefs available for holding, domicile, and auxiliary companies, see item 34.

3. Capital Gains Taxes

Capital gains realized or accounted for by a corporation are normally included in the taxable profits. In some cantons, capital gains realized on real property are taxed separately.

4. Branch Profits Taxes

A nonresident corporation carrying on business in Switzerland through a permanent establishment is taxed in the same manner and at the same rates as a resident corporation with respect to the net profits attributable to such permanent establishment. There is no withholding on branch profits remitted abroad.

The term "permanent establishment" is defined in a similar manner as in most tax treaties.

According to Swiss tax law, a part of the total net profits of the nonresident corporation should be attributed to the Swiss permanent establishment by applying specific factors such as turnover, capital invested, salaries paid and the like (so-called indirect method). In practice, however, the Swiss tax authorities take as a tax basis in most cases the profits shown in the books of the permanent establishment, which may be adjusted if necessary (so-called direct method). In this case, they may apply the maximum tax rate.

5. Foreign Tax Reliefs

In principle, no tax credit is available for taxes incurred by a resident corporation in countries outside Switzerland. As an exception to this rule, several tax treaties provide for a credit against Swiss tax for foreign withholding taxes on dividends, interest, and royalties that are not refunded. In other cases, a resident corporation, as a rule, may claim a deduction from taxable profits for taxes withheld at the source in a foreign country. This relief is not available for assessed taxes in certain cantons. Even if no tax treaty applies, unilateral provisions avoid international double taxation in certain cases as follows:

☐ Income (including capital gains) derived from real property situated outside Switzerland is not taxed.

☐ Income derived from a permanent establishment situated outside Switzerland is not taxed.

The tax due by a resident corporation is calculated tentatively on its total worldwide income and then reduced according to the ratio existing between the worldwide income and the exempt income. Thus, the latter is retained for determining the tax rate applicable in Switzerland. Dividends received by a resident corporation, whether from domestic or foreign sources, may be tax-exempt under special provisions more fully explained in item 28. If a Swiss corporation is granted the status of a so-called domicile company (as explained in item 34), international double taxation may also be alleviated.

6. Classification of Corporations

The Swiss Code of Obligations provides for the various forms of business enterprises in Switzerland, including corporations, limited liability companies, and cooperatives. From a tax point of view, a distinction can be made between normally taxed companies on the one hand and holding companies, domicile companies, and service companies on the other hand. For the privileged tax treatment of the second category of companies see items 28 and 34.

7. Payment of Taxes

The federal direct tax is paid annually although an assessment is made every two years (see item 32). Most cantons follow the two-year period similar to that of the confederation, but some cantons apply a one-year tax period.

8. Other Matters

Direct taxes are imposed at all three levels of government albeit under differing legislative frameworks. The Federal Constitution provides for the avoidance of intercantonal double taxation. The Federal Supreme Court has implemented this provision in numerous decisions which are precedents for similar cases. Double taxation between municipalities is avoided by express cantonal provisions usually reflecting the principles applied in intercantonal relations.

INCOME TAXES ON INDIVIDUALS

9. Rates

The federal direct tax on worldwide income is imposed at graduated rates. The maximum rate of 11.5% applies to income exceeding SFr.501,700 (single), and SFr.595,200 (married).

10. Local Income Taxes

The cantonal and municipal tax burden on worldwide income of an individual varies substantially. As explained in item 2, the basic tax rates are fixed in the applicable tax law, while the cantons and the municipalities decide annually by which percentage the basic tax rate shall be multiplied to arrive at the effective tax rate.

The following indicates the total (federal, cantonal, and municipal) tax burden in six Swiss cities of a married individual without children, as a percentage of a gross earned income of SFr.100,000. It should be noted that any income received by a married woman is incorporated in her husband's taxable income.

Basel	18.4%
Berne	19.7
Geneva	19.4
Lausanne	18.1
Zurich	14.5
Zug	10.1

These figures reflect the situation during the calendar year 1990. The figures are subject to change for any subsequent year.

Each individual is further liable to an annual cantonal and municipal tax on his wealth. This is more fully explained in item 25. The federal anticipatory tax also applies to individuals (see item 17).

11. Capital Gains Taxes

The federal direct tax is not charged on capital gains realized by an individual, provided he is not carrying on any business. If he does so, however, realized capital gains are added to his other taxable income. All cantonal tax laws provide for the taxation of capital gains realized on the disposal of real property. In a few cantons, these are included in the taxable income. In most cantons, however, they are taxed separately. Normally, the longer the period during which the taxpayer owned the real property, the lower the tax incidence. Only one canton taxes capital gains realized on the alienation of movable property, e.g., shares. It levies the special tax only if the capital gain is realized within a limited period of ten years after acquisition. Capital losses may be deducted from capital gains if the latter are taxable.

12. Foreign Tax Reliefs

See item 5.

13. Tax Period

An individual is required to use the calendar year but may select a different fiscal period of 12 months for the computation of business income.

14. Other Matters

Avoidance of Double Taxation within Switzerland. The information in item 8 also applies to individuals.

INCOME TAXES ON NONRESIDENTS

15. Liability to Tax

A nonresident company is liable to the federal direct tax on certain types of Swiss income only. The principal taxable items are income from real estate located in Switzerland, income from a Swiss permanent establishment, and income from debts secured by mortgages on Swiss real estate. A withholding tax of 35% is usually levied on dividends and bond and bank interest received by a nonresident company. Royalties are generally exempt from withholding tax. Liability for cantonal taxes is based on similar principles to those described above for the federal direct tax. A company is regarded as resident in Switzerland if it has its registered office or effective place of management in Switzerland. All companies incorporated under Swiss law must have a registered office in Switzerland and are, therefore, deemed to be resident in Switzerland for tax purposes. The cantons and municipalities generally apply similar rules for their own taxes.

A nonresident individual is liable to the federal direct tax on certain types of Swiss-source income only, those including the types of income that are subject to tax in the case of a nonresident company and, in addition, fees received as a director of a Swiss company and income from the exercise of a profession in Switzerland. Federal anticipatory tax of 35% is levied on dividends and bond and bank interest received by a nonresident individual. Royalties are generally exempt from tax. Liability for cantonal taxes is based on similar principles to those described above for the federal direct tax. An individual is regarded as resident in Switzerland for federal tax purposes if he or she lives there with the intention of staying permanently. Mere physical presence can also result in residence. An individual who is not employed in Switzerland is considered resident after remaining there for a certain period of time, usually from three to six months. An individual employed in Switzerland becomes resident there upon arrival. Similar factors are taken into account in determining whether an individual is resident in a particular canton for cantonal tax purposes. Anticipatory tax can be refunded pursuant to a tax treaty (see item 17).

16. Rates

Income tax rates for nonresidents are in principle the same as for residents. The cantons, however, replace the standard assessment for foreign employees without a resident permit with a withholding tax imposed at special and simplified rates (see item 18).

17. Withholding Tax Rates

Dividends (including constructive dividends and liquidation proceeds) from Swiss sources are subject to a withholding tax (federal anticipatory tax) of 35% on the gross amount which is deducted at source. The tax also applies to distributions from Swiss mutual funds, except distributed realized capital gains. Interest on private loans, whether or not secured by a mortgage, is not subject to anticipatory tax. On the other hand, interest on bonds and other certificates of indebtedness issued by a Swiss resident and interest paid by domestic banks are subject to anticipatory tax. Anticipatory tax law applies not only to banks and savings banks subject to Swiss banking law but also to anyone who publicly advertises to take interest-bearing deposits or is continuously in receipt of such. In this case the obligation to withhold anticipatory tax already exists where between 12 and 20 interest-bearing accounts are being kept. The tax is a prepayment for a Swiss resident who reports such income in his tax return, and any excess above his main tax liability is refundable. Federal anticipatory tax is, however, a final charge for a nonresident unless a refund can be claimed under a tax treaty.

The following rates are the treaty rates normally charged. They do not reflect special cases which may be provided for in particular tax treaties. Royalties are not taxed at the source in Switzerland.

Recipient	Dividends	Bond and Bank Interest
Nontreaty countries	35%	35%
Treaty countries:		
Australia	15	10
Austria	5	5
Belgium	15, 10	10
Canada	15	15
China	10	10
Denmark	0	0
Egypt	15, 5	15
Finland	10, 5	0
France	15, 5	10
Germany	15, 5	30, 0
Greece	15, 5	10
Hungary	10	10
Iceland	15, 5	0
Indonesia	15, 10	10
Ireland	15, 10	0
Italy	15	12.5
Ivory Coast	15	15
Japan	15, 10	10

Recipient	Dividends	Bond and Bank Interest
Korea	15, 10	10
Malaysia	15, 5	10
Netherlands	15, 0	5
New Zealand	15	10
Norway	15, 10	0
Pakistan	35, 15	35, 15
Portugal	15, 10	10
Singapore	15, 10	10
South Africa	7.5	35, 10
Soviet Union	35	35
Spain	15, 10	10
Sri Lanka	15, 10	10, 5
Sweden	5	5
Trinidad and Tobago	20, 10	10
United Kingdom	15, 5	0
United States	15, 5	5

The withholding tax is normally deducted at the full rate of 35% and adjusted to the treaty rate upon filing a refund claim with the federal tax authorities.

18. Special Withholding Provisions

As a great number of nonresidents work in Switzerland, most cantons apply a system whereby the employer is required to pay the income tax due by his nonresident employees. Some of the systems are similar to P.A.Y.E. (wage withholding); some give the right to ask for a normal assessment at year's end. The graduated rates include federal, cantonal, and municipal income tax.

Some cantons have in certain cases replaced the tax assessment explained in item 15 by a withholding tax. Thus, the Canton of Zurich applies the following rates on the gross amounts of:

	Rate
Director's fees and similar remuneration	22%
Remuneration of self-employed artists, sportsmen, actors, etc.	8
Interest income on secured real estate	15

The withholding tax is paid in final settlement of the tax liability arising under federal, cantonal, and municipal tax law.

19. Tax Treaties

See item 17.

20. Other Matters

Special Provisions for Foreign-Controlled Legal Entities Using Swiss Tax Treaties. Special requirements must be met by foreign-controlled legal entities resident in Switzerland which make use of Swiss tax treaties. A foreign-controlled resident corporation is excluded from the benefits of the Swiss income tax treaties, unless the corporation:

☐ Has a reasonable capital structure (generally the total of all interest-bearing loans should not exceed six times the company's equity).

☐ Distributes, as a dividend, a reasonable amount of the treaty-favored income, i.e., at least 25% of gross treaty-favored income.

☐ Does not use more than 50% of such gross income for payments (interest, royalties, management fees, and the like) to nonresidents.

☐ Does not pay interest exceeding a maximum rate of actually 8% on loans received (the rate may change from time to time).

OTHER SIGNIFICANT TAXES

21. Sales (Value Added)

Federal turnover tax is imposed upon sales or importation of goods and merchandise, but not on services. It is not a value-added tax; the tax is levied at one stage only.

The rates are as follows:

	Rate
Wholesale level (for resale)	9.3%
Retail level	6.2%

In addition, the federal government levies excise duties on beer, alcohol, and tobacco. Customs duties, mostly based on weight, are charged on imported goods and merchandise. Special rules apply for imports from EEC and EFTA countries.

22. Inheritance and Gift Taxes

The federal government does not impose any estate or gift tax. However, estate tax is imposed by 25 cantons, and a gift tax by 24 cantons. Except in a few cases, the municipalities do not share in taxes on estates or gifts. In the cantons levying both an estate and a gift tax, the latter is normally imposed on the same tax basis and on the same scale as the inheritance tax.

Normally, the cantons impose an inheritance tax in respect of estates (except real property situated outside Switzerland) of residents and of nonresidents to the extent they own real property situated in Switzerland. The applicable graduated tax scales take into account the relationship between the deceased and the heir, the amount of the inheritance and, in a few cases, the net wealth of the heir. In several cantons, transfers to children and the surviving spouse of the deceased remain tax-free. On the other hand, heirs not related to the deceased are charged at the highest rates.

23. Taxes on Payrolls (Social Security)

There are several federal social security schemes. With respect to four of them, all employers and all self-employed individuals are required to pay contributions. These are based on the total wages or professional remuneration paid, with no upper limit (except for the unemployment scheme). An employer may charge half of his contributions to the employees by deducting the appropriate amount from the wages paid. The collection of the contributions due is completely separate from the collection of taxes. The social security contributions are as follows:

	Wage Earners	Self-Employed Persons
Federal old age and survivor insurance scheme	8.4%	7.8%
Federal disability insurance scheme	1.2	1.2
Federal military service compensation scheme	0.5	0.5
Federal unemployment scheme (wages in excess of SFr.81,600 are not charged)	0.4%	
Total contributions	10.5%	9.5%

The cantons usually levy additional contributions for family and child allowance schemes.

The federal direct tax law permits the deduction of premiums paid by an employee or self-employed person to qualifying insurance companies for old age, widow's, and orphans' pensions (subject to certain limitations). The proceeds are fully taxable at special rates. The cantons have adopted similar rules.

24. Taxes on Natural Resources

The profit connected with the exploitation of natural resources is under certain circumstances taxable under income or capital gains federal and cantonal tax rules.

25. Other Taxes

Capital Tax on Corporations. A corporation pays annually the federal direct tax on its capital at a flat rate of 0.0825%. The cantons and the municipalities also impose such a tax normally at the flat rate, but in some cases at graduated rates. There is a basic tax rate which is then multiplied by a percentage fixed annually to arrive at the effective tax rate. The total tax burden shown in item 2 includes this tax.

Wealth Tax on Indiviuduals. Individuals pay a tax on capital to the canton and the municipality at graduated rates fixed as explained in the above paragraph. The annual tax burden in six Swiss cities of a married individual without children and a net wealth of SFr.500,000 is as follows (as a percentage of net wealth):

	Rate
Basel	0.620%
Berne	0.397
Geneva	0.387
Lausanne	0.612
Zurich	0.154
Zug	0.281

These figures are for calendar-year 1990 and are subject to change for any subsequent year.

Land and Property Taxes. Several cantons and municipalities impose an annual tax on the officially determined values of real property. A transfer tax is charged on the transfer of real property independently of taxing a capital gain derived from the same transaction.

Stamp Duties. If a Swiss corporation or a Swiss mutual fund issues new shares, a federal stamp duty (Capital Issue Tax) is charged on the amount of consideration received or the face amount, whichever is higher. The rates are as follows:

Share	Rate
Corporation	3%
Mutual fund	0.9
Issued in a merger or spin-off	1

Securities purchased through a Swiss professional security dealer (i.e., a bank, broker, holding or management company, depositary bank of a mutual fund) bear a federal stamp duty (Transfer Tax). The rates are as follows:

	Rate
On Swiss securities	0.15%
On foreign securities	0.30

The rates are 0.1% or 0.2%, respectively, on securities, bills of exchange, and the like issued for a period of less than three months.

COMPUTATION OF TAXABLE INCOME

For both a corporation and an individual carrying on a trade or business, the balance of the profit and loss account determined according to generally accepted accounting principles forms the tax basis. This balance may be adjusted by the tax authorities if transactions which are not at arm's length or not commercially justified (e.g., excessive depreciation) are discovered. Taxes on income and capital paid by corporations are a deductible item for federal tax purposes and under the law of most cantons.

26. Capital Gains

If capital gains are taxable, they are normally subject to tax in full. In the case of taxable gains realized on the alienation of real property, the taxable amount may be reduced for each year during which the seller owned the real property. Losses may be used to set off capital gains. In some cantons, a carryover is permitted for a few years.

27. Depreciation and Depletion

Depreciation of an asset is only permissible if it is used for business purposes. The rates must reasonably reflect the normal period of exhaustion and/or wear and tear. The federal tax authorities have indicated depreciation rates for many types of assets on the basis of the declining-balance method. If the straight-line method is used, depreciation at one-half of these rates is permissible. As a rule, the cantonal and municipal tax authorities accept the same rates. Recaptured depreciation constitutes ordinary income.

Under certain conditions, it is permissible to write down inventories by one-third of the purchase or manufacturing value or, if lower, of the market value without further justification.

There are no special depletion provisions.

28. Treatment of Dividends

Dividends are added to taxable income. Corporations receiving dividends from Swiss or foreign subsidiaries may claim for federal tax purposes, and under most cantonal tax laws, a proportional tax reduction calculated according to the ratio existing between the adjusted gross income and dividends received, or between net income and dividends received. As a rule, this reduction is granted if the parent corporation owns at least 20% of the paid-in capital of the subsidiary or if such an interest has a market value of at least one or two million Swiss Francs (substantial interest). In a few cantons, the capital tax is reduced in a similar way.

All cantons have a so-called holding privilege under which the total amount of dividends remains tax-free (see item 34).

29. Loss Carryovers

A loss occurring in any year of the same computation period of two years (see item 32) is automatically carried over to the other year within the period.

For federal tax purposes, the loss shown for one computation period (see item 32) may be carried forward to the three following periods. Most cantons apply similar rules.

30. Transactions between Related Parties

Revenue transactions must be carried out at arm's length. If the fair market value is not paid or received, adjustments may be made by the tax authorities for the taxation of one party without regard to the related party, particularly if it is a nonresident. The reallocated income is not only subject to federal, cantonal, and municipal income tax but also to federal anticipatory tax if it is considered to be a constructive dividend to the shareholder.

The arm's length principle also applies if a capital transaction is not carried out at fair market value. The consequences are the same as described in the prior paragraph. In specific cases, such as reorganizations between residents (in some cases only of the same canton), incorporation of a sole proprietorship or partnership, merger, and the like, the tax authorities may grant a tax exemption, provided the book value of the assets remains unchanged.

31. Consolidation of Income

Consolidated tax returns are not permitted.

32. Tax Periods

The federal direct tax and most cantonal and municipal taxes are assessed over a period of two years (assessment period) but collected annually. The tax is assessed on the average income derived by the taxpayer during the two years (computation period) immediately preceding the assessment or tax period. This may be illustrated as follows:

Computation Period	Assessment Period
Years 1987 and 1988	Years 1989 and 1990
Years 1989 and 1990	Years 1991 and 1992
Years 1991 and 1992	Years 1993 and 1994

A new taxpayer is taxed on the income attributable to the first tax year.

Some cantons assess income annually. Only the canton of Basel-City and, in the case of corporations, seven other cantons follow the system whereby the income tax is calculated, as in most other countries, on the income of the tax year but is levied in the following year.

The capital tax is based on the situation existing on the first day of the assessment period.

The fiscal period of an individual is explained in item 13. Corporations may select a financial year of 12 months other than the calendar year. In this case, the results of the financial year(s) ending during the computation period determine the tax liability.

33. Other Matters

Provisions. The following provisions are recognized for tax purposes:

☐ Liabilities arising in the current year but the extent of which cannot yet be determined.

☐ Risks of loss on current assets (e.g., doubtful debts for which a provision of 5% on domestic receivables and 10% on foreign receivables can normally be made).

☐ Other imminent risks of loss.

Provisions which are made for possible future risks are considered part of taxable profit. Provisions that were previously recognized for tax purposes but are no longer necessary are added back to taxable profit.

RELATED CONSIDERATIONS

34. Incentives and Grants

Individuals resident in Switzerland who are not Swiss nationals and have never exercised any activity in Switzerland have the option to be taxed for federal tax purposes and in certain cantons on a lump-sum basis instead of paying taxes on income and capital. The lump-sum basis takes into account annual expenditures or certain items of income, whichever is higher. The rates are generally the same as for normal income tax.

As mentioned in item 28, all cantons grant exemptions from income tax to corporations ("holding companies") exclusively or predominantly active in administering substantial interests in other corporations. The exemption applies to all income received. They pay only a capital tax, normally at reduced rates. This holding privilege is not available for federal tax purposes. However, relief is granted for this tax as explained in item 28. Corporations having only their registered office there but not carrying on any active business in Switzerland may qualify as so-called domicile companies and, therefore, pay none or a reduced cantonal or municipal income tax. They normally pay a reduced capital tax only. Federal direct tax, however, is imposed in full on such domicile companies. Similar privileges may be available in some cantons for auxiliary or service companies, i.e., corporations exclusively or predominantly rendering services to related corporations outside Switzerland only. Here, too, federal direct tax is charged in full.

Charitable organizations and certain qualified employee benefit or retirement plans are exempt from tax under certain conditions.

35. Exchange Controls

None.

36. Investment Restrictions on Nonresidents

Acquisitions of real estate by nonresident aliens or legal entities controlled by nonresidents require a license, which are limited.

37. Other Matters

Work Permits. Foreigners who intend to work in Switzerland need an official work permit, which may be difficult to obtain.

SELECTION OF BUSINESS ENTITY BY NONRESIDENTS

Nonresident investors can operate in Switzerland either through a branch or by forming a local subsidiary corporation. Both branches and foreign-owned corporations are taxed in the same way as residents.

Branch profits are determined and taxed as explained in item 4, and dividends of foreign-owned corporations are subject to withholding tax as noted in item 17. In a general way the situation of a subsidiary versus a branch may be summarized as follows:

	Branch	Subsidiary
Taxable entity	Branch and head-office constitute a single taxable entity	Two separate taxpayers
Liability of the head office or parent company for Swiss taxes	Liable	Not liable
Foreign withholding taxes on dividends, interest and royalties	No reduction or exemption; treaties do not apply	Reduction or exemption under a treaty

	Branch	Subsidiary
Federal stamp duty (capital issue tax)	Not due	Due
Profit remittance to the head office or parent company	No Swiss withholding tax	Swiss withholding tax of 35%

Many nontax considerations may influence the decision as to whether business in Switzerland should be carried on through a branch or through a subsidiary.

SPECIMEN TAX COMPUTATION

Information:

□ The corporation's headquarters are in Zurich. It is engaged in sales activities.
□ The shareholder's equity is SFr.3,000,000 and includes the paid-in share capital, reserves, and retained earnings.
□ The corporation's statement of income for the year follows:

	SFrs. '000'	
Sales in Switzerland	4,500	
Cost of sales	(2,500)	1,950
Dividends from Swiss subsidiaries		100
Dividends from foreign subsidiaries	100	
Foreign withholding taxes charged by treaty countries (not recoverable but tax credit)	(5)	95
Capital gain on sale of fixed assets		100
Total earnings		2,245
Sales expenses	650	
Administration expenses	250	
Interest paid	100	(1,000)
Income before Swiss taxes		1,245
Taxes		
Federal direct taxes	83	
Cantonal and communal taxes	231	
Tax credit for foreign withholding taxes not refunded	(5)	(309)
Income after Swiss taxes		936

	SFrs. '000'
Computation:	
Federal direct taxes	
Income after taxes	936
Federal income tax at 9.8% (1)	92
Reduction for substantial interests (2)	(11)	80
Federal capital tax at 0.0825%		3
Total federal direct tax		83
Cantonal and communal taxes	
Income after Swiss taxes	936
Cantonal and communal income tax at 28.554%(3)	267
Reduction for substantial interest (4)	(47)	220
Cantonal and communal capital tax at 0.3569%		11
Total cantonal and communal taxes		231

Notes:

(1) Maximum rate: 9.8%; minimum rate 3.63%.

(2) $\dfrac{\text{SFr.200,000 (gross dividends received)}}{\text{SFr.1,600,000 (gross income: 2,245 + 5 − 650)}} = 12.5\%$

(3) Maximum rate: 28.554%; minimum rate: 9.518%

(4)
Dividends received (gross)	200
5% for administration expenses	(10)
Portion of interest paid (relation of investment value to total assets)	(25)
Net income from dividends	165
As percentage of income after taxes	17.6%

TAIWAN
REPUBLIC OF CHINA

Editor's Note: The following information is reprinted from the 1991 edition.

INCOME TAXES ON CORPORATIONS

1. Rates

The regular rates of corporation income tax are 15% on income of not more than NT$100,000 and 25% on income over NT$100,000. See item 34 for possible maximum rates of tax on income.

2. Local Income Taxes

None.

3. Capital Gains Taxes

The income tax law does not provide for any special treatment of capital gains and losses. Capital gains are taxable at ordinary income tax rates. Currently, gains on land transactions are generally exempt. Effective January 1, 1990, gains on security transactions are tax-exempt. See item 25, Securities Transfer Tax.

4. Branch Profits Taxes

Branches of foreign corporations are subject to corporation tax on branch profits at the same rates as domestic corporations.

5. Foreign Tax Reliefs

Corporations based in Taiwan that have branches abroad are subject to income tax on their total profits regardless of source. To provide relief from double taxation, a tax credit is allowed for income tax paid to foreign countries by such branches.

7. Payment of Taxes

Corporations must pay a provisional income tax in the seventh month of the current fiscal year. While, in the normal course of business, interest and dividends are subject to withholding tax at the time they are received. The balance of the current year's income tax is due when their income tax return is filed. The deadline for filing the return is the last day of the third month of the following year, extendable with approval to the fifth month. A representative (liason) office is not required to file the return as it does not generate any operating income. However, it must file the return if it generates any nonoperating income such as interest income.

8. Other Matters

Business Tax. A business tax, which is more commonly referred to as value-added tax (VAT), is imposed at 5% of the invoice amount on the sale of goods, including sale of all types of capital assets except land, or services within Taiwan and on the importation of goods and services into Taiwan. Zero-rate VAT, however, applies to exporting goods and services related to export. VAT paid on purchases is generally creditable against any VAT payable on sales. A foreign branch is taxed with respect to VAT exactly the same as a domestic company. A liaison office not engaged in business needs no registration nor is subject to VAT. For industries such as small-scale enterprises, banking, insurance, securities, and special food and drink industries that apply gross-amount business tax, the input VAT is not refundable nor creditable.

INCOME TAXES ON INDIVIDUALS

9. Rates

The rates of individual income tax on taxable income for 1991, which are applied after deducting personal exemptions, allowances for dependents, and other deductions, are as follows:

Taxable Income		Tax on	Percentage
Over	Not Over	Lower Amount	on Excess
NT$ 0	NT$ 300,000	NT$ 0	6%
300,000	800,000	18,000	13
800,000	1,600,000	83,000	21
1,600,000	3,000,000	251,000	30
3,000,000		671,000	40

Individuals who are domiciled and reside in Taiwan, or who are not domiciled but have resided for more than 183 days in a calendar year in Taiwan, are considered residents for tax purposes. Residents are taxed on their Taiwan-source income only, regardless of the place where the income is paid or received. Husbands and wives are required to file joint returns.

Foreign nationals employed in Taiwan are permitted to remit their salaries received in Taiwan to their home countries subject to certain limitations.

10. Local Income Taxes

None.

11. Capital Gains Taxes

Capital gains realized by an individual are taxed at the same rates as ordinary income. Currently, gains on security transactions and land transactions are exempt; only one-half of the gain on transactions of registered stock of nonlisted companies, corporate bonds, government bonds, and approved financial debentures held by an individual for more than one year are subject to tax. However, see item 25, Securities Transfer Tax.

12. Foreign Tax Reliefs

Limited tax reliefs are available to citizens of Singapore under the tax treaty between Taiwan and Singapore.

13. Tax Period

The tax year for individuals is the calendar year.

INCOME TAXES ON NONRESIDENTS

15. Liability to Tax

Nonresidents are liable to tax on income generated from Taiwan sources. Nonresidents who have resided in Taiwan for less than 90 days in a calendar year are liable to tax only on income received in Taiwan. Nonresidents who have resided in Taiwan for more than 90 days but less than 183 days in a calendar year are liable to tax on income from sources both within and without Taiwan for services rendered in Taiwan.

Foreign corporations that do not have any fixed place of business in Taiwan are subject to income tax only on their Taiwan-source income; i.e., income from business activities conducted in the Taiwan. The withholding income tax rate is 20% on such income as dividends (with special approval), interest, rental, commissions, royalties, professional fees, etc., and 35% on dividends (without special approval) and gains from disposals of assets, etc. Certain foreign companies, such as those engaged in international transportation, engineering and construction, provision of technical services, and equipment leasing, which have generated Taiwan-source income, may apply to the Ministry of Finance for specific approval to fix a percentage (10% in the case of international transportation and 15% in the case of all others) of their Taiwan-source revenue as taxable income and pay 25% income tax thereon.

16. Rates

Salaries and wages, practitioners' fees, interest, rentals, royalties, commissions, and any other income earned by nonresidents are subject to withholding tax at 20%. Dividends earned by nonresidents are subject to withholding tax at 20% if from investments approved by the Investment Commission or at 35% if from investment not approved by the Investment Commission.

19. Tax Treaties

A tax treaty has been concluded with Singapore. In addition, tax treaties on international transportation business have been concluded with Japan, Korea, Singapore, South Africa, and the United States.

OTHER SIGNIFICANT TAXES

23. Taxes on Payrolls (Social Security)

A variety of insurance benefits are provided to employees under the government-administrated labor insurance program. Labor insurance coverage consists of insurance for ordinary risks and occupational risks. The cost of ordinary risk insurance is 7% of the employee's monthly salary or wages up to NT$22,800, 80% of which is borne by the employer. The cost of occupational risk insurance is paid entirely by the employer. A government agency prescribes which industries must obtain occupational risk coverage as well as the premium rates.

Certain welfare funds must be set up by larger businesses. Contributions to these funds are as follows:

□ 1% to 5% of paid-in capital when the business is established.

□ 0.05% to 0.15% of monthly operating revenues.

□ 20% to 40% of the proceeds from the sale of discarded materials.

25. Other Taxes

Land Value Tax. Land value tax is levied on both rural and urban land on the basis of the official assessed value of the land. A fixed yearly rate of 1.5% of the official assessed value applies to urban land for industrial use and 0.2% of the official assessed value for residential housing. Urban land for other than industrial use is subject to tax at progressive rates from 1% to 5.5%, rising with the official assessed value of the taxpayer's holdings of urban land located in a jurisdictional area.

Land Value Increment Tax. The land value increment tax is levied on the increase in the assessed value of land. The increment is subject to tax at progressive rates from 40% to 60%, increasing with the land value increment, which is expressed as a percentage of the official assessed value (40% imposed on value increment less than 100%, 50% on value increment more than 100% inclusive but less than 200%, and 60% on value increment more than 200% inclusive). The rate on residential housing is 10%. The tax is payable by the seller when ownership is transferred.

Stamp Tax.   Documentary stamps must be affixed to cash receipts, contracts for sale of personal property, job contracts, and contracts for sale, exchange, donation, or division of real property, etc. Stamp tax rates may be a percentage of the amount of a document or a fixed amount. The rates are 0.4% for the amount on receipts, 0.1% for the amount on contracts for transfer of real estate, 0.1% for the amount on job contracts, and NT$12 on each contract for sale of personal property.

Building Tax.   The building tax paid by the owner of the building is 3% of the official assessed value if the building is used for business, 1.38% if used as a residence, 1.5% if used as a factory or if used as an office of professional practitioners or public organizations and institutions.

Securities Transfer Tax.   Transactions on sale of stock and other securities issued by corporations are subject to a securities transfer tax of 0.6%, paid by the seller, based on the selling price of stock or securities sold. The securities transfer tax for bonds and certain other securities is 0.1%.

Import Duties.   Import duties are based on the dutiable value of imported goods or at a fixed monetary amount per unit. Various rates apply to different kinds of goods (see item 34).

Commodity Tax.   Commodity tax is an excise tax on selected domestically produced and imported commodities. Commodity tax rates are ad valorem, ranging from 2% to 60%.

Harbor Dues.   Harbor dues are levied on both imports and exports at 0.5% of the dutiable value or selling value.

Title Deed Tax.   Title deed tax is levied on the transfer of title of real property. It is payable by the buyer when ownership is transferred. The tax rate is 7.5% on property transferred through sale, gift, or occupancy, 5% if transferred through dien (the right to possess and use real property of another person by paying a price), and 2.5% if transferred through exchange or partition.

Estate Tax.   The estate within and without Taiwan of a regular resident (an individual either having a residence in Taiwan, or having no residence but a lodging in Taiwan and having lived in Taiwan for more than 365 days in the aggregate during the two years prior to his death) and the estate within Taiwan of a non-regular resident are subject to an estate tax at progressive rates ranging from 2% to 60%. The tax is paid by the heir.

Gift Tax.   A transfer of property within or without Taiwan by a regular resident and a transfer of property within Taiwan by a non-regular resident are subject to gift tax at progressive rates ranging from 4% to 60%. The tax is paid by the donor.

COMPUTATION OF TAXABLE INCOME

26. Capital Gains

The income tax law does not provide for special treatment of capital gains and losses. Any such gain is taxed at the ordinary income tax rates. Gains on land transactions are exempt. Losses thereon are not deductible. Gain from transactions in property is measured by the difference between the recorded value of the property and the value received, after deducting the incidental expenses. In addition, the appreciation or revaluation of depreciable fixed assets is exempt. Stock dividends received from a capital surplus account are exempt but are subject to income tax based on the selling price at disposal.

27. Depreciation and Depletion

All fixed assets (except land) used in a business are depreciable under one of three methods: straight-line, fixed-percentage-on-declining-balance, or working-hour. The service lives and residual values of assets are prescribed by the Government and must be used in computing depreciation.

28. Treatment of Dividends

Taiwan companies are required to withhold 15% tax, which is creditable, from both cash and stock dividends declared out of earnings.

Investment income earned by a company from another company which is not exempt from corporation income tax may be exempt from income tax to the extent of 80% of such income.

If a productive enterprise issues new stock from its undistributed earnings for qualified reinvestment purposes, the shareholders receiving the stock will not be taxed thereon until they dispose of the stock.

If undistributed earnings exceed 50% (100% for all productive enterprises or 200% for strategic industries and government-approved important industries) of paid-in capital, capital must be increased or dividends distributed, otherwise each shareholder will be assessed dividends tax applicable to his share of all undistributed earnings. Alternatively, the company may choose to pay a 10% corporation income tax on the excess earnings to avoid imposition of the imputed dividend income tax on shareholders.

29. Loss Carryovers

Carryover of net operating losses for five years may be allowed if a company's income tax return is examined and certified by a certified public accountant, or if the company maintains complete and adequate accounting books and records and has received approval from the tax office to use a blue form income tax return.

30. Transactions between Related Parties

If the income, costs, expenses, or profit distributions of the related companies are determined to be out of line with ordinary business practices, and hence constitute a tax evasion, the tax office may report the case to the central government for adjustment of the income to reflect regular business practices. Penalties may be imposed where tax evasion can be proved.

31. Consolidation of Income

No group relief is provided in the income tax law. Each company of a group of related companies is treated as a separate entity and is required to file its own income tax return.

32. Tax Periods

The tax year for companies is the calendar year. Companies may, however, request a different fiscal year if there are special supporting circumstances.

33. Other Matters

Income Liable to Tax.   Companies incorporated in Taiwan are liable for corporation income tax on their income from worldwide sources. Branches of foreign corporations are liable for corporation income tax only on their Taiwan-source income.

Deductions for Taxes Other than Income Taxes.   In computing the liability for income tax, corporations may deduct stamp tax, land value tax, building tax, etc., which are related to the corporation's business.

Deductions for Bad Debts.   Deductions based on the reserve method are allowed for estimated bad debt losses on accounts and notes receivable. The reserve may not exceed 1% of the year-end outstanding accounts and notes receivable not secured by collateral.

Inventory Valuation.   For tax purposes, inventories may be valued at cost or market, whichever is lower. The valuation of inventory at lower of cost or market must be consistent. Cost may be determined by any one of the following methods: specific identification, first-in first-out, last-in first-out, weighted average, moving average, and simple average. If the last-in first-out method is used, the rule of the lower of cost or market cannot apply.

Employee Benefit Provisions.   A retirement pay reserve not exceeding 4% of the corporation's total salaries and wages paid during the year is deductible, if the governing retirement plan is approved by the tax office. Such 4% may be increased up to 8% if the retirement plan is funded and the maintenance of the fund is handled in accordance with the prescribed regulations. For enterprises governed by the Labor Standards Law, the 8% is increased to 15%. Actual retirement payments shall be made according to the retirement plan and charged to the retirement reserve or paid out of the retirement fund, which must be deposited with a bank specified by the government. Any excess of actual retirement payments over the accumulated retirement reserve or the retirement fund shall be charged to current expenses in the year the excess occurred. Other types of employee benefits are deductible only when payments have actually been made to employees.

RELATED CONSIDERATIONS

34. Incentives and Grants

The major incentive of tax holidays expired in 1990 with the expiration of the Statute for Encouragement of Investment. The following incentives and grants were extended under the Statute for Upgrading Industries, which expires June 30, 1998.

Accelerated Depreciation. A ''company limited by shares'' may elect to use accelerated depreciation on certain qualified fixed assets. Accelerated depreciation allows the total service life of fixed assets, as prescribed by the Income Tax Law, to be shortened by one-half on machinery and equipment of specifically designated industries.

Investment Tax Credit. Investment tax credit may be granted to a company limited by shares on its purchases of qualified pollution control equipment or technology and automation equipment. The investment tax credit is 5% to 20% of acquisition cost. The investment tax credit may be applied against the enterprise's income tax liability. Any unused credits may be carried forward for four years. The annual credit amount, except for the last carryforward year, is limited to 50% of the enterprise's income tax payable for the current year. Expiring tax credits in the last carryforward year may be used to the extent of income taxes payable.

Research and Development Tax Credit. Twenty percent of the funds used in research and development, professional personnel training, and creation of internationally acceptable brand(s) of product(s) may be taken as credit against the income tax payable for that year. Any unused credit may be carried forward for four tax years. However, the credit, except for last year, cannot exceed 50% of the income tax payable.

Important Technology Tax Credit. Twenty percent of the amount invested in important technology enterprises may be claimed as tax credit against income tax. The tax credit, however, may not exceed 50% of the income tax for that year. The unused credit may be carried forward for the next four tax years.

Export Encouragement. Export sales of a company may qualify for a zero rate under the VAT system; that is, VAT paid on purchases related to export sales is completely refundable.

Venture Capital Tax Credit. Twenty percent of the amount invested in venture capital enterprises may be claimed as tax credit against income tax. The tax credit, however, may not exceed 50% of the income tax for that year. The unused credit may be carried forward for the next four tax years.

Merger Encouragement. Profit-seeking enterprises specifically approved by the Ministry of Economic Affairs for merger, to promote efficient operation and management, may qualify for exemption from corporation income tax, stamp tax, and deed tax created by the merger. In addition, the land value increment tax resulting from transfer of land from the merger can be registered as tax payable until the title to the land is transferred again.

Incentive for Investment in Areas with Limited Natural Resources or with Slow Development. Twenty percent of the qualified investment can be taken as a credit against the income tax payable of that year. The unused credits may be carried forward for the next four years.

Other Incentives.

☐ Royalties received from certain qualified patent rights or copyrights on computer software are tax-exempt.

☐ Qualified outward investment in response to ROC government policy by a company may result in 20% of such investment to be claimed as ''a loss reserve from outward investment'' deductible from taxable income. If after three years, such losses have not occurred, the reserve must be reversed for tax purposes.

☐ Relocation of facilities to certain industrial zones may qualify for the lowest tax rate in determining the land value increment tax.

35. Exchange Controls

Effective July 15, 1987, the controls over foreign exchange transactions conducted in or with the ROC have been relaxed. Under the new rules, a qualified importer/exporter may remit out/in unlimited funds for the import/export of goods. An ROC national, a foreigner with an ROC alien resident certificate, a registered business entity, or a nonbusiness organization may remit out unlimited funds for noncommodity trade expenditures such as freight, insurance premiums, commission, agency fees, and royalty and technical service fees, and remit in unlimited funds for services provided. In addition, an ROC national, a foreigner with an ROC alien resident certificate, a registered business entity, or nonbusiness organization may remit out up to US$3,000,000 yearly for such other expenditures as repatriation of invested principal, remittance of profits, purchase of foreign real properties, purchase of corporate stocks and bonds, loans to foreign borrowers, and donations, and remit into the ROC up to US$3,000,000 a year for such purposes as borrowing from abroad or receiving gifts. Each outward remittance, however, should not exceed US$1,000,000.

36. Investment Restrictions on Nonresidents

Investment-Commission-approved companies may be wholly owned subsidiaries of their foreign parents, and their chairmen and vice chairmen of directors may waive domicile and nationality requirements imposed by the Company Law. They can also repatriate their invested capital and remit profits without any restriction.

After the liberalization in July 1987 of the foreign exchange regulations, foreigners whose investments were not approved by the Investment Commission are now permitted to repatriate their invested capital, if any, that exceeds the minimum required capital and to remit profits up to US$3,000,000 a year.

SELECTION OF BUSINESS ENTITY BY NONRESIDENTS

In the promotion of foreign investment, the Investment Commission puts major emphasis on productive enterprises (capital-intensive and technology-intensive industries). The following industries are prohibited and restricted by the Investment Commission.

□ Prohibited industries:
—Industries that may endanger public security
—Industries that are contrary to local custom
—Public utilities
—Industries that are by nature monopolies or are prohibited by law

□ Restricted industries:
—Industries that may cause high pollution
—Banking and insurance industries
—Broadcasting, newscasting, and publication industries
—Industries that are restricted by law

Foreigners may also set up a local subsidiary company not approved by the Investment Commission in the ROC. Such a subsidiary, if set up as a company limited by shares, is required to have at least seven shareholders, at least half of whom must be Chinese residing in Taiwan. Under the existing regulations, the foreign shareholders, although in the minority, may hold majority shares.

Foreign companies may also set up a branch in Taiwan. However, a branch is prohibited from engaging in some types of businesses such as restaurants, consigned processing, investment, travel agency, shipping agency, leasing, container terminal, construction, etc. The branch is required to pay a corporation income tax at the same rates as domestic corporations (see item 1), and its after-tax profit is generally not subject to any further tax, except for a branch (equivalent to the form of company limited by shares of Taiwan, set up through approval of the Investment Committee, engaged in productive types of activities) that is qualified for those tax benefits specified in the Statute for Encouragement of Investment. Such a branch is taxed the same as a subsidiary organized through approval of the Investment Committee.

Presently, sale of goods of the foreign head office directly to customers in Taiwan—not through its branch—will not be considered as sales of the branch and will not be subject to taxes. Services rendered in Taiwan by the foreign head office will be considered as the revenue of the branch and will be subject to taxes.

Generally, a foreigner who wants to establish a nonproductive type of operation in Taiwan will have better tax benefits if such an operation is set up in the form of a branch rather than a local subsidiary. One major advantage of forming a branch is that the net income of the branch is subject only to corporation income tax, whereas the net income of a subsidiary is first subject to corporation income tax and then to dividend withholding tax. Under the existing regulations, a local company (including the subsidiary of a foreign company) is required to either distribute or capitalize its earnings once such earnings have exceeded one-half (increased to 100% for a productive enterprise and 200% for a strategic industry or government-approved important industries) of the company's paid-up capital, and both cash and stock dividends are subject to withholding tax.

SPECIMEN TAX COMPUTATION

Information:

□ The corporation is resident in Taiwan. The computation is for the fiscal year ending December 31, 1991.

Computation:

Gross Profits		NT$2,000,000
Add		
Excess depreciation provision	150,000	
Excess bad debt allowance	80,000	
Excess retirement pay reserve	10,000	
Travelling expenses not adequately supported (1)	4,500	244,500
		2,244,500
Less		
Preoperating expenses (2)	5,000	5,000
Taxable income		NT$2,239,500

□ Income tax payable by a nonproductive corporation is NT$549,875 ((NT$100,000 × 15%) + (NT$2,139,500 × 25%)).

□ Income tax payable by a productive corporation not qualified for the income tax exemption is NT$559,875 (NT$2,239,500 × 25%). Since the highest marginal corporate income tax rate was reduced from 30% to 25% effective January 1, 1986, the 25% maximum rate for productive corporations is no longer significant. Thus income tax payable by a productive corporation not qualified for the income tax exemption is the same as the amount for a non-productive corporation. In this computation, the tax is NT$549,875.

□ No income tax is payable by a productive corporation entirely exempt from income tax.

□ A venture capital enterprise, a "large trading company," an important productive enterprise, or an important scientific enterprise designated by the government is eligible for rates not exceeding 20% of its taxable income.

Notes:

(1) Expenses must be adequately supported. For airfare, the supporting documents are the passenger's copy of air tickets or boarding certificates issued by the airline company.

(2) Preoperating expenses must be amortized over five years.

TANZANIA

INCOME TAXES ON CORPORATIONS

1. Rates

The income tax rate on company profits is 45%.

2. Local Income Taxes

None.

3. Capital Gains Tax

A capital gains tax is imposed on the profit on sale of any interest in real property (see item 11).

4. Branch Profits Taxes

Branches (permanent establishments) of nonresident companies are taxed at the rate of 50%, unless limited by a double taxation agreement.

5. Foreign Tax Reliefs

Income properly derived from outside East Africa (Kenya, Tanzania and Uganda) is not liable to tax in Tanzania, whether remitted or not. Under the Tanzania Income Tax Act, 1973, there are provisions for relief in respect of tax charged also in Kenya or Uganda; in addition, there are the usual provisions for double taxation treaty relief.

INCOME TAXES ON INDIVIDUALS

9. Rates

Tax is charged on total income on a monthly basis. For an individual whose income is not solely derived from employment, the tax is calculated by dividing his annual income by 12, determining the tax on that income from the monthly tax rates, and multiplying this tax by 12. The monthly tax rates are as follows:

T-13

| Monthly Income | | Tax on | Percentage |
Over	Not Over	Lower Amount	on Excess
Shs. 3,250	Shs. 3,500	Shs. 0	7.5%
3,500	5,000	18.75	10.0
5,000	7,500	168.75	15.0
7,500	10,000	543.75	17.5
10,000	12,500	981.25	20.0
12,500	15,000	1,481.50	22.0
15,000	17,500	2,043.75	25.0
17,500	20,000	2,668.75	27.5
20,000	22,500	3,356.25	30.0
22,500	25,000	4,106.25	35.0
25,000		4,981.25	40.0

Personal allowances are Shs. 100 per month for a married taxpayer and Shs. 10 for each child to a maximum of four children. The insurance relief is 5% of a person's monthly salary or Shs. 400, whichever is the lesser. There is no single person's allowance. The relief is afforded against tax payable rather than gross income.

Expatriate Employees.   An employee on an expatriate contract is granted a tax-free allowance when calculating his monthly tax liability under P.A.Y.E. This allowance is only granted to an employee whose contract stipulates the payment of an inducement allowance in addition to his basic salary and whom the Bank of Tanzania allows to remit part of his salary overseas each month. The allowance is the lesser of the inducement allowance and Shs. 2,400 per month. Before such a tax-free allowance is granted, the recipient must register with the Treasury as an approved expatriate employee.

10.   Local Income Taxes
None.

11.   Capital Gains Taxes
Capital gains tax is imposed on the gain from the sale of any interest in real property.

| Amount of Gain | | Tax on | Rate |
Over	Not Over	Lower Amount	of Tax
Shs. 100,000	Shs. 500,000	Shs. 0	20%
500,000	1,000,000	80,000	25
1,000,000		205,000	30

The sale of any interest in real property must be at arm's length. The Commissioner of Income Taxes has a first option to buy the property from the seller if he feels that the transaction is not at arm's length.

12. Foreign Tax Reliefs

In principle these are the same as for corporations (see item 5), and apply only to residents.

13. Tax Period

The tax year is the calendar year. Business income may be based on the accounting year ended within the calendar year.

INCOME TAXES ON NONRESIDENTS

15. Liability to Tax

See item 9 with respect to expatriate employees.

16. Rates

Individual income tax rates are the same for nonresidents as for residents.

17. Withholding Tax Rates

Withholding taxes are levied on the following payments:

	Nonresident	Resident
Management or professional fees	30.0%	—
Royalties	30.0	—
Rents, etc.	40.0	—
Dividends	10.0	10.0%
Interest	20.0	12.5
Pension or retirement annuities	15.0	—
Insurance commission	7.5	7.5

If a nonresident recipient of a pension or retirement annuity resides in a country that has double taxation relief with Tanzania, the tax rate is 12.5%.

19. Tax Treaties

Tanzania has tax treaties with Denmark, India, Italy, Kenya, Sweden, Uganda, and Zambia.

OTHER SIGNIFICANT TAXES

21. Sales (Value Added)

A sales tax is imposed on local manufactures and most imports. The rate varies according to the item.

23. Taxes on Payrolls (Social Security)

National Provident Fund contributions are payable monthly in respect of most employment at the rate of 10% by both employer and employee.

25. Other Taxes

Capital Taxes. None.

Excise Duty. Reintroduced beginning July, 1989. The duty is imposed on both local products and imports of luxuries. The basis of the tax is both ad-valorem and specific.

Training Levy. A levy of 10% is payable on the total emoluments of noncitizen employees.

Payroll Levy. A levy of 4% is payable every month on the gross salary (including benefits-in-kind) paid to all employees (whether citizens or noncitizens).

Transport Levy. A 2% levy is deductible from all hire charges for the transport of goods by road except for goods in the course of export from Tanzania. This levy is payable monthly to the Tax Department. An individual may not deduct this levy unless the hire charges exceed Shs. 10,000.

Windfall Tax. A windfall profits tax is payable on the importation and sale of petroleum products. The tax is 100% of the windfall profit.

Car Benefit Tax. Employers, whether commercial companies or parastatals who purchase motor-vehicles (saloon cars, pick up or station wagon) weighing up to two tons, are liable to a car benefit tax amounting to Shs. 80,000 per car per annum.

Withholding Tax on Government Contractors and Tenderers. A levy of 2% is payable on the gross fees, charges, or like consideration payable by the Government, government agency, local government, or parastatal organization to any contractor or tenderer for the supply of goods or services.

Housing Fund. Employers must set aside and utilize 20% of after-tax profits for building houses for employees.

Single Trading Transaction Tax. A 30% tax on 75% of the gross proceeds (CIF value of imports including import duty and sales tax) is payable with effect from April 8, 1987. A single trading transaction is defined as "a transaction or series of transactions not carried out in a regular trading establishment."

COMPUTATION OF TAXABLE INCOME

26. Capital Gains

The capital gain is the difference between the sale proceeds and the capital cost of such interest or, where tax allowances are claimed, on the written-down tax value as adjusted for inflation and devaluation (see item 11).

27. Depreciation and Depletion

Accounting depreciation is ignored for tax purposes. Instead, there is a system of annual capital allowances which are calculated on the reducing-balance method (no alternative). Rates are 37.5% for heavy earth-moving equipment, tractors, trucks, etc.; 25% for cars, pickups, and aircraft; and 12.5% for all other machinery and plant, including ships. These allowances are deductible in computing taxable income. There are no initial allowances, but a one-time investment deduction of 20% in addition to normal allowances is granted on industrial buildings, installed machinery, and agricultural or livestock development farms. Industrial buildings as defined (similar to U.K.) qualify for 4% "straight-line" annual allowance. Farm works (as defined) qualify for a 20% straight-line annual allowance. There are no balancing allowances or charges on the cessation of trade, except for plant, machinery, cars, etc.

28. Treatment of Dividends

A withholding tax on dividends of 10% is deducted at the source for residents and for nonresidents. In the case of intercompany dividends, the recipient is exempt if it owns at least 25% of the voting capital of the paying company; otherwise, it pays 50% on the receipt. In a voluntary liquidation, all proceeds in excess of paid-up capital are treated as dividends. Bonus issues of debentures or redeemable preference shares are treated as dividends.

29. Loss Carryovers

Losses can be carried forward for set off against future profits.

30. Transactions between Related Parties

Sales of capital assets, where tax allowances are involved, between companies under common control are dealt with by offering an election to transfer over a written down tax value, instead of adopting open market value. There are sections in the Act to prevent avoidance in dealings between resident and nonresident concerns, and special provisions to deal with transfers of assets at the end of a lease-hire agreement.

31. Consolidation of Income

Taxpayers, individuals and companies resident in Tanzania, are liable to tax on all income accrued in or derived from East Africa (foreign income is exempt). All taxable income from whatever source is aggregated into total income, and only one assessment is issued, on an "actual" basis.

32. Tax Periods

The term "year of income" means a calendar year. Business income may be based on the accounting year ended within the year of income. There is no preceding year basis. This applies to both individuals and companies.

33. Other Matters

Bank Deposit Interest. Beginning July 1, 1990, the first Shs. 250,000 of bank deposit interest is exempt from tax.

RELATED CONSIDERATIONS

34. Incentives and Grants

Half of the gratuity or commuted pensions gratuity payable to any resident individual is exempt from taxation as well as non-East African income. Otherwise, the only exemptions granted are by Ministerial action after special negotiations; e.g., statutory corporations and certain foreign interest. The only special allowance is that referred to in item 27.

For the first four years, a company's taxable income derived from the mining of specified minerals is taxed at only 22.5% so that the rate reverts to 50% from the fifth year. Other than this and the special withholding tax rates, there are no special tax rates or concessions.

Investment Promotion Policy. Under the new National Investment Promotion Policy, Act No. 10 of 1990, both foreign and local private investors are highly encouraged. Approved investments in priority areas enjoy various incentives under the new Act: five-year tax holiday, exemption from indirect taxes, generous foreign exchange retention scheme, repatriation of profits, etc. An Investment Promotion Centre has been established to approve all applications for investment with a minimum bureaucracy.

35. Exchange Controls

All transactions between residents of Tanzania and nonresidents, and transactions by residents related to foreign currencies and to assets situated outside of Tanzania, require the approval of the Bank of Tanzania. Approval is based on policy guidelines laid down from time to time by the Ministry of Finance. It is important to note that Government policy in this area is constantly changing and investors should obtain detailed advice before entering into transactions that may involve exchange control rules. Currently, resident corporations that are wholly owned or controlled by a foreign parent company may remit capital and income to their parent companies only with the approval of the Bank of Tanzania. Nonresident individuals may remit funds to Tanzania for permanent capital investment with approval from the Bank of Tanzania. Similar approval is required to borrow funds within Tanzania.

36. Investment Restrictions on Nonresidents

Restrictions are imposed on entities owned by foreigners, whether a branch of a foreign company or a locally incorporated subsidiary of a foreign company. The restrictions concern the appointment of directors, the allotment of shares and, generally, all issues that will involve, at some stage, the transfer of funds from Tanzania to a foreign country.

SELECTION OF BUSINESS ENTITY BY NONRESIDENTS

Nonresident investors can operate in Tanzania either through a branch or by forming a local company. If a branch is used, branch profits are taxable at 55%, and no additional tax is levied on the remittance of branch profits, which must be approved by the Bank of Tanzania. Foreign expenses charged to the branch are not deductible for tax purposes. No withholding tax applies on such foreign expense charges.

The locally registered company is the common entity for foreign investors. The company pays corporation tax at 50%, and the company is not entitled to dividend rebate on its dividend income. Dividends paid by the company are subject to withholding tax of 10%. Remittance of both profits and dividends requires Bank of Tanzania approval.

SPECIMEN TAX COMPUTATION

Information:

□ The operating profit for the year is:

Trading results in Tanzania	Shs.	600,000
Trading results in Kenya and Uganda (taxed in country from which derived)		100,000
Dividend income from Kenya and Uganda		100,000
Dividend income from the United Kingdom		100,000
Capital profit on sale of long-term investment in shares		100,000
	Shs.	1,000,000

□ The Tanzanian trading results were arrived at after charges of:

Accounts depreciation	300,000
Transfer to provisions for employee benefits	200,000

□ Allowable tax depreciation for the year was Shs. 200,000, and payments debited to the provisions for employee benefits were Shs. 100,000. During the year, plant costing Shs. 500,000 was installed in an industrial building costing Shs. 100,000.

Computation:

	Resident Company (Shs.)		Branch (Shs.)	
Operating profit per accounts		1,000,000		1,000,000
Add				
Accounts depreciation	300,000		300,000	
Transfer to provision for employee benefits	200,000	500,000	200,000	500,000
		1,500,000		1,500,000
Less				
Tax depreciation allowed	200,000		200,000	
Actual payments debited to provision for employee benefits	100,000		100,000	
Industrial building deduction	4,000		4,000	
Investment deduction	120,000		120,000	
Capital profit			100,000	
Gross dividends from Kenya and Uganda			100,000	
Gross dividends from U.K. (exempt)	100,000		100,000	
Trading results in Kenya and Uganda	——	624,000	100,000	824,000
Taxable income		876,000		676,000
Corporation tax (45%, 50%)		394,200		338,000
Less				
Corporation tax borne on trading results in Kenya and Uganda		50,000		—
Tax payable		344,200		338,000

THAILAND

INCOME TAXES ON CORPORATIONS

1. Rates

The tax rate is 30% for companies listed on the Securities Exchange of Thailand and 35% for other companies, effective for the account period beginning on or after January 1, 1986. The term "corporation" means a company or juristic limited partnership incorporated under Thai laws and under foreign law, including: (a) commercial and profitable businesses operated by a foreign government, an agency of a foreign government, or other juristic persons set up under foreign law; (b) joint ventures (i.e., joint commercial and profitable businesses engaged in by companies, by a company and juristic partnership, a juristic partnership and a juristic partnership, or by a company and/or juristic partnership and natural person, a body of non-juristic persons, ordinary partnership or other juristic persons); (c) foundations or societies with income other than from their normal activities (the tax rate for foundations and societies is 10% of gross receipts, exclusive of such income as membership registration fees and donations or gifts, or 2% of gross receipts, exclusive of such income as membership registration fees and donations or gifts, if the income is from business, commerce, agriculture, industry, or transport); and (d) juristic persons prescribed by the Director-General under the approval of the minister and published in the Government Gazette.

2. Local Income Taxes

None.

3. Capital Gains Taxes

Capital gains are taxed as ordinary income.

4. Branch Profits Taxes

Branch profits are taxed at the rates specified in item 1. If branch profits are remitted abroad, tax at the rate of 20% is levied on top of the corporate income taxes.

5. Foreign Tax Reliefs

Taxes, including income taxes, paid to foreign countries are deductible expenses. Any gain on depreciable property is taxed as ordinary income. Stock dividends are taxed as ordinary income.

7. Payment of Taxes

Every juristic company or partnership (account period) must pay tax twice yearly. Interim tax payments are due within two months from the end of the first six-month period. The taxpayer must estimate total net profits or losses for the year and, in the case of profits, pay 50% of the tax so computed. This does not apply to a juristic company or partnership where the first or last accounting period is for less than 12 months. The filing of the annual returns and payment of tax on business income and income from international transport must be made within 150 days from the end of the accounting period. Any fiscal year may be selected.

INCOME TAXES ON INDIVIDUALS

9. Rates

Income is taxed at each of the following rates:

Taxable Income		Tax on Lower Amount	Percentage on Excess
Over	Not Over		
Bht 0	Bht 50,000	Bht 0	5%
50,000	200,000	2,500	10
200,000	500,000	17,500	20
500,000	1,000,000	77,500	30
1,000,000	2,000,000	227,500	40
2,000,000		627,500	50

In computing income the following deductible expenses are allowed:

☐ Income from Employment and Services Rendered. Deduction of 40% to a maximum of Bht 60,000.

☐ Income from Dividends, Interest, and Royalties. No deduction allowed, except for income from a copyright which is entitled to a deductible expense of 20%, up to a maximum of Bht 20,000.

☐ Income from the Rental of Property, Liberal Professions, Contracting, and Business and Industry. The standard deduction ranges from 10% to 85% in lieu of which the taxpayer may elect to itemize expenses.

In addition, taxpayers may deduct the following allowances:

□ Personal Allowances.

For taxpayer	Bht 20,000
For taxpayer's spouse	Bht 20,000
For each child	Bht 10,000
Additional for each child studying in Thailand	Bht 2,000

□ Life Insurance Premium Allowance. Up to Bht 10,000 for the premium of a life insurance policy whose term is 10 years or more and which was issued by an insurer carrying on business in Thailand.

□ Dividend Allowance. Up to Bht 10,000 and 30% of dividends from Bht 10,001 to Bht 400,000 received from a mutual fund or financial institution established under an ad hoc law for the purpose of providing loans to promote agriculture, commerce or industry. Dividends from companies registered under Thai laws will receive 30% tax credits in lieu of an allowance.

□ Provident Fund Contribution Allowance. Up to Bht 10,000 for contributions made by the employee to the Provident fund under the Revenue Code.

□ Social Security Allowance. Employee contributions to the social security fund are tax-free equal to the amount contributed.

□ Interest Allowance. Up to Bht 10,000 for interest paid on loans from banks, other financial institutions, life insurance companies, cooperatives, or employers used to purchase, hire-purchase, or construct a residential building by mortgaging them as a loan guarantee.

□ Charity Allowance. Up to 10% of the adjusted (gross) income minus deductible expenses and other allowances.

10. Local Income Taxes
None.

11. Capital Gains Taxes
None.

12. Foreign Tax Reliefs
No specific reliefs are prescribed in the Revenue Code. However, a Thai resident who in the course of the preceding year derived assessable income from a post or office held, or business carried on, abroad, or from a property situated abroad shall, upon bringing such assessable income into Thailand, pay tax thereon.

13. Tax Period
The calendar year is the tax period for individuals. Normally, individual income tax is payable once on March 31 of the following year. Individuals with the following

types of income must also pay tax in September on their income from January through June:

- [ ] Income from leasing property.
- [ ] Income from law, medicine, engineering, architecture, accounting, and the fine arts.
- [ ] Income from a contract of work where the contractor provides essential materials as well as tools.
- [ ] Income from businesses and commerce.

14. Other Matters

Exemptions from Taxes. The following are tax-exempt:

- [ ] Proceeds from the sale of movable property acquired by bequest or acquired without a view to trading or profits.
- [ ] Maintenance income derived under normal obligation, corpus of a legacy or inheritance, or gifts made in a ceremony or on occasion in accordance with established custom.
- [ ] Awards for educational or scientific research.

INCOME TAXES ON NONRESIDENTS

15. Liability to Tax

Nonresidents are not subject to income tax on income derived from foreign sources. For tax purposes, a nonresident is a person who resides in Thailand for less than 180 days.

16. Rates

On income derived from Thai sources, the tax rates in item 9 apply.

17. Withholding Tax Rates

Payments to foreign corporations are subject to the following withholding taxes:

- [ ] Fees. 25% after deducting 20% (up to Bht 20,000).
- [ ] Dividends, Interest, and Royalties. 20% for dividends remitted abroad. However, interest paid to a foreign corporation engaged in banking, insurance, or a similar financial business is subject to a 10% withholding tax.
- [ ] Lease of Property. 25% after a deduction of 10%. The rate is 1% for assessable income from the lease of oceangoing vessels transporting international goods, if the lease was approved under the law Promotion of Commercial Navy and the lease payments are between June 1, 1986 and September 30, 1991.
- [ ] Liberal Professions. 25% after a deduction of 40%.

	Dividends	Interest	Royalties
Nontreaty countries	25%(1)	25%(2)	25%
Treaty countries:			
Australia	15(3)	25(2)	15
Austria	20(4b)	25(2)	15
	15(4a)		
Belgium	20(5)	25(2)	15(6)
	15(3)		
Canada	20(4b)	25(2)	15(7)
	15(4a)		
China	15(8)	25(2)	15
	20(1)		
Denmark	20(8)	25	15
Finland	20(4b)	25(2)	15
	15(4a)		
France	20(4b)	25(9)	15(6)
	15(4a)		
Germany	20(5)	25(10)	15
	15(3)		
India	25(1)	25(2)	15
	15(11)		
Indonesia	25(12)	25(2)	15(13)
Italy	20(5)	25(10)	15(6)
	15(3)		
Japan	20(14)	25(2)	15(15)
	15(16)		
Korea	20(5)	25(2)	15
	15(11)		
Malaysia	20(17b)	25(2)	15
	15(17a)		
Netherlands	25(18)	25(2)	15(6)
Norway	20(8)	25	15
Pakistan	25(19)	25(2)	20(13)
Philippines	20(17b)	25(2)	25(20)
	15(17a)		
Poland	20(8)	25(2)	15(6)
Singapore	20(8)	25(2)	15
Sweden	20(8)	25	15
United Kingdom	20(5)	25(2)	15(6)
	15(3)		

Notes:

(1) 20% according to Royal Decree No. 95 issued under the Revenue Code in 1980.

(2) 10% rate on interest paid to financial institutions and insurance companies.

(3)   If the payor company engages in an industrial undertaking and the recipient company owns at least 25% of the voting shares of the company paying the dividends.

(4)   A company, excluding a partnership, which holds directly at least 25% of the capital of the Thai company:
   (a)   If the Thai company paying the dividend engages in an industrial undertaking; or
   (b)   In other cases.

(5)   If the payor company engages in an industrial undertaking or the recipient company owns at least 25% of the voting shares of the company paying the dividends.

(6)   5% on literary, artistic, or scientific copyrights.

(7)   5% on copyright and other like payments with respect to the production or reproduction of any literary, dramatic, musical, or artistic work (but not including royalties with respect to motion picture films and works on film or videotape for use in connection with television).

(8)   A company that holds at least 25% of the shares that has, under the circumstances, full voting rights.

(9)   3% on loans or credits granted for four years or more with the participation of a financing public institution to a statutory body or to an enterprise of Thailand in relation to the sale of any equipment or to the survey, installation, or supply of industrial, commercial, or scientific premises and of public works. 10% on interest paid to any financial institution.

(10)   10% on interest paid to any financial institution and insurance company and the payor of interest engages in an industrial undertaking.

(11)   If the company paying the dividends engages in an industrial undertaking and the recipient of the dividend owns at least 10% of the voting stock of the payor company.

(12)   20% rate similar to the nontreaty countries and 15% on dividends paid by a company engaging in an industrial undertaking, and the recipient company, excluding a partnership, owns at least 25% of the voting shares of the company paying dividends.

(13)   10% on literary, artistic, or scientific copyrights.

(14)   20% if the payor of dividends engages in an industrial undertaking.

(15)   Excluding any royalty, rental, and other amount paid with respect to a motion picture film and the operation of a mine, quarry, or any other place of natural resource extraction.

(16)   15% for payments to the parent corporation of the payor company.

(17)   A company which holds not less than 15% of the voting shares of the payor company:
   (a)   If the company paying the dividends engages in an industrial undertaking, or
   (b)   In all other cases.

(18)   10% if the recipient company owns at least 25% of the shares of the paying company. If the tax rate on company profits from which dividends are dis-

tributed is not more than 30%, then the dividend rate withheld may be 15%, but it is 20% in other cases, if the paying company is an industrial undertaking. If the tax rate on company profits is more than 30% but not more than 40%, the tax is 15% if the paying company is an industrial undertaking.

(19) 20% rate similar to the nontreaty countries and 15% if the company holds directly at least 25% of the capital of the payor company which is engaged in an industrial undertaking.

(20) 15% on royalties paid by an enterprise promoted by the Board of Investments of Thailand or with respect to cinema films or tapes for television or broadcasting.

19. Tax Treaties
See item 17.

OTHER SIGNIFICANT TAXES

21. Sales (Value Added)
Thailand levies a business tax on the gross receipts of the categories of businesses listed below:

Categories of Business	Tax Rate	Person Liable
Sales of goods	0.1% to 50%	Importer or manufacturer
Rice milling	3.5	Operator
Saw milling	4.0	Operator
Sales of securities*	0.1	Seller
Hire or work	3 to 10	Contractor
Leasing of movable property	2.5 to 3	Lessor
Warehousing	2.5	Operator
Hotels, restaurants, and night clubs	2 to 15	Operator
International transport		
Passenger	2.0	Operator
Cargo	0.5	Operator
Brokerages and agencies	5.5	Broker, agent, or performer of service
Sales of immovable properties as a business or profit	3.5	Seller
Banking	3 to 15	Operator
Insurances	2.5 to 3	Insurer
Entertainment	15 to 20	Operator

* Temporary exemption from January 1, 1991 until December 31, 1992.

A surtax of 10% of the business tax is levied as a municipal tax. Every "trader," which means any person carrying on a business in Thailand in one of the listed categories, must keep records of all gross receipts and must file business tax returns by the 15th of each month. The business tax on sale of goods is collected, with few exceptions, from importers and manufacturers. Retailers generally are not liable for the tax. The liberal professions, if practiced by individuals, are not included in the category "hire of work" and are exempt from the tax. Business tax is generally collected by the Revenue Department. For imported goods, the tax is collected by the Customs Department at the time import duty is paid and the tax is based on the total of the CIF price plus import duty and standard profit.

22. Inheritance and Gift Taxes

Gifts, other than those made in ceremonial or other occasions in accordance with established custom, are taxed as ordinary income. There is no tax on estates in Thailand.

23. Taxes on Payrolls (Social Security)

Effective March 1, 1991, for employers having 20 or more employees, the employees and the employer each contribute a monthly sum to the Social Security Fund at the rate of 1.5% of the employees' wages. The maximum wage for the contribution computation is Baht 500 per day or Baht 15,000 per month. The employee and employer contributions are to be remitted to the Social Security Fund by the employers within 15 days following the month in which wages were paid to employees.

24. Taxes on Natural Resources

A tax is levied on certain natural resources, such as swallow nests, fisheries, teak woods, mines and petroleum. The tax is paid by the holder of the concession for exploitation of such resources. Various Government agencies, such as the Revenue Department, Department of Fisheries, Department of Forestry, and Department of Mineral Resources are responsible for tax collections.

Petroleum Income Tax.   This tax is imposed upon a company as defined by the Petroleum Act B.E. 2514 (a company holding a petroleum concession from the Ministry of Industry or having a joint interest therein; or one purchasing crude oil, all of which is intended for export, from such a company). The tax rate is 50% of net profits.

25. Other Taxes

Land and Property.   There are two kinds of property taxes:

☐ Local Development Tax. This tax is imposed upon owners of land and persons in possession of land of a value ranging from 50 Stangs to Bht 400 per rai (about one-half acre) as prescribed in the tax schedule of the local Development Tax Act B.E. 2508. The tax is levied annually.

□ House and Land Tax. This tax is imposed upon the owner of a house, building, and land. The rate is 12.5% of the assessed annual lease value of the property.

□ Excise Taxes. Excise taxes are levied on certain goods, such as liquor, beer, soft drinks, matches, tobacco, snuff, cement, and petroleum products. The Excise Department is the collecting agency.

□ Customs Duty. Duties are imposed mainly on imported goods but also on some exports. Goods are classified into some 2,000 items. Both specific and ad valorem rates are prescribed. The majority of items fall within the range of 5% to 100%. The export tariff comprises only eight items: rice, metal scraps, raw hides, rubber, wood, raw silk, etc.

□ Signboard Tax. This tax is levied on signboards showing the name, symbol, or mark of a business and on advertisements, whether in the form of letters, pictures, sculptures or anything else. The rates specified in the Signboard Tax Act B.E. 2510 are calculated on the basis of the signboard's size and range from 1 to Bht 20 per 500 square centimeters.

COMPUTATION OF TAXABLE INCOME

26. Capital Gains

Capital gains are regarded as ordinary corporate income.

27. Depreciation and Depletion

Depreciation is allowed to be deducted from corporate income at the annual rates that follow. Depletion of natural resources through exhaustion is not deductible.

Depreciation Allowable	Rate
Buildings	
Durable	5%
Temporary	100
Cost of acquisition of depletable	
natural resources	5
Cost of acquisition of lease rights	
Indefinite duration	10
Defined duration	100 (1)
Cost of acquisition of patent,	
formula, goodwill, and copyright	
Unlimited period	10

Depreciation Allowable	Rate
Limited period of use	100% (2)
Any depreciable properties not mentioned above (excluding land and stock-in-trade)	20

Notes:

(1)   Over lease (and renewal) period.

(2)   Over period of use.

Either straight-line or an accelerating method of depreciation is allowed.

28.   Treatment of Dividends

No specific provision of law requires a company to declare dividends annually. Dividends can be accrued in the company's books of account for an indefinite period. If dividends are paid to a Thai resident shareholder amounting to Bht 10,000 or more, although the dividends are paid in installments and each payment does not exceed Bht 10,000, the company shall withhold income tax at the rates specified in item 9. Dividends remitted abroad to companies not carrying on business in Thailand are subject to withholding tax of 20%.

However, a Thai-incorporated company can exclude from taxable profits 50% of dividends received from other Thai-incorporated mutual funds and certain Thai-organized finance companies created to promote agricultural, commercial, and industrial activities. If the company is registered with the Securities Exchange of Thailand, it can exclude from taxable profits 100% of the dividends. The above exclusions apply if the company has income in the form of dividends not exceeding 15% of its gross income and investments are held for a certain period of time.

29.   Loss Carryovers

Losses may be carried forward for five years. No carryback of losses is permitted.

30.   Transactions between Related Parties

No specific provision is prescribed in the Revenue Code but certain transactions between related parties may receive special treatment. The Revenue Department reserves the right to arbitrarily assess the transfer price of imported goods.

31.   Consolidation of Income

No specific provision is prescribed in the Revenue Code. Tax must be computed for each separate entity.

32.   Tax Periods

Although the fiscal period is normally 12 months, the fiscal period of a newly incorporated company or a liquidating company may be for less than a 12-month period.

RELATED CONSIDERATIONS

34. Incentives and Grants

Companies qualifying under the Investment Promotion Act B.E. 2520 may be exempted from import duties and/or business taxes on machinery required to be imported for their business. Additionally, they may be exempted from corporation income tax on net profits for from three to eight fiscal years.

35. Exchange Controls

There are no restrictions on the importation of currency and negotiable instruments into Thailand. However, the foreign currency imported must be sold to a commercial bank, or deposited into a foreign currency account with a commercial bank in Thailand, within 15 days of the date of receipt.

The repatriation of capital, loans, profits, and interest can be made freely.

The commercial bank can freely sell foreign currency in relation to goods and services without limitation.

36. Investment Restrictions on Nonresidents

Two laws restrict an alien from investing and/or working in Thailand. These are:

□ Alien Business Law (N.E.C. Announcement No. 281). Under this law, an "alien" means a natural person or juristic person without Thai nationality. Alien businesses falling into Categories A, B or C are controlled by law. Category A comprises 12 types of businesses, including rice farming, salt mining, land trade, and accounting and legal services. Category B comprises 37 types of businesses, including timber, fishing, rice milling, retailing (with some exceptions), travel agency, and domestic transport. Category C comprises 14 types of businesses, including domestic wholesaling (with some exceptions), all exporting, manufacturing of animal feed, and mining. Generally, Category A and B businesses are closed to aliens. Category C businesses are open provided that a permit is obtained from the Department of Commercial Registration.

□ Alien Occupation Law (The Alien Work Permit Act 1978). Under this law, all aliens working in Thailand must obtain work permits from the Labor Department (with the exception of certain persons, such as diplomatic and consular personnel, etc.). Certain occupations are closed to aliens. Such occupations are divided into 39 types and include accounting and legal services, shoemaking, wood carving, etc.

SELECTION OF BUSINESS ENTITY BY NONRESIDENTS

The principal business entities are a partnership, limited private company, public company, joint venture, and branch of a company.

☐ Partnership. There are three types of partnerships: unregistered ordinary partnerships, registered ordinary partnerships, and limited partnerships. The liabilities for each type are different but the rules governing them are the same.

☐ Private Limited Company. Their characteristics are similar to those in U.K. law in that they are registered with a Memorandum and Articles of Associations and liability is limited to the value of shares.

☐ Public Company. A public company is one which has 100 or more shareholders. There are restrictions on the amount of shares that can be owned by individual and corporate investors.

☐ Joint Venture. A joint venture is when two or more persons join together to conduct business. It is not recognized under the Civil and Commercial Code although it is recognized by the Petroleum Act and Revenue Code.

☐ Branch of a Foreign Company. A branch office is treated as the same legal entity as its head office. Thailand does not recognize representative offices as corporate entities.

The most common corporate entities are the private limited company and the branch. The advantages of a company are that, subject to the conditions of the Alien Business Law, it can be quickly formed and has limited liability. It is regarded for taxation purposes as a separate legal entity and its shareholders are not regarded as doing business in Thailand solely by virtue of their equity holdings.

At present, the main disadvantage for a foreign branch is that the head office is subject to Thai law on business conducted in Thailand. Because the head office and branch are viewed as one and the same legal entity, certain transactions between the head office and its branch are subject to Thai tax law; for example, the recovery of head office expenses against the branch's income would generally be disallowed.

There is a tax advantage for a branch with respect to the remittance of profits. A company is required to withhold 20% on all foreign dividends, whereas a branch applies this 20% tax to the net amount remitted, which results in an effective tax rate of 16.67%.

TRINIDAD AND TOBAGO

INCOME TAXES ON CORPORATIONS

1. Rates

The standard corporate tax rate for resident and nonresident corporations is 40%. In addition, companies whose profits are assessed to tax under the Petroleum Taxes Act are charged to unemployment levy of 5% and national recovery impost. The national recovery impost rates are:

Taxable Profits	Tax Rate
Less than TT$5,000,000	1%
TT$5,000,000—TT$15,000,000	2%
Over TT$15,000,000	3%

The tax rate is 15% on the long-term insurance business of an insurance company, except, if the profits are transferred to the shareholder's account, a corresponding amount of the profits of the accounting period ending in the year of income in which the transfer is made is chargeable at the rate of 40%.

A tax credit equal to 15% of the chargeable profits is granted to the following companies:

☐ An approved small company.

☐ An approved company carrying on business in a regional development area.

☐ An approved activity company.

In the case of an approved company carrying on business in a regional development area and of an approved activity company, the tax credit is granted for a period of five years, from January 1 of the year in which the certificate of approval was issued.

2. Local Income Taxes

None.

3. Capital Gains Taxes

There are no capital gains taxes in Trinidad and Tobago. However, short-term capital gains are deemed to be income and are liable to tax. Such gains are defined as chargeable gains accruing on the disposal of an asset within 12 months of its acquisition or the reacquisition of an asset within 12 months of its disposal. Assets include options, debts and incorporeal property generally, currency other than that of Trinidad and Tobago, and any form of property created by the vendor or otherwise owned without being acquired.

Losses accruing on disposal of an asset which would be taxable as a short-term capital gain may be allowed against a short-term capital gain of the same year or, to the extent that it cannot be fully utilized, carried forward and set off against short-term capital gains of future years. Capital losses cannot be utilized to reduce income from any trade, business, profession, or vocation.

4. Branch Profits Taxes

Branches of foreign corporations are subject to corporation tax at the full rate on profits accruing in or derived from Trinidad and Tobago. The profit, less taxes, of a nonresident company carrying on trade or business through a branch or agency is deemed to be remitted in full and, therefore, is liable to withholding tax (see item 17) except to the extent that the profits have been reinvested in Trinidad, other than in the replacement of fixed assets.

5. Foreign Tax Reliefs

Residents of Trinidad and Tobago receiving income from foreign sources are entitled to a foreign tax credit under double taxation arrangements, reciprocal relief, or unilateral relief provisions. Where double taxation arrangements exist (see item 17), taxpayers resident in Trinidad and Tobago for the relevant year of assessment are entitled to a tax credit in Trinidad and Tobago for the tax payable in that other country on income arising there.

Unless a double taxation arrangement exists, unilateral relief is allowed to residents of Trinidad for income tax paid on income in the other country which is also subject to Trinidad and Tobago tax. For the purpose of allowing credit against corporation tax for dividends paid by a nonresident company to a Trinidad and Tobago company which controls not less than one-quarter of the voting power of that company, any foreign tax and Trinidad and Tobago income tax or corporation tax payable by the nonresident company on its profits is taken into account as if it were tax payable in the nonresident company's country.

6. Classification of Corporations

Corporations are classified for Trinidad and Tobago tax purposes as either resident or nonresident. A resident corporation is one whose central management and control is in Trinidad and Tobago. The distinction between resident and nonresident corporation is important in that resident corporations are subject to tax on their worldwide income whereas nonresident corporations are subject to tax only on their income directly or indirectly accruing in or derived from Trinidad and Tobago.

7. Payment of Taxes

Corporations are required to pay tax in four equal installments based on the estimate of taxable income made in the company's return for the preceding year. Installments are due by March 31, June 30, September 30, and December 31 in the year of income. Any remainder of tax is payable by April 30 of the following year.

8. Other Matters

Relief for Certain Companies. See item 1. For a company to obtain the relief, certain requirements must be observed before the Minister responsible for industry issues a certificate of approval.

INCOME TAXES ON INDIVIDUALS

9. Rates

Income tax is payable by residents of Trinidad and Tobago on all income wherever derived. Individuals who are resident but not domiciled in Trinidad and Tobago are taxable on all income derived from Trinidad and Tobago wherever received and on other income received in Trinidad and Tobago. The tax rates are as follows:

Taxable Income		Tax on	Percentage
Over	Not Over	Lower Amount	on Excess
TT$ 0	TT$12,000	TT$ 0	5%
12,000	20,000	600	15
20,000	40,000	1,800	30
40,000		7,800	35

A resident is entitled to claim certain tax credits against the amount of tax assessed. However, unused tax credits will not generate a tax refund.

10. Local Income Taxes

None.

11. Capital Gains Taxes

The information in item 3 also applies to individuals.

12. Foreign Tax Reliefs

The information in item 5 also applies to individuals.

13. Tax Period

The taxation year for individuals is the calendar year. However, a different fiscal period may be chosen for an unincorporated business carried on by the individual, in which case the individual's taxable income must include the income of the business for the 12-month accounting period ending within the year.

14. Other Matters

Tax Relief for Certain Investors. An individual ordinarily resident in Trinidad and Tobago is eligible to invest a maximum of TT$200,000 in approved business ventures and qualify for tax relief. The individual will be allowed to claim a rebate equal to his or her marginal rate of personal income tax applied to 50% of the amount so invested.

Health Surcharge Tax. The Finance Act 1987 imposed a tax called the Health Surcharge on employed and self-employed persons. The tax is not payable by individuals under age 16 or over age 60.

INCOME TAXES ON NONRESIDENTS

15. Liability to Tax

Where a nonresident individual is employed in Trinidad and Tobago or where a corporation carries on business in Trinidad and Tobago, the income accruing or derived from the activity is subject to tax. Tax is not payable on the external income of a person who is in Trinidad and Tobago for some temporary purpose and with no intention of establishing residence. A nonresident's income subject to tax includes income arising directly or indirectly through an agency or branch.

16. Rates

Nonresident individuals and corporations are taxed on their Trinidad and Tobago–source income at the same rates as resident individuals or corporations. However, nonresident corporations are subject to withholding tax on profits remitted or deemed to be remitted abroad.

17. Withholding Tax Rates

Withholding tax is applicable when remittances are being made to nonresidents in respect of dividends, other distributions, branch profits (net of corporation tax and reinvestment), interest and royalties etc.

	Dividends	Interest	Royalties
Nontreaty countries	15%/25% (1)	25%/30% (2)	20%/30% (2)
Treaty countries:			
Canada	15	15	15

	Dividends	Interest	Royalties
Denmark	10%/20% (3)	10%/15%/20% (3)(4)	20%
France	10/15 (5)	0/10 (6)	10
Germany	10/20 (3)	10/20 (3)(7)	20
Italy	10/20 (3)	10/20 (3)(7)	20
Norway	10/20 (3)	10/15/20 (3)(4)	20
Sweden	10/20 (8)	10/15 (7)	20
Switzerland	10/20 (3)	10/20 (3)(7)	20
United Kingdom	10/20 (3)	10/20 (3)(7)	20
United States	10/25 (3)	10/25 (3)(9)	25
Venezuela (10)			

Notes:
(1) The lesser rate applies only where recipient corporation owns 50% or more of the voting control of paying corporation.
(2) The lesser rate applies to individuals.
(3) The lesser rate applies when the recipient is the parent company.
(4) The 15% rate applies to bank interest.
(5) The lower rate applies if less than 10% of the issued share capital is owned.
(6) Interest earned on a loan or credit extended to an institution with responsibility for public financing of external trade is exempt from tax.
(7) The lesser rate also applies to bank interest.
(8) The lower rate applies if more than 25% of the issued share capital is owned.
(9) The 25% rate applies to bank interest.
(10) The profits derived from the business of air transport are exempt from tax.

18. Special Withholding Provisions

Branch profits, net of tax and reinvestment, are subject to withholding tax at a rate of 15% for non-treaty countries and 10% for treaty countries (except the applicable rate for Canada is 15%).

OTHER SIGNIFICANT TAXES

21. Sales (Value Added)

Value-added tax (VAT) at 15% is payable by registered persons on the value of goods and services supplied. VAT also is payable on imports of goods. Certain basic foods, exports, and certain services supplied to nonresidents are taxed at 0%. Registered persons can recover VAT paid on inputs, including capital expenditure, so that the tax is borne by the ultimate consumer. Generally, persons producing supplies of less than TT$120,000 annually are not required to be registered.

Certain transactions, such as insurance, certain banking services, stock brokerage, education, and medical and dental services, are exempt from VAT. The tax does not apply to the sale or transfer of real estate.

23.   Taxes on Payrolls (Social Security)

Weekly national insurance contributions are payable in respect of employed persons; part is payable by individual employees and part by employers. Contributions by the employer are treated as an allowable expense. Individual employees can claim 70% of their contribution as a deduction against their income for that year.

The rates of contribution are:

Weekly Earnings		Employee Contribution	Employer Contribution
Over	Not Over		
TT$ 0	TT$ 50	TT$1.10	TT$ 2.20
50	65	1.60	3.20
65	85	2.10	4.20
80	110	2.75	5.50
110	140	3.50	7.00
140	180	4.50	9.00
180	230	5.75	11.50
230		6.45	12.90

A health surcharge is payable by employees on their earnings. The rate applicable to employees earning less than TT$110 per week is TT$4.25 per week. Employees earning over TT$110 per week pay TT$8.25 per week.

24.   Taxes on Natural Resources

Supplemental petroleum tax (SPT) is charged on gross income derived from the disposal of crude petroleum. SPT is computed separately for land and marine operations. Certain deductions and allowances are available in computing gross income. SPT is deductible for purposes of the petroleum profits tax.

The base rate of SPT is 15% for land operations and 55% for marine operations. The rate applicable to additional production is 5% for land operations and 20% for marine operations.

Petroleum profits tax is charged on the profits of production, refining, and marketing of petroleum. The profits are determined by applying the provisions of the Income Tax Acts; however, particularly in the case of production profits, there are a number of provisions that materially affect the profits on which tax is payable.

25.   Other Taxes

Land and Property Taxes.   Taxes on property are levied by local authorities. The rates are normally paid by the occupier and are based on the assessed rental value of the property.

COMPUTATION OF TAXABLE INCOME

26. Capital Gains

Taxable capital gains (see item 3) are calculated as the difference between the cost of the asset and the sale proceeds net of related expenses. There are separate provisions for the treatment of partial disposals. Dispositions by way of gifts or in other circumstances that are not at arm's length are treated as disposals at market value.

27. Depreciation and Depletion

Capital cost allowances are generally provided on the diminishing balance basis for qualifying capital expenditures. On the sale, destruction, or obsolescence of an asset, a balancing allowance or charge is made for the deficiency or excess of the unallowed expenditure below or over the proceeds of sale. In addition, deduction of a reasonable amount is also allowed for the wear and tear of plant and machinery and of buildings used solely for housing plant and machinery. The rates vary according to the type of asset.

Depletion allowances, known as submarine well allowance, submarine production allowance, and land production allowance, may be claimed against income from the production of oil or gas.

28. Treatment of Dividends

Residents of Trinidad and Tobago must include all dividends received in their assessable income. No withholding taxes are deducted from dividends paid to residents; however, residents obtain a tax credit on dividends received. An individual resident or ordinarily resident is required to include in his taxable income 165% of any resident company distribution received, other than:

☐ Preference dividends.

☐ Distributions out of long-term insurance business profits that have borne tax at special rates.

☐ Distributions out of profits or gains on which no corporation tax was paid.

A credit is provided against the individual's tax liability on the grossed-up distribution of 65% of the distribution received; any excess of credit over tax liability is refundable.

Dividends received by resident companies from other Trinidad and Tobago companies are tax-exempt.

29. Loss Carryovers

Trading losses may only be carried forward to be offset against profits of the same trade as that in which the losses arose, but subject to this limitation they may be carried forward indefinitely. Capital losses (see item 3) may only be set off against capital gains arising in the same or future years.

30. Transactions between Related Parties

Provisions exist to restrict the use of "artificial or fictitious" transactions between related parties. The Board of Inland Revenue is empowered to disregard transactions between related parties where the Board is of the opinion that full effect has not been given to such transactions. In this context, transactions include dispositions or settlements. When a transaction has been set aside, the Board of Inland Revenue then makes an assessment on the basis of an arm's-length transaction.

31. Consolidation of Income

There is no provision for the filing of consolidated tax returns by related corporations.

32. Tax Periods

The basic period for computing liability to corporation tax is the company's own accounting period. Corporation tax is payable in quarterly installments based on the taxation of the preceding year. However, where a company expects to incur a loss in that year, the Board of Inland Revenue may permit a reduction or non-payment of the quarterly installments. Corporation tax returns are required to be filed on or before April 30 for the accounting year ending in the preceding calendar year. On commencement of business, the ending date for the accounting year is required to be agreed with the Board of Inland Revenue and no changes to the accounting year can be made without their consent. On cessation of business, tax returns are prepared to the date of cessation which may be greater (or less) than 12 months.

33. Other Matters

Management Fees. Management fees, defined as fees for the provision of management and personal services and technical and managerial skills paid to a nonresident are limited to a deduction equal to 1% of total expenses when computing chargeable income.

Scientific Research. Expenditures of a capital nature incurred in scientific research related to the taxpayer's business is deductible to the extent of 60% for the year of assessment for which it was incurred and 10% for each of the four succeeding years.

Promotional Expenses. Companies incorporated and resident in Trinidad and Tobago are allowed a deduction with respect to promotional expenses wholly and exclusively incurred in promoting the expansion of foreign markets for the export of goods produced in Trinidad and Tobago and shipped in commercial quantities. The deduction is equivalent to 150% of the amount actually expended. The Act defines promotional expenses, countries to which the allowance applies, and excluded industries.

RELATED CONSIDERATIONS

34. Incentives and Grants

There are various incentives and tax concessions to encourage investment in qualifying industries. These concessions are embodied in the following legislation:

☐ The Income Tax (In Aid of Industry) Ordinance Ch. 33 No. 2.

☐ Aid to Pioneer Industries Act Ch. 33 No. 3 (applicable only to taxpayers enjoying concessions under this act).

☐ Hotel Accommodation Act 1972.

☐ The Petroleum Taxes Act 1974.

☐ Fiscal Incentives Act 1979 (this Act has replaced the Aid to Pioneer Industries Act).

☐ The Petroleum Production Levy and Subsidy Act 1974.

The above legislation stipulates the nature of the industry and the type of expenditure which qualifies for tax concessions. Included in the legislation is an export allowance and duty-free concession.

35. Exchange Controls

All transactions involving foreign currency between nonresidents and residents require prior exchange control approval. At the present time approval is normally granted for all bona fide commercial transactions. Approval will normally be granted for dividends and profits on investments made by nonresidents to be remitted abroad provided applicable taxes have been paid and the investment was reported to the Exchange Control Authorities at the time the investment was made. Approval will also normally be granted for nonresident individuals employed on work permits to remit their savings abroad provided applicable taxes have been paid.

Borrowing by nonresidents from resident financial institutions is subject to regulation by the Central Bank.

36. Investment Restrictions on Nonresidents

Under the provisions of the Foreign Investment Act, a foreign investor may acquire issued shares of a local public company without prior approval provided that the total cumulative shareholding of the company held by foreign investors does not exceed 30%. Foreign investors incorporating a private company or acquiring shares in a private company need only supply the government authorities with certain information prior to making the investment. There are certain exemptions from obtaining licenses for residential, commercial, and industrial property. Apart from these exemptions, generally, other investments by foreign investors will require the prior approval from the Government.

TURKEY

INCOME TAXES ON CORPORATIONS

1. Rates

The rate of corporation tax is 46%, and supplemental levies amounting to 7% are imposed on the corporation tax.

2. Local Income Taxes

No income taxes are imposed by the provincial or municipal authorities.

3. Capital Gains Taxes

There is no special provision for capital gains. Gains resulting from sales of fixed assets subject to depreciation are taxed at the normal rate (which can be deferred for three years), and gains are not taxable to the extent the proceeds are reinvested in new fixed assets. However, the gains on the sale of real estate and securities for 1990, 1991, and 1992 are taxed unless the company's new shares are registered shares and are listed on the stock market. These gains should be retained (i.e., added to capital in the year of sale) for five years.

4. Branch Profits Taxes

A foreign company maintaining a permanent establishment in Turkey is subject to limited tax liability on the income received from the permanent establishment. The branch's income in Turkey is taxed in the same way as resident corporations.

5. Foreign Tax Reliefs

A credit is granted to the resident company against Turkish tax payable on its income from foreign sources in respect of foreign tax payable on the same income. This credit is limited to the Turkish tax payable on the foreign income. Tax treaties exist with Austria, Belgium, Finland, France, Germany, Italy (air and sea transportation only), Jordan, Korea, the Netherlands, Northern Cyprus, Norway, Pakistan, Romania, Sweden, Tunisia, and the United Kingdom.

6. Classification of Corporations

For tax purposes, companies are grouped as limited liability companies (corporations and limited companies) and personal companies (limited and ordinary partnerships). Corporation tax applies to limited liability companies and, beginning in 1986, joint venture partnerships engaged in construction or repair work extending for more than one year where at least one partner is a corporation. State economic enterprises and business entities owned by societies, foundations, and local authorities are also subject to corporation tax.

7. Payment of Taxes

The corporation tax return must be filed in the fourth month after the end of the company's own accounting period, and is paid in three equal installments starting with the month in which the tax return is filed. If the accounting period is the calendar year, the tax return must be filed in April and tax is payable in April, July and October.

Advance Payments. Payments on account of corporation tax due must be made at the rate of 50% of the previous year's tax liability. The advance payments are deducted from the corporation's ultimate tax liability as shown on the return for the tax year, and any balance is due by the end of the filing period. Any excess is carried forward against payment of advance tax due for the following year.

INCOME TAXES ON INDIVIDUALS

9. Rates

Income tax is levied on taxable income at progressive rates after deducting various allowances.

Taxable Income		Tax on	Percentage
Over	Not Over	Lower Amount	on Excess
TL 0	TL 12,000,000	TL 0	25%
12,000,000	24,000,000	3,000,000	30
24,000,000	48,000,000	6,600,000	35
48,000,000	96,000,000	15,000,000	40
96,000,000	192,000,000	34,200,000	45
192,000,000		77,400,000	50

Salaries paid in foreign currency by a nonresident employer from income earned abroad are exempt from income tax. However, such salaries are taxable if the employer has a commercial earning in Turkey.

A portion of the income taxes paid qualifies as a rebate, which is based on the taxpayer's monthly expenditures. The rebate is claimed monthly, but it cannot exceed the net income earned in that month. The rates of the rebate are:

Basis (Expenditures)	Rate
First TL 60,000	10%
Next TL 60,000	20
Next TL 80,000	12
Over TL 200,000	5

In addition, stamp duty of 0.04% is levied on gross salaries and wages.

Employment income is taxed by accumulating monthly salaries and wages and applying progressive rates, after deducting:

☐ The employee's share of social security.
☐ A general allowance of TL 54,000 per month.

An individual with income in addition to employment income must file a tax return. In such case, the incomes of a husband, wife, and children under 18 are aggregated, except to the extent that the wife's income is from assets inherited or acquired prior to marriage. Resident individuals are taxed on their worldwide income.

10. Local Income Taxes

No taxes are imposed by the provincial or municipal authorities; localities receive a share of the taxes collected by the state.

11. Capital Gains Taxes

Gain derived from the sale of business-related capital assets is included in taxable income (see item 3). The first TL 200,000 of gain derived during the calendar year from the sale of a privately owned asset is exempt from tax, except for certain assets (i.e., real estate, stock, and securities) held for less than one year. Gain from the sale of certain registered securities is exempt from tax regardless of the length of the holding period. However, foreign exchange gain derived from the sale of foreigners' share-capitals and share-certificates is not subject to tax.

12. Foreign Tax Reliefs

Credit for foreign tax paid is granted, limited to the Turkish tax applicable to the foreign-source income.

13. Tax Period

Income tax is assessed on the calendar-year basis. At the end of March, following the assessment year, a tax return must be filed and income tax is payable in three equal installments in March, June, and September.

INCOME TAXES ON NONRESIDENTS

15. Liability to Tax

Turkish law does not distinguish between Turkish citizens and foreigners with respect to taxation. Taxpayers with unlimited tax liability are taxed on their worldwide income. Taxpayers with limited tax liability are taxed only on various types of Turkish-source income.

A company whose statutory domicile and place of management are in Turkey and a person resident in Turkey have unlimited tax liability. A person whose residence and company whose statutory domicile and place of management are outside Turkey are considered to have limited tax liability. Since a company organized under Turkish law is required to specify in its articles a statutory domicile located in Turkey, all Turkish companies are resident taxpayers. If a nonresident company conducts business in Turkey through a branch, engages in activities in Turkey, or becomes a partner in a Turkish company, it will be taxed on branch profits (or the income of the company) in Turkey.

Individuals whose customary place of abode is not in Turkey are subject to limited tax liability. Persons who spend more than six continuous months in a calendar year in Turkey are considered residents except for individuals arriving in Turkey on temporary assignments.

The limited tax liability extends to trade or business income from a permanent establishment, salaries for work done in Turkey (regardless of where paid or whether or not remitted to Turkey), rental income from real property in Turkey, Turkish-source interest, and income from the sale of patents, copyrights, and similar intangible rights.

Income of limited taxpayers derived from exporting goods manufactured or purchased in Turkey is exempt from tax.

16. Rates

Income of nonresidents is taxed at the same rates as residents (see item 11), but nonresidents are not entitled to the general allowances and the income tax rebate. Various levies amounting to 7% (5% for nonresidents' salaries) of income tax are also imposed.

17. Withholding Tax Rates

Income of nonresidents, except for commercial and agricultural profits and income received by individuals with respect to the sale, transfer, or assignment of intangible property, is subject to a withholding tax that is deemed to have been deducted at source despite such income being connected with a permanent establishment in Turkey. Companies may choose to declare such income and deduct the withholding tax from the tax computed on the basis of the declaration. Thus, expenses incurred in generating the income would be deductible. Unless reduced by a double taxation convention (see item 5), depending on whether the recipient is a corporation or a person, the withholding tax rates are:

Type of Payment	Rate Corporations	Individuals
Independent professional services.	15%	15%
Oil exploration activities	5	15
Leasing	0.5	—
Other rentals (including royalties, patents, copyrights)	20	20
Securities income		
Interest on state bonds and treasury notes	0	0
Income from profit-sharing certificates	0	0
Interest on bearer bonds	10	10
Interest on nonbearer bonds	10	10
Other	10	10
Bank deposit interest		
Foreign exchange deposits	10	10
Other	10	10
Dividends and branch profits	0	0
Sales proceeds of patents and copyrights	25	25
Interest	10	10
Interest on government bonds	10	—
Trading activities in Turkey	0	0

A 5% defense industry promotion tax is applied to the withholding tax.
Withholding tax rates are reduced by the following treaties:

	Dividends	Interest	Royalties	Technical Assistance Fees
Austria	25%, 35% (1)	15%	10%	10%
Finland	15, 20 (2)	15	10	15
France	15, 20 (3)	15	10	15
Germany	15, 20 (3)	15	10	15
Jordan	10, 15 (1)	10	12	15
Korea (South)	15, 20 (1)	10, 15 (4)	10	15
Netherlands	15, 20 (2)	15	10	15
Northern Cyprus	15, 20 (2)	10	10	5, 15
Norway	25, 30 (1)	15	10	10
Pakistan	10, 15 (5)	10	10	10
Romania	15	10	10	15
Tunisia	12, 15 (6)	10	10	15
United Kingdom	15, 20 (2)	15	10	15

Notes:
(1) 25% if recipient company owns at least 25% of payor company.

(2)   15% if recipient owns at least 25% of payor company.
(3)   15% if recipient company owns at least 10% of payor company.
(4)   10% if debt matures in more than two years.
(5)   10% if recipient owns at least 25% of payor company.
(6)   12% if recipient owns at least 25% of payor company.

OTHER SIGNIFICANT TAXES

21.   Sales (Value Added)

The sales and production taxes were replaced by a value-added tax effective January 1, 1985. The VAT is levied at a general rate of 12%, but is not applied to exports. Banking and insurance companies transactions are exempt from VAT. VAT paid on the acquisition of capital assets is recoverable over a three-year period. The VAT may be deferred against collateral under certain investment incentive programs.

Service Tax.   A service tax is levied on banking and insurance transactions at 5% for 1991.

Fund Tax.   This special tax is levied on the CIF value of imports, and the rate is 6%.

22.   Inheritance and Gift Taxes

Recipients of property through inheritance or donation are subject to inheritance and gift tax at rates from 3% to 44%.

Tax paid in a foreign country on inherited property is deducted from the taxable value of the asset. Inheritance tax is payable in two installments each year over five years.

23.   Taxes on Payrolls (Social Security)

All employees must belong to the social security system, which includes insurance for work-related accidents and illness, sickness, pregnancy, disability, and old age and death. Contributions are payable by individual employees and employers. For citizens of countries with which Turkey has bilateral social security agreements, full contributions are imposed. Where there is no social insurance agreement, contributions for work-related accidents and illness, pregnancy, and sickness are paid. On earnings exceeding TL 801,000 per month, employees pay 14% and employers 19.5% up to an upper earnings level of TL 3,008,010 per month. Rates currently applied are as follows:

	Employee	Employer
Work-related accidents and illness (1)	—	1.5%
Pregnancy	—	1
Sickness	5%	6
Disability, old age, and death	9 14%	11 19.5%

Notes:
(1)   The rate varies between 1.5% and 7% based on the degree of risk inherent to the work.

24.   Taxes on Natural Resources

No special taxes are levied on the exploitation of natural resources except for a royalty, which is paid on the petroleum extracted.

25.   Other Taxes

Property Taxes.   These taxes are paid on the tax values of land and buildings at rates varying from 0.3% to 0.6%.

Stamp Duties.   Stamp duty is levied on a wide range of transactions, including contracts, agreements, notes receivable and payable, letters of credit, financial statements, and payrolls. The largest stamp duties are those related to setting up a new company's share capital and subsequent increases therein.

COMPUTATION OF TAXABLE INCOME

26.   Capital Gains
See item 3.

27.   Depreciation and Depletion
The cost of immovable property, installations and machinery, ships and other transports, and intangible assets with a limited useful life of more than a year can be depreciated on either the straight-line or declining-balance method. A change from straight-line depreciation to the declining-balance method is not permitted, but the contrary change is possible. Tax authorities have issued statutory rates of straight-line depreciation for a wide range of assets (e.g., buildings 2% to 4%, machinery and equipment 6% to 20%).

Taxpayers may select rates for depreciable assets purchased after January 1, 1983, subject to maximums of 25% for straight-line depreciation and 50% for the declining-balance method.

28. Treatment of Dividends

There is no additional tax on dividends paid by companies.

29. Loss Carryovers

Losses may be carried forward for five years but may not be carried back.

30. Transactions between Related Parties

Transactions between related parties, especially international transactions, must be on an arm's-length basis.

The profit from the liquidation of a company is taxed as if it had been earned in the ordinary course of business (see item 1). Any loss from the liquidation of a company may be carried back to the number of years within the period of liquidation, and any taxes paid in excess can be claimed.

Reconstruction and amalgamation of companies do not entail tax when the assets and liabilities are transferred at balance sheet values; otherwise, the rules for liquidation apply.

31. Consolidation of Income

All companies are regarded as separate taxpayers, and the profits and losses of affiliated companies generally may not be combined. However, a company merging with a loss company can deduct the accumulated losses from its income for a five-year period if approved by the Minister of Finance. Such losses are taxed at the rate of 10%. Profits transferred as dividends are deductible by the recipient company to avoid double taxation.

32. Tax Periods

The period for income tax assessment is normally the calendar year. However, companies may adopt a different 12-month fiscal period appropriate to their business, subject to the approval of the Ministry of Finance.

RELATED CONSIDERATIONS

34. Incentives and Grants

Tax Incentives. The two major incentives are the investment incentive allowance and the export incentive allowance. All activities qualify for the investment incentives, except those listed by the government. However, all investments made in priority development areas are eligible for the investment incentives.

Turkey is divided into four regions for purposes of the investment incentives. Projects must receive an "incentives certificate" from the State Planning Organization to qualify for the investment incentives. Project investments must be of over TL 250 million (priority development areas) and TL 2.5 billion (other incentives) to qualify for the certificate. Investment incentives include exemption from customs duties and taxes on imported machinery and equipment, investment allowances of up to 100% for approved projects, low-interest loans, and exemption from the construction tax. Sixteen percent of industrial goods export revenues exceeding US$250,000 are exempt from corporation income tax.

Free Zones. Free-trade and export processing zones have been created and are scheduled for completion in 1990 and 1991.

35. Exchange Controls

The Foreign Investment Department (FID) regulates foreign capital in Turkey. Current foreign capital rules include the following:

□ Each foreign partner must provide a minimum $50,000 in cash as capital.

□ Requests for transfers of profits and dividends may now be handled by the banks without delay.

□ The transfer of money acquired through a liquidation has been facilitated immediately following an examination.

□ Work permits can be granted for as many foreign personnel as are required for the efficient functioning of enterprises.

□ Previously blocked funds denominated in foreign currency may be invested in their entirety in start-up companies. Such funds held in Turkish Liras may not be so used unless a cash investment of foreign currency is made equal to 50% or more of the blocked amount.

□ The right to bring in capital-in-kind has been continued.

□ The FID grants permission to import patents, know-how, and similar intangible rights, and the Central Bank issues permits for the foreign exchange required for the payment.

□ Certain foreign credits-in-kind (or in cash) will require permission. The credit agreement will dictate the bank's payment of interest and principal with respect to these credits. Interest expense and other various costs are not restricted except in accordance with established banking practices.

□ Foreign capital companies are required to submit to the FID by May of each year a copy of their annual reports.

Law No. 6224. Law No. 6224 regulates all foreign investments benefiting from investment incentives (including banking) other than those involving the exploration for and extraction, processing, and distribution of petroleum (which are governed by petroleum law). The criteria used for granting the incentive certificate are similar to those for granting the investment permit. An investment certificate is provided by FID with the investment permit at the same time and does not require an extra application.

Law on Promotion of Tourism. In order to qualify for incentives, foreign corporations must obtain a Tourism Investment Certificate or a Tourism Facility Certificate from the Ministry of Culture and Tourism.

Petroleum Law. Investments in the area of petroleum are governed by this law and the related petroleum regulations and decrees issued by the Council of Ministers.

37. Other Matters

Nontrading Offices. Foreign companies are permitted to establish nontrading offices in Turkey with the permission of FID. Foreign exchange must be imported to finance the expenditures of these offices.

SELECTION OF BUSINESS ENTITY BY NONRESIDENTS

Existing legislation does not prescribe any particular legal structure for nonresident investors to operate in Turkey. Thus, all legal forms available to Turkish private-sector investors are also available to foreign investors, but most nonresidents establish a branch, corporation, or limited company.

The effective tax rate on branch profits or a nonresident company's dividends is the same:

☐ All earnings derived from Turkey by foreign companies that operate through branches are determined in accordance with the provisions of the income tax law governing commercial earnings. The rate of corporation tax on branch profits is the same as for corporations.

☐ Dividends received by a nonresident company from a subsidiary (a corporation or a limited company) in Turkey are not subject to tax.

SPECIMEN TAX COMPUTATION

	Type of Income	
	Taxable	**Exempt**
Profits	TL 100	TL 100
Corporation tax	(46)	—
Profit after corporation tax	54	100
Withholding tax (1)	—	(10)
Funds levy	(3.22)	(0.5)
Profit after withholding tax and funds levy	TL 50.78	TL 89.5
Tax rate	49.22%	10.5%

Notes:

(1) Income exempt from corporation tax is taxed at 10%.

TURKS AND CAICOS ISLANDS

1. Taxes

There are no taxes on income, dividends, capital gains, corporations, gifts, or inheritance. The Government does levy a probate fee on estates of 2% of their value but only to a maximum of $550.00. Guarantees against future taxation are available under a variety of Ordinances, with each application being considered individually by the Executive Council apart from those granted to exempted companies as set out in item 5; such guarantees are usually granted for projects and undertakings that will contribute to the development of the Islands. The Islands have no tax treaties with any other countries.

2. Exchange Controls

There are no exchange controls and no regulations to affect the free movement of funds into and out of the Islands. Dividends, interest, royalties, and other payments of all kinds may be freely remitted without the necessity for prior official approval.

3. Banking Facilities and Confidentiality

Two large international banks and a locally incorporated bank serve the commercial banking needs of the Islands. These, and a number of financial institutions are also involved in off-shore merchant banking and trust operations. Deposit accounts of any currency may be maintained by resident or nonresident persons or companies, subject only to the minimum deposit requirements of the particular banks. U.S. dollar current accounts may also be maintained and operated by residents and nonresidents alike. Banking in the Islands is regulated by the Banking Ordinance 1979 as amended by the Banking (Amendment) Ordinance 1989. The amending legislation has introduced the concept of captive banking aimed particularly at multinational companies.

The Confidential Relationships Ordinance 1979 imposed a duty of non-divulgence of information imparted under express or implied conditions of business or professional confidence. Accordingly, the complete confidentiality of the business and financial affairs of all customers and clients is protected by law.

4. Approximate Costs

The incorporation of a company costs approximately US$1,200, and annual fees for fulfilling basic statutory requirements range from US$700 to US$1,200 depending upon the time involvement for additional services requested and whether or not nominee directors are required. The cost of establishing a trust varies with the length and complexity of the trust deed, but averages about US$2,000. The fees for servicing a trust are about 0.025% of the gross asset value, with a minimum of US$500, but these costs may vary considerably with trust activity.

5. Corporate Law

The Companies Ordinance 1981 provides for two types of corporate entities: the local or non-exempted company and the off-shore or exempted company. An exempted company is one whose business is conducted mainly outside the Islands and, as such, is entitled to a number of privileges not available to local companies. There is no disclosure of ownership (beneficial or registered) or of directors and officers at the time of incorporation or afterwards. Bearer and redeemable shares may be issued. An exempted company may apply to the Governor of the Islands for a written guarantee that no fee increases shall apply to the company for a 20-year period nor shall any future taxes if any should be levied. The Companies Ordinance also permits a company incorporated outside the Islands to register to continue in the Islands as if it had been incorporated in the Islands as an exempted company. Similarly, an exempted company may transfer to another jurisdiction, assuming such transfer is permitted by the other jurisdiction.

6. Insurance Industry

Insurance companies are regulated by The Insurance Ordinance 1989. The legislation is specifically designed to encourage, within a flexible regulatory environment, captive insurance companies.

UGANDA

INCOME TAXES ON CORPORATIONS

1. Rates

Corporate tax rates are as follows:

Type of Company	Rate
All companies	40%
Insurance (income attributable to life insurance activities)	40
Mining (certain minerals)	25
Nonresident company with a permanent establishment in Uganda	55

The Finance Decree 1976 introduced measures to enforce the collection of tax from companies that had operated without submitting returns or paying taxes. The Decree requires every business to make a provisional payment at the beginning of each calendar year before a trading license will be issued by the local authority. The amount payable varies with the location and nature of the business. The rates are set down in the Decree. These measures have been extended by subsequent finance decrees and acts to cover more and more trading centers and businesses.

2. Local Income Taxes

None.

3. Capital Gains Taxes

None.

4. Branch Profits Taxes

When any trade, profession, or vocation is carried on partly inside and partly outside Uganda by a resident body of persons, the whole of any gains or profits shall be deemed to have accrued or have been derived from Uganda and shall be taxed at the rate of 55%.

5. Foreign Tax Reliefs

Uganda has double taxation agreements with Denmark and Zambia. There is no other legislation or agreements with regard to double taxation relief.

INCOME TAXES ON INDIVIDUALS

9. Rates

The resident individual income tax rates are as follows:

Taxable Income		Tax on	Percentage
Over	Not Over	Lower Amount	on Excess
Shs. 480,000	Shs. 620,000	Shs. 0	10%
620,000	870,000	14,000	20
870,000	1,310,000	64,000	30
1,310,000	2,620,000	196,000	40
2,620,000		720,000	50

The nonresident individual income tax rates are as follows:

Taxable Income		Tax on	Percentage
Over	Not Over	Lower Amount	on Excess
Shs. 0	Shs. 620,000	Shs. 0	10%
620,000	870,000	62,000	20
870,000	1,310,000	112,000	30
1,310,000	2,620,000	244,000	40
2,620,000		768,000	50

Dividend income of residents is liable to a 20% withholding tax which is allowed as a credit against the taxpayer's tax liability.

Foreigners employed in Uganda are deemed to be residents for tax purposes if they either have permanent home in Uganda and were present in Uganda for any part of the year of income or, if having no home in Uganda, were present in Uganda for a period or periods aggregating 183 days or more in the year of income or were present in the year of income and in each of the two preceding years of income for periods averaging more than 122 days in each such year of income. Persons leaving Uganda are required to obtain a tax clearance certificate before departure.

10. Local Income Taxes

Graduated personal tax is imposed on every person 18 years or over residing in a local authority and having income from farming, business, or employment. Assessments are issued by urban and rural local authorities based on annual salaries or wages or other income, and the tax is payable to the assessing local authority. The standard rate is Shs. 3,000 and rises over 24 bands of income to a maximum of Shs. 30,000. The tax is an allowable deduction for purposes of the individual income tax. Aside from graduated tax, there are no state or provincial income taxes.

11. Capital Gains Taxes
None.

12. Foreign Tax Reliefs
See item 5.

13. Tax Period
The fiscal year is from July 1 to June 30. The measures introduced by Finance Decree 1976 (see item 1) also apply to sole traders.

INCOME TAXES ON NONRESIDENTS

15. Liability to Tax
A withholding tax is imposed on nonresidents.

17. Withholding Tax Rates
Any management or professional fee, royalty, rent, premium, dividend, interest, pension or retirement annuity paid to a nonresident person (or body of persons) is subject to a withholding tax of 15%, which is calculated on the gross amount of the payment.

With regard to the income of a nonresident partner from a trade or profession, a 15% withholding tax is calculated on the gross income. In addition, Ugandan income tax is also calculated in accordance with the nonresident rates in item 9.

OTHER SIGNIFICANT TAXES

21. Sales (Value Added)
Sales tax is levied at varying rates contained in the Act on goods and services, which are also defined in the Sales Tax Act.

Customs Excise Duty. The above information also applies to customs duty on imported goods.

22. Inheritance and Gift Taxes
There is no estate duty in Uganda, but income from any estate is taxable at the corporation rate. There is no taxation of any type on gifts made or received.

23. Taxes on Payrolls (Social Security)

Social Security contributions are levied on employees at the standard rate of 15% of total monthly salary and wages. The employee and employer contribute 5% and 10%, respectively. Basically, this scheme only provides a refund of total contributions to the individual on retirement.

24. Taxes on Natural Resources

No special taxes are levied on the exploitation of natural resources. Normally, a royalty agreement is executed with the Ugandan Government. As a tax incentive, the income of mining companies is taxed at 25% instead of the normal corporation rate of 40%.

25. Other Taxes

Land and Property. The local administrations levy rates on property, which vary according to valuations.

Capital. There are no annual wealth or capital worth taxes.

Transfer Fees on Motor Vehicles. The transfer fee for motor vehicles varies depending on the type of vehicle and the period of ownership prior to the transfer. Transfers from deceased persons and registered hire-purchase companies are exempt from these provisions.

Withholding Tax. A 2% withholding tax is imposed on any sum in excess of Shs. 5,000 payable to any person in Uganda in respect of any goods or services supplied to or the execution of any contract with the Government, a local authority, an urban authority, a parastatal organization, or a corporation, company, or institution designated by the Minister. The deduction of this withholding tax is credited to the taxpayer as income tax paid.

Road User's Tax (Toll). A road user's tax is payable by vehicles using certain roads in Uganda. The amount of tax is determined by the type of vehicle.

COMPUTATION OF TAXABLE INCOME

26. Capital Gains Taxes

None.

27. Depreciation and Depletion

Depreciation adopted in the accounts is ignored for taxation purposes. Instead, there is a system of capital allowances for qualifying capital expenditures, which are deductible in computing taxable income. Annual deductions are allowed for certain classes of capital expenditure undertaken for business purposes, including industrial buildings at 4% (6% in the case of hotel buildings), and plant and machinery at rates of 37.5%, 25%, or 12.5%. Investment deductions are also available in respect of certain classes of capital expenditure, such as the construction of industrial buildings and the installation of machines (where the trade consists of the manufacture of goods and materials of local origin) and on new hotel buildings and extensions thereto. The deduction is a once-and-for-all 20% of capital expenditure. Offices, shops and residential buildings do not qualify for industrial buildings allowances.

28. Treatment of Dividends

Dividends payable to resident companies are not chargeable to Uganda income tax. However, dividends paid to any persons are subject to withholding tax of 20% and 15% for residents and nonresidents, respectively. For residents, this withholding tax is allowed as a credit against Uganda income tax.

29. Loss Carryovers

Trading losses may be offset against profit and carried forward to the next year. There is no carryback of losses to previous years, nor is any subvention or group relief available.

31. Consolidation of Income

Companies that are resident in Uganda are liable to corporation tax or withholding tax, whichever is applicable, on their income from all sources. There are no provisions for the filing of consolidated tax returns by related corporations.

32. Tax Periods

The assessment period is the period of 12 months that commences on the first day of July each year. The year of income is the fiscal year preceding the assessment year, but:

☐   If the assessee opts for his or her own accounting period ending within a fiscal year, the year of income shall be the period of 12 months ending on that date.

RELATED CONSIDERATIONS

34. Incentives and Grants

Exempt Income.   The Minister of Finance is empowered to sign an order exempting any class of income from income tax. There are also certain Government loans on which interest is paid free of tax. Certain bodies and classes of persons are also exempted from income tax; e.g., qualifying pension funds and provident funds. Twenty-five percent of the emoluments are exempt from tax of a non-Ugandan citizen or a temporary resident who has been granted a work permit for employment of a technical, managerial, or expert nature (after the Immigration Board certifies no Ugandan citizens or permanent residents are capable of such work).

Special Grants or Allowances. As a policy reform, the Uganda Government enacted The Investment Code 1991, which establishes the Uganda Investment Authority to promote, facilitate, and supervise investments for both local and foreign investors in Uganda. The new law replaces the Foreign Investments (Protection) Act, 1964, and the Foreign Investments Decree, 1977, but existing certificates of approved enterprises issued under those laws remain valid.

The Investment Code aims to rationalize the various procedures for investment approval and introduces additional incentives for investors.

The Uganda Investment Authority is designed as a ''one-stop shop'' for investors and is authorized to issue investment licenses, certificates of incentives, registration of agreements for transfer of foreign technology or expertise, and certificates of approval for externalization of funds.

The Investment Code specifies 24 priority areas of investment but forbids foreign investment in crop production, animal production, or the leasing of land for crop and animal production. The code also specifies seven activities, mainly services, for which a foreign investor is not eligible for investment incentives.

Facilities and incentives available to investors include exemption from import duties and sales tax, corporation tax, withholding tax, and tax on dividends for between three to five years, depending on the value of the investment, and to credit from domestic sources solely for carrying out the activities specified in the investment license.

Businesses licensed under the Investment Code are protected against compulsory acquisition outside the provisions of the Constitution of Uganda.

Special Tax Rates or Concessions. There is a special tax rate which applies to mining companies, whose income is taxed at 25% (see item 24). Mining companies are also able to charge capital expenditure to revenue. There are similar provisions for agricultural enterprises whereby capital expenditure incurred in the clearing of land for crop utilization may be allowed against revenue. The income of a life insurance company is taxed at 40%. The income of a nonresident company having a permanent establishment in Uganda is taxed at 55%.

35. Exchange Controls

Uganda has a comprehensive exchange control system under the authority of the Exchange Control Act. Circulars and regulations are issued to the private banks from time to time.

The dual exchange rate regime was abolished, and the exchange rate now is subject to periodic review. Within this system, no payment in foreign currency can be made to a nonresident without the sanction of the Central Bank.

Companies controlled overseas may remit dividends, subject to certain restrictions. At the present time, there are severe restrictions on the remittance of such items as management and professional fees. No individual may remit money (such as savings) outside Uganda without Exchange Control consent, apart from expatriate employees employed on contract with overseas terms of service. Such persons are normally allowed to remit one-third of their monthly salary to their country of origin, subject to a maximum of US $605 per month.

A locally incorporated company which brings in capital from overseas may be able to obtain a certificate of investment in an approved enterprise in accordance with the provisions of the Foreign Investments (Protection) Act 1964 as amended. Approved enterprise status can also be obtained in respect of fixed loans from an external account. A certificate, under the Act, carries with it a guarantee that profits may be remitted to the country from which the capital originated, and the capital itself may be repatriated if the company is wound up. Experience shows, however, that the possession of a certificate has in fact brought no special benefits to its holder.

A foreign controlled company incorporated in Uganda cannot normally borrow locally in excess of 20% of its paid-up capital. While a foreign company operating here would also have to obtain exchange control approval for any borrowings, the limit to those borrowings is not so clearly defined. In either case, experience indicates that the exchange control is likely to authorize a higher level of local borrowing if it can be satisfied that such borrowing is reasonable in the circumstances.

Remittances to South Africa are blocked.

Forex Bureau. The Finance Statute 1990 introduced the forex bureau authorized to deal in the purchase and sale of foreign currency on a spot basis. The authorized dealer banks also are permitted to operate forex bureaus, but all bureaus must be autonomous entities by registration and operation.

All Government business will be transacted at the officially fixed exchange rate, which also will apply to international loans and diplomatic missions.

The introduction of the bureaus will ease the past restrictions on remittances, provided supply of foreign exchange can be increased and sustained.

SELECTION OF BUSINESS ENTITY BY NONRESIDENTS

A foreign investor may either register a branch of a foreign company or incorporate a local limited company under the provisions of the Companies Act (Cap. 85). The registration of a branch is easy, audits are not required by law (and the scope of any audit can be negotiated), and the filing requirements for the Registrar of Companies are minor (but the company accounts as a whole may have to be filed).

However, the branch profits tax rate of 55% is higher than the resident company rate of 40%. Payments by the branch to the parent company for management or professional fees, royalties, dividends, and interest are subject to a withholding tax of 15% (calculated on the gross amount).

On the other hand, the incorporation of a local subsidiary company provides the advantages of limited liability, local investment, and the lower corporate tax rate of 40%. It is, however, more costly to incorporate and operate a company, a company secretary is required to file the necessary returns with the Registrar of Companies, and a full annual audit is required by law. Moreover, the Central Bank requires documentation that the nonresident share capital is paid in convertible currency and usually stipulates that no foreign exchange will be approved for payment of nonresident director's fees.

SPECIMEN TAX COMPUTATION

Information:

☐ The company is resident in Uganda and its year-end is December 31, 1990.

☐ The company's operating profit for the year is Shs.15,000,000.

☐ Operating profit is stated after charging:

Depreciation	Shs. 1,500,000
General provision against doubtful debts	700,000

and after crediting:

Dividends from a wholly-owned subsidiary	Shs. 2,000,000
Interest on Treasury Bills	1,600,000
Profit on disposition of fixed assets	420,000

☐ Movement on fixed assets:

Written-down value of motor vehicles brought forward from previous year	Shs. 2,000,000
Additions as restricted	1,500,000
Sales proceeds of a motor car as restricted	600,000

☐ Leave pay provision brought forward from the previous year is Shs. 750,000.

☐ Leave pay provision at December 31, 1990 is Shs. 900,000.

☐ Withholding tax was deducted at source on the dividend at 20%.

Computation:

Operating profit		Shs. 15,000,000
Add		
Depreciation	1,500,000	
General provision against doubtful debts	700,000	
Increase in leave pay provision	150,000	2,350,000
		17,350,000

Less

Dividend	2,000,000	
Interest on Treasury Bills	1,600,000	
Wear and tear allowance (1)	725,000	
Industrial buildings allowance (2)	6,000	
Profit on disposition of fixed assets	420,000	4,751,000
Adjusted profit		Shs. 12,599,000
Tax liability (at 40%)		Shs. 5,039,600

Less

Tax suffered at source on dividends (20% of Shs.2,000,000)		400,000
Net tax payable		Shs. 4,639,600

Notes:

(1) The wear and tear allowance is computed as follows:

Written-down value at beginning of year	Shs. 2,000,000
Additions	1,500,000
	3,500,000
Sales proceeds	(600,000)
	2,900,000
Wear and tear allowance (at 25%)	725,000
Written-down value at year end	Shs. 2,175,000

(2) The industrial buildings allowance is calculated as follows:

Cost	Shs. 150,000
Residue (January 1, 1990)	120,000
Annual allowance (4%)	6,000
Residue (December 31, 1990)	Shs. 114,000

UNION OF SOVIET SOCIALIST REPUBLICS

Editors Note: As this edition went to press, dramatic changes continue to occur in the Soviet Union. Prior to August 1991, the Soviet Union was a federation of 15 republics, each with a separate government. Since then, Union authority over the republics has all but disappeared. Each republic has or is in the process of adopting foreign investment and tax laws.

Tax law in the Soviet Union is constantly changing; its fragmentary nature reflects the ad hoc manner in which the existing legislation developed. Taxation has been a contentious issue between the Union and the republics, primarily concerning the split of tax revenues. In general, the republics have implemented laws more favorable to foreign investors than the Union laws.

The following chapters reflects the Union tax system in place prior to the coup in August 1991.

INCOME TAXES ON CORPORATIONS

1. Rates

A consolidated corporate tax system imposes a 35% tax rate on all domestic enterprises. This replaces a system in which taxes and Government payments varied among enterprises. Note that a 30% tax rate applies to joint ventures that are more than 30% foreign-owned (see item 34). The all-Union profit tax was to be repealed effective January 1, 1992. At such time, all enterprises, including those with foreign participation, were to pay a tax of 10% on the sale value of goods and services.

An excess profits tax, defined by the Council of Ministries, applies to all enterprises except qualified foreign enterprises (30% foreign ownership). Excess profits are defined on an industry-by-industry basis as profits in excess of two times the average profit earned by state enterprises in a particular industry. Excess profits are taxed at 80% for amounts up to 10% above the prescribed level and at 90% thereafter. This tax may be repealed according to legislation recently introduced.

2. Local Income Taxes

A substantial portion (23%) of the consolidated corporate tax is allocated to republic and local budgets. New tax legislation is being considered in several republics, including Estonia, Latvia, Lithuania, and Byelorussia.

3. Capital Gains Taxes

There are no specific taxes on capital gains.

4. Branch Profits Tax

Branches of foreign corporations are taxed on their income from activities, permitted by Soviet law, in which they engage either directly or indirectly. Such foreign legal entities are distinct from joint ventures, who are subject to a different tax rate (see item 34).

The rate of tax on income received by foreign legal entities carrying on activities in the USSR is 40%, unless such income is exempt or reduced by treaty or other international agreement.

5. Foreign Tax Reliefs

Relief is provied for foreign taxes paid under a system of bilateral tax treaties that avoid double taxation of income and property. In addition, tax on income subject to tax abroad can be reduced if such taxes are paid to the other country.

6. Classification of Corporation

Major changes in the economic system, including changes in the tax system, will affect the types of enterprises that can operate within the Soviet economic system. The definition of corporate taxpayers now includes specified state, republic, and local enterprises, leased enterprises, joint stock entities, joint ventures, and other entities that are legal persons.

7. Payment of Taxes

Taxes are paid quarterly in advance, based on an estimate of assessable profits, subject to readjustment in the subsequent period. Taxes are collected in advance from a joint venture on the fifteenth day of the last month of the quarter (however, see discussion of tax holidays in item 34). The tax authorities must receive by mid-January of the following year an estimate of current-year profits. The final tax statement must be submitted by March 15. A financial statement must be prepared and audited by Inaudit, the Soviet auditing organization, by this date. Any additional tax due must be paid by April 1.

Interest for late payments is imposed at a rate of 0.05% per day (18.25% per year).

8. Other Matters

Consolidated Tax Returns. It appears that enterprises with wholly owned subsidiaries may file consolidated tax returns if the entities report in consolidated financial statements.

INCOME TAXES ON INDIVIDUALS

9. Rates

A new law on individual taxation was introduced in June 1991. All citizens, both resident and nonresident in the USSR, are subject to tax. Non-permanent residents (those who stay less than 183 days in a calendar year) are liable for tax only on income arising in the USSR.

All income is subject to tax. Monthly income from salaries is subject to tax, with rates ranging from a minimum of 12% on income up to 1,000 rubles per month to a maximum of 30% on income over 3,000 rubles per month.

Monthly salary tax is withheld by the employer. Other sources of income, such as trading profits and rental income, are subject to tax, which must be paid quarterly.

10. Local Income Taxes

New tax legislation is under consideration in several republics. Several republics, including Estonia, Latvia, Lithuania, and Russia, have proposed both income tax and foreign investment laws.

11. Capital Gains Taxes

There are no special capital gains taxes.

12. Foreign Tax Reliefs

Taxes paid abroad by USSR permanent residents are allowed as a credit to offset tax liability. Such taxes may not exceed the total amount of tax due in the USSR. In any conflict between Soviet law and international double taxation treaties, the treaties prevail.

13. Tax Period

Individuals must use the calendar year.

14. Other Matters

Recently enacted tax reform also provides tax rates and rules for part-time workers, authors, and individuals engaged in agriculture.

INCOME TAXES ON NONRESIDENTS

15. Liability to Tax

Foreign legal entities and joint ventures are subject to tax in the USSR. Joint ventures are subject to tax at 30% (see item 34).

Foreign partners may be liable for withholding at 15% if the foreign partner is not exempt or eligible for an incentive.

17. Withholding Tax Rates

In general, a 15% withholding tax applies to profits attributable to a foreign partner and that are repatriated to a country with which the USSR does not have a tax treaty covering dividends. A withholding tax of 20% is levied on interest income, rents, and royalties.

Treaties have been concluded between the USSR and the following countries:

	Withholding Tax Rates		
	Dividends	Interest	Royalties
Austria	0%	0%	0%
Canada	15	15	10
Cyprus	0	0	0
Finland	0	0	0
France	15	10 (1)	0
Japan	15	10	10
Netherlands	15	0	0
Norway	20	0	0
Spain	18	0	5
Sweden	15	0	0
United Kingdom	0	0	0
United States	— (2)	0	0
West Germany	15 (3)	5 (4)	0

Notes:
(1) 0% for bank loans and commercial credit.
(2) No article covering dividend payments.
(3) 25% for certain partnerships.
(4) 25% for profit participation loans.

Treaty Definitions

Period of Time

	Construction Site (1)	Employment (2)
Austria	no article	less than 183 days
Canada	less than 12 months	less than 183 days (3)

Treaty Definitions

Period of Time

	Construction Site (1)	Employment (2)
Cyprus	less than 12 months (4)	less than 183 days
Finland	less than 36 months	less than 183 days
France	less than 24 months (5)	less than 183 days (6)
Japan	less than 12 months	less than 183 days
Netherlands	less than 12 months (4)	less than 183 days (7)
Norway	less than 12 months	less than 183 days (4)
Spain	less than 12 months	less than 183 days (6) (7)
Sweden	less than 18 months (8)	less than 183 days (6) (7)
United Kingdom	less than 24 months	less than 183 days (6) (7)
United States	no article	less than 183 days
West Germany	less than 12 months	less than 183 days

Notes:
(1) Period before a construction site becomes a permanent establishment.
(2) Period before employment becomes taxable for a resident of a treaty country.
(3) Under 183 days or 365 days in two consecutive calendar years for technical specialists.
(4) Period may be extended by agreement.
(5) If sites exceed 24 months, profits will be determined by mutual agreement.
(6) There are further detailed provisions with respect to time limits.
(7) There are detailed provisions for certain types of employment.
(8) Longer periods by negotiation.

19. Tax Treaties

In addition to bilateral tax treaties, the USSR also is party to several multilateral tax treaties and agreements on such issues as shipping and air and surface transportation.

OTHER SIGNIFICANT TAXES

21. Sales (Value Added)

Tax reform under consideration would impose a sales or value-added tax at rates varying from 10% to 30%.

22. Inheritance and Gift Taxes

There are no inheritance or gift taxes.

23. Taxes on Payrolls (Social Security)

A contribution must be made for social insurance by employers at the rate of 11% of salary.

24. Taxes on Natural Resources

There are no special rules on the taxation of natural resources.

25. Other Taxes

Entertainment Taxes. A 70% tax is imposed on net income from casinos, video arcades, and other types of entertainment.

COMPUTATION OF TAXABLE INCOME

26. Capital Gains

Although there are no special taxes on capital gains, the concept of gain as the measurement of income exists. Certain expenses may be deducted from income, including material expenses, depreciation, rent, labor expense, social security costs, property insurance, interest costs, repair costs, and other related expenses.

27. Depreciation and Depletion

The rules for depreciation are established under Soviet accounting rules. In general, depreciation and amortization are the same for accounting and tax. Depreciation follows a straight-line method over lives that are generally longer than those in Western countries. Land, minerals, forests, and other natural resources are subject to recovery through depletion allowances.

Faster depreciation allowances and recoveries may be permitted under joint venture agreements (see item 34).

29. Loss Carryovers

Recent tax changes provide for a five-year carryforward of net operating losses.

RELATED CONSIDERATIONS

34. Incentives and Grants

Since 1986, the Government has taken steps to encourage foreign investment in the USSR. Companies wishing to do business in the USSR should consider a variety of economic and commercial issues, including the foreign investment laws (and incentives) that apply in the individual republics. Below are some of the major tax implications affecting foreign corporations and joint ventures in the USSR.

Foreign Corporations:

☐ *Activities subject to tax*—taxes at the rate of 40% are imposed on persons carrying on business in the USSR for the following:

—profits derived from performing work in the USSR, including construction, assembly projects, transportation services, and the rendering of services within the country;

—profits from the use of authors' rights, patent rights, industrial designs, and other proprietary processes;

—profits derived from any other activity within the USSR.

□ *Deductions*—expenses related to carrying on the above activities in the USSR are allowed as deductions in determining taxable profit.

□ *Exempt income*—certain types of income may be tax-exempt if approved by the appropriate ministry of foreign trade organization. Types of income allowable for exemption include the following:

—interest from credit agreements and related operations;

—amounts paid for reprinting foreign scientific and technical materials;

—amounts paid by foreign trade organizations to import goods, equipment, or services;

—amounts paid to individual performers in art, music, or sports.

□ *Construction*—profits from construction are taxed at 40% of the site profit as shown on the site accounts. A withholding tax of 5% on the gross payment received from the Soviet customer may be levied instead. As with ordinary trading activities, it may be possible to negotiate a lower rate of tax that would be equal to the rate at which a similar Soviet entity would be taxed in the foreign participant's home country.

Joint Ventures. In general, a joint venture with more than 30% foreign participation pays a 30% tax on profits after certain deductions. Note that joint ventures with less than 30% foreign participation are treated as domestic enterprises and subject to tax at 35%. A 20% withholding tax is imposed on dividends paid to shareholders outside the USSR unless other provisions have been made in tax treaties between the USSR and the receiving country (see item 17). Also, the Council of Ministries can reduce the amount of tax on profits or wholly exempt the payment from tax.

□ *Joint venture agreement*—the joint venture agreement provides the total amount of contributions and the allocation of joint venture shares. Until recently, foreign partners' shares could not exceed 49%. As of December 1988, foreign investors may own up to 99%, and a foreign individual may be the chief executor. A partner's contribution can include currency as well as buildings, equipment, other tangible assets, the right to use land and resources, and intangible rights. There do not appear to be strict debt-equity limitations, although the USSR bank for external economic relations often is reluctant to guarantee credit if total equity is less than 30% of the total capital.

Additional or specific tax holidays and incentives often are negotiated between the foreign partner, the Soviet partner, and the Council of Ministries when the joint venture agreement is initiated.

☐ *Deductible expenses*—certain allocations to specific reserves from profits are allowed. Deductions are permitted for transfers to a reserve fund until the total of the reserve equals 25% of the capital of the joint venture. Other funds, in addition to the reserve, can be established for specific purposes, such as meeting the social needs of employees or for the development of production, science, and technology. Of these, however, only a fund for the development of production, science, and technology may be used for deductible transfers.

☐ *Balance sheet profit*—the computation of profit or loss in the USSR is determined under a balance-sheet approach, computed in accordance with Soviet accounting rules. Financial statements are prepared predominantly on a cash basis, supplemented with certain required timing and valuation adjustments.

Balance profit is determined before tax and includes the various components of the costs of sales, such as materials, wages, depreciation, insurance, lease costs, and interest. Transfers to the capital reserve fund (limited to 25% of capital) and a production and development fund (unlimited) then are deducted.

Taxable profit is subject to tax at a rate of 30%. Taxable profit is distributed 100% each year. Taxes represent the first distribution; the second distribution is to the social development fund for the workers (generally 10% to 15% of the balance profits); and the third distribution represents shareholder dividends.

☐ *Tax reliefs*—a joint venture with sufficient foreign investment generally is exempt from tax for the first two years, beginning with the first year in which it shows a taxable profit. Thus, this amounts to a tax holiday on three years' profits. Joint ventures operating in the Far East economic region are granted an additional year's tax exemption.

The Ministry of Finance can temporarily exempt from tax the share of profits that a joint venture's foreign shareholder intends to transfer out of the country or to lower the tax rate, unless otherwise specified in the tax agreement. At present, it is not clear how such an exemption or reduction will operate. According to recent regulations, it is to be applied primarily to joint ventures that manufacture consumer goods, hospital technology, pharmaceuticals, or certain technological products, or to those that are vital to the economy.

☐ *Foreign exchange gains and losses*—according to Government regulations, foreign exchange gains and losses are to be taken on profit and loss accounts. Unrealized exchange gains will be recognized and subject to tax.

☐ *Withholding tax*—in addition to the general 30% tax on profits, a 20% withholding tax applies to profits that are attributable to a foreign partner and that are repatriated to a country with which the USSR does not have a tax treaty or the treaty does not cover dividends. A withholding tax also can be levied on interest income and royalties. The withholding tax applies only to dividends transferred to foreign countries in currency. No withholding tax applies to dividends in the form of the joint venture's goods.

35. Exchange Controls

A foreign venture may repatriate profits in foreign or "hard" currency only to the extent of foreign currency revenue. Any remaining profits in rubles may not be remitted. Several options exist for dealing with unremitted profits and may be addressed in the joint venture agreement. They include counter-trade or barter, purchase of Soviet goods and services for export, import substitution (sale of goods of Soviet enterprises for hard currency), and investment in Soviet enterprises.

UNITED ARAB EMIRATES

1. Taxes

In general, no income or other tax is levied on companies or individuals. The main exceptions are taxes on the profits of oil companies and foreign banks at up to 55% and 20%, respectively. There are no official regulations prescribing methods of computing taxable income, but for banks, the taxes are usually calculated on the financial profits as reported in the audited financial statements and for oil companies, according to the tax clauses inserted in the formation or concession agreement.

2. Depreciation and Depletion

Depreciation allowances range from 4% to 33.33%.

3. Capital Tax

There is no capital tax or tax on capital gains.

4. Taxation of Dividends

There is no tax on dividends, royalties, fees, interest, and similar payments, except as invoked in the concession agreement for oil companies or separate agreement for foreign banks.

5. Tax Treaties

The United Arab Emirates have double taxation agreements with other members of the Arab Economic Unity Council, including Jordan, Sudan, Syria, Iraq, Kuwait, Egypt, and Yemen. Under these treaties, profits derived from shares or dividends, interest, royalties, and fees are taxable only in the contracting state where the income is earned. There is a tax treaty with France, regarding income and inheritance tax. National carriers are normally exempt from taxation on a reciprocal basis.

6. Exchange Controls

There are no exchange controls in force.

7. Banking Facilities

The UAE is said to have one of the highest number of banks and branches per capita in the world. Banks are either locally established, or consortiums with mixed local and foreign interests, or branches of foreign banks. No new branches of foreign banks are now allowed to be opened in the country and established foreign banks are limited to eight branches. The banking sector is controlled by the Central Bank of the UAE, established in 1981.

UNITED KINGDOM

INCOME TAXES ON CORPORATIONS

1. Rates

The rate of corporation tax for the financial year April 1, 1991 to March 31, 1992 (financial year 1991) is 33%. For financial year April 1, 1990 to March 31, 1991, the rate was retroactively reduced from 35% to 34%.

A 25% rate of corporation tax, known as the "small companies rate," applies to taxable profits where the company's total profits are £250,000 or less. There is marginal relief where total profits are between £250,000 and £1,250,000, although these limits are reduced for companies in a group or with associated companies (which includes foreign associated companies).

2. Local Income Taxes

There are no state or provincial income taxes in the United Kingdom.

3. Capital Gains Taxes

Gains realized on the disposition of capital assets are taxed at the corporation tax rate.

4. Branch Profits Taxes

Branches of foreign corporations are subject to corporation tax at the same rate as for resident companies. The lower rate (see item 1) may be available where the relevant double tax treaty contains a nondiscrimination clause. No withholding tax is levied on distributions of branch profits.

5. Foreign Tax Reliefs

All income from foreign investments is brought into the charge to corporation tax. Credit for foreign taxes on income (excluding taxes on capital, sales and property, and value-added taxes) is given under double taxation agreements and under unilateral provisions of U.K. law.

Credit is given separately for each source of income and is limited to the corporation tax payable on that income. Relief is given for withholding and other direct taxes on income received. In the case of dividends, where the recipient controls (directly or indirectly) at least 10% of the voting power in the paying company, credit is given for underlying taxes paid on profits under the gross-up method. There are no provisions whereby excess foreign tax credit attributable to one source of income may be used against another or carried forward for relief against income of future periods. Credit given to banks (and other financial institutions generally) for withholding tax on interest received on overseas loans is limited to 15% of the gross interest.

Credit relief is restricted to U.K. resident companies. United Kingdom branches of foreign banks are given credit for withholding tax payable on interest on overseas loans limited to 15% (but excluding tax charged by the country in which the bank is resident).

7. Payment of Taxes

Corporation tax is payable at an interval of nine months after the end of an accounting period (see item 32).

8. Other Matters

Controlled Foreign Companies (CFCs).   A CFC is a company that is resident in an overseas territory whose tax rate is less than half that of the United Kingdom and which is controlled by persons resident in the United Kingdom. The taxable profits of a CFC may be apportioned (provided they are more than £20,000 per annum) and added to the taxable profits of a U.K. resident company according to its interest. No apportionment is made where the interest is less than 10% of chargeable profits. A credit for the tax paid in the tax haven may be deducted from the U.K. corporation tax charge. The profits of a CFC will not be apportioned in any of the following circumstances:

□   The CFC pursues an acceptable distribution policy (i.e., it distributes at least 50% of its profits (excluding net capital gains) if it is a trading company or 90% if it is not carrying on a trade).

□   The CFC is engaged in exempt trading activities in its territory of residence.

□   The CFC satisfies a bona fide purpose or motive test.

□   The CFC satisfies a public quotation condition.

INCOME TAXES ON INDIVIDUALS

9. Rates

The rates of income tax on individuals' taxable income from April 6, 1991 are as follows:

| Taxable Income | | Tax on | Percentage |
Over	Not Over	Lower Amount	on Excess
£ 0	£23,700	£ 0	25%
23,700	—	5,925	40

Taxable income is computed after deducting the individual's personal and other allowances. The income of a husband and wife is taxed independently. The liability of individuals to income tax in the United Kingdom depends on a number of factors, including their residence status, domicile status, the nature of the income, and the source of the income.

Employment Income.   In general, individuals resident and ordinarily resident in the United Kingdom are liable to tax on their worldwide employment income. Persons who are resident but not domiciled in the United Kingdom and who are employed by a nonresident employer and perform no duties in the United Kingdom are liable to tax on earnings from that employment only if they are remitted to the United Kingdom.

Individuals resident but not ordinarily resident in the United Kingdom (generally those persons whose stay is for less than three years and who do not own property in the United Kingdom) who perform duties in the United Kingdom are liable to tax on earnings in respect of those duties.

An individual's assessable earned income will include his or her salary plus the value of any benefits in kind or expenses received as a result of his or her employment. Expenses incurred wholly, exclusively, and necessarily in the course of performing the duties of employment are deductible.

Trading and Professional Income.   Individuals resident in the United Kingdom are liable to income tax on profits arising from trades and professions carried on alone or in partnership. Profits generally are taxed on a preceding-year basis. Special rules apply to profits arising on the commencement and cessation of trades and partnerships. Income tax is payable in two installments: on January 1 during the tax year and on July 31 following the end of the tax year.

Investment Income.   Individuals resident, ordinarily resident, and domiciled in the United Kingdom are liable to tax on income from all sources, whereas individuals not domiciled in the United Kingdom are liable to tax on income arising in the United Kingdom and income with respect to foreign assets that is remitted to the United Kingdom. The law governing remittances of income is complex, and foreign nationals proposing to take up residence or employment in the United Kingdom are advised to obtain detailed guidance before arrival.

10.   Local Income Taxes
None.

11. Capital Gains Taxes

Capital gains derived by individuals who are resident in the United Kingdom are charged to tax. Effective April 6, 1991, the first £5,500 of chargeable gains are exempt. Gains are taxed as if they were the top slice of an individual's income, although income tax deductions and reliefs cannot offset them. Gains arising to a non-domiciled but resident individual on assets situated outside the United Kingdom are liable only on a remittance basis. Credit is given for foreign taxes paid on gains from non-U.K. assets.

12. Foreign Tax Reliefs

Credit is given for taxes paid in territories outside the United Kingdom in respect of income from sources outside the United Kingdom either under double taxation agreements or under unilateral provisions of United Kingdom law. Relief is given only to residents of the United Kingdom and is limited to direct overseas taxes payable by the individual.

13. Tax Period

The tax year runs from April 6 to April 5.

INCOME TAXES ON NONRESIDENTS

15. Liability to Tax

Nonresidents of the United Kingdom are liable to tax on income derived from:

□ Property situated in the United Kingdom.

□ Any trade or profession carried on through a branch or agency in the United Kingdom.

□ Any employment the duties of which are performed in the United Kingdom.

Certain income (e.g., interest on certain government securities) is not taxed in the hands of nonresidents. By concession, interest on bank deposits and building society deposits held by nonresidents is not assessed in certain circumstances.

17. Withholding Tax Rates

	Dividends (1)	Interest	Royalties
Nontreaty countries	A	25%	25%
Treaty countries:			
Antigua and Barbuda	A	25	Nil (4)
Australia	B (2)	10	10 (4)
Austria	B	Nil	Nil (3)

	Dividends (1)	Interest	Royalties
Bangladesh	A	10% (5,6)	10% (4)
Barbados	B	15	Nil (4,7)
Belgium	C	15	Nil
Belize	B	25	Nil (4)
Botswana	B	15 (6)	15
Brunei	B	25	Nil (4)
Bulgaria	A	Nil	Nil
Burma (Myanmar)	A	25	Nil (4,8)
Canada	D	10 (6)	10 (9)
China	A	10 (6)	10 (10)
Cyprus	B	10	Nil (11)
Denmark	E	Nil	Nil
Egypt	A	15 (6)	15
Falkland Islands	B	10 (6)	Nil (4)
Faroe Islands	B	Nil	Nil
Fiji	B	10	15 (4)
Finland	E	Nil	Nil
France	B	Nil	Nil
Gambia	B	15 (6)	12.5
Germany (Federal Republic of)	A	Nil	Nil (4,8)
Ghana	A	25	Nil (4)
Greece	A	Nil	Nil (4)
Grenada	A	25	Nil (4)
Guernsey	A	25 (12)	25 (12)
Hungary	A	Nil	Nil
India	B	15 (13,6)	25 (4)
Indonesia (14)	B	15 (15,6)	10
Irish Republic	B	Nil	Nil
Isle of Man	A	25 (12)	25 (12)
Israel	A	15	Nil (4,7)
Italy (16)	E	10 (6)	8
Ivory Coast	A	15 (6)	10
Jamaica	B	12.5 (6)	10
Japan	B	10	10
Jersey	A	25 (12)	25 (12)
Kenya	B	15 (6)	15
Kiribati and Tuvalu	B	25	Nil (4)
Korea (Republic of)	B	15 (17,6)	15 (18)
Lesotho	A	25	Nil (4)
Luxembourg	E	Nil	5
Malawi	B	Nil (19)	Nil (4,8,19)
Malaysia	B	15	15 (4,8)

	Dividends (1)	Interest	Royalties
Malta	B	25%	Nil (4)
Mauritius	B	25 (20,6)	15%
Montserrat	A	25	Nil (4)
Morocco	A	10 (6)	10
Namibia	A	20	Nil (4,11)
Netherlands	E	Nil	Nil
Netherlands Antilles (21)	—	—	—
New Zealand	B (2)	10 (6)	10
Nigeria	A	12.5 (6)	12.5
Norway	D	Nil	Nil
Pakistan	A	15 (6)	12.5
Philippines	F	15 (22,6)	25 (7)
Poland	B	Nil	10
Portugal	A	10	5
Romania	B	10	15 (23)
St. Christopher and Nevis	A	25	Nil (4)
Sierra Leone	A	25	Nil (4)
Singapore	B	15	15 (4,8)
Solomon Islands	B	25	Nil (4)
South Africa	A	10	Nil (4)
Spain	B	12	10
Sri Lanka	A	10 (20)	10 (24)
Sudan	B	15	10
Swaziland	A	25	Nil
Sweden	E	Nil	Nil
Switzerland	E	Nil	Nil
Thailand	B	25 (13,6)	15 (25)
Trinidad and Tobago	G	10 (6)	10 (4,9)
Tunisia	A	12 (13)	15
Turkey	A	15 (6)	10
Uganda	A	25	Nil (4)
U.S.A.	E	Nil	Nil (8)
U.S.S.R.	A	Nil	Nil
Yugoslavia	B	10	10
Zambia	B	10	10
Zimbabwe	G	10 (6)	10

Notes:

(1) No withholding taxes are levied on dividends paid, and nonresidents do not receive the tax credit which is associated with dividend payments to U.K. residents. These rules are frequently varied by double tax treaty, with the result that U.K. treaties fall into the following general categories:

(A) Treaties that give no tax credits to nonresidents and therefore levy no withholding taxes.

(B) Treaties that give no tax credit for nonresident companies owning 10% or more; a full credit is given to other nonresident shareholders, subject to a 15% withholding tax on the combined total of the dividend and the tax credit.

(C) As in (E) but subject to a 20% withholding tax on the combined total dividend and tax credit given in (E).

(D) As in (E) but subject to a 10% withholding tax on the combined total of the dividend and the tax credit given in (E).

(E) Treaties which give:
  (i) A half tax credit to nonresident companies possessing 10% or more of the voting power of the company paying the dividend, subject to a 5% withholding tax on the combined total of the dividend and that credit.
  (ii) A full credit to other nonresident shareholders subject to a 15% withholding tax on the combined total of the dividend and the tax credit.

(F) As in (B), but subject to a 25% withholding tax on the combined total of the dividend and the tax credit.

(G) As in (B), but subject to a 20% withholding tax on the combined total of the dividend and the tax credit.

The Taxes Act 1988 empowers the Government to introduce regulations to deny the treaty credit in E(i) above to a nonresident company if the company, or companies associated with it, have a qualifying presence in a state operating a unitary system of taxation.

(2) No tax credit for companies.

(3) 10% rate on royalties if recipient company owns over 50% of shares in paying company.

(4) 25% rate on certain mineral royalties.

(5) 7.5% rate on interest paid to a bank or financial institution resident in Bangladesh.

(6) Nil rate on interest paid to certain government bodies.

(7) 15% rate on film and certain other royalties.

(8) 25% rate on film and certain other royalties.

(9) Nil rate on copyright royalties, except on films.

(10) 7% for royalties with respect to industrial, commercial, or scientific equipment.

(11) 5% rate on film and certain other royalties.

(12) Credit given unilaterally in United Kingdom for tax paid in Guernsey, Jersey or Isle of Man.

(13) 10% rate on interest paid to banks.

(14) Notice of termination given with effect from April 1984. A new treaty is under negotiation. The old treaty will remain in force during negotiations.

(15) 10% rate on interest owed between banks, financial institutions, and certain other business enterprises.

(16) New treaty effective April 1991, except that for petroleum revenue tax and Italian tax the effective date is January 1991.

(17) 10% rate on loans for period exceeding two years.

(18) 10% rate on certain industrial royalties.

(19) 25% rate if recipient company controls over 50% of the voting power of the paying company.

(20) Nil rate on interest paid to a bank or certain similar entities.

(21) Treaty terminated effective April 1989.

(22) 10% rate on company bonds, debentures, etc., issued publicly.

(23) 10% rate on copyright royalties.

(24) Nil rate on copyright royalties.

(25) 5% rate on copyright royalties.

19. Tax Treaties

The United Kingdom has concluded an extensive range of double taxation agreements with over 80 countries throughout the world. These agreements may reduce the liability of nonresidents.

OTHER SIGNIFICANT TAXES

21. Sales (Value Added)

In common with other EC countries, VAT is charged on the supply by registered business of most goods and services. The standard rate is 17.5% effective April 1, 1991 (15% prior to April 1, 1991), which also applies to imported goods and certain services rendered by overseas persons. Exports of goods and certain services, domestic supplies of basic necessities, and some services of a social nature have a nil VAT rate. VAT-exempt supplies include insurance, banking, and certain property transactions. Fully taxable businesses recover VAT paid on most business costs including capital expenditure. VAT recoverable by businesses whose supplies include exempt transactions is restricted.

Foreign business concerns that make supplies of goods or services in the United Kingdom are required to register and charge VAT under the same rules as for domestic business. Foreign businesses that incur VAT on business costs but make no taxable supplies in the U.K. may apply to reclaim the VAT that a U.K. business can recover.

22. Inheritance and Gift Taxes

Inheritance tax applies to gifts (and similar transfers that reduce the value of the transferor's estate) and the value of assets passing on death. The tax is assessed by reference to the circumstances of the transferor rather than the transferee.

Where a lifetime gift is made to an individual or to certain trusts, no tax is payable provided the transferor lives for seven years after the date of the gift. Should the transferor fail to do so, the maximum tax is imposed on the transferee but taper relief is available if death occurs four to seven years after the gift is made.

Other lifetime gifts are taxable when made at 50% of the full rates, and if the transferor pays the tax, it is chargeable on the gift's grossed-up value. Additional tax (subject to taper relief) may become payable if the transferor fails to survive seven years.

The rate of tax payable on all lifetime gifts is determined by reference to the cumulative value of the transferor's taxable lifetime gifts in the seven-year period prior to the gift.

Tax is levied at full rates on the value of the deceased's estate on death, which is cumulated with the value of all taxable lifetime gifts within seven years of the death in order to ascertain the tax rate.

The full rates of inheritance tax on chargeable transfers made on or after April 6, 1991 are as follows:

Aggregate Value		
Over	Not Over	Rate
£ 0	£140,000	0%
140,000		40

Taper relief for gifts within seven years of death is calculated as follows:

Years between gift and death	0–3	3–4	4–5	5–6	6–7
Percentage of full rate of tax	100%	80%	60%	40%	20%

Inheritance tax charges extend to:

☐ All property, wherever situated, owned by an individual domiciled or deemed to be domiciled in the United Kingdom.

☐ Property situated in the United Kingdom owned by individuals domiciled elsewhere.

☐ Certain gratuitous transfers by close companies.

There are certain exemptions (e.g., transfers between spouses and transfers to charities) and an annual exemption of £3,000, which if unused can be carried forward one year. In addition, relief in the form of reduced rates of tax is available with respect to transfers of certain types of property (e.g., agricultural land or buildings and certain businesses) in which the transferor has an interest.

23. Taxes on Payrolls (Social Security)

National Insurance contributions are payable in respect of employed and self-employed persons. For employed persons, part is payable by individual employees and part by employers.

From April 6, 1991, employees earning £52 or more per week will pay 2% on £52 and 9% on the remainder up to £390 per week.

Employers pay at the following rates on employee earnings, which include certain benefits in-kind for higher-paid employees and directors:

Weekly Earnings

On or Over	Under	Rate
£ 0	£ 52	0 %
52	85	4.6
85	130	6.6
130	185	8.6
185		10.4

The above employee and employer rates apply in respect of employees who are not contracted out of the State Earnings Related Pension Scheme (SERPS). Amended rates apply if the employee is contracted out of SERPS. There is no upper limit on an employer's contributions. Self-employed persons pay a flat rate of £5.15 per week and 6.3% on business profits in excess of £5,900 per annum, up to a maximum payment of £905.94.

Credit is given for similar social security payments made out of earnings in certain other countries.

24. Taxes on Natural Resources

Petroleum revenue tax is levied on revenue derived from the extraction of oil and gas in the United Kingdom, including the territorial seas and continental shelf of the United Kingdom. It is an allowable deduction for corporation tax purposes. There are no special taxes levied on the exploitation of other natural resources.

Capital allowances are given for mineral extraction expenditures.

25. Other Taxes

Local Taxes. Local authorities raise revenue by levying a flat-rate community charge (''poll tax'') on most adult residents and by charging a property tax (''uniform business rates'') on non-domestic land and buildings. The rate of poll tax is set by each local authority for residents in its own area. The uniform business rate is set by the central Government at a fixed national rate, which is applied to the annual rental value of all business property.

Stamp Duty. Stamp duty is chargeable on transfers of property other than gifts. The rate of duty is ½% on the value of stocks and shares and 1% on real property worth more than £30,000. Stamp duty reserve tax is charged at a rate of 0.5% on certain share transactions. The Government has made a commitment to abolish stamp duty and stamp duty reserve tax on transfers of most property other than land and buildings from a date expected to be around May 1992.

COMPUTATION OF TAXABLE INCOME

26. Capital Gains

The chargeable gain or loss is the difference between the cost of the asset (after being indexed for inflation) and the sales proceeds. Dispositions by way of gift and transactions that are not at arm's length are treated as dispositions at market value. Gains on assets held at March 31, 1982 and disposed of after April 5, 1988 are, with some exceptions, restricted by reference to a base market value at March 1982. Hold-over relief may be available for the gift of business assets from an individual to any other individual or one or more trustees, in which case the transferee inherits the base value of the transferor.

Transfers of assets within a U.K. resident group of companies (a parent and its 75% subsidiaries) are deemed to be for an amount such that no loss or gain arises. The transferee company inherits the base value of the transferor. There are no provisions for making consolidated group capital gains returns.

Certain gains are exempt, including gain on the disposition of an individual's main residence. Gains on disposal of certain assets used in a trade may be deferred if reinvested in qualifying trading assets within a specified period.

27. Depreciation and Depletion

Depreciation adopted in the accounts is ignored for taxation purposes. Instead, capital allowances based on the cost of plant and machinery and industrial buildings are given as deductions in computing taxable income. Allowances are also available for capital expenditures on scientific research, patent rights, know-how, and agricultural buildings.

The primary capital allowance rates are:

	Percent	Method
Plant and machinery	25	DB
Private cars (maximum allowance per car £2,000 p.a.)	25	DB
Other vehicles	25	DB
New industrial buildings and hotels (excluding land)	4	SL
Agricultural buildings (excluding most forestry)	4	SL
Patent rights and know-how	25	DB
Scientific research	100	

Method:

DB = Declining balance
SL = Straight line

There are special rules permitting allowances to be wholly or partially disclaimed and special provisions for leased assets and for plant with a life of less than five years.

28. Treatment of Dividends

No withholding taxes are deducted from dividends paid by United Kingdom companies. Companies become liable, on payment of dividends, to make an advance payment of corporation tax (ACT) equal to 25/75 of the dividend which is paid to the shareholders. ACT is treated as a payment on account of the ultimate liability to corporation tax on profits (including capital gains) for the period in which the dividend is paid, subject to an overriding limitation on set-off of 25% of the profits.

United Kingdom resident shareholders obtain a tax credit against their personal income tax liability equivalent to the ACT attributable to the dividend they receive. Certain double tax treaties give part of the credit to nonresident shareholders (see item 17). Capitalization of profits or bonus issues of shares or stock (other than redeemable stock) are not normally treated as taxable distributions unless issued as an alternative option to a cash dividend. U.K. resident corporate shareholders are not liable to corporation tax on dividends from U.K. resident companies. The tax credit may be used to reduce the ACT which a company is required to account for on payment of dividends.

29. Loss Carryovers

Trading losses of companies may be set off against total profits (including capital gains) for the year in which the losses arise. For accounting periods ending on or after April 1, 1991, trading losses of companies may be carried back to offset total profits of the preceding three years. For accounting periods ended before April 1, 1991, the maximum permitted carryback period was one year. Trading losses carried forward may only be offset against profits of the same trade as that in which the losses arose, but subject to this limitation the normal rule is that they may be carried forward indefinitely. Trading losses and certain other amounts may be surrendered to other group companies (see item 31.) There are anti-avoidance provisions which operate where the ownership of a company with unused trading losses changes hands. Capital losses may only be set off against capital gains arising in the same year or in future periods. Other rules cover the treatment of income tax losses of individuals and partnerships. An individual's capital losses may offset only capital gains arising in the same and subsequent tax years. Income tax losses of individuals and partnerships sustained after April 5, 1991 may be relieved against personal capital gains.

30. Transactions between Related Parties

Transactions between companies resident in the United Kingdom and companies not resident in the United Kingdom under common control which are not carried out on an arm's-length basis may be subject to a direction, the effect of which is to levy tax as if the transactions had been on an arm's-length basis.

Reorganizations of companies in the United Kingdom may involve disposals of capital assets. There are a number of relieving provisions that enable tax-free reorganizations to be achieved.

31. Consolidation of Income

Companies resident in the United Kingdom (i.e., companies either managed and controlled in the United Kingdom or incorporated in the United Kingdom) are liable to corporation tax on their worldwide profits from all sources, including capital gains. Consolidated returns are not submitted for related companies, although a trading loss incurred by a group company may be offset against the profits of other members of the group for the same accounting period. For this purpose, a group is defined as a parent company together with its 75% subsidiaries which are resident in the United Kingdom. Relief for losses is also available where at least 75% of a company's ordinary share capital is owned by a consortium of U.K. resident companies (minimum holding 5%).

32. Tax Periods

The basis period for computing the liability to corporation tax is the company's own accounting period.

RELATED CONSIDERATIONS

34. Incentives and Grants

Investments in Manufacturing and Certain Service Industries. Cash grants and other incentives are available for the purpose of encouraging new investment in designated "assisted" areas in the United Kingdom. In most cases the award of a grant is discretionary and must be negotiated before becoming committed to the project. The detailed rules are complex and advice should be taken by persons proposing to invest in the United Kingdom.

Enterprise Zones. Certain areas are designated "enterprise zones" for a period of ten years. Expenditure incurred on industrial, commercial, or hotel buildings in these areas qualifies for 100% capital allowances on buildings and plant installed in buildings. Businesses operating in such zones qualify for other benefits, including exemption from the uniform business rate.

Free Zones. A number of zones adjacent to seaports or airports have been designated as free zones. Goods may be stored in these zones for an unlimited period free of customs duties and VAT.

35. Exchange Controls

There are no exchange controls operating in the United Kingdom.

36. Investment Restrictions on Nonresidents

There are no investment restrictions on nonresidents, although Government consent will be required in certain circumstances before a nonresident can obtain control of a company in a strategic industry. There also are restrictions on overseas shareholdings in certain strategic industries.

SELECTION OF BUSINESS ENTITY BY NONRESIDENTS

All nonresident companies which have a place of business in the United Kingdom are required to file their accounts with the Registrar of Companies in the same form as domestic companies. Although there may be tax or commercial reasons for setting up branch operations in the United Kingdom, the normal form of business entity is the limited company.

In general, foreign-owned companies are taxed in the same way as domestic companies. A point of special difficulty arises if the company is financed by loan capital, as interest paid on the loan to a nonresident parent company (or affiliate) having 75% control will be treated as a distribution. This means that the interest attracts liability to ACT and does not rank as a deduction for corporation tax purposes unless it is relieved by a double tax treaty. The relief given in certain tax treaties is subject to provisions against thin capitalization.

On the payment of dividends by a U.K. company, certain treaties allow a tax credit to the nonresident shareholder (see item 17). A nonresident who carries on business in the United Kingdom through a branch or agency is liable to tax on his U.K. trading profits and on any capital gains on U.K. assets used by the branch at the same rate as U.K. companies (see item 1). The lower rate of 25% only applies where there is treaty protection.

SPECIMEN TAX COMPUTATION

Information:

□ The company's operating profit for the accounting year ended December 31, 1991 of £260,000 comprises:

U.K. trading profits	180,000
U.K. dividend income (including tax credit £5,000)	20,000
Profit on sale of investment	60,000
	£260,000

□ The U.K. trading results are arrived at after charging:

Annual interest payable (£6,000 paid)	5,000
Depreciation	25,000
General provision for bad debts	5,000
Entertaining (other than staff)	2,000

□ The company purchased plant in September 1991 costing £140,000, which qualifies for the writing down allowance of 25%.

□ The company paid a dividend of £162,000 during the year. ACT thereon was £54,000 which, after deduction of £5,000 tax credit on dividend income, gives ACT of £49,000 to set off against the company's corporation tax liability.

□ The small companies rate of 25% (see item 1) does not apply since the company is a member of a large group of companies.

Computation:

	£	£
Profit per accounts, before tax		260,000
Add		
Depreciation	25,000	
General provision	5,000	
Entertaining	2,000	
Interest payable	5,000	37,000
		297,000
Less		
Dividend income	20,000	
Profit on sale of investment	60,000	
Writing down allowance (£140,000 × 25%)	35,000	115,000
		182,000
Add		
Capital gain (after indexation relief of £5,000)		55,000
		237,000
Less		
Interest paid		6,000
		£231,000
Corporation tax payable		
(Financial year 1990: £231,000 × 3/12 @ 34% = £19,635)		
(Financial year 1991: £231,000 × 9/12 @ 33% = £57,172)		76,807
Less		
Maximum ACT set-off		
(£231,000 × 25%) (1)	57,750	
ACT paid (net)	49,000	49,000
Tax payable October 1, 1992		£27,807

Note:

(1) The restriction is equal to the basic rate of income tax (see items 9 and 28).

UNITED STATES

INCOME TAXES ON CORPORATIONS

1. Rates

U.S. corporations are taxable on their worldwide income at the following rates:

Taxable Income		
Over	Not Over	Rates
$ 0	$ 50,000	15%
50,000	75,000	25
75,000		34

The benefit of the lower rates is gradually phased out by imposition of a 5% surtax on income between $100,000 and $335,000.

For corporations primarily engaged in providing services, taxable income is taxed at a flat 34% rate.

Minimum Tax.   In addition to the regular tax, corporations may be subject to a 20% alternative minimum tax (AMT). The AMT is imposed on taxable income increased by tax preference items and certain other adjustments. It is imposed on AMT income in excess of $40,000, but only where the AMT is more than the regular corporate tax. The $40,000 exemption is phased out for corporations with income over $150,000. Some significant preference and adjustment items include: accelerated depreciation, certain installment sales, tax-exempt interest on certain private activity bonds, and 75% of the difference between adjusted current earnings and taxable income.

S Corporations.   S corporations are hybrid business entities that combine the flexibility of the partnership format with the advantages of operating in a corporate form. Corporate shareholders must elect S corporation status, which remains in effect until revoked or terminated.

Items of corporate income, loss, deduction, credit, and tax preference pass through to the shareholders on a pro rata basis. Shareholders are taxed on such corporate income, whether distributed or not. Deductibility of losses is restricted by at-risk rules, basis rules, and passive loss limitations.

2. Local Income Taxes

Various state and local taxes are levied. The taxable bases and the tax rates vary widely. Taxes may be based on income, which generally is allocated to a state or locality determined by an apportionment formula that measures business activities based on property, payroll, and sales or gross receipts. The income tax rates may reach 12% or more but the average is substantially less. In addition, a state may impose corporate franchise taxes based on the capital employed in the state. State and local income taxes are deductible in determining taxable income for purposes of the federal income tax.

3. Capital Gains Taxes

Capital gains are defined as gains or losses arising from the sale or exchange of designated capital assets. Short-term capital gains (assets held for one year or less) are taxable at the regular income tax rates. (See item 1.) Long-term capital gains (assets held for longer than one year) also are taxed at the same rates as ordinary income. The distinction between capital and ordinary gains and losses continues to be relevant because capital losses can be offset only against capital gains. Such losses may be carried back three years and forward for five years. All such losses carried back or forward are grouped with other capital losses for that year and are used to offset any capital gains. However, the losses carried back are limited to an amount that will not cause or increase a net operating loss in the carryback year.

A loss resulting from the sale of depreciable property or from land used in a business is generally an ordinary deduction from income. However, any net gains from such sales may be taxed as capital gains after complex depreciation recapture rules are taken into account. Due to the repeal of preferential treatment of capital gains, this recharacterization will no longer be significant.

4. Branch Profits Taxes

Branches of foreign corporations are taxed on their income from U.S. sources, and on income from foreign sources that is effectively connected with the conduct of a U.S. business (see item 15) in the same manner and at the same tax rates as U.S. corporations.

In addition to tax at the corporate rates, a tax of 30% is imposed on the earnings of the U.S. branch that are deemed to be available for distribution. A similar levy is imposed on the interest expense attributable to the branch and considered paid to foreign lenders. The branch level tax on earnings deemed repatriated and interest paid may be reduced by income tax treaties.

5. Foreign Tax Reliefs

Comprehensive relief is provided for foreign taxes paid, both under double taxation treaties and under U.S. law. A tax credit is provided for direct foreign taxes paid on income. An indirect tax credit is also provided when dividends are received from first, second, and third tier related foreign corporations, for the taxes paid on the profits from which the dividends were paid. Provided a U.S. corporation owns at least 10% of the voting shares of the foreign corporation, the indirect credit is computed under the gross-up method, whereby the creditable taxes are included in the income of the U.S. corporate shareholder. The foreign tax credit is subject to limitations. First, foreign source income items, and their accompanying taxes, must be separated by categories (e.g., passive, financial services, shipping income, interest subject to a high withholding tax, dividends from foreign corporations in which the ownership is between 10 and 50%, and overall operating income). Within each category the tax credit cannot exceed the U.S. tax that would be payable on the net foreign-source taxable income within that category.

In lieu of a credit for foreign income taxes, a U.S. taxpayer may choose to deduct from taxable income all such taxes imposed directly. Foreign taxes other than income taxes are deductible even if the credit is claimed.

The foreign tax credit is generally available to a foreign corporation for foreign income taxes it pays on income that is effectively connected with a U.S. business.

7. Payment of Taxes

Corporations must pay estimated income tax in quarterly installments. Their annual income tax returns are due, with the unpaid balance of the income tax, within two and one-half months after the close of their tax year. Automatic extensions of up to six months for filing the tax return can be obtained, but not for the payment of tax due.

Foreign persons (corporations and nonresident aliens) are denied the benefit of tax deductions and credits unless tax returns are filed timely.

8. Other Matters

Controlled Foreign Corporations (CFC)—Subpart F Income. A CFC is a foreign corporation more than 50% controlled (voting power or value) by 10% U.S. shareholders. Although the U.S. may have no jurisdiction over a foreign corporation not engaged in business in the U.S., it uses its jurisdiction over U.S. shareholders to tax certain income, known as Subpart F income, directly to U.S. shareholders whether or not such income is actually distributed to them. For this purpose, a U.S. shareholder generally is a U.S. person owning 10% or more of the foreign corporation's voting power. The investment income earned by a CFC, as well as certain sales or services income derived by a CFC from transactions with related persons, generally will be taxed directly to its U.S. shareholders if such income is 5% or more of the CFC's gross income or $1 million. Also taxed to its U.S. shareholders is any increase in a CFC's earnings invested in certain property in the U.S., and the income earned by a CFC from insuring certain risks.

INCOME TAXES ON INDIVIDUALS

9. Rates

For 1991, the tax rates are as follows:

Married, Filing Jointly

Taxable Income		Tax on	Percentage
Over	Not Over	Lower Amount	on Excess
$ 0	$34,000	$ 0	15%
34,000	82,150	5,100	28
82,150		18,582	31*

Single

Taxable Income		Tax on	Percentage
Over	Not Over	Lower Amount	on Excess
$ 0	$20,350	$ 0	15%
20,350	49,300	3,053	28
49,300		11,159	31*

For 1992, the tax rates are as follows:

Married, Filing Jointly

Taxable Income		Tax on	Percentage
Over	Not Over	Lower Amount	on Excess
$ 0	$35,800	$ 0	15%
35,800	86,500	5,370	28
86,500		19,566	31*

Single

Taxable Income		Tax on	Percentage
Over	Not Over	Lower Amount	on Excess
$ 0	$21,450	$ 0	15%
21,450	51,900	3,218	28
51,900		11,744	31*

*Note:

Higher effective rates will apply if adjusted gross income (AGI) exceeds $100,000 in 1991 ($105,250 in 1992). Itemized deductions will be reduced by 3% of the excess AGI over this amount. This cutback, however, does not apply to medical, casualty, or investment interest deductions, and the amount disallowed cannot exceed 80% of total deductions. In addition, the benefit of the $2,150 personal exemption ($2,300 in 1992) is phased out at the rate of 2% for each $2,500 (or portion thereof) of AGI in the $150,000–$275,000 range for joint returns ($100,000–$225,000 for single returns).

Income Earned Abroad. U.S. citizens and resident aliens must pay federal income tax regardless of where they live or work, subject to a foreign tax credit for foreign taxes on the foreign portion of their income (item 12). U.S. citizens and resident aliens working overseas may elect to exclude up to $70,000 of qualified foreign earned income. Qualified housing expenses that exceed a base figure may also be excluded. In addition, the value of meals and lodging provided by an employer for those living in a qualifying camp outside the U.S. may also be excluded. Excess qualified housing expenses may be deducted if they are not borne by an employer. To qualify for the income and housing exclusions, the taxpayer must either be a bona fide resident of a foreign country who resides abroad for a full taxable year (generally, available to U.S. citizens) or be present outside the U.S. for 330 days out of 12 months (available to U.S. citizens and residents).

The foreign earned income and housing exclusions are elective and, if made, are binding on all subsequent tax years until revoked. If revoked, a new election cannot be made for the next five taxable years unless the consent of the IRS is received for the reelection.

Minimum Tax. Individuals may be subject to a 24% alternative minimum tax. The tax applies to alternative minimum taxable income in excess of specified exemption amounts, $30,000 (single) and $40,000 (joint). These exemption amounts are subject to phase out at certain income levels. Individuals are subject to the alternative minimum tax only if the alternative minimum tax is greater than the regular tax.

Alternative minimum taxable income is computed starting with regular taxable income determined with certain adjustments and preference items. Some significant adjustment and preference items include accelerated depreciation on certain real and leased personal property placed into service before 1987, depreciation of tangible property placed into service after 1986, depletion, incentive stock options, miscellaneous itemized deductions, and taxes.

10. Local Income Taxes

The information in item 2 generally applies to individual taxpayers.

11. Capital Gains Taxes

The maximum tax rate on net capital gains (long-term capital gains less short-term capital losses, if any) is 28%. The distinction between capital gains and ordinary income assets and the differentiation between long-term and short-term capital gains and losses are retained because the character and type of gain will affect the computation of tax.

Capital losses that exceed capital gains are allowed up to $3,000 and can offset gains dollar for dollar. Unused losses may be carried forward to future years until absorbed.

12. Foreign Tax Reliefs

Comprehensive relief is provided under double taxation treaties. In addition, under U.S. law, a tax credit or deduction is provided to citizens and residents of the United States for the direct taxes paid by the individual. The credit allowed is limited by categories (see item 5) to the same proportion of total U.S. tax that the taxable income from sources outside the United States bears to worldwide taxable income. A tax credit or deduction for such taxes is given to nonresident alien individuals on income effectively connected with the conduct of a trade or business within the United States.

13. Tax Period

Generally, individual taxpayers use the calendar year. However, an individual may elect a fiscal year, under certain circumstances, if such election is made for his first tax year. Fiscal-year taxpayers must maintain a set of books and records. Annual returns must be filed on or before the fifteenth day of the fourth month following the close of the tax year (April 15 for the calendar-year taxpayer). Extensions of up to six months are available. The extension does not extend the time for payment of any taxes due on the return. Individuals may be liable for penalties if sufficient estimated taxes have not been paid.

INCOME TAXES ON NONRESIDENTS

15. Liability to Tax

A foreign corporation or nonresident alien that is engaged in a U.S. business is taxed on income that is effectively connected with that business, in general, in the same manner and at the same rates as apply to domestic corporations and resident individuals. U.S. source income of both foreign corporations and nonresident aliens that is not effectively connected with a U.S. business, usually passive income such as interest or dividends, is generally subject to withholding taxes on the gross amount, as noted in item 17, and capital gains are generally exempt from tax. An election is available to treat income from U.S. real property as effectively connected with a U.S. business. Such an election enables the foreign owner to be taxed on net, rather than gross, income; thus, deductions for depreciation and other expenses may be obtained.

No U.S. withholding tax is imposed on interest paid by a U.S. corporation which had at least 80% of its gross income from an active trade or business outside the U.S. during the three taxable years preceding the payment of interest.

Proceeds from the disposition of a U.S. real property interest (which includes stock of a U.S. corporation owning predominantly U.S. real property) generally is subject to withholding of 10%, which is a credit against the tax ultimately due when tax return is filed.

Record Maintenance Requirements for Foreign-Controlled Corporations. U.S. business operations with foreign owners must maintain certain records relating to transactions with foreign related parties and generally must maintain those records within the United States. Noncompliance penalties may be imposed.

U.S. withholding tax is required on effectively connected income of U.S. partnerships that is allocable to foreign partners, regardless of whether the income is distributed. The withholding rate is 34% for corporate partners and 28% for individuals, partnerships, trusts, and estates. Partnerships are required to make quarterly withholding installments on the income subject to tax.

17. Withholding Tax Rates

The following table gives the basic provisions of how U.S. tax treaties apply to withholding on outward remittances of dividends, interest, and royalties. Under several treaties, the exemption or reduction in rate applies only if the recipient is subject to tax on such income in its country of residence; otherwise a 30% rate applies. So many exceptions and conditions apply, which are too numerous and detailed to list here, that the specific treaty must be reviewed in each case.

Certain U.S. portfolio interest and interest from U.S. banks may be exempt from U.S. withholding tax under domestic law.

| | Dividends | | | Industrial |
	To Parent	Other	Interest	Royalties
Nontreaty countries	30%	30%	30%	30%
Treaty countries:				
Aruba*	30	30	0	30
Australia	15	15	10	10
Austria	5	15	0	0
Barbados	5	15	12.5	12.5
Belgium	5	15	15	0
Canada	10	15	15	10
Cyprus	5	15	10	0
Denmark	5	15	0	0
Egypt	5	15	15	0
Finland	5	15	0	0
France	5	15	0	5
Germany	5	15	0	0
Greece	30	30	0	0
Hungary	5	15	0	0

	Dividends			Industrial
	To Parent	Other	Interest	Royalties
Iceland	5%	15%	0%	0%
India	15	25	15	20
Indonesia	15	15	15	15
Ireland	5	15	0	0
Italy	5	15	15	10
Jamaica	10	15	12.5	10
Japan	10	15	10	10
Korea	10	15	12	15
Luxembourg	5	15	0	0
Malta	5	15	12.5	12.5
Morocco	10	15	15	10
Netherlands	5	15	0	0
Netherlands-Antilles*	30	30	0	30
New Zealand	15	15	10	10
Norway	15	15	0	0
Pakistan	15	30	30	0
Peoples Republic of China	10	10	10	10
Philippines	20	25	15	15
Poland	5	15	0	10
Romania	10	10	10	15
Spain	15	15	10	10
Sweden	5	15	0	0
Switzerland	5	15	5	0
Trinidad & Tobago	30	30	30	15
Tunisia	14	14	15	15
United Kingdom	5	15	0	0
U.S.S.R.	30	30	0	0

* Termination (in part) effective January 1, 1988. Note that the treaty with South Africa also has been terminated.

19. Tax Treaties

Foreign persons relying on a tax treaty to reduce their U.S. taxes must disclose that information.

OTHER SIGNIFICANT TAXES

21. Sales (Value Added)

No sales or value added tax is levied by the U.S. government except for some selective taxes at the manufacturing level (gasoline, tires, trucks, alcohol, tobacco, etc.). State and local governments levy sales taxes on varying goods and at varying rates, which range up to 8%. These are normally paid by the ultimate consumer.

22. Inheritance and Gift Taxes

A federal estate and gift tax is imposed on transfers of an individual's estate at death. The unified tax ranges from 18% to 55%, depending on the value of the taxable estate.

The maximum federal rate bracket for the unified estate and gift tax for gifts made and for decedents dying after 1987 is 55%, applying to taxable transfers over $3,000,000.

The estate of a U.S. citizen or resident includes all property wherever located. U.S. citizens and residents are entitled to a unified credit of $192,800, which is applied after determining the combined cumulative tax liability for lifetime transfers and transfers made at death. The effect of this credit is to eliminate federal tax on estates below $600,000.

A generation-skipping tax is imposed if large amounts of property (in excess of $1 million) are given or transferred at death to a beneficiary more than one generation younger than the donor or decedent unless a gift or estate tax has been imposed on a person in the intervening generation.

Decedents who are neither U.S. citizens nor residents (nonresident citizens) are taxed only on the transfer of property located within the United States. Such property generally includes debts owed by a U.S. person and shares in a U.S. corporation, but does not include bank deposits. The estate and gift tax rates applicable to U.S. citizens and residents apply to nonresident noncitizens. An estate tax "unified credit" of $13,000 is provided to nonresident noncitizens. A higher credit may be allowed to the extent required by any U.S. tax treaty.

Nonresident noncitizens are subject to gift tax on the gift of tangible property located in the United States. Gifts of intangible property (such as stocks and bonds) are not subject to gift tax. There is no unified credit available for gift tax purposes.

Foreign death taxes or duties are creditable against the estate tax imposed on U.S. citizens and residents, but are not creditable or deductible for property included in the U.S. estates of nonresident noncitizens. An unlimited marital deduction is available, which generally permits the transfer of property from a decedent to a surviving spouse free of federal estate tax. The marital deduction generally is not available if a U.S. citizen or resident bequests property to a non-U.S. citizen spouse; it is available for bequests by a nonresident noncitizen to a surviving spouse who is a U.S. citizen. Transfers of a decedent's share of community property to a surviving spouse will qualify for the marital deduction.

Additionally, many states levy an estate or inheritance tax. A limited credit against the federal estate tax is available for these taxes.

23. Taxes on Payrolls (Social Security)

The U.S. social security system provides retirement and other benefits. The separate contributions payable equally by both employer and employee are 7.65% of the first $53,400 in 1991 ($55,500 in 1992) of gross wages. Further, a medicare tax at the rate of 1.45% on the employer and on the employee is imposed on wages between $53,400 and $125,000 in 1991 ($55,500 and $130,200 in 1992).

The tax rate for a self-employed person is 15.3% and applies to a $53,400 earnings base in 1991 ($55,500 in 1992). The medicare tax, at the rate of 2.9%, applies to wages between $53,400 and $125,000 in 1991 ($55,500 and $130,200 in 1992).

A separate tax is levied for unemployment insurance, which is paid by the employer as are premiums for workman's compensation insurance. The federal unemployment tax rate is 6.2% on the first $7,000 of wages paid.

25. Other Taxes

Personal Holding Company Tax. Broadly, a corporation is a personal holding company if (1) 60% or more of its gross income is derived from dividends, interest, income from personal services performed by a substantial shareholder, royalties, and rental income; and (2) if it is a closely held corporation (five or fewer individuals own directly or indirectly more than 50% of the stock). In addition to regular income tax, personal holding companies pay a penalty tax of 28% on undistributed personal holding company income. They are exempt from the tax on accumulated earnings.

Foreign investors with diverse interests in the U.S. frequently form a U.S. holding company to hold the shares of the various U.S. subsidiaries. Although such holding companies may meet the definition of a "personal holding company," the penalty tax does not apply if income is almost exclusively from dividends from subsidiaries that are actively engaged in business and are included in a consolidated income tax return. This matter requires the continual attention of a qualified tax advisor. Foreign corporations are not subject to the personal holding company provisions when the shares are all owned directly or indirectly by nonresident aliens, except for personal service contract income.

Property Taxes. The federal government imposes no property tax. However, taxes on real and personal property are levied by state and local governments. These taxes are generally based on the assessed value of the property (which is not necessarily the fair market value), vary widely, and are usually not significant.

Capital or Net Worth Tax. The federal government has no tax on capital or net worth. Some states and localities impose such taxes. No federal taxes are levied on the exploitation of natural resources, except for a windfall profit tax on producers of crude oil.

Accumulated Earnings Tax. Income accumulated in excess of the "reasonable needs of the business" is subject to a penalty tax of 28%. A cumulative exemption of $250,000 of undistributed earnings and profits is allowed. The cumulative exemption for corporations whose principal activity consists of the performance of certain services is $150,000.

Environmental Tax. Corporations with alternative minimum taxable income (see item 1) in excess of $2 million will be liable for an environmental tax at the rate of .12% of income above that amount. Certain environmental excise taxes also apply, such as the tax on ozone-depleting chemicals.

Luxury Excise Tax. Effective January 1, 1991, a new 10% excise tax is imposed on that portion of the cost of certain "luxury" items that exceeds a specified amount. The tax applies to automobiles costing more than $30,000, aircraft costing over $250,000, and jewelry and furs costing over $10,000.

COMPUTATION OF TAXABLE INCOME

26. Capital Gains

Capital gain or loss is measured by the difference between the tax basis (usually cost with adjustments for depreciation) of a capital asset and its sales proceeds.

Although preferential capital gains treatment has been repealed for corporations, the distinction between capital assets and ordinary income assets has been retained, and the character of the gain may affect tax computations. Note that a nominal 28% maximum rate will apply to long-term capital gains for individuals (see item 11).

27. Depreciation and Depletion

The Accelerated Cost Recovery System (ACRS) applies to assets placed in service after December 31, 1980 and before 1987. The cost of tangible depreciable property is recovered (deducted) at accelerated rates specified in tables over 3-, 5-, 10-, 15-, or 18-, or 19-year periods, depending upon the classification of property under the system. Longer lives are prescribed for property used predominantly outside the United States. Use of the accelerated rates may result in the imposition of the minimum tax (see item 1). Alternatively, taxpayers may elect to use the straight-line method over the specified period of the class or two other specified extended periods provided for each class. In addition, part or all of the gain upon the disposition of a depreciated asset may be "recaptured"; i.e., taxed at ordinary, not capital gain, rates.

The ACRS has been modified for most property placed in service after 1986. The new rules ("modified ACRS") apply to both new and used property. The major modifications include: certain assets are reclassified according to their present class life or "Asset Depreciation Range (ADR) midpoint life"; depreciation methods have been prescribed for each ACRS class, replacing statutory tables; real property will be depreciated on the straight-line method over 27½ years (residential) or 31½ years (all other); eligible personal property will be assigned a 3-, 5-, 7-, 10-, 15-, or 20-year class.

The revised 3-, 5-, 7-, and 10-year classes of property will be depreciated using a 200% declining balance method, with a later switch to straight-line. Property in the 15- and 20-year class will use a 150% declining balance method, switching to straight-line.

An alternative cost recovery system providing longer lives and using the straight-line method is mandatory for property used outside the U.S. The alternative systems can be elected by taxpayers.

Exhaustible natural deposits and timber qualify for the deduction of a reasonable allowance for depletion, which is normally based on the taxpayer's cost. Mines and certain interests in oil and gas wells may calculate depletion as a specified percentage of gross income, if such provides a greater deduction than cost depletion.

28. Treatment of Dividends

Dividends paid by taxable domestic corporations to U.S. citizens and resident aliens are taxable to such individuals. Dividend income of a nonresident alien is generally subject to the withholding rates discussed in item 17. Stock dividends, with certain exceptions, are not taxable.

A corporation may deduct from gross income 70% of the dividends received from a taxable domestic corporation, with certain limitations (80% if the recipient corporation owns at least 20% of the distributing corporation). Affiliated corporations may elect to deduct 100% of dividends received from other members of the affiliated group (consent of all members is required).

29. Loss Carryovers

Net operating losses may generally be carried back three years and forward fifteen years, with longer periods for certain types of income. An election may be made to waive the carryback period. Special rules apply to the computation of net operating loss carryovers of individuals.

30. Transactions between Related Parties

Gross income, deductions, credits, and allowances may be reallocated to clearly reflect income among businesses owned or controlled by the same interests. Comprehensive regulations provide guidelines for certain transactions.

A corporation's current deduction for interest paid or accrued to related persons is limited if the related person is not fully taxed by the United States on interest income.

Capital Transactions. The following capital transactions may be tax-free: organization of a corporation; exchange of property for stock provided the control requirements are satisfied; reorganizations through mergers, consolidations, and acquisitions of stock or assets in exchange for stock. However, when one or more of the corporations involved is a foreign corporation, permission may be required and a "toll charge" may be imposed with respect to the transaction. Losses from transactions between certain related persons are not deductible.

Corporations generally will be required to recognize gains and losses in connection with liquidating distributions of property. In addition, most nonliquidating distributions of appreciated property by corporations will be subject to tax at the corporate level.

31. Consolidation of Income

An affiliated group of corporations may file a consolidated return and be taxed as one corporation. Subsidiaries which may not be consolidated include foreign corporations, life insurance companies, certain corporations doing business in a U.S. possession, regulated investment companies, real estate investment trusts, and a domestic international sales corporation (DISC) or a former DISC. Life insurance companies may be included if they have been a member of the group for five years.

32. Tax Periods

The company's own accounting period may generally be used for income tax purposes.

RELATED CONSIDERATIONS

34. Incentives and Grants

The interest income from state and municipal bonds is generally exempt from federal taxation. The following tax incentives are also available:

☐ Credits are available for the substantial rehabilitation of certified historic structures and nonresidential structures first placed in service before 1936.

☐ For employing members of "target" groups, employers may obtain credits against income tax based on first-year wages.

☐ Taxpayers may elect to write off in five years the costs of certain pollution control facilities and certain other expenditures.

☐ Taxpayers may elect to deduct research and experimental expenses either currently or ratably over five years beginning with the year in which benefits are first realized. An additional credit is applicable for certain incremental research expenditures for activities conducted in the United States.

Foreign Sales Corporations (FSC). United States exporters who establish a foreign corporation in selected jurisdictions can exempt from U.S. tax a portion of their earnings from the sale of export property. For many U.S. manufacturers the exemption will be approximately 15% of export earnings. For U.S. wholesalers of export property, the exemption can reach 30% of export income. The FSC must maintain an office outside the United States and certain management functions must be performed outside the United States. The corporation must perform certain economic processes outside the United States and meet basic foreign presence requirements.

Domestic International Sales Corporation (DISC). For export sales up to $10 million, U.S. exporters may form a DISC corporation. For many U.S. manufacturers, the U.S. tax on approximately 47% of export earnings can be deferred by using a DISC, provided the deferred income is invested in qualified assets and other requirements are met. For U.S. wholesalers of export property, the income deferred from U.S. tax can reach 94% of export earnings. An annual interest payment, based on the 1-year U.S. Treasury bill rate, must be paid on the deferred tax. A DISC permits a larger percentage of export profit to escape current U.S. tax than does a FSC. Utilization of a DISC results in a tax deferral only, and not a permanent tax exemption as is the case with a FSC.

Manufacturing in a U.S. Possession. Under certain circumstances, a U.S. corporation may elect to take a credit equal to the portion of its U.S. tax that is attributable to its taxable income from the active conduct of a business in a U.S. possession and from certain possessions source investment income. To obtain the credit, the corporation must have 80% or more of its gross income from sources within a possession, and 75% of its gross income must be from a business actively conducted within a possession. Nonqualifying income is taxed currently, subject to the usual foreign tax credit. Special rules apply to the transfer of intangibles to a possessions corporation, as well as income generated from the intangibles.

35. Exchange Controls

There are no exchange controls in general effect for residents and nonresidents. Remittances abroad for any purpose are not restricted, except to a limited number of countries and their nationals (North Korea, Vietnam, Cambodia, and Cuba). All nonbanking U.S. businesses, including U.S. subsidiaries of foreign companies, are required to file periodic reports to the Federal Reserve Bank on assets, liabilities, and forward positions in foreign currencies. Additionally, persons who mail, ship, transport, or receive more than $10,000 of currency or monetary instruments in or out of the United States must file Customs Form 4790.

36. Investment Restrictions on Nonresidents

There are few federal restrictions on investments by nonresidents although there are certain reporting and withholding requirements (see item 15). Note, however, that the U.S. government may suspend or prohibit any merger or acquisition by a foreign person of a U.S. business enterprise if there is a national security threat.

SELECTION OF BUSINESS ENTITY BY NONRESIDENTS

A local subsidiary that is incorporated in one state is considered a foreign corporation in other states and must obtain permission to do business in other states, which is normally a routine matter. Similarly, an overseas corporation that establishes a branch operation must obtain permission to operate in any state. These matters are not crucial in selecting the form of entity in which to do business, which is a matter that requires considerable study. Some of the most important factors that enter into the selection are:

□ An overseas corporation is exposed to liability for the debts of its branch, while a subsidiary corporation does not expose its parent to such liability.

□ A local subsidiary is taxed at regular rates on its worldwide income while a branch is taxed at regular rates on its income effectively connected with a U.S. business.

□ A branch may expose the parent company to examination of its records by the Internal Revenue Service, while the examination of a local subsidiary generally involves only its own records.

□ A withholding tax is generally imposed on dividends paid by a subsidiary to its overseas parent. A comparable tax is imposed on the earnings of a U.S. branch available for distribution. However, investors from certain treaty countries may be able to avoid the branch taxes.

Numerous other factors enter into the decision to operate as a branch or a subsidiary including the ease of, and type of, financing that may be required, and the tax considerations in the foreign country. In practice, the majority of foreign investment is in the form of a local corporation.

In addition, a branch level tax will be imposed on the amount of interest deducted that exceeds the amount actually paid.

SPECIMEN TAX COMPUTATION

Information:

□ The specimen tax computation compares the tax consequences of the following cases:

Case
(A) A foreign individual, non-U.S. citizen or resident, owns a U.S. corporation.
(B) A foreign individual, non-U.S. citizen or resident, owns a U.S. corporation through a foreign parent corporation.
(C) A foreign individual, non-U.S. citizen or resident, owns a foreign corporation with a U.S. branch.
(D) A foreign individual, non-U.S. citizen or resident, acquires or starts a U.S. business directly and operates through a partnership or a sole proprietorship. The assumed profits from U.S. operations are the only source of U.S. income.

Computation:

	Cases			
	(A)	(B)	(C)	(D)
Profits before U.S. income tax	$100	$100	$100	$100
U.S. state tax (assume 6%)	6	6	6	6
	94	94	94	94
Federal income tax (1)	32	32	32	29
Profit after taxes	62	62	62	65
Dividend	62	62		
U.S. withholding tax (15%)	9	3(2)	3(3)	
Net transfer	$ 53	$ 59	$ 59	$ 65

Notes:

(1) Assumes top 1991 tax rate (34% corporations; 31% individuals).

(2) In most treaty countries, dividends paid to foreign shareholders are subject to a 15% withholding tax. However, many treaties provide for a withholding rate as low as 5% for substantial holdings.

(3) The U.S. imposes a tax on the deemed repatriated earnings of the U.S. branch. For most branches of foreign corporations, the rate will be comparable to the dividend withholding rate.

URUGUAY

INCOME TAXES ON CORPORATIONS

1. Rates

The income tax rate for corporations is 30%.

2. Local Income Taxes

There are no state or provincial taxes on income in Uruguay.

3. Capital Gains Taxes

There is no separate capital gains tax in Uruguay. Capital gains are treated as ordinary income.

4. Branch Profits Taxes

The income tax rate for branches is 30%. Profits credited or paid to nonresident head offices by Uruguayan branches and to nonresident partners (including dividends) are taxed only if they are taxed in the foreign country and if there is a tax credit for the tax paid in Uruguay.

5. Foreign Tax Reliefs

There is no provision for foreign tax relief.

6. Classification of Corporations

All companies are taxed on their total Uruguayan income. A company is taxed at the 30% rate when capital and labor combine to produce its income. Agricultural production is treated in a special manner (see item 33). Taxable income is determined at the company level.

Partnerships are not taxed on income earned primarily from capital investments or labor.

INCOME TAXES ON INDIVIDUALS

9. Rates

No income tax is levied on personal income in Uruguay, except for tax on income derived from agricultural activities (see item 33) and tax on commissions (see item 25).

10. Local Income Taxes

None.

11. Capital Gains Taxes

See item 3.

INCOME TAXES ON NONRESIDENTS

15. Liability to Tax

Uruguay's income tax (see item 1) applies only to income from Uruguayan sources.

17. Withholding Tax Rates

Technical assistance fees credited or paid to nonresidents, if the beneficiaries of the assistance are subject to income tax, are subject to withholding at a 30% rate. These fees are exempt if they are taxed in the foreign country and there is no tax credit in the foreign country for the withholding tax paid in Uruguay. Royalties credited or paid to nonresidents are subject to withholding at a 30% rate.

19. Tax Treaties

Uruguay has no tax treaties with other countries.

OTHER SIGNIFICANT TAXES

21. Sales (Value Added)

The standard value-added tax (VAT) rate is 22%; it is expected to be reduced to 21% effective October 31, 1991. A reduced rate of 12% applies to necessities, medicine, and other food products. Certain items are exempt from VAT, including farm products, real estate, agricultural machinery, tobacco, milk, oil-processed fuels, newspapers, periodicals, and books. Some services are also exempt from VAT—for example, interest on bank deposits, personal transportation, real estate leases, and imports of nontaxed goods. Exports are not subject to VAT and may, in addition, recognize a tax credit for the VAT paid on purchases to be applied on the production of goods exported. The VAT paid on the goods employed for the production of agricultural goods is also recognized as a tax credit.

22. Inheritance and Gift Taxes

Since the Estate Tax Law was repealed in 1974, no taxes have been levied on inheritances and gifts.

23. Taxes on Payrolls (Social Security)

The main social security taxes are as follows:

	Employer Contributions	Employee Withholdings
Pension fund	16.5%	13%
Health insurance	4%	3%
Tax on salaries	1%	2, 4.5, or 7%

The employee withholdings on tax salaries are planned to be reduced in this year and in the next year.

Employees are entitled under social laws to a number of fringe benefits, whose effect in relation to their basic salaries and wages is estimated at the following rates:

Legal bonus	8.33%
Vacation pay	4.55, 4.42, 4.28%
Annual leave	5.56%

There is a compulsory workmen's compensation insurance, but premiums vary widely according to type of activity.

25. Other Taxes

Net Worth Tax. The net worth tax is levied on all assets located, placed, or economically used in Uruguay, less liabilities, both subject to special adjustments determined by the law. In connection with liabilities that can be deducted, there are important limitations determined by law.

Individuals, family units, and undivided estates are taxed on the progressive scale listed below, which is stated in terms of multiples of the basic nontaxable allowance which is currently N$ 55,600,000 for an individual taxpayer, or N$ 111,200,000 for a family unit. The basic nontaxable allowance is established annually at the end of each fiscal year.

Range of Multiples of the Basic Nontaxable Allowance	Tax Rate
Up to one time	0.7%
Between 1 and 2 times	1.1
Between 2 and 4 times	1.4
Between 4 and 6 times	1.9
Between 6 and 9 times	2.2
Between 9 and 14 times	2.7
Over 14 times	3.0

The net worth of companies and other juridical persons is taxed at a flat rate of 2%. Banks and financial institutions are taxed at a 2.8% rate. Bank accounts with an impersonal designation are taxed at a 3.5% rate.

Finance Investment Companies Tax. Companies whose main activity is investing, directly or indirectly, outside Uruguay in securities, deeds, drafts, notes, or real estate are subject to a special law that restricts their operations and participation in national activities. If the only assets in Uruguay held by such corporations are shares of other foreign investment corporations, their current account balances do not exceed 10% of their total assets, and their holdings of public debt securities do not exceed a further 10%, the only tax to which they are subject is a tax of 0.3% over net worth (if the loans are *less* than twice the net worth), or over the loans' deducted net worth (if the loans are *more* than twice the net worth). Foreign currency deposits held by these corporations in local banks are not considered to be investments in Uruguay and, if such funds are not employed in activities within the country, these corporations are exempt from all other taxes.

Offshore Banking Activities. Banks and other financial companies engaged solely in foreign financial operations are exempt from all taxes on their business activities, equity capital, or income.

Taxes on Commodities. These excise taxes are levied on the manufacturers or importers of various products (e.g., luxury items, vehicles, and petroleum products) when the product is initially sold. Exports are not taxed.

Tax on Sales of Foreign Currency. Sales of foreign currency, means of payment, government securities expressed in foreign currency, and shares of foreign companies are taxed if the payment is made in local currency and the payment occurs in Uruguay. Most sales of foreign exchange are subject to a 2% tax. The rate is 0.05% if foreign exchange sales are between banking, financial, and foreign exchange institutions.

Tax on Bank's Assets. The net amount between a bank's assets and offshore banking activities is taxed at rates of, depending on the type of assets, 0.75% or 1.75%.

Tax on Commissions. Commissions and other retributions derived from the activities of commissioners, agents, brokers, etc., are taxed at a 5% rate. Effective January 1, 1992, they will be taxed at a 7% rate.

COMPUTATION OF TAXABLE INCOME

26. Capital Gains

Capital gains are included in ordinary income.

27. Depreciation and Depletion

Assets must be depreciated on the straight-line basis over their useful lives. In the case of real estate, the following rates are mandatory for tax purposes:

	Annual Rate
Urban buildings	2%
Rural buildings	3%

28. Treatment of Dividends

See item 4.

29. Loss Carryovers

Fiscal losses may be carried forward for three years. There is no loss carryback. These losses are adjusted for inflations rates on the basis of the price index.

31. Consolidation of Income

The filing of group tax returns is not permitted.

32. Tax Periods

Companies, branches, and firms that keep proper accounting records may use their financial closing dates for tax purposes. In other cases, the calendar year must be used. The fiscal year for income derived from agricultural activities tax is July 1 to June 30, and banking activities tax period is January 1 to December 31.

33. Other Matters

Taxable Income.   Only Uruguayan-source income from industrial, trading, and similar activities is taxable, including:

☐ Income arising from regular earning activities developed by enterprises.

☐ Royalties for the use of trademarks, patents, industrial designs or franchises paid by income-tax payers to beneficiaries, unless the beneficiaries are subject to income tax.

☐ Fees for technical assistance rendered from abroad when the payer is a person or firm subject to income tax. These fees are exempt if they are taxed in the foreign country and there is no tax credit in the foreign country for the withholding tax paid in Uruguay.

☐ Dividends distributed to foreign corporations and individuals are taxed if they are taxed in the foreign country and there is a tax credit for the tax paid in Uruguay.

Income derived from agricultural activities is taxed on either a notional system or actual income as calculated for purposes of tax on income of Industry and Commerce (according to the decision of the taxpayer). If gross income is higher than N$ 45,600,000 (approx.), only the second system (i.e., real income) is accepted for the following fiscal year.

Revaluation of Fixed Assets. The revaluation of fixed assets is mandatory for determining the fiscal value of assets at the end of the fiscal year, for net worth tax purposes, and to determine current depreciation charges for income tax purposes. The indices used for revaluation purposes are set annually on the basis of price indices applied for the Inflation Adjustment.

Inflation Adjustment. The tax computation includes the economic changes derived from inflation. For that purpose, the percentage of change in the price indices is applied to the difference between the asset value adjusted at the beginning of the year (except for fixed assets and assets that produce tax-exempt income) and the liabilities at the beginning of the year (except the proportion corresponding to the assets that produce tax-exempt income). A loss arises when the adjusted assets exceed the adjusted liabilities. Conversely, a profit arises when the adjusted assets are less than the adjusted liabilities.

Financial entities can choose between fiscal rules or Central Bank regulations in relation to bad debts and accrued interest. The option cannot be changed until the fiscal year ended December 31, 1988.

Penalties for Infringement of Tax Regulations. The failure to pay a tax in the appropriate place when it falls due is subject to fines ranging up to 20% of the tax, plus default of compound interest computed at 8% per month (from January 1, 1991).

Transgressions which consist in the violation of laws or regulations imposing formal duties, and include actions that tend to hamper the Tax Authorities' assessment and control duties, are penalized by fines ranging from N$ 1,220 to N$ 106,000.

Any fraudulent act perpetrated with the intent to obtain unlawful enrichment at the expense of the State's right to collect taxes is penalized by fines that may range up to 15 times the amount of the tax involved.

Any acts not included within the aforementioned unlawful classifications, which lead to a reduction in the payment of taxes, are penalized by fines ranging up to five times the amount of the tax omitted.

Penal Implications of Tax Fraud. In addition to punitive measures a taxpayer committing fraud may be imprisoned a minimum of six months (up to six years).

Statute of Limitations. The normal period is five years, but it is extended to ten years in cases involving fraud, failure to register with the tax authorities, failure to file tax returns, etc.

RELATED CONSIDERATIONS

34. Incentives and Grants

Industrial Promotion Law No. 14,178 grants various benefits to industries declared to be of national interest by the Executive Power. These consist mainly of local and foreign currency credit facilities, tax benefits that include full or partial exemption from all taxes, rebates in rates for services rendered by the State, exemption from taxes on corporate net income, etc. In addition, special tax exemptions and benefits are available to specific industries; for example, national merchant marine and airlines, national fertilizers sales, oil explorations, and forestry.

35. Exchange Controls

There are no exchange controls, and there is one free exchange market.

36. Investment Restrictions on Nonresidents

Foreign Investment Law 14,179 guarantees the right to repayment of invested capital and remittance of profits to foreign investments approved by the Executive Power. The invested capital may not be withdrawn during the first three years following the date of the investment contract. Any profits not remitted abroad are deemed reinvested. Remittances to the foreign investors are allocated initially to profits, and any surplus beyond these to capital repayments.

SELECTION OF BUSINESS ENTITY BY NONRESIDENTS

Nonresident investors can operate in Uruguay through a branch, local subsidiary corporation, or local partnerships. There are no tax differences between a branch and a local corporation since both are taxed at the same 30% rate. The branch will generally not be allowed to deduct, however, interest or other charges from its overseas head office. In practice, the choice of entity is usually determined by foreign, rather than Uruguayan, tax requirements.

VANUATU

1. Taxes

There are no taxes on income, capital gains, dividends, wealth, estates, gifts, or inheritances. Because exempted companies and trusts need not advise details of ownership to any authorities, this lack of taxes will consequently continue. Exempted companies are those that do not engage in business within Vanuatu except in furtherance of their offshore business.

Tax Treaties. There are no tax treaties between Vanuatu and any other countries.

2. Exchange Controls

There are no exchange controls, and all currencies are freely convertible. The currency is the Vatu.

3. Banking Facilities and Secrecy Provisions

Branches of major foreign banks, trust companies, and other financial institutions provide all usual banking and trustee services, including investment portfolio management. Numbered bank accounts are available, and over 100 banks are registered in Vanuatu.

The Companies Act 1986 imposes strict secrecy provisions. Exempted companies need not disclose beneficial ownership to governmental authorities, need not be audited, and no accounts need be filed with the Registrar. Heavy penalties and jail terms may be imposed on any person who discloses beneficial ownership of either an exempted company or a trust.

4. Approximate Costs

The average cost of establishing a local company is about U.S. $1,700, about $1,850 for an exempted company, or about $900 for a trust. These costs include the provision of all nominee services for one year. The annual fees for servicing a company are about U.S. $1,200 (U.S. $500 for a trust), but these costs may vary significantly, depending on the extent of activity. Companies can normally be established within one week and trusts within one day. Exempted banks and financial institutions attract higher fees but are not expensive by international standards; the additional costs are about U.S. $2,600 for each company.

5. Free Flag Shipping Register

Vanuatu has a free flag shipping register based on the Liberian model. Ships may be registered either in Vanuatu or New York, where offices are maintained, at costs that are low by comparison with other countries. All major international conventions have been ratified.

6. Related Considerations

Persons wishing to establish a local business, whether they are residents or non-residents, are required to hold a business license. All expatriate employees in a local business must be granted a work permit and obtain a residency permit. Residency permits are granted for periods of up to ten years. All permits and licenses are readily obtainable provided the business itself is regarded as economically beneficial to the country. The government encourages all new investment in the country, and often customs duties can be waived for new capital investments, particularly in the tourism industry where significant growth is occurring.

7. Other Significant Taxes

Vanuatu imposes a 10% turnover tax on all hotel and restaurant sales, which is payable monthly to the government by the hotel or restaurant.

VENEZUELA

INCOME TAXES ON CORPORATIONS

1. Rates

Taxable Income		Tax Rate (1)	
Over	Not Over	Multiply By	And Subtract
Bs. 0	Bs. 2,000,000	20%	—
2,000,000		30%	Bs. 200,000

Notes:
(1) For corporations, limited liability companies, and other legal entities that resemble corporations, except:
—Legal entities engaged in oil and related activities, including state-owned companies, are taxed at a flat rate of 67.7%.
—Legal entities not engaged in mining, hydrocarbons, and related activities are taxed at a flat rate of 60% for their income derived from royalties and similar participations due to the exploitation of mines and other income derived from the cession of such royalties and participations.
—Income derived from agreements in connection with the exploitation and refining of heavy and extra-heavy crude oil or from the exploitation and processing of free natural gas that are approved according to the Organic Law, which reserves to the State the commerce and industry of hydrocarbons or contracts of national interest according to the Constitution, are subject to the above rates.

2. Local Income Taxes

None.

3. Capital Gains Taxes

No special treatment is provided for capital gains. The tax rates in item 1 apply to capital gains as well as to other taxable income.

4. Branch Profits Taxes

Branches and other agencies of foreign companies domiciled in Venezuela are subject to the same tax rates as Venezuelan corporations.

5. Foreign Tax Reliefs

The tax law does not provide any tax credit for taxes paid by a Venezuelan taxpayer to a foreign country or political subdivision thereof, nor are foreign taxes deductible from Venezuelan taxable income.

6. Classification of Corporations

Except for the special tax treatment applicable to oil and mining companies (item 1), all corporations constituted in Venezuela are treated alike for tax purposes. Foreign corporations operating through a branch are taxed only on the Venezuelan net income generated by the branch.

Each participating corporation in a joint venture (consorcio) is taxed on its share of the joint venture's taxable net income and subject to file their own income tax return. The joint venture itself is not taxed, but it is responsible for determining its taxable income and for filing an annual information return.

7. Payment of Taxes

Income tax, based on the annual tax return filed within three months after the company's fiscal year-end, must be paid in full before the tax return is filed.

Estimated Tax Payments. Taxpayers with taxable net income over Bs.500,000 in the prior fiscal year must file an estimated tax declaration during the last half of the ninth month of their current tax period. The estimated net income declared must be at least 80% of the taxable net income in the prior period (or written evidence must be submitted to justify a lesser amount). Only 75% of the estimated tax due in the estimated tax declaration will be payable. If the estimated tax due is less than Bs. 20,000, the tax must be paid in full before the declaration is filed. If more than Bs. 20,000 is due, it may be paid in up to four equal monthly installments.

Income tax withheld and payments of estimated tax are considered advance payments of the final income tax liability as determined in the annual tax return.

The timely payment of income tax is the taxpayer's responsibility; bills are sent only for deficiencies, fines, and interest on delayed payments.

8. Other Matters

Inflationary Adjustment. Effective December 31, 1992, an inflationary adjustment of non-monetary assets and liabilities, with the exception of securities, must be made to update their value and reflect the initial inflationary adjustment in the net worth for that date.

All taxpayers must register with the Register for Assets Revalued. A 3% tax rate applicable to the initial inflationary adjustment for fixed assets subject to depreciation must be paid in three equal portions in the subsequent fiscal periods following the registration. The basis for computation of the initial inflationary adjustment will be the variance in the index price for consumers in the metropolitan area of Caracas (published by the Central Bank of Venezuela) between the month of acquisition and the month the revaluation is made.

The initial inflationary adjustment made to a fixed asset will not constitute part of its cost when the asset is disposed of. Also, in the case of disposals or non-monetary assets other than fixed assets, the resulting value derived from the revaluation must be excluded when determining the profit or loss in such transactions. This regulation does not apply to liquidations.

The new resulting value—after revaluation—must be depreciated or amortized over the period of useful life already established. However, only the remaining depreciation or amortization expense will be deductible for income tax purposes.

Effective January 1, 1993, an inflationary adjustment for each fiscal year must be made for non-monetary assets and liabilities, with the exception of securities, according to the provisions established in the income tax law in order to determine the inflationary adjustment applicable to the computation of taxable income.

Non-monetary assets and liabilities will include such balance sheet accounts as land, construction, machinery, vehicles, installations, inventories, investments with the exception of securities, and credits and debts in foreign currency subject to adjustment.

Net worth will be adjusted for each fiscal period according to the provisions established in the law.

INCOME TAXES ON INDIVIDUALS

9. Rates

The taxable income of resident individuals, regardless of the type of income, is subject to the following rates:

Taxable Income		Tax Rate	
Over	Not Over	Multiply by	And Subtract
Bs. 300,000	1,000,000	10.0%	30,000
1,000,000	1,500,000	12.5	55,000
1,500,000	2,000,000	15.0	92,500
2,000,000	2,500,000	18.0	152,500
2,500,000	3,375,000	21.5	240,000
3,375,000	4,250,000	25.5	375,500
4,250,000		30.0	566,250

Resident individuals whose annual net income does not exceed Bs. 300,000 are exempt from tax.

Salaries and other types of compensation, such as special allowances, are subject to tax withholding at source. A number of deductions from taxable income (see item 14) and the following personal exemptions are allowed to resident individuals:

For the taxpayer	Bs. 2,500
For a spouse and each resident dependent	1,500

10. Local Income Taxes

None.

11. Capital Gains Taxes

No special treatment is provided for capital gains. That is, the tax rates in item 9 apply to capital gains as well as to other taxable income.

12. Foreign Tax Reliefs

The Venezuelan income tax law does not provide for any tax credit for taxes paid by a Venezuelan taxpayer to a foreign country or political subdivision thereof, nor are foreign taxes allowed as a deduction from Venezuelan taxable income.

13. Tax Period

Individuals whose principal income consists of salaries and wages, professional fees, rentals, interest, and certain other income must file on the calendar-year basis. Those whose principal income is from commercial or industrial activities, agriculture, cattle breeding or fishing, or mining activities may file on a fiscal-year basis.

14. Other Matters

Deductions. Resident individuals (see item 15) may claim deductions in computing taxable net income, of which the following are the more important:

- ☐ Municipal tax payments
- ☐ Electricity payments
- ☐ Water service payments
- ☐ Street cleaning service payments
- ☐ Telephone service payments
- ☐ Venezuelan social security taxes
- ☐ Interest payments in connection with the principal residence and rental payments

- ☐ Tuition paid to educational institutions in Venezuela for taxpayers' children not over 25 years of age and for themselves
- ☐ Payments for medicine ordered by physicians
- ☐ Vehicle repair payments
- ☐ Tuition paid to special educational institutions and social rehabilitation payments
- ☐ Twenty-five percent of noncommercial professional fees other than medicine noted above
- ☐ Premiums paid to Venezuelan insurance companies for life, surgery, hospitalization, and maternity insurance
- ☐ Car insurance premiums
- ☐ Medical, dental, and hospitalization expenses incurred in Venezuela for the taxpayer and his or her dependents
- ☐ Donations for educational, cultural, sport, scientific, political, religious, or welfare purposes
- ☐ Contributions by an employee to an employees' savings plan up to 10% of the employee's annual compensation.

INCOME TAXES ON NONRESIDENTS

15. Liability to Tax

Residents and nonresidents may be taxed differently, as noted in item 14. For income tax purposes, a nonresident is a person who spends 180 days or less in Venezuela during his tax year. However, a resident in the prior tax year remains a resident for tax purposes even if he spends 180 days or less in Venezuela in the current tax year.

17. Withholding Tax Rates

The following flat tax rates, subject to withholding, apply to income earned in Venezuela by nonresident individuals or nondomiciled legal entities:

	Tax Withheld
Salaries and other compensation paid to nonresidents	20%
Fees paid to nonresident individuals for noncommercial professional services rendered in Venezuela—(taxable income is 90% of the gross revenue)	30
Premium income, (as defined) of nondomiciled insurance companies (taxable income is 30% of net receipts from Venezuelan sources)	10

The following categories of income received by nonresidents are subject to the tax rates in item 1 for corporations, or the rates in item 9 for individuals. The respective tax must be withheld at source.

□ Royalty income other than that derived from mining activities—taxable net income if 90% of gross revenue.

□ Income received by contractors or subcontractors for certain projects or services rendered in Venezuela—payments over Bs. 12,500 are subject to 2% withholding in the case of corporations, and 1% withholding for payments over Bs. 25,000 in the case of individuals.

□ Interest received on loans utilized by the debtor for the production of income in Venezuela, if the recipient of the income is a foreign financial institution or a parent company—a special 5% tax rate applies.

□ Income received by nonresident individuals (other than from salaries and similar remunerations or fees for noncommercial professional services rendered in Venezuela, which are subvject to the above withholding tax rates)—a special flat rate of 20% applies.

□ Technical assistance fees for services rendered from abroad and used in Venezuela—taxable net income is 30% of the gross revenue.

□ Technological service fees for services rendered from abroad and used in Venezuela—taxable net income is 50% of the gross revenue.

□ Freight income from international transportation earned by nonresidents or companies not domiciled in Venezuela—the deemed gross revenue is equivalent to 50% of the freight income on trips between Venezuela and abroad and vice versa, and the deemed taxable net income is equivalent to 10% of the deemed gross revenue.

□ Income of foreign producers and distributors of movie and television films presented in Venezuela—taxable net income is 25% of the gross revenue.

□ Fees of nondomiciled entities for noncommercial professional services rendered in Venezuela—taxable net income is 90% of the gross revenue.

19. Tax Treaties

The following tax treaties for the avoidance of double taxation are in existence:

□ Dealing with air and sea transportation only:
　France
　Spain
　United Kingdom
　West Germany

□ Dealing with air transportation only:
　Argentina
　Brazil

Italy
Portugal
Switzerland
Trinidad and Tobago

☐ Dealing with Decision 40 under the Andean Pact, avoiding double taxation with regard to the following member countries:
Bolivia
Colombia
Ecuador
Peru

OTHER SIGNIFICANT TAXES

21. Sales (Value Added)

There is no value added or other sales tax imposed in Venezuela, apart from the license tax (see item 25), which is levied on sales.

22. Inheritance and Gift Taxes

Tax is imposed on gratuitous transfers of property by reason of death or by an inter vivos act or connected transactions and is payable by the beneficiaries. The tax rates follow:

Value of Property		Ascendants Descendants Spouse Adopted Children	Brothers Sisters Nephews Nieces	Other Collaterals 3rd and 4th Degrees (e.g., Uncle, Cousin)	In-Laws, Other Relatives, Nonrelatives
Over	Not Over				
Bs. 0	Bs. 15,000	1%	2.5%	6%	10%
15,000	50,000	2.5	5	12.5	15
50,000	100,000	5	10	20	25
100,000	250,000	7.5	15	25	30
250,000	500,000	10	20	30	35
500,000	1,000,000	15	25	35	40
1,000,000	4,000,000	20	30	40	45
4,000,000		25	40	50	55

Property whose value does not exceed Bs. 75,000 is exempt from tax when inherited by an ascendant, descendant, spouse, adopted parent, or child of the deceased. Gifts of up to Bs. 25,000 made within a five-year period are also exempt.

Reductions for both inheritances and gifts of 5% to 40% of the tax are granted to some categories of beneficiaries. These reductions are limited to Bs. 100,000 and are granted if the value of the inheritance or gift is less than Bs. 250,000. If the value is between Bs. 250,000 and Bs. 500,000, half of the reduction applies. In the case of inheritances, the net assets owned by the heir are added to the value of the inheritance to establish the limit of the reduction.

23. Taxes on Payrolls (Social Security)

Premiums are computed on the basis of the employee's salary to a maximum salary of Bs. 15,000 monthly. The premium is partially payable by the employer and partially by the employee, at the rates indicated below. Employers are divided into three risk categories.

Occupation	Rate	
	Employer	**Employee**
Low-risk	9%	4%
Medium-risk	10	4
High-risk	11	4

Unemployment Insurance ("Paro Forzoso"). Premiums are computed on the basis of the employee's salary to a maximum salary of Bs. 15,000 monthly. The premium is payable at the rate of 17% by the employer and 0.5% by the employee.

Housing Policy ("Politica Habitacional"). The purpose of this policy is to provide dwellings to workers. Contributions are payable by the employer and the employee. The basis for computing these contributions will be represented by ten minimum basic salaries (which, in effect, is Bs. 6,000). The maximum employee contribution is 1% of his or her monthly basic salary (Bs. 6,000 × 10 × 1% = Bs. 600), and 2% is payable by the employer (Bs. 6,000 × 10 × 2% = Bs. 1,200).

Labor Law. Most provisions concerning employment in Venezuela stem from this law. An important provision is the mandatory profit sharing with employees of at least 15% of each year's taxable income, with a minimum of 15 days of compensation and a maximum of four months. Many employers distribute the maximum or even more, voluntarily or based on a collective labor contract.

Another important provision is the obligation to pay indemnities on termination of employment. The indemnities to which employees have a vested right are payable at the rate of one month's compensation for each year of employment. Double indemnities are payable in cases of unjustified dismissal.

Payroll Tax. Employers of five or more workers who engage in commercial or industrial activities must pay a 2% payroll tax on all salaries and other compensation paid to employees.

24. Taxes on Natural Resources

An exploitation tax and certain other taxes are imposed on the state-owned petroleum industry. Mining operations are subject to various taxes, which vary with the particular item being mined, in addition to the regular income tax.

25. Other Taxes

Land and Property Taxes. Real property taxes, which vary from one municipality to another, are comparatively small in Venezuela. There is also a fee upon the transfer of real estate, which amounts to 1% of the consideration stated in the deed if the price is over Bs. 500,000. A lower fee is charged for lesser amounts.

Capital Taxes. Authorized capital, which must be fully subscribed, is taxed at the rate of one per thousand. The tax is levied only upon registration. As established by Decision 220 under the Andean Pact and its Venezuelan Regulations, a company's capital must be represented by nominative shares. Increases in capital are subject to the same tax.

The branch of a foreign corporation is subject to the same tax upon registration in Venezuela. Since the tax is based on the foreign corporation's authorized capital, it can be expensive to register a branch of a foreign company with substantial capital.

Municipal License Tax. The municipal license tax is levied on enterprises carrying on commercial, industrial or similar activities within the territorial jurisdiction of a Venezuelan municipality. The tax rate, applicable to a company's gross revenue reported in its annual declaration, is fixed by the municipal authorities in accordance with a list showing various tax rates for the different types of business. The tax varies from 0.25% to 10%, but in the majority of cases amounts to 0.5% or less. Some municipalities in the interior of the country levy the license tax at a flat amount. Exemptions or sizeable tax reductions for certain periods of time are sometimes granted.

COMPUTATION OF TAXABLE INCOME

26. Capital Gains

As indicated in items 3 and 11, gains and losses from the sale of fixed assets or investments are treated as ordinary income or loss, and are computed by deducting the adjusted cost basis of the asset from the selling price. The cost basis (see item 8) consists of the original cost plus the cost of any improvements, and is reduced by depreciation taken on assets used in the production of income and deducted from taxable income to the date of sale. In the case of real estate, registration fees are added to the cost.

Gains on the sale of a taxpayer's principal residence do not have to be declared for income tax purposes if certain conditions regarding reinvestment in a new principal residence are fulfilled.

On credit sales of real property, the gain or loss is reported proportionately as collections are made.

27. Depreciation and Depletion

Depreciation and amortization must be based on the cost of the asset (see item 8). No rates for the various categories of fixed assets have been set by the tax authorities, but the rates must be reasonable. The straight-line or unit-of-production methods of depreciation are allowed; the Income Tax Administration may allow other adequate depreciation methods. Salvage value of the depreciable assets need not be considered. The depreciation deduction is allowed only for assets located in Venezuela that are used in the production of the taxpayer's taxable income. Depreciation of real estate used in the production of rental income is not deductible. However, depreciation of real estate is allowed if the property has been rented to workers of the enterprise owning the real estate.

Intangibles whose useful life can be determined by law or contract can be amortized and the respective expense deducted from taxable income.

28. Treatment of Dividends

Dividends from Venezuelan corporations are not subject to any taxation.

29. Loss Carryovers

Net losses can be carried forward to reduce the net income of the next three years. There is no loss carryback.

30. Transactions between Related Parties

There are no special provisions for items of this nature.

32. Tax Periods

Corporate entities may elect any fiscal period. The tax period must comprise twelve months, except that the first or last return may be for a shorter period as may the result of a change in the fiscal year, which must be approved by the tax authorities. Taxable net incomes of such short periods are not subject to annualization.

33. Other Matters

Construction Income. Taxable income from construction contracts that extend over more than one year is determined on the percentage-of-completion method. When a construction contract takes less than one year to be completed, but the project extends over two tax periods, the taxpayer has the option of declaring the total income in the period during which the work is completed or, alternatively, declaring portions of the income in the two periods.

RELATED CONSIDERATIONS

34. Incentives and Grants

Venezuelan income tax law provides tax exemptions, tax credits, and special tax rates for certain taxpayers. Tax exemptions are automatic as they are in the income tax law. The most important categories of income exempt from income tax are:

- [ ] Income from agricultural, cattle breeding, and fishing activities.
- [ ] Certain interest income from Venezuelan government bonds, from savings and loan associations, and received by workers on accrued vested-right labor law indemnities.
- [ ] Retirement or disability pensions.
- [ ] Employer contributions to employees' savings plans.
- [ ] Severance indemnities received by employees.

Tax Credits. A wide variety of industries, including manufacturing, are granted a tax credit of 10% for investments in fixed assets for the five years following August 31, 1991.

Unused investment credits may be carried forward for three years. The credit is recaptured if assets are retired during the four years following the year of acquisition.

35. Exchange Controls

Since March 14, 1989, the local currency (bolivar) is floating freely.

36. Investment Restrictions on Nonresidents

Decision 220 under the Andean Pact governs the treatment of foreign capital invested in member countries. The provisions of the Andean Pact are important to the foreign investor and should be reviewed when contemplating an investment in Venezuela.

SELECTION OF BUSINESS ENTITY BY NONRESIDENTS

Investments made by foreign companies incorporated abroad involving the domiciliation of the foreign company in the form of a branch must be registered with the Superintendency of Foreign Investments. Foreign companies are authorized to establish subsidiaries in Venezuela. Foreign investors may receive the total annual profits, and the foreign company incorporated in this country is legally authorized to remit such profits abroad upon the foreign investor payment of Venezuelan income tax on such profits.

SPECIMEN TAX COMPUTATION

Computation:

□ Individual.

Compensation		Bs.900,000
Less		
Social security tax	Bs. 7,200	
Rentals	60,000	
School fees	20,000	
Car insurance	12,000	
	99,200	
Medical expenses	14,400	
Electricity	2,500	
Telephone	3,000	119,100
Taxable net income		780,900
Tax (Bs. 780,900 × 21%)		78,090
Less		
Differential for lower tax brackets		30,000
Tax before personal exemption		48,090
Personal exemptions (credits):		
Taxpayer	2,500	
Spouse and one child	3,000	5,500
Tax liability for the period		42,590
Tax withheld during the period		40,460
Balance of tax payable		Bs. 2,130

□ Corporation.

Net income per books		Bs.6,000,000
Add		
Expenses deductible when paid (timing differences)		
Provision for uncollectible receivables	Bs.200,000	
Provision for future inventory losses	500,000	
Provision for labor law indemnities in excess of vested-right indemnities	300,000	
Accrued taxes, other than income tax	8,000	
Nondeductible items (permanent differences)		
Travel abroad	65,000	
Other expenses incurred abroad	4,000	

Expenses of relocation from Venezuela to affiliated company abroad	45,000	
Expenses not considered normal nor necessary	14,000	
Fines	12,000	1,148,000
		7,148,000

Less

Taxes paid other than income tax	Bs.7,000	
Uncollectible receivables written off	140,000	
Inventory losses realized (previously reserved)	280,000	
Payment of labor law indemnities in excess of vested-right indemnities	180,000	
Payment of vested-right labor law indemnities accrued prior to 1978 (when they were deductible on the paid basis)	60,000	
Nontaxable income:		
Interest exonerated from income tax	80,000	
Dividend income	200,000	947,000
Taxable net income		6,201,000
Tax (Bs. 6,201,000 × 30%)		1,860,300
Less: Differential for lower tax brackets		200,000
Tax liability (before investment credit)		1,686,300
Less: Investment credit (10% of investment in fixed assets)		150,000
Tax liability for the period		1,536,300
Less: Estimated tax paid for the period		1,519,000
Remaining tax payable	Bs.	17,300

WESTERN SAMOA

INCOME TAXES ON CORPORATIONS

1. Rates

Companies are taxable annually on the worldwide taxable income, including the balancing charge arising from the sale of business assets and intercorporate dividends. No distinction is made between private or public companies for income tax purposes.

Taxpayer	Tax Base	Rate
Companies:		
Resident	Worldwide taxable income	39.0%
Nonresident	Western Samoan-source taxable income	48.0
Insurance companies:		
Resident	Non-Western Samoan-source reinsurance income	2.5
	life insurance fund investment income	10.0
Nonresident	Life insurance premiums income	7.5
	General insurance premiums income	15.0
	Reinsurance premiums income	7.5

Taxpayer	Tax Base	Rate
Shipping companies	Gross income	5.0
Nonresident film rental companies	Gross income	15.0

No special provisions exist for extractive industries.

Deductions from taxable income are allowed for all reasonable expenses incurred in gaining or producing income and for accumulated losses.

Certain income is exempted from taxation by investment incentives. Also tax-exempt is income derived by the producer of primary production from the sale and disposal of primary production. This income has been exempted since the tax year beginning January 1, 1975. Primary production includes farming, handicrafts, and fishing. Clergy income from donations have been exempt since January 1, 1988. Other exempt income includes National Provident Fund income and income derived from nonresident government securities, sports associations, charitable organizations, and others.

7. Payment of Taxes

Income tax is assessed on the preceding year's income. Companies pay an estimated provision tax based on that assessment.

INCOME TAXES ON INDIVIDUALS

9. Rates

A wage tax applies to the worldwide income of individuals resident in Western Samoa. Benefits-in-kind are included in income. The tax rates for individuals are:

Taxable Income		Tax Rate
Over	Not Over	
WS$ 0	WS$ 4,000	10%
4,000	8,000	20
8,000	12,000	30
12,000	16,000	40
16,000		45

Rebates may be taken against income tax based on the number of dependents claimed during the entire year:

Number of Dependents	Annual Rebate
0 dependents	WS$156
2–4 dependents	312

Number of Dependents	Annual Rebate
5–7 dependents	WS$468
8 or more dependents	624

Taxable income is gross income less deductions permitted by law. Deductions include reasonable business expenditures incurred to earn business income, but business losses are not deductible from wage income. Income derived from primary production is exempt from tax.

The tax on wages and salaries is withheld at source under the pay-as-you-earn (PAYE) scheme. Taxes are paid in installments during the year in which the income is earned. Except under special circumstances, PAYE tax is the final tax, with no refunds.

Dividend and other payments made by companies are subject to withholding tax at source, which is a final tax (see item 17). Dividends received from enterprises granted an income tax holiday are exempt from tax.

14. Other Matters

Partnerships. Partnerships are not subject to tax as a separate entity; the tax assessments are issued on each of the partners.

Trustees. Trustees are taxable at the flat rate of 50%.

INCOME TAXES ON NONRESIDENTS

15. Liability to Tax

Nonresident companies having assets or business in Western Samoa and nonresident individuals are taxable only on income from sources within Western Samoa.

See item 1 for the tax rates applicable to companies and item 9 for the rates applicable to individuals.

17. Withholding Tax Rates

Companies are required to withhold tax on dividends and other payments made to resident and nonresident shareholders.

Payment	Withholding Rate
Dividends	
Residents	10%
Nonresidents	15
Interest	15
Commissions	10
Director's fees	30
Royalties	15

The withholding taxes on interest and dividend payments is a final tax. Interest received by residents from sources outside of Western Samoa is subject to normal rates of tax (see item 9).

OTHER SIGNIFICANT TAXES

21. Sales (Value Added)

There are no general sales taxes in Western Samoa. Selective excise taxes are imposed on a wide range of locally produced goods and imports. The rates vary according to the product; some of the major rates are:

Tobacco products	130%
Beer	45
Whiskey	60
Soft drinks	20
Gems and precious metals	45
Motor vehicles (maximum)	70

Exports are exempt from the excise taxes.

Goods and Services Tax. Effective July 1991, a 10% goods and services tax applies to providers of certain professional services, such as accounting, architecture, engineering consulting, dentistry, insurance (except the provision of personal life insurance or superannuation), legal, medical and certain pharmaceutical, surveying, valuation.

The 10% consumer charge also is imposed on the provision of any service, including accommodations, meals or beverages, rental services, admissions to movie theaters or sporting or entertainment events, and lotteries and bingo.

Funds raised for charitable, religious, or educational purposes are exempted from this tax.

22. Inheritance and Gift Taxes

Effective January 1, 1987, there are no death or gift taxes.

23. Taxes on Payrolls (Social Security)

Effective 1972, social security contributions fund the National Provident Fund (NPF), an autonomous body under the Ministry of Finance. Contributions are payable by both employees and employers at the rate of 5% of monthly wages, including overtime pay, allowances, bonuses, etc. No contribution is payable by an employee or the employer on wages of less than WS$20 per month.

The employer is required to withhold employee and employer contributions and submit the withholding to the NPF within seven days of paying wages.

Individuals under the age of 15, nonresidents, and other persons determined by the Minister of Finance are exempted from social security contributions.

Accident Compensation. Two schemes provide rehabilitation and compensation assistance to injured individuals. In the event of death, benefits go to the deceased's dependents. One provides for compensation to workers injured on the job, the other to victims of motor vehicle accidents.

Employer's contribution to worker's compensation	1% of wages
Motor vehicle accidents	tax of 5 sene per gallon of imported motor fuel

25. Other Taxes

Business Use and Activity Licenses. Taxes on the use of goods or property or permission to perform activities are charged annually through licenses issued by the Department of Inland Revenue. Businesses may take out multiple licenses to cover the various aspects of trading; the charges are WS$200 a year or WS$4 for a special daily license.

Passenger Charge. All international travellers departing from the Western Samoan airport are liable to a charge of WS$5 for citizens or WS$20 for all others. Aircraft crew, children under the age of two, and transit passengers are exempted from the charge.

Import Duties. Import duties are imposed on cost, insurance, and freight of certain items at ad valorem rates. The predominant rate throughout the tariff is 35%. Examples of different rates are:

	Rate
Certain raw materials, building materials, equipment	20%
Certain agricultural supplies and equipment	5–20
Imported food	5–60
Certain chemical and allied products	50
Wood and wood products, certain paper products	60
Certain apparel and footwear	60
Televisions, certain radios	50
Certain vehicles	50

Certain items are exempted. Full exemption applies to approved materials for educational, cultural, or religious purposes; materials for socioeconomic development received under grants from the United Nations of foreign governments by Western

Samoan organizations for relief; supplies for diplomatic or consular services; and passenger baggage, within limits. Full or partial exemptions may apply according to the Enterprise Incentives (Amendment) acts (see item 34).

In addition to the import duty, an excise tax is payable, with the highest effective rate of 155%.

Export Duties. The following exported items are taxed on an ad valorem basis when the F.O.B. price exceeds a certain minimum.

	Rate
Cocoa	20%
Copra	5%
Copra meal	3%
Coconuts	3%
Coconut oil	WS$25 per metric ton
Fruits	3%
Veneer and sawn logs	20%
Rough timber (depending on thickness)	5%–15%
Taro	3%

Stamp Duties. Stamp duties are levied on selected documents at various rates, for example, WS$0.50 for Articles of Association, WS$1.25 for lease documents, 0.3% on the annual rental value of mortgages, and 1%–0.5% on the value of transferred shares.

Property Taxes. There are no taxes on real property.

COMPUTATION OF TAXABLE INCOME

26. Capital Gains

Capital gains are taxed at the rate of 30%.

27. Depreciation and Depletion

Depreciation allowances are granted for reasonable wear and tear of plant, machinery, equipment, and vehicles as prescribed by the Commissioner of Inland Revenue. Most plant and machinery is depreciated at 20% of the written-down value. Commercial buildings erected or first used after December 31, 1989 can be depreciated at the rate of 20%, other buildings at the rate of 1.5%. Special depreciation allowances may be granted by the Minister of Finance for purposes of encouraging economic development.

29. Loss Carryovers

Losses can be carried forward indefinitely.

RELATED CONSIDERATIONS

34. Incentives and Grants

Special depreciation allowances may be granted by the Minister of Finance for purposes of encouraging economic development.

Exemptions from import duties, full or partial, may apply to materials, equipment, and plant required for the stablishment or expansion of enterprises approved under the Enterprise Incentives (Amendment) acts of 1984 and 1986.

35. Exchange Controls

Every sale of foreign currency by a commercial bank is subject to a foreign exchange levy at the rate of 1% of the tala value of the foreign currency. There are no exemptions or deductions.

YUGOSLAVIA

Editor's Note: The unilateral declarations of independence by Slovenia and Croatia, two of the six republics, in June 1991, have precipitated a political, economic, and military crisis. The outbreak of hostilities has brought the economy close to the brink of collapse.

A fiscal reform commission was formed in 1990 to prepare a new tax system in Yugoslavia. It had planned to introduce new corporate and personal income taxes, as well as a European-style VAT. Some of the key components of the reform are:

☐ The corporate profits tax would apply to corporate joint stock companies, limited liability companies, and partnerships limited by shares.

☐ Taxable profits (after deduction of such items as labor costs, depreciation, and bad debts) would be subject to a tax rate of either 35% or 40%.

☐ Capital gains realized on the sale of fixed assets, real estate, and securities would be subject to tax.

☐ Tax consolidation within a group of companies would be permitted.

☐ A five-year loss carryforward rule would be introduced.

☐ Also contemplated is a progressive income tax on wages and salaries, fringe benefits, pensions, dividends and interest, capital gains, royalties, and rental income.

It should be noted that the federal government has no right to levy direct taxes, and such draft laws rather are model legislation for the republics to use in formulating their laws.

The information in this chapter is reprinted from the 1991 edition, and caution is advised as the future of the country as a unified nation is highly uncertain. Eventual resolution of political and ethnic conflicts may result in the formation of economically linked sovereign states, and the individual republics will require extensive economic reconstruction and rehabilitation.

OVERVIEW

There are three levels of government that determine taxes in Yugoslavia:

☐ **Federation.** The Federal government administers the sales tax and customs and import duties. In addition, it defines who is subject to tax, as well as the tax base for taxes imposed on enterprise profits, wages, and international transportation.

- □ **Republics.** The Republics further define the income tax system as well as the property tax and sales taxes.
- □ **Local and Provincial Governments.** The local and provincial governments fix the rate of income tax.

Thus, because there are three levels of government operating independently, there are significant differences in taxes in the various republics and municipalities. As a consequence, it is essential that the local, republic, and federal authorities be consulted before contemplating investment in Yugoslavia.

INCOME TAXES ON CORPORATIONS

1. Rates

All types of enterprises (e.g., corporations, limited liability companies, partnerships limited by shares, general partnerships and limited partnerships, socially owned enterprises, sole proprietorships that are registered as legal persons, banks and other financial institutions, and insurance companies) are subject to the tax on enterprise profits. For resident enterprises, the tax is imposed on worldwide profits (defined as the difference between the turnover and the total costs). The tax base for non-resident enterprises is the profits earned in the territory of Yugoslavia.

The tax is imposed at a flat rate, which varies by activity and republic. For example, see below for the range of tax rates applicable to income from the following activities:

- □ Construction—.98% to 1.55%
- □ Industry and mining—.21% to 5.36%
- □ Financial and business services—1.76% to 3.51%

Certain deductions are allowed in the determination of taxable income (see item 33).

7. Payment of Taxes

Social Accounting Service (SDK).   The SDK, which is organized on the federation, republic, and provincial levels, collects revenues paid by legal entities. Enterprises are required to calculate and execute tax payments to the appropriate SDK office. The SDK audits enterprise accounts and can require additional payments.

INCOME TAXES ON INDIVIDUALS

Individuals are subject to a number of taxes and contributions, including taxes on wages and salaries, agriculture, self-employment, royalties, property, and inheritance and gifts. See item 23 for contributions on salaries and wages.

9. Rates

Residents who earn income from employment in Yugoslavia or abroad (provided that the individual was sent to work abroad on the basis of employment in Yugoslavia) are liable for tax on wages and salaries. Nonresidents are liable for income tax on any income from employment in Yugoslavia.

Certain earnings, such as fringe benefits—meals, vacation subsidies—and compensation for retirement or employment lay-off, are not considered taxation income.

The tax rate is fixed by the republican government (for the republican tax) and by the local government (for the municipal tax). The municipal tax rates are determined in the republican agreement on tax policy. The tax rates vary from 1.28% if the employer pays the tax on enterprise profits and 2.17% if the employer does not pay the enterprise profits tax. The tax due is withheld by the employer at source.

14. Other Matters

Additional Personal Income Tax. Individuals earning annual total income in excess of three times the average annual net wages in the economy (Republic of Croatia) are subject to an additional personal income tax. Certain reductions to income are provided, such as for dependents, charitable donations, and certain other taxes and fees.

Property Tax. Individuals deriving income from renting or leasing land, buildings, or certain types of equipment are subject to a property tax at rates ranging from 15% to 70%, depending on the income generated. The tax is imposed on rental income collected during the year for which the tax is being assessed, after deducting necessary costs (including the sales tax paid on the rendered services). Certain low-income taxpayers are exempt from the property tax.

Public Revenue Service (PRS). The PRS, which is organized on the republic and local level, assesses and collects taxes paid by citizens. The PRS monitors all steps in tax assessment, including submission of the tax return, assessment, insurance of liability, appeal, and collection.

INCOME TAXES ON NONRESIDENTS

15. Liability to Tax

Foreign persons deriving income from economic activities in Yugoslavia are subject to tax on that income. The rate of tax varies in accordance with republic and provincial laws. Certain tax exemptions and reliefs are provided for foreign persons reinvesting profits.

Nonresident individuals are taxed on Yugoslav-source income at the same level as residents. In general, the tax rates range from 5% to 50%.

The tax base for nonresident enterprises is the profits earned in the territory of Yugloslavia; however, see item 34 for a discussion of incentives and grants provided to foreign investment. The tax rates range from 3% to 5%. Joint ventures are liable to tax at rates ranging from 10% to 35%.

19. Tax Treaties

Yugoslavia has concluded comprehensive tax treaties with the following countries:

Belgium	Italy
Cyprus	The Netherlands
Czechoslovakia	Norway
Denmark	Poland
Egypt	Romania
Finland	Sri Lanka
France	Sweden
Germany	United Kingdom
Hungary	

Negotiations are currently underway with Australia, China, Switzerland, and the United States.

OTHER SIGNIFICANT TAXES

23. Taxes on Payrolls (Social Security)

Employers are obliged to withhold contributions from wages and salaries to finance social security, social services, and certain activities (e.g., water supply, public utilities, etc.). The contribution rates vary from 8.8% to 43% if the employee works for the Government, the Chamber of Commerce, or National Bank, or is in the Army.

25. Other Taxes

In addition to the tax on enterprise profits, enterprises are required to make contributions to social security and various social services. Certain levies depend on business results (such as enterprise profits tax), while other do not depend on business results (health care contributions, special pensions).

COMPUTATION OF TAXABLE INCOME

33. Other Matters

Deductions. For purposes of the tax on enterprise profits, certain deductions are allowed in determining taxable income, including:

☐ Operational costs

—material costs, depreciation (up to levels prescribed by law);

—nonmaterial costs, such as rents, fees, per diem allowances, traveling expenses, meal expenses, entertainment expenses, insurance premiums, national defense expenses, environmental protection expenses, banking fees, membership fees, etc.;

—gross wages, but not exceeding the average level in the economy of the republic;

—acquisition price of commodities and materials.

☐ Financial costs

—interest;

—revaluation of debts;

—foreign exchange losses;

—other financial expenses.

☐ Extraordinary costs

—fines, penalties, damages;

—value of investments that is not written off;

—other extraordinary expenses.

RELATED CONSIDERATIONS

34. Incentives and Grants

An exemption is provided to the tax on enterprise profits for a period of five years if at least 30% of the invested capital is foreign. The exemption is proportional, based on the percentage of foreign capital in the joint venture.

SELECTION OF BUSINESS ENTITY BY NONRESIDENTS

Under the Foreign Investment Law, foreign persons may invest in economic and social activities in Yugoslavia. Foreign investors are permitted to manage or take part in the management of enterprises in proportion to resources invested; assign rights and obligations to other foreign or domestic investors; share profits in proportion to resources invested and transfer or reinvest those profits; and share net assets value and repatriation upon cessation of operations.

Enterprises with foreign investment are accorded the same status, rights, and obligations as domestic enterprises. Foreign investors are entitled to profit-tax deductions in the initial period of operation and tax deductions on assets reinvested or deposited in Yugoslavia under conditions provided by the federal republic, the various republics, and the autonomous provinces.

Foreign investors may invest in the following forms of business:

☐ Socially owned enterprise
☐ Mixed enterprise, such as a joint-stock company or a limited liability company
☐ Private enterprise
☐ Contractual enterprise
☐ Bank or other financial organization
☐ Cooperative
☐ Insurance organization
☐ Any other form of business activity provided by law.

Foreign persons also can set up wholly owned enterprises, except for enterprises in such activities as armaments and military equipment, rail or air transport, communications and telecommunications, insurance, and publishing or mass media.

Foreign investment, including the original investment agreement and any changes, must be reported to the federal administration agency in charge of foreign economic relations. In addition, any reinvestment of profit or additional investment made by a foreign investor, as well as any assignment of foreign investment, must be reported to the federal administration within a specified period.

ZAIRE
FEDERAL REPUBLIC OF

INCOME TAXES ON CORPORATIONS

1. Rates

All resident corporations formed under Zairian law, whether limited companies (S.A.R.L.) or private limited companies (S.P.R.L.), pay tax at the rate of 50% on taxable income. Tax exemption may be granted for new foreign investment under the law "Code d' Investissements."

2. Local Income Taxes

Regional and urban taxes ranging from 3% to 5% of sales are imposed on certain manufacturing companies.

3. Capital Gains Taxes

Realized capital gains are taxed at the same 50% rate that applies to other income.

4. Branch Profits Taxes

Branch profits are taxed at 50%. Taking into account the 20% withholding tax on remittance of profits, the effective rate of tax is 60%.

5. Foreign Tax Reliefs

None.

7. Payment of Taxes

Corporations are required to pay tax by installments based on the tax paid for the previous year. The installments are as follows:

☐ 40% prior to September 1 of the current financial year.
☐ 40% prior to December 1 of the current financial year.

If the current year's tax is greater than that of the preceding year:

☐ 20% prior to April 1 following the end of the financial year (at this stage, therefore, the tax paid equals that of the previous year).

☐ The balance of the tax is paid before the end of the following month in which the company is officially notified "enrolled" of its tax obligation for the financial year.

If the current year's tax is less than that of the preceding year:

☐ The balance of the tax for the financial year is due by April 1 of the following financial year.

☐ If the first two installments already exceed the current year's tax obligation, the tax authorities should be officially notified in order to obtain a tax credit that may be used to offset future liabilities.

INCOME TAXES ON INDIVIDUALS

9. Rates

The annual tax tables in force since 1991 are:

Taxable Income

Over		Not Over		Rate
Z.	600,000	Z.	900,000	5%
	900,000		1,200,000	10
	1,200,000		1,850,000	12
	1,850,000		2,300,000	15
	2,300,000		3,700,000	18
	3,700,000		5,000,000	20
	5,000,000		6,700,000	22
	6,700,000		7,800,000	25
	7,800,000		9,500,000	30
	9,500,000		10,500,000	35
	10,500,000		12,700,000	40
	12,700,000		15,600,000	45
	15,600,000		17,500,000	50
	17,500,000		22,800,000	55
	22,800,000			60

The excess over Z.22,800,000 will be taxed at 60%, but the total tax payable is limited to 50% of total taxable income. This is the principal benefit for high income earners arising from the change in the tax rates. In addition, there is a special tax of 33% on the gross salaries paid to expatriate employees. This is not considered when assessing whether the 50% overall tax ceiling has been reached. Taxes assessed on the rates are reduced by 5% for each of the income earner's family members. This reduction is applicable only to the portion of annual income not exceeding Z.75,000,000. Salaries and wages are subject to tax deductions at source and employers are required to make annual declarations for their employees prior to January 10th following the end of the fiscal year (December 31).

Such benefits as housing, car allowances, medical care, and paid transportation for annual home leave are not taxable.

10. Local Income Taxes
None.

11. Capital Gains Taxes
None.

12. Foreign Tax Reliefs
None.

13. Tax Period
The calendar year must be used by all taxpayers.

INCOME TAXES ON NONRESIDENTS

15. Liability to Tax
Foreign individuals and companies resident in Zaire are subject to tax on their income arising in or received in Zaire. Zairian citizens resident abroad are taxable as though they were in Zaire on income arising in Zaire. Income arising abroad of Zairian citizens resident abroad is not taxable in Zaire.

16. Rates
A 20% withholding tax, which is a final tax, is levied on all types of income paid to nonresidents.

19. Tax Treaties
None.

OTHER SIGNIFICANT TAXES

21. Sales (Value Added)
Sales tax is levied on the following transactions at rates that became effective July 8, 1986 (except for goods locally manufactured, for which the new tax rate is effective as of January 1989):

	Rate
Services	18%
Air and sea transport:	
domestic	6
foreign	25
Goods locally manufactured	18
Raw materials, spare parts, and	
agricultural products	3
Building and construction	18
Exports	6.75 to 7

The above tax is deductible for income tax purposes. The tax represents an addition to the selling price and is levied on the beneficiary of the goods and services. The liability of the tax and payment thereof, however, remains the responsibility of the person rendering such services.

22.   Inheritance and Gift Taxes

None.

23.   Taxes on Payrolls (Social Security)

Both employers and employees contribute to a national pension scheme. However, the contributions are low and, therefore, the benefits are negligible. As a result, many companies have established non-contributory retirement schemes. It is general practice for employers to subsidize substantial portions of employee housing and transportation costs. Also, workers and their families are fully covered for medical costs at the employer's expense.

Expatriates' gross salaries are subject to a special tax of 33% (see item 9). This tax must be added back to income for corporate tax purposes.

25.   Other Taxes

Property Tax.   The annual taxes on property are based on the location of the property. Locations are classified into four ranks.

☐   Rank one: Z.240,000 for residential housing; Z.60,000 to Z.5,000,000 for apartments and other buildings; Z.1,000,000 for land.

☐   Rank two: Z.120,000 for residential housing; Z.30,000 to Z.900,000 for apartments and other buildings; Z.150,000 for land.

☐   Rank three: Z.45,000 for residential housing; Z.25,000 to Z.480,000 for apartments and other buildings; Z.50,000 for land.

☐   Rank four: Z.50,000 for residential housing; Z.10,000 to Z.300,000 for apartments and other buildings; Z.50,000 for land.

Capital Tax (on new or increased investment). Ten percent for S.A.R.L. companies only.

Tax on Imports of Services. Thirty percent.

Tax on Imports Other than Services. The tax is 20% except for raw materials and semicompleted goods for production which are taxed at 3% because these are considered priority items. In addition, standard custom duties are payable at varying rates.

COMPUTATION OF TAXABLE INCOME

26. Capital Gains
See item 3.

27. Depreciation and Depletion
No standard rates of depreciation are provided in the tax law. Realistic actual depreciation is deductible but the rates must be agreed upon with the tax authorities. In practice, the following rates are generally accepted by the tax authorities:

Property	Rate
Buildings	2.5%–5%
Plant and equipment	10–15
Furniture, fixtures & fittings	10–15
Motor vehicles	25

Under the mining law, special rates are provided for mining and mineral exploration companies, which are generally higher than those above. In most cases, corporations in mining activities have specific agreements with the Government about their tax status and other matters.

28. Treatment of Dividends
A 20% tax is withheld by the payer of dividends. The net dividends received are reduced by 90% and only the balance is included in income. The 20% tax retained is not creditable against the tax payable by the recipient.

The income distributed to an "inactive" (sleeping) partner in a private limited company is subject to a withholding tax of 20% and the net amount is fully included in taxable income for income tax purposes. Even if no income is distributed by the company, any drawings on current account in the books of the company will be deemed a distribution of income and, hence, will be subject to withholding tax. A resident foreign corporation (i.e., a limited company formed under a foreign law but registered in Zaire as the branch of a foreign company) must pay 20% tax on 50% of its after-tax income, which is considered to be distributable whether or not actually distributed.

29. Loss Carryovers

Losses may be carried forward for offset against the taxable income of the five succeeding years; no carryback is available.

30. Transactions between Related Parties

No special treatment is accorded such transactions.

31. Consolidation of Income

Consolidation of income for tax purposes is not allowed.

32. Tax Periods

The calendar year must be used by all taxpayers.

33. Other Matters

Reserves. All provisions, whether of a general or specific nature, must be added back to income for tax purposes. Thus, bad debts are normally only deductible in the year in which written off and any provision for employee benefits is also not deductible until actual payments are made to the employee.

Inventory. Inventory valuation methods are not prescribed by the tax law. Inventory may be valued at cost or market selling price. In certain cases, such as large wholesalers or retailers, provisions for obsolete or damaged goods calculated as a percentage of total inventories have been agreed with the tax authorities. Generally, cost is calculated on a FIFO or weighted average basis. The LIFO method is specifically prohibited if it does not agree with actual stock movement. Nevertheless, LIFO is used by some companies, particularly in the mining industry.

Rental Income. Rental income is taxed on a basis comparable to income taxes on individuals. Eighty percent of the gross rental income is taxed on the progressive scale given in item 9, with the same proviso that the total tax will not exceed 50% of the taxable base.

    Legal entities must withhold 20% of each rental payment when paying it to the landlord. This withholding, which must be paid to the tax authorities within ten days, is creditable against the landlord's tax liability.

Statute of Limitations. The tax authorities may review company income and other tax returns for the preceding ten years, even though the tax returns for part of that period may have been reviewed previously.

Tax Reform. Tax reform is presently under study, but considering the actual political changes, it is difficult to foresee when existing tax laws will be modified.

RELATED CONSIDERATIONS

34. Incentives and Grants

New and existing investments being modernized or expanded generally receive exemptions from various taxes for the first 5 to 10 years of their operation. A new investment law has simplified the administrative procedures for investors and companies applying for benefits under the new investment code. The law emphasizes, by giving more fiscal benefits, development in certain designated regions. Investments in priority/strategic industries (e.g., agriculture, transportation, energy, mines, and pharmaceuticals) and certain training programs receive maximum tax incentives. The fiscal incentives vary depending on the importance of the investment. Generally, exemptions for 5 to 10 years are available from capital tax, import duties, withholding tax, corporation tax, and salary tax for labor intensive industries.

35. Exchange Controls

Most transactions in foreign currency require the approval of either or both the Central and commercial banks. All imports must be validated and supported by import licenses and letters of credit. Imports of services are permitted only for highly technical areas and, generally, where local expertise is not available.

The foreign exchange derived from exports all goes to the commercial banks. About 25% of the foreign exchange is used to pay for invisibles, and 75% is used for other imports.

The Central Bank's regulations permit foreigners working in Zaire to transfer abroad a portion of their net salaries, providing their employment contracts have been previously approved and the amount of the transfer falls within the total allocation—each expatriate employee also has an individual allocation which must be applied for each year. Considerable delays can be experienced in obtaining an allocation.

36. Investment Restrictions on Nonresidents

All investments by nonresidents require the approval of the President of the Republic of Zaire. Such approval normally requires that Zairian shareholders, which may be the State, hold 40% of the total investment. The Government's general policy is to keep selected industries under the control of the State or Zairian citizens. Land may be owned only by Zairian citizens. However, foreign investors may lease land for a renewable period of 25 years at a negligible rent.

ZAMBIA

INCOME TAXES ON CORPORATIONS

1. Rates

Income arising in the tax year ending March 31, 1992 is taxed at the following rates:

	Rate
Farming	15.0%
Manufacturing	45.1%
Rural manufacturing business for the first five years	30.0%
Export of nontraditional products	15.0%
Export of goods manufactured from domestically produced agricultural raw materials	Exempt
Banking	
—on income up to K10,000,000	45.0%
—on income over K10,000,000	52.5%
Other sources	45.0%

A resident company is liable to tax on income from sources in Zambia, except for dividends from another Zambian incorporated company. In addition, it is taxable on the following foreign-source income:

☐ Dividends.

☐ Interest.

☐ Profits derived from a business carried on partly within and partly outside Zambia.

A company is resident in Zambia if that is where its management and control is exercised. In practice, the tax authorities normally regard a company as being resident if it is incorporated in Zambia.

Government-controlled companies are required to pay the higher of 1.5% of the Government's equity holding or company income tax. Holding companies are exempt to the extent they hold equity in government-controlled operating companies. No tax is payable by a company if such payment would prove detrimental to the company's operations. The Minister of Finance is also empowered to exempt any government-controlled company from equity levy.

Companies are required to make a payment, treated as tax, on loans to an effective shareholder in excess of K5,000. An effective shareholder for this purpose is an individual who controls 5% or more of the company's shares or voting power. At current rates, a loan of K10,000 would give rise to a tax charge, on the excess of K5,000 amounting to K5,000. This is recoverable when the loan is repaid, but any penalties incurred for late payment of the tax are not recoverable.

The Commissioner of Taxes is authorized to make deemed distributions in the hands of shareholders where he considers that inadequate dividends have been declared. Such dividends will be taxed to the shareholders in the same manner as ordinary Zambian dividends (see item 28).

2. Local Income Taxes

None.

3. Capital Gains Taxes

None.

4. Branch Profits Taxes

Branch profits are taxed in the same manner and at the same rate as resident corporations. Zambian dividends, foreign dividends, and interest would normally be excluded from the assessment.

5. Foreign Tax Reliefs

A resident company will, as a general rule, receive a credit for foreign tax limited to the lesser of the foreign tax or the Zambian tax on the foreign income. Zambia grants unilateral relief on foreign income derived from a country with which there is no double taxation convention. Sources of foreign income affected are noted in item 1.

7. Payment of Taxes

Tax is payable on a current-year basis in four installments, which are due on July 14, October 14, January 14, and April 14. Heavy penalties can be imposed on late payments or underpayments.

INCOME TAXES ON INDIVIDUALS

9. Rates

The rates for the year ending March 31, 1992 are:

Taxable Income		Tax on	Percentage
Over	Not Over	Lower Amount	on Excess
K 0	K 5,000	K 0	5%
5,000	15,000	250	10
15,000	30,000	1,250	20
30,000	50,000	4,250	30
50,000	70,000	10,250	40
70,000	100,000	18,250	45
100,000		31,750	50

The maximum rate of tax on profits derived from farming and the export of nontraditional products is 15%, and profits derived from the export of goods manufactured from domestically produced agricultural raw materials are exempt from tax.

Personal allowances are deducted from the assessable income of residents in arriving at taxable income and for the year to March 31, 1991 the personal allowances are:

Primary allowance	K 12,000
Handicapped person	K 600
Life Assurance	K 800 (maximum)

The "pay-as-you-earn" system of tax collection applies to emoluments. Individuals ordinarily resident in Zambia are liable to tax on income from sources in Zambia. They are also liable on the following sources of foreign income:

☐ Dividends.
☐ Interest other than Building Society and commercial bank interests.
☐ Profits derived from a business carried on partly within and partly outside Zambia.

Individuals with income in excess of K500 from other than employment are required to pay tax on that other income on the same current basis as corporations (see item 7).

Inducement Allowance and Contract Remittances. Employers are permitted to pay an inducement allowance to expatriate employees who require work permits of up to $24,000 per annum in foreign exchange to each employee. Approval for this amount is unusual. The Bank of Zambia normally approves amounts of approximately half the maximum or less. At the end of a two-year contract, the employer can pay a gratuity of up to 25% of the inducement allowance paid during the contract.

The inducement allowance and gratuity are exempt from tax in the hands of the employee, but they are not an allowable deduction to the employer for income tax purposes. All contracts require Bank of Zambia approval.

10. Local Income Taxes

None.

11. Capital Gains Taxes

None.

12. Foreign Tax Reliefs

Same as item 5.

13. Tax Period

March 31 is the standard tax year-end, and applies to all income other than from business. Accounts for the latter may be prepared to a date other than March 31 (see item 32).

INCOME TAXES ON NONRESIDENTS

15. Liability to Tax

In general, the residence status of a taxpayer does not affect his liability to income tax on income from sources in Zambia. The exceptions to this arise from double taxation agreements.

Certain payments to nonresidents (see item 17) are liable to withholding tax but, subject to the provisions of double taxation agreements, no additional tax is charged and there is no refund or set off. However, rental income is subject to assessment at normal rates and a credit is allowed for withholding tax, which is deducted at the rate of 15% of gross income. Fees paid to nonresident public entertainers are also subject to withholding tax at the rate of 30% of gross income.

16. Rates

The rate for income included in an assessment of a nonresident company is the same as for a resident company. Nonresident individuals are also chargeable at the same rates as residents who do not receive the inducement allowance, but they do not qualify for personal allowances unless an election is made to be assessed on a "world income" basis.

17. Withholding Tax Rates

Certain double taxation agreements provide that dividends, interest, and royalties shall be taxed in accordance with the laws of Zambia if they are effectively connected with a permanent establishment which the nonresident has in Zambia.

Interest on bills of exchange drawn for 180 days or less is exempt from withholding tax. Withholding rates, expressed as a percentage, are detailed in the table below. It provides guidance on the amount deducted from payments to residents of the countries listed. It is however impractical to include all of the circumstances which may affect liability to withholding tax.

	Dividends	Interest	Royalties
Nontreaty countries	20%	15%	30%
Treaty countries:			
Denmark	15	10	15
Federal Republic of Germany	15 (1)	10	10
Finland	15 (1)	15	5/15
France	20	15	Nil
India	15 (1)	10	10
Ireland	Nil	Nil	Nil
Italy	15 (1)	10	10
Japan	Nil	10	10
Kenya	Nil	15	30
Netherlands	15 (1)	10	10
Norway	15	10	15
South Africa	20	15	30
Sweden	15 (1)	10	10
Switzerland	20	Nil	Nil
Tanzania	Nil	15	30
Uganda	Nil	15	30
United Kingdom	15 (2)	10	10

Notes:
(1) These rates are reduced to 5% where the recipient company has 25% direct control of the paying company.
(2) The rate is reduced to 5% if the recipient controls, directly or indirectly, at least 25% of the voting power of the paying company.
(3) Management fees paid to nontreaty countries are subject to withholding tax at 30% of the gross amount. The profit derived from such fees is subject to assessment at normal rates, and credit is allowed for the withholding tax. The taxation of management fees paid to treaty countries depends on the provisions of the relevant agreement. Some agreements provide for a nil rate.

OTHER SIGNIFICANT TAXES

21. Sales (Value Added)

A fairly wide range of locally produced goods with tariff protection is subject to a sales tax as are dutiable goods. Sales tax is also charged on hotel accommodations, meals in restaurants, and various other services including professional services. The rates range up to 50%.

22. Inheritance and Gift Taxes

Estate duty is payable on estates valued in excess of K25,000 at rates ranging from 6% to 12% on amounts in excess of K595,000. There are no gift taxes except that gifts made within three years of death are liable to estate duty.

23. Taxes on Payrolls (Social Security)

Employees, other than most expatriates, are required to contribute jointly with their employers to the Zambia National Provident Fund. Contributions are 5% of salary, rising to K150 per month payable by each.

Local authorities charge an annual personal levy of up to K50 per employee, which employers are required to deduct from employees' wages. Workmen's compensation insurance is charged on the salary payroll at rates up to 1.75%. Salary in excess of K10,000 per annum is disregarded for purposes of this tax.

Selective Employment Tax. An employer is liable for 20% selective employment tax calculated on the emoluments of employees who require work permits. It is disallowable for income tax purposes. Qualifying gratuities, inducement allowances, and the emoluments of agricultural workers are exempt. A credit, up to 50% of the selective employment tax payable, is allowed against certain expenses incurred in training Zambian employees by professional firms engaged in accountancy, architecture, engineering, and quantity surveying.

24. Taxes on Natural Resources

Mineral Tax. Mining income is subject to mineral tax at the following rates:

☐ Copper, where the price is

Over (U.S. cents)	Not Over (U.S. cents)	Rate
	100	Nil
100	105	60%
105	110	70
110	115	80
115	120	95
120		100

☐ Other minerals, the rate is 20%.

25. Other Taxes

Land and Property.   Local authorities levy annual rates based on property values. Any transfer of land or shares is subject to property transfer tax at 7.5% of the realized value. Land includes buildings, structures, or improvements thereon. The tax is payable by the transferor. The realized value for land is the open market price and for shares is the open market price or nominal value, whichever is greater.

The Commissioner of Taxes can determine that no realized value is attached to a transfer within a group of companies if such transfer is carried out for the purpose of an internal reorganization.

International organizations approved by the Minister of Finance, some organizations which are exempt from income tax, cooperatives, and transfers by shareholders as a contribution to the equity of a company incorporated in Zambia are exempt from property transfer tax.

Education Levy.   Companies with a turnover (or gross income) in excess of K50,000 are required to pay an education levy. The rates are

Turnover		Levy
Over	Not Over	
K 50,000	K 100,000	K 750
100,000	200,000	1,500
200,000	500,000	3,000
500,000	1,000,000	7,500
1,000,000		1.5% of turnover up to a maximum of K75,000

This levy is payable on a current-year basis in four installments, which are due July 14, October 14, January 14, and April 14.

The charge is not an allowable deduction for income tax purposes.

Stamp Duty.   Various documents require stamping and there are duties on property transfers and share capital.

Transactions involving landed property must exclude any value attributable to the land all of which is owned by the State.

Withholding Taxes.   The Commissioner of Taxes can direct any person or partnership making a payment to any person engaged in construction or haulage operations (except employees) to deduct tax at 45% from the gross payment. If the contractor or hauler has a Certificate of Exemption, no tax is deducted. The tax deducted is allowed as a credit when an assessment is issued.

Every person or partnership is required to deduct tax at 30% from the gross payment to resident public entertainers. The tax deducted is allowed as a credit when an assessment is issued.

Withholding tax is deducted from the dividend payments at the rates specified in item 28. Every person or partnership is required to deduct tax at the rate of 15% from the gross payment of rents and at 30% from the gross payment of management fees. Rental income and management fees are subject to assessment at normal rates, and credit is allowed for the withholding tax when an assessment is issued.

The Commissioner of Taxes can exempt any person from deducting withholding tax from rent payments.

COMPUTATION OF TAXABLE INCOME

26. Capital Gains

None.

27. Depreciation and Depletion

Mining. Capital expenditure in relation to mining includes the cost of buildings, works, equipment, shaft sinking and expenditure prior to the commencement of production on preliminary surveys, boreholes, development or management. It is allowed on a life of mine basis or a new mine basis. The amount for life of mine is arrived at by dividing the expenditure by the estimated life of the mine as determined by payable ore reserves. Under a new mine basis, the expenditure is allowed in the year in which it is incurred.

Buildings. Farm buildings and improvements are written off in full in the year the expenditure is incurred.

Initial allowance is granted at 10% of the cost on new industrial buildings and additions to industrial buildings. The annual allowance is 5% of the cost.

Commercial buildings and structures qualify for an annual allowance of 2% of the cost if erected after March 31, 1969. Additions to pre-1969 buildings and structures do not qualify.

Plant. The annual allowance for plant and machinery varies from 30% to 50%, depending on the number of hours used during the year or whether used in farming. It is based on cost for the year in which first used and thereafter on each year's reduced balance except for plant and machinery used in farming, which is written off on a straight line basis over two years. For soft drinks manufacturers in rural areas, the annual allowance is 20% of cost.

The full proceeds of any sales during the year are deducted in arriving at the balance qualifying for annual allowances. This applies even though the asset is sold in excess of cost.

28. Treatment of Dividends

Every company incorporated in Zambia must deduct a 20% withholding tax on the gross dividends payable to companies resident in Zambia and all nonresidents. The rate for resident individuals is 30% of the gross amount.

The Commissioner of Taxes can issue a directive to apply a different rate to the dividends paid to nonresidents when a relevant double taxation agreement exists. Dividends paid out of farming profits are exempt from tax when paid by a company during its first five years of farming operations.

The withholding tax deducted by the company must be paid to the Collector of Taxes by the 14th of the month following declaration.

Dividends received by a company incorporated in Zambia are not subject to tax when paid by another Zambian incorporated company. The withholding tax on dividends received offsets amounts due to the Collector for withholding tax on dividends payable.

No additional tax is charged on dividend payments to resident individuals and there is no refund or set-off.

29. Loss Carryovers

A loss may be deducted only against profits from the same source. Losses can be carried forward indefinitely until so absorbed. When the shares of a company with an established tax loss change hands, there are antiavoidance provisions which may be invoked to disallow the losses.

30. Transactions between Related Parties

There are no special provisions for revenue transactions between related parties.

A depreciable asset may be sold to a related party for an amount equal to its depreciated value, even though the actual value of the asset may be higher or lower than its depreciated amount. There are antiavoidance provisions to counteract the sale of assets which qualify for annual allowances at other than market values.

31. Consolidation of Income

There are no provisions for the filing of consolidated tax returns by related corporations.

32. Tax Periods

The tax year ends on March 31 and applies to all income other than from business. Accounts for the latter may be prepared to a date other than March 31. The Commissioner of Taxes is empowered to assess the profits in respect of accounts prepared to a date other than March 31 for either the charge year ending before or after the date to which the accounts are prepared.

33. Other Significant Matters

Inventory. Stocks must be valued at the lower of cost or net realizable value. No value is placed on livestock purchased for stud and an election can be made to have other livestock brought to account on the basis of fixed standard values.

Bad Debts. Specific provisions for doubtful debts and actual bad debts which have previously been included in income are deductible. Recovered bad debts previously written off are includable in assessable income.

Exchange Gains and Losses. Taxable gains are taxed in the charge year in which they are realized. Allowable losses are deductible in the charge year in which they are realized.

Provisions. Specific provisions for employees benefits, e.g. leave pay, passages, and gratuities, are deductible.

Entertainment. No deduction is allowed for expenditure on entertainment, other than for purely staff functions.

Residence. The value of housing or furniture provided in the course of employment is exempt from tax unless the employee is an effective shareholder. A deduction is allowed for the mortgage interest on any one home used in Zambia as a private residence if neither spouse receives a housing allowance which qualifies for an exemption.

Employees who provide their own accommodation can be paid a tax-free housing allowance at rates ranging from K18,000 to K216,000 per annum depending on the basic salary of the employee.

Other Matters. When an employer pays education allowances for up to three children, who are attending school outside Zambia and are under 19 at the commencement of the charge year, there is an exemption of up to K350 for each child who is a boarder and K150 for each child who is attending school as a day pupil. Zambian citizens do not qualify.

Income received by way of gratuity is taxed separately from other income. The gratuity must be paid on termination of a written agreement after a minimum period of two years' completed service. An amount up to 25% of the basic salary earned in the period to which the gratuity relates is regarded as a qualifying gratuity. It is taxed at normal scale rates.

Commencement, termination, leave and education passages are normally exempt from tax if paid pursuant to a written agreement for employment. Zambian citizens do not qualify in respect of commencement, terminal, and leave passages. The advantageous tax treatment of passages, housing and education allowances, and gratuities does not apply to effective shareholders, i.e., those controlling 5% or more of the shares or voting power of the paying company or directors who are not full-time service directors.

Interest received by resident individuals on deposits in the Zambia National Building Society or any commercial bank in Zambia is exempt from tax.

An employer can pay employees a tax free allowance up to K51,600 per annum in lieu of providing a car.

Payments of up to K2,400 per annum from an approved pension fund are exempt from tax.

The first K40,000 of compensation for loss of office is exempt from tax. The excess can be spread forward over a period not exceeding five years.

Any taxpayer proposing to leave Zambia, no matter what the purpose of the journey, is required to have a Tax Clearance Certificate. Married women, visitors for 30 days or less, diplomatic staff, and persons in certain other categories are exempt.

RELATED CONSIDERATIONS

34. Incentives and Grants

A rural enterprise is a manufacturing business starting on or after April 1, 1976 in a rural area; or a hotel, motel, or lodge which commences business on or after April 1, 1981. The tax chargeable on the profits of a rural enterprise is reduced by two-fifths during the first five years it is in business.

Income derived from the export of goods manufactured from domestically produced agricultural raw materials is exempt from tax. Income derived from the export of nontraditional products is taxed at a maximum rate of 15%. Nontraditional products are anything produced or manufactured (other than electricity) and includes precious and semi-precious minerals exported through the Reserved Minerals Corporation.

The Minister of Finance can provide by Statutory Instrument for the granting of job credits in respect of each net addition to the number of employees of companies, partnerships, and individuals carrying on business as manufacturers.

An investment allowance of 10% of the cost is granted to manufacturers on new industrial buildings and additions thereto. This allowance is not deducted from cost for the purposes of calculating annual allowances. An investment allowance of 20% of the cost is granted on new or unused plant and machinery, other than motor vehicles, used in a manufacturing process. This allowance is not deducted from cost for the purposes of calculating annual allowances.

There are provisions for averaging income and losses from farming and fishing, on making a valid election.

Expenditure on growing tea, coffee, bananas, citrus or similar plants or trees qualifies for a development allowance at the rate of 10% of the expenditure, which is deductible from the profits of the business for the charge year in which the expenditure was incurred. In the case of a taxpayer growing them for the first time, the allowance can be carried forward until production starts but not for more than three years.

The Investment Act of 1986 details procedures for investing in Zambia. Various incentives are available depending on the nature of the investment. The rules are fairly complex and advice should be sought by potential investors.

Petroleum Exploration and Production. The determination of the assessable income from petroleum exploration and production is governed by separate regulations. Persons engaged in these activities enter into a contract with the state which provides for the expenditure and capital allowances which are deductible in determining the assessable income.

35. Exchange Controls

All persons requiring foreign exchange must submit documented applications through their commercial banks for submission to the Foreign Exchange Management Committee, which meets fortnightly to allocate the available foreign exchange. Priority is given to agriculture, mining, and export oriented manufacturing enterprises.

Prior Bank of Zambia approval must be obtained for the remittance of dividends, interest, loan repayments, and similar items.

Dividend remittances to nonresident shareholders are restricted on a pro rata basis to the lesser of 15% of the issued share capital or 50% of the profits after full provision for taxation. Remittances of branch profits are normally restricted to 50% of the profits after full provision for taxation.

36. Investment Restrictions on Nonresidents

Direct foreign investment by nonresidents requires sanction by the Bank of Zambia. Investors must also comply with the Investment Act 1986.

SELECTION OF BUSINESS ENTITY BY NONRESIDENTS

A nonresident individual or partnership or company can operate in Zambia either through a branch or a locally incorporated company. Apart from clearance of the investment by Bank of Zambia, licenses would need to be obtained for manufacturing or trading, as the case may be, import licenses if relevant, work permits for expatriate staff should they be needed, and comparisons made of branch profit remittances with dividends. Any or all of these can have a bearing on a decision whether to operate as a branch or a company. In respect of taxation, the only matters to be noted are the rates of tax in the case of an individual or partnership operating through a branch as compared to doing so through a company and, secondly, that there is no withholding tax levied on the remittance of branch profits.

SPECIMEN TAX COMPUTATION

Information:

□ A Zambia resident incorporated company's operating and other profits for the year of K500,000 consist of the following:

Manufacturing profits in Zambia	K350,000
Zambian dividends (gross)	100,000
Zambian interest (1)	10,000
Capital profit on the sale of an investment	40,000
	K500,000

□ The operating profits for the year have been arrived at after charging the following:

Depreciation	K150,000
General provision for repairs	K 30,000
Education levy	K 75,000

□ Capital allowances for tax purposes amount to K180,000.
□ An extension to the factory costing K100,000 was placed in service.
□ New plant costing K70,000 was installed and placed in service.

Computation:

		K
Trading profits		500,000
Add		
Depreciation	150,000	
General provision for repairs	30,000	
Education levy	75,000	255,000
		755,000
Less		
Zambian dividends (2)	100,000	
Capital profit	40,000	
Capital allowances	180,000	
Investment allowances:		
Buildings (K100,000 × 10%)	10,000	
Plant (K70,000 × 20%)	14,000	344,000
Assessable income		411,000
Tax payable (K411,000 × 45%)		184,950

Notes:

(1) Assuming that the interest is effectively connected with the Zambian business, a nonresident Zambian incorporated company would have the same tax liability. If the K10,000 of interest is regarded as derived from a separate source, the applicable rate of tax would be 45%.

(2) The gross dividends received will have incurred withholding tax amounting to K20,000, which will be available for set off against dividends payable.

ZIMBABWE

INCOME TAXES ON CORPORATIONS

1. Rates

Corporations are assessed income tax at the rate of 45% (however, see item 8) of their ordinary taxable income. Foreign dividends are taxed at 20%, but relief is given for tax withheld at source. Dividends received from local companies are excluded.

2. Local Income Taxes

None.

3. Capital Gains Taxes

There is a tax of 30% in respect of capital gains (aggregating more than $1,000) on sales of immovable property (real estate) and marketable securities (shares, stocks, bonds, and debentures) only, and on the redemption or maturing of stocks. In calculating the gain, the deduction for the original cost (plus cost of additions or alterations) is increased by 5% for each year since the expenditure was incurred. Overall capital losses exceeding $1,000 are carried forward for use in future years. This tax does not apply to sales of assets acquired for the purpose of resale (see item 26).

It is proposed that the 5% rate be increased to 10% effective April 1, 1991.

4. Branch Profits Tax

Corporations registered under the law of a foreign country are subject to a branch profits tax of 15% of 56% (i.e., 8.4%) of their taxable income. This is in addition to the regular corporate tax rates (however, see item 15). The total effective rate of combined income and branch profits tax is, therefore, 53.4% (45% + 8.4%).

5. Foreign Tax Reliefs

Unilateral relief is given for foreign taxes paid on foreign income deemed to be from a Zimbabwe source (see item 33).

6. Classification of Corporations

For tax purposes, there is no difference between public and private corporations.

7. Payment of Taxes

See item 32.

8. Other Matters

1991 Budget. It is proposed that, effective the year ending March 31, 1993, the corporation tax rate will be reduced to 42.5%.

Trusts. Trusts are taxed on the same basis and at the same rates as corporations.

INCOME TAXES ON INDIVIDUALS

9. Rates

The basic rates (but see item 8), before tax credits, of both married and single persons are:

Taxable Income		Tax on Lower Amount	Percentage on Excess
Over	Not Over		
$ 3,600	$ 6,000	$ 0	20%
6,000	12,000	480	30
12,000	18,000	2,280	40
18,000	30,000	4,680	50
30,000	45,000	10,680	55
45,000		18,930	60

These rates are applied to all taxable income except dividends, which are subject to tax at the special rate of 20%. In the case of local dividends, this is a withholding tax; foreign dividends are assessed together with other income, but at the special rate.

A husband and wife are taxed separately.

Tax Credits. The principal tax credits are:

□ Family—$360
□ Child—$120
□ Over 60 years of age (taxable income less than $5,000)—$100
□ Standard (all taxpayers)—$50
□ Insurance premiums—20% of premiums up to $2,000

□ Medical expenses—20% of expenses over $250
□ Other credits include credits for the blind, disabled, and full-time students under the age of 26.

Income tax payable is arrived at by deducting the aggregate of the tax credits from the basic tax payable.

10. Local Income Taxes

None.

11. Capital Gains Taxes

The same information applies as in item 3. A ''roll-over'' relief in respect of capital gains tax for principal private residences is available to individuals.

12. Foreign Tax Reliefs

Unilateral relief is given for foreign taxes, as in item 5.

13. Tax Period

See item 32.

14. Other Matters

Fringe Benefits. The value of any advantage or benefit from employment is taxable in the hands of the employee. The legislation is general in nature, except for two specific items:

□ Soft Loans (other than for educational or medical reasons). The taxable amount is the difference between the interest charged and interest at the rates of 12.5% (loans below $12,000) and 13.25% (loans above $12,000). The 1991 budget proposes to increase the rates to 13.0% and 14.5%, respectively, effective the year ending March 31, 1992.
□ Use of Employer's Motor Vehicle for Private Purposes. The taxable benefit is deemed the cost to the employer, which varies between $1,500 and $3,000 depending on the engine capacity. The 1991 budget proposes to increase benefits to between $2,400 and $4,800 effective the year ending March 31, 1992.

Tax-Free Income.

□ The first $2,400 of aggregated pensions received by persons age 60 or older.
□ The first $1,100 of aggregated bonuses or 10% of annual remuneration, whichever is the lesser.
□ The first $500 of aggregated taxable interest.

1991 Budget. Effective the year ending March 31, 1993, it is proposed that the tax-free band will be raised from $3,600 to $4,800 and the maximum rate, reduced to 55%, will be reached at a taxable income of $45,000.

INCOME TAXES ON NONRESIDENTS

15. Liability to Tax

All nonresidents in receipt of "taxable income" are liable to tax. Since a basic principle of "taxable income" is that the source must be in Zimbabwe (see item 33), it is not necessary to make many variations for nonresidents. In the case of corporations, the only material differences are the imposition of branch profits tax (see item 4) and the exemption (subject to certain restrictions) of interest received on loans made to mining concerns or to the government or a governmental body. This exemption also applies to nonresident individuals. In addition, interest received on Zimbabwe Government 4% disinvestment six-year bonds owned by nonresidents is exempt from tax; interest on Zimbabwe Government 4% 12-year (external) bonds and 4% 20-year (external) bonds held by nonresident individuals and corporations, respectively, also is exempt from tax. The tax credit for medical expenses is not granted to such individuals.

17. Withholding Tax Rates

The following withholding taxes apply:

	Dividends (1)	Interest (2)(3)	Fees (2) Directors'	Fees (2) Other	Remittances	Royalties (2)
Non-treaty countries	20%	10%	20%	20%	20%	20%
Treaty countries:						
Bulgaria	10	10	20	10	20	10
Germany	10	10	20	7.5	20	7.5
Netherlands	10	10	20	10	20	10
Norway	15	10	20	10	20	10
Sweden	15	10	20	10	20	10
So. Africa	20	10	20	20	20	20
United Kingdom	5	10	20	10	20	10

Notes:

(1) The concession to Bulgarian, Dutch, German, Norwegian, Swedish, and United Kingdom residents applies only when the recipient is a company controlling at least 25% of the voting power of the company paying the dividend. Otherwise the rate is 20%.

(2) No additional tax is payable on interest, other fees, or royalties in the case of Bulgarian, Dutch, German, Norwegian, Swedish, and United Kingdom residents. Others pay normal income tax with a credit given for tax withheld.

(3) Interest on Government disinvestment and external bonds is exempt from the withholding tax.

19. Tax Treaties

There are at present agreements for double-taxation relief with Bulgaria, the Netherlands, Norway, South Africa, Sweden, and the United Kingdom, but relief is given unilaterally for all foreign taxes paid on foreign income. Other treaties are being negotiated.

OTHER SIGNIFICANT TAXES

21. Sales (Value Added)

A sales tax is payable on sales and leasing of goods at the retail level; all sales at earlier levels are exempt.

Basic foodstuffs, motor fuels, prescribed drugs, beer, cigarettes, and livestock are exempt; vehicles and most electrical home appliances are taxed at 15%; computers, office machines, radios, televisions, and luxury items are taxed at 20%; all other goods, including furniture, ovens, and refrigerators, are taxed at 10%. Manufacturers, farmers, miners, and hoteliers operating in gazetted growth point areas may receive refunds of sales tax on certain capital goods. Refunds of sales tax also are granted for certain capital goods used in new agricultural, mining, manufacturing, or industrial projects that are specifically approved as such.

22. Inheritance and Gift Taxes

Estate (death) duty is levied on a sliding scale on the dutiable amount of an estate. The worldwide assets of a resident of Zimbabwe generally will be included in the dutiable amount, but certain assets, particularly with regard to those acquired before January 1, 1967, may be excluded depending on how and when those assets were acquired. The liabilities of the deceased and the costs of winding up the estate are allowed as deductions in arriving at the dutiable amount. Important exclusions from the dutiable amount are the family home of a deceased who is survived by a spouse or a minor child, and the proceeds of an insurance policy to meet the duty.

Due to the existence of rebates, estates of up to $50,000 with no surviving spouse and up to $100,000 with a surviving spouse are duty-free. On estates of between these amounts and $100,000 and $150,000, respectively, diminishing rebates reduce duty payable, until, at these levels the maximum duty rate of 20% is reached.

There is no donations tax, but donations made within five years prior to death are included in the estate for duty purposes. Capital gains tax does not apply to assets passing under a will to an heir (until the heir subsequently disposes of them).

23. Taxes on Payrolls (Social Security)

There are no social security taxes as such. Employers must pay (annually) workers compensation insurance premiums for all workers whose total annual earnings, including free benefits, are not more than $16,000. Private medical aid societies provide health facilities, and the Government provides relief to those completely destitute. Most employees are members of private pension schemes or are covered by mandatory retirement programs. It has been announced that effective April 1, 1992 a national pension scheme will commence. Contributions by both employers and employees will be 4% of employee earnings.

There are also the following mandatory taxes on payrolls (with limited exceptions):

☐ Training levy of 1%

☐ Standards development fund levy of 0.15%

25. Other Taxes

Property Rates. Both urban and rural local authorities levy rates, generally semi-annually, on real estate. The rates and basis of charge vary between authorities, and there is often differentiation between the rates charged for land and for buildings and the rates for residential and for business premises. Rural rates are lower than those for urban areas. Urban rates are usually in the range of 0.5% to 1.25% of a property's valuation.

Land Taxation. The central Government still plans to introduce a land tax to discourage the under utilization of commercial agricultural land. No details have yet been made public.

Transfer Duty. A duty is payable on transfers of real estate, which reaches a maximum of 5% on that amount of the value exceeding $15,000.

Stamp Duties. Stamp duties are payable on certain documents, including broker's notes, insurance policies, mortgage bonds, notarial bonds, checks, and transfers of mining locations.

Company Fees. Fees are payable on the registration of companies and on increases in authorized share capital. In addition, there is an annual return fee of between $30 and $300.

COMPUTATION OF TAXABLE INCOME

26. Capital Gains

Capital gains (i.e., the excess of sales proceeds over original cost) are not subject to income tax, unless the seller is held to have acquired the asset for the purpose of resale. Recoveries of capital allowances (see item 27) previously granted are included in taxable income. For the special tax on capital gains, see items 3 and 11.

27. Depreciation and Depletion

A special, initial allowance of 50% is claimable on industrial buildings (constructed by the taxpayer), plant, machinery, vehicles, etc, in the year the asset is first used. In subsequent years, allowances of 25% of cost will be granted. In the case of mining concerns, 100% of capital expenditures may be deducted in the year in which incurred; there is a depletion allowance of 5% on the sale value of minerals produced. An investment allowance of 15% is granted in respect of capital expenditure on new items in gazetted growth points, and 50% for equipment and buildings used in training (see item 33 for petroleum operators).

If the special, initial allowance is not claimed, wear and tear allowances are granted for capital assets used for the purposes of a trade. They range from 2.5% for new commercial buildings (e.g., blocks of offices or flats), 5% for industrial buildings, to 10%–20% for plant, machinery, vehicles, etc.

28. Treatment of Dividends

Dividends received from Zimbabwe companies, which are liable to income tax on their profits, are excluded from taxable income; those received by individuals will have already had a 20% withholding tax deducted at source. Foreign dividends are included in taxable income but are assessed at a special rate (see item 9).

29. Loss Carryovers

As indicated in item 33, losses can arise only if the aggregate permitted deductions exceed the aggregate gross income. Losses may be carried forward without time limit. More precisely, they are permitted as a deduction in determining the following year's taxable income from any source.

1991 Budget. It has been announced that, effective April 1, 1991, loss carryovers are to be restricted to six years, except for mining operations where losses may continue to be carried forward indefinitely.

30. Transactions between Related Parties

There are specific provisions relating to transactions not at arm's length, which enable the authorities to ignore such transactions. There is also authority to adjust the taxable sales proceeds of items sold for less than market value, and vice versa. Subventions and similar payments are not recognized.

31. Consolidation of Income

Every corporation and individual is treated as a separate taxpayer. Minor children are separately assessed provided their income does not arise from gifts made by their parents.

32. Tax Periods

A corporation (or any other taxpayer producing financial accounts) may apply to adopt an accounting year ending on any date. This will be regarded for all purposes as forming the basis of assessment to the following March 31, which is the fiscal year-end. Returns of income must be filed in August in respect of the fiscal year ended on the preceding March 31, although extensions beyond the filing date generally are granted if financial accounts have to be prepared. Assessments then are issued at any time during the ensuing 12 months, and the tax is payable within 30 days of assessment unless specific payment dates have been fixed. Three fixed payment dates generally are assigned to all self-employed individuals and to corporations. On each of these dates, part of the estimated (or assessed) tax for the preceding year must be paid. The first date is May 31 for all such taxpayers. The second date is set by the Commissioner of Taxes and may be any day between August 1 and December 31. The third date is four months after the second date. Half of the estimated (or assessed) tax for the preceding year must be paid on the first date (May 31), and the rest must be paid in two equal installments on the second and third dates determined by the Commissioner of Taxes.

33. Other Significant Matters

Inventory Valuation. Inventory may be valued at cost, replacement cost, or market value. Cost normally is determined on an actual, FIFO, or average basis. LIFO is not accepted.

Concept of Source. Basically, only income arising from sources within Zimbabwe is taxed. In most cases this presents no difficulty, but problems may arise where, for instance, a loan is made by a nonresident to a resident, or where a trade is conducted in two countries. There are two major exceptions to the basic principle: interest and dividends received from sources outside Zimbabwe are "deemed" to have been received from sources within Zimbabwe if received by a resident (but not otherwise); and royalties and similar payments for use in Zimbabwe of patents, showing of films, and imparting of "know-how" also are deemed to arise in Zimbabwe, irrespective of the residence of the recipient. A further basic principle is that taxable income is calculated by aggregating gross income from all sources (excluding capital gains but before any expense deductions are made), removing therefrom any income specifically exempted, and then deducting any permitted expenditure. Concepts of "net profit" and of separate sources of income are not relevant.

Permitted Deductions. The permitted deductions include practically all expenditure not of a capital nature incurred in the production of income or for the purposes of trade (which term includes employment, profession, and property leasing, as well as its usual meanings). Also, deductions are allowed for such items as bad debts, specific doubtful debts, contributions to pension funds, experiments and research, scholarships, etc. Specifically, a deduction is not allowed for business entertainment, dividends paid, alimony payments, domestic expenses, or donations, with very limited exceptions. The cost of earning dividends also is not allowed.

Tax-Free Interest. Interest from the Post Office Savings Bank, from certain building society investments, and on Tax Reserve Certificates (used to settle tax liabilities) is exempt from tax. Also tax-exempt (but only to individuals) is the first $500 of aggregated interest on loans or deposits.

Petroleum Operations. The taxable income of petroleum operators (i.e., those engaged in exploration) is calculated basically on the fair market value of petroleum disposed (sold or bartered, appropriated to refining, or exported without having been sold) during the year. Petroleum operators are allowed to deduct 100% of capital expenditures in the year in which incurred.

RELATED CONSIDERATIONS

34. Incentives and Grants

There are no incentives or grants to new businesses or prospective immigrants other than refunds of sales tax being granted in respect of plant and machinery or goods used in the construction of buildings utilized in new agricultural, mining, manufacturing, or industrial projects approved as such in advance.

To encourage exports, however, there is a tax-free 9% export incentive bonus payable on the value of the exports. This bonus will be reduced to 5% effective January 1, 1992, and will cease to be paid after July 1, 1992.

35. Exchange Controls

There is rigid exchange control. All proposed transactions that might involve payments outside Zimbabwe or the importation of goods into Zimbabwe (whether to be paid for or not) need prior approval. Normally, permission will be granted only if the type of goods to be imported is not made locally and is essential for the country's economy. As a result of the gradual implementation of the Structural Adjustment Programme, various items (mainly raw materials for use in manufacturing processes) can now be imported without prior approval.

36. Investment Restrictions on Nonresidents

No nonresident investment can be made without the approval of the Foreign Investment Centre. Approval generally will be granted only in cases where the investment can be shown to create employment and to benefit the country's balance of payments. Foreign investors are expected to provide for domestic equity participation within a reasonable period of time. Normally, nonresidents and nonresident corporations may not borrow from local sources. Borrowings by locally incorporated nonresident-controlled corporations are strictly limited. Prior exchange control approval also must be sought where remittance of investment income to nonresidents and nonresident-controlled organizations is contemplated.

SELECTION OF BUSINESS ENTITY BY NONRESIDENTS

From a tax viewpoint, the best form of nonresident trading up to March 31, 1991 is as an individual or as a partnership of individuals. This enables advantage to be taken of the lower tax rates before the maximum rate is reached at $40,000 (see item 9), and avoids the branch profits tax and the nonresident shareholders tax. However, if corporate status is required, a branch of an overseas corporation pays income tax and branch profits tax on all of its taxable income, whether retained for expansion or remitted; a locally registered subsidiary pays the same income tax but the nonresident shareholders tax is deducted only from such net profits as are declared as dividends.

Effective April 1, 1991 resulting from the decrease in company tax rates, it becomes more advantageous to trade as a locally registered company because of the difference between the company tax rates (45% and 42.5%, effective April 1, 1992) and the individual tax rates (maximum 60% reduced to 55%, effective April 1, 1992).

Another consideration is that loan capital is preferable to equity capital because interest is a permitted deduction to the payer and the recipient is subject only to income tax (with a minimum of the 10% withheld), whereas dividends are subject to withholding tax in addition to the income tax payable on the profits from which they are declared. These factors, of course, must be viewed also in the light of their tax treatment in the home country.

SPECIMEN TAX COMPUTATION

Information.

☐ A Zimbabwe-incorporated corporation has the following income for the year ending March 31, 1992:

Manufacturing profits in Zimbabwe	$500,000
Dividends from:	
Zimbabwe company	40,000
Foreign company (net, after deduction of $2,000 withholding tax)	18,000
Capital profit on sales of an investment	5,000
Zimbabwe interest (1)	29,000
	$592,000

□   Manufacturing profits were arrived at after charging:

Depreciation	$70,000
Provisions for doubtful debts	
Specific	13,000
General	7,000

□   Capital expenditure during the year was $160,000 for new machinery and $24,000 for new audio-visual aids used solely for training staff.

□   The investment was stock in a corporation, which was purchased in the tax year ended March 31, 1984 for $2,000 and sold for $7,000 (see note 1).

Computation of Income Tax.

Manufacturing profits		$500,000
Add		
Depreciation	70,000	
General provision for doubtful debts	7,000	
Zimbabwe interest	29,000	106,000
		606,000
Less		
Special initial allowance (50%)		
Machinery	80,000	
Audio-visual aids	12,000	
Training investment allowance (50%)		
on audio-visual aids	12,000	104,000
		502,000
Add		
Foreign dividends (gross)		20,000
Taxable income		$522,000
Tax ($502,000 at 45%)		225,900
Foreign dividends ($20,000 at 20%)		4,000
		229,900
Less		
Relief for withholding taxes on foreign		
dividends		2,000
Income tax payable		$227,900

Computation of Capital Gains Tax.

Proceeds from sale of investment		$7,000
Less		
Cost	2,000	
Permitted deduction (5% of cost for each		
of 9 years investment held; i.e., 45%		
of $2,000) (2)	900	2,900
Taxable capital gain		$ 4,100
Capital gains tax payable ($4,100 at 30%)		$ 1,230

Notes:
(1) If the interest had been from a foreign source, it would still be taxable as above. Relief would be granted for foreign withholding tax deducted from the gross interest.
(2) See item 3. The 1991 budget proposal, once law, would increase the deduction from $900 to $1,800, reduce the capital gain to $3,200, and reduce the tax payable to $960.

To \ From	Australia	Belgium	Canada	Denmark	France	Germany	Ireland
Corporate Income Tax	39	39	38	40	34	50	40
Statutory (Nontreaty)	30	25	25	30	25	25	0
United States	15	5/15	10/15	5/15	5/15	5/15	0
United Kingdom	15	5/10	10/15	0/15	5/15	15	0
Switzerland	15	10/15	15	0	5/15	10/15	0
Sweden	15	5/15	15	0/15	0/15	5/15	0
Spain	30	15	15	10/15	10/15	15	0
Netherlands	15	5/15	10/15	0/15	5/15	15	0
Luxembourg	30	10/15	10/15	5/15	5/15	10/15	0
Japan	15	5/15	10/15	10/15	10/15	15	0
Italy	15	15	15	15	15	25	0
Ireland	15	15	15	0	10/15	15	—
Germany	15	15	15/25	10/15	0	—	0
France	15	10/15	10/15	0	—	5/15	0
Denmark	15	15	15	—	0	10/15	0
Canada	15	15	—	15	10/15	15	0
Belgium	15	—	15	15	10/15	15	0
Australia	—	15	15	15	15	15	0